TEACHER'S MANUAL

Marketing Essentials

SECOND EDITION

Lois Schneider Farese
Marketing Education Teacher-Coordinator
Northern Highlands Regional High School
Allendale, New Jersey

Grady Kimbrell
Educational Consultant
Santa Barbara, California

Carl A. Woloszyk
Associate Professor
Department of Consumer Resources
    and Technology
Western Michigan University
Kalamazoo, Michigan

GLENCOE
McGraw-Hill

New York, New York   Columbus, Ohio   Mission Hills, California   Peoria, Illinois

Contents

Send all inquiries to:
GLENCOE DIVISION
McGraw-Hill
15319 Chatsworth Street
P.O. Box 9609
Mission Hills, CA 91346-9609

Printed in the United States of America.

ISBN 0-02-640602-0

2 3 4 5 6 7 8 9   RRW   03 02 01 00 99 98 97

Dear Marketing Teachers:

Welcome to the newly revised *Marketing Essentials, Second Edition,* a comprehensive text that captures the excitement and ever-changing elements of marketing in a global marketplace. If you liked the first edition of *Marketing Essentials,* you will thoroughly enjoy this new, updated edition.

The goal of this new text is to make your marketing classes come alive with excitement and to create an interest in marketing. To accomplish that goal, we have filled this text with real-life examples and practical marketing applications, and reorganized the text to make room for important new topics. You and your students will have fun discussing the new, as well as the familiar, topics that embrace the National Marketing Education Curriculum, all of which are creatively presented in *Marketing Essentials, Second Edition.*

Marketing is one of the most interesting business subjects in the curriculum. We see examples of marketing all around us every day of our lives. This text is designed to apply marketing concepts to current trends in the "real world." For example, the text stresses the multicultural nature of the U.S. domestic marketplace and workplace, as well as the move toward a more global economy. School-to-work transition exercises and application projects help students bring their work experience into the classroom and vice versa. Real-life case studies have students apply what they learned in the text to actual business situations. Every case study ends with an ethical question for students to ponder.

To prepare students for using computers in marketing, *Marketing Essentials* now has a chapter devoted to computer technology, as well as technology questions and optional computer applications activities for every chapter. Throughout the text, you will find examples of how computers are changing the way marketers are studying the marketplace and conducting business.

The special features and end-of-chapter activities were designed for the teacher who has students of varying abilities. They allow you to be flexible with your teaching strategies when trying to adapt to the various learning styles of your students.

To prepare students for marketing careers and DECA competition, every chapter offers alternative assessment exercises, one of which is always a role play. Every unit offers students the opportunity to select application projects for use in their personal portfolio, which can further demonstrate the students' comprehension and competency of the subject matter.

We have developed the most extensive support package available to marketing educators. New to this edition is the *Teacher's Wraparound Edition, School-to-Work Handbook, International Case Studies, Marketing Career Portfolio, Lesson Plans,* and *Marketing Software Binders.* These new supplements as well as the revised *Student Activity Workbook, Math Workbook, Transparency Binder,* and testing program address the learning styles of your students and your teaching needs.

This text is one you and your students will enjoy as much the last day of class as on the first day of class during this school year. Best wishes for a successful, exciting, and enjoyable school year teaching marketing!

The Authors

Lois Schneider Farese
Grady Kimbrell
Carl Woloszyk

►Welcome to Marketing Essentials!

Marketing Essentials provides a comprehensive, three-pronged approach to the subject matter suggested for marketing education classes by the National Marketing Educaional Association. First, it explores marketing practices and principles at both the retail and industrial level to give students an overview of the importance of marketing to the business world. Second, it stresses the mathematics fundamentals and applications they need to pursue marketing careers. Third, it helps students do the values clarification they need to identify their interests and aptitudes in the marketing career they will enjoy.

Marketing Essentials follows the curriculum model suggested by the National Marketing Educational Association and represented by this wheel.

Marketing Essentials is designed to:

- *teach students* **marketing foundations and functions,**
- *set the stage* **for further study of marketing in higher education,**
- *prepare students* **for participation in DECA activities, and**
- *introduce students* **to the real world of work to help them prepare for a marketing career.**

The three inner circles show the three foundations of the National Marketing Educational Association's core curriculum: *Economic Foundations of Marketing, Marketing and Business Foundations,* and *Human Resource Foundations.* The National Marketing Educational Association suggests that the remainder of a marketing program should be devoted to the nine functions of marketing, as shown on the outer wheel: selling, promotion, distribution, risk management, pricing, purchasing, marketing information management, product/service planning, and financing. *Marketing Essentials* covers all of the national curriculum.

The organization of the student text is designed for maximum flexibility. The text adapts well to a one-year or two-year high school marketing program.

At the beginning of the text, chapters contain material geared to helping students understand the foundations of marketing that they will need for further study and entry-level employment. These foundation areas cover the essentials of economics, business, marketing, and human resource development. The remainder of the book contains chapters devoted to the function areas of marketing shown on the chart below. The chapters of the book can be used in any order to match the needs of your curriculum. This chart shows the units and chapters where each foundation and function area can be found in the student text.

FOUNDATION OF MARKETING	UNIT	CHAPTERS
Economic Foundations of Marketing	1, 2	3–7, 13–40
Marketing and Business Foundations	3, 10	1, 2, 5–7, 13–40
Human Resource Foundations	4, 12	8–43

MARKETING FUNCTIONS	UNIT	CHAPTERS
Selling	5	13, 14, 15, 16, 17, 18
Promotion	6	19, 20, 21, 22, 23
Distribution	7	24, 25, 27, 28
Risk Management	11	38
Pricing	8	29, 30, 31
Purchasing	7	26
Marketing Information Management	9	32, 33
Product/Service Planning	10, 11	34, 35, 36
Financing	11	39, 40

Understanding the Lesson

The student text provides a constant structure that is easy for the students to use. New material is based on previous knowledge and the text instruction follows an organized flow of concept development, as shown here.

UNDERSTANDING THE UNIT

Marketing Essentials is divided into 12 Units, each of which begins with a two-page presentation. These two pages list the chapters included in the unit and present the marketing wheel with the foundations and/or functions that the student will be studying highlighted in color.

UNIT OPENER

CHAPTER REVIEW

CHAPTER OPENER

SECTION REVIEWS

CHAPTER OBJECTIVES

SECTION DEVELOPMENT

TERMS TO KNOW

INTRODUCTION

Totally new design and visuals motivate student learning. Exciting graphics encourage students to study the material. The readable type size and the vivid illustrations and examples invite student interest and participation.

Unit 6

Promotion

CHAPTERS

19
What Is Promotion?

20
Advertising Media

21
Preparing Print Advertisements

22
Visual Merchandising and Display

23
Publicity and Public Relations

Financing

Distribution

Risk Management

Product/ Service Planning

ECONOMIC FOUNDATIONS OF MARKETING

HUMAN RESOURCE FOUNDATIONS

Selling

Marketing-Information Management

MARKETING AND BUSINESS FOUNDATIONS

Promotion

Purchasing

Pricing

The highlighted color in the marketing wheel indicates the marketing foundations and functions students will study in the unit.

242

243

UNDERSTANDING THE SECTION

For the first time, *Marketing Essentials* uses a chapter-section organization. The purpose is two-fold: more flexibility for the teacher and shorter, easy-to-comprehend segments for the student.

Section Objectives tell students the skills and knowledge they can expect to master once the chapter is completed. They help students read with a goal in mind.

Sections are self-contained lessons on specific topics. Each section has its own objectives, Terms to Know, and review questions.

CHAPTER 4

World Economies

SECTION 4.1

Objectives

After completing this section, you will be able to
- explain what an economy is,
- identify the factors of production necessary to create goods and services, and
- list the three basic economic questions that must be answered by all economies.

Terms to Know

- economy
- resources
- capital
- entrepreneurship
- factors of production
- infrastructure
- scarcity

What Is an Economy?

An **economy,** or economic system, is the way a nation makes economic choices. The choices that must be made involve how the nation will use its resources to produce and distribute goods and services. Let's take a closer look at the resources a nation has.

Resources

Resources are all the things used in producing goods and services. Resources consist of land, labor, **capital,** and **entrepreneurship.** Figure 4-1 (pages 46-47) explains what economists mean by these terms.

Each of these resources presents its own set of problems and opportunities within an economy. The easiest way to appreciate this is to consider the plight of developing nations.

Such nations may want to attract certain kinds of industries. However, their options may be limited by the educational level of their workers. Are they skilled or unskilled? How much value an economic system places on education can profoundly impact one of its most important economic resources—its labor pool.

Capital is often an equally difficult problem for developing nations. At a national level, capital includes infrastructure. **Infrastructure** refers to the physical development of a country—to the state of its roads, ports, sanitation facilities, and utilities. These things are necessary for production and distribution of goods and services in an economy. Imagine trying to operate a modern factory without electricity. Imagine trying to run an international business without dependable phone service to keep in touch with the rest of the world.

Scarcity

All economies have different proportions of resources. Take the crown colony of Hong Kong, soon to be a part of China. It has a highly skilled and educated work force, a great deal of capital, an abundance of entrepreneurs—but very few natural resources. Many underdeveloped nations find themselves in just the opposite circumstances. They have natural resources to spare but not the capital or skilled labor to develop them.

So, nations have unlimited wants and needs (for growth and development), but only limited resources to meet them. In this respect they are much like people. Most people want more than they can afford. This difference between wants and needs on one hand and available resources on the other is called **scarcity.** Scarcity forces everyone—nations, businesses, and people—to make economic *choices.*

Real World

No One Said It Would Be Easy

Free enterprise came to Hungary in 1989. A new international airport was built to welcome tourists and business investors. Budapest's main shopping street became home to Benetton and Cartier. So, how did Hungarians feel about their new economy five years later? A 1994 Gallup poll of 1,000 Hungarians found that 57 percent believed they were worse off under the new economic system. Only 12 percent responded that they were better off, while 30 percent felt they had stayed the same.

Chapter 4 *World Economies* 45

Expanded content includes new chapters on computer technology, the global marketplace, and the relationship between marketing and our society.

The Terms to Know identify the key vocabulary terms to be presented in the section.

Figure 33-1
THE MARKETING RESEARCH PROCESS
There are five steps in the problem solving process.

1. Defining the Problem: The problem is identified and goals are set to solve the problem.

2. Obtaining Data: Researchers obtain data from secondary and primary sources.

SURVEY
Did you buy Brand X?
☐ Yes ☐ No

3. Analyzing Data: Researchers compile, analyze, and interpret the data.

4. Recommending Solutions to the Problem: Researchers come up with solutions to the problem and present them in a report.

5. Applying the Results: The research results are put into action.

New visual verbals highlight key points in the text. Visual verbals raise student interest and aid retention.

Focus on the Features

Each chapter contains special features designed to enhance students' abilities to relate to the real world of marketing. These special features fall into four categories: **Bright Ideas, Real World Marketing, Life in the Multicultural Marketplace,** and **Case Study.**

Bright Ideas tell how a particular marketing innovation came about and then offer a "Creativity Challenge" which asks students to develop related creative thinking skills.

BRIGHT IDEAS

Do the Opposite

Toshiba, the Japanese electronics company, once explained in an ad its formula for coming up with new product ideas. "Innovation is easy," stated the company. "You simply create the exact opposite of everything people wanted the day before."

To reinforce this point, the ad noted that in the 1950s miniaturization was popular. Everyone wanted smaller radios, smaller televisions, pocket-sized calculators. Now in the 1990s, big-screen TVs are turning people's living rooms into home theaters. Tongue-in-cheek, the ad suggested that Toshiba would next be developing a wrist-TV, followed somewhat later by a four-wall model that would provide 360-degree viewing.

Creativity Challenge Form teams of 3–5 people, and test the validity of Toshiba's approach. List all the products you can think of that seem to have cycled through the kinds of changes the ad described. Articles of clothing most readily suggest themselves—skirts, ties, sunglasses, etc. Don't stop there, however. Expand your list into as many different categories of things as you can. Then try to identify at least one item that seems immune to the pattern. Decide how it could realistically be made to fit.

Text fragments from adjacent page spreads (Unit 2, Economic Essentials, p. 38):

...air-conditioning...porated into te...goods to supp...computers, o...workers. The...accounting...

Businesses...must be able to offer...also be able to guarantee the quality...ucts, since they will become part of manufactured goods. For this reason, firms that sell to manufacturers usually establish strict quality control measures.

Wholesalers and Retailers Wholesalers obtain goods from manufacturers and resell them to industrial users, other wholesalers, and retailers. Wholesalers are also called distributors.

Wholesalers are common in certain industries, such as the food and auto industries. As consumers, wholesalers buy the products they resell. They also buy trucks...

by foreign as well as domestic companies. Patent infringement and industrial espionage (stealing ideas from other companies) are becoming more commonplace.

The government also regulates trade with other countries. U.S. companies are not permitted to sell certain products abroad if such sales might jeopardize national defense. To protect domestic industries, sometimes the U.S. government imposes trade restrictions on foreign-made products in that industry.

The government also passes laws to regulate how businesses operate. One of the most important of these laws, enacted to prevent monopolies, is the Sherman Antitrust Act (1890). It outlawed all contracts and agreements that would restrain trade or limit competition in interstate commerce.

A second law, called the Clayton Antitrust Act, was passed in 1914 to reduce loopholes in the Sherman Antitrust Act. In that same year, the Federal Trade Commission (FTC) was established to enforce both acts. The FTC's powers have since been expanded to include investigations of deceptive and misleading business practices, like false advertising.

To ensure economic stability for businesses, the government monitors our economy and controls our monetary supply through the Federal Reserve System. This is our nation's banking system. When the Federal Reserve Board of Governors thinks the economy is moving too fast or too slowly, it acts to correct the problem. For example, if prices are going up too fast, the board may increase interest rates to curb economic activity. Higher interest rates generally make it more difficult to borrow money and therefore discourage expansion by businesses.

Caption (italic): Government regulation protects businesses and individuals from unauthorized use of their personal property. What evidence of this practice do you see here?

protect businesses for a period of time from having others copy their creative ideas and identifying symbols. If one company wants to use another's name, symbol, or product, it must get permission to do so and pay a fee for the use.

You may have heard about businesses that produce products under a **licensing agreement**. Such an agreement protects the originator's name and products. For example, a T-shirt manufacturer might be granted an NFL licensing agreement so that it can produce T-shirts with NFL logos on them. For this privilege, the company will have to pay NFL Properties a fee. It will also have to agree to certain standards of operation imposed to protect the NFL's reputation.

With global competition getting more keen, businesses must try to protect their products from theft

---

Life in the Multicultural Marketplace

Where Do I Stand?

The envelope of space that people maintain around themselves and into which they can tolerate no intrusion without backing up or feeling uncomfortable is called personal space. Personal space varies with culture. People from the Middle East stand closer together in business situations than Americans. Men may even touch arms or hold hands as a sign of trust. The Japanese, however, stand farther away from each other than their Western counterparts and are not inclined toward physical displays of friendship. Nearer to home, many Mexicans and other Latin Americans practice the traditional embrace (abrazo) and stand closer together during conversation. Backing away from someone whose culture considers close personal contact to be preferable can be interpreted as impolite.

Life in the Multicultural Marketplace centers on the kinds of cultural differences that can make or break a product, company, or business relationship when one is doing business abroad.

Caption (italic): Government competes with private businesses in a very limited number of cases. In the instances shown here, who are the government's competitors?

Competitor

There are three business operations that our government runs. They are the Tennessee Valley Authority (TVA), the U.S. Postal Service, and Amtrak. The TVA provides electricity to parts of the rural South. It was established during the Great Depression when private companies were unwilling to invest in dams and power plants for the area. The U.S. Postal Service provides mail delivery nationwide. There are several specialized delivery companies that now compete with the Postal Service—DHL, United Parcel Service (UPS), and Federal Express. Amtrak is a passenger rail service that was established under the Rail Passenger Act of 1970. The act was necessary because rail line owners no longer wanted to offer passenger service.

In addition to these major businesses, the U.S. government also runs national parks and campgrounds. It charges fees to enter the parks and use the camp facilities. In some cases these tourist attractions are in competition with privately owned tourist attractions.

The Role of the Consumer

Most of the goods and services produced in the United States are bought by consumers for personal use. Therefore, the role of the consumer must be part of any discussion of our free enterprise system.

Consumers do two major things in the marketplace. First, they pick the winners—the products and businesses that will be in the marketplace tomorrow. Second, they determine how much demand there is for any given product and thereby help determine prices.

Deciding Which Businesses Survive

The United States is known as a consumer-oriented society. This reflects the power that consumers have in the U.S. marketplace. It is consumers who decide which products will be produced and which companies will stay in business.

Consumers do this by shopping. Every time they make a purchase, they are "voting" with their dollars. The more votes (or sales) a product gets, the more likely the success of that product and the company that produces it. This ability to pick the businesses that will and will not survive makes consumers very powerful indeed in a free enterprise system.

Real World MARKETING

Fine and Tandy

When Charles Tandy offered to buy out their chain of nine ailing Ft. Worth electronics stores in 1963, the owners of Radio Shack were only too happy to take the money. However, Tandy had the knack for changing base metal to gold. Under his careful direction, Radio Shack blossomed into the world's largest consumer electronics design and testing organization, with 31 plants and 7,000 retail outlets.

Real World Marketing highlights fun facts about recent or historical developments in marketing.

Horse-Care Products—for Humans

Caption (italic): **Straight Arrow,** a Pennsylvania-based producer of animal-care products, is targeting humans with its latest offerings. The company has repackaged its horse shampoo, Mane 'n Tail, to sell to people!

Straight Arrow made the move after learning that horse owners were using the product themselves. In fact, research indicated that 10 out of 12 bottles of Mane 'n Tail were finding their way into shower stalls rather than stables.

Straight Arrow repositioned its horse shampoo by stressing that human hair could now look as good as a horse's mane. The company developed two new brands. One, Equenne, is sold in salons where it competes with Nexxus products. The other, Conceived by Nature, is sold in the mass market to drugstores and other mass merchandisers. There it competes with Procter & Gamble products like Head & Shoulders. With this strategy, Straight Arrow's sales went from $500,000 to $30 million in five years.

The company planned a multimillion dollar print and TV campaign to support its two new brands. In addition, there were promotions featuring product displays at horse shows and giveaways of Ford Mustang convertibles. The aim was to double sales in one year to $60 million.

Straight Arrow's confidence was probably justified. The company had a precedent in another of its products, a muscle-relaxing liniment called Mineral Ice. Bristol-Myers Squibb had been selling Mineral Ice to people since 1990.

The trend of shifting products from the horse to the human market actually goes back nearly 20 years. In the late 1970s, Barielle, a company that had developed and sold an item called Hoof Care, moved the product into department stores. For that market, it was packaged in one-ounce jars and given a French name—Crème Fortifiante Pour Les Ongles (nail strengthener). Soon after this transformation, the horse-care version was taken off the market. That's a move that Straight Arrow says it will never make.

Case Study Review

1. How did Straight Arrow implement the marketing concept?
2. What psychographic characteristic would most likely help segment the market for Straight Arrow's shampoos?
3. Identify the marketing mix for Equenne and Conceived by Nature. (You will have to speculate about price.)

A MATTER OF ETHICS

4. Is it ethical for companies like Barielle to stop making animal-care products because they can make more money selling the same products to humans?

Case Studies focus on a product, person, company, or trend that has succeeded in a special way. This feature includes follow-up questions including an "A Matter of Ethics" question that asks students to engage in ethical decision making.

Reinforcing Chapter Concepts

Chapter Review activities are designed to be flexible and to address the varying levels of students' abilities. Each review page is color-screened to make it easy to find for quick review or thorough study.

Vocabulary Review helps develop vocabulary and writing skills.

Performance Assessment includes role-play and creative hands-on performance activities. Role plays provide practice for DECA competition.

Application Projects allow students to apply chapter concepts to real-life situations.

CHAPTER *Review*

Critical Thinking activities ask students to analyze, compare, interpret, and apply basic concepts encountered in the text.

Optional Computer Application activities allow students to use spreadsheet, database, and word processing software to solve situations and problems.

Vocabulary Review

For each group of terms, write a paragraph explaining what the listed items have to do with the heading.

International Trade
balance of trade
imports
exports

Trade Concerns
tariff
quota
embargo

General Agreement on Tariffs and Trade (GATT)
North American Free Trade Agreement (NAFTA)
European Union (EU)

Fact and Idea Review

1. Why do nations trade with one another? (Sec. 7.1)
2. What are the advantages and disadvantages of international trade for producers and workers? (Sec. 7.1)
3. How does the United States monitor and control imports from other countries? (Sec. 7.2)
4. Why is it surprising that the United States has a negative balance of trade? (Sec. 7.2)
5. Why might a country impose trade barriers? (Sec. 7.2)
6. Assume a foreign business customer wants to buy U.S. goods but does not have all the money needed for the transaction. What trade support is available from a U.S. organization? (Sec. 7.2)
7. How are GATT, NAFTA, and the EU related? (Sec. 7.2)
8. Given the complex import/export rules in the United States and other countries, what specialists might a business hire to handle those transactions? (Sec. 7.3)
9. How are multinationals and mini-nationals different from each other? How are they similar?
10. Cite three examples of communication cultural differences that can make serving a foreign country more difficult than serving it domestically. (Sec. 7.3)

100   Unit 8   *Business and Marketing*

11. Cite an economic factor and a political factor that could discourage a business from engaging in international trade. (Sec. 7.3)

Critical Thinking

1. How have you personally benefited from international trade? (Sec. 7.1)
2. React to the following statement: International trade benefits no one.
5. Do you see anything wrong with countries and U.S. states that offer incentives, such as reduced taxes, to foreign investors but not to local businesses?
6. When a Japanese investor bought New York City's Rockefeller Center in the 1980s, it brought out the xenophobia in many U.S. citizens. (Xenophobia is hatred or distrust of foreigners.) Since foreign investment is supposed to be good for a country, why do you think these people reacted this way?
7. What measures could a business that wants to get involved in international trade take to avoid cultural blunders?

Building Academic Skills

Math
1. Assume the currency exchange rate between the United States and Canada is 1.25, which means one U.S. dollar is equal to $1.25 in Canadian currency. How much would a $20 T-shirt cost a U.S. citizen shopping in Montreal?

Communication
2. Change a current magazine ad, billboard, television or radio commercial so that it is appropriate for use in a

Building Academic Skills provide realistic, creative applications of chapter content to academic areas.

Human Relations
3. A customer wants to buy a silk blouse that matches her outfit perfectly—until she learns that the blouse was made in China. Her dilemma? She thinks Americans should buy only American-made products. What would you do?

Application Projects
1. Summarize an article related to one of the topics in this chapter. Review publications such as *International Business*, the *Economist*, *Europe*, *U.S. News & World Report*, *Business Week*, *Forbes*, and *Fortune*.
4. Research the trend among multinationals to forge strategic alliances with foreign companies. What are the reasons for these alliances, and what have been the outcomes?
5. How are foreign teenagers alike or different from U.S. teens? Research one country to find out. Determine which products foreign teens buy and how businesses market those products to them. Based on your research, identify a U.S. product that could be used to target teens in the country you are researching. Decide on the marketing mix (product, place, price, and promotion) for this target market. Prepare a written report of your research and marketing mix decisions, complete with rationale for each decision.
6. Identify the Economic G-7 countries, and find out why they meet every summer. Present your findings in a written report.

Linking School to Work
Ask your employer if your company is involved in international trade. If it is, find out the particulars of its involvement. If it is not involved directly, are there any products manufactured by foreign companies sold by your business? Write a short report of your findings, and share it with your classmates.

Performance Assessment

Role Play
Situation. You are an intern in a marketing firm that specializes in international trade. You have been asked to be part of an extensive training program for firm employees doing business in Japan. Your task is to instruct people in the proper way to exchange business cards.
Evaluation. You will be evaluated on how well you do the following:
- Identify the purpose of the training.
- Stress the importance of business cards.

Complete the Chapter 7 Computer Application that appears in the Student Activity Workbook.

Portfolio

Consider the Application Projects that you have done for this unit. Select one that illustrates your mastery of the unit's content and might be of interest to potential employers. Reformat the activity as necessary, adding any explanatory text, and place it in your Portfolio. Consider using these activities:
- Chapter 6, Application Projects 2–5
- Chapter 7, Application Project 5

Chapter 7   *The Global Marketplace*   101

Fact and Idea Review questions require students to review and recall chapter material.

Linking School to Work relates marketing content to students' on-the-job experiences.

Portfolio encourages students to plan and prepare for future employment by creating a marketing portfolio. A separate teacher's portfolio provides guidelines and assessment suggestions.

Introduction

Today's marketing students bring to the classroom a variety of learning styles and needs. The *Teacher's Wraparound Edition* offers a new teaching tool for marketing educators and is designed to assist both new and experienced teachers by providing a wealth of teaching suggestions, resources, and professional notes on current trends and pedagogy in marketing education.

The Four-Step Teaching Plan

The new *Marketing Essentials* is the first marketing text to offer the convenience of a wraparound format. The structure of the *Teacher's Wraparound Edition* places a four-step teaching plan, text answers, critical thinking activities, discussion questions, cooperative learning activities, as well as additional teaching notes on the same page as the related student text. Each chapter in the *Teacher's Wraparound Edition* is divided into four instructional sections according

to a mastery approach designed to help you develop the chapter concepts and materials in an organized, consistent manner. This widely accepted instructional method develops students' understanding of subject matter while providing a consistent framework that makes it easy for you to teach the material. The four steps in the plan are **Focus, Teach, Assess,** and **Close.**

1 *Focus*

In order to introduce new material, you first need to gain students' attention and interest. Therefore, the first step in the four-step process is to focus student interest through an activity that makes the material relevant to them and encourages them to want to continue to explore the

chapter. The **Focus** activity is designed to be completed within the first several minutes of class and provides a motivational lead-in to the concepts that will be presented later in the section.

2 Teach

The second section contains the central core of the lesson, encompassing a teaching plan designed to give you maximum flexibility to meet the learning needs of your class. The suggestions offered in this section employ a wide variety of approaches to support your classroom instruction. For example, you will find discussion starters to get the class involved in a specific topic, cooperative learning activities, critical thinking activities, and appropriate teaching activities at three different levels to relate the chapter content to other key subjects such as math, communications, problem-solving, decision-making, and human relations. In addition, other activities suitable for independent practice are here for you to assign as needed.

3 Assess

Because students have different learning styles and learn at differing rates, the **Assess** section provides a variety of evaluation and reteaching activities designed to accommodate a wide range of learning abilities. Reteaching provides a means of presenting the same concept in a different manner, allowing you to help students who might have difficulty understanding the material. Enrichment activities found here will allow you to enhance the learning experience for those who have mastered the section content and are ready for more in-depth, experiential learning. The Section Review activities fall into this category and provide you with a method of assessing students' comprehension before continuing with new information. The evaluation found in this section supplies you with a complete testing program which includes a testbank that allows you to individualize your tests to meet your curriculum needs.

4 Close

The final step in the teaching plan is to allow students to demonstrate to you what they have learned. This is accomplished through a wide variety of activities including vocabulary review, review questions, and answering questions and solving problems about the material in the section. **Close** provides you with an activity to summarize the section's contents and be sure students have retained the key points of each section.

Unit Planning Guide

The information in the Unit Planning Guide gives you a comprehensive overview of the unit content along with the background information that will help you provide the best possible learning situation for your class. Using these pages, you can easily identify unit objectives, chapter learning objectives, and the resources available to you for each chapter in the unit. Refer to these pages as you plan each lesson in order to make the most of the numerous instructional material included with *Marketing Essentials*.

Unit Objectives An itemized list presents the performance-based objectives each student should be able to achieve once the unit is completed.

Teacher Classroom Resources A comprehensive list of chapter resources provides a quick reference for planning your instruction.

Unit 3 Planning Guide

Business and Marketing Essentials

Unit Objectives

After completing this unit, students will be able to achieve the following outcomes:

- Tell what a business is and explain its basic functions.
- Discuss business ethics and areas in which businesses are thought to have social responsibility.
- Identify demographic, geographic, and psychographic trends in the U.S. consumer market.
- Distinguish the consumer and industrial markets.
- Discuss the importance of international trade to nations and describe the ways governments can both thwart and encourage it.
- Explain how businesses can get involved in international trade and what factors they should consider before doing so.

Chapter 7

Chapter 5

Chapter 6

57a

Teacher Classroom Resources

CHAPTER	5	6	7
Transparency Binder	Transparencies 7a & 7b	Transparencies 8–11a & 11b	Transparency 12
Student Activity Workbook	pp. 25–30	pp. 31–36	pp. 37–42
Student Software	pp. 29–30	pp. 35–36	pp. 41–42
Marketing Math Workbook			Activity 3
School-to-Work Handbook	pp. 15–16	pp. 17–18	pp. 19–20
International Case Studies	pp. 15–16	pp. 17–18	pp. 19–20
Marketing Career Portfolio			Unit 3 activity, Student Text, p. 101
Test Booklet/ Testmaker Software	Chapter 5 test	Chapter 6 test	Chapter 7 test, Unit 3 test

KEY TO BASIC SKILLS ACTIVITIES

L1 Level 1 activities are basic activities and should be within the range of all students.

L2 Level 2 activities are average activities and should be within the range of average and above average students.

L3 Level 3 activities are challenging activities designed for the ability range of above average students.

Key to Basic Skills' Activities Explanation of the different levels of activities used throughout the *Teacher's Wraparound Edition* to allow you to customize activities to class competency level or to allow you to assign these activities to individual students on the basis of personal ability.

Performance Objectives Specific performance objectives for each section of every chapter in the unit.

Individual Course Objectives Local and state course objectives can be referenced for planning your instruction.

Features and Activities A thorough list of the features and activites that have been created for each chapter.

Unit 3 Organizer

CHAPTER	PERFORMANCE OBJECTIVES	OBJECTIVES state	local	FEATURES	ACTIVITIES
5 **Business and Social Responsibility**	5.1 1. Tell what a business is. 2. Explain the basic functions of a business. 3. Distinguish businesses from each other based on general characteristics. 5.2 1. Name the areas in which businesses are thought to have social responsibilities. 2. List some of the ways that business activities have impacted our environment. 3. Define ethics and suggest how marketers can make ethical choices. 4. Define consumerism and provide a brief history of the movement. 5. Describe current trends that are likely to improve the workplace for employees.			• Case Study: Newman's Own, p. 66 • Bright Ideas: Catch the Wave, p. 67 • Life in the Multicultural Marketplace: What's in a Name? p. 61 • Real World Marketing: Big Brother Is Watching (TV), p. 65	• Case Study Questions, p. 66 • A Matter of Ethics, p. 66 • Creativity Challenge, p. 67 • Section 5.1 Review, p. 63 • Section 5.2 Review, p. 69 • Chapter Review, pp. 70–71
6 **The Domestic Marketplace**	6.1 1. Identify demographic, geographic, and psychographic trends in the U.S. consumer market. 2. Suggest products and marketing strategies that can reach the diverse segments within that market. 6.2 1. Explain the concept of derived demand. 2. List the six major types of businesses that comprise the industrial market. 3. Suggest products that each major industrial market group might need to purchase.			• Case Study: Selling in a Multicultural Nation, p. 77 • Bright Ideas: Do the Opposite, p. 83 • Life in the Multicultural Marketplace: A Touchy Moment, p. 73 • Real World Marketing: A Woman's Touch, p. 79	• Case Study Questions, p. 77 • A Matter of Ethics, p. 77 • Creativity Challenge, p. 83 • Section 6.1 Review, p. 81 • Section 6.2 Review, p. 83 • Chapter Review, pp. 84–85
7 **The Global Marketplace**	7.1 1. Distinguish imports from exports. 2. Discuss the interdependence of nations. 3. Explain the advantages and disadvantages of international trade. 7.2 1. Discuss the U.S. balance of trade. 2. Identify three types of trade barriers. 3. Explain the various forms of trade support. 4. Name the major agreements governing world trade today. 7.3 1. Identify the three general types of activities businesses engage in when they get involved in international trade. 2. Explain some of the standard business practices involved in importing and exporting products. 3. Discuss the cultural, economic, and political factors that should be considered when deciding whether to do business abroad.			• Case Study: Pepsi Max, p. 92 • Bright Ideas: Expand Your Focus, p. 98 • Life in the Multicultural Marketplace: When Cards Are No Game, p. 96 • Real World Marketing: Do You Speak Capitalist? p. 87	• Case Study Questions, p. 92 • A Matter of Ethics, p. 92 • Creativity Challenge, p. 98 • Section 7.1 Review, p. 89 • Section 7.2 Review, p. 94 • Section 7.3 Review, p. 99 • Chapter Review, pp. 100–101

Using the Teacher's Wraparound Edition

The new *Teacher's Wraparound Edition* of *Marketing Essentials* provides you and your students with a wide range of activities to fit your classroom needs. The *Teacher's Wraparound Edition* also contains additional resource material "wrapped around" the actual student pages. It has been designed as a convenience for you and to allow you to maximize the program's effectiveness.

Unit Overview and Background Information previews unit content.

Introducing the Unit presents the unit content through activities that help spark student interest.

Unit Project offers a hands-on project related to the unit content.

Classroom Management lists all the resources available through the *Marketing Essentials* program.

Human Resource Essentials

Resources for Enrichment of Unit Content lists resources related to the unit content.

Unit Closure provides a concluding activity that summarizes the unit content.

Evaluation refers you to the Testmaker software or reproducible test provided for each unit.

Focus on the Photo/Cooperative Learning activities get students thinking about the first photo in the unit and how it relates to the material.

Guest Speaker Suggestions provide ideas of types of individuals you may consider inviting to speak to the class to further students' appreciation of unit materials.

Field Trip Suggestions offer suggestions on places to go to help students understand the real-world applications of unit content.

Understanding the Lesson

Each chapter contains two or three sections. You will find lesson plans for each section in the *Teacher's Wraparound Edition*. Lesson plans consistently follow the four-step teaching plan (Focus, Teach, Assess, and Close).

Focus

Bell Ringer Activity helps students "switch gears" from their previous class and focus on the task at hand.

Introducing the Section gives you a way to dive into section material.

Section Review Answers provide answers to section review questions.

Assess

Evaluate provides an opportunity for you to assign and review the Section Review material.

Reteaching activities help reinforce section concepts.

Enrichment activities extend students' understanding of the section.

Bright Ideas give additional information about this feature.

More About notes elaborate on chapter features.

Caption Answer provides answers to caption questions.

Teach

Guided Practice offers step-by-step strategies for teaching section material.

Discussion Starter helps you involve students in section material.

Critical Thinking and Cooperative Learning activities are designed to help students help each other and increase their critical thinking skills.

Skill Building Activities are offered in five subject areas: math, communication, human relations, problem solving, and decision making. They are written at three different levels.

Close

In the final exercise students summarize key concepts covered in the section.

Meeting Special Needs offers ways to teach students with special needs.

Lifelong Learning suggests ways students can further develop their skills.

 Did You Know features are short, factual blurbs about the chapter content.

Target Your Classroom Needs with Program Resources

The *Marketing Essentials* program offers a variety of teacher support materials to enable you to tailor the material to meet the needs of your students. These resources will allow you to meet your course objectives and maximize student learning.

New! Teacher's Wrap-around Edition is the first marketing text to offer a wrap-around format! The new format places a four-step teaching plan, text answers, critical thinking activities, discussion questions, cooperative learning activities, as well as additional margin notes, all conveniently located on the same page with the related student text. No more searching through the book for the information you need. It's all at your fingertips.

TEACHER'S WRAPAROUND EDITION

Marketing Essentials

SECOND EDITION

Lois Farese
Grady Kimbrell
Carl Woloszyk

LESSON PLANS
INCLUDES: • Chapter Lesson Plans
• Chapter Outlines

Marketing Essentials

SECOND EDITION

Lois Farese
Grady Kimbrell
Carl Woloszyk

MARKETING MATH WORKBOOK
TEACHER'S ANNOTATED EDITION
INCLUDES: • Marketing Math Pretest
• Math Activities for Each Unit
• Answers for Each Activity

Marketing Essentials

SECOND EDITION

Lois Farese

Marketing Math Workbook with Teacher's Annotated Edition offers supplementary math activities for every unit in the student text, plus convenient pretests and numeric key-pad drills.

New! Lesson Plans give you a preprinted listing of all the objectives and teaching options available for each chapter of the student text. This valuable resource simplifies lesson-planning and saves you time.

Student Activity Workbook with Teacher's Annotated Edition provides vocabulary, factual review, marketing applications, and optional computer activities using commercial spreadsheet, database, and word processing programs. Templates are available for both Macintosh and DOS environments.

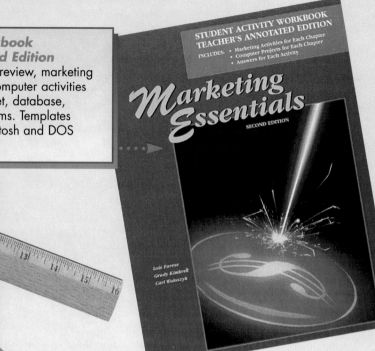

STUDENT ACTIVITY WORKBOOK
TEACHER'S ANNOTATED EDITION
INCLUDES: • Marketing Activities for Each Chapter
• Computer Projects for Each Chapter
• Answers for Each Activity

Marketing Essentials
SECOND EDITION

Lois Farese
Grady Kimbrell
Carl Woloszyk

MARKETING CAREER
PORTFOLIO
LINKING SCHOOL TO WORK
INCLUDES: • Portfolio Development and
Management Ideas
• Assessment Suggestions
• Transparency Masters
• Student Portfolio Contents
— Marketing Competencies
— Employability Skills
— Career Goals
— Service and Leadership
— Model Employment Letters
— Model Resume
— Job Application Form

Marketing Essentials
SECOND EDITION

Lois Farese
Grady Kimbrell
Carl Woloszyk

New! Marketing Career Portfolio features guidelines for helping students develop, assess, and manage portfolios that can showcase their employability skills gained in class using the *Marketing Essentials* components.

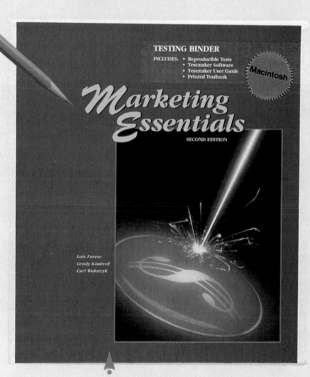

TESTING BINDER
INCLUDES: • Reproducible Tests
• Testmaker Software
• Testmaker User Guide
• Printed Testbank

Macintosh

Marketing Essentials
SECOND EDITION

Lois Farese
Grady Kimbrell
Carl Woloszyk

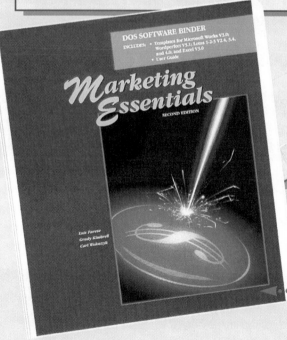

DOS SOFTWARE BINDER
INCLUDES: • Templates for Microsoft Works V3.0;
Wordperfect V5.1; Lotus 1-2-3 V2.4, 3.4,
and 4.0; and Excel V5.0
• User Guide

Marketing Essentials
SECOND EDITION

Lois Farese
Grady Kimbrell
Carl Woloszyk

New! Marketing Software Binder provides optional computer activities using spreadsheet, database, and word processing programs. Templates are available for both Macintosh and DOS.

Testing Binders provide you with a complete testing program in multiple formats. Each binder contains Testmaker software and documentation in DOS, Macintosh, or Apple format; a printed testbank of all test questions; and a booklet of reproducible chapter and unit tests.

New! International Case Studies combines international marketing news stories from major publications, such as *The Wall Street Journal* and *The New York Times,* with applications and critical thinking questions. Use this resource to provide students with practical applications on the important topic of international marketing.

New! Transparency Binder contains more than 70 transparencies of text illustrations with teaching suggestions. Transparencies are ideal for reteaching and reinforcing key text concepts.

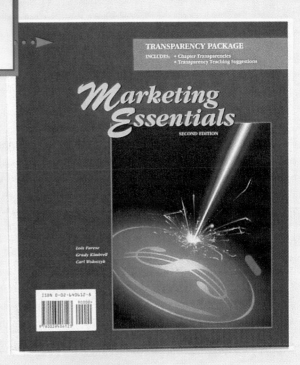

New! Marketing Simulation gives students the opportunity to bring the real world of marketing and decision making into the classroom. Optional software is available.

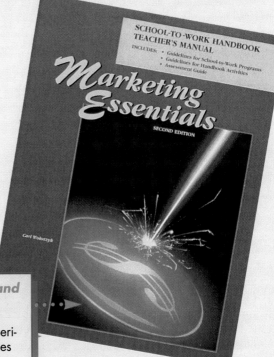

New! School-to-Work Handbook and Teacher's Manual provides reproducible worksheets for students to use to help them relate their class work to their on-the-job experience. An extensive *Teacher's Manual* provides you with guidelines for integrating marketing and school-to-work programs based on the Michigan School-to-Work program, a Rubic Assessment for each activity, and suggested student responses.

Integrating Computer Technology into Marketing Education

Pick up almost any newspaper or magazine today and you are sure to see headlines about computer technology—from the latest fad in computer games to how to do business on the Internet. Marketing is at the very heart of this technology, as manufacturers, software developers, and technology service providers all try to find new customers and new ways to use their products. Our economic society is rapidly changing from an industrial to an information-based society. As a result, your students' future marketing careers will all be touched by computer technology.

With an overwhelming variety of business and personal software programs, and enough "edutainment" software to fill the shelves of most computer stores, it is difficult to know what technology to use in your classroom. In addition, lack of time and money for hardware and software create limitations on integrating computer technology into your marketing program. The suggestions made here will get you started, and you will likely discover other ways of bringing technology to life for your marketing students.

> *Your students' future marketing careers will all be touched by computer technology.*

TEXTBOOK ACTIVITIES

New to this edition is an entire chapter on computers. Chapter 10, Computer Technology, gives students a thorough introduction to computers and provides information on the latest marketing uses for computers.

In addition, many chapters in the student textbook have technology-related activities in an end-of-chapter section called **Building Academic Skills**. By completing these activities, students will gain a greater awareness of the potential uses of technology in marketing. The activities give students an opportunity to learn how computer technology is used in gathering information and analyzing it for marketing decision making.

WORKBOOK ACTIVITIES

The *Student Activity Workbook* accompanying *Marketing Essentials* includes an optional computer activity for each chapter in the textbook. These computer activities require students to use commercial software programs for word processing, database, or spreadsheet applications. Template disks contain basic data for each of the activities, and students use this data plus the workbook directions and information to complete a marketing activity. In addition, activity questions require students to interpret their calculations or activity results and to extrapolate the information to broader marketing situations.

The spreadsheet activities are structured to allow students to learn basic functions and to input simple formulas to complete calculations. A quick reference guide to spreadsheet functions for popular commercial programs is included at the back of the *Student Activity Workbook*.

MATH WORKBOOK

Chapter 10 of the *Marketing Math Workbook* contains basic information about spreadsheets, including how to set up a spreadsheet, saving and retrieving spreadsheet files, and writing basic formulas. Activities give students an opportunity to apply their skills in designing spreadsheets and performing calculations using commercial software programs.

MARKETING SIMULATION

Completing a marketing simulation is another opportunity for students to apply their learning by developing marketing ideas and to use their creativity in competing with other students to solve marketing problems. Several activities within the simulation can be completed using commercial software programs. A teacher's guide includes suggestions for implementing and assessing the simulation.

OTHER RESOURCES

Several outside resources may be available to help you bring technology to your students. Among these resources are online services, newspapers and magazines, and school resources.

● *Online Services.* If your school has access to an online service, schedule a time to have the service demonstrated to your students. Online services are an excellent way of showing students how to access a database and conduct research. One online service to check out is the National Student Research Center. Using the National Public Telecomputing Network (TELNET), students can pay a visit to an electronic library and review abstracts on a variety of topics. If your school has access to TELNET and you want more information on the National Research Center, contact John Swang electronically at *nsrcmms@aol.com* or write to John Swang at the Mandeville Middle School in Mandeville, Louisiana.

● *Newspapers and Magazines.* Find newspaper and magazine articles that describe how technology has changed product development or the marketing of a product. For example, you might find an article about a local bank's electronic services or visit a local bank and ask for brochures describing its electronic services. Ask students to read the brochures and analyze how technology not only changed the services offered, but also the jobs of people in the bank. For example, with more automated services, fewer tellers are needed so the bank may be able to hire more people to provide financial planning and loan services.

Another way you might bring technology into the classroom is to find out whether local newspaper and magazine vendors would be willing to donate their unsold issues of computer magazines to your school. Have students find examples in the magazines of how technology affects the marketing of products. For example, many articles have been written about the information highway and how businesses are using it. In one case, the makers of Aquafresh toothpaste recently used the Internet to offer free samples of a new whitening toothpaste.

● *Shared School Resources.* Introduce your students to technology by planning shared activities with your school's computer, keyboarding, or accounting teachers. For example, when your students are studying financial planning and business plans, you might plan an activity with an accounting class that is also studying financial statements. Pair an accounting student with a marketing student and have them go through the process of entering accounting data and analyzing financial statements. Your marketing students will discover how financial records are kept via computer, while the accounting students will learn how financial data affects marketing decisions.

PLAN A "MARKET DAY"

Get your students involved in technology by having them plan a fund-raising event to raise money to buy either computer hardware or software for your marketing program.

Whether they actually conduct the event or not, students can use computers to create a plan, anticipate its results, and analyze what they can buy with the money. For example, students can use word processing software to write a description of their planned Market Day to be published in the school and local newspapers. They might also write letters to be sent to potential customers. Spreadsheet software can be used to list the products, their costs and sale prices, and the expected volume of sales. Students can analyze total potential earnings and decide what equipment or software to buy. If students plan telemarketing as part of their fund raising, they can explore databases by determining the best customers for their products and how they might find a database of these customers and their telephone numbers. For example, they might contact a local business organization and ask about their membership list.

PREPARE FOR DECA EVENTS

Encourage students to use computers in preparing for DECA activities. If you do not have classroom computers or your school does not have a computer lab, check with your local libraries. Many public libraries have computers available for patron use.

Using Cooperative Learning

Americans live and work in a heterogeneous society. Success and happiness in our professional and personal lives are largely dependent on our abilities to interact positively with others. Your marketing course provides many opportunities for students to learn and apply the skills necessary for positive interpersonal relationships. Cooperative learning allows students to work together toward a common goal as they take greater responsibility for their own learning and for the learning of others. They work in small groups of mixed-ability students, sharing ideas and learning academic material, and completing educational tasks. Cooperative learning enables you, the instructor, to empower your students for a life-long process of building, promoting, and sustaining positive interpersonal relationships.

> *Cooperative learning allows students to take greater responsibility for their own learning and for the learning of others.*

BENEFITS OF COOPERATIVE LEARNING

Cooperative learning offers many benefits including the following:

- People who help each other and work together toward a common goal generally begin to feel more positive about each other and interact constructively when performing collective tasks.
- Cooperative learning increases academic achievement and develops essential social skills.
- Students learn better when they are actively involved in the learning process.

- Students learn to work as a team. Not only must they learn the material themselves, but also they are responsible for helping everyone in the group master the skills and content.
- Students share equally the responsibilities for accomplishing a common goal. The successes or failures of the group are shared by all members of the group.
- While interacting with other students, individual learning and accountability is promoted.
- Students do not feel as isolated and they gain self-esteem.
- Students feel learning is important, valuable, and fun; and they like school. Often, attendance improves.
- Students draw upon their own creativity and on the strengths of their teammates.
- Schools with racially or ethnically mixed populations realize improved race relations among students and improved multicultural relationships.
- Students have the opportunity to perceive other students as colleagues rather than competitors. As a result, they recognize the value of helping others rather than working competitively.
- Students improve intergroup and interpersonal relationships. Specifically, they learn how to offer opinions, how to disagree with other team members, and how to work in cooperative environments. They learn to respect the opinions and feelings of others.

STRUCTURES

A variety of structures can be used to implement cooperative learning. Some of the most widely used learning modes in cooperative learning are described below. You can adapt these structures to fit the course content and your own teaching style.

- *Student Teams Achievement (STAD).* Students are assigned to teams, the teacher presents the lesson to the class as a whole, then the teams work together to make sure all members understand the information. Weekly quizzes assess student achievement.
- *Team-Games Tournament (TGT).* This learning mode is similar to STAD except that weekly quizzes are replaced with weekly tournaments (or competitions).
- *Jigsaw.* The teacher divides an assignment into separate and unique parts (one for each team member). Each team member works independently to gather the necessary information. Through the cooperation of everyone on the team, the information is collected, organized, and reported back to the class.
- *Jigsaw II.* This learning mode is more demanding for the students because the team is given the entire assignment and the team members determine how the tasks and responsibilities will be divided.
- *Learning Together.* Students work together to complete an activity and produce a finished product.
- *Group Investigation.* Students accept greater responsibility because they decide what they will learn, how they will organize their group to accomplish the task, and how they will share what they learn with the rest of the class.

TEACHER RESPONSIBILITIES

The teacher is responsible for preparing the students for the cooperative learning process. The following will help you establish an effective cooperative learning environment.

- Assign students to heterogeneous groups of four to six. Mix the group in ability, sex, and ethnicity.
- Coordinate the efforts of all participants in the group.
- Arrange the classroom so students can face each other as they work.
- Set the task and goal structure and make sure the team goal is well defined and understood.
- Provide the appropriate materials.
- Discuss cooperation and social skills, encourage all students to participate, and express the need to support team members.
- Monitor student interaction. Intervene when necessary to mediate or solve problems and teach skills.
- Evaluate student outcomes.

STUDENT RESPONSIBILITIES

Students also have responsibilities in cooperative learning. In order to accomplish a goal as a team, students must:

- work toward group goals, yet understand that individual accountability is expected;
- contribute their own ideas;
- understand that they are responsible for one another's learning as well as their own;
- have tolerance for individual differences;
- draw upon their own creativity and on the strengths of their teammates;
- communicate effectively with one another; and
- recognize that the differences among team members are a form of enrichment rather than deficits.

COOPERATIVE LEARNING IN THIS TEXT

Marketing Essentials provides many opportunities for cooperative learning. Activities in this text, such as **Bright Ideas**, are already designed as group activities. You can easily adapt others. For example, assign the students to work in pairs to discuss and complete the activities for the **Vocabulary Review** and the **Fact and Idea Review**. Cooperative learning is especially effective for more difficult learning tasks such as problem solving and critical thinking. Break students into groups of four and ask each group to complete the **Critical Thinking** and **Application Projects** activities and present their findings to the class.

The *Teacher's Wraparound Edition* also provides opportunities for cooperative learning. Each unit opens with an activity that asks students to work as a group to answer questions about the unit photo. These activities can be used to prepare the students for what they will be learning in the chapter; or they can be used as a follow-up to the chapter, reteaching the concepts or summarizing and applying what has been presented. In addition, suggestions for implementing a second cooperative learning activity are included for each chapter of the *Teacher's Wraparound Edition.*

EVALUATING COOPERATIVE LEARNING ACTIVITIES

After group assignments are completed, students can be evaluated through testing and applications and scored individually or as a group. Evaluation tools may include traditional tests or quizzes and group tests and quizzes. Students can be awarded points for both individual and team progress when they improve their own past performance, and cumulative team points can earn rewards for the entire group.

▶ Using Alternative Assessment

As a marketing educator, you help your students to gain an understanding of marketing and the role it plays in our economy. One of the traditional ways of measuring your students' progress toward meeting the course objectives is a written test that evaluates a student's recall and ability to answer questions about marketing content. In today's educational environment, however, there is a need to assess far more than students' rote learning skills. New curriculum objectives focus on the acquisition of knowledge and skills that will help students function in the work world, such as critical thinking, problem solving, communications, and human relations skills. The acquisition of those skills is not so easily evaluated using the traditional paper-and-pencil test.

In addition, your students have many different learning styles and different means of expressing their knowledge and skills. The combination of different learning styles and the need to evaluate students' skills calls for new, or alternative, methods of assessment.

Alternative assessment techniques require students to "do" something; that is, to demonstrate their knowledge by actually performing a task or creating a project. Observation of how the student performs the task or uses critical-thinking and problem-solving skills to complete a project constitute the assessment of performance.

> *Your students have many different learning styles and different means of expressing their knowledge and skills.*

PERFORMANCE ASSESSMENT

The assessment of performance evaluates how well a student performs a specific task. For example, in a simulated real-life role play, how does the student perform in responding to a customer's complaint? Or, how does the student handle a work-related conflict with another person? A paper-and-pencil test will not demonstrate your students' skills in this area.

The *Marketing Essentials* textbook provides a multitude of activities, projects, and situations that will help you to create opportunities for alternative assessment. Each chapter has a special feature entitled **Bright Ideas** that challenges students to use their creativity in developing new product or promotion ideas. Within the end-of-chapter activities is a section entitled **Performance Assessment** that contains suggested activities for role plays, oral presentations, computer applications, and demonstrations of marketing knowledge such as setting up a display or creating a graphic to communicate information. **Application Projects** and a chapter **Case Study** provide other opportunities for assessment. Suggestions for portfolio activities also are included in the student textbook. A separate publication, described below, provides suggestions to help you implement student portfolio activities.

STUDENT PORTFOLIO

Suggestions for helping your students develop an employability portfolio are contained in an ancillary called *Marketing Career Portfolio*. An employability portfolio is developed throughout the marketing course and is intended to be taken to a prospective employer to demonstrate a student's acquisition of marketing knowledge and general skills needed to succeed in a marketing career.

The *Marketing Career Portfolio* contains a teacher's resource booklet with suggestions for managing the portfolio development process, descriptions of each part of the suggested student portfolio, model documents, and suggestions for documents that students should include in their portfolios. Among the suggested materials for students to include in their portfolios are documents demonstrating marketing competencies, employability skills, career goals, service and leadership activities, employment letters, resume, and a job application form.

OBSERVATION AND QUESTIONING

You can observe each student's ability to work independently. You can also observe students' communication, human relations, and teamwork skills as they interact in cooperative learning groups or within a whole-class setting.

Questioning is also an excellent tool for assessing the competence of students and monitoring the development of meaningful understanding of concepts.

The *Marketing Essentials* program provides you with numerous opportunities to observe and question as part of the assessment process. Each textbook chapter includes activities to help you assess your students' progress in developing the following skills:

Critical Thinking Every chapter has "thought" questions that require students to apply reasoning and problem-solving techniques. Listening to students' comments and answers to these questions helps you gain insight into their understanding.

Cooperative Learning Use the **Bright Ideas** chapter feature to get students involved in generating ideas and developing solutions as a group. Other possibilities for small group work are the end-of-chapter application projects.

Problem Solving **Building Academic Skills** provides opportunities for students to analyze situations and information to solve problems. Computer applications also provide opportunities for students to analyze database, word processing, and spreadsheet problems.

Communications and Human Relations Textbook chapters also include activities requiring students to communicate orally—in small groups, in a role play, or in a class presentation—and to demonstrate their human relations skills through class interactions and role plays. In addition, specific suggestions for observing and questioning are included in the side columns of the *Teacher's Wraparound Edition.*

PRESENTATIONS AND PROJECTS

Among the skills students will need in their marketing careers are the ability to make oral presentations and to write reports. The *Marketing Essentials* textbook provides many suggestions for both oral and written presentations. Each student chapter has a section called **Application Projects** that includes a variety of activities that allow you to evaluate students' writing and oral communication skills. These projects also allow you to assess students' abilities in collecting information, organizing it in a logical flow, analyzing its meaning and applying it to the solution of a particular marketing situation.

Specific suggestions for projects are also included in the *Teacher's Wraparound Edition* in the **Guided Practice, Cooperative Learning, Enrichment,** and **Independent Practice** activities.

STUDENT SELF-ASSESSMENT

Another benefit of alternative assessment is the opportunity for your students to participate in assessing their own growth in learning. To help students participate in the assessment process, you must clearly explain the goals of the course and the criteria against which student performance will be measured.

At the beginning of the school year, you may want to develop a self-assessment form with your students. List the course goals and the evaluation criteria on the form. Help students to think in terms of evaluating their own course work, their attitudes and habits, their strengths and weaknesses, their accomplishments, and their own personal goals. Ask students to report to you periodically on their progress. You may want to have students write a short report (a page) describing their progress to include in a portfolio. For example, the report could explain why a document is included in the portfolio and how this document demonstrates the student's progress toward meeting a specific goal.

Tony Freeman/PhotoEdit

Teaching Critical Thinking Skills

The process of teaching students critical thinking skills is a goal of education in all disciplines and is of tremendous value to marketing students. Today's business environment—be it a corporate setting, self-employment, or a small business—is highly competitive and demands skilled employees. Your students will be a part of this business environment, competing for positions. One of the differentiating factors in achieving success in the workforce is an individual's ability to deal with the varied demands of the fast-paced world of business that requires insightful decision making, creative problem solving, and interactions with diverse groups, be it employees, management, investors, customers, or clients. By teaching your students critical thinking you are equipping them with essential skills necessary for acheiving success in today's workforce.

Critical thinking is the process of reasonably, or logically deciding what to do or believe. Critical thinking involves the ability to

- **compare and contrast,**
- **solve problems,**
- **make decisions,**
- **analyze and evaluate,**
- **synthesize and transfer knowledge, and**
- **conduct metacognitive exercises.**

> *By teaching your students critical thinking you are equipping them with essential skills necessary for achieving success in today's workforce.*

Critical thinking skills are important for the following reasons:
- Critical thinking skills help students investigate their own ways of solving problems and finding creative resolutions.

- Critical thinking skills lead students to investigations that compare and contrast what they know with unknowns.
- Critical thinking skills allow students to make decisions about their own learning and also make them aware of the processes they use.

HOW TO TEACH CRITICAL THINKING

How, then, do we teach critical thinking? Doesn't all learning require thinking? What is meant by higher-level thinking? These questions and questions like them require teachers to reflect on the instructional strategies used in daily lessons and include opportunities for students to reason and think about what is being learned.

All learning does require thinking. Benjamin Bloom's Taxonomy of the Cognitive Domain is probably the most widely recognized schema for levels of thinking.

Each of Bloom's cognitive categories includes a list of a variety of thinking skills and indicates the kind of behavior students are to perform at the objectives or goals of specific learning tasks. Here are some examples.

- *Knowledge:* define, recognize, recall, identify, label, understand, examine, show, collect
- *Comprehension:* translate, interpret, explain, describe, summarize, extrapolate
- *Application:* apply, solve, experiment, show, predict
- *Analysis:* connect, relate, differentiate, classify, arrange, check, group, distinguish, organize, categorize, detect, compare, infer
- *Synthesis:* produce, propose, design, plan, combine, formulate, compose, hypothesize, construct
- *Evaluation:* appraise, judge, criticize, decide

The wealth of activities and guidance provided both in the student text and this *Teacher's Wraparound Edition* will help you integrate critical thinking skills into your daily plans. Below are some guidelines for integrating and teaching these skills.
- *Let students know* they are engaging in aspects of critical thinking, be it comparison/contrast analysis, evaluation, synthesis, or determining relationships, such as cause-effect.

EXAMPLE: If you have groups of students analyze a business letter for its purpose (to inform, entertain, or persuade), as you might in Chapter 9, tell the students that they are analyzing. You should also broaden the application of this skill to other areas of the students' lives—they constantly analyze music, conversations with their friends, articles they read in magazines, television programs. This will help demonstrate to students that they have had experience in using the skill.

- *Use activities that focus* on open-ended problems. Activities with no "right answers" open up the possibilities and foster greater growth and a safe environment for using creative approaches to problem solving.

EXAMPLE: Have students in groups compare and contrast two reports written by an employee, to a supervisor, offering suggestions for improving the time it takes to respond to customer orders in a mail-order business. Then, have the groups draft their own report which could be a presentation, a cause-effect study, a report in a different format. In this way, you introduce several major skills: comparison/contrast, evaluation of a product, creation of a better product (creative problem solving).

- *Organize your students* in cooperative learning groups so that they can see how others solve problems, give each other feedback, and try out new ideas in a safe environment.

Joe Cornish/Tony Stone Images

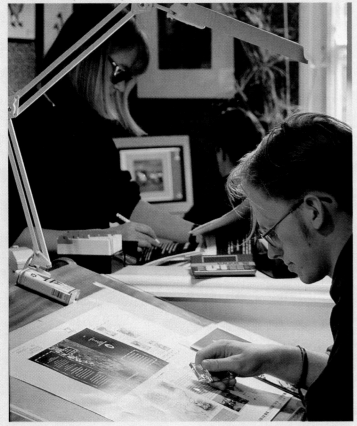

EXAMPLE: Have students in groups prepare a statement that will accompany a presentation to a client. Assign different organization patterns to each group (enumeration, generalization with examples, cause and effect, comparison/contrast). After each group completes its statement, have the entire class analyze the effectiveness of the statements and discuss ways that presentations can be hampered or helped by these materials.

- *Provide feedback* and use assessments that measure students' growth and performance in their newly acquired skills. Your feedback is important in encouraging students to feel comfortable experimenting with new ideas and new ways to look at problem solving and critical thinking.

EXAMPLE: Using the above example, each student could write his or her own written statement. In this way you allow an individual response which will better measure each student's growth and understanding of the skills.

Examples of questions that promote thinking at various levels are shown below. Questions such as those listed can be used to promote and stimulate critical thinking.

Knowledge—the identification and recall of information:
- **Who, what, when, where, how…?**
- **Describe…**

Comprehension—the organization and selection of facts and ideas:
- **Retell in your own words…**
- **What is the main idea of…?**

Application—the use of facts, rules, principles:
- **How is…an example of…?**
- **How is…related to…?**

Analysis—the separation of a whole into component parts:
- **What are the parts or features…?**
- **Classify…according to…**
- **How does…compare/contrast with…?**

Synthesis—the combination of ideas to form a new whole:
- **What would you predict/infer from…?**
- **What might happen if you combined…with…?**

Evaluation—the development of opinions, judgements, or decisions:
- **What do you think about…?**
- **Prioritize…**

All these suggestions, and others you find throughout this resource, will help you guide your students to a more productive and successful performance in their professional lives through the use of critical thinking.

Building Academic Skills

To succeed as marketing professionals students need a range of specific skills and training. Among the skills your students will need in order to compete in the Workforce 2000 are general strengths in communications, human relations, technology, and math. For example, all marketing professionals need to know how to write letters, scripts for presentations, work orders, or proposals; how to read memos, letters, and reports; how to speak coherently with a purpose or goal in mind; how to interact effectively with co-workers, and how to perform simple mathematics functions. Basic academic skills will support your students in completing tasks and roles, such as these, that their jobs will demand.

ACADEMICS IN THE MARKETING CURRICULUM

It is as important to foster your students' learning in academic areas as it is to make sure they have a firm foundation in marketing. Integrating academic skills into the marketing classroom can easily be done by making them a regular part of your classroom activities. For example, by having students read class assignments and texts, write letters and reports, give presentations, and perform mathematics exercises you are helping them improve their academic skills. All these activities include the academic skills that we want to foster in our students and are a natural part of the marketing curriculum.

Class assignments should include a component of these skills as part of your on-going evaluation of students' progress. For example, if you ask your students to prepare a report, and a requirement is that there are no typographical errors, you have built accuracy and attention to detail in the technical area of word processing or data entry into your assessment requirements.

Below are some specific ways in which you can effectively emphasize the academic skills your students need.

- *Identify students who need extra help* in academic areas. Early identification of students who need help in academic areas increases their chances of success in your course. Taking a writing sample the first day of class, giving a preliminary reading comprehension exercise, asking students to tell about themselves during your first class— all will give you indications of your students' levels of experience. Writing clinics, developmental courses, tutoring, and peer counseling are all formal ways to assist your

students in areas of weakness.

EXAMPLE: On the first day of class, have students write about their previous and current job experiences and how they might relate to marketing. In these samples you will collect information about individual students that will help you relate to them better, you will collect information about their previous experiences that can help them relate course content to their prior learning and you can determine who has difficulties with writing.

- *Incorporate academic skills* in your class assignments and activities. Emphasizing the importance of academic skills in your classroom will impress upon your students that these skills are necessary. As you talk about assignments, identify for students which academic areas they will be using. In this way they can identify the tasks required and the strategies they will need to complete the assignment satisfactorily.

> *It is as important to foster your students' learning in academic areas as it is to make sure they have a firm foundation in marketing.*

EXAMPLE: To help students learn how to market themselves, have them prepare a written description of their abilities that they would use as a basis for an interview. Tell them the description will also be part of a written application, and they will be evaluated on 1) a mock interview and 2) the written statement. Discuss the qualities of an effective written statement and positive interview skills before they begin the assignment, and evaluate them on how well they meet the standards.

- *Use assessments* that require and incorporate academic skills. For example, when you require that students comprehend what they're reading, write coherently, or adhere to principles of public speaking when they give a presentation, you are again reinforcing the skills needed to be successful in these academic areas.

EXAMPLE: Have students prepare a presentation, with a written summary and visuals, that explains a training process for implementing a new sales strategy or system. As part of the evaluation, give students a checklist prior to the presentation that defines the criteria for assessment of their speech. The checklist should contain categories such as the following: clear statement of purpose, effective speaking, organized presentation, appropriate use of visuals, etc. Also give them the requirements for the written summary—clearly organized, structured appropriately for the purpose, grammatically correct, accurate physical presentation (no typos) and format. By building these assessments into the assignment, you emphasize the importance of the skills, and also make the students aware of the necessity for competence in these areas.

Using these practical guidelines in your classroom will assure that your students are well prepared for the challenges of their careers. Giving them the tools, requiring that they use them, and giving them honest feedback offer them the greatest chance for success in the workplace—regardless of their professional goals.

CLASSROOM RESOURCES

To help you enhance your students' academic skills and integrate academic skills into your classroom, we have provided numerous academic activities and teaching strategies in this text.

The end-of-chapter activities include **Building Academic Skills** activities. These activities provide realistic, creative applications of chapter concepts to communications, technology, math, and human relations so students can gain minimum- through higher-level competence in these areas.

In addition, the side margins of the *Teacher's Wraparound Edition* include a variety of activities on applied academics that give students additional opportunities to strengthen their skills. These activities are written at three skill levels so that they may be adapted to the competency levels of your students.

Integrating Multicultural Awareness

The McDonald's corporation is opening restaurants in India as part of its global expansion. What do its marketers need to know about the culture of India in deciding what food products to offer in their Indian restaurants? How does an understanding of the culture of India affect their decisions?

Describe this scenario to students and ask for their opinions. Many students may be unaware that the cow is sacred to many Indians who do not eat beef. What then are the marketing obstacles for a hamburger restaurant? Armed with knowledge of Indian culture, the McDonald's marketers are creating a vegetarian menu for their restaurants in India. Their cultural knowledge may be the difference between success and failure in expanding into a new market.

> *Your students will be faced with a diverse marketplace.*

As future marketers, your students will be faced with a diverse marketplace in which people of many different cultures are both workers and consumers. Today's students need to understand and value the richness of the cultural heritages of the many people who make up the U.S. population. Such appreciation helps to create an environment in which people are able to live and work without hostility and misunderstanding.

James A. Banks, author of *Multicultural Curriculum Reform,* has described the need for multicultural education in this way: "A major goal of an effective multiethnic curriculum is to help students develop the ability to make reflective decisions on personal and public issues and to take successful action. Integrating the curriculum with ethnic content can be viewed as a process of curriculum reform. During this process, the entire curriculum is changed to enable students to view events, concepts, and issues from diverse ethnic perspectives."

TEXTBOOK RESOURCES

Every chapter of *Marketing Essentials* contains a special feature called **Life in the Multicultural Marketplace.** This feature highlights different aspects of ethnic culture. Use the feature for class discussion or for small group discussion. Also, assign research projects based on the ethnic groups identified in the feature.

Have students collect their own examples, from newspaper and magazine articles, of ethnic diversity. Have them explain how the different cultural groups may affect their personal and work lives in the future.

CURRENT ARTICLES

Use current news stories or advertisements to call students' attention to cultural differences that influence the marketing of a product. For example, an advertisement for a makeup product may focus on the special needs of women with dark skin. This advertisement ties into market segmentation and how different products are tailored to the needs of different groups of people.

Integrating Global Marketing

The environment that American businesses of every size are operating in is rapidly becoming more international. Thus, it is vital that we integrate an international perspective into all of our marketing courses. We can't treat the topic of "international marketing" as a separate entity any more. Consider these trends and events:

- Countries like the former Soviet Union and China moving from being command economies to market-driven economies. This transition brings many new consumers and producers into the world economy.
- Major trade regions being formed including the North America Free Trade Agreement, the European Community, and the Pacific Rim. These regions are breaking down trade barriers between countries within the region and unifying the region in trade from outside the region.
- Global opportunities for small and startup companies taking advantage of technological changes. International business is no longer the sole domain of multinational corporations. Many small, flexible, and innovative companies are now major global players.
- Multicultural forces bringing together lifestyles from all over the world. Businesses and individuals are faced with dealing with others from significantly diverse backgrounds and cultures.
- Faster communication and distribution makes competition possible from farther and farther distances. While a business needed only to be concerned with a competitor ten blocks away a few years ago; in a global economy, a serious competitive threat may now be ten time zones away.

Just as businesses are operating more and more globally, students preparing to enter business must be ready to operate in an international arena in the future. As the world gets smaller and communication gets faster, we can't remain comfortable in doing what has been done in the past. Without an international perspective, tomorrow's marketers may as well not even enter the game.

Why is global business so important? Two factors—the U.S. market is becoming more diverse with people from other countries, and businesses must look to foreign markets. Consider the following:

- The Hispanic population within the United States grew seven times faster than the general population between 1980 and 1990. It is expected to reach 31 million by the year 2000 with most coming from Mexico, Puerto Rico, and Cuba. Many marketers are adapting their products specifically for this market (see Chapter 6).
- The Asian-American population is expected to grow by 20 percent between 1992 and 2000. Marketers are very interested in this segment because it has a higher median household income than any other ethnic group. It is easy to reach geographically because it tends to be located in certain areas. Communicating can be difficult, however, because of language differences within the market (see Chapter 6).
- Many global markets are currently under-served. For example, American Express realized that people were travelling twice as much to other countries than domestically. That realization led to it offering Global Moneypac foreign travelers checks (see Chapter 2).
- Government and economies in transition are changing the way marketing is done. Privatization is occurring in Italy, Brazil, and Chile. In these and other countries, governments are selling assets and businesses to private owners (see Chapter 4).
- Not all international trade goes through smoothly. Marketers must be aware of and know how to deal with trade barriers such as tariffs, embargoes, and quotas (see Chapter 7).

The second edition of *Marketing Essentials* not only integrates global topics throughout the text but also includes a new international chapter called **The Global Marketplace.** This chapter provides your students with the international perspective that is so important in marketing. Also, included in this edition is a new feature that appears in every chapter of the text entitled **Life in the Multicultural Marketplace.** The feature helps create global awareness and clearly relates *Marketing Essentials* to the international marketplace.

An exciting new resource that was added to the *Marketing Essentials* program is the *International Case Studies Workbook.* This workbook combines international marketing news stories from major publications, such as *The Wall Street Journal* and *The New York Times,* with applications and critical thinking questions. It provides students with practical applications on the important topic of international marketing.

Integrating Ethics

One of your students who has a part-time job comes to you with a question about a situation at work. The student recently saw a supervisor mark down merchandise that was not on sale and not damaged so that friends could purchase the merchandise at a lower cost. The student asks you if that is acceptable business behavior. What will you answer?

During their marketing careers, your students will encounter many situations that will require them to make decisions about their own actions. Often, the ethical aspects of a decision are not even considered until after the decision has been made. However, this is often too late to consider the consequences and how the decision will affect the people involved. Helping students learn about ethical behavior and how to consider the effects of a decision before it is made are important topics for your marketing course.

The goal of introducing ethics into your course is not to teach values, but rather to help students clarify their own ethical beliefs and to learn how to evaluate ethical situations in light of their personal beliefs. Students need to learn how to evaluate their own actions and to ask themselves questions such as, "Will I think well of myself if I take this action?" "Would I want others to know about my actions?"

THE ETHICAL DECISION MODEL

Your students will learn to analyze ethical situations better if they have a model to use in deliberating the issues and the people affected by a decision. Several decision models exist, but the basic steps for an ethical decision model are as follows:

1. Determine the ethical issue.
2. Identify the actions for handling the situation.
3. Identify the people affected by the situation.
4. Analyze how the situation affects the people involved.

CASE STUDY

CD-ROM: The Hot New Research Tool

CD-ROM technology is the latest tool being used by marketing researchers. CD-ROM makes hard-to-find data easier to acquire. In addition, it can be obtained for less money than traditional marketing research studies.

Although CD-ROM publishing is a $1.7 billion industry, the technology is only a small part of the estimated $29 billion spent by marketers for business information. Compared to other forms of information delivery, though, CD-ROM is the second fastest growing medium.

CD-ROM is becoming increasingly popular with researchers because the cost of CD-ROM drives is decreasing, and there are more comprehensive marketing databases that are available on CD-ROM disks. In addition, information once stored on many diskettes or reels of computer tape can now be stored on a single compact disk.

Currently, more than 6,000 CD-ROM titles are available. These titles cover almost every marketing subject, including census data and demographics, advertising, telephone and mailing lists, and general marketing topics.

Companies, such as The Standard Rate and Data Service, have placed their business and consumer magazine directories on separate single compact disks. Now media buyers can find circulation numbers, reader demographics, and ad size specifications in minutes. This information is then used to buy advertising space in magazines targeted toward their customers.

The data on CD-ROMs can help companies learn more about their customers and the marketplace. Marketing researchers can find information on consumer purchase behavior and consumer attitudes. They can also search business data for Standard Industry Codes, employee size, sales volumes, and persons to contact for additional information. Reports that once took months to complete can now be done in a matter of hours.

Demographic and lifestyle information can be obtained by state, county, zip codes, and metropolitan statistical areas. Using commercially available Windows software with the CD-ROM databases, companies can conduct market research, advertising and media appraisals, site and territory evaluations, and direct marketing.

Business software titles can range from $200 to more than $5,000. Many can be purchased for a one-time fee or leased on a subscription basis.

While the costs of using sophisticated CD-ROM databases may be high, the ease and speed of obtaining the information needed may be worth the price. Many marketing researchers believe that CD-ROM technology is worth the cost because it saves time that would otherwise be spent in libraries or searching for information on online data services.

CD-ROMs are improving the way we conduct research. They allow researchers to access large databases, perform analysis, and, ultimately, make more intelligent marketing decisions.

Case Study Review

1. What is the primary advantage to CD-ROM technology?
2. Why are some businesses willing to pay high costs for subscription service software systems coupled with CD-ROM technology?

A MATTER OF ETHICS

3. Many people are wary of marketers having vast databases on customer characteristics. What ethical obligations do you think the marketing research industry has to the public?

Chapter 32 *Marketing Research* **427**

5. Decide which of the actions to take.

Each chapter in the textbook contains a **Case Study** which asks students to answer **A Matter of Ethics** question. You may want to use these cases for class discussion or have your students develop their writing skills by requiring short reports analyzing the ethical aspects of a case.

CLASSROOM STRATEGIES

Several methods may be used to integrate discussions of ethical issues into your marketing course. You may use the chapter **Case Study** or collect current articles that portray an ethical dilemma. Have students analyze the situations in class or write short reports of their analyses and conclusions.

- *Case Study Approach.* Using case studies from the textbook, have the entire class use the ethical decision model to analyze the issues and the possible actions to take. Make sure your students feel free to voice their opinions about the issues and the possible actions. If a full-class discussion becomes unwieldy, you may want to use small groups in a cooperative learning activity.

- *Cooperative Learning Groups.* Small groups of students are especially well suited to discussing cases and sharing their ideas about ethical issues. Divide students into groups of four to five. Observe groups to be sure that all students are participating. Allow each group to reach its conclusions, then ask a member of each to share that group's ideas with the class.

- *Role Plays and Debates.* Have your students role play ethical situations, using their own ideas about how to respond to a given situation. Discuss class responses to the role play, guiding students in using the ethical decision model. Set up debate teams to present different sides of an ethical issue.

Meeting Individual Needs and Special Needs

One of your greatest challenges as a teacher is to provide a positive learning environment for *all* students in your classroom. Because each student has his or her own unique set of abilities, perceptions, and needs, the learning styles and physical abilities of your students may vary widely.

ASSISTING STUDENTS WITH INDIVIDUAL NEEDS

To ensure that each student is challenged and motivated, you need to present the best possible learning opportunities and experiences. In order to help you provide all your students with a positive learning experience, this text provides a variety of activities for students to learn and apply the concepts of marketing. The diversity of these activities will stimulate the students' interest, motivate their learning, and facilitate their understanding.

In the *Teacher's Wraparound Edition,* additional individualized activities are provided. Each of these activities is specifically designed and coded for student ability levels.

- *Level 1* designates basic activities designed for the ability range of all students.
- *Level 2* activities provide practical applications designed for students who have mastered the concepts presented. Average to above-average students should be able to complete Level 2 activities.
- *Level 3* activities challenge students to expand their perspectives on the basic concepts learned. Level 3 activities are designed for the ability range of above-average students.

Also included in the *Teacher's Wraparound Edition*, are **Independent Practice** activities. These activities provide additional reinforcement and allow students to progress at their own pace.

TEACHING STUDENTS WITH SPECIAL NEEDS

Students in your classroom may be physically challenged. They may have impaired hearing or vision, learning disabilities, or behavior disorders (all of which may interfere with their ability to learn in your classroom). The learning styles

Richard Hutchings/PhotoEdit

of your students can also vary. Some students may be visual learners; others may learn more effectively through hands-on activities. Some students may work well independently while others need the interaction of working with others in groups. Your students may come from a variety of cultural backgrounds, and some students may have limited English proficiency.

Once you determine the special needs of your students, you can identify the areas in the curriculum that may present barriers to some students. In order to remove those barriers to learning, you may need to modify your teaching methods.

Suggestions to help you address different learning styles are provided on the bottom margins of every chapter of the *Teacher's Wraparound Edition.* These suggestions describe various strategies you can use for teaching students with special needs. You can select those strategies that are appropriate for the special needs and abilities of your students.

The chart shown on the next page describes some of the special needs you may encounter with students in your classroom and identifies sources of information. Also provided are tips for modifying your teaching style to accommodate the special needs of your students and locations of teaching tips within the *Teacher's Wraparound Edition.*

SUBJECT	DESCRIPTION	SOURCES OF INFORMATION
English as a Second Language	Multicultural and/or bilingual students often speak English as a second language or not at all. Customs and behavior of people in the majority culture may be confusing for some of these students. Cultural values may inhibit some of these students from full participation.	*Teaching English as a Second Language Reporter* *Mainstreaming and the Minority Child.*
Behaviorally Disordered	Children with behavior disorders deviate from standards or expectations of behavior and impair the functioning of others and themselves. These children may also be gifted or learning disabled.	*Exceptional Children* *Journal of Special Education*
Visually Impaired	Children who are visually disabled have partial or total loss of sight. Individuals with visual impairments are not significantly different from their sighted peers in ability range or personality. However, blindness may affect cognitive, motor, and social development.	*Journal of Visual Impairment and Blindness* *Education of Visually Handicapped* *American Foundation for the Blind*
Hearing Impaired	Children who are hearing impaired have partial or total loss of hearing. Individuals with hearing impairments are not significantly different from their peers in ability range or personality. However, the chronic condition of deafness may affect cognitive, motor, social development, and speech development.	*American Annals of the Deaf* *Journal of Speech and Hearing Research* *Sign Language Studies*
Physically Challenged	Children who are physically disabled fall into two categories—those with orthopedic impairments (use of one or more limbs severely restricted) and those with other health impairments.	*The Source Book for the Disabled* *Teaching Exceptional Children*
Gifted	Although no formal definition exists, these students can be described as having above average ability, task commitment, and creativity. They rank in the top 5 percent of their class. They usually finish work more quickly than other students, and are capable of divergent thinking.	*Journal for the Education of the Gifted* *Gifted Child Quarterly* *Gifted Creative/Talented*
Learning Disabled	All learning disabled students have an academic problem in one or more areas, such as academic learning, language, perception, social-emotional adjustment, memory, or attention.	*Journal of Learning Disabilities* *Learning Disability Quarterly*

TIPS FOR INSTRUCTION	CHAPTER NOTE
• Remember that students' ability to speak English does not reflect their academic ability. • Try to incorporate the student's cultural experience into your instruction. The help of a bilingual aide may be effective. • Include information about different cultures in your curriculum to help build students' self-image. Avoid cultural stereotypes. • Encourage students to share their cultures in the classroom.	5, 8, 9, 14, 23, 29, 33, 36, 43
• Work for long-term improvement; do not expect immediate success. • Talk with students about their strengths and weaknesses, and clearly outline objectives and how you will help them obtain their goals. • Structure schedules, rules, room arrangement, and safety for a conducive environment. • Model appropriate behavior for students and reinforce proper behavior. • Adjust group requirements for individual needs.	3, 28
• Modify assignments as needed to help students become independent. • Teach classmates how to serve as guides; pair students so sighted peers can assist in cooperative learning work. • Tape lectures and reading assignments. • Encourage students to use their sense of touch; provide tactile models whenever possible. • Verbally describe people and events as they occur in the classroom. • Limit unnecessary noise in the classroom.	7, 10, 15, 21, 31, 38, 42
• Provide favorable seating arrangements so students can see speakers and read their lips (or interpreters can assist); avoid visual distractions. • Write out all instructions on paper or on the board; overhead projectors enable you to maintain eye contact while writing. • Avoid standing with your back to the window or light source.	2, 13, 17, 27, 32, 37
• Determine with the student when you should offer aid. • Help other students and adults understand physically-disabled students. • Learn about special devices or procedures and if any special necessary safety precautions are needed. • Allow students to participate in all activities including field trips, special events, and projects.	6, 20, 22, 30, 35, 41
• Emphasize concepts, theories, relationships, ideas, and generalizations. • Let students express themselves in a variety of ways including drawing, creative writing, or acting. • Make arrangements for students to work on independent projects. • Utilize public services and resources, such as agencies providing free and inexpensive materials, community services and programs, and people in the community with specific expertise. • Make arrangements for students to take selected subjects early.	12, 19, 24, 40
• Establish conditions and create an environment that lead to success. • Provide assistance and direction; clearly define rules, assignments, and duties. • Allow for pair interaction during classtime; utilize peer helpers. • Tape lecture material. • Practice skills frequently. • Distribute outlines of material presented in class. • Maintain student interest with games and drills. • Allow extra time to complete tests and assignments.	1, 4, 11, 16, 18, 25, 26, 34, 39

The Importance of Teaching Entrepreneurship

The one job category predicted to produce the most *net new jobs* in the next 15 years is that of retail salesperson. According to the United States Department of Labor this job and 13 of the other top 20 jobs expected to provide employment opportunities in the 1990s and beyond require at most a high school diploma and do not pay a living wage. While retail selling is an important opportunity to learn about marketing, the simple fact is that relatively few adults support themselves through retail selling as a career. The exceptions are those who move into management or sell high-ticket items (appliances, women's and men's couture fashion, automobiles, etc.). Beyond retailing, the Fortune 500 companies that presently employ about 41 percent of all workers in the United States have not created a *net new job* in more than 20 years. So, where will your students work in the 21st century? More than anytime in the past century, the likelihood is that your students will need to work for themselves, not for someone else.

Presently, the U.S. Department of Labor estimates that between 15 and 20 percent of employed workers are self-employed—entrepreneurs. These percentages will grow and your students will be part of that growth. Knowing what it takes to find market opportunity, organize a business, and operate at a profit will be more important to future generations than it has been to past.

Learning about entrepreneurship is important for another reason. The U.S. economy, often defined as a mixed economy, has been built upon the energy and the drive of entrepreneurs over the years.

WHY TEACH ENTREPRENEURSHIP?

As a famous politician once said, "If not now, when; if not us, who?" While he was talking of greater societal issues, this rhetorical question can be asked of marketing and business teachers in relation to entrepreneurship. Because of the economic imperative for building entrepreneurial skills in all of our young people, there are at least three reasons for incorporating an entrepreneurial focus within your curriculum. By incorporating entrepreneurship in your curriculum you will add an important set of skills to your students' portfolio of business competencies. You will be introducing your students to a way of thinking about how they approach their careers. Finally, a focus on entrepreneurship offers the opportunity to build or reinforce the traditional academic skills of reading, communication, and computation.

> *Where will your students work in the 21st century?*

ENTREPRENEURSHIP AS A SET OF SKILLS

Entrepreneurship introduces students to aspects of business: from production to finance to marketing to management. The cognitive component of entrepreneurship education includes understanding of the relationship between micro and macro economic factors, market analysis, legal requirements and taxes, strategies for forms of business ownership, risk assessment, and finance. Skills that can be developed through the study of entrepreneurship include planning, higher order analysis, decision making, advanced mathematics, computer literacy, and bookkeeping.

ENTREPRENEURSHIP AS A WAY OF THINKING

Perhaps as important as the knowledge and specific skills associated with incorporating entrepreneurship is the way of thinking your students will learn. Entrepreneurship is truly about how one views the world around them. Entrepreneurs see the world as opportunity. It is their spirit of independence, curiosity and, most importantly, their initiative that drives our economic system. What better gift to give your students than the spirit of the entrepreneur.

ENTREPRENEURSHIP AS A STRATEGY FOR IMPROVING ACADEMIC SKILLS

One of the more powerful movements in education today is academic integration. Educators of all kinds are realizing that the artificial separation of "academic" and "vocational" subject matter is more harmful than helpful to students. Spurred by federal and some state legislation, many schools are experimenting with ways to make learning more holistic and less compartmentalized. With entrepreneurship as a focus, especially when combined with a *school-based enterprise*, there are wonderful opportunities to integrate mathematics, English, social studies, and science competencies in an activity that engages students' interest.

PREPARING FOR THE DECA ENTREPRENEURSHIP EVENT

The *Marketing Essentials* text provides a framework for helping students develop competitive entries for the DECA Entrepreneurship event. The following chart should help you assist your students who choose to pursue this exciting and educational activity.

**PREPARING FOR THE
DECA ENTREPRENEURSHIP EVENT**

Entrepreneurship Event Component	*Marketing Essentials* Chapter Reference
Self-Analysis	37, 42
Trading Area Analysis	6, 32, 39
Market Segment Analysis	13, 33, 39
Business Organization	37, 39
Product/Service Offering	34, 35, 39
Marketing Strategies	24, 29, 30, 39
Projecting Income and Expenses	40
Meeting Capital Needs	40

In addition to *Marketing Essentials*, Glencoe/McGraw-Hill offers two additional, excellent resources for teaching entrepreneurship: *Entrepreneurship and Small Business Management* by Meyer and Allen and from the CCM series, *Entrepreneurship* by Ely, Berns, and Popo.

Preparing for the School-to-Work Transition

Helping young people make the transition from school to work has become an educational and political issue in recent years. This has led to legislation supporting new programs like tech prep, youth apprenticeship, school-based enterprises, school-business partnerships, and service learning.

There are two recent Acts of Congress that already or will soon affect you and your curriculum—*The Carl D. Perkins Vocational Act and Applied Technology Education Act* of 1990 and *The School-to-Work Opportunities Act* of 1994.

THE CARL D. PERKINS VOCATIONAL ACT AND APPLIED TECHNOLOGY EDUCATION ACT

The Perkins Act was passed in 1990 in direct response to the many calls for educational reform and because of concern over the competitiveness of the U.S. economy. In the preamble to the act, the Congress said: "It is the purpose of this act to make the United States more competitive in the world economy by developing more fully the academic and occupational skills of all segments of the population. This purpose will principally be achieved through concentrating resources on improving education programs leading to academic and occupational skill competencies needed to work in a technologically advanced society."

The act included three components of particular interest to Marketing Educators. These are *tech prep and applied academics, integrated curriculum*, and *teaching all aspects of the industry.*

TECH PREP AND APPLIED ACADEMICS

Tech-prep education is a four-year, planned sequence of study for a technical field, beginning in the eleventh grade of high school. At the end of the four-year, marketing tech-prep program, students should be prepared to enter the workplace as technically skilled employees or for further education leading to two-year or four-year degrees in marketing or a related major. In some marketing tech-prep programs, postsecondary marketing curriculum is moved to the 12th grade

allowing for more advanced studies in the two-year college. In others, postsecondary credit is given for high school work so that students begin with an advanced standing in the two-year college. The following table illustrates a marketing tech-prep program including new applied courses designated by an asterisk. While many programs include courses beginning in the 9th grade, the following example begins with 11th grade as described in the legislation and concludes with a two-year degree in marketing.

Model Tech-Prep Program

11th Grade	12th Grade	1st Year	2nd Year
Algebra 1	Marketing Math*	Statistics	Analysis
Business Writing	Public Speaking	Marketing Literature*	Group Process
Principles of Technology		Marketing Research	
Geography	History of Marketing*	Economics	Government
Word Processing	Computer Applications	Accounting I	Accounting II
Marketing I		Principles of Marketing	Total Quality Management
	Professional Selling	Consumer Behavior	Marketing Communications
	Visual Merchandising	Principles of Retailing	Buying

(*New applied courses.)

The tech-prep program should place an emphasis on academic skills. Academics can easily be integrated into the marketing classroom. For example, when you teach the mathematics included in Chapters 18, 28, 31, and 40 in *Marketing Essentials*, you are teaching applied math. When teaching Chapters 9, 10, and 11 you are teaching applied communications. In addition, at the end of each chapter are Vocabulary Review and Building Academic Skills exercises. Both of these are opportunities to enhance the development of traditional academic skills in an applied setting.

INTEGRATED CURRICULUM

Integrating academic education with occupational education is at the heart of most school-to-work efforts. School-based learning is more effective when students can see that what they are learning in math, for example, applies to what they are learning in marketing. Or, that what they are learning in marketing applies to what they are learning in English. An integrated curriculum provides an opportunity for teachers to work together to blend the best instructional practices from each other's discipline.

There are a variety of ways in which academic and marketing subject matters can be integrated. The simplest strategy involves two or more teachers who agree to work as a team to create integration activities. For example, a history teacher may assign students to study the history of the companies for which they work. A marketing teacher may assign students to study the effects of an historical event on marketing, or even write a poem about customer service! Teachers may arrange to co-teach certain classes, swap classes, or become involved in evaluating each others' class activities. The possibilities are unlimited.

In one school, the senior creative writing teacher had the students write children's stories and test marketed them in the elementary schools! The graphic arts teacher had the same students prepare the illustrations and book covers. The marketing teacher worked with the students to develop a marketing plan for the books. In this quarter-long project, students and the teachers worked and learned together making this project a success.

TEACHING ALL ASPECTS OF THE INDUSTRY

The Carl D. Perkins Act requires any comprehensive vocational education program to include *all aspects* of a particular industry in which a student is planning to work. These skills should include: planning, management, finance, technical and production skills, underlying principles of technology, labor and community issues, economic development and health, safety, and environmental issues.

THE SCHOOL-TO-WORK OPPORTUNITIES ACT OF 1994

The School-to-Work Opportunities Act of 1994 is designed to help young people move from school to work. It encourages states to create *systems* of school-to-work transition. Unlike other educational legislation, this act is focussed on getting states to bring the various kinds of transition programs under one umbrella. This includes youth apprenticeship, traditional vocational education (including marketing education), JTPA, tech prep, and other job-related programs that are funded through the U.S. Department of Education and the Department of Labor. There are three components to the act: *school-based learning, work-based learning,* and *connecting activities*. School-based learning refers to all of the ways in which schools can prepare young people for their occupational future. Work-based learning refers to ways in which students can learn and develop academic as well as vocational skills on the job. Connecting activities are the activities that connect school-based learning with work-based learning.

USING *MARKETING ESSENTIALS* TO IMPROVE SCHOOL-TO-WORK TRANSITION

Marketing Essentials provides you with several tools to help you implement the school-to-work transition. Each chapter of the student text includes **Linking School to Work** activities in the Chapter Review. These activities are designed to move the student into the work context to observe, interview, or research an aspect of marketing. Many of these projects are a useful addition to work-based learning training plans.

Also available to you is the new *School-to-Work Handbook* that contains activities designed to help students make a successful transition from school to work. These activities address one of the major themes in the new legislation: knowledge of the workplace and knowledge of self. Included with this handbook is a teacher's manual providing you with detailed instructions on using school-to-work activities. Also contained within this handbook is Michigan state's own detailed guidelines for implementing a school-to-work system.

SCANS and *Marketing Essentials*

In 1991, the U.S. Department of Labor released a report entitled, What Work Requires of Schools: A SCANS Report for America 2000. The SCANS report identified five competencies which, in conjunction with a three-part foundation of skills and personal qualities, lie at the heart of job performance and are needed by all workers in order to prosper in the emerging workplace. These skills and competencies have been integraed into the *Marketing Essentials* program.

THE FOUNDATION	MARKETING ESSENTIALS

Basic Skills—reading, writing, mathematics, speaking, and listening.	The following chapters deal specifically with mathematics.
	Chapters 8, 18, 28, 31, 33
	In the following activities, students demonstrate competency in basic skills.
	Building Academic Skills
	  Math (Chapters 1–43)
	  Communication (Chapters 1–43)
	Application Projects (Chapters 1–43)
	Performance Assessment
	  Role Play (Chapters 1–43)
	  Public Speaking (Chapters 3, 7, 9, 13, 16, 21, 23, 41–43)
	Written Report (Chapters 5, 11, 12, 22, 28, 39)
	Creative Problem Solving (Chapters 6, 30)
	Presentation (Chapters 10, 17, 18, 24, 31)
	Interview (Chapter 37)
	Research (Chapters 14, 19, 35)
	Pictorial Essay (Chapters 20, 38)
	Persuasive Speaking (Chapter 26)

Thinking Skills—creative thinking, decision making, problem solving, knowing how to learn, and reasoning.	The following chapters deal specifically with thinking skills.
	Chapters 1–43
	In the following activities, students demonstrate competency in thinking skills.
	Bright Ideas (Chapters 1–43)
	Critical Thinking (Chapters 1–43)
	Application Projects (Chapters 1–43)
	Performance Assessment
	  Role Play (Chapters 1–43)
	  Creative Problem Solving (Chapters 6, 30)
	  Creativity (Chapter 15)
	Case Study Review (Chapters 1–43)

Personal Qualities—individual responsibility, self-esteem, self-management, sociability, and integrity.	The following chapters deal specifically with personal qualities. Chapters 11, 12, 37, 42 In the following activities, students demonstrate competency in the development of personal qualities. Building Academic Skills *Human Relations* (Chapters 1, 3, 5, 6, 8–34, 37, 38, 40–43) Bright Ideas (Chapters 1–43) Application Projects (Chapters 1–43)

SCANS COMPETENCIES	MARKETING ESSENTIALS

Resources—allocate time, money, materials, space, and staff.

The following chapters deal specifically with resources.

Chapters 12, 37, 38

Interpersonal skills—work in teams, teach others, serve customers, lead, negotiate, and work with people from culturally diverse backgrounds.

The following chapters deal specifically with interpersonal skills.

Chapters 16, 17, 37

In the following activities, students demonstrate competency in interpersonal skills.

Bright Ideas (Chapters 1–43)

Building Academic Skills
Human Relations (Chapters 1, 3, 5, 6, 8–34, 37, 38, 40–3)

Life in the Multicultural Marketplace (Chapters 1–43)

Linking School to Work (Chapters 1–43)

Performance Assessment
Role Play (Chapters 1–43)

Application Projects (Chapters 1–43)

Information—acquire and evaluate data, organize and maintain files, interpret and communicate information, use computers to process information.

The following chapters deal specifically with information.

Chapters 13, 33

In the following activities, students demonstrate competency in information.

Performance Assessment
Display (Chapters 2, 4)
Public Speaking (Chapters 3, 7, 9, 13, 16, 21, 23, 41–43)
Written Report (Chapters 5, 11, 12, 22, 28, 39)
Prepare Visual Aids (Chapters 8, 29)

Presentation (Chapters 10, 17, 18, 24, 31)
Interview (Chapter 37)
Research (Chapters 14, 19, 35)
Create a Chart (Chapters 25, 27, 36, 40)
Concept Mapping (Chapter 32)
Develop a Survey (Chapter 33)
Diagram (Chapter 34)
Computer Application (Chapters 1–43)
Application Projects (Chapters 1–43)

Systems—understand social, organizational, and technological systems; monitor and correct performance; design and improve systems.

The following chapters deal specifically with systems.

Chapters 3, 4, 10, 11, 12, 14, 25, 27, 32, 33, 37, 38, 39, 43

In the following activity, students demonstrate competency in designing and improving systems.

Linking School to Work (Chapter 11)

Technology—select equipment and tools, apply technology to specific tasks, and maintain and troubleshoot technologies.

The following chapters deal specifically with technology.

Chapters 10, 18, 33

In the following activities, students demonstrate competency in technology.

Computer Application (Chapters 1–43)

Building Academic Skills
Technology (Chapters 2, 4, 6, 12, 14, 19, 23, 25, 29–32, 35, 39, 40)

Performance Assessment
Preparing Visual Aids (Chapters 8, 29)
Linking School to Work (Chapter 8)

Preparing for DECA

DECA is an association of marketing students. It is a co-curricular club with chapters in more than 6,000 high schools. The membership includes representation from all 50 states, four U.S. territories, the District of Columbia, and two Canadian provinces. All DECA activities further student development in one or more of the following areas: leadership development, social intelligence, vocational understanding, and civic consciousness. Through the integration of individual and group DECA activities with the marketing education instructional program, students' skills are cultivated to ensure they will become future leaders in the areas of marketing and management.

LEADERSHIP SKILLS

The structure of a DECA chapter encourages leadership development among its members. Each chapter elects officers who, with the membership, identify an annual program of work. The identified program of work often includes committee chairpeople to organize and execute the activities identified in the program of work. Local activities encourage all members to act responsibly as a leader or member of a group. Chapter activities typically focus on the advantages of participation in a free enterprise system, marketing research, and an individual's civic responsibility within the community.

National DECA provides opportunities for local chapter officers and members to receive additional training. Annual Regional Conferences are held in the fall. In the spring, students may attend the Leadership Development Academy at the Career Development Conference (CDC). During the summer, a State Officer Leadership Institute is available. All of these functions offer basic training in leadership and chapter development. The skills gained and leadership qualities acquired are shared with all members of the chapter upon return from one or more of these training sessions.

COMPETITIVE EVENTS

One part of the DECA program of student activities is the competitive events program. The events are both competency and curriculum based and assist students in the refinement of workplace skills required for entry and/or advancement in the field of marketing. All events are centered around those skills expected by employers in all marketing fields—effective communication skills, ability to solve problems, ability to make decisions, and ability to function responsibly as either a leader or member or a team. Some events are for individuals and others require students to function as members of a group. The competitive events program provides recognition for student excellence at the local, state, and national level of competition. The recognition received by both individuals and teams within a DECA chapter serve as a showcase of the marketing program to the local school and community.

The purposes of DECA's competitive events are:

- to contribute to the development of competencies needed for careers in marketing, merchandising, and management;
- to evaluate student achievement of the competencies through careful measurement devices;
- to provide opportunities for student and group recognition;
- to provide constructive avenues for individual or group expression, initiative, and creativity;
- to motivate students to assume responsibility for self-improvement and self-discipline;
- to provide a vehicle for students to demonstrate their acquired competencies through individual and/or group activities;
- to assist students in acquiring a realistic self-concept through individual and/or group activities;
- to help students to participate in an environment of cooperation and competition; and
- to provide visibility for the educational goals and objectives of marketing education.

INDIVIDUAL SERIES EVENTS

As participants in the individual series event program, students are evaluated on their proficiency in handling simulated business situations. Each event is directly related to competencies mastered through classroom instruction and/or related job experience. The following are the instructional areas included in both the competitive events program:

- *Economic Concepts and Principles* (economics, marketing, and business)
- *Basic and Social Skills* (mathematics, communications, human relations, and career development)

● *Marketing Functions* (buying and pricing, promotion, selling, physical distribution, support activities, management and supervision)

Students participate in the event category in their identified area of occupational interest within the field of marketing. A typical individual series event includes a comprehensive written exam and two role-play events. In each series students are presented with a business situation. Students must then use the skills acquired through participation in their marketing class to make decisions and spontaneously react to the situation. A business executive judges students' performance while playing the role of the second party in the role play. The following is a listing of the individual competitive event areas:

● Advertising and Visual Merchandising Services Series
● Apparel and Accessories Marketing Series
● Finance and Credit Services Series
● Food Marketing Series
● General Marketing Series
● Hospitality and Tourism Marketing Series
● Retail Merchandising Series
● Quick Serve Restaurant Management Series
● Full Service Restaurant Management Series
● Vehicles and Petroleum Marketing Series

TEAM EVENTS

Team projects and events may be completed by teams composed of one to three DECA members. These activities involve writing across the curriculum. When completed, the professional documents could be included in a student's portfolio and would be of significant interest to both educators and businesspeople reviewing the portfolio. To the right is a chart of DECA team events and the corresponding chapters in *Marketing Essentials* that will help students prepare for the event.

All team events require completion of a written manual. Through their research and writing, students are expected to: function as leaders or members of a group, prepare complex reports, demonstrate initiative and creativity, and communicate recommendations based on their research to business executives. Each year, a specific topic is identified by DECA. All events must include research related to the topic and follow the identified format. Excellence in the written events is evaluated on both the quality of the written report and performance during an interview conducted by a judge from the business community.

DECA Team Events

EVENT	CORRESPONDING CHAPTERS
Written:	
Business and Financial Services Marketing	All
Entrepreneurship	37–40
Food Marketing Research	32–36, 39, 40
General Marketing Research	32–36, 39, 40
Hospitality and Recreation Marketing Research	5–7, 32–36, 39, 40
Retail Marketing Research	19–23, 32, 33, 39, 40
Participating:	
Entrepreneurship	37–40
Fashion Merchandising Promotion Plan	19–23, 39, 40
Project:	
Civic Consciousness	3–7
Creative Marketing Research	32, 33
Learn and Earn	37–40
Public Relations	19–23
DECA Quiz Bowl	All
Free Enterprise	3–7
International Marketing	5–7

USING *MARKETING ESSENTIALS* TO PREPARE FOR DECA

The preparation for all competitive events begins in the marketing education classroom and *Marketing Essentials* is designed to be one of your primary preparation resources. Several parts of the text as well as end-of-chapter activities in *Marketing Essentials* are devoted to preparing students for DECA. For example, studying Unit 6, Promotion, will help prepare students for the Advertising and Visual Merchandising Services Series event. Unit 11, Entrepreneurship, will help students prepare for the Entrepreneurship event. In fact, Chapters 39 and 40 give students step-by-step instructions on how to prepare for DECA's entrepreneurship written event which requires students to write a business proposal for a new business.

In addition, the end-of-chapter material for each chapter in *Marketing Essentials* contains role-play activities. These activities provide opportunities for students to practice for DECA's participating events. The activities are based upon the same premise of a DECA role-play situation. Students are given a marketing situation to contemplate. For example, students may have to create a promotion plan for a product or make a distribution decision. Students are asked to come up with a plan or solution and present it to the teacher who, in the role-play situation, represents a manager, a staff member, or other marketing personnel.

Role-play activities provide the teacher with a list of competencies to use as criteria in evaluating students' abilities in their subsequent role playing. In addition, you may also choose the competencies listed in any related DECA competitive events handbooks to use as criteria.

SUPPLEMENTAL MATERIALS FOR DECA PREPARATION

In addition to *Marketing Essentials,* there are several resources available that provide added training for students preparing for competition. Two of these resources are the Career Competency in Marketing Series published by Glencoe/McGraw-Hill and the event-specific Student

Training Guides available through DECA Images located at National DECA.

The Career Competency in Marketing Series (CCM)

The Career Competency in Marketing Series can be used to assist students in their preparation for both performance and written events. The textbooks prepare students to move from a career sustaining level of competence to that of supervisor within a specialized marketing industry.

The activities and technical information outlined in each of the books in the series assist students in decision-making and problem-solving skills. Additionally, students' communication skills are strengthened by completing the exercises in each text. For example, after completing Unit 4, Human Resource Essentials, in *Marketing Essentials,* students could complete the corresponding chapters in the CCM text. The industry-specific information detailed in the CCM text may assist students in attaining competencies which may not be mastered on the job or through a general marketing course.

In addition to using the CCM Series as preparation for individual competition, you may find it valuable to students preparing for team event competition. For example, when preparing for the Fashion Merchandising Promotion Plan Event, students could first study Units 5 and 6 in *Marketing Essentials* and then complete the assignments in the Marketing Skills section of the *Apparel and Accessories* CCM Series. You may then have the students present the completed assignments to management-level businesspeople in the apparel industry for review and evaluation. In doing this, students would gain experience in presenting their written work to businesspeople and justifying it during an interview.

Whether viewed as many small projects or a large project with many components, the written events are easily integrated into the instructional program. Much as a textbook is divided into chapters, each written event may be divided into several parts with a timeline for completion of each component and the final product. You could ask students early in the school year to select a topic from the list of written events. Once a category is identified, all end-of-the-chapter activities in the *Marketing Essentials* text would be completed for that specific industry. A student would also complete some of the culminating exercises in the corresponding CCM Series text. You could then develop a student checklist which parallels the requirements for entry in the DECA event. The checklist would serve as both a completion check-off for the students and an evaluation sheet for the teacher and/or business executive evaluating the components and finished project.

If approached in this way, the task is not viewed as overwhelming, but as an assessment of the competencies taught through the delivery of curriculum. You might consider this method of incorporating DECA into the marketing curriculum. Once this method is used, it is then a natural next step for some students to choose to refine their projects for entry in a DECA competitive event. It is an excellent opportunity to involve an entire marketing education program in the DECA competitive events program.

When used in conjunction with this text, the series provides an in-depth study for those desiring further knowledge in a given area. The CCM Series includes the following titles:

- *Advertising Services*
- *Apparel and Accessories*
- *Entrepreneurship*
- *Financial Services*
- *Food Marketing*
- *General Merchandise Retailing*
- *Hospitality Marketing: Lodging*
- *Hospitality Marketing: Travel and Tourism*
- *Vehicles and Petroleum Marketing*
- *Restaurant Marketing*

The DECA Student Training Guide

The DECA *Student Training Guide* provides occupation specific training for the DECA written test and role-play situations for the identified event area. In addition to sample test questions and simulated business situations, an individual competency checklist is included in each Training Guide. Students may use this to record their individual progress with respect to competency completion both in the classroom and on the job. Each Training Guide provides descriptions of the procedures at each stage of DECA competition and details the process of completing a role-play event and comprehensive written test. After mastering the competencies in the *Marketing Essentials* text, a student may use a Training Guide for individualized or small group study and further preparation for DECA competition. Student Training Guides are available in titles and levels corresponding to the individual series event titles.

Any preliminary plans for integrating DECA into classroom assignments should include a review of the current DECA Guide. The Guide provides guidelines for all competitive events for the school year as well as the National DECA address and phone number. You should contact the staff if questions arise as you prepare students for competition and integrate DECA into your instructional program.

Course Planning Guide

One-Semester Course

Week	Chapter	Chapter Title
1	2	Basic Marketing Concepts
2	3	Our Free Enterprise System
	4	World Economies
3	5	Business and Social Responsibility
	6	The Domestic Marketplace
4	8	Fundamentals of Mathematics
	9	Communication Skills
5	11	Interpersonal Skills
6	13	What Is Selling?
	14	The Sales Process
7	15	Determining Needs and Product Presentation
	16	Handling Customer Questions and Objections
8	17	Closing the Sale and Following Up
	18	Math for Retail Sales
9	19	What Is Promotion?
	20	Advertising Media
10	22	Visual Merchandising and Display
	23	Publicity and Public Relations
11	24	Channels of Distribution
	25	Physical Distribution
	27	Stock Handling and Inventory Control
12	29	Price Planning
	30	Pricing Strategies
	31	Pricing Math
13	32	Marketing Research
14	34	What Is Product Planning?
	35	Branding, Packaging, and Labeling
15	37	What Is Entrepreneurship?
	39	Developing a Business Plan
	40	Financing the Business
16	41	Careers in Marketing
	42	Making Your Career Decision
	43	Finding and Applying for a Job

MARKETING MATH WORKBOOK
TEACHER'S ANNOTATED EDITION
INCLUDES:
• Marketing Math Pretest
• Math Activities for Each Unit
• Answers for Each Activity

Marketing Essentials
SECOND EDITION

Lois Farese

Full-Year Course
Six-Week Grading System

Full-Year Course
Nine-Week Grading System

Marketing Essentials

SECOND EDITION

Lois Schneider Farese
Marketing Education Teacher-Coordinator
Northern Highlands Regional High School
Allendale, New Jersey

Grady Kimbrell
Educational Consultant
Santa Barbara, California

Carl A. Woloszyk
Associate Professor
Department of Consumer Resources
  and Technology
Western Michigan University
Kalamazoo, Michigan

GLENCOE
McGraw-Hill

New York, New York   Columbus, Ohio   Mission Hills, California   Peoria, Illinois

i

Send all inquiries to:
GLENCOE DIVISION
McGraw-Hill
15319 Chatsworth Street
P. O. Box 9609
Mission Hills, California 91346-9609

ISBN 0-02-640601-2 (Student Edition)
ISBN 0-02-640602-0 (Teacher's Wraparound Edition)

Printed in the United States of America.

2 3 4 5 6 7 8 9   RRW   03 02 01 00 99 98 97

Lois Schneider Farese, a nationally recognized secondary marketing educator, has been the marketing teacher and DECA advisor at Northern Highlands Regional High School in Allendale, New Jersey, for more than 25 years. She has been involved in organizing and running New Jersey regional and state DECA conferences and has also participated as series director and event manager at state and national DECA conferences.

As a result of her outstanding teaching methods and involvement in numerous marketing-related activities, Farese was named "Teacher of the Year" in 1981 by the Marketing Education Association of New Jersey. In 1982 she was recognized by the New Jersey Division of the American Vocational Education Association. In 1986 she became the first recipient from her school of the prestigious New Jersey Governor's Teacher Recognition Program. In 1993 the State Officer Action Team presented Farese with the Outstanding Service Award for her dedication, professionalism, and commitment to New Jersey DECA.

Farese has a B.A. in business and distributive education and two M.A.'s (one in business and one in psychology) from Montclair State College in New Jersey. She has numerous additional credits in education, administration, and supervision.

Grady Kimbrell, a nationally recognized author and consultant on career education, began his career in education teaching high school business in Kansas. After relocating to Southern California, Kimbrell taught business courses and coordinated students' in-class activities with their on-the-job experience. He later directed the work experience program for the high schools of Santa Barbara, California.

A pioneer in the use of computers as a tool for educational research, Kimbrell has assisted school districts with a wide variety of research and evaluation activities. His research into on-the-job work activities led to the development of a new type of career interest inventory used in career guidance. In addition, Kimbrell has served on numerous state instructional program committees and writing teams, designed educational computer programs, and produced educational films.

Kimbrell holds degrees in business administration, educational psychology, and business education.

Carl A. Woloszyk is a university professor with an extensive background in marketing education. He currently teaches graduate and undergraduate courses in career and technical education at Western Michigan University in Kalamazoo. He also serves as a local chapter advisor to Delta Epsilon Chi, the postsecondary division of DECA.

Woloszyk has been a state consultant for marketing and cooperative education, Michigan DECA state advisor, an administrator of career and technical education for a regional education service center, and a secondary marketing teacher-coordinator. As a secondary teacher-coordinator, he supervised a school store, taught marketing education classes, placed cooperative education students, and served as a local DECA chapter advisor. His students have received numerous awards at district, state, and national DECA conferences.

Woloszyk has served on the board of directors for national DECA and is the current Michigan representative to MarkED, a national marketing education curriculum and research consortium in Columbus, Ohio. He is a charter and board member of the Michigan Marketing Educator's Association.

Woloszyk received his undergraduate degree in business administration and his doctorate in business and distributive education from Michigan State University. He also has an M.A. in business education from Eastern Michigan University and an Educational Specialist degree in occupational education from the University of Michigan.

iii

Anne Cocroft Agyemang
Teacher
Randoph Career Technical Center
Detroit, Michigan

Allen Buntin
Marketing Education Teacher-Coordinator
Cactus High School
Glendale, Arizona

Jackie Cink
Business Education Instructor
Crete High School
Crete, Nebraska

Judy J. Commers
Marketing Education Teacher-Coordinator
Porter County Career Center
Valparaiso, Indiana

Jackie Freeman
Marketing Education Teacher-Coordinator
Robert E. Lee High School
Houston, Texas

Dan J. Greaven
Consultant for Marketing Education
North Carolina Department of Public Instruction
Raleigh, North Carolina

Mary Beth Hollas
Marketing Education Teacher-Coordinator
Lamar Consolidated High School
Rosenberg, Texas

Dennis C. Lane
Teacher-Coordinator
Parkway North High School
St. Louis, Missouri

Debra J. Laughlin
Marketing Education Teacher-Coordinator
Centerville High School
Centerville, Ohio

Kay Masonbrink
Teacher
Mt. Carmel High School
San Diego, California

LouGene McKinney
Teacher-Coordinator, Marketing and Business
Laramie High School
Laramie, Wyoming

David F. Olmer
Marketing Instructor
Inglemoor High School
Bothel, Washington

Patrick J. O'Reilly
Work-Study Coordinator
Woodland Hills High School
Pittsburgh, Pennsylvania

Ellen Potere
Business Education Chairperson
Sayville High School
West Sayville, New York

Diane P. Pruner
Program Coordinator, Marketing Education
Fairfax County Public Schools
Falls Church, Virginia

Mark M. Rael
Teacher-Coordinator
Cooper City High School
Cooper City, Florida

Reginald K. Shoesmith
Coordinator, Business Education and
 Tech-Prep/School-to-Work
Davenport, Iowa

Contents

Unit 5
Selling   172

Shaq's Summer Cooler

A LINE ANNE KLEIN

CORVETTE

Unit 7
Buying and Distribution   306

XV

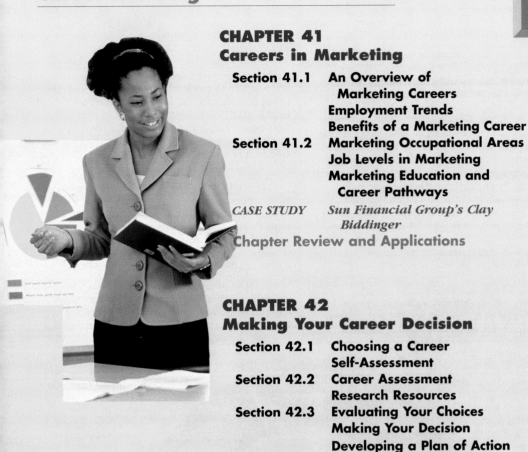

xvii

Have you ever seen a blueprint for a house or an office building? A blueprint is a plan of action drawn by an architect. It shows where each room will be, how big it will be, and the overall design of the structure.

How well the architect's "vision" is carried out, however, is really up to the builder. Two builders could look at the same blueprint for a house, but each could build a structure with its own unique character by using different bricks or paint or wood for the floors. The basic design of the two houses would be the same, but the two builders could put their own imprint on each.

Think of this book as your blueprint to marketing. It tells you what you need to know to start your career exploration and get a basic understanding of the principles and practices of marketing. It's up to you to put your own unique imprint on your career path.

Unit Opener Pages

Marketing Essentials is divided into 12 units, each of which begins with a unit opener. These two pages list the chapters included in the unit and present a graphic illustration of the "marketing wheel," shown here.

The three inner circles of the wheel show the three foundations of marketing—the *economic* foundations, the *marketing and business* foundations, and the *human resource* foundations. The outer segments of the wheel show the functions of marketing— selling, promotion, pricing, purchasing, marketing information management, product/ service planning distribution, financing, and risk management. The foundations and/or functions that you will be studying in the unit are highlighted.

Chapter Organization

The fundamental chapters at the beginning of the text will help you understand the foundations of marketing necessary for further study and entry-level employment. They cover the essentials of economics, business, marketing, and human resource development. The remaining parts of the text focus on the more specific areas of marketing. They will help you begin building your own unique marketing career.

CHAPTER OPENERS The chapter opener pages lay out the new information and applications of marketing principles the chapter holds. Each chapter begins with a photo that depicts a major concept discussed in the chapter. An introduction briefly outlines what you will learn and often gives a brief anecdote that relates the chapter concepts to your own life.

SECTION OPENERS Each chapter is divided into sections. These begin with an objectives list that tells you the skills and knowledge you can expect to have mastered once you have completed the section. The section's key terms are also listed.

CHAPTER REVIEWS Each section ends with a short review—usually 3–4 questions. These allow you to check your understanding of the section's most important concepts.

Chapter Features

Every chapter of *Marketing Essentials* contains four features. These provide examples of chapter concepts, extra information (often of an amusing or a surprising nature), and challenges to your creativity and imagination.

CASE STUDIES These full-page features give you real-life applications of chapter content. They focus on either current marketing trends or products, people, and companies that have been very successful. You'll recognize many of the companies and brand names discussed.

The case studies end with a short series of questions designed to help you see how the chapter's principles apply to the real-life marketing situations presented. Some questions even challenge those principles. Every Case Study Review ends with a special question that requires you to consider the ethical implications of some aspect of the case study.

REAL WORLD MARKETING Each chapter contains one or two of these short features. Many contain fun facts about such marketing-related topics as product and brand development, advertising, and successful entrepreneurs. They will give you an "I didn't know that!" thrill of discovery. Others focus on recent developments in marketing and speculate about likely future directions.

LIFE IN THE MULTICULTURAL MARKETPLACE This feature will help make you aware of the challenges of doing business in a global economy. The feature focuses on the kinds of cultural differences that can make or break a product, company, or business relationship when one is doing business across cultural boundaries.

BRIGHT IDEAS This feature focuses on the kinds of creative insights and problem solving that make for marketing success. It has two distinct parts. There's a narrative portion that tells how a particular marketing innovation came about—for example, how the Sony Walkman was created. The narrative is followed by a team activity that challenges you and your fellow students to think creatively.

End-of-Chapter Reviews

Each chapter ends with a series of activities designed to help you review content and prepare for a test or other form of assessment. They include these types of activities:

• **Vocabulary**—everything from formulating definitions to writing paragraphs or short essays using vocabulary words.

• **Fact and idea**—simple recall of chapter material.

• **Critical thinking**—questions that require more advanced thinking skills such as interpretation, analysis, comparison, making judgments, or applying concepts.

• **Basic skills**—realistic applications of chapter concepts involving math, communication, human relations, and technology.

• **Projects**—applications of chapter concepts designed to be done outside of class and involving real-life situations.

• **Linking school to work**—interview-based activities designed to be done on the job.

• **Performance assessment**—role-play, public speaking, and similar activities that offer ways of being assessed other than by traditional testing.

In addition, the last chapter in every unit features an ongoing Portfolio activity. It allows you to select the best of your marketing review projects for inclusion in a portfolio designed to go with you when you seek a job in the marketing field.

The World of Marketing

Unit Objectives

After completing this unit, students will be able to achieve the following outcomes:

- Describe the scope of marketing.
- Explain the economic value and benefits of marketing.
- Discuss the reasons for studying marketing.
- State the marketing concept.
- Define what constitutes a market, as well as how to identify one.
- Identify key methods used to reach potential customers, including developing a customer profile, target marketing, and positioning.

Chapter 1

Chapter 2

Teacher Classroom Resources

CHAPTER	1	2
Transparency Binder	Transparencies 1a & 1b	Transparencies 2–3a & 3b
Student Activity Workbook	pp. 1–6	pp. 7–12
Student Software	pp. 6–5	pp. 11–12
Marketing Math Workbook		Activity 1
School-to-Work Handbook	pp. 7–8	pp. 9–10
International Case Studies	pp. 7–8	pp. 9–10
Marketing Career Portfolio		Unit 1 activity, Student Text, p. 27
Test Booklet/ Testmaker Software	Chapter 1 test	Chapter 2 test, Unit 1 test

KEY TO BASIC SKILLS ACTIVITIES

L1 Level 1 activities are basic activities and should be within the range of all students.

L2 Level 2 activities are average activities and should be within the range of average and above average students.

L3 Level 3 activities are challenging activities designed for the ability range of above average students.

CHAPTER	PERFORMANCE OBJECTIVES

1
 	
Marketing Is All Around Us
	1.1 **1.** Define marketing.
	      2. Identify the nine functions of marketing.
	1.2 **1.** Define economic utility.
	      2. Name the five economic utilities and distinguish those related to marketing.
	      3. List the benefits of marketing.
	      4. Discuss the reasons for studying marketing.
	      5. Describe the trend in future employment opportunities for those trained in marketing.

2
 	
Basic Marketing Concepts
	2.1 **1.** State the marketing concept.
	      2. Distinguish customers from consumers and explain why the difference is important.
	      3. Describe what constitutes value for customers and consumers alike.
	2.2 **1.** Define what constitutes a market.
	      2. Suggest two basic ways to identify a business's potential customers and market products to them.
	      3. Describe some of the ways a market can be segmented.
	      4. Explain how to construct a customer profile.
	2.3 **1.** Identify the four P's of the marketing mix and explain how they are used to reach a business's customers.
	      2. Define positioning and illustrate its use.

Unit Overview and Background Information

Unit I provides students with a base of knowledge that they will use throughout the text. Chapter 1 defines marketing and provides an overview of the nine marketing functions that corresponds to MEA's National Marketing Curriculum (see graphic, page xviii). Chapter 2 lays the foundation for all future discussion of marketing principles and practices. It focuses on the marketing concept and such topics as market segmentation, target marketing, and positioning.

Introducing the Unit

Ask students to generate a list of products that come in different versions–models, styles, varieties, etc. (Possibilities include athletic shoes, jeans, cars, computers, ice cream, and health/beauty-care products.)

After students generate their list, ask why there are so many versions of one type of product. Then have students speculate about which types of people each product targets and how the manufacturer discovered those people's needs. Finally, have students consider how manufacturers determine how to reach the people for whom their products are intended. Tell students that answering these questions begins their journey into the world of marketing.

Unit Project

After reviewing the different marketing functions, have students select the DECA competitive area in which they want to compete this year. Then have them locate and interview a person who is employed in that area. To prepare, have students draft questions that relate to the information contained in Chapters 1 and 2. Review their questions to be sure they have covered all the important concepts. Require students to share their research with the class.

xx

Focus on the Photo/Cooperative Learning

Once students have completed this unit, divide the class into four groups. Ask each group to study the unit photo and decide which of the basic marketing concepts discussed in the unit they think it represents best. Have each group write a caption for the photo based on this analysis. Allow time for each group to present its caption along with the rationale behind it.

The World of Marketing

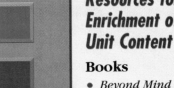

CHAPTERS

1

**Marketing Is
All Around Us**

2

**Basic Marketing
Concepts**

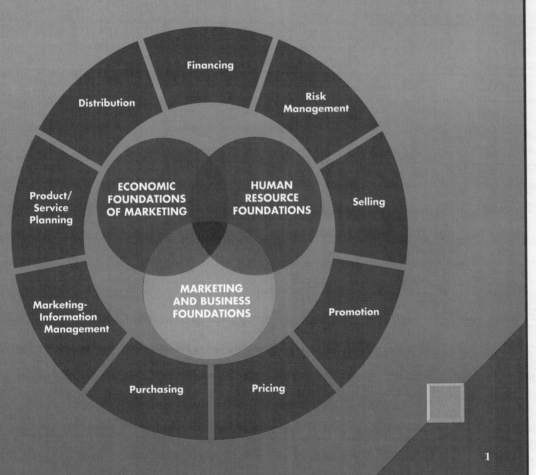

- Financing
- Risk Management
- Selling
- Promotion
- Pricing
- Purchasing
- Marketing-Information Management
- Product/Service Planning
- Distribution

ECONOMIC FOUNDATIONS OF MARKETING

HUMAN RESOURCE FOUNDATIONS

MARKETING AND BUSINESS FOUNDATIONS

Unit Closure

Have each student select a consumer item that can be demonstrated in class, such as a book, pen, grooming aid, or hat. Ask students to conduct library research to determine to whom their item was marketed to when it first appeared (original customer profile) and to whom it is marketed today (current customer profile). Have students determine how the product has changed over the years. Ask: What features have been added to the product and/or packaging that increase the product's usefulness? How have these changes added value to the product?

Evaluation

Administer the reproducible test for Unit 1, or construct your own using the Testmaker software.

Guest Speaker Suggestions

Since this unit is an overview of all marketing functions, anyone involved in marketing could qualify as a guest speaker. It would be best, however, if you could get people who are at the top of the career ladder—a director of sales, a vice president of marketing, a retail division manager, the creative director of an ad agency, or the owner of a company.

Field Trip Suggestions

Take your students for a bus ride around your community, and have them look for examples of the nine functions of marketing, the five utilities, target marketing, and positioning. At each stop along the way, require students to write down the connection between what they saw and the key concepts in Unit 1. This activity should prove to them that marketing is truly all around them.

Chapter Overview

Chapter 1 sets the stage for the students' study of marketing and their exploration of the area as a potential source of a career-sustaining job. It presents an overview of the marketing process in daily life, identifies the nine functions of marketing, and discusses the economic benefits of marketing. The chapter concludes with reasons for studying marketing.

Springboard

Ask students why they are taking the course. Write all answers on the chalkboard. Then to summarize and validate all of the reasons given, tell students that no matter what careers they choose, the course will help them become informed, proactive consumers who understand both the domestic and global economies. Explain that it will also develop in them the basic skills, thinking skills, and personal qualities necessary to succeed in both school and the workplace.

Prereading

List the section objectives to discuss with students. Have students skim the chapter, looking at the pictures, reading the captions, and noting the heads. Ask questions to ensure that students have a minimal understanding of the chapter structure.

Preteaching the Vocabulary

List the vocabulary words on the chalkboard. Then tell students to find each word where it is boldfaced in the chapter and, based on its definition, draw a picture or doodle that stands for the concept. Have students share and explain their pictures (and thus the concepts).

CHAPTER 1

Marketing Is All Around Us

In this chapter you will be introduced to the exciting world of marketing. You may not realize how much you already know about that world. As a consumer, you have been observing marketing practices your entire life. Now you will have the opportunity to explore the many facets of marketing, which are the basis for this text. You will also learn how marketing benefits you and how its study will personally help you in your career.

2   Unit 1   *The World of Marketing*

Classroom Management

For the Teacher
- Teacher's Annotated Editions for all workbooks
- Teacher's Manual for *School-to-Work Handbook*
- *Testing Binder*
- *Transparency Binder*
- *Marketing Software Binder*
- *Marketing Career Portfolio*
- *Lesson Plans*

For the Student
- *Student Activity Workbook*
- *Marketing Math Workbook*
- *School-to-Work Handbook*
- *Student Software*
- *International Case Studies*
- *Marketing Career Portfolio*

SECTION 1.1

Objectives

After completing this section, you will be able to

- define marketing and
- identify the nine functions of marketing.

Terms to Know

- marketing
- products
- goods
- services
- exchange

What Is Marketing?

Marketing is the process of developing, promoting, and distributing products in order to satisfy customers' needs and wants. **Products** include both goods and services. **Goods** are the kinds of things you can touch or hold in your hand. Hammers, automobiles, soda pop, clothing, and computers are goods. **Services** are the kinds of things you can't physically touch. They consist of a series of tasks performed for a customer. Dry cleaners, amusement parks, income tax preparers, and movie theaters provide services.

Marketing helps connect businesses to their customers and provides the means for the exchange process to occur. An **exchange** takes place every time something is sold in the marketplace.

If you consider the definition of marketing carefully, you will realize that you experience marketing principles and techniques daily. Let's take a normal school day and discover all the ways that marketing touches you.

Marketing and You

After you awake in the morning, you go to the kitchen for breakfast. You look in the cupboard at the many varieties of cereal, all with different ingredients and packaging. That is when you realize that all the products you will use this morning—shampoo, soap, toothpaste, and

---

BRIGHT IDEAS

First, Consider the Obvious

The project leader was frustrated and just a little panicked. He and his team of Sony engineers had been assigned the task of designing a miniature tape recorder with playback capability. Thus far, they had been only partially successful. Their first effort had yielded a tape player with reasonably good sound. (They listened to it now, even as they worked.) But they had been unable to squeeze a record mechanism into the device's palm-sized casing.

In the corridor, Masura Ibuka, the venerable cofounder of Sony, heard the music. Ibuka, seen as too eccentric to have a voice in the daily operations of the company, roamed the corridors looking in on various development projects. He liked the tape player and had an idea. On the other side of the building was an engineer who had developed a miniature stereo headset. Perhaps the team and that engineer could get together.

A detour—just what the project leader felt the team didn't need. What they needed was a smaller record mechanism! Still, one did not ignore a suggestion from the cofounder of Sony.

When Ibuka returned, the new version of the tape player was ready. He tried it and was delighted. The team leader could restrain himself no longer. The thing didn't record!

This was true, Ibuka admitted, savoring the obvious. But it made beautiful music. And, indeed, as the Sony Walkman, it continues to do so till this day.

Creativity Challenge Form teams of 3–5 people, and try to pick up on the obvious. Search your environment and experiences for items that are "products in waiting." These are the kinds of things about which people say, "Somebody could make a small fortune selling that."

Not too long ago, for example, sample sizes of new products would just be left at front doors. Now they're sold in stores right alongside the full-sized versions of the same items. That means that manufacturers are making a small fortune selling something that they had all along but never imagined people would buy.

FOCUS

Bell Ringer Activity

Ask students to tell you what the foundation of a building is. (Its underlying groundwork or base of support). Then ask students how you would create a building without first creating a foundation. (You can't—not if you want the structure to be solid and enduring.)

Explain that in this chapter they will begin to lay the groundwork (or foundation) for their knowledge of marketing. And they will start as any good builder does—with a blueprint, or plan.

Introducing the Section

Tell students that they will build their knowledge of marketing on not one but three foundations: *economic foundations* (basic economic principles and concepts of free enterprise and free market economics), *human resource foundations* (basic "people skills" critical to success on the job), and *marketing and business foundations* (basic skills and an understanding of the marketing concept, along with the business environment and management systems within which it is implemented). Draw each foundation in a separate circle (see the marketing "wheel" on page xviii for a model) while students do the same on a piece of paper. Tell students that they will look further at these foundations in Units 2, 3, and 4 but that the concepts are woven throughout the course.

Now draw the outer rim of the wheel and divide it into nine sections, per the model. Have students do the same on their papers. Tell them that all marketing activities are classified into nine functions that connect the people who make products (business) with those who buy them (customers). In this section, they will look at each function (and fill them in on their papers as the lesson progresses).

Meeting Special Needs

Learning Disabled

If you have students in your class with learning disabilities, they may require additional guidelines or even study aides to get the most out of the material presented in the textbook. For example, for students who find the written text difficult to use, you may wish to make chapter audio tapes so that such students can listen and read simultaneously. The tapes can be made with the help of other students in the class. Select those whose voices are clear and easy to follow. Set a relaxed pace for the reading, and use a bell or clicker to signal turned pages. Getting as many students as possible involved can make audio tape preparation a real class project in the best tradition of cooperative learning.

Teach

Guided Practice

1. Read Section 1.1 with students.
2. As you read through the material on the marketing functions, fill in each function on your chalkboard wheel. Have students do the same on their papers.
3. Introduce students to some of the publications that are standard references and resources in the marketing field. Possibilities include *Adweek's Marketing Week, American Demographics, Entrepreneur, Business Week, Forbes, Fortune, Inc., Nation's Business, Newsweek, Sales & Marketing Management, Time,* and the *U.S. Statistical Abstract. The Wall Street Journal* and the business section of the *New York Times* are also excellent resources. Encourage students to do all of the outside reading in marketing and business that they can fit into their schedules.

Discussion Starter

Ask: How have you used the nine functions of marketing in your activities inside or outside of school? (Answers will vary but could include advertising a car wash [promotion], selling candy or magazines [selling], setting a price on items for a bake sale [pricing], and buying items to make crafts for a fund raiser sale [purchasing]).

Critical Thinking

Ask: How are you part of the marketing process? (When you buy something you are in effect casting an "economic vote" to keep that product in the marketplace over one of its competitors. You are connecting yourself as a customer to a business by providing the exchange in the marketplace.)

toiletries—are created to meet your needs. Product planning and packaging are part of marketing.

You wonder what happened last night with your favorite sports team. You check the newspaper. It's filled with national and local retail advertising. One ad in particular catches your attention. So, you ask a few friends to go to the mall with you today after school. Advertising is part of marketing.

At the mall, scores of enticing store window displays encourage you to enter. Some of the stores are having sales featuring price reductions of 20–50 percent. Displays and promotional techniques are part of marketing.

In the mall store you enter, you are greeted by a sales associate who is ready to assist you with your purchase decisions. Personal selling is part of marketing, too, as are all the retail stores that help to distribute manufacturers' products.

You remember the trucks backed up to the loading docks that you passed on your way into the mall. All those trucks were moving goods from producers of products to consumers. You realize that someone had to sell those products to the businesses that purchased them for resale or use in their operations. During the buying-selling process, prices and delivery as well as credit terms had to be decided. All those selling and distribution functions are part of marketing.

As you are leaving the mall, a young man with a clipboard approaches you and asks if he can take five minutes of your time to ask a few questions about a new product. You are now participating in a marketing research study.

You wonder why the company doing the research wants your viewpoint. Then you realize that the product is one that you might consider buying.

On your way home, you come to the conclusion that marketing is truly all around us. You observe marketing practices every day.

Functions of Marketing

All the marketing activities you see daily can be classified into the nine functions of marketing. To see what those functions are, look again at the marketing wheel (page 1). The nine functions are the categories that make up the wheel's outer rim. Those functions help us appreciate the wide scope of activities involved in marketing.

Marketing Is Purchasing Purchasing is buying goods and services for a business's operation. For example, shirt manufacturers buy cloth and thread to make their products. Apparel retailers buy the finished shirts for resale in their stores.

Marketing Is Selling Selling is providing customers with goods and services they want to buy. This includes selling in the retail market to you, the final consumer of the product. It also includes selling in the industrial market where products are purchased for use in business operations.

Marketing Is Pricing Pricing means deciding how much to charge for goods and services. Most pricing decisions take competition into consideration, as well as how much a customer is willing to pay.

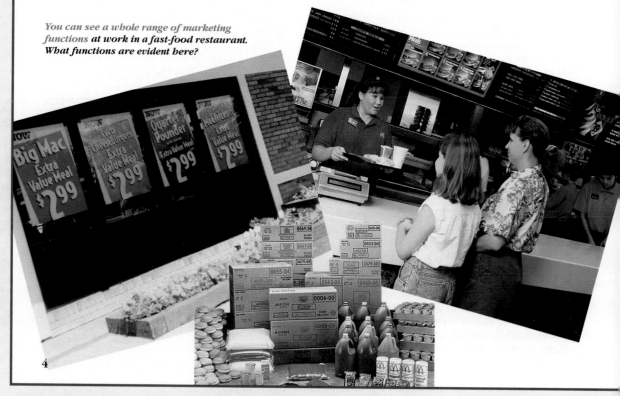

*You can see a whole range of marketing functions **at work in a fast-food restaurant.** What functions are evident here?*

4

Beverage Family Tree
PepsiCo beverages are available in 166 countries and territories through company-owned, joint venture and franchised bottlers.

Introduced 1991.

Introduced 1989.

Introduced 1992.

Distributed since 1991.

Introduced 1992.

Introduced 1984. Estimated 1993 Retail Sales: $610 Million.

Distributed since 1992.

Introduced 1992.

Acquired 1986. Estimated 1993 Retail Sales: $150 Million.

Acquired 1986. Estimated 1993 Retail Sales: $1.7 Billion. (PepsiCo owns brand 7UP outside the U.S.)

Introduced 1964. Estimated 1993 Retail Sales: $2.8 Billion.

Introduced 1993. (Sold outside the U.S.)

Introduced 1964. Estimated 1993 Retail Sales: $4.4 Billion.

Introduced 1957. Estimated 1993 Retail Sales: $1.1 Billion. (Sold outside the U.S.)

Introduced 1898. Estimated 1993 Retail Sales: $16.2 Billion.

Total Retail Sales: $28.2 Billion

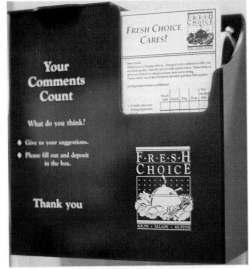

Planning, promoting, and researching—those are activities that producers of goods and services use to ensure the success of their products. What evidence of those functions do you see here?

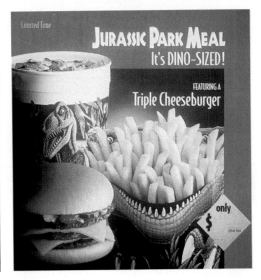

Marketing Is Product Planning Product planning involves all the decisions a business makes in the production and sale of its goods and services. Which products to carry is a major decision. Other decisions involve product packaging, labeling, and branding.

Marketing Is Marketing Information Management Marketing information management is the process of getting the marketing information needed to make sound business decisions. The basis for this process is marketing research. Did you ever complete a restaurant questionnaire that asked you to rate the service

you received? If so, you have participated in marketing research. Companies conduct marketing research to learn more about their customers, products, and promotions.

Marketing Is Promotion Promotion is any form of communication used to inform, persuade, or remind people about a business's products. Promotion is also used to improve a firm's public image. The TV and radio commercials you see and hear are forms of promotion called advertising. Specially designed drinking glasses or children's toys given away by McDonald's are a type of promotion, too.

Chapter 1 *Marketing Is All Around Us* **5**

Independent Practice

1. Assign and review the Chapter 1 Case Study in the *International Case Studies* workbook.
2. Have students take a mental walk through the local business district and list 20 products sold there. Then have them label each product as a good or a service. Review these lists in class.

Assess

Evaluation

Assign and review the Section 1.1 Review.

Reteaching

1. Assign and review the vocabulary terms for this section.
2. Assign and review Fact and Idea Review questions 1 and 2 from the Chapter Review.
3. Have students help you generate a chalkboard list of all the things they or their family purchased within the last week. Then have them help you label each as a good or service.

Enrichment

1. Assign and review the appropriate activities in the *Student Activity Workbook*.
2. Assign and review the appropriate Critical Thinking questions from the Chapter Review.
3. Have students choose three marketing functions and apply each to a real-life example in your local business community. (Answers will vary.)

Close

Have students complete this statement: Marketing is... (the process of developing, promoting, and distributing products in order to satisfy customers' needs and wants.)

6

Marketing Is Financing Financing is getting the money needed to finance the operation of a business. Business owners may request a bank loan in order to start a new business. Financing also includes decisions regarding offering credit to customers. Most retailers offer customers payment options such as MasterCard or Visa.

Marketing Is Distribution Distribution involves making decisions about where to sell your product. It also includes deciding on the method of transportation—truck, rail, ship, or air. How and where products are stored adds to the distribution decision

making. Some large retail chains store products in central warehouses for later distribution to member outlets.

Marketing Is Risk Management Risk management is preventing or reducing business loss. One economic risk that is out of a business's control might be a high local unemployment rate. Another might be the introduction of a new competing business in town. When Wal-Mart moves into a town, competing stores realize there is a risk customers will shop in the new store. Other risks include employee or customer accidents, as well as natural risks, such as floods or fires.

Function follows form—each of these buildings suggests a marketing activity that businesses pursue in order to sell their products. What are those activities?

Real World MARKETING

But Is It Still Good for What Ails You?

When Perkins Products Company brought out its "fruit smack" tonic in 1914, it was hoping the syrup's pleasant flavor would stimulate sales of the household remedy. The marketing hook worked so well that people began to drink the tonic even though they were feeling fine. They still do today. Only now they ask for it by a different name: Kool-Aid.

SECTION 1.1 Review

1. What is an exchange?
2. Which of the nine functions of marketing were illustrated in the typical school day described in this section?
3. Which of the nine functions of marketing were *not* illustrated in that same discussion?

Caption Answer

Obtaining *financing,* possibly from a bank; *distributing* their products, possibly by truck; *managing risk,* possibly by obtaining insurance against things like natural disasters.

Section Review Answers

1. The sale of something in the marketplace.
2. Product planning, promotion, selling, distribution, marketing research, purchasing, and pricing.
3. Financing and risk management.

SECTION 1.2

Objectives

After completing this section, you will be able to

- **define economic utility,**
- **name the five economic utilities and distinguish those related to marketing,**
- **list the benefits of marketing,**
- **discuss the reasons for studying marketing, and**
- **describe the trend in future employment opportunities for those trained in marketing.**

Terms to Know

- utility
- form utility
- place utility
- time utility
- possession utility
- information utility

Economic Benefits of Marketing

Have you ever questioned the benefits of marketing to businesses and to you personally? Marketing bridges the gap between you and the maker or seller of an item. In doing so, it helps make products more useful because you are able to purchase them when you want. Marketing makes buying easy for consumers. It also helps to create new and improved products, as well as lower prices.

Added Value

The functions of marketing add value to a product. In other words, they make it more useful. That added value in economic terms is called **utility**.

There are five economic utilities involved with all products—*form, place, time, possession,* and *information*. Of the five, form utility is the only one that is not directly related to marketing. The remaining four are marketing utilities.

Form Utility Form utility involves changing raw materials or putting parts together to make them more useful. In other words, it deals with making, or producing, things.

Let's look at a tree to determine its utility. In its original state, a tree has value as an object of beauty. It also prevents soil erosion and produces oxygen for us to breathe. When the tree is cut down to use in making other products, however, its usefulness increases. Lumber from the tree might be used to make pencils, paper, furniture, and buildings. The raw material (wood) becomes part of finished items that have more value to us than the raw material itself.

The same would be true if a manufacturer were assembling parts into a product. For example, the parts of a chair—the wood frame, the fabric used for the upholstery, the glue and nails used to hold the parts together, the reclining mechanism—are relatively useless by themselves. Putting them together adds form utility.

Place Utility Place utility involves having a product where customers can buy it. Businesses often study consumer shopping habits to determine where would be the most convenient location for consumers to shop. Some businesses decide on a direct approach by selling their products through catalogs. Others decide to rely on retailers for help in selling their products.

Time Utility Time utility is having a product available at a certain time of year or a convenient time of day. Marketers increase the value of their products by having them available when consumers want them. In order to achieve that goal, marketers must plan their operations well in advance.

Take, for example, toy manufacturers and retailers. Toy manufacturers introduce their new products to retailers each year in February at a toy fair held in New York City. That is when retailers decide which products they will sell during the holiday season *some nine months later!*

Retailers also offer convenient shopping hours to accommodate their customers. Mall stores are generally open 10 A.M.–9 P.M., while some convenience stores are open 24 hours a day.

Possession Utility How do you come into possession of the items you want? Unless they are given to you as a gift, you generally buy them for a given price. That exchange—of a product for some monetary value—is **possession utility.**

Retailers may accept alternatives to cash, like personal checks or credit cards, in exchange for their merchandise. They may even offer installment or layaway plans (delayed possession in return for gradual payment). Every one of these options adds value to the product being purchased. In fact, without these options, some customers would not be able to buy the items they want.

In business-to-business situations, companies also grant their customers credit. They may give them a certain period (say, 30 days) to pay a bill. This adds value to the products they sell.

Focus

Bell Ringer Activity

Have students help you generate a chalkboard list of at least five products that students and/or faculty in your school would want to buy at your school site and use daily or weekly. Once you compile the list, have students reach a consensus and choose one product for this activity. (Do not use a ballpoint pen, because this is used in Figure 1-1 on pages 8 and 9.)

Introducing the Section

Using the product chosen for the Bell Ringer Activity, ask students to answer the following questions. Write their answers on the chalkboard, dividing them into columns by economic utility.

1. What raw materials went into the making of this product? (Form utility.)
2. Where would you place this product so your customers would see it? (Place utility.)
3. When would be the best time of day to sell this product? the best time of year? (Time utility.)
4. How would students and/or faculty pay for this product—cash? personal check? school credit account? (Possession utility.)
5. How would you get information about this product to your potential customers—window displays? school newspaper ads? personal selling in the school cafeteria during lunch hours? (Information utility.)

Tell students that by answering the questions above, they have told how they would add economic value—or economic *utility*—to a product so that it can be sold. Mention that a producer initially added the economic value of *form utility* to raw materials to make them into a product in the first place. Then point out that even a quality product won't sell if consumers aren't made aware of it, and its features and benefits, through

Lifelong Learning

Marketing Is All Around Us

Employers frequently state that good interpersonal skills are required for even the most technical of jobs. This skill can be learned and improved over time in a variety of ways. Many classes are offered under a wide range of titles, such as Getting Along with Others, Communication Skills, Assertiveness Training, Customer Relations, Supervisory Skills, Listening Skills, or even Speech. Sometimes the courses are offered through adult education programs at local high schools or community colleges, or they may be part of the regular course offerings at a college or university.

advertising, product labeling, sales pitches, etc. (*information utility*). If it isn't made available to consumers in a place where they can see it (*place utility*), at a time when they need it (*time utility*), and in a way that they can conveniently pay for it (*possession utility*), they also won't buy it. Explain that this section looks at the ways marketers add value to products so that they will sell.

Teach

Guided Practice

1. Read Section 1.2 with students.
2. Have students read aloud the Case Study and review the answers in class.
3. Use the transparency for this section.
4. When discussing marketing careers on page 11, introduce the five levels of employment in marketing—*entry level, career sustaining, specialist, supervisor,* and *manager/ entrepreneur.* To be sure students understand the depth and breadth of skills required for each level, you might have them read the descriptions of these levels in Chapter 41, Section 2.
5. Assign and review the Chapter 1 Activity in the *School-to-Work Handbook.*

Discussion Starter

Have students describe which of the four utilities are created by the work they do in their co-op jobs. (Answers will vary. One possibility: "In my job, I arrange products in displays at the ends of aisles and by the cash registers. This adds place utility because the products are then positioned where customers will see them and perhaps buy them while they're waiting to pay for other goods.")

So, possession utility is involved every time legal ownership of a product changes hands. Possession utility increases as purchase options increase.

Information Utility Information utility involves communication with the consumer. Salespeople provide information to customers by explaining the features and benefits of products. Displays communicate information, too. Packaging and labeling inform consumers about qualities and uses of a product. For example, the label on a frozen food entree will tell you the ingredients, nutritional information, directions for preparation, and safety precautions. Advertising informs consumers of products and tells where to buy them, as well as how much they cost. Many manufacturers provide owners' manuals to explain how to use their products.

To sell products, then, businesspeople must transform materials into products that have value and use. They do this by employing the five economic utilities. Figure 1-1 presents an overview of this process using a single product as an example.

Figure 1-1

ECONOMIC UTILITIES

reflect the value that producers and marketers add to raw materials when they make them into products and offer them for sale to the public. Consider a ballpoint pen like the one you use for your schoolwork.

2. Place Utility

The manufacturer ships its pens to retail businesses— stationery stores, drugstores, supermarkets, mass merchandisers, and school stores—that make them available to consumers.

1. Form Utility

Plastic, metal, and ink are useless to a student in their raw form. However, once processed and put together, they have increased value (or utility) as a pen.

3. Time Utility

Retailers selling pens stock them regularly but may offer larger supplies in September, at the beginning of the school year.

Did You Know ?

Very few manufacturers do anything in real time. Fashion retailers buy at least six months to one year ahead of any given season. Magazines are produced six months prior to publication, requiring editors to celebrate the Fourth of July in December! Textbooks are traditionally published to be available the spring before the fall of their intended use in class. Ask students which utility influences these decisions. (Time utility.)

4. Information Utility

To encourage sales, retailers may offer special prices and let potential customers know about them through ads, signs, or displays.

5. Possession Utility

As part of the actual sales transaction, the customer pays for the pen (with cash, check, or credit card) and takes possession of it.

Lower Prices

Besides adding value to products, marketing activities also help increase demand for them. When demand is high, manufacturers can make products in larger quantities, which reduces the unit cost of each product. This is because there are fixed costs—such as the rent on a building—that remain the same whether the company produces 10 units or 10,000 units. When a company produces a larger quantity of a product, it spends less per unit on fixed costs. Thus, it can charge a lower price.

Here is an example using a fixed cost of $20,000.

Quantity Produced	Fixed Cost Per Unit
10,000	$2.00
200,000	.10

As you can see, the increased quantity significantly reduces the fixed cost per unit.

In addition, when products become popular, more competitors enter the marketplace. In order to be competitive, marketers find ways to lower their prices. Videocassette recorders were priced at more than $600 when they were first introduced. Now you can purchase a VCR for as little as $140. That's less than a quarter of the original price.

New and Improved Products

New and improved products are another result of increased competition generated by marketing. As businesses continue to look for opportunities to better satisfy customers' wants and needs, the result is a larger variety of goods and services for consumers. For example, personal computers have gotten smaller, more powerful, and less expensive. As more and more people become computer literate, this market continues to grow.

A review of detergents demonstrates the change in consumer preference and competition in that market. For years, consumers only had powder detergents available to them. Now consumers can choose between powder and liquid detergents. Easy-to-use containers with caps that measure the amount of liquid detergent to use for washing clothes demonstrate how marketers have responded to changing consumer trends.

Chapter 1 *Marketing Is All Around Us* **9**

More About

New Products

As the range of new products expands and competition for shelf space grows more intense, new product development becomes crucial for brand survival. Marketers must respond more quickly than ever to changes in consumer preferences. And thanks to computer technology, they can. In addition, even products that are doing well are often modified or made "new" in some way to stay fresh in consumers' minds.

Teach (Cont'd.)

You may also wish to have students look through the classified section of your local newspaper for ads seeking candidates for the career-sustaining jobs they chose to research.

Independent Practice

Choose a local business and describe how it provides the marketing utilities discussed in this chapter for three products.

Assess

Evaluation

Assign and review the Section 1.2 Review.

Reteaching

1. Assign and review the vocabulary terms for this section.
2. Assign and review Fact and Idea Review questions 3–9 from the Chapter Review.
3. Have students name two products to which marketers add time utility, place utility, possession utility and information utility. (Answers will vary but could include holiday merchandise [time utility]; soft drinks and workout clothing in a health club, batteries in a toy store [place utility]; layaway plans for clothing purchases, 90 days/same as cash deals on major appliances [possession utility]; written labels and warnings on over-the-counter medications, owner manuals from product manufacturers [information utility].)

CASE STUDY

Baking Soda—Genuine Improvement or Trendy Additive?

Baking soda is a derivative of trona, a naturally occurring mineral mined in Wyoming. As a consumer product, it dates back to 1846 when it was sold in one-pound bags as a baking ingredient. Today the baking soda box suggests using the product as a multipurpose household cleaner, an antacid, and a deodorizer for refrigerator and freezer.

It wasn't until 1970, however, that baking soda was used as an *ingredient* in other products. In that year Church & Dwight Co., Inc., added baking soda to its Arm & Hammer laundry detergent. Then, in 1988 the same company introduced Arm & Hammer toothpaste with baking soda. Major competitors like Colgate and Procter & Gamble (Crest toothpaste) quickly followed suit. In 1994 Chesebrough-Ponds introduced Mentadent—a toothpaste with fluoride, baking soda, and peroxide.

With the success of baking soda as a toothpaste ingredient, more and more companies began looking for ways to improve their products by adding baking soda. Western Pleasure added baking soda to its shampoo to reinforce its natural image. Baking soda was added to Scope mouthwash because research showed that

consumers believed it made their mouths feel clean. Odor-Eaters foot powder added baking soda as an ingredient because of its odor-destroying properties. For the same reason, Church & Dwight introduced Arm & Hammer deodorant antiperspirant with baking soda.

It will be interesting to see if adding baking soda continues to be the improvement of choice for established products. One company, Den-Mat, sees the trend as a fad. To reinforce that message, it included the words *baking soda-free* on the packaging of its Rembrandt brushing gel. Gillette's Oral-B Laboratories, which stresses the therapeutic nature of its products, agrees with Den-Mat. The division has not developed any oral-care products with baking soda.

In fact, both companies are supported by research. There is no clinical proof that baking soda actually makes the mouth cleaner. However, consumers don't seem to care about clinical studies. So, for the present it appears that using baking soda to enhance other products will continue. Just think, the baking soda you put in your refrigerator to kill odors can do the same—for your mouth, hair, shoes...

Case Study Review

1. Does adding baking soda to detergent, shampoo, foot powder, deodorant, toothpaste, and mouthwash add economic utility to those products? If so, what kind of utility? If not, why not?
2. How do the uses of baking soda described here support the theory that marketing helps create new and improved products?

A MATTER OF ETHICS

3. If there is no clinical proof that baking soda makes a person's mouth cleaner, is it ethical for the companies to suggest that it does?

Case Study Answers

1. Yes, adding baking soda adds to form utility of all named products by making them more useful to consumers.
2. When Arm & Hammer's detergent and toothpaste were successful, competitors tried to develop even better products using baking soda. Chesebrough-Ponds went a step further by adding peroxide to their Mentadent toothpaste.
3. Answers will vary. Most students will recognize that marketers should not make claims that cannot be substantiated. This particular claim, however, reflects how people *feel* when they use the product, not scientific fact.

Why Study Marketing?

By studying marketing, you will have the opportunity to evaluate marketing as a potential career. Even if you don't think marketing is for you, you will come to realize its importance for personal success. The skills and knowledge you gain from the study of marketing will help you in school and on the job.

Developing Marketing Skills

Marketing skills are useful in any career because they involve understanding business, as well as effectively relating and communicating with others. Let's look at the basic skills or foundations that employers expect from all levels of employees. From top management down to entry-level positions, these foundations are ones upon which a career in marketing is based.

Understanding Business You must understand how businesses operate in order to apply marketing practices in our free enterprise system. The more you learn about economics, business, and government's role in our economy, the better prepared you will be to advance in your career. In addition, this understanding will help you become a better-educated citizen. You will appreciate how government decisions impact your livelihood and be able to translate such information into intelligent voting decisions.

Understanding how businesses function on a day-to-day basis will help you develop the necessary attitude and skills required for successful employment. You will come to realize the importance of cooperation, competition, ethics, and teamwork.

Learning Interpersonal Skills Learning the techniques and principles of human relations will improve your ability to get along with others. This will help you in your dealings with supervisors, co-workers, customers, and friends.

Perfecting Communication Skills Do you ever find others asking you to explain something you said or wrote? If so, you may need to improve your oral and written communication skills. You will have that chance through the study of marketing. Marketing is communicating. How well businesspeople present their ideas to employees, customers, and others has a direct impact on a business's success or failure.

Is Marketing a Career for You?

According to the Bureau of Labor Statistics (BLS), employment in marketing and sales is projected to increase 20.6 percent in the period 1992–2005. A total of 2,671,000 new marketing and sales jobs is projected. Employment in service-related industries is expected to increase 33.4 percent (6,462,000 new jobs).

Another measure of employment opportunity in marketing is based on the type of employment, regardless of the industry within which it is done. The occupational structure of employment indicates that there has been an increase in managerial, sales, and service positions in all industries. Department of Labor projections indicate that managerial jobs in marketing-related fields will continue to be plentiful.

Throughout this text, you will have the opportunity to investigate marketing careers. Learning what careers you do not like is just as important as finding the career of your choice. By the time you have finished studying this text, you will have a good idea of the marketing careers that are right for you.

Life in the Multicultural MARKETPLACE

Two Translators Are Better Than One

Want to avoid translation problems when advertising outside the United States? Then hire a *backtranslator*. That's a second person to translate your ad copy *back into English* once it's been translated into a foreign language. Why the extra step? If the retranslated text differs from the original ad, you will know there are problems with the first translation. What can happen if you don't backtranslate? This:

- Pepsi issues an invitation to "come alive with the Pepsi generation"—only in Taiwanese it's a promise to "bring your ancestors back from the dead."
- Schweppes Tonic Water in Italian gets a market shift—to Schweppes Toilet Water.
- Kentucky Fried Chicken ("finger-lickin' good") tells the Chinese that its product is so good you will "eat your fingers off."

SECTION 1.2 Review

1. What is meant by the economic concept of utility?
2. Which economic utility is not classified as a marketing utility? Why?
3. Besides added value, what are two other benefits of marketing?
4. List the basic skills needed for success in a marketing career.
5. According to the Bureau of Labor Statistics, approximately how many new marketing and sales jobs will be created between 1992 and 2005?

Enrichment

1. Assign and review the appropriate activities in the *Student Activity Workbook*.
2. Assign and review the appropriate Critical Thinking questions from the Chapter Review.
3. Assign and review the Building Academic Skills Activities, Application Projects, Linking School to Work Activity, and Performance Assessment from the Chapter Review.
4. Many stores add possession utility by offering various payment plans so customers can enjoy their purchases (or at least have them held at the store) while paying for them over time. Have students survey the same type of department manager in at least three stores to determine what payment plans each offers. Then have them write a 100-word summary that explains the conditions of each store's payment plans and their own personal choice among those plans. *Note:* If a given store offers no payment plans, have students ask why and incorporate the answer in their reports as well.

Close

Have students complete the following statement: The functions of marketing add value to a product by making it more useful. This added value is also called _____ . (utility)

Section Review Answers

1. Utility means value added usefulness.
2. Form utility—because it is concerned with production of a product.
3. Lower prices and the creation of new and improved products.
4. Understanding of business, development of interpersonal and communication skills.
5. About 2.7 million.

11

Answers

Vocabulary Review

Paragraphs will vary. See Glossary for definitions.

Fact and Idea Review

1. Marketing is the process of developing, promoting, and distributing products through the exchange process in order to satisfy customers' wants and needs.
2. Purchasing, selling, pricing, product planning, marketing information management, promotion, financing, distribution, and risk management.
3. No, all are important for business success. Each contributes to making the product more useful to the consumer.
4. Place, time, possession, and information.
5. The raw materials that go into a pen are useless by themselves. However, once they are processed into parts and assembled in the production process, they have increased value, or utility, as a ballpoint pen.
6. By increasing demand for a product, which reduces the unit cost.
7. New and improved products are another result of increased competition.
8. Because it involves understanding business, as well as effectively relating and communicating with others.
9. Marketing jobs will continue to be plentiful.

Critical Thinking

1. A presidential campaign involves the process of planning and executing ideas (campaign promises). The exchange process involves votes instead of money.
2. One possibility: Marketing research indicates that people want fresher breath, and

Vocabulary Review

In a paragraph, define *marketing* and then explain the relationship of the following terms to it.

products
goods
services
exchange
utility
form utility
place utility
time utility
possession utility
information utility

Fact and Idea Review

1. What is marketing? (Sec. 1.1)
2. Identify the nine functions of marketing. (Sec. 1.1)
3. Of the four marketing utilities, is one more important than the other for business success? Explain. (Sec. 1.2)
4. Which of the five economic utilities are related to marketing? (Sec. 1.2)
5. Using a ballpoint pen as an example, explain the concept of form utility. (Sec. 1.2)
6. How can marketing help lower prices? (Sec. 1.2)
7. Explain marketing's role in developing new and improved products. (Sec. 1.2)
8. Why is the study of marketing helpful in any career? (Sec. 1.2)
9. What do Department of Labor projections predict for marketing jobs? (Sec. 1.2)

Critical Thinking

1. How is a presidential political campaign an example of marketing?
2. Provide an example of how marketing research could be related to product planning and promotion for a new or improved dental hygiene product. Assume your research revealed that "fresh breath" was important to the consumers studied.
3. How would you explain the following statement: Marketing is more than just promotion.
4. It is often said that marketing costs represent approximately 50 percent of the selling price of an item. Select a product of your choice to justify the need for marketing and its related costs in the sale of that product.

5. When handheld calculators were first introduced, they sold for $100. As they became popular, more and more companies introduced better, less expensive ones. Now you can purchase a handheld, solar-powered calculator for as little as $5. Provide several examples of other products that were more costly when they were first put on the market than they are now.
6. Why do you think employers want employees who have an understanding of business, as well as good interpersonal and communication skills?

Building Academic Skills

Math

1. Fixed costs for manufacturing widgets are $25,000. Determine the fixed cost per unit when the quantity produced is (a) 5,000 and (b) 75,000.

Communication

2. Write three questions that could be used to survey students' satisfaction with the prices, selection, and quality of food served in your school cafeteria.

Human Relations

3. Assume you are a salesperson in a computer store. A customer you are waiting on is hesitant about buying the midpriced laptop computer you've been showing her. Her objection? She's sure that with her luck she'll pay top dollar for the laptop now and in a year it will sell for less. Do you think she's correct? What would you say to her?

Application Projects

1. With 2–3 classmates, write a short story about a new fruit juice that you believe will be popular with teenagers. Assume you develop this new product and want to start selling it. Cover all nine marketing functions in your story. When you introduce each function, note this in parentheses.
   Example: The producers of Ocean Spray cranberry juice are trying to reach teenagers with a television commercial that uses upbeat music; an action shot of a large, breaking ocean wave; and a verbal invitation to "catch the wave." (Promotion)
2. Using the short story written in the first project, identify examples of the five economic utilities. Exactly what did your group do to create form, time, place, possession, and information utility?

---

baking soda is a means of achieving that goal. Therefore, toothpaste and mouthwash companies invent new formulas that include baking soda and promote those products by stressing the baking soda ingredient as the one that produces fresh breath.
3. Includes all activities from the conception of a product to its final consumption.
4. Students should use the marketing utilities to justify marketing costs.

5. Possibilities: big-screen televisions, CD players, portable cassette players, etc.
6. One possibility: Employers want employees who understand both their role in the total operation of a business and the importance of customers. Employees who realize that profit is necessary for businesses to survive will develop the type of attitude and skills needed for successful employment. Also, employees must be able to get along with co-workers and supervisors as well as

3. Summarize an article related to one of the nine functions of marketing or the five economic utilities. To find relevant articles, use business publications such as *Brandweek, Adweek, Business Week, Fortune, Forbes, Nation's Business, Sales & Marketing Management,* or *Marketing News.* Share your article summary with classmates. As a class, see if all nine functions and five utilities were covered by student presentations.
4. Design a bulletin-board display to depict the five economic utilities.

Linking School to Work

Ask your employer to identify 5–10 characteristics of an effective employee. Categorize those characteristics as a business understanding, an interpersonal skill, or a communication skill. Were there any characteristics that did not fit into one of those three categories? Which characteristic was regarded as most important to your employer? Why?

Performance Assessment

Role Play

Situation. You are employed as a cashier in the local supermarket. A disgruntled customer complains to

you about how manufacturers and retailers waste money on marketing. She thinks retail prices could be significantly reduced if manufacturers spent less money on marketing their products. As a high school marketing student, you take this opportunity to respond to the customer.

Evaluation. You will be evaluated on how well you do the following:

* Explain how marketing activities can actually lower prices.
* Show that marketing helps create new and improved products.
* Demonstrate the concept of economic utility.

Public Speaking

Prepare a two-minute speech to explain how form, place, time, possession, and information utilities contribute to the success of a product.

Complete the Chapter 1 Computer Application that appears in the Student Activity Workbook.

---

customers. Good communication skills are helpful in maintaining these relationships.

Building Academic Skills

Math
1. a. $25,000 \div 5,000 = \$5$
   b. $25,000 \div 75,000 = \$.33$

Communication
2. Possible questions include:

a. Our school cafeteria prices are fair. (Choices: Strongly Agree, Agree, No Opinion, Disagree, Strongly Disagree.)
b. I am pleased with our cafeteria's food selection. (Choices: Strongly Agree, Agree, No Opinion, Disagree, Strongly Disagree.)
c. I would rate the quality of food served in our school cafeteria as—(Choices: Poor, Fair, Good, Excellent.)

Human Relations
3. Students should be willing to concede that the customer is probably right about the laptop's selling for less in the future. The increased demand and competition created by marketing will likely bring prices down. In the interim, however, she will be doing without the convenience of a laptop. Making one available to her now, in a neighborhood store, with informative displays and sales support (time, place, and information utilities) makes the purchase worth the slightly higher price (possession utility).

Application Projects
1. Stories will vary.
2. Responses will depend on stories written for first project.
3. Summaries will depend on articles selected.
4. Displays will vary.

Linking School to Work
Answers depend on the work situation.

Performance Assessment
Refer to the *DECA Competitive Events Handbook* for evaluation guidelines.

Computer Application
Optional activity. Refer to the *Marketing Software Binder* for template and user information.

Evaluation
Administer the reproducible test for Chapter 1, or construct your own using the Testmaker software.

Chapter Overview

Chapter 2 introduces students to the marketing concept. It also describes how markets are segmented and discusses marketing strategies used to reach customers. Key concepts developed include target marketing, marketing mix (the four P's), and positioning.

Springboard

Tell students that in this chapter they will explore several different meanings for the word *market*. Have students write a series of sentences using the word in as many different ways as possible.

Prereading

List the section objectives to discuss with students. Have students skim the chapter, looking at the pictures, reading the captions, and noting the heads. Ask questions to ensure that students have a minimal understanding of the chapter structure.

Preteaching the Vocabulary

Before students begin reading the chapter, dictate each of the vocabulary terms and ask students to write them on a sheet of paper. When they finish, write the terms on the chalkboard. Then have students guess at the meaning of each. Write their guesses next to each term, but do not give the correct meaning. Leave this list on the chalkboard so that students can see how close their guesses were to the actual definitions as they work through the chapter.

Basic Marketing Concepts

CHAPTER 2

To be competitive and make a profit, businesses constantly try to improve their products. First, they study the market and identify their customers. Then they focus on the needs and wants of those customers. Finally, they use various techniques to reach those customers with their products.

This chapter will give you an overview of this process. Along the way, it will introduce you to some of the most important and basic concepts underlying all of marketing. These are concepts that you will find yourself using again and again as you proceed through this text.

Classroom Management

For the Teacher
- Teacher's Annotated Editions for all workbooks
- Teacher's Manual for *School-to-Work Handbook*
- *Testing Binder*
- *Transparency Binder*
- *Marketing Software Binder*
- *Marketing Career Portfolio*
- *Lesson Plans*

For the Student
- *Student Activity Workbook*
- *Marketing Math Workbook*
- *School-to-Work Handbook*
- *Student Software*
- *International Case Studies*
- *Marketing Career Portfolio*

Objectives

After completing this section, you will be able to

- state the marketing concept,
- distinguish customers from consumers and explain why the difference is important, and
- describe what constitutes value for customers and consumers alike.

Terms to Know

- marketing concept
- customers
- consumers
- value

Understanding the Marketing Concept

How do businesses become successful? They plan for it by following an idea called the **marketing concept.** That concept states that to make a profit a business must focus all of its efforts on satisfying the needs and wants of its customers.

Businesses were not always so consumer minded. At one time, most companies were *sales oriented*. That meant they made and sold their products without regard for what people needed or wanted. If potential customers were reluctant to buy, companies tried different or stronger sales pitches.

Today few, if any, firms would take this approach. That's because most are *marketing oriented*. This means that they focus on customer satisfaction and direct their resources toward offering the goods and services that people want. In other words, they follow the marketing concept.

Consumers vs. Customers

In order to use the marketing concept, you must first recognize the distinction between customers and consumers. **Customers** buy a product. **Consumers** use it.

BRIGHT IDEAS

Turning Conventional Wisdom on Its Head

Post-it notes are such a wonderfully simple and useful product. It's hard to imagine that they took 15 years to reach the market, but they did.

They started with a glue that failed. Spencer Silver, a chemist at 3M, created an adhesive that did stick—and didn't. Silver was fascinated by this quality, but no one else at 3M was. Conventional wisdom had it that the only good glue was one that stuck *permanently*. Silver walked the corridors of 3M for ten years but couldn't find anyone who could think of a thing to do with his halfhearted glue.

Eventually, though, someone did think of something. Arthur Fry, another chemist, came up with the actual idea for the Post-it note. Then he, too, ran into conventional wisdom. Post-it notes were just scrap paper. No one would ever buy them. Sure enough, when marketers floated the idea to potential customers by phone, it failed.

Post-it notes didn't take off until Fry and yet a third 3M employee actually put them in the hands of potential customers. Then they proved an unparalleled success. Virtually everyone sampled reordered. The Post-it note finally succeeded because three 3M employees dared to fly in the face of "conventional wisdom."

Creativity Challenge Form teams of 3–5 people, and challenge some conventional wisdom of your own. Select an item, process, or condition that is uniformly viewed as undesirable. Then try to think of a way—any way—to make it profitable. Find a use for "static cling," ballpoint pens that skip, fouled spark plugs. Afterward, offer your idea to the class as a whole. When all ideas have been presented, evaluate the originality of your collective thinking.

An adult who buys him- or herself a box of cereal is most likely both customer and consumer. However, if the adult is a parent, that might not be true. He or she could be buying the cereal for a child to eat. Think how that might complicate the cereal marketer's task. To appeal to children, the cereal might have to be heavily sweetened.

Chapter 2   *Basic Marketing Concepts*   **15**

Evaluation

Assign and review the Section 2.1 Review.

Reteaching

1. Assign and review the vocabulary terms for this section.
2. Assign and review Fact and Idea Review questions 1–4 from the Chapter Review.
3. To reteach the difference between consumers and customers, ask students why fragrance manufacturers advertise men's cologne in women's magazines and women's perfumes in men's magazines, especially during the months of November and December? (Ads are directed at the purchaser/customer who is buying the fragrance as a gift for the user/consumer.)

Enrichment

1. Assign and review the appropriate activities in the *Student Activity Workbook*.
2. Assign and review the appropriate Critical Thinking questions from the Chapter Review.
3. To help students better understand the concept of value and the controversies that surround it, have them read "It's the Myth of the '90s: The 'Value Consumer'" (*Brandweek* [Feb. 26, 1994], p.17). Have students who read the article explain what the author regards as misuse of the term *value* (to mean price) and its consequences (lower prices followed by lower quality).

Write the following three terms on the chalkboard and have students explain the relationship among them: profit, consumer value, marketing concept.

Appealing to adult standards of good nutrition, however, might rule that out. To be successful, the marketer would somehow have to satisfy both of these conflicting needs.

The customer-consumer distinction is even more significant in business-to-business marketing. In most firms, the person buying products for use in daily operations is not the one who will be using them. For example, the person responsible for purchasing office supplies might be buying them for 50 other employees. Those employees could request a certain type of pen or a particular brand of paper. In such situations, it is important to recognize the consumer's influence on the buying decision.

Customer Satisfaction

A second key element that users of the marketing concept must consider is customer satisfaction. What, ultimately, do customers look for? How do they judge a product? The answer is in terms of the product's value.

In general, **value** is the personal satisfaction gained from use of a good or service. Customers compare the price they pay for a product with all the benefits that come with it. Some of those benefits exceed what the product can do for them. They extend into the service and relationship areas.

With this extended definition, you can see that value would include everything from support services offered to how customers are treated by company personnel. Businesses that regularly deliver value of this type can achieve customer loyalty. Thus, value is not something defined by businesses. It is defined by the customer.

Consider some examples of firms interested in offering their customers value. Lexus offers new owners a four-year/50,000-mile limited warranty, 24-hour roadside assistance, and free lodging if a breakdown occurs more than 100 miles from home. These special services add value to the vehicle. Many supermarkets help the manufacturers of packaged food products provide value to their customers. The supermarkets keep records of customer purchases and pass the data along. Thus, where store memberships provide address data, manufacturers can mail coupons directly to their customers.

The goal of this kind of marketing is not just to make a sale but to develop a relationship with the customer. As customer demands for satisfaction of their needs and wants increase, the successful companies will be those that respond quickly and appropriately.

SECTION 2.1

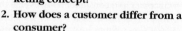

1. What is the marketing concept?
2. How does a customer differ from a consumer?
3. What does value mean to a customer?

Objectives

After completing this section, you will be able to

- define what constitutes a market,
- suggest two basic ways to identify a business's potential customers and market products to them,
- describe some of the ways a market can be segmented, and
- explain how to construct a customer profile.

Terms to Know

- market
- mass-marketing
- market segmentation
- geographics
- demographics
- psychographics
- customer profile

Identifying Your Customers

In order to respond to customers' needs and preferences, businesses must first know who their customers are. To find out, they must study the **market** for their product. That is the group of all potential customers who share common needs and wants, and who have the ability and willingness to buy the product. Consider an example. All the people who buy chewing gum are one part of the $2-billion chewing gum market. The other part consists of all those who have the ability to buy gum but don't. For the remainder of this chapter, we shall consider how businesses approach and ultimately reach their markets.

Mass-Marketing

Mass-marketing involves using a single marketing plan to reach all consumers. Today, this approach is not used very often. In fact, chewing gum (already cited) is one of the few products that is still mass-marketed.

---

1. To be profitable, a business must focus on satisfying its customers' needs and wants.
2. Customers buy products; consumers actually use them.
3. Price of a product compared to all the benefits that come with it.

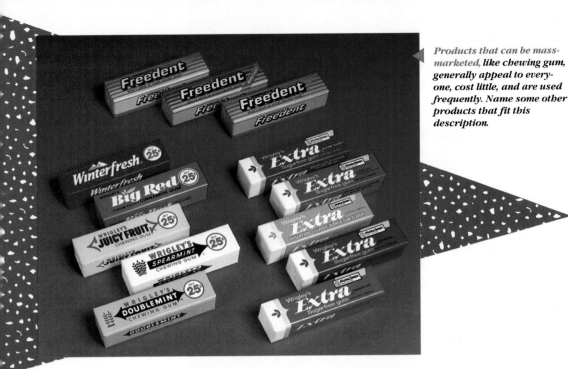

Products that can be mass-marketed, *like chewing gum, generally appeal to everyone, cost little, and are used frequently. Name some other products that fit this description.*

What makes a product a good candidate for this approach? Products that are mass-marketed generally have universal appeal. (In other words, virtually everyone likes them.) They also have few features to differentiate them from competitors.

To mass-market a product, businesses select a single, general advertising theme that appeals to most of the product's users. The theme is designed to keep the product's name before the general public. This is the approach used for years by the Wm. Wrigley Jr. Company. Wrigley sells its gum in over 100 countries, using a total of only six ad campaigns! The company's top-selling brand, Doublemint gum, has had the same campaign—"Double your pleasure, double your fun"—since the 1960s. (It has also used the same visual device—twins—to get its message across.)

Manufacturers of products that appeal to everyone still look for opportunities to "grow the market." Recall that though most people have the ability to buy chewing gum, not everyone does. So, chewing gum manufacturers pursue a dual marketing strategy. They market their product to people who do chew gum and, at the same time, look for opportunities to attract new customers who don't.

Wrigley did just that by developing an ad campaign directed at people who smoke. When the federal government banned smoking on domestic airline flights, Wrigley saw an opportunity to position its Spearmint gum as an alternative to smoking. Its advertising message—"When you can't smoke, enjoy gum-chewing satisfaction"—extends easily into any situation where smoking is frowned on or prohibited.

Market Segmentation

Today, mass-marketing is not as popular as it was in the 1950s and early 1960s. Back then consumers were hungry for products because of the shortages they experienced during World War II. Nowadays, there are so many different products on the market that companies must target a more specific group of potential customers if they want to be successful. If you think about it, most cereals, clothing styles, magazines, and car models don't appeal to everyone.

Dividing the total market into smaller groups of people who share specific needs and characteristics is the essence of **market segmentation.** The value of the technique lies in its allowing businesses to customize their product offerings and their marketing strategies.

To segment a market, you can use a variety of methods. Let's look at each one separately.

Geographics Geographics refers to segmentation of a market based on where people live. When segmenting a market geographically, you can refer to local, regional, national, or even global markets. Some businesses, by their very nature, segment their markets locally. For example, a small independent pharmacy generally caters to people who live in the vicinity of the store. Then there are products that are marketed nationally and internationally, such as Coca-Cola and Pepsi.

Some businesses use geographics to decide on new locations. Mountasia Entertainment International has a formula for selecting new sites for its amusement parks. The parks offer miniature golf, bumper boats, go-cart

Chapter 2 *Basic Marketing Concepts* **17**

 More About

Market Segmentation
Market segmentation is much easier for companies today—thanks to computers. For example, Kraft General Foods has an 800 number that receives roughly a half million calls a year. As each call is logged into a computer, so is data about the caller (age group, income level, geographic area, buying preferences).

model line. Ask students what that fact says about market segmentation vs. mass-marketing in the auto industry. (That the auto market is segmented.) Then have students try to identify as many of those market segments as possible and associate them with one or more car models.

Critical Thinking

Ask students why geographics and demographics would be important in the selection of a location for a new Toys "Я" Us store. (To be successful, such a store would need to be located in an area that is populated with enough families that have children to provide a steady stream of customers year-round.)

L1 Communication Skills

The day before you do this activity, have each student clip an article or ad that relates to this chapter from a newspaper or magazine. Each article or ad should be at least 200 words long. Divide students into pairs, and have each read his or her article while the other takes notes on content.

L2 Communication Skills

After students have finished their reading and note taking, have them prepare outlines of the articles or ads that were read to them, based strictly on their notes.

L3 Communication Skills

After students have created their outlines, have them write 100-word summaries of the articles that were read to them, based strictly on their outlines. Then have them evaluate how close they came to accurately reporting the contents of the piece. What do they need to improve about their listening and/or writing skills?

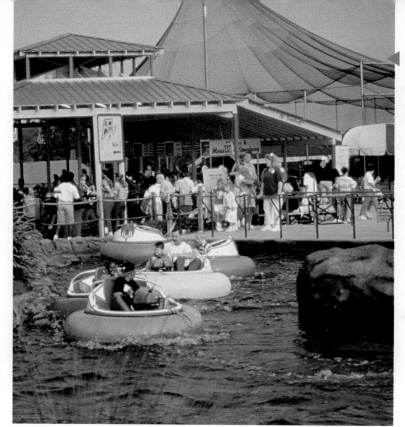

Mountasia's amusement parks are located near cities of at least 200,000. What market segmentation method does that requirement illustrate?

racing, batting cages, and indoor rollerblading rinks, as well as arcade games. Mountasia's formula requires that park sites be no more than 15–20 minutes from cities with populations of at least 200,000. This strategy helps

When Is a Paper Bag *Not* Disposable?

Life in the Multicultural MARKETPLACE

During the 1994 World Cup competition, McDonald's restaurants in Great Britain decided on a special promotion. They would package their Happy Meals in paper bags decorated with the flags of the 24 competing nations. One of the flags featured was Saudi Arabia's, with its graceful Arabic script. If the marketers at McDonald's had done their homework and had someone translate the script, however, they probably would have been shocked. They would have realized that they were about to use a passage from the Muslim holy book, the Koran, to sell burgers. Offended Muslims were quick to point out the mistake—a mistake that was made even worse by the ultimate fate of such packaging.

18   Unit 1   *The World of Marketing*

to ensure a constant stream of customers. People who live near a park are more likely to visit it often.

Demographics Demographics refers to statistics that describe a population in terms of personal characteristics. These include age, gender, income, ethnic background, education, and occupation. Once marketers know the demographics of a particular market, they can categorize and develop their products to appeal to its members.

Marketers can easily use age to segment the market in toys, toiletries, clothing, and food products. For example, toy manufacturers often identify the recommended age group for each toy or game right on the packaging. Jeans manufacturers create pants for toddlers, children, teens, and adults. Cap'n Crunch cereal is targeted to children, while All-Bran is marketed to adults.

Gender helps to create market segments as well. Jockey International, Inc., a men's underwear company, doubled its sales when it entered the women's market with Jockey for Her. Cosmetics companies have made successful crossovers going in the opposite direction. Beauticontrol, a Dallas-based direct-sales cosmetics company, learned that its alpha hydroxy acid (AHA) product called Regeneration was being used by women's husbands and boyfriends. So, it packaged the same lotion in a gray and black box and offered it as Regeneration for Men.

Cosmetics companies have also recently moved into ethnic markets. Maybelline has developed its Shades of You product line to offer new makeup alternatives to

Caption Answer

Geographics.

Feature Note

World Cup sponsors such as McDonald's were forced to find new ways to capitalize on their sponsorship. Why? Because the format of soccer matches does not allow for commercials at short intervals. Instead, the game is played in two 45-minute periods. Sponsors solved the problem by putting their logos on placards located at the base of the field where they could be seen during play.

She's one of those show-stopping types you remember. Even her **eyeshadow** lasts and **lasts.** Born to star? Tell me another.

New

Shades of YOU Eyeshadow

Rich, impactful shades created to complement your skin tone.

Stays true from compact to lid.

MAYBE SHE'S BORN WITH IT. MAYBE IT'S **MAYBELLINE.**

Cosmetics companies segment their market by ethnic group. What other market segmentation methods do such companies use?

minority women. Wet 'n Wild and Black Radiance are two cosmetics lines specially formulated for African-Americans.

Some companies attempt to appeal to ethnic markets by changing their product's packaging and promotional messages. For example, during the World Cup soccer competition of 1994, Coca-Cola made special efforts to reach the domestic Hispanic market. As part of its campaign, Coke designed bilingual (Spanish and English) packaging for its 2- and 3-liter bottles.

Psychographics **Psychographics** involves the study of consumers based on lifestyle, and the attitudes and values that shape it. Lifestyle is important to marketers because people who share interests and activities tend to have similar attitudes about products. Businesses have long recognized this fact. For example, magazine publishers and their advertisers count on such similarities among people interested in sports. It is sports enthusiasts who keep up the circulation of publications like *Golf Digest, Tennis, Ski,* and *Sports Illustrated.*

Besides interests, companies also watch for changes in personal attitudes about important topics in people's lives. These topics include health, physical fitness, eating, enjoyment, and living in general. When companies spot a new trend, they try to develop marketing strategies and products to tap into it. For example, in recent years there has been a trend toward "cocooning"—improving the

quality of life at home. As a result, all types of home products—furnishings, housewares, entertainment systems—have been flourishing.

Real World MARKETING

Dinner for the TV Generation

After World War II ended, an entrepreneur named Charles Swanson observed that 19 million women remained in the work force. He had the idea that they might need some help cooking meals—a notion that gave birth to Swanson TV dinners. The first 5,000 dinners hit supermarket frozen food sections in December 1953, a time when a new invention called television was becoming popular. The verdict from a Swanson panel of experts—1,200 housewives—was stomach-satisfying approval. The frozen TV dinner had found its target market. It went on to become an American institution.

Chapter 2 *Basic Marketing Concepts* **19**

3. In order to extend students' understanding of market segmentation, break the class into small groups. Give each group a product such as a bottle of vitamins, a hair-care product, a pair of sneakers, or a box of facial tissues. Have the groups develop the key benefit of their products to target a specific market that has been segmented by geographics, demographics, or psychographics. Then have the groups identify a different market segment that could be targeted with only minor changes to the product or packaging.

4. Ask students to identify a psychographic trend that is relevant to teenagers and the impact that trend is having on the sales of certain products. (Trends will vary. Possibilities include eating healthier foods, which has led to the development of a wide range of natural beverages, like teas and bottled waters; staying fit which has manifested itself through interest in new forms of exercise like in-line skating and the marketing of fashionable workout attire.)

Close

Ask students to differentiate between mass-marketing and market segmentation by using two different products to demonstrate those concepts.

Table 2–1

Both geographics and demographics are used to segment the snack food market. Explain how the data for pretzels supports this conclusion.

Regional Snack Food Preferences
(Annual Per Capita Consumption in Pounds–1992)

Region	Total Snack Foods	Potato Chips	Tortilla Chips	Pretzels
U.S.	20.6	6.6	4.2	2.0
Pacific	18.6	5.1	5.4	1.0
West Central	23.9	7.8	5.3	1.8
Southwest	21.3	6.5	5.9	.9
Southeast	18.6	6.5	3.1	1.3
East Central	23.2	8.6	4.0	2.6
Mid-Atlantic	19.2	5.8	2.6	4.0
New England	20.5	7.0	3.2	2.0

Sources: Snack Food Association (Alexandria, Virginia) and Nielsen Marketing Research

Lifestyle and attitude changes can occur in the workplace as well. Take the trend in corporate America to relax dress codes by letting employees dress casually one day a week—usually Fridays. The move has been good for employees, but it has harmed sales of certain clothing items. Sheer pantyhose sales, for example, have slid. In response, Hanes, a ladies' hosiery manufacturer, has developed alternate product lines. These include knee-highs and socks. The company hopes that the new products will recapture the 20 percent of sales lost to the casual trend.

Product Benefits A final way of segmenting a market is by product benefits. Companies usually build beneficial features into their products in response to consumer wants and needs. Consider sports shoe manufacturers. They divide their market into segments for people who jog, walk, play tennis, or do aerobics. Each of these activities makes different demands on footwear. So, manufacturers market different shoes for each segment. The various styles are designed to give wearers maximum support and comfort during their activity of choice.

Vitamin and Supplement Use (1992)

Region		Age		Education		Income	
East	36%	18–29	34%	Less than high school diploma	34%	Less than $15,000	34%
South	42	30–39	40	High school diploma	39	$15,000–$34,999	40
Midwest	38	40–49	43	Some college	41	$35,000–$49,999	43
West	47	50–64	43	College graduate	47	$50,000 +	48
		65 +	47				

Source: Louis Harris and Associates

Table 2–2

Consumers of vitamin pills and supplements can also be identified by using demographics and geographics. Assume you are considering production of a new vitamin product. Which areas/groups would you most likely avoid?

20   Unit 1   *The World of Marketing*

Shampoo manufacturers segment their market in a similar fashion. They offer different products to people with different types of hair (oily, dry, etc.); people who have dandruff; or people who wash their hair frequently.

Even some mass-marketers segment their markets. Consider the soda manufacturing industry. It uses mass-marketing but also segments by product benefits. It offers non-cola, diet, and caffeine-free soft drinks to customers with special needs. Indeed, if you think back to Wrigley, our other example of mass-marketing, you'll realize that it does something similar. It markets sugar-free gums in addition to bubble gum and its regular variety of flavors.

Developing a Customer Profile

If you combine geographic, demographic, and psychographic data, a remarkably complete picture of a prospective customer begins to emerge. This picture is called a **customer profile.**

As an example, consider snack food consumption. Who consumes what, where? Snack food manufacturers use geographics (regions of the country), demographics (ethnic ties), and psychographics (culture) to find out. Table 2-1 reveals patterns in regional snack food preferences. Notice, for example, that the primary market for tortilla chips is the Southwest. Further analysis suggests that there are ethnic and cultural influences on this food preference. Corn, which is what tortilla chips are made of, is a staple in the Hispanic diet. Not unexpectedly, then, the Southwest with its large Hispanic population has a high consumption of tortilla chips. Consumers in that region eat about six pounds of tortilla chips each year compared with an average of four pounds for the whole United States.

Trends in vitamin use can be uncovered and used in the same way. If you study the geographic and demographic data in Table 2-2, a profile of the typical vitamin user emerges. The person most likely to take vitamins is older, highly educated, earns $50,000-plus, and resides in the West.

SECTION 2.2

 Review

1. **What is a market?**
2. **What kinds of products can be mass-marketed?**
3. **What do geographics, demographics, psychographics, and product benefits have in common?**
4. **What marketing tool can be derived from geographic, demographic, and psychographic data?**

Objectives

After completing this section, you will be able to

- **identify the four P's of the marketing mix and explain how they are used to reach a business's customers, and**

- **define positioning and illustrate its use.**

Terms to Know

- **target marketing**
- **marketing mix**
- **positioning**

Reaching Your Customers

Assume you now know who your customers are. (You have a profile.) Assume also that you have a product, matched to the needs and wants of your customers. How do you bring the two—customer and product—together? The answer is through a series of key marketing decisions with the action-oriented names of *targeting* and *positioning*.

Targeting Your Market

Target marketing is focusing all marketing decisions on the specific group of people you want to reach. The more information you have on your target market, the easier it is to make these decisions.

There are four basic marketing decisions, collectively known as the four P's—*product, place, price,* and *promotion*. Together they comprise a product's **marketing mix.**

Let's consider one company's marketing mix choices for a new product line. For years Dana Perfumes has successfully marketed its Canoe cologne for men. Thus, when it recently decided to make a new niche for itself in the $415-million men's toiletries market, it had an established name to lead with. Figure 2-1 on pages 22-23 illustrates the marketing mix planned for Canoe Sport toiletries.

Chapter 2   *Basic Marketing Concepts*   **21**

Section Review Answers

1. All potential customers who share common needs and wants, and who have the ability and willingness to buy a particular product.
2. Those that have universal appeal and few features to differentiate them from competitors.
3. All are methods of segmenting a market.
4. A customer profile.

Focus

Bell Ringer Activity

Ask students to name five products that are specifically targeted to people their age. Then ask them to name five products that target children, and five more that target people over 50.

Introducing the Section

Use the responses to the Bell Ringer Activity to introduce the concept of target marketing. Explore the reasons why it was so easy for students to identify those products. (In most cases it will be because the products, prices, promotions, and places to buy those products are designed to meet the needs of those age groups—their target markets).

Teach

Guided Practice

1. Read Section 2.3 with students.
2. Have students read aloud the Case Study and review the answers in class.
3. Use the transparency for this section.
4. Use a visual aid to illustrate the concept and relationship between a target market and the four P's of the marketing mix. On the chalkboard, draw a circle with four arrows pointing toward it. Inside the circle write the name of a target market. Identify each arrow as one of the four P's. This illustration points up the importance of keeping the target market in mind while making all four decisions regarding the marketing mix. Change the direction of one of the arrows, and have it point away from the target market. Ask students what would happen in such a case. (The product would probably not sell well because one of the key marketing decisions would not be designed to

appeal to the target market. This would likely put off a certain number of potential customers.)

5. Assign and review the Chapter 2 Activity in the *School-to-Work Handbook.*

Discussion Starter

Show students an advertisement for a given product and tell them where you found the ad. Then ask them who the ad is targeting. This will help introduce the concept of target marketing. To explore the concept of positioning, ask students to state the ad's theme in one sentence. Expand the discussion by having students describe familiar ads and inviting their classmates to define both target market and positioning.

Critical Thinking

Ask students to respond to the meaning behind Hertz's slogan, "There's Hertz, and then there's Not Exactly." Ask: Why does Hertz, the market leader in the auto rental business, use that type of slogan? (Because it implies that Hertz is number 1 rather than saying so directly. The latter approach might offend some potential customers.)

Cooperative Learning

Have the class break into groups to explore a new business your DECA chapter/marketing club could run at school—a celebration service. The new business would deliver balloons and original cards to people in your school population for special occasions. These might include birthdays, holidays, and special events (like getting a driver's license, scoring the winning touchdown in a football game, getting into the college of one's choice, etc.).

Each group should target a different market segment in the school's population—parents, staff, students. For each market, the groups should prepare a customer profile and a plan that addresses

22

Figure 2–1

MARKETING MIX

The strength of a particular marketing mix depends on two things—how well the target market is defined and how well all marketing decisions are directed toward that market. How does the mix for Canoe Sport measure up to these two standards?

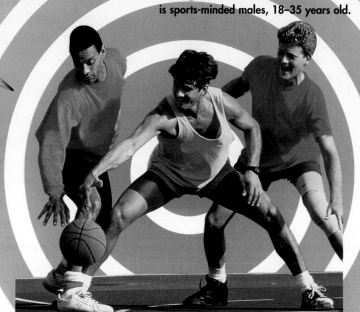

Target Market ▼

is sports-minded males, 18–35 years old.

Product Decisions ▲

include what product to make, how to package it, what brand name to use, and what image to project. Dana's choices: cologne, aftershave, sunscreen, and body shampoo—packaged in durable, shower-proof containers—carrying the Canoe Sport name—and appealing to sports enthusiasts.

Place Decisions ▼

determine how and where a product will be distributed. Dana's choices: to reach customers at drugstores and at mass merchandisers that are already selling Canoe men's cologne.

22 Unit 1 *The World of Marketing*

Most students should find Dana's marketing mix well and consistently focused. The target market is clearly defined—not all men, just a narrow range (18–35 year olds) with an interest (and possible actual involvement) in sports. Products suggest outdoor activity (sunscreen) and have locker-room convenience (shower-proof containers). Their prices are modest (in keeping with the modest means of most young men); likewise the places they're offered (mass merchandisers). The promotional campaign, with its mock cynicism, uses a kind of humor likely to appeal to younger consumers.

Note: Should students pick up on the fact that the shelf label price is lower than that recommended by the manufacturer, refer them to the discussion of resale price maintenance laws in Chapter 29.

Price Decisions ▲

should reflect what customers are willing and able to pay. Dana's choices: suggested retail price of body shampoo, $5.50; all other items, $7.50 each—trial sizes for line's launch, $1 each.

Promotion Decisions ▲

deal with how potential customers will be told about the new product—what the message will be, when and where it will be delivered, and with what inducements to buy. Dana's choices: print ads in national consumer and men's magazines—stressing a total body-care regimen for active, sports-minded young men—also, instant $1-off coupons offered in retail outlets.

Positioning Your Product

Al Ries and Jack Trout, authors of a book on the topic of **positioning,** define it as "what you do to get into the *mind* of the prospect." When you position a product, you try to get consumers to think of it in a certain way. You especially want them to distinguish it from the competition. Here are a few examples.

- Reach positioned its Wonder Grip toothbrushes for children as being fun and easy to use. The toothbrush design has rubber thumb grips to make it easier to teach children how to brush their teeth properly. The brush comes in five neon colors.
- Kodak positioned its Fun Saver cameras as single-use, throwaway cameras that can be used for any kind of outing.
- Gerber introduced its Graduates line and positioned it as food for toddlers, the next step up from infant products.

How do marketers decide where to position their products? Their inspiration can come from a number of different sources. Chief among them is the competition. Marketers often play to the weaknesses of their competitors. They also look for holes in the marketplace. These would indicate customers who are being underserved or whose needs are not being met at all. Let's consider some examples of these and other approaches.

Play to the Competition's Weaknesses
Because this is essentially a negative approach, marketers use it with care. It should be applied with a light touch. One way to do this is to reposition the competition.

Tylenol provides the classic case. McNeil Consumer Products Company positioned Tylenol as a substitute for people who could not tolerate aspirin (*that* product's weakness). The strategy worked so well that other pain reliever companies copied it. They positioned themselves against Tylenol as being more effective. Tylenol's response? It now depicts itself as the pain reliever of choice of doctors and hospitals.

Note from this example that a particular positioning is not a permanent identity. The way a product is characterized can change with time and shifts in the marketplace. For this reason, businesses must be vigilant. They must continually evaluate the effectiveness of their positioning and the attitudes of their target customers.

Look for Underserved Markets Another approach to positioning is to look for holes in the marketplace. What consumer needs and preferences are not being addressed? Are there any potential customers who are not being reached?

In an attempt to increase business, American Express looked for underserved customer segments. The niche it found was foreign travelers. (Research indicated that people were traveling twice as much abroad as domestically.) To serve that market, American Express introduced the Global Moneypac program to provide foreign denomination traveler's checks. Moneypacs eliminate

Chapter 2   *Basic Marketing Concepts*   **23**

the four P's of the marketing mix. Also, each should report its ideas to the rest of the class in an oral or written presentation.

L1 Human Relations Skills
Tell students to assume they are sales associates in a jewelry store. They have just overheard a new employee lose a sale because she did not realize that the person buying a watch was not the intended consumer. Ask students what they would say to this employee to explain the difference between a customer and a consumer. (The customer is the person who actually buys the item. The consumer is the person who uses it.)

L2 Human Relations Skills
Tell students to further assume that when they attempt to explain the difference between a customer and a consumer, the employee says she knows the difference and gets angry at them for eavesdropping on her. Ask students how they would diffuse the new employee's anger. (First, let the employee finish talking. Then explain that they made the same mistake when they first started. Finally, express their hope that the employee understands they were just trying to be helpful.)

L3 Human Relations Skills
Ask students to consider how they could have handled the above situation more effectively from the beginning. Ask: If you had it to do over again, what would you have said and done differently? (Answers will vary. One possibility: They might have approached the new employee as a friend and simply struck up a conversation about other work-related subjects. Then at an appropriate moment, they could have recounted a similar situation they had when they were new on the job. That way the new employee would have an opening to share her own experience without self-consciousness over the lost sale.)

Lifelong Learning

Basic Marketing Concepts

Staying informed about marketing practices requires students to keep up with legislation that deals with such issues as the regulation of unsolicited telephone calls. These bills, called Data Privacy Bills, are pending in such states as California, Massachusetts, Missouri, New Hampshire, Pennsylvania, Washington, West Virginia, Wisconsin, and Wyoming. Urge students to get in the habit of reading articles in local and state publications when they deal with such issues. Also, urge them to write or call their elected officials at the local, state, and national levels to find out where they stand on such issues and why.

CASE STUDY

Horse-Care Products—for Humans

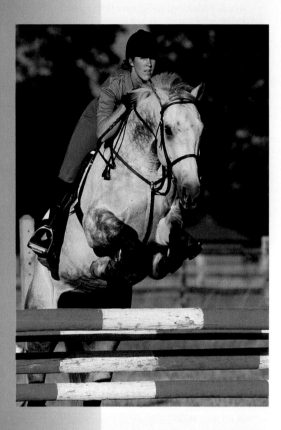

Straight Arrow, a Pennsylvania-based producer of animal-care products, is targeting humans with its latest offerings. The company has repackaged its horse shampoo, Mane 'n Tail, to sell to people!

Straight Arrow made the move after learning that horse owners were using the product themselves. In fact, research indicated that 10 out of 12 bottles of Mane 'n Tail were finding their way into shower stalls rather than stables.

Straight Arrow repositioned its horse shampoo by stressing that human hair could now look as good as a horse's mane. The company developed two new brands. One, Equenne, is sold in salons where it competes with Nexxus products. The other, Conceived by Nature, is sold in the mass market to drugstores and other mass merchandisers. There it competes with Procter & Gamble products like Head & Shoulders. With this strategy, Straight Arrow's sales went from $500,000 to $30 million in five years.

The company planned a multimillion dollar print and TV campaign to support its two new brands. In addition, there were promotions featuring product displays at horse shows and giveaways of Ford Mustang convertibles. The aim was to double sales in one year to $60 million.

Straight Arrow's confidence was probably justified. The company had a precedent in another of its products, a muscle-relaxing liniment called Mineral Ice. Bristol-Myers Squibb had been selling Mineral Ice to people since 1990.

The trend of shifting products from the horse to the human market actually goes back nearly 20 years. In the late 1970s, Barielle, a company that had developed and sold an item called Hoof Care, moved the product into department stores. For that market, it was packaged in one-ounce jars and given a French name—Crème Fortifiante Pour Les Ongles (nail strengthener). Soon after this transformation, the horse-care version was taken off the market. That's a move that Straight Arrow says it will never make.

Case Study Review

1. How did Straight Arrow implement the marketing concept?
2. What psychographic characteristic would most likely help segment the market for Straight Arrow's shampoos?
3. Identify the marketing mix for Equenne and Conceived by Nature. (You will have to speculate about price.)

A MATTER OF ETHICS

4. Is it ethical for companies like Barielle to stop making animal-care products because they can make more money selling the same products to humans?

Case Study Answers

1. By giving customers what they wanted—horse shampoo repackaged for humans.
2. Involvement with horses.
3. *Product:* Both products will have the same ingredients as Mane 'n Tail. Equenne's packaging will have an upscale look; Conceived by Nature's, a more functional look. *Place:* Equenne will be sold in salons, Conceived by Nature in drug-stores, mass merchandisers. *Promotion:* Both products will be advertised in print/broadcast media and through car giveaways. *Price:* Equenne will be priced higher.
4. Students will probably find the decision ethical. In our economic system, businesses have the right to make a profit—and dropping less profitable lines is one way to do that.

the need to change U.S. traveler's checks into foreign currency immediately upon arrival in a foreign country.

This approach is a good one to try if your company is small, new, or relatively unknown and competing against an established market leader. The idea is to find a small niche that is not of interest to the leader. For example, a specialty sausage maker in New York makes sausages for the Hispanic market. These contain seasonings that appeal to Hispanic tastes and set them apart from the major competitor's products.

Lead with Your Strengths   A business that is considered a market leader will often use that strength to position its products. When a company has the highest sales volume in a market, it wants everyone to know that it is number one. Saying so directly, however, might be offensive to some consumers. So, the company infers it. For example, Coca-Cola says its products are the "real thing." (What is inferred is that its competitors' products are not.)

Being first in the marketplace with a new concept or technology is a strength that companies use to show that they are innovators. Polaroid Corporation carved a niche for itself in the camera market by being the first to offer a camera that produces instant photos. More recently, Sharp introduced ViewCam, a new camcorder that allows users to watch the video on a screen while they are filming it.

If a business is clearly not the market leader, it must find another strength upon which to build a position. After studying the cola market, Seven-Up Company found that its product was the choice of people who did not want to drink cola. So, it positioned 7-Up as the "uncola." Avis faced a similar challenge when it had to position itself against Hertz, the market leader in the car rental field. Avis found that its primary strength was its competitive spirit. Hence the slogan, "Avis isn't number one, so we try harder."

Target Different Market Segments   Many marketers position their products by targeting different market segments. Godiva chocolates are positioned for an upscale market, whereas Hershey chocolates are positioned for the value-oriented customer. This kind of positioning is often used to differentiate similar products made by the same company. For example, Sara Lee has two divisions for hosiery. Hanes is positioned for the upscale market, while L'eggs targets the value shopper. Hanes hosiery is sold in department stores, while L'eggs hosiery is sold in grocery stores and mass merchandisers. Clearly, the two are positioned to reach entirely different socio-economic groups. This practice helps to grow several markets at the same time.

Putting It All Together

Let's look at one more example that ties together all the different decisions involved in reaching one's customers. Consider the case of Borden, which recently introduced a low-fat ice cream. The niche it identified fell between light ice creams with their 5 percent fat content and nonfat ice creams.

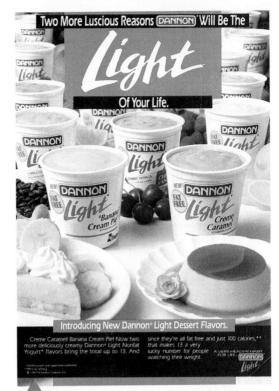

Positioning is what marketers do **to get into the minds of potential customers. How is Dannon positioning its two new flavors? Who are its target customers?**

The target market is people who are health conscious but not dieters. The *product* is an ice cream with only a 3 percent fat content. The *place* to find it is in supermarket freezer cases alongside light and nonfat ice creams. Its *price* is about $3 per half gallon (less than premium brands.) Its *promotion* proclaims its *positioning*—"low-fat that doesn't taste like lowfat."

SECTION 2.3 Review

1. What is target marketing?
2. What are the four P's?
3. Name a positioning approach that can be used in each of the following circumstances:
   a. Your product is the market leader.
   b. Your product is not the market leader.
   c. Your company makes two similar products.

Chapter 2   *Basic Marketing Concepts*   **25**

Assess

Evaluation

Assign and review the Section 2.3 Review.

Reteaching

1. Assign and review the vocabulary terms for this section.
2. Assign and review Fact and Idea Review questions 9 and 10 from the Chapter Review.
3. To reteach the concept of the marketing mix, select a simple product and review the characteristics that make it what it is. Consider name, packaging, ingredients, etc., and the other P's of the marketing mix (price, place, and promotion). Each time you cover a new P, write it on the chalkboard with an arrow pointing the a profile of the target market for the product.

Enrichment

1. Assign and review the appropriate activities in the *Student Activity Workbook*.
2. Assign the Unit 1 Activity in the *Marketing Math Workbook*.
3. Assign and review the appropriate Critical Thinking questions from the Chapter Review.
4. Assign and review the Building Academic Skills Activities, Application Projects, Linking School to Work Activities, and Performance Assessment from the Chapter Review.

Close

Distribute actual advertisements to two-person teams. Have them identify the target market, product, place, price, and promotion decisions (if they are all present), as well as how the company is trying to position the product in the consumer's mind.

Answers

Vocabulary Review

Paragraphs will vary. See Glossary for definitions.

Fact and Idea Review

1. The marketing concept.
2. Sales-oriented companies make products without regard for what people want and need. Marketing-oriented companies follow the marketing concept.
3. Situation: Parent (customer) buys a cereal for a child (consumer). Marketer must satisfy the wants and needs of both.
4. Trying to increase the value of products to customers by providing extended services.
5. Who its customers are.
6. Using a single marketing plan to reach all consumers.
7. Categorizing the market into smaller groups who share characteristics. It is used to customize product offerings and marketing strategies.
8. • Geographics: where people live.
   • Demographics: age, income, ethnic background, occupation, education.
   • Psychographics: lifestyle, attitudes, and values.
   • Product benefits: features that satisfy the wants and needs of consumers.
9. The strength of the marketing mix depends on how well all of the four P's are directed to the target audience.
10. Positioning is getting into the minds of potential customers. Products can be positioned by playing to competition's weaknesses, looking for underserved markets, and targeting different market segments.

Vocabulary Review

For each group of terms, write a paragraph explaining what the listed items have to do with the heading.

Marketing Concept
customers
consumers
value

Target Marketing
marketing mix
positioning

Market
mass-marketing
market segmentation
geographics
demographics
psychographics
customer profile

Fact and Idea Review

1. Ensuring a profit by focusing on the needs and wants of customers is an idea that has been given a special name. What is that idea called? (Sec. 2.1)
2. What is the difference between companies that are sales oriented and those that are marketing oriented? (Sec. 2.1)
3. Describe a situation in which the consumer of a product and the customer are not the same. Tell why that information would be significant to a marketer. (Sec. 2.1)
4. What are today's companies doing to develop customer loyalty to their products? (Sec. 2.1)
5. Before a business can respond to its customers' needs and wants, what must it know? (Sec. 2.2)
6. What is mass-marketing? (Sec. 2.2)
7. What is market segmentation, and how is it used by businesses? (Sec. 2.2)
8. List the general types of data developed using each of the following: geographics, demographics, psychographics, and product benefits. (Sec. 2.2)
9. How are the four P's used in target marketing? (Sec. 2.3)
10. Define positioning and suggest at least three techniques marketers can use to decide where to position their products. (Sec. 2.3)

Critical Thinking

1. Procter & Gamble has historically marketed its soaps and other household products to women. How can P&G capture the emerging male market for these products? What problems might P&G encounter trying to segment the market by gender?
2. Many women's magazines like *Glamour* and *Elle* publish advertisements for men's cologne. Explain the rationale for this practice.

3. How would you position a product like Ben-Gay ointment to make it appeal to young adults? to senior citizens? Would you use the same appeal? Why or why not?
4. What factors would you use to segment the market for a new exercise video? sports car? hair spray?
5. Identify a product positioned for a changing consumer lifestyle pattern *not* mentioned in the text.
6. "Relationship marketing" is becoming popular as more and more businesses become marketing oriented. These companies look for ways to develop relationships with their customers to ensure customer satisfaction, which leads to increased profit. What could record companies do to keep in touch with teenagers? What could computer and computer program companies do to keep in touch with their customers?
7. Explain the following statement with which you may agree or disagree: Although many products are sold by mass-marketers (such as discount drugstore chains, supermarkets, and mass-merchandising chains like Wal-Mart and Kmart), very few are really mass-marketed.

Building Academic Skills

Math

1. Baking soda toothpastes presently represent 25 percent of the $1.4-billion toothpaste market. What does that percentage represent in dollar sales?

Communication

2. Assume you work at the Gap. During a recent employee meeting, your manager requested that all employees come up with ideas on how to develop customer relationships. The thrust of the meeting was that the sale is just the beginning of a relationship that should be developed between the buyer and the seller. Write 3–4 paragraphs presenting your ideas on how this might work at the Gap.

Technology

3. One way of developing a relationship with customers is to learn as much as you can about their buying habits. What information could be assembled in a computer database to help you do this?

Application Projects

1. Summarize an article that demonstrates any of the key concepts in this chapter. In the summary,

Critical Thinking

1. Answers will vary. How to reach market: advertise in men's magazines, during sports events; develop products targeting men, like car soaps or heavy duty hand soaps. Problems: customer confusion because such products are universal in terms of use.
2. Men's colognes are frequently purchased by women for the men in their life. Cologne companies recognize that women are often the customers and men the consumers.
3. Answers will vary. Position for seniors as relief agent for arthritis symptoms, for young adults as antidote for muscle aches resulting from strenuous exercise. Reason: different markets require different appeals.
4. Factors should include demographics such as gender and age, as well as psychographics and geographics.

identify the specific concepts in parentheses. Use business publications such as *Brandweek, Adweek, Business Week, Fortune, Forbes, Marketing News,* or *Nation's Business* to find an applicable article.

2. Only 27 percent of all children aged 6–12 eat yogurt. The marketing challenge for yogurt makers is how to increase that percentage. Yoplait has Trix yogurt for children and Dannon has Sprinkl'ins. Describe the marketing mix you would use for a new yogurt for children. Remember to develop an appeal for both the consumers and customers of your new product.

3. People are drinking all types of cold beverages today, soft drinks, bottled waters, fruit juices, and sports drinks, to name a few. Evaluate the positioning of three brands of similar beverages in the marketplace. For example, compare the positioning of Nestea iced tea in a bottle, Arizona iced tea, and Snapple iced teas. If possible bring sample ads to class to demonstrate the respective marketing strategies of the three products.

4. Visa's positioning of "It's everywhere you want to be" was used to counter American Express's positioning of "Don't leave home without it." Research what these two credit card companies and others are presently doing to position their cards in this competitive market. Cut out magazine ads and recount television commercials to support your findings. What trends and conclusions can you draw from your findings about the marketing strategies used in the credit card market?

5. Conduct a survey of your classmates to determine the effectiveness of the positionings used by companies making teen-oriented products. For each product, ask your classmates to name the brand that comes to mind first and why he/she thought of it. Use products like jeans, toothpaste, cereal, sneakers, cologne, cosmetics, shampoo, and portable audio-cassette players. Analyze the marketing effectiveness of the more popular brands. Note their market segmentation, target marketing, and positioning strategies.

Linking School to Work

1. Observe how your employer positions itself in the marketplace. Report your findings.
2. Develop a profile of your company's customers based on their geographic, demographic, and psychographic characteristics.

Performance Assessment

Role Play

Situation. You are a sales associate in a jewelry store and in the process of training a new employee. The new employee observes, as you explain to a customer that the inexpensive Lorus watches are produced by a subdivision of Seiko. (Seiko watches are quality watches that are more expensive.) The customer seems pleased to learn this information and buys the Lorus watch. The trainee asks you why Seiko uses a different name to market its lower-priced watches. She also questions the ethics of such a practice.

Evaluation. You will be evaluated on how well you can do the following:

- Explain the marketing concept.
- Describe what constitutes value for customers.
- Define a market and suggest ways a market can be segmented.
- Explain target marketing and positioning.
- Justify Seiko's marketing strategy.

Display

Use products, advertisements, and your own materials to design a bulletin-board display that demonstrates one or more of the key concepts in this chapter.

Complete the Chapter 2 Computer Application that appears in the Student Activity Workbook.

Portfolio

Consider the Application Projects that you have done for this unit. Select one that illustrates your mastery of the unit's content and might be of interest to potential employers. Reformat the activity as necessary, adding any explanatory text, and place it in your Portfolio. Consider using these activities:

- Chapter 2, Application Projects 2 and 5 ■ ■

up a database with customer preferences and developing a frequent-buyer program.

Technology

3. Customer database should include name, address, telephone number, occupation, age, size, brand preferences.

Application Projects

1. Summaries will depend on articles selected.
2. Answers will vary.
3. Evaluations and sample ads will vary.
4. Credit card companies are looking for niches in the marketplace and tie-ins with other businesses.
5. Answers will vary.

Linking School to Work

Answers depend on the work situation.

Performance Assessment

Refer to the *DECA Competitive Events Handbook* for evaluation guidelines.

 Computer Application

Optional activity. Refer to the *Marketing Software Binder* for template and user information.

Evaluation

Administer the reproducible test for Chapter 10, or construct your own using the Testmaker software.

Portfolio

Refer to the *Marketing Career Portfolio* for development ideas and portfolio management and assessment.

5. New Age drinks like Fruitopia, Healthy Choice foods, and all brands of yogurt that stress healthy eating as a lifestyle choice.
6. Record companies could publish a newsletter written by and for teens. Computer companies could run an on-line bulletin board and send updates to customers.
7. Most student will agree that even products that have universal appeal are positioned to meet certain customer needs. Example: all the different

cold remedies that target particular consumers— adults and children, aspirin sensitive and aspirin tolerant, etc.

Building Academic Skills

Math

1. $350 million ($1.4 billion $\times$ .25)

Communication

2. Students' answers will vary. One possibility: setting

Economic Essentials

Unit Objectives

After completing this unit, students will be able to achieve the following outcomes:

- Summarize the key principles on which a modified free enterprise system is based.
- Explain how supply and demand interact to set prices.
- Discuss the consumer's role in a market economy.
- Identify the factors of production and relate them to the three basic questions that all economies must answer.
- List the goals of a healthy economy and explain how they are measured.
- Describe the four phases of the business cycle.

Chapter 3

Chapter 4

CHAPTER	3	4
Transparency Binder	Transparency 4	Transparencies 5–6
Student Activity Workbook	pp. 13–18	pp. 19–24
Student Software	pp. 17–18	pp. 23–24
Marketing Math Workbook		Activity 2
School-to-Work Handbook	pp. 11–12	pp. 13–14
International Case Studies	pp. 11–12	pp. 13–14
Marketing Career Portfolio		Unit 2 activity, Student Text, p. 57
Test Booklet/ Testmaker Software	Chapter 3 test	Chapter 4 test, Unit 2 test

KEY TO BASIC SKILLS ACTIVITIES

L1 Level 1 activities are basic activities and should be within the range of all students.

L2 Level 2 activities are average activities and should be within the range of average and above average students.

L3 Level 3 activities are challenging activities designed for the ability range of above average students.

CHAPTER	PERFORMANCE OBJECTIVES

3

**Our Free
Enterprise System**

3.1 **1.** Identify the basic principles of a free enterprise system.
2. Explain the role competition plays in such a system.
3. Discuss the importance of profit to free enterprise.

3.2 **1.** Describe the various roles government plays in our free enterprise system.
2. Explain how supply and demand interact to set prices.

4

World Economies

4.1 **1.** Explain what an economy is.
2. Identify the factors of production necessary to create goods and services.
3. List the three basic economic questions that must be answered by all economies.

4.2 **1.** Tell how command and market economies answer the three basic economic questions.
2. Explain why all economies are mixed.
3. Compare and contrast the economic approaches of capitalist, socialist, and communist societies.

4.3 **1.** List the goals of any economy.
2. Identify the various measurements used to analyze an economy.
3. Describe the four phases of the business cycle.

Unit Overview and Background Information

Unit 2 discusses some of the most basic principles of economics. Chapter 3 deals with the economic system the students are familiar with—our own free enterprise system characterized by private ownership, competition, profit, and risk. Chapter 4 launches students on a comparison of that system with other world economies and the various political systems that go with them.

Thus, this unit provides students with basic economic and political knowledge. The principles and practices explored will be used throughout the text to help students understand and appreciate why marketing is necessary in a market economy.

Introducing the Unit

Ask students why so many immigrants see the United States as the land of opportunity. (Because of the freedoms U.S. citizens enjoy. These include but are not limited to economic freedoms like opening one's own business, making a profit, competing, and owning private property.)

Unit Project

Have students prepare the National DECA Chapter Free Enterprise Project and/or the Individual Free Enterprise Project. Project guidelines may be obtained from National DECA, 1908 Association Drive, Reston, Virginia 22091.

As an alternative, have students conduct a survey of local business owners. The survey should focus on why they opened their own businesses and how the current economy and government are helping or hindering their success at the present time.

Unit

2

28

Focus on the Photo/Cooperative Learning

Once students have completed this unit, divide them into teams. Have each team write a statement reflecting how the unit photo illustrates the concepts presented in both chapters. They may select a topic of their own or address any of the following topics: monopolies, profit, global business, government regulation, or supply and demand.

Economic Essentials

CHAPTERS

3
Our Free Enterprise System

4
World Economies

Financing

Distribution

Risk Management

ECONOMIC FOUNDATIONS OF MARKETING

HUMAN RESOURCE FOUNDATIONS

Selling

Product/ Service Planning

Marketing-Information Management

MARKETING AND BUSINESS FOUNDATIONS

Promotion

Purchasing

Pricing

29

Chapter Overview

Chapter 3 describes the operation of the U.S. free enterprise system. The chapter identifies the basic principles of such a system. It also elaborates on government's role in our economy and the power of consumers.

 ### Springboard

Have students pretend they are would-be restauranteurs. Tell them to consider their options (type of restaurant, location, hours, menu prices, etc.) and write down their choices as they are made. Then have the class share their decisions. As students offer their plans, note for later reference when the concepts of competition, profit, monopoly, and supply and demand are mentioned in any form.

Prereading

List the section objectives to discuss with students. Have students skim the chapter, looking at the pictures, reading the captions, and noting the heads. Ask questions to ensure that students have a minimal understanding of the chapter structure.

Preteaching the Vocabulary

Before students begin reading the chapter, dictate each of the vocabulary terms and ask students to write them on a sheet of paper. When they finish, write the terms on the chalkboard. Then have students guess at the meaning of each. Write their guesses next to each term, but do not give the correct meaning. Leave this list on the chalkboard so that students can see how close their guesses were to the actual definitions as they work through the chapter.

30

CHAPTER

3

Our Free Enterprise System

Have you ever wondered why we have such a variety of businesses in the United States, from small mom-and-pop stores to huge multinational corporations? One reason is our economic system. Under that system, everyone is free to open his or her own business.

In this chapter, you will develop an understanding of how our economic system operates. You will come to appreciate how prices are determined, as well as what roles the government and consumers play in that system.

Classroom Management

For the Teacher
- Teacher's Annotated Editions for all workbooks
- Teacher's Manual for *School-to-Work Handbook*
- *Testing Binder*
- *Transparency Binder*
- *Marketing Software Binder*
- *Marketing Career Portfolio*
- *Lesson Plans*

For the Student
- *Student Activity Workbook*
- *Marketing Math Workbook*
- *School-to-Work Handbook*
- *Student Software*
- *International Case Studies*
- *Marketing Career Portfolio*

SECTION 3.1

Objectives

After completing this chapter, you will be able to

- identify the basic principles of a free enterprise system,
- explain the role competition plays in such a system, and
- discuss the importance of profit to free enterprise.

Terms to Know

- free enterprise system
- competition
- price competition
- nonprice competition
- monopoly
- risk
- profit

Basic Principles

In the United States, we have the freedom to make decisions about where we work and how we spend our money. We also have the freedom to elect the people we want to represent us in our government. These freedoms came about because our nation's founders believed that individuals should have freedom of choice. The **free enterprise system,** our economic system, was an outgrowth of that philosophy.

In theory, a free enterprise system encourages individuals to start and operate their own businesses without government involvement. The free enterprise system we have today is somewhat modified because the government does intervene on a limited basis. Most of that intervention, however, is to support the basic principles of free enterprise.

Businesses have many of the same freedoms that we have as individuals. For example, all of us have the freedom to own property and to compete in the marketplace.

As workers we compete for jobs. Businesses compete for customers. Businesses and workers alike face the risks associated with the decisions they make. We might risk our savings by investing in a friend's business. A business might risk the money it has made by investing it in a new product. When we invest in a business or a business invests in itself, it is with the same object—to make a *profit*. Profit is the essence of a free enterprise system. It is profit that motivates people and businesses to take risks.

Owning things, competing, taking risks, making profits—these freedoms are the foundation of a free enterprise system. Let's take a more detailed look at them.

Freedom of Ownership

In our free enterprise system, you are free to own your home, car, and clothing, as well as natural resources, such as land and oil. We tend to take this freedom for granted. However, there are a few countries in the world where government controls most of the property. People in those countries own their clothing and other personal belongings. However, the government owns most of the natural resources, housing, and businesses.

In the United States people are free to own their own businesses. There are, however, some restrictions on how and where those businesses may operate. For example, businesses that make things may be forced to comply with certain environmental measures. They may also be restricted in where they can locate. (Most kinds of businesses are zoned out of areas intended for private housing.)

Think about all the private property you own. In our free enterprise system, you have the right to buy anything you want, as long as it is not prohibited by law. You can also do what you want with your property. You can give it away, throw it away, lease it, sell it, or use it yourself. You decide because the United States has a free enterprise system. Under that system and our Constitution, you are granted that right.

Competition

Competition is present in many things you do. In school you compete for grades. In the workplace you compete for jobs and wages. Competition is healthy and vital to our free enterprise system. It helps motivate people to improve themselves.

Businesses that operate in a free enterprise system are no different. They try to attract new customers and keep old ones. Other businesses try to take those same customers away. This struggle between companies for customers is called **competition.**

Competition is an essential part of a free enterprise system. It forces businesses to produce better-quality

Focus

Bell Ringer Activity

Ask students if they have earned money baby-sitting, cutting lawns, making decorations or holiday gifts, or selling lemonade or iced tea. Tell them that all those who raised their hands were taking advantage of our free enterprise system.

Introducing the Section

Ask students if any one of them could start their own business if they wanted to. Once they agree, ask why that is possible. (Because of the economic system we have in the United States.) This will help you introduce the freedoms of our free enterprise system.

Teach

Guided Practice

1. Read Section 3.1 with students.
2. Go around the room asking students simple questions that reflect the freedom of choice they enjoy in a free enterprise system. Ask: Do you have the freedom to decide
   - if you want to work for someone or work for yourself?
   - if you want to go to college or go directly to work after high school?
   - which goods and services you are going to buy in the marketplace?
   - if you want to invest in a friend's new business or save your money in a bank?

   Answers (all of which are yes) will help introduce the freedoms of ownership, competition, profit, and risk.

Behaviorally Challenged

Students with behavior disorders can at times struggle to maintain the level of attention needed to deal with challenging material such as that presented in this chapter. To assist these students and encourage them to persist, you may wish to speak to them on an individual basis about their strengths and weaknesses. It might also be helpful at this time to outline chapter objectives with an eye towards helping them feel successful. This may require a more or less rigorous assessment program and enrichment material that capitalizes on their interests.

3. Have students read aloud the Case Study and review the answers in class.

Discussion Starter

To emphasize the concepts of profit and risk, tell students that their class is going to start a new business selling T-shirts to students in your school. Go to several individual students and ask them how much of their own money they are willing to invest in that new business. Start off by asking if they are willing to invest $100. If there are few "investors," reduce the amount (and consequent risk) and keep reducing it until it is very low—possibly as little as $5 or even $1.

You will probably find that some students will not be willing to invest even at $1, while others might be willing to invest more. After all students called on have committed themselves to a given amount, ask them why they decided on that figure. Then ask the class what they observed in their classmates' responses to the investment opportunity. (The main point is that with potential for profit comes risk. But most people don't fully appreciate what that means until it is personalized by having them put their own money on the line. More astute students may bring up other important issues, such as competition; the proportionality of investment and risk (the greater the risk, the greater the chance for higher profits if successful); and the fact that not all businesses succeed.)

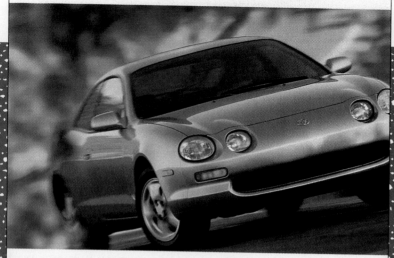

A Message To Your Heart.

A Message To Your Brain.

$259/mo.*
The Celica ST Coupe Lease.
Down Payment	$1,000
Refundable Security Deposit	$300
First Month's Payment	$259
Due At Lease Signing	$1,559

Think about it. Dual air bags** A 4-speaker stereo system. Air Conditioning. Tilt steering wheel. Precision handling. The most technologically advanced Celica Toyota has ever produced. All within your reach.

It defies logic, but it's true. Introducing the Celica ST Coupe Lease. It's a financial option that makes the all-new 1994 Celica even more attractive. So, for once, both your heart and your brain can say, "Yes. Yes. Yes."

The Celica ST Coupe Lease. One message you'll immediately respond to.

THE TOYOTA TOUCH LEASE

TOYOTA Celica
"I love what you do for me."

*Celica ST Sport Coupe with 5-spd. trans. Closed-end lease. $15,960 capitalized cost based on $1,000 down and dealer participation which may vary. MSRP $17,853 including freight. Monthly payments total $9,324. Lease-end purchase option $9,105. Your payments may vary depending on final price. Taxes, license, title, insurance, regionally required equipment and dealer charges extra. Lessee pays maintenance, excess wear & tear and $0.10/mi. over 15000/yr. Disposition fee, not to exceed $150, may be due at lease end. To qualified lessees through Toyota Motor Credit Corporation. Similar lease in AL, FL, GA, NC & SC through World Omni Financial Corporation. **Payments higher in AR, CT, LA, MA, MO, MS, OK, RI, TX, VA & WV.** Retail delivery by 7/5/94. See your participating dealer for details. ** Always use your seatbelts. Driver- and passenger-side air bags are a Supplemental Restraint System (SRS). Buckle Up! Do it for those who love you. © 1994 Toyota Motor Sales, U.S.A., Inc.

Most businesses compete by making price or nonprice appeals to potential customers. Which type of appeal is Toyota using in this ad? Explain.

goods and services at reasonable prices. Because of the struggle to attract new customers, businesses constantly look for ways to develop new products and improve old ones. Marketing helps in those endeavors by determining what customers want and how best to get products into their hands. Thus, competition results in a wider selection of products from which to choose. It also provides an incentive for businesses to operate in the most efficient manner possible. The results of these efforts help to increase the nation's output of goods and services, as well as its standard of living.

Marketing strategies determine how business will compete with one another. There are two basic ways businesses compete—through price competition and nonprice competition.

Price and Nonprice Competition Price competition, as the name implies, focuses on the sale price of a product. The assumption is that, all other things being equal, consumers will buy the products that are lowest in price.

The marketing strategies used by the Wiz, a discount electronics store, and Wal-Mart, the national discount store chain, are examples of price competition. The first insists, "Nobody beats the Wiz," while the second promises, "Always the lowest price—always." Both stress price as the primary focus of their competitive advantage.

In **nonprice competition,** businesses choose to compete on the basis of factors that are not related to price. These include the quality of the products, service and financing, business location, and reputation. Some nonprice

---

Caption Answer

Both types—the nonprice appeal is based on the sleek, stylish appearance of the car; the price appeal on the monthly payment which is low, the small print asserts, for all the "technologically advanced" features the car offers.

competitors also stress the qualifications or expertise of their personnel. Businesses that use nonprice competition may charge more for products than their competitors.

Nordstrom is a fine clothing specialty retailer that prides itself on providing complete customer satisfaction. Nordstrom's personnel are empowered to do whatever it takes to satisfy their customers. In addition to offering high-quality goods and customer service, the store also provides a unique shopping environment. Live music, courtesy of a strategically placed piano player, floats through the store.

The examples for price and nonprice competition would seem to suggest that businesses adopt one or the other strategy. However, it is not uncommon in our value-oriented society for businesses to try to do both. As competition gets more keen, you may see more price-oriented competitors offering services they never offered in the past.

Monopolies When there is no competition and one firm controls the market for a given product, a monopoly exists. A **monopoly** is exclusive control over a product or the means of producing it.

Monopolies are prohibited under a free enterprise system because they preclude competition. Without competition, a company can charge whatever it wants. It can also control the quality of a product and who gets it. Without competition, there is no mechanism to keep a company from acting without regard to customer wants and needs.

In the United States, the government permits a few monopolies to exist, mainly in industries where it would be extremely wasteful to have more than one firm. These monopolies, however, are regulated by the government. Utility companies are an example of this type of monopoly. Gas and electric companies must apply to government agencies for rate increases and provide financial data to support their applications.

Telephone service was a government-regulated monopoly until the breakup of American Telephone and Telegraph (AT&T). At that time, the government decided that long-distance telephone service could be deregulated and that the competition would be beneficial to consumers. Now many different communication companies—MCI, Sprint, etc.—compete for our long-distance telephone business.

Risk

Along with the benefits of private ownership of property and competition, businesses also face risk. **Risk** is the potential for loss or failure. Risk is generally perceived in relation to the potential for improved earnings. As the potential for earnings gets greater, so does the risk.

For example, you might decide to put your savings in the bank because they would be safe there. Other people might decide to invest their savings in the stock of a corporation. If the corporation were successful, those

people would probably make more money than you. However, their risk would be much greater because the corporation could also do badly. In that case, the value of the stock would go down, and the stockholders might lose money.

Businesses take risks all the time. Simply starting up is a risk. Let's say you wanted to open your own business. In that case, you would most likely put your savings into the enterprise. If the business were successful, you would make money. If the business failed, you could lose all your savings—and more.

As a matter of fact, one business in three in the United States fails after one year of operation. And risk continues, even if a business survives the first few years. When an industry develops and profits are great, more people enter that industry, thus increasing competition and the risk of failure for individual firms.

Risk is also involved in the development of new products. Product introductions are costly and risky. Up to 85 percent of new products fail in the first year. As a case in point, General Mills spent $34 million on a new cereal called Fingos, only to pull it off the market in less than a year because of poor sales. Sales of Fingos only reached $23 million, which did not cover the cost to market the new product.

Profit

Profit is the money earned from conducting business after all costs and expenses have been paid. Profit is often misunderstood. Many people think the money a business earns from sales is its profit. That is not true. As a matter of fact, the range of profit for most businesses is 1–5 percent *of* sales. The remaining 95–99 percent goes to pay costs, expenses, and business taxes.

Nonetheless, profit provides the incentive for people to risk their money on business ventures. It is the driving force in our free enterprise system. Without it, businesses cannot survive.

Real World

When a Failure Isn't

Henry Ford tried five times before he succeeded in inventing the Model T. Thomas Edison did 9,000 unsuccessful experiments before he finally created the electric light. Powdered gelatin (Jell-O) was around, owned and disowned by various patent holders for 105 years, before it became a kitchen staple. In a free enterprise system, failure isn't the last word. Often failure is just a step on the way to success.

Critical Thinking

Ask students why competition is such an essential element in our free enterprise system. (Without it, there would be monopolies that would control the prices, quality, and variety of goods and services available in our country. With competition, companies are forced to improve those things because otherwise they will go out of business.)

Suggest a type of business (fast-food restaurant, supermarket, cinema, or music/video store). Have students identify 3-5 establishments in the community that compete directly with each other for customers. (Answers will vary. McDonald's, Burger King, and similar businesses are likely examples of competitors.)

L1 Math Skills

Ask students to determine if the following businesses made a profit, suffered a loss, or broke even. (In the case of profit/loss responses, have students give a dollar amount.)
- Business A had revenues of $100,000 and expenses of $95,000. (Profit of $5,000)
- Business B had revenues of $2,000,000 and expenses of $2,025,000. (Loss of $25,000)

Did You Know ?

On average, U.S. businesses earn (after taxes) net profits of 5 percent or less.

Feature Note

Ask students to think about instances in which they tried and failed at something. Often, these experiences have been pivotal in their lives. Remind them that it is really how you react that counts. People who are paralyzed by failure may thereafter spend energy avoiding situations in which there is a threat of failure. People who are challenged by failure are motivated to try again.

L2 Math Skills

Ask students to determine if the following business made a profit, suffered a loss, or broke even. (In the case of profit/loss responses, have students give a dollar amount.)

Business C had sales revenue of $50,000 and sales returns of $3,000; a cost of goods sold of $22,000; and expenses of $20,000. [Profit of $5,000: $50,000 − $3,000 = $47,000 net sales; $47,000 − ($22,000 + $20,000) = $47,000 − $42,000 = $5,000.]

L3 Math Skills

Ask students to determine if the following business made a profit, suffered a loss, or broke even. (In the case of profit/loss responses, have students give a dollar amount.) Business D had sales revenue of $1,500,000 and sales returns of $50,000; a cost of goods sold that was 60 percent of net sales; and expenses of $580,000. [Broke even: $1,500,000 − $50,000 = $1,450,000; $1,450,000 × .60 = $870,000; $1,450,000 −($870,000 + $580,000) = $1,450,000 − $1,450,000 = 0]

Also, ask: What percentage of net sales did the expenses represent? (40 percent: $580,000 ÷ $1,450,000 = .4 = 40%)

Independent Practice

1. Assign and review the Chapter 3 Case Study in the *International Case Studies* workbook.
2. Tell students to select a local business and list the ways that the owner competes using price and/or nonprice competition.

■ **CASE STUDY** ■

For the Love of Golf

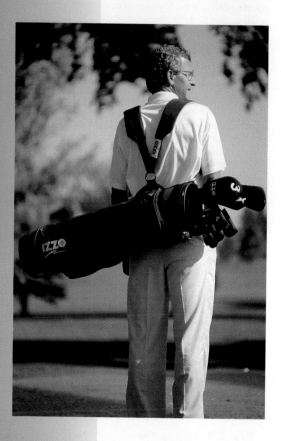

T. J. Izzo, a Denver home builder, had a love/hate relationship with golf. He loved the game but hated what it did to his aching back. The problem for Izzo was lugging a heavy golf bag, slung over one shoulder, through 18 holes of golf. Then Izzo had a brainstorm. Why couldn't golfers carry their heavy load the same way backpackers did? Thus was born the Izzo, a harness-like dual strap that distributes the weight of a golf bag evenly across the shoulders and down the spine.

A friend put up $15,000 so Izzo could patent his strap. As additional protection for his patent, Izzo negotiated a licensing agreement with Wilson Sporting Goods Company in return for their help in defending the patent against knockoffs. Another friend, a golfing buddy, invested $15,000 so Izzo himself could produce 1,500 sample straps.

34   Unit 2   *Economic Essentials*

To promote his new concept, Izzo sent sample straps to golf publications, which immediately endorsed it. Doctors recommended it, too. The only problem seemed to be that golfers thought the strap would be difficult to put on and take off. Izzo, however, had already thought about that potential problem. He lined one of his dual straps with velour to grip the shoulder and the other with nylon to slide off easily.

Despite all of Izzo's careful analysis and planning, no one was beating down his door to purchase his new strap. So, Izzo started attending golf tournaments with his golf bag strapped on. J. Michael Carrick, Tom Kite's caddie, was the first to notice the new concept. He now wears the strap to reduce back pain and muscle spasms. The strap got more help when Nick Faldo's caddie, Fanny Sunesson, began wearing it. She credits the strap with nothing less than "saving my career." Izzo promptly signed Sunesson up to promote his strap on the Professional European Golf Association tour.

To accelerate operations, Izzo raised another $380,000 by selling 10 percent of the company to a group of Wyoming investors. He also signed up independent sales representatives and foreign distributors. The first groups they will be targeting are college teams and top junior players. It is these groups that the company's vice president of marketing believes are the trendsetters.

All of this seems to be working. In 1993, Izzo made his first profit—$12,000 on revenues of $1 million from 75,000 straps. Revenues for 1994 were $1.7 million from the sale of 92,000 straps.

■■ *Case Study Review*

1. How does Izzo's invention reflect the four basic principles of our free enterprise system?
2. Why did Izzo allow Wilson Sporting Goods to manufacture his new golf bag strap?

A MATTER OF ETHICS

3. Was it ethical to have Fanny Sunesson, Nick Faldo's caddie, promote the strap on the European golf tour? Why or why not?

Case Study Answers

1. *Ownership of property:* Izzo owns his own business and the patent on his invention. *Competition:* Only competition Izzo has is from the traditional golf-bag strap. His job is to get the word out about the benefits of his version. *Risk:* Izzo is risking his time and money, as well as the investments of his two friends and the Wyoming investors. There is no guarantee of success. *Profit:* In 1993, Izzo made his first profit ($12,000).
2. Because Wilson agreed to help Izzo defend his patent against knockoffs.
3. Yes, because she used the strap and genuinely credited it with saving her career. Her endorsement was based on personal experience, not just lip service paid for with cash.

Product failure is a great risk for businesses that manufacture goods—up to 85 percent of new products fail. How many of these unsuccessful products do you recognize? Why do you think they failed?

SECTION 3.1

Assess

Evaluation
Assign and review the Section 3.1 Review.

Reteaching
1. Assign and review the vocabulary terms for this section.
2. Assign and review Fact and Idea Review questions 1–4 from the Chapter Review.
3. To review the difference between price and nonprice competition, ask students to name their favorite retail store. Then ask them why they shop there. If students mention any reasons other than price, write them on the board. Once no further answers are forthcoming, ask students what the listed reasons represent. (Nonprice competition.)

Enrichment
1. Assign and review the appropriate activities in the *Student Activity Workbook*.
2. Assign and review the appropriate Critical Thinking questions from the Chapter Review.

Close

Have students name the four key principles of our free enterprise system. (Ownership, competition, risk, and profit.)

Economic Cost of Unprofitable Firms Unfortunate things happen when businesses are not profitable. One of the first things businesses do when their profits begin to decline is lay off employees. When businesses are not profitable, their investors can lose money if the value of their stock falls below what they paid for it. As more and more investors sell their stock in the poorly performing company, the fewer resources the company has with which to conduct business. It begins to cut back on research and development for new products, as well as on the purchase of goods and services it needs to operate. This, in turn, affects the profitability of the suppliers and transportation companies that depend on those business transactions.

Government also suffers when business profits decline. Poorly performing businesses pay less in taxes. With unemployment up, the cost of social services rises. In short, everyone loses when businesses are not profitable.

Economic Benefits of Successful Firms Now let's look at what happens when businesses are profitable. Profitable businesses hire more people and pay them well. Investors earn money from their investments, which they in turn spend or reinvest. Vendors and suppliers make more money, too. As employment and profits climb, the government makes more money from taxation of individuals and businesses. Companies and individuals are also more likely to contribute to charities when they are doing well.

Finally, remember that profitable companies attract competition, which is beneficial to the consumer. More and more products are developed to better satisfy consumer wants and needs. Also, companies learn to operate more efficiently in order to lower prices.

SECTION 3.1 *Review*

1. Provide an example of how one's freedom of ownership may be limited by government.
2. Provide an example of a business that uses price competition and one that uses nonprice competition.
3. What principle of free enterprise provides the incentive for people to risk their money on business ventures?
4. What is risk, and why is it relevant to a free enterprise system?

Chapter 3 *Our Free Enterprise System* **35**

Caption Answer

Answers will vary. Some possibilities: Fingos has an unappealing name, loud and possibly off-putting package graphics. New Coke was marketed based on inadequate marketing research—few people actually wanted the taste changed.

Section Review Answers

1. Answers may vary. One possibility: limits on where businesses can locate.
2. Answers may vary. Price competition—Wal-Mart, nonprice competition—Nordstrom.
3. Freedom to make a profit.
4. Risk is potential for loss. Under free enterprise, greater risk usually translates into greater profit potential.

Focus

Bell Ringer Activity

Ask students how they are personally benefiting from the government's role in our free enterprise system *even as you speak to them.* Emphasize the qualification at the end of the question to lead students to the correct answer.

Note: For private school students, reword the question to focus on how "most young people ages 5 to 18" benefit from the government's role in our free enterprise system.

Introducing the Section

Students should recognize that they are receiving an education at public expense. Next ask what other services local, state, and federal governments provide. (Police and fire protection, military protection, Medicare, Medicaid, welfare, etc.) Ask students how the government is able to provide these services. (Through taxation.) Then ask how all of us can have a say in how our tax dollars are spent. (Through voting for government representatives who have views similar to our own.)

Teach

Guided Practice

1. Read Section 3.2 with students.
2. Tell students that the name of the government agency in charge of workers' safety is the Occupational Safety and Health Administration (OSHA). Ask them to supply examples of how businesses provide a safe working environment for employees under the law. (Answers will vary. Two possibilities: By providing hard hats for people who work in construction and proper ventilation for people who work in industries where there are toxic fumes.)

36

SECTION 3.2

Objectives

After completing this chapter, you will be able to

- describe the various roles government plays in our free enterprise system and
- explain how supply and demand interact to set prices.

Terms to Know

- licensing agreement
- demand
- supply
- equilibrium
- surpluses
- shortages

The Role of Government

Government plays four roles in our free enterprise system:

1. It provides general services.
2. It supports businesses to promote the growth and development of our nation.
3. It regulates businesses to ensure fair business practices and safety for consumers.
4. On a very small scale, it competes with private businesses.

Because of this government involvement in its economy, the United States is said to have a *modified* free enterprise system. To understand what that means, we have to take a closer look at government's various roles.

Provider of Services

To ensure the safety and general welfare of people in the United States, our government provides military, police, and fire protection, as well as free public education. In some cases, government expands its educational role to provide retraining for people who have lost their jobs as a result of changes in the marketplace and/or foreign competition. The Joint Training Partnership Act (JTPA) is one example of this sort of activity.

36   Unit 2 *Economic Essentials*

To improve transportation facilities in the United States, our government builds or supports the building of roads and bridges. The public library is paid for with government funds, as is our social welfare system. Medicare and Medicaid are two programs that are part of that system. Both provide medical care, the first for the elderly and the second for the poor.

Supporter of Business

Businesses are also served by our government. This is especially true in times of crisis. For example, when Chrysler Corporation was in danger of going bankrupt,

BRIGHT IDEAS

Wrap It

Anthony Seraphin was watching televised reports of earthquake damage in Armenia when he got an idea. To protect homes from further damage by aftershocks and weather, why not wrap them with plastic? Seraphin already knew how to manipulate plastic to seal smaller objects. He had used a technique similar to shrink wrapping to protect pleasure boats during winter storage.

Since Seraphin had his creative insight that houses could be wrapped, he has been involved in earthquake recovery efforts in both Armenia and Iran. His company, Global Wrap and Services, has also negotiated with the Florida state insurance department to offer disaster services in case of hurricane or flood. (Insurance companies have long lacked a quick and easy method to seal up damaged homes to protect them from further destruction.)

Creativity Challenge   Break into teams of 3–5 students, and try to think of something equally unconventional to "wrap." Ask yourselves what other problem could be solved by shrink wrapping. Better still, expand the possibilities by considering bagging, boxing, bandaging, canning, tenting, or covering something with paper. If it suits your group, don't work toward a problem solution. Back into one. Start with the object and/or the wrap, and try to think of a problem it would solve. Don't even feel compelled to be consistent. Swap objects or wraps midstream and see where it leads you.

Bright Ideas

Discuss with students the phenomenon of making a discovery while not really trying. Creative moments often occur when people are engaged in some kind of diversion entirely unrelated to the creative thought. They may be exercising, driving a car, or (as in the case of Anthony Seraphin) watching TV. Ask students if this has ever happened to them and, if so, what the end result was.

the federal government intervened by guaranteeing loans to the company. Chrysler rebounded and was able to repay the loans, as well as save the jobs of thousands of workers. In more recent years, floods and earthquakes have devastated communities nationwide. Government provided disaster assistance to help both businesses and home owners rebuild in the affected areas.

To support and encourage our free enterprise system, our government also runs the Small Business Administration (SBA). The SBA provides counseling and educational materials to prospective business owners to help ensure their success. Additional support comes in the form of loan guarantees for business owners who cannot get conventional loans.

Lastly, to encourage more global business activity, our government establishes trade alliances and agreements with other countries. Those agreements make it easier for U.S. companies to do business in foreign markets.

Regulator

Making laws is one of the principal functions of government. In the United States, most laws are designed to protect the safety, health, and welfare of individuals and the freedom of businesses to operate in our free enterprise economic system.

Consumer and Worker Protection   At the federal level, laws are carried out by regulatory agencies.

Several of these agencies have been set up specifically to protect workers and consumers. They include the Food and Drug Administration (FDA), the Equal Employment Opportunity Commission (EEOC), the Occupational Safety and Health Administration (OSHA), and the Consumer Product Safety Commission (CPSC).

At the state and local levels, government agencies require licensing of people who perform certain services, such as hairdressers and barbers. Also, health departments inspect restaurants and other food-handling businesses to protect consumers. Finally, to ensure that all workers have a certain standard of living, both state and federal governments mandate a minimum wage.

To protect our environment, the Environmental Protection Agency (EPA) was established in 1970. Local zoning ordinances help to maintain the value of residential real estate and provide for uses that are consistent with the public good.

The Securities and Exchange Commission (SEC) regulates the sale of securities (stocks and bonds). It is responsible for licensing brokerage firms and financial advisers. This type of regulation helps protect investors from deceptive practices. It also protects corporations whose stock is traded by requiring that all information provided about them to investors be truthful.

Business Protection   To protect our private property rights, government provides laws and regulations regarding patents, copyrights, and trademarks. These laws

Providing loans through the SBA **is one way government supports businesses in crisis. What are some others?**

3. List the initials of a few government agencies on the chalkboard. Possibilities include the FDA, EPA, SEC, FTC, EEOC, and CPSC. Ask students if they know what those agencies regulate. (FDA—food, drugs, cosmetics, and medical implants; EPA—environment; SEC—securities; FTC—interstate commerce and advertising; EEOC—hiring and firing practices; CPSC—consumer products other than those covered by the FDA.)
4. Use the transparency for this section.
5. Assign and review the Chapter 2 Activity in the *School-to-Work Handbook*.

Discussion Starter

To introduce the concepts of supply and demand, ask students how much they would be willing to pay for a concert ticket for their favorite musical artist or group. After asking several students and coming to a consensus on the amount most will pay, raise the price of a ticket and ask how many students would pay the higher amount. Keep probing until you reach a peak amount and only a few students still have their hands raised. Ask students what this line of questioning says about consumer demand. (As prices go up, fewer people are willing to pay them. This is the law of demand in supply and demand theory.)

Critical Thinking

Ask students if they would consider the U.S. government a competitor because it charges fees for people to visit or camp in national parks, such as Glacier National Park. (Answers will vary. Many will agree that national parks are in competition with private tourist attractions and campgrounds.)

Caption Answer
Provides loan guarantees, negotiates trade agreements that may help U.S. companies enter foreign markets.

Did You Know
OSHA has reorganized and increased its fines for companies that fail to comply with its restrictions. In cases of willful noncompliance, fines can now rise as high as $50,000 per occurrence. In addition, OSHA has added a free consultation service, mainly to help small businesses cope with its regulations. The service also helps firms develop safety standards and safe work environments.

Cooperative Learning

Put students into groups and assign each group one product with which they are familiar, such as a CD Player, Compact Disc, pair of jeans, a soft drink, etc. Have them develop the following: a demand schedule, a supply schedule, and a graph that depicts the equilibrium point for that product. Have each group present and defend its supply and demand graph to classmates in an oral presentation.

L1 Communication Skills

Ask students to prepare an outline for a one-minute speech about one of the four basic principles of our free enterprise system.

L2 Communication Skills

Have students use outlines they have prepared to make a one-minute oral presentation on one of the four basic principles of our free enterprise system.

L3 Communication Skills

Ask students to prepare an outline for a three-minute speech that includes all four principles of our free enterprise system. Then have the students orally present their ideas to the class.

*Government regulation protects businesses **and individuals from unauthorized use of their personal property. What evidence of this practice do you see here?***

by foreign as well as domestic companies. Patent infringement and industrial espionage (stealing ideas from other companies) are becoming more commonplace.

The government also regulates trade with other countries. U.S. companies are not permitted to sell certain products abroad if such sales might jeopardize the national defense. To protect domestic industries, sometimes the U.S. government imposes trade restrictions on foreign-made products in that industry.

The government also passes laws to regulate how businesses operate. One of the more important of these laws, enacted to prevent monopolies, is the Sherman Antitrust Act (1890). It outlawed all contracts and agreements that would restrain trade or limit competition in interstate commerce.

A second law, called the Clayton Antitrust Act, was passed in 1914 to reduce loopholes in the Sherman Antitrust Act. In that same year, the Federal Trade Commission (FTC) was established to enforce both acts. The FTC's powers have since been expanded to include investigations of deceptive and misleading business practices, like false advertising.

To ensure economic stability for businesses, the government monitors our economy and controls our monetary supply through the Federal Reserve System. This is our nation's banking system. When the Federal Reserve Board of Governors thinks the economy is moving too fast or too slowly, it acts to correct the problem. For example, if prices are going up too fast, the board may increase interest rates to curb economic activity. Higher interest rates generally make it more difficult to borrow money and therefore discourage expansion by businesses.

protect businesses for a period of time from having others copy their creative ideas and identifying symbols. If one company wants to use another's name, symbol, or product, it must get permission to do so and pay a fee for the use.

You may have heard about businesses that produce products under a **licensing agreement.** Such an agreement protects the originator's name and products. For example, a T-shirt manufacturer might be granted an NFL licensing agreement so that it can produce T-shirts with NFL logos on them. For this privilege, the company will have to pay NFL Properties a fee. It will also have to agree to certain standards of operation imposed to protect the NFL's reputation.

With global competition getting more keen, businesses must try to protect their products from theft

Where Do I Stand?

Life in the Multicultural MARKETPLACE

The envelope of space that people maintain around themselves and into which they can tolerate no intrusion without backing up or feeling uncomfortable is called personal space. Personal space varies with culture. People from the Middle East stand closer together in business situations than Americans. Men may even touch arms or hold hands as a sign of trust. The Japanese, however, stand farther away from each other than their Western counterparts and are not inclined toward physical displays of friendship. Nearer to home, many Mexicans and other Latin Americans practice the traditional embrace (*abrazo*) and stand closer together during conversation. Backing away from someone whose culture considers close personal contact to be preferable can be interpreted as impolite.

Caption Answer

Sports team and organization logos are probably licensed to clothing and souvenir manufacturers under federal law.

Feature Note

The reverse is also true. If someone invades the space of a person who is not comfortable with close proximity, the "invader" is considered rude. So, whose standard of personal space governs? There are no firm rules. However, in sales situations, the salesperson usually adapts to the customer's preference.

Government competes with private businesses in a very limited number of cases. In the instances shown here, who are the government's competitors?

Competitor

There are three business operations that our government runs. They are the Tennessee Valley Authority (TVA), the U.S. Postal Service, and Amtrak. The TVA provides electricity to parts of the rural South. It was established during the Great Depression when private companies were unwilling to invest in dams and power plants for the area. The U.S. Postal Service provides mail delivery nationwide. There are several specialized delivery companies that now compete with the Postal Service—DHL, United Parcel Service (UPS), and Federal Express. Amtrak is a passenger rail service that was established under the Rail Passenger Act of 1970. The act was necessary because rail line owners no longer wanted to offer passenger service.

In addition to these major businesses, the U.S. government also runs national parks and campgrounds. It charges fees to enter the parks and use the camp facilities. In some cases these tourist attractions are in competition with privately owned tourist attractions.

The Role of the Consumer

Most of the goods and services produced in the United States are bought by consumers for personal use. Therefore, the role of the consumer must be part of any discussion of our free enterprise system.

Consumers do two major things in the marketplace. First, they pick the winners—the products and businesses that will be in the marketplace tomorrow. Second, they determine how much demand there is for any given product and thereby help determine prices.

Deciding Which Businesses Survive

The United States is known as a consumer-oriented society. This reflects the power that consumers have in the U.S. marketplace. It is consumers who decide which products will be produced and which companies will stay in business.

Consumers do this by shopping. Every time they make a purchase, they are "voting" with their dollars. The more votes (or sales) a product gets, the more likely the success of that product and the company that produces it. This ability to pick the businesses that will and will not survive makes consumers very powerful indeed in a free enterprise system.

Real World

Fine and Tandy

When Charles Tandy offered to buy out their chain of nine ailing Ft. Worth electronics stores in 1963, the owners of Radio Shack were only too happy to take the money. However, Tandy had the knack for changing base metal to gold. Under his careful direction, Radio Shack blossomed into the world's largest consumer electronics design and testing organization, with 31 plants and 7,000 retail outlets.

Chapter 3 *Our Free Enterprise System* **39**

L1 Human Relations Skills

Tell students to assume they work as cashiers in a retail store and have been approached by a customer who wants to buy a scarf. The item is clearly marked $25, but the customer demands that it be sold to her for $5 because she found it on a table designated for sale merchandise of that price. (A sign on the table indicates that all scarves there are only $5.) Ask students what they would do in this situation.

L2 Human Relations Skills

Use the same scenario described in the L1 Human Relations problem. Ask students what they would actually say to the customer.

L3 Human Relations Skills

Use the same scenario described in the L1 Human Relations problem. Have students role-play the situation. Tell the student playing the customer to act very upset and demand that he or she be allowed to purchase the scarf for $5. Tell the student playing the cashier that he or she cannot sell the scarf for less than the ticketed price of $25 but must nonetheless maintain the customer's goodwill.

L1 Decision-making Skills

Have students suggest prices for T-shirts that their school marketing club might sell to other students and what the demand for those shirts would be at those prices. Ask how many students they think would buy the T-shirts at each price.

Caption Answer

For Amtrak (railroad passenger service)—bus and airline companies; for TVA—local electric utilities.

Feature Note

Ask students why they think Radio Shack has kept its original name, even though these days its merchandise has very little to do with radios. (Most likely the name's recognition level is so high that to change it now would be costly in terms of both money and customer goodwill.)

L2 Decision-making Skills

Ask students to prepare a supply and demand curve for the T-shirts that their marketing club plans to sell. Tell them to identify the equilibrium price and provide a rationale for their curve.

L3 Decision-making Skills

Ask students to defend their supply and demand curve and tie their T-shirt pricing decisions to the following principles: competition, risk, and profit.

Independent Practice

1. Tell students to investigate local ordinances dealing with the following subjects:
   - Type and size of signs allowed businesses in your community
   - Zoning laws in your immediate area
   - Blue laws (laws that stipulate businesses must be closed on Sundays)
   Have them present their findings in both oral and written reports.
2. Have students list products that have experienced changes in supply and demand and corresponding changes in price that support supply and demand theory.
3. Have students develop their own supply and demand curves with the equilibrium point identified for a hypothetical or real good or service.

Assess

Evaluation

Assign and review the Section 3.2 Review.

Figure 3-1

SUPPLY AND DEMAND THEORY

Supply and demand interact to determine the price customers are willing to pay for the number of products producers are willing to make.

Demand ▼

refers to consumer willingness and ability to buy products. According to the law of demand, if the price is low enough, demand for a product usually increases. This is reflected in the demand schedule below. It provides the points to plot a demand curve (see graph on page 41).

Demand Schedule for Sweaters Sold at Retail

Price per Sweater	Number Demanded
$35	600
34	800
33	1,100
32	1,500
31	2,000
30	2,600
29	3,400
28	4,600
27	6,200

Supply Schedule for Sweaters Sold at Retail

Price per Sweater	Number Supplied
$35	6,000
34	5,800
33	5,600
32	5,400
31	5,000
30	4,400
29	3,400
28	2,000
27	1,000

Supply ▲

is the amount of goods producers are willing to make and sell. The law of supply states that at a higher price, producers will offer a larger quantity of products for sale. At a lower price, they will offer fewer products. This is reflected in the supply schedule above. It provides the points to plot a supply curve (see graph on page 41).

Determining Prices

In addition to deciding the fate of products and businesses, consumers also decide the prices of goods and services sold in the marketplace. Consumers play a major role in supply and demand theory, which is used to control prices in a free enterprise system. Figure 3-1 illustrates how this theory works.

When the laws of supply and demand interact in the marketplace, they create conditions of *surplus, shortage,* or *equilibrium*. These conditions often determine whether prices will go down, up, or stay the same.

Surpluses of goods occur when supply exceeds demand. When this happens, businesses respond by lowering their prices in order to encourage people to buy more of the product.

One of the best examples of surpluses can be found in the produce section of a supermarket. A large supply of peaches, apples, broccoli, or other produce may be priced very low one week. The low price is often attributed to the supply of the crop. When there is an excess of a given crop (usually when it is in season), farmers lower their prices to sell large quantities. Supermarkets, buying large quantities of the crop at the low price, do the same. Thus, the surplus affects the price all the way down the line—by lowering it.

When demand exceeds supply, **shortages** of products occur. When shortages occur, businesses can raise prices and still sell their merchandise. For example, when Super Soaker water guns first became popular, the manufacturer raised the price $1–$2 per unit to capitalize on the increased demand and limited supply.

Lifelong Learning

Our Free Enterprise System

Students need to realize that studying consumer issues is an ongoing process. New issues arise and new products are introduced every day. Staying on top of these developments can help students become involved consumers—those who buy and use products that are safe, reasonably priced, and good for the environment.

In order to remain current on consumer issues, students should read magazines such as *Consumer Reports.* Encourage students to use their marketing education as a springboard to lifelong study of consumer issues. By continuing their reading in the field, they will be better able to make purchases that improve the quality of their lives.

Demand and Supply Curves for Sweaters Sold at Retail

Graph showing Demand Curve and Supply Curve intersecting at the Equilibrium Point. Y-axis: Price per Sweater ($27 to $35). X-axis: Number of Sweaters Demanded/Supplied (0 to 7,000).

Equilibrium ▲

exists when the amount of product supplied is equal to the amount of product demanded. On the graph above, this is the point where the supply and demand curves meet. It is also the point where both producer and consumer are satisfied with the price. The equilibrium price, therefore, is the price at which customers are willing to buy and producers are willing to sell.

Another toy, the Power Rangers action figures, provides a more pointed example. In 1994, when the figures became the rage, the manufacturer and retailers did *not* capitalize on the shortages that arose. However, other enterprising individuals did. How? They went from store to store and bought the figures when retailers got in new deliveries. They then sold the toys at much higher prices in flea markets and independently. These individuals understood the theory of supply and demand and used it to capitalize on the shortages.

When the amount of a product being supplied is equal to the amount being demanded, equilibrium exists. Customers buy all of the product that is available. Retailers clear their shelves of merchandise. Everyone's needs and wants are satisfied in the most efficient manner possible.

SECTION 3.2

Review

1. Name four ways government is involved in our free enterprise system.
2. Why is the United States said to have a *modified* free enterprise system?
3. What is the FTC, and what does it do?
4. In the U.S. free enterprise system, who decides which businesses will survive and what prices will be charged for the goods sold?
5. What is the equilibrium point in supply and demand theory?

Answers

Vocabulary Review

Captions will vary. See Glossary for definitions.

Fact and Idea Review

1. Freedom of ownership, competition, risk, and profit.
2. Because it forces businesses to produce better-quality goods and services at reasonable prices.
3. Provides the incentive for people to risk their money on business ventures.
4. Unprofitable businesses lay off employees, lose investors, and cut back on operations. The last adversely affects their suppliers and distributors. All pay less in taxes, thus lowering government revenues.
5. SBA provides counseling and educational materials to prospective business owners and loan guarantees to help business owners who can't get conventional loans.
6. FDA, EEOC, OSHA, Consumer Product Safety Commission, EPA, and SEC.
7. Both are laws passed to prevent monopolies.
8. Increase interest rates to curb economic activity.
9. TVA, Amtrak, and U.S. Postal Service.
10. When supply exceeds demand, there is a surplus and prices go down. When demand exceeds supply, shortages of products occur, which allows businesses to raise prices. The price at which buyers will buy and sellers will sell is the equilibrium price.

Critical Thinking

1. Answers will vary. Those who oppose government action might suggest that smaller stores use a variety of nonprice techniques to compete.

Vocabulary Review

Design a bulletin-board display based on this chapter's content. In your display plan, block out and briefly describe the illustrations you will use. Then write captions for them using at least ten of the following terms:

free enterprise system
competition
price competition
nonprice competition
monopoly
risk
profit
licensing agreement
demand
supply
equilibrium
surpluses
shortages

Fact and Idea Review

1. What are the four basic principles of a free enterprise system? (Sec. 3.1)
2. Why is competition an essential part of the free enterprise system? (Sec. 3.1)
3. What role does profit play in our free enterprise system? (Sec. 3.1)
4. What happens when businesses are not profitable? (Sec. 3.1)
5. How does the Small Business Administration support and encourage our free enterprise system? (Sec. 3.2)
6. Name a few government regulatory agencies that protect consumers and workers. (Sec. 3.2)
7. What do the Sherman Antitrust Act of 1890 and the Clayton Antitrust Act of 1914 have in common? (Sec. 3.2)
8. What might the Federal Reserve do if it sees prices going up too fast? (Sec. 3.2)
9. What three major businesses make our government a competitor in the marketplace? (Sec. 3.2)
10. How do supply and demand interact to determine price in our free enterprise system? (Sec. 3.2)

Critical Thinking

1. What, if anything, do you think government should do to help mom-and-pop retailers compete with retail giants like Wal-Mart, Home Depot, and Staples?
2. Do you think the government should control prices charged by your local telephone company? Why or why not?
3. Are new businesses guaranteed success in our free enterprise system? Explain your answer, and give examples to support your viewpoint.
4. Is there any such thing as a company's making too much profit? Explain.
5. Do you think our government should make it a practice to bail out failing businesses like Chrysler Corporation? Why or why not?
6. Why are patents and copyrights allowed in a free enterprise system? Aren't they in direct conflict with the concept of competition? Explain.
7. If three of the large automobile manufacturers wanted to merge into one large corporation, do you think the U.S. government would allow them to do so? Why or why not?
8. Provide examples from your own experience of supply and demand theory at work. Then try to think of one example each to illustrate surplus, shortage, and equilibrium.

Building Academic Skills

Math

1. Determine the profit a company makes with sales of $2,456,700; costs of $1,246,100; and expenses of $1,112,332. What percentage of sales does the profit represent?

Human Relations

2. A customer questions you about the fact that your video store's rental fees are 50 cents higher than those of the video store in the next town. You know the competing store does not carry the selection you do and its late charges are double yours. Given these facts, prepare a response for the customer.

Those who support government action might advocate using zoning laws to keep the Wal-Marts, etc., outside city limits.
2. Yes, because phone companies are monopolies and hence subject to regulation.
3. New businesses are *not* guaranteed success. Competition, consumers, economic conditions—all can change in ways that reduce business, force price cuts, and trim profits—even to the point of failure.

4. Answers will vary. Students should discuss the merits of the various uses to which high profits can be put—expansion, research and development, increased dividends.
5. Answers will vary. Discussion will likely pit those supporting the idea of survival of the fittest businesses against those who emphasize the social and financial costs of unemployment, bankruptcy, etc.

Communication

3. Write a story about a country that did away with competition as part of its economic system. Tell what life would be like in that country.

Application Projects

1. Using current business publications like *Fortune, Forbes, Business Week, Inc., Nation's Business,* or the business section of your local newspaper, find an article related to the content of this chapter. Summarize the article and explain how it illustrates, reinforces, or extends one or more of the chapter's concepts.
2. Select a federal regulatory agency to research. Write a report on your findings, which should include when the agency was established, its responsibilities, and a current issue facing that agency.
3. Research Avis Rent-a-Car to learn why its employees are also owners of the company. Find out if any other businesses have followed Avis's lead in the formation of employee-owned companies and what precipitated that decision.
4. Interview a local business owner about the government's involvement in the free enterprise system. Ask if any governmental policies have cost the business owner any money or caused any problems.
5. Conduct a debate on the pros and cons of government involvement in business.

Linking School to Work

Ask your employer to share the OSHA and EEOC rules that must be followed where you work. Some businesses post them in the employee lounge, dining area, or entryway. Share your findings with the class.

Performance Assessment

Role Play

Situation. You are employed as a salesclerk at the Lakeview Drugstore. This local establishment has been serving the residents of your town (which has a population of 30,000) for more than 25 years. In one month, however, a new discount drugstore is scheduled to open just two miles away. The owners of the Lakeview Drugstore have asked their employees for help. What would you suggest they do to meet the new competition?
Evaluation. You will be evaluated on how well you do the following:

- Explain the role competition plays in our free enterprise system.
- Elaborate on the concepts of price and nonprice competition.
- Incorporate the economic concept of risk into your presentation.
- Demonstrate creative problem-solving ability.

Public Speaking

An alien from outer space arrives in your high school and wants to know about our free enterprise system. Prepare an oral presentation of 2–4 minutes for your guest. Explain the main components of the free enterprise system in such a way that the alien will understand them. Stress the reasons why those features work so well in providing goods and services to U.S. residents.

Complete the Chapter 3 Computer Application that appears in the Student Activity Workbook.

6. Patents and copyrights do interfere with competition to a degree. But they also help inventors and creative people (owners) get the benefits (profit) of the time and money they invested (risk) in their work.
7. The government would not allow such a merger because it would violate antitrust laws.
8. Student examples will vary.

Building Academic Skills

Math

1. Profit: $2,456,700 - (1,246,100 + \$1,112,332) = \$98,268$
   Percentage of sales: $\$98,268 \div \$2,456,700 = .04 = 4\%$

Human Relations

2. Responses will vary. Students should explain that the additional cost affords a better selection and lower late fees.

Communication

3. Stories will vary but probably depict monopoly control and its likely consequences— poor-quality products, stagnant product development, high prices, and lack of response to consumer or social responsibility concerns.

Application Projects

1. Summaries will depend on articles selected.
2. Reports will vary.
3. Avis employees decided to buy the company when it was facing bankruptcy. Other worker groups that have followed suit include the employees of United Airlines.
4. Interviewee responses will vary.
5. Debate arguments will vary. Pro: Government intervention has been necessary to protect workers, the environment, and the public from business excesses. Con: Consumers can let businesses know what they do and don't like through their purchases.

Linking School to Work

Answers depend on the work situation.

Performance Assessment

Refer to the *DECA Competitive Events Handbook* for evaluation guidelines.

Computer Application

Optional activity. Refer to the *Marketing Software Binder* for template and user information.

Evaluation

Administer the reproducible test for Chapter 3, or construct your own using the Testmaker software.

Chapter Overview

Chapter 4 introduces students to different economic systems. In the course of comparing market, command, and mixed economies, it develops key economic concepts like resources, scarcity, and the basic economic questions.

The chapter also presents an overview of the different economic measurements countries use to determine how well their economies are doing. These include productivity, GDP, inflation and unemployment rates.

 ## Springboard

To introduce the concepts of economic resources and scarcity, ask students to imagine what life would be like in an underdeveloped country—say, in a small village in Africa, India, or South America.

Prereading

List the section objectives to discuss with students. Have students skim the chapter, looking at the pictures, reading the captions, and noting the heads. Ask questions to ensure that students have a minimal understanding of the chapter structure.

Preteaching the Vocabulary

Before students begin reading the chapter, dictate each of the vocabulary terms and ask students to write them on a sheet of paper. When they finish, write the terms on the chalkboard. Then have students guess at the meaning of each. Write their guesses next to each term, but do not give the correct meaning. Leave this list on the chalkboard so that students can see how close their guesses were to the actual definitions as they work through the chapter.

CHAPTER 4

World Economies

In Chapter 3 you learned about our free enterprise system. With that information as background, you can now study how other countries make economic decisions.

In this chapter, you will learn about alternate economic systems. You will also develop a general concept of what an economy is. Lastly, you will learn how economic systems measure success.

Classroom Management

For the Teacher
- Teacher's Annotated Editions for all workbooks
- Teacher's Manual for *School-to-Work Handbook*
- *Testing Binder*
- *Transparency Binder*
- *Marketing Software Binder*
- *Marketing Career Portfolio*
- *Lesson Plans*

For the Student
- *Student Activity Workbook*
- *Marketing Math Workbook*
- *School-to-Work Handbook*
- *Student Software*
- *International Case Studies*
- *Marketing Career Portfolio*

SECTION 4.1

Objectives

After completing this section, you will be able to

- explain what an economy is,
- identify the factors of production necessary to create goods and services, and
- list the three basic economic questions that must be answered by all economies.

Terms to Know

- economy
- resources
- capital
- entrepreneurship
- factors of production
- infrastructure
- scarcity

What Is an Economy?

An **economy,** or economic system, is the way a nation makes economic choices. The choices that must be made involve how the nation will use its resources to produce and distribute goods and services. Let's take a closer look at the resources a nation has.

Resources

Resources are all the things used in producing goods and services. Resources consist of land, labor, **capital,** and **entrepreneurship.** Figure 4-1 (pages 46-47) explains what economists mean by these terms.

Each of these resources presents its own set of problems and opportunities within an economy. The easiest way to appreciate this is to consider the plight of developing nations.

Such nations may want to attract certain kinds of industries. However, their options may be limited by the educational level of their workers. Are they skilled or unskilled? How much value an economic system places on education can profoundly impact one of its most important economic resources—its labor pool.

Capital is often an equally difficult problem for developing nations. At a national level, capital includes infrastructure. **Infrastructure** refers to the physical development of a country—to the state of its roads, ports, sanitation facilities, and utilities. These things are necessary for production and distribution of goods and services in an economy. Imagine trying to operate a modern factory without electricity. Imagine trying to run an international business without dependable phone service to keep in touch with the rest of the world.

Scarcity

All economies have different proportions of resources. Take the crown colony of Hong Kong, soon to be a part of China. It has a highly skilled and educated work force, a great deal of capital, an abundance of entrepreneurs—but very few natural resources. Many underdeveloped nations find themselves in just the opposite circumstances. They have natural resources to spare but not the capital or skilled labor to develop them.

So, nations have unlimited wants and needs (for growth and development), but only limited resources to meet them. In this respect they are much like people. Most people want more than they can afford. This difference between wants and needs on one hand and available resources on the other is called **scarcity.** Scarcity forces everyone—nations, businesses, and people—to make economic *choices.*

Real World

No One Said It Would Be Easy

Free enterprise came to Hungary in 1989. A new international airport was built to welcome tourists and business investors. Budapest's main shopping street became home to Benetton and Cartier. So, how did Hungarians feel about their new economy five years later? A 1994 Gallup poll of 1,000 Hungarians found that 57 percent believed they were worse off under the new economic system. Only 12 percent responded that they were better off, while 30 percent felt they had stayed the same.

FOCUS

Bell Ringer Activity

Ask students to name some of the things they or their families have bought in the last two weeks.

Introducing the Section

Note the variety of items named in the Bell Ringer Activity. Tell students that all of them as consumers benefit from our economy because they are able to buy goods and services like these produced by our economic system.

Teach

Guided Practice

1. Read Section 4.1 with students.
2. Use the transparency for this section.
3. To introduce the concept of infrastructure, ask students to cite differences in the roads, telephone service, and living conditions of a poor vs. an industrialized country like the United States. Ask students how a manufacturing business could function in such an environment.

Discussion Starter

Give students five minutes to develop lists of things they would most like to buy for themselves or their families. Then tell students to pretend that you gave each of them $100 on the condition that they buy something on their "wish lists." Ask them what that would be and why. Also, ask them if the $100 was enough to get everything on their wish lists. After they have responded, note that they have just made an *economic choice* because of *scarcity.*

Independent Practice

Have students research the resources of different developing countries by referring to the

---

Meeting Special Needs

Learning Disabled

Students with learning disabilities can have difficulty processing information in either written or verbal form or both. It is important that a learning-disabled student receive and give information in a way that works best for his/her specific disability.

Students who have difficulty processing written work often find it helpful to have the text tape-recorded. Obtaining information from visual representations such as graphs, charts, tables, and headings also helps. Students who have problems with verbal processing are advised to read materials before class discussion. They should also read notes taken in class by other students to ensure that they are not missing any valuable information.

Teach (Cont'd.)

World Almanac and locating recent articles from business publications. Have them report their findings to the class in oral and written report forms.

Assess

Evaluation

Assign and review the Section 4.1 Review.

Reteaching

1. Assign and review the vocabulary terms for this section.
2. Assign and review Fact and Idea Review questions 1–3 from the Chapter Review.
3. To reteach the concept of economic resources, ask students to identify everything that would be used to make and sell a pair of jeans. Keep probing until all four economic resources were identified in some manner.

Enrichment

1. Assign and review the appropriate activities in the *Student Activity Workbook*.
2. Assign and review the appropriate Critical Thinking questions from the Chapter Review.
3. Select an article that discusses a country's resources and infrastructure from a recent business or news publication and photocopy it for the class. Have students read the article in class and note the chapter concepts that they found in it.

Close

Ask students to name and provide examples of the four resources of all economies and to tell which of them, if any, they are part of at the present time. (Those with part-time jobs are labor; those who run their own summer enterprises are entrepreneurs.)

46

Figure 4–1

FACTORS OF PRODUCTION

is the technical term economists use for resources. Economists also attach special meanings to the four categories that comprise the factors.

Land ▲

refers to everything on the earth that is in its natural state—to natural resources, in other words. Land includes everything contained in the earth or found in the seas. Thus, coal and crude oil are natural resources. So are fish in a lake, and the lake itself. So are trees and plants, and the soil in which they grow.

Labor ▲

refers to all the people who work in the economy. Labor includes full- and part-time workers, managers, professional people, and public employees.

Capital ▶

includes the money needed to start and operate a business. It also includes the goods used in the production process. Factories, office buildings, computers, and tools are all considered capital resources. Raw materials that have been processed into a more useful form (such as lumber or steel) are also considered capital.

46   Unit 2   *Economic Essentials*

▶ More About

Infrastructure

Infrastructure can also refer to such things as banks and stock markets. *Financial* infrastructure can be just as important as physical infrastructure, but it is often the last requirement for industrial development to be put into place. Almost all former communist countries have to work especially hard in this area.

Basic Economic Questions

In deciding how to use their limited resources, nations, businesses, and people answer three basic questions:

1. *What* goods and services should be produced?
2. *How* should the goods and services be produced?
3. *For whom* should the goods and services be produced?

The means by which they answer these questions is an economic system.

SECTION 4.1 *Review*

1. What is an economy?
2. Name the factors of production necessary to create goods and services in an economy.
3. Because of scarcity, what three questions must be answered by all economies?

▼ Entrepreneurship

refers to the skills of people who are willing to risk their time and money to run a business. Entrepreneurs organize the other factors of production to create the goods and services desired in an economy.

Section Review Answers

1. An economy is how a nation makes decisions for using its resources to produce and distribute goods and services.
2. Land, labor, capital, and entrepreneurship.
3. *What, how,* and *for whom* should goods and services be produced?

SECTION 4.2

Objectives

After completing this section, you will be able to

- tell how command and market economies answer the three basic economic questions;

- explain why all economies are mixed; and

- compare and contrast the economic approaches of capitalist, socialist, and communist societies.

Terms to Know

- **market economy**
- **command economy**
- **capitalism**
- **socialist**
- **communist**
- **privatization**

How Does an Economy Work?

Economists have studied the way nations answer the three basic economic questions and have classified their economic systems into two broad categories. They are *market* (or capitalist) systems and *command* (or planned) systems.

As you will see, however, no economy can be called purely market or purely command. Elements of both systems can be found in all economies, making all economies *mixed*. To establish this, let's consider the two basic types of economic systems in their purest form. Then we can demonstrate how all economies are mixed.

Market Economies

The United States is a market economy, so you already know much about how a market economy operates. However, in a pure **market economy** there is *no* government involvement in economic decisions. The government lets the market answer the three basic economic questions.

Focus

🕐 Bell Ringer Activity

Ask students who decides what goods and services they can buy; if they are going to further their education by going to college; in what type of job they will be employed; and where they are going to live.

Introducing the Section

In response to the Bell Ringer Activity, students should acknowledge that they decide all those things for themselves. Tell them that isn't the case in some other countries. Explain that there are two types of economic systems— a market system (like the one they live under) and a command, or planned, economic system. In the latter type of system, the government makes some or all of those decisions for people.

Teach

Guided Practice

1. Read Section 4.2 with students.
2. Have students recall the three questions that all economies must answer. (What? How? For whom?) Tell students to use what they know about the differences between market command economies to guess who makes such decisions in each. Prepare a chart on the chalkboard to record correct responses. (In a market economy, *what* gets made and *for whom* is decided by consumers; *how* it is made is left up to businesses. In a command economy, all three economic questions are answered by the government.)
3. Ask students what they recall from Chapter 3 about how our government gets involved in our lives. (As a supplier of services, regulator, and supporter of business.) Tell them because of all that government

involvement, the United States really has a mixed economy. In fact, today all the world's economies are mixed.

Discussion Starter

Tell students that just as there are different kinds of economic systems, there are also different kinds of political systems. Ask students to name some of these systems and characterize the differences among them. (Minimal listing to build on should include democracy, socialism, and communism.)

Critical Thinking

Ask students if it is possible to have economic freedom without a democratic form of government. If the class has difficulty with the theoretical nature of this question, have them work toward an answer from the other direction. Let them start with a specific example—perhaps a communist nation like the Peoples Republic of China or Cuba—and review what they know about life there.

Once they have discussed a number of examples like these, then have them formulate a response to the initial, broader question. (Answers should acknowledge that in this era of mixed economies there are some repressive governments that do preside over successful market-oriented economies—Singapore and South Korea being examples.)

Cooperative Learning

Have students work in groups to research world economies in transition. Assign each group a country. Options include Poland, Hungary, Czechoslovakia, Argentina, Chile, Brazil, Mexico, Vietnam, China, and Russia. Tell students to use the school or a public library to learn what their country has been doing since 1990 to shift its economy over to a capitalist model. Have students report their findings in written and oral form.

1. *What?* Consumers decide what should be produced in a market economy. They do this through the purchases they make in the marketplace. Only those items that satisfy consumers' needs and wants are purchased, so only those products succeed. Products that do not satisfy consumers' needs and wants are not purchased and so fail.
2. *How?* How products will be produced is left up to businesses in a market economy. In such an economy, businesses must be competitive. They must produce quality products at lower prices than their competitors. To do that, they must try to find the most efficient way to produce their goods and services.
3. *For whom?* In a market economy, the people who have more money are able to buy more goods and services. To obtain money, people are motivated to work and invest the money they make.

Command Economies

In a **command economy** the government answers the three basic economic questions.

1. *What?* One person (a dictator) or a group of government officials (a central planning committee) decides what products are needed. In most cases, their decisions are dictated by what they believe is important. For example, the former Soviet Union was more interested in creating products for military use than in producing consumer goods for its people. Thus, there were always shortages of consumer goods in that nation.
2. *How?* Since the government owns all means of production in a command economy, the government runs all businesses. It decides how goods and services will be produced. It employs all workers

The few command economies **in the world today have sacrificed consumer needs and wants to military spending. What evidence of this choice do you see here, in this Cuban grocery store?**

and controls all employment opportunities. In fact, in the most extreme command economy, the government tells people where they will work and how much they will get paid. Bargaining for wages is not permitted.
3. *For whom?* In a command economy, the government decides who will get what is produced. In principle, all the people in the nation share equally in its wealth. In that way, everyone's basic needs are met. The government provides subsidies for housing and food so that everyone has a place to live and food to eat. It provides medical care and education. It provides jobs for everyone who wants to work. There is much security for people in such a system—but at the cost of individual freedom and choice.

Mixed Economies

As you already learned in Chapter 3, our free enterprise system is not a pure market system. There is some government involvement in the economy. Government enforces regulations to protect businesses, consumers, and workers. It supports businesses through agencies like the SBA. It even competes directly with private businesses in a few instances. Technically, then, the U.S. economy is a mixed economy.

In fact, all economies in the world today are mixed. Therefore, the most meaningful economic classification is based on how *much* government interferes with the free market. That, in turn, is determined by the society's philosophy of government. There are three political philosophies that have shaped world economies—democracy, socialism, and communism.

Capitalist Model   Nations that practice democracy believe that political power should be in the hands of the people. In democratic countries there is usually more than one political party from which to choose representatives to run the government. People in a democracy are free to elect those candidates who agree with their philosophy on how the government and the economy should be run.

The economic system most frequently associated with democracy is capitalism. **Capitalism** is an economic system characterized by private ownership of businesses and marketplace competition. In other words, capitalism is the same as free enterprise.

Government in a capitalist society is concerned about its people and cares for those who cannot care for themselves. However, the number of social services does not match that of a socialist country. The United States and Japan are two examples of countries that are classified as capitalist and have a democratic form of government.

Socialist Model   Today most countries that are characterized as **socialist** also have democratic political institutions. What makes them different from capitalist nations is the increased amount of government involvement in people's lives and in the economy.

Did You Know ❓

In September 1994, the *Moscow Times* introduced its own stock market index as a way to regulate Russia's new stock exchange. Prior to this daily account of the day's trading, the country had no centralized stock exchange report, such as the U.S. Dow Jones Industrial Average. Information about stock prices was inconsistent and inadequate, making people hesitant to invest.

In socialist countries, the government tries to reduce the differences between rich and poor. Key industries are run by the government with the object of keeping prices low for all people and providing employment for many. (Those state-controlled, noncompetitive companies are generally found in industries such as telecommunications, mining, transportation, and banking.) Socialist countries also tend to have more social services to ensure a certain standard of living for everyone. These services cover people from "cradle to grave." Medical care is free. In most socialist countries, so is education from elementary school through college. Pensions and systems to take care of the elderly are also in place.

To pay for all these "free" government services, businesses and individuals pay taxes. Indeed, in socialist countries people tend to pay much higher taxes than in capitalist countries. (See Figure 4-2.) Countries that are generally characterized as socialist are Germany, Great Britain, Sweden, Australia, and France.

Communist Model Communist countries have a totalitarian form of government. This means that the government runs everything, and one political party— the Communist party—runs the government. This is done ostensibly to ensure that all people share common economic and political goals.

In a communist country all people who are able to work are assigned jobs. Theoretically, there is no unemployment. Even if employees don't go to work, they continue to get paid under this system. The government decides the type of schooling people will receive and also tells them where to live. Housing accommodations are assigned according to need. Food and housing subsidies keep prices low, so everyone has a place to live and food to eat. Medical care is free.

There are very few totally communist countries left in the world today. In recent years, the economies of such countries have tended to collapse. This is because there is no incentive in such a system for people to increase their productivity.

The few countries that can still be classified as communist include Cuba and North Korea. Even China, which is politically still dominated by a communist party, is liberalizing its economic practices. As a result, China is moving toward a more capitalist economy.

Economies in Transition The breakup of the former Soviet Union probably provides the best examples of societies making the difficult change from command to market economies. Most Eastern European countries that were once communist satellites have embraced capitalism. They have also moved to more democratic forms of government.

In many of these nations, the state-owned industries have been privatized. **Privatization** refers to the process of selling government-owned businesses to private individuals. As a practical matter, this process generates much needed revenue for the governments involved. It also demonstrates a high level of commitment to making the transition to a market system.

Today even socialist countries are selling off some of their state-run businesses. They are doing so to help them balance their budgets as the costs for national health care, unemployment, and retirement programs soar. For example, from 1993 to 1995 Italy sold off close to $46 billion worth of state assets. Latin American countries are also privatizing state-owned businesses. Brazil now allows investment in state-owned businesses such as Telebras, its communications monopoly, as well as mining and energy concerns. Chile also has privatized its state-owned industries.

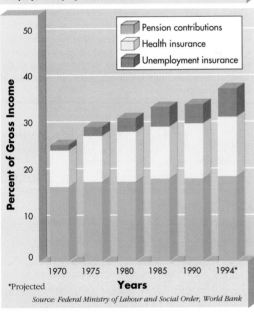

West German Welfare System
Employer/Employee Contributions

Legend:
- Pension contributions
- Health insurance
- Unemployment insurance

Percent of Gross Income vs. Years (1970, 1975, 1980, 1985, 1990, 1994*)

*Projected

Source: Federal Ministry of Labour and Social Order, World Bank

Figure 4–2

"Free" government services provided by most socialist states cost a great deal. What percentage of gross income were West Germans paying for their health and pension system in 1994?

SECTION 4.2

Review

1. **Explain how command and market economies answer the three basic economic questions.**
2. **Why are all economies mixed?**
3. **How do capitalist, socialist, and communist economies differ from each other?**

Chapter 4   *World Economies*   **49**

SECTION 4.2

Independent Practice

1. Have students research socialism and communism—not just the theories but the history and the problems as well as the benefits inherent in each system. Require students to prepare written reports with bibliographic references.
2. Assign and review the Chapter 4 Case Study in the *International Case Studies* workbook.

Assess

Evaluation

Assign and review the Section 4.2 Review.

Reteaching

1. Assign and review the vocabulary terms for this section.
2. Assign and review Fact and Idea Review questions 4–6 from the Chapter Review.
3. To reteach the distinction between command and market economies, prepare a table with heads for each one at the top and the following topics down the side: What? How? For Whom? Help students to complete the table.

Enrichment

1. Assign and review the appropriate activities in the *Student Activity Workbook*.
2. Assign and review the appropriate Critical Thinking questions from the Chapter Review.
3. Have students discuss reasons why communist countries had problems with low productivity. (Lack of incentive among workers.)

Close

Ask: What are the main distinctions between market and command economies? among democratic, socialist, and communist philosophies of government?

Caption Answer

Projected at close to 40 percent.

Section Review Answers

1. Market economy—government lets the market answer. Command economy—government answers.
2. All have both market and command elements.
3. Socialist governments are more involved in the economy than capitalist; communist governments run the entire economy.

Bell Ringer Activity

Ask students if they have heard of the 1929 stock market crash and the Great Depression of the 1930s. Ask what life in the United States was like during that period of time.

Introducing the Section

Responses to the Bell Ringer Activity should paint a picture of high unemployment, bankrupted businesses, and bread lines. Ask: If a depression is the worst of all economic times, what would be the best of times? (Responses should spell out the goals of a successful economy—low unemployment, high productivity, and stable prices.)

Teach

Guided Practice

1. Read Section 4.3 with students.
2. Have students read aloud the Case Study and review the answers in class.
3. To illustrate the term *economic measurement*, ask students how they would measure their own performance if they were asked to make pizza pies for three hours. (Their answers should help define the meaning of *worker productivity*, or output per worker hour—in this case, the number of pizzas made per hour.)
4. To introduce the concept of GDP, tell students that all nations measure their productivity, too. Ask students if they know what the letters *GDP* stand for. (Gross Domestic Product.) Then have them speculate about what they think would be included in the measurement of GDP.

■ CASE STUDY ■

Red Capitalism in China

The Tiananmen Square massacre in June 1989 told the world that China's government was determined to keep that country communist. At the time, staying in the communist fold was not seen as a recipe for success, either political or economic. Today, however, China has one of the world's fastest-growing economies. Why? Because of what some economists call "red capitalism."

Deng Xiaoping, China's chief ruler, launched his economic reforms by freeing China's 800 million peasants. The peasants were allowed to farm the land for personal profit. With this incentive, the peasants' productivity increased along with their standard of living. Deng also encouraged entrepreneurship, helped to create modern financial institutions, and welcomed foreign investment.

Deng's plans to modernize China's economy, however, did *not* include changes in its culture or politics. There would be no challenges to Communist party rule. As China opened its doors to foreign investors, however, its communist ideology underwent a change.

Today, even prominent Communist party members are capitalists. Take Huang Yantian, President of Guangdong International Trust & Investment Corp. (GITIC). GITIC is an arm of the government that has tried to attract foreign investors to help in China's economic transformation. By 1994, under Huang's leadership, GITIC had developed joint ventures with U.S. companies like McDonald's and Chrysler Corporation.

The new red capitalism combined with the effects of double-digit economic growth have transformed China's society as well, despite its leader's intentions. Today, few of China's 1.2 billion people follow the traditional communist ideology. People decide for themselves where they want to live and work. They are no longer told by the government when they should marry or have children. At state enterprises, workers spend less time reciting Marxist ideology and more time discussing production and bonuses. Illegal trade unions are springing up to protest layoffs, workplace conditions, corruption, and taxes. Even the media have become freer as the demands of commerce have created a need for accurate reporting.

While the government still arrests anyone it wants, China is clearly moving away from totalitarianism. As the country continues its economic modernization, social change appears inevitable. How the government will deal with it remains to be seen. It could lash out as it did in 1989—or it could give its people some of the political freedom that economic freedom has taught them to expect.

Case Study Review

1. What is the best way to describe China's economy?
2. Why do you think China is attempting to create a market economy?

A MATTER OF ETHICS

3. The United States has a policy of granting most-favored-nation status to developing countries that are moving toward market economies. Should China's poor human rights record bar that nation from receiving such preferential treatment?

Case Study Answers

1. China has a mixed economy. Both government and people are embracing capitalist model in terms of land ownership, creation of financial institutions and unions, and freedom of personal economic decision making (career, family, where to live). However, these changes do not extend to the political system, which is still firmly single party (communist).

2. To motivate its people to produce more and enable it to compete in the global market.
3. Answers will vary. Those supporting MFNS for China believe that market reforms will eventually transform the political system. Those against believe that withholding MFNS and similar economic incentives is the best way to force political reform.

Objectives

After completing this section, you will be able to

- list the goals of any economy,
- identify the various measurements used to analyze an economy, and
- describe the four phases of the business cycle.

Terms to Know

- productivity
- gross domestic product (GDP)
- gross national product (GNP)
- standard of living
- inflation
- consumer price index (CPI)
- business cycle

When Is an Economy Successful?

It is the goal of all economies to increase productivity, decrease unemployment, and maintain stable prices. All nations analyze their economies to see how well they are doing in these terms. The results of their analyses help to determine which phase of the business cycle their economies are in. This determination, in turn, allows businesses, consumers, and governments to make appropriate economic decisions.

Economic Measurements

Accurate information about an economy is essential to this whole process. Let's look at the economic measurements nations routinely use to determine their economic strength. These include various measures of productivity, inflation, and unemployment.

Productivity Productivity is output per worker hour. It is usually measured over a defined period of time, like a week, month, or year.

Businesses can increase their productivity in a number of ways. They can invest in new equipment or facilities that

---

allow their employees to work more efficiently. They can provide additional training or financial incentives to the same end. Finally, they can reduce their work force and increase the responsibilities of the workers who remain.

Moves such as these have in recent years helped to increase the productivity of American workers. For example, suppose a steel manufacturer with an aging plant could produce 1.25 million tons of steel a year with a work force of 550. If that manufacturer retooled to double its output and reduced its work force by 150, what would happen? The calculations would look something like this:

$$\text{Productivity} = \frac{\text{output per year (in tons)}}{\text{workers} \times \text{hours} \times \text{weeks}}$$

$$= \frac{2,500,000}{400 \times 40 \times 52}$$

$$= \frac{2,500,000}{832,000}$$

$$= 3 \text{ tons of steel per worker hour}$$

The resulting figure is nearly triple the old productivity rate (1.09 tons per worker hour).

Gross Domestic Product (GDP) Most governments study productivity by keeping track of an entire nation's production output. Today the principal way of measuring that output in the United States is **gross domestic product.** GDP is a measure of the goods and services produced using labor and property located in this country.

Note that under this standard both the laborers and the property owners can be foreign. What counts is that their output is generated domestically. For example, a BMW plant located in North Carolina would be a foreign-owned facility. And it would probably employ both foreign and domestic workers. The fact that the plant was

Life in the Multicultural MARKETPLACE

Take the Weekend Off

The world over, working people take the weekend off. It's just that what constitutes "the weekend" can vary. In the Middle East, for example, weekends are observed on Thursday and Friday. This is because Friday is the Muslim day of rest. That makes Thursday the equivalent of our Saturday. It is just as difficult to contact businesspeople in Middle Eastern countries on their weekend as it is to contact businesspeople here on ours. That makes Monday, Tuesday, and Wednesday the most opportune days for business contacts between the two regions.

Chapter 4 *World Economies* **51**

(Amount of consumer spending [two-thirds of GDP], business investment, net exports [exports - imports], and government spending—federal, state, and local.)
5. Use the transparency for this section.
6. Assign and review the Chapter 4 Activity in the *School-to-Work Handbook*.

Discussion Starter

Do a simple exercise to demonstrate the high standard of living we enjoy in the United States. Ask for a cumulative showing of hands in response to this question: How many of you have one working TV in your household? two? three? etc. Ask students if they think households in other parts of the world have that many TV sets? Then have them suggest other indices of a high standard of living.

Critical Thinking

Ask students which they would prefer—high or low inflation rates, and why. (Answers can vary. Those concerned with purchasing power and borrowing will likely favor low inflation. Those more concerned with savings and investments that earn interest, however, might be more tolerant of at least moderate inflation.)

L1 Math Skills

Have students calculate the productivity of a worker who produces 160 widgets in an eight-hour workday. (160 ÷ 8 = 20 widgets per worker hour)

L2 Math Skills

Tell students to assume that the manufacturing plant that makes widgets has 500 employees, all of whom work eight-hour shifts, five days a week. The total number of widgets they produced in one week was 424,000. Have students calculate the productivity for that week. [424,000 ÷ (500 × 8 × 5) = 424,000 ÷ 20,000 = 21.2 widgets per worker hour]

Productivity

To reinforce both the concept and computation of productivity rate, have the students do the math behind the steel mill's old productivity rate: 1,250,000 ÷ (550 × 40 × 52) = 1,250,000 ÷ 1,144,000 = 1.09.

L3 Math Skills

Tell students to assume that the widget manufacturing plant bought new equipment and laid off 10 percent of its workforce in order to improve productivity. If the plant produced 405,000 widgets in one week after these changes were made, what percentage of improvement, if any, was there in productivity. [Total workers: $500 \times .90 = 450$. Productivity: $405,000 \div (450 \times 40) = 405,000 \div 18,000 = 22.5$ widgets per worker hour. Percentage increase: $(22.5 - 21.2) \div 21.2 = 1.3 \div 21.2 = .06 = 6\%$.]

L1 Communication Skills

Tell students that they have been asked to suggest ways to increase productivity in the mail room of a medium-sized company. Each day the mail room handles approximately 500 pieces of mail. These are sorted and delivered to approximately 50 different people within the organization. Ask students to suggest ways to improve the process and to communicate those ideas to you in memorandum form. (Possible suggestions include improved sorting methods [by floor or department first] and robotic delivery of mail to eliminate kibitzing.)

L2 Communication Skills

Tell students to present their ideas to you in a role-play situation. Tell them that they should be prepared to talk from their memos rather than read them. They should also be prepared to answer any questions you may have about their suggestions.

located in the United States, however, would dictate that its production be included in the U.S. GDP.

GDP, then, is everything produced in this country in a year. What else would it be? It could be everything produced by U.S. citizens here or abroad. There is, in fact, such a figure. It's called **gross national product (GNP)**, and until December 1991 it was this country's principal way of measuring its productivity.

Note the difference—it's not where the production takes place but who's responsible for it. Consider a Ford plant located in England. Since Ford is a U.S. corporation, its production—even if it occurs in England—would be included in the U.S. GNP. It would not, however, be included in the U.S. GDP.

So, which figure is better, more useful? Today, GDP. That's because most other nations have opted for it as their principal measure of productivity. And that's why the United States has switched. The change makes it much easier for us to compare our economic performance with theirs (Figure 4-3).

Standard of Living Closely related to production measurement is a nation's **standard of living.** This is a measurement of the amount of goods and services that a nation's people have. It is a figure that reflects their *quality* of life.

To calculate the standard of living, you divide the GNP of a country by its population. Most industrialized nations enjoy a high standard of living because they have a high level of production.

Inflation Rate **Inflation** refers to rising prices. A low inflation rate (1–5 percent) is good because it shows that an economy is stable. Double-digit inflation (10 percent or higher), on the other hand, devastates an economy. When inflation gets that high, the money people have does not buy as much as it did a short time before. The period from the mid-1960s to the early 1980s was a highly inflationary period. Prices went up threefold in the United States during that time.

Controlling inflation is one of a government's major goals. When inflation starts to go up, many governments

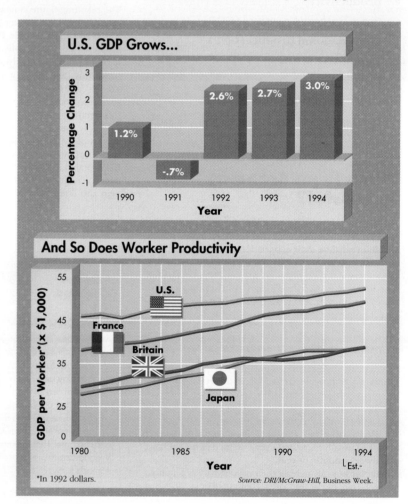

Figure 4-3

Trends in GDP growth tell whether a nation's economy is expanding or contracting. How would you characterize the U.S. economy based on the GDP figures in the top graph?

GDP per worker is a measure of productivity obtained by dividing a nation's annual output by the number of people in its work force. Of the nations represented in the bottom graph, which had the highest productivity?

Reprinted from June 27, 1994 issue of *Business Week* by special permission, copyright © 1994 by McGraw-Hill, Inc.

52   Unit 2   *Economic Essentials*

Caption Answers

Top graph: Except for one year (1991), the U.S. economy has been experiencing sustained growth.

Bottom graph: United States.

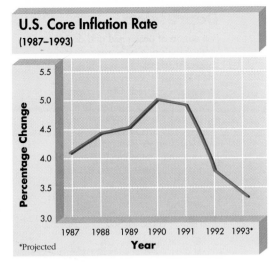

U.S. Core Inflation Rate
(1987–1993)

*Projected

Figure 4-4

The core inflation rate, graphed here, is based on the CPI minus food and energy costs, which tend to fluctuate more than other index components. Characterize the core inflation rate for the years shown.

raise interest rates, which reduces everyone's ability to borrow money. The result is a slowdown in economic growth, which helps to bring inflation down.

One measure of inflation used in the United States is the **consumer price index (CPI).** The CPI measures the change in price over a time of some 400 specific goods and services used by the average urban household. Food, housing, utilities, transportation, and medical care are a few of its components. The CPI is also called the cost-of-living index because it charts the cost of necessities and inflation. The CPI is often used as the basis or standard of comparison for other measures (Figure 4-4).

Unemployment Rate All nations chart unemployment rates (Figure 4-5). The higher the unemployment rate, the greater the chances of an economic slowdown. Conversely, the lower the unemployment rate, the greater the chances of an economic expansion. It is easy to see why this is true. When more people work, there are more people spending and being taxed. Businesses and government both pull in more money. Government, however, gets a bonus. It doesn't have to provide as many social services like unemployment compensation and food stamps.

The Business Cycle

Governments keep all of these statistics in order to determine the stage their economies are in at any given time. History shows that sometimes an economy grows, and at other times it slows down. These recurring changes are called the **business cycle** (see Figure 4-6, page 54).

Economies in the 1990s Early in the 1990s there was a global recession. This means that countries all around the world were in the throes of a recession at the same time. For countries like Germany and Japan, it was the worst recession since World War II. The United States was affected as well.

The recovery phase for the United States began in March 1991, but this recovery was different from others. Job growth did not increase as quickly. Businesses did not hire new employees as conditions improved. Instead, they asked existing employees to work longer hours.

In 1993, U.S. manufacturing workers who escaped layoff during the recession were working an average of 41 hours a week. This increased worker productivity. Increased investment in equipment, which displaced workers but increased output, also contributed to this trend. By mid-1994, U.S. workers were rated the most productive in the world.

Factors That Affect Business Cycles Business cycles are affected by the actions of businesses, consumers, and the government. In turn, businesses, consumers, and the government are affected by business cycles.

Businesses tend to react to business cycles by expanding their operations during periods of prosperity or recovery and curtailing their operations during recessionary periods. Expansion may involve investments in new properties, equipment, and inventories, as well as hiring more employees. When the economy moves into a recession, one of the first things businesses do is lay off workers.

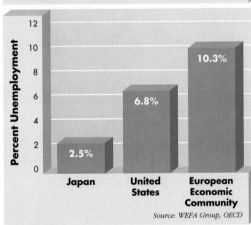

Unemployment Rates Compared
(Mid-1993)

Source: WEFA Group, OECD

Figure 4-5

Nations use employment rates as an indicator of economic health. Compared to Japan and the European Economic Community (EC), how is the United States doing according to these figures?

Chapter 4 *World Economies* **53**

L3 Communication Skills

Tell students they must make a formal presentation of their ideas to the class, who will be sitting in session as the board of directors of the company. Tell the speakers that they must be prepared to speak persuasively, field questions from multiple sources, and defend their proposal. Members of the "board" should feel free to ask questions at any point in the presentation.

L1 Decision-making Skills

Tell students they work for a small company that makes a component needed in the manufacture of automobile air bags. The company is thinking of borrowing $1 million to expand. However, the federal government just increased interest rates by 3/4 percent to control inflation. Ask students what affect that increase in interest rates might have on the economy. (Might slow it down.)

L2 Decision-making Skills

Tell students that the economy appears to be in recovery, but that the recent increase in interest rates may slow down economic activity. Ask them to decide whether they would recommend that the owners continue their plans for expansion. Have them write up their recommendation and rationale in memorandum form. (Recommendations will vary. Some will indicate that the owners should borrow the money now, before interest rates go any higher. Others may suggest pulling back just in case the increase in interest rates causes a recession. That would mean that demand for cars might go down as consumers stop buying.)

More About

Economies in the 1990s

Improvement in the U.S. economy following the global recession came gradually and was not felt by all parts of the country at the same time. The East Coast felt the recovery first. Parts of the West Coast, however—especially Los Angeles and its environs, damaged further by earthquakes and floods—had not pulled all the way out of recession as of 1995.

Caption Answers

Figure 4-4: Core inflation rate for the period was consistently low—under 5 percent.

Figure 4-5: Answers can vary. U.S. unemployment rate is worse than Japan's but better than the EC's.

Have students orally present and defend their written recommendation and rationale from the L2 Decision-making activity. Tell students to be prepared to answer questions and defend their proposal.

Independent Practice

1. Have students use newspaper and magazine articles to research and report on the current economic climate in the United States and other countries. Suggest that they check economic indicators like GDP, unemployment, inflation, and standard of living. Also, have them consider using a bulletin-board display of news articles as a visual aid for their report.
2. Have students research the interest rates for home mortgages for the past five years to determine their trend and to study the effect those rates have had on the real estate market.
3. Have students research inflation, its causes and the methods used to control it. Suggest that they compare how the government intervened to control inflation during the Carter administration (1976–1980) with how the government tries to control inflation now.
4. Have students chart U.S. business cycles from 1920 to the present.
5. Have students research how the 1990 recession and subsequent recovery were different from all others.

Assess

Evaluation

Assign and review the Section 4.3 Review.

54

Figure 4-6

THE BUSINESS CYCLE

Economists have identified four phases that comprise the business cycle.

Prosperity
is a period of economic growth. Nationwide there is low unemployment, an increase in the output of goods and services, and high consumer spending. Sometimes this period is called peak prosperity.

Depression
is a period of prolonged and deep recession. During a depression, consumer spending is very low, unemployment is very high, and production of goods and services is down significantly. Poverty results because so many people are out of work and cannot afford to buy food, clothing, or shelter. The Great Depression of the early 1930s best illustrates this phase of the business cycle.

Economic Activity

PINK SLIP

Time

Recession
is a period of economic slowdown. Unemployment begins to rise, fewer goods and services are produced, and consumer spending decreases. Recessions can end relatively quickly or last for a long period of time.

Recovery
is a period of renewed economic growth following a recession or depression. Recovery is characterized by reduced unemployment, increased consumer spending, and moderate expansion by businesses. Periods of recovery differ in length and strength.

NOW HIRING

Lifelong Learning

World Economies

The study of international economics can be useful to students in helping them identify information about the U.S. job market. Privatization of corporate assets in a distant country can have repercussions in the United States. For example, years ago General Motors had its property privatized by Argentina's government. That did not stop the company from recently reinvesting in the country, encouraged by its more stable economy. Whether that decision proves to be wise or not, the rest of GM will be affected by it. Regularly reading a major newspaper like the *Wall Street Journal* can help student's stay informed on such matters.

BRIGHT IDEAS

Look at Old Things in a New Light

In 1994 the people of the Russian town of Arhepovka began to starve—literally starve—for the lack of a good idea. Their cotton mill, which had supplied fabric for government uniforms for nearly a century, closed down when the Soviet Union split apart. The townspeople who had worked at the mill were now part owners of a defunct enterprise, and they had a choice. They could reopen under the leadership of the former plant manager. He was a young man with new ideas about making products they knew nothing about. Or they could reopen under the former communist directors of the mill. These men promised that they would use their influence to get new government business.

The townspeople made their decision in a very traditional manner. The plant manager was not one of them—he was not from Arhepovka. The directors, on the other hand, were people they had known and trusted their whole lives. The people of Arhepovka chose the old directors and the economic system they knew.

Unfortunately, that system no longer existed. Hundreds of miles away in Moscow, old officials were being replaced by reformers. Even more importantly, government-directed industry was giving way to consumer-driven enterprises.

Of course, no new work appeared. After more than a year without pay, the former mill workers began leaving to look for jobs elsewhere. The directors were still waiting for government help. A lifetime in a command economy had simply not prepared most people in Arhepovka to use what they had to solve their own problems, to innovate, and to see the possibilities in both.

Creativity Challenge   Break into teams of 3–5 students, and take the test that Arhepovka failed. Select a vacant facility in your own or a neighboring community. (If there are no vacant buildings, select a vacant piece of land.) Then try to come up with the most imaginative use for the property that your group can think of. Keep in mind the community's need for jobs and the income and tax revenues they generate. Keep in mind costs and what's already on the site. Finally, try to factor in social and environmental concerns.

And, to match lowered demand for goods and services in a recession or depression, they also cut back on inventories. This has a ripple effect in the economy as suppliers of those businesses feel the effects of lost revenues, too.

During a recessionary period, *consumers* fear loss of their jobs at worst and lower wages at best. This fear results in a loss of consumer confidence in the economy, which tends to reduce consumer spending. Reduced consumer spending causes businesses to reduce their operations in response to lower demand. The opposite is true during periods of prosperity and recovery. During those periods, consumers are more optimistic. They spend more, and businesses respond by producing more. Consumers are very important to an economy. In the United States, for example, consumer spending makes up two-thirds of GDP.

Government influences business cycles through its policies and programs. Taxation has a strong bearing on what happens in an economy. As the government requires more money to run programs, higher taxes are needed. When taxes are raised, businesses and consumers have less money with which to fuel the economy. The same effect occurs when the government raises interest rates. Higher interest rates discourage borrowing by businesses and consumers. This, in turn, reduces spending that would have occurred if they were able to borrow. When the economy needs a boost, the government may reduce interest rates, cut taxes, or institute federally funded programs to spark a depressed economy. For example, in 1993 Great Britain reduced interest rates on mortgages. This freed up $4.5 billion for consumers to spend in the economy. Also in 1993, to get out of a recession, Japan cut taxes and developed public works projects to fuel economic activity.

SECTION 4.3

1. What are the goals of any economy?

2. Name four measurements used to gauge the success of an economy.

3. Describe in the briefest terms what each of the following stands for:

   a. GNP

   b. CPI

   c. core inflation rate

   d. $\dfrac{\text{Output per year}}{\text{Workers} \times \text{hours} \times \text{weeks}}$

4. Describe the four phases of the business cycle.

SECTION 4.3

Reteaching

1. Assign and review the vocabulary terms for this section.
2. Assign and review Fact and Idea Review questions 7–12 from the Chapter Review.
3. To reteach productivity, ask students how they could increase their productivity in preparing typed reports that may need several revisions over a period of time. (Use a word processor.)
4. To reteach the concept of inflation, ask students to total the money they have in their pockets and to mentally go shopping today using only half of it. Ask them to describe how difficult it would be to buy what they want to buy, what they would have to do without, how else they would have to adjust their purchases.

Enrichment

1. Assign and review the appropriate activities in the *Student Activity Workbook*.
2. Assign the Unit 2 Activity in the *Marketing Math Workbook*.
3. Assign and review the appropriate Critical Thinking questions from the Chapter Review.
4. Assign and review the Building Academic Skills Activities, Application Projects, Linking School to Work Activity, and Performance Assessment from the Chapter Review.

Close

Have students complete this statement: An economy is most healthy when. . .(prices are stable, unemployment is low, and worker productivity is high.)

Section Review Answers

1. To increase productivity, decrease unemployment, and have stable prices.
2. Possibilities: productivity, GDP, standard of living, inflation rate or CPI, unemployment rate.
3. (a) Everything produced by U.S. citizens here and abroad; (b) Cost-of-living index—charts cost of necessities and inflation; (c) CPI minus food and energy costs; (d) productivity.
4. Prosperity—period of low unemployment, increased output, and high consumer spending. Recession—economic slowdown during which unemployment rises, production falls, and consumer spending decreases. Depression—deep and prolonged recession. Recovery—period of renewed growth after a recession/depression.

4 CHAPTER *Review*

Answers

Vocabulary Review

Essays will vary. See Glossary for definitions.

Fact and Idea Review

1. Yes, labor.
2. Infrastructure—roads, ports, sanitation facilities, utilities, etc.—is necessary for the production and distribution of goods and services in a nation's economy.
3. Scarcity.
4. Market and command systems.
5. Market system.
6. Because the former Soviet Union's central planning committee decided that the country should spend more of its resources on creating military products.
7. Possibilities include investing in plant and equipment or providing employee training and/or incentives.
8. Gross Domestic Product.
9. Standard of living.
10. When inflation gets that high, the money people have does not buy as much as it did a short time before.
11. When more people work, there are more people spending and being taxed. Businesses and government pull in more money, and government does not have to provide as many social services.
12. Business, consumers, and government.

Critical Thinking

1. Answers will vary. Possibilities: Could encourage foreign investment to make better use of natural resources; put more money into education to improve the quality of the work force; pass laws to encourage development of capital investment in

Vocabulary Review

Incorporate all the terms below into a one-page essay explaining how an economy functions.

economy
resources
capital
entrepreneurship
factors of production
infrastructure
scarcity
market economy
command economy
capitalism
socialist
communist
privatization
productivity
gross domestic product (GDP)
gross national product (GNP)
standard of living
inflation
consumer price index (CPI)
business cycle

Fact and Idea Review

1. If you had a part-time job, would you be considered an economic resource in the United States? If yes, which resource would you be? (Sec. 4.1)
2. Explain how the infrastructure of a country is related to the factors of production. (Sec. 4.1)
3. What economic principle forces everyone—nations, businesses, and people—to make economic choices? (Sec. 4.1)
4. Into what two broad categories have economists classified all economic systems? (Sec. 4.2)
5. In which economic system does the government let the market answer the three basic economic questions? (Sec. 4.2)
6. Why were there always shortages of consumer goods in the former Soviet Union? (Sec. 4.2)
7. How do businesses try to increase productivity? (Sec. 4.3)
8. What economic measurement does the U.S. government use to report the nation's production output? (Sec. 4.3)
9. Which government measure most closely reflects the amount of goods and services that a nation's people have? (Sec. 4.3)

10. Why is double-digit inflation bad for an economy? (Sec. 4.3)
11. Why is a low unemployment rate good for a nation? (Sec. 4.3)
12. Name three factors that affect business cycles. (Sec. 4.3)

Critical Thinking

1. What can developing countries do to improve their economies with regard to the factors of production?
2. How is it possible for a place like Hong Kong, with few natural resources, to develop a strong economy?
3. What would happen in the United States if the government were no longer involved in regulating business?
4. Why do you think almost all world economies are moving to a market system?
5. Would you like to live in a country where the government guaranteed employment, housing, food, and medical care for all its people? Why or why not?
6. Until the recent global recession, Japanese companies followed a policy of lifetime employment for their workers. Do you think U.S. companies should consider offering their workers such an arrangement? Why or why not?
7. To encourage economic growth and foreign investment, China gives outsiders tax breaks. State corporations pay a 55 percent tax rate. Foreign companies, however, pay no taxes the first two years of operation, 16.5 percent the next two years, and only 33 percent thereafter. What are the positive and negative effects of such a policy?
8. In 1993, 50 percent of Germany's labor costs of $27 per hour were attributed to social security, health, unemployment compensation, disability, and other taxes. Labor costs were close to Germany's in France, Italy, Spain, and Sweden. The United States and Japan's labor costs were approximately 25 percent lower, and those of Korea and Taiwan, even lower still. Why are labor costs so much higher for the European countries?

Building Academic Skills

Math

1. If inflation is up 2.5 percent from last year and last year the price of a loaf of bread was $1.59, how much would it be selling for now?

the country's infrastructure, businesses, and entrepreneurs.
2. By having a highly skilled and educated work force and a great deal of capital investment in the country.
3. Answers will vary. Some will say that large companies would become so powerful that they would no longer have to follow equal opportunity, environmental, and similar policies intended to protect the public. Believers in a pure market

economy would say that businesses and individuals would follow their own self-interest, which would ultimately be in the interest of the nation as a whole.
4. Most will acknowledge that the market system seems to work the best, mainly because it provides an incentive for people to work and open businesses.
5. Most students will recognize that all those government guarantees cost money (taxes) and

56

Communication

2. Assume you are writing a letter to a pen pal in a communist or socialist country. You have been asked how people in the United States afford vacations and medical care and retirement. In your response, compare the U.S. mixed economy with the economic system your pen pal lives under.

Technology

3. Access information on the 1993 recession in Japan and Europe from an on-line computer service or other computer database. Prepare a list of your findings. Note all resources, complete with author, article title, name of publication, date of publication, and page numbers.

Application Projects

1. Summarize in writing an article that addresses one of the topics in this chapter. In your summary link the article to specific chapter content. Use business publications such as *Business Week, Forbes, Fortune,* or the *Economist* to find an appropriate article.
2. Read the Business Outlook feature in *Business Week.* Write a summary that ties the concepts in that feature to topics in this chapter.
3. Research the current U.S. GDP and inflation, interest, and unemployment rates. Use the figures you gather to determine the business cycle phase of the U.S. economy at the present time. Summarize your findings in a one-page written report.
4. Assume the United States is in a period of rising inflation. Research the ways the government could intervene to help control or reduce inflation. Report your findings in both written and oral form.
5. Study the global recession of the early 1990s. Research the factors that contributed to the recovery period that followed. Present your conclusions in a two-page report. Note any controversies or differences of opinion that may exist among the experts regarding any particular factor.

Linking School to Work

Ask your employer about labor costs above and beyond wages paid to employees. What government taxes and employee benefits cost your employer additional money? Ask your employer what can be done to cut down on labor costs? Share your findings with the class.

Performance Assessment

Role Play

Situation. Assume you are an employee in a local family restaurant. A few homeless people come to the back of the restaurant every evening to see if there are any scraps of food that you can give them. A few regular patrons of the restaurant have commented on their presence. The owner, who is from Sweden, is fearful that the homeless people will chase away customers. He approaches you about the situation, noting that where he came from the homeless were taken care of by the state. Why, he asks with exasperation, does this situation exist in a prosperous capitalist country? How would you respond?

Evaluation. You will be evaluated on how well you do the following:

* Identify the three basic economic questions that must be answered by all economies.
* Explain how command and market economies answer those questions.
* Compare capitalist, socialist, and communist economies.
* Describe the goals of any economy.

Display

Design a bulletin-board display that accurately depicts the factors of production for the United States compared with those of another country.

COMPUTER APPLICATION

Complete the Chapter 4 Computer Application that appears in the Student Activity Workbook.

Portfolio

Consider the Application Projects that you have done for this unit. Select one that illustrates your mastery of the unit's content and might be of interest to potential employers. Reformat the activity as necessary, adding any explanatory text, and place it in your Portfolio. Consider using these activities:

* Chapter 3, Application Project 3
* Chapter 4, Application Projects 3-5 ■■

Communication

2. Students will need to identify the country and research the economic system in order to formulate a comparison.

Technology

3. Resource lists will vary, with most references being to publications like *Business Week* and the *Economist*.

Application Projects

1. Summaries will depend on articles selected.
2. Summaries will depend on feature selected.
3. Answers will vary.
4. Answers will vary. Possibilities include wage and price freezes, raising interest rates through the Federal Reserve.
5. Answers will vary. Key factors that contributed to the recovery were low interest rates; capital spending on computers, equipment, and facilities; and increased global competition that kept prices and wages in check.

Linking School to Work

Answers depend on the work situation.

Performance Assessment

Refer to the *DECA Competitive Events Handbook* for evaluation guidelines.

 ### Computer Application

Optional activity. Refer to the *Marketing Software Binder* for template and user information.

Evaluation

Administer the reproducible test for Chapter 4, or construct your own using the Testmaker software.

 ### Portfolio

Refer to the *Marketing Career Portfolio* for development ideas and portfolio management and assessment.

---

mean a loss of individual freedom. However, some may be willing to pay higher taxes and sacrifice some freedom to ensure social fairness.

6. Such a policy would force businesses to keep employees who might not be productive. That situation would be costly both to the businesses and to other employees who might have to take up the slack.

7. Positive effect: tax breaks attract foreign investors. Negative effect: badly needed taxes are lost.

8. Because of their socialist system of taking care of people from the cradle to the grave.

Building Academic Skills

Math

1. $\$1.59 \times 1.025 = \$1.62975 = \$1.63$

Business and Marketing Essentials

Unit Objectives

After completing this unit, students will be able to achieve the following outcomes:

- Tell what a business is and explain its basic functions.
- Discuss business ethics and areas in which businesses are thought to have social responsibility.
- Identify demographic, geographic, and psychographic trends in the U.S. consumer market.
- Distinguish the consumer and industrial markets.
- Discuss the importance of international trade to nations and describe the ways governments can both thwart and encourage it.
- Explain how businesses can get involved in international trade and what factors they should consider before doing so.

Chapter 7

Chapter 5

Chapter 6

Teacher Classroom Resources

CHAPTER	5	6	7
Transparency Binder	Transparencies 7a & 7b	Transparencies 8–11a & 11b	Transparency 12
Student Activity Workbook	pp. 25–30	pp. 31–36	pp. 37–42
Student Software	pp. 29–30	pp. 35–36	pp. 41–42
Marketing Math Workbook			Activity 3
School-to-Work Handbook	pp. 15–16	pp. 17–18	pp. 19–20
International Case Studies	pp. 15–16	pp. 17–18	pp. 19–20
Marketing Career Portfolio			Unit 3 activity, Student Text, p. 101
Test Booklet/ Testmaker Software	Chapter 5 test	Chapter 6 test	Chapter 7 test, Unit 3 test

KEY TO BASIC SKILLS ACTIVITIES

L1 Level 1 activities are basic activities and should be within the range of all students.

L2 Level 2 activities are average activities and should be within the range of average and above average students.

L3 Level 3 activities are challenging activities designed for the ability range of above average students.

Unit 3 Organizer

CHAPTER	PERFORMANCE OBJECTIVES

5
Business and Social Responsibility
	5.1 **1.** Tell what a business is.
	         2. Explain the basic functions of a business.
	         3. Distinguish businesses from each other based on general characteristics.
	5.2 **1.** Name the areas in which businesses are thought to have social responsibilities.
	         2. List some of the ways that business activities have impacted our environment.
	         3. Define ethics and suggest how marketers can make ethical choices.
	         4. Define consumerism and provide a brief history of the movement.
	         5. Describe current trends that are likely to improve the workplace for employees.

6
The Domestic Marketplace
	6.1 **1.** Identify demographic, geographic, and psychographic trends in the U.S. consumer market.
	         2. Suggest products and marketing strategies that can reach the diverse segments within that market.
	6.2 **1.** Explain the concept of derived demand.
	         2. List the six major types of businesses that comprise the industrial market.
	         3. Suggest products that each major industrial market group might need to purchase.

7
The Global Marketplace
	7.1 **1.** Distinguish imports from exports.
	         2. Discuss the interdependence of nations.
	         3. Explain the advantages and disadvantages of international trade.
	7.2 **1.** Discuss the U.S. balance of trade.
	         2. Identify three types of trade barriers.
	         3. Explain the various forms of trade support.
	         4. Name the major agreements governing world trade today.
	7.3 **1.** Identify the three general types of activities businesses engage in when they get involved in international trade.
	         2. Explain some of the standard business practices involved in importing and exporting products.
	         3. Discuss the cultural, economic, and political factors that should be considered when deciding whether to do business abroad.

Unit Overview and Background Information

This unit first introduces students to what businesses are all about and then explores the marketplaces in which they compete. Chapter 5 spells out the three major functions of business—production, marketing, and management. It also discusses the responsibilities of business to society at large in areas like the environment, consumerism, and business ethics. Chapters 6 and 7 repeat the pattern of the previous unit, exploring the domestic marketplace in depth and then widening the focus to the global marketplace.

Introducing the Unit

Tell students that you are going to give them $10,000 to invest in one corporation listed on the New York Stock Exchange, American Stock Exchange, or NASDAQ (over-the counter) stock exchange. Have them prepare a list of factors that they would consider when making their decision about where to invest this money. (Possibilities include business sector, price of the stock, current economy, and market[s] served.) After a class list is compiled on the chalkboard, note that all of the included factors are ones they will study in this unit.

Unit Project

Have students select a company to research. It should be a U.S. firm that does business abroad or a foreign-owned company that does business in the United States. To begin their research, tell students to get a copy of the firm's annual report. As the class proceeds through the unit, have students review their annual reports to learn if and how their selected company is involved in the topics covered.

Unit 3

58

Focus on the Photo/Cooperative Learning

Before students begin this unit, divide them into teams and have each team suggest a headline for the unit photo. Post their suggestions on a bulletin board. After the class has completed the unit, repeat the exercise, and invite students to discuss any differences between the before and after headlines. Ask what those differences say about what they have learned in studying the unit.

Business and Marketing Essentials

CHAPTERS

5
Business and
Social Responsibility

6
The Domestic
Marketplace

7
The Global
Marketplace

Financing

Distribution

Risk Management

Product/ Service Planning

ECONOMIC FOUNDATIONS OF MARKETING

HUMAN RESOURCE FOUNDATIONS

Selling

Marketing- Information Management

MARKETING AND BUSINESS FOUNDATIONS

Promotion

Purchasing

Pricing

59

Resources for Enrichment of Unit Content

Books

- *The Baby Bust—A Generation Comes of Age* by William Dunn
- *Capturing Customers* by Peter Francese
- *Do's and Taboos Around the World* by Roger Axtell
- *How to Do Business with the Japanese* by Boye DeMente
- *The Insider's Guide to Demographic Know-How* by Diane Crispell
- *Made in Japan* by Akio Morita and Sony
- *The Master Trend—How the Baby Boom Generation is Remaking America* by Cheryl Russell
- *Segmenting the Mature Market* by C. Morgan and D. Levy
- *Targeting Families* by Robert Boutilier
- *U.S. Statistical Abstract* and government publications reporting U.S. Census data

Magazines/Journals

- Current issues of *Adweek, American Demographics, Brandweek, Business Week,* the *Economist, Forbes, Fortune,* the *Harvard Business Review, Inc., International Business, Marketing News, Nation's Business,* and *Sales & Marketing Management.*

Unit Closure

Have students prepare a bulletin-board display of products, ads, and articles related to doing business in the domestic and global marketplaces. Ask students to supply materials and captions that present a complete picture of the following key concepts: current business practices (including ethical and social issues), targeting specific market segments in the domestic marketplace, and doing business in the global marketplace.

Evaluation

Administer the reproducible test for Unit 3, or construct your own using the Testmaker software.

Guest Speaker Suggestions

- Arrange to have a product manager for a large company explain how demographic and psychographic trends affect product planning and sales.
- Have the director of international sales for a large company speak to the students about the economic, cultural, and practical challenges of selling goods or services abroad.

Field Trip Suggestions

- If there is a foreign trade zone located near your school, arrange a visit. Ask a representative of the zone to provide the students with an overview of what happens there. Also, if possible, have the group visit one of the businesses located in the zone.
- Arrange for students to visit a store or mall that caters to a specific ethnic group.

BUSINESS AND SOCIETY

Pages 60–71

Chapter Overview

Chapter 5 discusses the types of businesses in the United States and the function of each. It also looks at the key issues of social responsibility that businesses face in marketing their goods and services.

Springboard

The day before you begin this chapter, ask each student to bring to class a list of three local businesses that provide a good or service to the community. The next day, generate a chalkboard list of these businesses, eliminating duplicates. (You should only have one restaurant, one dry cleaner, etc.) Have students characterize each entry as large or small, profit or nonprofit, provider of goods or services. Leave the list on the chalkboard for ongoing use.

Prereading

List the section objectives to discuss with students. Have students skim the chapter, looking at the pictures, reading the captions, and noting the heads. Ask questions to ensure that students have a minimal understanding of the chapter structure.

Preteaching the Vocabulary

Before students begin reading the chapter, dictate each of the vocabulary terms and ask students to write them on a sheet of paper. When they finish, write the terms on the chalkboard. Then have students guess at the meaning of each. Write their guesses next to each term, but do not give the correct meaning. Leave this list on the chalkboard so that students can see how close their guesses were to the actual definitions as they work through the chapter.

60

Business and Social Responsibility

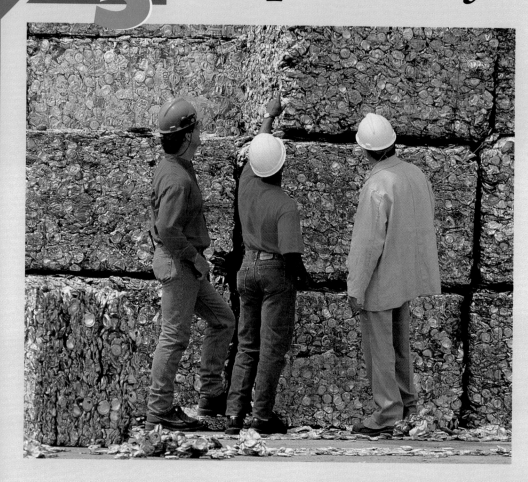

You learned in Chapter 1 about the needs that people have for goods and services. Now you will discover how individuals and groups work both to satisfy those needs and to make a profit by going into business.

Specifically, you will look at the range and functions of businesses in the United States. You will also consider some of the social issues involved in their operation.

60   Unit 3   *Business and Marketing Essentials*

Classroom Management

For the Teacher

- Teacher's Annotated Editions for all workbooks
- Teacher's Manual for *School-to-Work Handbook*
- *Testing Binder*
- *Transparency Binder*
- *Marketing Software Binder*
- *Marketing Career Portfolio*
- *Lesson Plans*

For the Student

- *Student Activity Workbook*
- *Marketing Math Workbook*
- *School-to-Work Handbook*
- *Student Software*
- *International Case Studies*
- *Marketing Career Portfolio*

SECTION 5.1

Objectives

After completing this section, you will be able to

- **tell what a business is,**
- **explain the basic functions of a business, and**
- **distinguish businesses from each other based on general characteristics.**

Terms to Know

- **business**
- **production**
- **marketplace**
- **management**
- **finance**
- **nonprofit organizations**
- **public sector**
- **private sector**

What Is Business?

Business is all of the activities involved in producing and marketing goods and services. Organizations involved in such activities are called companies, or simply *businesses*. Every business seeks to satisfy economic needs by planning, organizing, and controlling resources in order to produce and market goods or services.

The Functions of Business

Business has two primary functions—the *production* and the *marketing* of goods and services. These primary functions depend on an important support activity—*management*. Management is used to plan, organize, and control all available resources to reach company goals.

Production Production is creating, growing, manufacturing, or improving on something produced by someone else. A songwriter *creates* a song. A farmer *grows* wheat. Ford Motor Company *manufactures* cars.

What's in a Name?
Life in the Multicultural MARKETPLACE

In the United States, businesspeople move very quickly from formal introductions to a first-name basis. Regular use of titles (even a simple Mr. or Ms.) are reserved for only those holding the highest positions.

Elsewhere, this is not the case. In most other countries, first names are never used in business situations. However, figuring out what is a first name can be a problem. In Asian countries, including China and the Koreas, a person is introduced with three names, as Gong Kwan Ho. You might assume this person's first name is Gong, but Gong is the family (or last) name. You would call this person Mr. Gong. Suppose, however, a Latin American is introduced to you as Javier Morales Agredano. He would be Señor Morales to you. Agredano is his mother's maiden name.

Van conversion companies *improve* newly manufactured vans to make them more suitable for camping and travel.

Now consider an extended example. Weyerhauser Lumber Company produces lumber by cutting down tall trees and slicing them up in sawmills. The raw goods, freshly cut trees, are thus processed into usable lumber and shipped all over the country. Mobile home manufacturing companies buy the processed lumber, which serves as one of the main materials in their product. Harvesting the trees, cutting them into lumber, and making the lumber into buildings are all production activities.

Marketing When goods or services are created, grown, or manufactured, they must be sold in the marketplace. The **marketplace** exists wherever a product is sold to a buyer. It may be in a store, an outdoor market, or simply wherever two or more people agree to buy and sell a product.

Recall that the selling of something in the marketplace is the essence of the exchange process. The exchange process occurs when customers *exchange* their money (or their promise to pay) for the goods and services offered. The lumber processed by Weyerhauser in the example above earns no profit for the company and cannot be used for building anything until the exchange process has taken place. The exchange process is the focus of the broad range of activities that we call marketing.

Management Businesses use natural resources, labor, and capital to produce and market goods or services. These resources must be brought together through good management.

Focus

Bell Ringer Activity

Draw two large circles on the chalkboard. Above the circles, write Functions of Business. Have students draw the circles on a sheet of paper and write in each what they consider to be one function of business.

Introducing the Section

Solicit students' answers from the Bell Ringer Activity until you get the correct ones—*production* and *marketing* (of goods and services). Then ask how students think a company's resources are planned, controlled, and organized to produce and market goods and services. (You will probably have to coach them on this function, which is *management*.) Write the word *management* between the two circles. Tell students that this diagram will help them remember the functions of business.

Teach

Guided Practice

1. Read Section 5.1 with students.
2. Ask students to add their co-op jobs to the list on the chalkboard. Next to each new entry, indicate whether the business is large or small, profit or nonprofit, and what type of good or service it provides.

Discussion Starter

Have students generate some reasons why, as the text states, "more of the growth will be concentrated in service industries than in manufacturing." (Two-income households require services to make life easier; America is growing older, requiring more health-related services; private companies are taking over government services at all levels; high-tech manufacturing techniques require fewer workers.)

Teach (Cont'd.)

Critical Thinking

Give some examples of non-profit businesses that are not mentioned in the text. (Churches, homeless shelters and missions, meals-on-wheels projects, student vocational organizations such as DECA, Special Olympics.) Then ask: Why would anyone want to work for a business that does not have profit as a motive for operation? (Emotional satisfaction, less pressure to produce a product or meet sales numbers, enjoyment of people attracted to such work.)

L1 Math Skills

Tell students that the number of employed women will increase to 66 million by the year 2000 from 57 million in 1990. Ask: How many more women will be in the workforce in the year 2000? (9 million)

L2 Math Skills

Continuing with the figures given in the L1 Math Skills activity, pose this question: In what year between 1990 and 2000 would the number of women in the workforce be expected to have increased by 5 million? (Somewhere in calendar year 1995: 9 million ÷ 10 years = 900,000/year; 5 million ÷ 900,000 = 5.55 years.)

L3 Math Skills

Given the above figures, what is the percentage increase of the number of women in the workforce from 1990 to the year 2000? (Approximately 16 percent: 9 million ÷ 57 million = 0.1578.)

*These two very different marketplaces **exist** thousands of miles apart in different countries and cultures. Yet they have something very fundamental in common. What?*

Management is the process of achieving company goals by effective use of resources. Management functions include planning, organizing, and controlling. Because resources must be managed very carefully for a company to earn a profit, good financial planning and accurate records are necessary. Of course, federal and state tax laws require proper accounting procedures. Large businesses have finance and accounting departments to provide financial planning and accounting support for management.

The word *finance* has several meanings in business. It can mean money or anything that can be sold very quickly to get money. It can also mean borrowing money. You may have heard someone talk about financing a car. This means borrowing money to buy the car.

As a supporting function for management, **finance** means money management. Proper accounting procedures provide information needed for controlling financial resources. In small companies, financial planning and accounting are often combined into one department. In larger companies, the finance department is responsible for planning the use of money to reach company goals. Using accounting department records to show what has occurred in the past, the finance department prepares financial forecasts for the company's future.

Who are the people who manage a business's resources? The chief executive officer of a large company is a manager. So is the owner of a small business. Heads of departments (such as personnel, purchasing, and sales) are managers, too, but at a lower level. Their titles will vary, depending on the type of business and the individual company. In some businesses, top-level managers are called administrators.

Types of Businesses

Businesses come in a variety of shapes and sizes. In order to understand their differences, it is useful to divide

them into categories. Businesses can be categorized in the following ways:

- *By size.* Is the business large or small?
- *By profit orientation.* Is the business a profit or nonprofit concern?
- *By kind of product provided.* Does the business provide goods, services, or something else?

Large vs. Small For more than 100 years, the free enterprise system of the United States has nourished some of the most successful businesses in the world. One of the most dramatic success stories in modern American business is that of McDonald's Corporation, the fast-food giant.

Founder Ray Kroc, who sold restaurant equipment for a living, borrowed most of the money to start the company. The first McDonald's opened in 1955. By 1962, the company had sales of $76 million. Twelve years later in

---

Independent Practice

1. Assign and review the Chapter 5 Case Study in the *International Case Studies* workbook.

 More About

Small Businesses

What qualifies as a "small" business varies from industry to industry. Usually size is determined by annual revenue or gross receipts. For example, service businesses with receipts under $2 million dollars generally qualify for Small Business Administration (SBA) loans.

While usually nonprofit, public-sector institutions like public schools still operate much as for-profit businesses do. Explain how.

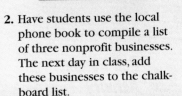
1974, sales had reached $2 billion. In 1994, the company sold $7.4 billion worth of hamburgers, french fries, and soft drinks! McDonald's Corporation is now the 30th largest corporation in the United States, valued at $22.5 billion.

While some new businesses like McDonald's grow rapidly, many continue to operate successfully as small concerns. A small business is one that is operated by only one or a few individuals. Nationwide, there are thousands of these "mom-and-pop" operations. They include neighborhood grocery stores, florists, gift shops, photocopy and print shops, and secretarial services. About 95 percent of all U.S. businesses are classified as small businesses. They employ over half of the private-sector (nongovernment) work force.

Profit vs. Nonprofit In a free market economy like that of the United States, people in business may earn a profit for efficiently satisfying the needs and wants of consumers. Thousands of new businesses are started in the United States each year. Many of them are established by people who want to work for themselves and make at least a moderate profit. Some of these new owners, however, do much better than that.

Microsoft, the computer software company, was started by Bill Gates in 1980 when he was just 18 years old. By 1994, the company had profits of $953 million! Profit is the motivating factor in starting most businesses. Most people want to earn as much profit from their business efforts as possible. But there are many service organizations operated with no intention of earning a profit for those who initiate or manage them. Examples include the Boys/Girls Clubs of America, and the YMCA and YWCA.

Like any business, **nonprofit organizations** must hire employees and pay the costs and expenses of running the organization. That means they must generate income. But all the income remaining after expenses are paid goes for the charitable cause outlined in the organization's charter.

In addition to charitable institutions, there are other organizations that operate as businesses do but are not intended to earn a profit. Many government agencies and services, such as public schools, fall into this category. These organizations are said to be part of the **public sector.** Businesses not associated with government agencies are part of the **private sector.**

Goods, Services, Etc. A final way to classify businesses is by looking at the type of products they provide. There are businesses that provide goods, like the bread sold in the supermarket or the flour used to make it. There are businesses that provide services, like dry cleaning for your clothes or security for the mall where you work.

Some classification systems make finer distinctions. They may single out businesses, such as newspapers and magazines, that provide information and ideas. They may also provide separate categories for businesses that promote people or places. Political parties try to "sell" their candidates to the voting public. State or regional tourist boards try to attract visitors to particular geographic regions.

As we move into the 21st century, American business will continue to grow. The direction, however, will be different. More of the growth will be concentrated in service industries than in manufacturing.

SECTION 5.1 *Review*

1. What activity plans, organizes, and controls resources to produce and market goods and services?
2. What are the three functions of business?
3. List at least three ways that businesses can be categorized.

Chapter 5 *Business and Social Responsibility* **63**

Assess

Evaluation

Assign and review the Section 5.1 Review.

Reteaching

1. Assign and review the vocabulary terms for this section.
2. Assign and review Fact and Idea Review questions 1–6 from the Chapter Review.
3. By now you should have quite a list of local profit and nonprofit businesses on the chalkboard. Divide the class into two or three teams, and have them face away from the chalkboard list. Assign a scorekeeper. Call out the names of local businesses from the list, and ask if the firm is small or large, profit or nonprofit, and what major product it provides. (Give one point for each correct answer.) The team with the most points at the end of the questioning wins.

Enrichment

1. Assign and review the appropriate activities in the *Student Activity Workbook*.
2. Assign and review the appropriate Critical Thinking questions from the Chapter Review.
3. Have students create a mnemonic device like the one provided in the Section Bell Ringer Activity to help them remember the three ways that businesses can be categorized.

Caption Answer

They offer a product (education) to consumers (students). They receive payment for that product (in the form of tax revenues) and use it to pay their employees and suppliers (operating expenses).

Section Review Answers

1. A business.
2. Production, marketing, and management.
3. By size, profit orientation, and type of product provided.

Close

On the chalkboard redraw the diagram. Ask two or three students to share the diagrams they created to help themselves remember the three ways that businesses can be categorized.

63

Bell Ringer Activity

Write the terms *social* and *responsibility* on the chalkboard. Ask students to help you brainstorm some meanings for both terms. They should come to the conclusion that social means "of society" and responsibility means "moral or legal liability or accountability." Now ask students to brainstorm a general definition for the term *social responsibility*. They should arrive at a general definition of "a moral and/or legal liability or accountability to society."

Introducing the Section

Generate a chalkboard list as students brainstorm answers to this question: What responsibilities, if any, do businesses have to society? Accept all answers, trying to classify them as they're given into these categories: Ethics, Environment, Consumers, and Employees.

Teach

Guided Practice

1. Read Section 5.2 with students.
2. Have students read aloud the Case Study and review the answers in class.
3. Use the transparency for this section.
4. Have students add social concerns to the chalkboard list of jobs they began in the chapter Springboard activity. Again, categorize these as matters of ethics, environment, etc.
5. Assign and review the Chapter 5 Activity in the *School-to-Work Handbook*.

SECTION 5.2

Objectives

After completing this section, you will be able to

- **name the areas in which businesses are thought to have social responsibilities,**
- **list some of the ways that business activities have impacted our environment,**
- **define ethics and suggest how marketers can make ethical choices,**
- **define consumerism and provide a brief history of the movement, and**
- **describe current trends that are likely to improve the workplace for employees.**

Terms to Know

- **ethics**
- **consumerism**

Marketing and Social Responsibility

In a free enterprise system, anyone can choose to go into business. But everyone who chooses to do so must abide by state and federal laws that apply to businesses. Some of those laws encourage fair business practices. Others protect consumers, workers, and investors, as well as the environment.

Apart from following the law, should businesses have any further social responsibility? Some businesses feel they should.

For example, Ben & Jerry's Homemade, Inc. (the Vermont ice cream manufacturer), donates 7.5 percent of its pretax earnings to the disadvantaged and the needy. The company also contributes to groups that strive for social change and environmental protection.

McDonald's Corporation helps to fund Ronald McDonald Houses, facilities near children's hospitals. The parents of young cancer patients stay at these residences while their children are receiving medical treatment. There are more than 150 Ronald McDonald Houses across the United States. McDonald's founder, Ray Kroc, also

endowed a charitable foundation. It has funded millions of dollars in medical research and programs to combat alcoholism.

Let's look at some of the issues that concern socially responsible companies like these. Those issues include protection of the environment, ethical conduct in the marketplace, and treatment of both consumers and employees.

Environmental Issues

Many environmental issues that affect us are governed by laws. For example, improper disposal of medical, chemical, and other hazardous wastes is prohibited by law. Socially responsible businesses follow the laws and understand their role in helping to preserve our natural resources.

Air and Water Pollution The federal government established the Environmental Protection Agency to protect the environment from pollution. The EPA is probably best known for its efforts to reduce smog caused by automobile emissions. All automobile manufacturers have had to modify their engines to meet EPA emission standards.

Lead in gasoline is another dangerous pollutant. So, the EPA has required that all cars built since 1975 must use unleaded gasoline. The average level of lead in people's blood has gone down by 85 percent since the advent of unleaded gasoline.

Chlorofluorocarbons (CFCs) were used as propellants in most hair spray, insecticide, and paint cans until the late 1970s. But the CFCs drifted into the

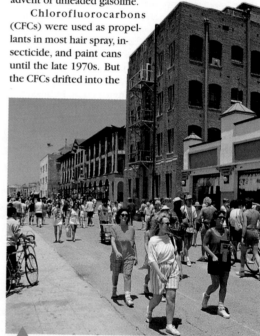

Years of using CFCs **in consumer products has damaged the ozone layer and put people at increased risk of skin cancer. What are businesses doing to avoid further damage to the environment?**

upper atmosphere where they destroyed a portion of the ozone layer. That layer had protected the earth from the sun's ultraviolet radiation for millions of years. As a result, scientists now say that when we expose our skin to the sun, we receive as much cancer-causing radiation in a few minutes as our parents did in six hours in the 1950s.

An international agreement was reached to phase out the use of CFCs by the end of the 1990s. But some socially responsible companies quit using fluorocarbon propellants on their own. They substituted different propellants or switched to pump sprays.

Freon, another CFC, was widely used in automobile and building air-conditioning systems. Federal law now requires manufacturers to use safer chemicals. All air-conditioning equipment sold in the United States after 1994, whether for vehicles or buildings, must use a freon substitute that will not harm the ozone layer. What about old air-conditioning units still in use? Garages and repair shops are being encouraged to recycle their freon.

Agricultural pesticides and chemical fertilizers have been used for years to grow bigger crops and more attractive fruits and vegetables. Some pesticides, though, have had harmful effects on animals and ultimately people. The EPA is constantly checking pesticides, some of which have already polluted our land, streams, lakes, and underground water supplies. When it determines that a pesticide causes cancer or has other harmful effects in humans or animals, the EPA prohibits its further use.

Industrial waste poses another problem for the environment. Industrial waste often finds its way through porous soil into the underground water supplies used by cities. According to the EPA, the greatest amounts of hazardous waste are generated by the chemical, electroplating, refining, rubber, textile, and plastics industries. Many states have passed laws controlling disposal of industrial wastes. In some areas, however, the most dangerous wastes are still not being disposed of safely. The EPA has increased its efforts to enforce proper waste disposal. The executives of some manufacturing companies have even been sentenced to prison for violation of safe disposal standards.

Conservation and Recycling   Concern for consumption of our natural resources reached a peak during the oil crisis of the 1970s. Car manufacturers responded by producing smaller, more fuel-efficient automobiles. Other businesses provided employees with vans and facilitated vanpooling arrangements. Employees left on their own set up car pools.

Into the next century, conservation of our natural resources will depend heavily on cooperation of business, government, and consumers. Some local governments now require consumers to participate in the recycling of glass, plastic, and aluminum through local trash collection. Many companies are making similar efforts. Alcoa, for example, recycles 15 billion cans a year. That represents a savings of about 60 percent of the aluminum the company uses for cans.

Nationally, the recycling of aluminum cans has been one of the most successful environmental efforts. From 1972 to 1994, Americans increased the percent of aluminum cans recycled from 15 percent to nearly 70 percent. The number of cans recycled each year increased from 1.2 billion in 1972 to more than 60 billion in 1994.

Business Ethics

Ethics are guidelines for good behavior. Ethical behavior is based on knowing the difference between right and wrong—and doing what is right. Ethical behavior is truthful and fair. It takes into account the well-being of everyone in the society.

In most situations, ethical concerns involving products or marketing are governed by laws. Such things as bait-and-switch advertising, price fixing, and selling unsafe products are prohibited.

Ethical questions that involve debate between our guaranteed freedom of speech and our guaranteed freedom to compete are not as easily answered. Consider an example. If it is ethical to make such products as tobacco and liquor, shouldn't the manufacturers be allowed to market them as glamorous, romantic, feminine, or manly?

To make the right ethical choices, marketers must answer these three basic questions:

1. Is the practice right, fair, and honest?
2. What would happen if the product were marketed differently?
3. What practice will result in the greatest good for the greatest number of people?

In making ethical choices, businesses sometimes look at the legal issues involved in addition to their perceived social responsibility. For example, sometimes firms face government recall of a product. To reduce losses that could arise from future lawsuits, a socially responsible business will recall an unsafe product *before* the government forces it to do so. Those irresponsible businesses who will not recall a product on their own will be forced to do so by a government agency like the Consumer Product Safety Commission.

Real World

Big Brother Is Watching (TV)

Sometimes advertisers overstep their bounds to sell a product. When they do, the Federal Trade Commission (FTC) usually steps in. Such was the case in a famous incident in 1964 when Lever Brothers, makers of Lifebuoy soap, had an actor in a TV spot shower with Dove because its own product wouldn't make enough lather. The FTC forced Lever Brothers to cancel the ad.

Chapter 5   *Business and Social Responsibility*   **65**

SECTION 5.2

Discussion Starter

Most large concert tours of major rock groups have enormous corporate sponsorship—often from beer companies. Is such sponsorship ethical when (a) many people in the audience may be below the legal drinking age and (b) when the advertising might encourage over-indulgence of those legally old enough to drink? (Some may feel that the First Amendment right of free speech includes the freedom to advertise, no matter the product or the consequences. Others may feel that any company has a moral and ethical obligation to monitor advertising to special populations or in special situations.)

Cooperative Learning

Divide your class into four groups. Have each group select one type of business, assume the roles of managers in that business, and formulate an employee policy based on the workplace trends listed in Figure 5-1. For example, if students choose a restaurant business, how would they accommodate male and female employees who have newborn babies or young children? Would they offer parents first preference on early shifts? on-site child care?

Have students present their policy statements to the class for comment and questions. Be sure the discussion includes a look at the downside of some of these workplace trends. (Flextime, for example, makes meetings difficult to schedule.)

Feature Note

Ask: How does this type of regulation limit advertisers? (Requires them to be accurate in depicting their product's attributes.) Why might this make radio advertising an attractive alternative? (No need for visuals. Verbal claims would still have to be truthful, but it would be harder to dispute a soap maker's assertion that its product lathers well without a visual standard.)

L1 Problem-Solving Skills

Present students with this problem: Your supervisor has asked you to keep track of the number of times one of your co-workers comes in late during the week. Would you agree to do this? Is it ethical of the supervisor to ask you to do this? Why or why not? (Answers will vary. Some students may agree to it, feeling that it is ethical since their coworker is breaking company rules and the supervisor should know about it. Other students may refuse to do it, feeling that it is unethical of the supervisor to put one employee in a position of spying on another.)

L2 Problem-Solving Skills

Tell students that unfortunately people in business sometimes do get caught in situations like the one described above, situations that will probably have undesirable consequences, no matter what they do. Ask: What are the undesirable consequences if you agree to keep track of the number of times your co-worker is late? What are the undesirable consequences if you do not agree to do it? (Answers will vary. If you agree to do it, your coworker may find out about it and your relationship will probably never be positive again. If you refuse your supervisor's request, however, you may damage your relationship with him or her, which will probably affect your work.)

Newman's Own

Conducting a business ethically, being concerned for your employees as well as the larger community, is admirable. But imagine starting a business whose sole purpose is to make money for charities. That's about as socially responsible as you can get!

Paul Newman, the movie actor, did just that. Newman has always been a philanthropist, making large donations to charitable, educational, and political causes. He has also always prided himself on his secret recipe for salad dressing. One story tells of his washing the dressing off a restaurant salad so he could dress it according to his own secret recipe. In the early 1980s, Newman decided to combine his salad-dressing skills with his desire to help others and start Newman's Own.

In the beginning, the company was small and made only his salad dressing. The dressing sold well, and soon

people were asking for more. Newman was surprised by the success but enjoyed his new role as entrepreneur. Within two years, the company introduced its Old Style Picture Show Popcorn and a line of pasta sauces, starting with Industrial Strength Spaghetti Sauce.

All of the Newman's Own products carry Newman's picture. He also writes the product legends for each item. These reflect his sense of humor, which has shoppers literally laughing in the (supermarket) aisles as they read his labels.

The company was profitable from the start, attributing its success to marketing high-quality products with all-natural ingredients and donating all profits to charity. Most of the money has been donated to local organizations often overlooked by mainstream contributors. Large donations have been made for relief efforts in Ethiopia and Somalia, and cleanup assistance after Hurricane Andrew.

In 1988, with proceeds from Newman's Own and private donations, Newman began a summer residential camp for children with serious or life-threatening illnesses. The camp is named the Hole in the Wall Gang Camp, after the gang in Newman's 1968 hit movie, *Butch Cassidy and the Sundance Kid.* Since 1988, three additional "Gang" camps have been founded in New York, Florida, and Ireland.

As of 1995, Newman's Own offered 18 products— 5 pasta sauces, 4 kinds of salad dressing, 5 varieties of popcorn, 3 salsas, and lemonade. As of 1994, Paul Newman himself had donated over $60 million to charitable and educational causes. This represented 100 percent of the after-tax profits from Newman's Own.

Case Study Review

1. What advantages and disadvantages do you see to the idea of having humorous labels on food products?

2. Would it make sense for most businesses to operate like Newman's Own? What made it possible for Newman to give away all the company profits?

A MATTER OF ETHICS

3. Is a company like Newman's Own, which supports causes, ethically required to tell the public which causes? Why or why not?

Case Study Answers

1. Answers will vary. Humor is attractive because it is friendly, doesn't take the product too seriously. Some people may think it's a gimmick.

2. Answers will vary. It would not be practical for a normal business to operate without profits. Newman has other income sources that make it possible for him.

3. Answers will vary. One view: The same question could be applied to all businesses asking whether the customer has a right to know how the profits are spent. The company is ethically required to spend profits responsibly but has no ethical responsibility to report its choices to the customers.

In some cases, businesses may recall products even if they are not responsible for design flaws or other problems. For example, in 1982 McNeil Consumer Products had its Tylenol capsules pulled off store shelves nationwide after someone was fatally poisoned by product that had been tampered with. The company also immediately alerted all Tylenol users to return their capsules to the stores where they had purchased them. The manufacture of Tylenol capsules was temporarily discontinued while McNeil worked with other drug companies to develop tamper-resistant packaging. Thanks to their efforts, today most over-the-counter drugs are packaged with a seal around the bottle top or around the entire package.

The American Marketing Association has developed a code of ethics for marketers. All members of the association agree to follow the code guidelines. These include detailed provisions about the truthfulness and fairness of marketing activities such as advertising, selling, pricing, marketing research, and product development and use.

Consumerism

Social responsibility involves the relationship of marketing with all of society. Consumerism, however, involves the relationship of marketing only with those who buy a company's goods or services. **Consumerism** is the societal effort to protect consumer rights by putting legal, moral, and economic pressure on business. This effort is shared by individual consumers, consumer groups, government, and socially responsible business leaders.

Consumerism had its beginning in the early 1900s. At that time it focused on product purity, product shortages, antitrust concerns, postal rates, and banking. From the 1930s to the 1950s, consumerism concentrated on product safety, labeling, misrepresentation, deceptive advertising, consumer refunds, and bank failures.

The greatest growth in consumerism took place from the early 1960s until about 1980. It involved all areas of marketing. The beginning of this consumer period was dominated by President Kennedy's Consumer Bill of Rights. It stated that consumers have four basic rights:

1. To be informed and protected against fraud, deceit, and misleading statements, and to be educated in the wise use of financial resources
2. To be protected from unsafe products
3. To have a choice of goods and services
4. To have a voice in product and marketing decisions made by government and business

Several widely read books gave impetus to consumerism during the 1960s and 1970s. Ralph Nader's *Unsafe at Any Speed* focused public attention on what the automobile industry could do to make cars safer. Rachel Carson's *Silent Spring* detailed how marketing contributed to a decaying environment. Vance Packard's *Hidden Persuaders* revealed marketing's influence on people.

Consumers were increasingly dissatisfied with poor-quality products, deceptive business practices, and the lack of concern for consumer complaints. They got angry and demanded action. The Federal Trade Commission responded by expanding its role in consumer issues.

In the 1980s, consumerism became less active than in the two previous decades. It has now achieved many of its goals. The quality of products and services has improved. More businesses listen to customer complaints and try to satisfy their concerns. Some companies now maintain 24-hour customer telephone service.

In the 1990s, companies are more responsive to customer complaints and environmental concerns than they

BRIGHT IDEAS

Catch the Wave

In 1984 Fran Rodgers founded a company called Work/Family Directions. Its purpose was to provide child-care referral services to companies that wanted to offer that benefit to their employees with children. Little did Rodgers know that she was riding the crest of a wave that would take her to $44.2 million dollars in sales by the end of her tenth year in business.

Work/Family now offers companies a wide variety of family referral and information services. These include help with adoption and after-school care. Elder-care referrals have also turned into a large portion of its business. That's because changing demographics have left many employees responsible not only for their school-age children but also for their aging parents. Work/Family helps employees make such complex decisions in the shortest time possible and with the least amount of stress. For companies, this means less work disruption and more productive employees.

Work/Family owes its existence to Fran Rodgers's alertness. She saw early on that peoples' needs were changing. She also spotted the surge in expectations that employers would help in meeting those needs. For Work/Family, the wave is still rising.

Creativity Challenge Form teams of 3–5 people and try to "catch the wave" yourself. Using Figure 5–1 on pages 68–69 as a jumping-off point, search for unmet business or consumer needs. Then design a solution in the form of a viable business. For example, Work/Family was founded to meet the needs of working parents. Since they often don't have money to spare, Work/Family looked to companies as clients.

L3 Problem-Solving Skills

Continue with the line of questioning followed in the L1 and L2 activities. Ask: If a supervisor or coworker requests that you do something at work that you feel is morally or legally wrong, what recourse do you have? (Answers will vary. One possibility: Tell the person that the request goes against your personal code of ethics. If he/she persists, document the incident and speak to your personnel director. If your company is small and there is no personnel department, speak to the owner.)

Critical Thinking

1. Consumer advocates such as Ralph Nader have become well recognized nationally for their work, as have some news reporters who, like Nader, investigate consumer issues. Should we accept the reports of consumer advocates without question? (Answers will vary. The safest course of action is to acknowledge that consumer advocates have their place but that they, like anyone else (including the people who run businesses), are only human and have their biases. Before making decisions about any product, you should read several reports about it, both pro and con, before drawing your conclusions.)

2. Some corporations such as Kmart are now including the physically challenged in their television commercials. Ask students what they think this says about the sense of social responsibility of these companies. (Practice shows a sensitivity to the physically challenged and their needs; also, an awareness that they are as vital a part of the consumer population as those who are not physically challenged.)

Bright Ideas

Ask: Why should businesses absorb the cost of providing services that really are part of their employees' personal lives? (Answers will vary, but businesses were the ones suffering the effects of ignoring employees' family needs. Also, once such needs were met, businesses stood to gain profits from greater productivity as well as lower employee turnover.)

Continue: Would you be more likely to buy the products of a company that shows the physically challenged in its commercials? (Answers will vary.)

Independent Practice

Have each student find a cigarette or alcohol ad and analyze it, in writing, in terms of the three basic questions for making ethical choices that are listed on page 65. Have students bring their ads to class with their analyses.

Show each ad to the class. Ask: How is the product presented— as glamorous? romantic? feminine? manly? Does it appeal to a particular ethnic group? to a particular age bracket? Or is the product simply presented in a straightforward manner? Which type or types of presentation are more ethical than the others? Why?

Assess

Evaluation

Assign and review the Section 5.2 Review.

Reteaching

1. Assign and review the vocabulary terms for this section.
2. Assign and review Fact and Idea Review questions 7–12 from the Chapter Review.
3. Draw a large circle on the chalkboard and write in it the term *social responsibility*. Draw four "spokes" from the circle, and ask students to name the four areas in which businesses have social responsibility (business ethics, environment, consumers, and employees). Then, have students brainstorm anything they can recall from the text about the chapter content dealing with these areas. Add these to the diagram, coming off of the spokes.

Figure 5–1

WORKPLACE TRENDS

Today's socially responsible businesses are offering their employees a more user-friendly workplace and even redefining the term *workplace* itself. Here are some of the changes they are making.

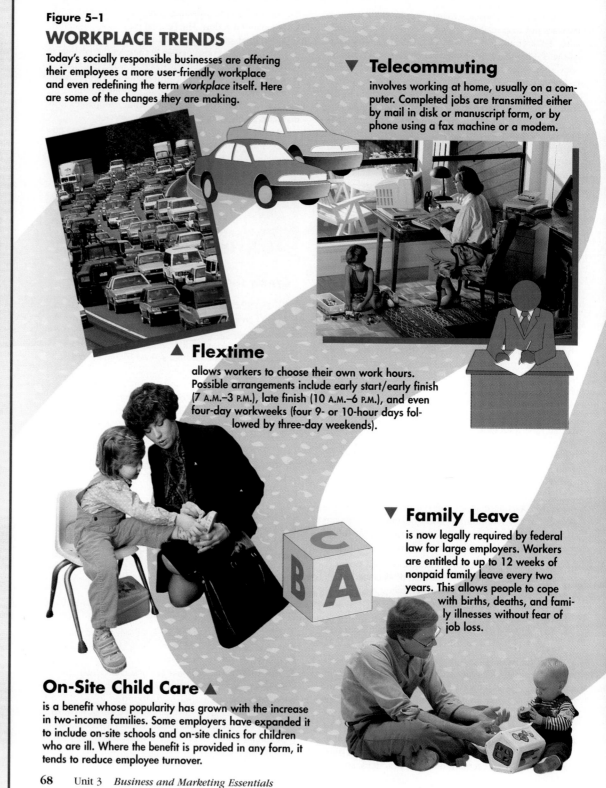

▼ Telecommuting

involves working at home, usually on a computer. Completed jobs are transmitted either by mail in disk or manuscript form, or by phone using a fax machine or a modem.

▲ Flextime

allows workers to choose their own work hours. Possible arrangements include early start/early finish (7 A.M.–3 P.M.), late finish (10 A.M.–6 P.M.), and even four-day workweeks (four 9- or 10-hour days followed by three-day weekends).

▼ Family Leave

is now legally required by federal law for large employers. Workers are entitled to up to 12 weeks of nonpaid family leave every two years. This allows people to cope with births, deaths, and family illnesses without fear of job loss.

On-Site Child Care ▲

is a benefit whose popularity has grown with the increase in two-income families. Some employers have expanded it to include on-site schools and on-site clinics for children who are ill. Where the benefit is provided in any form, it tends to reduce employee turnover.

68 Unit 3 *Business and Marketing Essentials*

Lifelong Learning

Business and Social Responsibility

Learning about marketing and social responsibility is the first step in a lifelong commitment to make choices based on information. When students make consumer decisions, the information they need is available to them if they make a conscious effort to become informed about a given topic. What products to use and how to dispose of them affect the student's personal environment as well as the environment at large. By reading a variety of publications and joining in community and school activities designed to educate consumers, students can make a difference.

▼ Help for the Physically Challenged

is mandated by the Americans with Disabilities Act (1990). Employers must provide physically challenged people with the same job opportunities and work site access that others have. To make this possible, employers may have to alter their workplaces physically, change the way a job is done, or provide individual assistance.

Health-Care Reform ▼

at the national level is an employee issue because so many Americans have received health insurance benefits through their jobs. Of the 37 million Americans who have not, however, virtually all who work are employed by small businesses or hold minimum-wage jobs. How to cover these people and how to hold the line on costs for those who have coverage are key issues in the national health-care debate.

have been in the past 30 years. Many companies now consider consumer concerns when developing their marketing plans. Product containers that can be recycled, for example, are a direct response to consumers' environmental concerns. When McDonald's restaurants switched from difficult-to-recycle styrofoam packaging to biodegradable paper, it was in response to pressure from consumers.

Employee Issues

As interest in traditional social responsibility concerns has receded, other concerns have replaced them. During the 1980s, employee issues began to attract public interest. It is these issues in the 1990s that are moving both business and government to action. Figure 5–1 presents an overview of the areas in which improvements have been made and are likely to continue in the near future.

SECTION 5.2 *Review*

1. **What term is used to describe businesses that show concern for the environment, their employees, consumers, and ethical behavior?**
2. **What are CFCs, and what have businesses done about them?**
3. **What are the characteristics of ethical behavior?**
4. **What is meant by consumerism?**
5. **Name three trends that are transforming today's workplace for employees.**

Chapter 5 *Business and Social Responsibility* **69**

SECTION 5.2

Enrichment

1. Assign and review the appropriate activities in the *Student Activity Workbook*.
2. Assign and review the appropriate Critical Thinking questions from the Chapter Review.
3. Assign and review the Building Academic Skills Activities, Application Projects, Linking School to Work Activity, and Performance Assessment from the Chapter Review.
4. Divide the class into at least four groups. Have each group generate an ethical problem that can occur at work, perhaps one that they have encountered on their co-op jobs. Problems could include such things as employee theft, having someone else punch your time card after you leave work, etc. Have each group prepare a dramatization of the problem and present it or, depending on the level of the group, role-play it to the class. Once each group has finished, lead a discussion on the ethical considerations of the situation and how the problem could be solved.

Close

On the chalkboard, draw the circle with four spokes radiating from it that you drew for the Reteaching exercise. Have students fill in the term that belongs in the circle (social responsibility) and the terms that belong on each spoke (business ethics, environment, consumers, and employees). Then, have students write one or two things next to each spoke that they can recall about chapter content.

Section Review Answers

1. Socially responsible.
2. Chlorofluorocarbons, chemicals that were used but are now banned as propellants. Businesses substituted chemicals that didn't damage the ozone layer or switched to pump sprays.
3. Ethical behavior is truthful, fair, and takes into account the well-being of society.
4. Consumerism is the effort to protect consumer rights through legal, moral, and economic pressure on business.
5. Any of the following: flex time, telecommuting, on-site child care, family leave, accommodation of the disabled, health-care reform.

5 CHAPTER *Review*

Answers

Vocabulary Review

Sentences will vary. See Glossary for definitions.

Fact and Idea Review

1. Seeks to satisfy economic needs by planning, organizing, and controlling resources to produce and market goods or services.
2. The production of goods and services and the marketing of goods and services.
3. Planning, organizing, and controlling.
4. About 95 percent.
5. Nonprofit organizations generate income to pay their costs and expenses, but anything left after expenses are paid goes to the charitable cause they sponsor. In a profit-making enterprise, these "leftover" funds would go to the owner(s) of the business.
6. Private-sector businesses could include McDonald's, Microsoft, and Weyerhauser. Public-sector organizations include public school systems and government agencies.
7. The environment (pollution, conservation, recycling); business ethics; consumer concerns; and employee-related issues.
8. Answers will vary. One possibility: Release of CFCs into the atmosphere where they have damaged the ozone layer. Governments worldwide agreed to phase out CFCs by the end of the 1990s.
9. • Is the practice right, fair, and honest?
   • What would happen if the product were marketed differently?
   • What practice will result in the greatest good for the greatest number of people?

Vocabulary Review

Use each of the following words in a sentence that demonstrates you know its meaning.

business
production
marketplace
management
finance
nonprofit organizations
public sector
private sector
ethics
consumerism

Fact and Idea Review

1. What does a business do? (Sec. 5.1)
2. Name the two primary functions of business. (Sec. 5.1)
3. What are the three major functions of management in business? (Sec. 5.1)
4. What percentage of American businesses do small businesses account for? (Sec. 5.1)
5. Explain how the operation of a nonprofit organization differs from a profit-making enterprise. (Sec. 5.1)
6. Provide an example of both a private-sector and a public-sector organization. (Sec. 5.1)
7. In what areas are businesses thought to have some degree of social responsibility? (Sec. 5.2)
8. Name one area in which business activity has had an unfavorable impact on the environment. Then explain how government and/or businesses have moved to remedy the situation. (Sec. 5.2)
9. What are the questions that marketers must ask themselves to make ethical business choices? (Sec. 5.2)
10. How has consumerism affected the way that businesses conduct themselves? (Sec. 5.2)
11. What rights do consumers have according to the Consumer Bill of Rights? (Sec. 5.2)
12. How does flextime differ from telecommuting? (Sec. 5.2)

Critical Thinking

1. Why would someone want to start a small business? Describe the success of a small business with which you are familiar.
2. How should industries that pollute the environment be handled by local, state, or federal governments?

3. What unexpected benefits might a company receive if it believes in and practices social responsibility?
4. Do consumers have a duty to be socially responsible in their purchasing? What might be some examples of this sort of conduct?
5. How are business ethics related to personal ethics?
6. Employee benefits like on-site child care tend to stabilize a company's work force. Given this fact, why do you think more companies don't offer such benefits?

Building Academic Skills

Math

1. If the local recycling center pays $.06 per pound for aluminum cans, how many pounds of cans would it take to get back $10?

Communication

2. Write a letter to a local government official describing the importance and benefits of recycling.
3. Conduct a telephone interview of a representative of your local chamber of commerce. Ask what new businesses have joined the organization in the past year. Also, try to get an evaluation of the economic, political, and other conditions facing businesses in your community.

Human Relations

4. You work for a company that produces textiles, and you have just discovered that the company has been disposing of its wastes in a manner that is unsafe for the environment. How will you handle your concern?
5. You are the manager of a retail office supply store. You have set a high standard for customer service, yet you've noticed one of your employees acting rudely with the customers. Have a classmate play the part of the employee. Then talk with him or her about the situation.
6. While working in a garage, you overhear the shop manager telling a mechanic to charge a customer for a new part, even though he used a reconditioned part for the repair. How do you respond?

Application Projects

1. With a group of other students, research the recycling centers in your community. Make a chart with information about the centers, including their locations, their hours of operation, the materials they

10. Consumerism has put legal, moral, and economic pressure on businesses to protect consumer rights.
11. • To be informed and protected against fraud, deceit, and misleading statements, and to be educated in the wise use of financial resources.
    • To be protected from unsafe products.
    • To have a choice of goods and services.
    • To have a voice in product and marketing decisions made by government and business.

12. Flextime allows workers to choose their own work hours, while telecommuting allows them to choose where they work (namely, at home).

Critical Thinking

1. Reasons will vary. Some possibilities: to be one's own boss, to make more money, to gain recognition in the community. Business descriptions will vary.

accept, and the rates they pay for those materials. Then make copies of your chart for distribution.

2. Find a local mom-and-pop business and interview the owners. Ask them to give you a brief history of the business. Also, find out what they like and dislike about having their own business. Then give a five-minute oral report telling the rest of your class what you learned.

3. Think of a project that would help your school conserve resources and protect the environment. Then write an editorial for the school newspaper. Explain your idea, and try to persuade other students to participate in your project.

4. Do an oral book report on one of the consumer classics described in this chapter (page 67) or on one of the titles listed below. Include a 200-word summary of the book and tell what you think makes it important.

   Environmentalism:
   • *Earth in the Balance* by Al Gore
   • *Deep Ecology* by Bill Devall and George Sessions
   • *The End of Nature* by Bill McKibben

   Social responsibility:
   • *The Ecology of Commerce* by Paul Hawken
   • *Ben and Jerry's, the Inside Scoop* by Fred Lager

   Consumerism:
   • *The Product Safety Book* by Stephen Brobeck
   • *The Green Consumer* by John Elkington

5. Study the scene in the picture below. Then write an explanation of what is happening with respect to products, the marketplace, the exchange process, and marketing.

6. Many companies in the United States take a special interest in social responsibility. Among the large companies known for such interests are McDonald's, Johnson & Johnson, John Deere, Dayton-Hudson, Control Data, Motorola, and NCR. Choose one of these companies or select another company—

small or large—with a particular interest in social responsibility. Research that company's policies and practices, and then write a 150- to 200-word report about the company's social responsibility.

Linking School to Work

Ask your employer whether he or she believes business has social responsibilities, and why or why not. Report back to the class, and discuss the answers you and your classmates received.

Performance Assessment

Role Play

Situation. The plant where you work has a serious problem with productivity. Much of the problem can be traced to days lost by employees with very young children. When their day-care arrangements don't work out or when their children are taken ill, these employees must leave early or take a day off. As a result, production and quality drop. Everyone is unhappy about the situation. The production workers, however, have a solution—and they've selected you as their spokesperson. They want you to make the case to your employer for an on-site child-care facility. What will you say in your presentation?

Evaluation. You will be evaluated on how well you do the following:

• Incorporate the general functions of business into your presentation.
• Discuss the extent to which businesses have social responsibilities in our society.
• Explain how businesses can make ethical choices.
• Justify workplace improvements of the type your fellow workers are recommending.

Written Report

Write a 400-word report about a local nonprofit organization, such as the YMCA. Describe how the functions of business apply to your nonprofit. Is there production? marketing? management? What forms do they take?

Complete the Chapter 5 Computer Application that appears in the Student Activity Workbook.

Chapter 5   *Business and Social Responsibility*   **71**

---

3. Have students write a brief summary of their interviews.

Human Relations

4. Students may suggest first going to their supervisor to complain and then moving higher up in the company if no satisfactory action is taken. Notifying government authorities is another possibility.

5. Students role-playing the manager should criticize constructively.

6. Answers will vary but likely include securing the cooperation of the other employee in documenting the incident, contacting a consumer agency, and looking for another job.

Application Projects

1. Charts will vary.
2. Oral reports will depend on businesses selected.
3. Editorials will vary.
4. Reports will depend on books selected.
5. Stand is a marketplace where customer is exchanging her money for a product—the farmer's produce.
6. Reports will depend on companies selected.

Linking School to Work

Answers depend on the work situation.

Performance Assessment

Refer to the *DECA Competitive Events Handbook* for evaluation guidelines.

Computer Application

Optional activity. Refer to the *Marketing Software Binder* for template and user information.

Evaluation

Administer the reproducible test for Chapter 5, or construct your own using the Testmaker software.

---

2. Answers will vary but likely include fines and cleanup costs. Encourage students to come up with more imaginative alternatives.

3. Increased sales.

4. Most students will probably say yes. Buying recycled products, buying from socially responsible companies, and buying in bulk to save excess packaging.

5. Business ethics are based on personal ethics—they are an expression of *shared* personal ethics.

6. The high cost of running an on-site child-care facility prevents many companies from offering this benefit.

Using Basic Skills

Technology
1. About 167 pounds.

Communication
2. Letters will vary.

Chapter Overview

Chapter 6 gives students an overview of the two broad U.S. markets—the consumer market and the industrial market. The consumer market is examined by age group, ethnic background, income, geographics, and psychographics; the industrial market, by type of business.

Springboard

Have students analyze their own families to decide how many markets (groups to which businesses might target their products) are represented. Later compile a chalkboard listing for the whole class, maximizing the number of entries to stress both the possibilities and complexities of marketing.

Prereading

List the section objectives to discuss with students. Have students skim the chapter, looking at the pictures, reading the captions, and noting the heads. Ask questions to ensure that students have a minimal understanding of the chapter structure.

Preteaching the Vocabulary

Before students begin reading the chapter, dictate each of the vocabulary terms and ask students to write them on a sheet of paper. When they finish, write the terms on the chalkboard. Then have students guess at the meaning of each. Write their guesses next to each term, but do not give the correct meaning. Leave this list on the chalkboard so that students can see how close their guesses were to the actual definitions as they work through the chapter.

CHAPTER **6**

The Domestic Marketplace

For businesses to be successful, they must know who their customers are. In other words, they must know their markets. This chapter is designed to introduce you to the U.S. marketplace and the different ways businesses classify and characterize its segments.

In the very broadest sense, there are two basic markets for products—a consumer market and an industrial market. This chapter will distinguish those two markets for you. It will also explain how businesses identify their opportunities within both.

72   Unit 3   *Business and Marketing Essentials*

Classroom Management

For the Teacher

- Teacher's Annotated Editions for all workbooks
- Teacher's Manual for *School-to-Work Handbook*
- *Testing Binder*
- *Transparency Binder*
- *Marketing Software Binder*
- *Marketing Career Portfolio*
- *Lesson Plans*

For the Student

- *Student Activity Workbook*
- *Marketing Math Workbook*
- *School-to-Work Handbook*
- *Student Software*
- *International Case Studies*
- *Marketing Career Portfolio*

SECTION 6.1

Objectives

After completing this section, you will be able to

- identify demographic, geographic, and psychographic trends in the U.S. consumer market and

- suggest products and marketing strategies that can reach the diverse segments within that market.

Terms to Know

- **consumer market**
- **whoopies**
- **baby boomers**
- **Generation X**
- **baby boomlet**
- **disposable income**
- **discretionary income**
- **family life cycle**

Consumer Market

The **consumer market** involves all people who make purchases for *personal* use. Presently the U.S. population is about 270 million. By the year 2025, that figure is expected to grow to 335 million. This increase plus expected demographic shifts will make the consumer market very different from what it is today.

To fully appreciate these changes, it is necessary to examine the current makeup of the U.S. population. The three most frequently studied demographic variables in the U.S. consumer market are age, ethnic background, and income. Geographic and psychographic trends are often considered as well. Together all of these factors provide a comprehensive picture of the U.S. consumer market.

Age

When marketers study age, they classify people by generation. The reason for this practice is that each generation tends to share certain characteristics. Therefore, generations make good market segments to target.

Whoopies   Well-heeled older persons—**whoopies**—are the 50-plus market. By the year 2000, adults aged 65 and older will number 35 million—an increase of 4 million since the 1990 census.

Marketers generally break down the over-50 market into three subgroups:

1. *Ages 50-64.* Most members of this group are still working and are at their peak earning power. Marketers like this group because of its high income and newfound freedom from the responsibilities of child rearing.

2. *Ages 65-74.* This group is considered the young elderly. In 1990, there were 18 million people in this age group. Most are financially secure, active, and healthy. They are prime targets for the leisure market, including travel and recreation.

3. *Age 75-plus.* This, the oldest elderly group, consists primarily of women. The group is characterized by poor health, less mobility, and (for some) even complete disability. Activities like shopping and driving become too difficult to manage or are unsafe. Members of this group are prime targets for nursing homes and other services for the elderly, like home health care.

As the numbers in this older generation increase, so will marketing to them. Already many marketers are getting experience selling to today's smaller groups of seniors

Life in the Multicultural MARKETPLACE

A Touchy Moment

When different cultures meet, touching (particularly during conversation) is a frequent source of misunderstanding. In one study, people of different nationalities were monitored in a variety of casual outdoor situations. In San Juan, Puerto Rico, a total of 180 casual touches of self or other party were counted in an hour. In Paris, France, there were 110 touches an hour. In Florida, a conversation between two Americans yielded only 2 touches an hour, while in London two English people didn't touch at all in the same period.

Thus, a Puerto Rican and an English person trying to do business together might feel uncomfortable with each other's style. The Puerto Rican might consider the English person cold. The English person might think the Puerto Rican pushy or presumptuous.

Chapter 6   *The Domestic Marketplace*   **73**

Meeting Special Needs

Physically Challenged

If you have students who are physically challenged in some way, making sure they have access to the classroom can be one of the first steps you take to ensure their full participation in the class. Be aware that a barrier can be a stair, a curb, a narrow walkway, a heavy door, or an elevator door that does not allow time for a wheelchair exit. Classroom tables need at least 27½ inches of clearance for a student in a wheelchair to pull up under them.

Also, keep in mind that some students in wheelchairs have full use of their hands while others do not. Never assume that a physically challenged student can or can't do something based on previous experience with another student.

Focus

Bell Ringer Activity

Put two sets of questions to students, and have them make brief notes on their answers:

- How many people live in the United States? Of what significance is that figure to marketers?

- How often is the U.S. Census taken? What kinds of information is gathered? Why is that information important to marketers?

Introducing the Section

Discuss the questions from the Bell Ringer Activity. Write the numbers that students suggest for the total U.S. population on the board. When a response comes close to the correct number (270 million), get students' responses to the second question in that set. (All those people are potential consumers of goods and services.)

To develop the concept of that large number's being divisible into various groups, use the second question set from the Bell Ringer Activity. Establish that the census is taken every ten years and that the information gathered includes household size, age and ethnicity, education and income levels, occupational and housing data. Note that this is all valuable information about the consumer market and hence the kind of information that marketers rely on to target their products to specific markets.

Teach

Guided Practice

1. Read Section 6.1 with students.

2. Use the four transparencies for this section.

3. Have students read aloud the Case Study and review the answers in class.

Teach (Cont'd.)

4. Ask students if they know the term that is often used to describe people in their parents' age group—people born between 1946 and 1964. (Baby boomers.) Then ask students what distinction that age group has within the whole U.S. population. (In terms of percentage of the total population, it is and has been the largest group for years.)

Discussion Starters

1. Ask students why their age group is one that marketers like to target. (Young people are viewed as trendsetters who like to try new things. Also, since many of them work and/or get an allowance, they have their own money to spend. Finally, marketers seek to build brand loyalty among consumers when they are young in hopes that they will stick with favored products when they are older.)

2. Ask students if they think senior citizen discounts are fair. Have students support their positions. (Answers will vary. Some will point out that retirees and other older people lack jobs and hence have lower income levels. This makes them logical recipients of a discount. Others, however, might point out that today's elderly are very well off as a group compared to former generations. These students might suggest a children's discount, since today children are the fastest-growing group among the nation's poor.)

3. To introduce the concept of ethnic market segments, ask the students what ethnic foods they like to eat. (This will help to make students aware of the number and variety of ethnic groups residing in the United States.)

*Older consumers **are increasingly being targeted by marketers who realize the tremendous opportunities this market segment will offer in the near future. What other products could effectively target this group? What sort of appeals could they make?***

SORRY, BUT CHILDREN UNDER 60 NOT ELIGIBLE FOR OUR 25¢ COFFEE.

There are some advantages to being a grown-up. If you're 60 or over, you can get a small coffee or soft drink at McDonald's® for just 25¢. If you're under 60, you'll just have to do something you youngsters have always had a hard time doing…be patient and wait.

What you want is what you get.

Finally a powerful pain reliever that's not a pain to open.

DRINK TO YOUR HEALTH WITH ENSURE.

The #1 Doctor Recommended Source of Nutri

$1.00 OFF ENS

---

as they wait for the baby boomers (see below) to reach 50. For example, drug companies are developing new packaging that targets older consumers. Tylenol bottles with FastCaps are specifically designed to be easy for arthritis sufferers to open.

Baby Boomers   For 18 years after World War II, the birth rate soared in the United States. The result was the **baby boomers,** 76 million babies born between the years 1946 and 1964. In 1990, people 26-44 years old numbered more than 77 million (taking into consideration deaths and immigrants). This large group should peak in 1997 at close to 78 million, at which time its members will be ages 33-51. By the year 2011, the oldest baby boomers will be 65 years old. From that point on, the generation will begin to decline rapidly as a result of deaths. (See Figure 6-1.)

Baby boomers have had the distinction of being the largest percentage of the population for many years. Tracking this group pays off for marketers because of its large size. Also, as baby boomers get older, their income and spending power increase. They are prime targets for all types of luxuries and recreational items.

Generation X   After 1964 the birth rate declined for years, which created the baby bust generation. This group is commonly referred to as **Generation X** (1965-1980). At a total of 44 million, Generation X is small compared to others.

Baby busters are the latchkey children who grew up to be self-sufficient. Members of Generation X have a high level of education. In 1993, 47 percent of the 18-24 year olds had some form of higher education. (In 1980 that percentage was only 31 percent.) As a result of their experiencing the 1990 recession, members of this generation are more financially cautious and conservative than people have been in the last 20 years.

Generation Xers are prime consumers of cosmetics, fashionable clothing, movies, and electronic items. To reach this group, marketers must use sharp images, music, a sense of humor, and a little irreverence. Reebok, for example, tries to attract Generation Xers with its casual Boks brand. Its ad states, "Hey man, if you're not careful, people will be saying, 'Hey, mister.'" The copy then explains that Dress Treads are "shoes you can wear to a real job without looking like a stiff."

Baby Boomlet   The **baby boomlet** era occurred in the 1980s and peaked in 1991. Many attribute the boomlet to baby boomers who finally started having children. For example, in 1990 women aged 30 and older accounted for 30 percent of total births. Census data reveal that the number of births started declining in 1992 and will continue to decline until Generation Xers decide to start their families.

The oldest members of the baby boomlet generation are now teenagers. The teenage market is important to

74   Unit 3   *Business and Marketing Essentials*

 More About

Generation X

The term *Generation X* was coined by writer Douglas Coupland in 1989, in his novel of the same name. Coupland felt that the generation was disappointed by difficult economic times. He theorized that all that held it together was TV trivia and endless credit-card debt.

The Baby Boom Ages

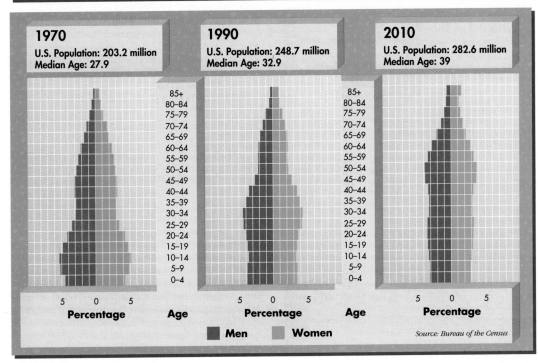

1970
U.S. Population: 203.2 million
Median Age: 27.9

1990
U.S. Population: 248.7 million
Median Age: 32.9

2010
U.S. Population: 282.6 million
Median Age: 39

Men   Women

Source: Bureau of the Census

Figure 6–1

The progress of the baby boom generation through the U.S. population is easy to see using a set of special graphs called population pyramids. How can you spot the boomers?

marketers because it is growing. By the end of the decade, teens should total 26.7 million—and they have money to spend (see Figure 6–2 on page 76). This is because most of their parents are in their peak earning years and are indulgent with their children. Things once considered luxuries for teens—cars, computers, and video games—are now considered necessities. In 1994 teens spent $89 billion.

Marketers realize that they can build brand loyalty by attracting consumers when they are teens. Frito-Lay has seen a rise in chip snacking by adults. It attributes this increase to teenage consumers they attracted years ago. So, Frito-Lay continues to draw 15 percent of its sales from teens. MasterCard is banking on the same phenomenon by offering teens their own credit cards. So is Sony, which has learned that 60 percent of 12–17 year olds have their own CD players. Other companies have recognized that teens buy their own deodorants, shampoos, and toothpastes.

Like teens, children are a key market segment for certain businesses. Kimberly-Clark's attention was attracted when its research indicated that American children aged 4–12 increased about 10 percent from 1990 to 1994. So, the company developed Kleenex for Kids—tissues in a box that's a toy. The line has six designs. One is a dinosaur box with stickers, another a train engine with a pop-up smokestack.

Although younger children may not have the purchasing power of teens, they spend money on snacks, toys, fast food, and entertainment. In addition, children influence their parents' purchases. Estimates as high as $132 billion a year are given for children's influence on household purchases. It is no mystery, then, when fast-food giants develop special programs to target children. Pizza Hut runs Kid's Nite. McDonald's offers Kid's Meals, as well as tie-ins with children's movies and their characters, to ensure its success in the children's market. *Sports Illustrated for Kids* appeared in 1989. Besides helping to fight illiteracy, the publisher hopes to create lifelong readers.

Ethnic Background

The U.S. population is becoming more diverse, mainly as a result of increased immigration. The white population is declining, while other ethnic populations are increasing. After the white market, the next three largest ethnic markets in the United States at present are African-Americans, Hispanics, and Asian-Americans.

Chapter 6   *The Domestic Marketplace*   **75**

4. To introduce the concept of lifestyle, have students consider how they and their family spend their leisure time. Ask: What products are marketed specifically for those leisure activities? (Answers will vary but certainly include TVs and other home electronics devices, board and computer games, athletic gear, books, pool supplies, camping equipment, and vehicles of various types, as well as travel and tourism services.)

5. Put this question to students: A rich person is just a poor person with money—true or false? Why or why not? (Answers will vary. Those students who qualify their responses by specifying a person who has been rich for some time are more likely to disagree because psychographic characteristics do not change that quickly, regardless of financial status.)

Critical Thinking

1. Select a product typically marketed to older people— say, an over-the-counter painkiller or a retirement village. Ask students if they would use the same product packaging and/or advertising message to market the product to all people over 50. Have them explain their reasoning. (Answers will vary, depending on whether students break up the over-50 age group into the three subgroups noted in the text.)

2. Have students brainstorm a list of cultures that might have significantly different orientations from our own on demographic or psychographic characteristics. As a starting point, use our own national preoccupation with youth. Have students suggest some cultures that value old age and summarize the likely effect of such a cultural attitude on product marketing. (Cultures that value age over youth might include various Asian and African cultures.

Consequences for marketing: more older people in ads for all products; slower, calmer, more reflective pace in ads; emphasis on respect for older people and the life experience they have accumulated. Other cultural attitudes that students might consider include value placed on material wealth, extended families, and preservation of nature.)

L1 Communication Skills

Have students form groups of 3–4.Then suggest a product that is generally linked with older people—like prunes. Ask students to think of ways to make that product appealing to teenagers and write these down in list form. (List entries will vary. Possibilities:

- Make the prune "cool" as marketers did with California raisins.
- Concentrate on the prune as a natural or healthy food.
- Use an Avis-type campaign for the fruit that has to "try harder."
- Appeal to the savvy skepticism and determination to "be their own person" that characterizes many young people today.)

L2 Communication Skills

Have students select one of the approaches they listed in the L1 activity and write an actual ad or other promotional piece using that approach.

L3 Communication Skills

Have students critique each other's ads or promotional pieces. Suggest that they note both what is most as well as what is least effective about each. If there is time and students are receptive to the idea, have them vote on the best effort of the groups (or best three) and present those to the class as a whole.

76

The Baby Boomlet Generation

Where Are They?

Projected Graduates (in millions)

High School

College

'90 '92 '94 '96 '98 '00 '02 '04
Year
Source: National Center for Education Statistics

How Much Do They Spend?

Average Dollars Spent (per week)

18–19 Years Old

16–17 Years Old

12–15 Years Old

$80, 60, 40, 20

1987 1990 1994
Year
Source: Teenage Research Unlimited

What Do They Buy?

Athletic Shoes — $3.0
General Clothing — $2.0
Blue Jeans — $1.5
Groceries* — $1.0
Health and Beauty Aids — $0.7

0 1 2 3
Billions of Dollars
Per week   Source: Simmons Market Research Bureau

Figure 6–2

Today's teens are an important market segmant because their numbers are growing and they have money to spend. How many of them are there now? On average, how much do they spend per week? What is the main item they spend their money on?

African-Americans African-Americans number approximately 33 million and spend roughly $350 billion annually. To reach the market, businesses have learned that they must back up their promotional activities with community support. For example, Maybelline runs Black

76 Unit 3 *Business and Marketing Essentials*

History Month promotions. It has also worked with the Coalition of 100 Black Women, a national organization that dedicates its efforts to improving the lives of women. Revlon has supported the United Negro College Fund.

Nia Direct offers marketers a database of African-American householders with average incomes over $31,000. Some big companies that have used Nia include Procter & Gamble, Kraft General Foods, Lipton, Lawry's Foods, and Quaker Oats.

Hispanics The Hispanic population was approximately 26 million in 1994. It grew at seven times the rate of the general population between 1980 and 1990 and is expected to reach 31 million by the year 2000.

About three-fourths of Hispanic-Americans identify their countries of origin as Mexico, Puerto Rico, and Cuba. Food marketers who sell products in these countries are following the migration and now marketing their brands to Hispanics in the United States. In 1994 Nestlé introduced Nido, a powdered milk it sells in Mexico, and Nestum, a breakfast cereal it sells in Venezuela. Goya is one food distributor that has been catering to the Hispanic population for a long time. Marketers of other kinds of products are also looking to gain a share of the $170-million Hispanic consumer market. Chase Manhatten Bank, Colgate-Palmolive, and Eastman Kodak all advertise in publications that target the U.S. Hispanic population.

Marketers who want to reach this ethnic group might consider using Spanish-language television. Hispanics watch television approximately 3.6 hours on weekdays, and most of that time is spent with Spanish-language programming. Marketers would also be wise to gain a thorough understanding of Hispanic culture. Seventy percent of Hispanics are Roman Catholics. Hispanic life centers on the family, and these families tend to be larger than the U.S. average (3.4 people vs. 2.6 for all U.S. families).

*Hispanics, who are extremely family oriented, **often shop as a family group. How could a supermarket make itself more appealing to such shoppers?***

CASE STUDY

Selling in a Multicultural Nation

To reach an increasingly diverse U.S. population, businesses are doing their homework. They are making a variety of efforts to learn about and appeal to the needs of different cultural groups. This is not only good policy but also a matter of necessity. Those same groups increasingly comprise the firms' customer base, work force, and business colleagues.

Wells Fargo Bank in San Francisco, for example, surveyed its Asian employees in order to develop guidelines for selling to Asian customers. They used that research to target their services to the Asian-American community.

Sprint gives employees of its new international division cross-cultural training. The program includes segments on respecting cultural differences, avoiding stereotypes, handling language problems, and understanding the value systems of different cultural groups. The company is also a partner in the Asian-American Association. The association markets Sprint's

international long-distance services to immigrants. It also explains schools, stores, medical care, and other aspects of U.S. life.

Other businesses have taken similar advantage of our diversified work force. Daniel's Jewelers, a chain based in California, makes it a practice to hire salespeople from the immediate neighborhood. Thus, stores located in predominately Hispanic and African-American neighborhoods have salespeople who understand the culture and the customers.

This process of reaching out by consumer product manufacturers and retailers is being duplicated in the industrial market. As ethnic segments in the population increase, so do the number of ethnic business owners. As a result, trade associations have been developing their own cross-cultural programs. For example, the Textile Care Allied Trade Association (TCATA) has engaged cross-cultural speakers for its annual meetings. The association includes businesses such as manufacturers and distributors of dry-cleaning and laundering equipment. Employees of such firms need cross-cultural training because many of their new customers are Koreans and Indians who have entered the dry-cleaning business.

In the years to come, attracting and retaining multicultural customers will be the focal point of many progressive businesses. Learning how to market to different cultures will result in increased profits.

Case Study Review

1. What is cross-cultural training, and why is it becoming so important to U.S. businesses?

2. Besides training, how else might businesses develop a work force qualified to deal with different ethnic markets?

A MATTER OF ETHICS

3. In many immigrant communities, non-English-speaking residents may be reluctant to say no to someone who speaks their language and shares their ethnic background. Under these circumstances, is it fair to target such communities using bilingual sales reps?

Chapter 6   *The Domestic Marketplace*   **77**

L1 Human Relations Skills

Have students compare their own family traditions for celebrating Thanksgiving and note any cultural differences.

L2 Human Relations Skills

Once students have a feel for cultural differences associated with Thanksgiving, ask how marketers catering to different ethnic groups might change their approaches to make the most positive appeal when promoting products sold in conjunction with the holiday. (Answers will vary depending on the cultural differences uncovered. Changes could be as minor as terminology [stuffing vs. dressing] or as major as adjusting recipes to meet culturally-based dietary restrictions.)

L3 Human Relations Skills

Have pairs of students role-play this sales situation: deli clerk takes a catering order from a customer who needs a whole Thanksgiving dinner for eight. Try to pair students of different cultural backgrounds to see how well the clerk handles questioning and order taking when it cuts across cultures. (Note: If all students are of the same ethnic background, play the role of customer yourself and assume different ethnic backgrounds from your students.)

L1 Math Skills

Refer students to Figure 6-4 (p. 79) and ask them to identify the percentage of families that had incomes of less than \$10,000 in 1993. [3.5% (under \$5,000) + 6.1% (\$5,000 − \$9,999) = 9.6%]

Case Study Answers

1. Training that teaches employees to respect cultural differences, avoid stereotyping, handle language problems, and understand the value systems of different cultural groups. Important because of increased diversity of U.S. domestic market.

2. By hiring people of the same ethnic background.

3. Answers will vary. However, it doesn't make business sense to seek new customers through a language barrier that can be easily overcome. High-pressure tactics or taking advantage of a potential customer's lack of sophistication would be unethical even without the language difference.

L2 Math Skills

Refer students to Figure 6-4. Ask them how the percentage of families earning less than $10,000 compares with the percentage of families earning $75,000 or more. [There are 5.9 percent more families making $75,000 than there are families earning less than $10,000: 8.2% + 7.3% = 15.5% (over $75,000); 3.5% + 6.1% = 9.6% (under $10,000); 15.5% − 9.6% = 5.9%.]

L3 Math Skills

Refer students to Figure 6-4 for further analysis of income distribution. Tell them that there are 68,506,000 households in the United States. Then have them calculate how many families are making less than $25,000. (Approximately 22,196,000 households make under $25,000: 3.5% + 6.1% + 7.2% + 15.5% = 32.3%; 68,506,000 × 32.3 = 22,195,940)

Independent Practice

1. Have students research the current population reports on consumer income published by the Bureau of the Census and U.S. Department of Commerce. Suggest that they compare their information (which will probably reflect updated data) with the information in the book and describe any trends that seem to be developing. In particular, suggest that they look for changes in population and income distribution.

2. Have students conduct demographic research on their own neighborhoods. Suggest they obtain information from the U.S. Census, county or regional planning board, local real estate agencies, or even the local newspaper.

This type of information has practical consequences for marketers. Food marketers, for example, know that when they sell products in Hispanic neighborhoods, the package sizes must be large.

A word of caution, though—generalizing across a culture has its limits. Some factors may differ depending on the country of origin. For example, a business that wants to sponsor a sporting event in order to reach the Hispanic market would be wise to study the differences among Mexicans, Cubans, and Puerto Ricans. Mexicans play soccer, but Cubans and Puerto Ricans play baseball.

Asian-Americans The Asian-American population in 1992 was 7.9 million. By the year 2000, that figure is expected to jump to 10 million. According to the 1990 census, the median household income of Asian-Americans was higher than that of any other ethnic group including whites. The likely reason for this? Asian-Americans have proportionally more college graduates than any other ethnic group and hold proportionally more professional jobs.

Asian-Americans make it easy for marketers to reach them by concentrating themselves in certain geographic areas (see Figure 6-3). As a result, marketers are able to use local media to reach the group rather than more costly national media.

Ten Largest Asian-American Markets

Ranking	Metropolitan Area	Asian Population (x 1,000)
1	Los Angeles–Long Beach	1,132.4
2	New York	631.4
3	Honolulu	608.8
4	San Francisco	375.9
5	Oakland	317.5
6	San Jose	300.4
7	Orange County, CA	295.3
8	Chicago	291.5
9	San Diego	240.8
10	Washington, D.C.	239.3

Source: Sales & Marketing Management's 1993 Survey of Buying Power

Figure 6-3

Most Asian-Americans live in the suburbs surrounding major metropolitan areas. According to the numbers and rankings shown here, in which section of the country are they concentrated? in which state?

78 Unit 3 *Business and Marketing Essentials*

Communicating with Asian-Americans is more difficult because there are 16 different classifications within the ethnic group, according to the U.S. Census Bureau. Some of those classifications include Chinese, Japanese, Vietnamese, Filipino, Asian Indian, Korean, and Hawaiian. Another startling statistic is that close to two-thirds of all Asian-Americans are foreign-born. Under these circumstances, being able to speak their language becomes the primary way of reaching these consumers.

Income

Marketers want to know how much money individuals or groups are likely to have available for spending on different products. For this reason, they look at two types of income—*disposable* and *discretionary*.

Disposable income is the money left after taxes are taken out. Marketers who produce and distribute products that are necessities are interested in changes in consumers' disposable income. **Discretionary income** is the money left after paying for basic living expenses such as food, shelter, and clothing. Marketers that sell luxury products are interested in changes in consumers' discretionary income.

Marketers also study the different income levels in the United States (Figure 6-4). In many cases, income levels help to distinguish different socioeconomic groups from one another.

The affluent, for example, are a small percentage of the population. In 1993, only 7.3 percent of households reported a pretax income of $100,000 or more. Nonetheless, they account for upwards of half of all discretionary spending in the United States. According to the Bureau of Labor Statistics, most affluent consumers spend their money on household operations, new cars and trucks, education, household furnishings and equipment, and women's and girls' apparel and services.

At the other end of the spectrum, about a third of U.S. households had incomes of less than $25,000 in 1993. Until recently, many businesses were more interested in the affluent market than in the low-income markets. However, retailers like Dollar General and Wal-Mart are flourishing by catering to this downscale market. The lower income group still needs food and clothing, and welcomes the lower prices offered by the large discounters.

Geographics

Where people live is often studied in relation to age, ethnic background, and income. To assist in such study, the U.S. government created Metropolitan Statistical Areas (MSAs). These are specially defined geographic areas used by the government in the distribution of federal aid, such as Medicare payments and grants for urban development.

Marketers also use MSAs—to target consumers and launch promotional campaigns. *Sales & Marketing Management* magazine reports on where people are

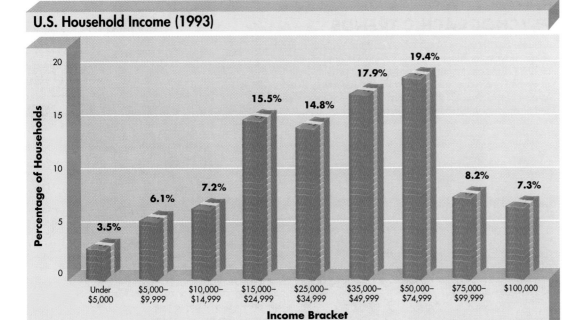

U.S. Household Income (1993)

Y-axis: Percentage of Households

- Under $5,000: 3.5%
- $5,000–$9,999: 6.1%
- $10,000–$14,999: 7.2%
- $15,000–$24,999: 15.5%
- $25,000–$34,999: 14.8%
- $35,000–$49,999: 17.9%
- $50,000–$74,999: 19.4%
- $75,000–$99,999: 8.2%
- $100,000: 7.3%

X-axis: Income Bracket

Source: Bureau of the Census

Figure 6–4

This graph shows the income distribution for U.S. households. Are the income brackets expressed in pretax or after-tax dollars? How do you know?

moving and how much spending power residents of the various MSAs have.

In general, the geographic trend in the United States has been for people to move to the South, the West, and the Southwest. Many retirees are relocating to those parts of the country. Industry has also moved to the same areas in search of lower land and labor costs.

Studying geographics in relation to ethnic groups is especially significant, since most immigrants tend to cluster around certain metropolitan areas. For example, the five key cities for Hispanics are New York City, Los Angeles, Miami, San Francisco, and Washington, D.C. Many Asian-Americans have located in U.S. suburbs.

Psychographics

Psychographic trends tend to follow demographics. For example, U.S. household trends reflect the changes in the general population. As each generation ages, its attitudes and stage in life are reflected in the data.

U.S. Households and Families Between 1990 and 1995, the number of households in the United States increased 6 percent. From 1995 to 2000, the projected increase is 11 percent. These changes are directly related to the differing sizes and habits of the baby boom, baby bust, and baby boomlet generations. As each group moves through the family life cycle, its needs change.

The **family life cycle** refers to the evolution of a family from the young single adult stage to retirement. In general, the traditional stages are *single, newly married, full nest* (when children live at home), *empty nest* (when children leave home), and *sole survivor* (widowed). Each stage in the family life cycle represents opportunities for marketers and makes market segmentation easy.

Real World

A Woman's Touch

When Louisa Knapp Curtis took a look at the women's section of the new *Tribune and Farmer* in 1879, she had to laugh. It was clear that her husband, publisher Cyrus Curtis, did not know women's tastes. Cyrus challenged his wife to do better—and she did. Under her direction, the section drew so much mail that in 1883 he converted it to a separate eight-page supplement. Today we know it as the *Ladies' Home Journal*.

Chapter 6 *The Domestic Marketplace* **79**

report (oral or written) have them address how marketers are capitalizing on the trend. If this article is not available, ask students to research the current trends in the entertainment industry or another trend related to the activities that fill their free time.

5. Assign and review the Chapter 6 Case Study in the *International Case Studies* workbook.

Assess

Evaluation

Assign and review the Section 6.1 Review.

Reteaching

1. Assign and review the vocabulary terms for this section.
2. Assign and review Fact and Idea Review questions 1–7 from the Chapter Review.
3. To reteach the concept of psychographics, ask students how they would describe the "typical" U.S. family today compared to the traditional family of the 1950s. (The fifties model of stay-at-home mom with dad providing the family's single income is much rarer today.) Then ask students what the significance of these changes would be for marketers. (More need for household and family services, as well as convenient and easy-to-prepare food products.)

Enrichment

1. Assign and review the appropriate activities in the *Student Activity Workbook*.
2. Assign and review the appropriate Critical Thinking questions from the Chapter Review.
3. Have students research current psychographic trends prevalent in the United States today. They can find these

---

Figure 6–5

PSYCHOGRAPHIC TRENDS

Attitudes are changing about what constitutes a better quality of life. Striving for balance in one's life is the goal of the 1990s. People are looking for activities that provide both enjoyment and ways to stay mentally and physically healthy. As part of this process, they are also looking for more natural and environmentally sound products and solutions.

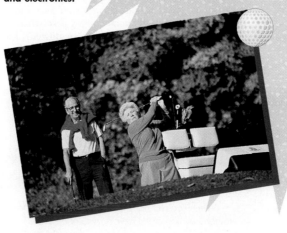

Having Fun ▲

Enjoying one's leisure time has become paramount. Proof of this trend can be seen in increased spending on entertainment, including theme parks, sports, toys, and electronics.

Eating What Comes Naturally

There is a trend in food products toward natural ingredients. For example, New Age drinks like Snapple and Fruitopia have become very popular. Nutritional concerns remain important, with new food product labeling making information on fat, cholesterol, salt, and calories even more accessible to consumers.

◀ Exercising at Any Age

Exercising is still important, but doing it to keep physically fit is limited to younger people. Older groups, for example, tend to see physical activity as a release from tension and/or a social activity. With more varied motivations have come new forms of exercise and new equipment.

In 1990 married couples made up 56 percent of all households and accounted for 70 percent of all consumer spending. The key to reaching this group is convenience. Households with adult children spend more money than their counterparts with younger children. Their highest expenses are for food, entertainment, personal-care products and services, and education. This group is at its peak earning years and can afford these higher expenses.

Increasingly, though, nontraditional family life cycles are reshaping our culture. The number of families headed by single parents is growing. So are the numbers of families with stepchildren, married couples without children,

80 Unit 3 *Business and Marketing Essentials*

Lifelong Learning

The Domestic Marketplace

Learning a second (or third) language is a long process that can take many years for the average student. High school and college are good times to spend a significant amount of time on introductory and intermediate language studies. However, learning a language is a lifetime process, as the language must be practiced regularly outside the classroom for the speaker to gain and maintain fluency. Also, time spent in a country or area that uses the language studied can be of lasting value. For those interested in a marketing career (domestic or international), Spanish and/or an Asian language (such as Japanese, Chinese, Korean, or Vietnamese) could be a valuable tool.

Shopping for Value ▶

Consumers in the 1990s are seeking value and quality more than ever. Businesses have responded with warehouse club stores and manufacturers' outlets. Restaurants now offer value meals and various kinds of discounts. Even big consumer products companies like Procter & Gamble have cut prices so that retailers can pass along the savings to consumers.

◀ Green Marketing

This term refers to the trend among businesses to consider the environment in their marketing decisions. The result has been efforts to reduce packaging, recycle, and conserve natural resources.

and divorced people. All have altered the traditional life-cycle pattern and created new needs for marketers to meet. For example, the increase in childless couples and single-person households has created demands for single-serving food products and small-scale furniture for smaller residences.

Even within traditional households, there have been significant changes. For one, most parents with children are both working. Two-income families have more buying power but many additional needs as well. Businesses that cater to such families include child-care facilities, restaurants, and housekeeping and gardening services. All simplify life by relieving working parents of traditional household duties.

Other Trends   Figure 6–5 presents some other psychographic trends that cut generally across the whole population. How many are reflected in your own life? Can you think of any others?

SECTION 6.1

Review

1. **Identify four different market segments by age and one demographic trend that is reflective of each.**
2. **After the white ethnic market, what are the next largest ethnic markets in the United States, and why are they important to marketers?**
3. **According to the last census, what has been the geographic trend in the United States?**
4. **Identify two current psychographic trends, and explain how marketers have capitalized on them.**

Chapter 6   *The Domestic Marketplace*   **81**

trends in current business and trade publications, as well as in issues of *American Demographics* magazine.
4. Write the following statement on the chalkboard and ask students what they think it means: Advertisements reflect the society at any given time. Then have students use a library's magazine stacks to find examples of advertisements from the 1950s and 1960s. Have students compare these ads to those in current publications and use their findings either to validate or invalidate the statement.
5. Tell students it is a fact that 75 percent of the elderly have close to four hours of leisure time a day, twice as much as any other age group. Ask students to develop a new good or service to take advantage of this fact and explain how they would market their product to its target consumer.
6. Have students research an ethnic market (Hispanic or Asian, for example). Tell them to find out what strategies marketers use to reach this market in general and pinpoint specific segments within the market. Have them present their findings and conclusions in a written report.
7. Tell students that by the year 2000, the number of consumers earning more than $50,000 is expected to double. Ask students to research how marketers are gearing up to respond to this level of affluence in America.

Close

Have students complete the following sentence: Studying the U.S. consumer market requires analysis of three different kinds of data. . .(demographic, geographic, and psychographic.)

Section Review Answers

1. Whoopies—will continue to grow as a group; baby boomers—the largest percentage of the total population for many years; Generation X—latchkey children who grew up to be self-sufficient; baby boomlet generation—teens and young children who spend money on themselves and influence their parents' purchases.
2. African-American, Hispanic-American, and Asian-American markets. Important because their numbers and purchasing power are growing.
3. Movement to the South, West, and Southwest.
4. Answers will vary. One possibility: Emphasis on quality of life has marketers striving to provide recreational outlets.

Focus

Bell Ringer Activity

Name a local retail store that is likely to be well known to the students. Then set a time limit of three minutes, and ask the class within that time to list all the things they can think of—other than inventory—that the store purchases to operate its business.

Introducing the Section

After students have generated a purchase list in the Bell Ringer Activity, ask them from whom businesses buy those items. Use the same line of questioning to get students to trace the purchases of wholesalers from manufacturers, and manufacturers from suppliers of components and raw materials.

Teach

Guided Practice

1. Read Section 6.2 with students.
2. To teach portions of the industrial market not related to the making and distributing of goods, have students identify doctors and dentists as businesses, and suggest some of the supplies and services that they buy to operate their businesses. Do the same for the government and institutions (like their school).
3. Assign and review the Chapter 6 Activity in the *School-to-Work Handbook*.

Discussion Starter

Tell students that DECA is a nonprofit organization. Ask them to which market it belongs—consumer or industrial—and why.

Cooperative Learning

Have students work in groups to identify at least three local businesses that fall into each of the six categories of organizations that make up the industrial market.

82

SECTION 6.2

Objectives

After completing this section, you will be able to

- explain the concept of derived demand,
- list the six major types of businesses that comprise the industrial market, and
- suggest products that each major industrial market group might need to purchase.

Terms to Know

- industrial market
- derived demand
- wholesalers
- retailers

Industrial Market

When we think of goods and services, most of us think of the consumer products that satisfy our own needs and wants. But another side of marketing that is even larger than the consumer market is the industrial, or business, market.

Doing business in the **industrial market** is often called business-to-business marketing. It involves all the customers who make purchases for *business* purposes.

Derived Demand

The industrial market is based on, or derived from, the demand for consumer goods and services. For this reason, the demand for industrial goods is called **derived demand.**

Marketers of industrial goods need to be aware of how their markets will change as a result of changes in the consumer market. For example, if consumers decide to buy more automobiles, the derived demand for auto components (tires, radios, batteries, electronic parts, etc.) will increase. That is exactly what happened in 1994 when machine tool and electronic components companies benefited from increased consumer demand for autos, computer equipment, and telecommunications services.

82   Unit 3   *Business and Marketing Essentials*

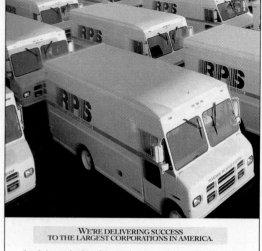

WE'RE DELIVERING SUCCESS
TO THE LARGEST CORPORATIONS IN AMERICA.

Smart business people understand it's not just the package, it's the customer that counts. That's why RPS delivers special services to meet their special needs. Like our same day delivery confirmation for every package. It lets you find out when your package was delivered and who received it, often within minutes of delivery. And there's no extra cost. It's just another way RPS helps you keep your promise to your customers.

No wonder America's largest corporations trust RPS to deliver more than just small packages. And that never changes, no matter what size you are. Call 1-800-762-3725.

We take care of business ...to business.

A Roadway Services Company

*RPS, a package delivery service, **is part of the industrial market. How do you know?***

Business Segments

All organizations that buy products from or sell products to one another for business purposes are part of the industrial market. Even businesses that are associated with consumers can be incorporated into the industrial market if they target businesses. For example, recently major hotel chains have been targeting the business traveler. Airlines did the same thing when they created a new class of travel called business class.

There are six major groups or types of business organizations that comprise the industrial market. Let's look at each of them in detail.

Extractors   Extractors are businesses that take something from the earth or sea. They include agricultural, forestry, fishing, and mining businesses. Extractors buy equipment such as tractors, trucks, saws, and drills, as well as supplies to conduct their business operations.

Construction and Manufacturing Businesses   Construction companies build structures like houses, office buildings, and manufacturing plants. They buy construction equipment, such as bulldozers for excavation work, and building supplies, such as lumber and nails. They may also subcontract for the services of such specialists as electricians, engineers, and architects.

Manufacturing involves producing goods to sell to other manufacturers or to wholesalers and retailers. Manufacturers buy raw materials, such as ore, wood, cotton, and grain. They buy components, such as steel, flour, textiles, and chemicals, as well as fabricated parts. (The last are items that are placed in products without further change. Fabricated parts may include fans put into

---

Caption Answer

Headline states that the company serves other businesses—"the largest corporations in the world."

air-conditioning equipment or electronic circuitry incorporated into television sets.) Manufacturers also purchase goods to support their operations. They buy machinery, computers, office supplies, and protective gear for their workers. They also buy business services like insurance, accounting, advertising, and delivery.

Businesses that sell products used in manufacturing must be able to offer prompt and efficient shipping. They must also be able to guarantee the quality of those products, since they will become part of manufactured goods. For this reason, firms that sell to manufacturers usually establish strict quality control measures.

Wholesalers and Retailers   Wholesalers obtain goods from manufacturers and resell them to industrial users, other wholesalers, and retailers. Wholesalers are also called distributors.

Wholesalers are common in certain industries, such as the food and auto industries. As consumers, wholesalers buy the products they resell. They also buy trucks, forklifts, warehouse services, and business services such as insurance, accounting, and delivery.

Retailers buy goods from wholesalers or directly from manufacturers and resell them to the consumer. As consumers themselves, retailers must buy the products they resell, as well as the supplies they need for providing services. In addition, retailers spend money on interior design elements (such as display fixtures and carpeting) to provide attractive, comfortable environments for their customers.

Business and Professional Services   Business services include financial planning, insurance, real estate, transportation, shipping, communications, utilities, sanitation, data processing, and advertising. Businesses buy other services for their operations, as well as office supplies, cars, trucks, vans, and computers.

Professional services include those of doctors, dentists, and lawyers. They buy office supplies specific to their businesses (syringes for a doctor's office, for example). They also use the services of accountants, insurance agents, and janitorial companies.

Institutions and Nonprofit Organizations Institutions include organizations such as private schools, universities, and hospitals. Nonprofit organizations include those such as the American Red Cross, the American Heart Association, and the Boy Scouts and Girl Scouts of America. All these organizations buy goods and services for their operations. Goods might include computers as well as office supplies. Services might include advertising, insurance, and accounting.

Local, State, and Federal Governments Federal, state, and local governments spend about $2 trillion annually. They buy a vast array of products—everything from the complex computers used in space exploration to pens and pencils for schools.

To market goods and services to the government, businesses must follow special guidelines. For example, the government is usually required to buy the least expensive goods and services that meet its written minimum specifications. So, to be considered by the government, a business must submit a bid quoting its prices.

When the bid system is not feasible, as in the case of a newly designed piece of military equipment, the government may negotiate a contract with a supplier. Such transactions are controlled by legal and budgetary regulations to help ensure the proper use of public funds.

BRIGHT IDEAS

Do the Opposite

Toshiba, the Japanese electronics company, once explained in an ad its formula for coming up with new product ideas. "Innovation is easy," stated the company. "You simply create the exact opposite of everything people wanted the day before."

To reinforce this point, the ad noted that in the 1950s miniaturization was popular. Everyone wanted smaller radios, smaller televisions, pocket-sized calculators. Now in the 1990s, big-screen TVs are turning people's living rooms into home theaters. Tongue-in-cheek, the ad suggested that Toshiba would next be developing a wrist-TV, followed somewhat later by a four-wall model that would provide 360-degree viewing.

Creativity Challenge   Form teams of 3–5 people, and test the validity of Toshiba's approach. List all the products you can think of that seem to have cycled through the kinds of changes the ad described. Articles of clothing most readily suggest themselves—skirts, ties, sunglasses, etc. Don't stop there, however. Expand your list into as many different categories of things as you can. Then try to identify at least one item that seems immune to the pattern. Decide how it could realistically be made to fit.

SECTION 6.2

Review

1. What constitutes the industrial, or business, market?
2. Why is demand for industrial goods called derived demand?
3. List the six major groups or organizations in the industrial market.

CHAPTER 6 *Review*

Answers

Vocabulary Review

People and products suggested will vary. See Glossary for definitions.

Fact and Idea Review

1. Age, ethnic background, and income.
2. Baby boomers have the distinction of being the largest percentage of the population.
3. Young elderly: leisure products, such as travel and recreation services. Generation X: clothing, athletic shoes. Children: toys and apparel.
4. African-Americans: back up promotional efforts with community support. Hispanics: use Spanish-language TV. Asian-Americans: use local media.
5. Disposable income: businesses dealing in necessities, like food and clothing. Discretionary income: businesses dealing in luxury items, like jewelry and luxury autos.
6. Evolution of a family, from a young single adult to retirement.
7. Possibilities: green marketing, exercising, shopping for value.
8. Because the demand for industrial products is derived from demand for consumer products.
9. Extractors are businesses that take something from the earth or sea. Manufacturers buy raw materials (that may be purchased from extractors) for use in producing goods to sell to other manufacturers or to wholesalers or retailers.
10. Submit a bid quoting its prices for the particular product or service needed.

84

Vocabulary Review

Identify people and/or products that would help explain the following terms to a person from another country.

consumer market
whoopies
baby boomers
Generation X
baby boomlet
disposable income
discretionary income
family life cycle
industrial market
derived demand
wholesalers
retailers

Fact and Idea Review

1. What are the three most frequently studied demographic variables in the U.S. consumer market? (Sec. 6.1)
2. What distinguishes the baby boom generation from others typically considered by marketers? (Sec. 6.1)
3. For what types of products are the young elderly prime targets? members of Generation X? children? (Sec. 6.1)
4. What must businesses do to target the African-American population? Hispanics? Asian-Americans? (Sec. 6.1)
5. For which types of businesses would changes in disposable income be important? changes in discretionary income? (Sec. 6.1)
6. Describe the family life cycle. (Sec. 6.1)
7. Name three current psychographic trends that are not related to households and families. (Sec. 6.1)
8. How can the change in consumer buying habits affect the industrial market? (Sec. 6.2)
9. How do extractors differ from manufacturers? wholesalers from retailers? (Sec. 6.2)
10. To be considered as a supplier by the government, what must a business do? (Sec. 6.2)

Critical Thinking

1. Research indicates that Americans aged 65 and older are less likely to buy from catalogs. They fear loss of their money and the inconvenience of having to return products by mail. What would you suggest to sell successfully to the elderly through direct marketing?

84 Unit 3 *Business and Marketing Essentials*

---

2. U.S. culture is youth oriented, equating such desirable traits as beauty with youth. This value has created a challenge for cosmetic companies that want to target older people. What would you tell such companies to do in order to negate this problem?
3. Create a package design and advertising slogan for a new soft drink that targets Generation X.
4. Evaluate teens in relation to children as a potential market for a new CD player. Which group would you target and why?
5. Take an existing product and reposition it for a different ethnic group. What changes would have to be made to the product, its packaging, and its advertising campaign? Why are those changes so important?
6. Show how a current psychographic trend capitalizes on current demographic trends.
7. Name a trend you see in the marketplace that was not mentioned in the chapter.
8. Use the concept of derived demand to explain what might happen to sales of synthetic fabrics in the industrial market if final consumers decided to buy only clothes made of wool, cotton, and other natural fibers.
9. Cite examples of how hotels and airlines might be considered part of the industrial market.

Building Academic Skills

Math

1. Teenaged boys are said to spend 17 percent of their money on clothing. Assuming the total amount spent nationwide by teenaged boys each year is $4 billion, what dollar amount do they spend on clothing?

Communication

2. Assume you are working as a sales associate in the shoe department of Nordstrom, an upscale specialty store. Your customer does not speak any English. Role-play with a classmate to demonstrate how you would handle this situation.

Human Relations

3. A shabbily dressed couple enters a luxury automobile showroom. None of the sales associates is eager to approach them. A younger associate finally does, however, and eventually sells them a $50,000 car. The couple puts down $20,000 cash as a down payment. What is the moral of this story? What does it say about how lifestyle characteristics can be misleading?

Critical Thinking

1. Facilitate returns, provide toll-free telephone number, use operators instead of a complicated computer message system.
2. Use older models and spokespersons, develop anti-aging products and products better suited to older skin and hair types.
3. Campaigns should include music, sharp images, a sense of humor, and/or a little irreverence.
4. Answers will vary. Those supporting children market may argue the teen market is saturated. Those supporting teens will look to their relative independence and spending power.
5. Answers will vary.
6. Psychographic trend of exercise goes hand in hand with the general aging of the population.

Technology

4. You have been hired by a stockbroker to research the geographic areas in the country that include high-income households. What technology is available to help you in this endeavor?

Application Projects

1. Summarize an article related to this chapter. In the summary reveal the connection between the article's content and specific trends or ideas presented in the chapter. Suggested periodicals include *American Demographics, Business Week, Sales & Marketing Management,* and *Marketing News.*
2. Research a specific age segment of the U.S. consumer market, such as the over-50 market or the baby boomers. Collect ads for products specifically targeting that group. Then take an existing product that is currently marketed to another age group and reposition it for the group you are researching. Prepare a written report, and share your work with classmates in an oral presentation.
3. Select a specific business that could market its products to an ethnic market but does not do so at the present time. Research a specific ethnic population in order to develop guidelines for targeting that group. Then prepare a report that summarizes the guidelines you would recommend.
4. Clip ads that target an upscale market and those that target a downscale market. Compare the products and marketing strategies used.
5. Using the edition of *Sales & Marketing Management* that reports buying power in the United States, research your MSA (the geographical area in which you reside). Report on the average household income and spending power in your area. How does it compare with the rest of the country?
6. Select one psychographic trend in the text to poll your classmates about. For example, ask them to tell you which beverages they prefer from a list you prepare. Make sure the list is well balanced, with half the choices all-natural beverages and the other half beverages that have artificial ingredients. Report your findings to the class. Is the trend toward all-natural ingredients evident in your sample? How do you account for your results?
7. Look through magazines and select two ads that illustrate a trend sweeping through the U.S. consumer market. In a two-minute presentation, show the ads to the class, and explain how they reflect the trend you have identified.
8. Find out what procedures are followed by educational officials in charge of purchasing your school's teaching supplies and equipment. Make both written and oral presentations reporting your findings.

Linking School to Work

Tell what business your training station does. What goods and services does it buy for its operation? Who are its customers? How might a change in the consumer market affect that business?

Performance Assessment

Role Play

Situation. You work for a new restaurant that targets senior citizens. Business is slow, and the owner has asked you and other employees to provide some suggestions on how to bring in more customers. What is your response?

Evaluation. You will be evaluated on how well you do the following:

- Identify demographic, geographic, and psychographic trends in the U.S. consumer market.
- Suggest products and marketing strategies for reaching the ever-changing U.S. population.
- Communicate your ideas in a convincing manner, complete with examples of your suggestions.

Creative Problem Solving

A local food store is experiencing tremendous competition from a large wholesale warehouse club. The club sells food at prices too low to match. Knowing that they cannot compete based on price, the owners of the local store are determined to attract customers by giving them a truly different shopping experience. Demographic data indicate that the area has been attracting upscale parents who have young children. Prepare a written report suggesting products and marketing strategies the local store could use to reach this market.

Complete the Chapter 6 Computer Application that appears in the Student Activity Workbook.

Lifestyle variables are not always the same for different socio-economic groups as one would imagine.

Technology

4. You can purchase CD-Rom disks that include this information or you could go on-line with a computer service to see if its data base has such information.

Application Projects

1. Summaries will depend on articles selected.
2. Reports will vary.
3. Guidelines will vary.
4. Strategies will vary with ads chosen.
5. Results will depend on MSAs selected.
6. Reports will vary depending on subject.
7. Explanations will vary with ads selected.
8. Presentations will vary.

Linking School to Work

Answers depend on the work situation.

Performance Assessment

Refer to the *DECA Competitive Events Handbook* for evaluation guidelines.

Computer Application

Optional activity. Refer to the *Marketing Software Binder* for template and user information.

Evaluation

Administer the reproducible test for Chapter 6, or construct your own using the Testmaker software.

---

7. Answers will vary.
8. Sales of synthetics would decline because clothing manufacturers would stop buying that type of fabric.
9. Hotels offer corporate housing, convention services for businesses, and suites equipped with speakerphones and fax machines for the business traveler. Airlines offer a special class of travel called business class.

Building Academic Skills

Math
1. $60,000 \times .17 = $10,200$

Communication
2. Role plays will vary.

Human Relations
3. Moral: you can't judge a book by its cover.

CHAPTER 7

THE GLOBAL MARKETPLACE

Pages 86–101

Chapter Overview

In Chapter 7 students learn about the global marketplace. The chapter explains the need for international trade, discusses government involvement in international trade, and introduces students to the practical side of doing business abroad.

Springboard

Write this question on the chalkboard: Is trading with foreign countries good or bad for the U.S. economy? Have each student write a list of points supporting his or her opinion. Then, through discussion, try to formulate a class position to serve as a standard of comparison for what students will learn throughout this chapter.

Prereading

List the section objectives to discuss with students. Have students skim the chapter, looking at the pictures, reading the captions, and noting the heads. Ask questions to ensure that students have a minimal understanding of the chapter structure.

Preteaching the Vocabulary

Before students begin reading the chapter, dictate each of the vocabulary terms and ask students to write them on a sheet of paper. When they finish, write the terms on the chalkboard. Then have students guess at the meaning of each. Write their guesses next to each term, but do not give the correct meaning. Leave this list on the chalkboard so that students can see how close their guesses were to the actual definitions as they work through the chapter.

86

CHAPTER 7

The Global Marketplace

The global marketplace makes all the people and businesses in the world potential customers, as well as potential employees or employers. In the United States, you have undoubtedly experienced this firsthand. Many products you are familiar with are produced by foreign-owned companies. Your Sony Walkman, Toyota automobile, Lipton tea, and Nestlé Crunch candy bar are all produced by foreign-owned companies. However, Sony, Toyota, Lipton, and Nestlé all have operations in the United States, where they employ U.S. citizens. In this chapter you will explore the key concepts that govern international trade and help create this global marketplace.

86 Unit 3 *Business and Marketing Essentials*

Classroom Management

For the Teacher
- Teacher's Annotated Editions for all workbooks
- Teacher's Manual for *School-to-Work Handbook*
- *Testing Binder*
- *Transparency Binder*
- *Marketing Software Binder*
- *Marketing Career Portfolio*
- *Lesson Plans*

For the Student
- *Student Activity Workbook*
- *Marketing Math Workbook*
- *School-to-Work Handbook*
- *Student Software*
- *International Case Studies*
- *Marketing Career Portfolio*

SECTION 7.1

Objectives

After completing this section, you will be able to

- distinguish imports from exports,
- discuss the interdependence of nations, and
- explain the advantages and disadvantages of international trade.

Terms to Know

- international trade
- imports
- exports
- absolute advantage
- comparative advantage

Why International Trade?

International trade involves the exchange of goods and services between nations. Goods and services purchased from other countries are called **imports.** Goods and services sold to other countries are called **exports.** These exchanges occur between businesses but are controlled by the governments of the countries involved. Let's take a look at the reasons why nations trade with one another.

Interdependence of Nations

Most countries are not self-sufficient. They need to obtain some of their goods and services from other nations. This is called *economic interdependence,* and it occurs because different countries possess unique resources and capabilities.

Unique resources may include a country's weather, raw materials, labor force, capital sources, and location. Some countries, such as the United States and Canada, have favorable climates for agriculture. The Middle East, Africa, and Mexico have crude oil, while Russia has coal. Some countries, like those in Eastern Europe and Asia, have inexpensive labor forces. Others, like the United

States and Japan, have the capital and technology necessary for manufacturing.

Because nations need different things, they find it advantageous to trade with each other. There are two types of advantages in international trade—*absolute* and *comparative*.

Absolute advantage occurs when a country has special natural resources or capabilities that allow it to produce a given commodity at a lower cost than any other nation in the world. For example, China produces close to 80 percent of all the silk in the world. In that case, China has an absolute advantage.

Even when absolute advantage does not exist, it can still be valuable for nations to conduct trade. This is because of comparative advantage. **Comparative advantage** refers to the value that a nation gains by selling the goods it produces more efficiently than other goods. Comparative advantage may be gained in international trade when countries specialize in products well suited to their production capabilities.

At present, U.S. businesses are well suited to producing high-tech goods and services. Their specialties lie in products such as airplanes, computers, high-tech machinery, entertainment, and telecommunications. (See Table 7–1 on page 88.) These products are ones for which the United States has a comparative advantage over less developed emerging nations.

What do emerging nations have to offer? Some have large, unskilled labor forces with low labor costs. Labor-intensive industries thrive in such an environment. (Labor-intensive means that it takes more labor than machinery to make something.) Thus, emerging nations can produce

Real World

Do You Speak Capitalist?

The Moscow office of Sea-Land, an international shipping company, wanted a brochure describing its customer service policies. Asked a Russian staffer, trying to be helpful, "Is that the same as customs service policies?"

Finding Russian words to describe all the new economic options available in the country is proving difficult. Since many of the terms have no equivalent translation in Russian, it can take three sentences to convey a concept like cash flow. The solution? Borrow the English terms. What's *detekuityrash*? You mean you don't recognize debt-equity ratio? You're excused. It's a tough concept even in English.

Chapter 7   *The Global Marketplace*   **87**

SECTION 7.1

Focus

⏰ Bell Ringer Activity

Ask students to list products that they enjoy because the United States allows international trade with other countries.

Introducing the Section

On the chalkboard, write the products (with brand names) that students listed in the Bell Ringer Activity. This activity will help students develop an appreciation of the variety of goods U.S. citizens have available to them because of international trade.

Teach

Guided Practice

1. Read Section 7.1 with students.
2. Ask students why most of the tea and coffee we buy comes from outside the United States. Their answers will help introduce the concept of interdependence of nations.

Discussion Starter

Have students explain why they agree or disagree with the following statement: International trade is beneficial to everyone in the United States—consumers, producers, and workers. The answers generated will help introduce the advantages and disadvantages of international trade for consumers, producers, and workers.

Independent Practice

Have students use the *World Almanac* to research a country of their choice—its major industries and natural resources, as well as what the country normally imports and exports.

Meeting Special Needs

Visually Impaired

Coping with the mass of printed material in class can be a challenge for visually impaired students. To meet this challenge, such students often use a combination of resources—readers, brailled books, recorded books, and class lectures.

To make the last more helpful to visually impaired students, you need to think carefully about

what you say in class. Consider writing on the chalkboard while talking through a computation. Use examples that are clear and specific and don't require interpretation. "This (pointing) plus that (pointing) equals 11" requires clarification; "4 plus 7 equals 11" doesn't. Sensitivity to student needs is the key.

Assign and review the Section 7.1 Review.

Reteaching

1. Assign and review the vocabulary terms for this section.
2. Assign and review Fact and Idea Review questions 1 and 2 from the Chapter Review.
3. To reteach the concept of interdependence of nations, break the word *interdependence* into its two component parts, and ask students to define them. (*Inter-* means "between"; *dependence*, "relying on someone else.")

Enrichment

1. Assign and review the appropriate activities in the *Student Activity Workbook*.
2. Assign and review the appropriate Critical Thinking questions from the Chapter Review.
3. Have students research the concept of protectionism—protecting domestic products by restricting imports or making them too expensive for consumers to buy. Students should learn that most proponents of a pure market system oppose protectionism, while many labor unions favor it to protect domestic jobs. Have students take a stand pro or con on protectionism for the United States and support their positions with facts gathered in their research.

Close

Have students complete this statement: Countries need to trade with each other because ...(most are not completely self-sufficient—they need to obtain goods and services from other nations.)

Top 20 U.S. Exporters (1992)

Rank Company	Major Exports	Export Figures ($ millions)	(% of total sales)
1. **Boeing** Seattle, WA	Commercial aircraft	17,486.0	57.5
2. **General Motors** Detroit, MI	Motor vehicles and parts	14,045.1	10.6
3. **General Electric** Fairfield, CT	Jet engines, turbines, plastics, medical systems	8,200.0	13.2
4. **Intl. Business Machines** Armonk, NY	Computers and related equipment	7,524.0	11.6
5. **Ford Motor** Dearborn, MI	Motor vehicles and parts	7,220.0	7.2
6. **Chrysler** Highland Park, MI	Motor vehicles and parts	7,051.8	19.1
7. **McDonnell Douglas** St. Louis, MO	Aerospace products, missiles, electronic systems	4,983.0	28.5
8. **Philip Morris** New York, NY	Tobacco, beverages, food products	3,797.0	7.6
9. **Hewlett-Packard** Palo Alto, CA	Measurement and computation products, systems	3,720.0	22.6
10. **E.I. Du Pont De Nemours** Wilmington, DE	Specialty chemicals	3,509.0	9.4
11. **Motorola** Schaumburg, IL	Communications equipment, semiconductors	3,460.0	25.9
12. **United Technologies** Hartford, CT	Jet engines, helicopters, cooling equipment	3,451.0	15.7
13. **Caterpillar** Peoria, IL	Heavy machinery, engines, turbines	3,341.0	32.8
14. **Eastman Kodak** Rochester, NY	Imaging, chemicals, health products	3,220.0	15.6
15. **Archer Daniels Midland** Decatur, IL	Protein meals, vegetable oils, flour, grain	2,700.0	28.9
16. **Intel** Santa Clara, CA	Microcomputer components, modules, and systems	2,339.0	39.1
17. **Digital Equipment** Maynard, MA	Computers and related equipment	1,900.0	13.5
18. **Allied-Signal** Morristown, NJ	Aircraft and automotive parts, chemicals	1,810.0	15.0
19. **Unisys** Blue Bell, PA	Computers and related equipment	1,795.8	21.3
20. **Sun Microsystems** Mountain View, CA	Computers and related equipment	1,783.6	49.2

Source: Fortune

Table 7–1

High-tech goods and services are the chief U.S. export. Of the top 20 exporting firms in the country, how many derive at least half of their sales from exports? How many derive at least a fourth of their sales from that source?

toys, clothing, and shoes (which are all labor-intensive products) at a lower cost than most industrialized nations. Where those products are concerned, emerging nations have a comparative advantage. It pays for high-wage countries like the United States to buy those items from emerging nations rather than make them themselves.

Advantages of Trade vs. Disadvantages

Consumers, producers, workers, and nations benefit from international trade in different ways. *Consumers*

benefit from the competition generated by foreign companies. That competition forces domestic producers to improve their quality and lower their prices. The variety of goods also increases as more and more foreign producers market their goods in the other countries.

As an example, consider the Hard Rock Cafe, with its global operations. Recently, the cafe opened its doors in East Asia, with branches in Singapore, Bangkok, Kuala Lumpur, Jakarta, Taipei, Bali, and Beijing. Thus, it joins McDonald's, Burger King, and Kentucky Fried Chicken in much of urban Asia. For Asians, the introduction of hamburgers and french fries is a change from their customary diet.

Caption Answer

Half—one firm (Boeing); fourth—seven firms.

Producers have the opportunity to grow their businesses by conducting operations in other countries. Some producers have found that the bulk of their business now takes place abroad. For example, Coca-Cola derives 80 percent of its total revenues from foreign operations.

Not just large corporations are benefiting from doing business abroad. Molex, a midsized midwestern firm that makes electrical connectors and cables, derives a third of its sales from its Japanese operations.

Workers are another group that benefits from trade. Increased trade helps businesses employ more people both at home and abroad. Companies that expand their businesses through exporting need more employees to increase their production. Domestic workers also benefit from foreign-owned companies that set up operations in their country. The United States is a case in point. Four million U.S. jobs are linked to foreign investment.

Lastly, nations as a whole benefit from international trade. Increased investment in a country by foreign businesses helps improve the standard of living for that country's people. Such economic alliances, in turn, often translate into political alliances. Think of the consequences of cutting off relations with a country that is a large market for U.S. exports or one that has many business investments here.

Although international trade is largely beneficial, there are some drawbacks for both producers and workers. Some domestic businesses cannot compete, given the cheaper labor and raw materials available in foreign countries. Such businesses often reduce their operations. Some even close down or move their operations to foreign countries. Their U.S. workers join the ranks of the unemployed. If they are not skilled in other areas, their prospects for making the kind of money they once made are low. For many, retraining may be necessary before they can again be gainfully employed.

SECTION 7.1

Review

1. What is the difference between imports and exports?
2. Explain the concept of economic interdependence of nations.
3. Define comparative advantage, and list three products in the production of which the United States has such an advantage.
4. Name one advantage consumers derive from international trade and one that nations derive.
5. What disadvantages, if any, does trade have for producers, workers, and nations?

SECTION 7.2

Objectives

After completing this section, you will be able to

- discuss the U.S. balance of trade,
- identify three types of trade barriers,
- explain the various forms of trade support, and
- name the major agreements governing world trade today.

Terms to Know

- balance of trade
- tariff
- quota
- embargo
- most-favored-nation status (MFNS)
- foreign trade zones
- Export-Import Bank (Eximbank)
- International Monetary Fund (IMF)
- General Agreement on Tariffs and Trade (GATT)
- North American Free Trade Agreement (NAFTA)
- European Union (EU)

Government Involvement in International Trade

All nations control and monitor their trade with foreign businesses. The U.S. government monitors imports through the customs division of the U.S. Treasury Department. All people and goods that enter the United States from a foreign country are subject to search and review by U.S. customs officials. Just as the United States checks incoming goods, so do other countries. All U.S. citizens and firms must conform to the customs requirements of foreign countries when visiting or exporting goods to them.

SECTION 7.2

Focus

🕐 Bell Ringer Activity

Ask students to identify the country with which the United States trades more than any other.

Introducing the Section

Once a student provides the correct response to the Bell Ringer Activity (Canada is our number one trading partner), ask the class why they think this is so. (Most will note our common border, and some will mention NAFTA.) The latter will help introduce the concept of government involvement in international trade.

Teach

Guided Practice

1. Read Section 7.2 with students.
2. Use the transparency for this section.
3. Have students read aloud the Case Study and review the answers in class.
4. Ask students which is better and why—when a country imports more than it exports or when it exports more than it imports. (It's better when a country exports more than it imports because that means the country's businesses are selling more abroad than its consumers and businesses are buying from foreign producers.) This discussion will help introduce the concept of balance of trade.

Discussion Starter

Ask: With all the new international trade agreements that are designed to promote free trade, will there still be a need for a country to impose tariffs and quotas on foreign-made goods? (Answers will vary. There still may be a need in certain situations, but the trend is to reduce and in many cases eliminate them.)

Section Review Answers

1. Imports are goods and services purchased from other countries. Exports are goods and services sold to other countries.
2. Since most nations are not self-sufficient but do possess unique resources, they trade the things they have to get what they need from other nations.
3. Advantage a country gains by selling goods it produces most efficiently; airplanes, computers, high-tech machinery.
4. Consumer advantages—lower prices, better-quality goods; national advantages—improved standard of living, political alliances.
5. Loss of jobs/companies to foreign competition for workers/producers, respectively; loss of tax revenue for nations.

L1 Math Skills

Have students study Figure 7-1. Call their attention to the first graph. Ask: By how many percentage points did U.S. imports grow from 1991 to 1992? (Approximately 10 percent.) During this same period, while U.S. imports were trending sharply upward, what was happening to other nations' imports? (They were continuing a gradual but steady decline.)

L2 Math Skills

Have students again look at Figure 7-1. This time call their attention to the second graph as well as the caption. Ask: From 1992 to 1993, what effect did excess imports have on the U.S. gross domestic product? How do you know? (More imports than exports created a trade deficit that pulled the U.S. GDP down. Graph shows trade deficit's "contribution" to be in negative numbers—bars extending below the zero level.)

L3 Math Skills

Have students study Figure 7-1 again, this time to analyze the relationship of the two graphs to each other. Tell students to concentrate on the entire period from 1988 to 1993, comparing the trend in imports with its effect on the nation's GDP. (In general the relationship is inverse—when the import line moves up, the GDP bars tend to fall into negative numbers; when the import line goes down, the GDP bars surge into positive numbers. Clearest correspondences are for the years 1990 and 1991.)

Nations keep track of their trade with each other. This gives them a key indicator of their economic health.

Balance of Trade

The difference in value between exports and imports of a nation is called its **balance of trade.** A positive balance of trade occurs when a nation exports more than it imports. (It has a *trade surplus*.) A negative balance occurs when a nation imports more than it exports. (It has a *trade deficit*.) At present, the United States has a negative balance of trade. The merchandise deficit alone was over $100 billion in 1993.

This negative balance of trade is surprising because the United States is the world's largest exporter. Some analysts believe the reason for this situation is that Americans like to buy more goods and services than people of other nations. Others believe the reason is that the United States has switched its emphasis from manufacturing and farming to providing services. Therefore, as a nation it imports many of the goods it once manufactured but now finds more economical to purchase abroad. In fact, European countries export more than 20 percent of their gross domestic products. The comparable figure for the United States is only 10 percent.

An unfavorable balance of trade has a number of unfortunate effects on an economy. For one, it reduces a nation's revenue. When more money leaves a country than comes in, that country becomes a debtor nation. Thus, a negative balance of trade reduces a nation's Gross Domestic Product. The combined graphs in Figure 7-1 illustrate this effect.

Increased unemployment can be another effect of a negative balance of trade. A nation's people may lose their jobs as foreign competitors take business away from domestic firms. Domestic businesses must become competitive or risk failure.

Japan is a country with which the United States has had a negative balance of trade for many years. In 1994, the U.S. trade deficit with Japan was close to $60 billion. Autos and auto parts accounted for over 60 percent of that figure.

Trade Barriers

When a nation's government wants to limit trade, it imposes trade barriers. These are controls that restrict the flow of goods and services among nations.

Why would a government want to limit trade? For a variety of economic reasons. It might be concerned with its balance of trade or with protecting domestic jobs. It might wish to shield new domestic industries from foreign competition.

There could also be security reasons. For example, a nation might want to avoid relying on foreign companies for products critical to its national defense. For similar reasons, it might avoid selling potential military technology to other countries.

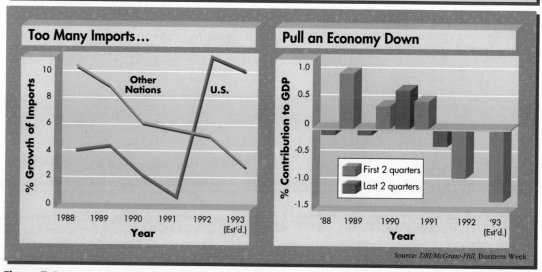

Why a Trade Deficit Hurts

Figure 7-1

The U.S. trade deficit rose from $72 billion in 1992 to $112 billion in 1993. That increase lowered the nation's GDP by 1.5 percent, the largest trade-based loss since the early 1980s. Name one factor that, according to the graphs, was responsible for this situation.

Reprinted from September 6, 1993 issue of *Business Week* by special permission, copyright © 1993 by McGraw-Hill, Inc.

90 Unit 3 *Business and Marketing Essentials*

Caption Answer

Other nations were not importing as much, perhaps because their economies were in recession.

Tariffs are assessed by officials of the U.S. Customs Service. At what point in the export/import process does this occur?

Some countries, such as the United States, are concerned with controlling both imports and exports. Let's look at import control first. The two most significant barriers used for this purpose are *tariffs* and *quotas*.

Tariffs   A **tariff** (sometimes called a *duty*) is a tax on imports. Tariffs may be used to produce revenue for a country. In the United States, revenue-producing tariffs were used as a primary source of income before income taxes were established in 1913. Today, these tariffs are generally low. They may be as little as 25 cents or less per item or pound.

Another type of tariff is protective. A protective tariff is generally high. Its purpose is to increase the price of imported goods so that domestic products can compete with them. This kind of tariff can keep foreign businesses that want to trade with the United States from doing so.

You may wonder how the government collects tariffs. When a plane, ship, or truck arrives in the United States from abroad, it goes through the same process you would go through. You would pass through customs and declare in writing what you were bringing into the country. A business does the same thing, only its declaration is called a *manifest*. From the manifest, customs officials can determine if the cargo is admissible under the law. They can also identify the recipient of the cargo and levy any applicable duties.

Quotas   An import **quota** limits either the quantity or monetary value of a product that may be imported. For example, the United States government might place a quota on foreign automobiles limiting the number that may be imported. It might also say that only $1 million worth of Irish crystal may be imported.

Sometimes, to improve their relations, one trading partner might voluntarily put quotas on the goods it sells

to another. For example, Japan voluntarily placed quotas on its auto exports to the United States in order to improve trade relations between the two countries.

Embargoes   An **embargo** is a total ban on specific goods coming into and leaving a country. For example, in 1989 the U.S. government embargoed Chilean grapes as a precaution after inspectors found poisoned fruit in a shipment. That embargo was lifted within a week.

Embargoes are often used for political reasons. During the Persian Gulf war, for example, the United Nations imposed an embargo on Iraq. The goal of this sanction was to end the war through economic rather than military means. The United States still observes that embargo.

Embargoes based on political differences can continue for a very long time. In 1994, the United States lifted its 20-year embargo on Vietnam so that trade relations could be cultivated between the two nations. The U.S. embargo against Cuba, however, still remains in effect after more than 35 years. It was imposed in 1960 when Fidel Castro made Cuba a communist state.

Trade Support

Nations wishing to encourage foreign trade have even more options than those wishing to discourage it. They can provide financial, advisory, and other assistance as an incentive. They can also join international organizations that support free trade.

Most-Favored-Nation Status (MFNS) The United States grants **most-favored-nation status (MFNS)** to countries with which it wants to encourage trade. This privilege is generally granted to emerging nations like China on a yearly basis. It benefits recipients by subjecting them to lower tariffs and quotas.

Chapter 7   *The Global Marketplace*   **91**

Did You Know ❓

As soon as President Clinton had signed the executive order ending the 19-year trade embargo with Vietnam, Pepsi released a photo of a giant Pepsi can being placed in a main square of Ho Chi Minh City. In the same spirit, Coca-Cola flew a 30-foot-tall inflatable Coke bottle to a celebration. Both companies are vying for dollars in a country where per capita income is $200 a year.

L1 Communication Skills

Have students make a written list of all the things they would like to know about U.S. foreign trade zones. Possibilities include foreign companies that are taking advantage of them, the way tariffs are levied on goods processed or assembled and distributed there, and if any of the new international trade agreements will reduce the need for such zones.

L2 Communication Skills

Have students write three paragraphs for a letter they will send to a U.S. foreign trade zone requesting the information specified in the L1 Communication Skills activity. Tell students that in the first paragraph they should introduce themselves, telling the reader that they are marketing students researching foreign trade zones as a requirement of their course work. The second paragraph should detail the information they would like to receive. The third paragraph should thank the person in advance for his/her cooperation and help.

L3 Communication Skills

Have students incorporate the paragraphs they developed in the L2 Communication Skills activity into correctly formatted business letters. These should include return address, date, inside address, salutation, message, complimentary close, and signature block. (See Chapter 9, Communication Skills, for format details and model.)

When the letters are complete, have students exchange them for proofreading and any recommended alterations in format, content, spelling, etc. Tell students that letters cannot be mailed if they have errors in them.

To complete the assignment, have students bring stamped, addressed envelopes to class. That way you can mail the letters to the various zones to ensure that they get off in a timely fashion.

Critical Thinking

Ask: How could an embargo against a foreign country hurt U.S. businesses? (It could open the door for competing companies from other nations to establish themselves in a foreign market by doing the business U.S. companies might have done had they been able to trade with the country. For example, by the time the United States lifted its embargo against Vietnam, many European and Asian companies had been doing business with that country for years. As a result, it was more difficult for U.S. companies to enter that market.)

Independent Practice

1. Assign and review the Chapter 7 Case Study in the *International Case Studies* workbook.
2. Have students research the current U.S. balance of trade with its top trading partners and present their findings in written report form.
3. Have students research the current status of the European Union. Specifically, have them determine how much progress has been made toward developing a single European currency. Also, instruct them to find out if additional members have joined since 1991.
4. Have students research the impact to date of GATT and/or NAFTA on U.S. workers and producers.

Assess

Evaluation

Assign and review the Section 7.2 Review.

Reteaching

1. Assign and review the vocabulary terms for this section.
2. Assign and review Fact and Idea Review questions 3–7 from the Chapter Review.

92

CASE STUDY

Pepsi Max

Pepsi, which gets outsold by Coke around the world, is moving aggressively into foreign markets. The reason? Earnings of its parent company, PepsiCo, are flat. To boost them, the company needs to grow, and that means expanding its foreign operations.

PepsiCo is pinning its hopes for expansion on a number of new products that are specifically designed for non-American tastes. The standout among the group is called Pepsi Max.

Pepsi Max was first introduced in Europe in 1993 and later (in 1994) in the Far East and Latin America. Though the beverage has only one-calorie, PepsiCo has been careful not to tout it as a diet drink. This is because typically, international consumers do not like such beverages. However, research indicated that consumers in Britain, Germany, and Australia did want to reduce their sugar consumption. More importantly, male cola drinkers surveyed indicated that they would try a no-sugar cola—on two conditions. The beverage could not have either a diet taste or a feminine image. Since males drink more cola than females, PepsiCo saw this as an opportunity to develop a product to compete with Coca-Cola. Thus was born Pepsi Max.

Scientists experimented for two years with sweeteners and flavor oils until they came upon acesulfame-K. It provided the flavor that passed a Pepsi/Coke taste test. The sweetener, which is manufactured by Hoechst (a German company), is still awaiting approval here by the FDA. In the meantime, Pepsi Max with acesulfame-K is being sold in foreign countries with great success.

Because Pepsi Max has a full-calorie taste without the full-calorie count, naming it presented a dilemma. PepsiCo used surveys and interviews to help in the process. From the data, two features that impressed potential consumers emerged—no sugar and *maximum cola taste*. The second feature gave the product its name—Pepsi Max.

Promotional campaigns targeting young people were developed around the name. They featured daredevils who surfed, snowboarded off cliffs, and lived life "to the max." Sampling events featured Maxmobile jeeps and men and women who glided through crowds on inline skates, handing out free cans of the product.

To get closer to its expanding foreign markets, PepsiCo invested in bottling companies outside the United States. It now has joint ventures and five outright acquisitions in 40 percent of its bottling network outside North America. A major move occurred in September 1993 when the company took a 26 percent stake in Baesa, a publicly held bottler in Buenos Aires, Argentina. This superbottler will eventually cover 400,000 retail accounts in South America.

In Spain, PepsiCo acquired Kesa (another bottler) and Kas (a local beverage company). As part of the deal, PepsiCo now owns Bitter Kas, a fruity carbonated drink that has widespread distribution throughout Spain. Bitter Kas is sold in as many Spanish stores, restaurants, and other outlets as Coke is—and in twice as many as Pepsi is. Pepsi has been developing new products for Kas. They include Pepsi Max and grapefruit- and orange-flavored Bitter Kas, as well as various juices.

Case Study Review

1. In its research, what did PepsiCo learn about foreign beverage tastes?
2. Besides developing new products for non-American tastes, what else did PepsiCo do to secure its foreign markets?

A MATTER OF ETHICS

3. Given the fact that acesulfame-K has not been declared safe for consumption in this country, do you think it is ethical for PepsiCo to use it in products sold abroad? Why or why not?

Case Study Answers

1. PepsiCo learned that some foreigners would like to reduce their sugar consumption. However, many like neither the taste nor the (feminine) image of diet drinks.
2. It invested in bottling companies outside the United States.
3. Answers will vary. Those most supportive of PepsiCo's decision to use the new sweetener will likely be people who are skeptical of the FDA's procedures and regulatory reach. They will emphasize that the sweetener's use is legal in the countries where Pepsi Max is being sold. Those opposed to the decision will probably argue a company obligation to proceed with caution in the face of an unknown risk.

Foreign Trade Zones Foreign trade zones are designated areas of a country where foreign businesses benefit from reduced tariffs. In these special areas, the businesses can store, process, assemble, and display products without first paying a tariff. The tariff is levied only when the goods leave the zone.

This arrangement has two advantages for foreign businesses. First, if the goods are eventually imported into the United States, the tariff is lower. This is because the United States taxes finished goods at a lower rate than raw materials. Second, if the goods are exported to other countries, they incur no U.S. tax at all.

Export-Import Bank (Eximbank) The **Export-Import Bank (Eximbank)** is an independent agency of the U.S. government. The bank was founded in 1934 in hopes that exporting would help the United States out of the Great Depression. Today its purpose is to foster trade between the United States and other countries. It does this by making or guaranteeing loans to foreign customers who want to buy U.S.-made products.

International Monetary Fund (IMF) The **International Monetary Fund (IMF)** is a multinational agency with more than 150 member nations. Its purpose is to help stabilize exchange rates among the currencies of its members. The IMF does this by attempting to avoid sudden shifts in the value of currencies based on international debt.

For example, the IMF helps debtor nations by lending them money for their trade deficits. This keeps their currencies stable. In such instances, the IMF acts as an international bank. Its operations also help alleviate fears businesses might have about getting paid in foreign currencies.

Trade Agreements

Governments negotiate agreements with each other to establish guidelines for international trade and set up trade alliances. Some of the most recent of these agreements have been milestones in the progress toward worldwide free trade. They include the *General Agreement on Tariffs and Trade,* the *North American Free Trade Agreement,* and the *European Union*.

General Agreement on Tariffs and Trade (GATT) The **General Agreement on Tariffs and Trade (GATT)** is an international trade agreement designed to promote global free trade through the reduction of tariffs and the use of a common set of rules for trading. Discussions on the agreement began in 1986 and lasted for seven years. The result was a 26,000-page treaty that was approved by 117 nations, including the United States, on December 15, 1993. GATT slashed tariffs on 8,000 categories of manufactured goods and established the World Trade Organization (WTO). The WTO was created to police the agreement.

Besides tariff reductions, GATT included some nontariff provisions. Patent protection, for example, was increased. However, it will be phased in over several years, which worries U.S. pharmaceutical firms whose products are commonly pirated in Third World countries. GATT also opened up agricultural markets around the world. Japan, for example, will import at least some rice and citrus. As the standard of living in Asian countries rises, it is expected that their people will eat more dairy, meat, fruit, and vegetable products. U.S. farmers hope to be the ones who meet those needs.

Within the GATT framework, nations are free to negotiate additional agreements among themselves. For example, the United States hopes to continue discussions with Asian countries regarding their invisible trade barriers. One target will be Japan's *keiretsu* system which links domestic suppliers together for production and distribution of products. Such practices exclude foreign competition from the Japanese marketplace. Other areas of discussion may involve human rights, antitrust policies, and global environmental concerns.

North American Free Trade Agreement (NAFTA) The **North American Free Trade Agreement (NAFTA)** is an international trade agreement among the United States, Canada, and Mexico. It went into effect on January 1, 1994. At that time, the United States already had a trade agreement with Canada, its largest trading partner. So, the principal benefit of NAFTA was increased trade with Mexico, its third largest trading partner. (See Table 7-2 on page 94.)

Over the next 15 years, all trade barriers and investment restrictions among the three countries will be eliminated. Indeed, on more than half of the 9,000 goods traded between Mexico and the United States, tariffs were eliminated immediately. Other benefits relate to fair and reliable rules governing trade, intellectual-property protection, and dispute resolution.

The U.S. entertainment industry was one of the immediate beneficiaries of NAFTA. Tariffs on all compact disks, which averaged 15 percent, were eliminated. Piracy of recordings became a federal offense in Mexico. Permits for rock concerts, granted sparingly before NAFTA, are now granted more freely.

Economically and politically, NAFTA is important for the United States. Since other regional trading blocs have emerged in Europe (see below) and Asia, North American countries needed to unite. Compared with those alliances, North America's is the largest and richest. It has about 360 million people who produce and consume $6.7 trillion in goods and services annually. That surpasses Europe's trading bloc with its 340 million people.

European Union (EU) Europe's trading bloc is called the **European Union (EU)**. It includes 12 countries—Belgium, Denmark, France, Germany, Greece, Ireland, Italy, Luxembourg, the Netherlands, Portugal, Spain, and the United Kingdom. From the start, the EU was intended to be a political as well as an economic union.

The EU was established by the Maastricht Treaty. In addition to free trade among the original 12 member

3. To reteach the concept of protective tariffs, ask students what a tax is. Then ask them to consider how a tax like a sales tax works to deter people from buying. Finally, have them compare this effect if the tax is only 5 percent of the item's price vs. 50 percent.
4. To reteach the concept of quotas, ask students what this statement means: The quota for fund-raising projects per club this year is two. Explain how nations set up quotas in the same manner to restrict trade.
5. To reteach the concept of trade alliances, have students describe how the states of the United States trade with one another. (Freely, without placing tariffs or quotas on goods sold from one state to another.)

Enrichment

1. Assign and review the appropriate activities in the *Student Activity Workbook*.
2. Assign and review the appropriate Critical Thinking questions from the Chapter Review.
3. Have students research the history of free trade zones to find out how many there are in the world and how many there are in the United States.

Close

Have students cite evidence supporting the following statement: During the next century, the United States will be more involved than ever in international trade because of the positive steps that have been taken by it and many other nations around the world. (Answers will vary, but students should cite the trade support the U.S. government offers through most-favored-nation status, foreign trade zones, Eximbank, the IMF, and international trade agreements such as GATT and NAFTA.)

Lifelong Learning

The Global Marketplace

Keeping up on international trade is a challenge for those not directly working in the field. The rules of the game are complex, and they can change overnight. So can the players. Think of the fall of the Berlin Wall in 1990 and its aftermath.

To help your students keep up with such changes, encourage them to find at least one business periodical that they enjoy and read it on a regular basis. Also, suggest watching television news coverage of international affairs on a regular basis.

**Bell Ringer
Activity**

Ask students how U.S. businesses can get involved in international trade. To guide their thinking, tell them to consider the case of a U.S. automobile manufacturer and what it could do to trade internationally.

Introducing the Section

Most students will be able to come up with the correct answers to the Bell Ringer Activity (importing, exporting, setting up shop abroad).

Teach

Guided Practice

1. Read Section 7.3 with students.
2. Ask students if they ever traveled to another country and/or crossed a U.S. border. (Select the terminology most familiar to your students.) Ask them what that experience involved. (For some it simply meant passing through a customs checkpoint. For others it might have involved filling out a customs declaration and having customs officials check their luggage.).

Ask students why there is such concern over comings and goings between countries. (Keeping track of the people and products that enter and leave a country can be a matter of public welfare, national security, or economics. Some items, like agricultural products, require special inspections or handling. Other items, like purchases made abroad, require payment of a duty.) This discussion will help students see the connection between what they were asked to do and what businesses must do if they want to get involved in importing and exporting goods.

94

nations, the treaty called for a single European currency and a central bank. Other treaty provisions related to fair competitive practices, environmental and safety standards, and security matters.

The appeal of something like the EU for businesses is understandable. Having one set of guidelines for all the different member nations makes it easier for businesses to operate throughout the EU.

Top 10 Importers of U.S. Products
(1993)

Rank	Country	U.S. Imports ($ billions)
1	Canada	100.1
2	Japan	47.9
3	Mexico	41.6
4	United Kingdom	26.3
5	Germany	18.9
6	Taiwan	16.2
7	South Korea	14.7
8	France	13.2
9	Netherlands	12.8
10	Singapore	11.6

Sources: Nation's Business; *Global Trade Information Services, Inc.*

Table 7–2

Even before NAFTA, Canada and Mexico ranked high on the list of major importers of U.S. goods. According to the table, do any geographic regions other than North America account for more exports?

SECTION 7.2

Review

1. What is the current status of the U.S. balance of trade?
2. Name three types of trade barriers.
3. How do foreign trade zones benefit foreign businesses?
4. What is the common goal or purpose of GATT, NAFTA, and the EU trade agreements?

94   Unit 3   *Business and Marketing Essentials*

Objectives

After completing this section, you will be able to

- identify the three general types of activities businesses engage in when they get involved in international trade;
- explain some of the standard business practices involved in importing and exporting products; and
- discuss the cultural, economic, and political factors that should be considered when deciding whether to do business abroad.

Terms to Know

- customs brokers
- letter of credit
- draft
- time draft
- multinationals
- mini-nationals
- joint ventures
- nationalize

Business Involvement in International Trade

While governments negotiate trade agreements, it is businesses that actually trade with one another. This section is designed to give you some idea of who or what these businesses are and how they operate across international boundaries.

Ways of Getting Involved

There are three basic means of getting involved in international trade—importing, exporting, and setting up shop abroad. The standard practices involved in these activities are complex. In fact, many businesses hire trade specialists to help them cope. Let's look at those practices, as well as the types of businesses that rely on them.

Caption Answer

No. Canada and Mexico together import $148 billion of U.S. products. By contrast, Southeast Asia (Japan, Taiwan, South Korea, and Singapore) accounts for only $90.4 billion; Europe (United Kingdom, Germany, France, and the Netherlands), only $71.2 billion.

Section Review Answers

1. The U.S. balance of trade is negative, which means the United States imports more than it exports.
2. Tariffs, quotas, and embargoes.
3. Foreign nations pay lower taxes on imported goods assembled in zones, no taxes on goods exported from zones.
4. To promote free trade among nations.

Importing In the United States, imports are subject to more than just the requirements of the U.S. Customs Tariff. They must also meet the same standards as domestic products, such as those imposed by the Food and Drug Administration. If these standards are met, however, most products can be imported without prior approval of the government. Only special items, such as alcoholic beverages and drugs like opium, require such approval. Quotas (discussed earlier) can also limit entry of certain goods into the country.

With the new international trade agreements, such as NAFTA and GATT, some imported products are subject to reduced duties while others are not. Knowing all the nuances of importing is always difficult. So, U.S. businesses usually hire **customs brokers,** specialists who are licensed by the U.S. Treasury Department. Customs brokers know the different laws, procedures, and tariffs. Over 90 percent of all imports are handled by customs brokers because of the complex procedures that must be followed.

Exporting Other nations have similar means of controlling and documenting imports. So, U.S. businesses must follow special procedures when exporting their goods. They must know the laws and procedures for each country with which they are dealing. Most businesses, therefore, hire international *freight forwarding companies* to handle export details. These companies are licensed by the U.S. Maritime Commission for ocean shipments.

You can imagine the risks involved in transporting goods from one country to another. The costs of transportation and insurance needed for these shipments vary greatly depending on the type of merchandise. Shipping mink coats would require different handling from shipping steel. To insure these international shipments, most businesses purchase special insurance (called marine insurance, although it may apply to air shipments as well as vessel shipments).

Credit risks are also greater than when dealing with domestic businesses. Each country has different laws,

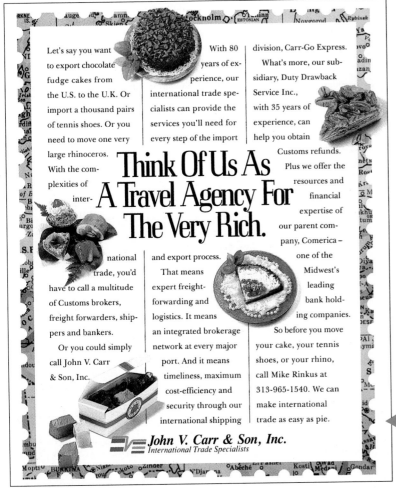

Some companies specialize in helping other companies cope with the complexities of doing business abroad. According to its ad, how does John V. Carr & Son help?

Chapter 7   *The Global Marketplace*   **95**

SECTION 7.3

3. Assign and review the Chapter 7 Activity in the *School-to-Work Handbook.*

Discussion Starter

Have students take the Multicultural Quiz on page 97. Discuss the correct answers (page 98) at length. This will help introduce the special considerations companies must face when doing business in a foreign country.

Cooperative Learning

Have students break into 3–4 teams in order to research an emerging country of their choice, such as China, Vietnam, Singapore, Brazil, Argentina, Hungary, or Czechoslovakia. Based on their research, students should identify at least three U.S. products that would sell well in that country and provide a rationale for their choices.

L1 Human Relations Skills

Ask students if they have ever had a supervisor at work who did not speak English very well because it was not his or her primary language. Have them identify some of the problems this situation caused. *Note:* If no one has had such an experience, ask students to imagine the difficulties that might arise. (Answers will vary. Some possibilities: employee errors resulting from failure to understand key instructions, high levels of frustration arising from efforts needed to understand whatever the supervisor says.)

L2 Human Relations Skills

Ask students to imagine what it would be like to be the supervisor described in the L1 Human Relations Skills activity. Have them identify the problems and frustrations they would have in that situation.

Caption Answer

By doing the jobs of customs brokers, freight forwarders, shippers, and bankers. Clients need deal with only one firm instead of several.

L3 Human Relations Skills

Have students break into pairs or small groups. Tell them to select a problem that might arise when employees and supervisors do not speak each other's primary language. Then instruct them to write two scripts. The first should illustrate poor handling of the problem; the second, effective handling. Suggest that students draw upon their own experiences to make the situations they depict realistic.

L1 Decision-making Skills

Have students brainstorm a general list of challenges (or problems) firms face when doing business either abroad or in areas of the United States where the work force includes people of many different ethnic groups. List all responses on the chalkboard. When the listing is complete, have students break it into major categories. (These might include company policies that infringe on employee customs or traditions, problems with ethnic prejudice, and communication/language difficulties.)

L2 Decision-making Skills

For each challenge listed in the L1 Decision-making Skills activity, have students identify a source or cause. Write each of those ideas next to the related challenge on the chalkboard, and have students record the list in their notes. (List entries will vary. Some possibilities: A key source of prejudice may be past experience with a particular ethnic group or simply fear of the unknown. Problems with communication often arise from a language barrier.)

languages, and currencies. Arranging payment for goods shipped to a foreign country can be accomplished in different ways, depending on past experience with a foreign customer and the degree of risk a business is willing to take.

If you have never dealt with a particular foreign customer before, you will probably want the most secure method of payment, which is a **letter of credit.** Letters of credit protect the exporter from foreign customers who decide they don't want the goods after they have been shipped. This is how letters of credit work. The foreign customer gets a letter of credit from a bank in his or her country that will guarantee payment. That letter of credit is then confirmed by a U.S. bank. As soon as the exporter can prove that it shipped the goods, it can be paid by the U.S. bank.

A second option that protects the exporter is the use of a **draft,** which is like a reverse check. In this method, the exporter sends the foreign bank documentation showing that it has shipped the goods. The documentation includes an invoice describing the merchandise and amount due, shipping documents, and a draft. The draft tells the bank to collect the money owed for the shipment from the foreign customer. Once the foreign customer pays the bill, the shipping documents are released by the bank so that the customer can pick up the goods. The money collected is converted to U.S. dollars and sent through the bank to the exporter.

A more liberal credit arrangement is for the U.S. company to send the documentation through a bank on a **time draft.** The customer signs the time draft, which is a promise to pay in the future, and receives the documentation. This allows the customer to take delivery of the goods without paying. The foreign bank, however, makes sure the customer pays the bill when promised. Generally, this method is used only after a relationship has been established with a foreign customer.

Setting Up Shop in a Foreign Country

Multinationals are large corporations that have operations in several countries. According to *International Business,* about one-third of the world's private-sector assets are controlled by some 37,000 transnational corporations with over 170,000 foreign affiliates. **Mininationals** are midsized and smaller companies that have operations in foreign countries.

One key characteristic sets multinationals and mininationals apart from domestic businesses—their foreign investments. Such businesses invest in factories, offices, and other facilities abroad that they use for their operations. These investments are referred to as *foreign direct investments (FDI).* Some countries attract more FDI than others.

In some countries, direct investment can only occur if you have a domestic partner. This is because foreigners are not permitted to own 100 percent of a business. Such partnerships, which are commonly called **joint ventures,** are a good idea even when not mandated by law. Domestic business partners know the market and procedures for conducting business in their countries. That is why

many U.S. fast-food chains have granted franchises to companies in foreign countries.

Special Considerations

To do business in a foreign country, businesspeople must keep in mind a number of special considerations. Some of these concerns are basic, such as differences in language and customs. Other concerns are political and legal.

Cultural Factors Differences in language and culture make international trade more difficult than doing business at home. As an example, consider the difficulty General Motors encountered when it tried to sell its Chevrolet Nova in South America. Sales did not meet expectations. The reason? The words *no va* in Spanish mean "No go!"

Cultural differences can lead businesses to stumble into even more sensitive areas. In 1994, Karl Lagerfeld, a German clothing designer, created a low-cut dress from fabric printed with Arabic script. The script turned out to be a passage from the Koran, and its use offended Muslims. Lagerfeld apologized, destroyed the dress, and asked fashion photographers to destroy their photos.

Sometimes language and culture can combine to create problems. In Japan when businesspeople say something will be "difficult," they really mean the answer is no. What is behind the indirect response is a cultural trait— the Japanese reluctance to be blunt. Japanese prefer to be subtle and nonconfrontational.

Custom and tradition are other areas rich in possibilities for misunderstanding. For example, in certain Asian countries, the customary greeting is a nod of the head,

When Cards Are No Game

Life in the Multicultural MARKETPLACE

The exchange of business cards is taken far more seriously in other parts of the world than it is here in the United States. In Southeast Asia, the process rises almost to the level of ritual.

In Japan, for example, cards are always offered with two hands. The person receiving the card accepts it the same way (with two hands), studies it carefully, and then bows slightly to it. The card is then placed in a leather card holder or metal card case and slipped carefully into a shirt or jacket pocket. It is never put in a wallet or back pants pocket. (The symbolism here is all important. The recipient shows respect for both the businessperson and his company by placing the card near the heart. To place it where it might literally be sat upon would show the greatest disrespect.)

Feature Note

It is also considered the height of disrespect to write on a business card in Japan, even if the information is relevant to the person or the company. To make notes on a card is to deface it. (A comparable action in this country would be taking notes on a person's photograph.) People doing business abroad should carry tablets or notebooks for taking down information or writing reminders.

Multicultural Quiz

Directions: Select the choice that best completes each statement (or follow the instructions given in the question).

1. In Saudi Arabia, you should never pass business papers with
   a. your left hand.
   b. your right hand.
   c. both hands.

2. In Hong Kong, Korea, and Taiwan, the shape that should be avoided on product packaging and in advertising is the
   a. circle.
   b. square.
   c. triangle.

3. In which of the following countries is punctuality very important when conducting business?
   a. Italy
   b. Guatemala
   c. Japan

4. Match the meaning of the okay sign to the country:

Country	Meaning
France	a. Symbol for money
Japan	b. Zero
United States	c. Vulgar connotation
Brazil	d. Everything is fine.

5. In which of the following countries are gifts expected on an initial visit?
   a. Germany
   b. United States
   c. Japan

6. In which country would you *not* send white chrysanthemums as a gift?
   a. Mexico
   b. Brazil
   c. Belgium

7. In which country would you *not* use a person's first name during business meetings?
   a. Great Britain
   b. Australia
   c. China

Figure 7–2

For answers, see page 98.

For answers, see page 98.

not a handshake. In some Middle Eastern countries, public gift giving is expected, but gifts must be given privately in some Asian countries. Maintaining good eye contact during a conversation is paramount in American, Canadian, British, Eastern European, and Jewish cultures. However, many Asians, Puerto Ricans, West Indians, and African-Americans tend to avoid direct eye contact. As a matter of fact, prolonged eye contact is considered impolite and even rude in Japan, Korea, and Thailand. To test your own awareness of such differences, take the multicultural quiz in Figure 7-2.

Economic Factors When deciding whether or not to set up shop in a foreign country, you should consider the key factors that contribute to the cost of doing business. These include infrastructure, cost of labor, and taxes. If you are anticipating selling goods in the country, you should also consider the standard of living of the population.

Infrastructure can be an initial and deciding factor. For some businesses, things like undependable telephone service or inadequate roads would rule out a location. For other businesses, they would represent an

Chapter 7 *The Global Marketplace* **97**

Did You Know ?

Multinational corporations that manufacture items abroad face some difficult ethical dilemmas. One of the biggest arises from differences in child labor laws. In many developing nations, children leave school at an early age to contribute to the family income. American companies that employ some of them provide on-site classrooms so they can continue their educations.

L3 Decision-making Skills

Have students rank the challenges annotated in the L2 Decision-making Skills activity, beginning with the one they would address first, next, etc. Then ask them to develop a written plan for the top three items on their list. The plan should take the form of a memo or short report and contain a rationale for each program suggested. (For example, to improve communications, students might suggest hiring language instructors for managers and employees. Classes could be conducted before, after, or during working hours, as feasible.) *Note:* This exercise may be completed in teams to encourage cooperative learning and team-building skills.

Independent Practice

1. Have students look through issues of *International Business* to find ads for customs brokers, freight forwarding companies, or other firms serving businesses involved in international trade. Tell them to list all the services these companies offer businesses, and compare those services to the activities involved in exporting and importing described in the chapter. In particular, have them note any services not mentioned in the text.

2. Have students read "The New Global Consumer" in the Autumn/Winter special edition of *Fortune* magazine that identifies opportunities in the global marketplace. After students have read the article, have them draw their own conclusions about which findings would be of interest to U.S. manufacturers of consumer products.

3. Tell students to research the current exchange rate for the U.S. dollar and some other currency. Have them explain why that rate would or would not be good for U.S. companies doing business in the country issuing the selected currency. Finally, as extra credit, ask students to research how companies protect their profits from swift and sharp fluctuations in the value of foreign currencies.

4. Have students write to various multinational corporations and ask for copies of their annual reports. Have students review the reports of several of the companies to see what their plans are for expansion in other countries. Have students report their findings to the class orally.

5. Have students look through *Inc.* magazines for a special supplement, a small booklet from AT&T titled "Going Global." Each supplement focuses on a different country. (For example, Mexico is supplement No. 3.) Have students share the information contained in these booklets.

Assess

Evaluation

Assign and review the Section 7.3 Review.

Reteaching

1. Assign and review the vocabulary terms for this section.
2. Assign and review Fact and Idea Review questions 8–11 from the Chapter Review.
3. To reteach the concept of cultural factors that should be considered if one is planning to do business abroad, ask students how they would greet someone they know in the United States. Follow up by asking them what they would do differently if they were in China or Japan. (Bow instead of shake hands.)

BRIGHT IDEAS

Expand Your Focus

Sometimes a company can keep doing exactly what it does best but, by shifting its target market, dramatically alter its sales and profits. Take Bonas Machine Company, an English manufacturer of textile machines. It enhanced its revenues by broadening its market from England to the whole world. By focusing on exports, the company now sells its looms in over 75 countries worldwide. These overseas sales now account for 90 percent of its production!

The shift to global marketing required a number of significant changes. The company had to go into the hiring of multilingual personnel in a big way. It had to prepare promotional materials in all relevant languages. It also had to participate in trade shows worldwide. Had Bonas not done these things, it is unlikely that the world would have beaten a path to its door. But with this type of commitment, Bonas earned an award from the Queen of England for outstanding effort in exports.

Creativity Challenge Form teams of 3–5 people, and plan a strategy to take a small company into the global marketplace. Select an actual local company or hypothesize the producer of some distinctively American product. Then build your strategy around key questions. For example, if a surfboard company in Southern California wanted to expand abroad, what new markets might it consider and why? What kinds of places and customers should it look for? What kinds of problems would it face, and how might it solve them?

---

opportunity. Companies involved in building roads, energy plants, and telecommunications systems would actively look for countries that have infrastructure development as their top priority.

The quality and cost of the labor force also requires review. You would want to know the educational and skill levels of the workers, as well as the customary wages and laws governing employment. Customary wages can vary greatly. For example, an average male worker in West Germany earned $33.21 per hour in 1994. The comparable figure in Poland was $2.36 and in the Czech Republic $1.76. In some countries (primarily in Western Europe),

employers are responsible for paying substantial amounts for mandated employee benefits above and beyond wages.

Other costs of doing business must be determined as well. These include taxes. Taxes on property and profits are common. Countries that want to attract foreign investment will sometimes offer reduced taxes for a period of time as an incentive.

Finally, standard of living can be a consideration if a business is eyeing a country as a market rather than a manufacturing site. When Honda wanted to enter China's consumer market, it recognized that most Chinese could not afford cars. So, the company targeted the motorcycle market instead and was very successful. As the Chinese become more affluent and a market for automobiles develops, this presence will prove doubly beneficial.

At present, the number of middle income workers is increasing in poorer nations. As that group grows, the demand for all types of ordinary consumer goods will increase. U.S. consumer products like soaps, detergents, breakfast cereals, snack foods, and soft drinks are popular among consumers in emerging nations.

Political/Legal Factors A government's stability is an important factor to consider when deciding whether to do business in a foreign country. If a country is subject to military takeover or popular revolution, there is always the possibility that new rulers might **nationalize** private property. When a country nationalizes property, the government takes ownership, and the owners generally get nothing in return. Bolivia, for example, nationalized all of its businesses in the early 1950s. You can well imagine how costly such an occurrence would be today when businesses routinely invest millions of dollars in buildings and equipment.

An unstable government can create problems for a business's employees as well. Business executives may be

Multicultural Quiz Answers

1. **a.** Because the left hand has historically been used for hygiene purposes and is therefore considered "unclean."
2. **c.** Because the triangle is considered a negative shape in those countries.
3. **c.** The Japanese consider it rude to be late for a business meeting. However, for social occasions it is all right to be fashionably late.
4. France **b.** Zero
   Japan **a.** Symbol for money
   U.S. **d.** Everything is fine.
   Brazil **c.** Vulgar connotation
5. **c.** In Japan gift giving is an important part of doing business. If a gift is presented to you, you are expected to respond with a gift. Also, exchanging gifts signifies the relationship's depth and strength. In contrast, gifts are not appropriate in Germany.
6. **c.** In Belgium, as in most of Europe and the United Kingdom, white chrysanthemums are reserved for use at funerals.
7. **a.** In Australia it is all right to use a person's first name because Australians are informal. In China, the first name *is* the surname. That leaves Great Britain, where it would not be appropriate to use a person's first name during business meetings.

 Bright Ideas

Ask: Why would the Queen of England issue an award to a company for focusing time and energy on exports? (To reward those who help Great Britain achieve a healthy balance of trade. Any country that does not focus on exports risks a growing trade deficit, which can pull its economy down.)

YUCATAN

THE CLIMATE FOR BUSINESS IS PERFECT IN YUCATAN

Blue water, soft sands, gentle breezes— and warm sunshine. These are just some of the impressions Yucatan leaves on its visitors. But, the State and its capital city of Merida are also home to a growing number of international firms like yours who are setting their sites here.

Our excellent infrastructure is one of many reasons why companies find Yucatan so appealing. With three major industrial parks in operation and three new parks recently developed, our building blocks are firmly in place. All have nearby rail service and excellent highway linkage to Merida's international airport and the Port of Progreso. And, capacity of utilities supporting industry— electricity, water, industrial fuels, communication— far exceeds current demand.

In Yucatan, it is easy to feel the warm spirit of industrial progress and partnership. We invite you to experience it firsthand— by visiting soon! For more information and a free brochure, call us at:

1-212-758-4015

YUCATAN
The New Frontier for Business

Government of the State of Yucatan, Mexico. Department of Industrial and Commercial Development.

*Countries worldwide **are looking for foreign investors. What selling points are made in this ad that might appeal to a U.S. company interested in setting up a manufacturing facility abroad?***

kidnapped in return for huge ransoms that help fuel political unrest. Political corruption can be difficult to handle. In some countries, payoffs to government officials are the only means of getting necessary licenses or approval to conduct business.

On the other hand, governments may be stable and helpful to businesses. They may be moving toward a market economy by *privatizing* state-run industries. Countries that want to be part of the global marketplace may also encourage foreign investment. They may reduce tariffs, develop laws for protection of intellectual property, and increase the percentage of business ownership permitted foreign investors.

SECTION 7.3 *Review*

1. How can a business get involved in international trade?
2. If a U.S. exporter has never dealt with a foreign customer before, which method of payment would be the most secure? Why?
3. Name a cultural, an economic, and a political factor that should be considered when deciding to do business in foreign countries.

Chapter 7 *The Global Marketplace* 99

Answers

Vocabulary Review

Paragraphs will vary. See Glossary for definitions.

Fact and Idea Review

1. Because they are not self-sufficient (must obtain certain products from other nations).
2. Advantages: expanded markets abroad mean more business, higher revenues, more job opportunities. Disadvantages: inability to compete with cheaper labor and raw materials available abroad.
3. Through the customs division of the U.S. Treasury Department.
4. Because the United States is the world's largest exporter.
5. To improve its balance of trade, protect domestic jobs or new industries, or safeguard its national security.
6. Loans or loan guarantees from the Export-Import Bank (Eximbank).
7. All are recent international trade agreements or alliances that encourage free trade among nations.
8. To handle importing, customs brokers; to handle exporting, freight forwarding companies.
9. Differences: multinationals are large corporations, while mini-nationals are smaller, midsized companies. Similarities: both engage in FDI.
10. Possibilities: product names can have embarrassing connotations in another language (Chevy's Nova); eye contact can be misread; social gestures like gift giving may be governed by different rules as to when, where, what, and how.
11. Economic factors: labor costs, infrastructure, taxes.

100

CHAPTER *Review*

7 CHAPTER

Vocabulary Review

For each group of terms, write a paragraph explaining what the listed items have to do with the heading.

International Trade
balance of trade
imports
exports
absolute advantage
comparative advantage
multinationals
mini-nationals

Trade Concerns
tariff
quota
embargo
joint ventures
customs brokers
letter of credit
draft
time draft
nationalize

Trade Support
most-favored-nation status (MFNS)
foreign trade zones
Eximbank
International Monetary Fund (IMF)
General Agreement on Tariffs and Trade (GATT)
North American Free Trade Agreement (NAFTA)
European Union (EU)

Fact and Idea Review

1. Why do nations trade with one another? (Sec. 7.1)
2. What are the advantages and disadvantages of international trade for producers and workers? (Sec. 7.1)
3. How does the United States monitor and control imports from other countries? (Sec. 7.2)
4. Why is it surprising that the United States has a negative balance of trade? (Sec. 7.2)
5. Why might a country impose trade barriers? (Sec. 7.2)
6. Assume a foreign business customer wants to buy U.S. goods but does not have all the money needed for the transaction. What trade support is available from a U.S. organization? (Sec. 7.2)
7. How are GATT, NAFTA, and the EU related? (Sec. 7.2)
8. Given the complex import/export rules in the United States and other countries, what specialists might a business hire to handle those transactions? (Sec. 7.3)
9. How are multinationals and mini-nationals different from each other? How are they similar? (Sec. 7.3)
10. Cite three examples of communication and/or cultural differences that can make doing business in a foreign country more difficult than doing business domestically. (Sec. 7.3)

---

11. Cite an economic factor and a political factor that could discourage a business from engaging in international trade. (Sec. 7.3)

Critical Thinking

1. How have you personally benefited from international trade?
2. React to the following statement: International trade benefits everyone and hurts no one.
3. What problems occur when trade between nations is not equal, as in the case of the United States and Japan? What measures could the United States take in order to reduce its trade deficit with Japan?
4. Assume South Korea broke a trade agreement with the United States by selling its automobiles here at below market prices. If the United States retaliated with trade sanctions (increased tariffs or quotas), how could that action hurt trade relations between the two countries?
5. Do you see anything wrong with countries and U.S. states that offer incentives, such as reduced taxes, to foreign investors but not to local businesses?
6. When a Japanese investor bought New York City's Rockefeller Center in the 1980s, it brought out the xenophobia in many U.S. citizens. (Xenophobia is hatred or distrust of foreigners.) Since foreign investment is supposed to be good for a country, why do you think these people reacted this way?
7. What measures could a business that wants to get involved in international trade take to avoid cultural blunders?

Building Academic Skills

Math

1. Assume the currency exchange rate between the United States and Canada is 1.25, which means one U.S. dollar is equal to $1.25 in Canadian currency. How much would a $20 T-shirt cost a U.S. citizen shopping in Montreal?

Communication

2. Change a current magazine ad, billboard, television or radio commercial so that it is appropriate for use in a foreign country. Translate the words into that country's language, and make any other changes necessary to promote the product effectively. Present your new ad to your classmates, and report on any problems you encountered in making the changes.

Political factors: political corruption, government instability, failure to protect a business's intellectual property.

Critical Thinking

1. Answers will vary. Most students will note foreign-made products they enjoy.
2. Most students will probably take issue with the absolute tone of the statement by citing instances of people or firms that have been

hurt by international trade.
3. Problem: one trading partner consistently suffers a negative balance of trade, which hurts its GDP and employment rate. Possible solutions: the consistently hurt nation could impose tariffs or quotas on its partner's key exports; both nations could negotiate a settlement.
4. South Korea could answer with its own trade sanctions on U.S. imports. That could hurt businesses not party to the original dispute.

Human Relations

3. A customer wants to buy a silk blouse that matches her outfit perfectly—until she learns that the blouse was made in China. Her dilemma? She thinks Americans should buy only American-made products. What would you do?

Application Projects

1. Summarize an article related to one of the topics in this chapter. Review publications such as *International Business,* the *Economist, Europe, U.S. News & World Report, Business Week, Forbes,* and *Fortune* to find an appropriate article. In your summary, be sure to relate the chapter topics to the content of the article.
2. Research the most-favored-nation status granted to China in 1994. What criteria was eliminated from the approval process? Why?
3. Read articles in business publications to find examples of U.S. companies that are involved in international trade. Learn which companies are this country's largest exporters and which have direct investments in foreign countries.
4. Research the trend among multinationals to forge strategic alliances with foreign companies. What are the reasons for these alliances, and what have been the outcomes?
5. How are foreign teenagers alike or different from U.S. teens? Research one country to find out. Determine which products foreign teens buy and how businesses market those products to them. Based on your research, identify a U.S. product that could be used to target teens in the country you are researching. Decide on the marketing mix (product, place, price, and promotion) for this target market. Prepare a written report of your research and marketing mix decisions, complete with rationale for each decision.
6. Identify the Economic G-7 countries, and find out why they meet every summer. Present your findings in a written report.

Linking School to Work

Ask your employer if your company is involved in international trade. If it is, find out the particulars of its involvement. If it is not involved directly, are there any products manufactured by foreign companies sold by your business? Write a short report of your findings, and share it with your classmates.

Performance Assessment

Role Play

Situation. You are an intern in a marketing firm that specializes in international trade. You have been asked to be part of an extensive training program for firm employees doing business in Japan. Your task is to instruct people in the proper way to exchange business cards.

Evaluation. You will be evaluated on how well you do the following:

- Identify the purpose of the training.
- Stress the importance of business cards.
- Demonstrate how to exchange business cards properly.
- Answer questions during the training session.

Public Speaking

You have been asked to make a presentation on international trade to the foreign language club in your school. The purpose of the presentation is to demonstrate the need for bilingual employees in business. You will want to provide information on how businesses get involved in international trade. You will also want to discuss the need to understand different cultures (especially when marketing products in foreign countries).

Complete the Chapter 7 Computer Application that appears in the Student Activity Workbook.

Portfolio

Consider the Application Projects that you have done for this unit. Select one that illustrates your mastery of the unit's content and might be of interest to potential employers. Reformat the activity as necessary, adding any explanatory text, and place it in your Portfolio. Consider using these activities:

- Chapter 6, Application Projects 2–5
- Chapter 7, Application Project 5 ■■

---

5. Answers will vary. Those with reservations will most likely object that domestic businesses are not being given the same opportunities as foreign businesses.
6. Possible reasons include fear of the unknown and concern about the nation's losing its economic independence.
7. Answers will vary. Possibilities include hiring executives with international trade experience,

diversifying the firm's workforce, and providing language and cross-cultural training for employees.

Building Academic Skills

Math

1. $20 ÷ 1.25 = $16

Communications

2. Ads and problems encountered will vary. Give special attention to how well students captured

the spirit as well as the substance of the ads they translated.

Human Relations

3. Answers will vary. Some students might try to convince the customer that such trade makes goods more affordable for consumers. Others will simply look for another blouse to match the outfit.

Application Projects

1. Summaries will depend on articles selected.
2. The MFN status granted to China in 1994 was based on economic criteria only. Human rights policies and practices were eliminated as considerations. U.S. position was influenced by its need for China's support in nuclear arms reduction negotiations with North Korea.
3. Answers will vary.
4. Principal reasons for alliances are time and cost savings.
5. Answers will vary.
6. Economic G-7 countries are the United States, Germany, Canada, Italy, Japan, France, and England. Their leaders meet annually to discuss economic and trade policies.

Linking School to Work

Answers depend on the work situation.

Performance Assessment

Refer to the *DECA Competitive Events Handbook* for evaluation guidelines.

 Computer Application

Optional Activity. Refer to the *Marketing Software Binder* for template and user information.

Evaluation

Administer the reproducible test for Chapter 7, or construct your own using the Testmaker software.

Portfolio

Refer to the *Marketing Career Portfolio* for development ideas and portfolio management and assessment.

Human Resource Essentials

Unit Objectives

After completing this unit, students will be able to achieve the following outcomes:

- Perform essential math functions with whole numbers, fractions, and decimal numbers.
- Effectively communicate by speaking, listening, writing, and reading.
- Discuss the uses of computers in business and in marketing.
- Facilitate understanding of others through personal attitude and interpersonal skills.
- Explain the basic functions of management and discuss effective management techniques.

Chapter 8

Chapter 9

Chapter 10

Chapter 11

Chapter 12

Teacher Classroom Resources

CHAPTER	8	9	10	11	12
Transparency Binder	Transparencies 13–15	Transparencies 16–17			Transparencies 18–19
Student Activity Workbook	pp. 43–48	pp. 49–56	pp. 57–62	pp. 63–68	pp. 69–74
Student Software		pp. 55–56	pp. 61–62	pp. 67–68	pp. 73–74
Marketing Math Workbook					Activity 4
School-to-Work Handbook	pp. 21–22	pp. 23–24	pp. 25–26	pp. 27–28	29–30
International Case Studies	pp. 21–22	pp. 23–24	pp. 25–26	pp. 27–28	29–30
Marketing Career Portfolio					Unit 4 activity, Student Text, p. 171
Test Booklet/ Testmaker Software	Chapter 8 test	Chapter 9 test	Chapter 10 test	Chapter 11 test	Chapter 12 test Unit 4 test

KEY TO BASIC SKILLS ACTIVITIES

L1 Level 1 activities are basic activities and should be within the range of all students.

L2 Level 2 activities are average activities and should be within the range of average and above average students.

L3 Level 3 activities are challenging activities designed for the ability range of above average students.

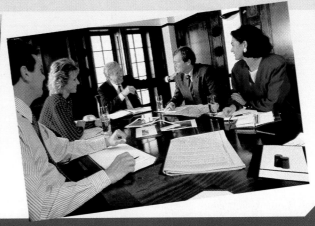

CHAPTER	PERFORMANCE OBJECTIVES
8 **Fundamentals of Mathematics**	**8.1** **1.** Write numbers in words, using commas and hyphens correctly. **2.** Understand the meaning of fractional amounts. **3.** Perform basic math operations with decimal numbers. **4.** Round answers, especially amounts of money. **5.** Convert fractions to decimal equivalents. **8.2** **1.** Use a calculator to solve math problems. **2.** Convert percentages to decimals and decimals to percentages. **3.** Read different types of graphs used to present mathematical data.
9 **Communication Skills**	**9.1** **1.** Explain the six primary elements of communication. **2.** Describe how to arrange the setting for a business meeting. **3.** Use listening skills to improve your understanding of messages. **4.** List three blocks to listening with understanding. **5.** Practice the three skills that will help you read with understanding. **9.2** **1.** Describe the three most common purposes for speaking. **2.** List four basic patterns for organizing a formal speech. **3.** Define parliamentary procedure and its purposes. **4.** Describe proper telephone skills. **5.** Explain the three basic considerations in writing.
10 **Computer Technology**	**10.1** **1.** List the major ways computers are used to save businesses money. **2.** Name types of computers. **3.** Discuss the functions of basic pieces of computer hardware. **4.** Define software. **10.2** **1.** Describe six types of popular software programs. **2.** Explain how these programs are used in business. **10.3** **1.** Name types of computer systems that are affecting the world of marketing. **2.** Discuss the future of computer technology.
11 **Interpersonal Skills**	**11.1** **1.** Explain the importance of understanding others. **2.** Discuss the personal traits that can help you be more effective in relations with other people. **3.** Identify three personal skills to master for successful interpersonal relations in the marketing world. **4.** Describe how interpersonal skills may be used in marketing. **11.2** **1.** Explain the importance of teamwork in the business world. **2.** Discuss six aspects of successful teamwork.
12 **Management Skills**	**12.1** **1.** Describe how horizontally organized companies differ from traditionally organized companies. **2.** Identify the three levels of management. **3.** Explain how a self-managing team functions. **12.2** **1.** Name the three functions of management. **2.** Identify the management techniques used by effective managers. **3.** Explain how to motivate employees through a system of rewards.

Unit Overview and Background Information

Once students have been introduced to economics, business, and marketing, they need to explore the real-world skills they will use in their co-op jobs and in career-sustaining jobs in marketing.

Chapters 8 and 9 review basic skills in mathematics and communication. Chapter 10 provides a valuable overview of computer technology. Chapters 11 and 12 stress the importance of interpersonal and management skills.

Introducing the Unit

Ask students why it is important to deal well with people, particularly in marketing careers. Next, ask students to define the term *foundation*. Also ask them to define the term *human resources*. Finally, point out the "Human Resource Foundations" circle on the Marketing Wheel and tell students that this unit covers the basic skills they will need in dealing with others, not only in their marketing careers but in their co-op jobs and in their personal lives.

Unit Project

Have students work together as a class to develop a training and policy manual to be used in running the school store. The manual should be set up like those issued by a human resources department to new employees. For models, ask students to bring in policy and training manuals they received as part of their co-op training.

After you finish studying each chapter in this unit, have students decide which concepts from the chapter apply to the manual.

Unit

4

102

Focus on the Photo/Cooperative Learning

After the class has completed this unit, divide them into five teams and have each team write a caption explaining why people are so important to business and marketing. Ask each group to consider this question: "Why can't computers run companies without people?" Allow time for each group to share their answer and compare similarities and differences in their approach to the question.

Human Resource Essentials

CHAPTERS

8
Fundamentals of Mathematics

9
Communication Skills

10
Computer Technology

11
Interpersonal Skills

12
Management Skills

Financing

Distribution

Risk Management

Product/Service Planning

ECONOMIC FOUNDATIONS OF MARKETING

HUMAN RESOURCE FOUNDATIONS

Selling

Marketing-Information Management

MARKETING AND BUSINESS FOUNDATIONS

Promotion

Purchasing

Pricing

Resources for Enrichment of Unit Content

Books

- *The Fifth Discipline: The Art and Practice of the Learning Organization* by Peter M. Senge
- *The Fifth Discipline Fieldbook: Strategies and Tools for Building a Learning Organization* by Peter M. Senge, Charlotte Robert, Richard B. Ross, Bryan J. Smith, and Art Kleiner
- *In Search of Excellence: Lessons from America's Best-Run Companies* by Thomas J. Peters and Robert H. Waterman, Jr.
- *Management: Tasks, Responsibilities, and Practices* by Peter F. Drucker
- *A Passion for Excellence* by Tom Peters and Nancy Austin
- *What They Don't Teach You at Harvard Business School* by Mark H. McCormack

Magazines/Journals

Current issues of *Byte, Journal of Small Business Management, Management Review, Modern Office Procedures, PC Magazine,* and *Psychology Today.*

Unit Closure

Discuss with students the management structure of the marketing class. How is the class organized? Compare its organization to that of local small businesses. Which communication, interpersonal, and management skills are used to make the class run smoothly? Through this discussion, students should understand that management as a process is not limited only to the business setting. They can practice their management skills now and thus be better prepared for their careers.

Evaluation

Administer the printed test for Unit 4, or construct your own using the Testmaker software.

Guest Speaker Suggestions

- Ask a tutor from a remediation program at a local vocational school or community college to speak to your class about how to improve basic math skills.
- Have a representative from Toastmaster's or another organization that teaches public speaking talk to your class about its programs.

Field Trip Suggestions

- Have students visit a computer store. They should look at various models of computers and printers, and peruse the available software. Have a salesperson demonstrate the capabilities of the computer equipment.
- Have students attend a meeting of a local chapter of the American Society for Training and Development.

Chapter Overview

Chapter 8 reviews the basic math skills that students will use in their marketing careers, as well as in daily life. In addition to discussions of number concepts and basic operations, the chapter includes instructions on how to use a calculator and an introduction to charts and graphs.

Springboard

Divide the class into two groups—those who have jobs and those who don't. Ask those who are employed to list on a sheet of paper the ways they use math in their jobs. Have those who don't work do the same assignment based on the ways they use math in their daily lives. Have the two groups share their listings.

Prereading

List the section objectives to discuss with students. Have students skim the chapter, looking at the pictures, reading the captions, and noting the heads. Ask questions to ensure that students have a minimal understanding of the chapter structure.

Preteaching the Vocabulary

Before students begin reading the chapter, dictate each of the vocabulary terms and ask students to write them on a sheet of paper. When they finish, write the terms on the chalkboard. Then have students guess at the meaning of each. Write their guesses next to each term, but do not give the correct meaning. Leave this list on the chalkboard so that students can see how close their guesses were to the actual definitions as they work through the chapter.

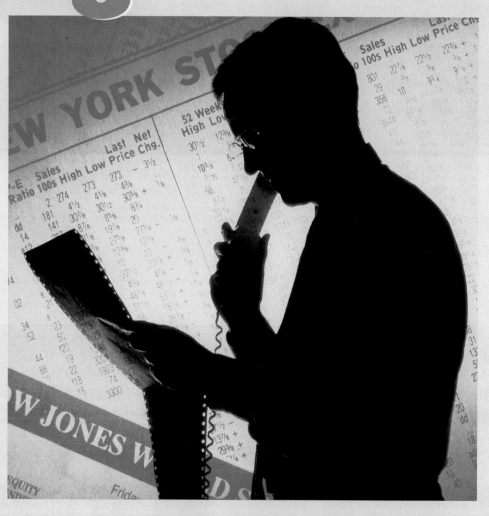

CHAPTER 8

Fundamentals of Mathematics

In a recent survey, employers in marketing careers agreed that entry-level workers need a much better grasp of the fundamentals of mathematics. So in this chapter, you will review computations involving fractions, decimal numbers, and percentages. You will also improve your skills in reading graphs and using a calculator.

Classroom Management

For the Teacher

- Teacher's Annotated Editions for all workbooks
- Teacher's Manual for *School-to-Work Handbook*
- *Testing Binder*
- *Transparency Binder*
- *Marketing Software Binder*
- *Marketing Career Portfolio*
- *Lesson Plans*

For the Student

- *Student Activity Workbook*
- *Marketing Math Workbook*
- *School-to-Work Handbook*
- *Student Software*
- *International Case Studies*
- *Marketing Career Portfolio*

SECTION 8.1

Objectives

After completing this section, you will be able to

- write numbers in words, using commas and hyphens correctly;
- understand the meaning of fractional amounts;
- perform basic math operations with decimal numbers;
- round answers, especially amounts of money; and
- convert fractions to decimal equivalents.

Terms to Know

- digits
- fractions
- numerator
- denominator
- mixed number
- decimal number

Writing Whole Numbers

The numbering system we use is composed of ten basic symbols: 0, 1, 2, 3, 4, 5, 6, 7, 8, and 9. These symbols are called **digits.** Each digit represents a number and can be combined to represent larger numbers, such as 14; 215; 4,237; and 36,852.

The numbers above are all whole numbers because they can be written without fractions or decimals. Each digit in a whole number represents *how many* of something. The digit on the right represents the number of *ones*. The next digit represents the number of *tens*. So, in the number 25, there are five *ones* and two *tens*.

Knowing the placement name for each digit and for groups of digits is necessary for reading numbers and writing them in words. You use this skill, for example, when you write a check. The check format requires that

amounts be written in both figures and words. Follow these five steps when you read whole numbers or write them in words.

1. Separate the number into groups of three digits: units, thousands, and millions. Very large numbers may include groups of digits for billions, trillions, and so on.

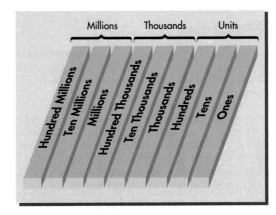

2. Separate the groups with commas.

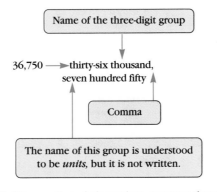

3. When writing whole numbers, never use the word *and*.

360 ⟶ three hundred sixty

No *and*

4. Use hyphens in numbers less than 100 that are written as two words.

29 ⟶ twenty-nine

Use a hyphen.

FOCUS

Bell Ringer Activity

As a test of basic math skills, write each of the following numbers on the chalkboard and have students respond to the questions:

1. 25 (Which digit represents the number of tens? the number of ones?)
2. 11456789 (Place commas correctly in the number. Which number groups represent millions, thousands, and units?)
3. 580; 31; 5,000,675 (Write these numbers in words.)
4. 7/8 (Which number is the numerator? the denominator?)
5. 5/5 (Convert this fraction to a whole number.)
6. 8/5 (Convert this fraction to a mixed number.)
7. 16.07 (Write this decimal number in words.)
8. 16.891 and 67.63 (Add these decimal numbers.)
9. 1.578 from 896.57 (Subtract these decimal numbers.)
10. 10.3 and 5.6 (Multiply these decimal numbers.)
11. 17.889; 14.842 (Round these numbers to the nearest tenth.)
12. 1.80 by 1.60 (Divide these decimal numbers.)
13. 1/8 (Convert this fraction to a decimal.)

Introducing the Section

Review the correct answers to the Bell Ringer Activity to get a better idea of the level of your class's basic math skills:

1. The 2 represents the number of tens; the 5, the number of ones.
2. With commas: 11,456,789. From left to right, 11 represents millions, 456 thousands, and 789 units.
3. Five hundred eighty; thirty-one; five million, six hundred seventy-five.
4. Numerator is 7, denominator 8.
5. 1
6. 1 3/5

Meeting Special Needs

English as a Second Language

Students whose native language is other than English face special challenges when class work turns to large numbers. Often when native speakers discuss numbers, they speak very quickly, blurring the sounds.

If the nonnative speakers are experiencing any difficulty, write the numbers under discussion on the chalkboard along with the sign indicating the operation being performed. It is usually not the calculation that causes the problem but the indistinct sounds involved in processing a string of numbers. Most adult bilinguals revert to their primary language to perform the calculation mentally in their heads and then translate the answer into English.

FOCUS *(Cont'd.)*

7. Sixteen and seven-
   hundredths, or sixteen
   point zero seven.
8. 84.521
9. 894.992
10. 57.68
11. 17.9; 14.8
12. 1.125
13. 0.125

Teach

Guided Practice

1. Read Section 8.1 with
   students.
2. Throughout the chapter, continually stress how important
   math skills are in every occupation. Remind students that
   today competition for jobs is
   fierce and that those hired
   will be required to have good
   technical skills, including
   math skills.

Discussion Starters

1. Ask: Which computations discussed in this section do you
   use most often and thus feel
   that you understand the best?
   (Answers will vary.)
2. Ask: Which computations discussed in this section do you
   use the least and thus feel
   that you need to understand better? What course of action
   would best help you become
   more familiar with those computations? (Answers will vary.)

Critical Thinking

Ask: What do we mean when
we say that acquiring math skills
is a *cumulative* process? (*Cumulative* means "increased by successive additions." Explain to
students that they will increase
their knowledge of how to perform math functions by starting
with the basics, as this chapter
does, and building on that basic
knowledge to learn more advanced functions.)

5. When a three-digit group is made up of only zeros,
do not write the name of the group.

3,000,375 ⟶ three million, three hundred
seventy-five

No words are written
for the thousands group.

Fractions

You learned about fractions when you were in grade
school, but you may not have had much practice using
them. Many jobs in business, especially in marketing, require a good understanding of fractions.

Fractions are numbers used to describe a part of
some standard amount. The top number, the **numerator,**
represents the number of parts being considered. The bottom number, the **denominator,** represents how many
parts in a whole or how many *total* parts are being considered. For example, the shaded area in the following
rectangle is ⅗ (three-fifths) of the total rectangle.

Numerator, the number of parts being considered

$$\frac{3 \text{ shaded parts}}{5 \text{ total parts}} = \frac{3}{5}$$

Denominator, the number of parts in a whole

In the example below, the number of circles is ⅖
(two-sevenths) of the total number of shapes.

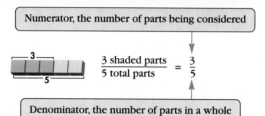

$$\frac{2 \text{ circles}}{7 \text{ shapes}} = \frac{2}{7}$$

Here are more examples illustrating the same principle.
The answers represent the number of *shaded* parts.

$$\frac{\text{Number of shaded parts}}{\text{Total number of parts}} = \frac{3}{8}$$

$$\frac{3 \text{ shaded parts}}{\text{Total number of parts}} = \frac{3}{3} = 1$$

One whole circle
is shaded.

$$\frac{5 \text{ shaded triangles}}{4 \text{ triangles in a square}} = \frac{5}{4} \text{ of a square}$$

A fraction can describe a
number greater than 1.

When the numerator is greater than the denominator, the fraction describes a number greater than 1. It can
be written as a **mixed number,** a whole number and fraction together.

$$\frac{6}{5} = 1\frac{1}{5}$$ Mixed number

Numerator is greater
than denominator.

Practice 1

What fraction of the total number of shapes
are triangles?

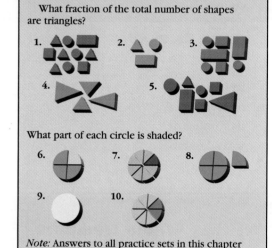

1. 2. 3.

4. 5.

What part of each circle is shaded?

6. 7. 8.

9. 10.

Note: Answers to all practice sets in this chapter
appear on page 117.

Decimal Numbers

A **decimal number** is a fraction or mixed number
whose denominator is a multiple of 10. The decimal number 5.3 means 5 + 0.3 or 5 + ³⁄₁₀ or 5³⁄₁₀. The decimal number 935.47 can be broken down as 900 + 30 + 5 + ⁴⁄₁₀ + ⁷⁄₁₀₀.

Knowing placement names is necessary for reading
decimals and writing them in words. Decimal placement
names apply to digits to the right of the decimal point.

More About

Fractions

Point out that fractions written in words are
hyphenated, the same as whole numbers under
100 consisting of two words. What happens when
such a number and a fraction occur in the same
amount, as with certain decimals? See Practice 2,
items 7 and 8, and the answers on page 117. Have
students formulate a rule.

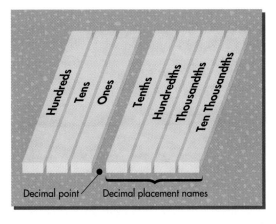

Decimal point | Decimal placement names

To read a decimal number or write it in words, follow the steps below. Use 15.083 as an example.

1. Begin with the whole number to the left of the decimal point *(fifteen)*.
2. Read or write *and* for the decimal point.
3. Read or write the number to the right of the decimal point as a whole number *(eighty-three)*.
4. Use the name of the decimal place of the final digit *(thousandths)*.

The result is *fifteen and eighty-three thousandths*.

You may also hear decimal numbers read using the whole number and only the names of the digits in the decimal places, with *point* for the decimal point. For example, 15.083 might be read as *fifteen point zero eight three*.

Understanding the relationship between decimal numbers and fractions is important when you are writing

Real World

MARKETING

Can You Say *Thaler*?

In the United States of America following the Revolutionary War, there was a backlash against years of colonial rule. American patriots rejected everything English. This included the English monetary system, with its pounds and shillings and awkward divisions of 12. Instead, the newly independent Americans embraced a decimal system based on a unit of Bohemian origins—the *Thaler*. (The word was a shortened form of *Joachimsthaler*, the name given to silver coins minted in the Joachimsthal region of Bohemia.) The only problem with the choice was that the Americans couldn't easily pronounce it. So, *Thaler* was quickly "Americanized" to *dollar*.

---

a check. After writing the amount in decimal form, you must write it again, using words for the dollars and a fraction for the cents.

Decimal form

Pay to the
order of XYZ Company $324.57

Three hundred twenty-four and $^{57}/_{100}$ Dollars

Dollars written in words | Cents written as a fraction

Practice 2

Write the decimal numbers in words. Write the amounts of money (as indicated by $) as you would on a check.

1. 5.6	**5.** 3.12	**8.** 25.48
2. 0.7	**6.** 9.05	**9.** $155.87
3. 14.5	**7.** 10.33	**10.** $545.67
4. 0.09		

Adding and Subtracting Decimal Numbers

To add or subtract decimal numbers, first list the numbers vertically, keeping the decimal points in line with each other. Then add or subtract as you would with whole numbers. Sometimes you may need to write zeros to fill a column.

$$1.45 + 3.4 = ?$$

Align decimal points vertically.

```
  1.45
+ 3.40  ←  Write 0s as needed.
------
  4.85  ←  Add as with whole numbers.
```

$$13.4 - 7.56 = ?$$

Align decimal points vertically.

```
 13.40  ←  Write 0s as needed.
- 7.56
------
  5.84  ←  Subtract as with whole numbers.
```

L1 Communication Skills

A journal is a written account that students keep to record what they have learned. Encourage your students to write a short (50-word) paragraph in their journals for each period you spend on this chapter. For a Level 1 Skill, have them explain in their own words what they learned in each lesson and give one example.

L2 Communication Skills

In their journals, have students answer one open-ended question about the day's class work in addition to their paragraphs. Examples:
- What relationship do you see between the things you learned today and the things you learned yesterday?
- Where else in your life or on your job have you used the information that you learned today?

L3 Communication Skills

When students have finished studying this section, have them write a 100-word paragraph in their journals that summarizes the concepts and skills they learned.

L1 Math Skills

Duplicate an entire newspaper ad or a portion of one that lists the prices for many products. (Ads for grocery stores or electronics outlets are particularly good for this purpose. The latter will feature higher prices and thus provide more difficult problems.)

Give students copies of the ad. Have them write the price of each product in words and fractions, as they would on a check.

Feature Note

According to his autobiography, Thomas Jefferson proposed during a meeting of the Continental Congress on July 6, 1785, "Resolved that the money unit of the United States of America be one dollar." Trade with the West Indies was facilitated by this measure because the Spanish peso (used at that time in the region) was patterned on the *thaler*.

L2 Math Skills

Using the ad provided in the L1 Math Skills activity, have students add and subtract dollar amounts of your choosing to each price. (Examples: If a cordless telephone is advertised at a price of $129.95, have students add $20.95 to this base price, for an answer of $150.90. Have them subtract $13.95 from the base price, for an answer of $116.)

L3 Math Skills

Using the ad provided in the L1 Math Skills activity, have students multiply and divide prices in the ad and round to the nearest cent. *Note:* When creating multiplication problems for themselves, students should drop the dollar sign from one of the amounts. (Examples: $109.95 × 29.95 = $3,293.0025 or $3,293; $109.95 ÷ $29.95 = 3.671 or 3.67.)

Independent Practice

1. Assign and review the Chapter 8 Case Study in the *International Case Studies* workbook.
2. Tell students to look in their local phone books, choose 10 seven-digit numbers at random, and write them on a separate sheet of paper. Then have students do the following:
- Separate each number into groups of units, thousands, and millions by using commas.
- Write each number in words.
- Calculate 25 percent of each number, and round the answer to a whole number if it doesn't already come out to one.
  (Answers will vary.)

Practice 3

Complete the following addition and subtraction problems with decimal numbers.

1. 5.4 + 8.6 =
2. 7.5 + 9.6 =
3. 9.8 + 7.5 =
4. 18 + 7.7 =
5. 17.5 + 4.75 =
6. 7.04 + 71.5 =
7. 6.7 + 0.6 + 2.67 + 7 =
8. 4.6 − 3.3 =
9. 45.9 − 7.76 =
10. $8 − $3.76 =
11. 5.7 − 1.11 + 14.078 =
12. 23.6 − 8.431 =
13. Bob's Bicycle Shop paid the following bills in September: $86.45 for gas, $114.86 for electricity, $187.58 for telephone, $98.36 for insurance, and $875 for rent. What is the total?
14. From a 40-yard bolt of fabric, Carol sold the following pieces: 3.33 yards, 4.5 yards, 2.25 yards, 2.125 yards, and 3.875 yards. How many yards are left?

Multiplying Decimal Numbers

To multiply decimal numbers, use the following two-step process.

1. Multiply the two numbers as if they were whole numbers. Pay no attention to the decimal points yet.
2. Add the number of decimal places in the two numbers being multiplied. Then, *working from the right,* count off the same number of decimal places in the product and insert the decimal point. *Note:* When counting off places from the right, you may have to add a zero in order to place the decimal point.

$$9.05 \times 4.31 = ?$$

9.05 has two decimal places.
4.31 has two decimal places.

```
  9.05
× 4.31
   905
  2715
 3620
390055  ⟶  39.0055
```

The answer must have four decimal places.

$$0.25 \times 0.3 =$$

0.25 has two decimal places.
0.3 has one decimal place.

```
  0.25
× 0.3
0.075
```

Write a 0 in the product in order to have three decimal places.

Multiply amounts of money as you would other decimal numbers. Remember to include the dollar sign in your answer.

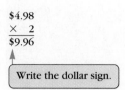

```
$4.98
×    2
$9.96
```

Write the dollar sign.

Rounding Decimal Numbers

Sometimes you may have to round a decimal number. This is especially common when multiplying with amounts of money, as when figuring tax amounts, discounts, and so on.

Use the following steps to round decimal amounts. Round 16.842, 16.852, and 16.892 to the nearest tenth.

1. Find the decimal place you are rounding to.

16.842   16.852   16.892

Tenths place

2. Look at the digit to the right of that place.

16.842   16.852   16.892

Digit to the right

3. If the digit to the right is less than 5, leave the first digit as is. If the digit is 5 or greater, round up.

16.842 rounds to 16.8

Less than 5

16.852 rounds to 16.9

5

16.892 rounds to 16.9

Greater than 5

When you are working with amounts of money, use the same steps to round your answer to the nearest cent (the nearest hundredth).

▶ **More About**

Rounding Decimal Numbers

What seems like an insignificant detail can end up being a very expensive mistake. For example, even a small mistake in rounding on a purchase order can cause a computer to kick it out for hand processing. This can cause further delays. Always double-check rounded amounts.

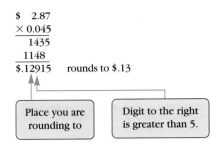

$
\begin{array}{r}
\$\ 2.87 \\
\times\ 0.045 \\
\hline
1435 \\
1148 \\
\hline
\$.12915 \quad \text{rounds to } \$.13
\end{array}
$

Place you are rounding to

Digit to the right is greater than 5.

Practice 4

Complete the following multiplication problems with decimal numbers. Round any amounts of money to the nearest cent.

1. $\begin{array}{r}5.2\\ \times\ 7\\ \hline\end{array}$ **2.** $\begin{array}{r}6.1\\ \times\ 4.6\\ \hline\end{array}$ **3.** $\begin{array}{r}31.4\\ \times\ 7.8\\ \hline\end{array}$ **4.** $\begin{array}{r}31.6\\ \times\ 6.3\\ \hline\end{array}$

5. $\begin{array}{r}5.08\\ \times\ 0.68\\ \hline\end{array}$ **6.** $\begin{array}{r}7.75\\ \times\ 3.2\\ \hline\end{array}$ **7.** $\begin{array}{r}0.687\\ \times\ 8.02\\ \hline\end{array}$

8. $8.5 \times 7.2 =$
9. $0.83 \times 0.04 =$
10. If you earn \$8.75 an hour, how much pay should you receive for 39.5 hours of work?
11. At Big Al's Pizza, the cost of delivering orders is \$.41 per mile. If the delivery van averaged 458.7 miles per day last week, what is the average daily cost of making deliveries?

Dividing Decimal Numbers

Division of decimal numbers is similar to division of whole numbers. Follow the steps below to divide decimal numbers.

1. Set up the division problem as you would with whole numbers.

69.7 divided by 1.7 = $1.7\,\overline{)\,69.7}$

69.7 divided by 1.724 = $1.724\,\overline{)\,69.7}$

2. Shift the decimal point in the divisor so that the divisor becomes a whole number. Then shift the decimal point in the dividend the same number of decimal places. Write zeros in the dividend, if necessary, in order to place the decimal point.

$1.7\,\overline{)\,69.7} \longrightarrow 17.\,\overline{)\,697.}$

Shift the decimal point one place to the right.

Write 0s.

$1.724\,\overline{)\,69.700} \longrightarrow 1724.\,\overline{)\,69700.}$

Shift the decimal point three places to the right.

3. Place a decimal point in the answer space directly above its new position in the dividend. Then divide as with whole numbers.

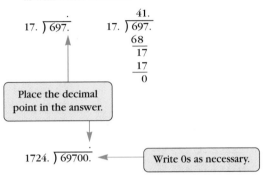

$17.\,\overline{)\,697.}$

$
\begin{array}{r}
41. \\
17.\,\overline{)\,697.} \\
\underline{68} \\
17 \\
\underline{17} \\
0
\end{array}
$

Place the decimal point in the answer.

$1724.\,\overline{)\,69700.}$ Write 0s as necessary.

Sometimes you may need to write extra zeros after the decimal point in order to have a remainder of zero.

$$16.38 \div 6.5 = ?$$

$
\begin{array}{r}
2.52 \\
6.5\,\overline{)\,16.380} \\
\underline{13\ 0} \\
3\ 38 \\
\underline{3\ 25} \\
130 \\
\underline{130} \\
0
\end{array}
$

$65 \times 2 = 130$
$65 \times 5 = 325$
$65 \times 2 = 130$
Remainder is 0.

Some decimal answers will continue indefinitely as you write zeros to the right of the decimal point. *Repeating decimals* will repeat a number or pattern of numbers.

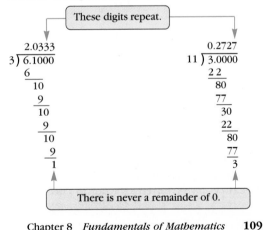

These digits repeat.

$
\begin{array}{r}
2.0333 \\
3\,\overline{)\,6.1000} \\
\underline{6} \\
10 \\
\underline{9} \\
10 \\
\underline{9} \\
10 \\
\underline{9} \\
1
\end{array}
$

$
\begin{array}{r}
0.2727 \\
11\,\overline{)\,3.0000} \\
\underline{2\ 2} \\
80 \\
\underline{77} \\
30 \\
\underline{22} \\
80 \\
\underline{77} \\
3
\end{array}
$

There is never a remainder of 0.

Assess

Evaluation
Assign and review the Section 8.1 Review.

Reteaching
1. Assign and review the vocabulary terms for this section.
2. Assign and review Fact and Idea Review questions 1–5 from the Chapter Review.
3. Do an oral review of Practices 1–5. By now, students should have a good grasp of all of the concepts. If they do not, however, reviewing the practices will help you determine where you need to give additional instruction.

Enrichment
1. Assign and review the appropriate activities in the *Student Activity Workbook*.
2. Assign and review the appropriate Critical Thinking questions from the Chapter Review.
3. Have students keep track of all the purchases made in your school store for one week, or make these figures available to students. For each type of item sold, have them calculate the total cost of the items, the total sales, and the difference between the two.

Close

Have students complete these statements:
- A whole number is written without...(fractions and decimals.)
- In a fraction, the numerator expresses _____ , and the denominator expresses _____ . (number of parts being considered; number of parts in a whole)
- A decimal number is...(a fraction or mixed number whose denominator is a multiple of 10.)

Lifelong Learning

Fundamentals of Mathematics

Taking basic courses in business math and accounting can give students an advantage in such diverse areas as completing income tax returns, buying groceries, computing interest paid on loans or credit cards, investing in retirement plans, and receiving the maximum benefits offered at work. Often benefits that employers offer go unused because individuals don't take the time to calculate their value. For example, many employers offer to match an employees' savings deduction up to a certain percentage, usually 4% of annual salary. Encourage students to master the calculations presented in the text and to find applications in real life that give them reason to exercise their knowledge.

FOCUS

Bell Ringer Activity

Write the following on the chalkboard:

Gross Monthly Sales for 1995

Metro Pet Emporium

January	$ 8,670
February	7,955
March	8,995
April	11,690
May	13,200
June	13,567
July	14,688
August	16,780
September	16,555
October	14,500
November	15,600
December	17,800

Tell students to imagine they work at Metro Pet Emporium and their co-op supervisor has asked them to present to the staff a comparison of the above sales figures for 1995. How would they do it?

Generate a chalkboard list of students' answers. If they don't arrive at the conclusion themselves, suggest that they present this information visually. Then ask them how they would do this.

Introducing the Section

Most students will be familiar with graphs. Some may even have used them for reports or presentations. Ask some of those students to assist you by drawing two sets of axes on the chalkboard—one for a bar graph and one for a line graph.

Then have the students label each vertical axis with the words *Sales (in thousands)* and the numbers 1–20. Have them label each horizontal axis with the word *Months* and abbreviations for the 12 months of the year. (See Figure 8-2 on page 116 for an example.)

Once the graph structures have been laid out, explain the concepts of bar and line graphs. Then ask students to help you plot the above figures on each.

110

Practice 5

Do the following division problems. Round answers to the nearest hundredth.

1. $0.75 \div 1.8 =$
2. $4.76 \div 3.8 =$
3. $1.758 \div 4.64 =$
4. $8.4 \div 0.015 =$
5. $0.063 \div 2.1 =$
6. $6.002 \div 0.3 =$

7. Software Corporation paid $2,366.05 for computer paper. If the paper costs $29.95 per box, how many boxes did the corporation buy?

8. Edward averages 80 questions per hour when typing test questions into a computer testbank. How long will it take him to enter 1,800 questions?

Converting Fractions to Decimals

As you read in the section on fractions, decimal equivalents of fractions are important in many jobs in marketing. To convert any fraction to a decimal, simply divide the numerator by the denominator.

Numerator

Denominator

$$\frac{1}{4} = 1 \div 4 = 4\overline{)1.00}$$
$$\begin{array}{r} 0.25 \\ \underline{8} \\ 20 \\ \underline{20} \\ 0 \end{array}$$

$$\frac{2}{3} = 2 \div 3 = 3\overline{)2.000}$$
$$\begin{array}{r} 0.666 \\ \underline{18} \\ 20 \\ \underline{18} \\ 20 \\ \underline{18} \\ 2 \end{array}$$

There is never a remainder of 0.

In its decimal form, ⅔ is a repeating decimal. When working with repeating decimals, you may round to the nearest hundredth for most applications. Thus, ⅔ = 0.67.

SECTION 8.1

Review

1. When writing numbers in words, when do you use a hyphen?
2. What is the numerator of a fraction?
3. When rounding numbers, how do you know whether to round up or down?
4. When multiplying two decimal numbers together, how do you know the number of decimal places in the answer?
5. How do you convert a fraction to a decimal?

110   Unit 4   *Human Resource Essentials*

SECTION 8.2

Objectives

After completing this section, you will be able to

- use a calculator to solve math problems,
- convert percentages to decimals and decimals to percentages, and
- read different types of graphs used to present mathematical data.

Terms to Know

- percent
- bar graph
- line graph
- circle graph
- pie chart

Using a Calculator

Nearly everyone in marketing and business uses calculators. There are two basic types. The most widely used type employs the *algebraic entry system*. This is the type of calculator used in the problems that follow. The other type uses the *reverse-entry system*.

The basic difference is that with the reverse-entry system, you enter the first amount, then the second amount, and then the operation (added to, subtracted from, multiplied by, or divided into the first amount). If you have a calculator that uses the reverse-entry system, read the instruction book that accompanies your calculator very carefully.

If you expect to be hired in sales or any other marketing job, you will almost certainly use a calculator. Besides simply knowing which buttons to press, you will be expected to work with accuracy, know how to work with fractions and amounts of money, and have an understanding of how the calculator computes with multiple operations.

Estimate, Then Operate

When using a calculator, many people follow the *guess-and-check method*. They estimate first, then enter

---

Section Review Answers

1. In numbers less than 100 that are written as two words.
2. The top number, which represents the number of parts being considered.
3. Look at the digit to the right. If it is less than five, leave that digit as is. If it is five or more, round up.
4. By counting the decimal places in the numbers being multiplied.
5. By dividing the numerator by the denominator.

the problem in the calculator. Finally, they check the displayed answer against the estimate.

$$388 + 995 = ?$$

Estimate: $400 + 1,000 = 1,400$

Enter the problem:

 1383

Check: 1,388 is reasonably close to the estimate of 1,400.

Displayed answer

$$480 \times 112 = ?$$

Estimate: $500 \times 100 = 50,000$

Enter the problem:

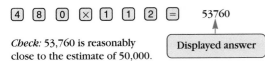 53760

Check: 53,760 is reasonably close to the estimate of 50,000.

Displayed answer

You may wonder why it is important to estimate your answers when you use a calculator. Surely the calculator is more accurate than your estimate. Sometimes, though, you may make errors when entering numbers or even press the wrong operation key. So, it's important to have an estimate of the answer in mind. For example, if you're expecting an answer of about 300, you'll know something is wrong if the displayed answer on your calculator is 3,300.

Another way to ensure accuracy when using a calculator is to check the display after you enter each number and before you press the operation key. If you have made an error, press the Clear Entry key [CE] to remove the last entry. Suppose you want to multiply 5.8×7.2, but you enter [5] [.] [8] [×] [7] [2]. Press [CE] to delete the last two keystrokes. Then you can reenter the second number correctly. The first number will remain in the calculator. Press the Equals key [=], and the answer will be displayed: 41.76.

How to Make Entries

Keep in mind as you enter digits that you can disregard leading zeros to the left of the decimal point (as in 0.6 or 0.375) and final zeros after the decimal point (as in 9.250 or 41.500). You don't need to enter these zeros. The calculator will display all the digits needed.

Number	Keystrokes Entered	Display
0.785	[.] [7] [8] [5]	0.785
5.10	[5] [.] [1]	5.1

When dealing with mixed numbers or fractions, you must first convert the fractions to decimal form. Do this by dividing the numerator by the denominator. For example, to enter 5¼, first enter [1] [÷] [4]. Then add the whole number by entering [+] [5].

When solving problems dealing with money, remember to write the dollar sign in the answer. You may also have to round the displayed answer to the nearest cent.

Display	Answer Written as Money Amount
5.25	$5.25
25.368216	$25.37 (Round to nearest cent.)
46.0194	$46.02 (Round to nearest cent.)
76514.1	$76,514.10 (No commas shown in large numbers on most calculators.)

A calculator can operate on only two numbers at a time. However, you can perform a string of involved calculations on more than two numbers if you are very careful. When only addition and subtraction are involved, the calculator will perform these operations as they are entered.

[8] [.] [6] [+] [.] [2] [5] [+] [1] [1] [.] [9] [−] [3] [.] [6] [2] [=] 17.13

When only multiplication and division are involved, the calculator will also perform these operations as they are entered.

[7] [7] [5] [×] [.] [9] [6] [÷] [5] [×] [1] [.] [9] [6] [=] 291.648

However, when a calculation involves a combination of addition or subtraction with multiplication or division, not all calculators work the same way. You will need to check how your calculator performs the operations in this type of problem. Most calculators will do the operations as they are entered.

$6 + 4 \times 6$ will be calculated as

$\boxed{6 + 4} \times 6 =$

↓

$10 \quad \times 6 = 60.$

$6 \times 4 + 6$ will be calculated as

$\boxed{6 \times 4} + 6 =$

↓

$24 \quad + 6 = 30.$

$9 - 5 \times 2 + 6 \div 7 =$ will be calculated as

$\boxed{9 - 5} \times 2 + 6 \div 7 =$

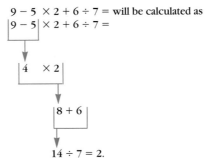

$\boxed{4 \quad \times 2}$

$\boxed{8 + 6}$

$14 \div 7 = 2.$

Finally, draw a circle on the chalkboard, and ask students how they would plot the same information on a circle graph. You may have to help them come to the conclusion that the circle represents the whole (the total for the year of $160,000) and that they will have to divide it into 12 slices to show each month's figure as a percentage of the whole.

Ask if any students know how to find percentages of a whole. If they do, ask them to provide the formula. If they do not, tell students that you will return to this concept later in the lesson. For now, it's enough that they know the three types of graphs and how they show information visually.

Teach

Guided Practice

1. Read Section 8.2 with students.
2. Use the three transparencies for this section.
3. Have students read aloud the Case Study and review the answers in class.
4. Assign and review the Chapter 8 Activity in the *School-to-Work Handbook*.

Discussion Starters

1. Ask: Which concepts discussed in this section do you use most often and thus feel that you understand the best? (Answers will vary.)
2. Ask: Which concepts discussed in this section do you use the least and thus feel that you need to understand better? What course of action would best help you become more familiar with those concepts? (Answers will vary.)

Critical Thinking

1. Ask students to list occasions when they routinely estimate numbers. (Answers will vary but probably include estimating travel mileage, number of yards gained in a football play, number of cookies that a recipe will produce, and how much a date with dinner and a movie will cost.)

Did You Know ❓

The most common error made when using a calculator or adding machine is transposing. In a transposing error, a person inputs the reverse of a given pair of numbers. For example, 798 would be entered as 789.

If you are entering a long string of numbers, it is advisable to enter it twice to see if the totals agree. If the difference of the two sums is devisable by 9, it is likely that you have transposed one or more numbers.

Teach *(Cont'd.)*

2. Have students speculate about why they are taught to estimate and do math computations by hand when they could use a calculator instead. (Answers will vary but should include the following: A calculator may not always be available for a computation. Also, knowing how to perform a math operation without a calculator helps you understand the logic of the process and thus apply it better.)

L1 Math Skills

For this activity, students will need a watch with a second hand or a stopwatch. Have each student select a 30-minute evening entertainment or news program. As they watch the program, they should record the following:

- Total number of minutes devoted to commercials during the program
- Total number of minutes devoted to news updates
- Total number of minutes given over to public service announcements
- Total number of minutes the program itself actually aired

L2 Math Skills

Using the information gathered in the L1 Math Skills activity, students should calculate what *fraction* of the half-hour program was made up of commercials, news updates, public service announcements, and the actual program itself. (Answers will vary.)

L3 Math Skills

Using the results of the L2 Math Skills activity, students should convert the fractions they developed to percentages and convert the percentages to decimals. (Answers will vary.)

112

BRIGHT IDEAS

When in Doubt, Go with a Number

When the first Datsun sports car arrived in the United States in 1970, it bore the sporty name *Fair Lady*. It had been named by a high-level executive in Japan as a tribute to the musical *My Fair Lady*. Possibly the executive thought that since Americans liked the play, too, they would find the name as appealing as he did. In fact, they never got a chance to consider it.

The executive's subordinate in the United States saw the nameplates on the cars and realized immediately they were a mistake. In Japan, where people liked their cars named for things like flowers, such a designation might be accepted. But in America, where people favored large "muscle" cars with huge engines and "horsepower," he knew it would be a disaster. In an act of unthinkable rebellion by a Japanese subordinate to his superior, the executive had all the nameplates removed.

That left him with a problem, though—what to call the car. There was no time for brainstorming or concensus building. The executive went with the company's internal designation for the car, the one the technicians had been using while waiting for a name to be assigned. The car made its debut in the United States as the 240Z.

The designation stuck. Today the company (now Nissan) still names the sportscar with numbers. It's the 300ZX. Chalk up one for the technicians!

Creativity Challenge Form teams of 3–5 people, and test the limits of number names. Brainstorm two lists—one of products for which number names would be ideal and another of products for which they would be wildly inappropriate. For the first list, try to include at least three items that do not currently use number designations for model names. Explain why such a name might have special appeal for consumers.

Percentages

Percent means parts per hundred. Thus, a number expressed as a percent represents the number of parts per hundred.

112   Unit 4   *Human Resource Essentials*

To write a whole number or a decimal number as a percent, multiply it by 100. A simple way to do this is to move the decimal point two places *to the right*.

$$0.70 = 0.7 \times 100 = 70\% \qquad \text{or} \qquad 0.70 = 70\%$$
$$0.05 = 0.05 \times 100 = 5\% \qquad \text{or} \qquad 0.05 = 5\%$$
$$2.5 \; = 2.5 \times 100 = 250\% \qquad \text{or} \qquad 2.50 = 250\%$$

> Move the decimal point two places to the right.

> Write 0s as needed.

You can use a calculator to do this operation.

. 7 × 1 0 0 =   70 = 70%
2 . 5 × 1 0 0 =   250 = 250%

Converting Fractions to Percentages

To write a fraction or mixed number as a percent, first convert the fraction to decimal form. Do this by dividing the numerator by the denominator. If there is a whole number, add it to the converted fraction. Then multiply by 100. You can use a calculator to do this operation.

½ = 1 ÷ 2 × 1 0 0 =   50 = 50%
⅜ = 3 ÷ 8 × 1 0 0 =   37.5 = 37.5%
4⅖ = 2 ÷ 5 + 4 × 1 0 0 =   440 = 440%

Converting Percentages to Decimals

You can change a percent to a decimal number by dividing by 100. A simple way to do this is to move the decimal point two places *to the left*.

> Move the decimal point two places to the left.

$$24.8\% = 24.8 \div 100 = .248 \qquad \text{or} \qquad 24.8\% = 0.248$$
$$0.5\% = \; 0.5 \div 100 = 0.005 \qquad \text{or} \qquad 0.5\% = 0.005$$

> Write 0s as needed.

You can use a calculator to do this operation.

12.6% = 1 2 . 6 ÷ 1 0 0 =   0.126
1.4% = 1 . 4 ÷ 1 0 0 =   0.014

You can also convert a percent with a fraction or mixed number to a decimal by using a calculator.

7¼% = 1 ÷ 4 + 7 ÷ 1 0 0 =   0.0725

Bright Ideas

Would the 240Z have been such a popular car if the internal designation had been the 222P or the 155E? There was something that intrigued car buyers about the "Z," as it was often called. Datsun's Stateside executive was very lucky that the internal designation happened to have been one that consumers embraced so readily.

CASE STUDY

A Really, Really Big Show

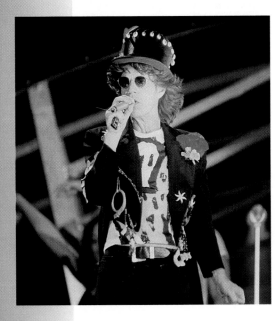

Rock concert tickets can cost a fortune. What's behind the sky-high prices? Besides supply and demand, lots of costly preparation.

Before highly popular musicians go on tour, they spend up to a year rehearsing and designing the stage sets and lighting for their shows. This can cost millions of dollars. When they finally do get on the road, they take a huge crew with them—everyone from piano tuners and truck drivers to cooks and lighting experts. Employee salaries, rental of arenas, utility and transportation expenses all add to the cost.

In 1994, pop singer Janet Jackson started off on a six-month tour. Her crew was made up of 115 people riding in nine specially fitted buses. It took 17 semitrailers to haul the sound and lighting equipment and the stage sets. Each week on tour cost $400,000.

If top-priced tickets to Janet Jackson concerts were $32, how many tickets would tour promoters have to sell to break even each week? You figure it out. If you divide $400,000 by $32, you arrive at a figure of 12,500. That's 12,500 tickets each week. For the musicians to have any income, they would need to sell thousands more!

Some other tours are much more expensive. The Rolling Stones' Voodoo Lounge tour in 1994–95 featured a stage set that cost $4 million to build. The set was lit by 1,200 light bulbs. It took 50 semitrailers to haul the Stones' equipment and sets and 17 buses for the crew.

The most expensive tickets for the Rolling Stones concerts cost $50. Other tour income came from the sale of T-shirts and promotional items. The Stones projected the 18-month tour would bring in $300 million. Of that, they earmarked more than $70 million for themselves. All of which proves that really big shows are really big business!

Case Study Review

1. Assume the average ticket price for the Rolling Stones tour was $40 and each concertgoer bought an average of $20 worth of merchandise. How many people would have had to attend the concerts for the tour to gross $300 million?

2. Assume that the Stones tour went on for 75 weeks and took in $300 million. Assume further that the profit was $70 million.
   a. What was the cost per week?
   b. Compare the weekly costs of the Stones tour and the Janet Jackson tour. What percentage of the Stones figure is the Jackson figure?

A MATTER OF ETHICS

3. Fifty dollars for a concert ticket is less than half of what some big-name acts are charging. Most of the fans of these musicians are young people with limited incomes. Do you think it is ethical for bands to charge so much for tickets? Defend your answer.

Chapter 8 *Fundamentals of Mathematics* **113**

L1 Communication Skills

Have each student take one concept presented in this section and teach it to someone outside the class—perhaps a friend or family member. Once the friend or family member firmly understands the concept, the student should make a journal entry about how he or she handled the instruction.

L2 Communication Skills

Have students consider the following questions about the L1 Communication Skills activity and record their responses in their journals:
- What was easy about trying to teach someone a math concept? What did you like about the process?
- What was difficult about trying to teach someone a math concept? What did you dislike about the process?

L3 Communication Skills

Tell students to give some thought to the act of teaching and what it takes to do it well. (They have probably already taught siblings, relatives, or friends such things as how to play a video game, use a computer, tie their shoes, etc.) In their journals, have students jot down some of the things they have discovered that make it easier for people to learn. (Answers will vary but may include learning in context, building skills one upon another, and having empathy for the person learning.)

If you have time, you may wish to discuss these things in class and even get some feedback on your own teaching style. If you do not have the class time, you may also ask students to give you some feedback in their journals. You may learn something new about how students perceive and react to your teaching style.

Case Study Answers

1. $300,000,000 ÷ $60 = 5,000,000
2. a. $300,000,000 − $70,000,000 = $230,000,000;
   $230,000,000 ÷ 75 = $3,066,667
   b. $400,000 ÷ $3,066,667 = .13 = 13%
3. Answers will vary. However, bands wouldn't be able to charge so much if the market could not bear the price. This is a classic example of supply and demand. At a concert performance, there is only a certain number of tickets available. If consumers are willing to pay such a high price to be present at a concert, bands will continue to charge it, especially given the costs that go into the show.

L1 Problem-solving Skills

Have students arrange these decimal numbers in order, from smallest to largest: 2.57, .009, .998, 12.345, .10, .00067, 98.9, 100.50, .87, and .01. (.00067, .009, .01, .10, .87, .998, 2.57, 12.345, 98.9, 100.50)

L2 Problem-solving Skills

Have students tell which of these percentages is correctly converted to a decimal. Have them provide the correct conversion for any items that are wrong.

a. 35.89% = 0.3589

b. 98% = .098 (Incorrect— should be 0.98.)

c. 9.12% = 0.0912

d. 1.78% = 0.00178 (Incorrect—should be 0.0178.)

e. 5.8% = 0.58 (Incorrect— should be 0.058.)

L3 Problem-solving Skills

Pose this problem to students: A friend of yours is having a hard time remembering the five steps used to solve percent problems. Recall that these include the following.

1. Estimate the answer.
2. Translate the problem into a math statement.
3. Do the calculations.
4. Round money amounts to the nearest cent.
5. Check your answer.

Develop a mnemonic device (something intended to aid the memory) to help your friend remember these five steps. (Answers will vary. Students could draw diagrams or think of words that correspond to the first letters of each step.)

Cooperative Learning

Pair each student who is having difficulty with a student who has mastered the concepts presented in this section. Give the following problems to each pair.

Percent Problems

Percent problems are often encountered on a job. For example, you may be asked to figure a discount amount or the amount of sales tax. You may have to figure the total selling price, including the tax. Maybe you will be asked to figure the percent commission on your total sales.

Most percent problems will involve finding a percent of a number. To do that, multiply the decimal equivalent of the percent by the number.

> Decimal equivalent of $5\frac{1}{2}$%

$5\frac{1}{2}$% of $35 = 0.055 \times \$35$

> *Of* tells you to multiply.

Use these steps to help you solve percent problems.

1. Estimate the answer.
2. Translate the problem into a math statement.
3. Do the calculations.
4. If necessary, round money amounts to the nearest cent.
5. Check your answer.

Many calculators have a Percent key % that can simplify percent calculations. Read the instructions for your calculator to find out how to use this key.

Two types of percent problems are explained below. The problems can be solved with a calculator without the use of a Percent key.

1. Suppose you have sold a set of skis listed at $395.99 to someone eligible for a 15 percent discount. How much in dollars and cents will you allow as a discount on the skis?

   - *First: Estimate the answer.* Round the list price to $400. Figure that 10 percent of $400 is $40. Since 15 percent is $1\frac{1}{2}$ times 10 percent, estimate the discount at about $60 ($1\frac{1}{2}$ times $40).

   - *Second: Translate the problem into a math statement.*

     15% of $395.99 = 0.15×395.99

   - *Third: Do the calculations.*

     $0.15 \times \$395.99 = \$59.3985$

   - *Fourth: Round the answer to the nearest cent, if necessary.*

     $59.3985 rounds to $59.40

   - *Finally: Check the answer against your estimate.* The amount $59.40 is reasonably close to the estimate of $60. The discount is $59.40.

2. If sales tax is $6\frac{1}{2}$ percent, how much tax should you collect on the sale of the skis? Before you can figure the tax, you have to find out the net selling price.

   List price − discount = net price
   $395.99 − $59.40 = $336.59

Now you can proceed, following the guidelines given above.

- *Estimate:* Round $6\frac{1}{2}$ percent to 7 percent and $336.59 to $300. A 7 percent sales tax means that $7 tax is collected on every $100 in sales. So, you can estimate the tax to be $21 ($3 \times \$7$).

- *Translate:*

  $6\frac{1}{2}$ percent of $336.59 = $0.065 \times \$336.59$

- *Calculate:*

  $0.065 \times \$336.59 = \$21.8784$

- *Round:*

  $21.8784 rounds to $21.88

- *Check:* $21.88 is reasonably close to the estimate of $21. The sales tax to be collected is $21.88.

Reading Charts and Graphs

Often in marketing, people need to use numbers to describe market trends, growth of sales, and other data. Graphs are a way of presenting such information in a way that is easier to understand than a long series of numbers. Because graphs are drawings, they make it possible for people to *see* information and grasp it more readily. It's easier to tell that one bar is longer than another, or that a line is going up or down, than it is to try to understand data by reading. Usually a graph shows the relationship between two kinds of data, or statistical information.

Translators Must Be Good at Math, Too

To someone living in the United States, 3.5 million square miles is a great deal of territory. To a Latin American, however, those same square miles translate into something even more impressive sounding—*9,1 millones de kilómetros.*

Notice that a person translating these area figures has to know much more than just how to convert the words from English to Spanish. He or she must know the correct formula to apply to convert square miles to square kilometers. (This gets tricky because to convert miles to kilometers, you multiply the miles by 1.6. To convert square miles to square kilometers, you multiply by 2.6.) The translator must also know the conventions of writing metric numbers. This means knowing, among other things, to substitute a comma for the internal decimal point.

Feature Note

Other math calculations a translator must be familiar with differ according to the languages in question. For example, a Japanese translator must know the following: 1 kin = 1.323 pounds, 1 kwan = 8.27 pounds, 1 sun = 1.193 inches, and 1 koku = 47.6 U.S. gallons. And consider the Chinese translator who needs to know that 1 li = 705 yards or 1 catty = 1.33 pounds.

Bar Graphs

A **bar graph** is a drawing made up of parallel bars whose lengths are proportional to the qualities being measured. The bar graph shown in Figure 8-1 was used by Morning Glory Music in its market research. It shows the relationship between the number of compact disks people bought in May and the ages of the buyers. Along the bottom of the graph, the age groups that purchased compact disks are listed. Each group is represented by a bar of a certain height. There is a vertical line along the left side of the graph indicating the numbers of disks sold.

To discover how many disks 19 to 24-year-olds bought, simply draw an imaginary line across the top of the bar that represents that age group. Then note where that line intersects the left side of the graph. As you can see, 19 to 24-year-olds bought 800 disks that month, more than any other group.

Look at the bar representing 25 to 34-year-olds. The top of this bar is halfway between the 600 and 700 sales level. So, you can estimate that this group bought 650 CDs that month. You can also easily see that the younger group bought about 150 more CDs than the 25 to 34-year-olds and about 600 more than people over 60. The relative heights of the bars gives the store an instant picture of the age distribution of its customers.

Line Graphs

Another kind of graph you have probably seen often in magazines and newspapers is a line graph. A **line graph** uses a line that joins points representing changes in a variable quantity, usually over a specific period of time. It is very useful for charting sales, prices, profits, output—things that people expect to change over time. The information is useful in predicting future trends so that businesses can make plans to prepare for them.

The line graph shown in Figure 8-2 on page 116 charts the ups and downs in compact disk sales at Morning Glory Music over the course of 1994. Along the bottom of the graph are the months of the year. Along the left side are the number of units sold. As you can see by following the line, by far the most sales (10,000) occurred in December. There was also a big jump in sales at the beginning of the summer and smaller increases in April and September. These were all followed by declines. This kind of information can help the store decide how much merchandise to order the following year.

Circle Graphs

A **circle graph** is a geometric representation of the relative sizes of the parts of a whole. Businesses often choose such a graph to compare things like the costs of different aspects of manufacturing or the ways income from sales is used by a company.

A circle graph is better known as a **pie chart,** because it looks like a pie cut into slices of different sizes. The proportions of the different "slices" are sometimes expressed as percentages of the whole circle and sometimes as dollar amounts.

The pie chart in Figure 8-3 on page 116 shows a percentage breakdown of where the money from the

Morning Glory Music—Compact Disk Sales by Age Group
(May 1994)

Figure 8-1

Bar graphs help readers see data and understand how one piece of data is related to another. For example, according to this graph, how did Morning Glory Music's oldest customers compare with its youngest in terms of purchases?

Chapter 8   *Fundamentals of Mathematics*   **115**

1. Make these entries on your calculator by converting the fractions to decimals (divide the numerator by the denominator to convert to decimal form and add the whole number):
   a. 6 1/8 (6.125)
   b. 7 2/5 (7.4)
   c. 9 1/4 (9.25)
   d. 10 5/12 (10.42)
   e. 4 5/18 (4.28)
2. Write these amounts as money (round to the nearest cent):
   a. 7.622 ($7.62)
   b. 788.99876 ($789.00)
   c. 7.35 ($7.35)
   d. 366563.333 ($366,563.34)
   e. 8916.98 ($8,916.98)
3. Use your calculator to write these decimal numbers as percentages (multiply by 100):
   a. .89 (89%)
   b. 3.6 (360%)
   c. .005 (5%)
   d. 8.15 (815%)
   e. .0009 (0.09%)

While students are doing these problems, walk around the classroom, helping students as necessary and making sure that the less skilled students are participating fully.

Independent Practice

1. If students don't already know it, have them determine the rate of the sales tax in your area. Then have them figure the total cost of your classroom set of *Marketing Essentials,* including sales tax. (Answers will vary.)
2. Have students use a readily available career resource, such as the *Encyclopedia of Careers and Vocational Guidance,* the *Occupational Outlook Handbook,* or the *Dictionary of Occupational Titles,* to research one career in marketing that interests them. Working from the written profile that they find in their research, have them take notes on the basic duties of the job and try to determine if and how math is used as part of the job. Have students share their findings.

Evaluation

Assign and review the Section 8.2 Review.

Reteaching

1. Assign and review the vocabulary terms for this section.
2. Assign and review Fact and Idea Review questions 6–10 from the Chapter Review.
3. Get a group consensus from the class on some statistics that you want to show visually. It could be your school's football or basketball scores for the season, weekly gross sales of your school store for two months—anything that your students agree on and find interesting.

   Once you have the statistical information, write it on the chalkboard. Then have students help you create bar, line, and circle graphs summarizing the data. *Note:* If you wish to make this a cooperative learning activity, divide the class into three teams and have each create one of the graphs.

Enrichment

1. Assign and review the appropriate activities in the *Student Activity Workbook.*
2. Assign and review the appropriate Critical Thinking questions from the Chapter Review.
3. Assign and review the Building Academic Skills Activities, Application Projects, Linking School to Work Activity, and Performance Assessment from the Chapter Review.

Morning Glory Music Compact Disk Sales (1994)

Figure 8–2

Line graphs chart change over time—in this case, the change in sales figures over a period of 12 months. How would you summarize the progression of Morning Glory Music's sales over the course of a year?

Morning Glory Music Retail Price Distribution—Compact Disks

Artist royalties 12%
Manufacturing 8%
Packaging & promotion 11%
Record company profit 30%
Retailer costs 14%
Retailer profit 25%

Figure 8–3

A circle graph shows a whole—here, the price of a compact disk—divided into parts. Which two price components account for more than half of what Morning Glory Music charges for a CD?

retail sale of a compact disk went. You can see from the chart that twice as much of the sale price went to retail profit as to the artists who made the recording. The biggest portion of the "pie" went to the record company. Look at the area representing manufacturing costs. You can see that it accounted for the smallest portion of the retail price.

This kind of chart enables companies to see at a glance which costs take the largest bite out of their revenues. The companies can then determine whether this breakdown accurately reflects their priorities. If not, they can institute cost-cutting measures as they see fit.

SECTION 8.2 Review

1. What is the guess-and-check method of using a calculator?
2. How can you convert a percentage to a decimal number?
3. Why do people use graphs instead of a series of numbers to present information?

Caption Answers

Figure 8-2: Sales start the year extremely low following the peak holiday buying season, rise fairly steadily to a secondary peak in the summer, then fall off in advance of huge holiday sales.

Figure 8-3: Profits for record company and retailer.

Section Review Answers

1. Involves estimating an answer first, *then* using the calculator. Technique helps confirm that answer has been calculated correctly.
2. Divide the percentage by 100 (move the decimal point two places to the right).
3. Because a visual representation is easier for most people to understand than a series of numbers.

Answers to Practice Sets

Practice 1 (page 106)
1. $\frac{4}{10}$ (or $\frac{2}{5}$)
2. $\frac{1}{3}$
3. 0
4. $\frac{4}{4}$ (or 1)
5. $\frac{2}{7}$
6. $\frac{3}{4}$
7. $\frac{1}{8}$
8. $\frac{5}{4}$ (or $1\frac{1}{4}$)
9. No parts shaded.
10. $\frac{2}{8}$ (or $\frac{1}{4}$)

Practice 2 (page 107)
1. Five and six-tenths
2. Seven-tenths
3. Fourteen and five-tenths
4. Nine-hundredths
5. Three and twelve-hundredths
6. Nine and five-hundredths
7. Ten and thirty-three hundredths
8. Twenty-five and forty-eight hundredths
9. One hundred fifty-five and $\frac{87}{100}$
10. Five hundred forty-five and $\frac{67}{100}$

Practice 3 (page 108)
1. 14
2. 17.1
3. 17.3
4. 25.7
5. 22.25
6. 78.54

7. 16.97
8. 1.3
9. 38.14
10. $4.24
11. 18.668
12. 15.169
13. $1,362.25
14. 23.92 yards

Practice 4 (page 109)
1. 36.4
2. 28.06
3. 244.92
4. 199.08
5. 3.4544
6. 24.8
7. 5.50974
8. 61.2
9. 0.0332
10. $345.63
11. $188.07

Practice 5 (page 110)
1. 0.42
2. 1.25
3. 0.38
4. 560
5. 0.03
6. 20.01
7. 79 boxes
8. 22.5 hours

4. Return to Metro Pet Emporium's gross sales listed in the Bell Ringer Activity for this section. Ask students to determine the percentage of the store's gross annual sales ($160,000) that each month's sales figure represents. (Students would use this formula: monthly total ÷ yearly total = monthly percentage of the whole.)

Once students arrive at the monthly percentages given below, have them create a circle graph to present that data in visual form.

January	.054 or 5%
February	.050 or 5%
March	.056 or 6%
April	.073 or 7%
May	.083 or 8%
June	.085 or 9%
July	.092 or 9%
August	.105 or 11%
September	.103 or 10%
October	.091 or 9%
November	.098 or 10%
December	.111 or 11%

To close out consideration of the data, ask the following question: Based on the circle graph, what deduction can you make about Metro Pet Emporium's business overall? (It seems to do a steady business all year round, without such highs as the Christmas season or such lows as the January slump that many retailers experience.)

Close

Have students complete this statement: Charts and graphs make it possible to. . .(see information and thus grasp it more readily.)

Answers

Vocabulary Review

Puzzles will vary. Definitions should be short and can consist of examples, synonyms, opposites, plays on words, and other crossword conventions. Here are some possibilities.

digits: 1–9
fraction: part of a whole
numerator: opposite of
    denominator
decimal number: contains a
    point
percent: stands for parts per
    hundred
circle graph: pie chart

Fact and Idea Review

1. Millions, thousands, and units (ones).
2. A number that describes a part of some standard amount.
3. A fraction or mixed number whose denominator is a multiple of ten. Examples: .35, .4, 1.3, 17.9.
4. If the digit to the right of the one that is being rounded to is 5 or more, you round up. If it is less than 5, you leave it as is.
5. You would divide 5 by 9, which yields the repeating decimal .555, which can be rounded to .56.
6. Estimate before doing the calculation. Also, check the display after entering each number and before pressing an operation key.
7. Convert the fraction to decimal form, and then move the decimal point two places to the right.
8. a. Estimate the answer.
   b. Translate the problem into a math statement.
   c. Do the calculations.
   d. Round monetary amounts to the nearest cent.
   e. Check your answer.
9. A bar graph uses bars of different heights to represent

118

Vocabulary Review

Build a crossword puzzle around the terms below. Use graph paper to arrange your entries. Then write short definitions for them.

digits
fractions
numerator
denominator
mixed number
decimal number
percent
bar graph
line graph
circle graph
pie chart

Fact and Idea Review

1. You should separate whole numbers into groups when you write them in words. What are these groups? (Sec. 8.1)
2. What is a fraction? (Sec. 8.1)
3. What is a decimal number? Give some examples. (Sec. 8.1)
4. How do you decide whether to round a decimal number up or down? (Sec. 8.1)
5. Describe how you would convert ⅝ to a decimal number. Give your answer rounded to the nearest hundredth. (Sec. 8.1)
6. What can you do to increase your accuracy when using a calculator? (Sec. 8.2)
7. Describe how you would convert a fraction to a percentage. (Sec. 8.2)
8. What are the five steps in solving a percent problem? (Sec. 8.2)
9. How is a bar graph different from a line graph? (Sec. 8.2)
10. Where did the term *pie chart* come from? (Sec. 8.2)

Critical Thinking

1. A market researcher plans to present data about purchases of colas by age group. She can't decide whether to use a bar graph or to list her groups on a blackboard in order of size. What should she do, and why?
2. Estimating an answer before doing the math on a calculator is a good idea. What are some reasons for estimating before doing the same problem on paper?
3. Should students be allowed to use calculators when taking math exams? Defend your answer.

4. If the price of the CD in Figure 8-3 (page 116) is $15, how would you find out how much money each segment of the graph represents?

Building Academic Skills

Math

1. Use a calculator to compute the 7.25 percent sales tax on the following individual purchases:
   a. Trousers at $57.00
   b. Cotton sweater at $44.95
   c. Three pairs of men's socks at $2.49 each
   Now assume that one person purchased all of these items at one time. Compute the merchandise total for the purchase and the sales tax.
2. Use a calculator to solve the following problem: You want to start a word processing business. The equipment you want to purchase costs $6,700. If your charges to your customers average $22 per hour, how many hours of work will it take to pay for the equipment?

Technology

3. Use the calculator function of a personal computer to redo the first problem in the Math section above. This time, base your calculations on a sales tax rate of 6.5 percent. Finish by calculating the savings at the lower tax rate.

Communication

4. Each of the following numbers can be expressed in three ways. Fill in the blanks.

Fraction		Decimal		Percentage
⅗	=	_____	=	_____
2⁄70	=	_____	=	_____
1⁄1,000	=	_____	=	_____

5. A customer calls on the telephone to ask for a quote on a case of tennis balls. A case contains 24 boxes of three balls, and each box costs $4.50. You quickly use your calculator to compute the price—$1,080. The customer laughs and says he's sure he can do much better than that. What did you do wrong, and how could you have avoided the problem?

Human Relations

6. You are the supervisor of a telemarketing team. Your records show that the success rate of your workers varies from 10 percent to 70 percent. Do you think it would be helpful to display these percentages in a chart for everyone to see? Why or why not?

---

ferent heights to represent

differences in variables. A line graph uses points connected by a line to show growth or decline in one variable over time.

10. A pie chart is round like a pie, and the segments being compared are shaped like slices of the pie.

Critical Thinking

1. Answers will vary. A bar graph has the advantage of being much easier to understand than a list of data because it is perceived visually almost instantly.

2. The same reasons as when using a calculator—to be sure the final answer is consistent with common sense, so that you catch simple arithmetic errors.

3. Answers will vary.

4. You would calculate the value of each percentage listed by multiplying the decimal equivalent of the percentage by $15. For example, the record company's profit would account for $4.50 of the price (15 × .30).

Could such a chart be used to motivate workers? What incentives might you offer the more productive workers to get them to help the less productive workers?

Application Projects

1. Get some blank checks from a bank and practice filling them out. Write checks to the following:

Del's Ford Dealership	$2,010.05
General Telephone Co.	47.55
Great Food Restaurant	15.86
Radical Clothes	132.00

2. Make a list of 15–20 numbers representing dollar-and-cent amounts (like $23.56, $142.55, $3.09, etc.). Read the figures aloud while members of the class use calculators to keep a running total. What percentage of the class arrived at the correct answer?

3. Suppose you sell electrical parts. In January, you had $15,000 in sales. In February, you were able to increase your sales by 15 percent over the previous month. On a separate sheet of paper, draw a line graph to show the increase you made and a continued 15 percent increase monthly through June.

4. At the library, do some research on sales tax in the United States. Do all states have this tax? If not, which states don't? What is the highest percentage of sales tax and the lowest percentage? Are all purchased items subject to sales tax? If not, which items are nontaxable? Organize your material into a five-minute oral report to the class.

5. Talk to someone in your community who owns or manages a retail business. It might be a small store, a restaurant, or a gasoline station. Find out how much it costs that business every time a customer pays with a credit card. Does the percentage the credit card company gets vary from credit card to credit card? How would this influence some businesses about the credit cards they accept?

6. At the library, do some research on the history of the modern calculator. Trace the major changes in the device from the first one to modern models. What could the early calculators do? What size were they? How much did they cost? Were they designed to be used in business, at home, or both? Write your findings in a 300-word report.

7. Imagine that you have a terrific idea for a new business. If you're like most people, you'll need a loan to get your business started. Go to a bank and inquire about the cost of business loans. If you borrowed $10,000 to start your business, how much would you have to pay each month? What percentage of the monthly amount would be interest on the loan? What total amount would you have paid by the end of the loan term? What difference, if any, would it make if the term of the loan were longer or shorter?

Linking School to Work

Prepare a demonstration illustrating the way you use calculators in your work. Include electronic cash registers, if you work with one on the job.

Performance Assessment

Role Play

Situation. A new employee at the fabric shop where you work has been having difficulties writing up transactions. If a customer purchases an even amount of fabric—say, 3 yards—the new salesclerk has relatively little trouble turning out a sales slip. However, if someone purchases a fractional amount of fabric—say, 3¼ yards—then even a calculator does this new-hire no good. He makes errors at every step of the computation. Your boss has asked you to help him out. How will you instruct him in getting from fractional yardage to purchase total (including 4½ percent sales tax)?

Evaluation. You will be evaluated on how well you do the following:

- Explain how to convert both fractions and percentages to decimal equivalents.
- Describe how to perform basic math operations with decimals.
- Show how to use a calculator to do math problems.
- Evaluate the effectiveness of your instruction and respond accordingly.

Preparing Visual Aids

Assume the instruction described in the Role Play activity above was being given to a small group instead of an individual. Prepare a set of visual aids to illustrate the points you would want to make. Use the medium of your choice—posters, transparencies, or computer graphics.

COMPUTER APPLICATION

Complete the Chapter 8 Computer Application that appears in the Student Activity Workbook.

Building Academic Skills

Math

1. a. $4.13
   b. $3.26
   c. $.54
   Total price: $117.35
2. 304.55 hours

Technology

3. a. $3.71
   b. $2.92
   c. $.49
   Total price: $116.54
   Savings: $.81

Communication

4. 3/5 = 0.6 = 60%

2/70 = 0.029 = 2.9%
1/1000 = 0.001 = 0.1%

5. You should have checked your answer by estimating: $4 × 25 = $100, so clearly an answer over $1,000 would be far off.

Human Relations

6. Answers will vary. Students who are motivated by competition will probably support posting the percentages, while those who are pressured by competition will likely oppose it. Possible incentive for more productive workers to help less: group celebration or outing when *team's* performance floor raised to 50 percent.

Application Projects

1. Checks should show amounts in both words and decimal numbers.
2. Class percentages will vary.
3. Points defining graph's line:

Jan.	$15,000
Feb.	$17,250
Mar.	$19,838
Apr.	$22,813
May	$26,235
June	$30,170

4. Research and oral reports will vary.
5. Interview findings will depend on the businesses selected and the cards they accept.
6. Reports will vary.
7. Loan data will vary with bank, current interest rates, and terms specified.

Linking School to Work

Answers depend on the work situation.

Performance Assessment

Refer to the *DECA Competitive Events Handbook* for evaluation guidelines.

Computer Application

Optional activity. Refer to the *Marketing Software Binder* for template and user information.

Evaluation

Administer the reproducible test for Chapter 8, or construct your own using the Testmaker software.

COMMUNICATION SKILLS

Pages 120–133

Chapter Overview

Chapter 9 covers the basic communication skills essential to clear expression of thought in the business world and in daily life.

 Springboard

Ask students to help you list the various types of communication (listening, reading, speaking, and writing). Ask how they use any of these types of communication in their co-op jobs, in school, and at home. Accept all answers—even such things as listening to music, reading magazines or comic books, talking to friends on the telephone, etc. Tell students that this chapter will help them communicate better both on and off the job.

Prereading

List the section objectives to discuss with students. Have students skim the chapter, looking at the pictures, reading the captions, and noting the heads. Ask questions to ensure that the students have a minimal understanding of the chapter structure.

Preteaching the Vocabulary

List vocabulary terms on the chalkboard. Divide students into four groups and have each group generate meanings for the terms. Limit this exercise to 15 minutes. When time is up, have each group give its definitions. Where the groups disagree in their definitions, use this as an opportunity to clarify information.

CHAPTER
9

Communication Skills

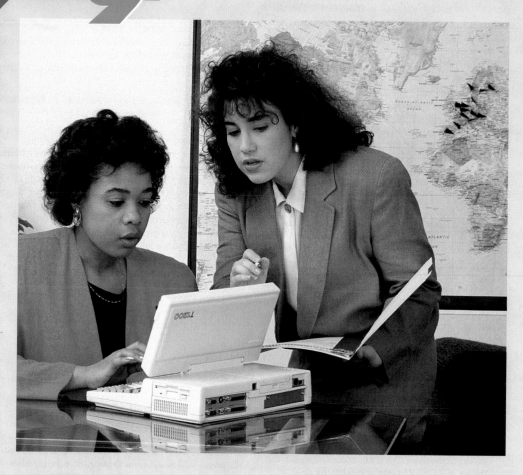

Studies show that, throughout your life, you will be involved in the communication process about 70 percent of your waking hours. Many of those hours will be spent on the job, where good communication skills are essential.

You will have to speak well to express yourself clearly to your employer and customers. You will have to listen well to get feedback from both. You will have to present your ideas in written form, so you must write well. You must read well to understand everything from office memos to employee manuals. This chapter explores all of these communication skills—speaking, listening, writing, and reading.

120   Unit 4   *Human Resource Essentials*

Classroom Management

For the Teacher
- Teacher's Annotated Editions for all workbooks
- Teacher's Manual for *School-to-Work Handbook*
- *Testing Binder*
- *Transparency Binder*
- *Marketing Software Binder*
- *Marketing Career Portfolio*
- *Lesson Plans*

For the Student
- *Student Activity Workbook*
- *Marketing Math Workbook*
- *School-to-Work Handbook*
- *Student Software*
- *International Case Studies*
- *Marketing Career Portfolio*

SECTION 9.1

Objectives

After completing this section, you will be able to

- **explain the six primary elements of communication,**
- **describe how to arrange the setting for a business meeting,**
- **use listening skills to improve your understanding of messages,**
- **list three blocks to listening with understanding, and**
- **practice the three skills that will help you read with understanding.**

Terms to Know

- **communication**
- **channels**
- **feedback**
- **blocks**
- **setting**
- **distractions**
- **emotional blocks**
- **jargon**

The Communication Process

Communication is the process of exchanging information, ideas, and feelings. This process is made up of the following primary elements:

- senders and receivers,
- messages,
- channels,
- feedback,
- blocks, and
- setting.

Senders and Receivers

Simply sending a message is not communicating. Every message must be sent, received, and understood. Both verbal and nonverbal means are used to send and receive messages. Speaking and writing are verbal means. Nonverbal means include facial expressions and *body language*—your physical actions that communicate your thoughts. (We will talk more about this in Chapter 11.)

In face-to-face conversations, you are often a sender and a receiver at the same time. Suppose that you have asked your employer, Mr. Simms, how he wants you to arrange a window display. As he explains the arrangement, he sends a message by talking. You receive the message by listening. As you listen, though, you may be sending a message at the same time—even if you don't say a word. The expression on your face may be saying, "I don't understand." Mr. Simms may receive this message and start over or he may rephrase the message.

Messages

The substance of any form of communication is the message—the information, ideas, or feeling the sender wants to share. Messages can be shared only if they are represented by symbols. Symbols can be anything that stands for something else. All communication is made up of verbal and nonverbal symbols.

Every word is a verbal symbol with a meaning that can be understood by others who know the same language. Avoiding nonstandard language, such as slang expressions and highly technical terms, will increase the probability that your message will be understood.

Channels

Channels are the avenues by which the message is delivered. In face-to-face conversations, the channels are sound and sight; the participants listen to and look at one another. In telephone conversations, the channel is the sound that is transmitted and received over the telephone lines. The participants speak to and listen to one another.

Another channel of communication is the written word. On the job, many messages are delivered in the form of letters, memoranda, and reports. The participants write and read each other's messages.

Feedback

Feedback is the receiver's response to the message. For example, when your employer explains your part in a new advertising program, you will probably ask some questions. This is feedback. You may restate some of the things your employer has told you. This assures both you and your employer that you understand the message.

Focus

Bell Ringer Activity

On the chalkboard, draw two people facing each other who appear to be talking. Have students imagine these two people in a business setting. What types of things will make it easy or difficult for them to listen and understand each other? Allow five minutes for students' responses.

Introducing the Section

Next to your chalkboard pictures, create one column labeled *Easy* and one *Difficult*. Solicit students' answers from the Bell Ringer Activity and list them in the appropriate columns. (Possibilities: interest level in each other's messages, type of business setting, distractions, feedback, and bias about the subject matter of each other's messages.) This section will help them to better listen and read with understanding.

Teach

Guided Practice

1. Read Section 9.1 with students.
2. This chapter deals with basic communication skills. As you work through it you may discover some students who need remedial help in reading and writing. Encourage students experiencing difficulties to speak with you privately so that you can refer them to the proper resources such as the school's guidance counselors or reading teachers for additional information and materials.

   Having good communication skills is more critical than ever for those entering the workforce. Encourage students to get help if they need it now rather than jeopardizing future career success. The MarkEd Resource Center in Columbus, Ohio (800-448-0398) also offers materials in communication skills.

English as a Second Language

If you have students who are not native speakers of English, the telephone can present special obstacles to their fully participating in the business world. Encourage these students to give extra special attention and practice to speaking on the telephone. Depending on the students' comfort level, they may begin these exercises either with someone they know, or for advanced students, by calling the library or directory assistance and asking for simple information. That way, when they must make calls, they will feel less intimidated. Advise students that it is appropriate to say "Would you mind repeating that last sentence, please."

Discussion Starter

Give some examples of body language in which physical actions and positions of the body communicate thoughts and tell what they mean. Bear in mind that sometimes such nonverbal cues can be positive or negative, depending on the person and the situation.

L1 Communication Skills

From the library, or from students' reading material at home, have them photostat a 200-word business-related or marketing-related article from a newspaper or magazine of their choice. After they read the article, have them answer the following questions:

- The purpose of this article is _____.
- Another title for this article could be: _____.
- List the vocabulary words and the jargon that you could not figure out by the way the terms are used. List the meaning you found in the dictionary for each term.
- Did you know anything about the subject of this article before you read it? Did it help you understand the article better?

L2 Communication Skills

Have students either outline the entire article they used for the L1 activity above, or write the main idea of each chapter.

L3 Communication Skills

Have students use the same article they used for the L1 and L2 activities above. Have students find another article on the same subject and compare and contrast the two pieces. How did understanding the first article help them evaluate the second article? Explain that the more they know about a subject, the more critical they become in evaluating communication about that subject.

Feedback is important in communication because it allows participants to clarify the message and know that it was understood by both (or all) parties.

When reading reports, you have little opportunity for feedback. Of course you can respond to a letter or memorandum, but it takes more time than giving feedback in a conversation. The greatest opportunity for feedback is in a face-to-face conversation with another person.

Blocks

Blocks interfere with understanding the message. The three primary blocks to understanding are *distractions, emotional blocks,* and *planning a response.* These will be discussed further under "Blocks to Listening with Understanding."

Setting

The **setting** is where the communication takes place. Outdoor settings are varied and often hard to control. Indoor settings in a job situation may vary from a large hall to a small office. However, you may have control over choosing the room, arranging the furniture, and so on.

When you choose the setting for a group meeting, think first of a room large enough to accommodate those expected to attend. Be sure there will be enough chairs and that they are arranged so everyone can see the main speaker. Check for adequate lighting. If you are giving an

---

Life in the Multicultural MARKETPLACE

When in Rio

Brazilian business customs offer a glimpse of life in Latin America's only Portuguese-speaking country. Business conversations frequently begin with small talk about the weather, local sights, and other pleasantries. It is not uncommon for this small talk to go on for 30 minutes or more. It may be accompanied by another important ritual—the serving and drinking of coffee.

Such drawn out preliminaries have their origins in Brazilian culture, which is polychronic. This means that a Brazilian businessperson may be more comfortable doing several things at once rather than focusing on a single topic or activity. He or she may call a business meeting, then take phone calls, review documents, or make other business decisions in its course. To monochronic Americans and northern Europeans, this can seem rude if not understood for the cultural trait that it is.

audiovisual presentation, arrange for and check the equipment, electrical outlet, and extension cord. You may also want to bring in coffee, soft drinks, and snacks.

When discussing something with one other person in a face-to-face conversation, a small room is more comfortable than a large one. You will also be more comfortable in your own workplace than in someone else's. If you want to make a person feel comfortable in a conversation, go to his or her workplace.

Listening

Earlier, you learned that about 70 percent of your waking hours are spent communicating. Of that 70 percent, studies show that some 45 percent is spent listening. So nearly as much time is spent in listening as in speaking, reading, and writing combined.

Some people never learn the difference between hearing and listening. Hearing is mostly a physical process that takes place in the ears. Listening is a mental process that requires using the brain. Learning to use listening skills is a vital part of being an effective communicator.

Listening Skills

Listening skills help you better understand the messages you receive. These skills involve what to listen for and what to think about as you listen. These same skills help you understand written messages, too.

Identify the Purpose If a meeting has been scheduled to discuss a particular topic, then you know the purpose of the message before the speaker begins to talk. At other times, when meeting with customers, for instance, you don't have advance notice of the purpose of the message. Then you have to identify the purpose from the content of the message. The sooner you can do this, the easier it will be for you to understand the whole message.

Look for a Plan When you listen to a structured speech, try to identify a plan of presentation. Knowing the plan makes it easier to see how different components of the message fit together to convey the whole message. For example, sometimes a speaker makes generalizations and then supports them with specific evidence or the speaker may use contrasts and comparisons or show cause-and-effect relationships. When you know the plan, you can often anticipate what the speaker will say next. You will also be able to sort out relevant and irrelevant information.

Face-to-face conversations between two (or even several) people are usually not as well planned as a formal speech. In these informal conversations, as long as you know the purpose of the message, it is not important to know the plan.

Give Feedback If you are conversing with another person or even in a small group, give feedback to

---

Feature Note

According to anthropologist Edward Hall, the cultures of the world divide into monochronic (single-focus), and polychronic (multi-focus). He classifies Americans, Germans, and most Europeans as the former and southern Europeans, Middle Easterners, and Latin Americans as the latter.

Listening to customers **is an important part of being an effective salesperson. What is one thing this salesperson can do to make sure he has understood the customer's message correctly?**

Cooperative Learning

Divide the class into three groups, and give each group a different verbal message to transmit from student to student throughout the group. The idea is for each student to explain the message to the next in his or her own words. Make the messages complex enough that students cannot simply memorize and repeat them by rote. Give the students 10 to 15 minutes to completely circulate the message. Then have the last student in each group report the message to the class. Discuss what obstacles prevented the message from coming full circle in its original form, or what tools the students used to keep it intact.

Independent Practice

1. Assign and review the Chapter 9 Case Study in the *International Case Studies* workbook. *

2. Have each student take notes on the content of a half-hour talk radio program or a half-hour television show that they only listen to instead of watch. From their notes they should write a 50- to 100-word summary of the contents. They should also answer these questions:
   - What made this assignment difficult or easy for you?
   - Since you could not give any feedback to the television or radio, how did you clarify the intended messages?
   - What blocks, if any, did you experience that interfered with your understanding of the content?
   - Did the setting help or hinder your understanding of the message?

show whether you understand the message. Without interrupting, you can nod your head, raise an eyebrow, or frown. You may have an opportunity to ask questions when the speaker pauses. When the speaker has completed the message, summarize in your mind your understanding of it. If your understanding of the message is different from that intended by the sender, ask the speaker to clarify it for you.

Search for an Interest On the job, many of the messages you receive from your employer or from co-workers relate to your job performance. Since you want to succeed at your job, show an interest in anything that will improve your performance.

You may attend meetings or conferences where you will hear messages that are so uninteresting you want to tune them out. This can become a habit that will cause you to miss important information. Remember, you can learn valuable information from even the most uninteresting message. Listen carefully to find something that interests you.

Evaluate the Message There are times for listening with empathy and times for listening and making judgments. You will need to be able to distinguish which type of listening is appropriate.

Sometimes a friend will express a need to share his or her innermost feelings. This is a time to listen with empathy and understanding. To make any judgment would be inappropriate and cause your friend to feel that you do not care or understand.

In most other conversations and when listening to messages, making judgments can help you listen with understanding. Your mind becomes more actively involved in the listening process when you make logical judgments. However, if you let your emotions get in the way, you will not understand messages you do not like. Always keep an open mind.

As you listen, evaluate the validity of the message. Try to distinguish between fact and opinion and evaluate whether the information presented is relevant to the purpose of the message.

Listen for More Than Verbal Content You know that there is more to the speaker's message than the meaning of the words. The manner in which the speech is delivered affects the meaning of the message. The rate of speech, pitch, volume, and voice quality can add and change meaning. Some experts estimate that 39 percent of the meaning of oral communication is due to vocal cues—not the actual words spoken but the way they are said.

Listen for a Conclusion You may want or need to take action based on the speaker's conclusion, so listen for it. If the speaker doesn't reach a conclusion, summarize the main points and then draw your own. Don't jump to a conclusion before the speaker has presented the facts or opinions to support it.

Take Notes If you are in a business discussion or meeting with one or several people, take notes on the main points presented. Employers appreciate employees who care enough to write down what the employer says.

Follow Directions It is very important to listen carefully when someone gives you directions. If there are several steps to undertake, be sure you understand each one. Give frequent feedback to the person instructing you, so that he or she knows you have understood each step.

Chapter 9   *Communication Skills*   **123**

Caption Answer

The salesperson can give feedback to make sure that he has understood the customer's message correctly.

Assess

Evaluation

Assign and review the Section 9.1 Review.

Reteaching

1. Assign and review the vocabulary terms for this section.
2. Assign and review Fact and Idea Review questions 1–8 from the Chapter Review.
3. Using the vocabulary words and the chapter content for Section 9.1, have students draw a simple diagram of the communication process and label each part. Allow them to draw the process with any types of symbols they choose.

Enrichment

1. Assign and review the appropriate activities in the *Student Activity Workbook.*
2. Assign and review appropriate Critical Thinking questions from the Chapter Review.
3. Choose two high-interest readings that would take about 10 minutes for students to read in class. Give the first reading to half of the class and the second reading to the other half. Have students read their selections and take notes on the content. Then pair each student from group one with a student from group two. Using only their notes, have each student relate the contents of his or her reading to the other student, who in turn, takes notes on the presentation. Have students note how closely the presenter's notes match the original readings. What feedback can the partners give each other about their presentation skills?

Close

Ask students to give you definitions for this section's vocabulary words without looking at their books.

124

Blocks to Listening with Understanding

Some things interfere with or *block* effective listening. Avoid these blocks, and you will be able to concentrate on the message.

Distractions Distractions are blocks to effective listening. They include noises and other environmental factors, interruptions by other people, and competing thoughts that creep into your mind.

Have you tried to listen to a person speak while someone is operating a power lawn mower outside your window? Other environmental factors, such as rooms that are too cold or too hot, can distract you, too. To avoid the distraction, you may decide to postpone a meeting or move to a different area.

Have you ever been listening intently to a message only to have a ringing telephone or a knock at the door interrupt you at a critical moment? When a message doesn't interest you much, has your mind ever wandered? On the job, most messages will be important. So exercise the discipline necessary to keep your mind on the message, despite distractions or occasional boredom.

Emotional Blocks Emotional blocks are biases against the opinions expressed by the sender that block your understanding. If you don't agree with the sender's ideas, it is especially important to listen and understand. Otherwise, you will not be able to give a meaningful response.

Planning a Response Planning your response blocks understanding because you can't concentrate on the message and your response at the same time. When the speaker says something that you want to respond to, it's tempting to think about your response and tune out the speaker. In doing this, you will probably miss some key points in the message and thus respond inappropriately. So, listen to the entire message before you plan your response.

Reading

Reading, like listening, is a process of trying to understand a message. In all careers, reading with understanding is a necessity. For example, to find and apply for most jobs, you have to read help-wanted ads and job applications.

Know the Purpose of Your Reading

You will be a more efficient reader if you determine why you are reading before you begin. For example, when you read a novel or magazine, you are reading for pleasure so you can read as fast or as slowly as you want. When

you read a job application form or a company memo, you have to read every word to be certain you understand all the information.

Read for Meaning

One of the many things required to succeed on the job is reading and understanding written messages. These three skills will help you do both:

- focus your mind,
- form pictures, and
- improve your vocabulary.

Focus Your Mind No one's mind focuses on a subject automatically without effort. Your mind will focus only through constant concentration. When you don't concentrate, the message will be unclear. As you read, monitor your thoughts. If your mind wanders when you are reading, refocus on the subject.

Form Pictures Try to form pictures of the people, places, things, and situations described. When you see elements of the message in your mind, the message is easier to understand.

Improve Your Vocabulary When you read, don't simply skip over unfamiliar words without giving them any thought. If you do, you may miss key points in the message. Try to figure out the meaning by the way the word is used in the sentence or paragraph and then look up the word in a dictionary. This will broaden your vocabulary and improve your understanding of written communication.

In your job-related reading, you will come across some technical terms called *jargon.* Jargon is made up of words that have meaning only in a particular career field. Many of these words aren't even listed in most dictionaries. Most marketing jobs have their own jargon. You will learn many of these words as you study this book.

SECTION 9.1 Review

1. What are the six primary elements of communication?
2. Describe how to arrange the setting for a business meeting.
3. Name the listening skills that help you to better understand messages you receive.
4. Name three blocks to listening with understanding.
5. What are the three skills to help you read better?

Section Review Answers

1. Senders and receivers, messages, channels, feedback, blocks, setting.
2. Think first of a room large enough to accommodate attendees. Have enough chairs. Check for adequate lighting. If you are giving an audiovisual presentation, arrange for and check equipment, electrical outlet, and extension cord.
3. Identify the purpose, look for a plan, give feedback, search for an interest, evaluate the message, listen for more than verbal content, listen for a conclusion, take notes, follow directions.
4. Distractions, emotional blocks, planning a response.
5. Focus your mind, form pictures, improve vocabulary.

SECTION 9.2

Objectives

After completing this section, you will be able to

- describe the three most common purposes for speaking,
- list four basic patterns for organizing a formal speech,
- define parliamentary procedure and its purposes,
- describe proper telephone skills, and
- explain the three basic considerations in writing.

Terms to Know

- parliamentary procedure
- quorum

Speaking

Many jobs in marketing require better than average speaking skills. Whatever your job in any career field, you will need to express yourself clearly so your employer, customers, and co-workers can understand the messages you are sending.

Know the Purpose

Before you formulate what you will say, know the purpose of the message you will send. In most cases, you will speak to inform, persuade, or entertain.

Speaking to Inform In most informal conversations and in many business meetings, the main purpose is to inform. The participants exchange information, frequently changing roles from sender to receiver and back again. When you are speaking to inform, get right to the point. Say what you want to say clearly and concisely.

Speaking to Persuade On any job there will be times when you will need to persuade others to see or do things your way. Perhaps the most important skill in persuading others is determining the listener's needs, then showing how you can satisfy at least some of those needs. This is a salesperson's most important skill. You will look at this more closely in Unit 5, Selling.

BRIGHT IDEAS

Say It with a Smile

How did Southwest Airlines get to be the only consistently profitable major airline in the United States? Certainly not by taking itself too seriously. Southwest flight attendants have been known to wear Groucho Marx glasses while serving in-flight snacks and to sing the safety regulations. When criticized for having too much fun, Southwest points to its excellent safety record (no fatal crashes in 23 years of service). It also has top scores for baggage handling, responding to customer complaints, and on-time performance.

Even though the Federal Aviation Administration has requested (but not ordered) Southwest employees to refrain from singing the safety regulations, it is not likely that they will comply. Southwest claims that the unusual presentation of material enhances passengers' attention to it. In any case, humor has helped Southwest reach the top of its field, and chances are it will keep using humor on board for many flights to come.

Creativity Challenge Form teams of 3–5 people, and make a list of likely candidates for the humorous treatment. Would a singing bank statement work? Would knock-knock jokes improve the VCR instructions? Would rhyme make those utility rate hike requests any more palatable? From your list, select the group favorite and try your hands at the technique.

Speaking to Entertain Sometimes the purpose of speaking is to entertain others. If you are a salesperson, for example, you may need to entertain clients. You don't have to be a comedian to enjoy joking and telling stories. This kind of speaking is usually quite informal.

Using Your Voice

You will need to use your voice effectively to be a good communicator. With practice, you can develop a pleasant voice that is neither too high nor too low. Your voice will sound relaxed if you speak in a medium, even tone. When you are tense, your voice may sound shaky and high.

Chapter 9   *Communication Skills*   **125**

Bell Ringer Activity

Tell students to imagine that the class has been visited by a friendly space alien. The space alien can understand English. However, she has no understanding of the concept of shoes. No one on her planet wears them because all of the soil there is sandy and soft; there are no hard floors or cement streets. Obviously, she must wear shoes while here on earth to protect her tender feet. You and your students must decide what type of shoes she would be most comfortable in. Then have students help you generate the following: (a) a succinct definition for shoes so the alien understands the concept, (b) a list of instructions that tell her how to put on her shoes, (c) tips for taking good care of her shoes.

Introducing the Section

Marketing jobs often require supervisors to train employees in tasks of which the latter have little prior on-the-job experience. Some employees find it as difficult to grasp new concepts as it will be for our space alien to learn about shoes. It takes clear communication and empathy not only to train employees but also to deal with customers from other cultures who may not understand English well. This deceptively simple exercise probably took students longer than they thought and prompted some disagreement and good discussion.

Have students answer the following questions:

1. What was the purpose of this communication? (to inform)
2. How could you use your voice and body language to let the alien know you are friendly and sincerely want to help? (Use a pleasant, relaxed voice and nondefensive body language.)

Bright Ideas

Monotony is the enemy of effective communication. While entertainment can be used effectively in situations such as reciting safety regulations, it is not so much because safety is a laughing matter (it is not) but because it is unexpected and gets the listeners attention.

SECTION 9.2
Teach

Guided Practice

1. Read Section 9.2 with students.
2. Have students read aloud the chapter Case Study and review the answers in class.
3. As you work through the information on speaking skills, ask students what strategies they would use to deal with customers who are not native speakers of English. For example, how would they explain features and benefits of a product, why a product is priced as it is, or a store's return or layaway policies to a person with limited knowledge of English?

Remind students that listening with empathy is important in dealing with people from other cultures because their frustration level is likely to be higher than that of the average customer.

You may wish to supplement this lesson with a discussion of some of the noticeable cross-cultural differences that occur when two cultures engage in business. For example, the Japanese style of doing business has been widely studied and commented upon. The Japanese tradition is to say "yes, we'll see," even when a proposal is being rejected outright. This presents American businesspeople with the task of determining when "yes" means "yes" and when it might mean "no." Japanese businesspeople rely on other cues to determine the meaning of the word.

Have students discuss other examples they may be familiar with. Remind them that cross-cultural differences can also occur within the U.S. such as when more than one cultural group live and work together in close proximity.

■ CASE STUDY ■

Tickling the Business Funny Bone

We all love to laugh. We enjoy remembering and sharing funny lines from movies or good jokes. However, business is serious business. There is no room for funny stuff.

Or is there?

Advertisers know you will remember their products better if they can make you laugh. Now humor consultants are beginning to teach managers the value of laughter in office communication.

"Humor bonds people together," says Robert Orben, who has written numerous books on humor in business. "If you can laugh together, you can work together," he adds.

Humor relaxes people and makes them more open to your ideas. Laughter (even a smile) reduces tension and hostility. It can motivate people. (Which teachers do you work the hardest for?)

But this doesn't mean your business conversation should be an endless stream of one-liners. Humor must be used sparingly and thoughtfully. Getting the message across to others—not getting a laugh—is the most important thing.

Malcolm Kushner (who has taught humor classes to the Internal Revenue Service) says humor should be brief and relevant to the point you want to make. You should not be afraid to poke fun at yourself. So even in the business world, don't leave home without your sense of humor.

Case Study Review

1. Why does humor improve communication with others? Give some examples of business situations in which you might use humor successfully.
2. When can humor hurt your ability to communicate with others? What kinds of humor might keep you from getting your point across?

A MATTER OF ETHICS

3. If a salesperson in your department was habitually telling customers jokes that insulted a social group or were offensive to people, how would you handle the situation?

Case Study Answers

1. Humor can put people at ease, which helps communication. It can be employed in advertising, office communication, sales situations, and even to ease tension at business meetings.
2. Humor can hurt when it is used at inappropriate times—for instance, when someone is angry or having a difficult time in a situation.

Humor that is offensive to the listener for any reason will prevent the message from getting across.
3. Students should feel that they can safely ask the person to stop, or go to a supervisor to help solve the problem.

Speak loudly enough to be heard without blasting your listeners. Vary your inflections by stressing certain words and syllables. Variations of speed and loudness, along with inflections, will make you sound interesting and help you communicate your message.

Speaking Formally

Many jobs in marketing and other careers will require you to deliver structured messages usually sent to inform or persuade. There are four basic patterns you may use to organize a structured message.

Enumeration *Enumeration* is listing several items in order. For example, when instructing a new worker on how to perform a certain task, you may begin by saying, "There are four steps in performing this task." The new worker will listen for four separate but related things to do. The steps will be easier to understand because the listener is expecting them. Use *signal words,* such as *first, second, third,* or *next,* to help the listener. (*Signal words* show the relationship between what you have already said and what you will say next.)

Generalization with Example Many speakers use *generalizations*—statements that are accepted as true by most people—to make a point. Then they support the generalizations with examples and evidence to show that the statement is true. For instance, if you make a general statement such as, "Everybody agrees that the new digital televisions have much better picture quality than the old televisions and will take over the market soon." You should follow it with a statement such as, "The market share of these digital televisions has grown from 20 to 40 percent in the past year. A Sony survey reported 87 percent of owners say the picture clarity is worth the price difference." Using evidence to support your generalization clarifies your message and helps your listeners remember the main points. Use signal words, such as *for instance* and *for example.*

Cause and Effect When you discuss an issue in terms of cause and effect, you lead the listener from the cause of something to the effect. This is an effective way to explain many topics. You can reverse this method by first presenting the effect and then considering possible causes. Use signal words, such as *therefore, consequently,* and *as a result.*

Comparison and Contrast Another good method of explaining something is to use comparison and contrast. You can explain new concepts by showing how they are similar to or unlike those your listeners already know. Use signal words, such as *similarly, however, nevertheless,* and *on the other hand.*

Parliamentary Procedure

If you have ever been a member of the student council or other student organization, you are probably familiar with parliamentary procedure. **Parliamentary procedure** is a structure for holding group meetings and making decisions. It is meant to make meetings democratic and decision making orderly. Parliamentary procedure is used in government, in business, and in social clubs. The rules that govern it vary depending on the contexts. However, certain elements are almost always present. Learning about them will help prepare you for formal business meetings.

A Quorum For a meeting to take place, there must be a quorum present. A **quorum** is a proportion of the membership—usually more than half.

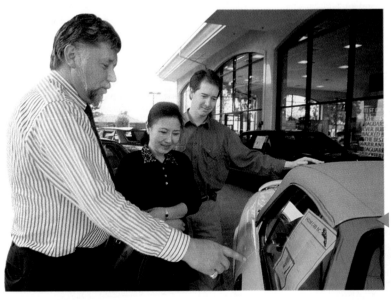

Enumeration **may be used to organize a structured message intended to persuade customers. How would this salesperson use enumeration to persuade this couple to buy this car?**

4. Use the transparencies for this section.
5. Assign and review the Chapter 9 activity in the *School-to-Work Handbook.*

Discussion Starter

Which is easier for you to understand and remember: a verbal message or a written message? (Answers will vary.) Admittedly, most of us have varying levels of attention at different times and in different situations, and students may mention this. However, they are also likely to express a preference for one over the other. A verbal message tends to engage the listener because the latter is in the same room with the person delivering the message and, in most cases, has the opportunity to give feedback for clarification. A written message, on the other hand, allows the receiver to have a permanent record of the message for further study and clarification if need be.

Critical Thinking

Ask students whether the purpose of each message that follows is to inform, entertain, or persuade. (Each message may have more than one purpose.)
- a sales presentation to a customer (to inform and to persuade)
- a report to your supervisor on ways to improve your department's customer service (to inform and possibly to persuade if you want your supervisor to take your recommendations)
- beginning a speech with a funny anecdote (to entertain and catch people's attention, which will thus persuade them to listen more closely)

Tell which of the basic patterns for organizing a structured statement (enumeration, generalization with example, cause and effect, and comparison and contrast) each of the following statements illustrates:
- First-quarter sales far exceeded sales estimates. As a result, all employees received a 1 percent bonus. (cause and effect)

Caption Answer

Answers will vary. The salesperson might use it to list the features of the car or he may list the process that the couple should follow to buy a car.

Did You Know

The term *quorum* comes from the Latin "of whom." In modern legal language, a quorum is defined as the specific number of persons needed to act on behalf of a committee, board of directors, shareholders, or legislative bodies. For example, in order for a law to pass in Congress, a specific number of representatives must vote or the vote is not valid.

Teach (Cont'd.)

- There are four steps in tying your shoes. First, take one lace in each hand. Second, place the right lace under the left. Third, loop the left lace under the right. Fourth, tie the ends of the right and left lace into a knot. (enumeration)
- Belker Department Store switched its retail sales associates from an hourly wage to straight commission on all sales in the department. As a result, employees' salaries increased in proportion to sales increases. (cause and effect)

Cooperative Learning

Have students review the section on Telephone Skills while you write these situations on the chalkboard:

1. An irate customer calls to complain that your company has failed to deliver his new refrigerator for the third day in a row.
2. A customer that does not speak English calls to ask for information on your store's annual three-day sale.

Divide students into pairs. Have each pair choose one of the above situations and generate a five-minute phone conversation between the caller and the receiver. Then have each pair role play the script for the class. Let the class be the judge of how effectively each situation was handled and give suggestions on alternative ways of handling the situation.

Parliamentary procedure is a structure often used to hold meetings. What is the purpose of using it?

Order of Business The meeting follows a standard *order of business,* which is called an agenda. The standard format for a meeting is as follows:

1. **Call to order.** The president or chairperson opens the meeting by saying, "I now call this meeting to order." This statement alerts all members that the meeting is beginning and that they should be quiet. The chairperson's job is to make sure the meeting runs according to the rules.
2. **Minutes of the meeting.** The secretary reads the minutes, which are a written record that outlines the decisions that were made at the last meeting. The president or chairperson asks the membership if there are any additions or corrections to the minutes. If there are no corrections, the minutes are accepted as a permanent record of the organization. If there are corrections, they are amended as necessary.
3. **Treasurer's report.** The treasurer reports the money that the organization received since the last meeting and the money it spent, as well as the current balance.
4. **Committee report.** Committees report on the status of their activities. Committees are set up in organizations to do research or plan events. Each committee presents a report at a meeting to let the entire membership know what they have done, as well as what they plan to do. Committees that exist year after year are called *standing committees.* Other committees may be established as the need arises for them.
5. **Old business.** Any issues that were discussed at the previous meeting but were not decided on become old business. Old business is reported at this point in the meeting.
6. **New business.** New ideas that members would like to have considered are brought up at the end of the meeting.

The Motion After being recognized, or allowed to speak, by the chairperson, one member makes a *motion,* or a proposal. Then, another member must second the motion. If no one seconds the motion, it dies, and no discussion takes place. Once a motion has been made by a member and seconded by another member, a period of discussion follows. Each member must be recognized by the chairperson before speaking. Then he or she has the right to speak for a certain length of time without

Caption Answer

Parliamentary procedure is used to make meetings democratic and decision making orderly.

 More About

Public Speaking

Toastmasters, a nationwide organization dedicated to helping individuals give effective presentations, can provide continued opportunity for practice after students graduate. Members meet on a regular basis and support each other by serving as an audience for the speaker to present a speech on a chosen subject.

being interrupted. When the time for discussion is up, the chairperson asks for a vote. This is known as *calling the question.* A majority vote is usually enough to carry the motion.

Telephone Skills

If you take a job in marketing, you will probably speak to many people on the telephone. A pleasant voice is even more important on the telephone than in face-to-face conversations. Your listener can't see you, so you can't rely on facial expressions and body language to help get your message across. However, you should talk with a smile in your voice.

Answer the telephone with a greeting that is cheerful but formal. Your greeting should also confirm with the caller that he or she has reached the right number. For example, you might answer, "Good morning. AKOA and Company. This is Eddie. May I help you?" If you work in a particular department, you may answer the phone by stating the department name. You might say, for example, "Customer relations. This is Jack speaking. May I help you?"

When speaking on the phone, use your most pleasant tone, enunciate clearly, and speak directly into the mouthpiece. Speak loudly enough for the other person to hear, but don't shout. Listen as well on the telephone as you do in a face-to-face conversation. Develop the habit of being courteous and never interrupt when the other person is speaking.

Be prepared to take a message. Have a pencil and paper ready to write down the time of the call, the caller's name and message, and the return phone number. Repeat the telephone number to the caller to make sure it is correct. Some businesses have phone logs in which to record every call that comes in.

Real World

Well Spoken

Frank Perdue's chicken business was doing well, but not as well as it might, its founder reasoned. So, starting in the early 1970s, the "tough man who makes tender chickens" became his own spokesperson. As a result, his business increased by 500 percent. Today, Perdue Chickens is worth in excess of $720 million.

Writing

Writing a message takes more time and thought than simply having a conversation. However, there are times when it is more appropriate to write your message so you can organize your thoughts, review, and revise your message before it is sent.

Many people forget most of the message in a conversation within the first 24 hours but a written message is a permanent record. A written message can be read and reread until it is clearly understood and then filed for future reference and review.

It's hard to ignore a written message. The person receiving it is more likely to take appropriate action than if the same message were delivered in a conversation.

Basic Considerations in Writing

In every type of writing, there are three basic considerations:

* know your reader
* know your purpose
* know your subject

Know Your Reader Before you begin writing even your first draft, think about the people who will receive your message. Who are they? Why will they read your message? What do they know about the subject? Answer these questions and any others that will help you know your reader. You can write a more meaningful message when you understand your reader's needs.

Know Your Purpose The second consideration before you begin writing is the purpose of your message. Most of your writing will be done to inform, request, confirm, persuade, inquire, or complain. Some messages, of course, combine two or more of these purposes.

Know Your Subject You will need to know your subject well to write a clear message about it. You may learn enough on the job so that you won't have to do further research on many of the subjects you will write about. While you are still new on the job, though, you will probably improve your written messages by researching the topic first.

Develop a Writing Style

Executives usually set the style and tone of writing for their companies. You will probably have opportunities to read company letters, memos, and reports before writing any yourself. This will help you determine your company's style.

The trend in business writing is toward a direct, conversational style. Remember, you are writing to communicate a message to one or more receivers. Use a crisp, clear style that is easy to read. Don't use your business writing to impress others with your extensive vocabulary.

Chapter 9   *Communication Skills*   **129**

Using Your Voice

The phone presents special challenges to those who work in a multicultural environment. Native speakers of English need to think about how some idiomatic expressions sound to those who are not native speakers of English and to practice refraining from gum chewing and speaking idiomatically when they answer phones in a business setting. They also might benefit from knowing what their voice sounds like on the phone. All answering machines have tape recorders that can be used to practice different speeds of talking as well as different phrases.

L1 Communication Skills

Robert's Rules of Order by Henry M. Robert is the classic guide to parliamentary procedure. Bring three or four copies to class. Divide students into three or four groups. Give each group a copy of *Robert's Rules,* and have students find definitions for the following terms:

1. acclamation
2. aye
3. ballot
3. call to question
4. Chair
5. convene
6. have the floor
7. motion
8. nay
9. point of order
10. second table

L2 Communication Skills

Using *Robert's Rules* as reference once again, have each group find definitions for the following types of motions: motion to reconsider; motion to postpone; motion to limit/extend debate; motion to table; motion to appeal; and motion to withdraw.

L3 Communication Skills

Have students hold a meeting on some relevant group project. Act as an observer, taking notes on the things they do well and on the areas in which they need to improve. Ask such questions as:

* If one of you decided to abstain from voting on an issue, would that vote go with the minority or the majority? (the majority)
* What happens to a motion if no one seconds it? (it dies)

MarkEd Resource Center (800-448-0398) offers materials on parliamentary procedure.

National DECA (703-860-5000) offers a concise booklet called *Guide for DECA Chapter Officers.* It provides a good synopsis of parliamentary procedures, motions, and orders of business.

Independent Practice

Look through your local want ads for jobs that interest you, preferably in marketing and sales. Choose one for which you might like to apply and write a formal letter of application that incorporates the eight standard parts of a business letter pictured in Figure 9-1. Write the letter as though you have the relevant experience, discussing the reasons you believe yourself suitable for the job. (You can combine this activity with Application Project 7 in the Chapter Review.)

Assess

Evaluation

Assign and review the Section 9.2 Review.

Reteaching

1. Assign and review the vocabulary terms for this section.
2. Assign and review Fact and Idea Review questions 9–14 from the Chapter Review.
3. Have students tell whether they would write a letter, a memo, or a report in each of these situations:
   - an apology to a customer for defective merchandise she received (letter);
   - an analysis of the features and benefits of two competing products (report);
   - a warning to all employees that they must not ring sales on anyone else's cash register key (memo);
   - a list of your department's safety regulations in case of an emergency (memo);
   - an analysis of a recent marketing survey done on customer satisfaction with your customer service department (report); and
   - a request for product information from another company (letter).

Figure 9–1

BUSINESS LETTERS

Most business letters include eight standard parts.

1. The Return Address is the address of the letter writer. Most companies have their address printed on stationery called letterhead. When you type a business letter on blank paper, type the return address at the top of the page.

3. The Inside Address is the name and address of the person who will receive the letter. The same address is typed on the envelope.

4. The Salutation is the greeting. The most commonly used salutation is, "Dear (Mr., Mrs., Miss, Ms.)." If you usually call the person by his or her first name, you can use it in the salutation: "Dear Adam." A colon always follows the salutation in a business letter.

5. The Body is the message of the letter.

6. The Closing is a respectful goodbye. Formal closings for business letters are, "Yours very truly" and "Yours truly." Less formal, more friendly closings are, "Sincerely" and "Cordially." A comma should follow the closing.

8. Reference Initials are the initials of the writer and sometimes the initials of the typist. They are typed two spaces below your typed signature, beginning at the left margin. The writer's initials are always typed first.

2. The Date Line shows the reader when the letter was written. In business, it is important to document when you write a letter.

7. The Signature Block includes the handwritten and typed name of the writer. Sign your name in ink above your typed name. Write both your first and last name, unless you are on a first-name basis with the reader.

Southland Office Supply

11061 West Olympic Boulevard
Los Angeles, California 90064

August 30, 19–

Mr. Dan Provost
3119 South Barrington Avenue
Suite G
Los Angeles, California 90066

Dear Mr. Provost:

Today we received your written request for four (4) reams of Pale Yellow 24-pound writing bond. We do not regularly stock this special color. Nevertheless, we have taken the liberty of ordering it for you from our supplier, who promises to have it to us in five (5) days. I will call you as soon as it comes in.

Thank you for thinking of Southland for your office supply needs. We look forward to filling this order and to doing business with you in the future.

Sincerely yours,

Jessica H. Johnston, Manager

jhj/seg

Lifelong Learning

Communication Skills

There are many ways for students to improve their voice and their ability to communicate effectively with both small and large groups of people. Many working adults say that early grounding in a Speech or Debate class helped them to get over a fear of speaking in public. By speaking in Speech, Debate, and Drama groups on a regular basis, students experience the wide range of emotions that public speaking can bring on. Most, but not all, students find that this practice leads to increased comfort later on when they must speak in front of a group. For those who still find the experience anxiety producing, speech coaching is another possibility.

Using a word processing program with spelling and grammar checkers helps to eliminate common errors.

Personalize your message by using the name of the person who will receive it. The receiver will have a warmer feeling toward you if you do.

You will probably need to use some jargon in your messages to people in your career field. However, avoid jargon or explain any jargon you must use when writing to those outside your field.

Letters, Memos, and Reports

There are many types of written communications. In business, most written messages are in the form of letters, memos, or reports.

Business Letters The main form of written communication with people outside your own company will be business letters. Business letters are always typed. (See Figure 9-1.)

Memos *Memo* is an abbreviated form of the word *memorandum*. Memos are written messages to someone in your company. They are usually brief and cover only one subject. Look at the sample memo on this page, Figure 9-2.

Like business letters, most memos are typed. However, memos are written in a much simpler format than business letters. They begin with a standard set of headings. Next to the appropriate headings you should fill in the sender's and receiver's names, the date, the subject, and then write your message in paragraph form. Often the language of memos is clipped and informal, since they stay within the company.

Reports Business reports cover such topics as yearly sales, survey results, or problems that need attention. Some are called *in-house reports* because they are to be read only by company employees. Others, such as reports to stockholders, are written for a wider audience. Often an in-house report is written by a company department to let management know the results of a project, or a report might move from one department to another. For example, the sales department may produce a report to tell the design department how customers like a product. Normally several people give input to produce the report. One person is usually responsible for the final writing of the report.

Company Publications

Many marketing companies produce internal publications for their employees. These might include employee handbooks giving policies and procedures, or newsletters. Company newsletters are a good way for management to communicate with all employees.

Companies also produce promotional brochures about the company or about individual products. Such

---

Southland Office Supply
Memorandum

To: All Office Employees
From: Jessica Johnston
Subject: Filling Special Stationery Requests
Date: August 30, 19--

Over the last three weeks, we have received three (3) customer requests for 24-pound writing bond in unusual colors that *we do not regularly stock*. Please fill any such orders from South Bay Suppliers in Santa Monica at 391-4300.

Let me know if you have any questions.

JHJ

Figure 9-2
Business memos are intended for internal company use rather than outside correspondence. How does the format of a business memo differ from the format of a business letter?

---

brochures are often slickly produced and colorful. Employees who help produce them need sophisticated language skills.

SECTION 9.2

Review

1. What are the three most common purposes for speaking?
2. What are the four basic patterns to use to organize a spoken message?
3. What is parliamentary procedure? Why is it used?
4. What types of information should you write down when taking a telephone message?
5. What are the three basic things you should consider when writing?

Enrichment

1. Assign and review the appropriate activities in the *Student Activity Workbook*.
2. Assign and review the appropriate Critical Thinking Questions from the Chapter Review.
3. Assign and review the Building Academic Skills Activities, Application Projects, Linking School to Work Activities, and Performance Assessment from the Chapter Review.
4. Have students write five-minute speeches using enumeration, generalization with example, cause and effect, or comparison and contrast. As students read their speeches aloud, have the class identify which technique was used and whether it was used correctly. Some high-interest topics to consider include the technological developments in personal computer technology, the "hottest" jobs for the year 2000 and beyond and where to find them, and cultural differences in doing business.

Close

Have students write one sentence that accurately summarizes the contents of each topic in the section. (Answers will vary.)

Caption Answer

The memo format merges the date, address, and signature blocks into a single heading. It also dispenses with the sender's full signature.

Section Review Answers

1. To inform, to persuade, to entertain.
2. Enumeration, generalization with example, cause and effect, comparison and contrast.
3. A structure for holding group meetings. It is meant to make meetings democratic.
4. The time of the call, the caller's name and message, and the return phone number.
5. Know your reader, know your purpose, know your subject.

Answers

Vocabulary Review

See Glossary for definitions.

Fact and Idea Review

1. Process of exchanging information, ideas, and feelings.
2. A message must be sent, received, and understood to make communication complete.
3. Feedback ensures that you have understood the directions and that the person giving directions is able to explain any step you don't understand.
4. A smaller room makes people feel more comfortable.
5. Identify purpose, look for a plan, give feedback, search for an interest, evaluate the message, listen for more than verbal content, listen for a conclusion, and take notes.
6. Some situations call for listening with empathy, without making any judgments.
7. It indicates that you think what is being said is important.
8. Try to figure out the meaning of the word from context. Then, look up the word in the dictionary.
9. The call to order, minutes of the last meeting, treasurer's report, committee reports, old business, and new business.
10. With a greeting and the company name and/or your name and department.
11. More opportunity to organize thoughts, review, and revise message before it is sent. Many people forget verbal messages within 24 hours, a written message is a permanent record.
12. Return address, date, inside address, salutation, body, closing, signature, and reference initials.

CHAPTER 9 Review

Vocabulary Review

Use each of the following in a 250-word paper on communication.

- communication
- channels
- feedback
- blocks
- setting
- distractions
- emotional blocks
- jargon
- parliamentary procedure
- quorum

Fact and Idea Review

1. What is communication? (Sec. 9.1)
2. Describe how the communication of a message is a two-way process. (Sec. 9.1)
3. Why is it important to give feedback when someone is giving you directions? (Sec. 9.1)
4. Why is a small room a good setting for a meeting with one other person? (Sec. 9.1)
5. Name the eight listening skills that will help you understand messages. (Sec. 9.1)
6. Discuss when and how making judgments as a listener can be helpful. (Sec. 9.1)
7. Discuss why taking notes is part of being an effective listener. (Sec. 9.1)
8. What should you do if you encounter a word you don't know while you are reading? Why? (Sec. 9.1)
9. Name the six standard parts of a meeting agenda. (Sec. 9.2)
10. How should you answer a business telephone? (Sec. 9.2)
11. What are some of the advantages of a written rather than a verbal message? (Sec. 9.2)
12. Name the eight parts of a business letter. (Sec. 9.2)
13. What style of writing do most companies prefer? (Sec. 9.2)
14. Why would you send a memo instead of a letter? (Sec. 9.2)

Critical Thinking

1. Describe an appropriate setting for an in-home cosmetics presentation and for a stockbroker's meeting. How and why should the two settings be different?

---

2. Why is it important to be a good listener? Which listening skills could help you most in school? How?
3. Describe a situation in which it would be appropriate and helpful to make judgments as a listener. Describe another situation in which it would not be helpful.
4. Choose a career that interests you. Describe how being a good reader could help you in that job.
5. If you were to instruct a fellow employee on how to complete a task, which of the four patterns discussed in this chapter would you use to organize your message? Explain.
6. Your co-worker has asked you to review a letter he has written to a customer. What elements will you look for in his business letter?

Building Academic Skills

Math

1. Communication via the telephone can be expensive. If the rate from 8 A.M. to 5 P.M. for a call from Chicago to Dallas is $.25 for the first minute and $.022 for each additional minute, how much would a ten-minute call cost? If the rate were 35 percent less between 5 P.M. and 11 P.M., how much would you save by waiting until after 5 P.M. to make the call?
2. To send a fax anywhere in the United States, a local business charges $4 for the first page and $1 for subsequent pages (plus the cost of the long-distance telephone call). If a fax machine costs $600 to purchase, how many single-page documents could you send commercially for the same price?

Communication

3. Using a word processing program, write a business letter to the principal of your school, describing a plan to raise funds for new football uniforms. Include all the standard parts of a business letter, and use the spelling and grammar checker feature of your program.
4. Watch the television or a video with the sound turned off. What nonverbal messages do you observe? What can you interpret from them?
5. Using the words peanut butter, experiment with changing the pitch, volume, and intensity of your voice to communicate various messages, such as disbelief, awe, confusion, and uncertainty.
6. Compose a memo telling all employees how to answer the telephone on the job. Follow standard memo format.

---

13. A direct, conversational style.
14. A memo is for informal communication within the company. A business letter is more formal, and goes outside the company.

Critical Thinking

1. Answers will vary.
2. We spend nearly as much time listening as we do speaking, reading, and writing combined. In school, you probably know the speaker's

purpose: to inform. If you are given an opportunity to ask questions, providing feedback to clarify the message is one of the most important of the listening skills. Taking notes improves your learning as you listen.

3.–5. Answers will vary.

6. Student should look for the return address, the date, the inside address, a salutation, a well-written body, a closing, a signature, and reference initials if appropriate.

Human Relations

7. You are a manager of a home electronics store. You observe a new salesperson who is obviously trying to impress a customer with his technical expertise and terminology. You can see that his overuse of jargon is offensive to the customer. What should you do?

8. You have been hired as an accounts receivable clerk at an auto parts store. Another clerk spends a great deal of time browsing through computer bulletin boards for classic car lovers, so that you end up doing most of the work. Because you are new on the job, you don't want to seem like a complainer. How do you handle the situation?

9. Your boss asks you to train a new employee in telephone answering procedure. This person doesn't take your instruction very seriously, insisting that everybody knows how to answer the phone. How do you respond?

Application Projects

1. Observe a conversation among friends. What examples of feedback do you notice?

2. Listen to a structured speech or read a short essay. What was the purpose of the communication? How do you know that? What pattern or structure was used? Make a brief outline of how the speech or essay was organized.

3. Research a marketing career to discover some of the jargon used in that field. List the terms and their definitions.

4. Pretend you are telephoning classmates to enlist them to work at a car wash to raise money for your school. Prepare your telephone speech and act out your phone call in front of the class.

5. Using the eight standard parts discussed in the text, write a formal business letter from your company, Jack's Construction, to Acme Hardware. The hardware store has delivered some faulty pipe to you, and you are writing to correct the situation.

6. Choose a marketing field you are interested in. Use a personal computer to write a business letter to an executive of a company in this marketing field. (Your librarian can help you find the correct address.) Request information about preparing for the career that interests you.

7. In a local paper, read the help wanted ads for a career that interests you. Become aware of the special task involved in reading classified ads:

decoding abbreviations. List the abbreviations you found in ads for jobs in your field. Write what each of these abbreviations means.

8. Telephone your local Chamber of Commerce. Request information about the types of marketing businesses that operate in your area and what proportion of the local economy they represent.

9. Imagine you received Jessica Johnston's memo (see Figure 9-2 on page 131). As a conscientious employee, write a memo to give her some feedback. First confirm that you received her memo and are carrying out her request. Then inform her of four more orders for the special paper. Ask whether this trend might call for Southland to begin stocking the special paper in the near future.

Linking School to Work

Interview your employer to find out how often written communication is necessary at your workplace. How often does he or she need to write a business letter, report, or memo? What other types of writing does he or she need to do? Share your findings with the class.

Performance Assessment

Role Play

Situation. You are a supervisor for a large marketing company. You have just hired an employee and must instruct him on how to write a business letter. How would you explain this task to your employee?

Evaluation. You will be evaluated on how well you can do the following:

- Demonstrate that you understand the purpose of your speech.
- Organize your speech.
- Explain the standard parts of a business letter.

Public Speaking

Prepare a two-minute speech to explain why the communication process is important to marketing.

Complete the Chapter 9 Computer Application that appears in the Student Activity Workbook.

8. Going to the employee with the complaint, trying to get his/her cooperation before going to a supervisor.

9. Explain that procedures for answering the phone at work are more formal and need to follow a routine, to make caller feel at ease and to reflect well on the company. Training often includes motivating a person to want to learn a new skill.

Application Projects

1. Examples might include asking questions or restating what was said.

2. The purpose will vary but in most cases speeches inform, persuade, or entertain.

3. Jargon will depend on the career.

4. Telephone calls should be well organized and clear.

5.–6. Letters should follow the format outlined in the chapter.

7. Review the abbreviations by writing the examples on the board and having students explain them.

8. Answers will vary.

9. Students should construct memos using the format outlined in the chapter.

Linking School to Work

Answers depend on the work situation.

Performance Assessment

Refer to the *DECA Competitive Events Handbook* for evaluation guidelines.

 Computer Application

Optional activity. Refer to the *Marketing Software Binder* for template and user information.

Evaluation

Administer the reproducible test for Chapter 9, or construct your own test using the Testmaker software.

Building Academic Skills

Math
1. $2.23; $1.45
2. 240

Communication
3. Letters should include all key parts of a business letter.

4. Students should list and compare the nonverbal messages they observe.

5. Have various students demonstrate how they would communicate various messages as they say peanut butter.

6. Memos should include top portion with to, from, subject, date, body, and signature.

Human Relations
7. Students should provide well thought-out responses.

Chapter Overview

Chapter 10 introduces students to the world of computers and popular software. It also discusses both current and anticipated uses of specialized computer technology in marketing.

Springboard

Ask students to help you create a chalkboard list of all the occupational areas in which computers are used, along with the ways they are used in each area. (For example, computers are used in retailing and wholesaling operations to process transactions and to scan and store information such as inventory.) Note how many of these occupational areas, activities, and services relate to marketing careers.

Prereading

List the section objectives to discuss with students. Have students skim the chapter, looking at the pictures, reading the captions, and noting the heads. Ask questions to ensure that the students have a minimal understanding of the chapter structure.

Preteaching the Vocabulary

Place a personal computer in your classroom. Point to each part of the computer and ask the class to help you name each element as one student writes the terms on the chalkboard. This activity will serve as a pretest to see how much students already know.

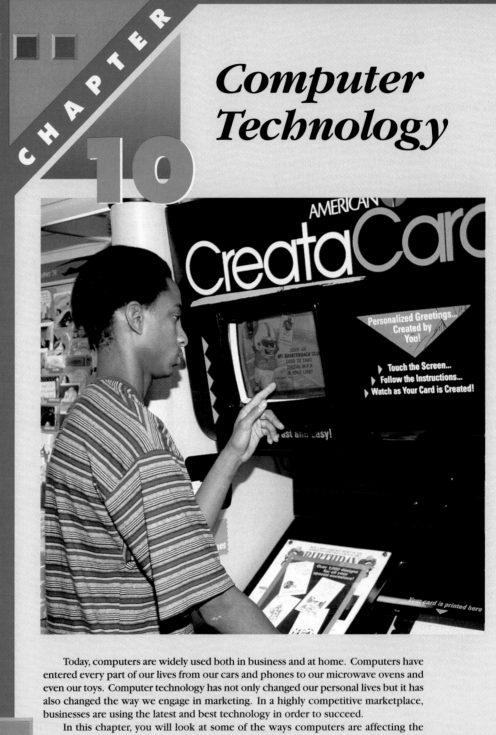

CHAPTER 10

Computer Technology

Today, computers are widely used both in business and at home. Computers have entered every part of our lives from our cars and phones to our microwave ovens and even our toys. Computer technology has not only changed our personal lives but it has also changed the way we engage in marketing. In a highly competitive marketplace, businesses are using the latest and best technology in order to succeed.

In this chapter, you will look at some of the ways computers are affecting the world of marketing. You will explore the ways in which computer technology can be used in marketing to increase efficiency and effectiveness.

134 Unit 4 *Human Resource Essentials*

Classroom Management

For the Teacher
- Teacher's Annotated Editions for all workbooks
- Teacher's Manual for *School-to-Work Handbook*
- *Testing Binder*
- *Transparency Binder*
- *Marketing Software Binder*
- *Marketing Career Portfolio*
- *Lesson Plans*

For the Student
- *Student Activity Workbook*
- *Marketing Math Workbook*
- *School-to-Work Handbook*
- *Student Software*
- *International Case Studies*
- *Marketing Career Portfolio*

SECTION 10.1

Objectives

After completing this section, you will be able to

- list the major ways computers are used to save businesses money,
- name types of computers,
- discuss the functions of basic pieces of computer hardware, and
- define software.

Terms to Know

- **mainframe**
- **microcomputer**
- **hardware**
- **disk drive**
- **CD-ROM**
- **software**

Computers in Marketing

Businesses use computers for numerous reasons. They use them to generate correspondence, maintain lists of customers or clients, and control inventory. They also use computers to create advertising materials, calculate and produce financial reports, and communicate electronically with other computers. Many businesses in today's world could not function without the use of computer technology.

Computers make it possible for businesses to process a large quantity of information with enhanced speed, ease, and accuracy—and at a reduced cost! Computers allow businesses to reduce the number of staff they require, improve their profit margins, enhance inventory control, and come to a better understanding of customer sales patterns. Most businesses find that their investment in computer technology is money well spent.

We are in the midst of a worldwide shift toward expanded use of technology. Fueled by the power of the tiny microprocessor, the silicon chip, we have entered the Information Age. In the early 1990s, U.S. industry spent more money on computers and communications equipment than on all other types of capital equipment combined. This included all machinery needed for manufacturing, mining, agriculture, construction, and all other fields of production. In today's business world, the use of computer technology has become the competitive means of survival.

One effect of the growth in computer technology is that boundaries between industries and professions are blurring. Technological advances in one industry are frequently adopted by others. One example of "borrowed technology" began in the mid-1970s when filmmaker George Lucas (while he was making *Star Wars*) created the special-effects company, Industrial Light & Magic. Industrial Light & Magic began working with digital film editing. In 1984, the Defense Department, while researching the Star Wars missile defense program, contracted with Silicon Graphics Inc. (SGI) to develop workstations. Soon afterward, Industrial Light & Magic was using the same SGI workstations with 3-D computer graphics to create an exciting new generation of special effects for movies. Then SGI passed on some of this technology to other clients like Ford Motor Company. Ford used the technology for the liquid molding of automobile parts. In 1993, Industrial Light & Magic used special effects to create the synthetic, yet realistic, high-resolution dinosaurs for the movie *Jurassic Park*. Ford designers then used exactly the same software to design features of prototype vehicles, thus reducing the need for blueprints. This reduced the time needed for prototype production by 30 weeks! The chain of events described above is just one example of progress through technological sharing.

Computer technology has the potential to revolutionize the world of work. Theorists have predicted that jobs, as we have known them in the industrial age, may disappear. William Davidow, co-author of *The Virtual Corporation,* sees computer information replacing some of what is now familiar in the marketplace. He says, "Much of the current economy is there because of a lack of information. If all the information you need is on your PC, you don't come into the office. That allows you to cut back on office space, secretaries, and file cabinets. This, in turn, displaces the janitor, the heating bill, and the construction worker."

Indeed, statistics show that effective organizations are decreasing in size. Increased efficiency through computer technology has allowed many businesses to reduce their clerical and managerial staff. The types of jobs are changing, too. There is an overall shift away from manufacturing toward services. By the year 2000, it is expected that white collar jobs will make up 60 percent of the work force.

FOCUS

Bell Ringer Activity

Have students take a moment to think of a name for their computers. If you only have one or two computers in class for demonstration, have the class reach a consensus on names for these computers.

Introducing the Section

Naming a computer transforms it from a nameless piece of equipment to a friend with whom you feel a connection. Ask some of the students to share their computer names. Tell them that this exercise will help them see their computers as friends. Students' futures, whatever career they choose, will involve computers. The more they learn now, the more comfortable they will be with advancing computer technology.

Ask students if they can describe the following while you write them on the chalkboard: *mainframe, CD-ROM, word processing, database programs, spreadsheet programs, desktop publishing programs, graphics and design programs, communications programs, point-of-sale (POS) systems, online services,* and *E-mail.*

Meeting Special Needs

Visually Impaired

Sound enhancements in modern computers can be of special interest to your visually impaired students. In fact, many special computerized machines have been designed especially for the visually impaired. One such innovation, the Kurzweil Reading Machine, uses a computer to convert standard written English text into spoken English. The U.S. Bureau of Education for the Disabled has made much use of these machines and they can often be found in libraries and schools. Ask if there are any that you may have access to in your area. Voice-activated computers are also available in some areas.

Guided Practice

1. Read Section 10.1 with students.
2. Use the transparency for this section.
3. If you need extra materials to reinforce and extend the concepts taught in this chapter, Glencoe (800) 334-7344 offers an entry-level computer program for high school students which includes software, videos, and student resource books entitled *Understanding Computers Through Applications.* Glencoe also offers computer proficiency texts designed to apply learning and increase skills, along with business applications software.
4. MarkEd Resource Center in Columbus, Ohio, (800) 448-0398, offers *Computer-EZ,* a 12-video series that introduces the major software packages used by business. Most videos feature a hands-on demonstration of the package. You can use these videos in class or as independent study assignments. MarkEd also offers software entitled *Business Quiz,* and a text-workbook for beginners entitled *Introduction to Microcomputers.*

BRIGHT IDEAS

Envision a New Technology

The computer that you use to produce your resume may be the same computer that helps you find a job. The information superhighway is attracting job seekers in droves with such services as E-Span, Career Connections, and Help Wanted USA. These online employment services and bulletin boards offer job seekers information on job openings at no or low cost. (Some services charge the employer a fee to list the job, while others charge the user but only for the time spent online.) The services also offer employers a special benefit—they help target computer-literate job candidates.

Creativity Challenge Form teams of 3–5 people, and continue your trip down the information superhighway. As a starting point, use a job search or perhaps the "day in your life" described in Chapter 1. Speculate about how computers could transform every activity you engage in or come in contact with.

Types of Computers

Computers range widely in size, cost, speed, and power. The largest and most powerful type of computer is called a **mainframe.** These machines fill a whole room and can be used by hundreds of people at the same time. Mainframe computers are generally used by large corporations, universities, and government organizations.

The smallest type of computer is the **microcomputer,** or personal computer. Since its introduction, this desktop machine has thrived as a business tool. A smaller, portable personal computer called the *laptop* or *notebook* has become popular with salespeople and other people who travel.

In the 1990s, partly due to the ever-plunging cost, the personal computer moved into the home. In 1994, some 32 million U.S. households had personal computers. John Maxwell, a brokerage analyst in Stamford, Connecticut, believes that home computing will be "the biggest growth area we'll see in our lifetime, in any industry."

Computer Components

The components of computer technology are hardware and software. Hardware and software work together to enable a computer to function. Let's take a closer look at these components.

Hardware

Hardware is the equipment—the computer and all the other pieces attached to it that make up a computer system. The major pieces of hardware include a system unit, keyboard, monitor, and printer. All these parts work together.

The *system unit* is the main part of the computer. Most system units contain one or more disk drives. A **disk drive** is used to store information on a disk or read information from a disk. The storage capacity of these disks varies, but rapid developments in technology continually make it possible to buy more storage capacity for less money.

The *keyboard* is used to type information into the computer and to control its action. It looks like the keys on a typewriter with a numeric key pad and function keys added.

A *monitor* displays computer output, such as a letter or computer graphics. A monitor is either a cathode ray tube (CRT) similar to a TV set or liquid crystal display (LCD) similar to digital display clocks or watches. The display is either monochrome (one color), shades of gray (as in LCD monochrome), or multicolored.

A *printer* reproduces an image from the computer onto paper. The image could be a picture, typed text, or a fancy combination of both.

Computer hardware may also include other options. (See Figure 10–1.)

Real World

MARKETING

The Vid Kid

You're never too young to start developing your talents. At a young age, Rawson Stovall bought a computer and became an expert at using it. At the age of 10, he began reviewing video games for the Abilene Reporter-News. Today his column, originally called "The Vid Kid," appears in about 20 newspapers.

 Bright Ideas

Ask students why employers might consider utilizing this new technology. (Recruiting costs are high and all companies are looking for ways to reduce expenses. Online ad costs may be less than the cost of newspaper ad costs. Candidates also prove to be computer literate.

More About

Computers

Computers make it possible for the employees of a company to work productively at home. Many companies have instituted telecommuting positions for those whose work is computer based. Writers, data processors, computer programmers, and insurance claims processors are among those careers where telecommuting is a reality.

136

Figure 10-1

OPTIONS

Typical options include CD-ROM, a mouse or trackball, a scanner, and a modem.

A Mouse or Trackball

is a small handheld part with a button or a ball on it. It is used to move a locator symbol around on the computer screen.

CD-ROM

drives provide high resolution graphics, animation, video, and digital sound. CD-ROMs can turn a computer into a multimedia adventure. They can also handle very large amounts of information, such as an entire encyclopedia on one disk.

A Scanner

takes an image from a piece of paper and translates it into computer information. It can capture a whole page of text or a photo and reproduce it on the computer screen.

A Modem

allows a computer to communicate through the telephone lines with other computers. With a modem, you can send and receive information internationally.

Chapter 10 *Computer Technology* **137**

SECTION 10.1

Discussion Starter

Ask students why they think computers were developed. (Answers could include that as the population grew, as advances in technology demanded more sophisticated ways to process information, and as life became more hurried and complex, the need arose for more sophisticated ways to store and process information quickly and accurately.)

Independent Practice

1. Assign and review the Chapter 10 Case Study in the *International Case Studies* workbook.
2. Students should research the features and benefits of various types of personal computers now available. Ask them to determine the difference between IBM and Apple products, and the features and benefits of both that effect the price and performance of each.

Assess

Evaluation

Assign and review the Section 10.1 Review.

Reteaching

1. Assign and review the vocabulary terms for this section.
2. Assign and review Fact and Idea Review questions 1–4 from the Chapter Review.
3. Using one of your classroom computers, point to each part of the computer and have students name it.

More About

DOS and Windows

Make sure students know the difference between DOS and Windows. DOS is the most common disk operating system. Until recently, most PC programs were written to work with DOS. (Apple and Macintosh computers have their own operating systems.) Microsoft Windows, which runs on top of DOS, is not an operating system but a graphical-user interface. With Windows you can display and switch between two different applications in two window frames on the monitor at the same time. To take advantage of this feature you need applications programs written specifically to work with Windows.

Software publishing is a growing industry. What is the function of software?

Software

Software controls the functioning of the hardware and directs its operation. Without software, a computer would not know what to do. Software is also referred to as programs or applications. Software is written to perform a number of different functions, such as word processing or production of graphics. These functions will be described in Section 10.2.

Some companies need to create specific software to meet their needs. Most common applications, however, are available commercially. In fact, software publishing has become America's fastest growing industry. Major software publishing companies, such as Microsoft, Lotus, Novell, Borland, and Oracle, continually compete to produce the newest, slickest products in this booming market. What an advantage for the consumer!

SECTION 10.1

1. What are three ways that computers can save businesses money?
2. Name two types of computers.
3. What is hardware?
4. Name the four major pieces of computer hardware.
5. What is software?

Objectives

After completing this section, you will be able to

- describe six types of popular software programs and
- explain how these programs are used in business.

Terms to Know

- **word processing programs**
- **database programs**
- **spreadsheet programs**
- **desktop publishing programs**
- **graphics and design programs**
- **communications programs**

Software Programs

Software has been developed to help us manage just about every facet of our lives. There are programs to help us manage our time and money. Some programs keep track of billable hours, then generate invoices that can be sent to clients. Medical practices use software to schedule patients and manage billing. Hotels use software to manage room assignments and generate bills. Universities use software to keep track of thousands of students and their class schedules. Farmers use software to manage their livestock and crops. Architects use computer assisted drafting (CAD) to design buildings. There is even software available to help programmers write more software!

As you can see, there are endless types of software available to meet our needs. In this section, we will discuss six popular types of software commonly used in marketing. These types include *word processing, database management, spreadsheets, desktop publishing, graphics and design,* and *communications.*

Word Processing Programs

Word processing programs are software programs used to create text documents. Although word processing documents are primarily text, they may also contain some graphics.

The uses for word processing programs in business include to

- write letters and memos,
- produce research papers and reports,
- write business plans,
- create contracts,
- record meeting minutes, and
- create announcements.

Word processing makes editing documents quick and easy. Changes can be made on the screen before printing a document. Word processing programs also offer other time-saving features, such as a built-in outliner to help you organize your thoughts, automatic line and paragraph numbering, sorting, and word counting. These features enable users to produce sophisticated, polished documents in a fraction of the time it used to take on a typewriter.

Many word processing programs contain a thesaurus and a dictionary. These features allow you to find synonyms for words and to check and correct your spelling. Some programs include a "grammar checker" that corrects punctuation and grammar errors. These features help users produce more accurate documents.

There are many word processing programs, with a variety of the features discussed above, available in the commercial market. Among the more popular word processing programs are WordPerfect and Microsoft Word.

Database Programs

Database programs are software programs used to collect related data, which can be sorted, searched through, and printed as needed. Imagine the kinds of information you keep track of using a set of 3" x 5" index cards. This is the kind of information you could put into a database instead. Once your information is entered in the computer, the database program allows you to organize and analyze the information quickly and easily. Instead of going through the cards by hand to find information or arranging the cards in a certain order, the database program does it in the blink of an eye!

Database programs can be used to complete many business functions. For example, businesses use database programs to

- maintain customer lists for automated mass mailings,
- keep information about guests and vendors for parties and events,
- catalog furniture and assets for insurance records,
- manage time and track billable hours, and
- catalog personnel records.

Suppose you have entered into the computer your company's mailing list which contains the names and addresses of 3,000 of your customers. With a keystroke or two you could alphabetize all the names or group the addresses by zip code. With another couple of keystrokes, you could display on the screen only those customers who live in a certain location. If you had entered your customers' birthdays, at the first of each month you could easily pull up all the customers with birthdays during that month and send them birthday cards. If you also entered information about customer purchase history, you could quickly pull up all those customers who made purchases during a certain month or who purchased a certain dollar amount of merchandise. Consider the following example of one business' use of database software.

Tim Hilton, owner of Top Dog, a small business that breeds pedigreed labrador dogs, uses a database to keep information about each of his dogs. The database information includes size of litter, gender, name of the mother and father, the color, weight, date born, and feeding record. It also includes the selling price and information about the owner who purchased the dog. Hilton can use his database to quickly analyze his sales records and use the data for future planning.

There are numerous types of database software programs. Some popular commercial database programs are D-base IV, Filemaker Pro, DataEase, and Fox Pro.

Spreadsheet Programs

Spreadsheet programs are software programs used to organize, calculate, and analyze numerical data. With a spreadsheet, you can perform financial and scientific calculations, organize numeric information, and create professional-looking reports. You can also illustrate the data with charts and graphs. Spreadsheets can be used in business to

- develop a budget,
- analyze financial performance,
- track loans or mortgages,
- track stock and bond performance,
- schedule projects,
- manage business assets,
- produce profit-and-loss statements, and
- calculate and produce payroll.

Thanks for the (Better) Memory

Like many immigrants, An Wang came to the United States in the 1940s with little money and a limited knowledge of English. In six years, however, he had a Ph.D. from Harvard and had invented a magnetic core memory that expanded a computer's ability to store information. He sold his invention to IBM and started Wang Laboratories. In 1988, Wang joined Thomas Edison, Alexander Graham Bell, and the Wright Brothers in the National Inventors Hall of Fame.

Bell Ringer Activity

Ask students what is directing their physical actions at this very moment. For example, what makes them able to turn their heads, raise their hands, stand up, sit down, etc. (Answer: they are directing their own actions with their thoughts.)

Introducing the Section

Software programs direct computers to do specific tasks just as your thoughts direct your body. Without software, the computer is useless. So think of software programs as "directors" that tell a computer to do specific tasks such as word processing or desktop publishing.

In this section students will look at six popular software programs used in business—programs that they may decide to purchase for home or office use at some future point.

Teach

Guided Practice

1. Begin by asking students if they have used software programs at home or in their co-op jobs. If they have, ask them to name the programs and tell what they use them for (for example, desktop publishing to create newsletters, etc.).
2. Read Section 10.2 with students.

More About

Computer Related Injuries

Using computers to work and study has made injuries of the wrist and fingers (cumulative-trauma disorders) much more prevalent, but they can be prevented or lessened by learning about correct finger positioning, adding such enhancements as wrist-support pads to the keyboard, and adjusting both chair and monitor.

Feature Note

Wang's invention came to life as a dedicated word processing computer, one of the first of its kind to allow the user to type, store, and retrieve a large amount of text. It featured a menu-based command system that did not assume that the user knew anything about programming a computer. Many of the features of the Wang word processor are alive today in PC software.

Discussion Starter

There are many types of software programs available. Ask students to prioritize the key factors that would influence their buying decision for each of the software applications discussed in this section.

Critical Thinking

Ask students why software programs are called application programs. *(Application means an act of applying or putting to use.* Application programs put computers to use by supplying the "intelligence" that makes them function.)

Cooperative Learning

Divide students into six groups. Assign each group one of the software programs discussed in this section. Have each group research four to eight popular software programs currently on the market and make a chart comparing the costs, features, and benefits of each program. You may wish to combine this with the Chapter Review Performance Assessment Activity entitled "Presentation."

Independent Practice

Allow students time in class to practice on their own with the software your school offers. Meet with each student individually to assess his or her level of confidence and competency with computer and keyboarding skills. You may wish to assign a word-processing exercise in which students must complete several tasks successfully such as using boldface and italics, changing margins, creating numbered and bulleted lists, creating superscript and subscript, etc. Adjust the difficulty of this activity to the level and needs of your class.

140

On the computer screen, a spreadsheet looks like a large grid formed by columns and rows. Data is entered into the squares, or cells, of the grid. A spreadsheet program calculates the data mathematically with amazing speed and accuracy. It can add together a hundred numbers in a column in a fraction of a second. Imagine having to do that by hand, or even with a calculator! Working with a grid like this, you can easily change any numbers you want in the column, and the new total will appear automatically.

One common use of a spreadsheet is to produce a financial statement. For example, many businesses and organizations use spreadsheet programs to analyze their annual income and spending. The data can be used to produce a graphic picture, such as a line graph or a pie chart. A pie chart, for example, might represent a company's spending for the year. Each section of the pie, sized proportionately, represents the percentage spent in a certain way. For example, the chart might depict what percent of the total outlay went toward salaries, building maintenance, research and development, or even toward phone bills! This pie chart illustration might be included in the annual report or in a presentation to potential investors or to a Board of Directors. Spreadsheet programs produce meaningful illustrations that are professional looking and easy for people to read.

Using a spreadsheet program can sometimes reveal information you may not have known. Take the following case for example. James is an area sales representative for Bella hair products. He spends most of his time in the field, visiting beauty salons and other customers in his geographical area. When his manager entered James's sales performance data into the computer, it was clear that there was a dramatic slump during January and February over the last couple of years. Since these were normally slow months, the manager hadn't thought too much about it. However, when he saw the data in a line chart on the computer, it was obvious that the drop in James's sales was much more than that of other salespeople. This led

*Shown here is a **typical spreadsheet screen.** What are two uses for spreadsheets?*

140 Unit 4 *Human Resource Essentials*

---

the manager to wonder what factors might be contributing to James's poor performance during those two months. He called James in to show him the chart and discuss it. James then admitted that during January and February of each year he took a second job as a temporary stand-in for a friend. Working late hours tired him out and affected his energy and attitude for his sales job. James and his manager discussed the situation and came up with a plan to prevent this from happening in the future. The spreadsheet program allowed James's manager to detect a problem he might not have seen otherwise.

There are various spreadsheet programs available to suit different needs. Some popular commercial spreadsheet programs are Lotus 1-2-3 and Microsoft Excel.

Desktop Publishing Programs

Desktop publishing programs are software programs used to design and produce professional printed materials. These programs allow you to combine word processing and graphics. Examples of how businesses may use desktop publishing include to

- create layouts for newsletters, books, brochures, advertisements; and
- create professional-looking forms, such as invoices and project planning sheets.

Many businesses have learned to save large amounts of money by using desktop publishing programs. In the past, they paid a graphic design or printing firm to work for them. Now they can produce the work themselves. Take the following business for example.

Mass Potential is a business that promotes and produces training seminars nationwide. It offers one-day seminars, such as "How to Deal with Difficult Employees," "Time Management," and "Stress Reduction." Using desktop publishing, it produces an elaborate course catalog. It sends out its catalogs in mass mailings (with mailing labels created from its enormous database mailing list). At the seminars, each participant receives a name tag and a map of the area. Both items are produced with desktop publishing. During the seminars, instructors often use overlays on an overhead projector and distribute handouts, both, of course, produced with desktop publishing!

Desktop publishing has become a valuable tool for professionals in all fields. It helps a company put its best foot forward and make a good impression. Desktop publishing produces documents that are creative, eye-catching, attractive, professional, and easy to read. Some popular commercial desktop publishing programs are PageMaker and Corel-Ventura Publishing.

Graphics and Design Programs

Graphics and design programs are software programs used to produce drawings and designs. Graphics programs can be used by businesses to

- create professional-looking illustrations,

More About

Communications Programs

A function of communications software is to link computers through a network. In 1994, Novell Inc., a leader in this technology, signed a deal with AT&T to enable its network software to operate over AT&T's long distance network. This allows smaller companies to link computers via the phone line rather than having to add physical cables.

*Desktop publishing **can make dynamic company publications. What other uses can you think of for this powerful software?***

- design a logo or letterhead,
- illustrate floor plans and furniture arrangements, and
- make flowcharts or seating and organizational charts.

Graphics and design programs can be used to produce simple drawings or elaborate designs. For example, they can be used to create a simple flowchart of the structure of an organization. They can also be used to create stunning artwork, 3D images, technical drawings, engineering graphics, and elaborate diagramming. Sound and animation can be added for multimedia presentations.

You can purchase professionally created art to use with your graphics and design program. You can buy a computer disk containing hundreds of art images or a CD-ROM with thousands of images! This art is generally called *clip art* and is available in black and white or color. The images are usually grouped together in categories like business, food, sports, people, places, animals, cartoons, or holidays. These images come ready-to-use, and you can use them in any document you choose. You can also easily add clip art to your desktop publishing program.

There are many graphics and design programs. Some popular ones include Adobe Illustrator, Aldus Freehand, and Corel Draw.

Communications Programs

Communications programs are software programs used to establish communication between your computer and other computers. They are often referred to as telecommunications. To run a communications program, you need a modem which allows the computer to send information through a telephone line. You can use communications software to transfer files directly from one computer to another. A few of the popular commercial communications programs are ProComm, Smartcom, and Microsoft Mail.

Communications software enables you to access online services which provide users with information and services. Online services include noncommercial bulletin board services (BBS); more sophisticated commercial online services, such as Prodigy, CompuServe, or America Online; and Internet. Some current and future uses of online services will be discussed in Section 10.3.

SECTION 10.2

Review

1. **Name six types of software programs commonly used by businesses.**
2. **Give an example of how each type of software program you listed in question #1 can be used in business.**

Evaluation

Assign and review the Section 10.2 Review.

Reteaching

1. Assign and review the vocabulary terms for this section.
2. Assign and review Fact and Idea Review questions 5–10 from the Chapter Review.
3. Have students orally review the purpose of the six software programs discussed in this section.

Enrichment

1. Assign and review the appropriate activities in the *Student Activity Workbook*.
2. Assign and review the appropriate Critical Thinking questions from the Chapter Review.
3. Have students research how a computer runs software. Specifically, they should describe the microprocessor, random-access memory (RAM), and hard disk capacity.

Close

Have students complete this statement: The six popular types of software programs discussed in this section include...(word processing, database management, spreadsheets, desktop publishing, graphics and design, and communications.)

Section Review Answers

1. Word processing, database programs, spreadsheet programs desktop publishing programs, graphics and design programs, communications programs.
2. Word processing: type letters and documents; Database: maintain address lists; Spreadsheets: develop a budget; Desktop publishing: create newsletters; Graphics and design: design a logo.

Caption Answer

Magazines, newspapers, books, and advertising can all be typeset using desktop publishing software.

141

SECTION 10.3

Objectives

After completing this section, you will be able to

- name types of computer systems that are affecting the world of marketing and

- discuss the future of computer technology.

Terms to Know

- point-of-sale (POS) system
- online services
- E-mail

Specialized Computer Technology for Marketing

The uses for computer technology in marketing are endless. In addition to the software programs discussed in Section 10.2, there are several computerized systems helping to shape the way we conduct business today. These include *point-of-sale systems, online services, electronic mail, interactive videodiscs,* and *interactive TV.*

Point-of-Sale Systems

A common use of computers in retailing is the **point-of-sale (POS) system.** This system uses light pens, hand-held laser guns, stationary lasers, or slot scanners to feed information directly from merchandise tags or product labels into a computer. This information can be used to update inventory and give a business detailed information about purchasing patterns. POS systems will be discussed further in Chapter 18 and Chapter 27.

Online Services

Online services allow people to use computers to access services and information. As you read in the previous section, online services include noncommercial bulletin board services, commercial online services, and Internet.

Bulletin Board Services Noncommercial bulletin board services (BBS) allow people to use their computers to exchange information at no charge or for a minimal fee. Across the world, there are thousands of noncommercial bulletin board services (BBS). If you have a modem and communications software, you can access a BBS. Some bulletin boards are set up to focus on certain interest groups. Some are school run bulletin boards. Noncommercial bulletin board services usually provide less extensive information and services than commercial online services, but allow people to send and receive information nevertheless.

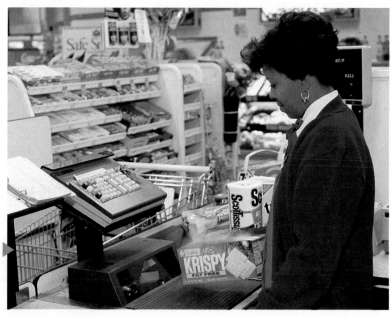

POS systems have revolutionized the grocery business. Besides giving the customer detailed information about products, what else can a POS system do?

142   Unit 4   *Human Resource Essentials*

Internet Shopping Network

File Edit View Go Bookmarks Options Directory   Help

Location: http://www.internet.net/

Internet Shopping Network

GUIDED TOUR   MEMBERS ONLY   MEMBERSHIP OFFICE

SELECT A DOOR ABOVE OR A LINK BELOW

http://www.internet.net/cgi-bin/imagemap/front

The number of Internet users is growing rapidly. What are the major features of Internet that make it popular with users?

Commercial Online Services Commercial online services provide services and information to their subscribers for a monthly fee. Commercial online services give customers access to news, shopping, weather forecasts, airline schedules, databases for research, and bulletin boards for communicating with other users. Using an online service, a subscriber could reserve airline tickets, shop for a car, purchase some flowers, preview movies, and check the weather—all from the comfort of home!

Commercial online services are playing a growing and exciting role in marketing. As of 1994, Prodigy, CompuServe, and America Online had 3.5 million subscribers collectively. The dollar volume on CompuServe's Electronic Mail is growing 30 percent to 40 percent annually. These subscribers have demonstrated that online services are a viable marketing tool for purchasing products.

Commercial online services are also widely used to promote products. Companies regularly provide presentations and demonstrations online. Movie makers provide clips of new movies for subscriber preview. Music publishers provide samples from upcoming albums. In 1993, the Ford Motor Company used Prodigy's National Football League Stadium Club forum to build excitement about the upcoming release of its new Mustang. Months before its release, Ford began showing on the computer the stages of the Mustang being built. It started by showing the wheels and frame, then every other week more parts were added. Finally, the fully assembled vehicle appeared on the same date as the new Mustang's official introduction.

Savvy marketers feel that commercial online services are also the perfect avenue for building customer relationships. Online, a business can communicate with customers on an ongoing basis, bring them into the planning phases, and find out how they liked a product after they have purchased it.

Online services allow marketers to measure consumer response to a product. When users access a presentation or a demo online, marketers instantly know it. A company gets instant feedback. If the feedback is negative, that allows the company to change the product accordingly. Some marketing agencies perceive online services to be the marketing medium of the future.

Internet You've probably heard about the Internet, called the information superhighway. It is the world's largest computer network and connects smaller networks to each other. A U.S. military research network founded Internet in 1969. Later, it was expanded to connect mostly academic institutions. Today, all kinds of people, including businesspeople, researchers, educators, consumers, activists, students, and military personnel, use the Internet to exchange information daily. In 1994, there were approximately 18,000 separate computer networks on the Internet, connecting more than 20 million computers! Analysts predict that by the beginning of the 21st century there will be about 100 million Internet users.

Using the Internet, you can connect with other computers, search databases, sell and purchase products, and participate in international discussion groups. For example, you could look up information in the library at the University of Madrid, Spain, or you could receive an interesting piece of information from a person in Hong Kong.

There are international discussion groups on every topic from quantum physics to motorcycle repair. There

Chapter 10   *Computer Technology*   **143**

Caption Answer

The Internet allows you to connect with other computers, search databases, sell and purchase products, and participate in international discussion groups.

Did You Know ?

Add to the list of things you can do online the prospect of getting a degree. The university of Phoenix allows students the option of attending classes online to receive both undergraduate and graduate degrees. Students' classes are online by modem. Such programs require good work habits and a self-motivated individual but can be a boon to people who have full-time jobs.

Teach

Guided Practice

1. Read Section 10.3 with students.
2. Have students read aloud the Case Study and review the answers in class.
3. You or someone in your school may already subscribe to an online service and/or use E-mail. If so, set aside class time or set up a demonstration time with your colleague to show students how online services and E-mail work.
4. Assign and review the Chapter 10 Activity in the *School-to-Work Handbook*.

Discussion Starters

Students should understand the proper care and maintenance of computer equipment in the workplace. (This is also a required competency in many tech-prep programs.) Discuss some of the ways to care for computers, printers, and disks. (Answers will vary but could include the following. Use a dust cover on PCs and printers. Don't touch the shiny parts of floppy disks and always return disks to a dust-free box. Never allow anyone to smoke, eat, or drink near your computer. Never leave floppy disks near your computer or printer because the magnetic waves in the motor of each can destroy information on your disk. Don't jar or jiggle computers because you may loosen soldered joints or electronic cards that have been snapped into the computer. Never remove or disconnect cables while the computer is turned on. Never turn off a computer or remove a disk from a disk drive while the drive is still turning. Don't pile books on top of your monitor. *Never try to fix a computer yourself.)*

As you have read in this chapter, computerization of the business world has eliminated many jobs once done by people instead of machines. This may greatly minimize your "people contact" in the workplace. Ask students to discuss the positive and negative consequences of interacting with few people throughout the day in the course of your job. (One positive consequence is that contact with fewer people means fewer distractions and more work accomplished. It could also possibly mean less conflict with other workers. Negative consequences include a sense of isolation along with loss of the opportunity to share ideas, brainstorm, and solve problems.)

L1 Communication Skills

Although software programs contain spell checkers and grammar checkers, nothing takes the place of proofreading when it comes to correcting your letters, memos, reports, and manuscripts. Tell students to look in a dictionary or editorial style book for the common proofreader's marks and copy them on a sheet of paper to keep permanently in their notebooks. Review each of the marks with your students and tell them that this "shorthand" is a common "language" that proofreaders have used for decades.

L2 Communication Skills

Give students an editing test with many errors in it to check their understanding of proofreaders' marks and their current level of editorial skill. When they have finished, review the test with the class and have students assess their own level of editorial skill. What common errors did they always seem to miss? Punctuation? Grammar? Spelling? Where do they need to improve?

---

are discussion groups, for example, for singles, for environmentalists, and for people with disabilities. There are even discussion groups for people who want to talk about the most recent television episode of "Friends" or about "Star Trek" trivia! Users have conversations by selecting a discussion group from a list, then entering messages into their computers. These messages then appear on the computer screens of others who are tuned in to that discussion group.

Many of the discussion groups deal with the uses of particular products. By viewing these areas, marketers can learn what their customers are saying about their products, offer service information, and ask for feedback to improve the product. Television producers, for example, often tune in to get feedback on their programming.

Electronic Mail (E-mail)

A popular use of telecommunications is electronic mail (E-mail). **E-mail** is mail prepared on a computer and sent to someone else who has a computer. Each user has a personal address. Instead of going to the mailbox and picking up paper mail, the receiver goes to the computer and reads his or her E-mail on the screen. It can be printed out on a printer if needed. E-mail is fast. Depending on how much other mail is being sent at the same time, E-mail can be transmitted either instantly or within an hour.

E-mail can be sent using the Internet, a commercial online service, or a small private bulletin board. Some large corporations maintain their own E-mail systems for communicating instantly with other employees, whether they are in the head office or in a branch office on the other side of the world. These private systems give the company great control, because no one from outside the company can use them. Microsoft, for example, maintains a private E-mail system to exchange information with its team of Solution Providers (people out in the field who assist customers with Microsoft products).

Culturally Informed Computers

Life in the Multicultural MARKETPLACE

Kiss, bow, or shake hands— these are the three principal ways that people around the world greet each other. They are also the title of a software program that helps businesses sort out the cultural differences that could affect their operations abroad. The program contains detailed information on more than 60 different cultures. In addition to greetings, it provides information on foods, gestures, personal space, and customer behavior.

144   Unit 4   *Human Resource Essentials*

E-mail's advantage is its speed. For example, an appliance store employee can use E-mail to enter an order for new merchandise into a computer. The order is instantly sent to the electronic address of the shipper. The shipper can acknowledge the order within minutes, and the merchandise can be readied for shipping almost immediately. E-mail proponents also find it convenient, economical, and ecological—no envelopes, stamps, or long-distance phone calling are needed!

Interactive Videodisc— The Computerized Salesperson

In retail marketing, there is a strong move toward the greater use of interactive technology. Interactive technology allows consumers to correspond with the computer. Interactive computers are frequently placed on shelves in retail stores and in stand-alone kiosks in malls and airports. The customer reads questions on the touch-sensitive screen and answers the questions by touching the appropriate word or box. In this way, the "computerized salesperson" directs the customer to the correct product.

Cosmetic companies, such as Clairol and Cover Girl, use on-shelf computers to help consumers choose the right shade of hair color or eye shadow. Office supply stores provide an on-shelf computer to help customers select the correct replacement ribbon or cartridge for their computer printers. Did you ever want to buy a piece of music but couldn't remember the performer's name? Some music stores use an interactive computerized kiosk to assist customers in identifying a piece of music even if they can only remember a few words. Wedding registries in department stores are often computerized. By typing in either of the couple's names and pressing the appropriate boxes on the screen, you can find the perfect wedding gift.

Warner-Lambert's Canadian division, a maker of health care and consumer products, has installed on-shelf computers in the cough-cold sections of more than 600 drugstores. The computers help consumers choose the appropriate product for their symptoms. The computer asks a series of questions about symptoms before recommending one of 26 products, 16 of which are Warner-Lambert products. (Warner-Lambert's computer is unusual in that it sometimes recommends competing brands!) It then describes the packaging so consumers can find the product.

Interactive TV

During the 1994 Super Bowl, the Chrysler Corporation used a new interactive television system for the first time. The system was used to measure viewer response to ads for the Neon, Chrysler's new small car. Interactive viewers answered survey questions through the use of a wireless laptop device. Chrysler was very pleased with the results.

Lifelong Learning

Computer Technology

New computer improvements and developments happen weekly, monthly, and quarterly. In order to keep current of changes students should read at least one computer magazine on a regular basis. Two good general magazines are *PC World* and *PC Magazine*. Both offer industry updates and new information along with the results of consumer and industry surveys of new and existing products. In addition to reading, however, it is most important that students have a regular opportunity to try out new software and other products and to learn to use the most popular programs. This can be achieved by taking classes or by volunteering at work to attend training seminars.

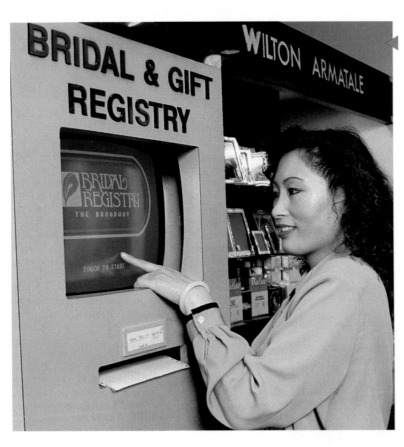

This interactive computer holds a database of bridal registries. Friends of registered parties can use the computer to select a wedding gift. What else are interactive computers used for?

L3 Communication Skills

After you have completed the L1 and L2 Activities, have each student make up an editing test, bring it to class, and exchange his or her test with another student. Then have each student review the other's test.

Independent Practice

What are the latest advances in computer technology and software for sales and marketing? Have students research current business publications and computer publications for at least one new product.

They should write a 50-word summary of what it is and what it does, and share it with the class. (Answers will vary. Sales and marketing software development has grown steadily since the mid-1990s. For example, Contact Management/Personal Information Managers help salespeople and managers keep track of whom they're talking to, when they're contacted, and what the customers want. Other products such as laptop and notebook computers have become not only helpful tools in the workplace but status symbols and coveted perks.)

Assess

Evaluation

Assign and review the Section 10.3 Review.

Today, companies are exploring the potential of interactive television. They are developing and testing ways in which interactive television can be used for advertising and promotion. Businesses are trying to determine what types of interactive TV work best and what consumers consider to be intrusive. Most agree, however, that this technology will play an important role in the future. Says Chrysler spokesman Scott Fosgard, "We're in the early stages of this new technology, and we know that it's going to revolutionize the way companies advertise."

The Future of Computer Technology

Computing power, which was once considered awesome, now seems trivial. Have you ever seen one of the greeting cards that plays a song, such as "Happy Birthday" or "Jingle Bells," when you open it? That little card has more computer processing power than what existed in the entire world before 1950! Today, a home video camera uses more processing power than the old IBM 360, the machine that launched the mainframe age. Sega, the game maker, will soon introduce a system called Saturn, which uses a higher-performance processor than the original 1976 Cray supercomputer, accessible only to the most elite physicists at the time.

We can expect this amazing increase in computer power to continue. What we can do on the phone now, we will be able to do with sight, sound, and motion on full-service networks in the future. Intel, a computer company, is already demonstrating its personal digital video-conferencing system. It is a personal computer with a camera on top and an earphone attached. It lets you talk with and look at someone as you transfer documents back and forth.

What more is to come? Marketers agree that we have seen only the tip of the iceberg.

In the world of banking, Charles Sanford, chairman of Bankers Trust, foresees "true global banking"—a financial marketplace in which everyone is linked through computer and telecommunications technology. Individual households, companies, investors, and governments will be connected with financial institutions. Transactions will be instantly received from anywhere in the world through voice recognition and DNA fingerprinting technologies.

Enormous technological strides are also predicted to occur in the automobile industry. Joe Groman, chief of

Chapter 10 *Computer Technology* **145**

Reteaching

1. Assign and review Fact and Idea Review questions 11–15 from the Chapter Review.
2. Have students write one or two sentences about each major section in this lesson to briefly summarize the concepts.

Enrichment

1. Assign and review the appropriate activities in the *Student Activity Workbook*.
2. Assign and review the appropriate Critical Thinking questions from the Chapter Review.
3. Students who work in an office are likely to work on a LAN (local-area network) which allows coworkers to share hard disk drives, printers, modems, and software. It's important to be LAN literate, particularly if you expect to run your own business and will someday be making the decision about whether to install one.

   Have students research the structure of a basic LAN, telling what it is and the elements it includes, and the pros and cons of working on one. (Answers will vary. A LAN connects any number of computers, printers, and peripheral devices in a local area. With the Internet, LANs can be linked to other LANs [for example, branch offices in the same firm]. A LAN includes

CASE STUDY

Predicting the Future

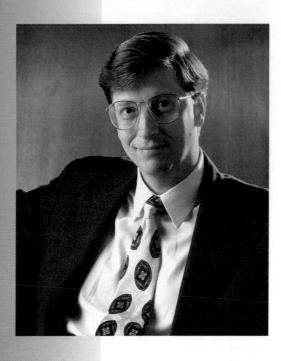

Microsoft Corporation has always been in the forefront of the microcomputer technology revolution. In 1973, Bill Gates and his classmate Paul Allen started the company. They were 18 years old and still students. Today, Gates is one of the wealthiest men in America with a net worth approaching $8 billion. Microsoft is the biggest software producer in the world. Its operating system, MS-DOS, is used in 85 percent of all microcomputers.

Often, technology companies become so good at making a certain kind of equipment or software that they stop looking at what new technologies may arise. When that happens, they get left behind. Gates and Microsoft don't want to make that mistake. Microsoft is making big investments in research and development of products that will give customers access to the information superhighway.

"The advances in communication will create new ways of using communication for learning, education, and commerce that go far beyond anything done to date," Gates says. The company has recently introduced a software project called Tiger, which will make digitized movies and television available to cable and phone subscribers with interactive television. It is also developing the

software people will need in order to hook up to Tiger's programming!

A division of the company currently produces CD-ROM disks for education and entertainment, but its eye is on the future, too. It is creating a market for the interactive services that the information superhighway will make available: its CD-ROM disks tie in to future interactive programming.

Another of Gates's ideas being developed is what he calls a "wallet PC." This is an electronic version of all the things you normally carry with you—shopping lists, calendars, credit cards, maps, even money! You would have a constant electronic connection to your bank account, so that you could pay for things without ever handing over a thing. Doing business on the Internet will one day require this kind of electronic money. Microsoft is trying to get a head start in the market.

At the same time, the company continues to upgrade its traditional software. The newest version of its popular Windows software, code named Chicago, includes many long-awaited improvements in ease of use and power. It also includes the capability to go on-line with the click of a mouse. That will eliminate the need for separate communications software among Windows users and give Microsoft a big advantage in the electronic mail business.

It's easy to see how Microsoft spends $500 million a year on research and development. Doing exploration on the future is expensive. It's risky. But in Microsoft's case, it is also likely to be quite profitable.

Case Study Review

1. Why might some companies decide to continue making the same computers for many years, rather than exploring new products for future markets?
2. What steps is Microsoft taking to make sure that it will not be left behind in terms of computer technology?

A MATTER OF ETHICS

3. When Microsoft introduced Windows software, many people felt it was a copy of Apple Computer's Macintosh operating system with its graphical display. What ethical concerns do you see in copying your competitors' products?

146   Unit 4   *Human Resource Essentials*

Case Study Answers

1. Answers will vary. Less risky. May be looking at profits only, instead of thinking of customer needs.
2. Microsoft is making big investments in research and development of products that will give customers access to the information superhighway.
3. Answers will vary. Copyright infringement is a possibility. Some may think Microsoft should pay a royalty to Apple.

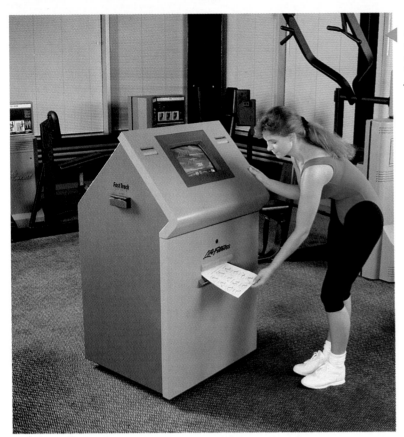

New uses for computers are continuously emerging. The LifeCenter, shown here, is used in gyms to monitor fitness levels. Name ways in which computers may be used in the future.

workstations [personal computers with a network interface card plugged into one of its expansion slots], a server [a computer that services the workstations], and the network tying them all together. Client server networks send large amounts of information to and from workstations. With peer-to-peer networks, every workstation is a peer because it has equal status and can exchange data with any other station. With LANs you share files, software programs, and equipment. This reduces your time and cost in purchasing separate units for each computer. When the network is down, however, all workstations are down and you lose time and sometimes information you have input. LANs are expensive to install and require a great deal of maintenance by trained personnel.)

4. Assign and review the Building Academic Skills Activities, Application Projects, Linking School to Work Activities, and Performance Assessment from the Chapter Review.

Close

Have students tell you how they plan to use computers in the course of their co-op jobs, at home, or in school. Ask them which computer skills they need to improve, what they want to learn more about, and how they plan to do both.

Help schedule practice time in school for those students who do not have computers at home.

TRW, the world's fourth-largest maker of auto parts, sees a bright future for the automobile. He says, "Think of the automobile as one big system filled with information technology. The future will hold all kinds of advanced systems." They will include smart cruise control with a single radar chip for receiving and sending signals to avoid hitting the car in front of you and radar for lane changing. They will also include diagnostic systems so the car can help fix itself. "Technology," says Groman, "is at the core of everything we're doing."

Dick Hammill, senior vice president for marketing and advertising for Home Depot, is sure that communications will also change retailing. On visions for Home Depot's future he says, "You've got a library, and it's on a chip. Number 489 is home improvement. Number 489A is how to refinish cabinets. Number 489B is how to plant tulips. It costs a nickel a minute to access this library online. You get all the information you need, and then all of a sudden, interactively, you can order the stuff." He also envisions an all-electronic catalog on CD-ROM with lines of Home Depot home improvement books and other products.

According to Bill Gates, founder and CEO of the megacorporation Microsoft, "In another ten years, most

decisions—hiring a part-time worker for your home, buying a consumer product, choosing a lawyer—will be made on a much more informed basis because of electronic communication. If I want to pick a bank, I cannot only compare [its] offerings with other banks', I can see what [its] customers have to say about [it]. I can ignore geographic limits to my shopping. It changes the nature of competition, which becomes pure because you can no longer benefit from customer ignorance. If you believe in markets—and I love markets—this is a good thing. It makes all markets work more efficiently."

SECTION 10.3 Review

1. Name five types of computer systems that are making an impact on business.

2. What is one change in computer technology that is expected in the future?

Chapter 10   *Computer Technology*   **147**

Caption Answer

Answers will vary. Computers will be used increasingly in interactive marketing situations.

Section Review Answers

1. These include point-of-sale systems, on-line systems, electronic mail, interactive videodiscs, and interactive TV.

2. Answers will vary. Some changes include an increase in computer power and computer use in all industries.

Answers

Vocabulary Review

See Glossary for definitions.

Fact and Idea Review

1. A mainframe is the largest and most powerful type of computer. A microcomputer is the smallest type of computer.
2. A CD-ROM.
3. A modem allows a computer to communicate through the telephone lines with other computers.
4. The software is what tells the computer what to do and how to operate.
5. Word processing is faster than typing, easier to edit, and you can check spelling and grammar.
6. It is a software program used to collect related data, which can be sorted, searched through, and printed as needed.
7. It is a software program used to organize, calculate, and analyze numerical data.
8. When you want to combine word processed text with graphic design elements.
9. It is used to produce drawings and designs.
10. When you want to establish communication between your computer and other computers.
11. It is used to feed information directly from merchandise tags or products into a computer.
12. Noncommercial bulletin board services, commercial online services, and Internet.
13. It is faster, cheaper, and more reliable.
14. Answers will vary. For example, it can be used to help a consumer select a product.
15. Chrysler used interactive TV to measure viewer response to ads for the Neon.

148

Vocabulary Review

Choose eight of the words below and write a 250-word paragraph explaining how you would use a computer in business.

mainframe
microcomputer
hardware
disk drive
CD-ROM
software
word processing programs
database programs
spreadsheet programs
desktop publishing programs
graphics and design programs
communications programs
point-of-sale (POS) system
online services
E-mail

Fact and Idea Review

1. What is the difference between a mainframe and a microcomputer? (Sec. 10.1)
2. What type of computer option do you need in order to produce high resolution graphics and animation on your computer? (Sec. 10.1)
3. What does a modem do? (Sec. 10.1)
4. Why is software necessary for using a computer? (Sec. 10.1)
5. Why would you use word processing rather than a typewriter when producing a business document? (Sec. 10.2)
6. What is a database program? (Sec. 10.2)
7. What is a spreadsheet program? (Sec. 10.2)
8. When would you use desktop publishing? (Sec. 10.2)
9. What is a graphic and design program used for? (Sec. 10.2)
10. When would you use a communications program? (Sec. 10.2)
11. How is a point-of-sale system used in business? (Sec. 10.3)
12. Name three types of online services. (Sec. 10.3)
13. What advantages does E-mail have over the post office? (Sec. 10.3)
14. Give an example of how interactive videodiscs can be used in retail marketing. (Sec. 10.3)
15. How did Chrysler first use interactive TV? (Sec. 10.3)

148 Unit 4 *Human Resource Essentials*

Critical Thinking

1. What are some advantages and disadvantages to businesspeople working from home and using computers instead of coming into the office?
2. Some people have discussed the possibility of everyone in the country being in one database with credit and income information and personal histories included. What kinds of concerns might this kind of database raise?
3. You have been asked to track the financial performance of your company. What type of software would you use to help you with this task?
4. What do you think might be the effect of desktop publishing software on the book and magazine publishing world?
5. Explain the possible effects of the widespread use of E-mail.
6. Through interactive videodisc and television systems, customers can obtain much of the information about products that salespeople would otherwise give them. Why would a company need salespeople if it uses these technologies?

Building Academic Skills

Math

1. Frank's Florist Shop uses a database to store all his customers' birthdays. His computer sends postcards to his customers on their birthdays, offering a free rose if they come in within a week. Frank says sales have increased by 12 percent since he began the giveaway program. His sales were $6,400 a month previously. What are they now? Use a calculator.
2. If there are 20 million users of the Internet now, and the number of users is expected to rise to 100 million by 2000, what is the percentage increase expected?
3. At your computer shop, orders are now always placed by E-mail messages to the suppliers. Your employer has estimated each E-mail message costs her 4 cents. If the cost of a telephone order was 72 cents, and the shop places eight orders a day, what are the savings per business week?

Communication

4. The supervisor who is training employees to use a new spreadsheet program goes through the instructions too quickly. In the following days, people seem to have trouble using the program. What could you say to the supervisor to help solve the problem?

Critical Thinking

1. Advantages include: savings of utility costs, cleaning costs, costs of office space. Disadvantages include: having less control over employee time, not knowing employees, their motivation, or work habits as well.
2. Answers will vary. Privacy would be an issue. Errors in information would be more serious if many users had access. People might be discriminated against because of the information.
3. Spreadsheet program.
4. Answers will vary. Should make process cheaper, allowing publishers to take more chances.
5. Since E-mail saves time and money, companies' profits should increase. And since order turnaround time is shorter, businesses can stay more responsive to customers' needs.
6. Answers will vary. Salespeople provide the human touch. Many people are uncomfortable with machines. Salespeople can answer questions

5. One of the assistants in your office is very fast with word processing, but his documents often have many spelling errors. What can you tell him to do to prevent these errors?

6. Every time your boss begins to explain the use of the new database program, your eyes glaze over, and you stop listening. How can you overcome this block to listening with understanding?

Human Relations

7. You have connected your company's computer system to a local area network with access to the Internet. Using Internet, employees can now do research and communicate with customers easily. Two employees, however, have become hooked on browsing through discussion groups. They spend most of their lunch hours online, and often stay after work. Though they assert they don't misuse the privilege during work, both have become less productive. How can you handle this situation?

8. In your drugstore, you have installed interactive videos in the cold medicine and hair dye departments. Some customers, especially older ones, seem intimidated by the machines, and you see them walking out without making a purchase. What might you do?

Application Projects

1. Interview a local businessperson who has installed a computer system within the past few years. Ask him or her to describe how the use of computers has changed the business. Write a 350-word report on your findings.

2. Choose a possible marketing career and research how computers are used in it. Speculate on what new uses computers might have in the future in that career. Give an oral report to the class.

3. Use the *Reader's Guide to Periodical Literature* to find magazine articles about the new CD-ROM and write a 350-word report about what can be expected in the use of interactive video in the next ten years.

4. Go to a travel agency and interview an agent about how the computer airline reservation system works. Ask about the past, when the system didn't exist. How has it changed the travel industry? Report your findings to the class.

5. Go on a class field trip to a local book publisher or newspaper and learn how these businesses use desktop publishing software. Ask for a demonstration. Try to arrange to have some hands-on practice producing a newsletter about class activities.

6. Write a 500-word history report on the major changes in microcomputers since they first became available. Include data on changes in speed, power, and ease of use. Use the school or public library to research your subject.

Linking School to Work

Find out from your employer how many different computer applications are in use at your workplace. List their names and what they are used for. Share your findings with the class. Tally which seem to be most popular.

Performance Assessment

Role Play

Situation. You are a computer salesperson. You are selling hardware and software to a record store owner. As a seller, you will be expected to choose hardware and software that would be appropriate to the record store owner's needs. Give a general explanation of the benefits of each part of the system.

Evaluation. You will be evaluated on how well you can do the following:

- Discuss the functions of basic pieces of computer hardware that would be appropriate for the record store.

- Describe the types of software programs that will help the record store owner conduct business on a daily basis.

Presentation

Visit a local software store and find out information about a popular software program. Ask what advantages the program offers over other programs. Choose either a word processing program, a database program, a spreadsheet program, a desktop publishing program, a graphics and design program, or a communications program. Present your findings to the class.

Complete the Chapter 10 Computer Application that appears in the Student Activity Workbook.

overcome it realizing that they need the information.

Human Relations

7. Answers will vary. Students should point out to employees that their production is down, and ask them to limit the use of online services to their own time. They should explain that if there's no improvement, it may be necessary to limit their access.

8. Answers will vary. Offer to assist them in using the equipment, or to help them yourself.

Application Projects

1.–6. Answers will vary.

Linking School to Work

Answers depend on the work situation.

Performance Assessment

Refer to the *DECA Competitive Events Handbook* for evaluation guidelines.

Computer Application

Optional activity. Refer to the *Marketing Software Binder* for template and user information.

Evaluation

Administer the reproducible test for Chapter 10, or construct your own using the Testmaker software.

---

the computer may not be programmed to answer. Salespeople can answer objections and be more persuasive than a computer.

Building Academic Skills

Math

1. $7168 ($6400 × 12% = 768; $768 + $6400 = $7168)

2. 500% (100,000,000 ÷ 20,000,000 = 5; 5 = 500%

3. $27.20 (72¢ − 4¢ = 68¢; (.68 × 8) × 5 = 27.20)

Communication

4. Students could ask for further instruction, pointing out the need to go over each step carefully, and making sure everyone understands.

5. He could use a computer spell checker or a dictionary.

6. Answers will vary. If students recognize they have an emotional block to listening, they can try to

Chapter Overview

Chapter 11 gives an overview of the key personal traits and interpersonal skills necessary for relating well to others, both on and off the job.

Springboard

Have students help you create a list of the people with whom they have interpersonal relationships (family, friends, etc.). Divide students into teams. Each team is assigned two groups of people from their list. Each team should list under their group, the interpersonal skills they feel are needed to deal well with this group. Was there overlap of interpersonal skills between each group? Discuss similarities and differences.

Prereading

List the section objectives to discuss with students. Have students skim the chapter, looking at the pictures, reading the captions, and noting the heads. Ask questions to ensure that the students have a minimal understanding of the chapter structure.

Preteaching the Vocabulary

Review the vocabulary. Then have students brainstorm definitions for each vocabulary word and give examples from their lives.

Discuss *agreement* and *consensus* in the context of teamwork.

CHAPTER 11

Interpersonal Skills

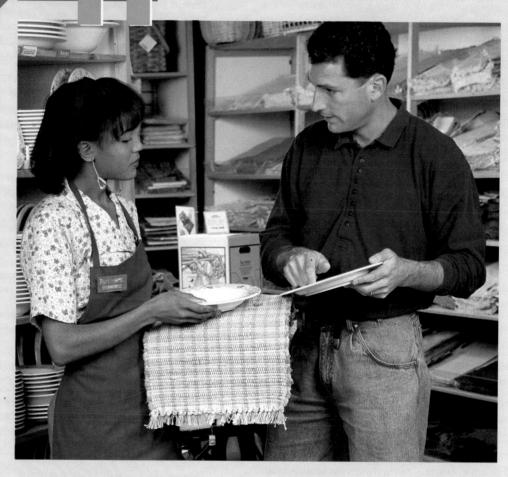

In classes, you and your teachers discuss new ideas. After school, you greet the bus driver as you head to your part-time job in a sporting goods store. Once there, you and a co-worker divide responsibilities for pricing new merchandise and checking stock.

Every day, a major portion of your time is spent relating to other people. Developing *interpersonal skills,* the skills you use in relating to others, helps you get along well with the many people you encounter. Using these skills is especially important on the job. Studies show that between 80 and 85 percent of a person's success in the world of work is due to having good interpersonal skills.

150   Unit 4   *Human Resource Essentials*

Classroom Management

For the Teacher
- Teacher's Annotated Editions for all workbooks
- Teacher's Manual for *School-to-Work Handbook*
- *Testing Binder*
- *Transparency Binder*
- *Marketing Software Binder*
- *Marketing Career Portfolio*
- *Lesson Plans*

For the Student
- *Student Activity Workbook*
- *Marketing Math Workbook*
- *School-to-Work Handbook*
- *Student Software*
- *International Case Studies*
- *Marketing Career Portfolio*

SECTION 11.1

Objectives

After completing this section, you will be able to

- explain the importance of understanding others,
- discuss the personal traits that can help you be more effective in relations with other people,
- identify three personal skills to master for successful interpersonal relations in the marketing world, and
- describe how interpersonal skills may be used in marketing.

Terms to Know

- body language
- initiative
- empathize
- assertive

Understanding Others

The first step in getting along with others is getting to know them. Finding out others' interests helps you understand them better. Interests often reflect values, and understanding people's values is helpful in most relationships.

Trying to understand the reasons for others' behavior also facilitates good relationships both on and off the job. You can learn to be sensitive to certain aspects of everyone's behavior. Observe the way a person deals with others. Does the person relate differently to different people in the same situations? Can you figure out why? Which of the person's personality traits might affect your relationship with him or her?

Observing body language is another key way to learn about a person. **Body language** is the physical movements and position of the body that communicate thoughts. For example, the person who leans slightly forward and nods in agreement with you is obviously paying attention. The person with an expressionless stare is looking but not listening.

Facial expressions are often good indicators of emotions and feelings. A pleasant, smiling expression, for instance, usually indicates a positive outlook.

Your eyes tell a lot about you, too. When you are happy, for example, your pupils get larger. When you are unhappy, the pupils constrict. In most people, this is an automatic response. So, if you are close enough to see a person's eyes clearly, you can learn more about him or her. Suppose you are interviewing a candidate to help you with an advertising campaign. As you explain the job responsibilities, look into the person's eyes for an indication of his or her feelings.

One study of body language found that people sometimes say one thing verbally and another through body language. Body language is often the more accurate indicator of the person's thoughts and feelings. By observing people in many different situations, you can learn to read body language with considerable accuracy.

Personal Traits

Understanding others is only the first step in getting along with them. It's also important to develop the personal traits that make getting along pleasant and productive. In the marketing world, the way you interact with others will determine to a great extent how successful and satisfied you are. The traits described here will help improve your interpersonal relations, both on the job and with your friends and family.

Personal Ethics

Demonstrating personal ethics is essential in every aspect of life, including the job. Ethical behavior includes honesty, integrity, and a sense of fair play. Everyone wants to be treated fairly, and to be told the truth. When you behave ethically, people trust you. This is particularly important on the job, where you may be giving people information to help them decide whether to buy something. Being untruthful or withholding negative information leads to customer dissatisfaction.

It's also important to demonstrate good personal ethics towards your employer and co-workers. Honesty is always a job requirement.

Creativity, Initiative, and Responsibility

Creativity, initiative, and responsibility are three traits that will help you achieve personal and marketing success. *Creativity* is using your imagination to be inventive. It allows you not only to come up with new products, but also to find new ways of doing your job.

Chapter 11 *Interpersonal Skills* **151**

FOCUS

Bell Ringer Activity

Ask students the difference between the words *subjective* and *objective*. Generate a chalkboard list of student definitions and arrive at a consensus. (*Subjective* means arising from conditions within the self that are not directly caused by external stimuli. *Objective* means dealing with facts or conditions as perceived without distortion by personal feelings, prejudices, or interpretations.)

Introducing the Section

Ask students what they find most difficult in their dealings with other people. Students might cite such issues as prejudice or personal dislike of a person's actions or beliefs. List these issues. Ask students what can make it easier to deal with difficult people. List these answers on the chalkboard.

Most students who have co-op jobs now or who will pursue marketing as a career will have heavy contact with people, which means a high potential for daily conflict. None of us will like everything everyone else does, says, or believes. However, tell students that their negative feelings about others can be minimized if they remain *objective* (focused only on the facts) instead of being *subjective* (allowing their personal feelings to affect and/or impair their judgment of people and situations).

Cite some examples where objectivity should be used (for example, an employment interview in which a supervisor puts aside his or her personal feelings for an employee and focuses on the employee's job performance).

Meeting Special Needs

Learning Disabilities

Students with oral expression difficulties often do not feel comfortable participating in exercises devoted to interpersonal skills because the physical difficulties they experience can make the exercises uncomfortable for them. Even so, these students can benefit from watching others and participating at a level they themselves select as comfortable.

Enforcing classroom rules regarding nonjudgemental behavior, and never allowing ridicule of any sort in the classroom can go a long way to encourage participation from all students. Allowing all students to submit written questions about material that they find challenging can also give students with oral expression difficulty an outlet.

Guided Practice

1. Read Section 11.1 with students.
2. Ask students for examples from their personal lives or on the job of how they exhibited the behaviors discussed in this section.
3. Ask students to think of times when they made snap judgments about people and they were wrong. Throughout the lesson, stress the importance of remaining objective, particularly in work situations where judging others not only affects your interaction with them but may impede your job performance.
4. Several texts are available in your local library on dealing with difficult personalities, particularly in the workplace. If students need to explore this issue further, include a discussion about it in this lesson.

Discussion Starter

You have a customer who has been verbally abusive to you. She returned a piece of merchandise saying it was "cheaply made and it fell apart the first day I used it." She says that you are "too slow" in ringing up her substitute purchase. The person who waited on her yesterday was "even slower than you—if that's possible." How would you handle this situation?

Critical Thinking

Ask students to suggest instances when a person's body language is not a good indicator of state of mind. (When someone has a physical disability or is aware of body language and is deliberately masking his or her feelings.)

Initiative means doing what needs to be done without being urged. Once you have used your creativity to come up with a new idea, it will go nowhere unless you use your initiative to act on it.

Responsibility is being accountable for your actions and doing your duty. After taking the initiative to begin a job, you must accept responsibility for completing it. Employers value responsible employees because they can be counted on to work without much supervision. They don't need prodding.

Attitude

Your attitude refers to the mental outlook you have toward people and situations. For good interpersonal relationships, you should develop a *positive attitude*. Try to see the good in the people you deal with. People with a positive attitude welcome a difficult assignment as a challenge. People with a negative attitude complain. A positive outlook makes you more likable.

Specific traits that foster a positive outlook are *interest* and *enthusiasm*. You can develop interest in a particular subject by learning more about it. For example, finding out why it's necessary to take inventory makes the process more interesting. It will help you do the job with more enthusiasm. Not only will you enjoy the work more, but you will be more productive. Maintaining a positive attitude is one of the keys to having a satisfying life.

Self-Control and Orderliness

People who exercise self-control are tactful and slow to anger. They don't indulge their impulses but behave in a disciplined way. This is important in marketing where you will be in contact with the public. Self-control and

orderly behavior inspire confidence in customers and in co-workers. They are essential qualities for managers and others in leadership positions. People who can't control themselves and do things in a sloppy, inattentive way, are not likely to be given much responsibility.

Self-Awareness and Willingness to Change

Knowing yourself is the first step to be willing to make personal changes. You can begin by making a list of all your personal strengths and weaknesses. Then decide which weaknesses you would like to work on first. Practice the traits that will help you improve your weaknesses. For instance, if you tend to put off difficult tasks, practice using your initiative. Make it a point to start your job by doing the hardest part first. You will find it becomes easier to practice the positive traits as days go on, and you will definitely notice a change in your attitude!

It's also important to be willing to listen to the feedback of others, and act on it. Sometimes we aren't aware of the effect we are having on other people. We can move ahead in our own personal growth if we are willing to change attitudes and behaviors that are negative.

Being willing to change also means being willing to adapt to changes around you. It's important to be flexible. Sometimes you may be asked to perform a task that isn't part of your job. Employees who are willing to adapt and be flexible are more valuable than those employees who cannot.

Self-Esteem

Self-esteem is your worth or value as seen by you. Having good self-esteem helps you see yourself as being able to do your job. It helps you get along with others.

To help others gain self-esteem, treat them with the respect and kindness that you would like to be treated with yourself. A cashier who looks a customer in the eye, smiles at him, and gives a friendly hello, is fostering that person's self-esteem. So is an employee who praises a co-worker's effort. Raising someone's self-esteem may be as simple as remembering his or her name.

Having a positive attitude will help make your work more enjoyable. What are two ways to foster a positive attitude?

Caption Answer

Develop an interest in the subject you are dealing with by learning more about it and show enthusiasm.

More About

Creativity

Many people assume that creativity refers to the act of creating art, music, or a written work. However, creativity can also be viewed as a function of putting ideas or items together in a novel or different way. The creative mind transforms items or ideas into something new. We all have the capability to be creative.

Empathy

You can earn a person's trust and respect faster by empathizing. To **empathize** means to understand a person's situation or frame of mind. Learn to respect the other person's point of view, even when you don't agree with it. This technique is especially important in dealing with customers.

Personal Skills

In addition to the personal traits described above, there are some personal skills that can help you get along with people on the job. Using the following skills can help you succeed in your career.

Assertiveness

Being **assertive** means standing up for your rights, beliefs, and ideas. People will respect you if you can be assertive without being pushy or aggressive. Show confidence and speak with authority. This does not mean you should sound like a know-it-all, but you do have to know what you are talking about.

Assertiveness is a skill that takes a while to learn. You will probably not have the opportunity to be assertive on the job until you have improved your knowledge and your skill level through experience. But as you gain more experience, you will gain confidence. Then you will be in a better position to influence others.

Time Management

Learning to budget your time for different tasks and to keep records of important deadlines or appointments are part of time management. It's not possible to be effective in your work unless you are able to use time wisely. A salesperson who misses an appointment with a client is not likely to make the sale—or any other sale to that client.

Goal Setting

Setting goals for your career and personal development is essential. If you don't know where you are headed, how can you ever expect to get there? Specific procedures for setting goals are outlined in Chapter 42.

Interpersonal Skills in Marketing

There are a number of interpersonal skills that are needed specifically to deal with the special relationship between marketing employees and their customers. You

BRIGHT IDEAS

Cut Your Product to Pieces

The first Band-Aids were created by Earle Dickson, a cotton buyer for Johnson & Johnson. Dickson's wife was accident-prone in the kitchen and frequently cut herself while cooking. Dickson knew what had to be done in such circumstances. The son of a physician, he had often watched his father bandage patients with dressing and surgical tape. The problem was that that method required a second person—or two hands. What Dickson needed, he reasoned, was some mechanism whereby his wife could bandage herself with one hand.

What he invented took the form of strips 3 inches wide by 18 inches long. The user determined the length by slicing off a piece to match the size of the wound. Dickson's wife was impressed, but the public wasn't. Sales were uninspiring. Then Johnson & Johnson came up with the idea of mechanically precutting the strips into more manageable (3 inch by ¾ inch) slices. Consumers have been stuck on Band-Aids ever since.

Creativity Challenge   Form teams of 3–5 people. Then brainstorm a list of products that have been improved by the Band-Aid solution—namely, by being cut up into smaller pieces and/or poked full of holes. You could start with bite-sized ice cream snacks and distressed jeans. Once you've listed a number of such "have beens," branch out into "could be's." Think of other items that would have increased potential if treated the same way. Reach for the most unusual possibilities.

---

will use these skills to carry out a variety of job procedures. The following is a list of some basic procedures you may be asked to handle that will require the use of your interpersonal skills:

1. *Handle customer requests and questions.* You will need to learn the proper procedures for handling customer requests and questions. You will also need to know to whom you should refer customers if you cannot answer their questions yourself.
2. *Provide customers with directions to your store location or other locations.* You will need to be able to give clear directions.

Chapter 11   *Interpersonal Skills*   **153**

SECTION 11.1

Cooperative Learning

Divide the class into four groups. Have each group generate one situation in which a person has to defend his or her actions. Sample situations:
- a teacher accusing a student of cheating on a test;
- a boss making unfair demands on an employee;
- a friend asking one more time to borrow something of yours when you would rather not lend it; and
- a store clerk trying to sell you something you don't want.

Have each group generate ways that each situation could be handled assertively and aggressively. Then have each group role play their scenario for the class. Did all groups agree with the way each situation was handled? (Remind students that what some people consider assertive, others consider aggressive.)

Independent Practice

1. Negotiating is a key interpersonal skill students will need in the workplace. Make sure students understand what negotiation is. Then list situations in which negotiation is used (for example, contract negotiation, negotiating salary, negotiating work hours, etc.). Allow students to pick one of the scenarios. Then have them write an analysis of the specific skills and traits mentioned in this lesson they would use in the negotiation situation they've chosen.
2. Assign and review the Chapter 11 Case Study in the *International Case Studies* workbook.

More About

Empathy

Using empathy on the job requires the listener to restate the customer's or co-worker's viewpoint in a clear way to demonstrate that the listener has received the message. For example, in responding to an irate customer, an employee could say, "Yes. I hear that you are unhappy with the purchase. I will work with you to solve the problem."

Bright Ideas

Relate the Bright Ideas feature to the old saying: "Necessity is the mother of invention." Ask students to explain the saying in their own words and to think of a time in their life when they have created or invented something because they had to given a situation. Their answers could be as simple as replacing a missing ingredient in a recipe or finding a substitute material for a project.

Assess

Evaluation

Assign and review Section 11.1 Review.

Reteaching

1. Assign and review the vocabulary terms for this section.
2. Assign and review Fact and Idea Review questions 1–5 from the Chapter Review.
3. Have students list on the board negative, poorly resolved incidents that they have observed in their personal life or on the job. Then have the class discuss ways in which the incidents could have been positively resolved.

Enrichment

1. Assign and review the appropriate activities in the *Student Activity Workbook*.
2. Assign and review the appropriate Critical Thinking questions from the Chapter Review.
3. Students will undoubtedly be dealing with people from many cultures in their marketing jobs of the future, or even in their co-op jobs now. To help with the communication process, they should become familiar with how body language differs from culture to culture. Have students do research on this and report their findings to the class.

Close

Have students write a 50-word paragraph telling how information from this lesson will help them deal more effectively with people both on and off the job.

Your interpersonal skills will help you solve problems on the job. What personal traits might help the employee shown here deal with this disgruntled customer?

3. *Understand management's role in customer relations.* You will need to know under what circumstances a manager should be called to talk to a customer. Policies differ from business to business.
4. *Understand procedures for handling difficult customers.* Having clear procedures helps to prevent you from becoming flustered or upset when dealing with customers who may be angry. These procedures can also protect your physical safety.
5. *Explain business policies to customers.* This includes return or exchange policies, and whether the business accepts checks or credit cards. You will need to be able to explain this information clearly and politely.
6. *Handle customer complaints.* If you have a specific procedure to follow, you will be better able to provide a customer with an acceptable response, whether positive or negative. You should always use empathy when listening to a complaint, but your response will depend upon company policy.

Life in the Multicultural MARKETPLACE

Fair Play

What happens when an idea or concept presented in one language for translation has no exact counterpart in the second, or target, language? Take the simple English expression *fair play*. According to Glen Fisher, a specialist in cross-cultural negotiation, there is no exact equivalent in any other language. For example, the term was brought into French as *le fer ple* but has no exact translation. In Spanish, the term *juego limpio* (literally "clean play") applies to various sports situations but does not extend into any other areas. Similarly, the everyday Spanish expression *simpatico* (literally "a nice or kind person") has no fully equivalent translation in English. These are the kinds of problems that give translators headaches—and prevent perfect comprehension on both sides of the negotiating table in business situations.

SECTION 11.1 Review

1. Explain the importance of understanding others.
2. Discuss the personal traits that can help you be more effective in relations with other people.
3. Identify three personal skills to master for successful interpersonal relations in the marketing world.
4. Name basic procedures you may be asked to handle on the job that require the use of your interpersonal skills.

Section Review Answers

1. Understanding others facilitates good relationships.
2. Personal ethics, creativity, initiative, responsibility, attitude, self-control, and orderliness.
3. Assertiveness, time management, and goal setting.
4. Handle customer requests and questions; provide directions; explain business policies.

Caption Answer

Personal ethics, creativity, initiative, responsibility, attitude, and self-control.

SECTION 11.2

Objectives

After completing this section, you will be able to

- explain the importance of teamwork in the business world and
- discuss six aspects of successful teamwork.

Terms to Know

- consensus
- agreements

Teamwork

You have probably been on many teams in your life. Perhaps you have played team sports at some time in school. If you have ever participated in a school or club car wash, or decorated the gym for a dance, you have been on a team. A team is a group of people who come together to achieve a goal. Teamwork is the skill they use to achieve that goal.

Teamwork is important in the business world. You will learn in Chapter 12 about new models of management where entire companies are organized into teams. Whether you work for one of these or not, however, teamwork skills are priceless. A manager at Sun Life Insurance Company said, "People rise and fall according to how they work with their peers."

Training

In order to be an effective team member, you must have training for all the tasks you will perform. You have probably heard of cross training in sports. That's a way of staying in shape that includes doing many different activities—swimming, running, and weight training, for example. Each one of the sports uses a different set of muscles and leads to a different kind of strength.

In the same way, people are cross trained for many tasks on a team. This gives the team flexibility and several strengths. Work becomes more enjoyable when you know you will not be doing the same thing every day.

At Hallmark Cards teams of editors, writers, artists, and production specialists oversee the entire process of making greeting cards. Twenty percent of the team's time during the first year is spent in training.

Team Goals

Before a team can begin to act, it has to be clear about what its goals are. In order for team members to feel committed to the goal, they must first feel involved in defining it. At Subway Sandwiches, for example, production teams set goals for time required to make each sandwich and for the quality of the product. Companies that involve employees in setting goals show that they respect and value employee opinions. This results in greater company loyalty and stronger team spirit.

In addition to having input into company goals, team members set specific goals for their teams. Usually, members must reach a **consensus** about goals. A consensus is a decision that each member agrees to. In order for this to happen, it is important that all team members are allowed to state their opinions. Other members must respect this right and not interrupt. Respectful discussion continues until the group reaches an agreement.

Assigning Roles

Even though individual roles may change from day to day, each person on the team needs to know which part of the process he or she is responsible for each day. Members are usually assigned tasks based on their skills and experience. Sometimes a less experienced member will be paired up with someone more skilled so he or she can receive training while completing the task.

Agreements

An **agreement** is a specific commitment that each member makes with the group. It is like a contract—a promise to perform a certain task, usually within a certain period of time. A team's agreements must be consistent with its goals.

For example, one of the production team goals in a pizza restaurant is to decrease the time it takes to make a pizza by 15 percent. Each affected member must complete his part of the process 15 percent faster. Sometimes this can be accomplished by cutting out unnecessary steps, or it may be that people have to work at top speed.

Because everyone has agreed on the goal to start with, each person is motivated to keep his or her agreement. If one person doesn't keep his agreement, the whole team's performance suffers. Team loyalty and peer pressure help to encourage people to keep their agreements.

Shared Responsibility and Shared Leadership

For a team to work, each member must feel responsible for the whole team's efforts. That's shared responsibility. It's not enough to do your own job well, and then complain if others don't seem to be doing theirs. That's where shared leadership comes in.

Chapter 11 *Interpersonal Skills* **155**

SECTION 11.2

FOCUS

Bell Ringer Activity

Ask students to first give you a definition of the word *team*. Ask which students work in teams at their co-op jobs or play team sports. Remind students that they have all participated in teamwork in this class with cooperative learning activities.

Based on their experiences, have students generate a list of the advantages and disadvantages of working on a team.

Introducing the Section

The workplace is now heavily oriented toward teamwork. This lesson provides a good starting point for reviewing some of the trends they will see in Workplace 2000:

- Our economy is increasingly driven by automation and high-tech inventions. Thus, workers must be more familiar with advanced manufacturing systems, which will require ongoing training.
- American job seekers will be competing with workers from all over the world to create the best products in a global economy that becomes more international every day.
- U.S. workers will change professions three times during their work lives and will change jobs six times. (These career and job changes will necessitate training.)*

This lesson will introduce students to the importance of training and to the skills they need to work in teams.

*(Source: Kleiman, Carol. *100 Best Jobs for the 1990s and Beyond*. Chicago: Dearborn Financial Publishing, 1992.)

Did You Know ?

The famous sales training leader Dale Carnegie coined the phrase, "Act enthusiastic and you'll be enthusiastic!" to point out that enthusiasm is like spontaneous combustion in that it feeds on itself and can grow into a regular behavior if practiced regularly. Similarly, research has shown that smiling promotes relaxation and a feeling of well-being.

Lifelong Learning

Interpersonal Skills

Living and working with others allow many opportunities to practice the topics brought up in this chapter. Topics that once were part of a psychology class are now included in workplace training. Employees may now receive instruction on conflict resolution, self-awareness, assertiveness training, and other related topics.

Guided Practice

1. Read Section 11.2 with students.
2. Have students read aloud the Case Study and review the answers in class.
3. Assign and review the Chapter 11 Activity in the *School-to-Work Handbook*.

Discussion Starter

You are in a training session with five other employees. You and four of the employees are getting along fine. But one member is asking too many unnecessary questions, arguing with the instructor, and resisting the training process. How would you and your co-workers handle this situation?

L1 Human Relations Skills

Have pairs of students role-play this scenario. Allow the class to give feedback.

An employee has asked to take a week's vacation because she has relatives visiting town. Although she has earned the vacation days and you cannot refuse to let her take the time, you are in a busy season and need all employees on hand. How would you handle this situation?

L2 Human Relations Skills

Follow the directions in the L1 Activity and ask students to consider this scenario.

One of your trusted employees tells you that John, another employee, is having someone else punch his time card at 7:00 P.M. each night, even though he leaves the stockroom at 6:45. How would you handle this situation?

L3 Human Relations Skills

Follow the directions in the L1 Activity and ask students to consider this scenario.

You observe one of your employees dealing with a customer in an extremely rude manner. How would you handle this situation?

156

CASE STUDY

The Remaking of Levi Strauss & Co.

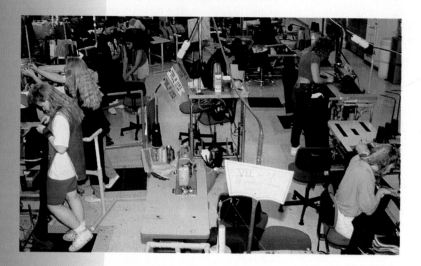

Levi Strauss & Co. has been making jeans for 150 years. The company has always been successful, but during the 1980s increased competition and a changing market meant Levi Strauss & Co. had to make some changes. It closed plants and laid off thousands of workers, but more was necessary.

The CEO of Levi Strauss & Co. is Robert Haas, great-great-grandnephew of Levi Strauss himself. In 1985 he and other family members bought Levi Strauss & Co. back from its stockholders. Then Haas began to remake the company using the team model.

Teamwork is now the name of the game at Levi Strauss & Co. Instead of learning one skill and doing that every day, workers learn 2–3 different tasks. Everyone does each task at different times. The same team is also involved in ordering supplies, setting production goals, and making personnel policies.

Instead of being responsible for one tiny part of production—sewing rear pockets on jeans, for instance—each member of the team is responsible for the whole process of jeans production. That includes cost, efficiency, and quality control.

Since instituting teams, in one Levi Strauss & Co. factory the time it takes to make a pair of jeans has been decreased in many cases by up to 80 percent. Team member's accomplishments add to team spirit.

Teams are also motivated to work well together because part of their pay is based on improved production. If some members of the team don't do their share of the work, the whole team suffers.

It hasn't been easy changing over to the team approach at Levi Strauss & Co. Many employees were glad to take orders and just do one job. They felt uncomfortable taking more responsibility. They also resented having their pay depend partly on other team members' work. But Robert Haas and the Board of Directors of Levi Strauss & Co. were committed to the teamwork model. Increased production, improved quality, and flexibility have confirmed their faith.

Case Study Review

1. What personal traits would be most important to working effectively on a production team at Levi Strauss & Co.?

2. If you were a manager at Levi Strauss & Co., how might you encourage teamwork?

A MATTER OF ETHICS

3. Levi Strauss & Co. bases part of employees' pay on improved work production among teams. Do you feel its ethical to have your pay based on others' work performance? Explain.

Case Study Answers

1. Creativity, initiative, responsibility, willingness to change, self-control, and orderliness are all important.
2. Answers will vary, but might include training, establishing team goals and agreements, assigning roles, and sharing responsibilities and team leadership.
3. Answers will vary.

*A team approach **helps Domino's operate more efficiently. Leadership is shared among the employees. Why is shared leadership an important part of teamwork?***

Independent Practice

Have students imagine that each one of them must function as an effective team leader and create a list of the qualities they think they would need to train others well. Have students share their answers with the class.

Assess

Evaluation

Assign and review the Section 11.2 Review.

Reteaching

1. Assign and review the vocabulary terms for this section.
2. Assign and review Fact and Idea Review questions 6–9 from the Chapter Review.

Enrichment

1. Assign and review the appropriate activities in the *Student Activity Workbook.*
2. Assign and review the appropriate Critical Thinking questions from the Chapter Review.
3. Assign and review the Building Academic Skills Activities, Application Projects, Linking School to Work Activities, and Performance Assessment from the Chapter Review.
4. Companies such as Nordstrom, IBM, Federal Express, etc. are well known for their excellent employee training. Have students research the training methods used by one of these companies or a company of their choice and write a 150- to 200-word report on the training methods the company uses.

In shared leadership, team members take action to bring the whole team's performance up to the standards the team has agreed on. Teams do this by having meetings at which they give feedback about individual performance and about specific parts of the team's work. If the feedback is about someone's performance, it must be given with respect. The atmosphere must be positive, not characterized by blaming.

If the feedback is about some aspect of the team process, it needs to be specific so team members can provide specific responses. For example, rather than saying, "We seem to be wasting a lot of time walking around," more specific feedback would be, "It takes two minutes to walk from my work station to the pizza oven." A team member might then suggest, "Could we move the work station closer to the oven to save time?"

Shared leadership allows all team members to perform some management functions. It makes employees feel more powerful, because it actually gives them more power. Shared responsibility and shared leadership are essential teamwork skills.

In your marketing career, you will certainly be a member of many teams. A department can act as a team. Any group that comes together to achieve something—reach a sales goal, perform an inventory—is a team. Teamwork skills will always be valuable interpersonal skills.

Real World

Reach Out and Touch Asia

Long-distance telephone calls to Asia are expanding at eight times the rate of domestic long-distance calls. For this reason, Sprint decided in 1992 to make a special effort to capture market share in the area. The company approached a group of Asian community leaders on the West Coast with a joint venture proposal. They would found the Asian-American Association, which would be funded primarily by Sprint. The main function of the group would be to help new Asian immigrants get settled in the United States. The association would offer information on medical care, education, and other services. It would also use sales representatives to encourage new immigrants to sign up with Sprint for long-distance telephone service. The association would thus enable Sprint to penetrate the $6-billion Asian market from the inside.

SECTION 11.2 *Review*

1. **What is teamwork? Why is it important in the business world?**
2. **Name and explain six aspects of successful teamwork.**

Chapter 11   *Interpersonal Skills*   **157**

Close

Have students complete this statement: Here are some ways in which I can anticipate further training in the workplace:...

Caption Answer

Shared leadership makes employees feel more powerful because it actually gives them more power.

Section Review Answers

1. Teamwork is the skill a team uses to achieve a goal.
2. Training, team goals, assigning roles, agreements, shared responsibility, and shared leadership.

CHAPTER 11 *Review*

Answers

Vocabulary Review

See Glossary for definitions.

Fact and Idea Review

1. If you know what other people are interested in, it can help you understand what motivates them and what their values are.
2. Creativity, initiative, and responsibility.
3. You can be interested and enthusiastic.
4. Self-awareness is the first step. Until you are aware, you cannot change.
5. To stand up for your rights, values, beliefs, without being aggressive.
6. Cross-training is learning many different skills so that you can fulfill many team functions.
7. Each member is allowed to speak with no interruptions, and respectful discussion continues until the group agrees.
8. Team members must have training, the team must have a goal, and members must know their responsibilities.
9. Shared responsibility and shared leadership help each member feel responsible for the whole team's efforts. Members take action to bring the whole team's performance up to the standards the team has agreed on.

Critical Thinking

1. Examples include the following: Shy person—eyes averted, head down, hands fidgeting. Defensive person—arms crossed, loud voice. Self-confident person—eyes straight ahead looking at person, arms at the side, head held high.
2. Examples include: Marketing manager—teamwork, understanding others, personal

Vocabulary Review

Write a paragraph that includes all the following words. Use them in ways that demonstrate you know their meaning.

body language
initiative
empathize
assertive
consensus
agreements

Fact and Idea Review

1. Why does finding out other people's interests help you understand them better? (Sec. 11.1)
2. What three personal traits allow you to come up with and follow through on new ideas? (Sec. 11.1)
3. What attitudes can you cultivate that will foster a positive outlook? (Sec. 11.1)
4. How can self-awareness help you to change weaknesses to strengths? (Sec. 11.1)
5. What does it mean to be assertive? (Sec. 11.1)
6. In a teamwork context, what is cross-training? (Sec. 11.2)
7. How does a team arrive at a consensus? (Sec. 11.2)
8. What must a team do before it can act? (Sec. 11.2)
9. Why does shared responsibility and shared leadership help a team to work well? (Sec. 11.2)

Critical Thinking

1. Describe the body language you would expect to see in a shy person, a defensive person, and a self-confident person.
2. Describe at least three interpersonal skills important to success in each of these careers: marketing manager, retail salesperson, cashier, and buyer.
3. Why is it necessary for people in the marketing world to behave ethically?
4. How do the personal traits of initiative and responsibility aid in building teamwork?
5. Describe some ways in which you can increase other people's self-esteem.
6. Describe the differences and similarities you believe exist between being assertive and being aggressive.
7. Why would employees be more motivated to perform well on a team than in an individual effort?

8. Why is it important for team decisions to be reached by consensus?
9. In teamwork, team members make agreements with the group. Describe some agreements you have made in your own life.
10. Would you prefer to work on a team where you do different tasks requiring different skills from day to day, or to work alone on the same sort of work each day? Explain your choice.

Building Academic Skills

Math

1. You have calculated that your idea to use plastic instead of metal in the manufacturing of your company's Gadget would save $.13 per Gadget. If your company can produce 600 Gadgets per day, and there are 250 production days in the year, how much will your idea save the company in a year?

Communication

2. There is a new manager in your department who repeatedly waits until just before the end of your shift to ask you to work overtime. How would you give feedback to the manager about this situation?
3. As an insurance agent, you have just met with a prospective buyer and discussed a particular health insurance plan. A brief written note would be an effective follow-up. What would you include in that note?
4. Write a memo to your production team setting up a meeting to talk about your goals for the next quarter. Include all the elements of a memo.

Human Relations

5. Go to a store and ask a salesclerk for assistance finding a type of product. Do not smile at the salesclerk. Go to another store. This time, make eye contact with the clerk and smile. Describe the two experiences and the reactions of each salesclerk.
6. You have an idea that you think will benefit your company, and you have an appointment to discuss it with your manager. At the beginning of the meeting, you discover that she has just read a report which shows the company's profits have dropped substantially this quarter. She is frowning and seems agitated. What would you do?

---

ethics. Salesperson—understanding others, initiative, assertiveness. Cashier—orderliness, personal ethics, positive attitude. Buyer—goal setting, assertiveness, teamwork.
3. Marketing depends on customers trusting the marketer. If marketers are not ethical, they will lose customer trust.
4. Both are necessary teamwork skills.
5. To help others gain self-esteem, treat them with respect and kindness.

6. Aggression is hostile, pushy, threatening. Assertion is self-confident, still respects other points of view.
7. Team spirit is a motivator.
8. Team members will be more committed to the decision if all agree to it.
9. Homework assignments, contracts with parents about chores, etc.
10. Answers will vary.

7. Delia, who is on your production team at Mega Sandwiches, is often two or three minutes late for her shift, and sandwiches tend to pile up at her workstation. The team's bonus pay is going to be threatened if the sandwich pileup doesn't stop soon. How do you approach Delia to talk about this?

Application Projects

1. Seeing and respecting another person's point of view is an important part of effective human relations. Suppose that you are involved in a company that is suffering financially. As a result, a number of jobs need to be terminated. Put yourself in the position of a manager who needs to do the job terminations. Describe how you might feel, your concerns, and your needs. Now put yourself in the position of an assistant who may lose his or her job. Describe how you might feel in his or her position.
2. Go to the personnel office of a local retail outlet and ask to see its policy manual. Research how each of the personal skills in marketing described in the chapter is handled in that business. Report your findings to the class.
3. Go to the library and research different systems for time management. Write a report comparing at least two of them. Point out similarities and differences.
4. Interview someone who works for an employment agency about the importance of interpersonal skills in business. Find out which skills come into play most often and which one skill your interviewee considers the most important. From the notes you take during the interview, report your findings in a five-minute speech to the class.
5. At the library, do some research on training in assertiveness or self-esteem. Find out what kinds of classes are available and how they relate to success in business.
6. Write a report comparing and contrasting the teamwork skills involved in playing a team sport with the teamwork skills used on the job. Describe how each type of team uses the six aspects of teamwork discussed in the chapter.

Linking School to Work

Are the employees at your workplace organized into teams? If they are, report to the class on how the teams work. If they aren't, write a 250-word description of how you would organize your co-workers into a team.

Performance Assessment

Role Play

Situation. You are an employee for a take-out pizza restaurant that serves pizzas, salads, and drinks. There are five other employees that work with you. Your manager has observed that customers currently must wait 15 minutes on average for their orders. She would like you to speed up the order process by five minutes by establishing a production team plan. Use teamwork skills learned in the chapter to devise the new plan. Include in your plan a discussion of how you will motivate your employees to work better as a team. Present your plan to your manager.

Evaluation. You will be evaluated on how well you can do the following:

- Describe the aspects of successful teamwork you will use as part of your new production plan.
- Discuss the personal traits and skills that will help your employees work better as a team.

Written Report

Conduct research at the library on a company that is organized around team processes. Write a short report describing how the processes are defined, what departments are involved in each, and exactly what tasks each team has responsibility for. Discuss how the team approach has affected profits and productivity in that company.

Complete the Chapter 11 Computer Application that appears in the Student Activity Workbook.

They should empathize with her but be assertive about the need for punctuality.

Application Projects

1. Students should describe their feelings from each point of view.
2. Students should compare how each business handles personal skills.
3. Students should share their answers with the class.
4. Students should discuss why these interpersonal skills are important.
5. Students should be encouraged to partake in self-esteem and assertiveness classes.
6. Students should include the six aspects discussed in the chapter.

Linking School to Work

Answers depend on the work situation.

Performance Assessment

Refer to the *DECA Competitive Events Handbook* for evaluation guidelines.

Computer Application

Optional activity. Refer to the *Marketing Software Binder* for template and user information.

Evaluation

Administer the reproducible test for Chapter 11, or construct your own using the Testmaker software.

Building Academic Skills

Math
1. $19,500 (.13 × 600 = 78. 78 × 250 = $19,500)

Communication
2. Employee should be assertive, not aggressive. Perhaps suggest that manager ask earlier in the day.
3. Notes should be cordial and should reiterate the details of the meeting.
4. Memos should follow the format outlined in Chapter 9.

Human Relations
5. By smiling students should receive a better response.
6. Students should wait until the manager will be more receptive to the proposal, then state the proposal's benefits to the company.
7. Students should approach Delia from the standpoint of team spirit and shared responsibility.

MANAGEMENT SKILLLS

Pages 160–171

Chapter Overview

Chapter 12 explores types of management structures and explains what managers do. It contrasts horizontal and vertical organization, and discusses self-managed work teams. It also looks at the basic management functions (planning, organizing, controlling) and discusses effective management techniques.

Springboard

Have students brainstorm definitions for the terms *managment* and *manager.* Then compare their definitions to the text's.

Once students have an understanding of both terms, invite them to describe decisions their co-op work station supervisors make daily and categorize them as *planning, organizing,* or *controlling.*

Prereading

List the section objectives to discuss with students. Have students skim the chapter, looking at the pictures, reading the captions, and noting the heads. Ask questions to ensure that students have a minimal understanding of the chapter structure.

Preteaching the Vocabulary

Before students begin reading the chapter, dictate each of the vocabulary terms and ask students to write them on a sheet of paper. When they finish, write the terms on the chalkboard. Then have students guess at the meaning of each. Write their guesses next to each term, but do not give the correct meaning. Leave this list on the chalkboard so that students can see how close their guesses were to the actual definitions as they work through the chapter.

160

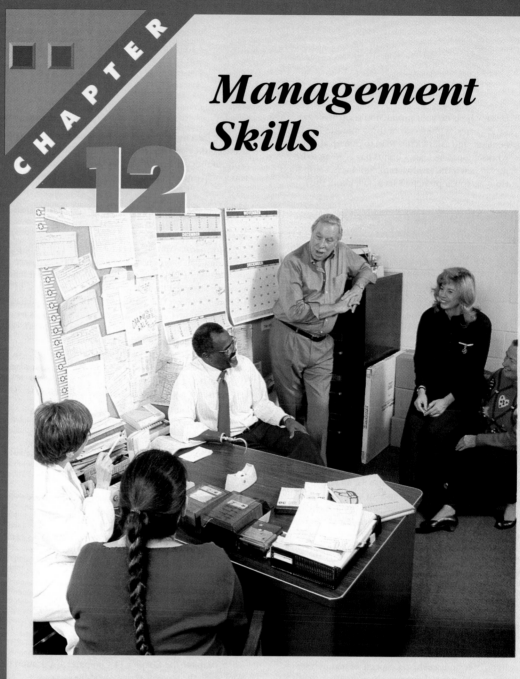

Management Skills

A position in management is one of the greatest challenges any employee can face. Management involves the communication and interpersonal skills we have looked at thus far, plus the abilities to plan, organize, supervise, and solve problems.

Does management appeal to you? More than likely you will have a chance to take a management job at some point in your marketing career. This is because the concept of management is changing. More and more employees will find themselves fulfilling management functions, whatever their job titles.

160   Unit 4   *Human Resource Essentials*

Classroom Management

For the Teacher

- Teacher's Annotated Editions for all workbooks
- Teacher's Manual for *School-to-Work Handbook*
- *Testing Binder*
- *Transparency Binder*
- *Marketing Software Binder*
- *Marketing Career Portfolio*
- *Lesson Plans*

For the Student

- *Student Activity Workbook*
- *Marketing Math Workbook*
- *School-to-Work Handbook*
- *Student Software*
- *International Case Studies*
- *Marketing Career Portfolio*

SECTION 12.1

Objectives

After completing this section, you will be able to

- describe how horizontally organized companies differ from traditionally organized companies,
- identify the three levels of management, and
- explain how a self-managing team functions.

Terms to Know

- vertical organization
- top management
- middle management
- supervisory-level management
- horizontal organization
- empowerment

Types of Management Structure

Management is the process of reaching goals through the use of human resources, technology, and material resources. To facilitate effective management, businesses are organized in two ways—vertically and horizontally.

Vertical Organization

In large, traditional companies managers look up to higher levels of management or down to employees, all within a single department. Their goal is to perform a particular department function well. Because of the up-and-down structure, this kind of organization is called **vertical organization.**

Within the traditionally organized company, there are three basic levels of management: **top management, middle management,** and **supervisory-level management.** Figure 12-1 (on page 162) distinguishes these three levels.

Horizontal Organization

Today, purely vertical organization is being displaced by new ways of structuring management. Management from the top down, with its three traditional levels, will continue to exist in many companies. It will not be the only option, however. It will exist side by side with new *self-managing* structures.

During the late 1980s and early 1990s, many corporations downsized in an attempt to increase their efficiency. These "lean and mean" firms, the reasoning went, could increase their productivity. With fewer workers producing as much if not more product, profits would rise. Unfortunately, for more than half of the companies that downsized, things didn't work out that way. Instead, employee morale suffered, customer dissatisfaction rose, and profits fell.

Clearly, more than staff cuts were needed to make companies more efficient. The answer was a new kind of management structure—**horizontal organization.** Horizontal organization has three key characteristics.

Self-Managing Teams   At the heart of horizontal organization is a restructuring of the traditional management hierarchy. Levels of management have been eliminated and the number of supervisors reduced. (This is called "flattening" the organization.) Instead of reporting up a chain of command, employees are organized into teams. These teams manage themselves.

Here's the way it works. Each team has someone called an "owner." This person is the nearest to an overall manager. He or she has ultimate responsibility for making sure the team meets its goals. The owner doesn't do this by issuing orders, however. He or she acts more like a coach than a boss. The owner works together with the whole team to define all the individual steps necessary to meet their goals.

What's behind this approach is the idea that the people actually doing the work are the best source of information about how it should be done. The team manages itself by sharing opinions and brainstorming. It also shares responsibility for the consequences of its decisions.

Encouraging team members to contribute to and take responsibility for the management process is known as **empowerment.** Empowerment reinforces team spirit and contributes to company loyalty. It thereby ultimately increases profits and productivity.

Organization by Process   A second characteristic of horizontal companies is organization by process. Self-managing teams are organized around particular processes, such as developing new products or providing customer support. Gone are functional divisions like the finance department or the engineering department. Rather, each process is handled by a team that includes people with many different specializations. The product development team, for instance, might include people from marketing

FOCUS

Bell Ringer Activity

Explain to students that the management structure of every company is slightly different. Some have strong leadership from the top and only allow midlevel and supervisory-level managers to execute orders from top executives. In other companies, self-managed work teams make many of the daily decisions that help the company function efficiently. With this information as background, ask students to jot down some answers to this question: Who or what determines the type of management in any company?

Introducing the Section

Make a chalkboard list of students' answers from the Bell Ringer Activity. Here are some factors that determine management structure:

- *Size.* Smaller companies are likely to have strong direction from an owner. Larger companies are likely to need several high-level managers who delegate their authority on order to make the many decisions it takes to run the business efficiently.
- *Type of product and time pressure.* Some businesses, such as restaurants, must work in self-managed teams in order to provide a great deal of product in a relatively short period of time.
- *Amount of government regulation.* The production of some products, such as canned foods, is subject to a strict government regulations. Thus, there must be strict guidelines for running the business.

Meeting Special Needs

Gifted

Gifted students may find that the material in this chapter offers them a first look at real-world organizational behavior. Encourage such students to take on a wide variety of enrichment and independant practice activities that will put them in contact with people in the business world and allow them to observe the daily practices that lead to success. Be sure they have the opportunity to present written summaries of their findings and explore with them what they observed.

Guided Practice

1. Read Section 12.1 with students.
2. Use the transparency for this section.
3. If you wish to do or assign further reading on management in the evolving workplace, consider adding these texts to your classroom library: *Management* by Drucker, *In Search of Excellence* by Peters and Waterman, *A Passion for Excellence* by Peters and Austin, and *The Fifth Discipline* by Senge.

Discussion Starter

If students haven't been a part of a self-managed work team at their co-op jobs, they will probably work on one at some point in their marketing careers. Ask them what they think the advantages and disadvantages of working on a self-managed work team might be. (Answers will vary. Advantages: shared responsibility, greater adaptability [because of all the different viewpoints]. Disadvantages: difficulty getting along, keeping everyone on goal.)

Critical Thinking

Ask students to describe the management structures of the following:
- Their co-op work stations
- Organizations and/or sports teams to which they belong
- Their marketing class
- Their school
  (Answers will vary.)

Independent Practice

1. Assign and review the Chapter 12 Case Study in the *International Case Studies* workbook.
2. Have students interview a manager or the owner of a local business to determine its management structure. Have them summarize their findings in an organization chart that shows the lines of

Figure 12-1

LEVELS OF MANAGEMENT

All managers perform the same basic functions, but their responsibilities differ according to their management level.

Top Management ▶

These are the men and women with the greatest responsibility. In large companies, top management consists of the chief executive officer (CEO) or president and other key executives who may have the title of vice president. These key executives make many company decisions and meet regularly with the CEO or president.

Middle Management ▲

These are the people who carry out top management's decisions. Middle managers provide the link between top management and supervisory-level management. They are responsible for motivating those at the supervisory level so that the company can reach the goals set by top management.

Supervisory-Level ▶ Management

These are the people who directly assign work duties and supervise employees on the job. The most common title at this level is supervisor. A supervisor is responsible for carrying out the plans of middle management.

Lifelong Learning

Management Skills

Today's work force requires participants to be responsible for managing their own careers. Given the central role of computer technology in many of the best-paying jobs, general education must be supplemented with actual hands-on computer knowledge. Encourage students to commit to developing and maintaining their computer skills by taking classes regularly, volunteering to learn new programs, and familiarizing themselves with as many computer applications as possible. Remind them that soon there will be no managers who are not computer literate.

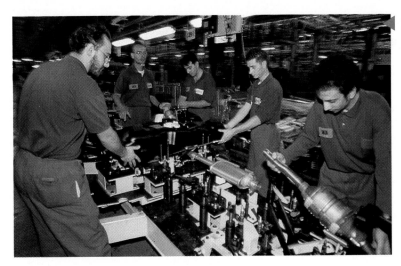

*Collaboration between employees **working in teams is at the heart of horizontal organization. Who manages such groups?***

authority and the titles of the managers involved. They should also include a brief statement of the owner's or manager's rationale behind that business structure.

Assess

Evaluation

Assign and review the Section 12.1 Review.

Reteaching

1. Assign and review the vocabulary terms for this section.
2. Assign and review Fact and Idea Review questions 1–5 from the Chapter Review.
3. Allow students to use their texts, if necessary, to write a 50-word comparison/contrast of how horizontally organized companies differ from vertically organized companies.

Enrichment

1. Assign and review the appropriate activities in the *Student Activity Workbook*.
2. Assign and review the appropriate Critical Thinking questions from the Chapter Review.
3. Total quality management (TQM) is a set of management principles and strategies based on the work of the late W. Edwards Deming. TQM emphasizes teamwork and having employees work to solve their own problems without intervention of a supervisor. Many businesses today, such as Xerox and Federal Express, successfully use TQM. Have students research TQM to learn about how it is being implemented in major companies today.

BRIGHT IDEAS

Draw It

Federal Express, the company that revolutionized the way people work, began as a doodle. Company founder Fred Smith was diagramming the distribution model used by major airlines to route flights—a hub and numerous connecting spokes. His idea was that if all mail were channeled through one major hub (say, Memphis, Tennessee), it could be sent out immediately to its final destination. As an organization plan, Smith's doodle worked so well that Federal Express was able to expand its guarantee to include any destination in the world.

Creativity Challenge Form teams of 3–5 people, and try drawing some organizational models of your own. Ignore straight lines (vertical or horizontal) and FedEx's hub and spokes. They've already been done. You're looking for something original. Try applying some really unconventional forms to an organization's structure. How would a company or a school operate if it were organized in a triangle? a tic-tac-toe grid? a spiral? What about something organic (like an amoeba) or manmade (like a series of hairpin curves)? What, if anything, do such forms have to recommend them as organizational models?

research, design, engineering, and finance. Instead of being department members reporting to department heads, however, they would be team members sharing opinions, decisions, and responsibility for the success or failure of the products they develop.

Customer Orientation The third characteristic of horizontal organization has to do with where teams get their direction. In vertical companies, the source of direction is management. In horizontal companies, it's the customer. If a company gives its customers what they want, the reasoning goes, everything else—large profits, high productivity, satisfied investors—will follow.

Wave of the Future? The movement toward horizontal organization in business is definitely a trend. For some companies, it has been extremely successful. Ford, for example, reduced the time it takes to develop and produce a new model from five years to three. That's a 40 percent reduction!

Not all companies, however, have been quick to jump on the bandwagon. Shifting from the familiar vertical model, with its levels of management, is a type of reorganization that can take years. For many companies, there will probably always be a mix of the two types. It will, therefore, be important for you to be familiar with the features of both.

SECTION 12.1 *Review*

1. **What is the principal difference between the structure of a vertical company and the structure of a horizontal company?**
2. **Name the three levels of management.**
3. **Describe the role of the owner in a self-managing team.**

Chapter 12 *Management Skills* **163**

Caption Answer

The team members themselves.

Section Review Answers

1. Vertical companies: organized in departments; orders come from management above. Horizontal companies: organized into self-managing teams that set own goals and make own decisions.
2. Top management, middle management, and supervisory-level management.
3. Coaches a team to help it meet its goals.

Close

To close the lesson, have students draw diagrams of the two types of management structures, label them, and write paragraph-length explanations of each.

Focus

Bell Ringer Activity

Ask students to think of a time when they acted as managers of a project at work, at school, at home, or in an extracurricular activity. The project need not have been complicated or long term. It could, for example, have involved managing a day of child care. Ask students to identify the situation and list some of the skills they used to accomplish their goals.

Introducing the Section

Have students share their answers to the Bell Ringer Activity. Those answers might include such things as planning, time management, resource management, scheduling, disciplining, evaluating work, goal setting, understanding the special needs of the physically challenged and people from other cultures, assessing people's potential and abilities, and evaluating quality of work. Students also probably needed good communication skills, good human resource skills, and the ability to solve problems and make decisions.

Point out that we all use management skills in our daily lives, if only to manage ourselves. We also all have the potential to manage well, which is an essential skill in today's competitive job market.

Teach

Guided Practice

1. Read Section 12.2 with students.
2. Use the transparency for this section.
3. Have students read aloud the Case Study and review the answers in class.
4. Invite a panel of 3–4 midlevel managers to speak to the class about their jobs. These people should discuss the pros and cons of management (including such things

164

SECTION 12.2

Objectives

After completing this section, you will be able to

- name the three functions of management,
- identify the management techniques used by effective managers, and
- explain how to motivate employees through a system of rewards.

Terms to Know

- planning
- organizing
- controlling
- mission statement

What Managers Do

All managers perform certain basic functions—planning, organizing, and controlling. Managers implement their decisions in these areas through the business's employees. This means that communicating and motivating people are especially important management skills.

Basic Management Functions

All managers, whether of the individual or team variety, perform the functions of planning, organizing, and controlling. They *plan* when they set goals and determine how to reach them. They *organize* when they decide who will do what and how they will do it. They *control* when they set standards and evaluate performance.

All three of these management functions involve making decisions. Some decisions will be fairly simple or routine. Other decisions will be difficult and complicated. In the latter cases, following the formal, six-step procedure shown in Figure 12-2 can be helpful.

Planning   The first step in the management process is planning. **Planning** involves deciding what will be done and how it will be accomplished.

Good management planning at any level is realistic, comprehensive, and flexible. It includes plans for the short- and long-range uses of people, technology, and material resources.

164   Unit 4   *Human Resource Essentials*

Decision-Making Process

✔ **1.** Define the problem.

✔ **2.** Identify the options available.

✔ **3.** Gather information and determine the consequences of each option.

4. Choose the best option.

5. Take action.

6. Evaluate results.

Figure 12-2

Complex problems having a large number of options, considerations, and consequences require a systematic approach—like this one—for a solution. What sort of approach do you think you would use for very simple problems?

To be an effective management tool, a management plan should be reduced to written form. When writing their plans, managers or management teams should not try to anticipate every possibility. An overly long and detailed document offers too many opportunities for misinterpretation.

Once the written plan is complete, it should be distributed to and discussed with everyone who needs to know about it. Managers should keep their management plans flexible so they can be easily revised in response to comment or change. They should also review and revise their plans often.

Organizing   **Organizing** is a coordinated effort to reach a company's planning goals. It involves assigning responsibility, establishing working relationships, staffing, and directing the work of employees.

Assigning responsibility and establishing working relationships (Figure 12-3) are functions usually carried out by top and middle management, even in horizontal companies. Staffing, which includes selecting and training new employees, is often shared by middle management and supervisors. Supervisors usually direct employees' work.

The organizing function in the largest companies is complex. There may be hundreds of middle-level managers, thousands of supervisors, and tens of thousands of employees. Since the work is divided among so many people, middle managers and supervisors in traditional companies are usually given a relatively narrow range of responsibilities.

In horizontal companies, middle management responsibilities are much wider. Because employees are empowered to do much of the organizing themselves,

---

Caption Answer

Make the decision on the spot, relying principally on prior experience as a guide.

Business Organization Chart

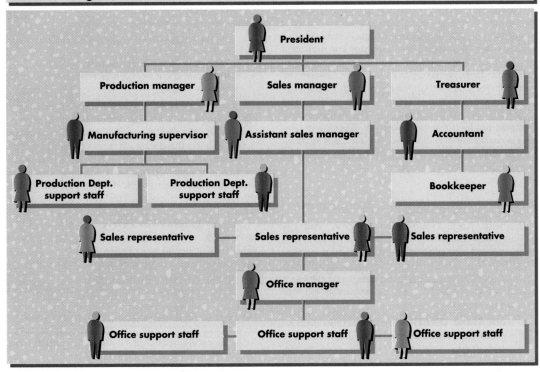

Figure 12–3

An organization chart shows the working relationships among the employees of a company. How has management organized this company—horizontally or vertically? How do you know?

managers are able to advise and troubleshoot rather than give orders. In smaller traditional companies as well, managers usually have a wide range of organizing responsibilities.

Controlling   Controlling is the process of comparing what you planned with actual performance. It involves three basic activities—setting standards, evaluating performance according to those standards, and solving any problems revealed by the evaluation.

Before setting standards, many companies compose a **mission statement.** It describes in a paragraph or so what the ultimate goals of the company are. For example, Federal Express Corporation organizes its statement around what it calls its people-service-profit philosophy.

The corporation begins by stating that its mission is to "produce outstanding financial returns by providing totally reliable, competitively superior, global air-ground transportation of…goods and documents that require rapid, time-certain delivery." The company then sets as service goals maintaining "positive control of each package…using real-time electronic tracking and tracing systems" and presenting "a complete record of each shipment and delivery…with our request for payment."

The mission statement concludes with its people-oriented goals: "We will be helpful, courteous, and professional to each other and the public. We will strive to have a completely satisfied customer at the end of each transaction."

Once a company has goals of this sort, it will adopt standards that are consistent with them. These standards will apply to all aspects of the firm's operation. Here are some possibilities:

*   *Financial standards*—profit, cash flow, sales
*   *Employee standards*—productivity, professional conduct, dress
*   *Customer satisfaction standards*—sales returns, customer complaints, repeat business, referrals
*   *Quality control standards*—production line checks for defects in materials or workmanship, repair requests, recalls

To arrive at such standards, managers work backwards from the overall goals in the company's mission statement. For example, an express carrier might have a standard requiring delivery of overnight packages by 10 A.M. of each day. Managerial thinking might go like this:

Chapter 12   *Management Skills*   **165**

Caption Answer

Vertically—chart shows the traditional three levels of management (president, managers, and supervisors) above line/support personnel.

Did You Know

The Bureau of Labor Statistics predicts that by 2005, professional, managerial, and technical positions will rise 12.4 percent, 3 percent, and 8.3 percent, respectively. The deficits show up in the crafts fields, as well as for operators of machinery and laborers. This prediction means more opportunities for those with education and the ability to solve complex problems.

---

as being paid a salary with a possible bonus as opposed to being paid hourly), the skills and training necessary to manage well, and what they consider to be their most effective management techniques. Also, have each manager discuss the management structure of his or her organization. Try to have managers from different types of businesses on the panel.

5. Assign and review the Chapter 12 Activity in the *School-to-Work Handbook*.

Discussion Starters

1. Ask: What would be our mission statement for this class? (Answers will vary. One possibility: Our mission is three-fold. First, to learn how marketing—through the production, pricing, promotion, and distribution of ideas, goods, and services—creates exchanges in order to satisfy individual and organizational wants and needs. Second, to explore the occupational area of marketing as a source of career-sustaining jobs. Third, to learn how we can become informed, proactive consumers who understand the domestic and international economic environment.)

2. Ask students to describe the orientation and training they received when they started their co-op jobs. What did they like about the training? What did they dislike about it? On what subjects or issues did they feel they needed more information? How would they convey their needs to their human resource manager? (Answers will vary.)

Critical Thinking

What special skills would a manager need in order to manage a highly multicultural staff? (Answers will vary. Some possibilities: a knowledge of the customs, business practices, language, and biases of the people that work for him or her; an ability to communicate clearly; patience; a true acceptance of people's differences.)

Cooperative Learning

Divide students into four groups. Give the groups one whole class period to decide on a small business that they would like to run for one day (for example, a pizza parlor, child-care center, catering service, or T-shirt store). Also, have them discuss the planning, organizing, and controlling phases of management for that business.

The groups are to assume that their businesses have at least five employees. These are the decisions the groups must make:

- First, they are to write a *mission statement* for their business. Then they are to adopt standards in planning, organizing, and controlling that are consistent with that mission statement.

- With regarding to *planning*, they need to decide on salaries and working hours for employees, prices of goods or services, hours of business operation, and company policies such as returns of merchandise.

- With regard to *organizing*, students will need to discuss advertising for employees, the skills and abilities new-hires must have, employee work shifts, job requirements, etc.

- With regard to the *controlling*, students will need to decide on procedures and time expectations for delivery of goods or services, standards for interacting with customers, how to handle the money, and how to maintain the workplace. They will also have to decide how they will evaluate employees to maintain the standards they set and how they will deal with problems that come up in the course of a day, such as employee absences, etc.

166

For 10 A.M. delivery, we must have packages slotted for next-day delivery leave the distribution center by 7 A.M. To have all packages leave by 7 A.M., they must be in the distribution center by midnight, and so on.

Once standards have been established, managers can then use them to evaluate both company and individual performance. When performance does not meet established standards, managers must identify and solve the problem. For example, employees may not be performing up to standard. Why? They may not be spotting production problems in the making. The defect rate in company products may be up sharply. Why? Equipment may be malfunctioning. Solutions in these cases might involve additional training for the employees and adjustment or replacement of the equipment.

Effective Management Techniques

Whether you find yourself a supervisor in a traditionally organized company or a member of a self-managing team, you will sooner or later have to develop management skills. That may sound intimidating, but it isn't. The most effective management techniques are really just a matter of common sense. Judge for yourself as you read through the suggestions that follow.

Give Clear Directions   Directing others requires good communication skills. Good communication is necessary at every level of management. Even the best employees won't be productive if they don't know what they are expected to do.

As a supervisor, give all the direction required for each job. Ask for feedback to determine whether your directions are fully understood. Usually you will need to repeat some of your directions, perhaps using a different approach. Encourage employees to ask questions about your directions. Communication will improve dramatically when they feel comfortable doing this.

Train New Employees Well   All new employees need some on-the-job training and orientation. As a supervisor, you may train new employees yourself or delegate the task. If you delegate the training to someone else, choose a person who knows the job well and is a good teacher. Then supervise the training. Make sure that all job duties are explained and that the new employees understand how to complete them.

Orienting new employees includes more than simply training them for their positions. New employees are often a little frightened at the prospect of a brand-new workplace and co-workers and perhaps new skills to learn as well. It is important to make new employees feel valued and welcome and to familiarize them with the working environment. Studies have shown that properly oriented employees are more satisfied with their work, more productive, and more likely to stay in the job.

Orientation may take as little as a couple of hours or as much as a few days. It commonly includes the following:

166   Unit 4   *Human Resource Essentials*

- Tour of the company and introduction to co-workers
- Discussion of the company's history and its mission and values
- Description of what the company does
- Training on equipment, such as cash registers and computers
- Information on where key facilities are located
- Information about payroll, benefits, and company policies

Be Consistent   When you have decided that a job must be done in a certain way, make certain that it is always done that way by every employee. Don't make exceptions unless there is a good reason to do so.

Always follow through on what you say. If you announce your intention to deduct part of an employee's salary for being late to work, do it. If you don't follow through on your decisions, employees will not respect what you say.

Treat Employees Fairly   Employees will be more productive if you treat them fairly. Set reasonable standards of performance that your employees can achieve, and apply those standards to everyone. Don't give special privileges to a few favorites.

Listen to suggestions from your employees, and consider acting on them. If someone thinks you are being unfair, look at the situation from the employee's point of view as well as your own. The employee may be right. If so, be honest enough to admit it and make changes. If you believe the employee is wrong, take the time to explain your reasoning. The person may understand your position and agree with you. If not, he or she will appreciate your effort to be fair.

Be Firm When Necessary   Sometimes supervising others requires a firm hand. Never let an employee take unfair advantage of you, the company, or another employee. Learn to be firm without losing your temper.

*New-employee orientation **often includes a tour of the workplace and introductions to co-workers. Why is this procedure preferable to letting a newly hired person explore and discover things on his or her own?***

Real World

A Kinder, Gentler Style of Management

The Family and Work Institute of New York recently surveyed 3,400 randomly selected men and women about what motivated them to take their current jobs. Management style proved to play a key role. Positions reporting to traditional hierarchical managers (variously characterized as "watchdogs" or "policemen") were disfavored. Instead, workers expressed a preference for "sensitive" and "supportive" employers displaying the following traits:

- Willingness to share information
- Concern for employees' personal/family life
- Recognition and acknowledgement of the value of employees' work

Why the emphasis on such traits? Apparently most workers feel that today's family and financial pressures are stressful enough without the addition of an unpleasant or inflexible work situation.

Each situation requiring disciplinary action is different. A friendly suggestion is all that is necessary to get most employees on the right track. Some people, though, don't respond to friendly suggestions. In these cases, you have to be direct and firm. Give whatever directions are appropriate, and be certain the employee understands what you expect. However, don't lose your temper.

Some employee problems are caused by the inappropriate behavior of one employee toward another. In such cases, it may be difficult to reason with one or both of them. Listen to what they have to say, and be reasonable but firm. In severe cases, you may have to move an employee to another department.

Consider Employees' Welfare Whenever possible, do what is best for your employees. Of course, you cannot and should not do everything they ask. You should, however, consider their welfare and show your willingness to treat them fairly. Do whatever you can to help them without sacrificing the amount or quality of work done. If appropriate, talk with your immediate supervisor about changes that will benefit your employees.

Set a Good Example Set a good example in everything you do on the job. Doing this one simple thing will make your supervisory job much easier.

For example, Frank, a department manager in a large retail store, wrote computer programs at night to earn extra money. He seldom went to sleep before 2 A.M., and he found it very difficult to arrive at the store on time.

Other employees in his department noticed that Frank was usually a half hour late. So, they decided they could sleep 20 minutes longer and still arrive at the store ahead of him. By following Frank's example, the whole department began arriving late for work. After several weeks of this, Frank was replaced.

Karen, the new department manager, always arrived at the store a few minutes early. When the other employees realized this, they reset their alarm clocks and began arriving early, too. Karen didn't have to say a word to anyone. She simply set a good example.

Delegate Responsibility

Some supervisors and many middle managers simply do too much work themselves. Some take work home almost every night. This may be necessary at times, but it usually means resources are not being managed well. Those who take work home are probably not delegating many tasks and responsibilities to others. Yet they often have capable employees with lighter workloads who would be willing to do more.

As a supervisor, don't try to do everything yourself. Organize your work responsibilities, and then decide which ones you can delegate to others. Decide which employee can best handle each task. If necessary, take time to teach some employees how to do new tasks.

Taking work home on a regular basis indicates that a manager may be assuming too much responsibility for too many things. In such a case, what is the solution?

In horizontal organizations, empowering employees is company policy. You will be expected to delegate. That way, you will do a better job with your remaining responsibilities. Your employees, in turn, will appreciate the chance to show that they can handle more responsibility. They will become more productive.

Foster Teamwork As you learned earlier in the chapter, teamwork is especially important in horizontally organized companies. As a manager or group "owner," you can foster teamwork in a number of ways. Encourage team members to step outside their areas of specialization and learn about other aspects of the process for which they are responsible. Try to promote honest and frank discussion before decisions are taken. Listen respectfully to the comments and opinions of other team members, and encourage others in the group to do likewise. Work toward consensus.

Although students' planning time for this exercise is limited and they will not be able to anticipate all of the possible situations about which they will have to make decisions as managers, this activity will help them see how complex management is. Have each group share its decisions in an oral presentation to the class. Class members may be able to suggest additional considerations in planning, organizing, and controlling.

L1 Decision-making Skills

Based on what they have learned about management in this section, ask students if they would make the decision to explore it further as a career option. Why or why not?

L2 Decision-making Skills

Pose this problem: You have just been offered a promotion to supervisory-level management in the store where you've worked for two years. You will receive about $25 more per week, be responsible for supervising five people, and work longer hours without getting paid for overtime. (At present, you work a straight 40-hour week and don't have to supervise anyone.) You plan to stay at the store another year, while you finish your education. Would you take the promotion? Why or why not?

L3 Decision-making Skills

Continue the problem posed in the L2 Decision-making Skills activity: You have been in a management position at the store for six months. While you like the company and had planned to stay in the field for several years, you are definitely not enjoying the additional burdens of your new position. You find yourself thinking a great deal about how much you enjoyed your old job. What would you do?

Feature Note

One of the things that motivates companies to study such issues is the high cost of replacing employees who are dissatisfied with their employment situations. High turnover rates can be lowered by paying attention to traits such as those listed if other factors (like working conditions and wages) are in line with industry norms.

Caption Answer

Delegating some tasks to capable employees.

Teach *(Cont'd.)*

Independent Practice

Being promoted from among a group of peers whom you now must supervise is a common occurrence in business. Tell students to imagine that they have just been promoted and now must manage three friends with whom they were originally hired. Considering this situation, have students write answers to these questions:

- What might be your friends' initial reactions to your promotion—jealousy or happiness that your hard work was rewarded?
- How would you deal with any negative reactions?
- What would be some issues that you yourself might have to deal with and overcome? (One possibility: insecurity at supervising people who were formerly your peers.)
- How will your relationship with your friends likely change?
- How can you keep your relationship with your friends professional?

Some students may already have had relevant experiences at their co-op jobs. For this reason, it will be beneficial to discuss their answers and their experiences in class.

Assess

Evaluation

Assign and review the Section 12.2 Review.

Reteaching

1. Assign and review the vocabulary terms for this section.
2. Assign and review Fact and Idea Review questions 6–10 from the Chapter Review.

CASE STUDY

Managing for Speed

Time is an essential resource that becomes more valuable as businesses pare down for efficiency. McKinsey and Company, a national business consulting firm, found that time is sometimes more valuable than money. Products that went to market six months behind schedule but within budget earned 33 percent less than the company expected. Products that went to market on time, even if their development costs ran 50 percent over budget, earned only 4 percent less than estimated!

Here are some management practices that help to speed business:

1. *Fighting red tape and bureaucracy.* Making approval and review procedures simple frees time for more productive work. Keeping organization simple, not allowing multilayered departments that slow the movement of projects, keeps employees focused on customer satisfaction.

2. *Streamlining business process and eliminating useless routine.* When something has always been done one way, people tend to keep doing it that way without thinking. Good managers should be on the lookout for tasks that can be eliminated or simplified, combined with other tasks, or done in a different order.

3. *Removing territorial barriers.* Employees in traditional companies are divided into departments that sometimes duplicate each other's work and pursue inconsistent goals. People within such departments also seldom communicate with each other. Sometimes they even try to make other departments look bad. All of these practices slow production. Creating team spirit by breaking down departmental walls saves time as well as frustration.

4. *Planning purposefully.* Sometimes planning becomes an activity for its own sake. The goal is forgotten. For planning to be effective, the people who make the plans should be the ones who execute them. Planning should involve people from every aspect of production, so that many perspectives are considered.

The one word that summarizes management activities that save time is *simplify.* An effective manager should ask him- or herself often, Can this be simplified?

Case Study Review

1. Which management structure—traditional or horizontal—do you think would be most open to simplification? Why?
2. Why do you think getting a product out faster can be more cost-effective than getting it out under budget?

A MATTER OF ETHICS

3. Sometimes in the effort to get a product out on schedule, manufacturers cut corners. They decide that they can correct any problems later. If you worked for this type of company, would you go along with this decision? Defend your position.

Case Study Answers

1. Horizontal—because these types of practices are at the heart of such a management structure.
2. Answers will vary. One possibility: Getting out into the marketplace first gives a new product a competitive edge. For at least a brief time, there is no competition. The product can become the consumers' choice by default, and competing products will have to work harder to overcome this preference.
3. Answers will vary. Gravest reservations will focus on products' being rushed to market before they have been thoroughly tested for defects or potential harm to users. Some students might distinguish these situations. Other students might disagree based on a belief in TQM.

Employee Motivation

The things that get rewarded get done. Keep this in mind when you become a manager. Follow these simple, yet effective, principles.

Reward Real Solutions, Not Quick Fixes Provide frequent feedback to employees and formally evaluate them each year. Identify goals to be achieved over a period of years. Then reward employees who contribute to these goals.

Reward Smart Work, Not Busy Work In many companies, people are rewarded for looking busy. Therefore, they invent all sorts of ways to look busy. If you reward results, however, you will get results.

Begin by putting the right people in the right jobs. Give them the tools they need, and fully explain what is expected of them. Tell everyone they will be rewarded for results. Encourage employees to spend a few minutes each morning organizing their time, including setting goals for the day.

Reward Simplification, Not Complexity In some companies, everything is complicated because complicators have been rewarded. Ordering a $2.79 pen from the supplies department at Intel Corporation, for example, used to take 95 steps and 12 pieces of paper. Intel recognized the problem and simplified the procedure. Now it takes 8 steps and 1 piece of paper.

Reward Quietly Effective People, Not Squeaky Wheels Many managers reward complainers and ignore those who actually do the work. Seek out those who quietly do a good job. Take a sincere interest in them, and they will perform even better. Ignore the chronic complainers.

Reward Quality Work, Not Just Fast Work Doing the job right the first time lowers costs, increases productivity, and increases worker pride. Identify those workers who value quality, not speed. Ask them to suggest ways to improve job performance. Reward employees who suggest improvements.

Reward Creativity, Not Mindless Conformity A reasonable amount of conformity is necessary in every company. However, some managers let conformity stifle creativity. The most important asset in any business is ideas. Encourage employees to be creative. Then reward them when they come up with good ideas.

A young engineer named Steve Wozniak was bored with his job working on computer chips. He asked on three occasions if he could work on designing a personal computer. His manager said no each time. So, he built the first Apple computer in his garage and became one of the most successful entrepreneurs in history.

Reward Loyalty Enthusiastic long-term employees are the key to success in most companies. Reward loyalty by investing in continuing education for employees and promoting from within. If the company is in a difficult financial position, avoid layoffs by cutting pay across the board, if necessary.

▲ *Awards are one way to recognize outstanding employee contributions or performance. What are some others?*

SECTION 12.2 *Review*

1. **What are the basic functions of management?**
2. **What does it mean to delegate responsibility?**
3. **What is the basic principle underlying the use of a system of rewards?**

Chapter 12 *Management Skills* **169**

3. First, have students decide on a type of business (for example, a stationery store). Second, write the words *planning*, *organizing*, and *controlling* on the chalkboard. Third, have students generate managerial duties for the three functions as they relate to the selected business. (For example, if the business is a stationery store, a planning duty might be to set goals for the first year's gross sales.) Continue until you have three or four managerial duties under each function.

Enrichment

1. Assign and review the appropriate activities in the *Student Activity Workbook*.
2. Assign the Unit 4 Activity in the *Marketing Math Workbook*.
3. Assign and review the appropriate Critical Thinking questions from the Chapter Review.
4. Assign and review the Building Academic Skills Activities, Application Projects, Linking School to Work Activity, and Performance Assessment from the Chapter Review.
5. Tell students that if they manage employees long enough, sooner or later they will have to terminate someone's employment. For those students who are now working at co-op training stations, have them discuss with their supervisors or personnel directors the company's grounds for dismissal. (Possibilities include nonperformance of duties, breaking company rules, violation of company policy on substance abuse.)

Close

Have students complete this statement: The three functions of management are. . .(planning, organizing, and controlling.)

Caption Answer

Possibilities include praise, bonuses, titles, promotions, and time off.

Section Review Answers

1. Planning, organizing, and controlling.
2. Delegating means giving jobs or duties to other people to do, rather than trying to do it all yourself.
3. Things that get rewarded get done.

Answers

Vocabulary Review

Explanations will vary. See Glossary for definitions.

Fact and Idea Review

1. Managers look up to higher levels of management or down to employees within a department structure.
2. Top management.
3. Assigns duties to and supervises workers on the job; carries out the plans of middle management.
4. To eliminate levels of management and reduce the number of supervisors.
5. Departments are organized by function, self-managing teams by process.
6. A good management plan is realistic, comprehensive, and flexible; written so that it is neither overly long nor overly detailed; distributed for both comment and revision.
7. Assigning responsibility, establishing working relationships, staffing, and directing the work of employees.
8. To determine whether the directions were understood or not.
9. Encourage team members to learn all aspects of the process for which they are responsible; promote honest and frank discussion; listen to the comments and opinions of group members and encourage others to do so; work toward consensus.
10. (a) Real solutions, not quick fixes. (b) Smart work, not busy work. (c) Simplification, not complication. (d) Quiet effectiveness, not complaining. (e) Quality work, not just fast work. (f) Creativity, not mindless conformity. (g) Loyalty.

170

Vocabulary Review

Study each pair of terms. Then in your own words, explain how they are related to each other. (*Hint:* Are they the same? Are they opposites? Is one part of the other? Are they both part of the same thing? Is one the result of the other?)

vertical organization—horizontal organization
top management—middle management
supervisor—supervisory-level management
planning—organizing
mission statement—company standards
controlling—empowerment

Fact and Idea Review

1. Describe how traditional management structure works. (Sec. 12.1)
2. A vice president in a vertically organized company would be part of which management level? (Sec. 12.1)
3. What does a supervisor do? (Sec. 12.1)
4. What does it mean to "flatten" an organization? (Sec. 12.1)
5. What is the principal difference between a company department and a self-managing team? (Sec. 12.1)
6. What are the characteristics of a good management plan? (Sec. 12.2)
7. What is usually involved in the organizing function of management? (Sec. 12.2)
8. Why is it important to ask for feedback after giving directions to an employee? (Sec. 12.2)
9. How can the owner of a management team foster teamwork in the group? (Sec. 12.2)
10. List seven work accomplishments or attitudes that should be rewarded. (Sec. 12.2)

Critical Thinking

1. Compare top-level management in a large company to what you think it would be in a small company.
2. Discuss why being fair is an effective and important management skill. Describe experiences you have had or heard about in which managers were not fair. What were the results of the unfair treatment?
3. Would you feel more comfortable in a traditional company where you had to answer to only one supervisor or in a horizontal company where you might have many people giving you feedback about your efforts? Compare the advantages of each organizational model, as you see them.

4. Why do you think rewards get better results than punishments?
5. Do you think a company's mission statement should include a commitment to doing business ethically? Should ethics be as important as profits? Defend your answer.
6. How could a manager's openness to suggestions from employees influence their loyalty to a company?

Building Academic Skills

Math

1. The vice president of a company makes an annual salary of $65,000 and works an average of 40 hours per week. The president of the company makes an annual salary of $100,000 and works an average of 60 hours per week. On a per-hour basis, who earns more money?
2. After reorganizing Smith's Sandal Inc. as a horizontal corporation, Bud Smith found that production increased by 20 percent. Before the reorganization, the company produced 2,300 pairs of sandals in a 40-hour work week. How many did it produce after the reorganization?

Technology

3. Use a computer on-line service to find information about management opportunities in the marketing field. (*Note:* Your school or local library may have access to such a service or be able to direct you to an on-line computer.)

Communication

4. Practice giving clear verbal directions. Ask another student to play the part of a new employee. Assume you are training the new employee whose job is to bag groceries in a supermarket. Make sure all the tasks of the job are covered and that the employee understands exactly what to do.
5. Imagine that you are the manager of a large bookstore. One of your salesclerks makes a suggestion about rearranging the children's section to include a few small tables and chairs. You like the idea and intend to carry it out. Write a thank-you note to the salesclerk for the suggested improvement.

Human Relations

6. Abe works as a travel agent for a small firm. The manager of the travel agency has just hired a new agent who happens to be a close personal friend.

Critical Thinking

1. In a large company, top management would consist of the chief executive officer (CEO) or president and other key executives, such as the vice president(s). Most small, locally owned businesses have only one manager.
2. Employees will be more productive, effective, and loyal under your supervision if you treat them fairly. Experiences offered will vary.

3. Responses will vary. Students should mention that managers are subject to more criticism in a traditional company. They also endure more stress because they share less responsibility with others. In a horizontal company, managers need to be more flexible and open to suggestions. They have less power.
4. Answers will vary. However, discussion should lead students to the conclusion that rewards encourage creativity and contribution while fear

The manager is showing her friend obvious favoritism. Abe likes his job, but he feels increasingly uncomfortable with the manager's unfair and inconsistent behavior. What should he do?

7. The athletic shoe manufacturing company where you work is organized in self-managing teams. You are the owner of the production team. One member of the group constantly interrupts during meetings, finishing other people's thoughts for them and arguing against their suggestions even before they have been fully offered. You fear that this behavior is limiting the team's effectiveness. How would you remedy the situation?

Application Projects

1. Describe what would go into the planning, organizing, and controlling of a school club car wash.
2. Describe what someone at a supervisory level might do in the following workplaces: (a) a women's clothing store, (b) a warehouse, (c) a tax preparation service, and (d) a family restaurant.
3. Rewarding good work on the job not only gets things done but also contributes to the morale and enthusiasm of employees. This, in turn, provides further benefits to the company. Brainstorm some creative ways that companies could reward their outstanding employees.

Linking School to Work

Ask your supervisor or employer what he or she thinks about the new management structures that emphasize teamwork and organization by process. Report back to the class on your findings. After everyone has shared the various responses they obtained, discuss any trends that are apparent and speculate about the reasons for them.

Performance Assessment

Role Play

Situation. You are an assistant manager at Hankton's, a very traditionally organized and run sporting goods store. During business hours, the store manager seldom leaves his office and speaks only with the assistant managers. The assistant managers and manager trainees mostly give orders to sales and stock personnel. They very seldom deal with customers. You believe the business could be more efficiently and successfully run with a team approach. You need to convince the manager that productivity and profits will increase with the proposed change. How will you present your argument for a more horizontal organization at Hankton's?

Evaluation. You will be evaluated on how well you do the following:

- Distinguish between vertical and horizontal business structures.
- Describe how management can help employees function as a team.
- Be persuasive in presenting the benefits of a team approach.

Paper

Write a paper describing your personal experiences working or playing on teams and speculating about the relevance of those experiences in the new self-managed workplace. What did you learn in your personal life that might be applicable to a work situation? What did you learn about your own behavior and that of others? How might this be significant to an employer?

Complete the Chapter 12 Computer Application that appears in the Student Activity Workbook.

Portfolio

Consider the Application Projects that you have done for this unit. Select one that illustrates your mastery of the unit's content and might be of interest to potential employers. Reformat the activity as necessary, adding any explanatory text, and place it in your Portfolio. Consider using these activities:

- Chapter 8, Application Projects 5 and 7
- Chapter 10, Application Projects 1, 3, and 6
- Chapter 11, Application Projects 3 and 6
- Chapter 12, Application Project 1

causes people to spend most of their time conforming and protecting themselves.

5. Students will likely agree that businesses should commit themselves to ethical practices. However, they will differ as to whether this commitment "goes without saying" or needs to be in writing.
6. If employees feel that their ideas are taken seriously and are important, they will feel more a part of the team and thus be more loyal.

Building Academic Skills

Math

1. The president, but only by about $.80 an hour.
2. 2,760 pairs of sandals

Technology

3. Information gathered will vary.

Selling

Unit Objectives

After completing this unit, students will be able to achieve the following outcomes:

- Use the eight steps of the sales process on the job.
- Explain the techniques that are applicable to both retail and industrial selling.
- Evaluate sales as a profession for career-planning purposes.
- Perform the functions of a cashier in a retail sales setting.

Chapter 15

Chapter 13

Chapter 14

Chapter 18

Chapter 16

Chapter 17

Teacher Classroom Resources

CHAPTER	13	14	15	16	17	18
Transparency Binder	Transparencies 20–21	Transparency 22		Transparency 23	Transparency 24	Transparencies 25–27
Student Activity Workbook	pp. 75–80	pp. 81–86	pp. 87–92	pp. 93–98	pp. 99–104	pp. 105–110
Student Software	pp. 79–80	pp. 85–86	pp. 91–92	pp. 97–98	pp. 103–104	pp. 109–110
Marketing Math Workbook						Activity 5
School-to-Work Handbook	pp. 31–32	pp. 33–34	pp. 35–36	pp. 37–38	pp. 39–40	pp. 41–42
International Case Studies	pp. 31–32	pp. 33–34	pp. 35–36	pp. 37–38	pp. 39–40	pp. 41–42
Marketing Career Portfolio						Unit 5 activity, Student Text, p. 241
Test Booklet/ Testmaker Software	Chapter 13 test	Chapter 14 test	Chapter 15 test	Chapter 16 test	Chapter 17 test	Chapter 18 test, Unit 5 test

KEY TO BASIC SKILLS ACTIVITIES

L1 Level 1 activities are basic activities and should be within the range of all students.

L2 Level 2 activities are average activities and should be within the range of average and above average students.

L3 Level 3 activities are challenging activities designed for the ability range of above average students.

CHAPTER	PERFORMANCE OBJECTIVES	
13 **What Is Selling?**	13.1	1. Define selling and state its goals. 2. Explain feature-benefit selling. 3. Identify sources of product information. 4. Discuss how customers make buying decisions.
	13.2	1. Explain how selling skills can be helpful in careers other than sales. 2. Distinguish different types of sales positions. 3. Identify the characteristics of effective salespeople.
14 **The Sales Process**	14.1	1. List the eight steps of a sale. 2. Explain how salespeople find customers. 3. Describe how the preapproach is used in industrial and retail sales.
	14.2	1. Explain the importance and purposes of the approach in the sales process. 2. Describe how industrial sales representatives conduct the initial approach. 3. List the three approach methods retail salespeople use and state when it is appropriate to use each.
15 **Determining Needs and Product Presentation**	15.1	1. Explain why determining needs is an essential step in the sales process. 2. Describe three methods used for determining needs.
	15.2	1. State the goal of the product presentation. 2. Explain how products are selected for the presentation. 3. Describe what to say during the product presentation. 4. Identify four techniques that will make for a lively and effective product presentation.
16 **Handling Customer Questions and Objections**	16.1	1. Distinguish between objections and excuses. 2. Explain why objections should be welcomed in the sales process. 3. Identify the five buying decisions upon which common objections are based. 4. List the four steps involved in handling customer objections.
	16.2	1. Identify six specific methods of handling objections. 2. Demonstrate the use of those methods in a variety of selling situations.
17 **Closing the Sale and Following Up**	17.1	1. Recognize customer buying signals. 2. List the rules for closing a sale. 3. Demonstrate specialized methods of closing a sale.
	17.2	1. Explain why suggestion selling is important. 2. List the rules for effective suggestion selling. 3. Demonstrate specialized suggestion selling methods. 4. Discuss the concept of relationship marketing and how it is related to the sales process. 5. Summarize the importance of after-sale activities.
18 **Math for Retail Sales**	18.1	1. List three general functions of all cash registers. 2. Describe the arrangement of currency and coins in a cash register drawer. 3. Demonstrate two methods of making change. 4. State the two most important rules for safeguarding money at the cash register. 5. Describe the general content of sales checks and the basic ways of generating them.
	18.2	1. Describe the various types of sales transactions. 2. Perform the math calculations necessary to fill out sales checks.

OBJECTIVES state	local	FEATURES	ACTIVITIES
		• Case Study: Become a Plumber—and Sell the World, p. 182 • Bright Ideas: Aim Low, p. 176 • Life in the Multicultural Marketplace: It's All in the Wrist, p. 181 • Real World Marketing: Sell Like Hotcakes, p. 179	• Case Study Questions, p. 182 • A Matter of Ethics, p. 182 • Creativity Challenge, p. 176 • Section 13.1 Review, p. 180 • Section 13.2 Review, p. 183 • Chapter Review, pp. 184–185
		• Case Study: Getting to Know Your Customers, p. 190 • Bright Ideas: Look for the Third Right Answer, p. 193 • Life in the Multicultural Marketplace: Talk Small Before You Talk Big, p. 192 • Real World Marketing: Don't Call Us—We'll Call You, p. 187	• Case Study Questions, p. 190 • A Matter of Ethics, p. 190 • Creativity Challenge, p. 193 • Section 14.1 Review, p. 191 • Section 14.2 Review, p. 193 • Chapter Review, pp. 194–195
		• Case Study: Salespeople + Computers = Increased Productivity, p. 202 • Bright Ideas: If You Make Them, They Will Come, p. 201 • Life in the Multicultural Marketplace: When They Laugh, Get Serious, p. 197 • Real World Marketing: A Lasting Look, p. 200	• Case Study Questions, p. 202 • A Matter of Ethics, p. 202 • Creativity Challenge, p. 201 • Section 15.1 Review, p. 199 • Section 15.2 Review, p. 203 • Chapter Review, pp. 204–205
		• Case Study: BT Wakes Up and Hears the Objections, p. 212 • Bright Ideas: Go Halfway, p. 210 • Life in the Multicultural Marketplace: When Yes Means No, p. 208 • Real World Marketing: A Change in Sales Personnel, p. 213	• Case Study Questions, p. 212 • A Matter of Ethics, p. 212 • Creativity Challenge, p. 210 • Section 16.1 Review, p. 210 • Section 16.2 Review, p. 213 • Chapter Review, pp. 214–215
		• Case Study: Just a Visit with the Family, p. 224 • Bright Ideas: Stay the Course, p. 218 • Life in the Multicultural Marketplace: It's Hard to Say Good-bye, p. 225 • Real World Marketing: Making Customer Satisfaction Count, p. 220	• Case Study Questions, p. 224 • A Matter of Ethics, p. 224 • Creativity Challenge, p. 218 • Section 17.1 Review, p. 220 • Section 17.2 Review, p. 225 • Chapter Review, pp. 226–227
		• Case Study: Reducing Credit Card Fraud, p. 237 • Bright Ideas: From the Hands of Babes, p. 232 • Life in the Multicultural Marketplace: One Will Get You Five, p. 233 • Real World Marketing: A Unified Currency for Europe? p. 238	• Case Study Questions, p. 237 • A Matter of Ethics, p. 237 • Creativity Challenge, p. 232 • Section 18.1 Review, p. 233 • Section 18.2 Review, p. 239 • Chapter Review, pp. 240–241

Unit Overview and Background Information

Selling is the first of the functions of marketing to be explored in the text. Chapters 13 and 14 provide students with a foundation by introducing the eight steps in the selling process and explaining the concept of feature-benefit selling. Chapters 15 and 16 discuss some of the most crucial issues involved in dealing directly with customers—how to determine their needs and how to handle their objections. Chapter 17 presents ways to close and follow up a sale, while Chapter 18 reviews the mathematics involved in selling.

Introducing the Unit

To introduce this unit, ask students to share their perceptions of salespeople with the class. (In most cases, their perceptions will be negative because their only exposure to selling has been through order takers or poorly trained salespeople in retail selling situations.)

To get students to change their perspective, ask questions like this one: Do you think Xerox or IBM salespeople would misrepresent their products' capabilities in order to make a sale to a Fortune 500 company? Why or why not? (The key follow-up question in such cases is, What happens when the salesperson shows up for the next sale call?)

Unit Project

The culmination of the unit should be an actual sales presentation based on the sales training manuals that students write as an ongoing project while working on the unit. To make the presentations more instructive, videotape them if possible, and play back the tapes for class evaluation.

172

Focus on the Photo/Cooperative Learning

Once students have completed the unit, divide them into teams. Have each team suggest a caption for the unit photo. However, instruct the teams to relate their group's caption to one of these themes, which you will assign to them: the sales process, determining needs and product presentation, and handling customer questions and objections.

Selling

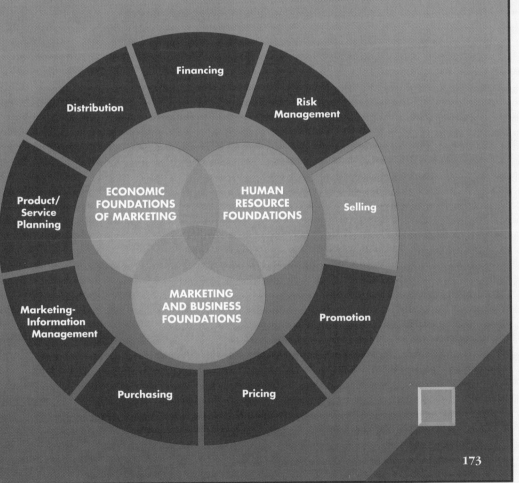

Financing

Distribution

Risk
Management

Product/
Service
Planning

ECONOMIC
FOUNDATIONS
OF MARKETING

HUMAN
RESOURCE
FOUNDATIONS

Selling

Marketing-
Information
Management

MARKETING
AND BUSINESS
FOUNDATIONS

Promotion

Purchasing

Pricing

173

Resources for Enrichment of Unit Conent

Books

- *Endless Referrals* by Bob Burg
- *The Sales Manager's Problem Solver* from the publishers of *Personal Selling Power*
- *Upside-Down Marketing* by George R. Walther

Magazines/Journals

Current issues of *Personal Selling Power* and *Sales & Marketing Management*.

Unit Closure

Have students brainstorm ways of evaluating salespeople based on the key principles learned for each step of the selling process. Tell them that the standards they compile will be used in some observation research.

Arrange with the managers of several local retail stores to have your students evaluate their salespeople's performance. Tell the managers to ask for volunteers for the project. Suggest they tell the volunteers when they will be evaluated (within a week) but not who will be doing the evaluating.

Students should work in pairs so that they can help each other remember exactly what was said during their sales encounter. They should analyze their findings carefully and report them in written form. The reports should then be passed along to the store managers.

Evaluation

Administer the reproducible test for Unit 5, or construct your own using the Testmaker software.

Guest Speaker Suggestion

Have the sales manager of a large industrial firm speak with your class about selling as a career. Ask the person to describe a typical day in a salesperson's life with the firm. Also, request that he/she provide background on educational requirements, in-house training, skills and attitudes necessary for success, salary ranges for entry-level and experienced personnel, and other incentives.

Field Trip Suggestion

Ask a local business that does in-house sales training if it would conduct a sales training session for your students to observe and/or participate in at the company's training center.

What Is Selling?

Pages 174–185

Chapter Overview

Chapter 13 introduces students to sales as a potential career choice. The link between selling and customer satisfaction is explored through detailed development of the concept of feature-benefit selling.

Springboard

Have students write brief summaries of the best and worst experiences they have ever had with salespeople. Then, based on those summaries, have them suggest characteristics they feel a good salesperson should have. Compile these into a single chalkboard listing to be retained for verification later in the chapter.

Prereading

List the section objectives to discuss with students. Have students skim the chapter, looking at the pictures, reading the captions, and noting the heads. Ask questions to ensure that students have a minimal understanding of the chapter structure.

Preteaching the Vocabulary

Before students begin reading the chapter, dictate each of the vocabulary terms and ask students to write them on a sheet of paper. When they finish, write the terms on the chalkboard. Then have students guess at the meaning of each. Write their guesses next to each term, but do not give the correct meaning. Leave this list on the chalkboard so that students can see how close their guesses were to the actual definitions as they work through the chapter.

174

What Is Selling?

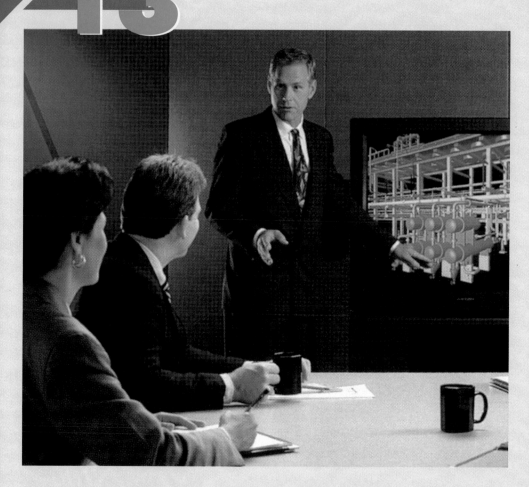

Selling involves providing customers with the goods and services they wish to buy. The selling profession is one of the oldest and most valued. This is particularly true in the United States, where businesses must compete for their share of the market.

In this chapter, you will be exposed to key selling concepts that link products to customers. You will learn what motivates people to buy. You will develop techniques for gathering relevant information about both products and customers. You will survey sales positions and the traits of successful salespeople. In the process, you may discover that selling is the career for you.

174   Unit 5   *Selling*

Classroom Management

For the Teacher

- Teacher's Annotated Editions for all workbooks
- Teacher's Manual for *School-to-Work Handbook*
- *Testing Binder*
- *Transparency Binder*
- *Marketing Software Binder*
- *Marketing Career Portfolio*
- *Lesson Plans*

For the Student

- *Student Activity Workbook*
- *Marketing Math Workbook*
- *School-to-Work Handbook*
- *Student Software*
- *International Case Studies*
- *Marketing Career Portfolio*

SECTION 13.1

Objectives

After completing this section, you will be able to

- define selling and state its goals,
- explain feature-benefit selling,
- identify sources of product information, and
- discuss how customers make buying decisions.

Terms to Know

- selling
- feature-benefit selling
- product feature
- customer benefits
- rational motive
- emotional motive
- extensive decision making
- limited decision making
- routine decision making

Knowing Your Product and Your Customer

Selling is helping customers make satisfying buying decisions—the kind they will be happy with after the sale. Salespeople accomplish this by communicating how products and their features match customers' needs and wants.

For example, one customer in a shoe store might need a comfortable pair of shoes because she stands most of the day at her job. Another customer might want a pair of dress shoes for a party. An alert salesperson will select one or several pairs of shoes appropriate to each customer's needs and wants. In this section, you will learn how to gain and use product knowledge of this sort to help customers make satisfying purchases.

Why is customer satisfaction so important? Because companies want repeat business. They will get it,

however, only if customers are happy enough with their purchases to return again and again.

The twin goals of selling, then, are to help customers decide on purchases and to ensure customer satisfaction so the firm can count on repeat business. To accomplish these goals, a salesperson needs to match the features of each product to a customer's needs and wants. This concept is called **feature-benefit selling.**

Feature-Benefit Selling

It is often said that customers do not buy products. They buy what the products will do for them. Here are some products and the possible reasons people buy them:

- Leather shoes are purchased for their appearance, easy care, comfort, and long life.
- A computer is purchased for increased productivity.
- Insurance is purchased for emotional and financial security.
- An automobile is purchased to travel safely and in comfort, as well as to impress others or to express one's good taste.

Product Features   A salesperson needs to learn how a product's features will benefit the customer. A **product feature** is a physical characteristic or quality of a good or service that explains what it is. The most basic feature of a product is its intended use. A person buys an automobile for transportation, a watch to tell time.

Beyond that, consumers look for certain qualities in products that differentiate competing brands and models. Those qualities are the physical characteristics of the product, or *tangible product features*. In a vehicle they might include color, price, automatic transmission, car stereo system, tires, air bag, and anti-lock brakes.

Additional features usually add more value to a product. For example, an iron that turns itself off after a few minutes of nonuse will cost more than a basic model that does not. Thus, physical features help provide the reasons for price differences among product models.

Then there are *extended product features*. These are not always physically part of the product, but they are important to the purchase decision. For a vehicle, extended features might be the warranty, service policy, and available financing. You might even consider the reputation of a company to be an extended feature. Why? Because there is reduced risk when dealing with a company that is known to stand behind its products.

Customer Benefits   When the features of a product are developed into customer benefits, they become selling points. **Customer benefits** are the advantages or personal satisfaction a customer will get from a good or service. It is a salesperson's job to analyze the product features from the customer's point of view to determine the benefits.

Chapter 13   *What Is Selling?*   **175**

Focus

Bell Ringer Activity

Have students attempt to write their own definition of selling. Encourage them to be more thorough in the development of this definition than they were with the vocabulary term guess already on the chalkboard.

Introducing the Section

Write the key concepts students generated in the Bell Ringer Activity on the chalkboard. Keep soliciting ideas from students until you have all the components of the definition—helping customers make satisfying buying decisions.

Ask students why it is so important to achieve this end. (Students should be able to recognize the need for repeat business as one of the primary reasons.) This discussion will allow you to introduce the two main goals of selling—to help customers decide on purchases and to ensure customer satisfaction so the firm can count on repeat business.

Teach

Guided Practice

1. Read Section 13.1 with students.
2. Use the transparencies for this section.
3. Use a simple product like a pencil to introduce the concept of feature-benefit selling. Have students identify the various features of the product. (In the case of the pencil, these would include attached eraser, #2 graphite, ribbed wooden construction, and yellow color.)

Next have students explain why each feature is a benefit to the user. (For example:
- Eraser makes correcting errors easy and convenient.

Meeting Special Needs

Hearing Impaired

Students with hearing impairments can and do participate in a wide range of classroom activities. To encourage their maximum participation, look at such students when you speak. Do this even if the student talks with the assistance of an interpreter. Not only is this more courteous, but it also allows

the hearing impaired student the option of viewing you and your lip movements directly. If class materials involve technical terminology, supply a list of these words in advance to the student and his or her interpreter. Unfamiliar words can be difficult to lip-read or sign without prior exposure.

- The #2 graphite is dark enough to be used to sketch or write; also recommended for use on standardized tests that are machine graded.
- Wooden construction makes it possible to sharpen the graphite.
- Ribbed design makes the pencil easy to grip and prevents rolling on flat surfaces.
- Yellow color makes the pencil easy to find in a pencil case or box.)

Discussion Starter

Ask students to share their last product purchase with the class and tell why they bought the item. This will allow you to introduce customer buying motives and the distinction between rational and emotional motives. Have students categorize their motives as one or the other.

Continue the discussion by asking students to share how long it took them to make their buying decisions. This line of questioning will help you introduce customer decision-making factors and levels of decision making.

Critical Thinking

1. Ask students what customers are really looking for (which benefits) when buying the following products: a piece of jewelry, most apparel, a winter coat, running shoes, a camera. (Answers will vary. Some possibilities:
   - Jewelry—makes purchaser (and recipient, if a gift) feel good.
   - Apparel—improves buyer's appearance.
   - Winter coat—keeps buyer warm.
   - Running shoes—makes running easier on the feet and legs.
   - Camera—helps purchaser take professional-looking photographs.)

BRIGHT IDEAS

Aim Low

Who would have guessed that a cable TV station with programming aimed directly at children could be successful? Yet Nickelodeon, carrying children's programming by day and reruns of popular situation comedies by night, is just that.

Now the station has found another great ignored market—preschool children and the people who care for them. For this market, Nickelodeon has come up with Nick, Jr.—programming during the morning hours when young children are not yet in school. The station will spend $30 million on this programming, which will occupy five full hours of its daytime lineup.

By capturing the preschool viewing time, Nick, Jr., hopes to attract increased revenue from advertisers targeting women aged 18–49. (They would be the caretakers of the children.) It's a story that should end happily for all—caretakers, children, advertisers, and Nickelodeon.

Creativity Challenge Form teams of 3–5 people. Then try to come up with a network of your own, unlike any other that exists. Start by brainstorming a list of markets that could potentially support their own cable TV station. (Keep in mind that it's advertisers that support a network, based on the viewers they can reach.) Describe the programming you would offer and the reasons you think it would succeed.

As a salesperson, you will need to answer two questions about each product feature:

1. *How does the feature help the product's performance?* The answer to this question represents the first step in developing a customer benefit. For example, the air pockets in the heel of a running shoe cushion its impact on the pavement.
2. *How does the performance information give the customer a personal reason to buy the product?* In other words, of what value is it to the customer? In the case of the running shoe, the cushioning effect of the air pockets gives the wearer more comfort when running or walking and helps protect the foot from injury.

After identifying the features of a product and their benefits, you should put together a *feature-benefit chart*.

The principles of selling **are reflected in advertising. How many tangible product features can you find in this ad?**

This is a chart in which each product feature is listed with its corresponding customer benefits. In preparing such a chart, remember that the more useful a feature, the more valuable the product to the customer. Figure 13-1 shows a feature-benefit chart for the Vivitar Series 1 500PZ camera.

Product Information

Product knowledge is essential for success in selling. Knowing about the product's price, composition, and manufacturing process helps a salesperson explain why one product is better than another. Knowing how to use and care for a product is essential when educating consumers and demonstrating a product during a sales presentation. Developing this product knowledge can be easy—if you know where to look for the information you need. Figure 13-2 on pages 178–179 suggests some possibilities.

Customer Buying Motives

Product knowledge, however, is not enough. To develop relevant consumer benefits for product features, salespeople must develop knowledge of customers. They must study what motivates customers to buy and what decisions customers make before finally purchasing a product.

Bright Ideas

Public television is Nickelodeon's closest competitor during the daytime. But while public television relies on donations and viewer sponsorship through pledge drives, Nickelodeon goes to the bank with advertiser-based revenue. They have more money to spend on children's programming, but they do have commercials. Some parents prefer PBS for that reason.

Caption Answer

Small size, red-eye reduction, power zoom, panorama capability, and electronic flash.

Feature-Benefit Chart

VIVITAR SERIES 1 500PZ CAMERA

Feature: 35–70 mm Power Zoom Auto Focus with Panoramic Adaptor

Benefits: Lets you take clear, sharp scenic photos in the panoramic mode, as well as zoom and ordinary photos. Such versatility makes the Series 1 500PZ the perfect camera for capturing both vacation sights and the special people in your life.

Feature: Auto Load and Auto Rewind

Benefits: Makes the camera easy to use. If the loading is not correct, the "0" in the film counter will blink, telling you that the film needs adjustment.

Feature: Automatic Flash Mode

Benefits: Allows for automatic operation of the flash in all conditions. Especially helpful in low-light situations or when the subject appears against a bright background, such as intense sunlight.

Feature: Flash-On Mode

Benefits: Creates a balanced shot by filling in unwanted shadows and bringing out all of your subject's details.

Feature: Flash-Off Mode

Benefits: Captures your subject using only available light. Especially useful in situations where flash photography is prohibited, such as in museums.

Feature: Red-Eye Reduction Automatic Flash Mode

Benefits: Reduces annoying red-eye in flash portraits. Allows the flash to emit a series of low-intensity pre-flashes that causes the subject's pupils to contract, thus reducing red-eye.

Feature: Fill-In Flash/Slow-Synchro Mode

Benefits: For night photography. Camera selects a slow shutter speed to capture background details and provides enough fill-in flash on the subject, using red-eye reduction.

Feature: Infinity Lock Mode

Benefits: For photographing distant views through windows. Automatically turns off flash to avoid reflections. Perfect for capturing that special photo when traveling by train, plane, or bus.

Feature: Self-Timer Mode

Benefits: Gets you into the picture. Delays release of the shutter button by 10 seconds. Self-timer lamp blinks to show the countdown.

Feature: Size–4.7 x 2.6 x 1.6 inches Weight–8.5 ounces

Benefits: Compact size and light weight make the Series 1 500PZ easy to handle. Especially convenient when traveling.

Feature: Limited One-Year Warranty

Benefits: Vivitar Corporation warrants the Series 1 500PZ to be free of defects in material and workmanship for a period of one year from original date of purchase. During the warranty period, Vivitar Corporation will repair or replace the product at no charge for parts and labor.

Feature: U.S. Authorized Service Centers

Benefits: For owner convenience, returns can be made to any of three service centers—in the East, South, and Pacific regions of the United States.

Feature: Suggested Retail Price–$309.95

Benefits: Good value for such a compact, easy-to-use, 35 mm zoom camera with auto focus, auto flash, auto load, and auto rewind.

Figure 13–1

The Vivitar Series 1 500PZ camera is perfect for someone who wants both a completely automatic camera and a variety of photographic capabilities. Which product feature allows the photographer to be in his or her own photo? What two questions help change that feature into a selling point?

Caption Answer

Feature: self timer mode. Questions: (1) How does the feature help the product's performance? (2) How does that information give the customer a personal reason to buy the product?

2. Tell students to assume they are selling ready-to-wear. Ask where they could find information on how to care for a particular garment. For example, how would they know whether to wash or dry-clean it? (Look at care labels inside the garment. Also, read hangtags.)

Cooperative Learning

Bring in owner's manuals, product labels, and some actual products. Have students break into groups, and give each group one or more items to study as a source(s) of product information.

At the end of 15 minutes, have each group report what kind of information the item provided. Then ask students what other information they would need to sell that product and where they could get it.

L1 Math Skills

Ask students to determine the net prices for the following two competing products:
- Camera A—sells for $139.99 and has a manufacturer's rebate of $10.
- Camera B—on sale for 15 percent off its original retail price of $159.99. (Camera A costs less: $139.99 − $10 = $129.99. Camera B: $159.99 × .85 = $135.99.)

L2 Math Skills

Have students determine the dollar amount of money saved by buying the less expensive camera. ($135.99 − $129.99 = $6).

L3 Math Skills

Have students determine what the percentage reduction in price would have to be for Camera B to match Camera A's net price. (Percentage of price difference: $6 ÷ $135.99 = .044 = 4%. Total percentage: 15% + 4% = 19%. Check: $159.99 × .81 = $129.59.)

L1 Decision-making Skills

Have students list three or four different kinds of products. Then have them write as many rational and emotive motives as they can think of for buying each of these products.

L2 Decision-making Skills

Using the rational and emotive motives developed for the three products in L1 Decision-making Skills activity, have students write selling sentences that connect product features with those motives for buying the products.

L3 Decision-making Skills

Lastly, have students select one of the products to use as the basis for a magazine ad, complete with headline (main buying motive) and ideas for illustrations (photos or artwork) that would help demonstrate the most important buying motives and their connection to specific product features. Have students defend their ads in an oral presentation to the class.

Independent Practice

1. Assign and review the Chapter 13 Case Study in the *International Case Studies* workbook.
2. Have students create a bulletin-board display of selected advertisements arranged according to buying motive. The ads on one side should depict rational motives; those on the other, emotional motives.

Figure 13–2

SOURCES OF PRODUCT INFORMATION

Salespeople can generally find all the product information they need through four main sources.

Direct Experience ▼

Using a product is probably the best source of direct experience. So, some businesses offer their salespeople discounts to encourage them to buy and use the company's merchandise. You can also get direct experience with a product by studying display models or visiting the manufacturing facility to see how the product is made.

▲ Printed Materials

These include user manuals, manufacturer warranties and guarantees, catalogs, and promotional materials. For clothing items or products that are packaged in boxes, bottles, or cans, labels provide important information.

Customers may have rational or emotional motives for making purchases. A **rational motive** is a conscious, factual reason for a purchase. Rational motives include product dependability, time or monetary savings, convenience, comfort, health or safety considerations, recreational value, service, and quality. An **emotional motive** is a feeling experienced by a customer through association with a product. Emotional motives are feelings such as social approval, recognition, power, love, affection, or prestige.

Both rational and emotional motives may be present in the same purchase decision. For example, people buy automobile tires for safety reasons (rational motive) because they care about loved ones who will share the vehicle with them (emotional motive).

Successful salespeople determine customers' rational and emotional motives in a potential buying situation. Then they suggest the features and benefits of the product that best match those motives.

Customers are individuals with different needs and wants that are constantly changing and shifting in relative importance. For example, teenagers may be motivated by

economy when purchasing a first automobile. As single, career-oriented adults, they may be motivated by recognition and social approval when buying a second. Later, as parents, they may be motivated by safety and convenience in selecting a car. Effective salespeople are sensitive to these changing needs and wants.

Customer Decision Making

Some customers need no help from salespeople. Others require significant time and effort. This difference has its roots in three distinct types of decision making—*extensive, limited,* and *routine.* Which type a person uses depends on these factors:

- Amount of previous experience with the product and company
- How often the product is purchased
- Amount of information necessary to make a wise buying decision
- Importance of the purchase to the consumer

Lifelong Learning

What Is Selling?

Sales skills are useful in life and should not be dismissed by those not interested in sales careers. For example, effective teachers "sell" their topic and convince students of features and benefits of learning. Parents "sell" new behavioral principles to children.

Supervisors "sell" new employees on doing work right the first time. Help students link the attributes of an effective salesperson to any role they think they may ever occupy and design a pledge to practice these skills in all areas of their lives.

Other People ▼

Friends, relatives, and customers can share their experiences with you. They can tell you what they liked about the product, as well as how they used it. Co-workers, supervisors, and manufacturers' representatives who have extensive product knowledge can share their expertise with you as well.

Formal Training ▲

Most industrial sales representatives receive much of their product knowledge through formal training sessions. (Some sales representatives spend several months attending classes and observing experienced sales representatives before going out on their own.) In retail settings, training is likely to be less structured. Information might be funneled informally to individuals or small groups as new merchandise is received or selected for promotion.

- Perceived risk involved in the purchase (fear that the product will cause financial loss or physical or emotional harm, or that it won't function properly)
- Time available to make the decision

Extensive Decision Making Extensive decision making is used when there has been little or no previous experience with the item because it is infrequently purchased. Goods and services that have a high degree of perceived risk and are very expensive or important to the potential customer fall into this category. Such products include expensive machinery used in manufacturing, land for a new building site, or an individual's first home.

Limited Decision Making Limited decision making is used when a person buys goods and services that he or she has purchased before but not on a regular basis. There is a moderate degree of perceived risk involved in the purchase. So, the person often needs at least some information to buy the product.

Consumer goods and services in this category might include a second car, certain types of clothing, furniture,

a vacation, and household appliances. Goods and services a firm might buy using limited decision making include accounting services, ad agency services, computer

Real World

MARKETING

Sell Like Hotcakes

The first thing to sell like hotcakes was, well, hotcakes. The expression is rooted in pioneer America, when settlers first discovered the joys of cornmeal batter fried on a griddle. The demand for griddle cakes was so great that cooks couldn't keep up with it. Today the notion of selling like hot cakes, used to refer to an item very much in demand, is still part of our language.

Chapter 13   *What Is Selling?*   **179**

Enrichment

1. Assign and review the appropriate activities in the *Student Activity Workbook*.
2. Assign and review the appropriate Critical Thinking questions from the Chapter Review.
3. Have students take a common product that they bring to school daily (like a knapsack) and prepare a feature-benefit chart for it. Allow time for students to present their finished charts to the class.
4. Have students examine a few issues of *Consumer Reports*. Ask students to determine what kinds of product information they can get from this periodical and when that information might be helpful.

Close

Ask students how feature-benefit selling is related to the two goals of selling. (Answer: In order to help customers decide on purchases and to ensure customer satisfaction so the firm can count on repeat business, a salesperson must uncover a customer's needs and wants. Once a salesperson knows what the customer needs or wants, he or she must communicate how the product's features match those needs and wants by changing the features into customer benefits.)

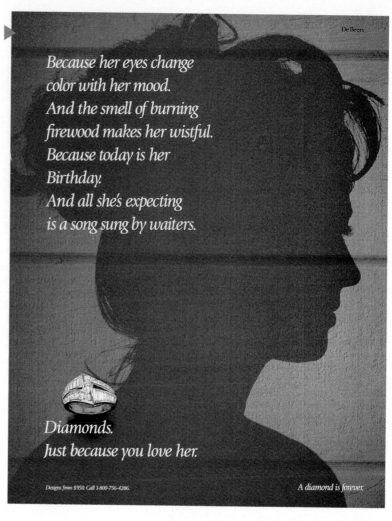

Some purchases require more thought than others. Which of the three types of decision making do you think this suggested purchase would involve? What sort of buying motive? Explain.

programs, office equipment, and certain products used in manufacturing or bought for resale.

Routine Decision Making Routine decision making is used when a person needs little information about a product because of a high degree of prior experience with it or a low perceived risk. The perceived risk may be low because the price is low, the product is bought frequently, or satisfaction with the product is high. Some consumer goods and services in this category are grocery items, newspapers, dry-cleaning services, hairdressing services, and certain brand name clothing and cosmetics. Customers who have developed brand loyalty for a product will use routine decision making. Even more expensive items, such as automobiles, may be purchased routinely if the customer has strong brand loyalty.

Businesses that simply reorder goods and services without much thought are using routine decision making. Products that businesses often buy routinely include raw materials, office supplies, maintenance services, and staple goods bought for resale. These products will continue to be routine purchases until a problem occurs with them or with the supplier. If this happens, limited decision making would be required to change suppliers or products.

SECTION 13.1 *Review*

1. What are the goals of selling?
2. Explain the concept of feature-benefit selling.
3. Name four sources of product information.
4. What are the three levels of decision making that help explain how customers make

Caption Answer

Decision making—probably extensive because of the expense and rarity of the purchase; buying motive—clearly emotional because of all the references to love, mood, and the occasion.

Section Review Answers

1. Helping customers make satisfying buying decisions and ensuring customer satisfaction so the firm can count on repeat business.
2. When features of a product are developed into customer benefits, they become selling points.
3. Direct experience, printed materials, other people, formal training.
4. Extensive, limited, and routine.

SECTION 13.2

Objectives

After completing this section, you will be able to

- explain how selling skills can be helpful in careers other than sales,
- distinguish different types of sales positions, and
- identify the characteristics of effective salespeople.

Terms to Know

- sales associates
- salesclerks
- telemarketing

Is Selling the Career for You?

The more you learn about selling, the more you will realize that the skills you need for that activity are the very same ones you use in your daily life. As a consumer, you evaluate the features and benefits of products you buy. As a student, you evaluate the features of the schools you choose to attend and how they measure up to your needs.

Now let's look at the other side of the coin—situations in which *you* are the product. Suppose you wanted to become president of your DECA chapter. You would present your qualifications (features) and tell how they would benefit both the chapter and its members. When you go on a job or school interview, you would do the same thing.

Examples of people who use selling as a tool abound in business. People in advertising regularly identify and communicate reasons for buying products. The chief executive officer of a corporation uses selling skills to get policies approved by the board of directors. It is not surprising, then, that many CEOs began their careers in sales.

How would you go about getting such experience? To give you some idea, let's look at the different types of sales positions and the characteristics of effective salespeople.

Types of Sales Positions

Sales positions are found in a variety of businesses. The situation with which you are probably most familiar involves working in a retail store. Retail sales personnel are often called *sales associates* or *salesclerks*. It is important to distinguish the two. **Sales associates** are expected to know their products and how to sell. **Salesclerks** are often simply order takers or cashiers.

For example, if you worked in a ski shop, you would probably be expected to know the various sizes and styles of skis, apparel, and accessories sold there. You would also be expected to help customers by explaining the features and benefits of the various items in a way that answers to their needs. In such a case, you would be considered a sales associate. However, if you worked in a self-service store where customers completed order forms and you simply retrieved the items listed, you would be considered a salesclerk.

There are many other sales positions that require extensive training and product knowledge. Think of all the large corporations and the products they sell. Companies like Sony, Johnson & Johnson, John Deere, and other less familiar manufacturers sell their products to other businesses. Sales representatives for those manufacturers are often college graduates. Some even have special degrees, such as chemical engineering. These sales representatives command high salaries and commissions, get bonuses for their efforts, and are trained to be highly professional.

Lastly, there is a specialized sales position that is growing in popularity—telemarketer. **Telemarketing** is the process of selling over the telephone. Consumer products that are frequently sold over the telephone include magazine subscriptions, service contracts for newly purchased televisions and computers, and lawn care services. Businesses are often solicited over the phone to purchase stationery supplies and cleaning supplies.

It's All in the Wrist

In many countries, the handshake is the traditional gesture of salutation. North Americans, however, tend to regard it as more than that. They use the handshake to form an opinion of a person based on the amount of pressure applied and whether or not eye contact is made. In the global marketplace, however, such a standard may be misleading.

In the Middle East, young businessmen are taught to use a gentle grip when shaking hands—to avoid suggesting aggression. In Islamic countries, a woman is not permitted to touch a man to whom she is not related. So, a handshake could cause a cross-cultural crisis. The French shake hands at every opportunity—when greeting, departing, returning—many times in a day, in both business and social situations.

Focus

Bell Ringer Activity

Tell students to think about the characteristics of an effective salesperson. Then compile a list based on the word itself—one characteristic for each letter. For example, *s*—sincere, *a*—articulate, etc.

Introducing the Section

Use a modified brainstorming technique to quickly get the Bell Ringer Activity lists onto the chalkboard. Call on students in a sequence that will ensure everyone has a chance to volunteer characteristics. (When students do not have any additional words to offer, they should be permitted to pass.) Continue until all words are listed on the chalkboard. Do not evaluate the students' responses at this point—that will be the next step in the process.

Teach

Guided Practice

1. Read Section 13.2 with students.
2. Have students read aloud the Case Study and review the answers in class.
3. Evaluate all the responses generated by students in the ongoing Bell Ringer Activity. Ask students to agree/disagree with each word and tell why they think it is/is not an important characteristic for salespeople to have.
4. Assign and review the Chapter 13 Activity in the *School-to-Work Handbook*.

Discussion Starter

Ask students if anyone in their family or circle of friends has a sales position. This question will help you introduce the different types of sales positions.

More About

Telemarketing

Telemarketers have had such negative press that even Miss Manners, the etiquette expert, advised people to hang up on them. New technology like caller identification and call-blocking can also work against telemarketers. Customers with these features are not as likely to pick up the phone if they see a phone number displayed on the screen that they don't recognize.

Did You Know

Many salespeople are periodically afflicted with a fear closely akin to stage fright. Theirs is a fear of self-promotion that inhibits the behavior that results in sales—namely, making sales calls. The *Journal of Training and Development* states that 40 percent of veteran salespeople suffer from this syndrome, called sales-call reluctance, at some time in their careers.

Present students with this scenario. A shoe salesperson is waiting on a mother and her three little boys. When one child starts crying uncontrollably, the mother is exasperated and wants to leave. But the salesperson has already found the shoes for the children and is ready to have them tried on. Ask: If you were the salesperson, what would you do to salvage the sale?

L2 Human Relations Skills

Using the scenario in the L1 Human Relations Skills activity, identify the traits that an effective salesperson would demonstrate in the situation. (Answers will vary. Most will suggest empathy, patience, problem-solving ability, good communication skills, and a positive attitude).

L3 Human Relations Skills

Have students role-play the L1 Human Relations Skills scenario, demonstrating the personal characteristics and skills identified in the L2 activity.

Independent Practice

Have students review employment want ads to find all the different ways a sales position can be listed. Suggest that they clip or highlight all ads they think are relevant and use them as the basis for a short written report. Possible topics for discussion: how terms used for industrial sales position differ from those used in retail selling, difference between inside and outside sales positions.

CASE STUDY

Become a Plumber—and Sell the World

The federal government deregulated the nation's natural-gas industry in 1992. Brooklyn Union Gas (BUG) was one of the many companies affected by this change. Until then, the utility was virtually unchallenged in the field of residential heating. With deregulation, however, its territory (Brooklyn, Queens, and Staten Island) was opened to competition. Some of its new competitors were Long Island's Lilco, California-based Pacific Gas & Electric, and a number of independent oil and gas entrepreneurs.

To meet this new challenge, BUG set three goals for itself: create customer satisfaction, enhance growth opportunity, and increase net profitability. To accomplish those goals, it restructured. Among other things, it eliminated its sales force, which was weak. For its former sales personnel, it substituted a presell qualification center—and lots of plumbers.

Now when potential customers call, telephone operators at the presell center handle much of the work that the sales force used to do. They qualify and categorize the callers, send out literature, answer general questions, and schedule appointments.

The appointments are handled by certified master plumbers, independently contracted and trained by BUG. They now explain the benefits of gas heat to prospects and sell boilers as well as install them.

BUG oversees the plumbers, whom they call installers. A seven-member team is in charge of training the installers in sales, safety, and new installation requirements, as well as BUG's performance standards. The goal is to encourage the installers to act as if they were representatives of BUG while still encouraging them to be entrepreneurial. (BUG customers pay the plumbers directly for boiler installations.)

The initial results of combining the sales and installer positions have been favorable. Closure rates per lead doubled during the pilot study.

Case Study Review

1. How do BUG's goals and actions relate to the general goals of selling identified in this chapter?
2. What trait(s) do plumbers already possess that make them good candidates for selling both boilers and the idea of using gas instead of oil for home heating? What skills might they still need to develop?

A MATTER OF ETHICS

3. BUG's decision to fire its entire sales force and replace them with independent plumbers could be viewed as ethically questionable—or not. Argue both sides of the issue.

Case Study Answers

1. BUG's goals are in accord with the text. Company restructured to give customers expert information and increase their satisfaction with the sales and installation experience.
2. Have: product knowledge and entrepreneurial spirit (independence, persistence, etc.). Need: selling skills.
3. Answers will vary. Some will defend BUG's restructuring as simply a matter of staying competitive. Others will argue that the company could have accomplished the same thing by retraining its salespeople instead of firing them.

Characteristics of Effective Salespeople

By now, you may be wondering if you have the qualities needed for success in a sales career. Don't be disillusioned by the cliché that a salesperson is born, not made. You can be an effective salesperson if you are willing to develop the following traits and skills.

Good Communication Skills Effective salespeople have excellent listening and speaking skills. When listening, they are even able to read between the lines in order to better understand their customers. Knowing proper grammar and having a pleasant speaking voice with clear diction further contribute to a salesperson's ability to interact well with customers.

Good Interpersonal Skills Effective salespeople know how to get along with different people. They can deal with customers who are demanding as well as with those who are reserved. They know what to say and how to say it. In particular, they are tactful. They can say something negative in a way that does not offend others.

Customers often have legitimate problems, and creative salespeople can solve them. They know how to ask the right questions to determine customer needs and develop appropriate solutions. This builds strong business relationships.

Solid Technical Skills Good math and computer skills coupled with product knowledge provide the technical foundation for a salesperson's career. Professional salespeople are experts in their field. They read industry trade papers and keep up with trends affecting their customers. To develop product knowledge, they study their company's products as well as the competition's.

Today's salespeople are also skillful computer users. They need to be because many now use laptop computers to stay in touch with their companies. This gives them access to up-to-date inventory and customer account information, among other things.

Positive Attitude and Self-Confidence In sales, maintaining a positive attitude is essential to success. A positive attitude involves learning from your mistakes and looking for something useful in all situations. Generally, people with high self-esteem and self-confidence are secure enough to accept rejection from lost sales and bounce back.

Goal Orientation Being motivated and ambitious are necessary in sales because many selling situations require salespeople to find new customers and generate new business. Being goal-oriented helps keep effective salespeople focused and striving for success.

Persistence is often necessary in sales. Some customers require more attention and more frequent calls before a sale can be made. Effective salespeople do not give up easily when confronted with customers of this sort. Rather, they view such situations as challenges and persist until they are successful.

Empathy Empathy is the essence of customer-oriented selling. Empathetic salespeople are able to see things from a customer's point of view and be sensitive to a customer's problems. For example, such a salesperson might say, "I can understand why you feel that way. If I were in your situation, I would feel the same." But the salesperson must be sincere in this. Customers are astute and can tell when salespeople don't mean what they say. When customers sense that you have their best interests at heart, they let down their defenses and begin really listening to you.

Honesty Successful salespeople are honest because they know integrity is the cornerstone of professional selling. To generate repeat sales and establish a sound relationship with customers, there must be trust. Customers do not welcome back salespeople who sold them goods they did not need or that did not perform up to their expectations.

Enthusiasm Lastly, all successful salespeople are enthusiastic about the products they sell. To be enthusiastic, you must believe in the products you sell and the company you represent. If you cannot convince yourself that the product you are selling is worthwhile or useful, you will not be able to convince your customers. Your lack of enthusiasm will come through. This means you must select products and represent companies that you believe in so your enthusiasm will come naturally.

Telemarketing is the process of selling over the telephone. What special skills and traits do you think telemarketers should have?

SECTION 13.2 Review

1. How can knowledge of selling help you in your everyday life?
2. Distinguish an order taker, a retail sales associate, an industrial sales representative, and a telemarketer.
3. Name six characteristics of effective salespeople.

Chapter 13 *What Is Selling?* **183**

Answers

Vocabulary Review

Paragraphs will vary. See Glossary for definitions.

Fact and Idea Review

1. So they become repeat customers.
2. A physical characteristic or quality of the good or service that explains what it is.
3. When they are changed into customer benefits.
4. How does the feature help the product's performance? How does the performance information give the customer a personal reason to buy the product?
5. A rational motive is a conscious, factual reason for a purchase. An emotional motive is a feeling of satisfaction a customer derives from a product.
6. College graduates, some with special degrees, who have extensive training and product knowledge.
7. Selling over the telephone.
8. Ability to deal with a variety of people and different personalities.
9. See things from the customer's point of view.
10. Select products and represent companies that you believe in so your enthusiasm will come naturally.

Critical Thinking

1. Answers will vary. Responses may be rational or emotional in nature; accept both.
2. **a.** Ability to get messages when away from home, which could be very important to businesspeople on the road.
   b. Makes camera easy to use and reassures customer of focused shots every time.
   c. Convenient because you don't have to change CDs as frequently.

184

Vocabulary Review

Construct a paragraph using the following word groupings as a guide.

Topic sentence: definition of *selling*

Supporting sentences:

- feature-benefit selling
  product features
  customer benefits
- rational motive
  emotional motive
- extensive decision making
  limited decision making
  sales associates

- salesclerks
  routine decision
  making
  telemarketing

Fact and Idea Review

1. Why is it so important for customers to be pleased with their purchases? (Sec. 13.1)
2. What is a product feature? (Sec. 13.1)
3. When do features of a product become selling points? (Sec. 13.1)
4. What two questions about a product feature does a salesperson need to answer to determine a customer benefit for that feature? (Sec. 13.1)
5. Explain the difference between a rational motive and an emotional motive. (Sec. 13.1)
6. What are some characteristics of manufacturers' sales representatives? (Sec. 13.2)
7. What is telemarketing? (Sec. 13.2)
8. What sorts of interpersonal skills do salespeople need to develop? (Sec. 13.2)
9. What are empathetic salespeople able to do? (Sec. 13.2)
10. What should you do in order to be an enthusiastic salesperson? (Sec. 13.2)

Critical Thinking

1. Think of a purchase you or your family recently made, and explain the meaning of the following statement: Customers do not buy products. They buy what the products will do for them.
2. Determine a customer benefit for each of the following product features:
   a. Remote access on a telephone message machine
   b. Automatic focus on a camera
   c. Capacity to hold ten CDs on a CD player
3. Where can a salesperson obtain product information to develop a feature-benefit chart for the following

184 Unit 5 *Selling*

items: a ski jacket? a bicycle? a camera? a copier? a computer?
4. You are the manufacturer of a unique jacket that can be made suitable for all seasons. The jacket is designed so that parts of it can be added or removed for changing weather conditions. What would you do to train your sales force? What would you do to help retailers train their salespeople to sell the jacket?
5. Assume you are a new sales associate for a retail store like the Gap that specializes in women's and men's clothing. Besides learning the types of products available, what additional information would you need to know to be an effective sales associate for that company? How would you get that information?
6. Explain your reasons for agreeing or disagreeing with the following statement: Customers love to buy but hate to be sold.
7. Think of a time when a telemarketer called your home. Was this person's selling effort successful or unsuccessful? Why?

Building Academic Skills

Math

1. In preparing a sales presentation for your company's all-purpose cleaner, you gather the following data on your own and competitors' products:

Cleaner	Fluid Ounces	Price
A	22	$ 3.79
B	28	4.29
C	40	6.99
Yours	44	7.19

Calculate the price per ounce for each cleaner. Then identify which, if any, product beats your own.

Communication

2. Write a classified advertisement for a sales position in the school store. Include a brief description of the job responsibilities, as well as the characteristics and skills required for the position.
3. In preparation for a sales demonstration with a product of your choice, write a letter to the product's manufacturer. In the first paragraph, introduce yourself and tell the reason for writing the letter. Include information on why you selected that company's product for your research. In the next paragraph, identify the specific information you are interested in. That might include product features, warranty information, related accessories,

3. Answers will vary. Responses that apply to all items: item itself, hang-tags, price tags, manufacturer's specification sheets, catalogs, brochures, owner's manuals, warranties, ads, other promotional materials, and sales representatives.
4. Manufacturer's sales force: have them visit the factory to see how the garment is made, give them a jacket to wear, and conduct formal sales training.

Retail salespeople: produce a video retailers can show their staffs that covers how the product is made and explains all the features and benefits of the product.
5. Company policies, such as special sales arrangements, credit cards accepted, as well as the return policy. You would learn these things during training and refer to operations guidelines given to you by the store manager.

construction and design of the product, as well as instructions for proper care and a list of service centers. In the last paragraph, request the information in a way that is courteous and makes it easy for the reader to comply.

Human Relations

4. One of the benefits of working as a salesperson for a retail store is receiving an employee discount. Assume you work for a local ski shop and receive a 20 percent employee discount, which can only be used by you and your immediate family members. Your friend is in the market for a new pair of skis and asks you to buy them for him so he can benefit from your discount. What would you do? Why?

Application Projects

1. Many different terms are used to identify sales positions. These include sales representative, sales associate, route sales representative, sales engineer, sales agent, sales trainee, sales/technical representative, sales consultant, direct marketing representative, and sales coordinator.
   - Using these terms as a guide, look through the classified section of a Sunday newspaper for sales want ads. Clip ten of them.
   - Review your ads to identify two sets of terms—those used to describe retail sales positions and those used to describe industrial sales positions.
   - Analyze the requirements for each position, giving special attention to previous experience and educational background. Also, note the starting salary.
   - On a piece of paper, mount the ads in sequence, starting with those having the least demanding requirements and ending with those having the most demanding requirements.

2. It takes special traits and skills to become a successful salesperson. See how well you meet the qualifications.
   - First, list all the traits you have that you think will help make you successful in sales. Then list all the traits and skills you think you need to work on.
   - Next, have a classmate make the same lists of your strong and weak points. Compare your own lists to those of your classmate. (You may be surprised at the differences.)
   - Then, working with the same classmate, brainstorm ways to turn your weaknesses into strengths.

3. Select a product and prepare a feature-benefit chart for it. The product should be one that would require limited decision making—that is, study and comparison before purchase. *Note:* You will be using this project to develop a sales training manual in later chapters.

Linking School to Work

Prepare a background report on your company. Include a brief history of the firm and how it sells its products. Also, discuss what types of salespeople are employed and what company policies related to sales are important for a new salesperson to know.

Performance Assessment

Role Play

Situation. You have been employed by a clothing store for three months. Every day when you arrive, your assistant manager tells you to check the incoming stock, return clothes left in the dressing rooms, and rearrange stock. You were hired as a sales associate, but you have not as yet met your weekly sales quotas. The problem is that you are spending so much time doing tasks that no one else wants to do that you are not able to help customers. At this point you are discouraged and decide you must speak with your manager.

Evaluation. You will be evaluated on how well you are able to do the following:
- Explain the importance of product knowledge and customer buying decisions.
- Discuss types of sales positions.
- Demonstrate characteristics of effective salespeople.
- Provide a creative solution to your problem of not having enough time to help customers.

Public Speaking

You have been asked to demonstrate the concept of feature-benefit selling for your company's new sales trainees. Using a product of your own choice, prepare and deliver an appropriate instructional presentation.

Complete the Chapter 13 Computer Application that appears in the Student Activity Workbook.

3. To get the addresses of manufacturers, students should look at product packaging or labels. Most will include a city and state for the home office. They should then call the home office to get the complete address, as well as the person to whom the letter should go.

Human Relations

4. Ethical choice would be to refuse. Students should realize the risks and consequences of buying the skis for a friend and explain them: If caught, they could get fired. Also, may be hard to stop if others ask the same favor.

Application Projects

1. Answers will vary. You may want to create a bulletin board display of the students' work.
2. Student lists will vary.
3. Suggest that students select products with which they are familiar. Check to be sure the product does *not* require routine or extensive decision making. Either of those extremes would make it difficult to prepare the sales training manual.

Linking School to Work

Answers depend on the work situation.

Performance Assessment

Refer to the *DECA Competitive Events Handbook* for evaluation guidelines.

Computer Application

Optional activity. Refer to the *Marketing Software Binder* for template and user information.

Evaluation

Administer the reproducible test for Chapter 13, or construct your own using the Testmaker software.

6. Most will suggest that customers don't like high-pressure sales tactics and/or salespeople who put their commissions before the needs and wants of customers.
8. Answers will vary.

Building Academic Skills

Math

1. A—$.17, B—$.15, C—$.17, Yours—$.16. B beats your price.

Communication

2. Answers will vary. Possible characteristics/skills: Good in math, likes people, responsible, punctual. No experience necessary.

Chapter Overview

Chapter 14 introduces students to all the steps in the sales process. It then explores the first two steps—the preapproach and the approach—in detail.

Springboard

To introduce the steps of a sale, have students think back to the last sales situation in which they used limited decision making. Then take them through the stages of a sale by asking questions designed to elicit each step (first a general description, then a name). For example, to illustrate approaching the customer, ask what happened when they walked into the store.

You should be able to elicit steps 2–7 in this fashion. However, you may have to supply additional examples for the pre-approach and follow-up steps if students do not have experience with these.

Prereading

List the section objectives to discuss with students. Have students skim the chapter, looking at the pictures, reading the captions, and noting the heads. Ask questions to ensure that students have a minimal understanding of the chapter structure.

Preteaching the Vocabulary

Before students begin reading the chapter, dictate each of the vocabulary terms and ask students to write them on a sheet of paper. When they finish, write the terms on the chalkboard. Then have students guess at the meaning of each. Write their guesses next to each term, but do not give the correct meaning. Leave this list on the chalkboard so that students can see how close their guesses were to the actual definitions as they work through the chapter.

186

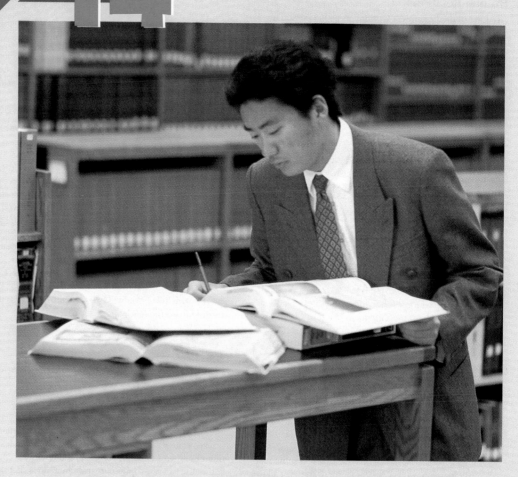

The Sales Process

Now that you have an understanding of product knowledge and customer decision making, you are ready to begin your study of the sales process. This chapter will give you an overview of the steps of a sale. It will also explain how salespeople find potential customers, how they get ready to sell, and how they approach customers in both retail and industrial sales situations.

186   Unit 5   *Selling*

Classroom Management

For the Teacher
- Teacher's Annotated Edition for all workbooks
- Teacher's Manual for *School-to-Work Handbook*
- *Testing Binder*
- *Transparency Binder*
- *Marketing Software Binder*
- *Marketing Career Portfolio*
- *Lesson Plans*

For the Student
- *Student Activity Workbook*
- *Marketing Math Workbook*
- *School-to-Work Handbook*
- *Student Software*
- *International Case Studies*
- *Marketing Career Portfolio*

SECTION 14.1

Objectives

After completing this section, you will be able to

- list the eight steps of a sale,
- explain how salespeople find customers, and
- describe how the preapproach is used in industrial and retail sales.

Terms to Know

- preapproach
- prospect
- referrals
- endless chain method
- cold canvasing

The Steps of a Sale

Professional salespeople go through eight steps when helping a customer make a purchase.

1. *Preapproach*—looking for customers and getting ready for the sale
2. *Approaching the customer*—actually greeting the customer face-to-face
3. *Determining needs*—learning what the customer is looking for in a good or service in order to decide what products to show and which product features to present first in the next step of the sale
4. *Presenting the product*—educating the customer about the product's features and benefits
5. *Handling questions and objections*—learning why the customer is reluctant to buy, providing information to remove that uncertainty, and helping the customer make a satisfying buying decision
6. *Closing the sale*—getting the customer's positive agreement to buy
7. *Suggestion selling*—suggesting that the customer buy additional merchandise or services to save money or better enjoy the original purchase
8. *Reassuring and following up*—helping a customer feel that he or she has made a wise purchase

In this chapter, we will concentrate on the first two steps—the *preapproach* and *approach*. In later chapters, we will examine the other six steps.

The Preapproach

The **preapproach** is getting ready to sell. In all selling situations, salespeople can prepare for the sale by studying their products and keeping abreast of industry trends. Reading periodicals related to their industry is helpful. In addition, they should pay careful attention to their personal appearance.

Beyond this basic preparation, retail and industrial salespeople get involved in specific activities. In some selling situations, the preapproach includes finding new customers.

Finding New Customers

Looking for new customers is called *prospecting*. A **prospect** (also called a lead) is a potential customer. Many types of businesses require salespeople to find prospects, while others do not. For example, most retail selling situations are not involved with prospecting because customers come to the store.

It is in selling situations where the sales representative visits the customer in the customer's home or business that prospecting is an important step in the sale. For that reason, prospecting is important in most business-to-business selling situations. As a matter of fact, in many industrial selling situations, salespeople are evaluated on how many new accounts they open and how much they sell. It is to the salesperson's advantage to open many new accounts to generate sales volume.

Real World

Don't Call Us—We'll Call You

Trade shows are a rich source of customer leads and contacts—provided exhibitors follow up. However, a recent survey suggests that companies rarely do. The average trade show visitor spends up to six hours looking at exhibits. He or she talks to more than 15 company or product representatives. Yet only about 20 percent of these potential customers are contacted afterwards.

Chapter 14   *The Sales Process*   **187**

Meeting Special Needs

English as a Second Language

If your class consists of students with differing levels of English fluency, the sales material can present several challenges—especially in the area of role-playing. Encourage active participation of all students in such activities, but keep in mind varying ability levels. Pair nonnative with native speakers for verbal exercises when appropriate.

In regular classroom activities, allow sufficient time for nonnative speakers to answer verbal questions. This will help them gain confidence in their communication skills. Also, note that there will be a big difference in students' English skills depending on how long they have been in the United States.

Focus

Bell Ringer Activity

Remind students that gold miners in the Old West were said to be "prospecting." Ask students what the term meant in that context.

Introducing the Section

Use the students' answers to the Bell Ringer Activity to introduce the concept of prospecting for customers as practiced by salespeople who must generate their own potential customer lists.

Teach

Guided Practice

1. Read Section 14.1 with students.
2. Use the transparency for this section.
3. Have students read aloud the Case Study and review the answers in class.
4. To introduce the preapproach, ask students what the prefix *pre-* means. (Before.) Then have students brainstorm to develop things that would be involved in the retail preapproach and the industrial preapproach.

Discussion Starter

Ask students if the following activities should be part of a salesperson's job:

- Checking in stock received from the manufacturer
- Rearranging stock
- Returning goods to stock from dressing rooms
- Putting price tickets on goods

Have students defend their answers. (Students should eventually arrive at the conclusion that all these activities help salespeople learn things they must know like the location, types, and prices of goods they sell.)

Critical Thinking

1. Ask students which type of prospecting they would prefer using—cold canvassing or the endless chain method—and why. (Most students would agree that the endless chain method is easier because it allows you to use the name of a mutual acquaintance to get a foot in the door.)

2. Tell students to imagine that they sell stationary bicycles and that they have an appointment with the buyer of a new sporting goods store. Ask how they might get acquainted with the store before their sales call. (Visit unannounced and note the location, merchandise mix, size, and amount of customer traffic.)

Cooperative Learning

Have students break into groups to brainstorm ways a new photographer can find customers. Tell students that this photographer's services include wedding photography, portraits, and commercial photography. (The latter classification includes photos for ads, brochures, annual reports, and the like.) Remind students to use all the possible prospecting methods discussed in this section. After ten minutes, have each group report its findings orally to the class.

L1 Math Skills

Tell students to assume that they work for a major department store and that they are working during a special one-day sale. During this sale, an additional 25 percent will be taken off the prices of items with red price tickets. Have students calculate the net purchase price for the following: three items priced at $99.99, $19.99, and $57.99 (only the first item has a red ticket). [($99.99 × .75) + $19.99 +

188

Sources and Methods of Prospecting

A rich supply of prospect sources is available to enterprising salespeople. Among them are various kinds of directories, periodicals, lists, and suggested leads.

Employer Leads   Some firms employ an entire telemarketing department for the sole purpose of generating leads for their sales staff. In such firms, telemarketers often qualify the leads. That way, the salespeople have a great deal of information about the prospects before ever meeting them. At the other end of the spectrum, other firms rely entirely on their salespeople to find new customers.

Most businesses probably fall somewhere between those two extremes. Many employers do what they can to help locate potential customers for their salespeople. Figure 14–1 provides some insight into how leads are created and acted on.

Telephone Directories   The White Pages of telephone directories provide names, addresses, and telephone numbers of potential customers in given geographic areas. The Yellow Pages list businesses that may be potential customers for certain industrial goods and services.

Trade and Professional Directories   Business-to-business sales representatives can use trade and professional directories to locate potential customers by type of business. A well-known directory is *Thomas' Register of American Manufacturers*.

Newspapers   Newspapers provide good leads for some salespeople. For example, birth announcements are good leads for insurance salespeople. Engagement announcements provide bridal shops, caterers, florists, and printers with prospects. Reports of business mergers and announcements of new personnel in business firms provide leads for industrial salespeople.

Commercial Lists   Salespeople may buy lists of potential customers from companies that specialize in categorizing people by such criteria as education, age, income, credit card purchases, and location. Lists of businesses categorized according to net sales, profits, products, and geographic locations are also available.

Customer Referrals   Satisfied customers often give salespeople **referrals**—the names of other people who might buy the product. Referrals give you the chance to talk to potential customers you might not have reached if they hadn't been recommended.

When salespeople ask previous customers for names of potential customers, they are said to be using the **endless chain method.** Some companies offer discounts or gifts to customers who give referrals.

Cold Canvasing   In **cold canvasing,** a salesperson tries to locate potential customers with little help other than a telephone directory. This is also sometimes called *blind prospecting*. Here are some examples:

- A real estate agent goes door-to-door in a neighborhood, asking people if they would like to sell their homes.
- A stockbroker selects peoples' names from a telephone book and calls them.
- A salesperson for a clothing manufacturer visits a new store in his or her sales territory.

Figure 14–1

HOW EMPLOYER LEADS ARE DEVELOPED

Employers often get leads from their involvement in trade shows and from advertising in trade journals and consumer magazines. Some firms send direct mail pieces to people in a given geographic area or to businesses in a given industry. The main thrust of their message is "Call us if you're interested." Other firms subscribe to computer database services to get names, addresses, and telephone numbers of prospective customers.

◀ **Prospective Customers Respond**

to this promotion by requesting further information.

Employers ▲ Pass On Leads

to the sales representatives responsible for the territories in which the prospects are located.

188   Unit 5   *Selling*

More About

Prospecting

Certain industries—namely, copier sales, temporary personnel sales, and local advertising sales—rely more heavily than others on the cold canvassing technique. Salespeople in these areas often walk into a prospective client's office with no appointment in order to gain information such as number of employees, decor (a key to financial resources), style of doing business, and level of professionalism. The disadvantage of this method is time and cost. There is a limit as to how many cold calls a salesperson can make in a day, as well as a limit to how effective these unplanned calls can be. The technique is most effective in high-density office buildings in major metropolitan areas.

Preparing for the Sale in Industrial Selling

In industrial sales, preapproach activities vary, depending on whether the sales call is with a previous customer or a new prospect. When dealing with previous customers, salespeople analyze past sales records. Knowing what and how much customers purchased in the past helps salespeople with new orders.

Knowledgeable salespeople also review their notes about the previous buyer's personality, family, interests, and hobbies. In general, people are pleased when others take the time to remember them as individuals, not just as accounts.

When dealing with a new customer, the salesperson must do some homework to qualify the prospect before going any further with the selling process. Questions that the salesperson should research include the following:

- Does the prospect need this product or service?
- Does the prospect have the financial resources to pay?
- Does the prospect have the authority to buy?

To find answers to these questions, you may make inquiries by calling other sales representatives who sell noncompeting lines. You may read the company's annual reports. You may visit the retail store or the manufacturing facility in question to get answers. To determine if the prospect has the financial resources to pay, you may subscribe to the credit services offered by Dun & Bradstreet

(D&B). D&B ratings suggest how good a credit risk your prospect is. Lastly, you may get the information directly from the prospect.

During your telephone conversation with the prospect, you may be able to answer some of the above concerns by tactfully asking questions. You could ask what competing products the prospect carries. This would give you an opportunity to determine if the person is satisfied with his or her present supplier and if your product could satisfy his or her needs. Other questions might help to determine how your product could help improve the prospect's business.

If a prospect is not a viable customer for your product, your research will have saved you time and money. However, if the prospect is a good lead, your research can be the basis for a strong sales presentation when you do finally meet face-to-face.

In order to make that contact, the final step in the preapproach for most industrial selling situations is making an appointment to see the prospect. This is true even when the customer is one you have dealt with before.

Preparing for the Sale in Retail Selling

Since the customer comes to you in retail selling situations, much of the preparation centers around the merchandise and work area. It involves stockkeeping and housekeeping activities such as those listed on page 191.

▼ Salespeople Act on Leads
by calling to qualify the prospects.

Salespeople ▶ Report Back

with information on the disposition of the prospects. That way the employer knows the salesperson has followed up on the leads sent to him or her.

More About

Dun & Bradstreet

As part of the process of qualifying a prospect, many businesses subscribe to credit reporting agencies such as Dun & Bradstreet to determine if prospects are creditworthy. Some companies receive their information from Dun & Bradstreet directly on-line to their computers. Others arrange to phone Dun & Bradstreet for the information, which is then mailed or faxed to their office.

$57.99 = $74.99 + $19.99 + $57.99 = $152.97].

L2 Math Skills

Tell students to assume that during the special one-day sale, management also offers a special coupon for 10 percent off one item of merchandise that has not been marked down. Tell them that the customer in the situation described the L1 Math Skills activity wants to apply that additional discount to the $57.99 item. Have them determine the total price the customer must pay, including 6 percent sales tax. [Merchandise: $74.99 + $19.99 + ($57.99 × .90) = $74.99 + $19.99 + $52.19 = $147.17. Sales tax: $147.17 × 1.06 = $156.]

L3 Math Skills

Tell students to assume that the person in the L2 Math Skills activity returns the $19.99 item and wants to exchange it for a $23.99 item. Have them calculate how much the customer owes the store. (Merchandise difference: $23.99 − $19.99 = $4. Sales tax difference: $4 × .06 sales tax = $.24. Total owed: $4 + $.24 = $4.24.)

Independent Practice

1. Assign and review the Chapter 14 Case Study in the *International Case Studies* workbook.
2. Have students interview an industrial salesperson or any businessperson who must generate his or her own sales leads. Have them ask the salesperson to describe the prospecting methods used and evaluate which were the most effective and why. Also, suggest they ask what the salesperson does with the leads once they are generated.

Evaluation

Assign and review the Section 14.1 Review.

Reteaching

1. Assign and review the vocabulary terms for this section.
2. Assign and review Fact and Idea Review questions 1–5 from the Chapter Review.
3. To reteach the steps of a sale, tell a story about a hypothetical sale. As you go along, have students identify each step of the sales process. (They should be able to name the step and tell when it starts in the sales process.)

Enrichment

1. Assign and review the appropriate activities in the *Student Activity Workbook*.
2. Assign and review the appropriate Critical Thinking questions from the Chapter Review.
3. Have students read issues of *Personal Selling Power* and *Sales & Marketing Management* magazines to find articles that pertain to prospecting and the preapproach. Ask students to summarize the articles they read in a written report and to share the key points orally with the class.

Close

Help students recite the eight steps of a sale by giving them the first letter of each step—P, A, N, P, O, C, S, F—as a clue. (Preapproach, approach, needs determined, presentation of product, objections overcome, closing the sale, suggestion selling, reassurance and follow-up).

CASE STUDY

Getting to Know Your Customers

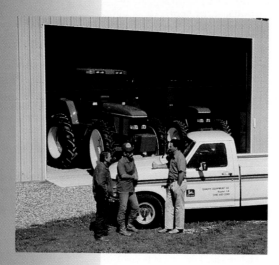

John Deere & Co., a producer of farm equipment, has developed a sales strategy that involves hourly workers in the sales process. Some of Deere's more experienced and knowledgeable assembly line workers make unscheduled visits to local farmers to discuss their problems. Deere's workers are also asked to attend regional trade shows throughout North America to explain Deere products.

To understand the significance of this sales strategy, let's look at some of the steps involved in the decision to buy a business-to-business product. We will assume that the potential customer already recognizes that he or she has a problem that requires a solution.

- *General need description.* The prospect determines the characteristics, specifications, and quantity of the needed item. When it is a complicated product, the prospect may solicit others with technical expertise. The John Deere workers have the technical expertise to supply this information.
- *Product specifications.* The prospect analyzes the product to decide whether it is a good value. Are its costs proportionate to its usefulness? Are all its features needed? The John Deere workers are invaluable at this stage because they can supply this information in a nonthreatening manner.
- *Supplier search.* Ways a prospect identifies a suitable supplier include past experience, recommendations, personal contact with salespeople, product literature and advertising, trade shows, and articles in publications. The John Deere workers fit into this list as part of the trade show option. However, they also add an option in the form of their informal, unannounced visits.
- *Supplier selection.* Many prospects use a rating system to help at this point. Typically they consider things like delivery capability, quality, price, and product service. The information gathered firsthand by Deere's low-key workers is highly valuable at this stage. It allows sales representatives to design a targeted sales presentation based on what the dealer or farmer deems most important.

Knowing a customer's buying decision process and inserting oneself into it early and skillfully in this fashion can give a firm a competitive edge. The proof? It has worked for John Deere. In 1994 the company's sales were up 5 percent, and its net income rose 35 percent.

Case Study Review

1. How is John Deere's use of hourly workers related to the preapproach step of the sales process?
2. Why is it important to know the prospect's buying decision process?

A MATTER OF ETHICS

3. Are customers being tricked by John Deere's "folksy" approach to salesmanship? Why or why not?

Case Study Answers

1. The hourly workers help salespeople prepare for the sale by gathering important information used to tailor the sales presentation for specific customers.
2. It creates opportunities to enter that process early, which gives an edge over competitors.
3. Answers will vary. Most will say no because the hourly workers are not deceiving the customers. They are simply trying to help the customers get what they need by communicating their needs to the Deere company. This method helps Deere produce products made to fit customer needs, which in fact should improve the quality of customer's work.

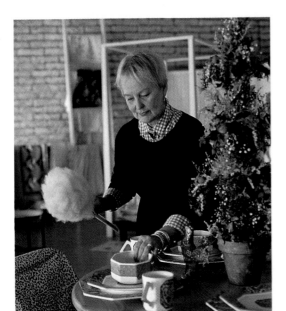

*Straightening, dusting, and replenishing **stock are more than just housekeeping tasks** for a salesperson. Explain why.*

- Straightening, rearranging, and replenishing the stock
- Adjusting price tickets before and after special sales
- Learning where stock is located and how much is available
- Taking inventory
- Arranging displays
- Vacuuming the floor, dusting the shelves, and keeping the selling area neat and clean.

All the above activities are important because they give you an opportunity to learn about the merchandise. You can learn what goods go well together, as well as the prices of the merchandise. Keeping all the merchandise in an orderly fashion is beneficial, too—especially when you go to look for a specific item requested by a customer.

SECTION 14.1

Review

1. List the steps in the sales process.
2. Name five sources and two methods salespeople use to find customers.
3. What key factor creates the difference in preapproach activities in industrial selling situations?
4. What is the focus of the preapproach in retail sales?

SECTION 14.2

Ojectives

After completing this section, you will be able to

- explain the importance and purposes of the approach in the sales process,
- describe how industrial sales representatives conduct the initial approach, and
- list the three approach methods retail salespeople use and state when it is appropriate to use each.

Terms to Know

- service approach method
- greeting approach method
- merchandise approach method

Approaching the Customer

The approach is the first face-to-face contact with the customer. Although different selling situations require the use of different methods in the approach, the importance and general purposes of the approach are the same in all selling situations.

Because salespeople can make or break a sale during their first few minutes with a customer, the initial approach is a critical part of the sales process. At this time, customers often pass judgment on salespeople. Customers who are turned off by the approach will be difficult to win over. Thus, the approach sets the mood or atmosphere for the other steps of the sale. As such, it has three purposes: to begin conversation, to establish rapport with the customer, and to focus on the merchandise. Let's look at how these purposes are accomplished.

To begin conversation, you need to be alert to what interests the customer. This is usually easier in industrial sales because you have time to conduct research prior to the initial meeting. In retail selling, you must be observant and perceptive from the moment the customer enters the store or department.

To establish rapport, treat the customer as an individual. There should be no stereotyping of a person because of age, sex, race, religion, or appearance. Moreover, you must be perceptive about the customer's buying style. Some customers like to do business quickly.

SECTION 14.2

Focus

Bell Ringer Activity

Ask students what most retail salespeople say to them when they initially approach them in a store.

Introducing the Section

Most students will answer the Bell Ringer Activity by saying that "Can I help you?" is the most common approach used by retail salespeople. Ask students what their normal reaction is to that approach. (Most will say, "No, I'm just looking.")

This line of questions will help introduce the importance of the initial approach and its main purposes. You also can use this information later in the chapter to show why the other two retail approaches are more effective in most cases than the service approach.

Teach

Guided Practice

1. Read Section 14.2 with students.
2. Ask students what a salesperson's goal should be during the initial approach to a customer. (Establish rapport with customer, focus on the merchandise, and begin conversation).
3. Assign and review the Chapter 14 Activity in the *School-to-Work Handbook.*

Discussion Starter

Ask students why they think so many retail salespeople greet customers as soon as they walk in the door, rather than waiting until the customer has had a chance to look around. (Company policy; for security purposes—to let customers know they are being observed; to help direct customers to the right location in the store.)

Caption Answer

Such tasks are part of the preapproach—they help a salesperson get ready to sell by allowing him or her develop product knowledge (where particular merchandise is located, its price, its compatibility with other items being offered for sale).

Section Review Answers

1. Preapproach; approach; determining needs, product presentation; handling questions, objections; close; suggestion selling; follow-up.
2. Sources: employer, phone book, professional directories, newspapers, commercial lists. Methods: endless chain and cold canvassing.
3. Whether customer is current or new.
4. Merchandise and work area.

Teach *(Cont'd.)*

Critical Thinking

Ask students what most business owners and managers expect to achieve with their business operations. (Students should identify profits, increased employee productivity, and lowering of expenses as important issues.)

Then ask students to use those key issues to develop an attention-getting line to use as part of an approach in an industrial selling situation. Students should assume they are selling a new computer or automated equipment for use in an office or a manufacturing facility. (One possibility: How would you like to increase your employees' productivity by 20 percent this year?)

L1 Communication Skills

Have students select and write down the major selling point for one of the products discussed and/or illustrated in Chapter 13.

L2 Communication Skills

Have students assume that they work in a retail store that sells the item they selected in the L1 Communications Skills activity. Ask them to write an effective retail merchandise approach for that product using the key selling point.

L3 Communication Skills

Tell students to assume they are the manufacturer's sales representative for the product selected in the L1 Communications Skills activity. Have them role-play the initial approach they would use when calling on a retail store buyer who is responsible for purchasing such items.

Others prefer a more methodical, slower pace. In any case, a customer likes to feel important.

To put a customer at ease and establish a positive atmosphere for the rest of the sale, do the following:

- Be courteous and respectful.
- Establish good eye contact.
- Be enthusiastic.
- Show a sincere interest in the customer.
- Be friendly and genuine.
- Use the customer's name (if known).
- Time the approach appropriately.

The Approach in Industrial Sales

In industrial sales the salesperson generally calls on the customer at his or her place of business, after having set up an appointment in the preapproach stage. Arriving early for your appointment will show your interest in the customer and give you time to organize your thoughts before walking into the customer's office. Introduce yourself and your company with a firm handshake and a smile. Use the customer's name. Some salespeople also give the customer a business card.

The initial approach depends on your prior dealings with the customer or the work you did in the preapproach. When meeting with customers you visit frequently, you can be more personal—within bounds. Some sales representatives keep records of their customers. They also read trade news. Comments on recent happenings in the customer's industry or personal recollections about the customer's family, interests, or hobbies can help make the initial approach a smooth one. Learning what is appropriate to say regarding personal matters, however, is critical. When used correctly, the technique puts the customer at ease and helps open lines of communication. Even if personal conversation is not appropriate, you should still engage in some small talk. It's good for establishing rapport and for building a relationship with the customer.

Talk Small Before You Talk Big

Sales presentations in Europe have a pace of their own. American salespeople who have been taught to "cut to the chase" may feel themselves bogged down in small talk. In fact, conversation about world events, sports, art, and other seemingly unrelated topics is considered an important part of the sales process in Europe. In such an atmosphere, the typical "hard sell" can destroy a developing rapport. Indeed, Europeans may conclude that there is something wrong with a product that is too aggressively sold.

When meeting a new customer, choose your words carefully. Comment on something important to the customer so that he or she will continue to listen. Reducing costs, increasing productivity, improving profits, generating more business, and being better than competitors are general concepts that many industrial salespeople use as a basis for their opening statements. Prior research on the prospect conducted in the preapproach will suggest other possible opening comments.

The Approach in Retail Selling

When and how you approach customers in a retail setting are important considerations. When customers are in an obvious hurry, approach them quickly. When customers are undecided, it is better to let them look around before making the approach. When customers are comparison shopping, encourage them to look around and ask questions. Many customers shop around before buying and appreciate helpful salespeople who take an interest in their buying problems.

There are three methods you can use in the initial approach to retail customers—the *service approach, greeting approach,* and *merchandise approach* methods. The selling situation and the type of customer determine which method is best.

Service Approach Method In the **service approach method,** the salesperson asks the customer if he or she needs assistance. For example, the salesperson might say, "May I help you with something?" This method is acceptable when the customer is obviously in a hurry or if you are an order taker for routine purchases.

In all other sales situations, this method is ineffective because it usually elicits a negative response, such as "No, I'm just looking." In this case, you lose control of the sales situation. In addition, the customer may feel awkward asking for help later after initially rejecting it.

Greeting Approach Method In the **greeting approach method,** the salesperson simply welcomes the customer to the store. The greeting can be formal or informal. Formal greetings are "Good morning," "Good afternoon," or "Good evening, Ms. Gonzales" (if you know the customer's name). Using customers' names makes them feel important.

When you know the customer, an informal greeting is appropriate with a personal comment specifically related to the customer. For example, you might say, "Congratulations on winning last week's tennis tournament, Alice." Small talk helps establish rapport.

After greeting the customer, pause for a few seconds. Out of courtesy, most customers will feel obligated to respond. Many customers will say why they are shopping. If they need help, they will tell you how you can assist them. If they are just looking, they will let you know. In any case, this approach method begins conversation, and it establishes a positive rapport. It does not, however, focus on the merchandise.

Lifelong Learning

The Sales Process

For students who choose a career in sales and marketing, the sales process will become an important part of daily life. But for those who choose other career directions, a knowledge of selling can still help them in many ways throughout their lives.

Not everyone sells products, but everyone buys them on a fairly regular basis. Knowledge of the steps a salesperson goes through can help a person avoid being pressured into unwanted purchases. It can also allow individuals to understand that a salesperson is simply doing a job and that a few minutes of social chatter is not a sign of friendship or false pretense.

Merchandise Approach Method In the **merchandise approach method,** the salesperson makes a comment or asks questions about a product that the customer is looking at. The only time you can use this method, of course, is when a customer stops to look at a specific item. Then you can open with a statement about the product's features and benefits.

Select the appropriate thing to say by noticing what interests the customer. For example, if a customer is looking at a label, you might say, "That shirt is made of a cotton and polyester blend, so it's machine washable." If a customer is simply looking at an item and you have no indication of the exact interest, you can talk about the item's popularity, its unusual features, or its special values.

BRIGHT IDEAS

Look for the Third Right Answer

How do people pay for telephone calls made from public phones? They deposit coins in the phone or use a telephone credit card—right? Wrong. There is, in fact, a third alternative that is fast becoming popular worldwide—pre-paid calling cards. These look much like credit cards but come in denominations of $1–$10. They are sold by local and long-distance phone companies and can be manufactured with decorative pictures of anything from a Big Mac to Spiderman. (This has made them popular as promotional vehicles for such companies as Kmart and McDonald's.) Sales of the cards have grown from an initial 12 million in 1992 to 325 million in 1994.

East-Coast phone giant Nynex recently installed 5,000 pay phones that accept no coins, only phone cards, in an effort to reduce vandalism. There is even a thriving secondary market for the cards as collectibles. A $1 Nynex card used as a promotion during the 1992 Democratic National Convention recently brought $1,700 at a collectors convention.

Creativity Challenge Form teams of 3–5 people, and try to create a new product by coming up with a "third right answer" of your own. You might begin by listing other examples that fit the model. Bicycle or motorcycle? (Moped.) Rent or own? (Timeshare.) Eat out or eat in? (Home catering service.) Then branch out into the unknown.

In business-to-business selling, the first face-to-face meeting generally occurs after contact has been made by telephone. What do you think the salesperson shown here said on the phone to get this appointment?

You can also ask a question about the item, such as "Is that the size you need?"

The merchandise approach method is usually the most effective initial approach in retail sales because it immediately focuses attention on the merchandise. It also gives you an opportunity to tell the customer something about the features and benefits of the merchandise. This helps arouse customer interest.

SECTION 14.2 *Review*

1. **What are the purposes of the approach in selling?**
2. **What three general things would an industrial sales representative say and do during the initial approach?**
3. **Name the three approach methods retail salespeople use, and suggest when it is appropriate to use each method.**

Answers

Vocabulary Review

See Glossary for definitions.

Fact and Idea Review

1. Study their products and keep abreast of industry trends.
2. Looking for new customers.
3. Selecting a new potential customer at random, as by going from door-to-door.
4. With a previous customer, analyze past sales records and review notes about customer's family, interests, hobbies. With a new customer, qualify the prospect by asking questions of other sales reps or reading the company's annual report.
5. Make an appointment to see the prospect.
6. Because first impressions are formed during the first few minutes of the sales call.
7. Treat the customer as an individual, be courteous, establish good eye contact.
8. Being more personal. It can smooth the way to say something about the person's family, interests, or hobbies, or about the company in particular.
9. Reducing costs, increasing productivity, improving profits, generating more business, and being better than the competition.
10. Customer will say, "No, I'm just looking."
11. Pause and wait for response.
12. Merchandise approach— because it immediately focuses attention on the merchandise and thus gives the salesperson a chance to arouse the customer's interest.

Critical Thinking

1. Person referred is more likely to be a potential customer.

194

Vocabulary Review

Work in small groups to develop a story about two salespeople, Chris and Jose. Incorporate the following terms into your story.

preapproach
prospect
referrals
endless chain method
cold canvasing
service approach method
greeting approach method
merchandise approach method

Fact and Idea Review

1. In all selling situations, what can salespeople do to prepare for the sale? (Sec. 14.1)
2. What is prospecting? (Sec. 14.1)
3. What is cold canvasing? Give an example. (Sec. 14.1)
4. What should you do to prepare for a meeting with a previous customer in a business-to-business selling situation? How would that differ if the appointment were with a new customer? (Sec. 14.1)
5. What is the final step of the preapproach in an industrial sales situation? (Sec.14.1)
6. Why is the approach a critical part of the sales process? (Sec. 14.2)
7. Tell at least three things a salesperson could do in the initial approach to put the customer at ease and establish a positive atmosphere for the rest of the sale. (Sec. 14.2)
8. When meeting with business customers you visit frequently, what is sometimes expected during the approach, and why is it important? (Sec. 14.2)
9. What general concepts do many industrial salespeople use as a basis for their opening statement when meeting a new customer? (Sec. 14.2)
10. What is the problem with "May I help you?" as a retail approach? (Sec. 14.2)
11. What should a salesperson do after using the greeting approach method with a retail customer? (Sec. 14.2)
12. Of the three retail approach methods, which one is considered the most effective? Why? (Sec. 14.2)

Critical Thinking

1. Why would a salesperson prefer using the endless chain method of prospecting rather than cold canvasing?

2. As a new sales associate for an independent insurance agency, what would you do to find ten prospects for life, car, and/or home insurance?
3. Given the opportunity to train new retail sales associates in the art of approaching customers, what three key concepts would you make sure you covered first. Why?
4. Why is important to learn about a customer's family, interests, hobbies, and personality traits? How can a salesperson determine what is appropriate and inappropriate to say about such personal matters?

Building Academic Skills

Math

1. Your customer is located 100 miles from your office. You can travel an average of 45 miles in one hour. If you have a 10:30 A.M. appointment and you want to arrive 15 minutes early, what time do you have to leave your office?

Communication

2. Introduce yourself to a teacher or classmate as a sales representative of Lane Copiers. Imagine this is the first time you are approaching this customer in an industrial sales situation. Be sure to use the prospect's name. Introduce yourself and your company while using a firm, businesslike handshake. Offer a catchy opening statement that will get your customer's attention. Smile! Was this easy or difficult for you? Why?
3. Write merchandise approaches that can be used in a retail selling situation for a camera, a pair of jeans, and a pair of work boots.

Human Relations

4. You are stuck in traffic and know you are going to be late for a very important appointment with a highly qualified prospect. What should you do? How could you prevent this situation from happening again?

Technology

5. Assume you are a sales representative for a shirt manufacturer and your customers are specialty and department store retailers. In order to keep track of your customers, you have decided to store all important information in a computer database. Besides the name, address, and phone and fax numbers of the retailers, what additional information would you include in the design of your database? Provide a rationale for each additional entry.

2. Answers will vary. Some possibilities: ask friends and relatives, check wedding and birth announcements, use telephone directory.
3. Answers will vary but should include stressing the importance of first impressions and using the proper approach method for the situation.
4. Why: Such information helps build a relationship—makes the customer feel regarded as a person, not just an account.
How: Answers will vary. Could test the waters slowly with inquiries based on such things as family photos in the office and move on from there.

Building Academic Skills

Math

1. 8 A.M. (100 ÷ 45 = 2.22 hours, or approximately 2¼ hours travel time, plus 15 minutes for early arrival = 2½ hours before appointment)

Application Projects

1. You are beginning an ongoing project for the sales unit—a sales training manual. For all aspects of this manual, you will use the product for which you prepared a feature-benefit chart in Chapter 13. Write the preapproach section of your sales training manual. In this section identify the selling situation as retail or industrial sales. Then discuss how a salesperson should prepare to sell the product. Provide specific examples and policies for your selling situation.

2. As part of your sales training manual, write the approach section. Explain how to approach a customer properly and provide a few suggested sample approaches in dialog form.

3. Pretending to be a customer, conduct your own informal survey of the professionalism of three retail salespeople. After your encounter with each, note what he or she did (or failed to do) to put you at ease and establish a positive atmosphere in the initial approach. Ask yourself these questions:
   - Was the person courteous, respectful, and enthusiastic?
   - Did the person show sincere interest in you?
   - Was the person friendly and genuine? Did he or she use your name (if known)?
   - Did the salesperson use a timely approach? Also, tell which of the three retail approach methods each salesperson used.
   Write a one-paragraph conclusion on your findings.

4. A local landscaper wants you to develop a system for prospecting, which includes businesses and home owners. Include all methods and sources that could be used to generate lawn service prospects.

Linking School to Work

1. Interview two sales representatives for your firm to determine the effectiveness of the training methods used by your company and how well the salespeople prepare for sales and approach customers. Ask them how they were trained for their jobs and what improvements (if any) they think are needed in the training materials and/or methods used. Additional questions should center around preapproach activities and sample approaches they use with previous and new customers. Share your findings with the class.

2. Ask your employer what your business does to generate new customers. Report your findings.

Performance Assessment

Role Play

Situation. You are employed by a photographer who wants your help in generating new clients. She has asked you to come up with a plan. The photographer specializes in weddings but also does commercial photography. Develop a plan for prospecting, as well as a script that can be used to call prospects. The goal of the phone call is for the photographer to make an appointment to show her work to the prospect at a later date.

Evaluation. You will be evaluated on how well you do the following:

- Explain how salespeople find customers.
- Describe how the preapproach is used in this sales situation.
- Create a telephone script that accomplishes the goal of making an appointment with a prospect.
- Effectively communicate your ideas to your employer.

Research

Assume your DECA chapter is running an art exhibition and auction sponsored by a professional art gallery. Your biggest challenge is finding viable prospects. To locate people who are likely to have "bare walls," research the following groups in the local newspaper and the offices of the recorder of deeds:

- People who recently bought homes or condominiums in your neighborhood
- People who recently got married
- Businesses that recently opened offices in your community

Try to accumulate a list of at least 30 prospects who might be in need of artwork.

COMPUTER APPLICATION

Complete the Chapter 14 Computer Application that appears in the Student Activity Workbook.

Technology

5. The database could also contain information about customers' families, interests and hobbies in order to assist with the approach phase of the sales process. Other items of interest would be the sales history of the client in order to help anticipate future needs and possibly data on changes in the store or its competitors.

Application Projects

1. Answers will depend on the product chosen.
2. The approach section will vary depending on the product but should include sample dialogs.
3. Paragraphs will vary depending on situations encountered by students.
4. Possible sources: telephone directories, commercial lists, customer referrals, and cold canvassing of neighborhood homes and businesses.

Linking School to Work

Answers depend on the work situation.

Performance Assessment

Refer to the *DECA Competitive Events Handbook* for evaluation guidelines.

Computer Application

Optional activity. Refer to the *Marketing Software Binder* for template and user information.

Evaluation

Administer the reproducible test for Chapter 14, or construct your own using the Testmaker software.

Communication

2. Possible introduction: "Hi, Mr./Ms. (name). I'm (name) from Lane Copiers. How would you like to improve productivity and cut costs at the same time?"
3. Answers will vary. Some possibilities:
   - "That camera is very easy to use—it's completely automatic."
   - "Those jeans are the ones shown in *Seventeen* magazine."
   - "Those boots are completely waterproof and long wearing."

Human Relations

4. If no car phone is available, pull off the road and call the client to advise that you are running late. (This will give you more credibility and will let the client know that you take your appointment seriously.) In the future, take a practice run, listen to traffic reports, and allow more time for travel delays or emergencies.

CHAPTER 15

DETERMINING NEEDS AND PRODUCT PRESENTATION

Pages 196–205

Chapter Overview

Chapter 15 covers two essential steps in the sales process—determining needs and presenting the product.

Springboard

Have students recall their last major purchase (one that required extensive or limited decision making) and what the salesperson asked them about the product they were looking for. Have students write those questions down in the order in which they recall their being asked. Also, have students write down anything special the salesperson did to impress them with the product's capabilities or features.

Prereading

List the section objectives to discuss with students. Have students skim the chapter, looking at the pictures, reading the captions, and noting the heads. Ask questions to ensure that students have a minimal understanding of the chapter structure.

Preteaching the Vocabulary

Before students begin reading the chapter, dictate each of the vocabulary terms and ask students to write them on a sheet of paper. When they finish, write the terms on the chalkboard. Then have students guess at the meaning of each. Write their guesses next to each term, but do not give the correct meaning. Leave this list on the chalkboard so that students can see how close their guesses were to the actual definitions as they work through the chapter.

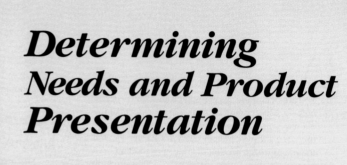

Determining Needs and Product Presentation

CHAPTER 15

In many ways, selling is like putting together a jigsaw puzzle. When you do a puzzle, you analyze the various parts by shape and size. Then you select the straight-edged pieces to use for the frame. When you sell, you analyze your customer's needs and buying motives. Then you use that information to begin framing your product presentation.

Determining customer needs and product presentation are critical to the sales process. In this chapter, you will be introduced to techniques that can help you with both.

196   Unit 5   *Selling*

Classroom Management

For the Teacher
- Teacher's Annotated Edition for all workbooks
- Teacher's Manual for *School-to-Work Handbook*
- *Testing Binder*
- *Transparency Binder*
- *Marketing Software Binder*
- *Marketing Career Portfolio*
- *Lesson Plans*

For the Student
- *Student Activity Workbook*
- *Marketing Math Workbook*
- *School-to-Work Handbook*
- *Student Software*
- *International Case Studies*
- *Marketing Career Portfolio*

SECTION 15.1

Objectives

After completing this section, you will be able to
- explain why determining needs is an essential step in the sales process and
- describe three methods used for determining needs.

Terms to Know

- nonverbal communication
- open-ended questions

Determining Needs

Customer needs are directly related to buying motives. Recall from Chapter 13 that these motives can be rational, emotional, or a combination of the two.

In this step of the sale, your job is to uncover the customer's reasons for wanting to buy. In some instances, these motives or needs will be quite obvious. In other instances, they won't be.

In either situation, taking a sincere interest in the customer is essential to this important step in the sales process. When the customer's needs are satisfied, everyone benefits. The business makes a sale. The satisfied customer often becomes a repeat customer. And you, as a salesperson, experience that welcome feeling of success.

When to Determine Needs

So that you can focus everything you do and say on your customer, you should determine his or her needs as soon as possible in the sales process. Here is an example of what can happen when a salesperson does not determine needs early on.

Salesperson: This is one of our most popular tennis racquets. *(This is the initial approach.)* It's perfect for you. The grip is the correct size. And the large sweet spot should help you improve your game.

Customer: That's very interesting, but I'm not buying the racquet for myself. It's a gift.

In the foregoing example, the salesperson went right into the product presentation before determining the customer's needs. After the initial approach, the salesperson could have asked, "Are you interested in a racquet for yourself?"

The answer to that simple question could have guided the salesperson into additional questions about the person for whom the racquet was being purchased. It also could have helped the salesperson decide which racquet to show the customer and which features to emphasize.

In retail selling, you should begin to determine needs immediately after the approach. This is the earliest you can start because you usually cannot research your customers before they come to your store. In industrial sales, needs can be determined in the preapproach. In both situations, you will continue determining needs throughout the sales process.

How to Determine Needs

Three methods will help you determine customer needs. They are *observing, listening,* and *questioning.*

Observing When you observe a customer, you look for buying motives that are communicated nonverbally. **Nonverbal communication** is expressing yourself through body language. Facial expressions, hand motions, eye movement, and other forms of nonverbal communication can give you clues about a customer's interest in a product and/or mood.

There are other details you can observe in retail and industrial sales situations that may provide even more clues about customers. When you observe how long a

When They Laugh, Get Serious

You're giving a report during a board meeting, and someone starts to laugh. If you were in the United States, you would probably assume that you'd said something funny. If you were in Japan, however, you would have to consider a very different possibility.

Among the Japanese, laughter is used to convey embarrassment, confusion, dismay, or shock. If you have indeed said or done something to embarrass or confuse your Japanese listeners, apologies are in order. If someone laughs when you make your apology, you must investigate further to discover your error.

Chapter 15 *Determing Need and Product Presentation* **197**

Meeting Special Needs

Visually Impaired

Students with visual impairments may not be able to maintain good eye contact. Depending on the severity of the impairment, they may in fact have no control over eye movement. This can put them at a disadvantage in some parts of the sales process. Note, however, that such students may excel at giving customers undivided attention because they are not distracted by visual images. And in telephone sales situations they may actually be at an advantage. Often listening skills are enhanced when visual impairment is present.

Focus

Bell Ringer Activity

Have students think about the various parts of their heads. Then tell them to complete the following statement: Nature gave us two _____ , two _____ , and one _____ . (ears, eyes, mouth)

Introducing the Section

Once students get the answers to the Bell Ringer Activity, connect those sense organs to the three ways we determine needs—by listening (ears), observing (eyes), and asking questions (mouth). You can also suggest that nature gave us *two* eyes and *two* ears (vs. one mouth) to help us remember to do more listening and observing than talking when determining the customers' needs.

Teach

Guided Practice

1. Read Section 15.1 with students.
2. Ask students to write ten questions that could be used to determine what type of cassette player a person might want to buy. Tell them to begin with general questions about past experience with such a product, intended use, and special functions they would like.

Discussion Starter

Ask students if they think it is a good practice to begin determining customers' needs by asking how much they want to spend. (Probably not—puts customer on the spot.) Then ask students how they could avoid asking this question. (By asking about intended use, past experience, etc. and deriving price from the answers.)

Teach (Cont'd.)

Independent Practice

1. Assign and review the Chapter 15 Case Study in the *International Case Studies* workbook.
2. Have students research the use of computer technology for determining customer needs.

Assess

Evaluation

Assign and review the Section 15.1 Review.

Reteaching

1. Assign and review the vocabulary terms for this section.
2. Assign and review Fact and Idea Review questions 1-6 from the Chapter Review.
3. To reteach the concept of determining needs, have students recall a visit to the doctor—the questions asked and how their answers helped in diagnosing the problem and prescribing a remedy. Then ask: How is that procedure similar to what salespeople do when working with customers during a sale? (Both procedures use questions to define problems/needs and knowledge of products to solve problems/meet needs.)

Enrichment

1. Assign and review the appropriate activities in the *Student Activity Workbook.*
2. Assign and review the appropriate Critical Thinking questions from the Chapter Review.

Close

Have students complete the following statement: You should begin determining needs...(as soon as possible in the sales process.)

One of the easiest ways to determine customer needs is to ask questions designed to uncover those needs. What sorts of questions might this salesperson ask his customers?

customer in a retail store looks at a product, you can get an initial idea about his or her interest in it. Also, how long the customer holds the product during a sales presentation (if he or she holds it at all) can indicate personal feelings for it.

In an industrial sales situation, you can generally get ideas about a buyer's interests by looking around his or her office. Trophies for winning company-sponsored tennis tournaments or paintings of horses, for example, probably indicate personal interests.

When calling on a retail buyer, walk through the store first. This will give you interesting information about the types of customers the retailer serves, the price levels of lines carried, complementary and competing products offered, and opportunities for additional sales.

The key to observing is proper selection of facts. You want only those that are important to the sales process. Avoid stereotyping people or drawing conclusions from your observations before getting additional facts.

Listening Listening helps you pick up clues to the customer's needs for use in the product presentation. Here's an example.

Customer: I want a camera so I can take pictures of my daughter while she's performing gymnastics. I have to admit, though, I'm not a very good photographer.

From these statements, you have learned that the customer is not an experienced photographer and therefore

needs an easy-to-use camera. He or she also needs a camera that has a fast shutter because it will be used in taking action shots.

To develop good listening skills, you must learn how to listen and understand. In Chapter 9 we explored listening skills and blocks to listening with understanding. So, if you need to brush up, reread the appropriate sections in that chapter. Remember, however, these five important listening skills when talking to your customers:

- Maintain good eye contact.
- Provide verbal and nonverbal feedback.
- Give customers your undivided attention.
- Listen with empathy and an open mind.
- Do not interrupt.

Questioning In order to listen to customers, you must get them talking. One way of engaging a customer in conversation is to ask questions.

When it comes to making a purchase, not all customers can clearly express their needs and motives. This sometimes occurs because of basic uncertainty and/or some difficulty in self-expression. In such a situation, well-chosen questions can help you uncover needs and buying motives.

When you begin determining needs, first ask general questions about intended use of the product and previous experience with it. Build your questions around words like *who, what, when, where, how,* and *why.* For example, you might ask the following:

198   Unit 5   *Selling*

- *Who* will be using the camera?
- *What* type of camera is the person presently using?
- *How* much experience has the person had with photography?
- *Where* does the person tend to do most of his or her photography—indoors or out?

Once you have an idea of the customer's general needs, then you can ask more specific questions relating to the product. These might include inquiries about size, color, and any special features desired.

Questioning is an important skill that must be done carefully. Always bear in mind that some customers will be protective of their privacy. They may resent even general, nonpersonal questions. For example, when selling skis it is often necessary to determine the customer's weight. In such a situation, you might have the various weight classes identified on a sheet of paper that you hand the customer. Then you can simply ask which category they fall into. In this way, you avoid asking the person, "How much do you weigh?"

Here are some other do's and don'ts of questioning.

1. *Do ask open-ended questions to encourage customers to do the talking.* **Open-ended questions** require more than a yes or no answer. For example, you might ask, "What do you dislike about the camera you're presently using?" The answer to such a question will provide valuable information about a customer's needs.
2. *Do ask clarifying questions to make sure you understand customers' needs.* To do this, use opening lines such as "Let me see if I understand you" or "Am I correct in assuming you're looking for a product that can...?"
3. *Don't ask too many questions in a row.* This will make customers feel as though you are cross-examining them.
4. *Don't ask questions that might embarrass customers or put them on the defensive.* For example, never ask, "How much do you want to spend?" Instead, ask about intended use and past experience. That should give you enough information to determine the correct price range on your own.

SECTION 15.1

Review

1. Why is determining needs an essential step in the sales process?
2. Name three methods used to determine customer needs.

SECTION 15.2

Objectives

After completing this section, you will be able to

- **state the goal of the product presentation,**
- **explain how products are selected for the presentation,**
- **describe what to say during the product presentation, and**
- **identify four techniques that will make for a lively and effective product presentation.**

Terms to Know

- **jargon**
- **layman's terms**

Product Presentation

During the product presentation phase of the sale, you show the product and tell about it. As you are determining the customer's buying motives, you will be displaying products that match the needs you have uncovered. The goal of the product presentation, of course, is to match the customer's needs with appropriate product features and benefits.

You can reach this goal by following certain guidelines that can make your product presentation smooth. These include careful selection of the products you show the customer, limiting the number of products you show, and knowing what to say and do during the presentation.

Selecting and Explaining Products

Your first decision in the product presentation step of the sale is what product(s) to show your customer. You must determine the price range and number of items to include. Then you must think about what you are going to say and how you are going to say it. Here are a few hints that will help improve your product presentation skills.

Which Products to Show After you have learned the intended use of the product, you should be able to select a few items that match those needs.

Chapter 15 *Determining Needs and Product Presentation* **199**

SECTION 15.1

Focus

Bell Ringer Activity

Ask students how the determining needs step is related to the next step of the sales process, the product presentation.

Introducing the Section

In response to the Bell Ringer Activity, most students will say that once you have some information regarding what a customer is looking for, you would immediately begin to show products that include those features.

Teach

Guided Practice

1. Read Section 15.2 with students.
2. Have students read aloud the Case Study and review the answers in class.
3. Ask students if they would always show the same product feature to all customers during the product presentation phase of a sale. Have them explain their answers. *Note:* If this question does not get a response, ask students how they would know which feature to present first in the product presentation. (In both cases, the one feature most important to that particular customer would be the one that would be shown first. Thus, the first feature shown will vary with the customer.)
4. Assign and review the Chapter 15 Activity in the *School-to-Work Handbook*.

Lifelong Learning

Determining Needs and Product Presentation

The chapter's techniques are useful for all circumstances involving persuasion, not just sales. To test this idea, have students try them out in these situations: convincing your family to vacation in the mountains rather than at the beach; asking for a raise after 6 months of exemplary work when company policy states that raises are to be given annually; asking a professor for an extension on a term paper because a key research source has been out of the library until today. Encourage students to apply the four steps to these situations and to think up other situations that they might encounter.

Discussion Starter

Ask students why all product demonstrations should be practiced before they are tried for customers. Have students speculate about what could happen if this were not standard procedure. (Mishaps of various sorts, demonstrations that don't work.) Ask students who have witnessed such unfortunate occurrences to share their experiences with the class.

Critical Thinking

Tell students to consider what kinds of demonstrations they could use for a rain jacket. Ask: What could you do to prove that the jacket was waterproof? (Pour water on it.) to show that the fabric was very strong? (Offer a swatch of fabric to the customer and have him/her try to rip it or poke a hole through it.)

Cooperative Learning

Refer students to the feature-benefit chart in Chapter 13 (page 177). Then have them break into small groups and develop a product presentation for the camera featured in the chart. Tell them to begin by brainstorming all the different techniques they could use to make the presentation come alive.

At the end of ten minutes, have each group present their ideas to the class in oral report form. (Suggested techniques will vary but should include ways of displaying and handling the camera, pointing out and demonstrating its features, using sales aids, and involving the customer in the sale.)

L1 Decision-making Skills

Ask students how many items they think a salesperson should display in front of a customer at one time. Ask them why they feel that way. (No more than three items at one time is recommended.)

Real World MARKETING

A Lasting Look

Shopping for furniture? Been to so many stores and talked with so many salespeople that you can't remember who was offering what? Domain Home Furnishings (Norwood, MA) has the answer. Its salespeople give potential customers a Polaroid photo of the piece of furniture they're interested in. When the salesperson writes his or her name and telephone number on the back, the photo becomes a business card—but with a difference. Domain reports that customers tend to keep the photos, whereas they tend to discard traditional business cards.

For example, if you learned that a customer wants a camera for professional use, you would select a technically advanced camera.

What Price Range to Offer   When you don't know the customer's price range and your knowledge of the intended use is insufficient to determine a price range, begin by showing a medium-priced product. That way, you can move up or down in price once you get the customer's feedback.

How Many Products to Show   To avoid overwhelming your customer, show no more than three products at a time. It is difficult for most people to remember all the features of more than three items during a presentation. When a customer wants to see more than three, remove the products that have been displayed and are no longer of any interest to the customer.

What to Say   In this step of the sales process, you talk about the product's features and benefits. Here is a good place to use your feature-benefit chart to tell your customer the product features that match his or her buying motives and needs.

When describing product features, use highly descriptive adjectives and active verbs. Avoid unclear words, such as *nice, pretty,* and *fine.* For example, you might say, "This full-cut sleeve allows complete rotation of the arm, making it extremely comfortable when skiing."

Choose your words carefully. Avoid slang and double meanings. For example, when selling an expensive suit to an executive, you would not say, "You're going to blow them away in that suit."

When selling industrial products, use the appropriate *jargon* so you communicate with industrial buyers at their level of expertise. **Jargon** is technical or specialized vocabulary used by members of a particular profession or industry. When selling products to retail customers, however, use *layman's terms.* **Layman's terms** are words the average customer can understand. Regardless of which terminology you use, try to show enthusiasm through your level and tone of voice as well as your facial expressions.

What to Do During the Presentation

To make a product presentation come alive, display and handle the merchandise effectively. Demonstrate the product in use, and use dramatic actions and sales aids to point out special features. Also, involve the customer in your presentation.

Displaying and Handling the Product
Creatively displaying the product is the first step in an eye-catching presentation. Some products, of course, lend themselves more naturally to visual display. Others will challenge your creativity. Diamond rings, for example, look best on a black velvet display pad. An attractive

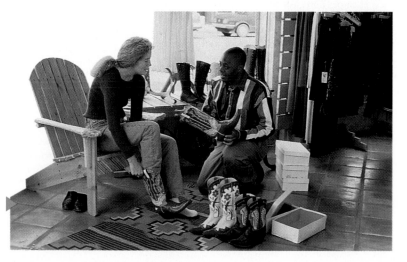

A good salesperson avoids overwhelming a customer with too many possibilities. What has this salesperson done to hold down the number of choices?

More About

Price

Sometimes a salesperson can make the wrong assumption about the price range the customer is interested in, especially with big-ticket items such as cars or computers. Often, customers require education about the different price categories before they can make a decision about how much they want to spend.

Caption Answer

Cleared away pairs of shoes that the customer has eliminated. Left only those that are still under consideration in view.

display of vacuum cleaners, on the other hand, takes more thoughtful planning.

The way you handle a product presents an image of its quality. Handle it with respect, and use hand gestures

BRIGHT IDEAS

If You Make Them, They Will Come

Doughnuts have been part of culinary history in many forms and many cultures for over 2,000 years. In Italy, they are called *zeppole,* in France *beignet.* However, it took the Americans to make doughnuts an actual industry, complete with franchises. What spurred the growth was part technology and part marketing genius.

During World War I, the Salvation Army had its cooks fry dough balls in hot oil as a treat for the troops. They called this form of doughnut a "doughboy" in honor of the men who were so fond of it.

After the war, a Russian immigrant to the United States named Adolph Levitt decided that doughboys would be just as popular with civilians. He tested his theory in Harlem, where he did his frying in the window of a bakery. The experience taught him something valuable—that people loved to watch doughnuts fry. A crowd would gather every time he made a batch, and that demonstration translated directly into sales. Once he started dunking, turning, scooping, and draining doughnuts, he couldn't make enough of them to keep up with demand.

To speed up production, Levitt came up with a conveyor belt that flipped the doughnuts during the frying process. His invention could produce 960 doughnuts an hour. It made him rich in a way doughnuts alone never could.

When World War II started, Levitt rented out his machines (at a patriotic discount, of course) to both the Salvation Army and the Red Cross. Those two organizations produced millions of doughnuts for troops in mess halls around the world.

Creativity Challenge Form teams of 3–5 people. Working together, try to identify one or two products not traditionally sold using demonstration that might benefit from use of the technique. In each case, describe the type of demonstration intended and provide a brief rationale for why you think it might be effective.

to show the significance of certain features. Expensive crystal goblets, for instance, should be held up carefully to the light.

Demonstrating Demonstrating the product in use helps to build customer confidence. This is especially true if you are showing an item that requires manipulation or operation, such as a television, camera, radio, food processor, clock, typewriter, or computer.

To prove selling points or claims made by the manufacturer, you may need to demonstrate a product in a more dramatic way. For example, you could drop an unbreakable dish on the floor to prove that it is durable.

Using Sales Aids When it is impractical to demonstrate the actual product or when you want to emphasize certain selling points further, you can use sales aids in your presentations. Sales aids include samples, reprints of magazine and newspaper articles, audiovisual aids, models, photographs, drawings, graphs, charts, specification sheets, customer testimonials, and warranty information. In addition, in today's technological society computers are playing an increasingly important role in product presentations.

Demonstration **is an especially helpful sales technique when dealing with complicated pieces of equipment. Why?**

Chapter 15 *Determining Needs and Product Presentation* **201**

Caption Answer

Encourages customer to have confidence in his/her own ability to handle the product.

Teach (Cont'd.)

Tell students that column A of the spreadsheet is for identification of each row, so they should begin their identification of columns with column B. (Columns and entries: B—item name, C—item number, D—regular price, E—discount percentage, F—discount amount, and G—price after discount. Math information /formulas: E—.25, F—D4*E4, G—D4-F4.)

L3 Math Skills

Have students revise the spreadsheet design from the L2 Math Skills activity to incorporate an additional discount. Tell students that along with the sale on selected items, customers will be able to redeem a coupon for an additional 10 percent off sale items. [Columns and entries: B-G—same as above, H—coupon, I—final price. Math information/formulas: H—.1, I—G4*(1-H4).]

Independent Practice

Have students read issues of *Personal Selling Power* and *Sales & Marketing Management* magazines to find articles that pertain to determining customer needs and product presentation. Ask students to summarize at least one relevant article in written form and share its key points with the class orally.

Assess

Evaluation

Assign and review the Section 15.2 Review.

Salespeople + Computers = Increased Productivity

More and more businesses are coming to realize how much computers can improve their salespeople's productivity. Consider some examples.

Becton Dickinson's AcuteCare division (which supplies hospital operating rooms with products such as gloves, scrubs, preps, and blades) decided to outfit its 90 sales representatives with IBM ThinkPads. The benefits of computer usage became apparent almost immediately.

One sales manager reported that his representatives didn't spend nearly as much time doing reports as they used to. In addition, the reports that were submitted arrived in a more timely fashion and contained information that was much more current. A sales representative reported that her time in front of customers was spent much more efficiently as well. She had been thumbing through pages of product specification and pricing sheets. Now she just pushed a button to give customers prices or product information. It made her look much more professional.

Pitney Bowes, the leading marketer of mailing systems, reinforced its move to computer usage by tying its sales managers' compensation to their computer literacy. One reason for such an emphatic approach was company image. Five years ago less than half of Pitney Bowes' new

products had a software base. Today all of them do. The sales force that sold such products needed to be more comfortable with computers and their applications.

Like Becton Dickinson, Pitney Bowes found that increased computer use improved productivity. Instead of looking through index cards for prospects, its sales representatives could now plug in the desired criteria and let the computer sort through customer lists for them. They could also develop account profiles, sales proposals, price books, and competitive reference guidebooks using similar techniques.

Colorado National Bank began using computers in an entirely different way. It equipped its service representatives with Apple PowerBook computers that had sound capabilities and overhead projectors. The service representatives then used the equipment to help corporate clients teach their employees about 401K savings plans. The result was presentations filled with music, color graphics, bulleted text screens, and charts. Still photos and narration also let satisfied plan members share their experiences with the audience.

It was NEC Technologies, the computer peripherals manufacturer, that created the most novel sales tool using computers. It started using computers for a custom-made interactive CD-ROM presentation. In the presentation, individual characters came to life and gave testimonials for NEC products. What was so novel was that the disc was not only the sales tool but also a sample NEC product. The successful use of this type of multimedia led to use of the program at trade shows and conventions as a self-running presentation.

Case Study Review

1. Why are computers considered sales tools?
2. What is so unique about NEC's custom-made interactive CD-ROM presentation?

A MATTER OF ETHICS

3. Do you think it was right for Pitney Bowes to link its sales managers' pay to computer proficiency? Why or why not?

Case Study Answers

1. Because they increase the productivity of salespeople.
2. It's both a sales tool and an NEC product.
3. By linking compensation to computer proficiency, Pitney Bowes ensured that salespeople would have a good reason to invest in becoming computer literate. It would have been less ethical had they simply insisted and offered no benefit.

Be creative when determining which sales aids will help you in your particular product presentation. For example, a manufacturer of industrial machinery might show a videotape of how quickly a machine performs. An insurance salesperson might use graphs and charts to show how dividends will accumulate or to compare the benefits of one policy with another. He or she might even use a computer to personalize the presentation of that information for each customer.

Involving the Customer   It is best to get the customer physically involved with the product as soon as possible in the sales presentation. In that way, you can appeal to the customer's senses. For example, you could have your customers hold and swing golf clubs, try on and walk around in a pair of shoes, use a computer keyboard or mouse, test-drive an automobile, or taste and smell food products.

You can also involve your customer verbally during the sales presentation by confirming selling points. For example, you might say, "This camera is extremely versatile with its power zoom *and* panorama feature. Did you ever feel torn between wanting a camera that could take great close-ups of the kids and one that could take wide-angle shots of a gorgeous view? *(Pause for customer's*

*Ford has pioneered **in the area of interactive marketing with its Ford Simulator software. The package allows potential customers to configure a vehicle to their own specifications—model, color, options package—and price it. How do you think the software helps Ford salespeople?***

answer.) Well, now you can have both those cameras in one." Getting agreement on several selling points helps to ensure that you are on the right track with the product selected for the customer.

If you use a computer for a presentation, it would be a good idea to incorporate an interactive element into it. For some portion of the presentation, have the customer respond to questions posed by the computer.

When you involve a customer in the sale, you help the person make intelligent buying decisions. You also help yourself because a customer is generally more attentive when doing more than just listening to what you say.

If you feel that you are losing your customer's attention, just ask a simple question. For example, say, "Now that you've seen the features of this camera, what do you think about it?" Regaining your customer's attention is essential if you are to continue with the sales presentation. The key is keeping the customer involved.

The marriage of computer and multimedia technologies is rapidly changing the sophistication of the sales aides salespeople have at their disposal. What possibilities do you see here?

SECTION 15.2   *Review*

1. **What is the goal of the product presentation?**
2. **Which products and how many of them should be selected for the presentation?**
3. **Give some guidelines for what to say during the product presentation.**
4. **Describe four techniques that will make the product presentation lively and effective.**

Chapter 15   *Determining Needs and Product Presentation*   **203**

15 CHAPTER *Review*

Answers

Vocabulary Review

Paragraphs will vary. See Glossary for definitions.

Fact and Idea Review

1. As soon as possible.
2. In retail selling: after the approach.
   In industrial selling: during the preapproach.
3. Retail situations: facial expressions, how customer looks at or holds product, and other forms of nonverbal communication. Industrial situations: buyer's personal interests through contents of office; store's customers, prices, and competing merchandise offered.
4. General questions about intended use and previous experience with the product.
5. Ask open-ended questions.
6. Avoid asking too many questions in a row and don't ask questions that will put the customer on the defensive or make him or her feel embarrassed.
7. Begin with the middle price range because you can go up or down from there.
8. Jargon is appropriate when selling to people in an industry who understand the jargon. Use layman's terms when the customer is not well versed in the technical vocabulary associated with the product.
9. Possibilities: samples, reprints of magazine and newspaper articles, audiovisual aids, models, photographs, drawings, graphs, charts, specification sheets, customer testimonials, and warranty information.
10. Physically: depending on the product, by having customer hold it, try it on, taste it, test it, etc.

204

Vocabulary Review

Write a paragraph incorporating the following terms:

nonverbal communication
open-ended questions
jargon
layman's terms

Fact and Idea Review

1. In general, when do you determine customer needs in the sales process? (Sec. 15.1)
2. Specifically, when should you begin determining needs in retail selling? in industrial selling? (Sec. 15.1)
3. What can you look for when you observe customers in retail situations? in industrial situations? (Sec. 15.1)
4. What questions should be asked first when determining customer needs? (Sec. 15.1)
5. What is one of the best ways to encourage customers to do the talking? (Sec. 15.1)
6. What two things should you avoid doing when questioning a customer? (Sec. 15.1)
7. When you are having a difficult time determining a customer's intended price range, what priced product should you show? Why? (Sec. 15.2)
8. When is it appropriate to use jargon? When should you use layman's terms? (Sec. 15.2)
9. Name five sales aids you can use in the product presentation. (Sec. 15.2)
10. How could you involve a customer in the product presentation physically and verbally? (Sec. 15.2)

Critical Thinking

1. Why is determining customer needs sometimes referred to as the *key* step in the sales process?
2. How would you use a feature-benefit chart in the product presentation step of a sale?
3. What is wrong with these two selling statements?
   - "You look great in that suit."
   - "This fabric is made of 420/420 denier nylon."
4. Explain why you should never ask a customer, "How much did you want to spend?" How can you avoid this situation?
5. How would you effectively display a set of china during a sales presentation?
6. Identify three features of a typewriter, and explain how you would demonstrate them.

7. Selling services is sometimes more difficult than selling goods, which can easily be seen. Explain what a landscape designer could do to sell landscape designs and maintenance services to a prospective customer.
8. What would you do to involve your customer if you were selling a bicycle? a pair of boots? a camera? a new business telephone system?

Building Academic Skills

Math

1. What is the total amount due from a customer who purchases three shirts at $25 each, two pairs of pants at $40 each, and four ties at $15 each? The sales tax on the clothing is 5 percent.
2. If your customer wants to buy 6 ¾ yards of fabric and the price per yard is $12.50, how much would you charge?

Communication

3. Role-play the determining needs and product presentation steps of a sale in the classroom by using a product such as a jacket, calculator, or purse. Begin by choosing a partner and deciding which of you will portray the customer and which will portray the salesperson. The rest of the class will observe and make notes on all the steps taken (both correctly and incorrectly) by the salesperson.
   Note: Before the enactments begin, the class should make a list of guidelines for listening, observing, asking questions, and presenting a product. During the role plays, those observing should place check marks next to the guidelines followed, take notes on those not followed, and then share their evaluations.

Human Relations

4. A woman begins looking at the size 8 dresses and says, "I used to wear size 8, but I've gained a few pounds." In reality, the customer is probably a size 12. What would you say in order to direct her to the correct size?

Technology

5. Decide which of the following products you would like to sell: investment services, an automobile, makeup and hair coloring, or a water purification system for industrial waste. Then identify the hardware, software, and audiovisual capabilities you would want to help you perform the determining

Verbally: by having customer answer questions, confirm selling points.

Critical Thinking

1. Everything you do from that point on is dependent on your customer needs.
2. As a resource for necessary product information and possibly even as a sales aid.

3. First is not descriptive enough; second uses language so technical customer is not likely to understand.
4. You may embarrass the customer, who may not know the price range. To avoid this situation, ask about intended use and/or previous experience with the product and infer price from answers.
5. On a simulated dining room table, complete with tablecloth, napkins and other pieces in the place setting.

needs and product presentation steps of a sale more effectively.

Application Projects

1. Continuing with your sales training manual, prepare the copy for the determining needs step of a sale. Include a brief description of the importance of this step and the techniques used in it. Finally, prepare a list of ten questions that could be used to determine a customer's needs. Begin with general questions regarding intended use and previous experience. End with specific questions about the particular features of the product, such as color, size, design, and quantity desired. Base your questions on the product for which you prepared a feature-benefit chart. *Note:* If you have not done a feature-benefit chart, select a product that would require a customer to spend time shopping for and comparing features. Some possibilities include a camera, a computer, a pair of running shoes, a microwave oven, and a bicycle.

2. Using the product for which you prepared a feature-benefit chart or the one you used to complete Application Project 1 above, prepare a detailed plan for the product presentation step of a sale. Use this plan as the next chapter in your sales training manual. For each product feature, include what you will say, how you will demonstrate that feature, what sales aids you will use, how you will use them, and how you will involve your customer with each feature. When appropriate, incorporate sample dialogue.

Linking School to Work

1. Ask your employer how the company's computer system provides the sales force with information and support for determining needs and making product presentations.
2. Interview a company salesperson. Ask what he/she does to determine customers' needs and otherwise make product presentations effective.

Performance Assessment

Role Plays

1. *Situation.* As the assistant manager of a shoe store, you are responsible for training and evaluating the sales staff. Chris, a new employee, is having difficulty.

Each time you observe him, you see 5–10 pairs of shoes in front of the customer he is helping. The sad part is that nine times out of ten, Chris's customers don't buy. You realize that you must speak with him.

Evaluation. You will be evaluated on how well you do the following:

- Explain why determining needs is an essential step in the sales process.
- Suggest three methods used to determine customer needs.
- Describe the goal of the product presentation.
- Explain how products are selected for the presentation.
- Motivate the new employee to improve.

2. *Situation.* You are employed as a sales associate for a home electronics store. Because you have one of the best sales records, your supervisor has asked you to take part in a company training program. The portion of the program for which you will be responsible is titled, "Making Product Presentations Come Alive." You are being asked to share your secrets for success.

Evaluation. You will be evaluated on how well you do the following:

- Discuss the goal of the product presentation.
- Explain how products are selected for the presentation.
- Cite guidelines regarding what to say during the product presentation.
- Explain the techniques that make your product presentations come alive.
- Communicate your ideas to the sales trainees with proper diction, voice quality, and continuity of thought.

Creativity

Prepare a list of creative ideas for presenting *and demonstrating* the product features of one of the following items: nonstick cookware, a snowboard, jet skis, cold-weather apparel, a universal gym, or a microwave oven.

COMPUTER APPLICATION

Complete the Chapter 15 Computer Application that appears in the Student Activity Workbook.

Human Relations
4. Answers will vary.

Technology
5. Investment services: computer and database program with capability to identify potential customers for specific investments; also, program that will enhance product presentations with personalized color graphics.

   Automobile: interactive computer program using CD-ROM to demonstrate various features of the car.

   Makeup and hair coloring: interactive program that can show customers what they would look like with different makeup and hair coloring.

   Purification system for industrial waste water: CD-ROM that would provide important information and testimonials from satisfied customers; also a database listing companies that would need such a system.

Application Projects
   Answers will vary.

Linking School to Work
   Answers depend on the work situation.

Performance Assessment
   Refer to the *DECA Competitive Events Handbook* for evaluation guidelines.

Computer Application
   Optional activity. Refer to the *Marketing Software Binder* for template and user information.

Evaluation
   Administer the reproducible test for Chapter 15, or construct your own using the Testmaker software.

6. Answers will vary depending on type of machine.
7. Show a rendering of the proposed landscape design on paper or a computer, use books or brochures to show samples of each tree, shrub, or flower that will be used in the suggested design, show photographs of previous jobs completed, and show copies of testimonials (letters) from satisfied customers.

8. Answers will vary. Bike—sit on, boots—try on, camera—hold and focus, phone system—use interactive computer program to answer questions.

Building Academic Skills
Math
1. $[(\$25 \times 3) + (\$40 \times 2) + (\$15 \times 4)] \times 1.05 = (\$75 + \$80 + \$60) \times 1.05 = \$215 \times 1.05 = \$225.75$
2. $6.75 \times \$12.50 = \$84.375 = \$84.38$

Chapter Overview

Chapter 16 involves handling customer questions and objections. It provides students with a basic understanding of how objections fit into the sales process. It also suggests a means to plan for them and a number of specialized ways to cope with them.

Springboard

Have students identify some of the techniques they use to convince their parents to let them do something out of the ordinary or to grant them a special favor. (Note that their requests must be ones that they expect their parents to object to, at least initially.)

Prereading

List the section objectives to discuss with students. Have students skim the chapter, looking at the pictures, reading the captions, and noting the heads. Ask questions to ensure that students have a minimal understanding of the chapter structure.

Preteaching the Vocabulary

Before students begin reading the chapter, dictate each of the vocabulary terms and ask students to write them on a sheet of paper. When they finish, write the terms on the chalkboard. Then have students guess at the meaning of each. Write their guesses next to each term, but do not give the correct meaning. Leave this list on the chalkboard so that students can see how close their guesses were to the actual definitions as they work through the chapter.

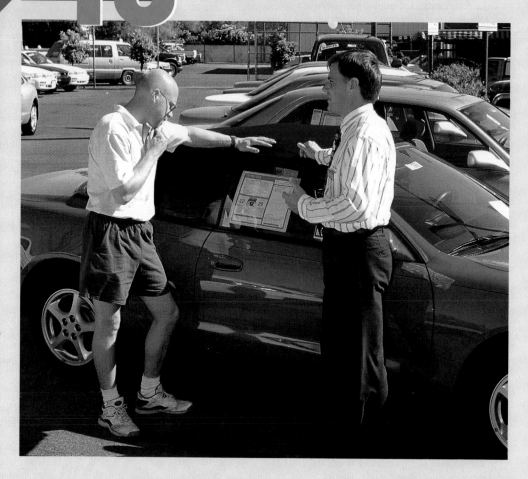

CHAPTER 16

Handling Customer Questions and Objections

In studying the sales process so far, you have learned how to prepare for the sale, approach a customer, determine customer needs, and present your product. Now it is time to look at handling customer questions and objections.

For example, a customer may like everything about a product except its color. Simply showing the same item in another color may solve the problem. Learning how to handle customer objections is an important part of your sales training because such objections are extremely useful in the sales process.

206   Unit 5   *Selling*

Classroom Management

For the Teacher

- Teacher's Annotated Editions for all workbooks
- Teacher's Manual for *School-to-Work Handbook*
- *Testing Binder*
- *Transparency Binder*
- *Marketing Software Binder*
- *Marketing Career Portfolio*
- *Lesson Plans*

For the Student

- *Student Activity Workbook*
- *Marketing Math Workbook*
- *School-to-Work Handbook*
- *Student Software*
- *International Case Studies*
- *Marketing Career Portfolio*

Objectives

After studying this section, you will be able to

- **distinguish between objections and excuses,**
- **explain why objections should be welcomed in the sales process,**
- **identify the five buying decisions upon which common objections are based, and**
- **list the four steps involved in handling customer objections.**

Terms to Know

- **objections**
- **excuses**
- **objection analysis sheet**
- **paraphrase**

Understanding Objections

Objections are concerns, hesitations, doubts, or other honest reasons a customer has for not making a purchase. Objections should be viewed as positive because they give you an opportunity to present more information to the customer.

Objections can be presented as either questions or statements.

Customer:	Do you carry any other brands?
Salesperson:	Yes, we have an extensive selection of brands available.
Customer:	These shoes don't fit right.
Salesperson:	Perhaps you would be more comfortable in a different style.

Excuses are insincere reasons for not buying or not seeing the salesperson. Customers often use excuses when they are not in the mood to buy or when concealing real objections. Here are some general excuses:

- "I'm too busy to see you today."
- "We don't need any more _____."

- "I'm just shopping around."
- "I didn't plan to buy anything today."

It is often hard to distinguish between objections and excuses. In some cases, a statement or question that seems to be an objection really means, "I don't want to buy today." This is an excuse.

When you are faced with this in a retail selling situation, be polite and courteous. Encourage the customer to look around and ask you any questions he or she may have.

In industrial sales, the procedure is different. If a potential customer refuses to see you when you make a call, leave a business card and ask if it is possible to see the person at a more convenient time.

There are cases when seeming excuses are actually attempts to hide real objections. "I didn't plan to buy today" may really mean, "I don't like the styles you have available." In that case, you may ask additional questions to get to the real reason for the disinterest in your product(s).

Welcome and Plan for Objections

Objections can occur at any time during the sales process and should be answered promptly. A customer who must wait to hear responses to questions or concerns tends to become preoccupied with the objection. When that happens, you may lose your purchaser's attention and confidence. So, answer objections when they occur.

Objections can guide you in the sales process by helping you redefine the customer's needs and determine when the customer wants more information. For example, a customer may say, "This item is very expensive." What the person may really mean is "Tell me why this product costs so much." In addition to letting you know why the customer is reluctant to buy, this objection gives you an opportunity to bring out additional selling points.

You should therefore welcome objections. They are not necessarily a sign that the sales process is going badly. In fact, research shows that there is a positive relationship between customer objections and a successful sales outcome. (See Figure 16–1 on page 208.)

You can prepare yourself for most objections that might occur in a sales situation by doing an **objection analysis sheet.** It enumerates common objections and possible responses to them. The actual objections, of course, may be slightly different from those you anticipated. However, the exercise of thinking through the responses gives you some idea of how to answer.

Sometimes you can incorporate anticipated objections into your product presentation so they do not become objections at all. You must be cautious about this, however. You don't want to include so many objections in your product presentation that you prevent your customer from talking. Remember, you still want your customer to be involved in the sale.

Bell Ringer Activity

Ask students if they have ever gone shopping without the intention of buying anything. Ask them to identify the statements they used in those circumstances when salespeople tried to help them.

Introducing the Section

The responses to the Bell Ringer Activity will help you introduce the difference between sincere objections and excuses for not buying. Note that some of the very same lines used as excuses can be used as sincere objections by other people wishing to buy. Have students identify some of those lines. Then ask students how they will be able to tell the difference between objections and excuses in those cases. (It's an ability that will come with experience.)

Teach

Guided Practice

1. Read Section 16.1 with students.
2. Use the transparency for this section.
3. Have students brainstorm objections a customer may have to any product with which they are familiar. (Product options include jeans, winter coats, snow skis, computers, etc.) List the objections on the board.

Use the chalkboard list to help students identify the five types of objections—those based on need, product, source, price, and time. (Most will be examples of product objections, although price objections may be represented well.) Have students generate examples of the other three common objections (need, source, and time).

Meeting Special Needs

Learning Disabled

If you have students who have attention difficulties, you may wish to take special care in presenting the steps required for handling customer objections. Attention difficulties can cause sequencing disturbances, depending on the severity of the difficulty. Thus, any material involving sequence of events can take longer for students to process and may even require visual reinforcement. Role-play once the students have the concepts firmly in mind, and allow them to determine the best way to remember the steps in the correct order.

Discussion Starter

Ask students when they think a salesperson should answer an objection—immediately, after some time has elapsed in the sale process, or after they have covered all selling points. (Answers will vary—each with appropriate rationale. However, as a general rule, it is best to answer objections promptly in order to avoid having a customer become preoccupied with them.)

L1 Math Skills

Tell students to assume that a camera is presently selling for $159.99, which is 20 percent less than the suggested retail price. Have students calculate the suggested retail price. ($159.99 ÷ .80 = $199.99.)

L2 Math Skills

Tell students that the camera noted in the L1 Math Skills activity is scheduled to go on sale at the beginning of next week. Consumers will be able to take advantage of a 15 percent discount on all items that retail for over $150. How much will the camera sell for during the special sale? ($159.99 × .85 = $135.99.)

Ask students what the sale price would be if the discount were taken off the suggested retail price instead of the actual retail price. ($199.99 × .85 = $169.99.)

L3 Math Skills

A salesperson applies the discount to the suggested retail price. The customer, seeing the result, objects strenuously. Explain why. (If applied to the suggested retail price, the discount would yield a "sale price" that's $10 higher than the actual retail price!)

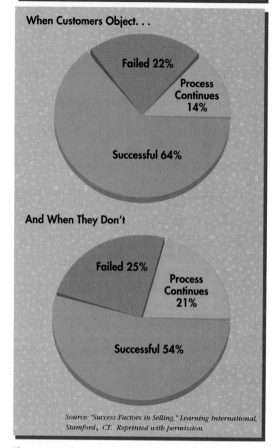

Sales Call Outcomes

When Customers Object...

- Failed 22%
- Process Continues 14%
- Successful 64%

And When They Don't

- Failed 25%
- Process Continues 21%
- Successful 54%

Source: "Success Factors in Selling," Learning International, Stamford, CT. Reprinted with permission.

Figure 16–1

Customer objections might be considered the "bad sign" that signifies ultimate success. What evidence of that conclusion can you find in the graphs shown here? What do you think accounts for such findings?

If you do include objections in the product presentation, always avoid introducing doubt—especially if none existed before. If you say, for example, "I guess you're worried about the safety of this snowmobile," you may introduce a fear that was not even a concern to the customer before you mentioned it.

A better way to handle the same situation would be to emphasize the safety features of the vehicle. For example, you might say, "The suspension on this snowmobile is specially designed to keep it stable. It's very safe to operate."

Common Objections

If you were to try to list all the objections a customer could have, you would probably find that they fell into

certain categories. Most would be based on key decisions the customer must make before buying—decisions about *need, product, source, price,* and *time.* You can use those same categories as a starting point for an objection analysis sheet.

Need   Objections related to need usually occur when the customer has a conflict between wanting something but not truly needing it. A comment such as "I really like this sweater, but it doesn't match anything I have" is an objection based on a conflict between a need and a want.

Product   Objections based on the product itself are more common. They include concerns about such things as construction, quality, size, appearance, or style. "I'm not sure this dress style is appropriate for work" is such an objection.

Source   Objections based on source often occur because of negative past experiences with the firm or brand. A buyer might say, "The last time I dealt with your firm, my order was three weeks late. How can I be sure this one will arrive on time?"

Price   Objections based on price are more common with high-quality, expensive merchandise. You might hear statements like "That's more than I wanted to spend."

Time   Objections based on time reveal a hesitation to buy immediately. These objections are sometimes excuses. At other times, however, customers have a real reason for not wanting to make a purchase on the spot. A customer might say, "I'm not in a position to make that type of purchase now. I won't be ready for at least two months."

Once you begin selling, you will probably hear all sorts of objections. You should note them for future reference. For now, Figure 16–2 can provide you with a few more examples.

When Yes Means No

Life in the Multicultural MARKETPLACE

There are virtually no gestures so basic that they cannot vary from one culture to another. What could be more commonplace and widely recognized than the gestures for yes (shaking your head up and down) and no (shaking your head from side to side)? In Bulgaria and Sri Lanka, however, nodding the head up and down means no, and shaking the head from side to side means yes! In other cultures, the gesture is much more subtle. In Greece, for example, no is conveyed by a slight upward nod of the head. To indicate yes, the Greeks tilt the head to either side.

Caption Answer

Success rates are 10 percent higher—64 percent as opposed to 54 percent—and failure rates a few percentage points lower when customers have objections. Reason may be that objections indicate a customer who is more serious about buying to start with.

Feature Note

Around the world, a nod of the head carries many other meanings besides yes. In Indonesia, for example, a slight nod of the head is the customary greeting for both men and women. It can also be used both to indicate congratulations and to acknowledge praise or congratulations received.

Figure 16–2

BUYING DECISIONS AND RELATED OBJECTIONS

Regardless of the buying situation or product involved, you can develop objections by thinking about basic buying decisions. Here are some possibilities in a business-to-business selling situation. In this case, the owner of a clothing store is discussing a potential order with a sales representative for a jeans manufacturer.

▼ Product
"My customers are beyond jeans. They want to see other things in denim. Shorts—definitely. Vests, dresses, hats, overalls—even better."

Need ▲
"I really don't need any more denim. It already accounts for nearly 20 percent of my floor space."

▼ Source
"The last time I placed an order with your company, it took two extra months to get here and four phone calls to straighten out the billing."

Price ▲
"At that rate, that's what I'd have to charge, and I can tell you my customers wouldn't pay it. They're savvy shoppers. They know where the discounters are— and when to use them."

Chapter 16 *Handling Customer Questions and Objections* **209**

L1 Communication Skills

Have students generate three product objections for a telephone answering machine.

L2 Communication Skills

Ask students to select one of the objections generated in the L1 Communication Skills activity to answer using the four-step method of handling objections. Have them prepare these responses in written form.

L3 Communication Skills

Pair students according to which objection they selected in the L2 Communications Skills activity. Then have the pairs try their hands at answering the objections they selected. After both members of each pair have had a chance to answer orally, have them read the written versions of the same responses prepared by their partners and evaluate how well their answers matched up.

Once this evaluation is complete, have the pairs work together to create an even better response than either one developed on his or her own. Have students submit these joint responses for your evaluation.

Critical Thinking

Ask students if the four-step process for handling objections could be used for any type of objection. Have them support their answers. *Note:* If they think the process cannot be used for a specific type of objection, have them brainstorm ways to make it work.

Independent Practice

1. Assign and review the Chapter 16 Case Study in the *International Case Studies* workbook.
2. Have students read issues of *Personal Selling Power* and *Sales & Marketing Management* magazines to find articles related to answering

---

Lifelong Learning

Handling Customer Questions and Objections

Like all parts of the sales process, the handling objections phase offers students an opportunity to learn valuable life skills. Some of the techniques used are just as effective when negotiating a dispute with a neighbor or co-worker or when presenting a rebuttal to a boss's denial of a raise.

Many companies recognize this and make training in such techniques available to nonsales employees. Your students, however, can duplicate the gist of this experience on their own. Encourage them to practice the four-step process in a variety of situations and then analyze why it did or didn't work for them.

Teach (Cont'd.)

objections or handling sales resistance. Ask students to summarize one relevant article in written form and discuss its key points with the class.

Assess

Evaluation

Assign and review the Section 16.1 Review.

Reteaching

1. Assign and review the vocabulary terms for this section.
2. Assign and review Fact and Idea Review questions 1–4 from the Chapter Review.
3. To reteach the five common types of objections, ask students to recall some of the objections they voiced regarding products that they or their families purchased in the last year. List the students' objections on the chalkboard. Then have students classify them according to buying decision.
4. To reteach the concept of welcoming objections, reenact several sales situations in which the salesperson gains useful information from the customer's objections. After each case has been presented, focus on the objections. Ask students how these objections were helpful to the salesperson.

Enrichment

1. Assign and review the appropriate activities in the *Student Activity Workbook*.
2. Assign and review the appropriate Critical Thinking questions from the Chapter Review.

Close

Have students complete the following sentence: An objection analysis sheet is. . .(a means of anticipating objections and planning responses to those objections in preparation for a sale.)

210

BRIGHT IDEAS

Go Halfway

If you've ever carried a briefcase, you know that it's next to impossible to locate anything in it without laying the case flat to open it. If you have no flat surface at waist level, you are sometimes forced to open the case on the floor.

To remedy this problem, Samsonite, the luggage company, invented the Smart Attaché™. It's a briefcase that automatically opens only halfway if you open it in the upright position. This means that you can get to important papers and other items while standing up. It also means you can carry out the maneuver without running the risk of dumping the whole case on the floor. Print ads for the Smart Attaché describe this feature as doing "twice the job by going half the distance."

Creativity Challenge Form teams of 3–5 people. Then develop a list of products that could be modified to make them more marketable. In each instance, briefly describe the nature of the modification, its benefits to consumers, and the ways it might lend itself to promotion.

Four-Step Process for Handling Objections

Successful salespeople have learned to use a very basic strategy when answering objections, regardless of type. Some call this strategy the "Old Faithful" method. It consists of four basic steps for handling objections—*listen, acknowledge, restate,* and *answer.*

Listen Carefully   To demonstrate sincere concern for your customer's objections, follow these key rules for effective listening:

• Be attentive.
• Maintain eye contact.
• Let the customer talk.

Acknowledge the Customer's Objections
Acknowledging objections demonstrates that you understand and care about the customer's concerns. Some common statements used to acknowledge objections are "I can see your point" or "I've had other customers ask the same thing." These acknowledgments make a customer

feel that his or her objections are understandable, valid, and worthy of further discussion.

In some situations you may feel like saying to the customer, "You're wrong." But this will probably put the customer on the defensive and destroy the rapport you have established up to that point. So, try to acknowledge a customer's objections in a positive way.

Restate the Objections   To be sure you understand the customer, you can restate his or her objections in a number of ways:

• "I can understand your concerns. You feel that… Am I correct?"
• "In other words, you feel that…"
• "Let me see if I understand. You want to know more about…"

Don't repeat the customer's concerns word for word. Instead, you should **paraphrase** the objections, or restate them in a different way. For example, a customer might say, "The style is nice, but I don't like the color." You could paraphrase the objection by asking, "Am I correct in assuming that you might be interested in the jacket if we could find your size in another color?"

When paraphrasing, don't change the meaning or content of what your customer says. Accurate paraphrasing shows the customer you understand his or her objections. It also helps you open the lines of effective communication when a customer has difficulty expressing concerns.

Answer the Objections   You should try to find a point of agreement with the customer before answering each objection. Then answer each objection tactfully, keeping in mind the customer's feelings. Never answer with an air of superiority or suggest that the person's concern is unimportant.

Think of yourself as a consultant, using the objections to further define or redefine the customer's needs. For example, if price is the objection, go back to determining the customer's needs. If a higher-priced item is warranted based on those needs, offer it. As you do, explain the features and benefits of the more expensive model and why that item is better suited to the customer.

SECTION 16.1

Review

1. Distinguish between objections and excuses.
2. Why should you welcome objections in the sales process?
3. Name the five buying decisions upon which common objections are based.
4. List the steps involved in the process for handling customer objections.

Bright Ideas

Ask: What customer objection could have been the catalyst for the innovation described in the feature? (A potential customer might have commented that she didn't want to buy a briefcase because it was too hard to find something in one. A salesperson may have been faced with laying his/her case on a client's desk to make such a search.)

Section Review Answers

1. Objections are honest reasons for not buying; excuses are insincere reasons.
2. Because they can uncover information the customer still requires to make a buying decision.
3. Need, product, source, price, time.
4. Listen carefully, acknowledge objection, restate it, and answer the objection.

SECTION 16.2

Objectives

After studying this section, you will be able to

- identify six specific methods of handling objections and
- demonstrate the use of those methods in a variety of selling situations.

Terms to Know

- boomerang method
- third party method

Specialized Methods of Handling Objections

There are six specialized methods for handling objections: *boomerang, question, superior point, direct denial, demonstration*, and *third party*. Some of these techniques are effective only in specific situations. Others are more commonly used.

Boomerang

Just as a boomerang returns to the thrower, an objection can be returned to the customer. With the **boomerang method**, the objection comes back to the customer as a selling point. Here is an example.

Customer: This ski jacket is so lightweight. It can't possibly keep me warm.

Salesperson: Actually, the lightness of the jacket comes from an insulation material called Thinsulate, which is lightweight and warm. The manufacturer guarantees that Thinsulate will keep you warmer, without the bulk, than comparable fiberfill insulation.

When using the boomerang method, you must be careful not to sound as if you are trying to outwit the customer. Instead, use a friendly, helpful tone when explaining how the objection is really a selling point.

Question

The question method is a technique in which the customer is questioned in an effort to learn more about the objections raised. Your questions may reveal hidden objections and/or help you learn more about the customer's needs and wants. While answering your inquiries, the shopper may even come to realize that the objections are not serious or valid.

Sometimes the question method can put the customer on the defensive. To avoid this, never ask questions in an abrupt manner. That may appear to be rudeness on your part. For example, suppose a customer comments, "I don't think my sister will like this purse." Never respond with a simple "Why not?" Instead, show courtesy and respect by asking a more complete question, such as "Why don't you think she'll like it?"

Superior Point

The superior point method is a technique that permits the salesperson to acknowledge objections as valid yet still offset them with other features and benefits. Because goods and services are not perfect, there are often trade-offs that take place when making a selection. The superior point method allows you to admit disadvantages in certain products but then present superior points to offset or compensate for them. This technique puts the customer in a position to decide between the different features and thus see additional reasons for buying. Here is an example.

Customer: Your prices are higher than the prices of your competitors.

Salesperson: That's true. Our prices are slightly higher but with good reason. We use better-quality nylon in our garments. Those garments will last 5–10 years longer than our competitors'. Plus, we guarantee the quality for life. If you ever have a problem with this garment, you can return it. We'll repair it free of charge.

Imagine the customer shown here has just pointed out some troubling irregularities in a garment's fabric. How would you use the boomerang method to respond?

Chapter 16 *Handling Customer Questions and Objections* **211**

Focus

Bell Ringer Activity

Have students recall the Springboard Activity and think about which methods they identified there worked best in which situations. List these on the chalkboard.

Introducing the Section

Using the methods list developed in the Bell Ringer Activity, look for similarities with the methods you will present in this section. If none exists, tell students that just as they have specialized methods for handling objections, so do professional salespeople. Explain that in this chapter they will study the methods professionals use.

Teach

Guided Practice

1. Read Section 16.2 with students.
2. Have students read aloud the Case Study and review the answers in class.
3. To introduce the boomerang method of handling objections, ask students what a boomerang does. (It comes back to you.) Tell students how an objection can come back to the customer as a selling point.
4. Assign and review the Chapter 16 Activity in the *School-to-Work Handbook*.

Discussion Starter

Describe a product such as a portable tape player or a laptop computer to the class verbally. Then describe it a second time with the item in hand, pointing out the features as you go. Afterwards, have students discuss which presentation was more effective and why.

Cooperative Learning

Have students work in groups to develop an objection analysis sheet for one of the following products: expensive snow skis, home/office copier, bicycle for two, portable CD player.

L1 Human Relations Skills

Tell students the exchange you are about to repeat is part of a planning session for a kitchen renovation.

Customer: I don't like the color you suggested for the kitchen cabinets.
Salesperson: Why don't we ask Mrs. Jones (another salesperson) if she likes that color.

Ask students what specialized method the salesperson's response demonstrates. (Third party.) Also, ask what was wrong with the way it was applied. (Third party wasn't neutral. Besides, the only person who really must like the color is the customer).

L2 Human Relations Skills

Ask students what method and response they would have used in the L1 Human Relations Skills activity. (Question method—to elicit customer's choice or help her arrive at it [*e.g.*, Would you prefer something lighter or darker for the cabinets?].)

L3 Human Relations Skills

Have students use the question method to respond to this objection: I don't think I really need a built-in microwave oven. I have a perfectly good free-standing model. (Response: Has there ever been a time when you could have used an additional microwave—say, when you were preparing several microwavable dishes and you had to wait for one to finish before you could begin cooking another?)

CASE STUDY

BT Wakes Up and Hears the Objections

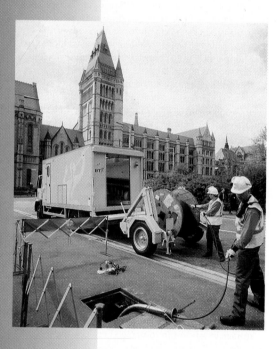

When Britain deregulated its telecommunications industry, its state-run monopoly, British Telecommunications PLC, faced competition from telecommunications giants from around the world. Since opening the market in 1991, Britain has licensed 146 companies. These companies are free to offer all types of services, from local phone service to advanced telecommunications systems.

Although British Telecommunications (BT) has 26 million phone lines and its nearest competitor only 500,000, BT has already lost 6 percent of its market share. In 1991 it had 100 percent of the market, but by 1994 that share had dropped to 94 percent. In fact, it is estimated that BT loses some 26,000 customers a day to its competitors. One analyst predicts that the new telecommunications companies could win up to 35 percent of the market by the year 2000.

Why are so many customers switching? The new companies are offering better service, lower prices, and more up-to-date technology. One competitor, Energis, supplies detailed calling reports for business customers. BT doesn't even itemize its bills for most of its customers, and it only bills them once every four months. Another competitor, Videotron Corporation, a Canadian cable-TV company, offers a system that carries voice, data, and video.

Faced with all this competition from advanced technological companies, BT sent representatives door-to-door to offer special deals. It is adding more fiber-optic lines and has cut its rates by $540 million since the beginning of 1994. Service is improving as well. Instead of waiting weeks for a new phone line, customers can now get one in a few days. More of BT's pay phones are now operational, too. Just a few years ago, six out of ten were out of order at any given time.

Even with all its problems, BT had revenues of $21 billion and pretax profits of $4.2 billion in 1993. Will it be able to report the same high figures for 1994 and the year 2000? That remains to be seen. Much will depend on how well it faces the objections and questions from customers who paid higher rates and received poor service for so many years when BT was a state-run monopoly.

Case Study Review

1. Which of the five buying objections do you think most BT sales representatives anticipate based on the information presented in the case study?
2. Suggest one objection and response for a BT sales representative's objection analysis sheet. Identify the method you used to handle the objection.

A MATTER OF ETHICS

3. Was it ethical for BT to wait until deregulation was a reality before lowering its prices and improving its service?

Case Study Answers

1. Product—BT did not offer the most up-to-date technology; source—its service record was poor (billed customers infrequently and didn't itemize calls); price—its prices were high (compared to its present competitors').
2. Answers will vary.

3. Arguably BT was more insensitive than unethical. A major problem of monopolies of all sorts is that lacking competition they have little incentive to improve their product since they are the customers' only choice.

Direct Denial

The direct denial method provides proof and accurate information in answer to objections. It is best used when the customer has misinformation or when the objections are in the form of a question. Consider an example.

Customer: I think this shirt will shrink.

Salesperson: Actually it won't because the fabric is made of 50 percent cotton and 50 percent polyester. The polyester will prevent shrinkage.

Note that when using the direct denial method, you must back up the negative reply with proof and accurate facts.

Demonstration

The demonstration method is a technique that answers objections by illustrating one or more features of a good or service. It exemplifies the adage "Seeing is believing." Here is an example.

Customer: I can't believe that food won't stick to the bottom of the pan if you don't use oil or butter.

"Objections Acknowledged and Answered" could be another title for this series of U.S. Postal Service ads. What objection was illustrated in this particular ad? Which method was used to answer it?

Salesperson: I'm glad you brought that up. Let me demonstrate how the Teflon coating lets you cook without fats of any kind.

The demonstration method can be quite convincing and should be used when appropriate. However, only conduct demonstrations you have tested. Make sure they work before using them on a customer in a sales situation.

Third Party

The **third party method** involves using a previous customer or another neutral person who can give a testimonial about the product. Some salespeople keep letters from satisfied customers to use as testimonials when handling objections. Others get permission from previous customers to allow prospective customers to call and verify the salesperson's claims. Here's how the method works.

Customer: I can't see how this machine can save me $1,000 in operating costs the first year.

Salesperson: Mr. Frank Smith, one of my customers, questioned the same point when he bought his machine a year ago. Now he praises its efficiency and says that his costs have gone down by $1,200. Here's a letter I recently received from him.

In any given sales situation, it is unlikely that you will use all six methods of handling objections. Over time, however, you will probably create some effective combinations.

SECTION 16.2 Review

1. Name six specific methods of handling objections.
2. Which specialized method exemplifies the adage "Seeing is believing"?

Caption Answer

Objection—overnight mail costs too much; method of handling—direct denial backed up with low rate quote.

Section Review Answers

1. Boomerang, question, superior point, direct denial, demonstration, and third party.
2. Demonstration.

SECTION 16.2

Independent Practice

Have students develop an objection analysis sheet for a product of their choice.

Assess

Evaluation

Assign and review the Section 16.2 Review.

Reteaching

1. Assign and review the vocabulary terms for this section.
2. Assign and review Fact and Idea Review questions 5–9 from the Chapter Review.
3. To reteach methods of handling objections, list the basic techniques on the chalkboard. Then provide students with sample dialogs that always end with an objection. Ask students to choose the most appropriate way to handle each situation.

Enrichment

1. Assign and review the appropriate activities in the *Student Activity Workbook*.
2. Assign and review the appropriate Critical Thinking questions from the Chapter Review.
3. Assign and review the Building Academic Skills Activities, Application Projects, Linking School to Work Activity, and Performance Assessment from the Chapter Review.
4. Have students role-play responses to objections that you, as a customer, propose.

Close

Have students complete the following statement: The most effective method to use when handling price objections is ____ because ____ . (Answers will vary, with the superior point method most likely favored because it allows a salesperson to acknowledge a high price and still offset it with a compensatory selling point.)

Answers

Vocabulary Review

Paragraphs will vary. See Glossary for definitions.

Fact and Idea Review

1. At any time.
2. Because a customer who must wait to hear responses to questions or objections tends to become preoccupied with them.
3. By preparing an objection analysis sheet.
4. Be sure not to cover so many objections that you prevent the customer from talking and being involved in the sale. Also, be aware that in anticipating an objection you don't create doubt about the product where none existed before.
5. The objection comes back to the customer as a selling point.
6. That the objections are not serious or valid.
7. Superior point method.
8. When the customer has misinformation or when the objection is in the form of a question.
9. Third party method.

Critical Thinking

1. Yes, it is possible—especially if the customer is presold.
2. a. Price
   b. Need
   c. Product
   d. Source
   e. Time
3. Answers will vary. Possibilities:
   a. Demonstration method— would allow customer to see the TV screen image and decide for him- or herself if it was clear enough.

16 CHAPTER Review

Vocabulary Review

Write one or two paragraphs on how to handle customer questions and objections. Incorporate these terms:

objections
excuses
objection analysis sheet
paraphrase
boomerang method
third party method

Fact and Idea Review

1. When can objections occur in the sales process? (Sec. 16.1)
2. Why should objections be answered promptly? (Sec. 16.1)
3. How can you be prepared for most objections? (Sec. 16.1)
4. What precautions must you take if you want to include anticipated objections in your product presentation? (Sec. 16.1)
5. What happens to a customer's objection when you use the boomerang method? (Sec. 16.2)
6. In using the question method for handling an objection, what does the salesperson hope the shopper will come to realize after answering the salesperson's inquiries? (Sec. 16.2)
7. Which specialized method of handling objections allows you to offset an objection with other features and benefits? (Sec. 16.2)
8. When is direct denial best used in handling objections? (Sec. 16.2)
9. Which specialized method of handling objections involves using a previous customer or another neutral person who can supply a testimonial about the product? (Sec. 16.2)

Critical Thinking

1. Do you think it is possible to go through the entire sales process without one customer objection? Explain.
2. For each of the following objections, identify the buying decision on which the concern is based. (The common buying decisions are need, product, source, price, and time.)
   a. "I'm really not sure I want to spend that amount of money on an automobile."
   b. I just love the shoes, but I'm not sure I'll have much use for them after the wedding."

c. "I don't like the assortment of rakes I received."
d. "I really don't know if I want to spend my money in this store. The last time I charged something and returned it, you didn't credit my charge account."
e. "I want to think about it. I don't usually buy the first thing I see that I like."
3. For each of the following objections, utilize one of the six specialized methods for handling objections. Identify the method with your response.
   a. "This is the smallest television I've ever seen. How can it possibly have a clear picture?"
   b. "I didn't think automatic focus cameras cost so much."
   c. "I'm not sure I need a copier that enlarges and reduces, especially at $300 more than the basic model."
   d. "Will this nylon and polyester fiberfill vest need to be dry-cleaned?"
   e. "These running shoes are so lightweight. Are you sure they're meant for avid runners?"
   f. "How can I be sure this copier won't break down all the time like my last one did?"
4. Is it possible to agree with a customer's objection and still sell that customer the product for which she or he has a legitimate objection? Provide an example to support your answer.

Building Academic Skills

Math

1. A customer is objecting to the price of a television set. As a sales associate, you are only authorized to offer a 10 percent discount. However, your sales manager can offer another 10 percent discount, when necessary. The television's retail price is $1,019.99. If you were to apply your discount and your sales manager agreed to let you offer the customer the additional 10 percent, what would be the final price you would offer the customer?
2. Your 5 percent sales commission is based on the price a customer actually pays. Based on the preceding question, how much commission do you lose when you sell the television with both discounts rather than at full price?

Communication

3. Acknowledge and then paraphrase the following objection: "I worry about radiation leaking from the door of a microwave oven. That can be dangerous."

---

b. Superior point method—acknowledge that automatic focus cameras do cost more but point out all the additional benefits they provide.
c. Question method—suggest some common situations in which reductions or enlargements are needed and ask if customer has ever encountered them.

d. Direct denial method—point out the care label and indicate that both fabrics are washable under normal circumstances.
e. Boomerang method—explain that light weight is a feature deliberately designed into the shoe to ease strain and fatigue over the long haul.
f. Superior point method—offer new extended warranty as proof of company's confidence in the superiority of its product.

Human Relations

4. Do a sales situation role play for your class in which you play the parts of both salesperson and customer. Tactfully answer each of the following objections:
   a. "This wool jacket costs more than I wanted to spend on a casual, everyday piece of clothing."
   b. "This Walkman has got to be too small to produce quality sound."
   c. "No shoes ever fit me properly. I doubt whether this pair will be any different."

Application Projects

1. As part of your continuing project, write the handling objections section of your sales training manual. Explain the importance of this step to the entire sales process. Include an objection analysis sheet for the product for which you prepared a feature-benefit chart.
   Note: If you did not prepare a feature-benefit chart, select a product like a pair of athletic shoes, a CD player, a computer, or a ski jacket. Present six objections, one for each of the specialized methods you learned in this chapter. Write your responses to the objections as though the customer were standing in front of you.
2. Interview two salespeople—one who sells in a retail setting and one who is involved in business-to-business selling situations. Ask these salespeople the following questions:
   a. What is the most common objection you hear?
   b. How do you usually handle that objection?
   c. What is the most absurd objection a customer ever raised, and how did you respond?
   d. How do you prepare for objections that occur during a sales presentation?
   Based on the responses of the two salespeople, what similarities did you find? what differences?
3. As a class, brainstorm all the objections the school administration might have to keeping the school store open during the entire school day, as well as during evenings when there are sporting events at the school. Work in teams to develop effective responses to those objections. Prepare an objection analysis sheet for this exercise. (*Note:* If the school store is open during those time periods, think of another request that the student body might make that would require analysis of possible objections by the school administration.)

Linking School to Work

Observe a co-worker who is selling a product to a customer or an idea to a colleague. Note the objections raised and the methods used to handle those objections. Summarize your findings in a written report.

Performance Assessment

Role Play

Situation. You are employed in the shoe department of a sporting goods store as a sales associate. One of the best-selling items is hiking boots that are waterproof, durable, and very lightweight. A customer you are helping is interested in the boots but is hesitant to buy. She thinks the price is too high, and she's not sure she wants to buy today. She has told you that she's a new hiker and has not as yet been out on any very long hikes. The mountain area where she has been hiking has several small streams and a rocky terrain. Use your skill in handling objections to help this customer make an intelligent buying decision.

Evaluation. You will be evaluated on how well you do the following:

- Distinguish between objections and excuses.
- Identify the buying decisions upon which objections are based.
- Demonstrate skill in using specific methods of handling objections.
- Effectively handle this customer's objections.

Public Speaking

Make an oral presentation supporting the idea that the same methods salespeople use to handle customer objections can be employed in everyday situations. To make your presentation relevant, base it on nonbusiness scenarios that are familiar to your classmates.

Complete the Chapter 16 Computer Application that appears in the Student Activity Workbook.

Communication

3. Suggested paraphrase: "Am I correct that you're worried about the safety of using a microwave oven?"

Human Relations

4. Answers will vary. Possibilities:
   a. Do you normally wear more casual or dressy clothing? If you wear more casual clothing, you'll find that this jacket offers you versatility. It goes with all types of outfits because of its neutral color and fashionable design.
   b. The small size of the Walkman is its major selling point. And if you listen to it with these headphones, you'll see how superb the sound is.
   c. These shoes are very popular with people who report having problems getting shoes to fit. Why not try them on to see if they fit you?

Application Projects

Answers will vary.

Linking School to Work

Answers depend on the work situation.

Performance Assessment

Refer to the *DECA Competitive Events Handbook* for evaluation guidelines.

Computer Application

Optional activity. Refer to the *Marketing Software Binder* for template and user information.

Evaluation

Administer the reproducible test for Chapter 16, or construct your own using the Testmaker software.

---

4. Yes. Examples will vary. One might be based on price. It is possible that the customer simply does not realize the value of all the features and benefits that warrant the higher price. Another example might be based on source. It is possible that past delivery problems have since been solved with new equipment or personnel.

Building Academic Skills

Math

1. With your discount: $1,019.99 \times .90 = $917.99. With manager's discount: $917.99 \times .90 = $826.19.
2. Full price: $1,019.99 \times .05 = $51. With discounts: $826.19 \times .05 = $41.31. Difference: $51 - $41.31 = $9.69.

Chapter Overview

Chapter 17 covers the last three phases of the sales process—closing the sale, suggestion selling, and following up. These steps should come naturally if the salesperson has determined the customer's needs and communicated the product's features in a way that shows how the product will satisfy those needs.

Springboard

Have the class think about the nature of buying signals, those actions that make it obvious a customer is ready to buy. Tell students to use their own behavior when making a difficult purchase decision as a guide. Compile a chalkboard listing of the group's suggestions.

Prereading

List the section objectives to discuss with students. Have students skim the chapter, looking at the pictures, reading the captions, and noting the heads. Ask questions to ensure that students have a minimal understanding of the chapter structure.

Preteaching the Vocabulary

Before students begin reading the chapter, dictate each of the vocabulary terms and ask students to write them on a sheet of paper. When they finish, write the terms on the chalkboard. Then have students guess at the meaning of each. Write their guesses next to each term, but do not give the correct meaning. Leave this list on the chalkboard so that students can see how close their guesses were to the actual definitions as they work through the chapter.

Closing the Sale and Following Up

At a certain point in the sales process, your customer will be ready to make a purchase. When this becomes apparent, it is up to you to close the sale.

Sometimes the decision to buy is quick and easy. At other times, it's more difficult. In this chapter you will learn how to recognize customer buying signals and how to close a sale. You will also learn how to suggest additional merchandise as part of a sale. Finally, you will be introduced to the follow-up procedures essential for customer satisfaction and repeat business.

216   Unit 5   *Selling*

Classroom Management

For the Teacher
- Teacher's Annotated Editions for all workbooks
- Teacher's Manual for *School-to-Work Handbook*
- *Testing Binder*
- *Transparency Binder*
- *Marketing Software Binder*
- *Marketing Career Portfolio*
- *Lesson Plans*

For the Student
- *Student Activity Workbook*
- *Marketing Math Workbook*
- *School-to-Work Handbook*
- *Student Software*
- *International Case Studies*
- *Marketing Career Portfolio*

SECTION 17.1

Objectives

After completing this section, you will be able to

- recognize customer buying signals,
- list the rules for closing a sale, and
- demonstrate specialized methods of closing a sale.

Terms to Know

- closing the sale
- buying signals
- trial close
- which close
- standing-room-only close
- direct close
- service close

Closing the Sale

Closing the sale is obtaining positive agreement from the customer to buy. All your efforts up to this step of the sale have involved helping your customer make buying decisions. So, closing the sale should be a natural part of the sales process. In fact, it is sometimes so natural that your customer closes the sale for you by saying, "I'll take it." In many sales situations, however, the customer waits for you to initiate the close. That is why it is important for you to learn when and how to close a sale.

Timing the Close

You close the sale when your customer is ready to buy. Since some customers are ready to buy sooner than others, you must be flexible. You may show a customer one product and almost immediately detect an opportunity to close the sale. At other times, you may spend an hour with a customer and still find that he or she is having difficulty making a decision.

In either case, do not feel obligated to complete an entire sales presentation just because you have planned

it that way. Remember, the key to closing the sale is customer readiness.

Buying Signals   To detect an opportunity to close the sale, look for **buying signals.** These are things a customer does or says to indicate a readiness to buy. They include facial expressions, actions, and comments. For example, a customer who is holding merchandise and smiling is usually sending you buying signals. So is a customer who has removed a jacket from its hanger and draped the garment over his or her arm. Comments that imply ownership are also buying signals. You know a customer is ready to buy when you hear comments such as "This is exactly what I was looking for."

Trial Close   To test the readiness of the customer and your interpretation of a positive buying signal, you can attempt a **trial close.** This is an initial effort to close a sale.

Trial closes are beneficial for two reasons. First, even if the close does not work, you will probably learn from the attempt. The customer will most likely tell you why he or she is not ready to buy. Second, if the trial close does work, you will reach your goal of closing the sale. Thus, in both situations you retain control of the sale and are in an excellent position to continue with the sales process. The rule, then, is always be ready to close.

General Rules for Closing the Sale

You will find it easier to attempt trial closes and to close more sales if you follow these general rules:

- *Rule 1—If you think the customer is ready to make a buying decision, stop talking about the product.* Continuing to sell to a customer who is ready to make a purchase may have a negative effect or even cause you to lose the sale.
- *Rule 2—When a customer is having difficulty making a buying decision, stop showing additional merchandise.* You should also narrow the selection of items by removing those things that are no longer of interest to the customer. You can do this by asking, "Which of these items do you like the least?" Once you get the selection down to two, you can concentrate on helping the customer make a decision.
- *Rule 3—Help a customer decide by summarizing the major features and benefits of a product.* You can also tell the advantages and disadvantages of the item being considered. Both methods help you to focus the decision making on important considerations.
- *Rule 4—Don't rush a customer into making a buying decision.* Be patient, courteous, polite, and helpful. Always remember that your primary interest is in customer satisfaction.

Chapter 17   *Closing the Sale and Following Up*   **217**

Focus

Bell Ringer Activity

Ask students when they think they should attempt to close the sale. Should they wait until they have covered all selling points before closing? Could they close immediately after the approach? What is the rule of thumb?

Introducing the Section

In response to the Bell Ringer questions, get students to realize that the time to close the sale is as soon as the customer is ready. This will help you introduce buying signals, timing the close, and rules for closing.

Teach

Guided Practice

1. Read Section 17.1 with students.
2. Ask students what the benefits of a trial close are. (If you fail to close, you have learned something; if you succeed, you reach your goal of making a sale.)
3. Tell students to imagine themselves in the following situations:
   - You have just finished an exceptionally effective product presentation.
   - You have just responded effectively to a key customer objection.
   Then ask students why these two situations present perfect opportunities to close the sale. (Customer is in a positive frame of mind.)

Discussion Starter

Have students react to the following statement: After closing the sale, it is best not to continue talking about the product. Ask students if they agree or disagree, and have them cite examples to support their positions.

Meeting Special Needs

Hearing Impaired

Students with hearing impairments ranging from complete loss to moderate loss communicate mainly by sign language. When it comes to written English, they are actually using it as a second language, much like students who are nonnative speakers.

Many factors affect the comfort level of hearing impaired students with English. These include

personality, intelligence, degree of deafness, residual hearing, age of onset of deafness, and family environment. This does not mean, however, that you should overlook errors in spoken or written English. Improvement can occur with increased use, correction, and exposure.

(Answers will vary. To keep the discussion on track, be sure to distinguish instances of suggestion selling [talking about *other* merchandise] from further talk about the product itself. Have the group carefully analyze instances in which further talk lost a sale. Be sure students understand the kind of talk that leads to problems and the nature of the problems caused. For example, praising the minimal shrinkage of a garment or noting how beautifully it dry-cleans could give the customer who hadn't considered shrinkage or dry-cleaning costs cause to rethink his/her purchase decision.)

L1 Math Skills

Ask students to calculate the total sale for a customer who has purchased the following items: three shirts priced at $29.99 each, six pairs of socks priced at $4.50 each or three for $12, and two pairs of pants priced at $59.99 each. (Shirts: $3 \times \$29.99 = \$89.97$. Socks: $2 \times \$12 = \$24$. Pants: $\$59.99 \times 2 = \$119.98$. Total: $\$89.97 + \$24 + \$119.98 = \$233.95$.)

L2 Math Skills

Ask students to determine the total amount due for the purchase described in the L1 Math Skills activity, assuming that the state sales tax is 6 percent. ($\$233.95 \times 1.06 = \$247.99$)

L3 Math Skills

Tell students that rather than the prices given in the L1 Math Skills activity, the shirts and pants are on sale at 20 percent off. Also, the socks are full price, so the customer has decided to buy only two pairs. Have students determine the total amount due for this purchase, including sales tax. [Shirts and pants: $(89.97 + \$119.98) \times .8 = \$209.95 \times .8 = \$167.96$. Socks: $2 \times \$4.50 = \$9$. Total: $(\$167.96 + \$9) \times 1.06 = \$176.96 \times 1.06 = \$187.58$.]

*Ready to buy **or not? What is this person's body language saying? Explain.***

- *Rule 5—Use words that indicate ownership, such as* you *and* your. When presenting selling points, say such things as, "You'll enjoy using this camera on your vacation."
- *Rule 6—Use major objections that have been resolved to close the sale.* The effect of having a major obstacle removed usually makes a customer receptive to buying the product or service.
- *Rule 7—Use effective product presentations to close the sale.* Dramatic product presentations often prove important selling points and get a customer excited about owning the product. Take advantage of high customer interest at these times and attempt to close.
- *Rule 8—Look for minor agreements from the customer on selling points that lead up to the close.* Ask questions such as, "Those walking shoes are comfortable, aren't they?" In general, if you get

218 Unit 5 *Selling*

positive reactions from your customer throughout the sales process, that same positive frame of mind will help make the closing natural.

Specialized Methods for Closing the Sale

Once you recognize a buying signal, you should attempt to close the sale. How you go about this depends on the selling situation. Certain selling situations warrant the use of specialized methods, such as the *which, standing-room-only, direct,* and *service* closes.

BRIGHT IDEAS

Stay the Course

One of the longest running ad campaigns in history features the Jolly Green Giant. The character was created in 1935 by Leo Burnett for the Minnesota Valley Canning Company. It was so successful that the company renamed itself for its trademark, becoming the Green Giant Company. The giant survived the company's move into frozen foods and even spawned a spin-off, the Little Green Sprout, in 1973.

The key to the giant's longevity can be summed up in one word—consistency. Throughout its 60-year relationship with Green Giant, the Burnett agency has held fast to its belief that consistent portrayal of the character is what keeps him alive and well and doing his job for the company. There are actually rules that govern his behavior and regular meetings between ad agency and client to discuss updates to the campaign. At this rate, look for the giant to live to be 100!

Creativity Challenge Form teams of 3–5 people, and give the giant a new sponsor. Make whatever alterations you feel are necessary to match the character to its new product. Then devise a "code of conduct" designed to take the character well into the 21st century. (Note that you don't have to follow the Burnett agency's approach. Your giant might be consistently inconsistent. His former identity as a spokesperson for veggies might be part of his new character [or not]. His vocabulary might be larger than "Ho, ho, ho" [or not]. Whatever your changes, be ready to explain how they will extend the giant's life another 60 years.)

Which Close The **which close** encourages a customer to make a decision between two items. To accomplish that goal, follow these three steps:

1. Remove unwanted items to bring the selection down to two.
2. Review the benefits of each item.
3. Ask the customer, "Which one do you prefer?"

This method makes it easy for a customer because only one simple decision must be made.

Standing-Room-Only Close The **standing-room-only close** is used when a product is in short supply or when the price will be going up in the near future. Because it can be perceived as a high-pressure tactic, this close should be used infrequently and only when the situation honestly calls for it. For example, a shoe salesperson might say, "This is the last pair of shoes I have in your size."

Direct Close The **direct close** is a method in which you ask for the sale. If you followed the rules for closing the sale, you have already obtained agreement from the customer on some selling points. So, it should seem natural to get confirmation on one more point.

However, it is sometimes necessary to ask non-threatening questions or to make statements to get the customer ready for the close. Here are a few:

- "Based on what I've shown you, how do you feel about this product?" If the customer answers in a positive way, you should be ready to take the order.
- "Can I assume that we're ready to talk about the details of your order?" or "It appears that you're pleased with what you've seen. Am I correct? Well then, shall we get started?" You would use these statements if a buying signal is very strong.
- In other instances, a simple statement such as "That should wrap it up" might be all that is necessary to see if the customer is ready to make a decision.

Positive statements by the customer in any of the above situations let you know that the direct close is in order. You can continue the closing with a few questions that relate directly to the purchase. Start with simple questions regarding the shipping address and delivery dates. Then get down to the specifics of the order such as styles, colors, and quantities of each. In a retail situation, you might simply ask a question regarding payment, such as "How would you like to pay for this purchase—cash, check, or credit card?"

Service Close Sometimes you run into obstacles or instances that require special services in order to close the sale. The **service close** explains services that overcome obstacles or problems. Such services include

*Your customer is considering **two items** and seems to be leaning toward one. If you were to attempt a close at this point, how would you handle it?*

Chapter 17 *Closing the Sale and Following Up* **219**

L1 Problem Solving

Set this scene for students: Assume you are a sales associate for an electronics store where you earn $7 per hour plus a 5 percent commission on all sales. It's the last day of our workweek, and you are $300 short of your weekly sales quota. However, there is hope you may still make it. You have just spent 30 minutes with a couple buying a portable TV for their daughter at college. They're having difficulty choosing between one model that's on sale for $349 and another that sells for $399.

At this point your supervisor tells you to take your lunch break because she expects the store to get very busy around noon. It's 11:30 a.m. when you attempt your first close, which is unsuccessful.

What are your options in this situation? List each on a separate sheet of paper.

(Answers will vary. Possibilities: Ask to take the next lunch break or to forgo lunch until after the noontime rush. Explain the situation to the couple, and ask again for a decision. Hand off the couple to a co-worker, and either ask to share the commission or resign yourself to losing it.)

L2 Problem Solving

Based on the situation described in the L1 Problem Solving activity, have students evaluate the alternatives available and choose one. Then have them explain their choices in written form. (Answers will vary. However, asking to take a later lunch is probably the most satisfactory solution. It would give students the opportunity to close, earn full commission, and make their weekly sales quota.)

L3 Problem Solving

Based on the decisions they made in the L2 Problem Solving activity, have students role-play exactly what they would say to their (a) supervisor, (b) co-worker, and/or (c) customers. (Role plays will vary.)

More About

Salespeople

Positive attitude can be an indicator of sales success. To predict which candidate might have the best shot at becoming a superior salesperson, one sales manager routinely asks candidates to describe an early childhood memory. Those who recall a positive experience have a better chance, to his mind, of success.

Independent Practice

1. Assign and review the Chapter 17 Case Study in the *International Case Studies* workbook.
2. Have students read issues of *Personal Selling Power* and *Sales & Marketing Management* magazines to find articles related to closing the sale. Have students summarize the articles in a written report and share their key points with the class orally.

Assess

Evaluation

Assign and review the Section 17.1 Review.

Reteaching

1. Assign and review the vocabulary terms for this section.
2. Assign and review Fact and Idea Review questions 1–6 from the Chapter Review.
3. To reteach the specialized methods of closing a sale, write the four methods on the chalkboard. Provide scenarios illustrating each method, and have students identify the method used to close in each situation.

Enrichment

1. Assign and review the appropriate activities in the *Student Activity Workbook.*
2. Assign and review the appropriate Critical Thinking questions from the Chapter Review.

Close

Ask students what they would do if a customer has four items in front of him/her and is confused about a purchase decision. (Get the selection down to two items by asking the customer which one he/she likes least. Then use the which close.)

220

---

gift wrapping, a return policy, special sales arrangements, warranties and guarantees, and bonuses or premiums.

For instance, you could offer gift wrapping when you know the purchase is a gift. You could explain the store's return policy when a customer is hesitant about a purchase. This is an especially good idea when the item is being purchased for someone else.

Special sales arrangements are used to close the sale when the customer needs help in paying for the item or order. In an industrial selling situation, the sales representative would talk about the terms of the sale, discussing such points as when payment is expected. (It might, for example, be 30–60 days after the date of the invoice.) A customer may also need information about credit terms to help him or her decide to buy. In a retail selling situation, acceptance of credit and checks, as well as special buying plans such as installment or layaway agreements, can be suggested. These make it easier for a customer to buy. When a customer questions the quality of the merchandise, you can explain that a warranty, or guarantee, is offered on the product.

Offering something special can also be an effective closing technique, particularly if the customer will save money and/or time as a result. Some enticements might include a free roll of film with the purchase of a camera or free alterations on a dress.

When your business offers the same quality merchandise at the same price as your competitors, your service may be the *only* factor that affects the buying decision. In such a case, promising better service than the customer is presently getting may help close the sale.

Failure to Close the Sale

Don't despair if your initial attempts to close a sale are unsuccessful. You will have many more opportunities,

Real World

Making Customer Satisfaction Count

Today more than a quarter of all companies link the pay of their salespeople to customer satisfaction levels. For example, IBM bases 40 percent of its salespeople's commissions on how well they have met customer needs. Indianapolis Power & Light goes even further. It has its customers *grade* its salespeople using the A–F scale common in schools. It then factors the results into their incentive pay.

Number of Close Attempts Before Quitting

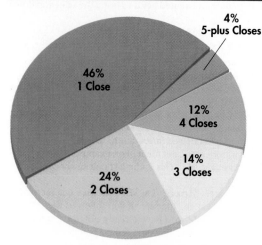

Source: Notre Dame University survey

Figure 17–1

More than 60 percent of all sales follow four or more attempted closes. Given this information, what does the pie chart suggest about the selling technique of the surveyed salespeople?

particularly if you treat your customer with courtesy and respect. Research suggests that perseverance is the way to succeed (see Figure 17–1).

In a retail setting, invite the customer to shop in your store again. In industrial selling, ask if you may call again. In both situations, remember that every sales contact has the potential to become a sale in the future.

SECTION 17.1	
	Review

1. What are customer buying signals?
2. When is it the right time to close a sale?
3. Provide examples for two of the following specialized closing methods:
   a. Which close
   b. Standing-room-only close
   c. Direct close
   d. Service close
4. Why is failure to close *not* a true failure?

Caption Answer

That 84 percent are robbing themselves and their companies of sales by failing to be more persistent in the face of unsuccessful close attempts.

Section Review Answers

1. Things a customer does or says to indicate a readiness to buy.
2. When the customer is ready to buy.
3. (a) Of the two remaining, which do you prefer? (b) That's the last one I have in your size. (c) That should wrap it up. (d) We accept credit cards if you don't want to pay cash.
4. Majority of sales follow a failed close.

SECTION 17.2

Objectives

After completing this section, you will be able to

- **explain why suggestion selling is important;**
- **list the rules for effective suggestion selling;**
- **demonstrate specialized suggestion selling methods;**
- **discuss the concept of relationship marketing and how it is related to the sales process; and**
- **summarize the importance of after-sale activities, such as departure, follow-up, and evaluation.**

Terms to Know

- **suggestion selling**
- **relationship marketing**

Suggestion Selling

Suggestion selling is selling additional goods or services to the customer. It does not mean loading down customers with unneeded or unwanted goods and services. Rather, it involves selling customers other items that will ultimately save them time and money or make the original purchase more enjoyable.

For example, consider the customer who buys a camera, takes it home, and only then realizes that he or she has no film for it. That means another trip to the store before the camera can be used. The salesperson would have had a sure sale by suggesting film as an additional purchase.

Benefits of Suggestion Selling

Suggestion selling benefits the salesperson, the customer, and the company. You benefit because customers will want to do business with you again. Your customer benefits because he or she is more pleased with the original purchase. The firm benefits because the time and cost involved in suggestion selling is less than the cost of making the original sale.

To illustrate the last point, consider the two purchases below. The second includes an extra item, a suggestion from the salesperson.

Pair of pants	$75	Pair of pants	$ 75
—		Shirt	35
Purchase total	$75	Purchase total	$110
Cost of goods	− 37	Cost of goods	− 55
Gross profit	$38	Gross profit	$ 55
Expenses	− 12	Expenses	− 15
Net profit	$26	Net profit	$ 40

Note that the extra time spent on suggestion selling significantly increased the firm's net profits. Expenses rose—but not in proportion to the sales volume. There are two reasons for this. First, less time and effort are needed for suggestion selling compared to the initial sale. Second, certain business expenses (like utilities and rent) remain the same despite the extra sales activity.

Rules for Suggestion Selling

There are five basic rules for suggestion selling.

- *Rule 1—Do suggestion selling after the customer has made a commitment to buy but before payment is made or the order written.* Introducing additional merchandise before the sale has been closed can create undue pressure on the customer. The only exception to this rule involves products whose accessories are a major benefit (like dolls with extensive outfit wardrobes). Salespeople who sell such products often introduce the additional items during the sales process to help close the sale.
- *Rule 2—Make your recommendation from the customer's point of view and give at least one reason for your suggestion.* For example, you might say, "If you want to use your camera immediately, you'll need film for it." A customer is usually willing to listen to your suggestion when it sounds as though you have his or her best interests at heart.
- *Rule 3—Make the suggestion definite.* Don't ask, "Will that be all?" Instead say, "This oil is recommended by the manufacturer for the engine." In most cases, general questions such as "Anything else?" take too much effort for customers to consider. They invite a negative response.
- *Rule 4—Show the item you are suggesting.* Merely talking about it is not enough. In some cases, the item will sell itself if you let the customer see and handle it. For example, putting a matching purse next to the shoes a customer just decided to buy can be quite effective, particularly with some commentary. You might say, "This purse matches your shoes perfectly, doesn't it?"
- *Rule 5—Make the suggestion positive.* For example, you could say, "This scarf will complement your coat beautifully. Look how perfectly it matches the color and how fashionable it looks on." You certainly would

Chapter 17 *Closing the Sale and Following Up* **221**

Focus

Bell Ringer Activity

Ask students what the counterperson at McDonald's or Burger King routinely asks after a customer orders a hamburger. (Would you like fries, a soft drink, etc., with that?)

Introducing the Section

Use answers to the Bell Ringer Activity to introduce the concept of suggestion selling. The example should make it easy for students to understand and appreciate the technique.

Teach

Guided Practice

1. Read Section 17.2 with students.
2. Use the transparency for this section.
3. Have students read aloud the Case Study and review the answers in class.
4. To introduce the benefits of suggestion selling, ask students if they think the technique is beneficial to the customer and/or the business. Have them explain their answers. (It's beneficial to both. Customers save time and money, and tend to be more pleased with their original purchases. Businesses make more money and have more satisfied customers.)
5. To introduce the rules for suggestion selling, invite students to recall their own experiences. Ask: As a buyer, when did you *least* appreciate suggestion selling efforts? Why didn't the technique work in that particular case? (Answers will vary.)
6. Assign and review the Chapter 17 Activity in the *School-to-Work Handbook.*

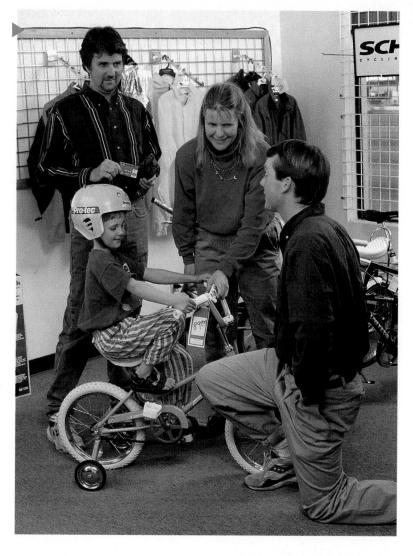

Evaluate this salesperson's suggestion-selling technique. What is he doing right?

never say, "You wouldn't want to look at scarves for your new coat, would you?" Such a negative statement shows a lack of enthusiasm or perhaps confidence on the part of the salesperson.

Suggestion Selling Methods

There are three methods used in suggestion selling. They are offering *related merchandise*, recommending *larger quantities*, and calling attention to *special sales opportunities*.

Offering Related Merchandise Related merchandise can be a good or service that a customer should have to increase the use or enjoyment of the original purchase. Introducing related merchandise is probably the easiest and most effective suggestion selling

method. For most purchases, there are accessory items that can be sold with the original purchase—a scarf to match a blouse or a special service contract for a new appliance.

Recommending Larger Quantities In retail selling, suggesting a larger quantity usually works with inexpensive items or when money, time, and/or convenience will be saved. For example, you may tell a customer who wants to buy one pair of pantyhose, "One pair costs $4, but you can buy three pairs for $10. That's a savings of $2. Buying three pairs will also save you a trip to the store next time you need a pair."

In industrial selling, the salesperson may suggest a larger quantity so the customer can take advantage of lower prices or special considerations. In addition to offering a better price per item, some manufacturers also

222 Unit 5 *Selling*

include special services. Buying a certain quantity, for instance, may allow a retailer to take advantage of free freight and/or free advertising.

Calling Attention to Special Sales Opportunities As a matter of customer service, salespeople are obligated to communicate special sales opportunities to their customers. This is so even if those opportunities are not related to the original purchase. Often they involve new merchandise, special sales, and holiday items.

In retail sales, routinely inform your customer of the arrival of new merchandise. Regular customers appreciate this special service because they like having the opportunity to see new merchandise before others do.

Most shoppers appreciate the opportunity to take advantage of a bargain. Salespeople are obligated to both the store and the customer to pass along such information. For instance, you could comment on a special sale by explaining, "We're having a one-day sale on all items in this department. You might want to look around before I write up your purchase."

Special occasions and holidays present an opportunity to sell more merchandise. You can suggest gift items to customers around such occasions as Christmas, Hanukkah, Valentine's Day, Father's Day, and Mother's Day.

Here's an example of what you can say: "If you haven't finished your holiday shopping for the men in your life, you may want to look at the special display of gift ideas we have here in the men's department. You'll be amazed at the variety and creativity of some of the items. If you would like to follow me over here, I can show you what I mean."

In industrial sales situations, sales representatives often show new items to their customers after they have completed the sale of merchandise requested. Thus, the salesperson has an opportunity to establish a rapport with the customer before introducing new merchandise.

After-Sale Activities

The big thrust among companies today is *relationship marketing*. **Relationship marketing** involves the strategies businesses use to stay close to their customers. In today's competitive marketplace, after-sale activities are an important part of this trend. They are used to develop and nurture customer relationships.

Today, with competition from all over the world, the loyalty of customers cannot be taken for granted. How

Goods that increase use or enjoyment of a purchase like a camera are ideal for suggestion selling. How many such items do you see here? List them.

Chapter 17   *Closing the Sale and Following Up*   **223**

L2 Communication Skills

Have students select one of the follow-up techniques generated in the L1 Communication Skills activity and use it as an on-the-job suggestion. Tell them to make their suggestion in the form of a written memo to the new vice president of sales for the auto dealership in which they are hypothetically employed as salespeople. Remind them to cite the benefits of the suggested course as well as describe it.

L3 Communication Skills

Have students write the letter (or cover letter) that would be sent to customers as part of the follow-up technique selected in the L2 Communication Skills activity. (This letter should be a sample of what students suggested in their memos to the vice president of sales.)

L1 Human Relations Skills

Ask students what they would include in the criteria for evaluating a salesperson's skills. (Possibilities: reaching or exceeding sales quotas; indicators of customer satisfaction (letters, phone log records); ability to communicate and desire to improve selling techniques.)

L2 Human Relations Skills

Have students develop a sales staff evaluation form that could be used at week's end to monitor sales activity and progress. Have students defend the items they included on their forms during a group discussion or series of oral presentations.

L3 Human Relations Skills

Have students use the tool they created in the L2 Human Relations Skills activity to evaluate a videotaped sales presentation. Then tell them that the person in the video tape is expecting an oral evaluation as well. Have pairs of students role-play the evaluation session.

Caption Answer

Possibilities include tripods, camera mounts, carrying cases, lenses, batteries, lights, and film.

Did You Know

According to Dartnell Corp. (a Chicago business organization), the average dollar volume a salesperson could bring into a company in 1994 was $1.1 million of revenue. There were, however, supersalespeople who sold 1.5 to 2 times that amount. These people by themselves often saved companies from red ink during the business downturn in the early 1990s.

L1 Decision-making Skills

Ask students if they think it would be ethical to use a voice-activated tape recorder to record their sales calls for evaluation purposes. (Answers will vary. Some will find the procedure ethical because the tape is being made for purely educational purposes. Others will find it unacceptable because the customers are apparently being given no choice about participation in the procedure.)

L2 Decision-making Skills

Ask students what problems could occur if a salesperson used a voice-activated cassette recorder as described in the L1 Decision-making Skills activity and a customer found out. (Possibilities: anger, distrust of not just the salesperson but the company as well, loss of pending and future sales, and even legal action.)

L3 Decision-making Skills

Have pairs of students role-play the situation described in the L2 Decision-Making Skills activity. Tell them to pretend that an irate customer, one who has just learned that all of his sales calls have been taped, is on the phone. Allow students some time to get in character. Tell them that "customers" will be evaluated on how well they articulate the reasons for their anger, "salespeople" on how well they mollify their callers.

Independent Practice

Have students read issues of *Personal Selling Power* and *Sales & Marketing Management* magazines to find one or two articles that demonstrate the topics discussed in this section. Have students summarize the articles they selected and present their key points to the class orally.

224

CASE STUDY

Just a Visit with the Family

In an attempt to reclaim a portion of the small-car market from foreign competition, General Motors established a wholly owned subsidiary. It gave this subsidiary a blank check to come up with a new car and new way of doing business. The result was Saturn Corporation.

Saturn's motto is "A Different Kind of Company. A Different Kind of Car." The company prides itself on customer relationships and service. Its goal is to build a unique relationship with its customers that results in customer enthusiasm and loyalty. That means giving its customers consistent treatment in all Saturn facilities.

To ensure this consistency, Saturn took special steps to see that the corporate philosophy made its way down to the retail level. Saturn dealers had to sign franchise agreements that contained the company's "no hassle, no haggle" concept of selling cars. This meant that they were required to be frank about all elements of a car's price and to adhere to their set prices. The Saturn retailers were also made responsible for building a special relationship with Saturn owners.

Saturn owners are made to feel like part of a family—the Saturn Family. It is not uncommon for new Saturn owners to be serenaded by the dealership sales staff when they accept delivery of their new cars. As they drive away from the showroom, balloons, music, and cheers follow them.

By far though, the Saturn Homecoming was the company's most ambitious effort at building a sense of "family" among its customers. In June 1994 Saturn invited all of its car owners to "come home" for a weekend to Spring Hill, Tennessee, the place where their cars were built. The

invitation was extended to nearly 700,000 owners nationwide—and 44,000 accepted.

Once in Spring Hill, the adults toured the plant where their cars were assembled, met the team members who assembled them, and shared their enthusiasm with other Saturn owners. The children went to Camp Saturn. In the evenings, everyone gathered for family-oriented concerts of popular and country and western music. Headliners included the Grammy-winning gospel duo of BeBe and CeCe Winans.

Case Study Review

1. Does the "no hassle, no haggle" concept of selling cars break any of the general rules for closing the sale? for suggestion selling?
2. How does Saturn demonstrate the concept of relationship marketing?
3. Would you prefer to buy a car the traditional way (by negotiating the price) or the Saturn way (by accepting a set price)? Why?

A MATTER OF ETHICS

4. What ethical problems do both the traditional and Saturn methods of buying a car present from the consumer's viewpoint? Given these concerns, what would be the most ethical method of arriving at a price for both consumers and auto manufacturers?

224 Unit 5 *Selling*

Case Study Answers

1. Closing rules are in line with concept—involve *not* talking, rushing customer, or showing more merchandise. There may be disagreement about suggestion selling—pushing additional merchandise could be seen as pressuring customer.
2. By building a sense of "family"—serenading customers, inviting them "home" to Tennessee.
3. Answers will depend on which is more important to students—getting the best price or avoiding conflict/haggling.
4. Either way customer left wondering whether he/she has been gouged on price. Suggested solutions will vary. One possibility: Use a disinterested third party to verify dealer cost and evaluate markup.

It's Hard to Say Good-bye

It's even harder when you've crossed the cultural divide. In Japan, for example, it is customary to escort guests from your home and wait until they are actually out of sight before shutting the door. While they are still in sight, it is customary to continue to wave or bow. Any host who fails to observe this ritual risks seriously offending a Japanese guest.

does a company stay close to its customers and keep them happy? By having the sale be the first step in developing a relationship, not the final one. So, think of after-sale activities as part of an ongoing dialog with customers in preparation for future sales.

Taking Payment/Taking the Order

Take payment or take the order with courtesy. Work quickly to complete the paperwork. Avoid saying or doing anything to irritate your customer at this stage of the sale. You have probably heard an annoyed customer say, "Forget the order. I don't want it anymore." If you are courteous and efficient, you can usually avoid this type of negative response.

Departure

Before the customer departs or before you leave your client's office, reassure the person of the wise buying choices that have been made. If an item needs special care or specific instructions, take the time to educate your customer about it. You may want to remind the customer, for example, that to get the best results from a Teflon-coated frying pan, it is best to preheat the pan. Helpful comments like this will make your customer feel you are interested and concerned. They also help ensure customer satisfaction.

Always thank your customers. Even when a customer does not buy, express your gratitude for the time and attention given to you. Invite him or her back to the store, or ask for permission to call again in the near future.

Follow-up

The follow-up includes making arrangements to follow through on all promises made during the sales process and checking on customer satisfaction with the purchase. If you promised a certain delivery date, call the shipping department to confirm it. Then check to make sure that delivery occurs as promised. If there is a problem, call the customer and explain the delay. If you promised to call back in one week, make that notation on your calendar. To check on customer satisfaction, phone the customer a week or two after the purchase to see if he or she is happy with it. You can also send a thank-you note with your business card attached.

In addition, you can use the time immediately after the sale to plan for your next encounter with the customer. Take notes on your conversation with the customer. Keep this in a file for future reference. In retail sales, note a customer's preference in color, style, and size, as well as the person's address and telephone number. In industrial selling, record personal information on the buyer's marital status, children, and/or hobbies to assist with future sales visits. Record changes in buying patterns that may lead to future sales.

Evaluation

In an effort to improve customer relations, some businesses send questionnaires or call customers to check on how well they were treated by the sales and service staff. The results of such surveys are passed on to salespeople so they can improve their technique.

Even if your company has such a formal method of reviewing your efforts, you should conduct your own evaluation. After the sales process is completed (even if you closed the sale), evaluate yourself. Consider everything you did. What were the strong points of your sales presentation? What did you do wrong? How could you have improved your performance? What would you do differently next time?

Such objective evaluations can help you improve your selling skills. They will enable you to look forward to your next sales opportunity. That kind of attitude will help you become more effective with each new sales contact. It will also help you become more successful.

SECTION 17.2 *Review*

1. What is suggestion selling, and why is it important?
2. Suggest two rules for suggestion selling.
3. Identify three methods used for conducting suggestion selling.
4. What is relationship marketing, and how is it related to the sales process?
5. Why are after-sale activities (such as departure, follow-up, and evaluation) important?

Evaluation

Assign and review the Section 17.2 Review.

Reteaching

1. Assign and review the vocabulary terms for this section.
2. Assign and review Fact and Idea Review questions 7–10 from the Chapter Review.
3. To reteach suggestion selling, describe sales situations that break one or more of the key rules for that type of selling (pages 221–222). After each description, ask students what went wrong, and have them tell you what the salesperson could have done to achieve a favorable outcome.

Enrichment

1. Assign and review the appropriate activities in the *Student Activity Workbook.*
2. Assign and review the appropriate Critical Thinking questions from the Chapter Review.
3. Assign and review the Building Academic Skills Activities, Application Projects, Linking School to Work Activity, and Performance Assessment from the Chapter Review.
4. Invite both a retail salesperson and an industrial salesperson to speak to the class about the kinds of suggestion selling and after-sale activities they perform in the course of their respective jobs. After the visits, have students compare and contrast the closing and follow-up techniques used in the two different sales situations.

Close

Have students complete this statement: When properly used, suggestion selling saves the customer…(time and money.)

Section Review Answers

1. Selling additional goods or services to the customer. Important because it helps create customer satisfaction.
2. (a) Do it after the close but before payment. (b) Make the recommendation from the customer's point of view. (c) Make the suggestion definite. (d) Show the item you are suggesting. (e) Make the suggestion positive.
3. Suggest related merchandise, larger quantity, and special sales opportunities.
4. Marketing that involves strategies businesses can use to stay close to their customers. Based on the idea that the sale is the first step in developing a relationship with customers.
5. Help salespeople prepare for future sales.

17 CHAPTER *Review*

Answers

Vocabulary Review

Stories will vary. See Glossary for definitions.

Fact and Idea Review

1. Initial attempts to close a sale. Even if they fail, you've still learned valuable information about why the customer is not ready to buy.
2. Because continuing to sell could have such a negative effect on the customer that it costs the salesperson the sale.
3. Remove unwanted items to bring the selection to two; review benefits; ask customer, "Which one do you prefer?"
4. When a product is in short supply or when the price will be going up in the near future.
5. Service close to offer other payment options.
6. Retail situation: invite customer to shop in your store again.
   Industrial situation: ask if you may call again.
7. Salesperson: customer will want to do business with salesperson again.
   Customer: more pleased with original purchase.
   Firm: increases net profits.
8. After customer has made a commitment to buy but before payment is made or the order is written.
9. By taking notes on conversation with the customer and keeping them for future reference. In retail selling, note customer's size, style, and color preference, as well as address and phone number. In industrial selling, record personal information about buyer's marital status, children, and/or hobbies, as well as any changes in buying patterns.

226

Vocabulary Review

Write a story about a sales situation in which you are asked to close the sale for a colleague. Incorporate all the terms below into your story.

closing the sale
buying signals
trial close
which close
standing-room-only close
direct close
service close
suggestion selling
relationship marketing

Fact and Idea Review

1. What are trial closes, and why are they beneficial to the sales process? (Sec. 17.1)
2. Why should a salesperson stop talking about a product once he or she detects strong buying signals from a customer? (Sec. 17.1)
3. What three steps should be followed when using the which close? (Sec. 17.1)
4. When should the standing-room-only close be used? (Sec. 17.1)
5. A customer in a retail store shows an interest in buying but is hesitant because he or she does not have the cash to pay for the purchase. Which closing method should the salesperson use? (Sec. 17.1)
6. What should you do if you did not close the sale in a retail situation? in an industrial situation? (Sec. 17.1)
7. How does suggestion selling benefit the salesperson, the customer, and the company? (Sec. 17.2)
8. When should you attempt suggestion selling? (Sec. 17.2)
9. How can a salesperson use the time immediately after the sale to plan for his or her next encounter with that customer? (Sec. 17.2)
10. Why should you evaluate yourself after the sales process is finished? (Sec. 17.2)

Critical Thinking

1. A customer seems to be frustrated because she likes three of the items you have shown her. What can you do to help make her buying decision easier?
2. Select the most appropriate closing method for each of the following situations, and provide a rationale for each of your choices.

226 Unit 5 *Selling*

a. "I can't wait until my friends see me in this outfit!"
b. "Now *these* boots are very comfortable."
c. "I really like this TV more than the others. The fact is, though, that I don't have enough money with me to buy it today."
d. "Your presentation was terrific, and I like those skis. But I think I'll wait until they go on sale."
e. "You've shown me so many pairs of gloves I like that I can't make up my mind."
f. "My parents are very fussy. What if I buy this clock for them and they don't like it?"
g. "I had such a bad experience with my last computer that I'm concerned about this one's reliability."
h. "All the flannel shirts you've shown me will sell well in my store. But I can't buy them now because my money is all tied up in my present stock. It's February, and your merchandise won't begin selling until next September."
3. List at least three related items that could be used for suggestion selling after a customer's decision to buy each of the following: a suit, a microwave oven, a video camera, and a bicycle.

Building Academic Skills

Math

1. Credit card customers are granted a 10 percent discount on all purchases (except sale merchandise) from November 5 through November 15. Calculate the total amount due from a credit card customer who wants to buy the following items during the discount period: two blouses at $50 each, four pairs of pantyhose at $4 each, and one sale item at $78.99. The 6 percent sales tax is applied after the discount is taken.

Communication

2. Prepare a memo explaining to all new sales employees the importance of suggesting related merchandise to customers making purchases. Include recommendations and guidelines so your readers are encouraged to attempt suggestion selling.

Human Relations

3. A customer wants to return a clock radio because he was not able to set the time or the alarm. The customer is probably not aware of a memory key that must be depressed while such settings are being

Critical Thinking

1. Ask customer specific questions to help get the selection down to two, and then summarize the major features and benefits of those items. If customer still cannot decide, suggest that she buy both.

10. To help you improve your selling skills and make you look forward to your next sales opportunity.

2. a. Direct close, customer indicated ownership.
   b. Direct close, strong buying signal.
   c. Service close, to suggest other means of payment.
   d. Standing-room-only close, to suggest skis may be unavailable for sale.
   e. Which close, to get selection down to two and help customer make decision.
   f. Service close, to reassure about returnability.
   g. Service close, to reassure with firm's willingness

made. How would you handle the return? How could the whole situation have been avoided?

Application Projects

1. For your continuing project, write an introduction for the closing step of the sales process. Include discussions of the step's importance and timing. Then write four different dialogs to demonstrate when and how to close the sale for your product. Each dialog must demonstrate a different specialized closing method.

2. For your continuing project, write an introduction for the suggestion selling step of a sale. Include discussions of the step's importance and timing. Finally, do the following:
   - List all the related merchandise you can use for suggestion selling with your particular product.
   - Write exactly what you would do and say to suggest one of the related items of merchandise. Remember to follow all the rules for suggestion selling.

3. Write the conclusion for your sales training manual. In it, stress the concept of relationship marketing.

4. Prepare an evaluation sheet to use in judging a sales demonstration. Include spaces to rate all the steps of the sale (including approach, determining needs, product presentation, handling objections, closing the sale, and suggestion selling), as well as departure and ability to communicate. Under each step of the sale, indicate items to be evaluated and points assigned to each. The evaluation sheet should total 100 points.

5. Plan a complete sales presentation for your product. Have your teacher select a classmate to role-play the part of the customer while you role-play the part of the salesperson. Make your presentation in class, and ask your classmates to evaluate your sales skills. *Note:* If possible, videotape the presentation.

6. Suggest ways the following businesses could both ensure customer satisfaction and develop ongoing relationships with their customers:
   a. Copier company that sells primarily to businesses
   b. Computer store that sells both to businesses and to consumers for personal use
   c. Robotics machinery manufacturer that sells to other manufacturers
   d. Automobile retailer that sells primarily to consumers for personal use

Linking School to Work

Interview a sales representative in your company to find out what closing technique/methods he or she uses. If you are a salesperson yourself, identify and analyze the closing methods you use in your sales position.

Performance Assessment

Role Play

Situation. You are a sales associate in a sporting goods store. You normally work in the footwear department, but because of the season you have also been asked to cover in the ski and other departments. A new store manager has asked all employees to share with her the sales practices they have found most successful. The goal is to develop a master plan that can be used storewide to ensure customer satisfaction through suggestion selling and relationship marketing. Even though you work in several departments, you need select only one to comply with her request.

Evaluation. You will be evaluated on how well you do the following:

- Explain why suggestion selling is important.
- State the rules for effective suggestion selling.
- Demonstrate specialized suggestion selling methods.
- Discuss the concept of relationship marketing and explain how it is related to the sales process.
- Describe the importance of after-sale activities, such as departure, follow-up, and evaluation.

Oral Presentation

You are employed as a sales associate for a local department store. The store manager is not pleased with the sales figures for the part-time associates. Since you have one of the best records among the full-time associates, the manager asks you to conduct a short training session on closing the sale. Prepare an oral presentation that includes material on how to recognize customer buying signals, when and how to close a sale, and demonstrations of specialized closing methods.

COMPUTER APPLICATION

Complete the Chapter 17 Computer Application that appears in the Student Activity Workbook.

to stand behind product with warranty or extended service contract.
   h. Service close, to suggest special payment plan.
3. Answers will vary. Possibilities: suit—shirt/blouse, tie/scarf, hose; microwave—cookbook, micro-wavable dishes, microwave accessories, service contract; video camera—tripod, video cassettes, carrying case; bicycle—water bottle, specially designed seat, cycling attire, helmet, basket for holding things.

Building Academic Skills

Math

1. Discounted (nonsale) items: $[(2 \times \$50) + (4 \times \$4)] \times .90 = (\$100 + \$16) \times .90 = \$116 \times .90 = \$104.40$.

   Purchase total: $(\$104.40 + \$78.99) \times 1.06 = \$183.39 \times 1.06 = \$194.39$

Communication

2. Memos will vary but should be done in correct format (with To/From/Subject/Date heading).

Human Relations

3. Answers will vary but should include demonstrating proper use of the memory key. Situation could have been avoided by doing this.

Application Projects

1. Introductions and dialogs will vary.
2. Introductions, merchandise lists, and suggestion selling pitches will vary.
3. Conclusions will vary.
4. Evaluation sheets will differ somewhat in content and format.
5. Presentations will vary.
6. Answers will vary. Here are a few possibilities.
   - Demonstrate copier for employees, check on satisfaction periodically, offer service contract.
   - Install software for customers, offer free classes on computer use, offer service contract.
   - Provide assistance in setting up equipment and training staff.
   - Offer extended service contract, check on satisfaction.

Linking School to Work

Answers depend on the work situation.

Performance Assessment

Refer to the *DECA Competitive Events Handbook* for evaluation guidelines.

Computer Application

Optional activity. Refer to the *Marketing Software Binder* for template and user information.

Evaluation

Administer the reproducible test for Chapter 17, or construct your own using the Testmaker software.

MATH FOR RETAIL SALES

Pages 228–241

Chapter Overview

This chapter looks at the important conclusion to the sales process—recording the transaction and presenting the customer with a sales receipt. It discusses the functions of cash registers, the arrangement of money in a cash register drawer, and do's and don'ts of making change. It also covers the various types of sales transactions and leads students through the steps involved in filling out sales checks.

Springboard

Begin the chapter by asking students what they still find challenging about such things as making change, transacting credit card sales, or conducting other types of transactions like returns. Tell students that with this chapter they will get a chance to improve their ability to do sales transactions accurately and skillfully.

Prereading

List the section objectives to discuss with students. Have students skim the chapter, looking at the pictures, reading the captions, and noting the heads. Ask questions to ensure that students have a minimal understanding of the chapter structure.

Preteaching the Vocabulary

Before students begin reading the chapter, dictate each of the vocabulary terms and ask students to write them on a sheet of paper. When they finish, write the terms on the chalkboard. Then have students guess at the meaning of each. Write their guesses next to each term, but do not give the correct meaning. Leave this list on the chalkboard so that students can see how close their guesses were to the actual definitions as they work through the chapter.

228

Math for Retail Sales

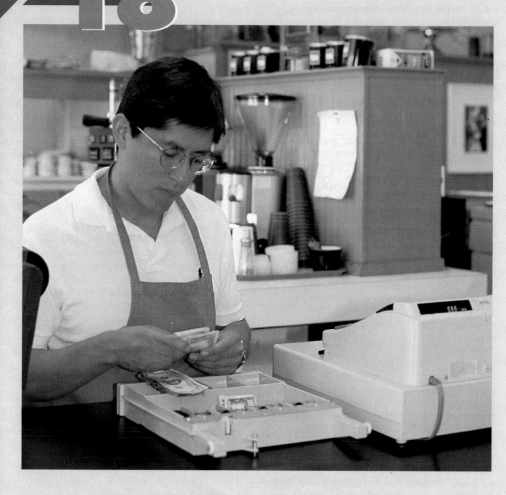

Your customer's decision to buy does not conclude the sales process. After you close a retail sale, you must record the transaction. You must also present the customer with proof of either payment or his/her promise to pay in the future.

In this chapter, you will explore two major areas—cash register operations and types of sales transactions. You will learn the basics of operating both manual and electronic registers, with special emphasis on recording sales and managing the cash drawer. You will also do the paperwork and calculations for both cash and credit sales.

228   Unit 5   *Selling*

Classroom Management

For the Teacher

- Teacher's Annotated Editions for all workbooks
- Teacher's Manual for *School-to-Work Handbook*
- *Testing Binder*
- *Transparency Binder*
- *Marketing Software Binder*
- *Marketing Career Portfolio*
- *Lesson Plans*

For the Student

- *Student Activity Workbook*
- *Marketing Math Workbook*
- *School-to-Work Handbook*
- *Student Software*
- *International Case Studies*
- *Marketing Career Portfolio*

SECTION 18.1

Objectives

After completing this section, you will be able to

- **list three general functions of all cash registers,**
- **describe the arrangement of currency and coins in a cash register drawer,**
- **demonstrate two methods of making change,**
- **state the two most important rules for safeguarding money at the cash register, and**
- **describe the general content of sales checks and the basic ways of generating them.**

Terms to Know

- **sales transaction**
- **Universal Product Code (UPC)**
- **Universal Vendor Marketing (UVM) code**
- **till**
- **opening cash fund**

Cash Register Operations

The **sales transaction** is the process of recording a sale and presenting the customer with proof of payment. Most retailers today use cash registers to record sales and provide customers with receipts. Cash registers fill three important functions of sales transactions:

1. *Recording sales.* Cash registers provide a convenient way to enter information about a sale. This usually includes the department, the type of transaction, the salesperson, and the amount of the sale. The salesperson also enters the amount tendered by the customer. The register responds with the amount of change due.

2. *Storing cash and sales documents.* Cash registers provide a convenient, organized way to keep cash, personal checks, credit sales checks, and refund slips. Coupons and other sales-related documents may also be kept in the cash register drawer.

3. *Providing receipts.* Cash registers automatically provide a receipt for the customer. This is the customer's record of the sale and proof of payment.

Most salespeople operate a cash register. In some retail stores, including many department stores and all supermarkets, cash register operations are the responsibility of a cashier or checkout clerk. Before you assume the responsibility of using a cash register and handling money, you will need to become familiar with all aspects of cash register operations.

Electronic Cash Registers

The electronic cash registers now in common use automatically perform many functions of a sales transaction. These include totaling quantity purchases, figuring sales tax, subtracting refunds and returns, and calculating the change due a customer.

Information on sales transactions can be entered into an electronic cash register in a number of ways:

- *Manual key entry.* Even with electronic cash registers, many businesses have their salespeople enter all sales transactions manually, using the register keys. All registers provide a numeric keyboard for entry in case other input devices don't work.

- *Electronic wand entry.* More and more retailers (especially department and clothing stores) are using electronic wands to enter sales transactions. The salesperson simply moves the point of the wand across the data printed on a tag attached to the article sold.

- *Optical scanning.* Many supermarkets have improved their efficiency in recording sales transactions by installing optical scanners at checkout counters. Salesclerks simply drag items across the scanner so it can read the bar codes on their packaging. If the scanner cannot read the code, the salesclerk keys the information manually.

Two types of codes are widely used for electronic entry. The **Universal Product Code (UPC)** is the bar code referred to above. It consists of a series of vertical bars and a row of numbers. Each item to be scanned has its own distinctive UPC. The **Universal Vendor Marketing (UVM) code** is the second type of code. It appears as a series of numbers across the top of a price tag. A UVM code is designed to be read by an electronic wand.

Once read and entered into a register, code information can be transferred to a mainframe computer for

---

Focus

Bell Ringer Activity

Have students read this lesson before you discuss it in class. The day you begin the lesson, bring an empty cash drawer to class. Have on hand "play" coins and currency, enough to constitute an opening cash fund. Call on volunteers to help you, and have students do the following:

- Count the opening cash fund. (Suggest appropriate amounts —say, $75 or $100 in coins and currency.)
- Place coins and currency in the drawer in the appropriate compartments. (Do not allow students to study the text diagram beforehand.)
- Tell you where such things as checks, food stamps, and coupons would go.
- Handle various small and large cash payments.

Introducing the Section

The Bell Ringer Activity will show you where students still need help in conducting cash transactions. As you work through this section, use the cash drawer for demonstration purposes.

Teach

Guided Practice

1. Read Section 18.1 with students.
2. Use the two transparencies for this section.
3. The MarkEd Resource Center in Columbus, Ohio, (800) 448-0398, has materials appropriate for use with this lesson.
4. For additional chapter resource material, you may wish to use Glencoe's program entitled *The Cashier,* which includes a textworkbook, a teacher's manual/key, and six sound filmstrips.

Meeting Special Needs

Learning Disabled

Because students with learning disabilities may have trouble with symbols, such as numbers, learning the material presented in the chapter could present challenges. Some students can more easily access the information when it is read aloud, either by a person or on tape. Students who have difficulty communicating effectively through printing or cursive writing may prefer to use a computer to perform calculations or to dictate their work to another person. In general, learning disabled students benefit from a classroom that incorporates a wide variety of learning modalities (visual, auditory, tactile, and kinesthetic).

Teach (Cont'd.)

5. Invite a representative from your local police department or a security company to talk to students about safety precautions one must take when dealing with money in a public venue, such as a store. (For example, what should you do if someone comes up to your cash register and demands money?)

Discussion Starter

Have students speculate about why some stores and other businesses will not accept currency larger than $20 bills. (Answers will vary but could include the following: The risk of getting a counterfeit bill increases with larger bills, such as fifties and one hundreds. Accepting larger bills forces you to keep higher levels of change in the cash drawer, which is a security risk. Finally, mandating that only smaller bills can be accepted is an employee theft deterrent, because it's easier for management to keep track of a smaller amount of money in the till.)

Critical Thinking

1. Ask: Why is good cashiering good customer service? (Answers will vary. Customers usually grow impatient if their sales transactions are not conducted in a timely fashion. In effect, they are being kept waiting in return for the privilege of giving their money to the store. If they are served rapidly and accurately, however, this increases their satisfaction with both the purchase and the business.)

2. Many businesses today, confronted with prospective employees who are math phobic, have poor math skills, or are less familiar with U.S. currency, are resorting to cash registers that minimize computation. Ask students to suggest some of the features that these registers have. (Keyboards with words and pictures instead of numbers and programs that compute cash back for the customer.)

230

Two types of codes **are used on merchandise for optical scanning purposes—UPCs and UVM codes. Of the two codes shown here, which is which? Explain.**

further processing. Many electronic cash registers are linked to such computers as part of a POS system. Using the register data, the computer can update inventory records with each sale and automatically reorder items in short supply. Under some circumstances, it can store customer information and make it available for marketing or credit-check purposes. It can also print out financial statements, sales trends, and reports of sales personnel productivity.

The Cash Drawer

Checks and currency collected in sales transactions are generally deposited in the till. The **till** is the cash drawer of a cash register.

Cash Drawer Arrangement The till normally has ten compartments—five in the back and five in the front. Although some companies vary the arrangement, bills are usually kept in the back of the drawer and coins in the front. The typical arrangement is shown in Figure 18-1.

In the section for bills, the first compartment on the left often remains empty. It is reserved for checks or other special items. The second compartment contains $20 bills, the third $10 bills, and the fourth $5 bills. The last compartment on the right is used for $1 bills. When a customer tenders a $2 bill, it is placed under the $1 bills.

230　　Unit 5 *Selling*

In the section for coins, the first compartment on the left is used for silver dollars and half-dollars. The next compartment is for quarters, the following one for dimes, and the one after that for nickels. The last compartment on the right is for pennies.

This arrangement facilitates making change because the bill and coin compartments are related. Each pair has at least one digit in common. The $20 bills are behind the quarters ($.25). The $10 bills are behind the dimes ($.10). The $5 bills are behind the nickels ($.05), and the $1 bills are behind the pennies ($.01).

Opening Cash Fund At the beginning of each business day, the manager or some other designated person will provide a limited amount of money for the cash register. This **opening cash fund** consists of the coins and currency designated for the register for a given day's business. To verify the fund, the assigned person first counts the coins and places them, one denomination at a time, in the correct compartment. Then he or she does the same with the currency.

As the coins and currency are counted, the amount is written down to make sure the total matches the amount planned for the register. If it matches exactly, the change fund is even. If there is more than planned, the fund is over. If there is less than planned, the fund is short. If the opening cash fund is short or over, it should be reported immediately to the person who supplied the money.

Cash Drawer Arrangement

Various uses:
- Checks
- Large bills
- Food stamps
- Rolls of change

$20　$10　$5　$1

50¢　25¢　10¢　5¢　1¢

Figure 18-1

The typical cash drawer has bills in the back and coins in the front. How does this arrangement facilitate making change?

Making Change If you are a salesperson who handles a large number of cash transactions during a business day, you may at some point run short of certain denominations. Check your cash drawer during any slack time you have to see if you need any bills and/or coins. If you do, request the change you need then. This preventive procedure can help you avoid delays when customers are waiting for service.

A customer who has made a decision to buy usually wants to pay quickly and move on. That is why accuracy and speed are of primary concern in recording sales. If you work as efficiently as possible, you will usually be able to keep your customer happy.

You should take special care with cash transactions. When making change, be thorough and accurate. Figure 18-2 illustrates the procedure you should use.

Figure 18-2
HANDLING CASH PAYMENTS

As soon as you have entered the transaction in the cash register, announce to the customer the total amount of the sale. Say, "That will be $17.65."

▲ Announce the Amount Tendered

when the customer offers payment in cash. Say, "Out of $20."

▲ Place the Money on the Cash Drawer Ledge

and leave it there until you have given change to the customer. This eliminates most disputes over the amount tendered.

Count Silently When ▲ Removing Change

from the cash drawer. The most common method is to count up from the purchase price, taking out the smaller denominations of coins and currency first. Use as few coins as possible in making change.

▲ Count Aloud When Handing Change

to the customer. Say, "That's $17.65 out of $20—$17.75 (giving the customer a dime), $18 (giving a quarter), $19, and $20 (giving two $1 bills, one at a time)."

Chapter 18 *Math for Retail Sales* **231**

Then have students speculate about the effects of such adjustments on wages. (Fewer skills and skills of a lower level translate into less money in workers' paychecks.)

L1 Math Skills

Give students this hypothetical situation: Assume you work as a salesclerk in an art supply store. Shortly before the store opens, you are given a cash bag containing one roll each of pennies, nickels, dimes, and quarters (50 coins to a roll) plus ten $1 bills, two $5 bills, and two $10 bills. This is your opening cash fund. You should start the day with $70.50 in your register. Do you have the correct amount? Verify your fund. [Bills: (10 × $1) + (2 × $5) + (2 × $10) = $10 + $10 + $20 = $40. Coins: (50 × $.01) + (50 × $.05) + (50 × $.10) + (50 × $.25) = $.50 + $2.50 + $5 + $12.50 = $20.50. Total: $40 + $20.50 = $60.50. Fund is $10 short.]

L2 Math Skills

Continue the hypothetical in the L1 Math Skills activity: The art supply store has just closed, and you must balance the cash drawer. Basically, this procedure involves totaling all the cash, checks, and credit slips in the drawer and then subtracting the opening cash fund and any refunds given to customers. The result is the day's receipts. If this figure matches the total on the register tape, the drawer is balanced.

You have $157.84 in cash, $212 in checks, and $325.50 in credit slips. There was one refund for $22.16. The register tape puts the day's receipts at $602.68. Does your drawer balance? [Yes: ($157.84 + $212 + $325.50) − ($22.16 + $70.50) = $695.34 − $92.66 = $602.68.]

More About

Handling Cash Payments

The most common trick played by con artists on unsuspecting cashiers is the "Can I have change for a $5 bill?" trick. Once change is given, another request is made and another. By the time the requests are finished, the con artist is richer and the clerk may not even realize there's a problem until the cash drawer is reconciled at the end of the business day. Cashiers of busy registers are the favorite prey of such con artists. Experienced cashiers know to slow down and complete each request for change as if it were the first of the day.

Teach *(Cont'd.)*

L3 Math Skills

Continue the hypothetical in the L2 Math Skills activity: Suppose the register tape reads $607.45. What does that mean, and what could account for it? (The drawer is $4.77 short—possibly because a customer was given too much change, a transaction was input incorrectly, or petty cash was removed without a petty cash slip's being placed in the register.)

Suppose the register tape reads $600.18. What does that mean, and what could account for it? (The drawer is $2.50 over—possibly because a customer was shorted on change, a transaction was input incorrectly, or the opening cash fund was miscounted.)

Independent Practice

1. Assign and review the Chapter 18 Case Study in the *International Case Studies* workbook.
2. Have students generate a list of five purchase amounts and corresponding amounts tendered. For example, if the purchase amount is $14.49, the customer might tender $20.50. (*Note*: Each purchase amount and amount tendered should be under $100.) Students will use the amounts in Reteaching Activity 3 below.

Assess

Evaluation

Assign and review the Section 18.1 Review.

232

Many customers try to avoid accumulating small change by tendering an odd amount of change to pay for their purchases. For example, if a sale totals $18.39, the customer might give you $20.39. You would use the 39 cents to cancel the "odd cents" of the sale and give change for the $20 bill. The same customer might also tender $20.50. Then you would count the odd cents first, starting at $18.39, as in Figure 18-2.

Most newer cash registers calculate and display the amount of change. If you are using such a machine, you may find it easier to begin with the largest denomination. For a $17.65 purchase, for example, the register will display $2.35 due the customer. Select the change from the cash drawer by taking out two $1 bills, a quarter, and a dime. Because the customer knows from the display what change is due, you can count it out the same way.

Practice 1

How would you make or arrange for change in the following situations?

1. A customer gives you a $50 bill to pay for a $22.61 purchase. What change would you give her? *Note:* Use the smallest number of bills and coins possible.
2. A customer is buying two audio cassettes that total $15.09, including tax. The smallest bill he has is $20, and he doesn't want to get back a great deal of change. What is your response?
3. You are a cashier at Long's Drugstore, and a customer gives you $20.75 to pay for a purchase of $13.63. Count the customer's change back to him. Why did he give you the change along with the $20 bill?

Note: Answers to all practice sets in this chapter appear on page 239.

Sales Tally At the close of each business day, salespeople and cashiers who use a cash register must account for the day's sales and money. This process goes by a number of names, including balancing the cash or balancing the till.

Most cash registers automatically keep a sales *tally*, or summary of the day's sales. This makes the job of balancing the cash much simpler. The person responsible for each register counts the money and fills out a brief closing balance report. Then he or she removes the tape from the cash register and sends the money, report, and tape to a central office.

Some older cash registers do not keep an automatic sales tally. If your company uses one of these registers, sales checks may be written for each sale and the information recorded on a tally sheet after each transaction. At the end of the day, sales must be reviewed to balance the cash.

Safeguards Against Theft Every employee who uses a cash register should be familiar with some safeguards against the theft of money. The first rule is always to close the cash drawer between transactions. Even while you are counting change to a customer, you should partially close the drawer. After giving change, remove the money tendered by the customer from the register ledge. Place the bill in the drawer and close it. The second rule is to lock the register if you leave it.

You may occasionally encounter a customer who interrupts you while you are counting change. In a rare case, the person might be trying to distract you in the hope that you will make incorrect change in his or her favor. More often, the customer has a genuine concern. It is best to ignore the interruption while you are making change. You can respond politely once the transaction has been completed.

BRIGHT IDEAS

From the Hands of Babes

When Howard Wexler saw his young son put his hand in his sock and *pretend* it was a puppet, he had an idea. Why not *make* it a puppet? So, he created a line of sock puppets—socks with funny characters painted or sewn to the toes—and marketed it. A child can wear one on each hand and put on a play. Two or more children can play with them together. Any number of children can wear them as socks.

Wexler, of course, is no ordinary parent. He's an inventor with a successful track record. The toys and games he has created have racked up retail sales of over $10 million. (His other products include Connect Four, a 3-D tic-tac-toe game, and the Crunch ball, an easy-to-catch indoor ball filled with styrofoam packing pieces.)

Wexler's genius is seeing potential in the obvious. What will he think of next? No doubt, something simple that will add to his fortune.

Creativity Challenge Form teams of 3–5 people. Using the lost and found or someone's junk drawer for inspiration, try to create a toy or entertainment product of your own that has marketable potential. Search and play and speculate for at least 15–20 minutes. Do not give up without a product, even if you have to go in search of fresh inspiration.

Bright Ideas

What's the difference between Howard Wexler and an ordinary person? He not only can recognize a marketable idea but has the skills to turn it into a salable product. How can a person learn the skills needed to get a product to market? By studying marketing and working for others who are already in the process of inventing and distributing products.

From time to time, counterfeit bills show up in almost every city. Every company has, or should have, printed information on how to identify counterfeit money. Legal bills, for example, have crisp portraits on the front side and tiny colored threads in the paper. The portraits on counterfeit bills are often not as crisp looking, and the paper usually does not have threads.

Sales Checks

A *sales check* is a written record of a sales transaction. At a minimum, it includes such information as the date of the transaction, the items purchased, and the purchase price. In this form, it is valuable to a customer as an itemized receipt. In its most complete form, a sales check can contain customer information (name, address, and phone number) and details like the time of the sale and the identity of the salesperson. This is additional information that a business would find valuable.

Today most larger businesses use electronic cash registers and POS systems. That means fewer handwritten sales checks. The electronic registers provide customers with a portion of the cash register tape as a receipt. The POS systems provide computer-generated sales checks. (Sales and customer information are input by keyboard. The computer then prints out a sales check for the customer and a duplicate for the store.)

With technological advances like these, why would you concern yourself with written sales checks? Because many small businesses do not have access to electronic registers and POS systems. Their salespeople record transactions by hand, in sales check books that contain 2-3 copies of each form. They also use *sales check registers*, metal or plastic devices that contain a supply of continuous sales checks in duplicate or triplicate form. (When a slip is completed, you simply pull a handle and eject one or two copies. A second or third copy is kept inside the sales register, and a new sales check moves into place for the next transaction.) In these instances, the written sales checks provide both customer and company with the details that the cash register tape cannot.

Since small firms account for such a large percentage of U.S. businesses, you may find yourself working for a company that does not use automated cash registers. That means you will have to prepare a handwritten sales check like the one shown in Figure 18-3 for every sale. Take the time now to familiarize yourself with its basic entries.

Sales Check—Single Purchase

Mason's
LUGGAGE & FINE LEATHER GOODS
15154 Ryland Avenue • Abington, PA • 19001

Date __5-11__ 19__

Sold to _____CASH_____

Address _____

Emp. # _____11335_____

Dept	Qty	Article	Price	Amount	
511	1	WALLET	24.99	24	99
			Mdse Subtotal	24	99
			Sales Tax	1	50
			Total	26	49

Figure 18-3

As a written record, a sales check provides a business with more than just the math of a transaction. What other information does it supply?

SECTION 18.2

Objectives

After completing this section, you will be able to
- describe the various types of sales transactions and
- perform the math calculations necessary to fill out sales checks.

Terms to Know

- cash sale
- debit card
- floor limit
- layaway
- on-approval sale
- cash on delivery (COD) sale
- return
- exchange
- allowance

Types of Sales Transactions

As a salesperson or cashier, you will handle several types of sales transactions. Most will be cash or credit sales. There will be layaway (or will-call) sales, on-approval sales, and COD sales as well. You will also be dealing with returns, exchanges, and allowances.

Cash Sales

A **cash sale** is a transaction in which the customer pays for his or her purchase with cash or a check. The simplest cash sale occurs when the customer tenders cash. In this case, you simply record the transaction on the register, give the customer change and a cash register receipt, and wrap the purchase.

Each business has its own rules about accepting checks. You will have to follow the check policy of the company or store where you work. When your customer writes a check, you will probably need to verify his or her identity. Most businesses request a driver's license and one other form of identification for this purpose.

234   Unit 5   *Selling*

To prepare handwritten sales checks, you will have to do some math. If a calculator is unavailable, that will mean performing the necessary math operations by hand. Usually at least four steps will be involved, as shown in Figure 18-4.

Occasionally, you will not be given a unit price. You will have to calculate it. This occurs when items are sold in multiple quantities, such as three pairs of stockings for $12.

To find the selling price of one item in an instance like this, you will have to divide the price instead of multiply it. Thus, one pair of stockings in the example above would be $4 ($12 ÷ 3).

Note, however, that when the division is uneven, *any* fractional amount is charged to the *customer*. The price of one pair of stockings when three pairs are $10.99 is calculated as follows:

$$\$10.99 \div 3 = \$3.663 \text{ or } \$3.67$$

Practice 2

Do the sales calculations indicated below.

1. Calculate the amount for each item by multiplying the unit price times the quantity purchased.

Dept.	Quantity	Item	Price
12	10	Vests	$85.00
16	5	Footballs	$15.95
18	11	Clocks	$26.50
21	20	Irons	$39.95

2. If all of the above items were part of a single purchase, what would be the merchandise total?
3. Assuming a sales tax rate of 6 percent, find the tax and total amount due for each purchase listed below. Round the tax to the nearest cent.

Item	Price
Tires	$315
Ski Boots	$185
Clock	$105
Books	$110
Washer	$429

4. Determine the price for one can of soda when a six-pack sells for $2.17.
5. Determine the price for two rolls of film when three rolls sell for $12.25.

Debit Card Sales

Many businesses now offer customers the option of using their automatic teller machine (ATM) cards to purchase products. These cards were originally designed to enable bank customers to make deposits and withdrawals from their bank accounts at an ATM. When a customer

Figure 18-4
SALES CHECK— MULTIPLE PURCHASES

Customers often buy more than one item and more than one unit of each item. This makes for a slightly more complicated sales check.

Step 1—Multiply Unit Price Times Quantity

for each item and extend the amounts to the last column. Remember that the last two digits on the right are cents. Place a decimal point to their left, or enter them to the right of the vertical line dividing the last column into two unequal parts.

Step 2—Add Item Amounts

to arrive at a merchandise subtotal. Enter this figure on the appropriate line.

Step 3—Calculate Sales Tax

or look it up in a tax table. Sales tax must be paid by the buyer on all retail sales. It is calculated as a percentage of the merchandise subtotal. In most states, food and prescription medicines are exempt from sales tax, as are shipping charges.

Step 4—Add Subtotal and Tax

to get the purchase total. This is the amount the customer will pay.

ODEL'S CAMERA, INC.
1329 Walnut Street • Santa Barbara, CA 93101

NEW CUSTOMER ☐ YES ☐ NO DATE 6/17/--

NAME CASH
COMPANY
ADDRESS
CITY & STATE
PHONE (RESIDENCE)   PHONE (OTHER)

SOLD BY — TYPE OF SALE: CASH / CHECK ✓ / C.O.D. / CARD TYPE / ACCOUNT / PURCHASE ORDER NO.

CODE	QTY.	DESCRIPTION	PRICE	AMOUNT	
U	1	MET2 45 CT-4 Flash	325.00	325	00
X	6	Konica 220 Color Film	6.19	37	14
X	12	Kodak 120 B&W Film	2.49	29	88

SPECIAL INSTRUCTIONS

HANDLING	—	—
SUB TOTAL	392	02
TAX	31	36
SHIPPING	—	—
TOTAL AMOUNT	423	38
PAID	423	38
BALANCE	0	

SHIP VIA:
PAID ON # _____ TC # _____
CC # _____

7932

uses an ATM card to make a purchase at a store, the card becomes a **debit card.** This means that the amount of the purchase is *debited* (or subtracted) from the customer's bank account.

To use an ATM card this way, a customer slides his or her card through a special sensing device. It reads the information stored in the magnetic strip on the back of the card. After the sale is totaled on the cash register, the customer enters his or her *personal identification number (PIN)* into a keypad. This authorizes the debit. If there is money in the customer's bank account to cover the purchase, the sale is approved electronically. The customer then receives a receipt.

There are many advantages for both customers and businesses in the use of debit cards. The business has access to its money much sooner than with a check. It doesn't have to be concerned about bad checks. The money cannot be stolen from the store, as cash can. For their part, customers don't have to carry large amounts of cash or checkbooks. It is also harder for thieves to use

a debit card because they can't make a purchase without knowing the cardholder's PIN number.

Credit Sales

Most businesses today accept one or more of the major credit cards, such as Visa, MasterCard, and American Express. Many large oil companies and department stores issue their own cards in addition to accepting the major ones. The goal is to make it easier for the general public to shop. This, of course, increases sales.

In many businesses now, the amount of each credit card sale is electronically deposited to the business's bank account as the sale is made. A combination credit card sales check and receipt is issued by the cash register. With this procedure, the credit card company is able to deduct its service charge from the store's bank account immediately. The store normally has access to its funds the next day. This is much faster than if credit card sales checks had to be delivered to a bank.

Chapter 18   *Math for Retail Sales*   **235**

SECTION 18.2

4. The MarkEd Resource Center, (800) 448-0398, has materials appropriate for use with this lesson.
5. Assign and review the Chapter 18 Activity in the *School-to-Work Handbook*.

Discussion Starter

Have students discuss the various return/exchange/allowance policies at their co-op training stations. Some stores, such as Nordstrom, have a nonrestrictive return policy and will take back any merchandise at any time. Other stores state that merchandise must be returned within a certain period of time and that the exchange will be made for store credit only. Have students discuss the uses and abuses they have observed of such policies. (Answers will vary.)

Cooperative Learning

Divide students into groups of four or five. Have each group of students discuss their employers' procedures and policies for accepting and cashing (a) checks, (b) traveler's checks, (c) foreign currency (for example, Canadian dollars), (d) special store redemptions such as bonus points that count toward the purchase of merchandise, and (e) $50 and $100 bills. For example, ask:
- Who must approve checks— a senior sales associate? a department manager?
- What type of identification do the various companies require of customers—picture ID? driver's license number?
- Are third-party checks allowed? Why or why not?

Have each group report its findings to the class.

L1 Math Skills

Give students this problem: Nancy returned a birthday gift (a sweater) to Brigg's Department store because it didn't fit her. The store gave her a credit for $78.75 to apply to another purchase. Nancy decided to buy a belt for $12.55, a scarf for $29.95, three pair of socks

Did You Know ?

How do people pay for merchandise when they shop on-line? In the future they might use cash. The newest concept in electronic payment, known as Ecash, functions as the electronic equivalent of cash and can be loaded on your computer and used in increments as small as 5 cents. One company, Digicash, is currently testing its version. Others will soon follow.

Buying computer cash is like buying a phone card for a specific amount. The benefit is that only one merchant, the one that sells you the Ecash, knows your credit card or checking account number. Other on-line merchants benefit from not having to worry about fraudulent use of credit cards.

at $5.99 each, and a jacket on sale for $25. Her state's sales tax is 5 percent. Once Nancy purchased these items, was there any money left on her store credit to apply to another purchase, or did she have to add money to make her purchases? {She had to add $10.99. Purchases: [$12.55 + $29.95 + ($5.99 × 3) + $25] × 1.05 = ($12.55 + $29.95 + $17.97 + $25) × 1.05 = $85.47 × 1.05 = $89.74. Difference: $89.74 − $78.75 = $10.99.}

L2 Math Skills

Pose this problem: J&W Hardware is having a one-day sale. A customer buys three combination padlocks at $3.29 each, four pocket screw drivers at $.99 each, 12 flashlight batteries at $1.89 per four-pack, and two rolls of electrical tape at $.89 each. The state's sales tax is 8.5 percent. How much did the customer pay? {Customer paid $23.09: [($3.29 × 3) + ($.99 × 4) + ($1.89 × 3) + ($.89 × 2)] × 1.085 = ($9.87 + $3.96 + $5.67 + $1.78) × 1.085 = $21.28 × 1.085 = $23.09.}

L3 Math Skills

Pose this problem: Sharon wants to put a winter coat that costs $599 on a 90-day layaway. Her state's sales tax is 4 percent. She must put down 30 percent of the entire purchase amount and pay the balance within 90 days. How much must she put down on her coat? How much must she pay within 90 days? (Purchase price: $599 × 1.04 = $622.96. Down payment: $622.96 × .30 = $186.89. Balance: $622.96 − $186.89 = $436.07)

Getting Credit Authorizations Credit cards have become an efficient, popular alternative to more traditional forms of payment. Some people, however, abuse the privilege of using a credit card by charging more than they can pay. So, many businesses (especially retail stores) have a set limit on credit card charges. The **floor limit** is the maximum amount a salesperson may allow a customer to charge without getting special authorization. Usually, the manager or someone in the credit department must approve charges that exceed the floor limit.

To confirm that a customer has been approved to charge the amount of a sale, most businesses use *electronic credit authorizers*. Many POS systems, in fact, include an integrated credit authorizer. Other electronic credit authorizers are separate pieces of equipment. These devices, smaller than a telephone, read data encoded on credit cards. The data is transmitted to a computer, and approval or disapproval is usually received in less than a minute.

Companies that do not use electronic credit authorizers check for approval of charges in other ways. With a major credit card, for example, you may wait while a salesperson calls a central authorization telephone number for approval of charges. The salesperson may also look for your credit card number on a list of delinquent account numbers.

Recording Sales If you are employed as a salesperson for a retail business, you will probably sell merchandise to customers who want to charge their purchases on a credit card. In this case, you will have to know how to complete credit card sales checks. This is not very difficult, since the math calculations are identical to those for a cash transaction. (See Figure 18–5.)

There are many variations in credit card sales checks. However, most have a few things in common. To start, there are usually at least three copies of each sales check—one for the customer, one for the seller, and one for the bank or credit card agency. You may use a mechanical imprinter to transfer the customer's name and account number to the sales slip, or you may write the information on the sales check by hand.

In many businesses, you may not use credit card sales checks at all. Instead, you will record all of the needed information electronically. Electronic recording of credit card sales is getting more common every day and will soon be standard procedure.

Obtaining Payment If you do use credit card sales checks for charges to bank cards (VISA, MasterCard, etc.), you (or someone in your company) may deposit them much as you deposit checks in your company account. A special deposit slip must be prepared to accompany the bank copies of the bank card sales checks. That way, they can be credited to your company bank account as quickly as the checks you deposit.

Copies of sales checks for travel and entertainment cards and oil company credit cards must be sent for payment to the company that originated them. So, it takes a little longer to turn these charges into cash in the bank.

If your company accepts credit cards, it will have to pay a fee to the bank or agency that handles the billing and record keeping. This is a percent of credit sales based on a sliding scale. For example, suppose your store had VISA sales of $100,000 during the same period that another store had VISA sales of only $2,000. Then your company would pay a smaller percentage for handling. The handling fee for travel and entertainment cards is usually slightly higher than for bank cards.

Credit Card Sales Check

Figure 18–5

Calculations for credit sales are the same as those for cash transactions. What additional information, however, does a credit sales check require? Why?

Caption Answer

Customer's name and address are *not* optional. Also required are the credit card account number and the customer's signature. Two reasons: to verify customer's identity and allow customer to be billed for payment at a later date.

Did You Know

What protects electronic payment such as credit or electronic checks against theft? Encryption technology can prevent computer hackers from stealing your account number when you make an on-line purchase. Merchants and card issuers get the information they need, but the public at large is prevented from accessing your account number by means of electronic scrambling.

CASE STUDY

Reducing Credit Card Fraud

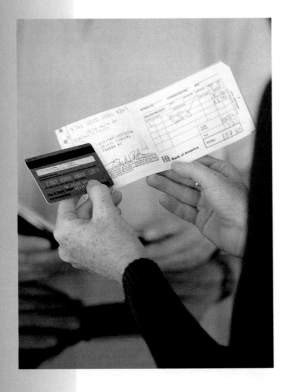

or verified that they were allowed to use the borrowed cards before okaying their purchases. Out of a total of 127 purchases made with the borrowed cards, only six were questioned! One purchaser bought a $1,200 computer printer with no questions asked. One man used a card with a woman's name on it to charge a $115 meal at a New York restaurant and then signed the charge slip "Daffy Duck." No one even raised an eyebrow!

When the magazine told credit card companies about their results, the companies were not surprised. They suggested that retailers don't want to risk losing sales by offending customers, who may not like having to prove their identity. Also, credit card companies usually pay stores for purchases as long as the card has not been reported lost or stolen. This means stores feel no financial incentive to be careful, as they do with personal checks.

In the end, everyone pays for credit card fraud. Credit card companies lose because they must absorb the huge losses. Customers lose because they must pay higher interest rates and annual fees to help repay the companies. Retailers lose because customers then have less money to spend on their merchandise. An ounce of prevention on the retailer's part could help save many millions of dollars every year. It's just good business sense.

Obtaining authorizations for credit card purchases assures that the accountholder is approved to make the purchase. It doesn't assure that the person using the card *is* the accountholder, however. Use of lost and stolen credit cards at retail outlets accounts for 50–80 percent of all credit card fraud—almost $600 million in 1993.

Retailers have a responsibility to help prevent credit card fraud. They should check the signature on the card against the one on the sales slip. They can also ask for photo identification, such as a driver's license. Mostly, however, they don't.

Money magazine recently conducted an experiment. The magazine sent 33 staff members shopping in 17 American cities. Each shopper was given someone else's credit card to use, but each signed credit card sales checks with his or her own name. The shoppers kept records of how many merchants checked the signatures

Case Study Review

1. Credit card companies could insist that retailers always check signatures and identification before approving credit sales. Why do you think they don't?
2. Customers are almost always asked to provide proof of identity when paying by check. Why do you think they would be offended if asked to provide identification for credit card sales?

A MATTER OF ETHICS

3. Assume retailers would lose sales by consistently verifying signatures and asking for identification. Is that an adequate reason *not* to do what they can to reduce credit card fraud? Why or why not?

Case Study Answers

1. Retailers do not want to risk sales by offending customers.
2. Answers will vary. One possibility: Unlike checks, credit cards carry a signature that can be verified and, in some instances, a photograph of the cardholder.
3. Answers will vary. Those opposing added precautions can argue that legally they are not

obligated beyond identifying cards reported lost or stolen. They already lose money by accepting cards for payment (card issuer's discount). Those supporting added precautions can argue in favor of an ethical obligation on the part of retailers to hold down costs for all those with whom they do business.

L1 Human Relations Skills

Give students this problem: You are in a theater management training program, and it's a busy Saturday night "walk in" before the prime-time movies start. A customer tries to use a movie ticket that was included in an entertainment coupon book he recently purchased. However, the book specifically states that such tickets are not to be used on a Saturday night. When you point this out to the customer, he says he was unaware of the restriction and protests that he wants to see the movie anyway. How would you handle this situation? (Answers will vary. Movie tickets and restaurant coupons are frequently included in such entertainment books with the restriction that they are not to be used at specific times. In this situation, you would probably allow the customer to use the ticket but explain that you cannot allow this again.)

L2 Human Relations Skills

Pose this problem: Some people refuse to show identification when asked—particularly to a young person. At your co-op training station, you ring up a sale for a man who writes a check for his purchase. When you ask to see his identification for check authorization, he refuses. How would you handle this situation? (Answers will vary, but no customer should be allowed to pay with a check without first showing identification. Thus, tell the customer that you are following standard store policy and that you must see his ID. If he still refuses, tell him you will take cash. If he says he has no cash and continues to protest, call a manager to handle the situation. Unless the manager knows the man personally, he or she will also probably refuse to take the check—the wisest course of action.)

L3 Human Relations Skills

Pose this problem: You do not work on commission in your co-op job as a retail sales associate. One of the full-time employees, who works on a base salary and commission, constantly asks you to ring your sales on her cash register key so she can get the credit for your sales and thus earn more commissions. When you balk at this, she says, "What does it matter to you? You're paid hourly. It doesn't matter how much you sell!" How would you handle this situation? (Answers will vary. However, the employee is asking you to do something dishonest—claim that she made sales she did not make. If you ring your sales on her key, she would be earning money because of your hard work. Also, even if you're not on commission, it does matter how much you sell. Your supervisor is probably monitoring your sales performance which, in turn, will be considered in your co-op review and in any future raises or promotions.)

Independent Practice

Have each student contact two local retailers to find out whether or not they have layaway plans. If the retailers contacted do not offer layaway, have students ask if they have replaced it with such plans as deferred payment or "90 days same as cash." Have students share their findings in class. Afterwards, conduct a discussion dealing with how such payment plans increase sales and what problems (if any) they present for retailers.

Practice 3

Calculate the impact credit card fees would have on the business described below.

1. At Rachel's Gifts, VISA sales are usually between $13,000 and $15,000 per month. The VISA handling charge for $10,000-$14,999 is 3 percent of sales; for $15,000-$19,999, 2.5 percent; and for $20,000-$29,999, 2 percent.
   a. If Rachel had $15,500 in VISA sales one month, how much more would she net than if sales were $14,300?
   b. How much would Rachel net in that month if her shop did $21,000 in VISA sales?
2. Rachel has decided to accept the Diner's Club card in her shop. The handling charges are 1 percent higher than for VISA at each sales level. If Rachel had $21,000 in Diner's Club sales, how much more would she pay in handling fees than she does for VISA sales?
3. Rachel had $13,600 in cash sales, $14,800 in Diner's Club sales, and $15,200 in VISA sales one month. What were her net sales after handling charges?

Layaway/Will-Call Sales

With **layaway** (also known as will-call), the merchandise is removed from stock and kept in a separate storage area until the customer pays for it. Many department stores sell clothing on layaway. Because this appeals to many shoppers, it often increases sales. Usually the customer makes a deposit on the merchandise. He or she must agree to pay for the purchase within a certain time period. The customer may have the merchandise when it is fully paid for. If it is not paid for within the agreed-upon time, the goods are returned to stock. Any money paid need not be returned to the customer.

On-Approval Sales

Some department and specialty stores extend a special privilege to their regular customers—**on-approval sale.** This is an agreement that permits a customer to take merchandise (usually clothing) home for further consideration. If the goods are not returned within an agreed-upon time, the sale is final. The customer must then send a check or pay for the merchandise at the store.

COD Sales

A **cash on delivery (COD) sale** is a transaction that occurs when a customer pays for merchandise at the time of delivery. Because the customer must be on hand when the merchandise is delivered, however, COD sales are not as efficient as other types of sales transactions.

238 Unit 5 *Selling*

Returns, Exchanges, and Allowances

A **return** is merchandise brought back for a cash refund or credit. Gifts that do not suit the recipient's taste are one of the most common categories of returns.

An **exchange** is merchandise brought back to be replaced by other merchandise. Items of clothing that are the wrong size or color are commonly exchanged.

An **allowance** is a partial return of the sale price for merchandise that the customer has kept. These are usually given when there is a defect in the merchandise, such as a missing button.

Each of these situations will require you to do a different type of sales transaction. Take a return, for example. Some businesses adopt a policy of no returns. Most, however, feel that accepting returns is an important part of good customer relations. Some businesses accept returns but don't give cash refunds. Instead, they issue credit slips that can be used to pay for other merchandise purchased from the same business.

Most businesses are happy to make exchanges because they want their customers to be satisfied. If the item returned and its replacement are priced the same, such a transaction is called an even exchange. If not, it is an uneven exchange.

For example, suppose John decides he needs a calculator for his personal use but wants a less expensive one than he was given for his birthday. Say, the original calculator was priced at $90, and John wants to exchange it for one priced at $60. You would refund the difference, $30, plus the sales tax on that amount. If a customer wants to exchange an item for one that is more expensive, then the procedure would be reversed.

Real World

MARKETING

A Unified Currency for Europe?

Even though the 12 member nations of the European Union have moved closer in many ways, they all still have their own currencies. Whenever a financial transaction takes place across any border, one currency must be changed into another. Having a single, unified currency would eliminate the time and labor expended on this process.

The British have been the most vocal opponents of a single European currency. They fear that loss of the pound sterling would jeopardize their control of internal banking matters. (It would, but that's the price of unity.) Onlookers compare the process the EU is going through now to what went on when the 13 colonies hammered out their relationship in the pages of the Federalist Papers.

Feature Note

The new currency was to have been launched in 1997. However, in mid-1995 EU finance ministers announced that there was no way this deadline could be met. The new target is 1999.

Obstacles to the new currency are many: German opposition (because of the strength of the mark), complex technical issues, and even the lack of a name. Suggestions for the latter range from *franken* to *shilling* and include the term *monnet* (after EU founding leader Jean Monnet). Whatever name is eventually selected, officials agree that it must be pronounceable throughout Europe.

Refund Slip

Nicky's Dress Shop — REFUND SLIP

STORE NO.	DATE 10/20/--	ITEM RETURNED	AMOUNT
		Dress	89 90
NAME Deborah Murchak			
ADDRESS 4322 Wenona Rd.			
CITY & STATE Everett, WA 98208			
TELEPHONE NO. 206-882-0252		TAX	5 84
CUSTOMER'S SIGNATURE Deborah Murchak		TOTAL AMOUNT	95 74
EMPLOYEE NO. 12A	AUTHORIZED BY L. Allen	REASON FOR RETURN Too small	
		CASH REGISTER RECEIPT TAPE MUST BE STAPLED TO THIS FORM	

Figure 18–6

Most businesses accept returns of one kind or another in order to maintain customer goodwill. What is Nicky's policy on returns?

When you refund cash to a customer on a return or an exchange, you will probably have to fill out a refund slip. One of these is shown in Figure 18-6.

Practice 4

How much will be returned to or paid by the customer in each of the following cases? Assume a sales tax rate of 7 percent.

1. Mrs. Smith returned a $150 dress that was too large and selected a smaller size in another style priced at $115. How much will you return to her?
2. Mr. Jordan returned a $45 radio because it was apparently defective. He selected another model priced at $75. How much more will you charge him?

SECTION 18.2 *Review*

1. **How is a credit card sale different from a debit card sale? a will-call sale? an on-approval sale?**
2. **Kim is considering the purchase of a new guitar for $950, plus $24 shipping. The state sales tax is 8 percent. Explain how he should go about figuring the total purchase amount.**

Answers to Practice Sets

Practice 1 (page 232)
1. Four pennies, a dime, a quarter, two $1 bills (or a $2 bill), a $5 bill, and a $20 bill. *Note:* If customer has the penny (for the $.61), then a nickel could substitute for the four pennies.
2. Ask if customer has $.09 in change or at least a dime.
3. "That's $13.63 out of $20.75 — $13.64, $.65 (handing off two pennies), $.75 (and a dime); $14, $15 (handing off two $1 bills), and $20 (handing off a $5 bill)." By tendering the $.75, the customer reduces the amount of small change to be returned to him.

Practice 2 (page 234)
1. Vests $850; footballs $79.75; clocks $291.50; irons $799
2. $2,020.25
3. Tires $333.90; boots $196.10; clock $111.30; books $116.60; washer $454.74
4. $.37
5. $8.17

Practice 3 (page 238)
1. a. $1,241.50
   b. $20,580
2. $210
3. $42,628

Practice 4 (page 239)
1. $37.45
2. $32.10

Assess

Evaluation

Assign and review the Section 18.2 Review.

Reteaching

1. Assign and review the vocabulary terms for this section.
2. Assign and review Fact and Idea Review questions 6–10 from the Chapter Review.
3. Review with students the major concepts in this section so they understand the various types of sales transactions.

Enrichment

1. Assign and review the appropriate activities in the *Student Activity Workbook*.
2. Assign the Unit 5 Activity in the *Marketing Math Workbook*.
3. Assign and review the appropriate Critical Thinking questions from the Chapter Review.
4. Assign and review the Building Academic Skills Activities, Application Projects, Linking School to Work Activities, and Performance Assessment from the Chapter Review.
5. Have each student create one math problem related to any of the concepts in this lesson (for example, multiplying unit price by quantity, figuring sales tax, determining the unit price on one item when merchandise is sold in multiple quantities, etc.). Have students work in pairs to solve each other's problems.

Close

Have students summarize in at least 50 words why they feel that conducting retail sales transactions accurately and efficiently is good customer service.

Caption Answer

Shop accepts returns and gives the customer cash rather than just a credit or an exchange.

Section Review Answers

1. Credit sale involves later payment; debit sale, immediate deduction from bank account. Credit sale gives customer immediate possession with later payment; will-call sale, later possession after gradual payment. Credit sale involves deciding to buy before possession; on-approval sale, deciding after possession.
2. ($950 × 1.08) + $24 = $1,026 + $24 = $1,050

Answers

Vocabulary Review

Explanations will vary. See Glossary for definitions.

Fact and Idea Review

1. Department, type of transaction, salesperson, amount of sale, amount tendered, and change due.
2. Manual key entry, electronic wand entry, and optical scanning.
3. Universal Product Code—bar code that can be read by a scanner.
4. Bills are kept in the back compartments, coins in the front. Denominations are arranged from larger to smaller, moving from left to right.
5. Accuracy and speed.
6. A driver's license and one other form of identification.
7. To use an ATM card to authorize the amount of a purchase to be debited (subtracted) from one's bank account.
8. Electronic device that reads data encoded on credit cards and transmits it for immediate approval or disapproval of a purchase.
9. In most states, food, prescription drugs, and shipping charges.
10. An exchange in which the returned item and its replacement are not priced the same.

Critical Thinking

1. There would most likely be an increase in register errors and a slowdown in transactions.
2. Speed, elimination of keying errors, reduction in training costs.
3. As a basis for relationship marketing—store could use such a list to announce sales,

Vocabulary Review

Study each pair of terms. Then in your own words, explain how they are related to each other. (*Hint:* Are they the same? Are they opposites? Is one part of the other? Are they both part of the same thing? Is one the result of the other?)

UPC—UVM code
till—opening cash fund
layaway—will-call
sales transaction—exchange
cash sale—personal check
debit card—PIN
credit sale—floor limit
return—allowance
on-approval sale—COD sale

Fact and Idea Review

1. What information does a cash register provide about a sale? (Sec. 18.1)
2. List the three methods of entering information into electronic cash registers. (Sec. 18.1)
3. What is a UPC? (Sec. 18.1)
4. What are some of the general principles according to which most cash drawers are arranged? (Sec. 18.1)
5. What two factors are most important to the customer about the way you make change? (Sec. 18.1)
6. When a customer pays for a purchase by check, what else is he or she usually asked to supply? (Sec. 18.2)
7. What does it mean to use an ATM card as a *debit* card? (Sec. 18.2)
8. What is an electronic credit authorizer? (Sec. 18.2)
9. What items are usually exempt from sales tax? (Sec. 18.2)
10. What is an uneven exchange? (Sec. 18.2)

Critical Thinking

1. What might happen if the money in a cash drawer were arranged differently each day?
2. What advantages do you think using an electronic wand would have over manually entering prices?
3. Why would a store be likely to want a list of all its customers' names and addresses?
4. How could having a POS system make taking inventory easier?
5. What do you think would be the effect on sales of a store's having a no-return policy?

6. People have suggested that as more buyers use debit cards, checks will become obsolete. Do you think this is likely? Why or why not?
7. What types of goods are you still likely to purchase COD?
8. A gas station allows customers to pay for their gas using debit or credit cards. Customers pump their own gas and use an electronic pay point near the pump to pay. They never directly interact with a station employee. What advantages and disadvantages might there be to allowing customers to complete sales without help?

Building Academic Skills

Math

1. Obtain or make a set of "play" money. Assume you work for a business whose cash register does not calculate the amount of change due customers. Count back the change aloud for the following transactions:
   a. $15 payment for a $13.22 purchase
   b. $40.50 payment for a $39.40 purchase
   c. $10.27 payment for an $8.27 purchase
2. A department store offers a 20 percent discount to senior citizens. If your grandmother purchased items at $17.99, $15.95, and $3.59, what would be her total bill?

Communication

3. Write a memo to all cashiers at Francisco's grocery explaining the reasons you are switching from manual to electronic cash registers.

Human Relations

4. You work as a cashier, and today has been exceptionally busy. You give change to a woman for a $10 bill. She claims she gave you a $20 bill. Unfortunately, you neglected to leave the bill out while making change. How would you handle this situation?
5. The children's clothing store where you work uses an old-fashioned cash register that requires entering the amount of each sale by hand. One of the salespeople often enters the amount incorrectly. This means you have to take extra time at the end of the day to reconcile the difference between the amount of money taken in and the amount of recorded sales. How would you approach this person about improving his or her accuracy?

target certain merchandise to certain customers. As a marketing research tool—store could survey customer reactions; do geographic, demographic, and psychographic studies.

4. By constantly updating inventory status with sales check data, a POS system eliminates the need for a physical count.
5. Such a policy would make customers more cautious in their purchase decisions and thus have a potentially chilling effect on sales.

6. Answers will vary, but the idea of a paperless system has appeal for many people and businesses.
7. Answers will vary but might include items that require the help of delivery people to move and the direction of the purchaser to place, such as large appliances or furniture. Another possibility is phone orders from businesses that do not take credit cards.
8. Advantages: stations reduce labor costs and crime risk, can increase their hours; customers don't

Application Projects

1. Get information at the library about grocery store conversion to optical scanners. How does the increased speed and accuracy of these systems affect a grocery store's profits?
2. Using a library and the school computer instructor as resources, research what the bars and numbers in a UPC represent.
3. Discuss the ways that a store manager might train employees to prevent loss through credit card fraud, bad checks, and counterfeit currency.
4. The next few times your family goes to the supermarket, check the accuracy of the scanned prices against the shelf prices of items you buy. List all errors and whether they were in the store's favor or yours. Share results with the class.

Linking School to Work

1. Report to the class what cash handling procedures are used in your workplace to avoid short-change artists. If someone has attempted to short change you or a fellow employee, describe what happened.
2. At work inquire about the payment methods customers prefer. Specifically, try to determine what percentage of customers use cash, debit cards, personal checks, and credit cards. Compare your findings with other class members, and discuss why you think there are differences between one kind of business and another.

Performance Assessment

Role Play

Situation. You are a cashier at Lydia's Bookstore, completing sales transactions by cash, check, credit card, and debit card. A customer asks to pay for a purchase by credit card. After tallying the merchandise on your cash register, you call for an authorization and discover the customer has gone over his credit limit. The customer has no cash or personal checks but is carrying his ATM card. He thinks he won't be able to buy the books and is upset. Suggest a way to complete the sale, and then do so.

Evaluation. You will be evaluated on how well you do the following:

- Tally merchandise, including calculating sales tax.
- Verify the customer's identity.
- Explain why the sale cannot be completed as a credit transaction.
- Describe to the customer how to use an ATM card as a debit card, and complete the sale using the card.

Oral Presentation

Give a six-minute oral presentation on one of the following topics:

- The growth in the use of electronic cash registers over the past ten years, with a description of the changes in the technology
- A history of credit card use in America, including a demonstration of how to use a credit card imprinter and an explanation of what each entry on a credit card sales check means

Complete the Chapter 18 Computer Application that appears in the Student Activity Workbook.

Portfolio

Consider the Application Projects that you have done for this unit. Select one that illustrates your mastery of the unit's content and might be of interest to potential employers. Reformat the activity as necessary, adding any explanatory text, and place it in your Portfolio. Consider using these activities:

- Chapter 13, Application Project 3
- Chapter 14, Application Project 4
- Chapter 18, Application Project 3
- Any relevant portion of the sales training manual you prepared as part of the ongoing project for this unit ■ ■

4. Ultimate answer will depend on store policy. If the customer is always right, then you would take her word about the $20 bill—unless you were very sure that you were right. If the store's policy is not so customer-oriented and you are unsure what she gave you, you should admit your mistake.
5. Answers will vary. It might be helpful to show the person the reconciliation process to establish the time being lost, then suggest some techniques that he/she could use to improve accuracy.

Application Projects

1. Decreased labor costs and better inventory control contributing to profit.
2. You might have students visit a grocery and have the manager explain the symbol system.
3. Manager might invite someone from the police department to talk to employees about the various ways con artists defraud businesses.
4. Students might do a class table, showing which store had the most errors.

Linking School to Work

Answers depend on the work situation.

Performance Assessment

Refer to the *DECA Competitive Events Handbook* for evaluation guidelines.

Computer Application

Optional activity. Refer to the *Marketing Software Binder* for template and user information.

Evaluation

Administer the reproducible test for Chapter 18, or construct your own using the Testmaker software.

Portfolio

Refer to the *Marketing Career Portfolio* for development ideas and portfolio management and assessment.

have to carry cash, can fill up more quickly. Disadvantages: stations more dependent on computer technology that could break down, may lose money on each transaction as a result of discounting; customers might miss human touch.

Building Academic Skills

Math

1. Answers will vary.

a. That's $13.23, $.24, $.25; $.50, $.75, $14; and $15.
b. That's $39.50, and a dollar makes $40.50.
c. That's $9 and $10.
2. ($17.99 + $15.95 + $3.59) × .8 = $37.53 × .8 = $30.02.

Communication

3. Memos will vary.

Promotion

Unit Objectives

After completing this unit, students will be able to achieve the following outcomes:

- Explain the role of promotion in marketing.
- Explain the purpose and types of advertising media.
- Prepare print advertising.
- Explain how to design, prepare, maintain, and dismantle displays.
- Tell what public relations specialists do.

Chapter 21

Chapter 19

Chapter 20

Chapter 22

Chapter 23

Teacher Classroom Resources

CHAPTER	19	20	21	22	23
Transparency Binder	Transparency 28	Transparenies 29-30		Transparencies 31a & 31b–32	
Student Activity Workbook	pp. 111–118	pp. 119–126	pp. 127–132	pp. 133–140	pp. 141–146
Student Software	pp. 117–118	pp. 125–126	pp. 132–133	pp. 141–142	pp. 147–148
Marketing Math Workbook					Activity 6
School-to-Work Handbook	pp. 43–44	pp. 45–46	pp. 47–48	pp. 49–50	pp. 51–52
International Case Studies	pp. 43–44	pp. 45–46	pp. 47–48	pp. 49–50	pp. 51–52
Marketing Career Portfolio					Unit 6 activity, Student Text, p. 305
Test Booklet/ Testmaker Software	Chapter 19 test	Chapter 20 test	Chapter 21 test	Chapter 22 test	Chapter 23 test Unit 6 test, Midterm

KEY TO BASIC SKILLS' ACTIVITIES

L1 Level 1 activities are basic activities and should be within the range of all students.

L2 Level 2 activities are average activities and should be within the range of average and above average students.

L3 Level 3 activities are challenging activities designed for the ability range of above average students.

Unit 6 Organizer

CHAPTER	PERFORMANCE OBJECTIVES	
19 **What Is Promotion?**	19.1	1. Explain the role of promotion in marketing. 2. Describe the characteristics of advertising and publicity.
	19.2	1. Explain the characteristics of sales promotion and personal selling. 2. Describe the concept of promotional mix.
20 **Advertising Media**	20.1	1. Define advertising and explain its purposes. 2. Identify the various types of media. 3. Explain the advantages and disadvantages of various types of media.
	20.2	1. Describe how various media rates are set. 2. Calculate print media costs. 3. Suggest some standards for selecting promotional media.
21 **Preparing Print Advertisements**	21.1	1. Describe how ads are developed. 2. Create advertising headlines. 3. Prepare advertising copy. 4. Select advertising illustrations. 5. Explain the significance of a signature.
	21.2	1. Explain the importance of advertising layouts. 2. Tell the advantages and disadvantages of using color in advertising. 3. Describe how typefaces and type sizes can be changed to add variety and emphasis to print advertisements. 4. Explain how to check advertising proofs.
22 **Visual Merchandising and Display**	22.1	1. Define visual merchandising and distinguish it from display. 2. Explain how exterior and interior features contribute to a store's image. 3. List the various kinds of displays.
	22.2	1. Describe the steps used in designing and preparing displays. 2. Describe the various artistic considerations involved in display preparation. 3. Summarize the proper procedures for maintaining and dismantling displays.
23 **Publicity and Public Relations**	23.1	1. Describe the nature and scope of publicity and public relations. 2. State the benefits of public relations activities. 3. Recognize the audiences for public relations.
	23.2	1. Explain the primary task of public relations specialists. 2. Explain the various duties performed by public relations specialists. 3. Describe the elements of a news release.

Shaq's Summer Cooler

241c

Unit Overview and Background Information

Businesses collectively spend a phenomenal amount of money annually on promotion and advertising. Thus, this is a key unit in *Marketing Essentials* that will help students see how important promotion and advertising are in selling goods and services.

Chapter 19 tells how all promotion must be coordinated through the appropriate promotional mix. Chapter 20 gives an overview of the types of advertising media, and teaches students how to calculate media costs. Chapter 21 details the parts of a print advertisement and discusses ad layouts. Chapter 22 tells how to design and prepare displays. Chapter 23 discusses the target audience for PR activities, and teaches students how to write a news release.

Introducing the Unit

Present students with an array of ads, press kits, news releases, and pictures of displays. Have them make a chalkboard list of the skills it takes to create these promotional pieces. Then ask students to look at the chalkboard list and identify some of their own personal abilities and aptitudes listed on the chalkboard.

Unit Project

Have each student interview three people involved in different aspects of promotion—for example, an advertising copywriter, an artist, and a marketing manager—and write a report comparing and contrasting the duties, career paths, and job satisfaction levels of each. The report should conclude with a summarization telling whether the student would or would not consider these professions as potential careers.

Unit

6

242

Focus on the Photo/Cooperative Learning

Once students have completed this unit, divide the class into four groups and assign each one of these four functions: advertising media, preparing print advertisements, visual and merchandising display, and publicity and public relations. Have each group work on a promotional strategy that could be used by a company, such as Corvette, at a sports event.

Promotion

CHAPTERS

19
What Is Promotion?

20
Advertising Media

21
Preparing Print Advertisements

22
Visual Merchandising and Display

23
Publicity and Public Relations

Resources for Enrichment of Unit Content

Books

- *Advertising Services* (CCM Series), Glencoe
- *The Career Directory Series*
- *Dictionary of Occupational Titles*
- *Encyclopedia of Careers and Vocational Guidance*
- *The Gregg Reference Manual*, McGraw-Hill
- *Occupational Outlook Handbook*
- *Reader's Guide to Periodical Literature*

Magazines/Journals

- *Advertising Age*
- *Broadcasting*
- *Business Week*
- *Channels*
- *Communication Arts*
- *Direct Marketing Magazine*
- *Inc.*
- *Journal of Marketing*
- *Marketing News*
- *Media Week*
- *Public Relations Journal*
- *Public Relations News*
- *Public Relations Quarterly*
- *Stores*

Unit Closure

Have students choose jobs in promotion that interests them, and shadow a professional working in that field for at least four hours during the person's typical work day. (Students can do this at their co-op training stations, or at a business of their choice.) Arrange a private conference with each student after this experience to discuss it and to determine whether the student wants to explore this area further. Give each student appropriate guidance and resources for further career exploration.

Evaluation

Administer the printed test for Unit 6, or construct your own using the Testmaker Software.

Guest Speaker Suggestions

- Have a graphic designer and a copy writer from an ad agency or local print publication talk about how they develop and create ads.
- Invite a local display designer or display director to talk about the image his or her store creates with its visual merchandising and displays.

Field Trip Suggestions

- Have students visit a local trade show to see how new products are introduced, how existing products are promoted, and how each company encourages continued customer support and loyalty.
- Have students visit an advertising agency, focusing their field trip particularly on the creative services department.

WHAT IS PROMOTION?

Pages 244–255

Chapter Overview

This chapter explores the role of promotion in marketing.

Springboard

Bring to class rival brands of two similar items. Place the items where students can see them. Tell students to imagine that they want to buy the item shown. However, there is no sales promotion or advertising available to help them make their buying decision. There are no ads, no salespeople, or displays to help sell the product. Students must make their buying decision based strictly on the items they see in front of them. Have them jot down some factors that would influence their buying decision.

Prereading

List the section objectives to discuss with students. Have students skim the chapter, looking at the pictures, reading the captions, and noting the heads. Ask questions to ensure that the students have a minimal understanding of the chapter structure.

Preteaching the Vocabulary

List and review the vocabulary terms with the students. Acknowledge students' correct answers by writing a brief definition next to the terms they know. Place an asterisk by terms they do not know and return to the vocabulary list later when you come across these unfamiliar terms in each section of the chapter.

What Is Promotion?

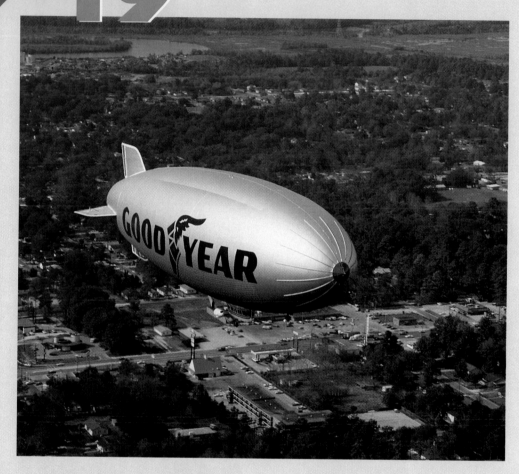

How do you find out about new movies, the latest clothing trends, new car models, or the good things an organization does for the community? Perhaps you read an advertisement in the newspaper. Maybe you received a flyer in the mail or a salesperson gave you information. These are all forms of promotion that businesses use to communicate.

In this chapter you will learn about the role of promotion in marketing. You will be introduced to the various forms of promotion that businesses use, and you will explore the concept and importance of promotional mix.

244   Unit 6   *Promotion*

Classroom Management

For the Teacher
- Teacher's Annotated Editions for all workbooks
- Teacher's Manual for *School-to-Work Handbook*
- *Testing Binder*
- *Transparency Binder*
- *Marketing Software Binder*
- *Marketing Career Portfolio*
- *Lesson Plans*

For the Student
- *Student Activity Workbook*
- *Marketing Math Workbook*
- *School-to-Work Handbook*
- *Student Software*
- *International Case Studies*
- *Marketing Career Portfolio*

SECTION 19.1

Objectives

After completing this section, you will be able to

- **explain the role of promotion in marketing and**
- **describe the characteristics of advertising and publicity.**

Terms to Know

- **promotion**
- **product promotion**
- **institutional promotion**
- **advertising**
- **publicity**

The Role of Promotion

Promotion is any form of communication a business or organization uses to inform, persuade, or remind people about its products and improve its public image. A business uses **product promotion** to convince potential customers to buy products from it instead of from a competitor. In doing this, the business also

- explains the major features and benefits of its products (especially in relation to the products of competitors),
- tells where those products are sold,
- advertises sales on those products,
- answers customer questions, and
- introduces new products.

A business uses **institutional promotion** to create a favorable image for itself (especially in relation to competitors). Institutional promotion does not directly sell a certain product. However, by creating a favorable image, institutional promotion may ultimately result in increased sales of a company's products.

Promotion is an important part of our economy. Each year, billions of dollars are spent on promotional activities and millions of people perform promotion related work.

There are four basic types of promotion: *advertising, publicity, sales promotion,* and *personal selling.* Each plays a vital role in promoting businesses and their products.

Advertising

Advertising is any paid form of nonpersonal presentation and promotion of ideas, goods, or services by an identified sponsor. Advertising is distinguished from other forms of promotion by three features:

1. The time or space devoted to it is paid for.
2. It uses a set format to carry the message rather than personal, one-on-one selling.
3. It identifies the sponsor of the message.

Nationally, businesses spent more than $126 billion on various types of advertising in 1992. Businesses spend so much on advertising because it offers these six advantages:

1. A large number of people usually see the advertiser's message.
2. Advertising costs per potential customer (whether that customer is a viewer, reader, or listener) are usually lower than other forms of promotion.
3. Businesses can choose the most appropriate media to reach their target market, since there are many different ways to advertise (billboards, newspapers, radio, and television, to name a few).
4. A business can control the content of an advertisement and adapt it to the medium and method of presentation.
5. Advertisements are subject to repeat viewing. This helps to keep the advertiser's message in people's minds.
6. Advertisements can "presell" products—that is, they can influence people to make up their minds about a purchase before they shop.

As overwhelming as its advantages might seem, advertising has four principal drawbacks:

1. Advertising cannot focus well on individual needs because the message is the same for all customers.
2. Some forms of advertising, such as television, can be too expensive for many businesses.
3. In certain respects, advertising is wasteful and inefficient. Many of the people that read magazine ads or view television, for example, are not potential customers for the advertised product.
4. Because of the cost involved and the need to attract and hold the attention of potential customers, advertisements often must be brief. Sometimes a page of advertising copy or a few words on a billboard, for example, are too brief to inform in depth. Other forms of promotion—personal sales presentations, for example—can be far more complete.

Chapter 19 *What Is Promotion?* **245**

A more detailed explanation of advertising, its purposes, and the various forms of advertising is given in Chapter 20.

Publicity

Publicity involves placing newsworthy information about a company, product, or person in the media. A business can use publicity to promote particular events, such as the groundbreaking ceremonies for a new store. A business can also use publicity to promote particular products, such as a new line of computers. The principal function of publicity, however, is building an image. Image is the way a business or organization is defined in people's minds. It is an impression based on a combination of factors—physical surroundings, personal experiences, and things written or said in the media.

The right kind of publicity can create a positive image for a company and maintain or improve that image within the community. Examples of business activities that are pure image builders include sponsoring cultural events such as concerts and art exhibits, awarding scholarships and prizes, and donating land or equipment for public use.

How does publicity differ from advertising? Publicity is free—at least in terms of its placement; advertising is not. A one-minute story about a company or one of its products on the evening news costs nothing. Fifteen seconds of advertising time on the same broadcast would cost a great deal.

Publicity has other advantages as well. The audience for news is huge, and the sources that produce it are

Publicity Soviet Style

When the Soviet Union collapsed, so did its system of subsidizing government-owned newspapers. On their own for the first time, many such publications were forced to look for new revenue sources. What did dailies like *Moskovskaya Pravda* do? Did they raise their prices or their advertising rates? Of course, but they also turned to something that would be a contradiction in terms to Western marketers. They offered businesses paid publicity. Newspapers sent staff writers to do feature stories on companies and then billed them $1,000. Clearly, the former Soviets are going to need some time to work out the finer points of marketing. In the meantime, forget the press releases. Just send money!

Real World

MARKETING

Call Direct to Collect

Entrepreneur Yuri Radzievsky had a hunch that marketers would want to know where all the Russian, Polish, and Israeli immigrants coming to the United States were living. So, he compiled a database. Using subscription lists from foreign-language newspapers and ticket purchases for performances by Russian, Polish, and Israeli entertainers, his company came up with a list of more than 150,000 names sorted by language. AT&T bought the list and used it to create both Hebrew- and Russian-language direct-mail campaigns. According to Sandra K. Shellenberger of AT&T, response rates for the database-directed offers ran as high as 20 to 30 percent. That represented a gold mine for marketers whose previous efforts were usually measured in single digits.

held in high esteem by the public. (Newspapers, news programs, and news reporters are usually viewed as more objective than advertisers.) This means that people are more likely to pay attention to news stories than to advertisements. They are also more likely to believe news stories.

It would be inaccurate, however, to say that businesses using publicity get something for nothing. Sometimes they get just what they pay for because they give up much of their control over their message. Not only the content but when and how the message is presented is determined by the media.

There is at least one other key risk associated with the use of publicity. Not all publicity is positive. Negative stories, such as an accident or an unsafe product, can hurt a company's image. You will learn more about publicity in Chapter 23.

SECTION 19.1

Review

1. What is promotion?
2. Why do companies spend billions each year on advertising?
3. What is publicity? How does publicity differ from advertising?

CASE STUDY

Winning with Event Sponsorships

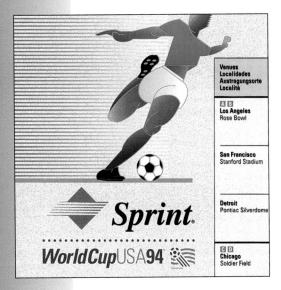

Experts predict that businesses which sponsor sporting and community events have a great future in the United States. Consumers love events, and businesses love consumers. More than $2.4 billion is spent annually by corporations to sponsor events.

During the 1994 World Cup soccer, major corporations, such as MasterCard, General Motors, Coca-Cola, and McDonald's, paid more than $20 million for international "official sponsorship." Other corporations, such as American Airlines, Sheraton, and Sprint, paid $7 million to become "marketing partners" of World Cup soccer. The World Cup was the largest international sporting event in recent history and was watched by about 30 billion viewers worldwide.

The summer and winter Olympic games, which occur on an alternating basis every two years, also provide great international sponsorship opportunities for U.S. corporations. Sponsoring the summer or winter Olympic games is important for major companies because statistics show that

- 64 percent of all American families watch the Olympic games,
- 94 percent of all Olympic viewers believe that the sponsors are successful companies, and
- more than 80 percent feel that the sponsors are dedicated to excellence and are energetic industry leaders.

Many companies annually sponsor national or regional sporting events, such as NFL and college football games, auto racing, rodeos, and golf tournaments. Companies are also looking at nonsporting sponsorships that are interesting, enjoyable, and family-oriented. Increasing diversity in the United States will mean that a greater number of businesses will be sponsoring cultural events, such as ethnic and community festivals.

Marketing experts are also predicting that companies will become more involved with "cause marketing." Environmental issues, such as the depletion of the ozone layer and the rain forests, improvement of air quality, clean oceans and lakes, and help for endangered species will be event marketing winners in the future. Companies which sponsor events that affect peoples' lives will be providing valuable public service and gaining a positive image among potential customers.

Case Study Review

1. Why do companies choose to sponsor sporting and community events?
2. Why was the World Cup so popular for corporate sponsorships in the United States?
3. What corporate image is projected to viewers by being a corporate sponsor?

A MATTER OF ETHICS

4. Why is it important for businesses to project an ethical image at an event such as World Cup?

Chapter 19   *What Is Promotion?*   **247**

SECTION 19.2

Objectives

After completing this section, you will be able to

- **explain the characteristics of sales promotion and personal selling and**
- **describe the concept of promotional mix.**

Terms to Know

- sales promotion
- slotting allowance
- sales incentives
- licensing
- promotional tie-ins
- premiums
- incentives
- promotional mix

Sales Promotion

According to the American Marketing Association, **sales promotion** represents all marketing activities, other than personal selling, advertising, and publicity, that are used to stimulate consumer purchasing and sales effectiveness. The objectives of sales promotion are to increase sales, to inform customers about new products, and to create a positive store or corporate image.

Sales promotion has the following three unique characteristics:

1. It usually involves short term activities (as opposed to advertising and publicity which tend to be longer in length).
2. It usually offers some type of incentive to make a purchase.
3. It can be successfully used in all channels of distribution with manufacturers, wholesalers, retailers, and consumers.

Sales promotions may be either consumer oriented or trade (business-to-business) oriented. Let's take a closer look at each of these types of promotions.

Trade Promotions

Trade promotions are sales promotion activities designed to gain manufacturers', wholesalers', and retailers' support for a product. More money is actually spent on promoting to businesses than to consumers. (See Figure 19-1.) Major trade promotions include slotting allowances, buying allowances, trade shows and conventions, and sales incentives.

Slotting Allowances   A **slotting allowance** is a cash premium paid by the manufacturer to a retail chain for the costs involved in placing a new product on its shelves. Slotting allowances can range from a few thousand dollars to more than $100,000 per product. In addition to buying space in the store, slotting allowances also pay for a retailer's cents-off specials on a product, charges for store shelves, penalties if a company's product doesn't sell, and store advertising and display costs.

Buying Allowances   A buying allowance is a special price discount given by manufacturers to wholesalers and retailers to encourage them to either buy a product or buy a larger quantity of a product. Because of the price discount wholesalers and retailers make more money on each product they sell. Thus, they are more likely to promote the product to customers.

Trade Shows and Conventions   Trade shows and conventions are designed to reach wholesalers and retailers. They provide businesses with opportunities to introduce new products, encourage increased sales of existing products, and gain continued company and product support.

Sales Incentives   Sales incentives are awards given to managers and employees who successfully meet or exceed their company's set sales quota for a particular product or line of products. Awards may include cash and prizes. For example, a John Deere Farm Implement dealer might receive an all expense paid trip for selling a certain number of tractors in a given sales year.

Consumer Sales Promotions

Sales promotion efforts designed to encourage customers to buy a product are called *consumer promotions*. Major consumer sales promotion devices include licensing, promotional tie-ins, visual merchandising and displays, premiums and incentives, and product samples. These forms of sales promotion help to encourage sales.

Licensing   An increasingly popular form of consumer promotion is **licensing.** In 1994 licensing was a $67 billion industry, generating $1 billion a year in retail sales with more than 225 licenses granted. Organizations, such as manufacturers, movie makers, sports teams, and celebrities, may license for a fee their logo, trademark, trade characters, names and likenesses, or personal endorsements to a business to be used in promoting the business's products. For example, the NFL, NBA, and NHL

Trade Promotion's Triumph
Estimated share of expenditures by packaged-goods manufacturers

	$29*	$32	$37	$42	$46	$52	$56	$61	$65	$69	$72
Trade promotion	34%	36%	37%	37%	38%	40%	41%	43%	46%	47%	50%
Advertising expenditures	43%	39%	37%	36%	35%	34%	34%	33%	29%	28%	25%
Consumer promotion	23%	25%	26%	27%	27%	26%	25%	24%	25%	25%	25%
	1981	1982	1983	1984	1985	1986	1987	1988	1989	1990	1991

*in billions

Source: Donnelley Marketing, Nielsen Marketing Research

Figure 19–1

During the 1980s businesses increased their spending on trade promotions. What effect does this increased spending on advertising and consumer promotions?

frequently grant licenses to apparel and equipment manufacturers allowing them to use particular logos and individual sport figure endorsements to promote their products. Warner Brothers' movie studio licenses *Looney Tunes* cartoon characters to be used to promote Nabisco, McDonald's, and Welch's products.

Promotional Tie-ins Promotional tie-ins involve sales promotional arrangements between one or more retailers or manufacturers. They combine their resources (advertising and sales promotional activities) to do a promotion that creates additional sales for each partner. Promotional tie-ins can be complex and involve several companies. An example is the Little Caesars Lucky Sevens sweepstakes game with prizes and savings provided by USAir, Sheraton Universal Hotel, Twin Towers Hotel, Hertz, and Toys "Я" Us. Successful tie-ins can also be done on a national, regional, or local basis with only a single partner. Tie-ins are designed to stimulate customer response to a product offered and combine the resources of each partner in the arrangement.

Visual Merchandising and Displays *Visual merchandising* refers to the coordination of all physical elements in a place of business so that it projects the right image to its customers. *Displays* refer to the visual and artistic aspects of presenting a product to a

target group of customers. Window, floor, counter, and other in-store display techniques are all forms of visual merchandising.

By exposing potential customers firsthand to a company's products, visual merchandising and display stimulate sales and serve as in-store advertising. A complete discussion of visual merchandising and display can be found in Chapter 22.

Premiums and Incentives The most popular and frequently used sales promotion devices are premiums and incentives. They are both designed to increase sales by building product loyalty and attracting new customers. **Premiums** have generally come to mean low-cost items given away free to consumers as a condition of purchase. There are four types of popular consumer premiums:

1. *Coupons* are certificates given to customers, entitling them to cash discounts on goods or services. Manufacturers use coupons to introduce new products, to enhance the sales of existing products, and to encourage retailers to stock and display both. Retailers and service businesses use coupons to introduce a grand opening, to invite new customers to visit or call, and to encourage repeat business by current customers. Coupons reach potential

Chapter 19 *What Is Promotion?* **249**

Why is it important to get people to come to the open house? (It is important for people to actually see the activities instead of just hearing about them. Their attendance will help build their loyalty and goodwill toward the program. This, in turn, will attract more students and will garner more support from the business community.)

Now have students consider promotional activities in relation to consumer merchandise. How have they (1) been induced to buy merchandise, (2) been informed about new products, or (3) changed or upgraded their image of a store or corporation? What were the promotional tools used to accomplish all three? What are the similarities between selling a program or an idea, and selling merchandise?

Tell students that this section looks at trade and consumer promotional activities that are designed to increase sales, to inform customers about new products, and to create a positive store image or corporate image. They will also look at personal selling and how promotional goals are achieved with the proper promotional mix.

Teach

Guided Practice

1. Read Section 19.2 with students.
2. MarkEd Resource Center (800) 448-0398 offers LAP Modules, videos, and text-workbooks that are ideal for use with this section.

Did You Know

At a Grocery Manufacturer's of America seminar in 1994, the fact emerged that although there are 1,100 coupons created for each individual in the United States each year, only 2.3 percent of them are ever redeemed. Meanwhile, printing costs, along with associated distribution and redemption costs continue to rise. Technological innovations may redefine the industry.

3. If possible, schedule a field trip to a local trade show so that students have a better understanding of the purpose of trade shows. (Those students who go to state and national DECA competition will have the opportunity to visit the trade show at the convention in which textbooks and other educational materials, DECA merchandise, and school store merchandise will be displayed.)

4. Invite a promotional events coordinator from a local shopping mall to discuss how the mall uses promotion to attract shoppers.

5. Assign and review the appropriate activities in the *Student Activity Workbook*.

6. Use the transparencies for this section.

Discussion Starter

Why does a business use a promotional mix instead of relying on one form of promotion only? (Different types of promotion appeal to and reach different members of a target audience. By using several types of promotion, a business can thus appeal to and reach a wider audience.)

Choose a product that is currently being promoted with several types of promotion. Ask students what each type of promotion contributes to selling efforts.

MFR COUPON · EXPIRES 6/4/95 · 00194

Save 40¢

when you buy
14 OZ. OR LARGER
Honey Nut Cheerios ®

RETAILER: General Mills will reimburse you for the face value of this coupon plus 8¢ if submitted in compliance with our redemption policy. Copies available upon request. Void if copied, prohibited or regulated. Cash value 1/100 cent. Send to GMI COUPON REDEMPTION. Box 900. MPLS., MN 55460 or an authorized clearinghouse. **ONE COUPON PER PURCHASE** — Good only in USA, APO's & FPO's.

A75984E   0495

Good Cereal Good Value

5 16000 71240 4   (8100)0 00194

Coupons are a popular type of premium. Why do manufacturers and retailers use coupons?

customers through a variety of routes. They are placed on or inside product packages, sent through the mail, and printed in newspapers and magazines. Sometimes they are placed by themselves into newspapers as free standing inserts. Coupons are probably the most popular type of premium.

2. *Factory packs,* or *in-packs,* are free gifts placed in product packages. This form of premium is especially popular with cereal manufacturers, who use it to increase their products' appeal to children.

3. *Traffic builders* are low-cost premiums, such as pens, key chains, and calendars, which are given away free to consumers for visiting a new store or for attending a special event.

4. *Coupon plans* are ongoing programs offering a variety of premiums in exchange for labels, coupons, or other tokens from one or more purchases. For example, a customer might send a manufacturer three soup can labels from a specific type of soup in exchange for a recipe book. Premiums available are often shown in special catalogs. A variation of this program is called the part-cash redemption whereby a customer returns fewer proof-of-purchase seals from a product plus a cash amount in exchange for a gift or rebate.

Of course, there are costs involved in using premiums. These costs are ultimately paid by the businesses offering them. With coupons, for example, the stores accepting manufacturers' coupons send them to their company headquarters or to a clearinghouse to be sorted and passed along to redemption centers. The centers, in turn, reimburse the stores for the face value of each coupon plus a handling charge of about 8 cents per coupon. They then bill the manufacturers.

Although often used in the same way as premiums, **incentives** generally refer to higher-priced products earned and given through contests or as sweepstakes awards. (See Figure 19–2.)

Product Samples   Another form of consumer sales promotion is the product sample. A *product sample* is a free trial size of a product that is sent through the mail, distributed door-to-door, or through retail stores and trade shows. Detergents, toothpastes, shampoos, deodorants, and colognes are frequently promoted this way.

Samples are especially important in promoting new products. Drug manufacturers frequently give samples to doctors and dentists to try with their patients. Teachers sometimes receive sample textbooks to encourage them to buy classroom sets.

Consumer sales promotions, such as premiums, incentives, and product samples, have several advantages in common. Each promotional device is unique and has special appeal to a potential customer. Each gives the

Real World

MARKETING

The First Coupon
Ever wonder how coupons got started? C.W. Post introduced the first one in 1895. The one-cent token was released to convince people in Battle Creek, Michigan to buy Grape-Nuts cereal.

Caption Answer

Manufacturers use coupons to introduce new products, to enhance the sales of existing products, and to encourage retailers to stock and display both.

Figure 19-2
INCENTIVES

Incentives include contests, sweepstakes, and rebates. Businesses use these activities to promote many products because they create customer excitement and interest and thus increase sales.

Announcing the 1st Annual Konica

IMAGE OF **PERFECTION**

COMPETITION
FOR PROFESSIONAL PHOTOGRAPHERS

- 1 GRAND PRIZE $5,000

- 4 CATEGORY WINNERS $1,000 EACH
  WEDDING, PORTRAIT, ACTION, ILLUSTRATIVE

- HONORABLE MENTIONS IN EACH CATEGORY

- TOURING EXHIBITION FOR FINALISTS & SEMI-FINALISTS

- AWARDS CEREMONY

Konica

◀ Contests

are games or activities that require the participant to demonstrate a skill. This can include writing a short story or essay about a product, naming a new product, or creating a new advertising slogan. Contest winners are awarded such prizes as scholarships, all-expense paid trips, and money.

Sweepstakes ▲

are games of chance. They require no skill. For example, customers at fast-food restaurants may be given a game card with or without a purchase. They must then scrape away a section of the card to win a free product or collect a number of cards to qualify for a prize. By law in most states, customers cannot be required to make a purchase in order to enter a contest or sweepstakes.

OFFICIAL MAIL-IN REBATE CERTIFICATE
$3.00 Refund Savings

To receive your $3.00 refund on *Merriam-Webster's Collegiate® Dictionary, Tenth Edition:* send this certificate along with the price sticker appearing on the shrink-wrap of your purchased dictionary and your original cash register receipt(s) showing a purchase date between August 15, 1994 and October 1, 1994 with the price of each *Merriam-Webster's Collegiate® Dictionary, Tenth Edition* circled to:

10th Collegiate Rebate Offer
P.O. Box 2633
Springfield, MA 01102-0560

NAME_____
ADDRESS_____
CITY_____ STATE_____ ZIP_____

Allow six weeks for delivery. Offer available in U.S. only. Offer void where prohibited, taxed or otherwise restricted by law. No reproductions allowed. Refund will not be honored without proof of purchase. Limit: 3 per customer. Certificates must be received by November 1, 1994.

Not just Webster. Merriam-Webster.™

Rebates ▲

are discounts offered by manufacturers to customers who purchase an item during a given time period. Auto and household appliance manufacturers frequently make use of rebates to encourage customers to buy their products.

L1 Math Skills

You receive a coupon in the mail for 50 cents off of a box of laundry detergent that normally costs $5.95. What percentage discount are you receiving if you use the coupon? (8 percent. .50 ÷ 5.95 = 0.084)

L2 Math Skills

Your store offers to double the amount of any coupon you bring in. What percentage would you save if your store doubled the amount of the coupon you used to buy the laundry soap in the L1 Activity? (Approximately 17 percent. .084 × 2 = 0.168)

L3 Math Skills

You buy the brand of laundry soap in the L1 and L2 Activities once every two months. If you use a 50-cent coupon each time you buy this particular laundry soap, what percentage will you save over six months if your store always doubles the amount of the coupon? Assume that the soap remains priced at $5.95 for the six-month period. (Approximately 17 percent. 5.95 × 3 = $17.85. 3 ÷ 17.85 = 0.168)

Independent Practice

1. Assign and review the Chapter 19 Case Study in the *International Case Studies* workbook.

More About

Promotion

Not only big businesses benefit from the promotional mix. *Pet Product News* ran an article suggesting that owners of small individually owned pet supply stores could improve sales by passing out promotional materials, transforming part of their floorspace into a collection center for charitable purposes, inviting local celebrities to participate in events, and improving employee sales and morale through education and incentive programs. The same techniques work no matter the size of the business, only the scale of the promotional activities changes.

2. Using such publications as *Advertising Age, Supermarket News, Mass Market Retailers, Stores, Chain Store Age, Business Week,* and *Inc.,* have students research the latest trends in sales promotion. They may need to limit this to one area only, such as trends in promoting food products. Have them develop an outline of their findings and then write a 250-word report based on their outlines.

3. Have students choose one local company and, based on their observations of that company's promotions, list five characteristics of its image. Then have them write a 50-word summary of the company's image.

Assess

Evaluation

Assign and review the Section 19.2 Review.

Reteaching

1. Assign and review the vocabulary terms for this section.
2. Assign and review Fact and Idea Review questions 6 – 10 from the Chapter Review.
3. Have students write one summarizing sentence about the content of each A and B Head section in this lesson.

Enrichment

1. Assign and review the appropriate activities in the *Student Activity Workbook.*

---

customer something of value and thereby helps maintain product loyalty. As a result, buying often increases. In certain cases, as with a contest or sweepstakes, the customer has fun in the process.

There are some disadvantages to sales promotions, however. They are often difficult to end without the customers becoming dissatisfied (or at least disappointed that the promotion is finished). If the promotion is not properly planned and managed, store image and sales can suffer. Finally, sales promotions are only designed to supplement other promotional efforts and cannot make up for poor products.

Personal Selling

Advertising, publicity, and sales promotion are forms of *nonpersonal selling*—communicating with customers in ways other than through direct contact. The remaining way for a business to communicate with its customers is through *personal selling*—making an oral sales presentation to one or more potential buyers. It is the principal responsibility of sales personnel.

There are two types of sales personnel—*order-taking* and *order-getting. Order-taking personnel,* such as cashiers, counter clerks, and sales associates, perform routine tasks. At the retail level, they set up displays, stock shelves, answer customer inquiries, and operate cash registers. Industrial order takers usually work with customers over the telephone.

Order-getting personnel, such as professional salespeople, are more involved in informing customers and helping them to buy. Generally, order-getting sales personnel sell big-ticket consumer items, such as real estate, automobiles, home appliances, and industrial goods and services. They usually receive more intensive training than their order-taking counterparts.

Personal selling, whether order-taking or order-getting, is designed to complete a sale once a customer is attracted to a business by advertising, publicity, or sales promotion. If the sales presentation is done well, personal selling improves customer satisfaction. This is because the salesperson can use information gained from the personal contact to address the customer's unique concerns and problems.

Personal selling, then, is the most flexible and individualized of the promotion devices available to business. However, it has some obvious disadvantages. First, a salesperson can help only one person at a time. This may mean a larger sales staff is needed. Second, businesses that rely on personal selling must make sure their employees completely understand the selling process to ensure continued sales and goodwill. This may mean additional training. As a result, the cost of personal selling is likely to be higher than, for example, the cost of self-service selling (selling in which no salesperson assists you).

BRIGHT IDEAS

Empty Pockets

What if you were a small skiwear manufacturer based in London and you had a great product (flashy neon ski clothing) but no money to spend on promotional activities? What if you could convince the world's top ski magazine photographers to use your clothes in photo shoots around the world? What if all of a sudden your clothes turned up in ads for skis, ski boots, ski resorts, and even in feature stories on skiing technique? What if your sales went through the roof to $60 million and you suddenly had market share in the United Kingdom, New Zealand, Australia, Europe, and even in the United States?

Then you would be Nevica, Ltd., a company whose future was transformed by sending product samples to just 30 influential photographers. Such results prove that money isn't everything. Imagination and invention are good substitutes for a lack of promotion dollars.

Creativity Challenge Form groups of 3–5 people, and see where you end up when you start with nothing. Select a product, either an unsuccessful one or one that doesn't yet exist. Then brainstorm the cheapest possible ways to get that product before the public. Discuss types of promotion you might use. Create visuals of the types of promotion you would use. Present your proposals to the class using your visuals to support your discussion.

The Concept of Promotional Mix

To achieve promotional goals it is important to decide on the right promotional mix. **Promotional mix** is a combination of different types of promotion. A business decides on the promotional mix that will be most effective in persuading customers or other businesses to purchase and support the business's products.

Most businesses use more than one type of promotion to achieve their promotional goals. For example, the

---

Point out that although Nevica, Ltd. did not have a great deal of money to spend on promotion, it did have a good product and a polished sales letter and knowledge of the market to know into whose hands to place the product. Ask students to think about the chances Nevica would have had for success had it sent out poorly prepared letters complete with spelling mistakes and grammatical errors to the wrong people. Remind students that it was not so much luck, but hard work and thorough research that made the difference.

*Personal selling **involves making an oral presentation to a potential buyer. Give one advantage and one disadvantage to personal selling.***

Walt Disney Company uses a combination of local and national advertising; publicity; sales promotions; and personal selling in the form of courteous, well-groomed employees. This promotional mix helps to attract and keep customers returning to Disney's entertainment complexes and stores.

Each type of promotion is designed to complement the other. For example, advertising creates awareness of a business's product, while publicity creates a favorable image for the business itself. Sales promotion efforts stimulate sales, reinforce advertising, and support selling efforts. Finally, personal selling builds on all of these previous efforts by helping the individual customer and completing the sale.

All types of promotion must be coordinated. For example, national advertising should be accompanied by local advertising so local businesses can take advantage of a national campaign. Decorations and in-store displays should be coordinated to back up the promotion. To ensure a smooth promotion, sales personnel should be made aware of coupons, rebates, contests, and other promotional tools that will be used. (Sales are lost and customer dissatisfaction created when products mentioned in ads are not available or the sales staff is uninformed about the promotion.)

In large companies, the marketing department usually establishes a promotion budget, allocates resources, coordinates the campaign, and determines the right promotional mix for the company. Large companies often have separate managers for advertising, personal selling, sales promotion, and publicity. In smaller businesses, these responsibilities often rest with the owner-operator or are shared with one or two people responsible for all the promotional activities.

SECTION 19.2 *Review*

1. Why do businesses use sales promotions?
2. What unique characteristics do sales promotions have?
3. Name and explain the two types of sales personnel.
4. What is meant by promotional mix?

2. Assign and review the appropriate Critical Thinking Questions from the Chapter Review.
3. Assign and review the Building Academic Skills Activities, Application Projects, Linking School to Work Activities, and Performance Assessment from the Chapter Review.
4. Have students work together to prepare a promotional calendar for your school store for each month of the school year. They should attempt to incorporate all four types of promotion into the calendar.

Close

Have students complete this statement: The three unique characteristics of sales promotion are:. . .(it usually involves short-term activities as opposed to advertising and publicity which tend to be longer in length; it usually offers some type of incentive to make a purchase; and it can be successfully used in all channels of distribution with manufacturers, wholesalers, retailers, and consumers.)

Caption Answer

Advantage: Improves communication and hence customer satisfaction. Disadvantage: Costs more because it requires a large sales staff and substantial training.

Section Review Answers

1. To create sales and increase market share.
2. They involve short-term activities, offer some type of incentive to make a purchase, used with all channel members.
3. Order-taking sales, order-getting personnel.
4. Types of promotional activities used to persuade customers to purchase products.

Answers

Vocabulary Review

See Glossary for definitions.

Fact and Idea Review

1. To explain major features and benefits of products, tell where products are sold, advertise sales, answer customer queries, introduce new products, and create a favorable image for business in relation to competitors.
2. Product promotion is used to convince people to buy or use a certain product. Institutional promotion does not directly try to sell a product but is used to create a favorable image, which can result in sales.
3. Advertising, publicity, sales promotion, and personal selling.
4. It is paid for and uses a set format to carry the message, rather than personal, one-on-one selling. It identifies the sponsor.
5. Advantages: Publicity is free—at least in terms of its placement, news audiences are large, and the sources that produce news (newspapers, news programs, and reporters) are often held in high esteem and viewed as more objective than most advertisers. Disadvantages: A business loses control over its message, such publicity may create a negative image if poorly presented.
6. Slotting allowances, buying allowances, trade shows and conventions, and sales incentives.
7. Coupon plans, factory packs (in-packs), traffic builders, and coupons.
8. Contests and sweepstakes are different kinds of games. Contests require participants to demonstrate a skill while sweepstakes are merely games

254

Vocabulary Review

Write a brief definition of each term, based on your reading of the chapter.

promotion
product promotion
institutional promotion
advertising
publicity
sales promotion
slotting allowance
sales incentives
licensing
promotional tie-ins
premiums
incentives
promotional mix

Fact and Idea Review

1. For what specific purposes do businesses typically employ promotion? (Sec. 19.1)
2. What is the difference between product promotion and institutional promotion? (Sec. 19.1)
3. List the four basic types of promotion. (Sec. 19.1)
4. What features distinguish advertising from other forms of promotion? (Sec. 19.1)
5. What are the principal advantages and disadvantages of using publicity as a promotional device? (Sec. 19.1)
6. List four types of trade promotions. (Sec. 19.2)
7. List four types of consumer premiums. (Sec. 19.2)
8. Explain the difference between contests, sweepstakes, and rebates. (Sec. 19.2)
9. How do the duties of order-taking and order-getting sales personnel differ from each other? (Sec. 19.2)
10. "The Walt Disney Company has a good promotional mix." What does this statement mean? (Sec. 19.2)

Critical Thinking

1. Some people think advertising is a waste of money that raises the prices of goods and services needlessly. What do you think? Is the money spent on advertising justified? Provide at least two arguments to support your position.
2. Identify an incident or event that brought a local or national business negative publicity. Could the business have avoided the unfavorable outcome? Could it have limited the damage to its image? If so, how?

254 Unit 6 *Promotion*

3. Why don't manufacturers who issue coupons simply lower the prices of their products to attract customers? What is the value of coupons to such businesses?
4. Some manufacturers are upset because they are forced to pay slotting allowances. Why do retailers feel that they are justified in charging the manufacturers the fees?

Building Academic Skills

Math

1. Promotional discounts are given to stores by manufacturers to place products in preferred locations or to pay for ads, displays, or in-store demonstrations. Calculate the store's cost to stock the following items and the percentage of the discount given.

Item	Purchase Amount	Discount Amount	Net Cost to Store	Percent of Discount
Ski apparel	$5,650	$847.50	_____	_____
In-line skates	$ 535	$ 42.80	_____	_____

Communication

2. Skim an issue of a newspaper to find stories dealing with local or national companies. Identify each company and then categorize the publicity received as either positive or negative. Support your conclusions in each case with a paragraph or two explaining what the facts are and how their publicity helps or harms the business.

Human Relations

3. Identify three businesses in your community that use order-getting sales personnel and three that use order-taking sales personnel. Interview someone in each kind of position. Ask them what they like most (and least) about their work. Have them describe the nature and duration of any training they received. Finally, ask them what things they have found that most impress (or disturb) the buying public. Report your findings in a 150-word paper.

Technology

4. Research and prepare a brief report on the advantages of electronic coupon machines as promotional devices.

---

of chance. Rebates are discounts offered by manufacturers to customers who purchase during a given time period.
9. Order-taking personnel set up displays, stock shelves, answer customer inquiries, operate cash registers, and work with customers over the phone. Order-getting personnel are more involved in informing customers and in helping them to buy. They sell big-ticket consumer items and industrial goods and services.

10. Disney uses a combination of local and national advertising, public relations and publicity efforts, sales promotions, and well-groomed salespeople to sell its products.

Critical Thinking

1. Answers will vary.
2. Answers will vary.
3. Manufacturers issue coupons for three reasons: to introduce new products, to enhance the sales

Application Projects

1. Plan a promotion for a product of your choice.
   a. As thoroughly as possible, describe the market you want to reach. Include information on people's ages, occupations, income, education, hobbies, etc.
   b. Describe what public image you would like your product to have.
   c. Choose a name for your product and explain why you think it will appeal to your market audience.
   d. Describe where you will sell your product (catalog, retail store, discount store, industry). Tell why this is the best outlet to reach your chosen market.
   e. Decide whether you will depend on order-taking personnel (cashiers and clerks) or order-getting personnel (salespeople) to sell your product. Explain your choice.
   f. What kind of premiums might you offer to promote your product? What kind of premiums would not be suitable?
2. Tell about an experience that you or your parents or guardians have had with a consumer sales promotion. Identify the product which you or they purchased and the consumer sales promotion device which caused the purchase.
3. Have your teacher or DECA advisor access the sales promotion plan event guidelines available from National DECA, Delta Epsilon Chi division. Develop a sales promotion plan using these guidelines.
4. Choose a product that is heavily promoted in the marketplace. Write a 250-word analysis of the product. Answer the following questions in your analysis:
   a. What market is being targeted?
   b. What type of image is the company trying to project?
   c. What types of promotion are used?
   d. Are the promotions effective? Why or why not?

Linking School to Work

1. Visit a local store or cooperative education training station to review products offered for sale. Photograph or bring examples to class of consumer sales promotions being used to sell products at the store.
2. Interview a store owner or manager to discover what trade promotions are typically offered to the owner or manager to encourage him or her to purchase a selected product or product line.

Performance Assessment

Role Play

Situation. Assume you are the assistant manager of a record shop. Your manager has recently asked you to develop a promotional mix to attract teenagers. Identify the proper promotional mix for your store by using various promotional devices (advertising, publicity, sales promotions, and personal selling) available in your area. Explain your ideas for the promotional mix.

Evaluation. You will be evaluated on how well you can do the following:

- Explain your ideas for the promotional mix.
- Describe how each type of promotion will address the target market.

Research Paper

Review a recent issue of a newspaper or business publication and find an article dealing with a consumer sales promotion. Clip out the article and develop a 150-word paper explaining the company's product and the type(s) of consumer promotions being used in the promotional campaign.

Complete the Chapter 19 Computer Application that appears in the Student Activity Workbook.

Human Relations

3. Papers will depend on the person selected. Papers should report information on order-taking and order-getting personnel.

Technology

4. Answers should mention customer convenience, increased product sales, elimination of redemption errors by store personnel.

Application Projects

1. Strategies should address six areas noted.
2. Student experiences will vary. Sales promotions might include premiums and incentives.
3. Sales promotion plans should follow the DECA guidelines.
4. Information about products should cover four areas noted in question.

Linking School to Work

Answers depend on the work situation.

Performance Assessment

Refer to the *DECA Competitive Events Handbook* for evaluation guidelines.

Computer Application

Optional activity. Refer to the *Marketing Software Binder* for template and user information.

Evaluation

Administer the reproducible test for Chapter 19, or construct your own using the Testmaker software.

---

of existing products, and to encourage retailers to stock and display both. Simply lowering prices would not accomplish all of these goals.

4. By requiring manufacturers to spend money to get products on shelves and support products with promotions, retailers make sure the products they carry will sell. Since there are more stock-keeping units (SKUs) than most stores can handle, retailers can't afford to have slow-moving inventory on their shelves.

Building Academic Skills

Math

1. *Ski Apparel*: Net Cost = $4802.50 (15% discount)
   In-line Skates: Net Cost = $492.20 (8% discount)

Communication

2. Answers will depend on the stories selected. Answers should be based on the publicity information in the chapter.

ADVERTISING MEDIA

Pages 256–269

Chapter Overview

This chapter introduces advertising media and explains how advertising rates are set.

 ### Springboard

Bring to class several print ads and hang them around the room. Include a mix of promotional and institutional ads with different target markets. Have students look at all of the ads, then close their eyes, and tell you which ads they remember best. What attracted their attention or aroused their interest? Tell students that they have just discovered the overall purpose of advertising: to attract attention and arouse interest so that people will buy a product or accept an idea.

Prereading

List the section objectives to discuss with students. Have students skim the chapter, looking at the pictures, reading the captions, and noting the heads. Ask questions to ensure that the students have a minimal understanding of the chapter structure.

Preteaching the Vocabulary

Ask students to define the word *media*. Have them name the three types of media. Point to the ads in the room that feature products. Ask students to give the purpose of these ads. Then point to a few of the institutional ads. Ask the purpose of these ads. Students have identified the two types of advertising.

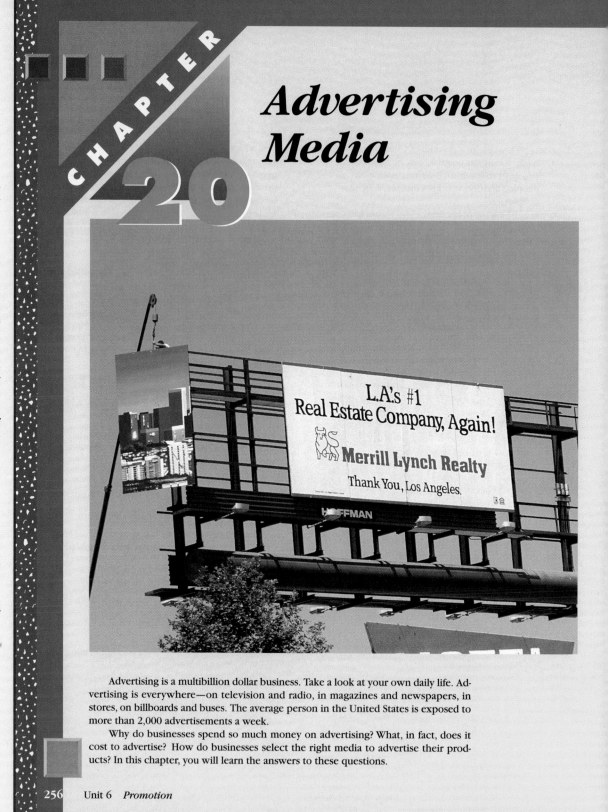

Advertising Media

CHAPTER 20

Advertising is a multibillion dollar business. Take a look at your own daily life. Advertising is everywhere—on television and radio, in magazines and newspapers, in stores, on billboards and buses. The average person in the United States is exposed to more than 2,000 advertisements a week.

Why do businesses spend so much money on advertising? What, in fact, does it cost to advertise? How do businesses select the right media to advertise their products? In this chapter, you will learn the answers to these questions.

256   Unit 6   *Promotion*

Classroom Management

For the Teacher

- Teacher's Annotated Editions for all workbooks
- Teacher's Manual for *School-to-Work Handbook*
- *Testing Binder*
- *Transparency Binder*
- *Marketing Software Binder*
- *Marketing Career Portfolio*
- *Lesson Plans*

For the Student

- *Student Activity Workbook*
- *Marketing Math Workbook*
- *School-to-Work Handbook*
- *Student Software*
- *International Case Studies*
- *Marketing Career Portfolio*

Objectives

After completing this section, you will be able to

- **define advertising and explain its purposes,**
- **identify the various types of media, and**
- **explain the advantages and disadvantages of various types of media.**

Terms to Know

- **promotional advertising**
- **institutional advertising**
- **media**
- **print media**
- **broadcast media**
- **specialty media**

Advertising and Its Purpose

Recall from the previous chapter that advertising is any paid form of nonpersonal promotion of ideas, goods, or services by an identified sponsor. To reach customers, advertising uses a set format that is defined in terms of time (a 30-second television commercial) or space (a half-page newspaper ad). In addition to product information, advertising always identifies the name of the business that paid for it.

The main purpose of advertising is to present its message so well that the customer will buy the product or accept the idea presented. In doing so, advertising also gives people the essential information they need to decide whether or not to buy. Advertising identifies the good, service, or idea and special features, such as price, benefits, and location. It may also tell when the business selling the product is open.

There are two main types of advertising—*promotional* and *institutional*. Advertising designed to increase sales is known as **promotional advertising.** It helps businesses by

- creating an interest in products,
- introducing new products and businesses,
- explaining a product,
- supporting personal selling efforts, and
- creating new markets.

Promotional advertising does have limitations, however. It cannot improve a bad product. Advertising is unlikely to change the mind of any customer who has already made a purchase decision.

Institutional advertising attempts to create a favorable impression and goodwill for a business or an organization. It does this by presenting information about a company's role in the community, important public issues, and topics of general interest, such as the environment, public health, and education.

Types of Media

Advertising messages are presented to the public through media. **Media** are the agencies, means, or instruments used to convey messages. There are three general categories of advertising media: *print media, broadcast media,* and *specialty media.*

Print Media

Print media include everything from newspapers and magazines to direct mail, signs, and billboards. Print media advertisements are done in written form. They are among the oldest and most effective types of advertising.

Newspaper Advertising Newspapers are a main form of print media for many businesses. Why? Because about 55 percent of U.S. adults read the paper every day. (See Figure 20–1 on page 258.) Most newspapers are local or national dailies or weeklies. Local newspapers are distributed to local subscribers or sold through local vendors. National newspapers, such as *USA Today* and *The Wall Street Journal,* are also sold to subscribers or through vendors. National papers are distributed to larger regional markets throughout the country.

Some community newspapers feature local news, but a majority of content is devoted to advertising. Community papers, along with special newspapers called shoppers which contain no editorial content, are delivered free to persons who live in certain areas. (Stores often use community newspapers and shoppers to advertise weekly specials and sales.)

Newspaper advertising has four advantages:

1. Newspapers have a large readership and a high level of reader involvement. These characteristics are an

FOCUS

Bell Ringer Activity

Ask students how many of them watch infomercials. Discuss the types of products generally featured in infomercials (exercise equipment, makeup, skin care products, kitchen appliances, etc.). Ask students these questions.

- What is an infomercial?
- Why are the above-mentioned products (and others that students generate) suited to infomercial advertising as opposed to print advertising or 30-second radio or TV ads?
- At what times of the day and on what days of the week are infomercials run?
- Why are infomercials appropriate for today's viewing audience?
- Are infomercials effective advertising tools?

Introducing the Section

Infomercials were developed in response to the lifestyle trends of the 1990s. They are appropriate to our times because people are staying home more and are watching much more television at odd hours of the day, seven days a week. Celebrities are ideal infomercial spokespeople because they are credible in the eyes of a significant portion of our society. Also, home shopping has become a popular way to purchase products. Thus, infomercials, have become effective advertising tools. Have students make predictions about other types of advertising that might be developed in the next century, given current societal trends.

Meeting Special Needs

Physically Challenged

If your class involves field research or field trips of any kind, encourage the physically challenged individuals to participate in site selection and transportation planning to ensure the access to all sites for all students. Access issues are of major concern for students who use wheelchairs and barriers such as stairs, curbs, narrow walkways, heavy doors, etc. and must be taken into account when planning an event. By making the field work accessible to all students you allow for a positive, rather than an exclusionary, situation. Awareness is the key issue, along with a willingness to learn of the daily problems faced by those with physical challenges.

Guided Practice

1. Read Section 20.1 with students.
2. As you review ads throughout this lesson, have students identify whether the ads appeal to people's wants, needs, or both. Discuss the societal trends reflected in advertising.
3. In recent years ads for such things as perfume, jeans, and even soft drinks have become controversial. Some people, for example, feel that Calvin Klein pushes the limits of good taste with his advertising for perfume and jeans. In the mid-1990s, Coca-Cola came under fire for a TV commercial that some branded as sexist. The commercial showed a male construction worker taking off his T-shirt to enjoy a Diet Coke during a break while several females in an adjacent building watch him.

   It's appropriate to discuss controversial ads with your students since they have already seen much of it in the popular media. The depth of your discussion will depend on the level of your class.
4. *Advertising Services* by Wray, available from Glencoe, (800) 334-7344, is an excellent supplement to this chapter and a good independent study aid for students preparing for DECA competition in advertising.
5. MarkEd Resource Center in Columbus, Ohio, (800) 448-0398, offers LAP Modules, videos, and text-workbooks on advertising and promotion that are appropriate for use with this section.

---

outgrowth of content. Newspapers carry a variety of high interest content that attracts readers including daily news, sports, and manufacturers' coupons.

2. Newspaper circulation is known, so businesses using newspapers can target their advertising to people living in certain geographical areas or with certain interests. Advertisers, for example, can target ads to selected locations within a region.
3. The cost of newspaper advertising is relatively low. This is because most of the paper is printed in black and white and the quality of paper is less expensive than that used in magazines and direct mail. Also, some of the publishing costs are paid for by the subscribers.
4. Newspaper ads can be timely and advertisers can easily change ads, often up to 24 hours before the paper goes to print.

Newspaper advertising has three limitations:

1. There is sometimes wasted circulation (as when papers are sent to a wider area than the target market).
2. The life of an advertisement is limited because in most households newspapers are thrown away daily.
3. The quality of reproduction is poor in relation to other media. The black-and-white format of most newspaper advertisements makes them generally less appealing than other print media. However, new designs and improvements in color production and quality are becoming more common, despite the increased costs.

Magazine Advertising Magazines can be classified into local, regional, and national weeklies, monthlies, and quarterlies. Local and regional magazines are often developed for cities or metropolitan areas. They usually promote local entertainment, restaurants, and businesses in their immediate geographical area. Many national magazines have regional editions and rates. *Field and Stream,* for example, has seven regional editions.

Examples of national weeklies include such news magazines as *U.S. News and World Report, Time,* and *Newsweek*. Examples of national monthlies include *Essence, Details,* and *Vanity Fair*.

Magazines can also be classified as consumer or business (trade) magazines. Consumer magazines are read for personal pleasure or interest and include such publications as *Reader's Digest, Vogue,* and *Sports Illustrated*.

Business magazines appeal to people with a general interest in business or a particular field within business. Examples of general business publications include *Business Week, Inc.,* and *Forbes*. Some business magazines or trade journals, such as *Marketing News, Adweek,* or *Stores,* are directed at a particular field of business.

Magazine advertising closely follows newspaper advertising in popularity because of the four major advantages it offers:

1. Businesses can target their audience because the circulation and characteristics of regular readers are known.
2. Magazines are often read more slowly and thoroughly than newspapers, so the information in an ad is more likely to be remembered.

Total U.S. Advertising Expenditures by Major Medium

Rank	Medium	1993 Volume in $Billions
1	Newspaper	$32.03
2	Television	30.58
3	Direct Mail	27.27
4	Yellow Pages	9.52
5	Radio	9.46
6	Magazines	7.36
7	Outdoor	1.09

Source: McCann-Erickson

Figure 20–1

Advertising is a multibillion dollar business. Given the figures here, calculate the total dollar amount that was spent on advertising in 1993. What percentage was spent on newspaper advertising?

Caption Answer

117.31 billion; 27 percent.

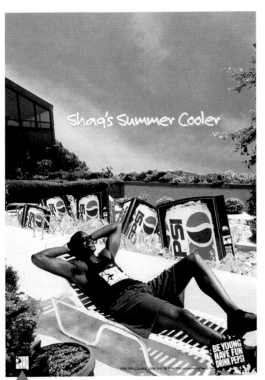

Shaq's Summer Cooler

BE YOUNG. HAVE FUN. DRINK PEPSI!

Some products are more effectively advertised in magazines than in newspapers. What are two advantages of advertising this product in a magazine rather than in the newspaper?

3. The print quality in magazines is generally better than that in newspapers.
4. Magazines have a longer life span because they are generally kept for an extended period of time, during which they (and the ads in them) may be reread.

Despite these advantages, there are three drawbacks to magazine advertising:

1. Compared to newspapers, magazines have less mass appeal within a geographical area.
2. Compared to newspaper advertising, magazine advertising is more expensive.
3. The ads in magazines usually are not as timely as those in daily newspapers because the deadline for inserting ads is often many months before publication.

Direct-Mail Advertising   Direct-mail advertising, as its name suggests, is sent by businesses directly through the mail to prospective customers. According to the Direct Mail Advertising Association, direct mail sells more than $80 billion in goods and services annually for local and national advertisers.

Types of direct-mail advertising include newsletters, catalogs, coupons, samplers, price lists, circulars, invitations to special sales or events, and postage-paid reply cards and letters. Businesses often enclose direct-mail

advertising with their monthly bills and statements. Large retailers and manufacturers often send direct-mail catalogs and price lists to prospective customers.

One of the most important considerations in direct-mail advertising is the mailing list used. It can be assembled by the advertiser from current customer records or purchased from a direct mail specialty firm that sells lists of potential customers. Whatever its source, however, the list must be accurate. Otherwise, a large part of the expense incurred for the mailing will be wasted.

Here are four advantages of direct-mail advertising:

1. The advertiser can be highly selective about who will receive the mailing.
2. The advertiser can be flexible about the timing of the mailing and can keep competitors from seeing the advertisements.
3. The advertiser has a wide choice of advertisement sizes and formats, such as letters, catalogs, and postcards, limited only by certain postal regulations.
4. The advertiser can use coupons or other incentives to get customers to try the product.
5. The advertiser can use direct mail, such as product catalogs or magazine or record club subscriptions, to actually make the sale. Customers can order or subscribe directly using an order form or a toll-free number.

Direct-mail advertising has three major limitations:

1. There is a low level of response in relation to the number of items sent—usually less than 1 percent. This problem is compounded when customer lists become dated and items are sent to the wrong target audience.
2. The cost of direct mail, including producing and printing each piece of the mailing, maintaining and buying mailing lists, processing, and postage are high and getting higher.
3. Many people think of direct-mail advertising as "junk mail" to be discarded without opening, or at least without careful reading.

Outdoor Advertising   Both local and national businesses use outdoor signs, or billboards, for advertising. There are two types of outdoor signs—*nonstandardized* and *standardized*.

Nonstandardized outdoor signs are used by local firms at their place of business or in other locations throughout the community. For the off-site signs, businesses usually pay rent to the owners on whose property the signs are displayed.

Standardized outdoor signs are available to local, regional, or national advertisers. Such signs are purchased from outdoor advertising companies, come in standard sizes, and are placed near highly traveled roads and freeways.

Three types of standardized outdoor signs are *posters, painted bulletins,* and *spectaculars. Posters* are preprinted sheets put up like wallpaper on outdoor billboards. They are changed three to four times each year.

Chapter 20   *Advertising Media*   **259**

6. Have students read aloud the Case Study and review the answers in class.
7. Use the transparency for this section.

Discussion Starter

Have you ever made a purchase based largely on an advertising campaign? What was the product, and what factors induced you to buy?

Critical Thinking

In what medium would you advertise the following products?

- African-American fashion dolls for children ages 7–12 (in African-American magazines like Ebony and on children's morning television programs).
- A new line of rain jackets (*Field and Stream* and other magazines related to outdoor sports, and the sports section of the newspaper).
- Vitamins (health-related publications such as *Shape and Muscle & Fitness*, radio spots, and televisions spots).
- A movie (billboards, newspapers, bus stops transit advertising).
- A watch that costs $1,150 (business magazines, *Town & Country,* and other publications that appeal to an audience with an above average disposable income).
- Computers and computer equipment (computer magazines, direct-mail advertising, business magazines, and the newspaper).
- Legal services (directory advertising; some lawyers and legal clinics also use billboard advertising and transit advertising).
- This textbook (direct mail to teachers, administrators, and state supervisors of marketing education;

More About

Outdoor Advertising

The latest gimmick offered by a company called Space Marketing Concepts, Inc. is the opportunity for companies to advertise on a large inflatable billboard which will orbit in space with a brand name or logo clearly visible to an observer on earth. The cost ranges from $15 to $30 million. Insurance is available to cover any disasters.

educational journals, particularly those related to marketing education; flyers and specialty media given way at conferences).

- Pre-owned cars (television, radio, and newspapers).

Cooperative Learning

Divide students into groups. Have each group develop an advertising poster for National DECA Week, Free Enterprise Week, or for your school's marketing program.

Independent Practice

1. Have students select a magazine that they like, and use it to do some research on magazine advertising. Ask students to determine the characteristics of the magazine's readership. Have students look at a few issues to see the kinds of goods and services that are advertised in the magazine. Students should write a brief report summarizing their findings.

Painted bulletins are painted billboards that are changed about every six months to a year. *Spectaculars* are outdoor advertising signs which use lights or moving parts and are situated in high traffic areas, such as in densely populated metropolitan cities.

Outdoor advertising is popular with some advertisers. However, its use is becoming more restricted because of environmental and traffic safety concerns. The signs are said to mar scenic views and distract drivers. In many urban areas outdoor billboards have size restrictions and spacing requirements between billboards. They also have to be a specified number of feet away from schools, parks, and playgrounds. Outdoor advertising is primarily used along roadways in areas zoned for commercial and industrial uses.

Four advantages to outdoor advertising are that it:

1. is highly visible,
2. is relatively inexpensive,
3. permits easy repetition of a message that works 24 hours a day, and
4. can be geographically tailored to reach specific target markets.

The three disadvantages of outdoor advertising are:

1. the message has to be short because of limited viewing time,
2. the makeup of the audience is largely unknown when placed along major roadways, and
3. advertisers must abide by increasing government regulations imposed to prevent outdoor advertising from being both a form of blight and a traffic hazard.

Directory Advertising Directory advertising is placed in alphabetical listings of households and businesses called *directories*. The best-known of these listings are telephone directories. They are commonly divided into the White Pages and a classified section known as the Yellow Pages.

In the White Pages, businesses receive a free alphabetical listing along with noncommercial telephone customers. In the Yellow Pages, businesses pay for an alphabetical listing and, if desired, a larger ad. These appear under general headings, such as florists, physicians, recreational vehicles, or travel agencies. The Yellow Pages help consumers find suppliers of goods and services.

Advertising in the Yellow Pages has several advantages:

1. Yellow Pages advertising is relatively inexpensive.
2. Telephone directories are found in 98 percent of American households, so they are used by all demographic groups.

*Outdoor advertising **permits easy repetition of a message that works 24 hours a day. What are three other principal advantages of outdoor advertising?***

3. Telephone directories are usually kept for at least a year and are seldom thrown away until another is provided.

The biggest disadvantage to Yellow Pages advertising is that directories are usually printed yearly. So, advertisers cannot adjust their prices, advertise sales, or change their message easily. Just as with any other medium, advertisers must make sure that the directory reaches the intended market to avoid advertising waste.

Service businesses like to use directory advertising. If you check your local Yellow Pages, you will see ads for such service providers as lawyers, electricians, plumbers, and physicians. Note that these are all people you are likely to call only when you have a particular need. Because people use them infrequently, such businesses often combine directory advertising with other forms of advertising to attract or inform customers before the service need occurs.

Transit Advertising *Transit advertising* uses public transportation facilities to bring advertising messages to people. It includes

- printed posters found inside business and commuter trains;
- exterior posters on the outside of taxis and buses; and
- station posters located near or in subways and in railroad, bus, and airline terminals.

Transit advertising has three key advantages:

1. It reaches a wide and (in the case of bus and train passengers) captive audience.
2. It is economical.
3. It has a defined market (usually an urban area).

There are three major disadvantages to transit advertising:

1. It is often unavailable in smaller towns and cities.
2. It is subject to defacement.
3. It is restricted to certain travel destinations.

Broadcast Media

Broadcast media includes radio and television. The average person over a lifetime of 70 years will spend nearly 10 years watching television and almost 6 years listening to the radio. So, you can see why advertising through broadcast media is popular.

People listen to radio and watch television not only for entertainment but also to get information. In fact, people are more likely to believe the information they get

260 Unit 6 *Promotion*

Real World

MARKETING

What You See Is Not Necessarily What You Get

When you see a scoop of ice cream in a TV or print ad, look again. You're probably looking at a scoop of mashed potatoes. The use of stand-ins to solve logistical problems (ice cream melts almost instantly under hot studio lights) is one of many tricks ad producers use to get the job done.

from television than the information they get from print media. Since they can both see and hear the television message, it comes alive for them.

In the United States, there are approximately 8,000 AM and FM radio stations. Most of the 800 commercial television stations are affiliated with one of the major networks—ABC, CBS, NBC, or FOX. In addition, there are some 5,000 cable television stations. Cable television networks such as Cable News Network (CNN), The Discovery Channel, MTV, TNT, and Black Entertainment Television are becoming increasingly more popular.

Given this tremendous availability and the popularity of broadcast media, it is no surprise that many businesses use it to sell their products, despite the higher advertising costs involved. Let's take a closer look at advertising on each type of broadcast media.

Radio Advertising It is estimated that radio reaches 96 percent of all people age 12 and over in any given week. This ability to reach a wide audience makes radio an extremely effective advertising medium.

The best times for radio advertising are in the morning, when people are driving to work, and during the afternoon or early evening, when they are coming home. These are called prime times for radio advertising because advertisers are guaranteed a more concentrated audience.

Radio advertisements are presented in 15-, 30-, or 60-second time slots. The messages are effective in encouraging people to buy because the announcer or actors (along with background music, jingles, slogans, and/or sound effects) add excitement, drama, or humor.

There are three key advantages to radio advertising:

1. With radio, the advertiser can select an audience, such as teenagers, various ethnic groups, and/or professionals, by advertising on stations targeting that particular market.
2. Radio is more flexible than print advertising because messages can be changed easily. For example, an advertiser can make changes in the script for an advertising message a few days or even just a few minutes before the message is recorded.

3. Radio is a mobile medium that can be taken just about anywhere, such as shopping, jogging, hiking, or driving.

Although there are numerous advantages to radio advertising, there are some disadvantages as well:

1. Radio advertising has a short life span. When the message is broadcast, it is gone—unless the business pays to have it rebroadcast later. In fact, radio advertisers usually buy several time slots instead of just one.
2. In markets where there are many stations, several stations often compete for the same audience. So, potential advertisers must decide on which radio station to advertise—or advertise on several.
3. Due to the lack of visual involvement, listeners might become distracted during radio advertisements and miss some or all of the message.

Television Advertising For many businesses, television is the ultimate advertising medium because it can communicate a message with sound, action, and color. Prime time for network and cable television is between 7 P.M. and 11 P.M., when millions of viewers are watching.

A widely used new form of television advertising is the infomercial. Infomercials are actually 30-minute commercials. They promote products such as cookware, makeup, and appliances using a talk-show type setting. Viewers can order the advertised merchandise by calling a phone number or writing to an address.

Television has several advantages for advertisers:

1. Perhaps more than any other medium, television can pull together all the elements necessary to produce a creative advertising message. (Think of the catch-phrases and jingles you know by heart simply from hearing them on TV commercials.)
2. People are more inclined to believe what they see happen rather than what they merely read about.
3. Because it comes directly into the viewer's home, television is like door-to-door selling. It somehow seems more personal and is therefore more effective.
4. Commercial television networks can reach a mass audience—millions of people nationwide. In the case of cable networks, television can be directed to an audience with a specific interest, such as news, comedy, sports, science, or movies.
5. A televised advertising message can be adapted to take advantage of holidays, seasonal changes, and special-events programming, such as the Super Bowl, other sporting events, or entertainment specials.

There are three major disadvantages to using television as an advertising medium:

1. Television has the highest production costs of any type of media and a high dollar cost for the time used. Prime-time costs, in particular, are sometimes prohibitive. They keep many smaller companies from using television advertising or force them to buy time in less desirable periods when fewer people are watching.

Chapter 20   *Advertising Media*   **261**

2. Have students find an example of a print ad that they do not like (or write a description of a television commercial or radio spot that they do not like). Have them answer these questions:
   - What elements of the ad don't you like?
   - What would you do to improve the ad?
   - Despite your dislike of the ad, do you think it is effective?

Assess

Evaluation

Assign and review the Section 20.1 Review.

Reteaching

1. Assign and review the vocabulary terms for this section.
2. Assign and review Fact and Idea Review questions 1–7 from the Chapter Review.
3. Bring in a magazine and a section of the newspaper that contain a great deal of full-page advertising. Choose several ads that are easy for all students to see and ask the following questions about each ad:
   - Is this a promotional ad or an institutional ad?
   - Is it appealing to a want, a need, or both?
   - Who is the target audience for this ad?
   - How do the elements in the ad (for example, color, visual images) appeal specifically to the target audience?
   - If the product is a familiar one, can you recall prior advertising campaigns for it? How does that ad campaign differ from this one? How does the current advertising reflect current societal trends?

More About

Television Advertising

Television advertising is such an important part of determining what gets seen on television, that the absence of soccer on major networks can be traced in part to the fact that soccer only has two periods of play, and unlike football or basketball, has no time outs, leaving little time for commercials. The rest of the world has coped with this fact by allowing sponsors to place billboards around the edge of the arena allowing viewers to see the name whenever the camera pans to that portion of the field. This in fact worked out well during the World Cup, which was televised to billions of viewers worldwide. It is not enough, however, to encourage the televising of national games, yet.

Enrichment

1. Assign and review the appropriate activities in the *Student Activity Workbook*.
2. Assign and review the appropriate Critical Thinking Questions from the Chapter Review.
3. Advertising offers many career-sustaining job opportunities. Research the field of advertising and write a 150- to 200-word report that outlines the job responsibilities of three career-sustaining positions in advertising that interest you. Also tell what educational, extracurricular, and volunteer activities will help you prepare now for each job. If you have the time and resources, contact people who are actually doing these jobs and ask them to discuss some of the things they do and do not like about the job. (Print resources include The *Career Directory* series, the *Dictionary of Occupational Titles*, the *Occupational Outlook Handbook*, and the *Encyclopedia of Careers and Vocational Guidance*. Also

CASE STUDY

Advertising in U.S. Schools

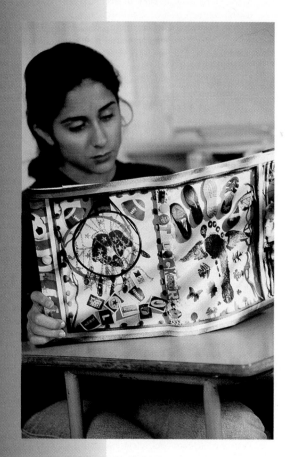

Many corporations are now plugging their products in U.S. classrooms. The largest and most controversial in-class marketing method started in 1989 with Channel One. Channel One provides daily news and other special TV programming to students in about 12,000 schools—almost 40 percent of the middle and high schools in the United States. By agreeing to have Channel One, schools receive televisions, satellite dishes, and VCRs worth more than $50,000.

However, Channel One includes not only current events and other educational programming, but also advertisements for a variety of products. Advertisers can pay more than $200,000 for a 30-second ad spot.

The National Parent-Teachers Association and the National Education Association oppose Channel One. Both organizations and many teachers believe that advertising products should not be done in school.

TV advertising is not the only form of corporate advertising going on in the schools. Some companies, such as Nike, Hershey, Foot Locker, Crayola, Mattel, Nintendo, and Warner Brothers, distribute bookcovers, a form of specialty advertising, free to students. These companies place on the bookcovers ads that promote their products. These ads can be targeted to any age level, region, ethnic background, or economic level. Depending on the size of the ad, companies can pay from $25,000 to more than $115,000 for every million bookcovers.

Other companies, such as American Airlines, Kellogg's, and Red Lobster, distribute maps, globes, and instructional materials for use in the classroom. In tight budget times, many schools appreciate the free support for their students and the extra equipment and educational materials.

Case Study Review

1. Why do some parent and teacher associations oppose Channel One in the schools? Do you think their arguments are valid? Why or why not?
2. What advantages and disadvantages are there to advertising on Channel One or to contributing free educational materials or supplies to students?
3. Name other types of advertising or promotional efforts that occur in your school.

A MATTER OF ETHICS

4. Why might some people see advertising in schools as an ethical problem?

262   Unit 6   *Promotion*

Case Study Answers

1. Some oppose Channel One because they believe the station misuses valuable educational time. Other people are offended by the commercialization of the school environment.
2. Advertisers hope students will become more aware of and ultimately buy their products. Disadvantages include the perception that the advertisers are forcing students to watch TV advertising, or use a particular product.
3. Examples include college recruiter presentations, yearbook ads, and candy sale posters.
4. Some people may see advertising in schools as forcing products on a captive audience or may perceive businesses as taking advantage of schools.

Make your ideas fly.

World's largest flying banners. Fine computer imaging.
Covering North America and the British Isles.

NATIONAL AERIAL ADVERTISING

Wayne Mansfield, President 1-800-223-7425
Los Angeles— Bruce G. Friedlander 310-792-8111
England— David Macdonald 011-44-243-551127

Businesses are constantly creating new forms of advertising to help them promote their products to consumers. Name one new form of advertising you have seen recently.

encourage students to use the *Reader's Guide to Periodical Literature* for current articles. Finally, they will also find many career books in the business or reference section of their local bookstores.)
4. Television and radio advertising both set their rates based on the time of day and the programming (which determine the target audience.) Ask students to identify the advertising which appears during their favorite television show and on their favorite radio station in general. Is the advertising similar? Are there similarities in the audience that advertisers are trying to reach?

Close

Have students complete this statement: The purpose of advertising is to. . .(present its message so well that the customer will buy the product or accept the idea presented.)

2. The audience size is not assured.
3. Many viewers consider television commercials to be a nuisance. Such viewers may switch channels or leave the room during commercial breaks. As a result, advertising dollars are wasted.

Specialty Media

Specialty media are relatively inexpensive, useful items with an advertiser's name printed on them. The items are usually given away with no obligation attached to receiving and keeping them.

To be successful as advertising tools, specialty items must be practical, subject to frequent use, and likely to be placed in locations where they will be seen often. Common items, such as calendars, pens, pencils, memo pads, and key chains, fit this description and are popular specialty items. When designed well, specialty items carry the name and address of the business sponsoring them and an advertising message urging the reader to action. Sometimes, however, the size of the item prevents the use of a message, and only the name and address of the business appear.

Specialty advertising has two limitations. First, the distribution of the items is usually somewhat limited. Second, the items might be given to people who would never consider buying the product or patronizing the business.

Other Advertising Media

Businesses are constantly creating exciting, innovative means of transmitting their messages to potential customers. Examples include sports arena billboards, commercials run in movie theaters and on home video rentals, ads placed on hot air balloons and blimps, skywriting, and airplanes pulling advertising banners.

Increasingly, in-store advertising techniques, such as electronic shelf ads, supermarket cart advertising displays, instant coupon machines, and TV infomercials, are being used to advertise products. You can probably add to this list as new media are designed to help advertisers get their messages out to potential customers.

SECTION 20.1 *Review*

1. What is advertising?
2. What is the main purpose of advertising?
3. List the six different types of print media.
4. What are two forms of broadcast advertising?
5. What is specialty media?

Chapter 20   *Advertising Media*   **263**

SECTION 20.2

Objectives

After completing this section, you will be able to

- **describe how various media rates are set,**
- **calculate print media costs, and**
- **suggest some standards for selecting promotional media.**

Terms to Know

- **cost per thousand (CPM)**
- **network radio advertising**
- **national spot radio advertising**
- **local radio advertising**

Media Costs

Media costs vary greatly, not just with type of media but with geographical location as well. For example, a quarter-page newspaper ad in a large-city daily could cost four to eight times more than the same size ad in a small-town weekly. Given such variation, it is virtually impossible to quote exact rates for each type of media advertising. It is possible, however, to generalize about how those rates are set.

When businesses want to access rates for the various media, they can look up the rates in the publications of Standard Rate and Data Service. It publishes rate cards for most major media according to general categories, such as print media or broadcast media.

Another advertising industry service important to both advertisers and print media is the Audit Bureau of Circulation (ABC). Print media publishers subscribe to the ABC to have it verify their circulation figures. This is important in print media because advertising rates are based on circulation. Circulation figures are important selling points for the media to use when trying to attract advertisers to the publication.

Newspaper Rates

Newspaper advertising rates are classified into two categories depending on whether the ad is a *classified ad*

or a *display ad*. Classified ads can advertise everything from services performed to houses for sale to job openings. They are called *classified* because they are grouped or classified into specific categories, such as help wanted, real estate, personals, and auto sales. People or businesses who buy classified ads usually pay by the word or line of type.

Display ads involve the creative illustration of the product being advertised. They are a mix of art or photographs, headlines, copy, and a signature or logo of the product or business. Display ads are generally larger than classified ads. Their cost is based upon the amount of space used.

Newspapers quote display advertising rates by the column inch. A column inch is an area that is one column wide by one inch deep. If a newspaper quotes a column inch rate, you simply multiply the number of inches by the number of columns to determine the total number of column inches. Then you multiply the total column inches by the rate. For example, if the rate for a column inch is $17, then an ad that measures 4 inches long by 3 columns will cost $204.

$$\$17 \times 4 \text{ inches} \times 3 \text{ columns} = \$204$$

A number of factors can change the regular newspaper rates charged to advertisers. Display ads are usually sold at *run-of-paper* rates. Run-of-paper allows the newspaper to choose where to run an ad in the paper. However, for a higher rate advertisers can run ads in guaranteed or preferred locations, such as the last page of a section or in the sports section.

The use of color also affects the advertising rate. Ads done in color are sold at a higher rate than those done in black and white.

The frequency of advertising lowers the rate charged for display ads. The more a business advertises, the less it pays per insertion.

Businesses that advertise in a newspaper infrequently generally pay an *open rate*. The open rate, often referred to as the noncontract rate, is the basic charge for a minimum amount of advertising space. The open rate varies depending on when an advertisement will appear in a paper. For example, a newspaper may charge a daily rate (Monday–Thursday) of $28 per column inch, a Friday rate of $29, a Saturday rate of $31, and a Sunday rate of $35 per column inch.

Businesses that advertise in the newspaper more frequently often contract with a newspaper to guarantee that they will use a certain number of column inches for a specified time period. Thus, they are granted *contract rates* which are discounted from the open rate. Contracts can be written in a number of ways. For example, a yearly frequency contract guarantees that an advertiser will use a minimum number of column inches each week, for 52 weeks. A bulk space contract guarantees that a minimum number of inches will be used when the advertiser chooses, within a 12-month period.

Lifelong Learning

Advertising Media

Since advertising affects so many decisions that students will make during their lifetime, it is to their advantage to understand its uses and applications as consumers as well as potential marketers. Following

this class, they can keep up with trends in advertising by reading a variety of publications including *Adweek, Advertising Age, Marketing News,* and other general interest publications.

BRIGHT IDEAS

Try the Worst Idea

You're stuck for an ad headline. You've tried all the good ideas and they haven't worked. So, what do you do? You try some of the bad ideas.

That's what Seth Werner and Dextor Fedor did when they were asked by a growers association to come up with an ad campaign for California raisins. The two copywriters racked their brains, trying all of their best ideas, their good ideas, and even their so-so ideas. In the end, hopelessly blocked, they were forced to consider their worst ideas. They resorted to puns, or plays on words. Suggested Werner, "We could always have a bunch of raisins sing, 'We Heard It Through the Grapevine.'" They laughed and groaned at the same time. It was so obvious, so trite, so bad. They couldn't—could they?

Today, for many people the vamp of, "I Heard It Through the Grapevine" summons up only one image—a long line of claymation raisins winding their way across a tabletop. It's an advertising classic. All of which goes to prove that sometimes by looking for the worst idea, you can find the best of the bunch!

Creativity Challenge   Form teams of 3–5 people, and try to come up with an ad headline that's so bad it's good. For a product, choose something that's familiar but has no widely recognized ad campaign. Consider other kinds of produce (such as lemons or watermelon), school or office supplies (such as lead pencils or typing paper), or a landmark (such as a road, bridge, or town). See if you can create an instant classic—or at least give yourselves and your classmates a good laugh.

Another rate that is important to advertisers is the **cost per thousand (CPM)** rate. The CPM rate is the media cost of exposing 1,000 readers to an ad. It is useful in comparing the cost of advertising to reach 1,000 readers in one newspaper to the cost of advertising to reach 1,000 readers in another newspaper. The comparison is made by using the formula:

$$\frac{\text{Cost of the ad} \times 1,000}{\text{Circulation}} = \text{cost per thousand (CPM)}$$

For example, if the cost of an ad in the *Times* is $500 and the paper has a circulation of 500,000, its cost per thousand rate would be calculated as follows:

$$\frac{\$500 \times 1,000}{500,000} = \frac{\$500,000}{500,000} = \$1 \text{ per } 1,000 \text{ readers}$$

If the cost of an ad in the *Tribune,* a competing paper, is $600 and the paper has a circulation of 300,000, its cost per thousand rate would be calculated as follows:

$$\frac{\$600 \times 1,000}{300,000} = \frac{\$600,000}{300,000} = \$2 \text{ per } 1,000 \text{ readers}$$

All things being equal, an advertiser would probably choose the *Times* over the *Tribune* because it would cost less per 1,000 readers.

Of course, all other things might not be equal. The *Tribune's* circulation could include more of the advertiser's target market, or the paper could offer a special placement for the ad. The point is that the cost per thousand (CPM) is a convenient measure that puts all newspapers on the same footing. It is a factor to be considered in the placement of advertising.

Magazine Rates

Magazine rates are based on circulation, quality of readership, and the production technique used in the advertisement. To calculate the actual cost of magazine advertising, you need to become familiar with some terms found on magazine advertising rate cards, including *bleed, black-and-white rates, color rates, premium position, discounts,* and the *cost per thousand rate* (CPM) discussed earlier.

Bleed means that half-page or full-page ads are printed to the very edge of the page, leaving no white border. Magazines generally charge between 15 to 20 percent extra for bleeds.

The lowest rates magazines offer for display ads are black-and-white rates for black-and-white advertisements. *Color rates* are offered for color ads. Each time the magazine adds color to the ad, the rates increase. Four-color advertisements, also called *full-color,* are the most expensive magazine ads.

Premium position refers to where ads are placed in the magazine. Ads placed in premium positions, such as on the first page, are more expensive to run.

Frequency discounts are offered to advertisers who want to run the same ad several times during the year. A special discount rate may be offered or the magazine may publish an entire schedule of rates for the number of times during the year an advertiser contracts to advertise. The rate per issue decreases as the frequency increases.

Another discount is a *commission*—a percentage of sales given by the magazine to the advertising agency for placing the ad for the advertiser. A typical commission is 15 percent.

Discussion Starter

Which advertising rate computations discussed in this section do you understand the best?

Which computations do you feel that you need to understand better?

What course of action would best help you become familiar with those computations you need to understand better?

L1 Math Skills

The *Williamstown Gazette* quotes a column inch, noncontract rate of $23 for Monday through Thursday placement, and $25 for Friday placement. If you want to run one 6-inch by 3-column ad on Thursday and one 6-inch by 3-column ad on Friday, how much will you pay? ($864. Thursday's ad is $414. $23 × 6 inches × 3 columns = $414. Friday's ad is $450. $25 × 6 × 3 = $450. $414 + $450 = $864.)

L2 Math Skills

You decide that you want to run a 6-inch by 3-column ad in the *Gazette* on the first Thursday and Friday of each month. Your Gazette salesperson offers you a 12-month contract for $7,257.60. What percentage discount has she given you? (30%. $864 × 12 = $10,368 [cost without discount]. $10,368 − $7,257.60 = $3,110.40. $3,110.40 ÷ $10,368 = 0.3 or 30%.)

L3 Math Skills

The cost of an ad in the *Gazette* is $650; it has a circulation of 475,000. The cost of an ad in the *Herald-News* is $600; it has a circulation of 560,000. Which has the lowest CPM rate? (The *Herald-News* at $1.07 per 1,000 readers versus the *Gazette's* CPM rate of $1.37 per 1,000 readers. *Gazette*: $650 × 1000 ÷ 475,000 = $650,000 ÷ 475,000 = $1.37. *Herald-News*: $600 × 1000 ÷ 560,000 = $600,000 ÷ 560,000 = $1.07.)

Bright Ideas

Tell students that being stuck in the creative process is a normal part of the process. Most writers experience "writer's block." There are a wide variety of tricks writers use to "unblock." In addition to trying the worst idea, some writers just write anything, even the same word over and over on a page; draw pictures instead of writing words; or take a break and do something active.

Did You Know

Why is cost per thousand referred to as CPM instead of CPT? In this case, M stands for *mille,* the Latin word for thousand. The word millennium comes from the same word, as does the word millenary, meaning a group of 1,000 units or things.

Teach (Cont'd.)

Independent Practice

1. Have students select a magazine that they like. They should first determine the circulation of the magazine.
   - Has the circulation decreased or increased over the past few years? Why?
   - What are the characteristics of the magazine's readership?
   - What kinds of products are advertised in the magazine?
   - Generally, how do the products advertised match the publication's target market? Students' findings should be summarized in 100 to 150 words.
2. Assign and review the Chapter 20 Case Study in the *International Case Studies* workbook.

Assess

Evaluation

Assign and review the Section 20.2 Review.

Reteaching

1. Assign and review the vocabulary terms for this section.
2. Assign and review Fact and Idea Review questions 8–12.
3. Go over each of the formulas for calculating newspaper and magazine rates. Stress to students that they should not hesitate to talk to you privately if they need more help in understanding the content of this section.

Finally, a cash discount may be offered for paying the bill earlier than its due date (this may be written 2/10, net 30). This cash discount would permit the advertiser or ad agency to take a 2 percent discount if the bill is paid 10 days from the date of the invoice. The payment, if the discount is not taken, is due 30 days from the date of the invoice.

Take a look at the rate card in Figure 20–2. You would calculate the cost of a full-page, four-color advertisement with bleed as follows:

$23,300	1 page, four-color rate
× .15	bleed
$ 3,495	extra for bleed

$23,300	1 page, four-color rate
+ 3,495	bleed
$26,795	for 1 page, four color, with bleed

If an ad agency placed the ad and it took the commission and the cash discount, the total cost of the above ad to the agency would be:

$ 26,795	1 page, four color, with bleed
× .15	ad agency's commission
$ 4,019.25	

$26,795.00	1 page, four color, with bleed
− 4,019.25	agency's commission
$22,775.75	net cost of ad to agency after commission
× .02	cash discount percentage if paid within 10 days of invoice
$ 455.52	cash discount

$22,775.75	net cost of ad to agency after commission
− 455.52	cash discount
$22,320.23	net cost to advertising agency for one full-page, four-color ad, with bleed after cash discount and agency commission.

As with newspapers, the cost per thousand rate can be used to compare the cost of advertising in several magazines. For example, if a magazine had a circulation of 2 million and its full-page, black-and-white ad rate was $35,000, the CPM rate would be $17.50.

$$\frac{\$35,000 \times 1,000}{2,000,000} = \$17.50$$

Radio Rates

After a business decides to buy radio time, it needs to decide what kind of radio advertising to use. There are three options—*network radio advertising, national spot radio advertising,* and *local radio advertising.*

The 3,000-Letter Alphabet

Life in the Multicultural MARKETPLACE

Japanese presents a major challenge for the manufacturers of typewriters and other keyboard-based machines. The written form of the language uses 3,000 separate characters, or ideographs, derived from ancient Chinese. The Japanese refer to these characters as *kanji.* In addition, the Japanese have two alternative alphabets with which to grapple. One (*katakana*) is used primarily for English and other foreign words. The other (*hiragana*) expresses the grammar and pronunciation of Japanese words and sentences. Increasingly, billboards and street signs in Japan are in dual script format, containing both the traditional *kanji* and the more modern *katakana.*

If a business is national in scope, it usually chooses network radio advertising or national spot radio advertising. **Network radio advertising** is a broadcast from a studio to all affiliated radio stations throughout the country. Network radio advertising allows an advertiser to broadcast an ad simultaneously to several markets through sponsorship of a special program, activity, or radio personality.

National spot radio advertising is used by national firms to advertise on a local station-by-station basis. It is used to target select markets in the country.

Local radio advertising is done by a local business for its target market. It is limited to a specific geographical area.

When selecting advertising it is important to know the difference between *spot radio* and *spot commercials. Spot radio* refers to the geographical area an advertiser wants to reach with its advertising. So, when selecting spot radio, businesses need to identify their target market and their potential customers. *Spot commercials* are advertising messages of one minute or less. It is important to realize that spot commercials can be carried on network or spot radio.

Each radio station determines actual advertising rates by time of day. Rates are generally higher during peak listening times, such as early mornings and late afternoons. Radio stations also offer less costly, *run-of-schedule (ROS)* air times. ROS air time allows a radio station to decide when to run the ad spot. Because target audiences, audience size, rates, weekly package plans, and discounts vary from station to station, a business should carefully review and compare the rates of the radio stations on which it might advertise.

Feature Note

Not only languages such as Japanese, but even less exotic languages such as Spanish or French require adjustment to the typical American keyboard. The need for additional characters and accent marks in all other languages prompted the development of a computer software program called *Accent.* This multilingual word processor allows the user to quickly and easily type letters, reports, or whatever is needed in the alphabet of the desired language. Currently the program supports even Greek, Turkish, Finnish, Icelandic, and other European languages, and Japanese is scheduled in the near future.

Magazine Rate Card

GENERAL RATES

RATE BASE: Rates based on a yearly average of 1,100,000 net paid A.B.C.
A member of the Audit Bureau of Circulation

SPACE UNITS	BLACK & WHITE	BLACK & ONE COLOR	FOUR COLOR
1 page	$16,000	$19,630	$23,300
2 columns	11,620	14,560	18,170
½ page	10,130	13,550	17,200
1 column	5,920	9,530	12,180
½ column	3,020		
Covers			
Second Cover			$25,520
Third Cover			23,300
Fourth Cover			27,020

BLEED CHARGE: 15%
AGENCY COMMISSION: 15%
CASH DISCOUNT: 2% 10 days, net 30 days

Bleed accepted in color, black & white, and on covers, at an additional charge of 15%. No charge for gutter bleed in double-page spread.

Premium Positions: A 10% premium applies to advertising units positioned on pages 1, 2, and 3. A surcharge of 5% applies to bleed units in premium positions.

Rate Change Announcements will be made at least two months in advance of the black & white closing date for the issue affected. Orders for issues thereafter at rates then prevailing.

ISSUANCE AND CLOSING DATES

A. On sale date approximately the 15th of month preceding date of issue.

B. Black & white, black & one color, and four-color closing date, 20th of the 3rd month preceding date of issue. Example: Forms for August issue close May 20th.

C. *Orders for cover pages non-cancellable. Orders for all inside advertising units are non-cancellable 15 days prior to their respective closing dates.* Supplied inserts are non-cancellable the 1st of the 4th month preceding month of issue. Options on cover positions must be exercised at least 30 days prior to four-color closing date. If order is not received by such date, cover option automatically lapses.

Figure 20–2

Based on this magazine rate card, what is the cost of a black-and-white half-page ad paid in ten days from issuance of the invoice?

Television Rates

Advertising rates for television also vary with time of day. It is more expensive, for example, to advertise during the prime-time hours of 7 to 11 P.M. (known as Class AA time) than during other hours. The rates charged for other time slots, such as Class A, Class B, Class C, and Class D,

are less because of diminishing viewership. Businesses try to place their advertisements in time slots during which their potential customers will most likely see them.

A business considering the purchase of television time contacts a television media representative. The representative helps the business determine coverage times available. He or she also arranges package deals that can be developed to give the advertiser more advertising spots, or volume or seasonal discounts.

Selection of Promotional Media

The choice of an advertising medium depends on the product to be advertised, the habits and lifestyles of the target audience, and the types of media available in the area. These questions can help determine what type of media to use:

1. Does the medium reach the greatest number of customers at the lowest cost per customer?
2. Does the medium provide opportunity for illustrating the product?
3. Does the medium provide an opportunity to present an adequate selling message?
4. Does advertising in this medium pose any special problems?
5. What is the medium's flexibility in terms of making last-minute changes in the message?
6. Does the medium provide an opportunity to sell the product or just announce its availability?
7. Does the medium provide enough excitement for special promotions?
8. Does the medium fit the image of the business and offer enough prestige and distinction?
9. Does the medium cover the targeted geographical area?

SECTION 20.2 *Review*

1. Name three factors that affect newspaper rates.
2. What is the difference between an open rate and a contract rate?
3. What is the formula for figuring cost per thousand?
4. What determines the rate TV and radio stations charge for advertising?
5. Name three factors that affect an advertiser's choice of promotional media.

Enrichment

1. Assign and review the appropriate activities in the *Student Activity Workbook*.
2. Assign and review the appropriate Critical Thinking questions from the Chapter Review.
3. Assign and review the Building Academic Skills Activities, Application Projects, Linking School to Work Activities, and Performance Assessment from the Chapter Review.
4. Have students watch television or listen to the radio for 20 minutes at three different intervals during the day: in the morning before you go to school or on your way to school, in the early afternoon from 2:00 to 6:00, and in the evening from 7:00 to 10:00. Have students write down what types of products are advertised during these three different time periods. Did the commercials differ at all in their general presentation or length of time from one time period to another? Why were these time periods chosen for these specific products? Have students bring their findings to class for discussion.

Close

Have students complete this statement: The choice of advertising media depends on. . .(the product to be advertised, the habits and lifestyles of the target audience, and the types of media available in the area.)

Caption Answer

The ad would cost $9,927.40 ($10,130 – [$10,130 × .02] = $10,130 – $202.60 = $9,927.40).

Section Review Answers

1. Location, color, and frequency.
2. Open rate is the basic charge. Contract rates provide a discount based upon volume.
3. $\dfrac{\text{cost of the ad} \times 1,000}{\text{circulation}} = \text{cost per thousand (CPM)}$
4. The time of day.
5. The product, the lifestyles of the target audience, and types of media available.

Answers

Vocabulary Review

See Glossary for definitions.

Fact and Idea Review

1. Promotional advertising creates interest in products, introduces new products, presents product information, etc. Institutional advertising creates a favorable impression and goodwill for a business.
2. Print media, broadcast media, specialty media.
3. Advantages: 1. Large readership, a high level of reader involvement. 2. Circulation is known, so businesses can target their advertising to certain geographical areas. 3. Cost is lower than other print media because quality of paper and print is less expensive. 4. Lead time can be as little as 24 to 48 hours. Disadvantages: 1. There is sometimes wasted circulation. 2. Ad life is short as newspapers are thrown away daily. 3. Quality poor in relation to other media.
4. You can select your audience because circulation and characteristics of regular readers are known. Magazines are often read more slowly and thoroughly than newspapers, so information in an ad is more likely to be grasped and retained. Print quality is higher in magazines. Magazines have a long life so ad may be reread.
5. Advertising sent by businesses directly to prospective customers. Examples include newsletters, catalogs, coupons, etc.
6. Outdoor signs are said to mar the scenic views and cause traffic safety concerns.
7. Because of their tremendous availability and popularity.

268

Vocabulary Review

Use the following vocabulary terms in a 250-word paper on advertising media.

promotional advertising
institutional advertising
media
print media
broadcast media
specialty media
cost per thousand (CPM)
network radio advertising
national spot radio advertising
local radio advertising

Fact and Idea Review

1. Explain the differences between promotional and institutional advertising. (Sec. 20.1)
2. Identify three general categories of advertising media. (Sec. 20.1)
3. What are the four principal advantages and three principal disadvantages of using newspaper advertising? (Sec. 20.1)
4. In what respect is magazine advertising superior to newspaper advertising? (Sec. 20.1)
5. What is direct-mail advertising? Give five examples of direct-mail advertising. (Sec. 20.1)
6. Why is outdoor advertising losing popularity in some areas of the country? (Sec. 20.1)
7. What is the major reason that so many businesses use broadcast media for advertising? (Sec. 20.1)
8. What are magazine rates based upon? (Sec. 20.2)
9. Why is a knowledge of cost per thousand rates helpful to newspaper and magazine advertisers? (Sec. 20.2)
10. How do network radio advertising, national spot radio advertising, and local radio advertising differ from each other? (Sec. 20.2)
11. For advertisers, what are the advantages and disadvantages of using run-of-schedule air rates? (Sec. 20.2)
12. What determines the rates charged for television advertising? (Sec. 20.2)

Critical Thinking

1. How would consumer buying habits be different if advertising in all of the forms discussed in this chapter did not exist?

2. Why is institutional advertising necessary? (*Hint:* Think of at least three situations in which promotional advertising would be either inappropriate or inadequate.)
3. Assume you are a member of a legislative committee considering a ban on "junk mail" advertising. What information would you like to have from people on both sides of the issue before making your decision?
4. Will a prime-time television slot always guarantee an advertiser the best results in selling a product? Why or why not?
5. With the advent of multiple TV cable and network channels, television advertisers are confronted with "channel grazers"—people who use their remote control to switch channels to avoid advertising. Come up with one creative way that advertisers might try to limit the amount of channel grazing.

Building Academic Skills

Math

1. Prepare a table or graph comparing the cost per thousand for each of the newspapers below:
   • *Chronicle:* Circulation 1,400,000; cost of ad $1,000
   • *News:* Circulation 750,000; cost of ad $900
   • *Post:* Circulation 575,000; cost of ad $150
2. Calculate the cost per thousand rate for a magazine that has a circulation of 1.5 million and charges $25,000 for a full-page black-and-white ad.

Communication

3. Gather information about a single product from three different advertising sources (for example, the Yellow Pages, a magazine, a newspaper, television, and a billboard). Write a two-page analysis of how these sources differ from each other in their presentation of the product and approach to the consumer.

Human Relations

4. Your company has a hard choice to make—to stick with your current radio ads or switch to a new approach. The current ads feature a humorous character popular with the public. The ads win awards, but they don't sell the product. The new approach features mind-numbing repetition of the product name in an irritating voice. Your market research shows that people hate the voice—and remember the ad (kids in particular like to imitate it). Make your best case for the approach you favor.

8. Circulation, quality of readership, and production technique used.
9. Cost per thousand rates are useful for comparing the relative advertising costs of different newspapers and magazines.
10. Network radio advertising is a broadcast from a studio to all affiliated radio stations throughout the country. National spot radio advertising is used by national firms to advertise on a local, station-by-station basis for selected target markets in the country. Local radio advertising is done by a local business for its target market and is limited to a specific geographical area.
11. A lower rate for air time.
12. Time of day.

Critical Thinking

1. Without the help of advertising, it would be difficult to compare the availability of desired products and to make price comparisons.

Application Projects

1. Look through newspapers and magazines to find examples of promotional and institutional advertising. Clip four appropriate ads and contribute them to a classroom display contrasting the two types of advertising.
2. Prepare an advertising log for one hour of your television viewing. List the products advertised, characterize the advertising approach taken, identify the sponsor as either a national or local advertiser, and describe what you believe to be the target market. Note any trends you see in terms of these factors.
3. For a product of your choice, make some decisions about how to advertise it. Assume that money is no problem.
   a. Bearing your target audience in mind, select the media through which you will advertise. Consider the times at which you would want television and radio ads to run and the size of ads in print media. Choose the publications you think are best suited to reaching your audience.
   b. Decide whether you will use institutional or promotional advertising or a combination of both. Describe your promotional advertising—such as humorous, informational, serious—and your institutional advertising. Explain why they are appropriate for the product and the audience.
   c. If your product will sell better during different seasons, decide when and in which media you will increase your advertising.
   d. At the library, research television and radio costs and the newspaper and magazine rates for the publications you have chosen. If you have chosen direct mail or specialty advertising, research the costs of those. Estimate your advertising budget per month and per year.
4. Using direct-mail advertising you have received as examples, write a direct-mail marketing letter for the following:
   a. a new condominium development,
   b. a record of the month club,
   c. a hiking magazine, and
   d. a charity or special interest group of your choice. As you write each letter, think about the market you would target. Decide what other pieces should go into the package with each letter, such as reply cards or testimonial letters from famous people.
5. Develop an individual advertising prospectus for the Advertising Campaign Event sponsored by National

DECA and used for the Delta Epsilon Chi division. Write National DECA, 1908 Association Drive, Reston, VA 22091-1594 for latest event guidelines.

Linking School to Work

1. Interview your training station sponsor or an immediate supervisor to discover the types of advertising media used to promote your employer's business. Write a short report detailing the results.
2. Bring to class examples of the print advertisements produced by your employer's business. Be prepared to tell the class how often the print ads are run and in what types of print media they appear.

Performance Assessment

Role Play

Situation. You are a sales associate in a newly opened apparel and accessories store. Your manager has asked you to develop a plan for a direct-mail campaign to target new and current customers. Since your store is new, procedures will have to be established to create a customer mailing list.

Evaluation. You will be evaluated on how well you can do the following:

- Explain the advantages of using direct mail.
- Explain how you propose to develop a customer mailing list.
- Identify your specific ideas for a direct-mail campaign including a discussion on the type of mailer you intend to send and your reasons for your choice.

Pictorial Essay

Direct-mail advertising comes to most homes every week. Start looking at the direct mail your family receives. Take five pieces that interest you. Analyze them in terms of artwork and description of the good or service and try to determine why they appeal to you. Create a pictorial essay by attaching your analysis and direct-mail advertising to a poster board.

Complete the Chapter 20 Computer Application that appears in the Student Activity Workbook.

---

2. Students should recognize that institutional advertising attempts to create a favorable impression and goodwill for a company.
3. Answers will vary. However, they should focus on determining what is junk mail and what is legitimate, useful advertising.
4. No. While prime-time viewership is the largest potential viewing audience, it may not be the target market your product needs to reach.
5. Answers will vary.

Building Academic Skills

Math

1. Chronicle:
$$\frac{\$1,000 \times 1,000}{1,400,000} = \$.714$$

News:
$$\frac{\$900 \times 1,000}{750,000} = \$1.20$$

Post:
$$\frac{\$150 \times 1,000}{575,000} = \$.260$$

2. CPM is $16.67
$$\frac{\$25,000 \times 1,000}{1,500,000} = \$16.67$$

Communication

3. Answers depend on the sources students select.

Human Relations

4. Students may suggest that selling the product is most important thus the ad should be changed. Or students may suggest that an entirely new ad be created.

Application Projects

1. Types of advertising will vary.
2. Student answers will vary but should include the elements listed. Students should compare ads with each other.
3. Advertising should be appropriate for the type of product. Students should keep in mind the target audience, type of advertising, seasonal appeal, and ad costs.
4. Direct mail letters should be similar in format to the direct mail examples.
5. Advertising prospectus should follow the latest event guidelines.

Linking School to Work

Answers depend on the work situation.

Performance Assessment

Refer to *DECA Competitive Events Handbook* for evaluation guidelines.

Computer Application

Optional activity. Refer to the *Marketing Software Binder* for template and user information.

Evaluation

Administer the reproducible test for Chapter 20 or construct your own test using the Testmaker software.

Chapter Overview

Chapter 21 introduces the development and execution of print advertisements.

Springboard

Write on the chalkboard:

- Ford Escort (or other car)
- IBM or Apple Computer
- Nike or Reebok Athletic Shoes
- Haagen-Dazs Ice Cream

Ask students to describe what a print ad looks like for each product, based on prior ads seen. Is it usually in color or in black and white? What is the basic mood of the ad? What types of slogans are used?

Prereading

List the section objectives to discuss with students. Have students skim the chapter, looking at the pictures, reading the captions, and noting the heads. Ask questions to ensure that the students have a minimal understanding of the chapter structure.

Preteaching the Vocabulary

Write vocabulary terms for the parts of a print ad in one column on the board and the rest of the vocabulary in another. Pin up a print ad and ask students to identify the parts of each ad and to generate definitions of each term. Help students generate definitions for the second column of vocabulary, using the Glossary as needed.

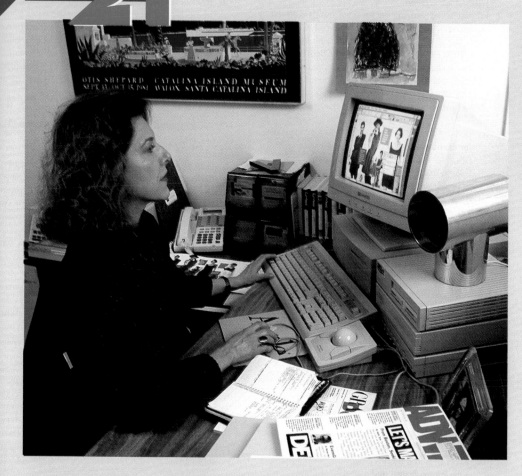

CHAPTER 21

Preparing Print Advertisements

Successful advertising campaigns help sell products. Think of all the ads you've seen in newspapers and magazines that made you want to buy such things as sporting equipment, cosmetics, or new clothes.

How are such ads developed? Who writes them? How do they know which approach to take, what will work, and what won't? How do they think of those catchy slogans and choose the illustrations to go with them?

In this chapter you'll discover answers to all these questions. You'll get information specific enough to allow you to try your own hand at ad writing.

270   Unit 6   *Promotion*

Classroom Management

For the Teacher

- Teacher's Annotated Editions for all workbooks
- Teacher's Manual for *School-to-Work Handbook*
- *Testing Binder*
- *Transparency Binder*
- *Marketing Software Binder*
- *Marketing Career Portfolio*
- *Lesson Plans*

For the Student

- *Student Activity Workbook*
- *Marketing Math Workbook*
- *School-to-Work Handbook*
- *Student Software*
- *International Case Studies*
- *Marketing Career Portfolio*

SECTION 21.1

Objectives

After completing this section, you will be able to

- describe how ads are developed,
- create advertising headlines,
- prepare advertising copy,
- select advertising illustrations, and
- explain the significance of a signature.

Terms to Know

- advertising agencies
- cooperative advertising
- headline
- copy
- illustration
- clip art
- signature
- slogan

The Advertising Agency

After a company decides which product to promote, which print media to use, and how much to spend, the next step is to develop the advertisement. The size and the financial resources of a business usually determines whether a business creates the ad itself or whether it uses an advertising agency.

Advertising agencies are companies that exist solely to help clients sell their products. There are about 10,000 such agencies in the United States, employing only about 100,000 people. So, you can see that advertising agencies represent a fairly small group of specialists—especially when you consider that General Motors, by comparison, employs about 700,000 people.

Most of the major U.S. advertising agencies (the ones that employ the most people and make the most money) are in New York City, Chicago, and Los Angeles. In 1991, one of the largest agencies, Leo Burnett, headquartered in Chicago, employed approximately 4,700 people, had offices in more than 40 countries, and had $3.9 billion in advertising billings.

Advertising agencies are usually organized into four service departments:

1. *Client service* works with agency groups and individual businesses to identify opportunities for advertising. (Many of these employees are called account executives.) This department looks at client needs, creates advertising plans, and coordinates advertising with other promotion activities related to the account.
2. *Creative service* develops the advertising messages and produces the ads. Graphic artists, copywriters, commercial designers, and art directors work together in this department to create advertisements.
3. *Research service* studies target markets, the attitudes of potential customers, and their buying behavior towards a company's products. This department helps determine what type of message will have the greatest appeal for a particular market segment.
4. *Media service* advises clients on their media choices. It suggests how much of the client's advertising budget should be spent on television, radio, newspapers, magazines, and other forms of advertising, such as billboards and direct mail. This department also decides on the timing, placement, and frequency of various advertisements. The media plans developed by this department for a company's products are based on the region, city, number of men and women, income, education, and the reading and television viewing habits of people in the target market.

Cooperative Advertising

Cooperative advertising is an arrangement whereby advertising is paid for by both a manufacturer and a local advertiser. Cooperative advertisements feature both the manufacturer's name or brand name along with the name of the local advertiser. The manufacturer pays part (most commonly 50 percent) of the cost of placing the advertisements.

In a cooperative advertising program, a variety of advertising and promotional materials are usually supplied to the retailer from the manufacturer. These might include the art for newspaper ads with space for the retailer's name and address, television and radio ads with time allotted to insert the retailer's name and location, in-store advertising displays, and posters.

To participate in cooperative advertising, a retailer must sign a contract with the manufacturer. The contract

Focus

Bell Ringer Activity

Tell students to imagine that they manage the Creative Services Department of an advertising agency. The department, which includes graphic artists and copywriters, is responsible for developing the advertising message and producing the ads.

Your client, Hart Manufacturing, has called a meeting for late this afternoon. Your job: generate some ideas for a magazine ad campaign on a night light that's activated by the sound of the human voice.

Have students name the product, and come up with an idea for a photo or illustration, and a catchy slogan. What predominant colors would they use? Would they have a great deal of written copy explaining the product, or very little? Who is the target audience?

Introducing the Section

Review students' answers from the Bell Ringer Activity, which should start them thinking in terms of how the elements of an ad combine to create message, mood, and image—the topic of this section. Tell students to hold on to the information they generate for the Bell Ringer Activity. They may wish to use it in conjunction with Application Project 1 in the Chapter Review or with the Cooperative Thinking Activity in Section 21.2.

Meeting Special Needs

Visually Impaired

Due to the visual nature of print advertising, you may wish to plan for some of the challenges faced by the visually handicapped individuals in your class. In discussing print ads that contain photos and/or illustrations, it may be useful to describe the pictorial portion of the ad out loud, giving verbal descriptions of the shapes and sizes in the picture along with clear descriptions of the total ad.

Teach

Guided Practice

1. Read Section 21.1 with students.

2. Invite a representative from a local ad agency to visit your class to explain the depth and breadth of the agency's business and to discuss the types of advertising it does for various client accounts (the focus on this guest speaker's talk should be print advertising). Particularly discuss the creative teamwork involved in developing ads.

   You may wish to ask the agency to send representatives from more than one department (for example, an account rep, a copywriter, and a graphic artist) to discuss the various aspects of their work. To further extend students' learning, have them take notes on the presentation and write a 150- to 250-word summary of it.

3. For those students planning to participate in DECA's competitive event in advertising, Glencoe's *Advertising Services* by Wray, one of the *Career Competencies in Marketing* series, is an ideal independent study aid. Or, you may wish to use selected chapters from *Advertising Services* to supplement teaching this chapter.

Discussion Starter

In which department in an ad agency would students prefer to work and in what capacity? Why? Based on their answers, what skills will they need to develop to better prepare for this type of work?

A cooperative advertisment **displays a manufacturer's products. It includes both the manufacturer's name or brand name along with the name of the local advertiser. How do manufacturers and retailers benefit from such an arrangement?**

gives the specific conditions for advertising the manufacturer's products in the media. After the advertising is completed, the manufacturer reimburses the retailer for the agreed-upon costs of the campaign.

Developing Print Advertisements

Print advertisements must contain certain essential elements. These include a *headline, copy, illustrations,* and a *signature.*

To communicate successfully, an ad must attract attention, arouse interest, create desire, and finally produce action. To accomplish all of this, each of an ad's key parts must be coordinated with the others.

Headline

The **headline** is the lettering, slogan, or saying that gets the readers' attention, arouses their interest, and leads them to read the rest of the ad. Headlines are responsible for 70 to 80 percent of the sale's effectiveness of most advertisements, so many experts consider them the most important part of a print ad.

Headlines must be attention getters. If they are not, the advertisement may not be read. Here are some innovative and attention-getting headlines:

Just Do It (Nike)

The Flue Season Is Here (St. Peters Chimney Sweep)

Watch What You Eat (Benihana Restaurants)

Sometimes headlines have a subheadline to clarify or expand on the main idea expressed in the headline. Subheadlines are normally found in smaller type close to the headline. Here are some examples of subheadlines used to expand on the headline:

Pride & Joy (headline)
Introducing Kids of Color from Playskool (subheadline)

13 Hour Sale (headline)
Hudson's Great Savings Storewide! (subheadline)

A headline stresses one primary benefit of a product. So, it should be brief, easy to understand, and powerful. Most headlines are brief because most people cannot take in more than seven words at one time. Here are some examples of well-written headlines that use seven or fewer words:

Kodak Film…Because Time Goes By (Kodak)

Life in the Multicultural MARKETPLACE

Follow the Bouncing Ball

Attempting to produce print ads for Arabic-speaking Middle Eastern countries can be a disorienting experience for the uninitiated. To start, Arabic is read from right to left, not left to right as English is. Pictorial sequences likewise must be shown in what an English speaker would consider reverse order. One U.S. maker of laundry detergent learned about these differences the embarrassing way. His company prepared an ad for an Arab client that contained a series of illustrations. The first box on the left featured soiled clothes; the middle box, detergent; and the last box on the right, clean clothes. To the client, it appeared that the manufacturer's product made clean clothes dirty!

Caption Answer

The manufacturers can promote their products and the retailers can promote their stores while sharing the cost of advertising.

Feature Note

While Arabic writing is read from right to left, Chinese writing reads from top to bottom. Ask students to imagine the implications of producing advertising for products to be exported to China. (Would need to be sure content would not be misconstrued if layout features a pictorial idea with a story line read in English from left to right.)

Do The Ripe Thing (California Tree Fruit Agreement)

In a recent study, creative directors from major advertising agencies analyzed award-winning print ads to determine what their headlines had in common. They discovered that 32 percent of the headlines used familiar sayings with a twist. For example, a headline used by a boot manufacturer stated,

> Most Boots Have a Hard Time
> Coping with the Realities of Life.

About 23 percent of the headlines made use of opposites, such as "up/down" and "lie/truth." For example, a ski lodge ran this headline on its print ad:

> After a Day of Downhill Skiing,
> Getting a Fine Meal Shouldn't Be an Uphill Battle.

Other headlines reviewed by the creative directors used these techniques to attract attention:

- news and information to announce a new product,
- shock or surprise treatment of a subject to arouse attention or emotion,
- questioning to get the reader involved, and
- arousing curiosity by using such phrases as "how to" or "you should know."

Real World

Filling the Bill

Inflated ad claims are at least as old as the Civil War. It was around that time in our country's history that traveling theater troupes put out word of coming attractions by tacking up posters, or bills, in towns where they would soon be appearing. The shows seldom lived up to the fantastic claims made in these ads. The expression *fill the bill,* meaning *deliver what was promised,* remains with us to this day.

Here are some other techniques you can use when writing headlines:

1. *Alliteration* (repeating initial consonant sounds)—Ruffles Have Ridges
2. *Paradox* (a seeming contradiction that could be true)—It Will Fill You Up, But It Won't Weigh You Down
3. *Rhyme*—Bounty…The Quicker Picker-Upper
4. *Pun* (a humorous use of a word that suggests two or more of its meanings or the meaning of another word similar in sound)—Every Litter Bit Hurts
5. *Play on Words*—For Soft Babies and Baby Soft Hands

More than 80 percent of the people who look at a print advertisement just read the headlines. Thus, you want your headlines to be powerful enough to draw potential customers into reading the copy. Here are some suggestions that will help you write powerful headlines:

1. Every headline should have a single focus or main idea. Before writing a headline, try to sum up the main idea in a single sentence. This technique will help you remain focused on the subject and thus produce a headline with impact.
2. Attract readers with one or more of the three most powerful words in advertising—*new, now,* and *free.*
3. Headlines should be directed to the reader and appeal to the self-interest of the potential customer.

A pun is used in this ad to creat humor. How might you rewrite this ad using alliteration, a paradox, rhyme, or a play on words?

Chapter 21 *Preparing Print Advertisements* **273**

L1 Communication Skills

Advertising copy should always be written in the active voice. Have students rewrite these sentences in the active voice.

1. SensorExcel™, the next revolution in shaving closeness, is brought to you by Gillette.
2. One Hundred Twenty images selected from Corel Professional Photos are profiled in *The World's Best Digital Photographs* (coffee-table book and companion CD-ROM).
3. A 3800 V engine, air conditioning, and many other luxury appointments are included as standard features of the Buick LeSabre.

L2 Communication Skills

Ask students to combine each group of sentences to create one sentence that is written in the active voice.

Group 1
1. The finest selection and quality of internationally sourced leather sofas and sectionals are now offered by Jennifer Leather.
2. Jennifer Leather also offers internationally sourced loveseats, chairs, and ottomans.

Group 2
1. Esquire is an extensive collection of handsome timepieces.
2. These timepieces have quality features and details.
3. The features and details of Esquire timepieces are rarely found in watches so affordable.

L3 Communication Skills

Have students collect and critique a variety of print ads discussing the use of active and passive voice.

Teach (Cont'd.)

Independent Practice

1. Assign and review the Chapter 21 Case Study in the *International Case Studies* workbook.
2. Have each student review your local newspaper for one example of cooperative advertising. For each ad they should identify the type of business, the local merchant, and the manufacturer who sponsored the ad. They should also identify each element of the ad (for example, headline, copy, signature, etc.).

Assess

Evaluation

Assign and review the 21.1 Review.

Reteaching

1. Assign and review the vocabulary terms for this section.
2. Assign and review Fact and Idea Review questions 1–7 from the Chapter Review.
3. Show students several ads from a magazine and a newspaper. Have them identify the parts of each ad and answer the following questions about each:
   - What technique does the headline use to get the reader involved (news and information to announce a new product, shock or surprise, etc.)?
   - What figurative techniques were used to create the headlines (for example, alliteration, rhyme, etc.)?
   - Read the ad copy to the students. Is it written in the form of a conversation or written to educate the consumer?

4. Make your headline long enough to feature one product benefit, but short enough (try to keep most headlines to seven words or less) to encourage people to read the rest of the advertisement.
5. Arouse reader curiosity by promising something—a free offer, more miles per gallon, better service, fewer cavities, etc.
6. Use simple language. Readers will mistrust or misunderstand ads with complex headlines. By using simple language in headlines, you can ensure that nearly everyone will understand your message and no one will resent it.

Copy

The **copy** is the selling message in a written advertisement. It should directly expand on the information in the headline or the product shown in the illustration. It should also stress the benefits and features of the product advertised.

Good copy, like a good headline, is simple and direct. Copy can vary from a few words to several paragraphs. Copy does not have to be extensive as long as it gets the message across.

Copy can be written in the form of a conversation, or it can be written as an educational tool. It can be a testimonial to the benefits of using the product, or it can describe how an institution can help you.

Copy should appeal to the senses. Through the words used, the customer should be able to see, hear, touch, taste, and/or even smell a product.

Your copy will be competing with hundreds of other advertisers for the reader's attention, so it must be dramatic. It should:

- establish contact with the reader,
- create awareness,
- arouse interest, and
- build preference for the product.

Give your copy news value by providing specific information. Tell the who, what, when, why, where, and how of your product. Remember, too, that

facts about your product are more powerful than claims. If possible, use case histories, statistics, performance figures, dates, and quotes from experts.

Key words used in copy, such as *compare, introducing, now, price, save, easy,* and *new,* establish immediate contact with the reader. They arouse interest and create awareness and desire.

Advertising copy should be written in the active voice to make it more immediate. In other words, you would write, "This item will help you," rather than "You will be helped by this item." Try to use warm, personal language and expressions familiar to your target audience.

Finally, the copy should ask for action. It helps to include a penalty for not acting now. Words such as *today, act now, before it's too late,* and *without delay* help create action.

An example of an ad with well-written copy is the National Wildlife Federation ad shown here. The copy explains that wildlife, like this baby tamarin monkey, is quietly disappearing. The ad urges readers to find out how they can protect endangered species by contacting the Federation. The copy is simple and direct. It is dramatic, establishes contact with the reader, creates awareness, and arouses interest. It is written in the active voice. Most importantly, it tells readers how to take action.

Illustration

The **illustration** is the photograph or drawing used in a print advertisement. Its primary function is to attract attention, arouse a desire to buy, and encourage a purchase decision for the advertised product. It should also tie into the headline and copy. The illustration, together with the headline, should lead the potential customer to read at least the first sentence of the copy.

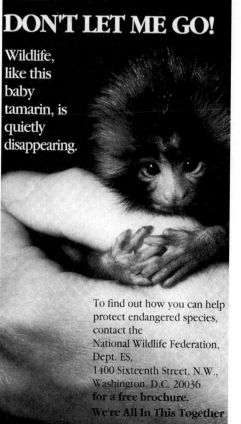

DON'T LET ME GO!

Wildlife, like this baby tamarin, is quietly disappearing.

To find out how you can help protect endangered species, contact the National Wildlife Federation, Dept. ES, 1400 Sixteenth Street, N.W., Washington, D.C. 20036 **for a free brochure. We're All In This Together**

Working for the Nature of Tomorrow®

NATIONAL WILDLIFE FEDERATION

The elements of a printed ad include the headline, the copy, the illustration, the signature, and sometimes a subheadline. Why do you think a subheadline was used in this case?

More About

Advertising Agencies

In 1994, the Leo Burnett Company Inc. won 15 first place statuettes at the 23rd Annual Mobius Advertising Awards. That same year it pioneered an innovation in television advertising during the Super Bowl in which it produced and broadcast a commercial during the game for its client, Reebok shoes.

Caption Answer

To expand on the main idea expressed in the headline.

THE RULES HAVE CHANGED.

Talk trucks and two names come to mind. Dodge is about to change all that, with a pick-up that challenges all the rules. Beginning with the new Dodge Magnum V-10† – with 450 lb ft of torque, 300 hp, and over 13,000 lbs of towing capability.

All this horsepower is just for starters. Because the same pickups that, overall, carry the most powerful line of engines also carry the most safety features – with a standard driver's airbag and available four-wheel anti-lock brakes.*

There's no law that says trucks have to ride like trucks. That's why we gave our new pickup a new frame and improved suspension travel. We just wouldn't hear of making a noisy pickup, either. Fact is, we worked very hard to make our new Ram a standard for quietness.

Pickups have always been workhorses. Now they're a convenient place to conduct business. With an available center console in the front seat. An ingenious storage system available behind the seats. And, in back, a set of tie downs so well engineered, they can support the weight of the entire truck.

We've provided an extra measure of protection, too – using more exterior galvanized steel than any other full-size pickup on the road, and making substantial use of anti-chip materials. The rules have changed.

DODGE RAM

THE NEW DODGE
A DIVISION OF THE CHRYSLER CORPORATION

For still more information, call 1-800-4-A-DODGE. *Now available for order. *Always wear your seat belt for a fully effective airbag. ABS available on all 1500 and 2500 pickups.

Illustrations are a major element of print ads. What function do the photos in this ad serve?

The illustration is usually the first thing a reader sees in the ad. So, it should transmit a total message that would be hard to communicate with words alone. Illustrations should show:

- the features of the product,
- how the product works,
- the advantages of owning the product,
- the safety features of the product,
- the possible uses for the product,
- the need for the product, and
- an image associated with the product, such as prestige, status, or leisure.

Photographs should be used in advertisements when a sense of reality is necessary. Sometimes it's important for the customer to know exactly what the product looks like or how it's used. For example, consumer products such as clothing, cosmetics, jewelry, furniture, or stereos should be illustrated with photographs.

Drawings are often used to show a part of a product that the reader would normally not see. For example, cutaway drawings of such products as cars, equipment, and tools help show important features not visible in a photo.

Businesses often get photographs from suppliers, manufacturers, or trade associations. In addition, professional photographers are often hired to photograph situations or products. The photos used in advertisements should be sharp and clear with good contrast between light and dark areas.

Although original photos and artwork are ideal for illustrations, businesses often use *clip art* in their print advertisements. **Clip art** consists of stock drawings,

Chapter 21 *Preparing Print Advertisements* **275**

Enrichment

1. Assign and review the appropriate activities in the *Student Activity Workbook*.
2. Assign and review the appropriate Critical Thinking questions from the Chapter Review.
3. Like everything else, the content and tone of print advertising has changed much since the turn of the century. Have students research the evolution of print advertising with respect to such things as illustrative style, style of typeface used, amount of copy in the ad, and trends in layout. (Ads in the early part of this century, for example, contained a great deal of copy in very small typeface, as compared to modern ads which contain relatively little copy. They were likely to be elaborately illustrated and thus appeared to be more art than advertisement. Ad copy was frequently written to educate.)

   Suggest to students that they make photostats of ads from each era for comparison and contrast. Have them make some predictions about how print advertising will further evolve as we head into the next century.

Close

Have students complete this statement: The six possible elements in a print ad are. . .(headline, copy, illustration, clip art, signature, and slogan.)

Lifelong Learning

Preparing Print Advertisements

Having the ability to dissect a written advertisement can be useful to students in a wide variety of situations both on and off the job. Knowing the components of written advertisements can help individuals evaluate a variety of products fairly, and teach them not to rely on the visual content alone.

Caption Answer

The photos illustrate the features of the product, how the product works, the safety features of the product, and the image associated with the product.

Bell Ringer Activity

In Chapter 10 students did proofreading exercises in the Communications Skills Activities in Section 10.3. They should still have the proofreader's marks they were instructed to find and copy in their notebooks. Give each student a copy of a print ad that you have rewritten to contain several errors, including an error in the price of the product. Make this a fairly difficult exercise with subtle errors. Allow 15 minutes for students to proofread the ad.

Introducing the Section

Review the Bell Ringer Activity. Tell students that this is not just a pedantic exercise; proofing ads for correctness is critical. Ask students to tell you some of the negative consequences of errors printed in ads. (Incorrect prices could result in customers demanding to be given a product at the advertised price if the price is incorrectly printed as lower than it is supposed to be. This results in lost revenue if the business acquiesces to giving the lower price, and poor public relations if it doesn't.)

In this section, students will look at how layout contributes to the overall print advertising message. They will also discover the critical importance of proofing print ads.

---

photographs, and headlines clipped from a printed sheet and pasted into an advertisement. Because clip art is ready for reproduction and printing, it is inexpensive, quick, and easy to use.

When designing advertisements, pay careful attention to where the reader's eyes will be directed. The best ads contain *lines of force* that guide the reader to the copy through illustrations. For example, the models in photos or drawings should be facing or looking at the copy. A model in an illustration that looks out of the ad space moves the reader's eyes away from the copy.

Whether photographs or drawings, illustrations determine the image a business projects to the public. After a business selects an illustration style, it normally does not change that style for a period of time. Thus, to maintain its image, a business should not only select its illustrations carefully but also periodically evaluate them for consistency.

Signature

No advertisement is complete without its sponsor. The **signature,** or logotype (logo), is the distinctive identification symbol for a business.

In national ads, the signature is the name of the firm. The signature in local retail ads usually includes the business's name, address, telephone number, business hours, and slogan.

A well-designed signature gets instant recognition for a business. Even though readers may not be interested in the particular product advertised at the moment, the signature should be so easy to remember that they will identify with it at a later time.

Slogans are often used with the signature to create a distinct image for the company, its products, or its corporate mission. A slogan is a catch phase or small group of words that are combined in a special way to present an advertising message. An example of an advertising slogan is, *"I love what you do for me—Toyota."*

SECTION 21.1 *Review*

1. Identify the four major service departments found in most advertising agencies.
2. Why are headlines considered by many to be the most important part of print advertisements?
3. What is the main purpose of advertising copy?
4. What should illustrations show about a product?
5. What is the signature in an advertisement?

276   Unit 6   *Promotion*

SECTION 21.2

Objectives

After completing this section, you will be able to

- explain the importance of advertising layouts,
- tell the advantages and disadvantages of using color in advertising,
- describe how typefaces and type sizes can be changed to add variety and emphasis to print advertisements, and
- explain how to check advertising proofs.

Terms to Know

- ad layout
- advertising proof

Developing Print Advertising Layouts

An **ad layout** is a rough draft that shows the general arrangement and appearance of a finished ad. It clearly indicates the position of the headline, illustration, copy, and signature.

Whether you are dealing with a newspaper salesperson, a magazine representative, or a printer, each will probably need only a rough draft to complete a print advertisement. So, you do not have to be an artist to develop an ad layout. You do need to make sure, however, that the information is correct.

Ad layouts should be developed with the following general ideas in mind:

1. They should be prepared in exactly the same size as the final advertisement.
2. Illustrations should be large enough to show all product features.
3. The ad should make generous use of white space for an uncluttered look.
4. The image projected in the layout should be appropriate for the target audience.
5. The *typeface* (style of printing type) and size should be easy to read and appropriate for the target audience.

Section Review Answers

1. *Client service:* Identifies opportunities for advertising. *Creative service:* Creates advertising messages and produces ads. *Research service:* Studies target markets, the attitudes of potential customers, and buying behavior. *Media service:* Makes decisions about client's advertising budget as well as timing and frequency of ads.

2. Seventy to eighty percent of sales effectiveness.
3. To stress the benefit of advertised product.
4. Product features, how it works, advantages, possible uses, safety features, need, and image associated with product.
5. Distinctive identification symbol.

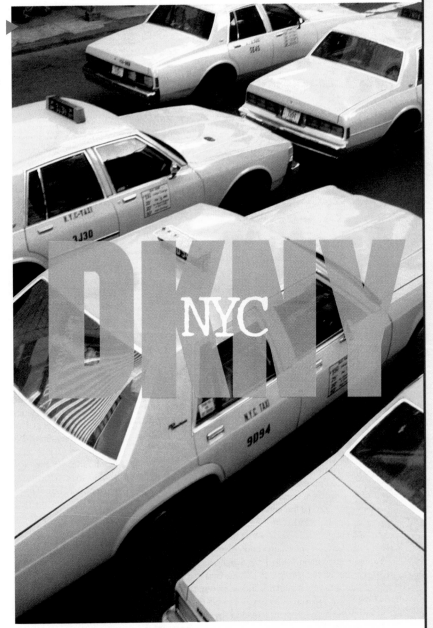

Color can make all the difference in an ad. This DKNY ad ran in full-color in magazines. Why don't all advertisers choose to run ads in color?

Using Color in Print Advertisements

A little color makes an advertisement stand out on the printed page. Also, color ads draw higher response rates than black-and-white ads because they are more realistic. In fact, research has proven that color newspaper ads can increase the reading of copy by as much as 80 percent over black-and-white ads. Studies have also shown that because of the response rates full-color ads are usually more cost effective than two-color ads (black plus a color).

Although color adds excitement and realism, each added color raises the cost of the advertisement. Adding a second color alone can increase costs by as much as 35 percent. Therefore, when businesses use color in advertisements, the added cost must be continually measured against the desired results.

Chapter 21   *Preparing Print Advertisements*   **277**

Teach

Guided Practice

1. Read Section 21.2 with students.
2. Have students read aloud the Case Study and review the answers in class.
3. MarkEd Resource Center, (800) 448-0398, offers LAP Modules and Videos appropriate for use with this lesson.
4. Assign and review the appropriate activity in the *School-to-Work Handbook*.

Discussion Starter

A serif typeface such as New Times Roman has a short light line projecting from the top and bottom of a main stroke of a letter. A sans serif typeface such as Modern is perfectly plain, with lines of uniform thickness and without serifs. Ask students if they can tell the difference between serif and sans serif.

Critical Thinking

Reds, oranges, and yellows are considered aggressive, intense, warm colors that make things appear to advance. Greens, blues, and violets are considered tranquil, cool colors that make things appear to recede. If you were creating a four-color ad for each of these new products, what predominant colors would you use and why?

- a new sports car whose selling points are its sleek design and its ability to go from 1 mph to 60 mph in a matter of seconds; backpacks for college students;
- boxed chocolate candy advertised as "fit for royalty";
- a shampoo and hair conditioner combined in one product and advertised as "gentle enough for the baby in you";
- room air freshener with the smell of springtime.

More About

Using Color in Print Advertisements

Use of color in ads is on the rise around the world. In Asia, consumer markets are rapidly expanding while the level of illiteracy remains high. This requires advertisers to communicate their messages in a way other than through words. Color is an ideal solution as it can be used to illustrate emotions in a way that is easily understood.

Caption Answer

Advertisers sometimes run ads in black and white because color ads are more expensive to run.

Cooperative Learning

Using a personal computer, create 10 to 15 sets of alphabets, each one in a different typeface and with three or four point sizes such as 12 pt., 18 pt., etc. Each set should contain:

- a Roman alphabet of upper-case and lower-case;
- an italic alphabet of upper- and lower-case letters;
- a sample of a block of ad copy.

For example:

Bookman Old Style 12 point

Aa, Bb, Cc, Dd, Ee, Ff, Gg, Hh, Ii, Jj, Kk, Ll, Mm, Nn, Oo, Pp, Qq, Rr, Ss, Tt, Uu, Vv, Ww, Xx, Yy, Zz.

Aa, Bb, Cc, Dd, Ee, Ff, Gg, Hh, Ii, Jj, Kk, Ll, Mm, Nn, Oo, Pp, Qq, Rr, Ss, Tt, Uu, Vv, Ww, Xx, Yy, Zz.

The battery just died. And Seiko Kinetic is born. The quartz watch that doesn't need a battery. Ever. Its tiny motion-powered generator gets its energy from the natural motion of your arm. Like when you scratch your head and say, *"How'd they do that?"*

Divide students into groups of four to six. Review the chapter section entitled "Selecting Typefaces and Type Sizes for Print Advertisements." Give each group one product for which they must develop the headline, a catchy slogan, and the copy for an ad. Then have them choose the typeface(s) that best evokes the mood, image, and message of the ad.

You may wish to give photostats of these alphabets to each student so they can use them in developing their ads for Application Project 1.

278

CASE STUDY

Newspapers in the Information Age

Newspapers have traditionally been a major form of advertising media in the United States. In fact, retail print advertising accounts for more than half of most local newspaper revenue.

However, newspapers today are facing some stiff challenges from other forms of media. Many advertisers now perceive broadcast media, direct mail, and interactive media as better vehicles for promoting their products. They believe these forms of media allow for greater advertising creativity. Newspapers by contrast, say the critics, offer advertisers little in the way of innovation.

Another problem confronting newspapers is reduced market penetration. At the end of World War II readership was at an all time high. In 1947, there were approximately 39 million households. Most households then subscribed to both a morning and evening newspaper. Newspaper circulation totaled 52.5 million. Newspapers enjoyed a market penetration of 135 percent, according to the Audit Bureau of Circulation. Today, newspaper market penetration has slid from 135 percent to 65 percent.

Furthermore, a study conducted by the American Society of Newspaper Editors found that 55 percent of U.S. adults read a paper nearly every day and have a high regard for daily news. But another 19 percent have little interest in newspapers and are poor new reader prospects. An additional 13 percent are nonreaders.

Attracting readers and convincing advertisers to stay with newspaper advertising is causing many newspapers to try new innovations. Newspapers are focusing on areas such as design, circulation, value-added programs, national advertising, and electronic technology and color production quality. For example, the *Spokesman-Review*

in Spokane, Washington, now offers two Cityline audiotex services and caller-paid 900-number lines for horoscopes and weather information. People can also call Cityline to order concert and special events tickets.

Another hot trend for newspapers is the voice personal system. Personal ads can be used for renting an apartment, job hunting, and finding a date. Unlike the more traditional classified ads, the newspaper voice personal ad is free to the customer. Respondents to the ad, however, pay the newspaper's ad charges which are directly billed to their monthly telephone bill.

Fax machines are also being used by some newspapers. Employment and real estate ads are available to readers by using a national fax service. Companies, such as Classifacts, headquartered in Denver, contract with newspapers to sell real estate information to a national audience. Newspaper readers who are moving can use the service and can find out about available real estate in other cities.

Newspapers are also working more with local retailers to build customer databases. For example, the *Denver Post* has created databases for editors and advertisers to selectively target potential customers.

Will these innovations be enough to save the newspaper industry from declining advertising revenues? Confidence in the industry by industry insiders seems shaky. In a 1994 survey of 1,000 randomly selected newspaper editors, publishers, and advertising managers, 70 percent of the respondents said they believe the industry is "somewhat healthy" now, but only 54 percent believe that this will be the case in 10 years.

278 Unit 6 *Promotion*

■■ *Case Study Review*

1. Why do some critics view newspapers as "ancient and obsolete"?
2. What strengths do newspapers have as an information and advertising source?
3. Speculate why industry insiders are somewhat concerned about future newspaper revenues.

A MATTER OF ETHICS

4. Do you think that it is ethical for newspapers and retailers to share information about customers to build databases? Explain.

Case Study Answers

1. Critics view newspapers as ancient and obsolete because they offer little in the way of innovation. Other forms of media allow for greater advertising creativity.
2. The strength of the newspaper is that it is published everyday, it has a high reader involvement, newspaper circulation is known, the cost of advertising is low, and newspaper ads can be timely.
3. Industry outsiders are concerned about stiff challenges from other forms of media and reduced market penetration.
4. Answers will vary. Some may feel it is ethical to use consumer information to build databases; others may feel it is an invasion of privacy.

BRIGHT IDEAS

The Improbable Spokesperson

Met Life is an insurance company. Snoopy is a cartoon dog, a creation of Charles Schulz of Peanuts fame. What could they possibly have in common? At first glance, there isn't much. Yet in print and television ads, they have enjoyed a long and successful partnership.

Snoopy is the official spokesperson for Met Life. He puts a warm and friendly face on what would otherwise be just another corporation dealing in an incomprehensible product. By doing this, he makes the company more accessible to the public. He gives it a personality. Snoopy, the cartoon character—loyal, honest, trustworthy—imparts those same characteristics to Met Life. If you doubt that, listen to the message: "If you're looking for an insurance company you can trust..." That's a lot of responsibility for a little dog.

Creativity Challenge Form teams of 3–5 people, and try some advertising matches of your own. Try to pair products that don't currently use spokespeople in their ads with the most unusual but effective personalities you can think of. Spokespersons can be real people, historical figures, fictional characters, or cartoon characters. Prepare a headline for an ad and any copy that helps establish the connection between the spokesperson you select and the product.

Selecting Typefaces and Type Sizes for Print Advertisements

There are a variety of typefaces and type sizes available for use in print ads. Advertisers should make sure that the size of the type and the typefaces they select are appropriate for the business and for the target audience, yet distinctive, too. Different typefaces and type sizes can affect the way a reader feels about an advertisement. For example, a typeface that is too small or difficult to read will lower the readership of an ad. A study done by the Newspaper Advertising Bureau found that nearly one-third of readers over 65 had trouble reading newspaper type. This means that some one-third of newspaper readers over 65 may not be reading ads at all unless they have large, simple type and a good, uncluttered design.

In general, print advertisers should use one typeface for headlines and prices and another typeface for copy. You can add variety and emphasis by using different sizes, italics, and boldface versions of the two basic typefaces selected for the advertisement.

Checking Advertising Proofs

When advertisements are given to a newspaper or magazine staff for preparation, an advertising proof is developed. The **advertising proof** shows exactly how an ad will appear when printed.

The advertising proof is sent to the advertiser for review and approval. The advertiser carefully checks the proof to make sure that the ad was done exactly as planned. It is particularly important to make sure that all prices are accurate and all brand names are correctly spelled. If errors are found in the proof, the errors are marked and returned to the newspaper or magazine publisher for correction.

Before giving final approval to a written advertisement, the advertiser should do one final evaluation on it by answering these questions:

1. Is the ad bold enough to stand out on a page, even if it is placed next to other ads?
2. Does the headline arouse interest and attract attention?
3. Is the illustration large enough and done well enough to highlight the product?
4. Is the signature plate apparent and distinctive?
5. Is the copy simple, direct, and understandable?
6. Does the layout guide the reader to and through the copy?
7. Are the typefaces and type sizes easy to read? Is the ad uncluttered?
8. Does the ad successfully communicate the intended message? Is the image projected appropriate for the target audience?

SECTION 21.2

Review

1. What is an ad layout? What are five things you should keep in mind when developing ad layouts?
2. What is one advantage to using color in print advertisements?
3. How can variety be added to the type selected for print advertising?
4. What should an advertiser check for on an advertising proof?

Chapter 21   *Preparing Print Advertisements*   **279**

Independent Practice

1. Assign and review the appropriate Case Study in the *International Case Studies* workbook.
2. Using *The Career Directory* series or the *Encyclopedia of Careers and Vocational Guidance*, have students explore a career-sustaining job in advertising. Have them write a 250-word paper describing the job.

Assess

Evaluation

Assign and review the 21.2 Review.

Reteaching

1. Assign and review the vocabulary terms for this section.
2. Assign and review Fact and Idea Review questions 8–11 from the Chapter Review.
3. Review with students the five points for creating good ad layouts that are given in the section.

Enrichment

1. Assign and review the appropriate activities in the *Student Activity Workbook.*
2. Assign and review the appropriate Critical Thinking questions from the Chapter Review.
3. Assign and review the Building Academic Skills Activities, the Application Projects, Linking School to Work Activities, and Performance Assessment from the Chapter Review.

Close

Have students complete this statement: Before giving final approval to a written ad, the advertiser should answer these questions:. . .(Questions are listed under the head "Checking Advertising Proofs.")

Answers

Vocabulary Review

Crossword puzzles will vary.

Fact and Idea Review

1. Creative services department develops words and art for ads.
2. Because both manufacturers and retailers take part in it and reap benefits.
3. Headline, copy, illustration, and signature.
4. Because most people cannot remember more than seven words at a time.
5. Possibilities include: alliteration, paradox, rhyme, pun, and play on words.
6. Photos are used when sense of reality is necessary. Drawings are used to show part of a product or technical feature that customer would normally not see in photo.
7. Signature in local ad usually includes business name/address, telephone number, business hours, and slogan. In national ads, signature includes name of firm and possibly trademark and slogan.
8. Layouts should be prepared the same size as final advertisement. Illustrations should be large enough to show all product's features. Ad should make generous use of white space for an uncluttered look. Image projected in layout should be appropriate for target audience. Typeface should be easy to read and appropriate.
9. Color makes an ad stand out, draws a higher response rate, and adds excitement and realism to an ad.
10. Typeface should be appropriate for both business and target audience.
11. Errors are marked and returned to the publisher for correction.

280

Vocabulary Review

Construct a crossword puzzle using all the following vocabulary terms. Below the puzzle, include appropriate clues for each term.

advertising agencies
cooperative advertising
headline
copy
illustration
clip art
signature
slogan
ad layout
advertising proof

Fact and Idea Review

1. What tasks are performed by the creative services department? (Sec. 21.1)
2. What is "cooperative" about cooperative advertising? (Sec. 21.1)
3. What are the four essential elements of a written advertisement? (Sec. 21.1)
4. Why should headlines consist of no more than seven words? (Sec. 21.1)
5. Identify three techniques you can use to develop attention-getting headlines. (Sec. 21.1)
6. What are the two types of illustrations used in print ads and when should each be used? (Sec. 21.1)
7. In an ad, what is included with a signature? (Sec. 21.1)
8. List four principles that should be followed in developing print advertising layouts. (Sec. 21.2)
9. Give three reasons for using color in print advertisements. (Sec. 21.2)
10. What should advertisers make sure of when selecting type? (Sec. 21.2)
11. What should an advertiser do if he or she finds an error on an advertising proof? (Sec. 21.2)

Critical Thinking

1. Discuss the advantages and disadvantages for both manufacturer and retailer in a cooperative advertising arrangement.
2. Why do you think supermarkets, local banks, and travel agencies frequently use print advertising?
3. Why would a business develop different print ads for the same product if it advertised that product in both newspapers and magazines?

4. What special concerns would you have in designing a print ad for a product used by senior citizens?
5. Advertisers often debate whether the price of the product should be included in an ad. How would you determine when price should or should not be included in print advertisements?

Building Academic Skills

Math

1. You are checking proofs for the advertising flyer your sporting goods store puts out monthly, a portion of which appears below. Do you have any corrections?

HORIZON
Wide Angle

Binoculars (with case)

Sale Price $169.99
Less Rebate (20%) 34.00

Price after rebate

$149.99

TUFFY
Tennis Balls

3 Tubes

$7.75

That's only $2.88 per tube!
(regularly $2.98)

PRICES VALID THRU SEP. 31

Communication

2. From your local newspaper or a magazine, select three ads that use illustration primarily to establish mood. Clip the ads and mount them on individual sheets of paper. Then, for each, write a paragraph describing the tone you think the ad's sponsor was trying to set.

Critical Thinking

1. Advantages and disadvantages are listed under the head Cooperative Advertising in Section 1.
2. The primary trading area is well-known, which allows these businesses to target customers effectively with print advertising. These businesses frequently run weekly and monthly specials, coupons, and discounts. Print media, such as newspapers, are read daily by many, so they provide a way to get an immediate response. These businesses also attempt to mass market their products, and print advertising can reach all classes of consumers.
3. Businesses might develop different print ads for the same product in an attempt to reach different target markets. Newspapers are mass marketed and are read by all types of people in a certain area, while magazines tend to attract certain target segments based upon the magazines content and reader interest.

3. Identify five household or consumer products you are familiar with and develop advertising headlines for each. Base your headlines on opposite words such as *up/down, hot/cold,* or *inside/outside.*

Human Relations

4. A customer wishes to purchase an item that was advertised improperly in a print advertisement. The item actually costs more than the advertised price. When told about the higher price the customer is upset and angry, but still wants the product. What procedures would you use to calm the customer and still complete the sale?

Application Projects

1. Select a product. Then develop an original headline and copy using the techniques and suggestions identified in this chapter.
2. Collect advertising slogans or advertising headlines for use in an unofficial class quiz. Write each slogan or headline on a note card, along with the name of the sponsoring company. Read each slogan aloud and have your classmates identify the business using it. Examples:

Don't Leave Home Without It (American Express)

Have It Your Way (Burger King)

We Try Harder (Avis)

3. There are five techniques that can help you write memorable headlines: alliteration, paradox, rhyme, puns, and play on words. Develop two headlines using each of these techniques.
4. Prepare an ad layout announcing the grand opening of a new sporting goods store in your community. Be sure to include the following information:
   a. the actual headline,
   b. the location of any illustrations,
   c. the location of copy,
   d. any introductory offers and special pricing that will be featured, and
   e. a signature plate including the store location and hours.

Linking School to Work

Collect a print advertisement from your place of business and evaluate the headline, copy, illustration, and signature for completeness and appropriateness. Be prepared to share your findings with the class.

Performance Assessment

Role Play

Situation. You are employed as a marketing ad coodinator for a restaurant chain. Currently your restaurant is running a print ad that shows a pair of elderly spinsters who bumble their way through the restaurant's menu, treating the daily specials as though they were classified by the military. The dialogue is filled with slips of the tongue, memory lapses, and muddled thinking— all of which the general public apparently finds both amusing and persuasive (purchase of the specials is up by 30 percent). However, members of a local senior citizens group are not amused. They have complained about the ad. You have been asked to create a new ad that targets senior citizens. After developing a layout of your ad you have been asked to present it to the marketing manager explaining the strengths of the ad.

Evaluation. You will be evaluated on how well you can do the following:

- Create an effective advertising headline.
- Prepare advertising copy.
- Select advertising illustrations.
- Use a signature.
- Explain the reasons why each element of your ad is effective.

Public Speaking

Go through magazines and newspapers you usually read. Pick out ads that do and do not appeal to you and separate them into two piles. Analyze the ads and write short paragraphs explaining why they did or did not capture your interest. Then give a five-minute speech to the class explaining how you would change the ads you didn't like in order to appeal to the market you represent.

Complete the Chapter 21 Computer Application that appears in the Student Activity Workbook.

tube. September only has 30 days.

Communication

2. Answers will vary depending on the ads students choose.
3. Headlines should be written according to the guidelines in the chapter.

Human Relations

4. The student should act professionally and try to meet the customers needs. The student should probably tell the customer that he or she will find the manager to help rectify the problem.

Application Projects

1. Headlines should be based on the guidelines in the chapter. Headlines should clearly be related to the product.
2. Slogans will vary. Ask students what elements make slogans memorable.
3. Students should identify the type of headline technique they have used.
4. Ad layouts will vary but should follow the guidelines discussed in the text.

Linking School to Work

Answers depend on the work situation.

Performance Assessment

Refer to *DECA Competitive Events Handbook* for evaluation guidelines for both Role Play and Public Speaking exercises.

 Computer Application

Optional activity. Refer to the *Marketing Software Binder* for template and user information.

Evaluation

Administer the reproducible test for Chapter 21, or construct your own using the Testmaker software.

4. You would have to pay careful attention to typefaces in order to make the ads legible for this audience. Seniors have difficulty in reading small print, so the advertising copy would need to be in larger type. Ad copy should appeal to safety, security, stability, and traditional values. It should also stress ease of operation and product use with seniors. The illustrations used in the ads should reflect the needs of the target audience and in no way be demeaning to senior citizens.

5. When you want customers to buy a product now include the price, but when you are presenting an image for a business or product do not include the price of the product.

Building Academic Skills

Math

1. The price of the Horizon Wide Angle Binoculars is $135.99. The Tuffy Tennis Balls are $2.58 per

Chapter Overview

This chapter explains the importance of visual merchandising in creating store image. It discusses types of store displays, and looks at the practicalities of creating and maintaining them.

Springboard

Ask students to imagine that they're in a local shopping area. Tell them to list the visual interior and exterior elements of any store which give clues as to the type of merchandise (discounted high-end) carried. List students' answers on the board. Elements listed should include exterior window displays; store location; store entrance; the marquee; store layout; etc. Tell students that one term comprises all of these elements—*visual merchandising*.

Prereading

List the section objectives to discuss with students. Have students skim the chapter, looking at the pictures, reading the captions, and noting the heads. Ask questions to ensure that the students have a minimal understanding of the chapter structure.

Preteaching the Vocabulary

Have students ask you to define the vocabulary words with which they are unfamiliar. If no one asks questions, choose students at random to give a definition for each term.

CHAPTER 22

Visual Merchandising and Display

You enter a new store for the first time. Immediately you know, without even looking at a price tag, that the merchandise is expensive. There are dozens of visual signals—the width of the aisles, the sophistication of the displays, the amount and look of the merchandise—that tell you that you are not in a discount store. Turning to the first shirt you see, you look at the price tag—$122. You are right about the store.

In this chapter you will explore the importance of visual merchandising. You will learn to identify the physical elements retailers use to create the right image. You will also learn how to design and prepare displays.

282   Unit 6   *Promotion*

Classroom Management

For the Teacher

- Teacher's Annotated Editions for all workbooks
- Teacher's Manual for *School-to-Work Handbook*
- *Testing Binder*
- *Transparency Binder*
- *Marketing Software Binder*
- *Marketing Career Portfolio*
- *Lesson Plans*

For the Student

- *Student Activity Workbook*
- *Marketing Math Workbook*
- *School-to-Work Handbook*
- *Student Software*
- *International Case Studies*
- *Marketing Career Portfolio*

SECTION 22.1

Objectives

After completing this section, you will be able to

- define visual merchandising and distinguish it from display,
- explain how exterior and interior features contribute to a store's image, and
- list the various kinds of displays.

Terms to Know

- visual merchandising
- display
- storefront
- marquee
- store layout
- fixtures

What Is Visual Merchandising?

Visual merchandising refers to the coordination of all physical elements in a place of business so that it projects the right image to its customers. The "right" image is one that invites interest in the merchandise or services being offered, encourages their purchase, and makes the customer feel good about where he or she is doing business.

Successful businesses create distinct, clear, and consistent images for their customers. A good image helps separate a business from others that offer similar products, making it appear unique. Such an image is a blend of customer characteristics, store location, products, prices, advertising, publicity, and personal selling. However, its most important component is sales promotion, of which visual merchandising is a form. This chapter primarily focuses on visual merchandising in retail stores. But it is important for you to know that manufacturers and wholesalers also use visual merchandising to sell their products. Visual merchandising is used extensively, for example, at trade shows and conventions.

The term *visual merchandising* is sometimes used interchangeably with the term *display*. The two are not the same, however. Display is a much narrower concept. It is only one part of visual merchandising. **Display** refers to the visual and artistic aspects of presenting a product to a target group of customers. Visual merchandising, by contrast, involves the visual and artistic aspects of the entire business environment.

With the growth of self-service retailing, visual merchandising has increased tremendously in importance. Consider the example of the supermarket. In such a retail environment, there is little personal selling. Products must largely sell themselves. This fact has spurred manufacturers of food and grocery items to develop innovative product designs, attractive packaging, and creative in-store displays. These visual merchandising activities have had a strong influence on the promotional activities of other self-service and full-service retailers.

People involved with visual merchandising, then, are responsible for the total merchandise or service presentation, the overall business image, and even the building and placement of design elements. Today's visual merchandiser is an active member of the decision-making team that promotes a business and its products.

Elements of Visual Merchandising

Visual merchandising is used to make a store and its merchandise so attractive that the customer will enjoy the shopping experience and want to return. To achieve this end, stores manipulate four key elements: *storefront, store layout, store interior,* and *interior displays.*

Storefront

The total exterior of a business is known as the **storefront.** The storefront includes the entranceways, display windows, marquee, window awnings, and the building itself (its design and setting).

The importance of an effective storefront cannot be overestimated. Well designed, it can project an appropriate image—discount or expensive, conservative or trendy. It can also attract potential customers by making the business stand out from its competition.

Marquee One of the first things customers see after they take in the general outlines of the building and any landscaping is the marquee. The **marquee** is a sign that is used to display the store's name. Such a sign can be painted or lighted. It can be used alone or with a recognized trademark. Marquees are designed primarily to attract attention and advertise a business's location. Like

Chapter 22 *Visual Merchandising and Display* **283**

Bell Ringer Activity

Have students choose one of the stores they frequent and write answers to the following questions about it.

- What type of merchandise is displayed in the windows?
- What is the quality and sophistication of these window displays? Crowded? Simplistic? Are the colors understated? Vibrant?
- Where is the store located? What does its location say about its exclusivity or lack thereof?
- What does the store's entrance look like?
- What does the marquee look like?
- How is the store laid out?
- What types of services are available?
- What is the general quality of the store's fixtures?
- What treatment is on the floors?
- What color is on the walls?
- What is the lighting like?
- What is the quality of the interior displays?
- How would you classify this store's overall image?

Introducing the Section

Review students' answers to the Bell Ringer Activity. Were there any disagreements among students regarding their perceptions? Explain that students should not judge a store negatively because it carries discount merchandise. Some of the most successful retailers in the U.S. (Wal-Mart for example) do some of the heaviest discounting and offer some of the most extensive product lines, thus drawing customers from all socioeconomic classes and making them feel good about finding substantial bargains. Wal-Mart's store image corresponds directly to its successful marketing strategies.

Meeting Special Needs

Physically Challenged

The Americans with Disabilities Act of 1990 makes it illegal for companies to deny employment opportunities to individuals who have real or perceived mental or physical disabilities. It also requires employers to make reasonable accommodations to enable disabled workers to perform their work. This includes access to entrances and exits and to the work itself. These factors influence workplace design and personnel space design as well as encourage companies to design buildings that all people can enter and exit without hardship. You may wish to consider these issues in chapter discussions.

Teach

Guided Practice

1. Read Section 22.1 with students.
2. Use the transparency for this section.
3. MarkEd Resource Center in Columbus, Ohio, (800) 448-0398, offers videos on visual merchandising appropriate for use with this section.
4. Show the class photographs or slides of store layouts. Have students identify and define selling space, merchandise space, personnel space, and customer space. Ask students to study each photo or slide and make suggestions for improving the layout of the store.

Discussion Starter

Promotional displays promote the sale of one or more of the store's items. Give some creative examples of special lighting, signs, and/or props you would find in displays for the following items:

- luggage (maps, a globe, a miniature airplane or train, sunglasses or anything evocative of a beach, a sunlamp, signs for certain cities or destinations);
- fine crystal goblets displayed during the holiday season (the goblets could be filled with confetti or clear marbles, a sign that says Happy Holidays! or Happy New Year!, streamers in various colors, party favors, holiday ornaments or wrapped gifts);
- a vacuum cleaner (a thick square of carpeting with [fake] dirt sprinkled on it);
- necklaces and other jewelry

any form of typeface, they can also be used to project a particular image. For example, a discount merchandiser, such as Wal-Mart, might use bold, blocklike capitals in its marquee. An upscale department store might use an elegant script.

Entrances Entrances are usually designed with customer convenience and store security in mind. Normally, smaller stores have only one entrance, while larger stores (such as department stores) have several. The average midsize business probably needs at least two entrances—one leading in off the street for pedestrians and another adjacent to the parking lot for patrons who drive to the business.

There are several types of entrances. There are revolving, push-pull, electronic, and climate-controlled entrances. (The latter are found in enclosed shopping malls.) Each of these projects a certain image. Electronically controlled sliding doors, for example, suggest a practical, self-service business. Push-pull doors, which often have fancy metal or wooden push plates or bars, suggest a full-service establishment.

Window Displays Display windows, when available on a building's exterior, are especially useful for visual merchandising. Displays placed in these windows can begin the selling process even before the potential customer enters the store.

Window displays are designed to attract the customer by suggesting both the type of merchandise and the type of atmosphere that lie within the store. Two basic kinds of window displays are promotional displays and institutional displays.

Promotional displays promote the sale of one or more of the store's items. They do so by presenting items with special lighting, signs, and/or props. A promotional display for skiwear accented by fir trees and fake snow is an example.

Institutional displays promote store image rather than specific products. Such displays are designed to build customer goodwill and enhance store image by showing that the business is interested in the welfare of the community. Institutional displays focus on public causes, worthy ideas, or community organizations. They might feature the activities of the national groups, such as the Muscular Dystrophy Association, or local volunteer efforts on behalf of the historical society or the "Students Against Drunk Driving" program.

Store Layout

Store layout refers to the way store floor space is allocated to facilitate sales and serve the customer. A typical layout divides a store into four different kinds of space:

1. *Selling space* is assigned for interior displays, sales demonstrations, and sales transactions.
2. *Merchandise space* is allocated to items that are kept in inventory.

284   Unit 6   *Promotion*

3. *Personnel space* is assigned to store employees for lockers, lunch breaks, and restrooms.
4. *Customer space* is assigned for the comfort and convenience of the customer. Such space may include a restaurant, dressing rooms, lounges, and recreation areas for children.

Once selling space has been allocated, visual merchandising personnel work closely with management to decide the best locations for particular kinds of merchandise. Typical questions that must be answered at this point include the following:

1. Where should general product categories and customer service areas be located in the store?
2. Which products should be located closest to doors, elevators, parking lots, and other exits?
3. Where should impulse and convenience goods be placed?

BRIGHT IDEAS

Talk to the Windows

If you could talk to a window display, what would you say? Well, you could ask, "How much *is* that doggie in the window?" And you might just get an answer, thanks to a company called MicroTouch Systems, Inc. MicroTouch has developed a device that will allow retailers to turn display windows into touch-sensitive screens. When combined with audio technology that transmits sound through glass, the device allows customers to hear information about featured merchandise at the touch of a hand, even when a store is closed.

Use of the device is not limited to exterior windows. It also has applications to merchandise display cases and museum exhibits.

***

Creativity Challenge   Form teams of 3–5 people, and design a store window that could make effective use of MicroTouch's new technology. Consider how that technology might affect the physical arrangement of the merchandise. Decide what sort of information you would program the system with. Finally, describe how and why your particular display would increase the store's business. (You might also note any disadvantages or drawbacks of the new technology that become apparent as the group works with the concept.)

More About

Self-service Retailing

Self-service retailing has become such a boon to fashion retailers such as shoe stores that industry specialists predict that self-service stores could account for up to 30 percent of department store business by 1999.

Bright Ideas

Ask students to think about other possible ways in which this new technology might be applied to other features such as promotional displays. What are the benefits of having inanimate displays talk? Would stores be able to get away with having fewer employees if devices could answer questions? Would the buying public accept the inanimate substitutes?

4. How should related items, such as shirts, ties, and belts, be displayed?
5. Where should seasonal and off-season products be located?
6. Where should bulky items be located?
7. How close should interior and window displays be to the related department or inventory?
8. What traffic patterns should be designed to promote extended shopping within the store?
9. How should merchandise be arranged to encourage purchases?

Store Interior

Once the general placement of merchandise has been determined, store personnel can begin developing the visual merchandising approaches that they will use on the building's interior. The selection of such diverse elements as floor and wall coverings, lighting, colors, and store fixtures can powerfully affect the store image.

Take flooring, for example. Many supermarkets use linoleum or tile floors to project an inexpensive, practical image. Many specialty stores use thick carpeting to send just the opposite message to their customers.

Colors and lighting can be used in a similar fashion. Bright colors and light pastels (or plain white) appeal to different types of customers. Stores catering to teens might favor bright colors and bright lighting. Stores catering to adults often choose pastels and soft, subtle lighting effects. Discount stores would choose simple fluorescent lighting, while prestige retailers might install expensive chandeliers.

The principal installations in a store, however, are the fixtures. **Fixtures** are store furnishings, such as display cases, counters, shelving, racks, and benches. These can be permanent or movable.

A business seeking an upscale image might enhance its fixtures by painting them or covering them with textured materials of various kinds (carpeting, fabric, cork, or reed, for example). A business catering to discount buyers would most likely leave its fixtures plain and exposed.

Walls are another interior feature that can be covered to reinforce store image. For example, small or subtly patterned paper is often used by women's specialty stores, while department stores tend to favor soft pastels. Walls are also used to display merchandise. For example, clothing can be pinned to the surface. This technique has the advantage of both saving space and attracting customers with higher-than-eye-level displays.

The width of a store's aisles probably influences behavior more directly than any other element of visual merchandising. Wide, uncluttered aisles create a more positive impression than narrow, cramped ones. Customers shop longer and are more relaxed when they are not pressed by crowds or delayed by long lines.

Finally, the size, variety, and quality of the merchandise assortment carried by a store affects its clientele. High-end, brand-name merchandise conveys a different image

A store's interior should reflect the store's image. How have visual merchandisers used floor and wall coverings, lighting, colors, and store fixtures in this store to create the proper image?

from low-end, generic (nonbrand) goods. Each will attract (or put off) a different kind of customer.

Interior Displays

Strictly speaking, interior or in-store displays are part of the general store interior. However, as elements of visual merchandising, they are so significant that they are commonly considered in a category by themselves. This is because such displays generate one out of every four sales. If interior displays are done exceptionally well, they enable customers to make a selection without personal assistance. Thus, they occupy an especially important place in today's selling environment where many stores are self-service.

Five types of interior displays are closed displays, open displays, architectural displays, point-of-purchase displays, and store decorations. (See Figure 22-1 on pages 286–287.)

Chapter 22 *Visual Merchandising and Display* **285**

displayed for Valentine's Day (a heart-shaped candy box with the jewelry inserted in the candy wrappers;
● a sign that says "A Treat for Your Sweet"; red, white, and pink ribbon; a cupid)
Have students generate other examples of products and display ideas.

Critical Thinking

Ask students where they have seen each kind of interior display discussed in this section. What type of store was it in? What purpose did the display serve?

Cooperative Learning

If your school has a school store, here are some suggested activities:
● Have students take pictures of window displays, organizing them for future reference in case you want to duplicate the displays next year.
● Have students take an inventory of all fixtures, recording the number of each item and rating its condition.
● Have students recommend other fixtures that would be useful for the store. Have students list all the types of interior displays that are used. Would they recommend any improvements? If so, have them list their recommendations, giving a rationale for each one. What else needs to be improved and updated in the store to better evoke its image?

More About

Fixtures

A current trend in fixtures is "ambiance" displays. For example, sporting goods retailers might create waterfalls, complete with the sights and sounds of an actual fishing location to complement fishing goods displays.

Caption Answer

Visual merchandisers have used an elegant rug as a floor covering and framed art on the walls, expensive looking lighting, wall columns, open space, and fine displays to project an up-scale image.

Figure 22–1

TYPES OF INTERIOR DISPLAYS

Retailers use interior displays to show merchandise, provide customers with product information, get customers to stop and shop at the store, reinforce print and other forms of advertising, and promote the store's image.

Closed Displays ▲

allow customers to see but not handle merchandise. They are found in catalog showrooms or businesses, such as jewelry stores where security or breakage is a concern.

Point-of-Purchase Displays ▼

are displays designed mainly to promote impulse purchases. In a recent survey conducted by the Point-of-Purchase Advertising Institute, a majority of retailers reported that point-of-purchase displays are more effective at supporting new products than established ones. Some of the more popular point-of-purchase displays include shelf talkers and danglers, mobiles and banners, illuminated and nonilluminated signs, testers/sampling devices, floorstands, and cash register units. They are usually supplied by a product manufacturer for use at or near the point of sale (checkstand, cash register, etc.).

Open Displays ▼

allow customers to handle and examine merchandise without the help of a salesperson. Hanging racks for suits and dresses or countertop and shelf displays for cosmetics are examples.

Architectural ▶ Displays

consist of model rooms that allow customers to see how merchandise might look in their homes. Such "rooms" need not be defined by walls or partitions. Area rugs or the arrangement of the furniture itself can be used to suggest the setting.

◀ Store Decorations

are displays that coincide with specific seasons or holidays. Banners, signs, props, and similar items used to invoke the spirit of Valentine's Day, Halloween, summer, or fall are examples.

Chapter 22 *Visual Merchandising and Display* **287**

L3 Human Relations Skills

Ask students to consider this scenario:

You have just observed a customer take a tie off the men's counter, put it in his pocket, and walk out of your department. What should you do? (More than likely, the person is shoplifting, although this might not be the case. Always follow your store's policy with regard to shoplifting. It's best to call security and your manager instead of confronting the shoplifter directly.

Independent Practice

1. Interview your co-op supervisor or the manager of a local retail store. Ask him or her how the decisions are made to create the store's image through visual merchandising. Ask if recent image changes have been made or are planned. If so, what changes were or will be made? Why was the decision made to change the store's image?

   Summarize your finding in a 250-word report. If possible, take photos of the various elements of the store's visual merchandising to accompany your report.

2. Assign and review the Chapter 22 Case Study in the *International Case Studies* workbook.

3. Have students make up a display rating sheet addressing the criteria discussed in this chapter. Tell them to take the rating sheet to the local mall and use the sheet to rate various displays in a wide variety of shots. If possible, have them photograph the displays they choose to rate. Have them pick the best display they found and present the photo, or a sketch if a camera is not available, to the class along with a brief discussion of why they rated the display above all the others.

Assess

Evaluation

Assign and review the Section 22.1 Review.

Reteaching

1. Assign and review the vocabulary terms for this section.
2. Assign and review Fact and Idea Review questions 1–8 from the Chapter Review.
3. Ask students to explain why display is only one part of visual merchandising. Then, for reteaching purposes, have them identify all aspects of visual merchandising that they have learned to date.

Enrichment

1. Assign and review the appropriate activities in the *Student Activity Workbook*.
2. Assign and review the appropriate Critical Thinking questions from the Chapter Review.
3. Have students write a report that compares and contrasts two types of retailers who sell the same types of items but who have two totally different images. They should comment on each item mentioned in this lesson that contributes to a store's overall image.
4. Arrange for students to tour a local retail store with one of the store's managers. Have the manager discuss how the interior and exterior elements contribute to the store's visual merchandising.

Close

Have students complete this statement: Visual merchandising refers to...(the coordination of all physical elements in a place of business so that it projects the right image to its customers.)

Interior displays use fixtures and props to showcase merchandise. Obviously, the types of fixtures and props visual merchandisers use will vary depending on the merchandise displayed.

Props used with interior displays are generally classified as *decorative* or *functional*. Decorative props include background scenery used to indicate a season or simply to create an interesting setting. Functional props include functional items for holding merchandise, such as mannequins and shirt forms. Display designers often look for unusual props or unusual ways to use common items as props. Imaginative jewelry display designers, for example, may use open candy boxes to display colored stone rings in the candy papers.

It's Not All Black and White

To create visual displays and packaging for the global marketplace, a knowledge of color and number symbology (what colors and numbers stand for in various cultures) is essential. Consider the case of the U.S. company that hoped to do well selling its products in Japan. The firm packaged its wares in white boxes and grouped them in lots of four. When sales proved disappointing, company managers looked for the reasons. Only then did they learn that their products' poor performance could be attributed at least in part to their packaging. In Japan and other Asian countries including China, white is the color of mourning. In addition, four is considered an unlucky number because in both Japanese and Chinese it sounds like the word for death. By contrast, in China at least, the color red and the number eight are considered lucky.

SECTION 22.1 *Review*

1. **What is visual merchandising?** Explain how it differs from display.
2. **How do exterior and interior features contribute to a store's image?**
3. **List two different types of window displays and give an example of each.**
4. **Describe the five different types of interior displays used by retailers and provide an example of each.**

Objectives

After completing this section, you will be able to

- **describe the steps used in designing and preparing displays,**
- **describe the various artistic considerations involved in display preparation, and**
- **summarize the proper procedures for maintaining and dismantling displays.**

Terms to Know

- **complementary colors**
- **adjacent colors**
- **proportion**
- **formal balance**
- **informal balance**

Display Design and Preparation

In the retail environment, a display has about three to eight seconds to attract a customer's attention, create a desire, and sell a product. This restricted time frame means that a business must target its displays carefully to appeal to its customers. If it fails to do so, it not only risks losing sales but ruining its image as well. For example, the traditional clothing store that suddenly begins showing abstract displays of trendy merchandise is likely to attract some new style-conscious customers. It is also likely to alienate many of its regular customers.

Thus, before displays are built, promotional and visual merchandising staffs should agree on the answers to these questions:

1. What is the image of our business?
2. Who are our customers?
3. What kind of merchandise concept is being promoted (trendy, conservative, formal, casual, etc.)?
4. Where will the display be built and located?
5. What merchandise will be displayed?
6. How will the selection of merchandise affect the display's design? How will it affect our business's image?

Section Review Answers

1. Visual merchandising involves the visual and artistic elements of the entire business while display relates to product presentation.
2. Well designed interior and exterior features can project an appropriate image and can also attract potential customers by making the business stand out from its competition.
3. Promotional displays promote the sale of one or more of the store's items. Institutional displays promote store image rather than specific products.
4. Closed displays, open displays, architectural displays, point-of-purchase displays, store decorations. Examples will vary.

Once the answers to these questions are decided upon, visual merchandisers can design and build the display by following five steps:

1. Selecting the merchandise for display.
2. Selecting the type of display.
3. Choosing a setting type.
4. Manipulating the display's artistic elements.
5. Evaluating the completed display.

Selecting Merchandise for Display

The first important step when building a display is to select the right merchandise. Merchandise selected for display must have sales appeal. For this reason, new, popular, and best-selling products are often selected for display. Display merchandise must also be visually appealing and have the ability to attract customers. In addition, it must be timely and current. It must be appropriate for the season and for the store's geographic location. Often it addresses the latest fashion or trend.

Selecting the Display

The type of display that is used is largely determined by the merchandise selected. There are four possibilities.

A *one-item display* is used to show a single item. An example would be Reebok Hardcourt tennis shoes displayed on a tennis ball-shaped stand with a promotional sign. One-item displays are usually constructed for a single product promotion or an advertised special.

A *line-of-goods display* shows one kind of product but features several brands, sizes, or models. An example would be a display unit showing car stereos by various manufacturers, such as Audiovox, Jensen, or Sony, or a display of different car stereos put out by a single manufacturer.

A *related-merchandise display* features items that are meant to be used together. For example, in an apparel store, a related-merchandise display might feature casual wear—shirts, pants, sweaters, and shoes that go together. Related-merchandise displays are designed primarily to entice the customers to buy more than one item.

A *variety display* (also called an *assortment display*) features a collection of unrelated items. Such displays usually emphasize price and tell customers that a wide variety of merchandise is available for sale. They are typically used by variety stores, discounters, and supermarkets to make a special appeal to bargain hunters.

Choosing a Setting Type

Displays can be presented in a number of different types of settings. The setting a business selects will depend largely on the image it is trying to project.

A *realistic setting* depicts a room, area, or recognizable locale. The scene could be a restaurant, a park, or a party. The details are provided by props, such as tables, chairs, plants, risers, books, dishes, and mannequins.

A *semirealistic setting* suggests a room or locale but leaves the details to the viewer's imagination. For example, a cardboard sun, beach towel, surfing poster, and a sprinkling of sand would be enough to invoke the rest of the scene—an oceanfront beach—in the viewer's mind. Businesses use semirealistic settings when either space or budget do not permit the construction of realistic settings.

An *abstract setting* does not imitate (or even try to imitate) reality. It focuses on form and color rather than reproducing actual objects. For example, wide bands of torn colored paper used as an accent behind or around merchandise can create an attractive visual image that has nothing to do with reality.

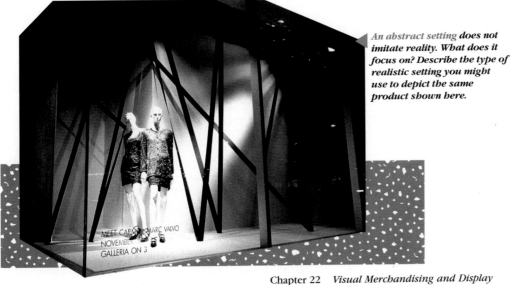

*An abstract setting **does not imitate reality. What does it focus on? Describe the type of realistic setting you might use to depict the same product shown here.***

Chapter 22 *Visual Merchandising and Display* **289**

289

SECTION 22.2

Focus

⏰ Bell Ringer Activity

Ask students this question: If you only had three to eight seconds to attract attention in a nonverbal way, how would you do it?

Introducing the Section

Review students' answers from the Bell Ringer Activity. Some of the things they mentioned might include using dramatic or loud colors, using signs, using physical motion, etc.—all things that are used in display to attract attention.

Tell students that in the retail environment, a display has about three to eight seconds to attract a customer's attention, create a desire, and sell a product. Thus, a business must create its displays carefully to appeal to its target customers. Ask students to describe displays that made a particularly lasting impression on them and tell why.

Teach

Guided Practice

1. Read Section 22.2 with students.
2. Have students read aloud the Case Study and review the answers in class.
3. MarkEd Resource Center in Columbus, Ohio, (800) 448-0398, offers videos on visual merchandising appropriate for use with this section.
4. Show slides or pictures to illustrate the various types of displays. Have students identify the type in each picture. Also have them tell what kind of store uses each type of display. Use slides or pictures to illustrate the use of realistic, semi-realistic, and abstract settings for displays. Ask students to evaluate the settings shown.

Caption Answer

It focuses on color and form. Answers will vary.

5. Use the transparency for this section.
6. *Visual Merchandising* and *Store Design* and *Stores* are excellent publications featuring the current national trends in visual merchandising. Have several copies available in your classroom for students to peruse. (They will be asked to use these two publications and other marketing-related magazines in the chapter's Performance Assessment Activity.)
7. Assign and review the Chapter 22 Activity in the *School-to-Work Handbook*.

Discussion Starter

Draw various types of lines on the chalkboard (straight, curved, diagonal, vertical, horizontal) and ask students what moods they evoke.

Critical Thinking

Describe related merchandise that could be displayed with the following items:

- ten-speed bicycles (bicycle locks, carrying pouches, additional reflectors, bicycle clothing);
- flower seeds (gardening supplies, books on planting flowers, flower pots, sun hats, gardening clogs);
- men's dress shirts (ties, cufflinks, suspenders, pocket squares);
- ice skates (heavy socks, scarves, stocking caps, mittens and gloves, blade protectors, carrying case);
- computers (printers, covers for the equipment, paper, paper holders, software, "how to" books such as *DOS for Dummies*, disks and disk cases); and
- this textbook (all of the ancillary materials, such as the workbooks).

Have students generate other products and related items.

Abstract settings are gaining popularity, mainly because they are inexpensive and do not require large amounts of storage space for accumulated props. Display specialists are increasingly accenting products with such items as cardboard, paper, string, yarn, ribbon, and paint in preference to more traditional and realistic items.

Manipulating Artistic Elements

The artistic elements of a display include *line, color, shape, direction, texture, proportion, motion,* and *lighting.* These elements influence your perception of a display in ways that you are probably not aware of.

Line   Since people read English from left to right, they also tend to read displays the same way. Therefore, visual merchandisers try to create lines within displays that travel from left to right over all the products featured.

Various types of lines create different impressions. Straight lines suggest stiffness and control; curving lines, freedom and movement; diagonal lines, action; vertical lines, height and dignity; and horizontal lines, width and confidence.

Color   Color can make or break a display. Displays whose colors match their surroundings too closely may not catch the customer's eye. Displays whose colors are too bright or contrasting may overwhelm the merchandise being presented.

The colors selected for a display should contrast with those used on the walls, floors, and fixtures around them. For example, a store done in pastels should have displays featuring darker, stronger colors.

Which colors make the most effective contrasts? The answers can be found in the standard color wheel (see Figure 22–2), which illustrates the relationships among colors. **Complementary colors** are found opposite each other in the color wheel and create the greatest contrasts. Red and green, blue and orange, and violet and yellow are examples of complementary colors.

Adjacent colors (also called analogous colors) are located next to each other in the color wheel and contrast only slightly. Successive adjacent colors (such as blue-green, blue, and blue-violet) form families, or groups of colors that blend well with each other.

Effective displays use these color groupings to advantage to create visual calm or excitement. For example, colors from the warm side of the color wheel, such as red and yellow, convey a festive, party mood that works well with lower-priced merchandise. Such colors must be used cautiously, however. Their contrast is so great that it can detract from the merchandise and even irritate customers. This problem can usually be avoided by varying the shades of the colors somewhat to lessen their contrast yet still retain their warmth and friendliness. Colors from the cool side of the color wheel, such as blue and green, connote calm and refinement. They are often associated with higher-priced merchandise.

Customers' expectations about color are also important in planning displays. People have come to expect certain color schemes at certain times of the year or for certain kinds of merchandise—for example, green for St. Patrick's Day, orange and brown for fall, and pastels for infant's clothing.

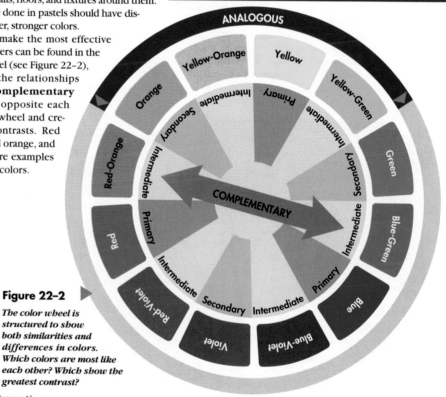

The Color Wheel

Figure 22–2
The color wheel is structured to show both similarities and differences in colors. Which colors are most like each other? Which show the greatest contrast?

Finally, customers' reactions to color also figure into planning displays. Red, for example, evokes excitement. So, you would not use it in a display designed to convey tranquility. The best way to learn about color use in displays is to visit stores with regularity and observe what color combinations are being used. Another way is to read visual merchandising, trade, and fashion magazines, such as *Visual Merchandising and Store Design, Stores,* and *Vogue*.

Shape   *Shape* refers to the physical appearance, or outline, of a display. It is important to consider shape when selecting display units and the merchandise used in a display.

Shape is determined by the props, fixtures, and merchandise used in the display. However, the shape of a display is not limited by the merchandise itself. Squares, cubes, circles, and triangles are some of the shapes that display units may resemble. Displays that have little or no distinct shape—called *mass displays*—are also possible. Mass displays are often used to display large quantities of merchandise and to convey a message of low price.

Direction   A good display guides the viewer's eye over all the merchandise, moving smoothly from one part of the display to another. It does not skip around. This smooth visual flow is called *direction*. Good displays create direction by using color, repetition, lighting patterns, ribbons, and by arranging merchandise in a pattern to guide the customer's eye.

Displays should have a *focal point*. A good method of creating a focal point is to build a display around an imaginary triangle (having more merchandise at the bottom of the display than at the top, for example). This arrangement helps keep the eyes moving up and center.

Displays that lack direction are said to be *unfocused*. Typically, they contain too many unrelated items, too many colors, or too many lines that both confuse the customer and detract from the merchandise.

Texture   Texture refers to the way the surfaces in a display look together. These surfaces can be either smooth or rough. The contrast between them creates visual interest.

Products that are smooth, such as flatware, should be placed against backgrounds or props that are rough. Items that are rough, such as jewelry, should be displayed against smooth surfaces (a dark velvet cloth is traditional).

Proportion   Proportion is the relationship between and among objects in a display. The merchandise should always be the primary focus of a display. Props and signs should be in proportion to the merchandise—they should never overshadow it in importance. Poor use of proportion creates a display that is either too crowded or too empty.

Balance   Placing large items with large items and small items with small items in a display is called **formal balance**. For example, if a large item is placed on one side of a display, an equally large item should be placed on the other side to balance the arrangement.

The opposite technique can also be exciting in a display. Balancing a large item with several small ones is called **informal balance**. An example would be a display in which an adult mannequin is juxtaposed with several short baskets of flowers raised to the mannequin's height.

Motion   Motion can be made part of a display through the use of motorized fixtures and props. For example, animated figures, such as mechanical mannequins, have been used for years in holiday displays.

Motion should be used sparingly to accentuate merchandise. Like color, it can become distracting if it is overdone.

Lighting   Proper lighting makes merchandise appear more attractive in displays. As a general rule, it is recommended that display lighting be two to five times stronger than a store's general lighting. The actual strength will depend on whether the display is interior or exterior.

Display lighting should follow three basic rules:

1. It should match the image of the business.
2. It should not cast shadows over the merchandise being displayed.
3. It should not create a glare.

Colored lighting can be used in displays to create dramatic effects. For example, tinted lamps can cast sharp black or grey shadows against a background. When using such lamps, however, you should keep in mind that the customer must always be able to see the merchandise in its true colors.

Evaluating Completed Displays

Once a display is created, visual merchandisers should evaluate it to make certain the display fulfills its purpose. In evaluating the display, visual merchandisers should ask themselves the following questions:

1. Does the display emphasize and enhance the store's image?
2. Does the display appeal to the store's customers?
3. Is the display attention grabbing? Does it make good use of the merchandise?
4. Does the display emphasize timeliness? Does it reflect the season?
5. Does the display use a creative theme which is appropriate for the merchandise?
6. Does the display use color effectively?
7. Were proper design principles used? Were they used in an imaginative way?
8. Is the display artistically pleasing?
9. Are display cards and signs easy to read? Do they coordinate with the display?
10. Is the display clean and orderly?

Display Maintenance

Once a display has been constructed, it needs to be maintained. The merchandise especially must be kept clean and attractive while on display.

L1 Math Skills

Ask students to consider the following:

You know that you need 15 yards of ribbon to complete your holiday window display. The length of each spool of ribbon you intend to purchase is 9 feet. How many spools will you need to finish your display? How much ribbon will you have left over? (You need 6 spools to complete the display, and you will have 7.5 feet left over. First, you need 46.5 feet of ribbon [15.5 × 3 = 46.5 feet]. 46.5 ÷ 9 feet per spool = 5.16 or 6 spools. 6 spools × 9 feet of ribbon on each spool = 54 feet of ribbon. 54 − 46.5 = 7.5 feet remaining.)

L2 Math Skills

Ask students to consider the following:

The ribbon you have just purchased in the L1 Activity is to be fastened around the perimeter of your store's largest display window, which is 13 feet by 10 feet. What is the perimeter of the window? (46 feet. P = 2 × [13 + 10])

L3 Math Skills

Ask students to consider the following:

What is the square footage of the store window in the L2 Activity? (130 square feet. A = width × length. 13 feet × 10 feet = 130 feet.)

Lifelong Learning

Visual Merchandising and Display

Although not all students will proceed along their career path to become in-store merchandisers you can help students connect the information to many varied occupations. Those who work in non-retail service businesses, such as medical offices, employment agencies, or even advertising or marketing services, need to be aware of the implications of display and use of interior space. Those operating their own businesses will find it helpful to know the terms that the specialists use. In decorating their own homes, students will find they can apply the same concepts of color, lighting, and use of texture and space.

Cooperative Learning

After you have finished reading through this lesson, divide students into four to six groups. Using only those things that they find in the classroom, have each group design and create a one-item, line-of-goods, related-merchandise, or variety display. Each group should agree on answers to the four questions that must be asked before a display is built. They should also create a setting type, and use whatever artistic elements are available to them in the room. When they are finished, have each group critique its own and the other groups' displays.

Independent Practice

Have students draw a color sketch of the following: a one-item display, a line-of-goods display, a related-merchandise display, and a variety display. They should identify the products in each display.

Assess

Evaluation

Assign and review the Section 22.2 Review.

Reteaching

1. Assign and review the vocabulary terms for this section.
2. Assign and review Fact and Idea Review questions 9–12 from the Chapter Review.
3. Show photographs and slides of displays. Have the students tell you: what type of display it is; the setting type; and whether it exhibits formal or informal balance. Also discuss whatever is appropriate about the line, use of color, shape, direction, texture, and lighting (if possible, given each photo), and proportion.

CASE STUDY

Changing an Image

Florsheim shoe company has traditionally been associated with wing tips and flashy dress shoes. The company is now attempting to change that image. The changes will reposition the shoe chain for the future.

To create this change, the company is introducing new casual shoe styles, changing its packaging design, and reformatting its stores. Aiming for a younger customer, the company recently opened a new store in downtown Chicago. It hopes that the new store will be a prototype for future Florsheim stores.

The new prototype store places an emphasis on a less formal, more laid-back style. There is a neon logo on the storefront with white bold letters, which matches the white elements within the store. Rather than the company's traditional mahogany woodwork and rich leathers, the new store is outfitted with maple wood and green carpeting.

New track lighting has brightened the store and dress standards for sales associates are more relaxed. The shoe displays are less formal, more contemporary, and more casual. Rather than display row upon row of oxfords and loafers, all merchandise is displayed on flat shelves or slatted walls. These types of displays are less formal and provide flexibility in displaying new and changing shoe styles.

Shoes are now grouped by category. Casual shoes are placed along the right side wall, formal footwear

along the back, and value-oriented footwear along the left side wall. The various shoe groupings tend to guide customers throughout the store.

Even with the changes, the company has kept some traditional store designs, such as wood columns and framed Early American graphics. The Florsheim crest, originally designed in 1892, still hangs near the sales terminal.

Case Study Review

1. Based upon your experience and from the Case Study information, who is the traditional customer for Florsheim shoes? Why is Florsheim attempting to change its image?
2. Why has the company kept its traditional wing tips and formal shoes along the back of the store?
3. What has the company done to maintain its traditional customer base?

A MATTER OF ETHICS

4. Do you think that a company with such a long tradition is being disloyal to its primary customers by changing its image? Explain.

Case Study Answers

1. Regular Florsheim customers have traditionally been 45 year-old and older professionals. Changing its image is an attempt to attract younger customers and to broaden the traditional customer base.
2. Traditional customers will be led through the store to purchase the higher-priced footwear.

It is hoped that they may also walk by and possibly purchase more casual shoes which are displayed along the side walls.
3. It has still kept the traditional wooden columns, early American graphics, and the company crest.
4. Answers will vary.

Evaluating a display **is part of the design and preparation process. Evaluate this display by asking yourself the evaluation questions listed in the chapter.**

Individual businesses have different policies regarding the duration of displays. Most businesses, however, observe the same general rules for display maintenance:

1. Displays should be checked daily for damage or displacement caused by customer handling.
2. Missing merchandise should be replaced immediately.
3. Lights should be checked periodically and replaced as necessary.
4. Display units and props should be cleaned and merchandise dusted on a regular basis.

Proper display maintenance can keep the merchandise fresh and attractive in the eyes of customers. Poor maintenance, on the other hand, can create a negative image not only of the merchandise but of the store as well.

Dismantling Procedures for Displays

Specific procedures for dismantling displays also vary with each business. Answering yes to the following list of questions ensures that materials, merchandise, fixtures,

Real World

MARKETING

What Color Is Your Label?

In a blind coffee tasting test, coffee from a yellow can impressed consumers as too weak. Coffee from a brown can struck them as too strong. Nevertheless, the coffee in the two cans was identical. This supports the theory, now common among market researchers, that the color of a product's packaging affects its sales. When Canada Dry switched its sugar-free ginger ale cans from red to green and white, sales shot up by 27 percent.

backgrounds, and props remain in good condition after display use.

1. Were the proper tools gathered before the display was dismantled?
2. Was the display dismantled safely?
3. Was the merchandise removed without damage?
4. Was the merchandise checked for problems before it was returned to stock?
5. Was any damaged merchandise properly recorded?
6. Was the merchandise returned to stock or to the selling area?
7. Was the background removed without damage?
8. Were the mirrors, if any, polished?
9. Was the display area cleaned?
10. Was the floor vacuumed or cleaned?
11. Were the props cleaned or polished?
12. Were the fixtures and props returned to display storage?
13. Were the lights checked to see if they needed to be replaced?

SECTION 22.2
Review

1. **Identify the five steps involved with display design and preparation.**
2. **Identify the artistic elements used in building displays.**
3. **Summarize the proper procedures to follow for maintaining and dismantling displays.**

Chapter 22 *Visual Merchandising and Display* **293**

Enrichment

1. Assign and review the appropriate activities in the *Student Activity Workbook*.
2. Assign and review the appropriate Critical Thinking questions from the Chapter Review.
3. Assign and review the Building Academic Skills Activities, Application Projects, Linking School to Work Activities, and Performance Assessment from the Chapter Review.
4. If your school has a DECA chapter, assign a team of students to design, construct, and build an institutional display promoting DECA and your chapter.
5. Have the students visit the display shop of a local retail store to see where and how items are stored and to discuss how they are reused in various displays throughout the year. Also have the display director discuss his or her career path with the students, including the educational and professional background that prompted him or her to go into display. To make this a Communication Skills Activity, have the students write a 200-word summary of the field trip.

Close

Have students write out or orally summarize the ten steps in evaluating completed displays. (Steps are listed in the chapter.)

CHAPTER Review

Answers

Vocabulary Review

See Glossary for definitions.

Fact and Idea Review

1. Storefront, store layout, store interior, and interior displays.
2. Effective visual merchandising provides a clear, consistent image for a store in physical terms; shows merchandise clearly and with excitement; and creates an atmosphere that convinces people to buy things.
3. A storefront is the total exterior of a business. A marquee is part of the storefront. It is the sign that is used to display the store's name on the outside of the building.
4. The way floor space is allocated to facilitate sales and serve the customer.
5. Selling space, merchandise space, personnel space, and customer space.
6. They generate one out of every four sales.
7. Point-of-purchase displays.
8. Decorative props include such things as background scenery used to indicate a season or simply to create an interesting setting. Functional props include such functional items for holding merchandise as mannequins and shirt forms.
9. Questions are listed on page 288.
10. Complementary colors lie opposite each other in the color wheel and create the greatest contrast. Adjacent colors lie next to each other in the color wheel and contrast only slightly.
11. Formal balance is achieved by placing large items with large items and small items with small items. Informal balance is achieved by balancing a large item with several small ones.

Vocabulary Review

Organize the class into two teams for a game of "Marketing Tic-Tac-Toe." One team will be the "X" team. The other will be the "O" team. Your teacher will call on members of each team, alternately, to provide the proper definition for the terms below. For every correct definition, the team will be allowed to place either an "X" or an "O" on the chalkboard tic-tac-toe grid.

visual merchandising
display
storefront
marquee
store layout
fixtures
complementary colors
adjacent colors
proportion
formal balance
informal balance

Fact and Idea Review

1. What four elements are manipulated by visual merchandisers to create a store image? (Sec. 22.1)
2. Summarize the expected outcome of effective visual merchandising. (Sec. 22.1)
3. What is the difference between a storefront and a marquee? (Sec. 22.1)
4. What is meant by the term "store layout"? (Sec. 22.1)
5. Name the four types of space found in most store layouts. (Sec. 22.1)
6. Why are interior displays an important aspect of visual merchandising? (Sec. 22.1)
7. Which type of interior display has been found to be most effective with new product introductions? (Sec. 22.1)
8. Explain the difference between decorative and functional props. (Sec. 22.1)
9. What questions must every business address before constructing displays? Why? (Sec. 22.2)
10. Locate complementary and adjacent colors on the color wheel and explain how the colors contrast with each other. (Sec. 22.2)
11. Describe how formal and informal balance are achieved in a display. (Sec. 22.2)
12. Summarize how displays should be evaluated. (Sec. 22.2)

Critical Thinking

1. Assume you are in charge of hiring visual merchandisers for a large full-service department store. What basic skills would you require in any display specialist you hired?
2. Explain why it is important to know your community and your customers when designing store displays.
3. Is it necessary for staff members who work with visual merchandising to know basic sales promotion techniques? Justify your response.
4. Entrances should be designed for customer convenience. However, retailers in some locations are limiting the number of functioning entrances because of concern over shoplifting and pilferage. Discuss some other strategies you think might be used in stores to reduce theft risks around or near entrances.
5. Manufacturers often provide point-of-purchase displays to retailers. If you were a retailer, what criteria would you use in deciding whether or not to accept such a display?
6. The newest colors in ready-to-wear clothing—hot pink, lime green, and irridescent orange—clash with your store's conservative, beige-on-brown decor. You must display the merchandise. How do you do so without creating jarring or irritating effects?
7. A new store is opening in your community. Flower beds, shrubbery, potted trees, and benches bracket the main entrance. Custom-made awnings with the store's logo are placed over the windows. There's even a two-story sculpture attached to the front wall below the store's marquee. What image is this business trying to project?

Building Academic Skills

Math

1. You must install carpeting covering in a store area. The surface to be covered is 15 yards by 20 yards. If you must pay $15.50 per square yard for carpeting, what amount would you budget for the job?
2. You must recondition a half dozen mannequins (two adult and four youth). If reconditioning a youth mannequin costs $150 and reconditioning an adult mannequin costs 50 percent more, what amount should you budget for the entire job?

Communication

3. You work as a visual merchandiser for the largest department store in your community. You would like

---

12. See page 291 for evaluation guidelines.

Critical Thinking

1. Possibilities include: a person who has education and/or experience in design, construction, lighting or animation, demonstrates initiative, creativity and flexibility.
2. Answers should indicate that the windows should appeal to the store's customers and be reflective of the community if they are to be effective.

3. Yes. Visual merchandising is a form of sales promotion. The purpose of everything a visual merchandiser does is to attract customers' attention, create a desire for a product, and ultimately sell the product.
4. Answers might include stationing greeters or security personnel at the entrances, keeping merchandise near entrances in closed displays or placing alarms at entrances.
5. Answers might include the type and degree of

294

the store to devote one of its main display windows to a public service that you strongly support. Write a formal proposal detailing your views. Be sure to name the public service, describe the nature of the display, and indicate how you believe the store will benefit. Also, be prepared to counter the argument that window space is too valuable to devote to public causes, and that less visible space will suffice and can be found inside the building.

Human Relations

4. Your store recently installed lock racks for all leather coats and jackets. This means that all the merchandise is secured with locks, keys, and metal cords that must be removed by store personnel before an item can be tried on. The fixtures have cut theft losses by half but are extremely unpopular with customers. Salespeople, who must deal firsthand with the public, are taking the brunt of the criticism. "Well, *I* don't steal," they're told, and "I don't have time for this." If you were one of these salespeople, how would you respond to these customers?

Application Projects

1. Draw a floor plan showing the layout of a local business. (If you choose a department store, diagram only one floor.) Color code those areas provided for merchandise, selling, customers, and personnel. Then critique the layout in terms of ease of entry, traffic flow, utilization of display space, and availability of customer conveniences.
2. Select a holiday or season as a theme. Then describe an effective window display based on that theme and suitable for use by one of the businesses listed below. Be sure to specify the kinds of merchandise you would feature.
   a. Clothing store
   b. Greeting card store
   c. Travel agency
   d. Florist
3. Visit a local department store to observe and rate the displays. For each display considered, do a simple sketch, indicate color, and briefly describe both the merchandise featured and any apparent theme. Evaluate each display in terms of the artistic elements discussed in this chapter.
4. Visit a local supermarket to observe the extent and variety of point-of-purchase displays. Using a camera, photograph at least five different displays and create a poster board collage.

Linking School to Work

1. Visit your cooperative education training station or a local retailer. Identify at least eight different types of interior displays and specify the kinds of merchandise featured. Examples: countertop—stationery; cases—pen-and-pencil sets; point of purchase—key chains.
2. Complete a career investigation by making arrangements to job shadow a person employed in the field of visual merchandising. If this is not possible, use information which may be available in your school's media center to investigate the duties, salary and benefits, training requirements, and future growth opportunities for visual merchandisers.

Performance Assessment

Role Play

Situation. You are employed as a sales associate in an apparel and accessories department. Your department manager has asked you to create a soft line display for the department. Using materials and merchandise, you are to construct an effective display within a specified time period. You will be given the following merchandise to be displayed: scissors, fish line, straight pins, safety pins, poster board, a small iron, and white tissue paper.

Evaluation. You will be evaluated on how well you can do the following:

- Utilize proper steps in designing and preparing a display.
- Manipulate artistic elements to create an effective display.

Written Report

Use a recent issue of *Stores, Visual Merchandising and Store Design,* or other marketing related magazines to complete a 250-word report on a new visual merchandising concept, store format, or display technique being used today.

Complete the Chapter 22 Computer Application that appears in the Student Activity Workbook.

Chapter 22 *Visual Merchandising and Display* **295**

---

support for maintaining and stocking the display, overall attractiveness of the display, and promotional discounts given to place the point-of-purchase display in the store.
6. Students should suggest types of displays, settings, and artistic elements that can be manipulated to create a pleasing effect.
7. Judging from the storefront, this business is expensive, conservative, elegant, and in a very exclusive part of the city.

Building Academic Skills

Math

1. $4,650 (15 × 20 = 300 square yards; 300 × $15.50 = $4,650)
2. $1,050 (4 × $150 = $600; 2 × $150 = $300; $150 × .50 = $75; $150 + $75 = $225; 2 × $225 = $450; $600 + $450 = $1,050).

Communication

3. Students should stress the importance of community relations and how it helps to promote the store. Letters should be professionally written according to the guidelines outlined in Chapter 9.

Human Relations

4. Students should explain that retailers must take measures to curtail shoplifting and should be readily available to assist customers by unlocking merchandise and showing it to them.

Application Projects

1. Individual floor plans will vary but should be well thought out in terms of traffic flow, ease of entry, utilizations of display space and availability of customer convenience.
2. Window displays will vary but should match the image each store projects.
3. Store displays that students observe will vary. Student's rating should include sketches, indicate color, and describe the merchandise.
4. Students should display their photos in class.

Linking School to Work

Answers depend on the work situation.

Performance Assessment

Refer to the *DECA Competitive Events Handbook* for evaluation guidelines.

Computer Application

Optional activity. Refer to the *Marketing Software Binder* for template and user information.

Evaluation

Administer the reproducible test for Chapter 22, or construct your own test using the Testmaker software.

Chapter Overview

Chapter 23 explores the ways that businesses create image and goodwill through publicity and public relations.

Springboard

The Marine Corps annually sponsors "Toys for Tots," National DECA supports the Muscular Dystrophy Association, and The Body Shop urges its customers to write letters on behalf of Amnesty International for prisoners of conscience. Ask students to list other worthy causes or public events sponsored by companies, and to discuss newsworthy information about a company, product, or person that they have seen in the media. The former, public relations, and the latter, publicity, are the subjects of this chapter.

Prereading

List the section objectives to discuss with students. Have students skim the chapter, looking at the pictures, reading the captions, and noting the heads. Ask questions to ensure that the students have a minimal understanding of the chapter structure.

Preteaching the Vocabulary

Write the vocabulary terms on the board. Have students silently choose two terms from the list and look up each term in the chapter without writing anything down. Have them close their texts and give the definition for each term to the person sitting next to them. Then review the entire list as a class.

CHAPTER 23

Publicity and Public Relations

The largest department store in town sponsors a marathon. In the main business district, stores put out donation containers for the United Fund. A bank volunteers some of its managers each week to be guest speakers at a high school.

None of these activities is likely to bring their sponsors a dime of profit. So, why do the businesses do it? The answer is simple: it's good public relations and creates positive publicity.

In this chapter you will explore publicity and public relations. You will discover what public relations specialists do and you will learn how to write news releases.

296   Unit 6   *Promotion*

Classroom Management

For the Teacher
- Teacher's Annotated Editions for all workbooks
- Teacher's Manual for *School-to-Work Handbook*
- *Testing Binder*
- *Transparency Binder*
- *Marketing Software Binder*
- *Marketing Career Portfolio*
- *Lesson Plans*

For the Student
- *Student Activity Workbook*
- *Marketing Math Workbook*
- *School-to-Work Handbook*
- *Student Software*
- *International Case Studies*
- *Marketing Career Portfolio*

Objectives

After completing this section, you will be able to

- **describe the nature and scope of publicity and public relations,**
- **state the benefits of public relations activities, and**
- **recognize the audiences for public relations.**

Terms to Know

- **public relations**
- **customer advisory boards**
- **consumer affairs specialists**
- **community relations**

Nature and Scope of Publicity and Public Relations

As you learned in Chapter 19, publicity involves placing newsworthy information about a company, product, or person in the media. The main purpose of publicity is to build an image.

The basic difference between advertising and publicity is that publicity is not paid for by the business, a fact that makes it more credible to many people. For this reason, publicity is an excellent way to spread information about a company, a product, or a person.

The disadvantage of publicity, of course, is that it cannot be controlled by the business. The bad stories are as likely to get publicized as the good. Thus, businesses work to generate positive publicity whenever possible. Often they do this by engaging in public relations. **Public relations** refers to any activity designed to create goodwill toward a business.

Public relations specialists attempt to get good publicity for their companies by creating public relations events. Here are some examples:

- The grand opening of a new store or remodeling of an existing one.
- An interview with a company official about the company's mission and philosophy.
- The launching of a new product or product line.
- The announcement of promotions or retirements.
- The presentation of an award to the company or one of its employees.
- A community activity, such as an exhibit or parade sponsored by the business.
- A charitable activity, such as a walkathon for a local charity, in which the business participates.

The goodwill generated by such public relations activities benefits a business by

- increasing sales;
- reinforcing the company's good reputation;
- spreading accurate information (from the business's viewpoint) to the public;
- increasing the receptivity of consumers to the company's advertising;
- conditioning customers to expect quality products from the company;
- reducing the impact of problems (complaints, critical news stories, employee disputes) when they do occur; and
- helping to obtain better treatment from government regarding zoning, licenses, and taxes.

The Audience for Public Relations

The types of activities that qualify as public relations and the audiences to which they are targeted are many and varied. Businesses are concerned with their employees, customers, and the general public.

Employee Relations

To customers, employees are the company. Successful businesses have loyal and well-motivated employees who feel they are important to the company. The public relations staff works with management and employees to design programs that foster such attitudes. These programs include

- tuition reimbursement for taking educational courses or additional job training,
- newsletters for and about the company and its employees (these are commonly called *house organs*),
- health and wellness programs,

Chapter 23 *Publicity and Public Relations* **297**

Focus

Bell Ringer Activity

Ask students to consider this question: "How do you want people to think of you?"

Introducing the Section

If students are willing to give their answers to the Bell Ringer Activity, make a list of them. Answers might include: a good friend, attractive, caring, compassionate, strong, sensitive, etc. So, too, companies have "images" and want to be regarded by the public as "caring, compassionate, concerned, etc."

The purpose of publicity is image-building. Public relations attempts to get good publicity by creating events that foster goodwill. A company is concerned with how its *employees, customers*, and the *general public* (including its stockholders) view it. This section explores the way public relations events are geared to all three.

Teach

Guided Practice

1. Read Section 23.1 with students.
2. Have students read aloud the Case Study and review the answers in class.
3. Make sure to discuss non-profit organizations' need for publicity and PR in this section. A museum, for example, uses publicity to increase attendance and interest in special events. Public relations events better explain the museum's work to the public. The goodwill generated by publicity and public relations efforts encourages the donations that nonprofit organizations need to continue their work and their research.

Meeting Special Needs

English as a Second Language

When preparing class materials for nonnative speakers keep in mind that some common use of pictorial language can be lost in the translation. Even if students can understand the words, idiom can present confusion. This can also include jokes, anecdotes, personal comments, or personification. You may wish to provide handouts in advance so that students can see key vocabulary before class. A second option is to have a list of key words or phrases on the board or on an overhead transparency that students can refer to while you speak.

Discussion Starter

Ask students to give examples of negative publicity that local or national companies have received within the last few years and how those companies attempted to counteract the effects of such publicity. (Example: in 1994, USAir received negative publicity because of the fatal crash of one of its flights and two emergency landings of USAir flights following just a few short weeks thereafter. USAir's efforts at counteracting the negative publicity included running full-page ads in major newspapers that touted its high safety standards.)

Cooperative Learning

Ask students to name the "publics" served by your marketing program. Then divide the class into five groups. Have each group brainstorm some PR events to promote goodwill and provide a positive image for your marketing program to one of the publics your program serves. Review their events in class. Tell students to keep their notes; they will be using them in Section 2.

L1 Communication Skills

First, have student differentiate between *opinion* and *fact*. Have students tell whether the following statements are fact or opinion: Ms. DeBeers is President of Mid-America Chemical Corp. (fact); Ms. DeBeers assumed this position after her father retired from the presidency of the company (fact); Ms. DeBeers is president of the company because her father was president before her (opinion); Ms. DeBeers feels that Mid-America is the best chemical company in the United States (opinion—until she backs up her statement with statistics.)

- strategies for open communication between management and employees,
- promotion programs from within, and
- employee suggestion programs and recognition awards for improvements in performance and efficiency.

The importance of good employee relations cannot be overestimated. Effective and well-run organizations can maximize employee relations by

- clearly identifying job descriptions and responsibilities,
- utilizing each employee's skills,
- informing employees as to how they will be rated for promotion and salary increases,
- instituting wage and benefit packages that are competitive with other businesses in the field,
- providing a formal motivation program for employees,
- avoiding discriminatory employment practices,
- informing employees in advance about events and plans that will affect their work,
- holding regular staff meetings, and
- explaining rules and regulations to employees.

Customer Relations

Good communication between employees and customers is vital in promoting a favorable business image. What you say and how you say it can make all the difference between a dissatisfied customer and a loyal patron.

Real World
MARKETING

Taking It Personally

"It's the personal touch that counts" is Mary Kay Ash's credo. It's also a major factor in the success of Mary Kay Cosmetics, which realizes sales each year in the hundreds of millions. Ash, who started her Dallas-based beauty empire in 1963, makes a point of never getting a name wrong. She also sends each of her beauty consultants a personally designed card every Christmas.

Courtesy, helpfulness, interest, tolerance, and friendliness bring customers back. This repeat business is what makes a company successful.

Many retail firms, however, go further than just friendliness and courtesy. They offer shoppers special services and amenities in order to maintain good customer relations. These services and amenities include restaurants, child-care facilities, gift wrapping, check-cashing services, fax and copying machines, and free delivery.

Other public relations efforts are less obvious. **Customer advisory boards** are panels of consumers who make suggestions about products and businesses. Customer advisory boards are used by manufacturers,

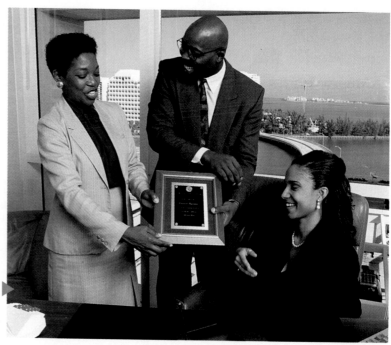

Companies design award programs to promote good employee relations. What are other ways of promoting employee relations?

298   Unit 6   *Promotion*

More About

Employee Relations

In many companies, employee relations are handled by the Human Resource department. The scope of employee relations tends to increase with the size of the company and the number of employees. For example, health and wellness programs can range from producing a flyer to overseeing an on-site fitness center.

Caption Answer

Other activities include providing tuition reimbursement, company newsletters, health and welfare programs, team strategies, promotion programs, and employee suggestion programs.

CASE STUDY

Building Effective Customer Relations

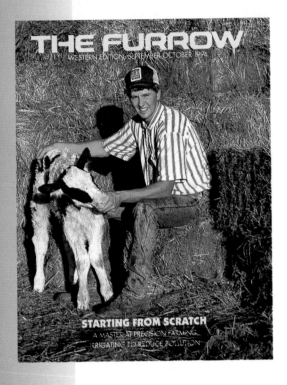

THE FURROW
WESTERN EDITION/SEPTEMBER-OCTOBER 1994

STARTING FROM SCRATCH
A MASTER AT PRECISION FARMING
IRRIGATING TO REDUCE POLLUTION

John Deere & Company, a U.S. manufacturer of farming equipment, has had a long history of creating a favorable business image by using a magazine to communicate with its customers. Since 1895, it has published a noncommercial magazine, called *The Furrow,* which serves the agricultural community.

The Furrow is directed at the company's farming customers. It covers both national and international farming trends and issues. While John Deere does not compete with other commercial publications for hard agricultural news stories, it does run feature stories which attract farmers' attention. The focus of the magazine is to give customers throughout the world valuable farming information.

John Deere publishes *The Furrow* in 18 overseas markets and in 11 different languages. *The Furrow* is published in nine U.S. editions and three Canadian editions. It is also published in Australia, South Africa, New Zealand, the Netherlands, Belgium, Norway, Sweden, Germany, Denmark, Italy, France, Portugal, and the

United Kingdom. Total worldwide circulation is 1,600,000, of which about 570,000 is in the United States, and 110,000 in Canada.

In the early years the magazine accepted advertising from other companies. Today, the magazine only advertises John Deere products. The magazine's editorial content, however, offers practical advice and does not promote John Deere products.

To make sure that the articles are valuable, the company conducts reader surveys and maintains close contact with its dealer network. The magazine has American and European editors and freelancers who write and edit articles about regional farming issues. The magazine is regionalized to reflect issues important to each region of the United States and to each country. According to company officials, editorial quality is the main reason for the magazine's success in satisfying its target audience.

The Furrow is free to John Deere customers, courtesy of the company and its dealers. John Deere picks up the production costs of the magazine. Individual local dealers maintain mailing lists because the company believes that local dealers know their customers best. By having dealers maintain the lists the company is assured that the magazine is sent to the correct target audience.

The Furrow successfully provides free, practical advice for John Deere customers. In doing so, it creates a positive public image for the company.

Case Study Review

1. Why does John Deere spend money to publish *The Furrow?*

2. How does John Deere ensure that *The Furrow's* articles are of interest to farmers from different regions within the United States and different countries?

3. Why does John Deere allow the dealers to maintain customer lists?

A MATTER OF ETHICS

4. In the early years John Deere allowed other advertisers beside itself to advertise in its publication. Today, only the company advertises in the magazine. Do you think that this is ethical? Explain.

Independent Practice

Assign and review the Chapter 23 Case Study in the *International Case Studies* workbook.

Assess

Evaluation

Assign and review the Section 23.1 Review.

Reteaching

1. Assign and review the vocabulary terms for this section.
2. Assign and review Fact and Idea Review questions 1–4 from the Chapter Review.

Enrichment

1. Assign and review the appropriate activities in the *Student Activity Workbook*.
2. Assign and review the appropriate Critical Thinking questions from the Chapter Review.
3. Using local print and broadcast media, have students identify five examples of local or national businesses that have received positive publicity within the last week. They should name the business, tell what products it produces, describe the publicity, and discuss what they think the publicity achieved.

Close

Have students complete this statement: The goodwill generated by public relations activities benefits a business by…(Answers on page 297. If students have a difficult time remembering the benefits, allow them to study the appropriate page in their books for two minutes, close their books, and try to recall how public relations activities benefit businesses.)

300

---

wholesalers, and retailers alike to test new products. For example, a supermarket might want to learn about customer preferences regarding store hours and cultural food items to stock. It may also want to learn whether in-store promotional devices, such as electronic coupons and videocarts, are well liked. By consulting with an advisory board, the supermarket can adjust or change policies, product lines, or promotional efforts to meet the needs of customers.

Some larger department stores also hire consultants to assist customers with their purchases. Fashion, cosmetic, travel, bridal, and interior decorating consultants, and personal shoppers, are examples of employees with specialized training who are hired by some retail firms.

National companies often employ **consumer affairs specialists** to handle customer complaints and to serve as consumer advocates within the firm. Consumer affairs specialists design programs to reflect customer needs for information on topics such as nutrition, health and wellness, and product safety.

Many businesses also sponsor special events to foster positive customer relations. An example is a fashion show to display store fashions.

Community Relations

Community relations refers to the activities that a business uses to acquire or maintain the respect of the community. Businesses foster good community relations by participating in and sponsoring activities that benefit the civic, social, and cultural life of a community. Some examples of community relations activities include sponsoring Special Olympics teams, awarding scholarships

Leave the Soles of Your Feet on the Floor

Sometimes what seems to be an inoffensive gesture or part of normal movement can cause problems for the uninformed traveler. In many parts of the world, for example, the bottom of the foot is considered the lowest and least clean part of the body. For this reason, it is the height of insult to position your feet in such a way that the soles of your shoes are visible to another person. Saudi Arabia, Egypt, Singapore, and Thailand all have long-standing taboos in this regard. Business travelers to these countries report that this taboo combined with the custom of sitting on cushions on the floor can turn you into a contortionist. (The trick is to tuck your feet under you while sitting.)

Ameritech is a sponsor of the Special Olympics. Why is this an example of community relations?

to deserving students, financing guest speakers for civic organizations, and matching employee donations to local charities.

Community relations is an important activity for many businesses. Employees who represent the company in the community are often encouraged to join and remain active in civic organizations, such as the Jaycees, Rotary Club, or the Lions. In addition, involvement with school and community organizations, such as athletic boosters, business and school partnership programs, economic development committees, or the local chamber of commerce, provide recognition for individual employees and present a favorable image for the business. Some companies release employees from normal job responsibilities for limited time periods to chair important charitable fund-raising efforts, such as United Way campaigns aimed at community improvement or enhancement.

Effective businesses need to be active participants in their communities. Although the primary aim of community relations work is to promote civic pride and help the local residents, these events also help create goodwill for their business participants. Customers and the general public do pay attention to the sponsors of community-wide activities.

SECTION 23.1

Review

1. What is the relationship between public relations and publicity?
2. Name three ways in which the goodwill generated by public relations can benefit a company.
3. What are the three audiences for public relations?

SECTION 23.2

Objectives

After completing this section, you will be able to

- explain the primary task of public relations specialists,
- explain the various duties performed by public relations specialists, and
- describe the elements of a news release.

Terms to Know

- news release
- press kit
- press conference

What Do Public Relations Specialists Do?

Companies often hire *public relations* firms or establish *public relations* departments. If you're employed in public relations as a public relations specialist, you will work with more than just customers, employees, and the media. You will also consult with civic and professional groups, legislators, government officials, consumer activists, environmentalists, stockholders, and suppliers.

You may work in the public as well as the private sector. The public sector includes schools, hospitals, universities, government agencies, charitable organizations, and the military. Like private businesses, public agencies also have a need to project a favorable image.

Your principal task as a public relations specialist is to publicize the good news about your company and its products—and to control the damage done by any bad news. Consider the following actual case.

In 1990, traces of dangerous benzene were found in Perrier, a French sparkling water. This prompted a nationwide recall of over 72 million bottles of Perrier. While no one died from drinking tainted Perrier, the company suffered a tremendous image problem. By acting quickly, apologizing, and monitoring consumer responses to new ads for the product, Perrier was able to overcome the bad publicity.

BRIGHT IDEAS

Try Going in Person

When the Pentagon ordered 400 boxes of their new product, a paper called REUSE-A-PAGE, Josh Shindler and Barry Davis were elated. When there were no further orders, however, the young entrepreneurs became concerned. They were sure they had a quality product that answered to both the environmental and cost concerns of government today. What was the problem?

A call to the East Coast brought a quick response. The paper was languishing on the shelves of the Pentagon because people weren't sure what it was or how to use it. They walked right past it and continued to reach for the paper they were familiar with.

Shindler and Davis decided it was time for a demonstration. They flew to Washington, seated themselves beside the shelves with their paper, and snagged anyone who walked by for a 30-second demonstration. Pentagon employees looking for paper watched them write on their product with a water-soluble pen and then erase that writing with a spray bottle of water.

Their quirky, personal approach not only impressed their customers but also made headlines. In fact, their personalities proved so useful as marketing tools their caricatures now appear in company literature. They're in the spotlight now—and they plan to stay there.

Creativity Challenge Form teams of 3-5 people, and try your own version of the Shindler/Davis approach. Select a product that the group feels is good but underexposed. Then brainstorm innovative ways to personally reach customers—and garner a little publicity on the side.

Writing News Releases

The public relations specialist's principal publicity tool is the news release. A **news release** is a prewritten story about a company that is sent to the various media. It usually contains information about the company's employees, stores, operations, products, corporate philosophy, or participation in an event or program. (See Figure 23-1 on page 302.)

A news release must contain a certain amount of newsworthy information in order to be picked up and carried by the media. To be successful, then, public relations

Chapter 23 *Publicity and Public Relations* **301**

Focus

Bell Ringer Activity

Obtain a copy of a one-page news release. Allow students to take notes as you read the release. Who sent this news release? Who was it sent to?

What is the subject of the release? When did the event occur? Did it contain any words or jargon that confused you or were unfamiliar to you?

Was this release successful in conveying its message? Why or why not?

Introducing the Section

The news release is the public relations specialist's principal publicity tool. If done well, a news release is an effective tool in disseminating information about a company, a person, or an organization. In this section, students will concentrate on how to write a news release. They will also look at public relations specialists' other duties.

Teach

Guided Practice

1. Read Section 23.2 with students.
2. Use the transparency for this section.
3. Assign and review the Chapter 23 Activity in the *School-to-Work Handbook*.

Discussion Starter

Is it ethical for companies to use public relations specialists to try to influence public opinion? Why or why not? (Some students may feel that public relations translates into "accentuate the positive and eliminate the negative"—which is only giving one half of the story. However, using PR to influence public opinion is only truly unethical when a company with fundamentally unethical business practices tries to pass itself off as ethical through its PR activities.)

Did You Know ?

Public relations plays a role in many things other than product promotion. During the 1994-1995 baseball player strike, public relations experts worked to make the best of a bad situation. When the smoke cleared and the players went back to work, Major League Baseball renewed all but one of its 20 major national TV advertising spots.

Bright Ideas

REUSE-A-PAGE has already come out with REUSEables for overhead projectors and it plans to sell reusable paper sheets to a grocery chain that intends to use the sheets for shopper's personal grocery lists. Ask students to think about additional products that reusable paper could be used for. For example, students might suggest using the reusable paper to make homework lists on a daily basis.

301

Critical Thinking

Have students think about the kinds of news releases each of the following businesses might generate: school, hospital, a university, a charity, the Navy, a government tourism agency. What will the direct benefit to each business be as a result of the publication of the news release?

Cooperative Learning

In the Section 1 Cooperative Learning Activity, students worked in groups to generate some PR events that would build the image of your marketing program. Have students return to their original groups and develop a specific plan with appropriate activities for reaching its target audience. Have each group present its plan to the class. Try to have students implement some of these activities.

Independent Practice

The text mentions that damage control, as in the case of the Perrier recall discussed in the chapter, is an important part of a public relations specialist's job. Within the last several years there have been several highly publicized cases in which public relations efforts helped overcome bad publicity. Have each student research one such case of damage control. Their 150- to 200-word papers should describe the situation, the company involved, the bad publicity and how it came about, and all major PR efforts taken to overcome it. Have students consult such publications as *Advertising Age*, *Adweek*, *Business Week*, *Marketing Management*, *The New York Times*, *The Reader's Guide to Periodical Literature*, and *The Wall Street Journal*.

Figure 23–1

NEWS RELEASE

News releases should be double-spaced and written on letterhead stationery. Margins should be about 1½ inches to allow the editor to make notes. Always type or word process copy which is clean, legible, and free of spelling errors.

For Immediate Release

Contact: Jennifer Barton Trifecta Entertainment (615) 320-0333
Dixie Pineda

**ALL-STAR ENTERTAINMENT
LINE-UP FOR SATURN HOMECOMING**

NASHVILLE, Tenn.--April 1994--A host of prominent entertainers, athletes and business executives recently gathered in Nashville to unveil details of a historic event scheduled to take place in Spring Hill, Tenn., on June 24-25, 1994.

U.S. Olympic gold medal speed skater Dan Jansen, country music superstar Wynonna and R&B and gospel singing sensations BeBe & CeCe Winans joined Saturn Corporation President Skip LeFauve to announce their participation in The Saturn Homecoming, a two-day customer appreciation event like no other in history. Seven hundred thousand Saturn car owners from across the U.S., Canada and Taiwan are being invited to visit Spring Hill, Tenn., the birthplace of Saturn cars.

Don Hudler, Saturn vice president of sales, service and marketing, announced what's in store for owners making the trip to Tennessee. "Customer relationships and service are at the heart of Saturn's philosophy. We have created The Saturn Homecoming as one more way to show our owners that they are our first priority. We are pleased to offer activities for the entire family during Homecoming including manufacturing plant tours, Camp Saturn for kids and a premiere entertainment lineup."

Saturn will present a state-of-the-art musical concert on Friday and Saturday evening featuring Wynonna and BeBe & CeCe Winans. A 50-foot stage fashioned after a 1950's American jukebox will be constructed on the grounds of the Saturn facility especially for The Homecoming Concert. Guests will enjoy the show in a natural amphitheater created by rolling hay and alfalfa fields surrounding the plant.

(more)

The Saturn Homecoming Program Headquarters • 3001 W. Big Beaver Suite 400 • Troy, Michigan 48084

1. The news release should always have the name, address, and phone number of the contact person sending out the release on the top of the page. All pages should be numbered except for the first page.

2. The first paragraph should answer the Who, What, When, Where, and Why questions.

3. The story with important facts should be developed within the next few paragraphs.

4. More information, which is slightly less important can follow. This information could be cut by an editor without losing vital information.

5. When identifying people in a news release include the full name and title or position of the person, but avoid using Mr., Ms., Mrs., Dr., etc. After you have used the complete name refer only to the last name in the remaining part of the news release.

6. The entire news release should be brief—usually one or two pages is enough. If the news release runs more than one page, write "more" at the bottom of each page except the final one. Identify and number each succeeding page at the top. On the last page, put "---30---" or "###" at the bottom to signify the end of the news release.

Lifelong Learning

Publicity and Public Relations

Students that want to work in public relations will need a strong foundation in business writing and personal communication along with specific job skills such as developing viable public relations campaigns. Those who are not pursuing jobs in public relations will still benefit by keeping aware of what companies are doing in their public relations strategies.

personnel must observe certain guidelines in planning and carrying out publicity projects:

1. Publicity projects should be selected for multiple uses. For example, information gathered for a news release should also be appropriate for use in a new company brochure or ad.
2. Public affairs staff should send only important news releases to the media. (For example, a news release telling of a shopping mall expansion that will result in many new jobs created in a community has a good chance of being run by the media.) If a media source is overwhelmed with submissions, it will tend to disregard them. By sending significant news releases periodically, a business has a better chance of having its material published.
3. News releases should be sent to all media, both print and broadcast, at the same time. The chances that one will use the material are greater when all are contacted.
4. News releases should have a continuity of theme extending over many months or even years. Similar repeat messages will achieve maximum impact on an audience. For example, a consistent message might be that a business is community minded. Such is the case with the Dayton-Hudson Corporation community involvement program. Since 1946, the company has contributed $200 million to the communities where it operates stores. The monies go to support local job training and dropout prevention programs, dance, music, theater, and arts groups. As a result, Dayton-Hudson and its family of stores (Target, Mervyns, Hudson's, Dayton's, and Marshall Field's) are known as good corporate citizens.
5. Remember that the media are interested in news, not publicity. Therefore, the word *publicity* should never be used when communicating with media personnel.

A news release should be properly formatted. It also must answer five basic questions:

1. Who said or did something? Try to avoid editorial comment and personal opinion. If an opinion must be included, attribute it to the originator by using quotes.
2. What was said or what happened? Use simple and accurate words. Words that are unfamiliar or jargon used in a business might confuse news personnel. Be as brief as possible but be sure to cover important facts about the event.
3. When was it said or when did it happen?
4. Where was it said?
5. Why was it said or why did it happen?

Other Public Relations Duties

While news releases are the major written document for which public relations specialists are responsible, they are not the only ones. Public relations staff also prepare

*Public relations specialists **use news releases to publicize news about their companies. Suppose your company were to sponsor this event. Write a news release to publicize it.***

annual reports, brochures, and responses to customer inquiries. Occasionally, they even write short feature articles for trade magazines. They also develop press kits.

A **press kit** is a folder containing articles, news releases, feature stories, and photographs about a company, product, or person. Press kits are given to the media to assist them in reporting on the intended news item.

Public relations personnel frequently meet customers and the public face-to-face. They attend public relations events and organize press conferences.

A **press conference** is a meeting in which media members are invited by a business or organization to hear an announcement about a newsworthy event. Examples of announcements usually covered in press conferences include corporate officer changes and reorganizations of corporate divisions. They also include new product developments, expansions, and closings of company plants or offices.

SECTION 23.2 *Review*

1. **What is the primary task of public relations specialists?**
2. **Identify at least five format rules for writing news releases.**
3. **Name three other duties besides writing press releases that are performed by public relations specialists.**

303

Answers

Vocabulary Review

See the Glossary for definitions.

Fact and Idea Review

1. Public relations is any activity designed to create goodwill toward a business. Publicity is newsworthy information, either good or bad, about the company which is neither paid for by the company, nor controlled by the company.
2. Employee relations: programs and activities conducted by a business to promote goodwill among employees. Customer relations: services, amenities, programs, and services provided to a business's customers. Community relations: activities that a business uses to acquire or maintain the respect of the community.
3. Possibilities include: tuition reimbursement, newsletters for and about the company and its employees, health and wellness programs.
4. Possible answers: the grand opening of a new store, an interview with a company official about the company's mission, the launching of a new product.
5. A customer advisory board is a panel of customers who makes suggestions on new products. A consumer affairs specialist is an employee of a business who handles customer complaints and serves as a consumer advocate within the company.
6. A prewritten story about a company that is sent to the various media. It contains information about the company's employees, stores, operations, products, or philosophy.
7. The question of who, what, when, where, and why must be addressed.

Vocabulary Review

Use the following vocabulary terms in a 150-word paper on public relations.

public relations
customer advisory boards
consumer affairs specialists
community relations
news release
press kit
press conference

Fact and Idea Review

1. Explain the difference between publicity and public relations. (Sec. 23.1)
2. Distinguish between employee, customer, and community relations. (Sec. 23.1)
3. List three programs or policies that businesses use to improve their image in the eyes of their employees. (Sec. 23.1)
4. Give three examples of public relations events. (Sec. 23.1)
5. How do the duties of a customer advisory board differ from those of a consumer affairs specialist? (Sec. 23.1)
6. What is a news release? (Sec. 23.2)
7. Name five basic questions that must be addressed when writing a news release. (Sec. 23.2)
8. Name two tools used by public relations specialists to generate publicity. (Sec. 23.2)

Critical Thinking

1. What is meant by the statement, "To the customer, the employees are the company"?
2. Besides working with customers and the media, public relations specialists also consult with civic and professional groups, legislators, government officials, consumer activists, environmentalists, stockholders, and suppliers. Explain why public relations specialists should respond to these groups.
3. Dayton-Hudson gives back 5 percent of its taxable profits to communities where it does business. The contributions are made in two areas: social service programs and local arts. Analyze the reasons for giving to these causes and why you believe the company concentrates its efforts in these two areas.
4. Identify local businesses that have community relations programs. What kinds of activities are they using to enhance their reputations in the community?

Building Academic Skills

Math

1. Assume that you must submit a budget for your marketing program's public relations activities over the next school year (ten months from September to June). You have $500 to spend. Identify the activities that you would schedule and the costs associated with each (by month). Then determine the percentage you are spending on each activity. *Note:* You can spend on special events, guest speakers, news releases, personal letters, and newsletters but not advertising.

Communication

2. Write a job description for a public relations specialist based on what you have learned in this chapter.
3. Write a news release announcing the grand opening of the school store for the upcoming school year.
4. Write a letter inviting a public relations specialist to speak to the class about publicity and public relations. (Consult your teacher for a list of speakers.) In your letter, be sure to describe the audience, any areas of special interest, the format to be used, and any scheduling requirements. Have your letter proofread by your teacher before you mail it.

Human Relations

5. As a rule, managers in your company participate in a program of corporate giving. Once a month, a certain amount is automatically deducted from each participant's paycheck and given to established charities. The vice president to whom you report asks you to participate. You are reluctant. You would prefer to pick your own charities and schedule your own donations. How would you explain your position to your superior?

Technology

6. One way that businesses communicate to the public is by sending news releases to the media. Use a computer to develop a database of local newspapers in your area to whom you would send a news release about the grand opening of your school store.

Application Projects

1. Watch a local television news program or read a local newspaper for one week. Keep a log of all stories relating to either local or national businesses. Note the gist of each story. Try to determine whether it had its origins in a news release. Note whether the publicity was positive or negative.

---

8. Press conferences and press kits.

Critical Thinking

1. This statement implies that the customer's image of a business is largely determined by the employees who directly interact with the customer. No amount of advertising or promotion can make up for employees who treat customers badly. The image that customers have of a company's employees will tend to translate into feelings about the company's products.
2. The principal reason for working with these diverse groups is to get out good news about the company and its product and to control the damage done by bad news.
3. The company wants its stores located in healthy thriving neighborhoods. This makes good business sense. The grants for social service programs encourage young people and adults to complete their education, be self-reliant, and find good jobs.

2. For each of the following businesses, describe the kinds of public events you might sponsor and the public projects in which you might participate. Explain why they would be good for each business.
   a. A small Hispanic-owned machine tool factory that employs many minorities.
   b. A large waste disposal company that provides a commercial and consumer trash pick-up service and maintains a landfill.
   c. A large corporation located near a YMCA.
3. Choose one event sponsored by each of the companies above and write a news release for it.
4. Your company sells a product that has been tampered with before reaching the stores. As a result, several people have become ill enough to need medical care. As public relations officer for the company, what steps would you recommend that the company take?
5. Choose an event that is sponsored by a community business. Contact the company's public relations department and ask a representative to speak to your class about the planning that goes into such an event.
6. National Geographic, Hallmark, and General Motors often sponsor TV specials. List three programs you have seen that were sponsored exclusively by these or other companies. Think about the program itself and the type and number of commercials for the sponsor. Describe what image you think the company is trying to project. Explain how you felt about the program. Tell whether or not you think the company succeeded in its goal.

Linking School to Work

1. Write a short paragraph on the company *house organ*, or employee newsletter, used in your business. Describe how frequently it is produced and how it is distributed to employees. Attach a copy of it to your paper. If your business does not have a newsletter, explain how the business communicates to its employees.
2. Investigate and compile a list of employee benefits provided to full-time employees in the business where you currently work or one of your choice.

Performance Assessment

Role Play

Situation. You are a public relations specialist for a large clothing company. Recently, the company has expanded and will open seven new stores in the next month. You have been asked to develop public relations activities to create positive publicity for the company's expansion plan. Your activities should generate good employee, customer, and general public relations. You will present your plans to the president of the company.

Evaluation. You will be evaluated on how well you can do the following:

- Describe appropriate public relations activities in terms of the audience they are intended for.
- Explain the benefits of the public relations activities you have chosen.

Public Speaking

Collect employee newsletters from relatives, friends, or acquaintances, and contribute them to a class display. After you have had a chance to study all the available publications, select the one that you feel projects the most positive image of the company publishing it. Defend your choice in a five-minute oral presentation by listing those features you found most impressive in the publication you selected. Also describe those features you found least impressive in the publications you rejected.

Complete the Chapter 23 Computer Application that appears in the Student Activity Workbook.

Portfolio

Consider the Application Projects that you have done for this unit. Select one that illustrates your mastery of the unit's content and might be of interest to potential employers. Reformat the activity as necessary, adding any explanatory text, and place it in your Portfolio. Consider using these activities:

- Chapter 19, Application Project 1
- Chapter 20, Application Projects 4 and 5
- Chapter 21, Application Project 4
- Chapter 22, Application Project 1
- Chapter 23, Application Project 3 ■ ■

---

4. Letters should follow the business letter format discussed in Chapter 9.

Human Relations

5. Students' responses should be courteous. Students should explain their position in a professional manner.

Technology

6. Databases will vary depending on the size of the community.

Application Projects

1. The news stories will vary. However, students should be able to determine whether the information was generated by a news release and whether the information is positive or negative.
2. Examples will vary.
3. News releases will vary.
4. Examples include reimbursing customers who have become ill, issuing a warning about the product, and issuing a new tamper proof package.
5. Answers will vary depending on the event and public relations agency.
6. These companies are trying to generate positive public relations by sponsoring programs.

Linking School to Work

Answers depend on the work situation.

Performance Assessment

Refer to the *DECA Competitive Events Handbook* for evaluation guidelines.

Computer Application

Optional activity. Refer to the *Marketing Software Binder* for template and user information.

Portfolio

Refer to the *Marketing Career Portfolio* for development ideas and portfolio management and assessment.

Evaluation

Administer the reproducible test for Chapter 23 or construct your own test using the Testmaker software.

In addition supporting local causes creates a positive corporate impression and encourages business from local citizens.

4. Answers will vary depending on the community.

Building Academic Skills

Math

1. Answers will vary. However, check to see that the activities associated with the ten-month plan do not exceed $500 and that the activities for each month are realistic and do not reflect advertising costs.

Communication

2. Ability to write press releases and produce press kits; being capable of conducting press conferences; having excellent writing, public speaking, and communication skills.
3. News releases should follow the format rules discussed in the chapter.

Buying and Distribution

Unit Objectives

After completing this unit, students will be able to achieve the following outcomes:

- Diagram the channels of distribution for consumer and industrial products.
- Explain the nature and scope of physical distribution.
- Distinguish purchasing agents and buyers.
- Describe the buying process.
- Trace the stock-handling process from receiving and checking to ongoing inventory management.
- Discuss the impact of technology on inventory systems.
- Calculate the major entries in a merchandise plan.
- Figure stock turnover rates.

Chapter 26

Chapter 27

Chapter 25

Chapter 24

Chapter 28

Teacher Classroom Resources

CHAPTER	24	25	26	27	28
Transparency Binder	Transparencies 33–36		Transparencies 37a & 37b–39		Transparencies 40–42
Student Activity Workbook	pp. 147–152	pp. 153–158	pp. 159–164	pp. 165–172	pp. 173–178
Student Software	pp. 151–152	pp. 157–158	pp. 163–164	pp. 171–172	pp. 177–178
Marketing Math Workbook					Activity 7
School-to-Work Handbook	pp. 53–54	pp. 55–56	pp. 57–58	pp. 59–60	pp. 61–62
International Case Studies	pp. 53–54	pp. 55–56	pp. 57–58	pp. 59–60	pp. 61–62
Marketing Career Portfolio					Unit 7 activity, Student Text, p. 375
Test Booklet/ Testmaker Software	Chapter 24 test	Chapter 25 test	Chapter 26 test	Chapter 27 test	Chapter 28 test Unit 7 test

KEY TO BASIC SKILLS ACTIVITIES

L1 Level 1 activities are basic activities and should be within the range of all students.

L2 Level 2 activities are average activities and should be within the range of average and above average students.

L3 Level 3 activities are challenging activities designed for the ability range of above average students.

Unit

7 Organizer

CHAPTER	PERFORMANCE OBJECTIVES

24

Channels of Distribution

24.1
1. Define a channel of distribution.
2. Identify channel members.
3. Discuss the different channels of distribution for consumer and industrial products.

24.2
1. Identify the key considerations in distribution planning.
2. Discuss the circumstances under which multiple channels of distribution are used.
3. Compare the costs and control involved in having a direct sales force vs. using independent sales agents.
4. Describe the three levels of distribution intensity.
5. Explain some of the challenges involved in distribution planning for foreign markets.

25

Physical Distribution

25.1
1. Explain the nature and scope of physical distribution.
2. Identify transportation systems for the distribution of products.
3. Give examples of transportation services.

25.2
1. Describe storage needs.
2. Identify various types of warehouses.
3. Discuss distribution planning for international markets.

26

Purchasing

26.1
1. Differentiate between purchasing agents and buyers.
2. List the three steps in the buying process.
3. Explain how determining needs is accomplished in both industrial and resale situations.
4. Discuss how wholesale and retail buyers analyze customers' needs and wants.
5. Identify three basic buying plans used to keep track of inventory for buying purposes.

26.2
1. List the criteria buyers use in selecting supply sources.
2. Compare and contrast the deals offered by suppliers and select the best one.
3. Explain how buyers order goods and evaluate the purchases made.

27

Stock Handling and Inventory Control

27.1
1. Explain the need for a stock-handling process.
2. Describe how merchandise is received and checked.
3. Discuss the methods used to mark merchandise.
4. Describe the procedure for transferring merchandise.

27.2
1. Define inventory management.
2. Explain the types of unit inventory control systems.
3. Discuss the impact of technology on inventory systems.

28

Purchasing and Distribution Math

28.1
1. Calculate and verify extensions on purchase orders and invoices.
2. Use appropriate tables to determine shipping charges.

28.2
1. Explain the significance of the major entries in a merchandise plan.
2. Calculate those entries.
3. Figure stock turnover rates.

Unit Overview and Background Information

Unit 7 presents the "nuts and bolts" involved in buying and distribution. Chapter 24 explores the place decision of the marketing mix (how products will be distributed and sold in domestic and foreign markets), while Chapter 25 concentrates on the nature and scope of physical distribution (transportation systems, storage, etc.). Chapter 26 considers the purchasing function in depth, after which Chapter 27 looks at the critical importance of stock handling and inventory control. Finally, Chapter 28 guides students through the math calculations used by buyers and vendors.

Introducing the Unit

Have students speculate about how your school cafeteria purchases the food supplies and utensils it uses. Ask: Who is responsible for purchasing? Where and how was the merchandise stored prior to distribution? By what means of transportation did it arrive at its final destination? How was the merchandise checked in and stored once it arrived? How often is merchandise reordered? As you discuss each aspect of the distribution process, write it on the chalkboard—purchasing, physical distribution, etc.

Unit Project

Have students investigate the policies, forms, and procedures used to receive, check, and route merchandise within a local business of their own choice. Students should prepare a written report based on their research, including their evaluation of the effectiveness of the policies, forms, and procedures used. They should draw conclusions and make recommendations for improvement.

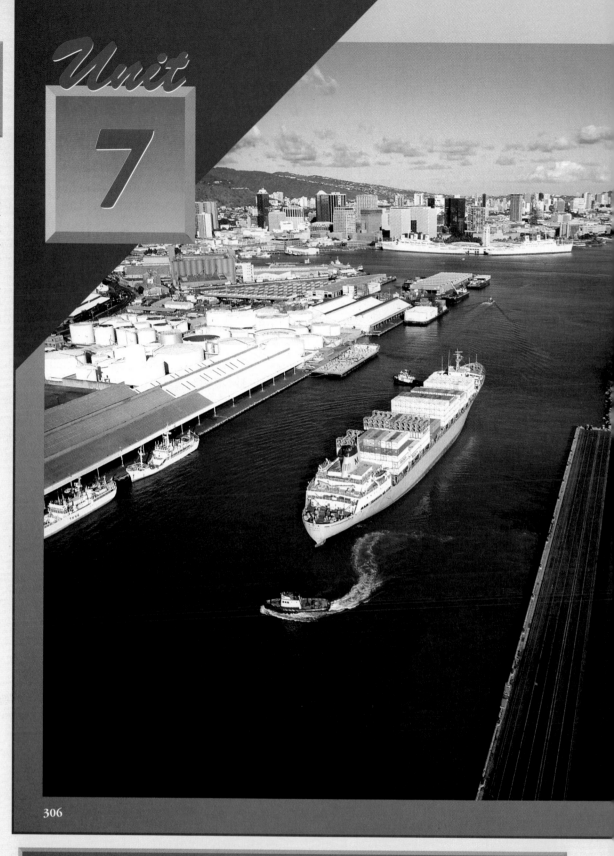

306

Focus on the Photo/Cooperative Learning

Once students have completed this unit, divide the class into four groups. Have each group study the unit photo to determine an appropriate headline for it. The only restriction is that the headline should relate in some way to buying and distribution. It need not, however, be rooted in fact. Have the headlines read aloud for comparison and discussion.

Buying and Distribution

CHAPTERS

24
Channels of Distribution

25
Physical Distribution

26
Purchasing

27
Stock Handling and
Inventory Control

28
Purchasing and
Distribution Math

Resources for Enrichment of Unit Content

Magazines/Journals

Current issues of *Chain Store Age Executive, Chilton's Distribution Magazine, Distribution and Traffic, Handling and Shipping, Inc., Industrial Purchasing Agent, Mass Market Retailers, Production and Inventory Management, Purchasing, Purchasing Management, Railway Age, Stores, Supermarket News, Traffic Management*, and *Transport Topics.*

Unit Closure

Have students select one product (for example, apples, meat, or auto parts) and trace its route from manufacturer, to storage, to distribution, to final inventory before sale.

Evaluation

Administer the reproducible test for Unit 7, or construct your own using the Testmaker software.

Guest Speaker Suggestions

- Invite a purchasing agent from a service business and one from a manufacturing business to discuss their jobs as well as potential careers in purchsing.
- Have a representative from each of the types of storage facilities discuss the considerations and costs involved when storing goods in each type of facility.

Field Trip Suggestions

- Take students on a tour of a local distribution center, if you have one nearby.
- Take students to a central market district, if you have one nearby, to talk with suppliers.
- Have students visit a local business that receives a substantial amount of merchandise daily to observe and talk with those who receive, check, and mark that merchandise.

CHAPTER 24

CHANNELS OF DISTRIBUTION

Pages 308–321

Chapter Overview

Chapter 24 presents fundamental information about channels of distribution, such as where they begin and end, and who their members are. It also distinguishes the types of channels typical of the consumer and industrial markets. Distribution planning in foreign markets rounds out the chapter.

Springboard

Hold up a 100-percent cotton T-shirt. Tell students to assume it's their latest purchase. Then have them write down the steps that were necessary to transform raw cotton from a farmer's field into a garment they could buy in a store. Suggest that the students retain their lists for later reference and discussion.

Prereading

List the section objectives to discuss with students. Have students skim the chapter, looking at the pictures, reading the captions, and noting the heads. Ask questions to ensure that students have a minimal understanding of the chapter structure.

Preteaching the Vocabulary

Before students begin reading the chapter, dictate each of the vocabulary terms and ask students to write them on a sheet of paper. When they finish, write the terms on the chalkboard. Then have students guess at the meaning of each. Write their guesses next to each term, but do not give the correct meaning. Leave this list on the chalkboard so that students can see how close their guesses were to the actual definitions as they work through the chapter.

308

CHAPTER 24

Channels of Distribution

Successful businesses identify their customers and call them their target markets. This identification is then used to create the marketing mix for a product, which includes decisions about product, price, place, and promotion.

In this chapter you will explore the *place* decision—that is, how the product will be distributed and sold in the marketplace. You will learn about the many considerations that go into making that decision. You will also be introduced to distribution planning for foreign markets.

Classroom Management

For the Teacher

- Teacher's Annotated Editions for all workbooks
- Teacher's Manual for *School-to-Work Handbook*
- *Testing Binder*
- *Transparency Binder*
- *Marketing Software Binder*
- *Marketing Career Portfolio*
- *Lesson Plans*

For the Student

- *Student Activity Workbook*
- *Marketing Math Workbook*
- *School-to-Work Handbook*
- *Student Software*
- *International Case Studies*
- *Marketing Career Portfolio*

SECTION 24.1

Objectives

After completing this section, you will be able to
- **define a channel of distribution,**
- **identify channel members, and**
- **discuss the different channels of distribution for consumer and industrial products.**

Terms to Know

- **channel of distribution**
- **intermediaries**
- **electronic retail outlets**
- **vending service companies**
- **agents**
- **direct distribution**
- **indirect distribution**

Distribution Basics

Marketers need to ask themselves how and where their target market will buy their products. This is the place decision, one of the four P's of the marketing mix. Toothpaste manufacturers, for example, know that customers like to buy such common personal convenience items in supermarkets and drugstores. A toothpaste manufacturer would therefore want its products to be sold to such stores.

To make a place decision, marketers must decide on their **channel of distribution.** This is the path a product takes from producer or manufacturer to final user.

Where a Channel Begins and Ends

The channel of distribution always begins with the producer or manufacturer. A producer might be a farmer or a craftsperson. A manufacturer could be a company that makes goods for people to use in their daily lives or a company that makes goods other manufacturers need

in their operations. In either case, the channel ends when the product changes form.

Let's use oranges and one product made from them to illustrate. Figure 24-1 on page 310 shows how the channels of distribution would look if we diagramed them. Note that one channel ends and another begins when the oranges change form. When the oranges are sold to someone who will turn them into juice, that is the start of a new channel. Thus, there are two separate and distinct channels involved—one for the oranges and one for the juice.

BRIGHT IDEAS

Change with the Times

When newspapers made the transition to computerized production, they did more than increase the efficiency of their operations. They also changed the form of their product from printed information to electronically stored information. With that transformation, they laid the groundwork for a new channel of distribution.

In the past, if you wanted to read a previously published article, you paged through bound volumes of back issues or scrolled through rolls of microfilm. Now computers house the archives of most newspapers, and some large dailies have begun to offer information services to their readers.

Specifically, previously published articles can be retrieved, printed, and for a fee sent by mail, fax, or computer to readers at home or in the office. The *Los Angeles Times,* for example, offers a service called Timeslink that allows readers to access information about past stories through a computer modem. The rationale of this service is simple. How much easier to let the computer find all the articles relevant to a topic than to plow through the archives oneself.

Creativity Challenge Form teams of 3–5 people. Then brainstorm a list of unusual services that could be offered through this new channel of distribution. For example, someone interested in sports could retrieve and sell recruiting statistics to students interested in obtaining sports scholarships.

Focus

Bell Ringer Activity

Have students recall the four P's of the marketing mix they learned in Chapter 2 (product, place, price, and promotion). Ask what they recall about the place decision.

Introducing the Section

If students have difficulty relating to the Bell Ringer Activity's abstract question, ask them where they buy their clothing, compacts disks, shampoo, and shoes. Remind students that in order to reach them, manufacturers of those products would have to had to decide to include those businesses in their place decisions. Tell them that the place decision in the marketing mix is the focus of this chapter on distribution planning.

Teach

Guided Practice

1. Read Section 24.1 with students.
2. Use the three transparencies for this section.
3. Have students read aloud the Case Study and review the answers in class.
4. Remind students of the T-shirt example used in the Springboard activity and the lists they made. Ask how many channels of distribution were involved there. (Four—cotton farmer to thread manufacturer, thread manufacturer to fabric manufacturer, fabric manufacturer to clothing manufacturer, and clothing manufacturer to retailer. *Note:* Some students might have included a wholesaler, but that would not change the number of channels, only the number of members in one channel.)

Meeting Special Needs

Gifted

Students in your class who consistently finish work more quickly than others and who have above average ability, task commitment, and creativity may be considered gifted. You may wish to challenge these students to work on an independent project related to distribution channels. For example, you may ask such students working either individually or as a group to research channels of distribution in foreign markets such as Russia or China. Ask students to imagine that they are a U.S. manufacturer of some success who is considering a new market for one or more products.

5. To teach the concept of agents, ask students to explain the job of a real estate agent. (Agents find buyers for sellers and sellers for buyers, for which they receive a commission.) Then ask students if, in general, the real estate agents own the properties. (No, they are sales agents for people who wish to sell their property.)

6. To teach the concept of channels of distribution in the consumer market, put a diagram on the chalkboard (Producer to Consumer), and identify it as direct distribution. Then ask students to name products they have purchased directly from producers and have them describe the circumstances of the purchase. (If necessary, remind them that if they bought in a retail store, the channel of distribution was probably *not* direct.)

7. To introduce the various indirect channels of distribution in the consumer market, draw each one on the chalkboard, beginning with the shortest and moving to the longest. For each one, describe the type of products generally sold using that channel. Ask students for examples of other types of products they think would use the same channel.

8. To teach the channels of distribution in the industrial market, follow the same described in items 6 and 7 above.

Discussion Starter

Ask students if they think the Hershey Foods Corporation in Hershey, Pennsylvania, would be willing to distribute their school store candy. (Most students will

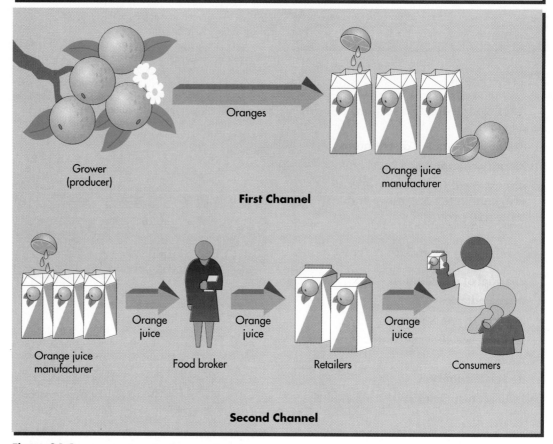

Channels of Distribution

Grower (producer) — Oranges → Orange juice manufacturer

First Channel

Orange juice manufacturer → Orange juice → Food broker → Orange juice → Retailers → Orange juice → Consumers

Second Channel

Figure 24–1

A new channel of distribution begins when the product changes form. Suppose the orange juice were made into Popsicles. How would that change the diagram?

Channel Members

A channel of distribution, then, includes producers, manufacturers, and final users of a product. When the product is purchased for use in a business, the final user is classified as an *industrial user*. When the product is purchased for personal use, the final user is classified as a *consumer*.

Apart from producers and manufacturers, there are other channel members called *intermediaries*. **Intermediaries** are channel members that help move products from the producer or manufacturer to the final user. They are also sometimes called *middlemen*. Intermediaries are a primary factor in providing place utility.

Intermediaries are classified on the basis of whether or not they take ownership (or title) to goods and services. *Merchant intermediaries* take title; *agent intermediaries* do not. Agent intermediaries, usually called

agents, are paid a commission to help buyers and sellers get together.

Merchant Intermediaries The two major types of merchant intermediaries are wholesalers and retailers. Special types of retailers include *electronic retail outlets* and *vending service companies*.

Wholesalers buy large quantities of goods from manufacturers, store the goods, and resell them to other businesses. Their customers may include retailers, professional or commercial users, manufacturers, governments, institutions, or other wholesalers.

Traditional retailers sell goods to the ultimate consumer through their own stores. Large retail chain stores, such as Sears, are sometimes so big they are able to take on the wholesaling functions of buying in large quantities, storing, and distributing in smaller quantities to their chain store branches. Smaller retailers may use the services of wholesalers.

310   Unit 7   *Buying and Distribution*

It would create a third channel. The second would end with the Popsicle manufacturer after food broker. The third would be Popsicle manufacturer to retailer to consumers.

Electronic retail outlets sell goods to the ultimate consumer through special television programs and computer linkups. *Home shopping networks* are television stations whose sole purpose is to sell products to consumers. These companies buy the products in set quantities and sell them via television programs. Consumers phone in their orders while watching the shows. Two of the more popular home shopping television shows are QVC and the Home Shopping Network.

Computer linkups are offered through special computer programs, like Prodigy. Consumers who have the program for their home computers can buy goods directly from offerings included in the program setup. Using a modem, they can place an order directly over the computer network.

Linking the television, computer, and telephone together creates an even more advanced electronic retail outlet, which is often referred to as an *interactive shopping vehicle*. Unlike home shopping television channels, the interactive shopping linkup puts customers in control of the images on their television screen. Consumers are able to look through catalogs, select products on the television screen by using a mouse or remote control, and arrange electronically to have the products delivered to their homes.

Vending service companies buy manufacturers' products and sell them through machines that dispense goods to consumers. Such companies often place their vending machines in stores, office buildings, restaurants, hospitals, schools, and other institutions for free. They make their money from the items sold through the machines, which they stock on a regular basis. In some colleges, you can purchase a variety of food and snacks—sandwiches, fresh fruit, cookies, candy, soda, and hot drinks—from vending machines.

Continued improvement in vending equipment has increased the variety of products that can be sold through vending machines. For example, two large vending service companies (Canteen Corp and Service America) have begun experimenting with offering frozen food entrees through vending machines. That would give manufacturers of frozen foods a new distribution channel to consider. ConAgra (Healthy Choice) and Stouffer's (Lean Cuisine) are two companies that are researching the possibilities of using this new channel for their frozen foods.

Agents Agents are a part of the channel of distribution because they negotiate the title of goods. They do not take title themselves but instead arrange agreements between channel members. Agents usually work strictly on commission. They receive a certain percentage of the sales by their principals, the manufacturers they represent.

There are two basic types of agents—*independent manufacturer's agents* and *brokers*. Both do the same basic job. Independent manufacturer's agents represent several related (but noncompeting) manufacturers in a specific industry. They are not on any manufacturer's payroll. They work independently, running their own businesses.

For example, an independent manufacturer's agent might carry a line of fishing rods from one manufacturer, lures from another, insulated clothing for hunters from a different manufacturer, and outdoor shirts from still another manufacturer. This manufacturer's agent would sell the merchandise to sporting goods wholesalers and retailers who specialize in hunting and fishing.

A broker also acts as a sales agent for different manufacturers. The broker's roles and responsibilities can be exactly the same as those of a manufacturer's agent, or they can be a little more involved. Most brokers sign agreements with their principals that outline their responsibilities. The broker may be responsible for merchandising and for selling the goods. For example, Pezrow is a food and nonfood broker in the Northeast. It follows plans from its principals regarding shelf position and other merchandising requirements when displaying and stocking the products in supermarkets.

Nonchannel Members Nonchannel members include transportation companies and independent storage warehouses. They are not considered part of the channel of distribution because they do not take title to the goods nor are they involved in negotiating that title. They are simply hired to facilitate the physical movement of the goods. You will learn more about businesses like these in Chapter 25.

Direct and Indirect Channels

In general, channels of distribution are classified as *direct* or *indirect*. **Direct distribution** occurs when the goods or services are sold from the producer directly to the final user; no intermediaries are involved. **Indirect distribution** involves one or more intermediaries.

Direct and indirect distribution are both common in marketing goods. For services, however, the channel of distribution is more often direct because most services are performed by the service business itself. For example, employees in a hair salon actually perform such services as cutting customers' hair. (In some instances, however, the channel for services can be indirect. This is the case when an independent insurance agent sells insurance to consumers or businesses.)

Channels in the Consumer and Industrial Markets

Different channels of distribution are generally used to reach the final consumer in the consumer and industrial markets. For example, a manufacturer of paper products might sell napkins to both markets by using two different and distinct channels. When selling to the industrial market, the company would sell napkins to industrial distributors

Chapter 24 *Channels of Distribution* **311**

recognize that Hershey would not want to deal with such a small operation because the paperwork and shipping would be too costly and time-consuming. The only way the school store could buy from the Hershey Company might be to buy a truckload, which would be impractical because the school store does not have the storage space or the sales volume to handle such a large order.) This example will help introduce the need for wholesalers and their role in the distribution process.

Critical Thinking

1. Ask students if they think that by the year 2010 electronic retail outlets will replace traditional retail store outlets. Have them support their opinions. (Answers will vary.)
2. Have students try to imagine what it would be like if all intermediaries were to disappear overnight. Ask: What would happen within a year to the variety of goods available to consumers? to production capabilities? (The former would be reduced, the latter limited.)

   Continue: Would manufacturers still mass-produce goods if mass distribution were no longer possible? (Probably not.) What could manufacturers do to sell their products to final users without intermediaries? (They could sell them from their own factory outlets or use print and broadcast media advertising to encourage orders by phone, mail, or fax.)
3. Ask students why small retailers tend to use the services of wholesalers. (Because they lack the storage space, capital, and customers to buy in large quantities.)

L1 Math Skills

Pose this problem: A manufacturer sells an item to a discount chain store at 50 percent off the list (or suggested retail) price. If the item has a list price of $75.59, what does the discount chain store pay for it? ($75.59 × .50 = $37.80)

L2 Math Skills

Continue the problem from the L1 Math Skills activity: Tell students to assume that the same manufacturer that sells the item to the discount chain store for 50 percent off the list price gives a regular retailer only 40 percent off. Ask students to determine the dollar savings enjoyed by the chain store over a regular retailer. (Retailer cost: $75.59 × .60 = $45.35. Difference: $45.35 − $37.80 = $7.55)

L3 Math Skills

Continue the problem from the L1 and L2 Math Skills activities: Tell students to assume that the chain store does not get 50 percent off the list price, but rather the standard 40 percent off and an additional 10 percent for doing its own distribution. Ask students if this arrangement is the same as a 50 percent discount, and have them explain their answers. (No, it's not the same because the discounts apply *in sequence:* $75.59 × .60 = $45.35; $45.35 × .90 = $40.82. Students should compare this answer with the one arrived at for the chain store in the L1 Math Skills activity—$37.80.)

Independent Practice

1. Assign and review the Chapter 24 Case Study in the *International Case Studies* workbook.
2. Have students interview a local broker, wholesaler, or retailer. Have them develop

---

who, in turn, would sell the napkins to restaurants. When selling to the consumer market, the company would sell napkins to a wholesaler or use brokers to sell to retailers. The retailers would then sell the napkins to consumers for personal use.

To get a clearer picture of how channels are structured in the consumer and industrial markets, study Figures 24-2 and 24-3. Note that while the individual channels may be different, both markets make use of direct and indirect distribution.

Figure 24-2

DISTRIBUTION CHANNELS FOR CONSUMER PRODUCTS

Most consumer goods are not marketed using direct distribution (channel A) because consumers have become accustomed to shopping in retail stores. Of the indirect channels available, Manufacturer/Producer to Retailer to Consumer (channel B) is the most commonly used.

Channel A

There are four key ways in which direct distribution is used for consumer goods.

1. Selling products at the production site. Examples: Farmer's roadside stand, factory outlet.

2. Having a sales force call on consumers at home. Examples: Avon, Tupperware.

3. Using catalogs or ads to generate sales. Example: Infomercials (30–60 minute TV commercials that explain a product in detail and tell viewers how to order it directly from the manufacturer).

4. Telemarketing. Examples: Magazine subscriptions and telecommunications services are often sold in this way.

Channel B

This is the most commonly used channel for merchandise that dates quickly or needs servicing. Fashion apparel and automobiles are sold this way. Chain stores also use this channel because they handle the physical distribution of the products they buy.

Channel C

This is the most common distribution method for staple goods (items that are always carried in stock and whose styles do not change frequently). The manufacturer sells to the wholesaler, who then handles the sales, warehousing, and distribution of the goods to retailers. Consumer goods sold this way include supermarket items, flowers, candy, and stationery supplies.

Channel D

This is the channel for manufacturers who wish to concentrate on production and leave sales and distribution to others. The agent sells to wholesalers who are involved in storage, sale, and transportation to retailers. The retailer then sells to consumers.

Channel E

This is the channel chosen by manufacturers who do not want to handle their own sales to retailers. The agent simply brings the buyer and seller together. Expensive cookware, meat, cosmetics, and many supermarket items are sold this way.

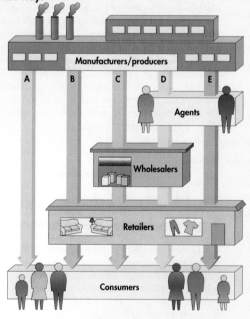

📁 **More About**

Manufacturers

Manufacturers provide retailers with more than just goods to sell. Since they are the best authorities on the use, quality, and contents of their own products, they often supply retailers with valuable product information, display materials, and even advertising ideas. These services can be especially important to smaller retailers or those with limited budgets for advertising and/or training sales personnel.

Figure 24–3

DISTRIBUTION CHANNELS FOR INDUSTRIAL PRODUCTS

Because industrial users shop differently and have different needs from consumers, they use different channels of distribution. In fact, the least commonly used channel in the consumer market—direct distribution (channel A)—is the most commonly used in the industrial market.

Channel A

This is the most common method of distribution for major equipment used in manufacturing and other businesses. The manufacturer's sales force calls on the industrial user to sell goods or services. For example, a Xerox sales rep sells copiers directly to manufacturers and commercial businesses. *Note:* All methods of direct distribution listed for the consumer market are used in the industrial market as well.

Channel C

Small manufacturers who do not have the time or money to invest in a direct sales force may prefer this channel. The agent sells the goods to the industrial wholesaler who stores, resells, and ships them to the industrial user. The advantage of this arrangement is that both agent and industrial wholesaler are likely to be experts well known in the industry. Their reputation and services may be impossible for a small manufacturer to duplicate on its own.

Channel B

This channel is used most often for small standardized parts and operational supplies needed to run a business. Industrial wholesalers take ownership of the products, stock them, and sell them as needed to industrial users. For example, a restaurant supply wholesaler buys pots, pans, utensils, serving pieces, and paper products from various manufacturers to sell to restaurant owners.

Channel D

This is another channel used when a manufacturer does not want to hire its own sales force. The agent represents the manufacturer for sale of the goods but does not take possession or title. The merchandise is shipped directly from the manufacturer to the industrial user. Construction equipment, farm products, and dry goods are often marketed this way.

Chapter 24   *Channels of Distribution*   **313**

questions that relate to current problems and/or challenges these businesspeople face today.

For example, many wholesalers and brokers are being left out of the distribution channel for very large retail operations like Wal-Mart because they buy only directly from the manufacturer. Small retailers are also getting hurt because they cannot command the deep discounts that operations like Wal-Mart can. Therefore, they can't offer their customers the same low prices.

3. Have students research the new forms of interactive channels of distribution in the consumer and industrial markets. Specifically, tell them to see how the information superhighway (the joining of computer technology and telecommunications) may impact the way business is done in the near future. *Note:* They can also research the impact QVC and other electronic retailers are having on traditional retailers.

Assess

Evaluation

Assign and review the Section 24.1 Review.

Reteaching

1. Assign and review the vocabulary terms for this section.
2. Assign and review Fact and Idea Review questions 1–6 from the Chapter Review.
3. To reteach the concept of agent intermediaries, have students think about professional athletes, actors and actresses, and other celebrities. Ask students if they have ever heard that such people have agents. Invite students to speculate about what an agent's job might be in such circumstances. (To find work and negotiate contracts for their clients.)

Assess *(Cont'd.)*

Tell students that some manufacturers are just like those actors and athletes. They want to sell their goods but don't want to go out and find customers. They, too, hire agents to do it for them.

Enrichment

1. Assign and review the appropriate activities in the *Student Activity Workbook*.
2. Assign and review the appropriate Critical Thinking questions from the Chapter Review.
3. Have students prepare a bulletin-board display showing the various channels of distribution used to get a given product into the hands of final consumers. They can select something as simple as a pencil or as complex as an automobile.
4. Have students research the different methods of distribution used by a company to get its product into the hands of consumers. For example, a company such as IBM has consumer, industrial, and electronic distribution.

Ask students to select a company and research all of the various channels of distribution it uses. Suggest they present their findings in chart form and share them with the class.

Close

Have students complete the following statement: The path a product takes from the producer or manufacturer to the final user is called. . .(a channel of distribution.)

314

Computer Companies Go Direct

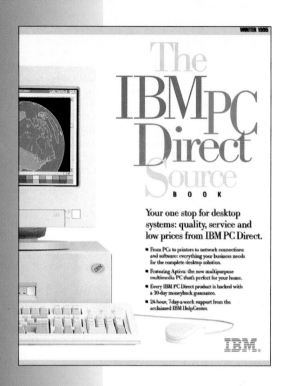

Dell is a company that provides its customers with build-to-order computer systems. The company is also a pioneer in selling computers directly to consumers, through telemarketing.

At one point Dell tried to sell its computers in retail outlets. It found, however, that retailers were not ideal distributors for its products. Retail salespeople thought it took too much time and effort to explain build-to-order computers. They preferred to sell and replace standard machines.

The big three—IBM, Compaq, and Apple—are now taking a page from Dell's book and getting into direct marketing. IBM's entry into direct marketing was through a mail order catalog, called *IBM PC Direct*. The catalog carried a full line of IBM personal computers, along with numerous non-IBM accessories and software.

The IBM facility that handles all direct marketing functions and builds computers for the catalog is in Raleigh, North Carolina. Its operators have taken another page from Dell's book. They custom-configure a

314   Unit 7   *Buying and Distribution*

system, provide price information, and set a shipping date—all while the customer is on the line.

Apple sales from its distributor network have declined in recent years. They slipped to less than 50 percent of total sales in 1994, down from 80 percent in 1991. The reason? The company changed its distribution strategy to include mass merchandisers and direct mail catalogs.

Apple has mailed millions of catalogs to both new prospects and previous customers who returned registration cards. Its catalogs emphasize computer solutions and hardware. Even though Apple says it offers its complete line through direct marketing, it often suggests that customers interested in higher-end computer systems visit an Apple dealer.

Compaq, worried about how its dealers would react to its direct distribution strategy, went so far as to purchase mailing lists rather than use the registration card data generated by dealers. It also decided not to offer its complete line through its catalogs.

In all these cases, the computer manufacturers are just trying to be where the customers are. The companies don't feel that they are effectively reaching small business and home computer buyers through distributors and dealers. So, they are reaching out to these customers directly.

Presently, however, the number one direct marketer of computers is Gateway 2000 of Sioux City, South Dakota. According to market researcher Dataquest, Gateway held a 5 percent share of personal computers shipped in the United States in the first quarter of 1994. Dell's share was only 4.6 percent.

Case Study Review

1. Diagram Dell's channel(s) of distribution, as well as the big three's. Which channels are direct, and which are indirect?
2. What distribution planning considerations were apparent in the big three's decisions to change their distribution strategies?

A MATTER OF ETHICS

3. Should computer companies be allowed to compete with their own customers—that is, their own dealers? Under all circumstances or just some? Explain.

Case Study Answers

1. Dell: manufacturer to consumer or manufacturer to industrial user (both direct). Big three: catalog sales—(same as Dell); retail sales—manufacturer to retailer to consumer or manufacturer to industrial distributer to industrial user (indirect).
2. The big three feared the competition from Dell, Gateway, and similar companies who are able to create custom-built computers at competitive prices.
3. Some will feel that the computer companies are treating their dealers unfairly, while others will see the move as smart marketing. The move, however, could backfire if the dealers no longer push the companies' lines because of the added competition from their own vendors.

Life in the Multicultural MARKETPLACE

Some companies do better than others when it comes to international expansion. J.C. Penney is one company that has done exceptionally well. How? By researching and then evaluating its potential in local markets worldwide.

For example, instead of opening full-line stores in Japan and Singapore, the company sells private label men's clothing in those markets. In other locations (like the Caribbean, Russia, and Iceland), it has licensed catalog stores. In Mexico, however, Penney will open seven regular stores. The company already knows from experience that this channel is ideal for that market. That's because Penney already does $100 million of business with Mexican shoppers in border stores.

Now let's consider a real-life example—PolyGram, the second largest record company in the world. It has three different types of customers and uses two different channels to reach them.

First, PolyGram sells to specialty chain stores like Sam Goody's and Tower Records. It doesn't need any intermediaries to reach these chains because they buy in such large quantities and do their own distribution. PolyGram's second type of customer is small, independent music stores. The company reaches these mom-and-pop operations through wholesalers. Finally, PolyGram sells to mass merchandisers like Wal-Mart. It uses specialized wholesalers called rack jobbers to reach these stores. Rack jobbers manage inventory and merchandising by counting stock, filling it in when needed, and maintaining store displays.

SECTION 24.1 *Review*

1. What is a channel of distribution?
2. Identify the first and last member in a channel of distribution, as well as two additional members who may be included in some channels of distribution.
3. Which type of distribution channel—direct or indirect—is used more frequently for consumer products? for industrial products?

Objectives

After completing this section, you will be able to

- identify the key considerations in distribution planning,
- discuss the circumstances under which multiple channels of distribution are used,
- compare the costs and control involved in having a direct sales force vs. using independent sales agents,
- describe the three levels of distribution intensity, and
- explain some of the challenges involved in distribution planning for foreign markets.

Terms to Know

- intensive distribution
- selective distribution
- exclusive distribution
- integrated distribution

Considerations in Distribution Planning

Distribution planning involves decisions regarding a product's physical movement and transfer of ownership from producer to consumer. In this chapter we are addressing only transfer of ownership concerns. You will study physical distribution concerns in Chapter 25.

Distribution decisions involve and affect a firm's marketing program. Some of the major considerations are the use of *nontraditional and multiple channels, control vs. costs,* and *intensity of distribution* desired.

Nontraditional and Multiple Channels

Businesses do not always follow the traditional channels of distribution. A classic example of a nontraditional

Chapter 24 *Channels of Distribution* **315**

FOCUS

⏰ Bell Ringer Activity

Ask students to name some nonfood products that have found their way into supermarkets. (Videotapes, carpet cleaners [rentals], flower arrangements.)

Introducing the Section

Use the answers from the Bell Ringer Activity to introduce the concept of nontraditional and multiple channels of distribution. Then have students think about hotels and how they are targeting the business traveler.

Tell students that whenever a business expands the sale of its goods or services to a different market, it must use multiple channels of distribution. Ask why that is necessary. (Because each market may have a distinct way in which goods and services are sold and distributed.)

Teach

Guided Practice

1. Read Section 24.2 with students.
2. Use the transparency for this section.
3. Ask students how soap, shampoo, hair conditioner, and facial tissue companies that generally sell their products to consumers through brokers and supermarkets could do business in the industrial market. To give students a hint, suggest they try to think of where all those products might be found *in miniature.* (Hotels and motels.)

Ask students if they would use the same brokers who sell to supermarkets to sell these miniature products to hotels. (No, because such brokers specialize in selling to supermarkets and would not know the ins and outs of selling to hotels.)

Teach (Cont'd.)

4. To introduce distribution planning in foreign markets, ask students what problems beyond language barrier they would foresee in trying to distribute and sell a company's products in a foreign market. (Answers will vary. Possibilities include breaking into an established system of doing business, taking business away from domestic firms that sell the company's products, and finding personnel who speak the language and know the cultural nuances well enough to sell in the country.)

5. Assign and review the Chapter 24 Activity in the *School-to-Work Handbook*.

Discussion Starter

To motivate students and get them thinking about nontraditional and multiple channels, recount this story: Two business executives are shopping for fishing gear for a vacation trip. While waiting to pay their bill, they spot a poster for insulated clothing designed to keep people warm at subzero temperatures. The executives have been looking for garments of just this sort for a research team they are sending to Antarctica in a few months. The retailer answers the executives' questions and allows them to inspect a sample garment. The executives like what they see and place an order with the retailer.

The retailer starts soliciting business from manufacturers and contractors who work in cold outdoor locations. He/she becomes an industrial distributor of the insulated garments. The new channel of distribution is manufacturer to industrial distributor (retailer) to industrial user.

Ask students to brainstorm a list of similar opportunities. Suggest they start with businesses that already carry, manufacture, or provide particular products. Then have them consider how those firms could expand their roles in present or new channels.

316

channel was created by L'eggs Products, a division of Hanes. L'eggs revolutionized the industry when it began selling panty hose in supermarkets. Before that time, panty hose were sold primarily through department stores and specialty shops. However, Hanes knew it could reach more women by placing its product where they shopped most often—in supermarkets. Recently, Xerox Corporation made a similar move. It began selling its office supplies (paper, envelopes, message pads) in supermarkets in an attempt to reach home office consumers.

Multiple channels are used when a product fits the needs of both industrial and ultimate consumers. For example, take Greenfield's Healthy Foods, a company that produces fat-free cookies and brownies. Presently Greenfield's sells its fat-free snacks to supermarkets and convenience stores, as well as to airlines. However, it is also looking to expand into other markets, such as schools and hospitals. Each new market poses questions regarding the exact channel of distribution needed to reach it.

Retailers also use multiple channels. A retail stationery store, for example, generally carries stationery supplies, greeting cards, and some convenience items for consumers. Much of its business, though, may involve selling office supplies to businesses in the local area. To cater to this industrial market, the stationery store might offer credit, trade discounts, and delivery services.

Some manufacturers use multiple channels to reach as many consumers as possible. For example, Patagonia, a manufacturer of outdoor clothing and accessories, sells its products in its own retail stores, through catalogs, and through independent retail dealers. This approach to distribution planning can cause problems if the retail dealers feel they are competing with their supplier (Patagonia, in this case) for consumer sales. If the manufacturer can prove there is no direct competition, however, retailers will accept a multiple-channel distribution policy.

Control vs. Costs

All manufacturers/producers must weigh the control they want to keep over the distribution of their products against costs and profitability. In some cases, this means deciding between using an in-house sales force or independent sales agents. In other cases, it means accommodating one's business to the dominant member in a particular channel of distribution.

Who Does the Selling? A manufacturer must make decisions regarding the amount of control it wants over its sales function. It can decide to use its own sales force or hire agents to do the selling.

A direct sales force is more costly because in-house sales representatives are on the company payroll, receive employee benefits, and are reimbursed for expenses. The manufacturer, though, has complete control over them. It can establish sales quotas and easily monitor each sales representative's performance.

When sales volume is very high and a company is well established in the marketplace, it may be less costly to use

an in-house sales force. That is because the selling effort is minimal and the company can hire sales representatives on a salary basis to service established accounts. However, when first starting out, a company may not be able to afford this alternative because of the costs outlined above.

With an agent, a manufacturer loses some of its control over how sales are made. But the cost of using agents can be lower than hiring an in-house sales staff. No employee benefits or expenses need be paid because agents are independent businesspeople. In addition, they are paid a set percentage of sales. So, the cost of sales is always the same in relation to the sales generated.

Who Dictates the Terms? In recent years, another cost/control consideration has emerged—the increasing power of retail giants like Wal-Mart, Toys "Я" Us, and Home Depot. Manufacturers that want to do business with such retailers must often adhere to strict criteria about selling direct and offering special services in areas like shipping, pricing, packaging, and merchandising. The added services cost manufacturers money. Because of the large volume of business generated by the retail giants, however, most manufacturers adhere to their wishes.

There are those manufacturers, however, that cannot (or choose not) to get involved with the giants. Instead, they distribute their products through smaller retailers.

As a case in point, Sashco Sealants, Inc., a manufacturer of caulking products, decided to sell only to small independent retailers instead of mass merchandisers. Sashco's two top-selling products, Lexel and Big Stretch, are doing well in this niche. One reason is that hardware cooperatives such as Ace Hardware, Service Star, and True Value are buying Sashco's products. (The cooperatives are corporations owned by hardware dealers.) Another reason is that Sashco did not have to lower its prices to a point where its profitability would be affected, as might have been the case if it had dealt with mass merchandisers. (Because major mass merchandisers buy in such large quantities, they often negotiate for extremely low prices from their suppliers.)

Distribution Intensity

Distribution intensity has to do with how widely a product will be distributed. There are three levels of distribution intensity—*intensive, selective,* and *exclusive.*

Intensive Distribution Intensive distribution involves use of all suitable outlets for a product. The objective is complete market coverage. The ultimate goal is to sell to as many customers as possible, wherever they might shop. For example, motor oil is marketed in quick-lube shops, farm stores, auto parts retailers, supermarkets, drugstores, hardware stores, warehouse clubs, and other mass merchandisers. Ceiling fans are sold in catalog stores, lighting specialty stores, hardware stores, bath and kitchen remodeling retailers, and do-it-yourself electrical/plumbing supply chains.

In the industrial market, industrial supplies fall into this category. One such product manufactured by 3M is

More About

Multiple Channels

The trend toward manufacturers opening their own stores is on the upswing. Sony Corporation has two such stores—Sony Style in New York City and Sony Gallery in Chicago, Illinois. Analysts claim that the trend helps independent retailers rather than harming them by increasing product awareness.

facial respirators. To reach all possible users of facial respirators, 3M has included welding supply channels, farm supply distributors, and specialty chemical channels in its distribution planning.

Selective Distribution Selective distribution means that a limited number of outlets in a given geographic area are used to sell the product. The objective is to select channel members that are good credit risks, aggressive marketers, and good inventory planners. With this type of distribution strategy, the manufacturer may exert some pressure on intermediaries to move the product. Frequent local advertising may be required of the intermediaries, as well as maintenance of a well-stocked and well-balanced inventory.

When retailers carry goods that are selectively distributed, they face less competition than with products that are distributed intensively. As a result, they are more willing to promote the manufacturer's products. The intermediaries chosen to sell these products are generally the best equipped to maintain the image of the product. They are also selected for their ability to cater to the final users that the manufacturer wants to attract. For example, Ralph Lauren selects only top department and specialty stores to appeal to the affluent target market that will buy its clothing and dry goods.

Exclusive Distribution Exclusive distribution involves protected territories for distribution of a product in a given geographic area. In this system, dealers are assured that they are the only ones within a certain geographic radius that have the right to sell the manufacturer's or wholesaler's products. Prestige, image, channel control, and a high profit margin for both the manufacturer and intermediaries are characteristic of this distribution strategy. When there is an exclusive distribution agreement, the retailer is usually tied by contract to the manufacturer. Franchised operations are examples of exclusive distribution planning.

In addition to manufacturer-sponsored franchise agreements, wholesalers may sponsor voluntary groups in which a retailer agrees to buy and maintain a minimum inventory of the wholesaler's products. The wholesaler services the account regularly by checking inventory, telling the retailer what needs to be reordered, and by sponsoring special promotions to help sell those products to final consumers. An example of a voluntary group sponsored by a wholesaler is the National Auto Parts Association (NAPA). Retail auto parts stores affiliated with NAPA buy most of their stock from that wholesaler and participate in its promotions.

Guidelines set forth by the manufacturer, franchisor, or the wholesaler cooperative ensure exclusivity of the product line to the retailer. The retailers have limited competition in the sale of the product, and the product's image is maintained through the exclusivity of distribution. It is assumed that buyers will seek the outlets that carry these products.

A variation on exclusive distribution is found in manufacturers that own and run their own retail operations.

Real World MARKETING

U.S. Catalogs Have Wide Appeal

U.S. catalog companies like L. L. Bean, Eddie Bauer, and Patagonia are among the most popular clothiers in Japan. Why? Because catalog buying cuts out wholesalers and other middlemen and makes prices affordable.

Except for the middlemen, everyone seems to benefit from this arrangement. Bean's sales in Japan are impressive—about $100 million in 1993. Japanese consumers get to order reasonably priced, quality clothing in a convenient and user-friendly way. (The company offers catalogs and order forms in Japanese.) Even the Japanese government looks favorably upon foreign catalog companies. It points to them as evidence of its campaign to increase imports and reduce the country's perennial trade surplus with the United States.

This is called **integrated distribution.** The manufacturer acts as wholesaler and retailer for its own products. (See Figure 24–4 on page 318.) For example, Sherwin-Williams sells its paints and Fanny Farmer Candies sells its candies in company-owned retail stores.

Distribution Planning for Foreign Markets

Distribution planning takes on a new dimension when businesses get involved in international trade. Here we will look at just two foreign markets—Japan and Latin America. The situations U.S. businesses encounter there should give you an appreciation of the problems businesses face abroad and the kinds of solutions available to them.

Japan

As a rule of thumb, distribution of products in Japan must begin with quality products. If a company has quality products, then it must still surmount three key barriers to get those products into the hands of final users: Japan's tight-knit distribution system, cultural requirements for maintaining business relationships, and difficulty dissolving distributor-supplier relationships.

Japan has a unique distribution system in which intermediaries are so powerful that they determine what products will get sold to which retailers and at what

Chapter 24 *Channels of Distribution* **317**

Lifelong Learning

Channels of Distribution

Having knowledge of different distribution channels can make students better consumers as well as better marketers. As technology makes home shopping easier, consumers must remain actively involved in evaluating products and their usefulness. That goes for the electronic retail outlets themselves. Perceiving the pros and cons of each channel can help students determine the best one for each product they buy. Continuing their computer studies will help students use the technology of the future in a critical and responsible way.

Cooperative Learning

Tell students that a new computer company has developed a revolutionary new laptop computer that is less expensive than those on the market today. The only problem is that the company is running short on funds. However, the owners believe that once the benefits of this new laptop get out to the industry, the laptop will be in demand.

Have students break into groups, and give them 15 minutes to discuss this scenario. Ask them to develop a comprehensive distribution plan that is realistic and fits the circumstances described. Tell them to concentrate on key factors used in distribution planning, costs and expenses involved in their plans, and the level of distribution intensity suggested.

At the end of fifteen minutes, ask each group to share its plan with the class. Be sure they provide a rationale for each component offered.

L1 Decision-making Skills

Tell students to assume that they work for a perfume manufacturer that wants to expand the market for its scents beyond perfumes and colognes for consumers. Company marketers are giving consideration to selling the firm's chemical formulas to the manufacturers of other products that require scents. They are also looking to place their existing products with businesses other than retail outlets.

Have students brainstorm two lists—the first, all the different types of products that require scents; the second, other businesses that could be markets for perfumes and colognes.

(Lists will vary. Here are some possibilities. Products: soaps, detergents, and other cleaning products; over-the-counter liquid medicines; makeup and other cosmetic products; deodorants and other personal hygiene products; room fresheners. Markets:

hotels and motels to use much as they do miniature containers of shampoo and conditioner, cruise ships and airlines that might want to provide a selection of colognes for first-class passengers, all businesses that use employee gifts as incentives.)

L2 Decision-making Skills

Have students review the lists generated in the L1 Decision-making Skills activity to select the one product/market they think has the most potential. Have them provide a written rationale for their choice.

L3 Decision-making Skills

Have students decide exactly how they would pursue the product/market selected in L2 Decision-making Skills activity. Tell them to develop a plan that includes selling points for that product/market, as well as strategies to inform their new target customers that they are in a new line of business.

Independent Practice

1. Have students analyze one of the catalogs that they or their families receive. Tell them to classify the catalog publisher as a direct or an indirect distributor. (The decision will rest on whether the catalog features only one company's products or several companies' products.)

2. Have students research distribution planning required in a country of their choice. Tell them to access their public or school library databases to find published articles that deal with the challenges and opportunities involved in selling goods abroad using foreign distributors.

Integrated Distribution

Figure 24–4

Manufacturers who own and control all the facilities making and handling their products are practicing integrated distribution. They include companies like McDonald's (fast food), Sherwin-Williams (paints), and Ethan Allen (furniture). What are some other possibilities?

prices. Some say that Japanese deregulation is helping to cut down on the many layers of intermediaries in Japan's distribution system, as well as on the power they have. Even so, distributors remain the main links into the marketplace. For example, Coleman Co., a maker of camping equipment, has reported that it sometimes had to cater to the desires of 120 distributors. It also had to hire local managers to work with them.

As if the sheer number of relationships were not enough, Japanese culture requires that such relationships be cultivated intensively. Foreign company executives must be willing to spend a great deal of time and money forging strong personal ties with distributors. Personal

relationships are developed through golf, entertaining, and eating out after business hours. In 1994 a day of entertaining that included golf and dinner could cost a company up to $1,000.

Once forged, such relationships are difficult to break. That can be a problem, too. Consider the case of Novellus, a semiconductor equipment maker in California. Its chairman visited Japan over six times before deciding on a suitable distributor. To seal the relationship, the executive played golf and ate sushi with the distributor's executives on many occasions. The resulting agreement was maintained by having Novellus's chairman continue his visits to the distributor at least bimonthly.

Caption Answer

Students should concentrate on firms that sell products carrying the company name or a recognized store brand like Kinney (shoes), Singer (sewing machines), Fanny Farmer (candy), Sears (Kenmore appliances), and Kentucky Fried Chicken (fast food).

More About

Japanese Distribution

The numerous layers of intermediaries also add tremendously to the prices Japanese customers pay for U.S.-made products. Each intermediary who handles a product adds to its price. As a result, a piece of china sold to an initial intermediary for $1.25 may end up costing a customer $25.

It is expected in Japan that business relationships will be cultivated intensively, both during and after business hours. What do you think is the rationale behind such a practice?

Once Novellus had a stronghold in the market, it decided to go it alone. The company discovered, however, that in Japan you cannot abruptly drop a distributor. You must devise a plan for a gradual withdrawal over many *years*. The relationship has to be kept up in order to prevent the distributor from losing face. So, the only way Novellus could keep from losing the trust of its Japanese customers was to slowly take accounts from its distributor. During that multiyear process, commissions paid to the distributor had to be higher than before because the number of accounts was dwindling.

Latin America

Japan is not the only country where there are problems breaking an agreement with distributors. In Colombia, for example, you cannot fire an independent sales agent without providing a settlement. The sales agent would be entitled to 10 percent of his average annual compensation, multiplied by the number of years he was your distributor.

In the past, Latin American distributors did very little for foreign exporters. They simply distributed sales literature. When sales occurred, they would help cut through the red tape required to import goods into their country. That service, however, often required payoffs to officials. How much? In Brazil, distributors charged up to 50 percent of the selling price! Exporters had little choice but to pay because Latin America had an underdeveloped and monopolistic distribution network.

Times have changed, however, thanks to competition. In some cases, foreign businesses that were not pleased with local distributors set up their own distribution networks. Others found global distributors in the United States that offered services in Latin America, thus bypassing the local distributors entirely. Nonetheless, local distributors are still important, and many are now improving their services in order to be more competitive.

If you were to select a local distributor in Latin America, you would have to evaluate its capabilities carefully. Many are not trained to sell highly technical products, nor do they have the finances to conduct business effectively. To ensure success, many foreign businesses keep managers on site to oversee the work of distributors. They also inquire about a distributor's finances to determine if the firm has the cash flow necessary to pay bills. For example, Master Lock, a U.S. hardware company, developed strict criteria for handling dealers. The company insists that distributors pay their bills in a more timely fashion than is average for the region.

As a last point of consideration when doing business in Latin America, it is important to restrict distributors to a single country or a few distributors to one country. The reason? Political rivalries are high between countries. Latin America is not a single, borderless market like the European Union. Each country requires special attention. There are very few distributors that have the ability to cross borders in order to conduct business.

SECTION 24.2 Review

1. To develop an effective distribution plan, what key factors must you consider?
2. When are multiple distribution channels used?
3. Give two reasons for using a direct sales force instead of independent sales agents.
4. What are the levels of distribution intensity?
5. Explain some of the challenges businesses face when getting involved with distribution planning in Japan.

Assess

Evaluation

Assign and review the Section 24.2 Review.

Reteaching

1. Assign and review the vocabulary terms for this section.
2. Assign and review Fact and Idea Review questions 7–10 from the Chapter Review.
3. To reteach distribution intensity, ask students where they have seen chewing gum sold. They should be able to identify a variety of locations, including but not limited to supermarkets, convenience stores, diners, candy stores, service station stores, etc. This will help reinforce the concept of intensive distribution, trying to reach customers wherever they might shop.
4. To reteach exclusive distribution, ask students how many Ford or Chevrolet dealerships they can name in the immediate area. The students will come to realize that the manufacturer offers those retailers the *exclusive* right to serve a certain geographic area of the community based on population density.

Enrichment

1. Assign and review the appropriate activities in the *Student Activity Workbook*.
2. Assign and review the appropriate Critical Thinking questions from the Chapter Review.
3. Assign and review the Building Academic Skills Activities, Application Projects, Linking School to Work Activities, and Performance Assessment from the Chapter Review.

Caption Answer

It strengthens business ties by making them more personal. It also helps participants understand each other better, which is very important in a society where direct speech or confrontation are avoided at all cost.

Section Review Answers

1. Use of nontraditional and multiple channels, control vs. costs, intensity of distribution.
2. Firms want to reach the most customers.
3. Gives complete control of sales function, lowers costs when sales volume is very high.
4. Intensive, selective, and exclusive.
5. Tight-knit distribution system, intensive cultivation of business relationship.

Close

Ask students to recall the three levels of distribution intensity that a business can consider in its distribution planning. (Intensive, selective, and exclusive.)

24 CHAPTER *Review*

Answers

Vocabulary Review

Stories will vary. See Glossary for definitions.

Fact and Idea Review

1. On the basis of whether they take title to the goods they sell—those that take title are merchant intermediaries (wholesalers and retailers), those that don't take title are agents (independent manufacturers' representatives and brokers).
2. No, they carry noncompeting lines to avoid conflict of interest (*e.g.*, fishing rods from one manufacturer, lures from another).
3. No, because they neither take nor negotiate title to goods.
4. Direct—no intermediaries involved; indirect—one or more intermediaries involved.
5. Direct.
6. Consumer market: manufacturer to agent to wholesaler to retailer to consumer. Industrial market: manufacturer to agent to industrial distributer to industrial user.
7. Manufacturers that want to sell to giant retailers often must adhere to strict criteria about selling direct and offering special services in the areas of transporting, pricing, packaging, and merchandising.
8. Because they want to sell to as many customers as possible, wherever they might shop for motor oil.
9. Because they would be assured of a protected territory for the products, as well as a high profit margin.
10. Because of political rivalries between Latin American countries.

320

Vocabulary Review

Using a product that you purchased recently, write a story about how that product found its way into your hands. Include all the following terms in your story.

channel of distribution
intermediaries
electronic retail outlets
vending service companies
agents
direct distribution
indirect distribution
intensive distribution
selective distribution
exclusive distribution
integrated distribution

Fact and Idea Review

1. How are intermediaries classified? Provide two examples of each classification. (Sec. 24.1)
2. Do independent sales agents carry competing products from different manufacturers? Why or why not? (Sec. 24.1)
3. Are transportation companies and independent warehouses part of the channel of distribution? Explain your answer. (Sec. 24.1)
4. What is the difference between direct and indirect distribution? (Sec. 24.1)
5. What channel of distribution is generally used for services? (Sec. 24.1)
6. A manufacturer wants to concentrate solely on production and leave sales and distribution to the experts. What channel of distribution would such a company use in the consumer market? in the industrial market? (Sec. 24.1)
7. In what ways are giant retailers becoming powerful in the channels of distribution? (Sec. 24.2)
8. Why is intensive distribution most often chosen by manufacturers of motor oil? (Sec. 24.2)
9. Why would retailers want to be part of an exclusive distribution agreement with a manufacturer? (Sec. 24.2)
10. Why would a foreign business restrict distributors to a single country in Latin America? (Sec. 24.2)

Critical Thinking

1. How significant do you think interactive shopping vehicles will be in the future? Will they change the way traditional retailers operate? If so, how?

2. Under what circumstances would an established business fire its independent sales representative order to establish a direct sales force?
3. If you were to make a decision regarding the intensity of distribution for the products listed below, which level (intensive, selective, or exclusive) would you select and why?
   a. IBM personal computers
   b. Expensive imported sweaters
   c. New brand of shampoo
   d. Automobile
4. What one aspect of establishing a Japanese distributor for your products would you find most appealing? What one would you find most troublesome? Why?

Building Academic Skills

Math

1. Calculate the savings, if any, for a manufacturer that uses independent sales agents instead of an in-house sales force. Here are the facts.
   - The manufacturer needs to cover 20 states, with a minimum of one sales representative for each state.
   - The manufacturer's sales over the past five years have averaged $2,000,000 per year.
   - Independent agents are paid 8 percent commission on sales.
   - If in-house salespeople were hired, they would each get paid a salary of $30,000, plus approximately $5,000 per year in bonuses.
   - Additional expenses for each in-house salesperson would include use of a car (monthly leasing cost, including gasoline and insurance, $700); health benefits per salesperson of $500 per year; and an expense account that generally averages $400 per month.
   - Total payroll taxes for all in-house salespeople paid by the manufacturer would be approximately $110,000.
2. Using the information in the preceding question, calculate the sales expense percentage for the in-house sales force. How does that percentage compare with the 8 percent commission (sales expense) for the independent sales agents?
3. Again using the information in the first math question above, determine the sales volume at which the manufacturer should switch from independent sales agents to an in-house sales force. Assume all

Critical Thinking

1. Key question is, Should traditional retailers join the interactive shopping movement or fight it? They've put a great deal of money into making their stores pleasant shopping environments. Do they now encourage people to shop from home? Students should suggest ways such retailers could tap into the interactive shopping market and still maintain or grow their sales volume.

2. If business were so good that the independent reps were making more than in-house sales personnel on straight salary; if the reps were used just to find new customers who could now be adequately served with less experienced sales personnel at lower cost.
3. **a.** Computers—probably selective or exclusive.
   b. Sweaters—probably selective or exclusive.
   c. Shampoo—could be any one of the three depending on rationale.

projected expenses for the in-house sales force would remain the same.

Communication

4. A new sporting goods apparel manufacturer wants to sell its products through catalogs to compete with Lands' End, Cabelas, Patagonia, and L. L. Bean. As the new marketing manager, you've just spent a great deal of money buying a specialized mailing list of prospective customers. However, you don't want to send catalogs to any of them until you know they want one. Write a letter to get prospective customers interested in receiving your catalog.

Human Relations

5. You are a salesperson for Fanny Farmer candies. A customer complains that the selection is small and that she would like to see candy made by other manufacturers sold in the store. What would you say to the customer?

Application Projects

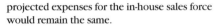

1. More and more consumers are shopping through catalogs. Here are some of the ways businesses obtain merchandise found in these catalogs:
   a. The manufacturer makes the goods found in the catalog.
   b. The manufacturer contracts with other manufacturers to make the goods found in the catalog under the private label of the catalog house.
   c. A catalog house, acting as an independent retailer, buys goods from different manufacturers and places those goods in its catalogs.
   d. A retailer prepares a catalog of goods sold in its store.

   Diagram the channel of distribution for each of the four ways goods are sold through catalogs. Bring one catalog to class and identify the channel of distribution used for the goods in the catalog.

2. Assume you are a small manufacturer of specially designed clothing for people who spend a great deal of time outside in cold weather. You currently sell this clothing yourself to retailers near your factory in Pennsylvania. You would like to expand your distribution to retailers in other northern states, but your budget does not permit you to hire the large sales force necessary to reach all the retailers in those states. What options are available to you? Explain their advantages and disadvantages.

Linking School to Work

1. Ask your employer to tell you from which channel members selected goods your firm buys are obtained. Trace those goods back to the manufacturer or producer in order to diagram their channels of distribution to the final user. Share your findings with your class in both oral and written reports.
2. Identify your firm's place in the channel of distribution for the products or services your firm provides to its customers.

Performance Assessment

Role Play

Situation. Assume your DECA chapter has developed a unique board game based on trivia about your state. You have identified two target markets within your state—consumers aged 12 years old through adult and businesses. (The businesses might be able to use the game as a premium for customers.) Your next step is to find investors who are willing to put up money to get the game manufactured. A local businessperson, Chris Greer, has given you a quote on manufacturing the game and suggested that you develop your distribution plan fully before asking people to invest. Greer volunteered to critique your plan as soon as you have it ready.

Evaluation. You will be evaluated on how well you do the following:

- Identify channel members.
- Explain key considerations used in distribution planning.
- Discuss the different channels of distribution for consumer and industrial goods and services.
- Communicate your ideas clearly and with conviction.

Oral Presentation

Make a creative, informative, and accurate presentation to the class to explain multiple channels of distribution and distribution intensity. Use one of the following products to explain both concepts: shampoo, computers, lifetime light bulbs, or ballpoint pens.

Complete the Chapter 24 Computer Application that appears in the Student Activity Workbook.

---

5. Answers will vary but should include a tactful explanation of integrated distribution and its benefits for customers.

Application Projects

1. a. Manufacturer to consumer.
   b. Two channels: manufacturer to industrial user and manufacturer to consumer.
   c. Manufacturer to retailer (catalog house) to consumer.
   d. Manufacturer to retailer to consumer.
   Other channels will depend on catalogs students bring to class.
2. Answers will vary. One option would be to negotiate with independent manufacturers' representatives who would act as the company's sales agents for the given territories. Advantage: Agents work on commission and pay their own expenses.

   Another option might be to hire a few in-house sales representatives who would sell the clothing to wholesalers in the desired states. Advantage: Wholesalers would do the more extensive and involved job of selling to numerous retailers. Potential disadvantage: Won't work if there are, in fact, no wholesalers dealing in such clothing.

Linking School to Work

Answers depend on the work situation.

Performance Assessment

Refer to the *DECA Competitive Events Handbook* for evaluation guidelines.

Computer Application

Optional Activity. Refer to the *Marketing Software Binder* for the template and user information.

Evaluation

Administer the reproducible test for Chapter 24, or construct your own using the Testmaker software.

---

d. Automobile—exclusive because of franchising agreements manufacturers make with retailers.
4. Answers will vary.

Building Academic Skills

Math

1. Cost of independent sales force: $2,000,000 × .08 = $160,000.

Cost of in-house sales force: ($35,000 × 20) + ($700 × 12 x 20) + ($500 × 20) + ($400 × 12 × 20) + $110,000 = $700,00 + $168,000 + $10,000 + $96,000 + $110,000 = $1,084,000. Difference: $1,084,000 − $160,000 = $924,000.
2. $1,084,000 ÷ $2,000,000 = .542 = 54.2%
3. $1,084,000 ÷ .08 = $13,550,000

Communication

4. Letters will vary.

PHYSICAL DISTRIBUTION

Pages 322–335

Chapter Overview

Chapter 25 discusses physical distribution—the process of transporting, storing, and handling of products on the way from seller to customer.

 ### Springboard

Read the chapter introduction aloud with students. Ask students to list the methods of transportation used in physical distribution and write this list on the board. Finally, ask students to define *product storage* and tell where most products are usually stored.

Prereading

List the section objectives to discuss with the students. Have the students skim the chapter, looking at the pictures, reading the captions, and noting the heads. Ask questions to ensure that the students have a minimal understanding of the chapter structure.

Preteaching the Vocabulary

Assign an equal number of vocabulary terms to each row of students. Have each row look up their terms in the chapter, write a short definition for them in their own words, and generate one symbol that will serve as a mnemonic to help all students remember the term. One student from each row should write abbreviated definitions on the chalkboard, along with the symbols, and review both with the entire class.

Physical Distribution

CHAPTER 25

Physical distribution is the key link between a business and its customers. It delivers the right product at the right time to the right place.

In this chapter you will learn about physical distribution and its relationship to marketing. You will explore transportation systems used by business. You will discover the importance of warehousing to the distribution process. You will also look at the types of warehouses businesses use to store merchandise.

322   Unit 7   *Buying and Distribution*

Classroom Management

For the Teacher
- Teacher's Annotated Editions for all workbooks
- Teacher's Manual for *School-to-Work Handbook*
- *Testing Binder*
- *Transparency Binder*
- *Marketing Software Binder*
- *Marketing Career Portfolio*
- *Lesson Plans*

For the Student
- *Student Activity Workbook*
- *Marketing Math Workbook*
- *School-to-Work Handbook*
- *Student Software*
- *International Case Studies*
- *Marketing Career Portfolio*

SECTION 25.1

Objectives

After completing this section, you will be able to

- explain the nature and scope of physical distribution,
- identify transportation systems for the distribution of products, and
- give examples of transportation services.

Terms to Know

- physical distribution
- transportation of goods
- common carrier
- contract carrier
- private carrier
- exempt carrier
- ton-mile
- carload
- freight forwarders

The Nature and Scope of Physical Distribution

Our economy is based on the buying and selling of many different products. Goods of all types are sold by manufacturers to buyers around the country and the world. **Physical distribution** is the process of transporting, storing, and handling goods to make them available to customers.

Physical distribution includes freight transportation, warehousing, materials handling, protective packaging, inventory control, warehouse site selection, order processing, and customer service. Given all these activities, you can see that physical distribution is an important link between a business and its customers.

Physical distribution must be coordinated with other business functions, such as purchasing, finance, production, and promotion. For example, since promotional activities are planned in advance, the distribution system must have the products at the right time and place for the promotion.

As you can imagine, transporting, storing, and handling goods are expensive. In fact, physical distribution is the third largest expense for most businesses. It is surpassed only by the cost of material and labor.

The actual cost of physical distribution differs from business to business. Department stores and specialty stores spend about 2 percent of their total sales on transporting, receiving, storing, and distributing merchandise. Printers, publishers, and clothing and machinery manufacturers spend between 4 and 5 percent of total sales on distribution costs. Petroleum refineries spend some 25 percent of their total sales for distribution.

Physical distribution involves three marketing functions: transporting, storing, and handling merchandise. In this chapter you will look at transportation and storage. In Chapter 27 you will explore merchandise handling.

Types of Transportation

Once something has been sold, it usually needs to be moved from the seller to the consumer. **Transportation of goods** is the marketing function of moving goods from a seller to a buyer. Manufacturers, wholesalers, and retailers all use some type of transportation to move goods.

Goods are moved by five major transportation forms: motor carriers, railroads, waterways, pipelines, and air carriers. Most businesses that transport goods are subject to federal and/or state regulations of the rates they charge and their operating procedures.

Trucking

Trucks (or motor carriers) are the most frequently used form of transportation. They are used primarily for lightweight shipments over moderate distances. Trucks handle nearly 80 percent of the shipments weighing less than 1,000 pounds each. Most businesses use trucks for local deliveries.

Motor carriers used for interstate commerce are regulated by state and federal transportation agencies. State transportation agencies regulate fuel taxes, safety issues, and rates charged for intrastate (within a state) trucking. A federal agency, the Interstate Commerce Commission (ICC) regulates transportation of goods between states. Prior to the passage of the 1980 Staggers Rail and Motor Carrier Act, the ICC had a great deal of authority. The ICC regulated all rates, routes, and operating procedures for interstate mail, train, and truck lines. The Staggers Act relaxed federal rules and regulations. It provided more freedom for interstate motor carriers and railroads to negotiate competitive rates and services.

Chapter 25 *Physical Distribution* **323**

FOCUS

Bell Ringer Activity

Write the following products on the chalkboard. Ask students to tell you which method of transportation they would use to transport them from seller to consumer, and the factors that would influence their decision.

- Coal (train, it's a heavy, bulky freight);
- a small overnight parcel (air or transportation service company, depending on the dollar value of the parcel and the time value of delivery);
- fruit (train or truck, depending on distance and time value of delivery);
- coffee to be shipped abroad (waterway, since it will not spoil in storage and thus doesn't need to be shipped by air); live fish from Maine to California (air, because of the time value of delivery);
- roses from France (air, because of the time value of delivery); and
- computer equipment (air, because of its fragility and dollar value).

Introducing the Section

Based on their answers to the Bell Ringer Activity, have students generate the main reasons for selecting certain types of physical distribution. Tell students that in this section they will look at the advantages and disadvantages of the various methods of physical distribution and the factors that influence the usage of each.

Meeting Special Needs

Learning Disabled

Students with oral expression disabilities benefit from an opportunity to make a contribution to the class in ways other than in-class discussion. For example, students might prepare a bulletin board display or a report on a topic that could be distributed to all students. Make assignments in accordance with students' interests and talents. The opportunity to participate is the key and involvement can take root if students are given regular opportunities. Keep in mind, these students do benefit from listening to class discussion even if they are not comfortable contributing.

Teach

Guided Practice

1. Read Section 25.1 with students.
2. When discussing water transportation, make sure to indicate on a map the key shipping routes such as the St. Lawrence Seaway, the Mississippi and the Ohio rivers, the Great Lakes, etc.
3. MarkEd Resource Center in Columbus, Ohio, (800) 448-0398, offers materials appropriate for use with this chapter.

Discussion Starter

Have students suggest products in addition to those mentioned in the text which might be processed in transit. (Answers could include crude oil, which can be processed into gasoline, heating oil, and jet fuel; or cotton, which can be processed into thread and then cloth.)

Cooperative Learning

Divide the class into two groups, Team #1 and Team #2. Have each team generate a list of 20 products and the type of physical distribution appropriate for each.

When students have finished, toss a coin to see which team goes first. The winner of the coin toss starts by giving the other team its first product. If the other team correctly identifies the method of distribution for the product, it gets a point and gets a turn. If it incorrectly identifies the method of distribution, it loses its turn and the querying team gets the point. Go through each team's 20 products. The team with the most points wins.

There are four types of motor carriers: *common carriers, contract carriers, private carriers,* and *exempt carriers.* Let's take a closer look at each.

Common Carriers Most motor carriers are **common carriers.** Common carriers provide transportation services to any business in its operating area for a fee. A common carrier receives a "certificate of convenience and necessity" from the state and federal governments.

Common carriers can specialize in handling a single *commodity* (good), such as household items, steel, or petroleum. Or they can handle a number of different commodities.

A common carrier must publish its freight rates. However, it can change its rates or the geographical area it serves, so long as it does not discriminate against a shipper of merchandise by charging rates that are different from its published rates or providing services that are different. More than one-third of all motor freight is handled by common carriers.

Contract Carriers A **contract carrier** provides transportation services on a selective basis, according to agreements between the carrier and the shipper. A contract carrier can provide services on a one time basis or on a continuing basis. Contract carriers do not provide transportation services to the general public.

Contract carriers negotiate their fees with each customer, and the fees may differ from agreement to agreement. Contract carriers often transport goods for more than one business, and they can charge different rates to each business. Contract carriers must file their contracts with the appropriate state or federal regulatory agency.

Private Carriers **Private carriers** transport goods for an individual business. The transportation equipment is owned and operated by the business, which transports only its own goods.

Every business is free to choose the type of transportation it will use. Cost is certainly a factor for most businesses. Starting a private carrier operation involves a large investment in equipment and facilities. A business that regularly ships a large amount of merchandise, though, may like the flexibility of owning its own means of transporting its goods.

Many businesses use a combination of motor carriers. For example, they may use their own trucks for local deliveries but use common or contract carriers for shipments beyond their local service areas.

Exempt Carriers **Exempt carriers** are free from direct regulation of rates and operating procedures. In most cases, they carry agricultural products. Their rates are lower than those charged by common carriers because of their exempt status. Exempt carrier status can also be granted to local transportation firms that make short-distance deliveries within specified trading areas in cities.

Advantages and Disadvantages of Truck Transportation Trucks are a convenient form of transportation. They can pick up products from a manufacturer, wholesaler, or retailer and deliver them to various

Real World MARKETING

Leave the Driving to Him

In 1914 Carl Eric Wickman had an idea. As one of the few car owners in the Minnesota mining town where he lived, he offered to drive miners to and from work for a small fee. Wickman painted his car gray to hide the mud and dust of the road, which led one observer to remark that the car looked like a "greyhound dog streaking by." Wickman liked the image so much that he adopted it as an emblem and a name for his company— the Greyhound Bus Company.

urban and rural geographical locations through our nation's extensive highway network.

Using trucks helps reduce the packaging costs for some products. A truck does not have to be unloaded until it reaches its destination; thus, the goods require less protective packaging.

Trucks can make rapid deliveries and therefore reduce the need to carry large inventories between shipments. This significantly reduces inventory costs.

Among the disadvantages of using motor carriers are their susceptibility to traffic jams, equipment breakdowns, and traffic accidents, all of which cause delays in delivery. In addition, businesses can generally ship products over long distances less expensively by other means.

Rail Transportation

Railroads are a major type of transportation in the United States. Trains move nearly one and a half times more *ton-miles* of freight than motor carriers. A **ton-mile** is the movement of one ton of freight one mile.

Trains are important for moving heavy and bulky freight, such as coal, steel, lumber, chemicals, grain, farm equipment, and automobiles over long distances. To compete with motor carriers, railroads have aggressively advertised the benefits of shipping by rail. They offer several specialized and innovative pricing and delivery services, including *piggyback service, fishyback service, specialized service, package cars, diversion-in-transit,* and *processing-in-transit.* Let's look at each of these services.

Piggyback and Fishyback Service *Piggyback service* gets its name from carrying (piggybacking) loaded truck trailers on railroad flatcars. *Fishyback service* is shipping loaded truck trailers on ships and barges. For this service, loaded trucks are carried piggyback on trains to a port where they are loaded onto ships or barges. Piggyback and fishyback services combine the

More About

The ICC

The oldest regulatory agency in the United States is also on top of Congress's list to be closed. Recently the agency averted closure by submitting a 220-page report justifying its existence. It remains to be seen what activities, such as safety inspection, could be added to its jurisdiction to make it a more attractive department.

More About

Trucking

In August 1991, Congress eliminated state regulation and interstate tariffs on motor carriers— except for carriers of household goods. Now the states only regulate insurance and safety so there are fewer distinctions between common or private carriers and exempt carriers than previously.

advantages of truck transportation with the lower costs of rail and water transportation.

Specialized Services Some products need to be hauled in special railroad cars. For example, refrigerated cars keep perishable products such as milk or fresh vegetables from spoiling over long distances. Other specially designed freight cars are used for hauling combustible or hazardous materials, such as chemicals.

Package Cars Shippers pay lower rail transportation rates if they fill an entire boxcar. A **carload** is the minimum number of pounds of freight needed to fill a boxcar. Carload weights are established for different classifications of goods. Once a shipment reaches the minimum weight, the shipper pays the lower rate, regardless of the size of the car. A *less than carload* is a shipment that falls short of minimum weight requirements for filling a freight car. Rates charged for *less than carload* shipments are more expensive because partial carloads have to be unloaded at each destination. Unloading time and the extra effort involved increase the rates charged to shippers.

In *package* (or *pool*) arrangements, goods from several shippers who are sending their items to a common destination are combined to fill an entire carload. If the goods were sent separately, each shipper would have to pay a higher rate since it would be shipping less than a carload.

Diversion-in-Transit *Diversion-in-transit* service allows the redirection of carloads already en route. For example, a vegetable grower in the South can send vegetables north and find the best price for them while they are en route. When the grower finds a buyer, the railroad will divert the shipment to the buyer—even if the buyer is not at the originally anticipated destination. Of course, the railroad charges a fee for this service.

Processing-in-Transit *Processing-in-transit* permits shippers to have products processed, repackaged, and assembled while in transit to their final destination. For example, wheat can be made into flour, stored, and then delivered when orders are received from customers.

Advantages and Disadvantages of Rail Transportation By handling large quantities, railroads can ship at relatively low costs. In addition, trains are seldom slowed or stopped by bad weather.

The biggest disadvantage of train transportation is its lack of flexibility. Trains cannot reach as many places as motor carriers. They can pick up and deliver goods only at stations along rail lines.

Water Transportation

Shipment by water is one of the oldest methods of moving merchandise. Ships carry merchandise from one part of the United States to others, as well as around the world. U.S. water transportation is regulated by the United States Maritime Commission.

Internal and Intracoastal Waterways *Internal shipping* is shipping from one port to another on connecting rivers and lakes. Waterways, such as the St. Lawrence Seaway, the Mississippi and Ohio rivers, and the Great Lakes, are important internal shipping routes. The St. Lawrence Seaway (a combination of rivers, canals, and lakes) as well as the Mississippi and Ohio rivers all

Rail transportation is a major means of transporting bulky freight. What two advantages does this type of transportation offer?

Chapter 25 *Physical Distribution* **325**

L1 Math Skills

Motor carriers ship 24 percent of the ton-miles of freight transported in the United States. If railroads ship one and one-half times more than this, what percentage of the ton-miles is shipped by train? (36%. 1.5 × .24 = 0.36)

L2 Math Skills

Pipelines carry about 24 percent of the ton-miles of freight transported in the United States. Air transportation is less than 1 percent of the ton-miles of freight shipped.

Given the percentage of ton-miles shipped by motor carriers and railroads, have students make a pie chart entitled "Freight Shipment by Carrier" that shows the percentage of ton-miles shipped by motor carrier, railroad, pipelines, air transportation, and waterways/other. They will have to determine the percentage for waterways/other, given the other statistics. (Graphs should reflect these percentages: motor carriers, 24 percent; railroads, 36 percent; pipelines, 24 percent; air transportation, 1 percent; waterways/other, 15 percent.)

L3 Math Skills

Parcel post is used for shipping small packages weighing between 16 ounces and 70 pounds. Have students tell whether the following packages would be shipped by parcel post:

- 1,200 ounces (No. This is 75 pounds. 1200 oz. × 16 oz = 75 pounds)
- 928 ounces (Yes. This is 58 pounds. 928 oz. × 16 oz = 58 pounds)

Caption Answer

The advantages are low cost and the fact that they are seldom slowed by bad weather.

Teach (Cont'd.)

- 1,088 ounces (Yes. This is 68 pounds. 1,088 oz. × 16 oz = 68 pounds)
- 32 ounces (Yes. This is 2 pounds. 32 oz. × 16 oz = 2 pounds)
- 1,120 ounces (Yes. This is 70 pounds. 1120 oz. × 16 oz = 70 pounds)

In Section 2 of Chapter 35, students will discuss English to metric conversion in product labeling. For now, briefly tell them that pounds convert to kilograms in the metric system. Have them imagine that the above products were weighed using the metric system. Have them convert the pound weight of each product to kilograms by multiplying by 0.454.

- 34.05 kilograms (75 pounds × 0.454 = 34.05)
- 26.33 kilograms (58 pounds × 0.454 = 26.332 or 26.33)
- 30.87 kilograms (68 pounds × 0.454 = 30.872 or 30.87)
- 0.91 kilograms (2 pounds × 0.454 = 0.908 or 0.91)
- 31.78 kilograms (70 pounds × 0.454 = 31.78)

Independent Practice

1. Assign and review the Chapter 25 Case Study in the *International Case Studies* workbook.
2. Have students create a map of the United States with the key waterway shipping routes marked, both internal and intracoastal. Also on this map, they should identify at least two products likely to be transported over each major waterway.

Waterways offer the transportation method of choice for large international shipments. Why?

give ocean-going vessels access to the heartland of America. Agricultural and industrial products of the Midwest are regularly shipped from the Great Lakes to other parts of the world.

Intracoastal shipping is shipping between ports along the Atlantic or Pacific coasts or from one coast to the other. For example, shipments can be sent from the New York Port Authority to the San Francisco Port Authority through the Panama Canal.

International Waterways International waterways are the oceans and rivers that connect continents and countries. Transportation by water is particularly important for international product shipments. Because of the low cost, almost all overseas freight is transported by ships and barges. Products commonly shipped by international waterways include heavy equipment, steel, forest products, rubber, coffee, and grain. As international trade continues to increase, so will the use of shipping by international waterways.

Advantages and Disadvantages of Water Transportation The biggest advantage of waterway transportation is low cost. Ships and barges are the cheapest form of freight transportation. They are also the slowest. Speed is not a problem when shipping bulky, nonperishable items, such as coal, forest products, and cement. For perishable goods such as dairy products, though, shippers need to use other forms of transportation.

Water transportation has some other disadvantages. If the buyers are located far from the port city, products must be off-loaded from ships onto railroad cars or motor carriers to reach their destination. This added cost of distribution reduces the cost advantages of water transportation.

Water transportation can also be affected by bad weather. Great Lakes shipping, for example, is generally closed for two to three months during the winter.

Pipelines

Pipelines are normally owned by the company using them, so they are usually considered private carriers. In the United States, there are more than 175,000 miles of pipelines.

Pipelines are most frequently used to transport oil and natural gas. For example, they move crude oil from oil field to refinery, where it is processed. The refined products, such as gasoline, are then trucked to retail outlets such as your local gasoline station.

Pipelines are more important in the physical distribution process than most people think. They carry some 24 percent of the ton-miles of freight transported in the United States. By comparison, trains carry about 36 percent and motor carriers about 24 percent.

Advantages and Disadvantages of Pipeline Transportation The construction of pipelines requires a high initial investment, but operation costs are small. The risk of a pipeline breaking is small, but that risk increases in areas that are prone to earthquakes.

Caption Answer

Low cost makes waterways the transportation method of choice for large international shipments.

Damage from pipeline leaks can be extensive. Pipelines are a dependable mode of transportation because they are not subject to delays due to such things as bad weather.

Air Transportation

Currently, air transportation is less than 1 percent of the total ton miles of freight shipped. High-value, low-weight items, such as computer equipment, are often shipped by air. Certain perishable products, such as fresh cut flowers and some medicine, are also shipped by air.

The Federal Aviation Administration (FAA) regulates air transportation. However, it does not regulate charges for air freight, so airlines and air transport companies set their own rates. Air freight carriers offer such things as wide-bodied jets that can ship more goods and specialized packaging developed to help prevent damage. Specialized freight planes now under development will allow air carriers to reach and serve more markets in the future.

Advantages and Disadvantages of Air Transportation The greatest advantage to air transportation is its speed. Many companies, such as Federal Express, advertise overnight delivery. This fast delivery time allows businesses to satisfy customers who need an item quickly. It also reduces inventory expenses and storage costs for warehousing products.

The greatest disadvantage of air transportation is its cost. It is the most expensive form of distribution. Air shipment rates are usually twice as costly as truck rates. For some shippers, however, the advantage of greater speed of delivery may outweigh the extra costs. Other disadvantages of air transportation include mechanical breakdowns and delays in delivery caused by bad weather.

Transportation Service Companies

Transportation service companies handle small and medium-sized packages. There are four kinds of transportation service companies: *the U.S. Postal Service, express carriers, bus package carriers,* and *freight forwarders*.

U.S. Postal Service

The U.S. Postal Service ships small packages by parcel post. *Parcel post* is classified as fourth-class mail, which includes packages weighing more than 16 ounces, newspapers and magazines, and printed matter that weighs less than 16 ounces (but *not* postcards and letters). Parcel post is used most often for shipping small packages weighing less than 70 pounds and not more than 108 inches in combined length and girth (distance around).

Parcel post can be insured against loss or damage or sent COD (cash on delivery). Parcel post can also be express-mailed at higher rates to guarantee next-day delivery.

BRIGHT IDEAS

If Buses Could Fly

People laughed at the Wright brothers when they talked about a flying machine, and now they're laughing again at the idea known as the Airbus. Conceived by Airbus Industrie, a European consortium consisting of members from France, Germany, Britain, and Spain, the Airbus is ready to move from the drawing board to the air.

The company recently unveiled plans for a double-decker long-range jet capable of carrying 850 passengers up to 7,000 nautical miles. The Airbus would weigh in at over 1 million pounds but theoretically be able to take off and land on regular airport runways.

The extra size of the aircraft would allow for some interesting innovations. Among the possibilities are rooms built in the cargo portion of the plane that could serve as fitness centers, business areas, or lounges for informal passenger functions. The planes would sell for $200 million each and would have their biggest market among carriers now flying routes into crowded Asian airports.

Creativity Challenge Form teams of 3–5 people, and come up with some improbable products of your own. For ten minutes brainstorm wildly, putting together random combinations of familiar objects, the odder the better: a wheelchair and a helicopter, a refrigerator and a TV remote control, a tape recorder and a translation dictionary. Afterwards, go through your list of "inventions" and decide which one has the most potential (practical, humorous, humanitarian—whatever). Briefly describe the purpose of the device, how it would work, who would be its principal users, and what its major features and benefits would be.

Express Carriers

Express parcel carriers specialize in transporting small, lightweight packages usually weighing less than 150 pounds. Express parcel carriers, such as United Parcel Service (UPS) and Federal Express, offer door-to-door pickup and delivery and COD service. Express shipments may be made nationally or internationally by airplane, truck, bus, or train. Rates are based on speed, weight, distance to be sent, size of package, and type of service used. Regular service usually takes from two to three days. A more expensive, next-day service is also available.

Chapter 25   *Physical Distribution*   **327**

Assess

Evaluation

Assign and review the Section 25.1 Review.

Reteaching

1. Assign and review the vocabulary terms for this section.
2. Assign and review Fact and Idea Review questions 1–10 from the Chapter Review.
3. List on the board the five methods of transportation used in physical distribution and have students generate at least five products normally transported by each.

Enrichment

1. Assign and review the appropriate activities in the *Student Activity Workbook*.
2. Assign and review the appropriate Critical Thinking questions from the Chapter Review.
3. If your school has a school store, have students identify how various merchandise arrived at the store. They should give the name of the carrier and also indicate the type of carrier—common, private, exempt, or contract.

Bright Ideas

Many products that we now take for granted were greeted with skepticism when they were first introduced. Have students list inventions both of this century and of earlier times that had this effect on the general population. What does this say about human nature?

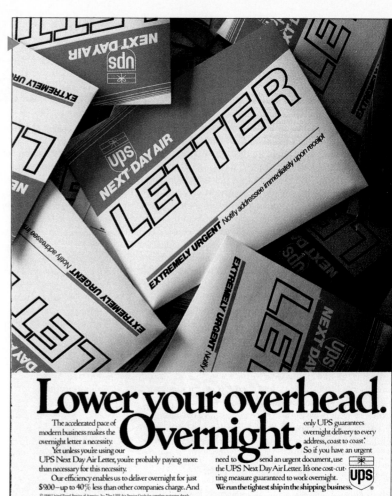

Express carriers, such as UPS, offer next-day delivery for packages. Why are express carriers most often used for small packages?

Express parcel carriers have several advantages over parcel post. These advantages include

- automatic pickup for customers who ship regularly,
- up to three attempts to deliver a parcel on consecutive delivery days,
- computerized tracking networks for tracing lost packages, and
- automatic loss and damage insurance.

Bus Package Carriers

Bus package carriers provide transportation services for packages weighing less than 100 pounds. Bus package carriers, such as Greyhound, can provide same-day or next-day service to cities and towns along their scheduled routes. As with other forms of shipping, the cost of bus package transportation depends on the weight of the package and the distance it will travel.

328 Unit 7 *Buying and Distribution*

Freight Forwarders

Freight forwarders are private companies that combine shipments from several different businesses and deliver them to their destinations. By combining shipments, freight forwarders can often obtain truckload or carload rates and lower transportation costs for shippers. Freight forwarders also use air and water carriers as needed.

SECTION 25.1 *Review*

1. What is physical distribution?
2. Identify five transportation systems for the distribution of products.
3. List four different examples of transportation service companies.

SECTION 25.2

Objectives

After completing this section, you will be able to

- describe storage needs,
- identify various types of warehouses, and
- discuss distribution planning for international markets.

Terms to Know

- storage
- private warehouse
- public warehouse
- distribution center
- bonded warehouse

The Storage of Goods

Storage is the marketing function of holding goods until they are sold. The amount of goods stored is called an *inventory*. We will talk more about inventories in Chapter 27.

Storing goods is an essential activity for marketers. Manufacturers need to store goods until they receive orders from purchasers. Wholesalers store merchandise before selling it to retailers. Lastly, retailers store merchandise to sell to customers. Merchandise might also be stored for these reasons:

- Production has outpaced consumption, and the surplus goods must be stored.
- Products such as agricultural commodities may be available only during certain times. Storage of excess production helps to stabilize prices.
- Some purchasers buy items in quantity to get discounts on their purchases and then store the items until they are needed.
- Merchandise is stored at convenient locations to provide faster delivery to customers.

Storing goods adds time and place utility to products by making them available when and where customers want them. The costs involved in storing products include space, equipment, and personnel. Storage also involves the cost of tying money up in inventory rather than investing it in

an activity that could provide a larger return for the business. Businesses try to balance the costs of holding merchandise in inventory against the possibility of not having enough merchandise available when customers want to purchase it.

Products are stored in a number of ways. For example, cars and trucks are stored in an outdoor lot, petroleum products in specialized storage tanks, and grain in grain elevators.

Determining *where* to store goods is an important decision. Efficient, adequate storage reduces the storage costs for a business and helps assure good customer service. Most products are stored in *warehouses*—facilities in which goods are received, identified, sorted, stored, and prepared and dispatched for shipment. Let's take a closer look at the type of warehouses businesses use.

Private Warehouses

A **private warehouse** is a facility owned by a business for its own use. A private warehouse is designed to meet the specific needs of its owner. Specialized conditions, such as a temperature-controlled environment, are built into the facility.

In addition to storing merchandise for the business, private warehouses often house other parts of the business operation, such as offices. Private warehouses are costly to build and maintain. In a recent survey, large retailers reported spending 51 percent of their total physical distribution costs on warehouse expenses; transportation costs accounted for the remaining 49 percent. Private warehouses should be considered only when a significant amount of merchandise needs to be stored, and the total operating costs are lower than those of public warehouses.

The storage function *is an essential part of marketing goods. What are four reasons why storage may have been used here?*

Chapter 25 *Physical Distribution* **329**

Focus

⏰ Bell Ringer Activity

Have students generate reasons why products need to be stored until they are sold, taking into consideration the needs of a manufacturer, a wholesaler, and a retailer.

Introducing the Section

Based on the list students generated in the Bell Ringer Activity, ask them how storage adds time and place utility to products. Tell students that in this section they will look at the marketing function of storage.

Teach

Guided Practice

1. Read Section 25.2 with students.
2. Have students read aloud the Case Study and review the answers in class.
3. Use the transparency for this section.
4. As you discuss the contents of this section, encourage students to identify the various types of storage facilities in your community and the types of goods each holds.
5. Assign and review the Chapter 25 Activity in the *School-to-Work Handbook*.
6. If you wish to further explore the operational and personnel issues related to warehouses and distribution centers, consult *Distribution Center Management*, a periodical published by the Customer Service Institute, 1010 Wayne Ave., Suite 440, Silver Spring, MD 20910, (301) 585-0730.

Caption Answer

Production has outpaced consumption, and the surplus needs to be stored. Some products, such as agricultural commodities, are available only during certain times. Storing helps to stabilize prices. Some purchasers buy items stored in quantity to get discounts on their purchases. Merchandise is stored at convenient locations to meet customer delivery needs better.

Have students speculate about why the need for personal or self-storage facilities is increasing. (Because of high construction costs, new homes and apartments are smaller and have less storage space. Also, our society is becoming increasingly mobile; people choose to move or are transferred in their work more often. Thus, people often store their furniture and other personal belongings rather than use them, in anticipation of moving again within a short period of time.)

Critical Thinking

Ask students to suggest some circumstances under which storage would not be appropriate.

Independent Practice

Have students research parcel post, one or more private parcel carriers, and one or more express carriers. They should get details about the services each provides, the time necessary for delivery, and the costs. Given this information, they should construct a chart that compares the features and benefits of each service in a ready-reference format.

Public Warehouses

A **public warehouse** is a facility available to any business that will pay for its use. Public warehouses not only rent space but also provide services to businesses. For example, many public warehouses provide shipment consolidation; barcode labeling; receiving, checking, and marking; order filling; and truck terminal operation services.

There are five types of public warehouses:

1. *Commodity warehouses* are used primarily for agricultural products, such as tobacco, cotton, or grain.
2. *Bulk storage warehouses* keep products only in bulk form, such as chemicals and oil.
3. *Cold storage warehouses* store perishables such as fruits, vegetables, and frozen products.
4. *Household goods warehouses* handle personal property storage, household articles, and furniture.
5. *General merchandise warehouses* store any item that does not require specialized handling.

Distribution Centers

A variation of the private and public warehouse is the **distribution center**—a warehouse designed to speed delivery of goods and to minimize storage costs. The main focus in a distribution center is on moving products, not on storing them. Since warehousing adds 5 to 7 percent to the cost of merchandise, there is no value added in keeping merchandise stored for very long.

Distribution centers consolidate large orders from many sources and redistribute them as separate orders for individual accounts or stores within a chain. Merchandise normally stays only a short time in a distribution center. It is bad business practice to store goods for long periods of time without good reason. Goods in storage do not make money for a business. (See Figure 25-1.)

Figure 25-1

THE J.C. PENNEY DISTRIBUTION CENTER

J.C. Penney's distribution center in Dallas, Texas helps the company fulfill the needs of individual J.C. Penney stores in the region. The purpose of its distribution center is to move products from the suppliers to the stores, not to store them.

1. Merchandise arrives at the distribution center from many transportation sources.

Did You Know ?

J.C. Penney can receive as many as 115,000 invoices a month at a cost of 30 cents per invoice to process. Penney is moving toward a paperless process in which merchandise is moved via electronic data at a cost of 5 cents per invoice. This results in a savings of $28,750 per month.

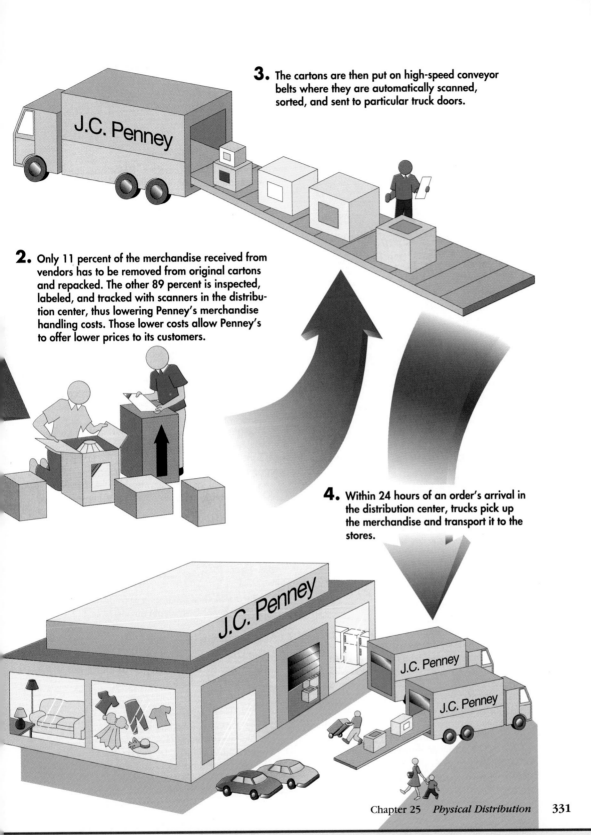

3. The cartons are then put on high-speed conveyor belts where they are automatically scanned, sorted, and sent to particular truck doors.

2. Only 11 percent of the merchandise received from vendors has to be removed from original cartons and repacked. The other 89 percent is inspected, labeled, and tracked with scanners in the distribution center, thus lowering Penney's merchandise handling costs. Those lower costs allow Penney's to offer lower prices to its customers.

4. Within 24 hours of an order's arrival in the distribution center, trucks pick up the merchandise and transport it to the stores.

Chapter 25 *Physical Distribution* 331

Assess

Evaluation

Assign and review the Section 25.2 Review.

Reteaching

1. Assign and review the vocabulary terms for this section.
2. Assign and review Fact and Idea Review questions 11–16 from the Chapter Review.
3. Write these products on the chalkboard and have the students tell you in which type of public warehouse each would likely be stored:
   - broccoli (cold storage),
   - cotton (commodity),
   - chemicals (bulk),
   - your personal bicycle and skis (household goods),
   - apples (cold storage),
   - washing machines (general merchandise),
   - wheat (commodity),
   - furniture (household goods),
   - oil (bulk), and
   - toys (general merchandise).

   Have the students generate additional examples of goods and quiz each other on the types of public warehouses where each would be stored.

Lifelong Learning

Physical Distribution

While students who are not planning for careers in the physical distribution area of marketing might not be exposed to new innovations and methods of transportation or new industry regulations and guidelines, as consumers these factors will have impact on them especially in terms of the prices they pay for goods and services. Therefore, it is beneficial for students to keep informed about these updates and changes as they occur by reading articles in general business magazines such as *Business Week* and *The Wall Street Journal*.

Enrichment

1. Assign and review the appropriate activities in the *Student Activity Workbook*.
2. Assign and review the appropriate Critical Thinking questions from the Chapter Review.
3. Assign and review the Building Academic Skills Activities, Application Projects, Linking School to Work Activities, and Performance Assessment from the Chapter Review.
4. Arrange for a one-day field trip to a private warehouse, public warehouse, and distribution center. Have the students take notes on the field trip, developing an outline from their notes, and further developing a 250-word paper on their outline.

   The final paper should include such things as why the goods are being stored and for whom; why this facility was chosen for storage; how the goods are received, identified, sorted, stored, and prepared and dispatched for shipment; and specialized vocabulary terms related to warehousing. (You may wish to combine this with Application Project #3.)

CASE STUDY

Partnering for Success

Mothercare is a 200-store maternity retailer based in Secaucus, New Jersey. Recently Mothercare has been experiencing difficulties with clothing vendors who were delivering merchandise in the wrong quantities, sizes, and colors to its stores. The deliveries of the wrong merchandise caused problems for the company because many items had to be returned. In addition, some shipments were not being delivered in a timely fashion.

Mothercare explored two options for correcting its shipping difficulties—to build its own distribution center or to use a distribution and transportation company. After considering these options Mothercare decided to contract with DMSI, a Charlotte, North Carolina distribution and transportation company.

DMSI provides retailers with shipment consolidation; barcode labeling; receiving, checking, and marking services; and delivery by truck. DMSI now handles all of Mothercare's distribution functions. It arranges transportation of Mothercare's products from the vendors into DMSI. It receives its store orders, checks the orders for accuracy, and distributes the merchandise

through DMSI private carriers. DMSI handles four to five million pieces of merchandise annually for Mothercare, as well as providing central warehousing for some of Mothercare's merchandise. Mothercare chose DMSI because the company offered economies of scale for a company of its size. For companies like Mothercare that do under $100 million in sales, DMSI offers shipping rates that are from 5 to 10 percent lower than smaller retailers could obtain on their own.

To save on distribution costs for Mothercare, DMSI consolidated deliveries into more economical full-truck deliveries rather than the smaller, twice-a-week shipments that had been sent by some vendors. In addition, DMSI merged its distribution labeling system with the barcoding system used by Mothercare. Shipping labels were automatically printed when the barcodes were scanned in the DMSI warehouse.

To ensure quality control, buyers from Mothercare sent product samples to employees at DMSI. The DMSI employees were trained by the Mothercare buyers to inspect shipments for quality by comparing the merchandise to the samples. Mothercare also hired a person to serve as a liaison between the buyers, the DMSI distribution center, and the company's headquarters.

As a result of this new partnership, the deliveries of Mothercare's products to its stores have improved. The company has also been able to avoid a costly investment in its own distribution center.

Case Study Review

1. Why did Mothercare decide to contract for distribution instead of building its own distribution center?
2. How was Mothercare able to save money by using DMSI?
3. What services are currently being performed by DMSI for Mothercare?

A MATTER OF ETHICS

4. Former vendors who had shipped directly to Mothercare stores now must send their merchandise to DMSI. Do you think Mothercare treated longtime vendors properly by requiring them to work with DMSI? Explain.

Case Study Answers

1. The company decided that the capital required to build a distribution center could best be used to concentrate on the main business.
2. Mothercare was able to save on shipping costs by consolidating shipments and avoiding more costly smaller deliveries from various vendors.
3. It arranges all of Mothercare's transportation into DMSI, receives its orders, checks orders for accuracy, and distributes merchandise.
4. The delivery system changed, not necessarily the vendors. Common carrier and transportation service companies were hurt by the new arrangement, but concern for profit and the overall survival of a company dictates that companies attempt to keep costs as low as possible.

Bonded Warehouses

Bonded warehouses store products that require the payment of a federal tax. Imported or domestic products cannot be removed from a bonded warehouse until the required federal tax is paid. Bonded warehouses can be either public or private. They are used because taxes do not have to be paid on products until they have been removed from storage. Businesses save on taxes by taking goods out of storage only when they are needed.

Distribution Planning for International Markets

Distributing products using the most efficient and least expensive methods available to meet the needs of the customer requires careful planning. Selling to customers in the international marketplace requires even more planning than for domestic markets. Businesses that sell internationally must follow U.S. export laws, as well as the import laws of the countries to which they are selling.

To deliver their goods successfully, businesses need to know about other countries' physical transportation systems. For example, in some less developed nations, the postal system may not be reliable enough to assure delivery of small packages by mail. Other countries may not have a particular distribution method, such as a national rail system. Some countries have legal restrictions about how products may be transported.

Another part of planning for international transportation may be to have shipping documents translated into other languages. Even in English-speaking countries,

different terms may be used. For example, in England, you might want to know that a truck is called a lorry.

The need for planning becomes even more obvious when you consider the many products whose parts are made in different countries. For example, car manufacturers often use parts made in several different countries. Those parts are shipped to the assembly plant where the final product is put together and is shipped to another destination. Planning for the best method of transporting parts from each country is the key to keeping the assembly lines running and the final products getting to buyers like you.

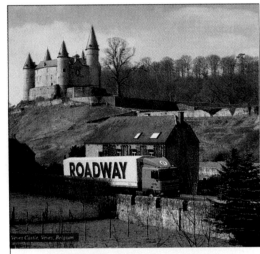

Five continents, One carrier...

Roadway Express now offers international door-to-door service to over fifty-five countries on five continents. With service through all major ports, you get the benefits of a single carrier, computerized tracking and only one invoice. So if you're thinking of shipping internationally, call your local Roadway representative or call our International Hotline at 1-800-INTL-REX.

ROADWAY
Working Expressly For You

Distributing products internationally requires extensive planning. What are some things that must be considered?

Answers

Vocabulary Review

See Glossary for definitions.
1. carload
2. physical distribution
3. common carrier
4. contract carrier
5. private carrier
6. transporting function
7. exempt carrier
8. ton-mile
9. freight forwarder
10. storage function

Fact and Idea Review

1. Moving goods from sellers to buyers. It is important because once something has been sold, it must be moved.
2. ICC.
3. Differences will vary.
4. Advantages: convenience, reduction in packaging costs, reduced inventory costs. Disadvantages: susceptibility to traffic jams, equipment breakdowns and traffic accidents, higher prices for long distances than other transportation.
5. Piggyback service, specialized service, package cars, diversion-in-transit, and processing-in-transit.
6. Advantages: Relatively low costs for items handled in large quantities, and few delays for bad weather. Disadvantages: Lack of flexibility.
7. Agricultural and industrial products and international shipments.
8. Because they are normally owned by the company using them.
9. Speed of delivery.
10. U.S Postal Service, express carriers, bus package carriers, and freight forwarders.
11. The storage function is the marketing function of holding goods. The amount of goods stored is called an *inventory*.

Vocabulary Review ▬▬▬

Write the term that best matches each definition given below.

1. Minimum number of pounds of freight to fill a boxcar.
2. Process of transporting, storing, and handling goods.
3. Provide transportation services to any business for a fee.
4. Do not provide transportation services to the general public.
5. Owned and operated by an individual business to provide transportation services.
6. Marketing function of moving goods from sellers to buyers.
7. Free from direct regulation with respect to rates and operating procedures.
8. The movement of one ton of freight one mile.
9. Private companies that consolidate shipments from several different businesses and deliver them to their destinations.
10. Marketing function of holding goods.

Explain the differences between the following vocabulary terms.

private warehouse
public warehouse
distribution center
bonded warehouse

Fact and Idea Review ▬▬▬

1. What is the transporting function and why is it an important aspect of physical distribution? (Sec. 25.1)
2. What federal agency regulates interstate commerce for motor carriers? (Sec. 25.1)
3. Explain the differences among the four types of motor carriers. (Sec. 25.1)
4. Identify the advantages and disadvantages of motor carriers. (Sec. 25.1)
5. Identify three of the six specialized services offered by railroads. (Sec. 25.1)
6. What are two advantages and one disadvantage of railroads? (Sec. 25.1)
7. What types of products are typically shipped by water? (Sec. 25.1)
8. Why are most pipelines classified as private carriers? (Sec. 25.1)
9. What is the single most important advantage in using air transportation? (Sec. 25.1)
10. What are the four kinds of transportation service carriers? (Sec. 25.1)

11. Explain the storage function of physical distribution. What term is used for the goods stored? (Sec. 25.2)
12. What is the difference between private and public warehouses? (Sec. 25.2)
13. List the five types of public warehouses and tell what they generally store. (Sec. 25.2)
14. How does a distribution center differ from a warehouse? (Sec. 25.2)
15. What is a bonded warehouse? (Sec. 25.2)
16. How might international distribution differ from distribution in the United States? (Sec. 25.2)

Critical Thinking ▬▬▬

1. Many retail distribution and transportation executives support federal legislation that would reduce state trucking regulations. What do you see as potential benefits and disadvantages of this effort?
2. From the following modes of transportation, identify six examples of merchandise that would be shipped by each. Tell whether this mode of transportation would be the only one used and give reasons to support your answer.
   a. motor carrier
   b. rail carrier
   c. air carrier
   d. water carrier
3. Identify the primary mode of physical transportation for each of these items:
   a. flowers from Holland to be transported to Detroit
   b. iron ore from Duluth, Minnesota to be shipped to New Jersey
   c. gasoline to be delivered to a local retailer
   d. farm equipment manufactured in Canada and shipped to the Midwest
   e. crude oil from the Southwest to be shipped to Boston, Massachusetts
   Tell why you think the mode of transportation you chose is best in terms of speed of delivery, dependability, capacity to handle heavy and bulky items, access to delivery location, and cost.
4. Most of the inland waterways were developed with federal funds, while pipelines were built by the oil companies themselves. Why do you think the federal government supports one mode of transportation and not the other?
5. Give two benefits and two disadvantages of a company owning its own warehouse.

12. A private warehouse is a facility owned by a company, manufacturer, wholesaler, or retailer for its own use. A public warehouse is a facility available to any business that will pay for its use.
13. See Section 25.2 for a description of what each of the five types of warehouses generally store.
14. Distribution centers focus on moving products rather than storing them.
15. A bonded warehouse stores domestic or imported products requiring the payment of a federal tax.

16. International businesses must follow not only U.S. export law but also relevant import law.

Critical Thinking

1.–2. Answers will vary.
3. (a) Air carrier
   (b) Waterways
   (c) Motor carrier
   (d) Railroad
   (e) Pipelines

Using Basic Skills

Math

1. A train has 35 cars. The average load per car is 104,500 pounds of grain. How many tons of grain is the train carrying? (*Hint:* There are 2,000 pounds in one ton.)
2. A private carrier's tractor-trailer rig has an empty weight of 24,500 pounds. It is carrying 22 tons of steel. How much more could the truck carry with-out exceeding an 80,000 pound limit?
3. A large manufacturer can save 28 percent by using a piggyback service. The cost of shipping the manufacturer's products without the piggyback service will total $65,550. How much will the manufacturer save by using the service?

Communication

4. Research and write a 100-word paper about the advantages and disadvantages of federal deregulation of the railroad industry.

Human Relations

5. You are working as a clerk in a warehouse. A carton of candy has been damaged during a shipment. As you are filling out a damage report for the damaged merchandise, a co-worker suggests you ignore the damaged goods and have some candy because the warehouse will never miss it. What would you say to your co-worker? How do you believe management would view your co-worker's suggestion?

Technology

6. Using trade or professional journals in your classroom or media center, research the latest technologies used by shipping companies to track merchandise from place of origin to final delivery.

Application Projects

1. Talk to a local businessperson about why his or her company uses the type of transportation it does for physical distribution. Write a 100-word report on your findings and share it with your class.
2. Visit a warehouse and observe its receiving, storing, and shipping processes. Write a short field trip report about your observations.
3. Choose a self-storage warehouse business in your area and write a 100-word report on how the business got started, its monthly fees, the type of merchandise stored there, and plans for business expansion.

4. Prepare a research report on the North American Free Trade Agreement (NAFTA) and its impact on shipping.

Linking School to Work

1. Research the methods of shipping used at your cooperative education training station or place of employment. Prepare a written report on your findings, including a description of the method(s) used most frequently and the rationale for using it.
2. Interview by phone or in person a manager employed in the transportation industry, a warehouse, or a distribution center. Ask about career oppor-tunities available in physical distribution.

Performance Assessment

Role Play

Situation. You are employed as a traffic manager for a large company that grows oranges. Your plant super-intendent has asked you to assist in the training of new employees. Specifically, she has asked you to give a 15-minute talk on various types of distribution methods approved for shipping oranges. You are to explain the advantages of each method, including the method you find most appropriate for shipping oranges. You should also explain why certain forms of transportation are not appropriate for shipping your product.

Evaluation. You will be evaluated on how well you do the following:

- Explain the nature and scope of physical distribution.
- Identify appropriate transportation methods for distributing oranges.

Flow Chart

Choose a product and construct a flowchart diagram tracing the product's path from a manufacturer to the retailer. Include the name of the manufacturer, the product, and the various carriers used to deliver the merchandise. Be sure to include where the product is stored before it reaches the final consumer.

Complete the Chapter 25 Computer Application that appears in the Student Activity Workbook.

---

3. $18,354. ($65,550 × 28% or .28 = $18,354.00)

Communication
4. Papers will vary.

Human Relations
5. Management would view this incident as possible grounds for dismissal, particularly if no attempt was made to prop-erly record the damage.

Technology
6. Answers should include a discussion of scanning equipment, bar codes, and electronic data interchange.

Application Projects
1. Papers will vary depending on the type of business.
2. Observations will vary depending on warehouse.
3. Papers will vary.
4. Papers should include the latest NAFTA information.

Linking School to Work
Answers depend on the work situation.

Performance Assessment
Refer to the *DECA Competitive Events Handbook* for evaluation guidelines.

Optional activity. Refer to the *Marketing Software Binder* for template and user information.

Evaluation
Administer the reproducible test for Chapter 25, or construct your own test using the Test-maker software.

---

4. Inland waterways were already there and that with relatively few improvements, they could be made into a major source of public transportation.
5. Benefits: Direct control over the facility, its inventory, its record keeping, its employees, and its service functions. Disadvantages: High initial cost of land, construction and equipment, and continuing operating expenses.

Using Basic Skills

Math

1. 1,828.75 tons (35 cars × 104,500 lbs. per car = 3,657,500 lbs./ 2000 lbs. in a ton = 1,828.75 tons)
2. 5.75 tons more (Step #1—22 tons = 44,000 lbs. + truck weight of 24,500 lbs. = 68,500 lbs. Step #2— 80,000 lb. weight limit − 68,500 lbs. truck and cargo = 11,500 lbs. Step #3—11,500/2,000 = 5.75)

Chapter Overview

Chapter 26 gives students an idea of what a career in purchasing would be like. It distinguishes purchasing agents and resale buyers and compares their different buying situations. It also discusses such pragmatic concerns as negotiating terms of sale with suppliers.

Springboard

Have students generate a chalkboard list of all the things they would need to purchase if they were to open a retail gift store. (Possibilities include everything from lighting fixtures, counters, and a sales register to the gift items themselves and the boxes and bags to hold them.) When the list is complete, help students determine which items would be purchased by the store's buyer. (Items for resale.)

Prereading

List the section objectives to discuss with students. Have students skim the chapter, looking at the pictures, reading the captions, and noting the heads. Ask questions to ensure that students have a minimal understanding of the chapter structure.

Preteaching the Vocabulary

Before students begin reading the chapter, dictate each of the vocabulary terms and ask students to write them on a sheet of paper. When they finish, write the terms on the chalkboard. Then have students guess at the meaning of each. Write their guesses next to each term, but do not give the correct meaning. Leave this list on the chalkboard so that students can see how close their guesses were to the actual definitions as they work through the chapter.

336

Purchasing

Who does the shopping in your household? How does that person know what to buy, how much to buy, and when and where to shop? Those questions are not very different for the people who do the purchasing for businesses.

What is different is what they buy and the quantity purchased. Manufacturers buy the equipment, machinery, raw materials, and supplies needed in the manufacturing of goods. Wholesalers and retailers buy goods for resale. Service businesses buy the supplies they need to perform their services. In this chapter you will learn who is responsible for buying these products and what is involved in the buying process.

Classroom Management

For the Teacher

- Teacher's Annotated Editions for all workbooks
- Teacher's Manual for *School-to-Work Handbook*
- *Testing Binder*
- *Transparency Binder*
- *Marketing Software Binder*
- *Marketing Career Portfolio*
- *Lesson Plans*

For the Student

- *Student Activity Workbook*
- *Marketing Math Workbook*
- *School-to-Work Handbook*
- *Student Software*
- *International Case Studies*
- *Marketing Career Portfolio*

SECTION 26.1

Objectives

After completing this section, you will be able to

- differentiate between purchasing agents and buyers,

- list the three steps in the buying process,

- explain how determining needs is accomplished in both industrial and resale situations,

- discuss how wholesale and retail buyers analyze customers' needs and wants, and

- identify three basic buying plans used to keep track of inventory for buying purposes.

Terms to Know

- purchasing agent
- buyers
- just-in-time (JIT)
- six-month merchandise plan
- resident buying offices
- basic stock list
- model stock list
- never-out list

Overview of the Purchasing Function

All businesses must have someone in charge of the purchasing function. In a small business, it might be the owner or manager. In larger businesses, it is often other management-level employees.

Regardless of the type of business, the general purchasing function includes determining what to buy and making arrangements with sources regarding final price, delivery, services expected, and method of payment. The employees who perform these tasks have a variety of titles, depending on the type of business in which they are employed. The difficulty level of their jobs is directly related to the types of purchases they make.

Who Does the Buying?

In manufacturing and service businesses, the people responsible for purchasing may be called *purchasing agents*, industrial buyers, or procurement managers. In wholesaling or retail businesses, they are simply referred to as *buyers*. Although the job titles may differ, the key function is to buy goods and services that are needed in the operation of a business. How they go about doing that is slightly different because of the goods they are responsible for buying. Let's look at how their roles differ.

Purchasing Agents A purchasing agent buys goods used in service and manufacturing businesses. This means the person is generally involved with the procurement of materials needed to provide a service or produce a manufacturer's goods. In manufacturing businesses, such people are often directly involved with *production planning*.

To get an idea of the responsibilities this entails, consider the case of an industrial purchasing agent for an outerwear apparel manufacturer. That purchasing agent would have to work closely with sales and marketing. Why? Because it is important to know what has to be produced to meet the sales goals of a company. This information is contained in the *master production schedule*.

Let's say that the marketing department predicts the company will sell 500 Style No. 1900 jackets in the coming months. The purchasing agent must know how much fabric, insulation, and thread and how many zippers it takes to produce 1 Style No. 1900 jacket. This is called a *bill of materials*. Then the total of all materials needed to make 1 jacket can be multiplied by 500 to determine exactly how much needs to be purchased to meet the sales goal.

To determine when to buy those items, the purchasing agent would be responsible for *materials requirement planning (MRP)*. MRP phases the purchasing to match the production schedule. For this reason, the purchasing agent must know the capacity of the manufacturing facility. He or she must be sure the company has room for the supplies and raw materials it needs and for enough inventory of finished goods to fill anticipated orders.

All these decisions are outlined in the master production schedule. Time lines and delivery of all supplies must be followed and checked on a regular basis to maintain that schedule. This ensures that everything is where it should be for manufacturing to progress at a rate sufficient to fill orders.

Focus

Bell Ringer Activity

Ask students if they would enjoy going shopping—with someone else's money. Then ask if any of them have ever considered becoming a buyer, either one who buys goods for a retail store or one who buys goods used to operate a business.

Introducing the Section

Once you have the students' responses to the Bell Ringer Activity, you can continue your questioning to help introduce the two types of buyers—purchasing agents and resale buyers. Here are a few more questions you can use to get to that point in the lesson. Ask:

- What do you think that type of job would be like? Would it be fun? interesting? challenging?

- Which type of buying appeals to you more—buying for resale or buying materials and supplies for use in the operation of a business? Why?

Teach

Guided Practice

1. Read Section 26.1 with students.

2. Use the two transparencies for this section.

3. Ask students to think about the resale and industrial buying situations. How would they be similar/different? What general kinds of tasks would be involved in both? What parts of the jobs would be different? Why?

4. Have students recount their experiences making their own purchases or participating in a family purchase decision. If necessary, suggest the following types of purchases to get the discussion going: jeans, athletic shoes, dress shoes, CD player, CDs, television, family automobile, and a family vacation.

Meeting Special Needs

Behaviorally Disordered

Students with behavior disorders of any type require a class environment that provides both support and structure so that they know both what to expect and what will be expected of them. Experiment to determine the best learning modality for each student, and structure activities accordingly.

For example, a visual learner would benefit from having material presented in the form of photographs or computer graphics. Students who act out in class may need assignments to match their learning style. Approaches like these will help such students comprehend the material and enable them to participate better in class discussions.

Ask students what makes certain buying decisions easier than others. This line of questioning should help to introduce the types of purchase situations—new-task, modified re-buy, and straight re-buy. Ask students to project how these three purchase situations would affect the way resale buyers and purchasing agents purchase goods for their businesses.

5. To lead the students through the 6-month merchandise plan, provide different scenarios for them to consider as you introduce each section of the plan:

- For *planned sales*, tell students that the economy appears to be in a period of recovery and continued growth is expected. Unemployment figures have dropped from 6.9 percent to 4.5 percent, and inflation is low at 3 percent. Ask students how they would use this general economic information to project planned sales for the next six months. (Answers will vary. However, most students will recognize that there should be an increase in sales for the coming season.) Then ask students to suggest a percentage for that increase. (Anything from 5 percent to 15 percent would be acceptable as long as students used the suggested economic information as part of their decision.)
- For *BOM inventory*, ask students how much inventory must be on hand to meet sales of $10,000 in a given month in a local retail store. To get their thinking started, ask if

Buyers In wholesaling and retailing operations, the purchasing function has a slightly different purpose. Wholesale and retail **buyers** purchase goods for resale. Their main role is to forecast the needs of their firms' customers and buy products that will meet those needs.

Wholesale buyers who cater to retailers must predict what the final customers are going to buy. If a wholesaler caters to the industrial market, the wholesale buyer must anticipate the needs of manufacturers and other businesses in that industry.

Retail buyers must decide what their customers will want. Let's look at a department store chain to get an idea of what that job would be like. In such a chain, most of the buying for all branches is done at a central location. Hence, this type of buying is called *centralized buying*.

Buyers involved in centralized buying generally buy all the items for a department or part of a department. For example, there may be three buyers for women's shoes. One may be in charge of casual shoes, another traditional shoes, and still another better shoes. To coordinate the efforts of those three buyers, there would be a merchandise

or division manager. This person would oversee all buyers for a given area of the chain store operation. In this case, all shoe departments in all branch stores would be under this person's supervision. That would include men's, children's, and women's shoes.

Chain stores use centralized buying in order to create a unified image for the chain. That way, customers can expect to find the same goods in every branch. There are a few instances, however, when chain stores want to have special goods in their stores that are not available elsewhere in the chain. In these cases, local store managers or their designated buyers are authorized to make special purchases for their individual stores. This would be considered *decentralized buying*.

You may be wondering how centralized retail buyers for national chains adjust for slight variations in customer preferences. With the advent of the computer, they are now able to study sales on a daily basis. They can determine where goods are selling quickly and slowly. For example, if a certain style of shoe is selling well in one branch store but poorly in another, the buyer can have the shoes transferred from one store to the other. Another

Figure 26–1

JUST-IN-TIME INVENTORY CONTROL

is an arrangement in which suppliers deliver parts and raw materials just before they are needed for production.

Parts Are Delivered ▼

on a schedule that conforms to production needs—just in time for use in the production process. If a shipment is late, it can bring a whole operation to a halt.

Order Is Placed ▲

when parts and supplies run low, which is frequently. Plants keep only small stocks on hand to avoid tying up money and space in inventory. Suppliers and transportation companies are informed by computer linkup which items are needed for production and when.

338　Unit 7　*Buying and Distribution*

More About

Purchasing Agents

A survey in *Purchasing* (September 1994) found that 70 percent of purchasing professionals report they have become more involved in product development since the last time the survey was taken in 1989. In addition, 26 percent of those responding to the survey said they got involved at the concept phase and another 26 percent during the design phase.

benefit of centralized buying is the quantity discounts that chain stores can negotiate with vendors because of the large volume of goods they purchase.

Types of Purchase Situations

How difficult is the task of a purchasing agent or a buyer? The answer depends on the type of purchase. There are three types of purchase situations: *new-task purchase, modified rebuy,* and *straight rebuy.*

New-Task Purchase In a *new-task purchase* situation, a purchase is made for the first time. Such purchases may be triggered by a formerly unrecognized need or a desire to change existing operations in a firm. For example, a retail or wholesale operation may be considering a new product line. A manufacturer may be considering a new way to make its product, such as using robots instead of people to handle one phase of the manufacturing process. Obviously, much research into the advantages and disadvantages of a new purchase is needed.

Modified Rebuy In a *modified-rebuy* situation, the buyer has had experience buying the good or service, but some aspect of the purchase changes. Perhaps the buyer is purchasing from a new vendor because the previous vendor went out of business or increased prices significantly. In a modified-rebuy situation, the buyer usually gets proposals from several vendors before making a buying decision.

Straight Rebuy In a *straight-rebuy* situation, the buyer routinely orders the goods and services purchased from the same vendor(s) as in the past. Staple goods fall into the straight-rebuy category for wholesale and retail buyers. The purchase of certain manufacturing supplies may be considered a straight rebuy for most purchasing agents.

In some manufacturing companies, *all* materials and parts needed to make a product are purchased in a straight-rebuy situation. This is because of an inventory control system called **just-in-time (JIT)**. With JIT, a company is linked via computer to its supplier so the supplier knows exactly what, how much, and when to deliver to meet production needs. In essence, the company is in a partnership with suppliers to guarantee frequent shipments of goods that keep pace with production needs. Figure 26–1 shows how JIT works.

▼ Finished Goods Are Shipped to Customers
as soon as they are assembled. Inventories of completed or partially completed products are kept to a minimum.

▲ Parts Go Straight to Production
where they are assembled immediately. No parts are stored.

RUSH DELIVERY

$10,000 in inventory would be sufficient. (Most students will recognize that you would have to have more than that amount of stock on hand. Otherwise the shelves would be bare.) This line of questioning will help introduce the concept of stock-to-sales ratios—how much stock is needed to cover sales. Suggest to students that in some businesses the stock-to-sales ratio would be low (*e.g.,* businesses that order merchandise for customers). In other types of businesses, it would be much higher (*e.g.,* stores that have a huge selection of merchandise).

- For *retail reductions,* ask students what they think would be included in this figure on the merchandise plan. (Employee discounts, markdowns, and shortages.) Ask students why this figure would be important to include when planning purchases? (Sales figures would not accurately reflect the merchandise needed to cover sales if these items were not considered. Sales projections would be too low.)

Discussion Starters

1. Ask students if they think large chain stores should allow local branches to buy some of the goods they sell or if they think central buyers should do all the buying for all the stores. (Answers will vary. Supporters of centralized buying will cite the need for a unified image. Supporters of local buying will suggest the need for some freedom to make each store a little unique and allow it to cater to its particular customers.)

Teach *(Cont'd.)*

2. Once students are acquainted with the concept of just-in-time buying and inventory control, ask if they think it is a good idea for wholesale and retail buyers to consider. Have them explain why or why not. (Answers will vary. At present there are a few large chains, like Wal-Mart, that use JIT inventory systems. As items are sold in the various retail stores, a computer transmits those records via satellite to a central location. Thus, all sales from every store are available to central buyers on a daily basis. Minimum and maximum levels of inventory are monitored by the computer system and re-orders are generated as needed to keep stock levels at the optimal level.)

Critical Thinking

Ask students who's job is easier in terms of determining user/customer needs—an industrial buyer's or a retail buyer's. (Answers will vary. Each job has its difficulties, depending on the type of buying situation involved [new-task, modified-rebuy, etc.] and the scope of the job's responsibilities.

For example, an industrial buyer who is involved in production planning would have to work closely with sales and marketing to determine what has to be produced to meet the sales goals of the company. He or she would help to analyze past sales and forecast future sales. Purchases of raw materials and supplies would be based on these projections.

Resale buyers (retail and wholesale buyers) must focus on the needs of the final consumer. They must predict what items will be popular well in advance of the buying season. Once items are purchased, they must monitor sales and reorder items that are selling well. How well they predict their customers' needs will be reflected in sales.)

The JIT system was first adopted by U.S. auto makers in the early 1980s. Since then, all types and sizes of manufacturers have adopted it, from computer companies to makers of molded plastic parts.

Steps in the Buying Process

Even companies that embrace the JIT philosophy must at some point decide on their suppliers. This is a key part of the purchasing process. That process can be broken down into three steps:

1. Determining what to buy
2. Selecting suppliers and negotiating terms
3. Placing the order and evaluation

For the remainder of this chapter, we will explore each of these steps in detail.

Determining What to Buy

There are two key differences between industrial and resale buying situations. The first is the purpose of the purchase. The second is how each type of buyer determines the needs of his or her firm.

Industrial Buying

As you learned earlier, purchasing agents buy goods and services that will be used in the manufacturing process or service operation of a business. Their involvement in making final decisions about what is purchased may differ, depending on the buying situation. In new-task purchases, other members of the organization, often referred to as *influentials*, will make the final decision. In modified-rebuy and straight-rebuy situations, the purchasing agents themselves will be responsible for determining the organization's needs.

New-Task Purchase Situations In a new-task purchase, many people in the organization may be responsible for determining the characteristics of the item(s) needed. For example, if new manufacturing equipment is to be purchased, the people who will use the equipment will be involved. So will the top executives in the manufacturing division. Depending on the situation, other influentials may dictate the standards to be used in evaluating vendors. They may also make the final buying decision for major purchases. The purchasing agent will generally be part of a team and will most likely be responsible for doing research into possible supply sources.

Modified-Rebuy and Straight-Rebuy Situations In modified- and straight-rebuy situations, the purchasing agent will be responsible for purchasing the items needed in the organization. If the purchasing agent is not directly involved with production, the

management-level employees who plan production would tell the purchasing agent what needs to be ordered. If the purchasing agent is responsible for production planning, those needs would be determined through analysis of the sales goals of the company. Sales forecasts planned by the marketing department would have to be reviewed, along with the facility's master production schedule, to make sure supplies were available when needed in the production process.

Resale Buying

Although most steps in the buying process are the same for purchasing agents and buyers, the determining needs step is a little different. That is because the purpose of the purchase is different. Rather than buying supplies and equipment for use in the making of products, retail

BRIGHT IDEAS

Make a Fashion Statement

Nylon stockings have been part of working women's wardrobes since 1942. During the 1960s, however, women's hosiery manufacturers began to notice a trend toward more casual dress. As part of that trend, teenagers especially started going barelegged.

To prevent their product from losing ground, hosiery manufacturers tried a new tactic. They came out with tinted and colored nylons. Eventually they added patterned and textured hose as well. In so doing, they converted nylon stockings from a neutral part of a woman's wardrobe into a fashion essential. The tactic worked. Sales continued upward. Since then, women's hosiery manufacturers have modified their product to keep pace with the ever-changing dictates of fashion.

Creativity Challenge Form teams of 3–5 people. Then put a product of your own choice on the fashion cycle. As a run-up to this selection, try to list as many nonclothing items as your group can think of that go through stylistic cycles. (Automobiles, for example.) Finish this process by adding one new item to the list—your choice for change, a product that as yet remains unaltered by fashion's fickle touch.

Six-Month Merchandise Plan

Spring Season 19—   Department _____

No. _____

		Feb.	March	April	May	June	July	Total
Sales	Last Year							
	Plan							
	Actual							
Retail Stock BOM	Last Year							
	Plan							
	Actual							
Retail Reductions	Last Year							
	Plan							
	Actual							
Retail Purchases	Last Year							
	Plan							
	Actual							

Figure 26–2

Buyers allocate their spending based on planning documents like this one. Why do you think planning is done six months at a time rather than yearly?

and wholesale buyers buy goods that will be resold to their customers. To accomplish that purpose, they must do the following:

- Plan far in advance of the selling season.
- Analyze customers' needs and wants.
- Decide which goods and quantities of goods to purchase.

Planning Buyers must plan their purchases far in advance of the selling season. They accomplish this by preparing a **six-month merchandise plan**—essentially a budget that estimates planned purchases for a six-month period. Figure 26-2 shows such a plan. Note that it is built around the following elements:

- *Planned sales.* This figure is basically last year's sales figure with adjustments for current economic conditions and competition. For example, if the economy is doing well and expected to improve, a buyer might want to increase planned sales for the coming season.
- *Beginning-of-the-month (BOM) inventory.* Buyers must be sure there is enough stock to accommodate

the sales volume planned. To project this figure, a buyer would check the previous year's records for how much stock in relation to sales was needed for each month. Say, in a given month sales were $40,000, and the BOM stock for that month was $120,000. That would be a *stock-to-sales ratio* of 3 to 1. If economic and market conditions are similar this year, the buyer could apply that same ratio to the planned figure for that month.

- *Planned retail reductions.* This figure takes into account employee discounts, markdowns, and shortages. (Shortages include clerical errors, employee pilferage, and shoplifting.) Such reductions are included in a merchandise plan because they affect the amount of money budgeted for purchases.
- *Planned purchases.* This entry shows the retail-dollar purchase figures a firm needs in order to achieve its sales and inventory projections for each month. All of the figures discussed above—planned sales, BOM stock, and reductions—are needed to determine this figure.

Chapter 26 *Purchasing* **341**

L1 Human Relations Skills

Tell students to imagine that a retail store chain operation has adopted a just-in-time inventory buying system but that it is not yet fully operational. Therefore, some popular goods are not on the store's shelves, and customers are asking for them. Ask students what they would tell those customers. (Explain the new system, and tell them that they will call them as soon as the items arrive.)

L2 Human Relations Skills

Tell students to assume that the situation explained in L1 Human Relations Skills activity has now been going on for one month. Many customers who have had items on order all that time are becoming annoyed. Have students develop a plan to deal with these angry customers.

L3 Human Relations Skills

Have students role-play an exchange with one of the customers described in the L2 Human Relations Skills activity. This customer has been waiting for over a month for a specially priced automatic camera. Observers of the various role plays should evaluate the effectiveness of the techniques used to mollify the customer.

L1 Decision-making Skills

Tell students to imagine that the class is going to open a holiday boutique for two weeks in December. Their job is to buy all the merchandise that will be sold in the boutique. Have them brainstorm all the steps they think they should follow in making those decisions.

L2 Decision-making Skills

Have students review the ideas generated in the L1 Decision-making Skills activity and arrive at the final process they will follow in making decisions about what to buy.

L3 Decision-making Skills
Have students use the process agreed upon in L2 Decision-making Skills activity to develop the list of items they will purchase for the holiday boutique.

Independent Practice

1. Assign and review the Chapter 26 Case Study in the *International Case Studies* workbook.
2. Have students research the career of buyer by reading about it in the *Dictionary of Occupational Titles,* by clipping help-wanted ads for buyers in their local newspaper, and by interviewing buyers in their community. From these sources, have them determine the positive and negative aspects of buying jobs, the recommended educational requirements, experience that would be helpful for someone interested in a buying career, and projections for employment in the field for the next five years. Have students present their findings in written reports.
3. Ask students to research the names of trade journals that are generally read by wholesale and retail buyers in given fields. There are trade journals for each area of specialization, such as *Women's Wear Daily* and *Sporting Goods Dealer.* If students can access the trade journals, have them read one article that reports a trend that would be important to a buyer/purchasing agent. Ask students to present oral reviews of the articles they've read and to submit a short written summary to you.

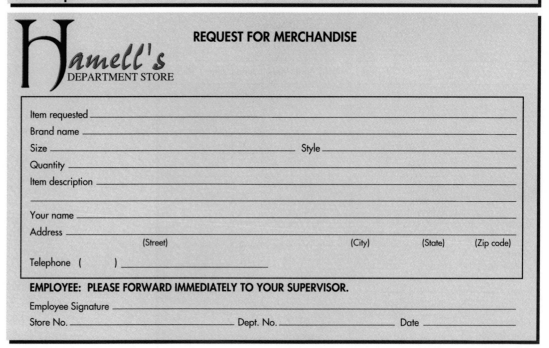

Want Slip

REQUEST FOR MERCHANDISE

Hamell's DEPARTMENT STORE

Item requested _____

Brand name _____

Size _____ Style _____

Quantity _____

Item description _____

_____

Your name _____

Address _____
(Street)   (City)   (State)   (Zip code)

Telephone ( ) _____

EMPLOYEE: PLEASE FORWARD IMMEDIATELY TO YOUR SUPERVISOR.

Employee Signature _____

Store No. _____ Dept. No. _____ Date _____

Figure 26–3
Information supplied to buyers through want slips is especially valuable. Why?

You will learn how to calculate all the figures in a merchandise plan in Chapter 28.

Analyzing Customer Needs and Wants
Wholesale buyers must anticipate the needs of the industrial businesses, service businesses, retail operations, or other wholesalers that are their customers. Retail buyers must anticipate the needs and wants of retail customers. How do they do it?

Many retail firms ask their salespeople to prepare *want slips* like the one shown in Figure 26-3. These are customer requests for items not carried in the store. Other firms may contact customers directly through professional market research studies, consumer panels, or direct questioning by sales personnel. So much time and effort is devoted to determining customers' needs because, as the saying goes in retailing, "Goods well bought are half sold." Retail buyers who buy goods that customers want will make the job of selling those goods much easier.

In studying industry trends and consumer buying habits, buyers analyze their previous sales records. They also gather market information in the following ways:

- *Reading trade journals and other business publications.* A *trade journal* is a business publication that covers a specific business. *Women's Wear Daily*, for example, covers the women's apparel industry.

Other good sources of business information are general business publications, such as *Forbes* and *Business Week.* Business sections of newspapers provide information about current local and national economic conditions that might impact on a business.

- *Comparison shopping of competitive stores.* This involves visiting those stores to see what goods and services they offer. Brands carried, prices, and quantities of items are all noted and compared. Besides direct competitors, catalogs that have competitive offerings may be studied and compared, too.
- *Talking with sales representatives.* Suppliers' reps are familiar with trends because they see what other businesses order. In some cases, they can predict the success of certain products because they have information about reorders of popular products from many stores.
- *Attending trade shows.* At *trade shows,* suppliers for a given industry present their goods for buyers to see. Trade shows are sponsored by trade associations, which charge suppliers for the space they use on the floor of a show. Suppliers display their goods and services and have sales representatives available to discuss the products with interested buyers. Many

Caption Answer
Reflects wants of actual customers; indicates that the merchandise, if stocked, would be "half sold."

More About

Trade Journals
Progressive Grocer and *Frozen Food Digest* are examples of trade journals read by buyers in the supermarket industry. In the field of sporting goods, buyers read *Sporting Goods Dealer, Sports Style,* and *Outdoor Retailer.* Industrial buyers can keep abreast of their field by reading a trade journal called *Purchasing.*

trade shows publish a directory of all participating vendors to make it easy for buyers to contact them at a later date.

- *Hiring the services of a resident buying office.* **Resident buying offices** are retailers' representatives in a central market. A *central market* is a geographic area where many suppliers of a given product are located. (New York City's garment district, for example, is a central market for apparel.) Resident buying offices send information to retail buyers on a regular basis. They inform buyers about new merchandise offerings, closeouts, fashion trends, special buys in the market, and market conditions.

Deciding on Goods and Quantities Deciding what to buy begins with a decision about a firm's merchandise assortment. *Merchandise assortment* is the amount of merchandise to stock for customers. It refers to both width (which products to carry) and depth (how many of each product to carry). Since risk increases as product assortment expands, buyers must have some idea of what products will sell. If the products stocked don't sell, the buyer must make adjustments in the merchandise assortment. To do this, the buyer considers merchandise image, brand policies, and the firm's pricing policy.

For example, suppose you are the buyer for a men's clothing store. To evaluate new sweaters for the fall line,

you need to determine whether the styles and quality of the garments match your store's image and prices. The quantity of goods you can purchase depends on what merchandise is on hand, what has been ordered, what has been sold, and what needs to be reordered.

To help keep track of that information and to make decisions about which items to buy, buyers use three basic buying plans. These plans are commonly referred to as *basic stock lists, model stock lists,* and *never-out lists.*

A **basic stock list** (Figure 26-4) is used for staple items—items that should always be in stock. Staple items include products such as groceries, hardware, cosmetics, housewares, china, and stationery. Based on expected sales for a given period, a basic stock list specifies the minimum amount of merchandise that should be on hand for specific products. It shows the quantity of items that should be reordered, as well as the colors, styles, and sizes that should be carried. For ease in recording those products when they are purchased and sold, retailers assign each product a code. That code is commonly referred to as its *SKU (stockkeeping unit).*

A **model stock list** (Figure 26-5 on page 344) is used for fashionable merchandise. Because fashion items change relatively rapidly, these lists are less specific than basic stock lists. The information contained in model

Basic Stock List

Stock	Description	Size	Packing Units	Cost	Retail	Min. Stock	October Sales		November Sales		December Sales	
							This Year	Last Year	This Year	Last Year	This Year	Last Year
1381	Skippy Peanut Butter	32 oz.	24			4						
1382	Skippy Peanut Butter	18 oz.	24			8						
1383	Skippy Peanut Butter	12 oz.	24			8						
1384	Jiff Peanut Butter	32 oz.	24			4						
1385	Jiff Peanut Butter	18 oz.	24			8						
1386	Jiff Peanut Butter	12 oz.	24			8						

Figure 26-4

Buyers use basic stock lists to plan purchases and keep track of items that should always be in stock. Where on this list is the SKU?

Caption Answer

First column shows the stockkeeping unit code.

4. To experience firsthand what comparison shopping involves, have students identify competing stores in the area and specific items of merchandise to compare. Then, working in teams, have them compare those items in the stores in terms of price, promotion, and merchandising/display. Have the student teams report their findings to the class in both written and oral form.

5. Have students prepare a basic stock list, a model stock list, a never-out list for your school store.

Assess

Evaluation

Assign and review the Section 26.1 Review.

Reteaching

1. Assign and review the vocabulary terms for this section.
2. Assign and review Fact and Idea Review questions 1–5 from the Chapter Review.
3. To reteach the different types of buyers, provide examples of several buying situations, and ask students to classify the type of buyer involved. For example, tell them that Toys "Я" Us has employees who are located in the central office. One group of employees buys all the toys for the chain. The other group of employees buys all the bags, tape for the sales registers, shelving, and display equipment needed in the operation of those stores. Ask: Which one is the resale buyer and which one is the industrial buyer? (Toys—resale buyer; supplies and equipment—industrial buyer).

Enrichment

1. Assign and review the appropriate activities in the *Student Activity Workbook.*

Assess (Cont'd.)

2. Assign and review the appropriate Critical Thinking questions from the Chapter Review.

3. Have students research the current economic climate of the nation and local community. Suggest that they get figures on unemployment, interest rates, and inflation, as well as some idea of the current business cycle and predictions for the coming months. Then have them use that information to decide on the percentage increase/decrease in sales that they would project for a six-month merchandise plan for a business of their choice.

4. Have students investigate buying trends in college bookstores and their possible application to high school bookstores. Require that they identify at least one new product to be added to the existing line of goods carried in their own school store. Students should base their suggestion on a careful investigation of students' needs and possible supply sources. Tell them to present their findings and the rationale for their suggestion in a written report.

Close

Have students identify the three steps in the buying process. (Determining what to buy, selecting suppliers and negotiating terms, and placing the order and evaluation.)

Model Stock List

PRODUCT CLASS _Misses Sportswear_   SEASON _Spring_

General Style	Specific Style	Price Range	Color	Total Units	Size 6	Size 8	Size 10	Size 12	Size 14
Blouse	Sleeveless Tailored	$25	White	12	1	3	3	3	2
			Black	12	1	3	3	3	2
			Blue	12	1	3	3	3	2
Blouse	Short-sleeve Oversize	$35	Pink	24	2	6	6	6	4
			Orange	24	2	6	6	6	4

Figure 26–5

Buyers use model stock lists for fashion merchandise. How and why does this type of list differ from a basic stock list in form and content?

stock lists identifies goods by general classes (blouses, skirts, dresses, slacks) and style categories (short sleeve, long sleeve); sizes; materials; colors; and price lines. Style numbers are not included because each manufacturer's style numbers change each year. Thus, although model stock lists identify how many of each type of item should be purchased, the buyer must actually select specific models at the market.

A **never-out list** is used for best-selling products that make up a large percentage of sales volume. Items are added to or taken off the list as their popularity increases or declines. For example, a video rental store will keep a popular movie on the never-out list and keep a large quantity of the video cassettes in the store. After the movie declines in popularity, only regular quantities of it will be maintained. It will be taken off the never-out list and other, more popular titles will be added to it.

Life in the Multicultural MARKETPLACE

Coffee, Tea, or Mud?

In many countries throughout the world, a polite offer of a cup of tea or coffee is part of the greeting ritual. The proper response is acceptance. (If you reject the offer, you are effectively rejecting your host's hospitality.)

Be forewarned, though. In "coffee cultures"—cultures in which coffee is the beverage of hospitality, such as the Middle East and Mediterranean countries—the coffee is strong and thick. In some cases, it resembles mud, and it doesn't come in decaf!

SECTION 26.1 Review

1. What is the primary difference between purchasing agents and buyers?

2. List the three steps in the buying process.

3. In an industrial buying situation, what must the purchasing agent monitor in order to determine what to buy?

4. In a retail buying situation, what does a buyer prepare in advance of the selling situation?

5. Name three things wholesale or retail buyers might use or do in order to analyze their customers' needs and wants.

6. In wholesale and retail businesses, what three basic buying plans may be used to keep track of inventory in order to decide what to buy?

Caption Answer

How: Contains general descriptions of merchandise rather than codes; lacks cost data, space for sales totals (past or present), and minimum stock figures. Why: For items that change so quickly they are unlikely ever to be reordered.

Section Review Answers

1. Purchasing agents buy goods needed for use in businesses. Buyers purchase for resale.
2. Determine what to buy. Select suppliers and negotiate terms. Place the order and evaluate.
3. Production and sales.
4. A six-month merchandise plan.
5. (See student text pages 342–343.)
6. Basic stock, model stock, and never-out lists.

Objectives

After completing this section, you will be able to

- list the criteria buyers use in selecting supply sources,
- compare and contrast the deals offered by suppliers and select the best one, and
- explain how buyers order goods and evaluate the purchases made.

Terms to Know

- consignment buying
- memorandum buying
- advance dating
- extra dating
- end-of-month (EOM) dating
- receipt-of-goods (ROG) dating
- purchase order
- invoice
- stock turnover

Selecting Suppliers and Negotiating Terms

Even though the purpose for buying is different for purchasing agents and for wholesale and retail buyers, the ways they find suppliers and the criteria they use to select them are the same. For the most part, purchasing agents and buyers rely on manufacturers' and wholesalers' catalogs and sales representatives.

For many staple items, catalogs provide sufficient information to decide which supplier is offering the best deal. When purchases are more involved, a sales representative generally meets face-to-face with the purchasing agent or buyer.

To locate these sources of supply, purchasing agents or buyers may respond to ads they see in trade journals or receive in the mail. They may also use directories published by trade associations and attend trade shows.

Real World MARKETING

Pricing Goes Global

A financial analyst studied the costs involved in building a Pontiac Le Mans. In the year he studied the vehicle, it sold for $20,400. The analyst determined that international suppliers accounted for 60 percent of that price, as follows: Korea—$6,000; Japan—$3,500; Germany—$1,500; Taiwan—$800; the United Kingdom—$500; and the Republic of Ireland—$100. The remaining amount—$8,000—represented Detroit's contribution to the vehicle's price.

Selecting Suppliers

The criteria for selecting suppliers fall into a few key categories. They include *production capabilities, past experience, product and buying arrangements*, and *special services*.

Production Capabilities When dealing with a source for the first time, buyers may request specific information about the source's production capabilities. They may even visit a facility in person to see it in operation. In addition, buyers may solicit business references to determine the source's reputation in the industry. These factors would be extremely important when selecting suppliers and transportation firms as partners in a just-in-time production arrangement.

Past Experiences Many buyers maintain resource files that document past experiences with vendors. All basic information, such as products carried, prices, delivery and dating terms, and the names of sales representatives, is recorded. Also noted are evaluations of products, delivery performance, and customer service.

Product and Buying Arrangements A major factor in selecting a supplier is the quality of goods it offers. Retail buyers keep accurate records of customer returns and the reasons for them. If the reason relates to the quality of the goods, that vendor may be dropped as a supplier.

Another deciding factor might be the services offered. Some suppliers have special policies regarding merchandise returns and special sales arrangements. Two special types of sales and return policies are called *consignment buying* and *memorandum buying*.

In **consignment buying**, goods are paid for only after they are purchased by the final consumer. This special arrangement is applicable to wholesale and retail buying situations. The supplier owns the goods until the wholesaler or retailer sells them. Many suppliers offer

Chapter 26 *Purchasing* **345**

Ask students what criteria they would use for selecting a vendor. (If that question is too general for the group, tell them to imagine that they are in charge of buying T-shirts for a DECA fundraiser. For vendors, they have a choice of three local and three out-of-state firms.)

Introducing the Section

Write the students' answers to the Bell Ringer Activity on the chalkboard. Keep soliciting responses until you have covered the key criteria—production capabilities; past experience with the vendor; product offerings; and buying arrangements (including price, dating terms, shipping terms, return policy, and any special services available).

Teach

Guided Practice

1. Read Section 26.2 with students.
2. Use the transparency for this section.
3. Have students read aloud the Case Study and review the answers in class.
4. When teaching the different dating terms discussed in this section, write their names on the chalkboard. Then provide several examples, and have students match each with the appropriate term.

   For further practice, go through all the examples and have students determine the following:
   - Last date to take advantage of discount
   - Last date for payment in full
5. Assign and review the Chapter 26 Activity in the *School-to-Work Handbook*.

Feature Note

Students may be surprised at the high foreign content of some of their favorite items. Have them pick a product, such as their athletic shoes, and research the materials and/or components that went into them. The Made in the U.S.A. label may mean that the product was merely assembled in the United States from parts made abroad.

Discussion Starter

Present this situation to students for their consideration: They are purchasing agents for a bicycle manufacturer. (They buy the components that go into bikes.) They have two principal vendors that offer the same quality components. Vendor A offers low prices with no shipping charges but is unreliable when it comes to meeting delivery schedules. Vendor B charges higher prices (also with no shipping charges) and guarantees its delivery dates. (Answers will vary.)

L1 Math Skills

Tell students they have a $15,000 invoice dated May 2 with terms of 3/10, net 30. Have them determine the date full payment is due, the last date for taking the discount, and the amount due if the discount is taken. (Full payment: $31 - 2 = 29$ days left in May $+ 1 =$ June 1. Discount deadline: $2 + 10 =$ May 12. Amount due with discount: $15,000 \times .97 = $14,550.$)

L2 Math Skills

Tell students to assume that another vendor is offering the same merchandise quantity and quality as in the L1 Math Skills activity, but the invoice amount is $15,300 with dating terms of 4/20/net 45. Determine the total amount due if the discount is taken, as well as the deadline dates for taking the discount and payment in full. (Amount due with discount: $15,000 \times .96 = $14,688. Full payment: $45 - 29 =$ June 16. Discount deadline: $2 + 20 =$ May 22.)

---

consignment buying as an incentive when introducing a new line of goods. Since a buyer pays for the goods only when they are sold, no money is tied up in inventory. Thus, there is virtually no risk. The problem with consignment buying occurs when merchandise is stolen or damaged. Then there is often a question about who was responsible for it and who must pay.

Memorandum buying occurs when the supplier agrees to take back any unsold goods by a certain date. The buyer pays for all the goods purchased but is later reimbursed for goods returned in accordance with the agreement. This buying arrangement allows for returns. Each agreement may be a little different with regard to time lines for accepting returns.

Special Services Besides return policies, retailers today are demanding more and more services from their suppliers. In some cases, only the suppliers that offer those services are considered.

One of the special services many retailers are requesting (and in some cases demanding) is the placement by manufacturers of Universal Product Codes (UPCs) on goods. Having the codes on all products saves the retailer time because individual items do not have to be marked with a price. Shelf or bin signs are sufficient.

When a coded item is purchased, an optical scanner at the sales register reads the UPC and identifies both product and price. How does the scanner know the price? The buyer or assistant buyer has the task of inputting the prices of the items into the computer. Another major benefit of having UPCs is evident when the buyer wants to run specials (like 20 percent off) on selected items. Pricing data can be revised quickly and easily using a computer system.

Research indicates that the cost of marking prices on items can run up to six cents per item when done by employees who have to attach price tickets to products. When a retailer uses bar codes, the cost is approximately half of one cent per item. That is a savings of $.055 per item. Multiply that savings on all the products in a store, and you can understand why many retailers will not even consider vendors who do not have UPCs on their goods.

Even the large boxes that hold products now have bar codes on them to identify the contents. Machines that read those codes can use them to route the products to various departments within a store or to different stores within a chain.

Many retailers and wholesalers have shelving requirements for their products that are identified through a computer program called Peg Man. Before this program was available, buyers had to measure the size of an item (or its packaging) and count the number of units that would fit on a peg board or a shelf. The number of facings (rows of items) then had to be considered to see how much total shelf space a product would use. With the Peg Man program, a supplier can tell a retailer exactly how much shelf space is required for a product. So, many retailers that use the program require that their suppliers have the same capability.

Some suppliers offer their customers merchandising services. Service representatives stop by the store to arrange special displays or check on stock. They may also provide special store displays, hangtags, or videos on the product for use in merchandising. Other suppliers may offer to train retail store employees in the features and benefits of their firm's products.

Negotiating Terms

To evaluate suppliers, buyers must know the terminology related to the negotiations. They should be able to compare and contrast deals offered by various suppliers to determine which is best for their firm. If you were negotiating the purchase of items for a local DECA chapter fund raiser, you would want to be familiar with *discounts, dating terms*, and *delivery arrangements*.

Discounts *Discounts* are reductions from quoted prices. Discounts that should be reviewed include cash, trade, quantity, seasonal, and promotional. All of these discounts are discussed in Chapter 30.

Dating Terms Dating terms state when a bill must be paid and the discount permitted for paying early. *Ordinary dating* occurs when the dating terms are based on the invoice date. Consider, for example, ordinary dating of 2/10, net 30. It specifies the percent of discount permitted for paying early (2 percent), the number of days within which you can take advantage of the discount (10 days), and the total number of days within which you must pay the invoice in full (30 days).

In addition to ordinary dating, you should also know several other dating terms. These include *advance dating, extra dating, EOM dating*, and *ROG dating*.

Advance dating occurs when manufacturers indicate a date other than the invoice date from which the dating terms take effect. It is sometimes offered to businesses as an incentive to buy before the buying season. For example, an invoice may be dated January 15 and include the following advance dating terms: 2/10, net 30—as of March 1. In this situation, the date of the invoice is disregarded, and March 1 is the date from which the billing terms take effect. If the bill is paid by March 11 (10 days from March 1), the buyer can take advantage of the 2 percent cash discount. If not, the buyer must pay the bill by March 31 (30 days after March 1).

Extra dating grants additional days before the dating terms take effect. In special deals, the manufacturer may offer extra dating to encourage a buyer to purchase new merchandise. Extra dating terms are written 3/10, net 30, 60 extra. Thus, the 3/10, net 30 stipulations apply after the 60 extra days have passed.

A simple way to determine the dates for payment is to add the extra days to the dating terms. Take, for example, an invoice dated July 15 with terms of 3/10, net 30, 30 extra. The terms could be changed to 3/40 (10 + 30), net 60 (30 + 30). Therefore, August 24 would be the date on which the discount expires and September 13 the last date for full payment of the invoice.

Purchasing

Consumers can be thought of as purchasing agents for their homes and/or businesses. Following many of the steps mentioned in this chapter can help students in this regard by encouraging them to plan major purchases, analyze and understand their own needs and wants, and decide on goods and quantities desired before shopping. Even tips such as keeping track of items purchased regularly and noting the various sources for these products can go a long way toward helping students become astute and well-informed consumers.

CASE STUDY

Looking for a Few Good Vendors

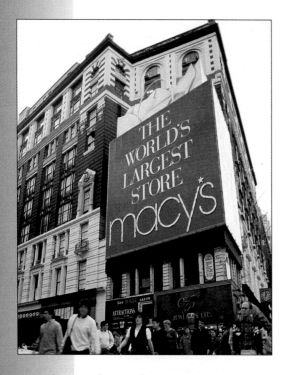

When Federated Department Stores, Inc., merged with R. H. Macy & Company, the new firm became the largest department store group in the United States. Before the merger, each firm utilized different buying systems. Federated was known for its team buying system in which all stores bought the same merchandise. Macy allowed each of its branch stores to do its own buying.

With the new merger, it will be interesting to see which buying system will be employed by the combined Federated-Macy firm. Federated has a Vendor Intensification Program designed to reduce the number of vendors from whom it buys. With fewer vendors, the ones chosen are being asked to do more for the company.

What do retail buyers look for in the vendors they choose? Consider the supermarket industry and how its vendors are responding to retailer demands. The current trend in the industry is for food-packaging companies to develop retailer-specific promotions and better service. The three companies that are the front runners in this form

of marketing are Coca-Cola, Procter & Gamble, and Kraft General Foods.

Coca-Cola's promotion agency goes on sales calls to assess retailer needs for promotions. The agency then develops promotions based on the suggestions of retail buyers. Kraft General Foods has streamlined order-taking and distribution between its divisions so that retail buyers can deal with one organization. Procter & Gamble has created a Brand Development Fund that tailors TV spots to key retailers.

The first move in the direction of these retailer-specific programs was accomplished through pricing options. Those options became available when some vendors introduced Everyday Low Prices as a way to get away from the prevalent high-low pricing strategy. (High-low pricing involves setting high prices and then running numerous promotions to lower them.)

What will retail buyers want next from their suppliers? They will be looking for account-specific business planning. The Marketing Corporation of America (MCA), a Connecticut-based management consultant group, conducted a survey of retailers to find out what that might include. MCA's study found that 71 percent of retailers want creative partners. Sixty-three percent want marketing and logistics expertise. Forty-two percent seek superior consumer knowledge. Flexibility was also noted as being important, as was how much suppliers spend on developing their brands.

■ ■ *Case Study Review*

1. If the new Federated-Macy firm decides to adopt the Vendor Intensification Program, what effects might this have on Macy's buyers and vendors?
2. How are packaged-goods manufacturers attempting to improve their relationships with supermarket buyers? What three areas are the focus of their efforts?

A MATTER OF ETHICS

3. Review the results of MCA's study. Do you see any potential problems that might develop between buyers and their suppliers if the retailers were to get what they wanted?

Chapter 26 *Purchasing* **347**

L3 Communication Skills

Have students role-play the negotiation to settle the dispute with the vendor described in the L1 Communication Skills activity.

L1 Decision-making Skills

Remind students of the decisions they made in the previous section regarding the holiday boutique. There they had to decide what to buy. Now ask them what criteria they would use for selecting vendors to supply those items.

L2 Decision-making Skills

Using the criteria developed in the L1 Decision-making Skills activity, have students research two or more vendors who can supply them with the goods they want to buy.

L3 Decision-making Skills

Using the criteria developed and information researched in the L1 and L2 Decision-making Skills activities, have students decide which vendors they would select to supply the holiday boutique merchandise. Ask them to provide a rationale for each of their vendor selections.

Independent Practice

Tell students that their local DECA chapter wants to buy a camcorder to record all their activities for the year. They will also use the camcorder to videotape role plays done by students in preparation for DECA competition. Some of their videotapes will be used for presentations to the administration and parents, and as recruitment tools for DECA.

With these varied uses in mind, tell students to research the camcorders available and recommend the best product for the chapter's needs. They should also be prepared to recommend the best vendor and back up that choice with a suitable rationale.

Table 26-1

To encourage purchases, vendors offer buyers and purchasing agents a variety of discounts and payment terms, as shown here. If an invoice's terms are simply net 30, what is the discount? If the invoice were dated June 10, when would final payment be due?

Dating Terms

Dating Terms	Example	Cash Discount	Final Payment
Ordinary	2/10, net 30	2% if paid within 10 days of invoice date	30 days from date of invoice
Advance	2/10, net 60 as of _____ date	2% if paid within 10 days from advance date	60 days from advance date in dating terms
Extra	3/15, net 30 Extra 30	3% if paid within 45 days of invoice date	60 days from invoice date
EOM	2/10, net 30 EOM	• Invoice dated on or before 25th of month: 2% if paid within 10 days after last day of month of invoice date	30 days from last day of month
		• Invoice dated after 25th of month: 2% if paid within 10 days after end of next month	30 days from last day of next month
ROG	4/20, net 60 ROG	4% if paid within 20 days of date goods were received	60 days from date goods were received

End-of-month (EOM) dating is changing the date from which the billing terms take effect to the end of the month. The exception to this occurs when the date of the invoice is after the 25th day of the month. In that case, the buyer is permitted to go to the end of the next month to begin the dating terms.

Here are two examples of end-of-the-month dating. In the first example, an invoice is dated March 2, with terms of 2/10, net 30, EOM. In this case, the dating terms begin on March 31, the last day of the month. Therefore, the date up to which the buyer can take advantage of the discount is April 10 (10 days after March 31). The last date to pay the bill is April 30 (30 days from March 31). In the second example, an invoice is dated April 27, with terms of 3/10, net 30, EOM. Here the terms begin on May 31 because the date of the invoice is after the 25th of the month. Therefore, to take advantage of the discount, the buyer's firm must pay this invoice by June 10. The final date for payment of the invoice is June 30 (30 days after May 31).

In **receipt-of-goods (ROG) dating**, the terms begin when the buyer's firm receives the goods. Therefore, you do not consider the invoice date when determining the dates for payment of the invoice. An example of ROG dating is 3/10, net 30, ROG. If the invoice is dated June 1 and the goods are received July 15, the end date for taking advantage of the discount is July 25 (10 days from July 15).

The last date for payment of the invoice is August 14 (30 days from July 15). Table 26-1 summarizes all of these dating terms.

Delivery Arrangements Delivery arrangements are important when a buyer is deciding on a source of supply for goods and services. The terms for delivery are all variations of FOB (free on board). There are four options:

1. *F.O.B. destination.* The title or ownership of the goods remains with the seller until the goods reach their destination. The seller pays the transportation charges and assumes the responsibility for the condition of the goods until they arrive at the buyer's place of business.
2. *F.O.B. shipping point.* The buyer pays the shipping costs and is responsible for losses for damages that occur in transit.
3. *F.O.B. factory freight prepaid.* The goods become the property of the buyer at the factory. The seller, however, pays the shipping charges.
4. *F.O.B. destination charges reversed.* The merchandise becomes the buyer's only when goods are received. The buyer pays for the transportation charges. If the goods are lost or damaged in transit, the buyer's investment is protected because the goods do not yet belong to the buyer.

348   Unit 7   *Buying and Distribution*

Caption Answer

No discount; final payment by July 10.

Placing the Order and Evaluation

Once the decisions have been made about what to buy and from whom, the next step is to actually order the goods. When the order arrives, the purchasing agent's or buyer's job moves into a new phase. He or she must check the order for accuracy, evaluate the quality of the goods, and get feedback from the people who work with them.

In retail settings, the buyer is responsible for pricing, merchandising, and promotion of the products purchased. The profitability of purchases is a key factor in evaluation of a buyer.

Purchase Order and Invoice

To place an order, most businesses prepare a **purchase order,** a legal contract between the buyer and the supplier that specifies the terms of the agreement. The purchase order includes information regarding the quantity, style, number, and unit price of each item purchased, as well as any special requests, such as shipping and delivery instructions. You will learn how to complete a purchase order in Chapter 28.

When a supplier ships the goods requested on a purchase order, an **invoice** (or bill) is sent to the buyer. The invoice contains much of the same information found on the purchase order.

However, there are some instances when this is not true. Occasionally a buyer does not get a complete shipment. That can happen when a supplier runs out of a given item or items. In that case, you will see the notation *B.O.* on the invoice, which stands for "back-ordered." Back-ordered items are temporarily out of stock and will be sent as soon as they are available. The buyer is not charged for back-ordered items until they are shipped. In other cases, the notation *Discontinued* or *O.S.* (out of stock) may be used. Discontinued and out-of-stock items are no longer carried by that supplier.

Evaluation

Industrial and wholesale/retail buyers solicit feedback to determine whether the goods and services purchased meet the purposes for which they were bought. In an industrial setting, the goods and services are evaluated on the basis of how well they perform in the manufacturing process or in the operation of the business. The costs of purchasing goods and services and their productivity are reviewed to see if they are in line with the buyer's expectations. Suppliers are evaluated on the basis of delivery promptness and service rendered.

Retail and wholesale buyers are concerned with the sales movement of their merchandise. Therefore, buyers talk with customers to get firsthand knowledge of their reactions to the items purchased. They also study sales records to determine fast-selling and slow-selling items. Fast-selling goods may need to be ordered quickly to avoid running out of stock. Slow-selling goods must be analyzed to determine why they are not selling faster.

With computers, buyers are able to determine the rate of sale of items and compare those rates with others. The results of such comparisons determine which products are "keepers" and which ones should be eliminated. To determine the rate of sales, the computer will divide the number of items sold weekly by the total on hand.

Another measure of stock activity is the stock turnover rate for individual items and for departments or stores. **Stock turnover** is the number of times the average stock has been sold and replaced in a given period of time. The higher the stock turnover rate, the more times the goods were sold and replaced. In retailing and wholesaling operations, the key is moving stock so there is cash available to buy more fast-selling stock. Stock that sits on the shelf is not making money. You will learn how stock turnover rates are calculated in Chapter 28.

Analysis of slower-selling items is needed before a decision is made to remove them from the store's inventory or to stop dealing with the supplier. It may be that the product is seasonal—it only sells when it is cold. If there was no cold weather this year, you have a plausible reason for that product's poor sales record. Another reason for slow sales might be the time and effort needed to sell an item. If it takes salespeople too much time to sell a given item, they may not like selling it. That would affect sales negatively. Late deliveries cause poor sales volume, too. If fishing season opens on Wednesday and your delivery of fishing lures arrives two days later on Friday, you can conclude that sales were down simply because the goods were not on the sales floor when customers wanted them.

As you can see, the purchasing function is more involved than buying goods for use in your household, but the basics are the same. Whoever is in charge of that function must be able to determine needs, research suppliers, decide where to shop, buy the goods, and evaluate the purchases afterwards. That evaluation helps you to determine what you would do differently the next time.

SECTION 26.2
Review

1. Name four criteria buyers use in selecting supply sources.
2. With what terms should a buyer be familiar in order to negotiate deals offered by suppliers?
3. What do buyers prepare to order goods?
4. When evaluating purchases made, what is the key concern of wholesale and retail buyers?

---

26 CHAPTER *Review*

Answers

Vocabulary Review

Paragraphs will vary. See Glossary for definitions.

Fact and Idea Review

1. • New-task purchase—a first-time purchase (*e.g.*, a new product line).
   • Modified-rebuy—prior purchase that has changed in some respect (*e.g.*, purchasing from a new vendor).
   • Straight-rebuy—purchase made repeatedly without change (*e.g.*, routinely ordering goods from the same vendor).
2. Suppliers deliver parts and raw materials just before they are needed for production.
3. Planned sales, BOM stock, planned reductions, and planned purchases.
4. They help buyers identify new purchases and ensure that those items are the ones customers want.
5. A retailer's representative in a central market; helps buyers by sending them information about product offerings, closeouts, fashion trends, special buys, and market conditions.
6. By responding to ads that they see in trade journals or that come by mail, by using trade association directories, and by attending trade shows.
7. Inclusion of Universal Product Codes on all goods to speed up shelving and marking.
8. Buyer may take a 2 percent discount if the invoice is paid in 10 days; otherwise the full amount is due in 30 days.
9. • Advance dating—terms take effect *as of* a specified date.
   • Extra dating—grants additional days before terms take effect.

350

Vocabulary Review

Write two or three paragraphs incorporating these vocabulary terms.

- purchasing agent
- buyers
- just-in-time (JIT)
- six-month merchandise plan
- resident buying offices
- basic stock list
- model stock list
- never-out list
- consignment buying
- memorandum buying
- advance dating
- extra dating
- end-of-month (EOM) dating
- receipt-of-goods (ROG) dating
- purchase order
- invoice
- stock turnover

Fact and Idea Review

1. Name and explain three kinds of buying situations in which all buyers may find themselves. Provide an example of each situation. (Sec. 26.1)
2. Explain the concept of just-in-time inventory control. (Sec. 26.1)
3. What figures are projected and calculated on a six-month merchandise plan? (Sec. 26.1)
4. Of what significance are want slips to retail buyers? (Sec. 26.1)
5. What is a resident buying office, and how might it help a local retail buyer? (Sec. 26.1)
6. How do purchasing agents and buyers locate sources of supply? (Sec. 26.2)
7. Name one special service that many retailers are demanding from suppliers, and tell why it is so important. (Sec. 26.2)
8. What do the numbers in ordinary dating (such as 2/10, net 30) specify? (Sec. 26.2)
9. What are the differences between the following dating terms: advance dating, extra dating, end-of-month dating, and ROG dating? (Sec. 26.2)
10. How are purchase orders different from invoices? (Sec. 26.2)
11. Name one measure of stock activity, and explain why buyers use that measure for evaluation of which goods to continue buying. (Sec. 26.2)

Critical Thinking

1. Do you think a just-in-time inventory control system could be used for a retail or wholesale operation? Why or why not?
2. If you were a buyer and given the options below for delivery of an order you placed with a supplier, which one would you choose? Why?
   • F.O.B. destination
   • F.O.B. shipping point
   • F.O.B. factory freight prepaid
   • F.O.B. destination charges reversed
3. If your high school were considering the purchase of a new copier, what people in the school system might be thought of as influentials? Explain what power and influence each might have on the purchase decision.

Building Academic Skills

Math

1. If sales were $250,000 last year and this year's sales goal is a 10 percent increase, what should planned sales be?
2. Calculate the July stock-to-sales ratio for a business that had a July opening inventory of $70,000 and sales of $35,000.
3. Determine the BOM stock figure for a merchandise plan by applying a stock-to-sales ratio of 4 to 1 to planned sales of $22,000.
4. Determine planned reductions for the merchandise plan by calculating the 10 percent reduction from last year's figure of $340.

Communication

5. You work in a men's clothing store. A customer approaches you and asks for a sweater that the store does not carry. You have received similar requests for the same sweater from other customers. What would you say to the customer? How would you communicate this information to the store buyer?

Human Relations

6. If you were a retail buyer of dolls for a toy chain store such as Toys "Я" Us that had more than 700 stores, what would you say to a supplier that has poorly designed packages? Let's say the packages break open easily and are difficult to stack on the shelves. How much power do you think you would have?

• End-of-month dating—moves the date terms take effect to the end of the month.
• ROG dating—terms begin when the buyer receives the goods.
10. Purchase orders are used by buyers to order goods. Invoices are used by suppliers to bill buyers for those goods.
11. Stock turnover rate (number of times average stock is sold and replaced in a given period of time)—a good measure because if stock is kept

moving there will be a flow of cash to buy new stock.

Critical Thinking

1. Yes, because computers already keep track of inventory on a daily basis in grocery and department stores. It would be just a matter of tying suppliers and carriers into the system.

Technology

7. Research commercial computer programs available for keeping track of inventory in a small-to-medium-sized business.

Application Projects

1. As a buyer, you have to select one of the following vendors from which to purchase 150 pairs of jeans:
   - *Vendor A.* Has a reputation for delivering goods two weeks later than promised. The price per pair of jeans is $20 each. There is a 1 percent quantity discount on all purchases over 100. Vendor A has dating terms of 2/10, net 30 and delivery terms of F.O.B. shipping point. Shipping charges are approximately $19.
   - *Vendor B.* Has an excellent reputation for delivering on time. The price per pair of jeans is $22 with dating terms of 2/10, net 30, 30 extra and delivery terms of F.O.B. store.

   Based on this information, determine the following:
   a. The unit price per pair of jeans for both vendors after all discounts and freight charges have been considered.
   b. With which vendor you would place your order—Vendor A or Vendor B. Explain the reasons for your answer.

2. Determine the date until which the buyer may take advantage of the discount and the date by which the invoice must be paid for the following:

Invoice Terms	Date Goods Were Received	Dating Terms
a. Jan. 22	Jan. 30	2/10, net 30
b. Feb. 15	Feb. 25	3/10, net 30, 60 extra
c. April 23	May 2	2/20, net 60, as of Aug. 5
d. May 10	June 10	3/10, net 30, EOM
e. Sept. 4	Sept. 30	2/10, net 30, ROG

Linking School to Work

Ask your supervisor who in your company is responsible for buying the things that are needed for the operation of the business. If possible, interview that person about his/her job responsibilities and the skills required. Share your findings with your classmates in an oral report.

Performance Assessment

Role Play

Situation. You are a management trainee in a retail operation, presently working as an assistant to the toy buyer. Your first job was to input all current purchase orders into the computer. You were also responsible for reviewing want slips sent in by local retail salespeople. A number of want slips you have reviewed indicate that customers are asking for a new product. You don't recall inputting any purchase orders for that item.

You decide to take the initiative and research possible suppliers of the new product and report back to the buyer. You learn that there are two suppliers—Fun Toys Manufacturing and Master Toys & Games. Fun Toys sells the toy for $2.50, requires a minimum order of 100, offers dating terms of 2/10, net 30 and delivery terms of F.O.B. store. Master Toys & Games sells the toy for $2.75 (no minimum order required), offers dating terms of 3/10, net 60 and delivery terms of F.O.B. destination. What will you say to the buyer?

Evaluation. You will be evaluated on how well you do the following:

- Identify the three steps in the buying process.
- Discuss how retail buyers analyze customer needs and wants.
- Compare and contrast the deals offered by suppliers, and select the best one.
- Communicate your ideas to the buyer.

Persuasive Speaking

As supervisor of cashiers in a retail store, you observe a cashier making mistakes when putting SKU codes into a POS terminal. When you mention this to the cashier, she responds, "There are too many numbers to record for each item. When a customer buys a lot of items, I don't worry if I make a mistake with the SKU. Customers appreciate my fast service, so why should the store care if I make a few mistakes?" As this employee's supervisor, what would you say to make her understand the importance of the SKU codes to the buying process?

COMPUTER APPLICATION

Complete the Chapter 26 Computer Application that appears in the Student Activity Workbook.

2. F.O.B. destination because the seller would pay for the transportation and retain responsibility for the goods until they arrived.
3. Answers will vary depending on school system.

Building Academic Skills

Math

1. $250,000 × 1.10 = $275,000
2. $70,000 ÷ $35,000 = 2

3. $22,000 × 4 = $88,000
4. $340 × .90 = $306

Communication

5. Answers will vary but should include filling out a want slip as a way of showing the customer how much his or her opinions and business are valued by the store.

Human Relations

6. You would tell the supplier to upgrade the packaging or lose the order. Given the size of the order (initial stock for over 700 stores), you would have a great deal of power.

Technology

7. Students might mention Peg Man. Other answers will vary.

Application Projects

1. a. Vendor A: Order—150 × $20 = $3,000; quantity discount—$3,000 × .99 = $2,970; cash discount—$2,970 × .98 = $2,910.60; shipping—$2,910.60 + $19 = $2,929.60; unit price—$2,929.60 ÷ 150 = $19.53.
   Vendor B: Order—150 × $22 = $3,300; cash discount—$3,300 × .98 = $3,234; $3,234 ÷ 150 = $21.56.
   b. Answers will vary depending on whether students place greater value on price or reliability.

2. a. Feb. 1, Feb. 21
   b. April 26, May 16
   c. August 25, October 4
   d. June 10, June 30
   e. October 10, October 30

Linking School to Work

Answers depend on the work situation.

Performance Assessment

Refer to the *DECA Competitive Events Handbook* for evaluation guidelines.

Computer Application

Optional activity. Refer to the *Marketing Software Binder* for template and user information.

Evaluation

Administer the reproducible test for Chapter 26, or construct your own using the Testmaker software.

Chapter Overview

Chapter 27 discusses the key functions in the distribution system of stock handling and inventory control.

Springboard

Ask students to imagine that they own a business. How would they know what merchandise is on order, is on hand, has been sold, and needs to be ordered?

A system of product tracking and storage is needed to be able to answer these questions. Ask students to define inventory. Have them tell how different goods would be checked, marked, and stored in inventory. Ask students who have worked in stock handling and inventory in their co-op jobs to tell the class how checking, marking, and storage are handled for various goods at their co-op training stations.

Prereading

List the section objectives to discuss with the students. Have the students skim the chapter, looking at the pictures, reading the captions, and noting the heads. Ask questions to ensure that the students have a minimal understanding of the chapter structure.

Preteaching the Vocabulary

Ask students to define the vocabulary. Write the accurate definitions students generate on the board. Then list the terms with which they are unfamiliar and write their correct definitions as you come to them in the chapter.

Stock Handling and Inventory Control

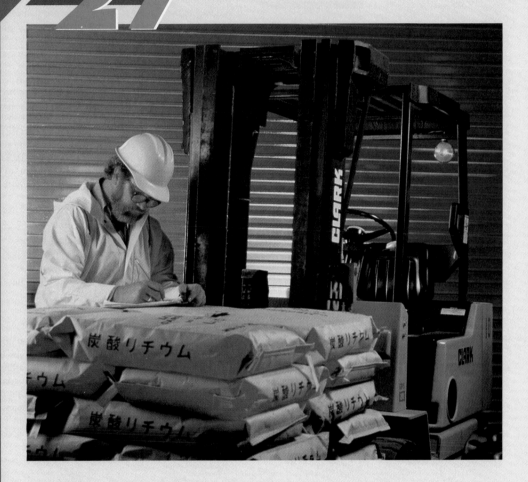

In Chapter 26 you learned about the buying function. Now you will learn about the importance and nature of stock handling and inventory control in the distribution system of any successful business.

In this chapter you will read about procedures for receiving, checking, and marking merchandise. You will learn about the importance of inventory management and the purpose of inventory control systems. You will also learn the importance of accurate inventory records and how computerized management information systems are being used to assist in inventory management.

352   Unit 7   *Buying and Distribution*

Classroom Management

For the Teacher
- Teacher's Annotated Editions for all workbooks
- Teacher's Manual for *School-to-Work Handbook*
- *Testing Binder*
- *Transparency Binder*
- *Marketing Software Binder*
- *Marketing Career Portfolio*
- *Lesson Plans*

For the Student
- *Student Activity Workbook*
- *Marketing Math Workbook*
- *School-to-Work Handbook*
- *Student Software*
- *International Case Studies*
- *Marketing Career Portfolio*

SECTION 27.1

Objectives

After completing this section, you will be able to

- explain the need for a stock-handling process,
- describe how merchandise is received and checked,
- discuss the methods used to mark merchandise, and
- describe the procedure for transferring merchandise.

Terms to Know

- receiving record
- blind check method
- direct check method
- dummy invoice check method
- spot check method
- source marking
- preretailing marking method

The Stock-Handling Process

Think about the hundreds of items of merchandise that are stocked in your local stores, such as Wal-Mart or Kmart. As merchandise is sold, new merchandise is received by the store. Imagine the confusion and the wasted time trying to find items if the store had no system for handling and organizing its stock.

Manufacturers also receive many different parts or raw materials for use in making finished products. These items are received in stock and must be tracked just as retailers track the merchandise they receive.

Whether a business receives raw materials, parts, or merchandise, a process is needed for handling items received. The steps in stock handling include receiving goods, checking them, marking the goods with information, and transferring them to a sales area.

Receiving Merchandise

Merchandise ordered by a store is received, checked, and marked with a selling price before it is transferred to the sales area. In larger businesses, several people may be needed to receive, check, and mark goods. In smaller businesses, a salesperson, manager, or even the owner may do the job.

Where merchandise is received depends on the type and size of the business. Smaller businesses may have a back room or may even use store aisles for receiving merchandise. Most stores, however, have enough space to devote a part of the basement, upstairs, or first floor to receiving.

Large businesses and chain stores usually have separate warehouses or distribution centers to receive and store merchandise before it is routed within the company. The specific area where deliveries are made by carriers is called a *dock*. Docks usually have platforms for the merchandise and are covered or enclosed to protect the merchandise from weather damage. They are large enough to accommodate the type and size of shipment the business normally receives.

Receiving Records Every business records the goods it receives in a receiving record or log. A **receiving record** is a form that is used to describe the goods received by a business.

The items on a receiving record depend on the needs of the business using it. They can include the following:

- person who received the shipment,
- shipper of the merchandise,
- place from which the goods were shipped,
- name of the carrier,
- number of the carrier,
- number of items delivered,
- weight of items delivered,
- shipping charges,
- department that ordered the merchandise, and
- date the shipment was received.

Some businesses use a short type of receiving record called an apron. An *apron* is a form attached to the invoice before the merchandise moves through checking and marking. The apron system helps prevent the payment of duplicate invoices because the apron is made out only when the shipment is received.

If a business uses an apron system, the receiving number may be called an apron number. For a retail business, the apron is prepared by a store's buyers. Apron forms stay with the merchandise until it reaches the sales floor. They list the steps the merchandise takes to reach the selling floor. The information found on the apron includes the receiving number, the department number, the purchase order number, any terms on the purchase order and on the invoice, routing, and the date the shipment was checked.

Focus

Bell Ringer Activity

Receiving inventory is the first step in inventory management. Copy a receiving record or an apron (check with a local business—a fast-food restaurant or a retail store are two good sources) and give each student a copy. Tell students the basic usage of the record or apron. Have them study the categories on each and deduce why the information in each category is essential to know when receiving merchandise.

Introducing the Section

Have students think about how they receive inventory in your school store. How do they check it to verify quantity and condition? How do they mark it and move it to the sales area? If you do not have a school store, how have students verified quantity and condition and perhaps marked such things as candy or other merchandise for a club sale?

Ask students why receiving, checking, and marking inventory are considered part of the physical distribution process (because distribution includes handling and storing products).

In Chapter 25, students looked at the general physical distribution process, which included warehousing. In this section they will further explore the physical distribution process by looking at receiving, checking, marking, and transferring.

Meeting Special Needs

Hearing Impaired

Students who wear hearing aids can be easily distracted by background noise so it is important to try and restrict unneeded interference. Each hearing aid has its own limited range of use. Therefore, you will need to discover how close you need to stand to the student in order for him or her to hear you. Keep in mind that comments made in the back of the room may prove inaudible to the student if the speaker is out of range. You may repeat questions or comments for the benefit of the hearing-impaired or include the question in your answer.

Guided Practice

1. Read Section 27.1 with students.
2. Use the transparency for this section.
3. Have students read aloud the Case Study and review the answers in class.
4. MarkEd Resource Center in Columbus, Ohio, (800) 448-0398, offers materials appropriate for use with this chapter.
5. Have students visit a local business which receives a substantial amount of merchandise daily to observe and talk with those who receive, check, and mark merchandise. Have these procedures changed and/or been streamlined over the years? Why or why not? If so, what changes have occurred? How do the procedures vary by type of merchandise received?

Discussion Starter

Have students generate some ways that receiving, checking, marking, and transferring would be handled on these products: flowers and plants; produce such as fruits and vegetables; and animals, birds, and fish received at a pet store. (All of these products will probably be more closely inspected than other products that are easier to check, such as canned goods.)

Critical Thinking

Have students generate some reasons why merchandise sometimes arrives damaged at a business. (Possibilities: poor packing of the product, either in its packaging or in the carrier itself; mishandling merchandise before or after it is shipped; and bad weather conditions that made the physical transport of the merchandise unusually rough.)

Checking Merchandise

After merchandise is received, it must be checked to verify quantity and condition. In larger businesses, checking is usually done in the receiving area. In small retail stores, it may be done in the aisles. (See Figure 27–1.)

There are four methods used to check merchandise. These methods include the blind check, direct check, dummy invoice check, and the spot check.

With the **blind check method,** a list is made from an invoice of only style numbers and descriptions. This list is then compared to the numbers on the actual invoice or purchase order for discrepancies. The blind check method is accurate but time consuming.

With the **direct check method,** the merchandise is checked directly against the actual invoice or purchase order. This procedure is faster than the blind check method, but errors may not be found if the invoice itself is incorrect. For example, some receivers do not completely check the total number of items once they see the amount listed on the invoice. If the amount looks correct, they may not bother to take an actual count.

The dummy invoice check is similar to the blind check method. With the **dummy invoice check method,** the count is made on a form similar to an invoice, but sizes and styles are omitted. The receiver writes the description of the merchandise and counts the quantities received. The merchandise is then checked against the actual invoice once it is received. The blind check method is used when the merchandise needs to be moved quickly to the sales floor and the actual invoice has not yet been received from the seller. Invoices often follow the shipment of goods by two or more days.

The **spot check method** is a random check of one carton in a shipment (such as 1 in 20). The carton is checked for quantity. One product in the carton is also inspected. If the contents are as stated on the invoice, the remaining cartons are assumed to be the same. Spot checking is often used for products such as canned goods, paper products, and pharmaceuticals.

Returning Merchandise Careful checking practices can save a business large amounts of money. All inaccuracies on invoices or damaged goods that have been received must be identified and reported according to the policies of the business. When this is done, the business can get proper credit or adjustments from the carrier or the seller.

Figure 27–1
CHECKING PROCEDURES

To increase accuracy and efficiency, specially trained employees called receivers inspect and record newly arrived merchandise.

1. All cartons and merchandise are checked for damage. All merchandise is sorted and counted.

354   Unit 7   *Buying and Distribution*

Stock Handling and Inventory Control

To students not pursuing marketing careers, the information in this chapter may seem removed from mainstream interest. However, one of the major benefits in taking a marketing course is to realize how many steps and how many people are involved in getting a product to consumers. This chapter's information on stock handling and inventory control demonstrates the vast array of steps that large and small businesses go through to make products available. Keeping up with changes in this area by reading the Business section of a daily newspaper or the *Wall Street Journal* or *Business Week* can help students in their role as consumers.

Apart from damage, there are many other reasons a business might return merchandise. Perhaps it received something it did not order, or decided to cancel an order after it was shipped. Perhaps the seller sent too many items or the merchandise arrived too late.

Upon return of the merchandise, the seller issues a *credit memorandum*. This piece of paper is notification that the buyer's account has been credited for the value of the returned merchandise.

Marking Merchandise

After it has been received and checked, merchandise must be marked with the selling price and other information. Different methods may be used for various kinds of merchandise.

Universal Product Codes (UPCs) are widely used in business today for tracking merchandise. Many businesses receive goods that are preticketed with prices and UPCs. As you learned in Chapter 18, UPCs are made up of parallel bars and a row of numbers printed on a package or a label. These codes describe the merchandise and its price. The codes are entered into a computerized inventory system for use in tracking sales and inventory levels.

UPCs are often used for **source marking.** With this method, the seller or manufacturer marks the price before delivering the merchandise to the retailer. Merchandise can be moved directly from the receiving area to the sales floor. This saves the retailer both money and time.

Stores using UPCs mark prices by placing a sign on a shelf or a bin. The UPCs are scanned at the checkout area, and the price stored in the computer for that code is entered for the sale.

Some businesses use a *preretailing marking method* of marking merchandise. With the **preretailing marking method,** pricing information is marked in advance by the seller or the buyer on the retailer's copy of the purchase order. This information is entered in the buyer's computer system, and prices are available for marking merchandise as soon as it is received. Preretailing marking is normally used for staple items unlikely to have price changes between the time of the order and receipt of the merchandise. It saves time because merchandise can be price marked immediately.

Merchandise can also be marked at the store with an electric or hand-operated pricing machine. Few stores use this method today because of the wide use of bar code scanners.

3. All incorrect items, damaged merchandise, and items ordered but not received are identified and reported.

2. Invoice and shipping tickets are verified against counts. The count is verified against the purchase orders.

Chapter 27 *Stock Handling and Inventory Control* **355**

More About

Marking Merchandise

UPC codes are now able to store more information per square inch than ever before. One product's UPC code can pack up to about 25 words into a one inch square.

Cooperative Learning

If you have a school store, have students work as a team to receive, check, and mark merchandise for a defined period of time (perhaps one month). After that time, they should assess how they could improve on the process of doing all three and present a written report of how they will implement changes in the present receiving/checking/marking system.

L1 Human Relations Skills

What skills, abilities, and personal qualities would you look for in a candidate that would be hired to receive, check, mark, and transfer goods? (Answers could include (1) honesty since he or she would have the opportunity to steal merchandise, (2) attention to detail and the ability to concentrate for extended periods of time, (3) accuracy and efficiency in recording information, (4) tact in dealing with suppliers whose goods arrived damaged, (5) physical stamina and the ability to lift potentially heavy merchandise, and (6) being bilingual if the business receives merchandise from a foreign country which sends merchandise transmittal documents that are not written in English.)

L2 Human Relations Skills

How would you test the above candidate to determine his or her suitability for the job? (Possibilities include having the person do the following: (1) demonstrate the ability to record goods on a receiving record or an apron, (2) tell you how he or she would check merchandise, (3) pass a physical exam, and (4) pass a test that assesses the depth of his or her second language skills. There are also various standardized tests for administration to potential employees that assess such things as honesty and level of attention to detail.)

CASE STUDY

Bar Codes: Improving Business Operations

The Universal Product Code was first adopted as a standard for the grocery industry in the United States during the 1970s. Today, bar codes are used by all kinds of businesses all over the world.

Bar codes are black-and-white coded strips that are printed directly on products or on labels that can be attached to items. The most common bar-code format is the Universal Product Code (UPC), which is used in the United States. An international version of the UPC is called the European Article Numbering System (EAN).

Bar codes have become so common that it may be difficult today to find products that do not use them. Even service companies have found a way to use bar codes to improve their operations. For example, United Parcel Service uses bar codes on its packages as a way of tracking them in transit.

Bar codes provide a great deal of information. The use of bar codes requires three things: scanners to read the codes, an electronic data interchange system (EDI) to transmit the coded information to a computer system, and a computerized database into which the information is read. Each bar code is unique. When scanned, the bar code connects the product to the computer database in which information about the product is stored. This system allows a great deal of information to be available quickly. In addition, people in many different locations can access the computer database, thus tracking a product as it moves from one place to another.

One U.S. company that has benefited from bar codes is the Chrysler Corporation. Its bar-code system has helped Chrysler save money and improve its operations. Chrysler invested over $2 million to install a bar-code system for tracking vehicles shipped from one place to another. The new system has cut down on the loss of vehicles in transit and also the amount of paperwork required to ship vehicles. Chrysler estimates its savings to be several million dollars a year.

Chrysler's system tracks cars in transit by sending electronic messages to distributors notifying them of incoming car deliveries. Through preestablished agreements, freight carriers only need to tell shippers of deliveries made, thus eliminating the need for freight bills. Chrysler's use of bar code technologies is no small affair. More than 50,000 import transactions and more than 70,000 export transactions are handled daily in its transportation system.

Many other companies use bar codes, for everything from tracking sales of merchandise to directing airline luggage to its destination. Bar codes are not only convenient; they are required in some businesses. For example, Wal-Mart and Toys "Я" Us either refuse to buy products without bar codes or charge for products that do not have them.

Bar codes provide many advantages in helping businesses to track their products whether they are going to the next state or to a country on the other side of the world.

Case Study Review

1. Why are bar codes being used more and more today in all areas of marketing?
2. Why does Wal-Mart and Toys "Я" Us charge for packages that are not bar coded?

A MATTER OF ETHICS

3. Consumer advocates argue that UPC-coded items should also be individually price marked to assist customers. Retailers, however, say that using UPC marking ultimately helps consumers by reducing overall merchandise costs. What do you think? Are businesses that mark prices only on a shelf on which a product is displayed and not on the product itself being fair to consumers? Is UPC marking enough, or should all products be marked with the actual price?

Case Study Answers

1. To improve shipping, reduce paperwork, and have more timely information about inventory on hand and knowledge about its location.
2. Non barcoded packages increase inventory costs and complicate the inventory control process for these retailers.
3. Students should be able to identify cost savings through UPC pricing. Errors do occur however, when UPC labels are not kept current with prices and by marking each item individually it allows the consumer to match the price on the label with the price charged through a scanner.

Invent Something You'd Like to Have

Most college students live in small quarters, two or three to a room, either in dormitories or off-campus housing. Such arrangements don't leave much space to spare.

To solve this problem, students have developed their own solutions. One of these is the loft bed (basically the top half of a bunk bed with the space beneath reserved for other furniture). Because such beds are usually hand built, however, many schools ban them as unsafe.

Lock White was one of the students who never had a loft bed. He liked their look and the space they created, but he had no aptitude for construction. What he needed was a prefabricated, easy-to-assemble loft bed that would pass the strict college safety standards. Since there was no such thing, he decided to invent it.

White and a friend, Rob Dameron, did an independent-study project to determine the feasibility of such a product. They then hired an architect to design the prototype, which included guard rails and could be sold by mail as a kit. To sell the kits, they set up their own company, Collegiate Designs, a mail-order furniture firm.

Their prefabricated bed was a resounding success. Today the line features 23 products, including futons, computer stands, and desks. All the furniture is reasonably priced, space efficient, and can be disassembled for easy storage. By acting to meet their own needs, White and Dameron founded a thriving business. It's a principle they intend to continue following. Next on the company agenda? A patented device to reduce textbook theft!

Creativity Challenge Form teams of 3–5 people, and brainstorm a list of common problems faced by team members. Then go back through the list, looking for one problem that might have a solution that could result in a marketable product. Describe its features.

Finally, merchandise can be marked with the familiar price tickets. In large stores, price tickets are prepared by hand or by machine in a marking room or in a stock room. *Gum labels* are used on merchandise with a flat, hard surface such as books. *Pin tickets* are used on merchandise that will not be damaged by the pinholes, such as socks or scarves. *String tags* are used for larger articles, such as dresses, shirts, and suits.

Price Ticket Information Price marking on the price ticket identifies the price of the merchandise. Other important information may also be included on the price ticket. Many businesses include information such as store numbers, model or style numbers, color, sizes, fabrics, manufacturer's number, and lot numbers. This information is useful for tracking merchandise. It also helps a business determine which items, sizes, and colors are popular with customers.

Transferring Merchandise

Once merchandise is received, checked, and marked, it is ready to be moved to the sales area. From there, it is often transferred to different departments within the business.

Stock transfer from a department or store to the warehouse occurs at the beginning of each season when old merchandise must be removed from the department sales area to make room for new merchandise. Old merchandise is put on sale for a short period of time. Merchandise that does not sell is transferred to a warehouse or a distribution center.

Transferred merchandise is accompanied by a form describing the items, style numbers, colors, sizes, cost, and retail prices. Duplicate copies of the transfer forms are retained as a record of merchandise on hand.

Stock transfers between departments can occur when merchandise is carried by more than one department or when the demand for merchandise in one department creates a need for additional merchandise. It can also occur when the merchandise is used for sales promotions, such as displays, advertising illustrations, or fashion shows, or when the merchandise is used for installation or repairs in various departments.

Stock transfers between stores can occur to fill orders or requests by customers due to inadequate stock in a store. Finally, stock transfers from store to distribution outlet can occur when off-season and nonsaleable merchandise is sold to surplus or discount stores.

SECTION 27.1

Review

1. **Describe the stock-handling process.**
2. **What is the purpose of a receiving record?**
3. **Describe the process for checking merchandise.**
4. **Discuss the methods for marking and transferring merchandise.**

Chapter 27 *Stock Handling and Inventory Control* **357**

SECTION 27.2

Objectives

After completing this section, you will be able to

- **define inventory management,**
- **explain the types of unit control inventory systems, and**
- **discuss the impact of technology on inventory systems.**

Terms to Know

- **dollar control**
- **unit control**
- **stockkeeping unit (sku)**
- **perpetual inventory system**
- **physical inventory system**

Inventory Management

For many businesses, inventory is one of the most costly parts of their business operations. As you learned in Chapter 25, *inventory* refers to an amount of goods stored. Examples of a manufacturer's inventory include such things as raw materials, goods in process, and finished goods. Retail inventory includes all goods for resale. Inventory represents a large business investment and must be well managed to maximize profits for the business.

Inventory management is the process of buying and storing merchandise for sale while controlling costs for ordering, shipping, handling, and storage. Inventories that are not properly controlled waste the resources of a business. Many businesses lose money because they manage their inventories poorly. For example, they may have the wrong merchandise in stock or may stock too many slow-selling items and too few fast-selling ones.

Inventory management is difficult because businesses have to anticipate the demands for various types of merchandise. For example, businesses are expected to

- maintain a wide assortment of popular merchandise that never runs out of stock,
- maintain a high amount of merchandise turnover without compromising on customer service,
- keep an adequate amount of merchandise to minimize investment without running out of stock,

358 Unit 7 *Buying and Distribution*

- purchase new merchandise at large enough volumes to gain the lowest prices but never buy too much merchandise that does not sell, and
- keep current products on its shelves without letting any merchandise become old and obsolete.

Good inventory management balances the costs of inventory with the benefits of maintaining a large inventory. The costs of inventory include not only the cost of the items in stock, but also storage, insurance, and taxes. Inventory ties up a business's *working capital*—money that could be used for other purposes. Successful inventory management helps increase working capital because the business does not have to borrow money to pay for other expenses.

Stock Turnover

The most effective way to measure how well inventory is being managed is to look at stock turnover. *Stock turnover* is the number of times the average inventory has been sold and replaced in a given period of time. High turnover rates mean that merchandise is selling quickly. That means higher profit for the business because its money is not tied up in inventory.

*Inventory must be well-managed **in order to maximize profits. How does inventory management help increase the availability of working capital?***

Stock turnover is a good measure of success for buyers to use in evaluating vendors and products from year to year. Buyers also use stock turnover rates to compare a store's entire operation with the operations of similar stores. For example, the stock turnover rate for a supermarket can be compared with rates of other supermarkets but not with the rate of a furniture store. You will learn how to calculate stock turnover rates in Chapter 28.

Stock turnover rates for selected retailers are available from trade associations and commercial publishers. One such publisher is Dun and Bradstreet Credit Services, which publishes *Industrial Norms and Key Business Ratios*.

Dollar Control and Unit Control

Inventory management involves both dollar control and unit control of merchandise held in inventory. **Dollar control** represents the planning and monitoring of the total inventory investment that a business makes during a stated period of time. A business's dollar control of inventory involves information about the amount of purchases, sales, dollar value of beginning and ending inventory, and stock shortages. With this information, a business can determine the cost of goods sold and the amount of gross profit or loss during a given period of time. By subtracting operating expenses from the gross profit, the business can determine its net profit or loss. Additional information about developing profit and loss statements is found in Chapter 40.

Unit control refers to the quantities of merchandise that a business handles during a stated period of time. Unit control allows the business to keep stock adjusted to sales and lets the business determine how to spend money available under a planned budget.

In a unit control inventory system, each item or a group of related items is referred to as a **stockkeeping unit (sku).** A unit control inventory system tracks merchandise by the merchandise's sku. Tracking the skus gives valuable sales information on the items that are or are not selling. A business can use this information to make better merchandising decisions. For example, sales promotions can be run to sell slow-moving items or to spotlight popular ones.

Unit control records also allow purchasing personnel to see what brands, sizes, colors, and price lines are selling. By keeping track of this information, buyers can understand customer preferences and order accordingly.

Finally, unit control records specify when items need to be ordered. When a minimum stock amount is reached, an order is placed for more stock. This system ensures that adequate assortments are available and helps avoid out-of-stock situations.

Types of Unit Control Systems

All merchandise bought and sold must be tracked to gain the information needed for effective inventory management. Two methods of tracking inventory are the *perpetual inventory system* and the *physical inventory system*.

Perpetual Inventory System

A **perpetual inventory system** tracks the number of items in inventory on a constant basis. The system tracks all new items purchased and returned, as well as sales of current stock. An up-to-date count of inventory is maintained for purchases and returns of merchandise, sales and sales returns, sales allowances, and transfers to other stores and departments.

With a perpetual inventory system, a business keeps track of sales as they occur. This information is collected manually or with a point-of-sale system.

Manual Systems With a manual system, employees gather paper records of sales and enter that information in the inventory system. These records include sales checks, price tickets, merchandise receipts, transfer requests, and other documents used for coding and tabulation.

Merchandise tags are used to record information about the vendor, date of receipt, department, product classification, color, sizes, and style. The merchandise tags from items sold are sent in batches to a company-owned tabulating facility or to an independent computer service organization where the coded information is analyzed by a computer.

Point-of-Sale Systems As you know from Chapter 10, a point-of-sale system uses hand-held laser

Independent Practice

1. Have students read an article on advances in inventory systems in one of the following sources: *Mass Market Retailers, Supermarket News, Chain Store Age Executive, Progressive Grocer,* or *Stores.* They should identify the article, write a 250-word summary of it, tell the magazine source from which it came, and the date of the issue. (You may wish to combine this with Application Project 8 in the Chapter Review.)
2. If your school has a store, do the following: (1) assign students in pairs to count inventory and (2) have students develop written procedures to be followed in the store when taking inventory. (If you already have written procedures, have students compare their suggested procedures to the existing ones and combine the two documents to create a more efficient inventory-taking process.)

Assess

Evaluation

Assign and review the Section 27.2 Review.

Reteaching

1. Assign and review the vocabulary terms for this section.
2. Assign and review Fact and Idea Review questions 5–13 from the Chapter Review.
3. Have the students list the reasons for inventory management and describe the difference between physical and perpetual inventory systems.

guns, stationary lasers, light pens, or slot scanners to feed information directly from merchandise tags or product labels into a computer. Point-of-sale systems are faster and more accurate than manual systems.

Physical Inventory System

Under a **physical inventory system,** stock is visually inspected or actually counted to determine the quantity on hand. A physical inventory is conducted on a periodic basis, usually once a year. Even if they use a perpetual inventory system, businesses complete a physical inventory at least once a year to calculate the value of their ending inventory.

Visual Inspection Visual inspection is used to monitor inventory levels. For example, hardware stores often place stock cards on pegboards with stock numbers and descriptions for each item displayed. The stock cards specify the number to be kept in stock. The amount to reorder is the difference between the number on hand and the specified number to be stocked.

Although a visual inspection system is easy for stock clerks and ordering personnel to use, it does not tell the

This employee is using a point-of-sale system to ring up purchases. What is one advantage of a point-of-sale system?

rate of sales for each item. The number to stock may be an estimate of sales for a typical period of time.

Counting Stock Businesses physically count inventory at least once a year. In many cases, the business will close so employees can count the inventory. Employees usually work in pairs—one counts merchandise while the other records. After the counting is finished, the total retail value of the inventory is determined. This value is reported on the business's financial statements.

Using Both Systems

A business does not have to choose between a physical inventory system or a perpetual inventory system. Many businesses use both. The perpetual system gives an up-to-date inventory record throughout the year. The physical system gives an accurate count that can be compared to the perpetual records to identify errors or problems.

The inventory records are used to help the business track sales and manage its merchandise. After a physical count is taken, the ending inventory that results becomes the beginning inventory for the year that follows. Purchases during the year are added to this amount, while sales are subtracted. Ending inventory is calculated in the example that follows.

	Number of items for 1/1/-- to 6/30/--
Beginning inventory, 1/1/19--	1,000
Net purchases (purchases less purchases and allowances returned)	+ 300
Merchandise available for sale	1,300
Less net sales (sales less returns and allowances)	− 1,050
Ending inventory 6/30/19--	250

Sometimes the ending inventory shown in the perpetual system does not match the physical count of inventory. Most often the physical count shows less merchandise in inventory. In that case, a *stock shortage* or *shrinkage* has occurred. Stock shortages are caused by theft, incorrect counting when merchandise is received, or errors at the cash register.

Using the previous example, if the perpetual system showed ending inventory of 225, a stock shortage of 25 would have occurred (250 − 25).

The Impact of Technology on Inventory Management

Electronic data processing using UPC product codes and computerized inventory systems are often used today to manage and improve inventory control. Sophisticated information-gathering systems can track items from the

More About

Technology and Inventory Management

Vendor managed inventory systems (VMI) in which manufacturers set up inventory tracking programs in retail stores are a new innovation in inventory management. VMI helps manufacturers by giving them information needed to produce what sells, and retailers by keeping out-of-stock inventories to a minimum.

Real World
MARKETING

An Apple a Day

At the time, building a computer the average person could use might have seemed like mission impossible. Nevertheless, that was the mission California computer whizzes Steve Jobs and Steve Wozniak set for themselves. They worked on the design for their machine in a lab at Hewlett-Packard. They built the prototype in the garage of Steve Jobs' parents. Today, Apple Computers, the company they founded, is a multimillion dollar enterprise.

SCM also helps to save time. SCM enables distribution centers to reduce processing time by about two days.

Manufacturers and retailers also are teaming up to implement Quick Response programs to improve inventory control in retail stores. The goal of Quick Response programs is to shorten the order cycle and to reduce excess inventory carried in stores. By shortening the order time, individual stores can reduce the amount of inventory on hand. This reduction requires less capital while also allowing for sufficient stock to meet customer needs.

Electronic data processing is no longer just for big businesses. Now even the smallest stores can get low-cost, computer-generated reports containing sales and inventory figures by product classifications. This type of information helps a business reduce the number of items that must be marked down for sale. It also helps to improve turnover and increase profits by pinpointing where inventory is too high or too low.

Most computer manufacturers offer free written information on the inventory management systems available for their equipment. Computer service companies also have materials available on such programs.

The use of technology and computerized systems has become increasingly important for businesses. The use of computerized systems has led to more efficient inventory management and thus to increased business profits.

Businesses physically count stock at least once a year. If the physical inventory requires more time and paperwork than the perpetual inventory, why do businesses use it?

purchase order to the final customer sale. Today, in general merchandising retailing, most of the larger retail chains and many smaller chains use computerized scanning equipment.

Today's technology is quickly changing the way in which stock is handled and controlled. The retail industry has created standards to take advantage of new technologies and computerized systems. These standards include:

- UPCs with standard product identifier bar code symbols to capture sku-level information at the point of sale,
- standard electronic data interchange (EDI) transactions to communicate electronically from business to business, and
- standardized shipping container marking (SCM) as a way to identify case and case contents.

EDI can help shorten order cycles. Some companies have reported that use of EDI has helped them save as much as five days in processing electronic purchase orders. Savings of two days are possible for manual orders. The savings in time between reorders allows businesses to carry one week less of inventory at their stores.

SECTION 27.2
Review

1. **What is inventory management and why is it important?**
2. **Name the different types of unit control systems for effective inventory management.**
3. **What impact have computers had on inventory management?**

Enrichment

1. Assign and review the appropriate activities in the *Student Activity Workbook.*
2. Assign and review the appropriate Critical Thinking questions from the Chapter Review.
3. Assign and review the Building Academic Skills Activities, Application Projects, Linking School to Work Activities, and Performance Assessment from the Chapter Review.
4. Application Project 9 asks the students to contact a company that makes computer-based inventory systems. Here are some companies to contact:
   - AW Computer Systems, Inc., 9000 A Commerce Pkwy, Mount Laurel, NJ 08054, (609) 234-3939 (makes point-of-sale computer systems for retailers);
   - American Business Computers Corp., 451 Kennedy Road, Akron, OH 44305, (216) 733-2841 (point-of-sale systems for restaurants, and other products);
   - Control Transaction Corp, 14 Industrial Rd., Fairfield, NJ 07006, (201) 575-9100 (computerized point-of-sale systems).

Close

Divide students into five groups. Assign one of the five major concepts covered in this lesson to each group (stock turnover, dollar control, unit control, perpetual inventory system, and physical inventory system). Have each group determine the best way to explain this concept using an outline, a symbolic drawing, etc. Then have each group explain its concept to the rest of the class.

Caption Answer

The physical inventory gives an accurate count that can be compared to the perpetual inventory.

Section Review Answers

1. See chapter for a complete description of the topic.
2. Physical inventory system and a perpetual inventory system.
3. Computers provide sophisticated information-gathering systems which can track items from the purchase order to the final customer sale.

Answers

Vocabulary Review

See the Glossary for definitions.

Fact and Idea Review

1. A form that describes the goods received by a business. See text for list of all items.
2. It helps prevent the payment of duplicate invoices because the apron is made out only when the shipment is received.
3. If it is received damaged, if it was not ordered by the business, if the business decided to cancel it after it was ordered, etc.
4. See Section 1 of text for list.
5. The number of times the average inventory has been sold and replaced in a given period of time.
6. Dollar control represents the planning and monitoring of the total inventory investment.
7. Unit control records help a business keep stock adjusted to sales and let a business determine how to spend money
8. By using manual systems and point-of-sale systems.
9. A point-of-sale system is the use of light pens, hand-held laser guns, stationary lasers, or slot scanners to feed information directly from merchandise tags or product labels into a computer. Point-of-sale systems are quicker and more accurate than are manual systems.
10. Visual inspection and counting stock.
11. See Section 2 for example and explanation.
12. The difference between the recorded sales and the sales based on the actual count of merchandise.
13. Developments include UPC codes, EDI transactions, and standardized shipping.

362

Vocabulary Review

Pair up with another student and quiz each other on the meaning and definition for each of the following vocabulary words.

receiving record
blind check method
direct check method
dummy invoice check method
spot check method
source marking
preretailing marking method
dollar control
unit control
stockkeeping unit (sku)
perpetual inventory system
physical inventory system

Fact and Idea Review

1. What is a receiving record? Identify ten things commonly found on receiving records. (Sec. 27.1)
2. What is the purpose of an apron system? (Sec. 27.1)
3. Explain why a business might return merchandise. (Sec. 27.1)
4. Identify four reasons for transferring merchandise between departments. (Sec. 27.1)
5. What is stock turnover? (Sec. 27.2)
6. What is the difference between dollar control and unit control as they relate to inventory management? (Sec. 27.2)
7. What advantage does unit control provide? (Sec. 27.2)
8. How is inventory counted in a perpetual inventory system? (Sec. 27.2)
9. What is a point-of-sale system? What are some of its advantages? (Sec. 27.2)
10. What methods are used to monitor inventory under a physical inventory system? (Sec. 27.2)
11. Explain how ending inventory is calculated. (Sec. 27.2)
12. What is a stock shortage? (Sec. 27.2)
13. Name three developments in the retail industry that take advantage of computerized systems and new technologies. (Sec. 27.2)

Critical Thinking

1. Explain why source marking is important for a small business.
2. Retailers sometimes code their actual cost of merchandise on price tickets. Do you think this

362   Unit 7   *Buying and Distribution*

information should be kept from customers? Why or why not?
3. Why do you think inventory management is so difficult? What expectations are placed on a business that complicate inventory management?
4. Why do stock turnover rates vary by the type of business? Give examples of businesses with high and low turnover rates.
5. What problems might occur if a business used only a perpetual inventory system and never made an actual count of its inventory?
6. Which inventory system requires more paperwork—the physical inventory system or the perpetual inventory system?
7. How can the use of computer technology assist in inventory management?
8. Explain why computers can be used effectively for inventory management, even in small businesses.

Building Academic Skills

Math

1. A sporting goods store calculated its cost in employee time of price marking all its merchandise to be $72,000 a year. The store estimates that it can save 28 percent of this cost by switching to source marking for all its merchandise. What is the amount of the savings?
2. A local retailer changed from price marking its merchandise with actual price stickers to using UPC labels. The use of the UPC labels saves the store $18,000 a year. In addition, the store estimates that last year's sales of $788,000 will be 3 percent higher this year because the scanned UPC labels help prevent checkout errors. What is the total gain?
3. If beginning inventory was $280,000, net purchases were $756,000, and net sales were $872,000, what is the amount of ending inventory?

Communication

4. Write a 50-word explanation of the importance of stock turnover rates and why they vary by type of retail institution.

Human Relations

5. You are working in the receiving room of a large supermarket. You observe a co-worker damaging incoming merchandise through careless behavior. You are concerned that your manager may suspect you, and you fear you might lose your job over the incident. Explain how you would handle this situation.

Critical Thinking

1. Source marking reduces the retailers' costs.
2. Because the average customer doesn't realize the difference between the actual cost and the retail price is not pure profit.
3. See text for discussion.
4. Some businesses rely on high sales volumes with low profit margins for their success while other businesses rely on high profit margins for each

item sold, placing less emphasis on high sales volume. Examples will vary.
5. It would have no way of identifying losses.
6. The physical inventory system causes more paperwork.
7. Technologies such as EDI, UPC codes, and SCM codes can assist with inventory management by keeping track of items from the purchase order to the customer sale.
8. Prices of computers, related hardware, and

Technology

6. Research the information contained on a UPC price label from a business of your choice to determine what the code lines represent.

Application Projects

1. Obtain a receiving record used by your cooperative education training station or one furnished by your instructor. Review the items detailed on the receiving record and explain what each represents.
2. Make a list of ten consumer products. Find examples of each and describe the type of price ticket used most frequently to price mark the item.
3. Working in small groups or individually, contact a retail business in your community. Ask for permission to visit the store and have someone explain the store's receiving, checking, and marking procedures. Give a five-minute oral report of your visit. With your classmates, discuss the differences you find between companies.
4. Choose a local retail store. Think about the types of products the store sells. Then write a short 150-word report recommending the best way for the store to track its inventory (for example, a POS system versus a manual system). Give reasons for your recommendation.
5. Make a line graph or bar chart of merchandise sales for your school store for each hour of the business day or for each day of one month. Analyze the chart for slow and peak sales times.
6. Research catalogs of merchandise (provided by your instructor) to be sold in a school store. Make a list of ten items and describe each by type, brand, style, and so on. List the cost and retail price for each item. Decide the quantities to stock for each item chosen. Justify all your selections.
7. Research business magazines and newspapers and find an example of a company that has improved its inventory management system. Write a brief 150-word report describing the situation and explain how improved management of inventory made the company more profitable.
8. Research computer-based inventory systems. Develop a list of five to ten questions you would ask a computer company representative if you were converting a small, family-owned toy manufacturing business from an old inventory system to a computer-based one.
9. Contact a company that makes computer-based inventory systems and invite a representative to

speak to your class. Ask him or her the questions you developed in Application Project #8.

Linking School to Work

Investigate the receiving process used at your place of employment or at your training station. List the job tasks that a receiver would perform from the time the merchandise is delivered until it is placed on the sales floor.

Performance Assessment

Role Play

Situation. You are employed as an assistant department manager in a large discount store. A problem has come up with inventory shortages. Your department manager has asked you to prepare a presentation about inventory shrinkage for an upcoming associates' meeting.

Your presentation must include a discussion of the possible causes of inventory shrinkage, inventory control procedures that could be used in your department, and steps that need to be followed to reduce inventory shortages.

Evaluation. You will be evaluated on how well you do the following:

- Identify the causes of inventory shrinkage.
- Explain the types of unit inventory control systems that are appropriate for your company.
- Identify a plan and procedures to reduce inventory shortages.

Create a Chart

A retail store had the following levels of inventory throughout the year:

January	1,890 units
March	3,920 units
May	3,450 units
July	4,500 units
September	2,980 units
November	4,260 units

Create a bar chart showing the inventory for each month.

COMPUTER APPLICATION

Complete the Chapter 27 Computer Application that appears in the Student Activity Workbook.

Technology

6. UPC code information will vary with the business but will contain product information.

Application Projects

1. Items will vary depending on form chosen.
2. Types of price tickets will depend on the consumer products students choose.
3. Interviews will vary. Students should discuss the differences in stock handling procedures.
4. Reports will depend on the types of retail stores the students select.
5. Slow and peak sales times will depend on the school store.
6. Costs of items will depend on the catalogs students use.
7. Research reports will depend on the companies the students select.
8. Students should ask how to establish a computer-based inventory system.
9. Guest speakers should provide additional information on computer-based inventory systems.

Linking School to Work

Answers depend on the work situation.

Performance Assessment

Refer to the *DECA Competitive Events Handbook* for evaluation guidelines.

Computer Application

Optional activity. Refer to the *Marketing Software Binder* for template and user information.

Evaluation

Administer the reproducible test for Chapter 27, or construct your own test using the Testmaker software.

---

software programs have been greatly reduced. This makes the use of computers for inventory management possible.

Building Academic Skills

Math

1. $72,000 \times 28\% = \$20,160$
2. $18,000 \times (3\% \times \$788,000) =$
   $18,000 + \$23,640 = \$41,640$

3. $280,000 + 756,000 = \$1,036,000 -$
   $872,000 = \$164,000$

Communication

4. Explanations will vary.

Human Relations

5. Students' responses to the situation will vary but should be well thought out and tactful.

CHAPTER 28

PURCHASING AND DISTRIBUTION MATH

Pages 364–375

Chapter Overview

In this chapter, students explore the math calculations buyers and vendors use. The chapter focuses on the preparation of three key documents— purchase orders, invoices, and merchandise plans.

 Springboard

Remind students of some of the forms they were introduced to in Chapter 26. Characterize each briefly, and challenge students to identify it. Allow them to refer to the earlier chapter, as necessary.

- Legal contract between buyer and seller. (Purchase order)
- The supplier's bill. (Invoice)
- Budget for planned purchases (Six-month merchandise plan)

Prereading

List the section objectives to discuss with students. Have students skim the chapter, looking at the pictures, reading the captions, and noting the heads. Ask questions to ensure that students have a minimal understanding of the chapter structure.

Preteaching the Vocabulary

Before students begin reading the chapter, dictate each of the vocabulary terms and ask students to write them on a sheet of paper. When they finish, write the terms on the chalkboard. Then have students guess at the meaning of each. Write their guesses next to each term, but do not give the correct meaning. Leave this list on the chalkboard so that students can see how close their guesses were to the actual definitions as they work through the chapter.

364

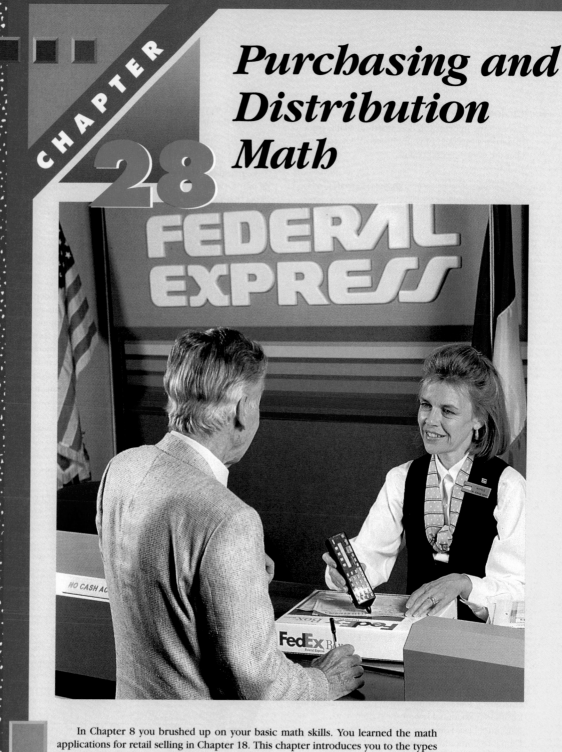

CHAPTER 28

Purchasing and Distribution Math

In Chapter 8 you brushed up on your basic math skills. You learned the math applications for retail selling in Chapter 18. This chapter introduces you to the types of math calculations used by buyers and vendors.

364   Unit 7   *Buying and Distribution*

Classroom Management

For the Teacher
- Teacher's Annotated Editions for all workbooks
- Teacher's Manual for *School-to-Work Handbook*
- *Testing Binder*
- *Transparency Binder*
- *Marketing Software Binder*
- *Marketing Career Portfolio*
- *Lesson Plans*

For the Student
- *Student Activity Workbook*
- *Marketing Math Workbook*
- *School-to-Work Handbook*
- *Student Software*
- *International Case Studies*
- *Marketing Career Portfolio*

Objectives

After completing this section, you will be able to

- calculate and verify extensions on purchase orders and invoices, and
- use appropriate tables to determine shipping charges.

Terms to Know

- extension
- parcel post

Purchasing Calculations

Much of the math that a buyer does is for purchase orders. For vendors the comparable form is the invoice. The calculations for both forms are very similar to those performed by retail salespeople on sales checks.

Purchase Orders

In industrial sales, the salesperson and the buyer agree on the terms of the sale and record the information in a legal contract. The most common type of contract is the purchase order. It lists the quantity, price, and description of the products ordered, along with the terms of payment and delivery.

If you were responsible for ordering goods for resale, one of your duties would be to prepare purchase orders, or PO's. In Figure 28-1 on page 366, notice the information routinely included in a PO.

- *Item number*—vendor's catalog designation; identifies the merchandise being ordered
- *Quantity*—the number of units ordered
- *Description*—explains precisely what is being ordered
- *Unit*—how the item is packaged and priced (individually, by the dozen, by the ream [500 sheets per package], etc.)
- *Unit cost*—price per unit
- *Total*—the **extension**, or result of multiplying the number of units by the cost per unit

BRIGHT IDEAS

Talk to This Package That Just Arrived, Will You?

The gizmo you ordered has at last arrived. You open the package and find an assortment of parts—but no instructions. Then, slowly and calmly, a voice from the box begins to tell you what to do.

You take some aspirin, snap the safety cap in place, and put the bottle back in the medicine cabinet. Before you can shut the cabinet door, the cap reminds you that you shouldn't take any more aspirin for at least four hours.

You're cooking dinner. You wonder aloud how long you should cook the frozen carrots—and the bag tells you.

Sound far-fetched? Not really. Prices of computerized voice chips are already plummeting. In the not-too-distant future, they will become economical enough to allow companies to incorporate them into products and packaging. Think of the possibilities!

Creativity Challenge Form teams of 3–5 people, and do just that. Consider all the different ways that talking products would change consumer and corporate responsibilities, market access, security arrangements, and any other aspects of business that you can think of.

Note that if you order several items on the same purchase order, the total of all extensions is entered at the bottom of the Total column. It is on this amount that any sales tax is figured and to this amount that it is added.

Invoices

When filling an order based on a PO, a vendor will include an invoice like the one shown in Figure 28-2 on page 366 with the delivered merchandise. The check marks indicate that the invoice has been checked to verify its accuracy. The numbers and amounts are correct (they match the PO and other documents), as are the extensions.

Chapter 28 *Purchasing and Distribution Math* **365**

FOCUS

Bell Ringer Activity

Give each student a blank purchase order similar to that shown in Figure 28-1 (page 366). Then read the following information aloud, and have students use it to fill out their purchase orders. They should calculate all extensions, total them, figure the amount due with sales tax. (Use your own state's sales tax rate for the last calculation.) This will serve not only as a gauge of listening ability but also as a pretest of students' ability to calculate extensions and totals.

Ship to:
Raintree Gifts
3219 Berwick Boulevard
Los Angeles, California 91106

Vendor:
Oak Park Office Supply
1313 Clough Road
Cincinnati, Ohio 45230

Assign your own *item numbers* to these purchases:

- 50 note pads @ $.99 each
- 100 boxes of paper clips (120 per box) @ $.49 each
- 2 leather portfolios @ $39.99 each
- 20 fountain pens @ $1.99 each

(Students' entries and calculations should yield the following result: $49.50 + $49 + $79.98 + $39.80 = $218.28. Tax and total due will vary with state.)

Introducing the Section

Review students' answers to the Bell Ringer Activity. Be sure students understand the meaning of each category on the purchase order.

Throughout the study of this section, stress the importance to both buyers and vendors of accurate recording of such information. Note that a PO serves as a written record of merchandise purchased and shipped.

Meeting Special Needs

Behaviorally Disordered

Students with behavior disorders need a structured learning environment. To provide such an environment, you may find it helpful to seek input from the students themselves. Ask about their strengths, their weaknesses, and the techniques that enhance the learning process for them.

You will also have to balance the individual needs of these students with the group's requirements. The class as a whole should not be made to suffer because of the behavior of one or two students. Reinforce appropriate behavior, and model it for students.

Teach

Guided Practice

1. Read Section 28.1 with students.
2. Use the two transparencies for this section.
3. For those students still experiencing difficulties with basic math skills, your procedure for teaching should include a great deal of guided practice and comprehension checking, as you did with Chapter 8, "Fundamentals of Mathematics."
4. You may wish to have representatives of the U.S. Postal Service, Federal Express, and UPS talk to students as a panel about the various services that each company provides, including corporate discount rates.

Discussion Starters

1. Have students discuss some ways that such services as Express Mail, UPS, and Federal Express have changed the way companies do business. (Answers will vary. All express mail services have enabled companies to do business more efficiently. They can send and receive merchandise more quickly. It may cost a little more, but it also generates more business by better satisfying customers' wants and needs.)
2. Have students speculate about the types of vendors (and their services) that would have received purchase orders from the publishing company that produced *Marketing Essentials.* (Answers will vary but could include typesetter, film house, and printer.)

Figure 28–1

Businesses use their own PO's to order goods from other firms. In this case, suppose Mountain-Air had also ordered two boxes of file folders at $18.50 each. How would that have changed the PO?

Purchase Order

Bicycle Shop

PURCHASE ORDER NUMBER: 1004

Invoice and ship to: Mountain-Air Bicycle Shop
123 State Street
Van Nuys, CA 91423

DATE: Oct. 15, 19 - -

Vendor: Channel Paper Distributors
436 Ocean Avenue
Mission Hills, CA 91345

ITEM NO.	QUANTITY	DESCRIPTION	UNIT	UNIT COST	TOTAL
K2007	10	Photocopy paper	500 ea.	$ 5.16	$ 51.60
K94	2	Calculators	ea.	19.95	39.90
J411	15	Binders	ea.	11.75	176.25

TOTAL AMOUNT:		$ 267.75
TAX		22.09
TOTAL DUE:		$ 289.84

Invoice

CHANNEL PAPER DISTRIBUTORS

SOLD TO: Mountain-Air Bicycle Shop
123 State Street
Van Nuys, CA 91423

INVOICE NO: K5005
DATE: Oct. 24, 19 - -

YOUR ORDER NO.	DATE SHIPPED	SHIPPED VIA	FOB	TERMS
1004	10/24/- -	UPS	M. HILLS	2/10, N30

ITEM NO.	QUANTITY	DESCRIPTION	UNIT	UNIT COST	TOTAL
K2007 ✓	10 ✓	Photocopy paper ✓	500 ea.	$ 5.16 ✓	$ 51.60 ✓
K94 ✓	2 ✓	Calculators ✓	ea.	19.95 ✓	39.90 ✓
J411 ✓	15 ✓	Binders ✓	ea.	11.75 ✓	176.25 ✓

TOTAL AMOUNT:	$ 267.75 ✓
TAX	22.09 ✓
UPS	14.22 ✓
TOTAL:	$ 304.06 ✓

Figure 28–2

Vendors bill their customers by including invoices with the orders they fill. In this instance, why doesn't Channel Paper's total agree with Mountain-Air's?

Caption Answer

Figure 28-1. There would have been an extra entry totaling $37, plus sales tax. For students proficient enough to work out the sales tax rate (8.25 percent), the extra tax would come to $3.05, for a new total of $329.89.

Caption Answer

Figure 28-2. Because Channel Paper has included shipping charges for the order.

Look carefully at the entries at the bottom of the invoice. In addition to the merchandise total (or subtotal), there are also places for sales tax, shipping charges, and the actual amount to be paid by the customer. For the remainder of this section, we will consider how these entries are calculated.

Sales tax is paid only once—by the final user. In other words, it does not apply to goods sold for resale. In Figure 28-2, Mountain-Air pays the tax because clearly its purchases are intended for use in the operation of its business. Were it buying ten bikes, however, there would be no sales tax entry. The sales tax would be paid by its customers.

Regardless of the nature of its purchases, Mountain-Air is entitled to take advantage of the specified payment terms (2/10, N30). Note, however, that discounts apply only to merchandise. Shipping charges are not discounted.

Practice 1

Use a separate sheet of paper to complete the following problems.

1. Calculate the extension for each purchase order entry. Then figure the total amount of the order.

ITEM NO.	QUANTITY	UNIT COST	TOTAL
K2007	6	$5.16	_____
J1012	6	1.15	_____
B0017	2	3.60	_____

2. The invoice entries below contain a number of computational errors. Find and correct them.

ITEM NO.	QUANTITY	UNIT COST	TOTAL
J1468 ✓	20 ✓	$ 4.95 ✓	$ 99.00 ✓
M140 ✓	50 ✓	1.25 ✓	6.25
M245 ✓	18 ✓	6.95 ✓	1,251.00
C001 ✓	5 ✓	318.00 ✓	1,590.00 ✓
K238 ✓	10 ✓	420.00 ✓	2,100.00
L012 ✓	25 ✓	22.50 ✓	1,125.00

Note: Answers to all practice sets in this chapter appear on page 373.

When Do We Eat?

The American custom of eating the main meal in the evening is not universal. In fact, people in most other countries eat their main meal at midday, usually between 1 P.M. and 3 P.M.

In countries where a large meal comes early in the day, a light meal usually suffices later. This meal can be anything from fruit and cheese to English high tea. (The latter isn't a formal tea but an informal supper offered at about 5 P.M. It is usually built around such items as eggs or tinned meats.)

Businesspeople should keep these differences in mind when traveling abroad or entertaining foreign visitors here. A visiting colleague from Italy or France who has just finished a large midday meal would be hard-pressed to enjoy a steak supper at 6 P.M.

Shipping Charges

Most manufacturers, distributors, and retailers use the United Parcel Service (UPS) or the U.S. Postal Service to deliver merchandise. Recall from Chapter 18 that delivery charges are generally exempt from sales tax. That is why they are added *after* the sales tax has been calculated.

Parcel Post The cost of shipping merchandise depends on the service used, the weight of the shipment, and the distance it is being sent. If you take your packages to the post office, you will probably send them **parcel post.** Parcel post rates are shown in Table 28-1 on page 368.

Zones 1 and 2 are within 150 miles of the post office where you mail your packages. Zone 3 is between 150 and 300 miles away. The farther away the destination, the higher the zone number and rate. The local zone, for packages mailed to addresses in the same city, has the shortest distances and the lowest rates.

When you weigh packages of more than a pound for shipping by parcel post, count any part of a pound as a full pound. That is, if a package weighs 4 pounds and 3 ounces, look up 5 pounds in the rate table. To find the cost of sending such a package to Zone 6, for example, you would read down the Weight column until you came to 5 pounds and then across to Zone 6.

COD Your company may send merchandise COD (cash on delivery). When you ship COD, the postal carrier will collect the amount due and forward it to your company. However, your company must prepay the shipping charges. The amount due may include both the total for merchandise and shipping costs. In addition, the customer must pay a fee for the COD service. The fee varies

L1 Math Skills

Have students work in pairs to create ten sets of purchase order entries using the quantity/merchandise description/unit cost format—for example, 2 sweaters @ $47.98 each. The unit cost for each item of merchandise should range from $1 to $100. The quantity of merchandise should range between 2 and 10.

When each pair of students has generated their own list, they should exchange it for another pair's list. Then both pairs should calculate the extensions for each other's "orders." For example, 2 sweaters @ $47.98 each = $95.96.

L2 Math Skills

After students have worked each other's problems, have each pair once again exchange lists. Each pair of students should work together to put the total amounts in order, from highest to lowest.

L3 Math Skills

Have each pair of students use Table 28-1 on page 368 to generate ten package weights and destinations (for example, a package weighing 16 pounds and 7 ounces, going to zone 8). When all pairs of students have generated such a list, have them exchange papers. Then, when you give the signal, have each pair work as quickly as they can to figure the final mailing cost for each package. The first pair of students to correctly identify the mailing costs for all their packages wins. (You determine the prize. Make sure, however, that winners' answers are correct.)

Feature Note

How much you eat can be as problematic as when you eat it. Food and acceptance are much more related in other cultures than in the United States. In such circumstances, failing to eat what you are served in sufficient quantity can be taken as an insult.

For example, if you sit down to eat at an Italian table and merely pick at the food, your host is likely to have the chef prepare you something you really enjoy! You can plead dietary restrictions for one dish, but you must be prepared to eat a substitute. The true Italian host will not be happy until you have eaten.

Teach *(Cont'd.)*

Critical Thinking

Ask students why post-office-to-post-office service costs less. (It saves the carrier the trip to the addressee's home or place of business.)

Cooperative Learning

Design a worksheet with problems in each of the areas covered in this lesson. Have students complete the worksheets in cooperative groups, including below-level, on-level, and above-level students in each group. Reward the groups in which all members are able to describe the steps taken to calculate each problem.

Independent Practice

1. Assign and review the Chapter 28 Case Study in the *International Case Studies* workbook.
2. Have students consult with their co-op training station supervisor to create a list of the vendors with whom the firm does business. Have students include in their lists the types of merchandise purchased, how often, and in what sorts of quantities. Have students share their lists with the class.

Assess

Evaluation

Assign and review the Section 28.1 Review.

Reteaching

1. Assign and review the vocabulary terms for this section.
2. Assign and review Fact and Idea Review questions 1–5 from the Chapter Review.
3. Working with the same blank form, repeat the Bell Ringer Activity using new information of your choice. Have students fill out the purchase order, calculating the various extensions and the final total due, including sales tax.

Parcel Post Rates (Fourth-Class Mail)

Weight (not exceeding ___ lbs.)	Local	1&2	3	4	5	6	7	8
2	$2.12	$2.19	$2.32	$2.46	$2.74	$2.85	$2.85	$2.85
3	2.19	2.29	2.49	2.70	3.12	3.54	4.00	4.05
4	2.25	2.39	2.65	2.94	3.50	4.06	4.35	4.60
5	2.31	2.49	2.81	3.17	3.88	4.58	5.20	5.40
6	2.38	2.59	2.98	3.41	4.26	5.10	6.33	8.55
7	2.44	2.68	3.14	3.65	4.64	5.62	7.06	9.60
8	2.50	2.78	3.31	3.89	5.02	6.14	7.78	10.65
9	2.57	2.88	3.47	4.12	5.40	6.67	8.51	11.70
10	2.63	2.98	3.63	4.36	5.78	7.19	9.24	12.75
11	2.69	3.08	3.80	4.60	6.16	7.71	9.97	13.75
12	2.76	3.18	3.96	4.83	6.54	8.23	10.69	14.80
13	2.80	3.25	4.08	4.99	6.79	8.57	11.17	15.85
14	2.85	3.32	4.19	5.16	7.04	8.92	11.65	16.90
15	2.89	3.38	4.28	5.27	7.23	9.17	11.99	17.95
16	2.93	3.43	4.36	5.39	7.40	9.40	12.31	19.00
17	2.97	3.48	4.44	5.49	7.56	9.62	12.61	19.91
18	3.01	3.53	4.51	5.60	7.72	9.83	12.90	20.38
19	3.05	3.58	4.59	5.69	7.87	10.03	13.17	20.83
20	3.08	3.63	4.65	5.79	8.01	10.22	13.43	21.26
21	3.12	3.68	4.72	5.88	8.15	10.40	13.68	21.66
22	3.15	3.72	4.79	5.97	8.28	10.57	13.91	22.05
23	3.18	3.77	4.85	6.05	8.40	10.74	14.14	22.43
24	3.22	3.81	4.91	6.13	8.52	10.90	14.36	22.78
25	3.25	3.85	4.97	6.21	8.64	11.05	14.57	23.13
26	3.28	3.89	5.03	6.29	8.76	11.20	14.77	23.46
27	3.32	3.93	5.09	6.36	8.87	11.35	14.97	23.78
28	3.35	3.97	5.14	6.44	8.97	11.49	15.16	24.09
29	3.38	4.01	5.20	6.51	9.08	11.63	15.34	24.39
30	3.41	4.05	5.25	6.58	9.18	11.76	15.52	24.68
31	3.44	4.09	5.30	6.65	9.28	11.89	15.69	24.96
32	3.47	4.13	5.36	6.71	9.37	12.01	15.86	25.23
33	3.50	4.17	5.41	6.78	9.47	12.14	16.02	25.50
34	3.53	4.20	5.46	6.84	9.56	12.26	16.18	25.75
35	3.56	4.24	5.51	6.91	9.65	12.37	16.34	26.01

Source: U.S. Postal Service

Table 28–1

Packages sent by parcel post travel by ground transportation for the rates shown here. What would it cost to send a package weighing 22 pounds and 3 ounces to Zone 7?

Caption Answer

The cost would be $14.14.

More About

Shipping Charges

Ask: What would it cost to send a 34-pound package to Zone 1? ($4.20) What would it cost to send that same package to Zone 8? ($25.75) Why is there such a big difference in price? (Because the Zone 8 package must be transported a greater distance and possibly handled more frequently in the process.)

Express Mail Rates

Weight (lbs.)	PO to Addressee	PO to PO
$\frac{1}{2}$	$ 9.95	$ 9.50
1	13.95	11.15
2	13.95	11.15
3	15.95	13.15
4	17.95	15.15
5	19.95	17.15
6	23.50	20.70
7	24.50	21.70
8	25.55	22.75
9	26.55	23.75
10	27.60	24.80
15	32.70	29.90
20	37.85	35.05
25	43.00	40.20
30	48.15	45.35
40	58.40	55.60
50	68.65	65.85
60	79.20	76.40
70	91.60	88.80

- 70 lbs. and 108" combined length and girth are the maximum weight and size per package.
- $4.50 charge per pickup stop (not per piece).

Table 28–2

Express mail ensures next-day delivery of packages weighing up to 70 pounds. If you had to get an 8-ounce package cross-country overnight, given the rates shown here, how would you send it and why?

depending on the amount collected. Up to $500 may be collected on delivery by a postal carrier.

For COD shipments, many businesses prefer using United Parcel Service. This is because UPS does not limit the amount that can be collected at delivery to $500 and the shipping charges do not have to be prepaid.

Express Mail When you need to ship something fast, you may use the express mail service provided by the U.S. Postal Service. There are two types of express mail service—post office (PO) to addressee and post office to post office (PO to PO).

PO-to-addressee service is available for most zip codes, and delivery by 3 P.M. on the next day is guaranteed in most areas. PO-to-PO service is less expensive, but next-day delivery is available to only a few zip codes. Express mail rates are shown in Table 28–2.

A number of private parcel carriers also provide such service. They include Federal Express, UPS, Airborne Express, and Emery Worldwide Courier.

Real World

Garbage In, Dollars Out

Big City Forest is a company that has its own "new math." Some companies look at broken wooden pallets and crumpled packaging materials and see garbage. Big City Forest sees dollars.

The Bronx, NY, company recycles wooden pallets and packaging materials. It turns salvageable wood into new pallets, butcher-block furniture, or wood chips. In the process, it diverts tons of trash from landfills, saves other companies hundreds of thousands of dollars in waste disposal costs, and gives close to 20 people a regular income.

Practice 2

Use a separate sheet of paper to complete the table entries below.

1. What would be the charges for sending the following packages by parcel post?

	Weight	Zone	Parcel Post Rate
a.	1 lb. 8 oz.	2	_____
b.	2 lb. 1 oz.	4	_____
c.	3 lb. 4 oz.	6	_____
d.	17 lb. 2 oz.	3	_____
e.	33 lb. 1 oz.	7	_____

2. Calculate the price difference for each pair of shipping alternatives described below.
   a. A 20-pound package sent by Express Mail PO to addressee vs. the same package sent PO to PO
   b. A six-pound package sent cross-country to a home address in Zone 8 by Parcel Post vs. the same package sent by Express Mail

SECTION 28.1

Review

1. **A customer orders six triple packs of adhesive tape at $1.79 each—6 × $1.79 on your invoice. What term describes this calculation?**

2. **How do parcel post and express mail rates compare?**

Chapter 28 *Purchasing and Distribution Math* **369**

4. Design a worksheet with problems in each of the areas covered by this section. Have students work in small groups to complete the worksheets. Be sure to include below-level, on-level, and above-level students in each group. Reward the groups in which all members are able to describe the steps taken to calculate each problem.

Enrichment

1. Assign and review the appropriate activities in the *Student Activity Workbook*.
2. Assign and review the appropriate Critical Thinking questions from the Chapter Review.
3. Bring to class samples of the shipping record forms provided by the U.S. Postal Service, UPS, Federal Express, and similar firms to their customers. Allow students to fill out a form for each, noting the specific information required.

Close

Have students complete these statements:
- Much of the math that a buyer does is for...(purchase orders.)
- Much of the math that a vendor does is for...(invoices.)

Caption Answer

Probably by Express Mail, PO to addressee. For a half-pound package, you would pay only $.45 more to have it delivered directly to the person for whom it was intended.

Section Review Answers

1. Extension.
2. Parcel post rates are much lower, mainly because packages are transported by surface carrier and take longer to arrive. Express mail moves by air for overnight delivery and thus costs much more.

SECTION 28.2

Focus

Bell Ringer Activity

Have students speculate about the answer to the following question: What factors must retail buyers consider before determining how much money is available to them for buying product at any given time? Have students list the possibilities on a sheet of paper.

Introducing the Section

Many of the factors students need for their response to the Bell Ringer Activity have been introduced in earlier chapters in this unit (notably Chapter 26). Retail buyers must consider *planned sales, beginning-of-the-month stock, retail reductions,* and *planned purchases.*

Students may recognize these items as the major entries in a merchandise plan. Briefly review each concept with students. If they are having a difficult time comprehending and remembering any or all of the concepts, help them create a mnemonic device for each.

Teach

Guided Practice

1. Read Section 28.2 with students.
2. Use the transparency for this section.
3. Have students read aloud the Case Study and review the answers in class.
4. MarkEd Resource Center in Columbus, Ohio, (800) 448-0398, has materials appropriate for use with this section.
5. This section involves a great deal of math calculation. As with the first section, you should include guided practice and comprehension checking as necessary, especially for those students still experiencing difficulties with basic math.

SECTION 28.2

Objectives

After completing this section, you will be able to

- **explain the significance of the major entries in a merchandise plan,**
- **calculate those entries, and**
- **figure stock turnover rates.**

Terms to Know

- **cost**
- **retail**
- **open-to-buy (OTB)**

Merchandise Plan Calculations

Marketing math for retail buying involves preparing a six-month merchandise plan. Recall that such a plan includes four key elements—projected sales, beginning-of-the-month stock, retail reductions, and planned purchases. All of these figures must be calculated. Once they are, the amount of money available for buying product at any given time within the planning period can be determined. In this section, all of these computations will be explained and illustrated.

Planned Sales

The first figure calculated on a merchandise plan is the planned sales figure. In most cases, this is determined by using the previous year's monthly sales figures and adjusting them to reflect the firm's current-year sales goal.

For example, suppose sales for a particular month last year were $100,000 and this year's goal is to increase sales by 10 percent. This year's planned sales for the month would be calculated as follows:

Desired increase: $100,000 × 10 = $10,000
Planned sales: $100,000 + $10,000 = $110,000

You could also reach the same result in a single step:

$$\$100,000 \times 1.10 = \$110,000$$

A firm's goal for the current year is derived from a study of last year's sales, current market and economic conditions, and an analysis of the competition. Projection

---

of an accurate planned sales figure is important because all other figures on the merchandise plan are computed on the basis of this figure.

Beginning-of-the-Month (BOM) Stock

To arrive at the planned beginning-of-the-month (BOM) inventory, you apply a stock-to-sales ratio to the planned sales figure. For example, suppose the stock-to-sales ratio is 2:1 (usually reported as 2). This means that to accommodate a given sales volume it is necessary to keep twice that amount of stock on hand. If sales of $5,000 are anticipated, BOM inventory should be twice that amount, or $10,000.

How does a buyer arrive at the appropriate stock-to-sales ratio? By analyzing the previous year's records. The buyer would divide the BOM stock figure for each month by the month's sales figure. For example, suppose the stock figure for a given month had been $15,000 with sales of $3,000. The stock-to-sales ratio would be figured as follows:

$$\$15,000 \div \$3,000 = 5 \text{ (or 5:1)}$$

You should realize that just as there is a BOM stock figure, there is also an EOM (end-of-month) stock figure. The two are very closely related. The BOM stock figure for any given month is the EOM stock figure for the *previous* month.

Planned Reductions

Recall that planned retail reductions take into account the kinds of things that either reduce merchandise or the ultimate amount it earns for a retailer. When employees are given discounts on merchandise or merchandise is put on sale, it brings in less revenue. Merchandise that disappears through pilferage or shoplifting brings in nothing. Such reductions in earnings ultimately affect the amount of money that must be planned for purchases.

Planned retail reductions can be calculated in two different ways. One is to calculate reductions as a percentage of planned sales. For example, suppose planned reductions have historically been 10 percent of planned sales. If planned sales for the month are $25,000, planned reductions for that month would be calculated as follows:

$$\$25,000 \times .10 = \$2,500$$

Some firms set goals of reducing planned reductions from the previous year. For example, assume a firm's goal is to reduce this year's planned reductions by 5 percent from last year's figure. If last year's reductions were $700, this year's planned reductions would be figured this way:

Desired decrease: $700 × .05 = $35
Planned reductions: $700 − $35 = $665

This result could also be reached in a single step:

$$\$70 \times .95 = \$655$$

Lifelong Learning

Purchasing and Distribution Math

One of the most striking changes in the way purchasing departments operate is that nearly all now use computers. In fact, software has been developed specifically for purchasing departments. The market stood at $250 million annually in 1994 and is expected to grow to $600 million by 1997.

Such projections indicate that tremendous importance is placed in the industry on computer skills. Students interested in marketing careers in general and purchasing careers specifically must be comfortable with computers. They should build up their keyboarding speed and accuracy and keep those skills well honed if they want to compete successfully for the best jobs.

Six-Month Merchandise Plan (Model)

Spring Season 19—   Department _Kitchenware_

                                                    No. _6124_

		Feb.	March	April	May	June	July	Total
Sales	Last Year	82,000	96,000	90,000	100,000	94,000	80,000	
	Plan	90,200	105,600	99,000	110,000	103,400	88,000	
	Actual							
Retail Stock BOM	Last Year	328,000	336,000	297,000	360,000	291,400	224,000	
	Plan	360,800	369,600	326,700	396,000	320,540	246,400	
	Actual							
Retail Reductions	Last Year	12,300	14,400	13,500	15,000	14,100	12,000	
	Plan	11,685	13,680	12,825	14,250	13,395	11,400	
	Actual							
Retail Purchases	Last Year	NA	NA	NA	NA	NA	NA	
	Plan	110,685	76,380	181,125				
	Actual							

Figure 28–3

This nearly completed merchandise plan is based on the following assumptions: (a) sales are expected to increase by 10 percent over last year; (b) last year's stock-to-sales ratios should be used to compute this year's BOM stock figures; (c) this year's planned reductions should be 5 percent lower than last year's; and (d) planned BOM stock for August is $264,000. What are the planned purchase figures for May through July?

Planned Purchases

Recall that planned purchases are the retail-dollar purchase figures a firm needs in order to achieve its sales and inventory projections. Note that this definition utilizes a distinction that we have not focused on till now—the distinction between *retail* and *cost* figures. This distinction will be explored in depth in Unit 8. For now simply note that **cost** refers to what a retailer pays for merchandise, while **retail** refers to what a retailer gets for it. Retail figures for the same merchandise would be higher since they would include the retailer's profit. The planned purchase figure is recorded as a retail figure on the merchandise plan because all figures on that plan are expressed in retail prices.

All of the figures discussed thus far are used in calculating planned purchases (P). That includes planned sales (PS), planned EOM/BOM stock, and planned reductions (R). Here is the formula:

(PS + EOM stock + R) − BOM stock = P

Assume that planned sales are $10,000, planned EOM stock $25,000, planned reductions $500, and BOM stock $20,000. Using the formula, planned purchases would be arrived at this way:

($10,000 + $25,000 + $500) − $20,000 =
$35,500 − $20,000 = $15,500

Figure 28–3 shows a nearly completed merchandise plan. Study it carefully. Then try to duplicate the buyer's computations based on what you have learned thus far in this section.

Open-to-Buy

At any given time during the buying season, a buyer may want to know the **open-to-buy (OTB).** This is the amount of money left for buying goods. It is calculated as follows:

P − (goods received + goods ordered) = OTB

Caption Answer

May—$48,790; June—$42,655; July—$117,000.

6. It may help students with comprehension if you write each of the basic formulas covered in this section on the chalkboard.
7. You may wish to have a Management Assistance Officer from the SBA talk to students about merchandise planning.
8. Assign and review the Chapter 28 Activity in the *School-to-Work Handbook*.

Discussion Starter

What social, economic, and market factors would you consider when determining a percentage increase with which to adjust your firm's current-year sales goals? (Answers will vary, but possibilities include the following, any of which might bring in new business:

- New and/or improved products that you intend to offer
- An increased focus on customer service
- An increase in the population in your area and/or a change in demographics
- A new business location that is more accessible
- An increase in the prices of your products
- Greater use of advertising and promotion
- A decrease in competition
- Good word-of-mouth from your established customer base)

L1 Math Skills

Below are the 1998 monthly sales figures for Hampton's Jewelry Store. Have students determine the monthly planned sales for 1999, based on the percentage increase planned for each month—2 percent for January through April and July, 30 percent for the remaining months.

	1998	1999
Jan.	$ 45,600	($54,720)
Feb.	65,112	(78,134)
Mar.	62,456	(74,947)
Apr.	62,200	(74,640)
May	80,766	(104,996)

June	82,998	(107,897)
July	44,332	(53,198)
Aug.	43,768	(56,898)
Sept.	42,998	(55,897)
Oct.	65,567	(85,237)
Nov.	134,100	(174,330)
Dec.	125,000	(162,500)

L2 Math Skills

Have students continue working with the Hampton's Jewelry Store figures from the L1 Math Skills activity. Ask: By what percentage does Hampton's hope to increase its sales in 1999 compared to 1998? (Total projected sales for 1999: $1,083,397. Total sales for 1998: $854,897. Difference: $228,499. Percentage increase: $228,499 ÷ $854,897 = 0.267 or 27%.)

L3 Math Skills

Have students work in pairs to generate two problems for each of the formulas for (a) BOM stock, (b) planned reductions, (c) planned purchases, and (d) open-to-buy. Once students have generated their problems, have them switch papers with another pair of students. Each pair of students should work together to solve the problems.

If this activity is too difficult for the level of your class, generate several problems each for BOM stock, planned reductions, planned purchases, and open-to-buy. Have students solve them at the chalkboard.

Independent Practice

Have students create a work sample for their portfolios that demonstrates they understand the important concepts discussed in this section. They can do this by creating a sample merchandise plan, perhaps based on school store sales figures from last year. (See Enrichment Activity 11 below.)

■ CASE STUDY ■

Turning a Giant Around

Sears, Roebuck & Co. is one of the country's biggest retailers. In recent years, though, it has been struggling with reduced sales and profits. The reason? The public sees Sears as boring and stodgy, and the company's famous catalog has been a money loser for years. In 1993, the company's merchandise group lost almost $3 billion.

Sears is turning around, however. In September 1992, the company named Arthur C. Martinez to head the merchandise group. Martinez closed 113 unprofitable stores and stopped publishing the catalog. Stores began to carry clothing lines that customers found more appealing. A $40 million advertising campaign targeted a more youthful, stylish customer. The year after Martinez took over, Sears Merchandise Group posted profits of $752 million. Another 18 percent increase in earnings was predicted for 1995.

But Martinez wasn't satisfied. "The turnaround is only 35 percent complete," he explained. The company

will continue renovating older, rundown stores to attract more customers. It is working hard to sign up popular women's clothing lines. Company buyers are learning to be good negotiators in order to make better use of planned purchase money. Employees are being trained to give better customer service.

Company database research showed that women between the ages of 25 and 50 are the company's biggest market. As a result, the company will be targeting them, adding 30 percent more floor space for women's apparel and carrying more expensive, higher-profit merchandise. Sears will follow the lead of J. C. Penney in creating its own private-label clothing lines.

Sears stopped selling cosmetics in the mid-1980s. Customers preferred the luxury marketing of department store cosmetics counters with their beautifully groomed makeup experts offering advice. Now Sears will follow this pattern in its new cosmetics departments, which will carry the store's own line of products.

Martinez is even trying to turn around the old catalog department. The newest versions of Sears catalogs have been pared down and targeted to specific markets. This is a strategy that has been successful for other modern direct mail marketers.

Sears is a 19th-century company that began by selling everything from inexpensive and sturdy clothing to farm tools and buildings through its huge catalog. In order to be successful into the 21st century, the retail giant recognized it had to make major changes. Arthur C. Martinez has proved a captain who can steer Sears into more profitable marketing waters.

■ ■ *Case Study Review*

1. If Sears expects an 18 percent increase in earnings this year, how would that affect the merchandise plan for the next year?

A MATTER OF ETHICS

2. Sears buyers were well known for being very friendly with their suppliers—so friendly, in fact, that they often paid higher prices for their products than other retailers did. Was this just a matter of poor business judgment or ethical misconduct? Explain.

Case Study Answers

1. It would raise the planned sales figures and change all those dependent on them.
2. Answers will vary, but it can be argued that both are true. As business judgments go, it was part of the buyers' jobs to get the best-quality merchandise at the lowest price. Indeed, keeping costs down would have been especially

critical in a firm having financial problems. In addition, ethically the buyers' first loyalty should have been to their employer in all business situations. However, by elevating personal friendship above job obligations, the buyers effectively favored the suppliers at the expense of Sears.

Assume that merchandise received against the planned purchase figure computed above is $6,500 thus far and merchandise on order against it is $2,000. The present OTB would be as follows:

$$\$15,500 - (\$6,500 + \$2,000) =$$
$$\$15,500 - \$8,500 = \$7,000$$

Practice 3

On a separate sheet of paper, do the following merchandise plan calculations for Granny's Gift Shoppe:

1. Last March the shop had sales of $4,200. The owner's goal is to increase sales by 7 percent. What would be the planned sales for this March?
2. Last year's stock-to-sales ratio for March was 1.5:1. What should be the BOM stock figure for this March?
3. The owner would like to cut planned reductions by 5 percent this year. If last year's reductions for the month were $500, what would be this year's target figure?
4. With the figures already given or calculated and an EOM stock figure of $5,000 for March, determine planned purchases for the gift shop.

Stock Calculations

Buyers are interested in stock activity. How well stock moves reflects not only on the products and their vendors but also on the buyer. One key measure that buyers use is stock turnover.

If a store keeps records of the retail value of its stock, it computes its stock turnover rates as follows:

$$\frac{\text{Net sales (in retail dollars)}}{\text{Average inventory on hand (in retail dollars)}}$$

For example, if net sales during a period are $49,500 and average inventory is $8,250, the stock turnover is 6:

$$\frac{\$49,500}{\$8,250} = 6$$

To determine the average inventory, use average inventory amounts for each of the months included in the time period being considered. Total these, as shown in the second column below.

Month	Average Inventory	Net Sales
January	$ 50,000	$ 10,000
February	55,000	15,000
March	68,000	20,000
April	64,000	19,000
May	63,000	21,000
June	60,000	20,000
Totals	$360,000	$105,000

To get the average inventory for the six-month period, divide by the number of months.

$$\frac{\$360,000}{6} = \$60,000$$

Finally, to calculate stock turnover, divide total net sales (see the third column above) by average inventory.

$$\frac{\$105,000}{\$60,000} = 1.75$$

This figure means that the average inventory was sold and replaced 1.75 times during the six-month period.

When only cost information about stock is available, stock turnover can be calculated with this formula:

$$\frac{\text{Cost of goods sold}}{\text{Average inventory on hand (at cost)}}$$

If a store wants to look at the number of items carried in relation to the number of items sold, it calculates its stock turnover rates in units with this formula:

$$\frac{\text{Number of units sold}}{\text{Average inventory on hand in units}}$$

Answers to Practice Sets

Practice Set 1 (page 367)

1. K2007 $30.96	2. *Errors:*
J1012 $ 6.90	M140 $ 62.50
B0017 $ 7.20	M245 $ 125.10
Total $45.06	K238 $4,200.00
	L012 $ 562.50

Practice Set 2 (page 369)

1. a. $ 2.19	2. a. $2.80
b. $ 2.70	b. $14.95
c. $ 4.06	
d. $ 4.51	
e. $16.18	

Practice 3 (page 373)
1. $4,494
2. $6,741
3. $475
4. $3,228

SECTION 28.2

Review

1. Why is planned sales the first figure written on a merchandise plan?
2. If the stock figure for last month was $28,000 and sales were $7,000, what is the stock-to-sales ratio?
3. What is the retail formula for calculating stock turnover?

Section Review Answers

1. Because all other figures depend on it.
2. 4:1, or 4.
3. Net sales (in retail dollars)
   Average inventory on hand
   (in retail dollars)

SECTION 28.2

Assess

Evaluation

Assign and review the Section 28.2 Review.

Reteaching

1. Assign and review the vocabulary terms for this section.
2. Assign and review Fact and Idea Review questions 6–10 from the Chapter Review.
3. To reteach the section's key concepts, have students write in their own words how to calculate planned sales, BOM stock, a stock-to-sales ratio, planned reductions, planned purchases, open-to-buy, and stock turnover rate.

Enrichment

1. Assign and review the appropriate activities in the *Student Activity Workbook*.
2. Assign the Unit 7 Activity in the *Marketing Math Workbook*.
3. Assign and review the appropriate Critical Thinking questions from the Chapter Review.
4. Assign and review the Building Academic Skills Activities, Application Projects, Linking School to Work Activity, and Performance Assessment from the Chapter Review.
5. Have students work together as a group to figure as many of the following as they can for the months that your school store is operational: (a) planned sales for each month of next year, (b) BOM stock, (c) planned reductions, (d) planned purchases, (e) open-to-buy, and (f) stock turnover rate.

Close

Have students complete this statement: Once projected sales, BOM stock, retail reductions, and planned purchases are calculated, _____ can be determined. (the amount of money available for buying product at any given time within the planning period)

373

Answers

Vocabulary Review

Math problems will vary. See Glossary for definitions.

Fact and Idea Review

1. Item, quantity, description, unit, unit cost, and total.
2. Multiply the number of units by the cost or price per unit.
3. Shipping charges, payment terms.
4. Service used, weight of shipment, and distance being sent.
5. Cash on delivery. Postal carrier collects the amount due and forwards it to the seller.
6. Those for planned sales, beginning-of-month stock, planned reductions, and planned purchases.
7. The BOM stock figure for any given month is the EOM stock figure for the previous month.
8. To know how much money he or she still had to spend on purchases.
9. Total monthly average inventory figures and divide by the number of months.
10. Retail formula, cost formula, and units formula.

Critical Thinking

1. To ensure that customers receive exactly what they ordered.
2. Answers will vary. Possibilities include lower printing costs because businesses can do larger runs, reduced errors when employees must learn to use only one form, simpler record keeping (only one series of form numbers to deal with instead of two).
3. Computer could fill out the form by merging information from various databases with it. Computer could also instantly update customer records.

Vocabulary Review

Write three math problems utilizing the terms below, either alone or in combination. In each problem, include a brief description of the situation and a sample calculation.

> extension
> parcel post
> cost
> retail
> open-to-buy

Fact and Idea Review

1. What information must the customer provide on a purchase order? (Sec. 28.1)
2. Describe how to calculate an extension. (Sec. 28.1)
3. What information does the vendor usually include on an invoice that is not part of a purchase order? (Sec. 28.1)
4. The cost of shipping is based on what factors? (Sec. 28.1)
5. What does COD stand for, and how does it work? (Sec. 28.1)
6. What computations are involved in preparing a merchandise plan? (Sec. 28.2)
7. Describe the relationship between BOM and EOM stock figures. (Section 28.2)
8. Why would a buyer need to know the OTB amount? (Sec. 28.2)
9. How does a buyer determine average inventory on hand? (Sec. 28.2)
10. What are the three versions of stock turnover that can be calculated? (Sec. 28.2)

Critical Thinking

1. Why is it so important to verify numbers and amounts on invoices?
2. Some businesses use combination purchase order/invoice forms. What advantages would there be to this?
3. How could using a computer to generate invoices save time?
4. Why wouldn't you prepare a new merchandise plan every month?
5. Why is it a good idea to keep a stock-to-sales ratio low?
6. What could happen if a buyer computed a planned sales figure for the next planning period that was 20 percent too high?

Building Academic Skills

Math

1. Calculate the extensions for these purchases:
   a. 6 chairs at $59.95 each
   b. 6 place mats at $6.95 each
   c. 6 napkins at $2.95 each
2. In the housewares department of Arley's department store, the buyer plans to purchase $35,000 in merchandise over the next six-month period. The store has already received $12,000 worth of housewares, and another $8,000 is on order. What is the buyer's OTB?
3. If your planned sales for the month are $22,000, and your stock-to-sales ratio is 4, what should your BOM stock figure be for your merchandise plan?
4. A merchandise plan has $45,000 in planned sales for February. If planned reductions are 5 percent, what is the planned reduction figure?
5. Compute planned purchases by using the following information:

Planned sales	$ 3,500
Planned EOM stock	9,000
Planned reductions	500
Planned BOM stock	8,500

6. Calculate stock turnover rates for the following retail institutions using the data provided.

Type of Institution	Net Yearly Sales	Average Inventory (Retail)	Stock Turnover Rate
Department store	$14,503,000	$3,085,744	_____
Shoe store	875,000	265,150	_____
Jewelry store	245,800	102,400	_____
Grocery store	1,542,875	96,430	_____
Service station	155,900	5,575	_____

7. Given the following information, calculate the stock turnover rates in units for the following situations.

   Units sold during the year:
   12,000; 2,500; 5,000; 1,580; and 3,475

   Average inventory on hand in units: 1,500

8. Given the following information, calculate the stock turnover rates in retail dollars for the following situations.

   Net yearly sales: $15,560; $17,500; $12,540; $16,000; and $11,575

   Average inventory on hand at retail: $6,000

4. Answers will vary. However, such a short lead time hardly allows for "planning" at all. It also might not be possible to get money allocated on such short notice.
5. So that too much money is not tied up in inventory at any given time.
6. Buyer would not meet his/her sales goals. He or she would also probably have bought too much inventory.

Building Academic Skills

Math

1. a. $59.95 × 6 = $359.70
   b. $6.95 × 6 = $41.70
   c. $2.95 × 6 = $17.70
2. $35,000 − ($12,000 + $8,000) = $35,000 − $20,000 = $15,000
3. $22,000 × 4 = $88,000
4. $45,000 × .05 = $2,250

9. Calculate the annual stock turnover at cost for the following situations.

   Cost of goods sold during the year: $55,700; $36,780; $64,975; $44,560; and $48,725

   Average inventory at cost: $13,475

Communication

10. You are the buyer for a men's retail clothing store. There have been repeated requests for a certain brand of trousers, but your manager doesn't like doing business with the company that makes them. Write a memo to your manager describing the increased sales that would result if you were allowed to buy these trousers.

Human Relations

11. In a meeting to work on the merchandise plan for your store, one of the department heads is anxious to set the planned sales figure at 15 percent over present sales. She believes this will "light a fire" under the salespeople. How would you explain to her the need for realistic planned sales figures?

Application Projects

1. Ask several local businesses for blank copies of their invoice and purchase order forms. Compare the formats for ease of use.
2. Bring a mail order catalog to class. Compare the way each company handles its shipping and handling charges. Do they all base their charges on weight and distance?
3. Call various private shippers and find out their rates for different types of service—surface, air, second day, next day. Also, find out about charges for insurance. Prepare a chart comparing the services offered by the various shippers, and present it to the class.

Linking School to Work

Ask your employer if you may look at the merchandise plan for your business. Analyze the plan, noting the planned sales, planned reductions, and stock ratio. Ask your employer to explain how he or she uses the plan to decide how much to buy and when it's time to reduce stock. Ask how he or she thinks planning effects the profits of the business. Report to the class on your findings.

Performance Assessment

Role Play

Situation. You will make an oral presentation of a merchandise plan for your business, which sells bicycles and related gear. Last year's sales were $175,000, spread evenly over the 12 months. This year sales are expected to increase. The stock-to-sales ratio last year was 3, and planned retail reductions were 10 percent of sales.

Evaluation. You will be evaluated on how well you do the following:

- Decide on a realistic planned sales number.
- Do the necessary computations to complete the merchandise plan.
- Evaluate and incorporate current economic considerations into your planning.
- Explain your recommendations in a way that shows a thorough understanding of the use and content of a merchandise plan.

Paper

Do research at local businesses on new technology for producing purchase orders and invoices. Write a two-page paper describing your findings.

Complete the Chapter 28 Computer Application that appears in the Student Activity Workbook.

Portfolio

Consider the Application Projects that you have done for this unit. Select one that illustrates your mastery of the unit's content and might be of interest to potential employers. Reformat the activity as necessary, adding any explanatory text, and place it in your Portfolio. Consider using these activities:

- Chapter 24, Application Project 2
- Chapter 26, Application Project 1
- Chapter 27, Application Project 4 ■ ■

- $64,975 ÷ $13,475 = 4.8
- $44,560 ÷ $13,475 = 3.3
- $48,725 ÷ $13,475 = 3.6

Communication

10. Memos will vary depending on additional circumstances that students hypothesize.

Human Relations

11. Answers will vary but should include a discussion of the effect that unreasonable goals or expectations have on a work force.

Linking School to Work

Answers depend on the work situation.

Performance Assessment

Refer to the *DECA Competitive Events Handbook* for evaluation guidelines.

Computer Application

Optional activity. Refer to the *Marketing Software Binder* for template and user information.

Evaluation

Administer the reproducible test for Chapter 18, or construct your own using the Testmaker software.

Portfolio

Refer to the *Marketing Career Portfolio* for development ideas and portfolio management and assessment.

---

5. ($3,500 + $9,000 + $500) − $8,500 = $13,000 − $8,500 = $4,500
6. • Department store: $14,503,000 ÷ $3,085,744 = 4.7.
   • Shoe store: $875,000 ÷ $265,150 = 3.3.
   • Jewelry store: $245,800 ÷ $102,400 = 2.4.
   • Grocery store: $1,542,875 ÷ $96,430 = 16.
   • Service station: $155,900 ÷ $5,575 = 28.
7. • 12,000 ÷ 1,500 = 8
   • 2,500 ÷ 1,500 = 1.67

- 5,000 ÷ 1,500 = 3.33
- 1,580 ÷ 1,500 = 1.05
- 3,475 ÷ 1,500 = 2.3
8. • $15,560 ÷ $6,000 = 2.6
   • $17,500 ÷ $6,000 = 2.9
   • $12,540 ÷ $6,000 = 2.1
   • $16,000 ÷ $6,000 = 2.67
   • $11,575 ÷ $6,000 = 1.9
9. • $55,700 ÷ $13,475 = 4.1
   • $36,780 ÷ $13,475 = 2.7

Pricing

Unit Objectives

After completing this unit, students will be able to achieve the following outcomes:

- Use pricing terminology correctly and effectively.
- Perform computations related to pricing theory and practice.
- Plan and implement a pricing strategy.

Chapter 31

Chapter 29

Chapter 30

Teacher Classroom Resources

CHAPTER	29	30	31
Transparency Binder	Transparencies 43–45a & 45b	Transparencies 46–47a & 47b	Transparencies 48–50
Student Activity Workbook	pp. 179–184	pp. 185–190	pp. 191–196
Student Software	pp. 183–184	pp. 189–190	pp. 195–196
Marketing Math Workbook			Activity 8
School-to-Work Handbook	pp. 63–64	pp. 65–66	pp. 67–68
International Case Studies	pp. 63–64	pp. 65–66	pp. 67–68
Marketing Career Portfolio			Unit 8 activity, Student Text, p. 417
Test Booklet/ Testmaker Software	Chapter 29 test	Chapter 30 test	Chapter 31 test, Unit 8 test

KEY TO BASIC SKILLS ACTIVITIES

L1 Level 1 activities are basic activities and should be within the range of all students.

L2 Level 2 activities are average activities and should be within the range of average and above average students.

L3 Level 3 activities are challenging activities designed for the ability range of above average students.

375b

CHAPTER	PERFORMANCE OBJECTIVES

29
Price Planning
	29.1 **1.** Define price and explain its importance.
	     2. State the goals of pricing.
	     3. Distinguish between market share and market position.
	29.2 **1.** Identify four market factors that affect price planning.
	     2. Explain demand elasticity in relation to supply and demand theory.
	     3. Discuss government regulations that affect price planning.

30
Pricing Strategies
	30.1 **1.** Apply the three basic pricing concepts (cost-oriented, demand-oriented, and competition-oriented) to pricing a product.
	     2. Describe the consequences for manufacturers of pricing forward and pricing backward.
	     3. Distinguish between a one-price policy and a flexible-price policy.
	     4. Explain the two main pricing policies that should be considered when introducing a new product.
	30.2 **1.** Identify various pricing techniques.
	     2. List the steps in setting prices.

31
Pricing Math
	31.1 **1.** Explain how a firm's net profit or loss is related to pricing.
	     2. Calculate dollar and percentage markup based on cost or retail.
	     3. Calculate markdown in dollars, as well as determine sale price and maintained markup.
	31.2 **1.** Describe the general procedure for figuring discounts.
	     2. Calculate various kinds of discounts.

Unit Overview and Background Information

Unit 8 is devoted to pricing principles and practices. Chapter 29 addresses the importance of price and broadens students' awareness of the various factors that affect it. Chapter 30 contains a plethora of basic pricing strategies that students are bound to recognize, from various forms of psychological pricing to cost-, demand-, and competition-oriented pricing. With all the theory in place, Chapter 31 focuses on the computational skills needed for pricing. Students are taught the basic formulas for determining markups, markdowns, and various kinds of discounts.

Introducing the Unit

Ask students what would happen to a local business that charged its customers the same amount it paid for the goods it sold. (Some students will say that the business would break even, while other more astute students will recognize that it would be losing money because there would be nothing left to pay operating expenses like rent, utilities, employee wages and benefits, and advertising.) This simple example should help students recognize how important price planning is to the financial success of a business.

Unit Project

Have students prepare a video or multi-media presentation on pricing principles and practices. Tell them that the presentation should be between five and ten minutes long, logically organized, and cover the key points from the unit. Have them work in groups to decide what they should include in the presentation (both audio and video).

Unit

8

376

Focus on the Photo/Cooperative Learning

Once students have completed this unit, divide the class into four groups. Tell them that they are going to reposition the jelly beans featured in the unit photo. Then assign each group a pricing strategy—odd-even, multiple, promotional, or price lining—and have them redo the price labels for the candy bins. *Note:* Groups can add extra signage to the display.

Pricing

CHAPTERS

29
Price Planning

30
Pricing Strategies

31
Pricing Math

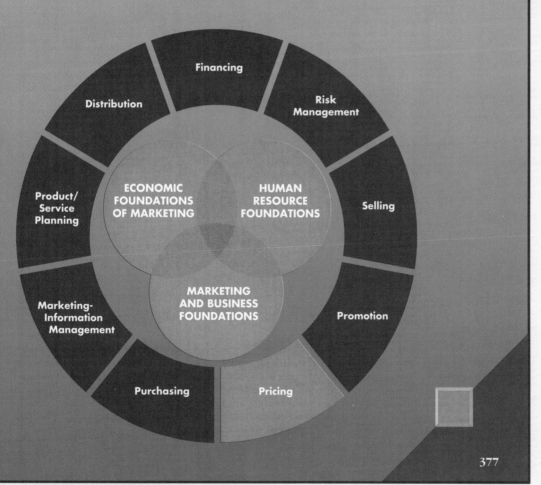

Resources for Enrichment of Unit Content

Books

- *Successful Retailing: Your Step-by-Step Guide to Avoiding Pitfalls and Finding Profit As an Independent Retailer* by P. Wardell
- *12 Simple Steps to a Winning Marketing Plan* by G. Larkin

Magazines/Journals

Current issues of *Brandweek, Business Week, Chain Store Age Executive, Men's Wear, Nation's Business,* and *Women's Wear Daily.*

Unit Closure

Have students revisit the work they did in determining the retail, wholesale, and manufacturer's price for Continental's Coconut Surprise cookies in Chapter 30. Have them write a short report on the steps they would suggest to a new employee responsible for pricing yet another new company product. Tell students to include sample calculations to cover concepts such as markup and break-even point.

Evaluation

Administer the reproducible test for Unit 8, or construct your own using the Testmaker software.

Guest Speaker Suggestions

- Have a product manager from a local firm speak to the class about the factors he/she considers when making pricing decisions.
- Some newspapers monitor price advertising to be sure advertisers don't deceive their readers. If your local paper has such a policy, have someone from the publication speak to the class about it.

Field Trip Suggestion

Have students visit a local retail shopping mall to find examples of pricing strategies and techniques in practice. Have students carry clipboards or notebooks to record exactly what price tickets, signs, or displays say that illustrates a given pricing theory.

Chapter Overview

Chapter 29 introduces students to price planning. The chapter discusses the goals of pricing, as well as the market factors that affect it. Government regulations that deal with pricing are also considered.

 Springboard

Have students think of items they value enough to buy even if it means foregoing other purchases. Students should then take turns asking their classmates how much they would be willing to pay for these goods or services. Answers should be listed on sheets of paper rather than announced. Only when all purchases have been considered should students compare their answers and note which products elicited the widest range of prices.

Prereading

List the section objectives to discuss with students. Have students skim the chapter, looking at the pictures, reading the captions, and noting the heads. Ask questions to ensure that students have a minimal understanding of the chapter structure.

Preteaching the Vocabulary

Before students begin reading the chapter, dictate each of the vocabulary terms and ask students to write them on a sheet of paper. When they finish, write the terms on the chalkboard. Then have students guess at the meaning of each. Write their guesses next to each term, but do not give the correct meaning. Leave this list on the chalkboard so that students can see how close their guesses were to the actual definitions as they work through the chapter.

CHAPTER 29

Price Planning

Let's play a version of *The Price Is Right*. What price would you pay for a one-pound box of candy—$6 or $50? What price would you pay for a used car with 10,000 miles on it—$100 or $7,000? If you picked $6 for the candy and $7,000 for the car, you evaluated the prices in relation to the value you would expect to get from each. You probably felt that $50 was more than you wanted to spend for the candy. You probably assumed that a $100 car was a lemon.

Just as you did in the above two examples, marketers consider price in relation to value when making pricing decisions. They also look at several other factors we'll explore in this chapter.

378   Unit 8   *Pricing*

Classroom Management

For the Teacher

- Teacher's Annotated Editions for all workbooks
- Teacher's Manual for *School-to-Work Handbook*
- *Testing Binder*
- *Transparency Binder*
- *Marketing Software Binder*
- *Marketing Career Portfolio*
- *Lesson Plans*

For the Student

- *Student Activity Workbook*
- *Marketing Math Workbook*
- *School-to-Work Handbook*
- *Student Software*
- *International Case Studies*
- *Marketing Career Portfolio*

SECTION 29.1

Objectives

After completing this section, you will be able to

- **define price and explain its importance,**
- **state the goals of pricing, and**
- **distinguish between market share and market position.**

Terms to Know

- **price**
- **market share**
- **market position**
- **return on investment**

What Is Price?

Price is the value of money (or its equivalent) placed on a good or service. It is usually expressed in monetary terms, such as $5.50 for a pen. It may also be expressed in nonmonetary terms, such as free goods or services in exchange for the purchase of a product.

Relationship of Product Value

The key to pricing is understanding the value buyers place on a product. Value is a matter of anticipated satisfaction. If consumers believe they will get a great deal of satisfaction from a product, they will place a high value on it. They will also be willing to pay a high price for it.

Thus, a seller must be able to gauge where a product with its given features will rank in the customer's estimation—valued much, little, or somewhere in between. This information can then be considered in the pricing decision. The seller's objective is to set a price high enough for the firm to make a profit and yet not so high that it exceeds the value potential customers place on the product.

Various Forms of Price

Price is involved in every marketing exchange, regardless of whether the term *price* is used. The fee you pay a dentist to clean your teeth, the amount you pay for a new pair of shoes, and minor charges such as bridge tolls and bus fares are all prices. Rent is the monthly price of an apartment. Interest is the price of a loan. Dues are the price of membership. Tuition is the price you pay for an education. Wages, salaries, commissions, and bonuses are the various prices that businesses pay workers for their labor. Price, then, comes in many forms and goes by many names.

Importance of Price

Price is an important factor in the success or failure of a business. It helps establish and maintain a firm's image, competitive edge, and profits.

Many customers, for example, use price to make judgments about products and the companies that make them. To some customers, a higher price means better quality from an upscale store or company. To other customers, a lower price means more for their money. In these cases, price is a vital component of a business's image.

Sometimes price is the main thrust of a firm's advertising strategy. Some retailers stress that they offer the lowest prices in town or promise that they will beat any other store's prices. In such cases, price plays an important role in establishing the edge a firm enjoys over its competition.

Finally, price helps determine profits. Marketers know that sales revenue is equal to price times the quantity sold. Thus, sales revenue can be increased either by selling more items or by increasing the price per item. That is in theory, however. In reality the number of items sold may not increase or even remain stable if prices are raised. Table 29-1 shows what may happen.

Projected Effects of Different Prices on Sales

Price per Item	x	Quantity Sold	=	Sales Revenue
$30		100		$3,000
27		120		3,240
24		130		3,120
21		140		2,940
18		160		2,880
15		200		3,000

Table 29-1

An increase in the price of an item may not produce an increase in sales revenue. Why?

Chapter 29 *Price Planning* **379**

Caption Answer

Because the number of people willing to buy at the higher price may decrease. In other words, sales volume may decline.

Discussion Starter

Have students discuss the adage that one person's junk is another person's treasure. Suggest they use their experience playing *The Price is Right* (Springboard Activity) as a starting point. Help them build toward the idea that the values people place on things vary with the individual.

Critical Thinking

Ask students if an increase in price will always help to increase profits. (No, not if costs and expenses increase more or if sales volume goes down because of the higher prices.)

Independent Practice

1. Assign and review the Chapter 29 Case Study in the *International Case Studies* workbook.

2. Have students poll their classmates regarding their favorite fast-food restaurant, toothpaste, deodorant, cologne, jeans, or any other type of product teenagers buy for themselves. Tell students to assume that the members of the class represent all the people who buy those products. Based on the data they collect, have students prepare two items:
   - A pie chart depicting market share for each brand (Students can use Figure 29-1 on page 380 as a model.)
   - A list of competitors ranked in order by market position.

Evaluation

Assign and review the Section 29.1 Review.

It is also important to remember that an increase in price can increase profits only if costs and expenses can be maintained. You will explore this limitation later in the chapter.

Goals of Pricing

While marketers are concerned primarily with earning a profit, they do have other pricing goals. Those other goals include *gaining market share,* achieving a certain *return on investment,* and *meeting the competition.* Let's look at each of these in a little more detail.

Gaining Market Share

Sometimes a business will forgo immediate profits for long-term gains in some other area. One goal, for example, might be to take business away from competitors. In this case, we say the business is trying to increase its market share. **Market share** is a firm's percentage of the total sales volume generated by all competitors in a given market. Businesses constantly study their market share to see how well they are doing with a given product in relation to their competitors.

Visualize the total market as a pie. Figure 29-1, for example, depicts the total market for breakfast cereals in the United States. Each slice of the pie represents each competitor's share of that market. The biggest slice of pie represents the firm that has the largest percentage of the total sales volume.

In addition to market share, marketers are interested in their relative standing in relation to their competitors, or their **market position.** To monitor market position, a firm must keep track of the changing size of the market and the growth of its competitors. For example, according to market position, the number one long distance telephone carrier in the United States is AT&T. It has the highest sales volume of all companies in the long-distance telephone market. In many markets, the number

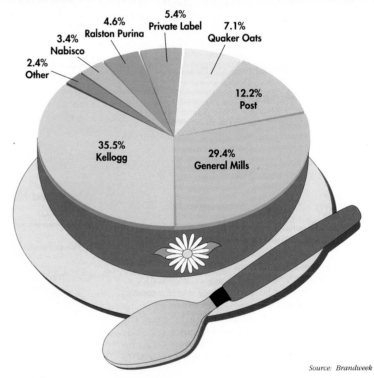

Breakfast Cereals—The U.S. Market

2.4% Other
3.4% Nabisco
4.6% Ralston Purina
5.4% Private Label
7.1% Quaker Oats
12.2% Post
29.4% General Mills
35.5% Kellogg

Source: *Brandweek*

Figure 29-1

Market share is a key measure of success in a competitive marketplace. Which company has the largest share of the market diagramed here? If that market represents $8 billion in sales, what are the leader's sales revenue?

Kellogg has the largest share—35.5 percent, or about $2.8 billion in sales.

one company often stands out as the market leader, while other companies scramble for second-, third-, and fourth-place positions.

Pricing may play a role in establishing and maintaining a firm's market share and market position. In order to maintain or improve both, businesses watch their competitors. When a company wants to increase its market share, it may engage in price competition in order to take business away from its competitors. (Of course, it may also use other competitive tools, such as increasing the frequency of advertising or using new advertising media and messages.)

Return on Investment

Return on investment is a calculation used to determine the relative profitability of a product. The formula for calculating return on investment is as follows:

$$\frac{\text{Profit}}{\text{Investment}}$$

Profit, of course, is just another word for return, which explains the expression *return on investment*.

Consider an example. Assume your company sells widgets for $8 each. Your costs to make and market the widgets is $6.50 per unit. If you recall from Chapter 3 that profit is money earned by a business minus costs and expenses, here is how you would calculate your return on investment:

$$\frac{\$8 - \$6.50}{\$6.50} = \frac{\$1.50}{\$6.50} = .23$$

This means that your rate of return on investment is 23 percent.

A company may price its products to achieve a certain return on investment. Let's say that your widget company wants to achieve a return on investment of at least 15 percent on a new model. To determine the price at which the new widgets would have to sell, you would work backwards. You would start with a target price, the price at which you want to sell the new widgets. Then you would determine what the company has to do to get costs down so that that price will generate your target return. You will learn more about target pricing in Chapter 30.

Marketers often resort to this same type of calculation when they are concerned about accusations of earning unreasonably high profits. For example, utility companies use it to *limit* their profits, which are scrutinized by the government to protect customers from rate gouging. Such companies are permitted to make a reasonable profit—enough to fund continued growth and stockholder dividends—but no more.

Meeting the Competition

Some companies simply aim to meet the prices of their competition. In so doing they either follow the

industry leader or calculate the average price and then position their product close to that figure. Two products priced in this manner are automobiles and soft drinks. Competing products in both these categories tend to be very similar and thus may be priced closely to one another.

How does one compete when there is no price competition? On the basis of other factors in the marketing mix. These might include quality or uniqueness of product, convenience of business location or hours, and level of service. For example, a television manufacturer might offer a longer-term or more comprehensive warranty than its competitors. A bookstore might engage a local drama group to do weekly readings from popular titles. A restaurant might stay open 24 hours a day. In all such instances, businesses would be trying to meet competition based on a marketing strategy that takes more than price into consideration.

SECTION 29.1 Review

1. Why is price an important factor in the success or failure of a business?
2. Name three goals of pricing in addition to making a profit.
3. Distinguish between market share and market position.

Bell Ringer Activity

To open discussion of this section and address the market factors affecting price, ask students to consider the following scenario. A family wins a raffle sponsored by a charitable organization. The prize is a sports car, which the family doesn't want. For legal reasons, however, the charity cannot take it back. So, the family decides to sell the car and donate most of the proceeds to the charity.

Ask students what the family should charge for the car, what would be a fair market price. Also, have them consider what factors would play a part in setting the price for the car.

Introducing the Section

The students' responses to the Bell Ringer Activity will help you introduce the market factors affecting price. They include the following:

- Costs and expenses. In the Bell Ringer Activity scenario, the family will have to pay income taxes on the value of the car they won. They may also incur charges to have the vehicle registered with the state.

- Supply and demand. How much the family can get for the car will depend in part on the popularity and general availability of that particular sports car in the marketplace. Consumers' perceptions of the car will also play a role.

- Competition. How much auto dealers are asking for the same type of car will also influence how much the family can get for it.

Teach

Guided Practice

1. Read Section 29.2 with students.
2. Use the transparency for this section.

382

SECTION 29.2

Objectives

After completing this section, you will be able to

- **identify four market factors that affect price planning,**
- **explain demand elasticity in relation to supply and demand theory, and**
- **discuss government regulations that affect price planning.**

Terms to Know

- **break-even point**
- **elastic demand**
- **inelastic demand**
- **price fixing**
- **price discrimination**
- **loss leader**
- **unit pricing**

Market Factors Affecting Prices

How do businesses make price decisions? The answer is not an easy one, as you have probably already realized.

To start, most price planning begins with an analysis of costs and expenses, many of which are related to current market conditions. For example, the cost of raw materials may increase a manufacturer's costs to make an item. Passing that increase on to customers may seem an easy remedy for the situation. However, it's not that simple. The manufacturer must consider the effect the higher price will have in the marketplace. How will it affect demand, consumer perceptions and buying habits, and the competition? We will take up these questions next.

Costs and Expenses

In today's competitive economic environment, businesses constantly monitor, analyze, and project prices and sales in the light of costs and expenses. They do this because sales, costs, and expenses together determine a firm's profit.

BRIGHT IDEAS

Label It

Today "branded" produce is not all that unusual. However, 50 years ago when United Fruit Company decided to attach its name and the image of Chiquita Banana to its produce, most people doubted it could be done.

In the first place, no one was sure how to brand something as easily bruised as a banana. Inked stamps, gummed labels—what? In the second place, no one was really sure how many imprints would be necessary. It was estimated to be an absolutely huge number. Third, the technology to do the job didn't exist. It would have to be invented. Fourth, the result of overcoming all these obstacles would be a process so expensive that United Fruit bananas would have to sell for $10 apiece!

None of these dire predictions ever came to pass—well, almost none. United Fruit decided to brand its produce with pressure-sensitive labels. When the company's supplier heard the size of the order—1 billion stickers—he passed out. (Fortunately for him, the figure was a crude estimate. In fact, the company needed closer to 3 billion stickers!) The machinery to apply the labels was eventually invented by a Honduran plantation worker. Bananas never sold for anywhere near $10 apiece. And United Fruit's labels were so successful at distinguishing its produce from others' that the company changed its name to Chiquita Brands International.

Creativity Challenge Form teams of 3–5 people. Try to identify a product that would be as difficult to brand today as bananas were when Chiquita Banana came on the scene. Note that the reasons for the difficulty do not have to be the same (that is, physical). Neither does the purpose of the branding (beating the competition) nor the method (pressure-sensitive labels).

Responses to Declining Profit Margins
What do marketers do when costs or expenses increase or when sales decline? How do they maintain their profit margins? Do they change their prices? Some do—and some find other ways to improve their profit picture.

Some businesses have found that price is so important in the marketing strategy of a product that they will

Bright Ideas

Since Chiquita began branding its fruit, the idea has caught on. Other fruits now bear pressure-sensitive labels not only to feature the name of the grower but also to deliver information about the variety. Apples, for example, are frequently branded according to varietal names—Rome, Granny Smith, Gala, etc.—to promote consumer awareness of varietal taste differences.

make almost any other change before that one. They will reduce the size of an item before they will change its price. For example, a candy manufacturer might reduce a candy bar from 4 to 3.5 ounces rather than increase its price. In such a case, the cost of making the candy bar would be reduced. So, the manufacturer could still make a profit at the established price—provided, of course, the same quantity continued to be sold.

In other cases, manufacturers drop features their customers don't value. In 1994 Reebok stripped down its best-known athletic shoe, the $135 "Shaq Attaq." Four versions replaced the one, starting with a basic model priced at $60 and ending with an option-packed shoe much like the original at $130. Thus, by eliminating features, the company could compete more effectively based on price.

Finally, some manufacturers respond to higher costs and expenses by improving their products. They add more features or upgrade the materials used in order to justify a higher price. The increase caused by higher costs or expenses is merged with the increase resulting from improvements in the product.

Goodyear Tire & Rubber Co. used this approach successfully with its Aquatred all-season radial tire, designed especially to be effective on wet roads. Aquatred tires sold for 10 percent more than Goodyear's previous premium-priced, mass-market tire. In the tire's first two years, Goodyear sold more than 2 million Aquatreds. Consumers perceived the improved tire as having more value and so were willing to pay a higher price for it.

Responses to Lower Costs/Expenses On occasion, prices may actually drop because of decreased costs and expenses. Aggressive firms are constantly looking for ways to increase efficiency and thus decrease costs. Improved technology and less expensive but better-quality materials may help create better-quality products at lower costs. For example, personal computers have fallen in price because of the improved technology of microprocessors that require less wiring and assembly time. Technological advances have also improved the durability and memory capability of computers.

Break-even Point Manufacturers are always concerned with making a profit. They are especially concerned, however, in two situations—when marketing a new product and when trying to establish a new price. In these circumstances, manufacturers carefully analyze their costs and expenses in relation to unit and dollar sales. They do this by calculating their break-even point.

The **break-even point** is the point at which sales revenue equals the costs and expenses of making and distributing a product. After this point is reached, businesses begin to make a profit on the product.

For example, suppose a toy manufacturer plans to make 100,000 dolls that will be sold at $6 each to retailers and wholesalers. The cost of making and marketing the dolls is $4.50 per unit, or $450,000 for the 100,000 dolls. How many dolls must the toy manufacturer sell to cover its costs and expenses? To calculate the break-even point, the manufacturer divides the total amount of costs and expenses by the selling price:

$$\frac{\$450,000}{\$6} = 75,000$$

To break even, the firm must sell 75,000 dolls. After 75,000 are sold, the firm will begin to make a profit.

Supply and Demand

You learned the basics of supply and demand theory in Chapter 3. Recall that demand tends to go up when price goes down and down when price goes up. This statement is accurate as a general rule. It does not, however, completely explain how pricing occurs in the marketplace. This is because demand for some products does not respond readily to changes in price.

The degree to which demand for a product is affected by its price is called *demand elasticity*. In terms of demand elasticity, products are said to have either *elastic demand* or *inelastic demand*.

Elastic demand refers to situations in which a change in price creates a change in demand. Changes in the price of steak can serve as an example. If the price of

To get around declining profit margins, many firms improve their products by adding features. How did Goodyear improve its basic all-season radial tire according to this ad?

Chapter 29   *Price Planning*   **383**

3. Have students read aloud the Case Study and review the answers in class.
4. To explain the concept of demand elasticity, ask students to suggest a product that is very popular with teenagers. Ask students how much they normally pay for the item. Then keep increasing the price until no one would be willing to buy the item.

At this point, change the hypothetical. Tell students to assume that there is only *one* manufacturer of the item and only one retailer selling it. (Select one brand and one store, and eliminate all others.) Then give students a number of alternatives. Ask:
- Would you be willing to pay a higher price if you learned that the retailer did not expect another shipment for two months?
- If a competitor were to produce a knockoff of the product at a lower price, would you buy it? Why or why not?

This line of questioning will help introduce the factors affecting demand elasticity. These include availability of substitutes, brand loyalty, price relative to income, luxury vs. necessity, and immediacy of purchase.
5. Assign and review the Chapter 29 Activity in the *School-to-Work Handbook*.

Discussion Starter

Tell students to assume they can manufacture and distribute perfume for $5 an ounce. Then ask: If you wish to sell this product in upscale department stores, is a suggested retail price of $10 appropriate? Why or why not? (It would not be appropriate because patrons of such stores would expect to pay much more—perhaps even hundreds of dollars an ounce.)

Critical Thinking

Ask students to ponder the following: If suppliers are always willing to produce more at higher prices and buyers are always willing to buy more at lower prices, what does this suggest about the general configuration of supply and demand curves? If students are perplexed by the abstract nature of this question, refer them to the supply and demand schedules and graph in Chapter 3, pages 40 and 41, to help them visualize it. (Supply curves will move higher from left to right; demand curves, lower.)

Cooperative Learning

Have students break into groups to discuss this situation: They run a company that manufactures cookies. They have just been informed by the company purchasing agent that the cost of flour will be going up. They must now decide how they can absorb the increase without raising prices to their customers.

Give students about ten minutes to brainstorm ideas, and then have each group report their suggestions. Have the class vote on the most creative, yet realistic, solution offered.

L1 Math Skills

Ask students to explain in their own words the formula for determining the break-even point. (Divide the total costs and expenses of making a product by the selling price. The result is the point at which the business begins to make a profit.)

L2 Math Skills

Have students calculate the number of backpacks All Outdoors Inc. (AOI) must sell to break even if the cost of making one backpack is $15 and AOI plans to produce 60,000. The selling price AOI would charge its customers per backpack is $24. [($15 × 60,000) ÷ $24 = $900,000 ÷ $24 = 37,500.]

384

steak were $8 per pound, few people would buy it. If the price were to drop to $5, $3, and finally $2 per pound, however, demand would increase at each price level.

These increases would not continue indefinitely, however. At some point, they would be limited by another economic law—the *law of diminishing marginal utility*. This law states that consumers will buy only so much of a given product, even though the price is low. For example, let's say that detergent went on sale, and you bought two cases of it because the price was low. If three weeks later a new sale is announced for the same detergent, you may decide that you already have enough to last for months. So, you will not take advantage of the new sale.

Inelastic demand refers to situations in which a change in price has very little effect on demand for a product. Certain food products, such as milk and bread, fall into this category. If the price were to increase sharply, most of us would not buy much less of these two items. If it were to decrease sharply, there would be just so much bread and milk we could use.

Figure 29-2

DEMAND ELASTICITY

varies with five factors. Most depend on the consumer's personal situation or attitudes about the purchase.

Availability of Substitutes ▶

When substitutes are readily available, demand becomes more elastic. In the case of detergents, there are many competing brands, all of which will clean your clothes about equally well. Demand for detergents would therefore be elastic.

▼ Price Relative to Income

Changes in price are relative to the income of the customer. If a price increase is slight and does not have a major impact on the customer's budget, he or she will probably buy the product. If the increase is large and far more than the customer's budget allows, he or she will probably not buy it. So, if the increase is significant relative to one's income, demand is likely to be elastic.

Brand Loyalty ▲

Some customers will not accept a substitute product, even though there are many competing brands. In such situations, demand becomes inelastic.

384   Unit 8   *Pricing*

Lifelong Learning

Price Planning

The concepts presented in this section of the chapter could constitute an entire course. Newspapers and magazines still carry stories dealing with companies that are under investigation for price fixing, price discrimination, or some other violation of pricing laws.

These issues should continue to be of interest to students long after they complete this course. As consumers, they will certainly be affected by pricing legislation, court decisions, and investigations. Those who enter careers in the various marketing areas will likely learn more about these issues as they pertain to the products for which they have responsibility.

What determines whether demand for a product is likely to be elastic or inelastic? Figure 29-2 suggests some answers.

Consumer Perceptions

Consumer perceptions about the relationship between price and quality or other values also play a role in price planning. Some consumers equate quality with price. They believe a high price reflects high quality. A high price may also suggest status, prestige, and exclusiveness.

For example, when new designer fashions are introduced, their prices are very high. Consumers who want to be seen wearing them are willing to pay the higher prices. As the availability and popularity of fashionable items increases, however, the prices tend to drop along with the prestige and exclusiveness.

Some businesses create the perception that a product is worth more than others by limiting the supply of

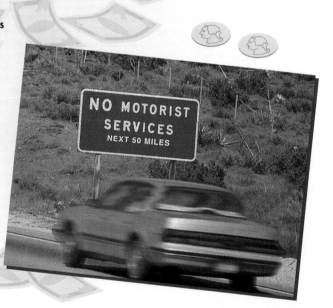

Luxury vs. Necessity ▲

When a product is a necessity (such as insulin for a diabetic), demand tends to be inelastic. When a product is a luxury, just the opposite is true. Note that here again the classification is relative. What is a luxury for one person may be a necessity for another.

Urgency of Purchase ▶

If you are running out of gasoline and the next gas station charges $.15 more per gallon than you usually pay, you will probably still stop and buy gas. If a purchase must be made immediately, demand tends to be inelastic.

Chapter 29 *Price Planning* **385**

Swatch Watches as Collectibles

L1 Decision-making Skills

Have students list all the features of a CD player or any other product that has several distinguishable features and with which students are familiar. Ask them which features are absolutely essential to the enjoyment they get from the product. Then ask them to identify additional features they would like to have. Finally, have them identify those features that are not that important to them.

L2 Decision-making Skills

Tell students to put a dollar value on all the features they identified in L1 Decision-making Skills activity. For example, the feature that allows a user to skip to the next song may be worth $10 of the $150 retail price of the CD player. Have them continue this process until they have reached the total dollar value of the product.

Next, have them place a dollar value on the additional features they would like to see on the product. Lastly, have them decide at what point they would stop adding features because the price would no longer reflect the value placed on them. Have students prepare a written report of their decision and rationale.

L3 Decision-making Skills

Using the information from the L2 Decision-making Skills activity, have students develop a three-tiered product line, as follows:

- One basic product with essential features priced at 25 percent below the average retail price
- One average product priced at the average retail price
- One top-of-the line product priced at 25 percent above the average retail price

When the first Swatch appeared in 1983, the theory behind the inexpensive watch was that people should have several watches. There would be one for the office, one for dress, one for doing yard work on weekends. Watches weren't just to keep time. They were fashion accessories.

As Swatch watches increased in variety, people began collecting them. Today there are more than 1,000 different kinds of Swatch watches, with approximately 125 new ones being added every year. Old Swatch designs are never copied. Once they sell out, that's it.

When the SMH Group, the company that produces Swatch watches, recognized the collector's desire for its product, it began producing more expensive models in limited editions. The result has been a craze that can be described as "Swatchmania."

For example, on the evening of October 12, 1993, people began gathering in front of the Tourneau watch store on Madison Avenue in New York City. Why? To get in line for the next day's sale of the Trésor Magique, a platinum Swatch with a $1,618 price tag. On

October 13, collectors snapped up all 1,500 Trésor Magiques that were on sale in 14 retail stores across the country. The December before, $100 Chandelier Swatch watches caused fights to break out after collectors paid homeless people to stand in line for them!

Basically, two Swatch collections of 60 watches each are introduced each year, in the spring and in the fall. The watches are priced from $40 for the basic Swatch to $80 for the Swatch Chronso. Then there are special limited editions that usually go for $80 each. Trésor Magique was the exception, being very expensive. Limited editions usually consist of 9,999 watches.

How much of a collectible can a Swatch be, given its short life span? That would depend on the Swatch. For example, in 1983, SMH gave 200 Jelly Fish Swatch watches to journalists at the very first press conference it held. Those free watches are now worth thousands of dollars. Most Swatch watches, however, have not appreciated that much. At an auction in Zurich, most ordinary Swatch watches went for under $200. Even the prized Jelly Fish sold for only $4,200.

Nonetheless, people are joining collectors' clubs. SMH has its own club with a worldwide membership of 100,000. Retailers, too, encourage Swatchmania. When a Boston store owner ran a Swatch exchange, more than 1,000 people came and purchased almost 10,000 new Swatch watches in one weekend. As the owner explained, "When people think they're investing, it makes the sale easier."

Case Study Review

1. How are customers' perceptions fueling Swatchmania?
2. How do the theories of demand elasticity apply to the practices of the SMH Group in producing Swatch watches?

A MATTER OF ETHICS

3. Do you think Swatch watches should be marketed as collectibles when in reality most ordinary Swatch watches have not gone up that much in value? Is this an ethical practice? Why or why not?

Case Study Answers

1. Customers believe they are investing in collectibles.
2. By limiting the supply of certain watches and never repeating a design, the SMH Group is creating a situation in which there are no substitutes for the Swatch watch. They are also fostering a perception of exclusiveness. Both situations allow them to charge higher prices.
3. It is impossible to judge today what the eventual value of limited edition Swatch watches will be. This is a risk that all buyers of collectibles take. It is not limited to the buyers of Swatch watches.

the item in the market. They do this by coming out with a limited edition of a certain model. In this way they can charge a higher price. Why? The reasoning is that the value of the item will increase as a result of its exclusiveness.

Personalized service can add to the consumer's perceptions about price. Many consumers are willing to pay more for items purchased from certain businesses because of the service those businesses offer. In these cases, marketers can charge slightly higher prices because consumers are willing to pay for the added service.

Thus, a marketer must be concerned with *subjective* price—that is, the price consumers see as the value they are getting for what they are buying. The perception of the price is what counts.

Competition

Because price is one of the four P's of the marketing mix, it must be evaluated in relation to the target market. When its target market is price conscious, a company can use a lower price to appeal to that market. When its target market is not price conscious, a company can resort to various forms of nonprice competition.

As you learned in Chapter 3, nonprice competition minimizes price as a reason for purchase. Instead, it creates a distinctive product through such means as product availability and customer service. The more unusual a product is perceived to be by consumers, the greater the marketer's freedom to set prices above those of competitors.

In price competition, marketers change prices to reflect consumer demand, cost, or competition. When products are very similar, price often becomes the sole basis on which customers make their purchase decisions. For example, if shoppers see no difference between Maxwell House coffee and Hills Brothers coffee, they are likely to buy the brand that costs less.

For this reason, competitors watch each other closely. When one company changes its prices, others usually react. For example, if the manufacturer of Tide detergent reduces its price, its competitors are likely to do the same. The benefit of this kind of competition is lower prices for consumers.

When competitors engage in a fierce battle to attract customers by lowering prices, a *price war* is the result. The problem with price wars is that firms reduce their profits while trying to undercut their competitors' prices and attract new customers. This may result in excessive financial losses and, in some cases, actual business failure.

Some industries seem more prone to price wars than others. Traditionally, the airline industry has been one that used prices as a means of meeting competition. Their price wars have taken a heavy toll throughout the industry in recent years. In the early 1990s, for example, U.S. airlines had combined losses of $10 billion.

McDonald's, Burger King, and other fast-food restaurants are known for their price wars. If McDonald's lowers its price on a Big Mac, Burger King generally follows suit on its Whopper.

In price competition, then, marketers influence demand through price. In nonprice competition, they emphasize other marketing factors.

Government Regulations Affecting Prices

Federal and state governments have enacted laws controlling prices. Therefore, marketers must be aware of their rights and responsibilities regarding *price fixing, price discrimination, resale price maintenance, minimum pricing, unit pricing,* and *price advertising*.

Price Fixing

Price fixing occurs when competitors agree on certain price ranges within which they set their own prices. Price fixing can be proved only when there is evidence of collusion. This means that there was communication among the competing firms to establish a price range. Price fixing is illegal because it eliminates competition, which is the cornerstone of the free enterprise system.

The federal law concerned with price fixing is the Sherman Antitrust Act of 1890, which outlawed monopolies. To better understand the act's purpose and how it operates, consider one recent example of how it has been used.

In 1992 the Justice Department filed an antitrust suit against eight major airline carriers for price fixing. The government explained that the airlines were setting fares via a jointly owned computer system. The computer system allowed each airline to know exactly what the others were doing with regard to pricing strategies. United Airlines and US Air immediately agreed to stop the practice of proposing future increases over the computer network. American, Delta, Northwest, Continental, TWA, and Alaska Airlines decided to fight the allegations of price fixing.

Price Discrimination

Price discrimination occurs when a firm charges different prices to similar customers in similar situations. The Clayton Antitrust Act of 1914 defines price discrimination, stating that it creates unfair competition. In 1936, the Robinson-Patman Act was passed to strengthen the provisions of the Clayton Act. In general, the Robinson-Patman Act prohibits sellers from offering one customer one price and another customer another price if both customers are buying the same product in similar situations.

The Robinson-Patman Act was intended to help smaller retailers compete with the large chain stores. It

Tell students to identify all the product features for each of the three models and to provide a rationale for their decisions. Have them summarize their decisions in chart form.

L1 Problem-solving Skills

Tell students to assume they work for a jeans manufacturer that wants to keep its prices low in order to be competitive. However, the firm has been losing money because its expenses and cost of doing business have been rising. If the company has another bad year, employees may be laid off, and the company may go bankrupt.

The management team has asked employees for suggestions on how they as employees can reduce the company's expenses. Have students brainstorm responsive ideas.

L2 Problem-solving Skills

Continue the L1 Problem-solving Skills activity. Have students work in groups to discuss the cost-cutting ideas generated in the brainstorming session. Tell them to select the three ideas they think are most feasible. Then have them identify the pros and cons of those ideas in a jointly written memo.

L3 Problem-solving Skills

Continue the L2 Problem-solving Skills activity. Have one student from each group defend the group's ideas to the rest of the class. The class will represent the firm's corporate board of directors. Tell the group representatives to be prepared to answer tough questions regarding the rationale and execution of their ideas.

L1 Human Relations Skills

Tell students to assume they work for a discount store whose circular for a big sale has been included in the most recent Sunday newspaper. There's a problem, though. The merchandise described in the circular has not yet arrived, and the sale starts today. In fact, since the shipment is overdue, no one at the store really knows when it will arrive.

Management has told salespeople that they should try to sell customers substitute items. Ask students why this is probably not such a good idea. (The store could be accused of bait-and-switch advertising, an illegal practice.)

L2 Human Relations Skills

Continue the L1 Human Relations Skills activity. Have students devise a response to customers who request an advertised item that is not in the store. Tell them to follow their management's directive but to be sure that customers do not perceive their gesture as bait-and-switch advertising.

L3 Human Relations Skills

Continue the L1 Human Relations Skills activity. Tell students that as marketing students who just studied the Robinson-Patman Act, they should alert their manager of the problems that could occur if salespeople try to offer substitute products. Tell them to plan what they are going to say to the manager and then actually role-play the exchange with you or another classmate.

Independent Practice

Have students select three products that are advertised at very low prices in their local newspaper. Have them go to the stores in question and explore the situations. Were the prices listed in the paper real, or were they

was presumed that bigger stores would be in a position to demand lower prices because of the volume of goods they could purchase. Smaller retailers would be at a competitive disadvantage.

Thus, the Robinson-Patman Act created restrictions on pricing and other price-related options, such as rebates, credit terms, warehousing, premiums, coupons, guarantees, discounts, and delivery. However, there are a few exceptions. Price discrimination within a channel of distribution is permissible under these circumstances:

- When products purchased are physically different
- If noncompeting buyers are involved
- If prices do not hurt competition
- If costs justify the differences in prices
- If production costs go up
- If prices are changed to meet another supplier's bid

In addition, discounts are permitted if the sellers can demonstrate that they are available to all channel members on a proportional basis, graduated to allow small and large buyers to benefit and qualify, or justified by savings incurred. Obviously, price discrimination is a complicated matter that must be studied carefully to be sure pricing is in line with the provisions of the Robinson-Patman Act.

As a case in point, in 1993 druggists charged the largest mail order seller, Medco (now owned by Merck), and five pharmaceutical manufacturers with violating the Robinson-Patman Act. According to the courts' interpretation of this law, a company must offer the same price to all buyers in the same "class of trade." Drug makers offer huge discounts to health maintenance organizations (HMOs) and mail order companies by saying that those companies are distinct types of customers that offer distinct services. Pharmacists don't agree. They claim that the drug manufacturers subsidize huge discounts to HMOs and mail order companies by charging drugstores much higher prices. The pharmacies want a ruling that puts them in the same class of trade as HMOs and mail order firms. That way they would be entitled to the same discounts offered

Real World

MARKETING

It Rings True

Early coins were so poorly made that counterfeiters had a fairly easy time substituting their bogus coins for the real thing. So, when offered a coin, a merchant would drop it on a stone slab and listen for the sound. A fake coin would make a flat, dull noise. A real coin would "ring true"— a phrase that is still used today to describe something genuine.

to those businesses. The burden of justifying the price differences is on the manufacturers.

Resale Price Maintenance

Manufacturers' resale price maintenance policies have come under scrutiny by legal authorities. Historically, manufacturers would set a retail price for an item and force retailers to sell it at that price. If a retailer sold the item at a lower price, the manufacturer would punish the retailer by withholding deliveries or refusing promised discounts or allowances.

Several Supreme Court decisions found such policies to be either unfair or deceptive business practices. The decisions concluded that suggested resale prices could not be used to mislead the public regarding a product's value or to take away a retailer's ability to determine its own prices.

How, then, can these policies be used? In general, a manufacturer may suggest resale prices in its advertising, price tags, and price lists. But it cannot coerce current customers into adhering to such prices. It can, however, tell customers in advance that they will not be permitted to sell its products if they break the established pricing policy. The difference between "coercing customers" and "telling them in advance" is the fine line manufacturers with such policies must walk. For that reason, many manufacturers have abandoned such policies.

Minimum Price Laws

Many states have enacted minimum price laws (also known as unfair sales laws). The laws were enacted to prevent retailers from selling goods below cost plus a percentage for expenses and profit. Some states have passed such laws that cover all products, while others have included only specific products (such as bread, dairy products, and liquor) in their laws.

In states where minimum price laws are not in effect, an item priced at cost to draw customers into a store is called a **loss leader.** Retailers select highly popular, well-advertised products to use as loss leaders. They do this in the hope of increasing customer traffic and sales of other goods carried by the store. Disposable diapers, for example, are often used as loss leaders because parents with young children need the product and may look for the best price. Although the item is on sale for only a limited period of time, retailers hope to attract new customers who will become steady customers.

Unit Pricing

A number of states have passed laws to make it easier for consumers to compare similar goods that are packaged in different sizes or come in different forms (such as frozen and canned foods). **Unit pricing** allows consumers to compare prices in relation to a standard unit or measure,

MCI, a principal challenger to AT&T's still preeminent position in the long-distance telephone market, took aim at one of the giant's advertising campaigns by asserting that AT&T's claims "just don't ring true." They thereby created a new double meaning for the phrase.

Supermarket shelf labeling **helps shoppers decide which brands and package sizes to buy. Of the two options shown here, which is the better buy? Explain.**

such as an ounce or a pound. Foods stores have been most affected by these laws. They have responded with shelf labels and computer records of unit prices.

Price Advertising

The Federal Trade Commission (FTC) has developed guidelines for advertising prices. Some of the more common standards applied to price advertising include the following:

- A company may not advertise a price reduction unless the original price was offered to the public on a regular basis for a reasonable and recent period of time.
- A company may not say that its prices are lower than its competitors' without proof of such comparison based on a large number of items.
- A premarked or list price cannot be used as the reference point for a new sale price unless the item has actually been sold at that price.

- *Bait-and-switch advertising* is illegal. In bait-and-switch advertising, a firm advertises a low price for an item it has no intention of selling. When a customer comes in and asks for the advertised item, salespeople switch the customer to a higher-priced item by saying that the advertised product is out of stock or of poor quality.

SECTION 29.2 *Review*

1. **Name four market factors that affect price planning.**
2. **What is demand elasticity, and how does it alter the theories of supply and demand?**
3. **What is the difference between price fixing and price discrimination? What laws govern each?**

Chapter 29   *Price Planning*   **389**

---

misrepresented? Were the products with the low prices being used as loss leaders? Was this a case of bait-and-switch? Students should present their findings in oral report form.

Assess

Evaluation

Assign and review the Section 29.2 Review.

Reteaching

1. Assign and review the vocabulary terms for this section.
2. Assign and review Fact and Idea Review questions 5–10 from the Chapter Review.
3. To reteach the factors affecting price, provide various examples in story form. After each story, have students identify the pricing factor being illustrated.

Enrichment

1. Assign and review the appropriate activities in the *Student Activity Workbook*.
2. Assign and review the appropriate Critical Thinking questions from the Chapter Review.
3. Assign and review the Building Academic Skills Activity, Application Projects, Linking School to Work Activities, and Performance Assessment from the Chapter Review.
4. Have students research five products that have actually gone down in price over the last 5–10 years. Tell students to uncover the reasons for the price reductions and explain them in relation to the concepts presented in this section.

Close

Ask students to recall the laws governing price discrimination and price fixing. (The Clayton Antitrust Act covers price discrimination; the Sherman Antitrust Act, price fixing. The Robinson-Patman Act covers both.)

Caption Answer

The canned corn is the better buy at only 6.8 cents per ounce compared to 12.5 cents per ounce for the frozen corn.

Section Review Answers

1. Costs and expenses, supply and demand, consumers' perceptions, and competition.
2. How demand is affected by price. Price changes have no effect on inelastic demand.
3. Price fixing—competitors agree on price ranges (Sherman Act). Price discrimination—a firm charges different prices to similar customers (Clayton, Robinson-Patman Acts).

Answers

Vocabulary Review

Explanations will vary. Here are some possibilities:

- Retail price of item vs. price per ounce, sheet, etc.
- Percentage of total market vs. rank among the competition
- Relative profitability vs. point at which a firm starts to turn a profit on a product
- Demand affected by price vs. demand not affected by price
- Competitors' agreeing on a price range vs. a firm's charging similarly situated customers different prices
- Selling an available item at cost to attract customers vs. offering an unavailable item at a low price to attract customers

Fact and Idea Review

1. If consumers believe they will get a great deal of satisfaction from certain product features, they will place a higher value on the product and will be willing to pay a high price for it. A seller, therefore, must be able to gauge where a product with its given features will rank in customers' estimation— valued much, valued little, or valued somewhere in between.
2. Market share is a firm's percentage of the total sales volume generated by all competitors in a given market (*e.g.*, AT&T may have a 75 percent share of the long-distance phone market). Market position is a business's relative standing in relation to its competitors (*e.g.*, AT&T is number one among long distance carriers in terms of sales volume).
3. $\dfrac{\text{Profit}}{\text{Investment}} = \dfrac{\text{price} - \text{cost}}{\text{cost}}$
4. On the basis of quality or uniqueness of goods and

390

Vocabulary Review

Explain the difference between each pair of words listed below.

price—unit price
market share—market position
return on investment—break-even point
elastic demand—inelastic demand
price fixing—price discrimination
loss leader—bait and switch

Fact and Idea Review

1. How does the role of product value play a part in price planning? (Sec. 29.1)
2. Provide one example each of market share and market position. (Sec. 29.1)
3. How is return on investment calculated? (Sec. 29.1)
4. Once businesses have met each others' prices, how else can they compete? (Sec. 29.1)
5. Name one business situation in which prices dropped because of decreased costs and expenses. (Sec. 29.2)
6. Name five basic factors that indicate whether a product is likely to have elastic or inelastic demand. (Sec. 29.2)
7. How do consumers' perceptions play a role in price planning? (Sec. 29.2)
8. How does competition play a part in price planning? (Sec. 29.2)
9. What are unfair sales laws? (Sec. 29.2)
10. What is unit pricing? Why have some states passed laws requiring businesses to post the unit prices of items? (Sec. 29.2)

Critical Thinking

1. Setting prices higher than the competition's will put your business on a fast track to failure. Is this statement true or false? Explain the reasons for your answer.
2. A firm expects to sell 10,000 widgets at $10 each. The cost of manufacturing and marketing the widgets is $7.50 each. Calculate the break-even point for the widgets. Of what significance is this analysis to the manufacturer?
3. Many diabetics depend on insulin to stay alive. If the price of insulin went up $10, would the demand for insulin go down as is suggested by the theory of supply and demand? Explain your answer in terms of demand elasticity.

Building Academic Skills
Math

1. Calculate the break-even point for a notebook that costs a business $1 to make and market and that will be sold for $1.50. The total quantity that will be sold at that price is 60,000.
2. Determine the return on investment for the following two video games:

	Morris Mania	Berto's Revenge
Manufacturing cost	$10.00	$ 8.75
Selling/marketing expenses	4.00	3.25
Selling price	17.00	14.75

Based on return on investment, which video game is more profitable for the company?

Communication

3. Deliver a two-minute talk explaining why knowledge of the consumer is so important in pricing decisions.

Human Relations

4. You are working in a snack shop. A steady customer approaches you to ask about a new package of chewing gum that contains ten sticks instead of the customary six. The customer is used to buying the six-stick pack for $.25 and is not happy with the new package, which sells for $.50. What do you say to this customer to maintain his/her goodwill?

Technology

5. Prepare a pie chart using a computer graphics program to depict market shares for the $800 million sports drink market. Use the following fictional figures to represent the sales for each competing brand.

Brand	Sales (× 1,000)
Gatorade (Gatorade Company)	$570,000
PowerAde (Coca-Cola)	93,000
Nautilus (Dr. Pepper)	55,000
Everlast (A&W)	33,500
Energade (Cadbury Beverages)	24,500
Hy-5 (Grey Eagle Enterprises)	15,000
Other	9,000

Application Projects

1. Your firm is thinking of entering the soft drink market. Your boss asks you to prepare a report analyzing Soda Manufacturer E's performance for

---

services, extra consumer benefits, and convenience of business location or hours.

5. Personal computer business.
6. Availability of substitutes, price relative to customer's income, brand loyalty, luxury vs. necessity, and urgency of purchase.
7. Customers may perceive a product to be worth more because of a high price, a limited supply, or the quality of service provided by the firm selling the product.

8. Firms can compete on either a price or non-price basis. (The latter emphasizes things like availability and customer service over price.)
9. Minimum price laws—laws that prevent retailers from selling goods below cost plus a percentage for expenses and profit.
10. Allows consumers to compare prices in relation to a standard unit or measure, such as an ounce or pound; helps consumers compare similar goods that are packaged differently.

the last two years. (The company's market share increased from 10 to 15 percent, and its market position went from fifth to third.) Include the following elements in your report:

- Draw a diagram of the change in E's market share. The first year's market shares for all companies competing in the soft drink market were as follows:

    Soda Manufacturer A—35 percent
    Soda Manufacturer B—25 percent
    Soda Manufacturer C—15 percent
    Soda Manufacturer D—12 percent
    Soda Manufacturer E—10 percent
    Soda Manufacturer F— 3 percent

- Explain how the change in market share affected E's market position.
- Explain how E could have used price to accomplish its goals of a 5 percent increase in market share and a change in market position from fifth place to third.

2. You are the manufacturer of a new shampoo called Hair Joy and must determine the price you should charge your customers (both wholesalers and retailers) for the product. Hair Joy promises users more manageable hair that is full of body. Market research indicates that consumers want this type of shampoo.
    - Visit one or two local stores and take down the prices of at least four comparable shampoos. Compare the unit prices (per ounce) for each.
    - Assume that your cost of manufacturing and distributing Hair Joy to wholesalers and retailers will be $1.85 per ten-ounce bottle. Assume also that retailers generally double the price they pay for shampoo from the manufacturer. What would you suggest as the price retailers should be charged?
    - Considering that you expect to make 200,000 bottles of shampoo at the price you decided upon, what will be your break-even point?

3. Research recent legal cases of companies that have been accused of breaking federal or state laws that govern pricing practices. Write a 200-word report of your findings.

Linking School to Work

Investigate the pricing goals of your firm. Ask your supervisor to rank the following goals in order of importance for your business:

- Earn a profit.
- Improve market share.
- Generate a satisfactory return on investment.
- Meet the competition.

Ask your supervisor to explain the significance of the top-ranked goal for your business. Write a report.

Performance Assessment
Role Play

Situation. You are employed as a management trainee for a unisex clothing store that specializes in jeans and trendy clothing. The sales rep for a designer jeans manufacturer has just made a presentation to you and the store buyer. The store buyer wants your opinion about whether or not to carry the jeans. The jeans are more costly than others you sell. However, the jeans manufacturer feels that your store could sell them for $80, which is $10 more than your most expensive pair of designer jeans. You agree with her because the jeans are very different. You think they will sell well, even at the higher price. In ten minutes, you will be meeting with the store buyer to share your thoughts and opinions. What will you say?

Evaluation. You will be evaluated on how well you do the following:

- Explain the importance of price.
- Discuss the goals of pricing.
- Recall four market factors that affect price planning.
- Explain demand elasticity in relation to supply and demand theories.
- Convince the buyer that these jeans should be carried in your store.

Visual Aids

You have been asked to make a presentation to a group of younger students (grades 6–8) who are studying pricing practices. Your partner will cover the basics of pricing theory, and you will be responsible for covering government regulations. To make your presentation come alive, you realize that you will have to rely heavily on visual aids. Plan the visual aids you will use and execute rough sketches of them.

COMPUTER APPLICATION

Complete the Chapter 29 Computer Application that appears in the Student Activity Workbook.

Communication
3. Talks will vary.

Human Relations
4. Answers will vary but should include references to any improvements that could justify the increased unit price.

Technology
5. Finished pie chart should show Gatorade with close to three-fourths (71 percent) of the total market, PowerAde with 12 percent, and all the others with "slices" representing single-digit percentages.

Application Projects
1. Students' diagrams need to reflect the increase in Manufacturer E's market share and position (most likely at the expense of Manufacturers C and D).
2. Competition's prices, students' retail prices, and students' break-even points will vary.
3. Reports will vary with latest cases and source material selected.

Linking School to Work
Answers depend on the work situation.

Performance Assessment
Refer to the *DECA Competitive Events Handbook* for evaluation guidelines.

Computer Application
Optional activity. Refer to the *Marketing Software Binder* for the template and user information.

Evaluation
Administer the reproducible test for Chapter 29, or construct your own using the Testmaker software.

Critical Thinking
1. False, since some businesses succeed competing on a nonprice basis.
2. ($7.50 × 10,000) ÷ $10 = $75,000 ÷ $10 = 7,500. Figure means that the firm will begin to make a profit after selling 7,500 widgets. This can help the firm set sales goals.
3. Demand would not go down because insulin is something diabetics need at any price to stay

alive. Since it's a necessity, demand for it would be inelastic.

Building Academic Skills
Math
1. ($1 × $60,000) ÷ $1.50 = $60,000 ÷ $1.50 = 40,000
2. Morris Mania: [$17 − ($10 + $4)] ÷ ($10 + $4) = ($17 − $14) ÷ $14 = $3 ÷ $14 = 21.4%.

Chapter Overview

Chapter 30 considers a wide variety of pricing strategies. There are accounting-oriented strategies, demand- and competition-oriented strategies, product life cycle strategies, psychological strategies, and discount-based strategies. Students will find this chapter easy to relate to because they have seen so many of these strategies in action when they have gone shopping.

Springboard

Have students read the opening paragraph of this chapter. Tell them that in the course of working on this chapter they will have to decide on a price for Continental's new cookie. Suggest they begin now by making some preliminary notes listing information they think they will need or questions they should have answered in order to reach a decision.

Prereading

List the section objectives to discuss with students. Have students skim the chapter, looking at the pictures, reading the captions, and noting the heads. Ask questions to ensure that students have a minimal understanding of the chapter structure.

Preteaching the Vocabulary

Before students begin reading the chapter, dictate each of the vocabulary terms and ask students to write them on a sheet of paper. When they finish, write the terms on the chalkboard. Then have students guess at the meaning of each. Write their guesses next to each term, but do not give the correct meaning. Leave this list on the chalkboard so that students can see how close their guesses were to the actual definitions as they work through the chapter.

Pricing Strategies

You have just been hired as a product manager for Continental Cookies, Inc. Your first assignment is to review the pricing structure used for all current products and to develop a price for a new cookie called Coconut Surprise that will be introduced shortly.

Continental is a small cookie manufacturer that sells half-pound, one-pound, and two-pound packages of cookies in decorative tins and specially designed paper packages. After reviewing all the factors that go into price planning, what strategy will you use to arrive at a price for the new cookies?

Classroom Management

For the Teacher
- Teacher's Annotated Editions for all workbooks
- Teacher's Manual for *School-to-Work Handbook*
- *Testing Binder*
- *Transparency Binder*
- *Marketing Software Binder*
- *Marketing Career Portfolio*
- *Lesson Plans*

For the Student
- *Student Activity Workbook*
- *Marketing Math Workbook*
- *School-to-Work Handbook*
- *Student Software*
- *International Case Studies*
- *Marketing Career Portfolio*

SECTION 30.1

Objectives

After completing this section, you will be able to

- apply the three basic pricing concepts (cost-oriented, demand-oriented, and competition-oriented) to pricing a product;

- describe the consequences for manufacturers of pricing forward and pricing backward;

- distinguish between a one-price policy and a flexible-price policy; and

- explain the two main pricing policies that should be considered when introducing a new product.

Terms to Know

- **markup**
- **cost-plus pricing**
- **one-price policy**
- **flexible-price policy**
- **skimming pricing**
- **penetration pricing**

Basic Pricing Concepts

As you start your analysis, remember that a major factor in determining the profitability of any product is price. You need to find the right price for your target market. Only then will you have a chance of being successful.

There are three basic concepts that you may want to consider in determining the price for Coconut Surprise cookies. They are *cost-oriented pricing, demand-oriented pricing,* and *competition-oriented pricing.*

Cost-Oriented Pricing

In cost-oriented pricing, marketers first calculate the costs of acquiring or making a product and their expenses

of doing business. Then they add their projected profit margin to these figures to arrive at a price. *Markup pricing* and *cost-plus pricing* are two of the most common methods of cost-oriented pricing.

Markup Pricing   Markup pricing is used primarily by wholesalers and retailers who are involved in acquiring goods for resale. A **markup** is the difference between the price of an item and its cost. It is generally expressed as a percentage. If a business is to be successful, the markup on its products must be high enough to cover the expenses of running the business and must include the intended profit. Details and calculations related to markup pricing are given in Chapter 31.

Cost-Plus Pricing   In **cost-plus pricing**, all costs and expenses are calculated, and then the desired profit is added to arrive at a price. Very similar to markup pricing, cost-plus pricing is used primarily by manufacturers and service companies. The method is more sophisticated than markup pricing because all fixed and variable expenses are calculated separately for different goods and services. For example, when a manufacturer is running at full capacity, the fixed expenses become a smaller percentage of total sales and thus permit the manufacturer to charge a lower unit price for goods. If a company receives a rush order and must pay overtime to employees in order to get out the job, the increased labor costs may be calculated into the price of the goods.

Service businesses, such as market research companies and accounting firms, determine the costs involved in each job and then add on a profit to arrive at a price. Many companies have specialists and use sophisticated

Real World

When Price Was Job One

In addition to being a legendary entrepreneur and inventor, Henry Ford was also a marketing pioneer. He believed that the way to succeed was to make a quality car that was affordable for the average person. To achieve that goal, he picked a price and declared that it was what his car would sell for. He then set about altering the manufacturing process to make that price possible.

In 1913, it took Ford workers nearly 11 hours to turn out a single chassis. By 1914, they had it down to 1 hour. When the Model T was introduced in 1908, it cost $950. By 1927, when the efficiencies of the assembly line had fully taken hold, it was only $290.

Focus

Bell Ringer Activity

Tell students to assume that their DECA chapter has decided to raise funds by making and selling decorative wreaths (or design-your-own T-shirts or costume jewelry). Have them list all the factors that must be considered in arriving at a price for the item they want to make.

Introducing the Section

On the chalkboard, list the factors students came up with in the Bell Ringer Activity. Then group the factors into cost-oriented, demand-oriented, and competition-oriented categories. Ask students why all three kinds of factors need to be considered when deciding on the price of the product. (To be sure the price is not so high or low that the company does not make enough money.)

Teach

Guided Practice

1. Read Section 30.1 with students.
2. Use the transparency for this section.
3. To introduce the influence of wholesalers and retailers, take the DECA scenario one step further. Suggest that instead of having a fund raiser, the local DECA chapter will sell the wreaths, T-shirts, or jewelry it makes to other DECA chapters and to local retailers. That would make the club a manufacturing business.

   Ask students what additional factors would have to be considered in determining prices under these new circumstances. (Who besides the manufacturer would need to make a profit? [Other DECA chapters and the local retailers.] Must costs be reduced so that discounts can be offered to these businesses?)

Meeting Special Needs

Physically Challenged

Students who use wheelchairs do so as a result of a wide variety of disabilities, ranging from spinal cord injury, cerebral palsy, post-polio, quadriplegia, muscular dystrophy, and even severe arthritis. Most wheelchairs are manually propelled by the student, but some students who have limited use of hands or arms may have an aide to assist them. Most

students who need other assistance will ask. Don't automatically assume that assistance is required. Do not insist on "helping" if your offer is turned down. Students who use wheelchairs will appreciate your awareness if you are not so aware of their disability that it becomes all you see of them.

4. To introduce the choice between a one-price policy and a flexible-price policy, continue to use the DECA scenario. Suggest that the club's products be sold in the school store as well. Ask students if they think the club should put price tags on the items, or if customers should be allowed to bargain. Encourage students from cultures in which bargaining is the norm to explain the process and the rationale for it. Have students name products for which bargaining is expected even in our culture.

5. To introduce pricing and the product life cycle, continue to use the DECA scenario. Tell students to consider the choice that must be made when introducing a new product to the market. Should the product's price be higher, lower, or in line with competing products? Have students discuss the advantages and disadvantages of each pricing option.

Discussion Starter

Tell students that their company, Realrock, is introducing a walking shoe for people who want jogging shoe construction without all the high-impact features. Ask student if they would use skimming or penetration pricing. (Answers will vary. With the proper rationale, either type of pricing would be acceptable.)

Critical Thinking

Have students support this statement: To some degree, price setting is beyond the control of the manufacturer. (Students should note that consumers ultimately determine the price by what they are willing to pay. Students could also cite the repeal of price maintenance laws. Wholesalers and retailers can raise or lower the price beyond what the manufacturer feels is ideal by adding their own markups.)

---

computer programs to study all fixed and variable expenses involved in each job. Figure 30-1 illustrates how cost-plus pricing can be used to calculate price.

Demand-Oriented Pricing

Marketers who use demand-oriented pricing attempt to determine what present consumers are willing to pay for given goods and services. The key to using this method of pricing is the consumer's perceived value of the item. The price set must be in line with this perception. If it is not or if the perceived value itself is misread, the item will be priced too high or too low for the target market. Either could cause the product to fail.

Another aspect of demand-oriented pricing involves demand differentials. When there are few substitutes for an item and there is demand inelasticity, demand-oriented pricing is effective. Consumers are generally willing to pay higher prices because they believe an item is different from its competitors. Companies try to achieve this status by developing brand loyalty.

In other cases, the prices do not reflect major differences in the good or service. They reflect only the demand for the good or service. For example, theaters often charge different prices for tickets on the basis of the location of the seats. Some seats will be more expensive than others. Everyone who buys a ticket will see the same performance but from a different vantage point. Telephone companies may charge higher rates for long-distance calls made during peak times. The cost of providing that service may not change, but the demand for the service increases.

Cost-Plus Pricing

Bradley's Print Shop

Paper (40 reams @ $10/ream)	$400
Labor (10 hours @ $10/hour)	100
Printing materials	60
Artwork	140
Expenses	50
Profit	50
Final price to customer	**$800**

Figure 30–1

Cost-plus pricing breaks a price down into its component parts. If you wanted to show the similarity between markup pricing and cost-plus pricing, how might you relabel the entries shown here?

394   Unit 8   *Pricing*

Manufacturers may also create prices for different styles on the basis of a demand differential that is not a reflection of the cost of making the item but rather the demand for a given style. For example, white washing machines may be priced at $300, while those that are yellow or beige may be sold for $350. The difference in price is not based on an increase in the cost of producing color machines. Rather, it is based on the demand for fashionable colors.

Competition-Oriented Pricing

Marketers who study their competitors to determine the prices of their products are using competition-oriented pricing. These marketers may elect to take one of three actions after learning their competitors' prices: price above the competition, price below the competition, or price in line with the competition. What is different about this method of pricing is that there is no relationship between cost and price or between demand and price. Marketers simply set prices on the basis of what their competitors charge. Two basic types of competition-oriented pricing strategies are *competitive-bid pricing* and *going-rate pricing*.

Competitive Bid Pricing Determining the price for a product on the basis of bids submitted by competitors to a company or government agency is called competitive bid pricing. Most government agencies are required by law to request bids based on certain specifications so they can select the company that offers the lowest price on the desired product. In such cases, some companies will elect to enter a very low bid in order to obtain the contract. They will accept a smaller profit in order to keep their employees working.

Going-Rate Pricing Almost all firms engage in some form of going-rate pricing. This involves studying the competition's prices to be sure one's own prices are in line. Going-rate pricing is especially important in businesses where the competing products are similar. The firm with the leading market share may be the leader in setting prices. How other companies elect to price their products (above, below, or in line with the market leader) depends on their philosophy of doing business and their market position in relation to the leader.

Combining Pricing Considerations

Even though the three basic pricing concepts just described were introduced as separate options, in reality most marketers use all three to determine prices. Cost-oriented pricing is helpful to marketers in determining the price floor for a product—that is, the lowest price for which it can be offered for sale and still earn the company a profit. Demand-oriented pricing may be used to determine a price range for the product. This range would be defined on one side by the price floor and on the other by a ceiling price (the highest amount consumers would be willing to pay). Finally, competition-oriented pricing may

---

Did You Know

Would you believe that the price of an accounting software program called Simply Money was *no* charge for the first million copies sold! Computer Associates International Inc. dared to risk the lowest price ever to encourage users to buy future upgrades and related programs.

Pricing Backward from Retail Price

Estimated retail price	$25.00
Retailer's markup (40 percent of retail)	– 10.00
Wholesaler's price to retailer	$15.00
Wholesaler's markup (30 percent of wholesale)	– 4.50
Manufacturer's price to wholesaler	$10.50

Figure 30–2

To arrive at a wholesale price, a manufacturer can subtract all markups from the retail price. Suppose in the example shown here that the manufacturer's cost was $11. What would the manufacturer have to do?

Pricing Forward from Manufacturer's Cost

Cost of producing item	$9.00
Manufacturer's expenses and profit (25 percent of cost)	+ 2.25
Manufacturer's price to wholesaler	$11.25
Wholesaler's markup (42.9 percent of cost)	+ 4.83
Wholesaler's price to retailer	$16.08
Retailer's markup (66.67 percent of cost)	+ 10.72
Retailer's price to consumer	$26.80

Figure 30–3

Adding markups to cost is another way manufacturers can price their goods. Suppose in the example given here market research had shown that consumers would pay as much as $30 for the item. What would the manufacturer's options be?

be used to examine the competition to make sure the final price matches the standing the firm wishes to have in relation to its competitors.

In addition to using the foregoing strategies to arrive at a price, manufacturers may also consider the prices they will charge wholesalers and retailers for their products. This means working backward from the final retail price or forward from costs and expenses to the final retail price. Figures 30-2 and 30-3 illustrate these two methods.

In Figure 30-2, which describes the steps in working backward, the retail price is set first, on the basis of consumer demand and competition. Next, the markups desired by the wholesalers and retailers are deducted from the suggested retail price. Finally, the price that the manufacturer will charge the wholesaler is determined.

In Figure 30-3, which illustrates the steps working forward from the manufacturer's cost, the wholesalers' and retailers' markups are added to the cost to arrive at the final selling price. If the price is set at this point, competition and consumer demand are left out of the pricing decision. When the marketer does not consider these two factors, the final retail price may be higher than a competitor's and higher than the price consumers are willing to pay. On the other hand, if the differentials in the product warrant a higher price, the company will enjoy an even higher profit margin than it would have if it had used the backward method.

Pricing Policies and Product Life Cycle

A basic pricing decision every business must make is to choose between a *one-price policy* and a *flexible-price policy*. A business also needs to consider how a new

product will be introduced into the marketplace. That choice will determine the pricing decisions that follow as the product moves through its life cycle.

One-Price vs. Flexible-Price Policy

A **one-price policy** is one in which all customers are charged the same price for the goods and services offered for sale. Under a one-price policy, prices are quoted to customers by means of signs and price tags, and no deviations are permitted. Most of the retail stores that you are familiar with employ this policy.

A **flexible-price policy,** on the other hand, permits customers to bargain for merchandise. In this type of situation, a price is quoted by either the buyer or seller, and then the bargaining begins. Most retail stores avoid using flexible pricing because it can cause legal problems and because many customers do not like it. However, customers do expect to find a flexible-price strategy in effect with such goods as used cars, antiques, furniture, and selected jewelry.

Product Life Cycle

Recall that products move through four stages: introduction, growth, maturity, and decline. When products are no longer profitable to a company, they may be dropped from the line. Pricing plays an important role in this sequence of events.

Chapter 30 *Pricing Strategies* **395**

L1 Decision-making Skills

Tell students to imagine that they will be introducing a new toy called Twinks to the marketplace. Ask them if they think new toys should be introduced with skimming or penetration pricing. Have them provide examples of each method based on their own experiences with toys.

L2 Decision-making Skills

Continue the L1 Decision-making Skills activity. Tell students that the cost to make and market Twinks is $10. Then ask them if the introductory price should be set at $35 (skimming pricing) or $12.50 (penetration pricing)? Ask what the advantages and disadvantages of each price would be.

L3 Decision-making Skills

Continue the L2 Decision-making Skills activity. Tell students to analyze the alternatives already discussed for the pricing of Twinks and set their own price. Have them prepare a memo to the marketing director that outlines the reasoning behind their decision.

Independent Practice

1. Assign and review the Chapter 30 Case Study in the *International Case Studies* workbook.
2. Have students identify a product that is new on the market and research its price. Have them also research the prices of similar competing products to see if they are higher, lower, or the same as the new product.

   When their research is complete, have students prepare a report stating their findings and conclusions regarding the pricing strategy used to introduce the new product. Part of those conclusions should include an explanation of whether penetration or skimming pricing was used.

3. Have students interview the owner or manager of an antique store or automobile dealership regarding the pricing policy used by their sales staff. Do they use a one-price or a flexible-price policy? Have students ask their interview subjects to explain why the chosen method is effective in their type of business. Have students report their findings in written form.

Assess

Evaluation

Assign and review the Section 30.1 Review.

Reteaching

1. Assign and review the vocabulary terms for this section.
2. Assign and review Fact and Idea Review questions 1–5 from the Chapter Review.
3. To reteach demand-oriented and competition-oriented pricing, ask students to recall some of their favorite toys from childhood. Ask if those toys were very popular at the time, the way that Cabbage Patch dolls were popular in the 1980s and Power Rangers were popular in the 1990s. Ask if there were many other toys that were similar to their favorites. Finally, ask if anyone remembers the price of their favorite toy—whether it was more or less than the price of the similar toys? This line of questioning should help reteach how demand can increase the price of an item and how competition can help to keep prices of similar products in line with each other.

*In many antique shops, **customers can bargain with salespeople or owners for a better price. What kind of pricing policy do such shops have?***

New Product Introduction Depending on the philosophy of the business and market conditions, one of two pricing methods may be used when a new product is introduced—*skimming pricing* or *penetration pricing*.

Skimming pricing is a pricing policy that sets a very high price for a new product. Such a policy is designed to capitalize on the high demand for a product during its introductory period. At this time, the high price is geared toward trendsetters. These are people who are generally willing to pay higher prices in order to be the first to own or avail themselves of a new product.

Businesses that use this method recognize that once the market for the product changes to more price-conscious customers, the price will have to be lowered. However, while the product is new and "hot," the business will enjoy a high profit margin. This margin will help cover the research and development costs incurred in designing the product and create a prestigious image for it. Another advantage of skimming pricing is that the price may be lowered without insulting the target market.

One disadvantage of skimming pricing is that the high initial price generally attracts competition. Once other firms begin to compete successfully, the price will have to be lowered. Another disadvantage becomes apparent if

the initial price is far above what consumers (even the trendsetters) are willing to pay. In that case, sales will be lost and profits diminished because the market will not take the item seriously.

Penetration pricing is the opposite of skimming pricing in that the initial price for a new product is set very low. The purpose of penetration pricing is to encourage as many people as possible to buy the product and thus penetrate the market. This type of pricing is most effective in the sale of price-sensitive products (items with elastic demand).

With this pricing policy, mass production, distribution, and promotion must be incorporated into the marketing strategy in order to penetrate the market quickly. The product should take hold in a short period of time. This allows the marketer to save on fixed expenses (through mass production) and to increase the profit margin (through volume sales).

The biggest advantage of penetration pricing is its ability to capture a large number of customers for a company in a relatively short period of time, thus blocking competition. Another advantage is its ability to move into a market in which the leaders are offering higher prices and lure away large numbers of customers.

396   Unit 8   *Pricing*

Flexible-price strategy.

Skimming Pricing

Most fashion apparel is introduced using skimming pricing. Price reductions then follow the article through the fashion cycle from introduction (high price) to popularity (competitive price) to decline (reduced price).

BRIGHT IDEAS

Try Some Dino-Light

Would customers plunk down $20 to buy a string of lights when it wasn't even Christmas? Sue Scott, a sculptor and art gallery manager, thought so. However, the bankers she asked for loans didn't. So, she set up her own company, Primal Lite, using cash advances from her credit cards.

Scott based her business on a simple observation: people like to decorate with lights. What used to be a Christmas tradition has become year-round household decoration. To capitalize on this trend, Scott decided to increase people's options. Instead of just plain bulbs, she began offering strings of tiny creatures—lizards, trout, lobsters, cattle—over 40 different designs, all lit from within.

From its inauspicious beginnings in 1986, Scott's business grew to sales of $4 million in 1994. (She has projected $20 million by the year 2000.) Although there's nothing new about strings of lights, by giving them her own personnel twist, Scott has been able to capitalize on an emerging trend.

Creativity Challenge Form teams of 3–5 people. Think of everyday products that could be modified by giving them the "light" treatment (that's lit from within, lit from without, lit for decoration, lit for practicality, etc.). Just for fun, try to concentrate on items that have not been lit before. Any potential for a dining room table that provides its own light? What about bedroom slippers with built-in night lights? See how many "dino-light" ideas you can come up with.

A major disadvantage of penetration pricing becomes apparent if the product is not in high demand by customers. In that case, the lower price will cause the marketer to suffer a bigger loss than it would have if a higher initial price had been set.

Other Product Stages Pricing during subsequent periods in a product's life cycle will be determined on the basis of which pricing method was originally used—skimming or penetration. During the growth stage, sales increase rapidly, and total costs per unit decrease because volume absorbs fixed costs. The main goal of marketers is to keep products in this stage as long as possible.

If the product was introduced with skimming pricing, sales should be monitored closely. Once sales begin to level off, the price should be lowered to appeal to the next target market, which is slightly price conscious. If the product is considered a fad, the price may be lowered drastically.

If the product was introduced with penetration pricing, very little price change will be made in the growth stage. Rather, other promotions will be used to keep sales high.

Once the product reaches the maturity stage, when sales begin to level off because demand is cut in half, competition is generally very keen. At this stage, marketers look for new market segments to hold the prices for their products. For example, a baking soda marketer may stress noncooking uses for baking soda, such as deodorizing or cleaning refrigerators.

The marketer's principal goal during the maturity stage is to stretch the life of a product. Some companies revitalize products in this stage by adding new features or improvements. Another option is to seek new markets in emerging nations. Products that have been made obsolete here by technological advances may be in the introductory or growth stage in other places. Photocopiers are an example. Older or superseded models are reconditioned and sold in emerging nations where they are considered state-of-the-art technology. By using techniques like these, marketers can significantly extend a product's life cycle. When such efforts are not successful, however, a product moves into its decline.

In the decline stage, sales decrease and profit margins are reduced. To maintain profitability, marketers therefore try to reduce the costs of manufacturing or carrying the product, or they cut back their advertising and other promotional activities. Once a product is no longer profitable, it is phased out.

SECTION 30.1

Review

1. **Explain how cost-oriented, demand-oriented, and competition-oriented pricing concepts can be combined to determine price.**
2. **What effects do pricing forward and pricing backward have on manufacturers' selling to wholesalers and retailers?**
3. **What is the difference between a one-price policy and a flexible-price policy?**
4. **Name and explain two pricing methods that may be used when a new product is introduced into the market.**

Chapter 30 *Pricing Strategies* **397**

Bell Ringer Activity

Tell students that they are to assume that a one-price policy will be used for the DECA fund-raising product (wreaths, T-shirts, or jewelry). Ask students to arrive at an exact price for the product, assuming it was going to be sold in the school store. Have them write that price on a piece of paper and note their reasons for selecting that amount.

Introducing the Section

Use the students' answers to the Bell Ringer Activity to discuss psychological pricing techniques. Provide students with the following additional information, and give them an opportunity to revise their original price figures in light of it:

* The cost of making one item (wreath, T-shirt, or piece of jewelry) is $10.23, plus expenses of $2.27.
* Going retail prices for similar wreaths, T-shirts, and items of jewelry are between $13 and $25.

Ask students if this information changed the way they felt about the original prices they set. Have them provide a rationale for their decisions.

Before proceeding with the chapter, tell students that they may change their prices at any point during the discussion of psychological pricing techniques. Also, encourage them to suggest any modifications of the DECA project that come to mind and might make it more profitable for all involved.

SECTION 30.2

Objectives

After completing this section, you will be able to

* identify various pricing techniques and
* list the steps in setting prices.

Terms to Know

* psychological pricing
* prestige pricing
* price lining
* discount pricing
* trade discounts
* seasonal discounts

Pricing Techniques

Now that we have looked at general pricing concepts and policies, it is time to look at specific pricing techniques that marketers use. These techniques include *psychological pricing* and *discount pricing*.

Psychological Pricing

Psychological pricing refers to techniques that create an illusion for customers or that make shopping easier for them. In either case, psychological pricing techniques appeal to particular market segments because of their shared perceptions and buying habits. Among common psychological pricing techniques are *odd-even pricing, prestige pricing, multiple pricing, promotional pricing,* and *price lining*.

Odd-Even Pricing A technique that involves setting prices that all end in either odd or even numbers is known as *odd-even pricing*. The psychological principle on which the technique is based is that odd numbers ($.79, $7.95, $59.99) convey a bargain image. Even numbers ($1, $10, $100) convey a quality image. Whether or not this is true, you will find that many marketers follow the odd-even technique in an effort to project a certain image.

Within the framework of the general principle, marketers have developed a few refinements:

* *When using round numbers, do not include the cents in the price.* For example, do not price an item at $50.00. Price it at simply $50, with no cents included.
* *When deciding on prices just above round amounts, price $3-$4 higher rather than slightly higher.* For example, it is better to price an item at $33 or $34 rather than $31 or $32.
* *When deciding on prices just below round amounts, price slightly lower.* For example, if an item is close to $40, it is better to price it at $38 or $39.

Prestige Pricing Another psychological technique is **prestige pricing,** the practice of setting higher-than-average prices to suggest status and prestige to the consumer. As noted in Chapter 29, many customers assume that higher prices mean higher quality. Thus, they are willing to pay more for certain goods and services. For example, Rolls Royce automobiles, Waterford crystal, and Lenox china are all prestige priced. By contrast, when prices are set very low, this target market perceives the products as "cheap" or of little value.

Even customers who are known to prefer higher-priced products, however, have limits on what they will spend for prestige goods and services. To avoid exceeding these limits, marketers must set ceiling prices very carefully.

Multiple Pricing Some businesses have found that pricing items in multiples, such as 3 for $.99, is better than selling the same items at $.33 each. Multiple pricing suggests a bargain and helps to increase sales volume.

Promotional Pricing The psychological technique of promotional pricing is generally used in conjunction with sales promotions when prices are lower than average. Two basic types of promotional pricing are loss-leader pricing, discussed in Chapter 29, and special-event pricing.

As you will recall, loss-leader pricing is used to increase store traffic by offering very popular items of merchandise for sale at cost or slightly above. Customers who are familiar with the prices of these items will be attracted by the bargain and will come to the store to shop. Marketers hope that while customers are in the store they will also buy other items at the customary markup and will return on subsequent occasions.

In special-event pricing, items are reduced in price for a short period of time. Some examples of this technique can be found in back-to-school specials, Presidents' Day sales, dollar days, anniversary sales, and the like. At the end of a season, businesses also run clearance sales to get rid of the old merchandise in order to make room for the new.

Other promotional pricing techniques involve rebates, coupons, and other special discounts, which will be covered later in this chapter. The main characteristic of promotional pricing is that it is temporary. After the promotion ends, prices go back to normal.

More About

Pricing Techniques

When Dillard's Department Stores, Inc., decided to adopt an "everyday low pricing" policy in the mid-1980s, it was in sharp contrast to the way other department stores priced merchandise (*i.e.,* with plenty of room for markdowns at sale time). Since then, Dillard's has suffered declining revenues, and analysts think that it is its pricing strategy that is responsible. Its customers seem to want cyclically reduced prices. The thrill of the bargain wins, at least in this instance. *Note:* For another view of everyday low prices, see the Chapter 31 Case Study on page 411.

CASE STUDY

Levi's Jeans Regain Their Pricey Image

Levi Strauss & Co., best known for its jeans and Docker's brand cotton slacks, has recently been selling its products in Europe and Asia. In these areas, Levi's retail prices are much higher than in the United States—sometimes as high as $80 per pair of jeans. In the United States, those same jeans can retail for as little as $29.99. That figure is $2 less than *cost* to foreign businesses.

As a result, in 1993 foreign sales represented 38 percent of Levi's $5.6 billion revenues and 53 percent of its $361 million profit. At the same time, sales of Levi's jeans were flat in the United States. Why the difference? One reason was that the Levi's name had more glamour abroad than at home.

Taking a cue from its overseas operations, Levi Strauss decided to change its image at home to a more prestigious one. Ironically, that was an image the company once had in the United States.

Over a decade ago, Levi's jeans were sold in upscale department stores, like R. H. Macy & Company. However, when Levi Strauss decided to sell its jeans to J. C. Penney, Macy's retaliated by dropping the Levi's line. By selling to a discount department store, the reasoning went, Levi Strauss had sacrificed the upscale image of its jeans.

Clearly, Macy's did not want to compete with Penney's on price.

By the mid-1990s, Levi Strauss's efforts to regain its upscale image had begun to take hold. R. H. Macy & Company was once again carrying its products—in stand-alone jeans boutiques. The most popular model, 501 jeans, was selling in Macy's for $42. Sears also carried 501s, again in stand-alone shops where they were positioned as a prestige product. In fact, retail prices on 501s rose 40 percent in three years at Sears.

To enhance the prestigious image it was developing for Levi's jeans, Levi Strauss opened its own retail store across from Bloomingdale's, the upscale department store in New York City. The new store sells basic 501s for $47, more than the Macy's price. These higher prices not only reflect a new pricing strategy but also add significantly to the profit margin.

Will Levi's new pricing strategy help or hinder the company in the long run? Only time will tell. For the moment, Levi Strauss continues to conquer the rest of the world. The company is starting to do business in India, Hungary, Poland, Korea, Taiwan, and Turkey. Next it hopes to expand into the Czech Republic, as well as Russia, South Africa, and China. What product will it lead with? Levi's jeans, of course—once again a prestigious product at home and abroad.

Case Study Review

1. Which of the basic pricing strategies (cost-oriented, demand-oriented, or competition-oriented) is Levi Strauss using with its 501 jeans?
2. Which psychological pricing technique is Levi Strauss using? Explain.

A MATTER OF ETHICS

3. Is it ethical for businesses to create prestigious images for products like jeans based simply on price? Do you feel the same way about high-priced colognes? cars? food products?

Chapter 30   *Pricing Strategies*   **399**

2. Ask students if they can think of a variation on cumulative discounts utilized by airlines. (Frequent flier plans that allow airline passengers a free ticket once they have flown a certain number of miles in a specified period of time.)

Cooperative Learning

Have students work in small groups to determine a price for Continental's Coconut Surprise cookies (the Springboard Activity). Tell students to go through the six-step pricing procedure for a new product. While the groups work, circulate among them and provide any information they require.

Note: The first Critical Thinking and Application Projects on pages 404–405 are designed to help students with this task. Later lead a discussion to compare the groups' prices and explore the reasons for any major differences.

L1 Communication Skills

Ask students to recall the text found on most pricing signs. Specifically, ask them what most signs look like when the store uses prestige pricing. (Script or small print for the price, or no price at all.) Ask what such signs look like when the store uses promotional pricing. (Big, bold letters.) Ask what such signs look like when the store uses multiple pricing. (Big, bold lettering with savings noted.) Finally, ask what such signs look like when pricing lining is used. (One sign for each rack stating that all items on the rack are one particular price.)

L2 Communication Skills

Ask students to design a pricing sign to go on top of a rounder (circular rack) of sweat pants and sweat shirts. Tell them that the items are on sale for $15 each, but if customers buy two they pay only $25, a savings of $5.

Price Lining Price lining is a special pricing technique that requires a store to offer all merchandise in a given category at certain prices. For example, a store might price all of its blouses at $25, $35, and $50.

When deciding on price lines, marketers must be careful to make the price differences great enough to represent low, middle, and high prices for the category of goods being offered. Price lines of $25, $26, $28, and $30, for example, would confuse customers because they would have difficulty discerning their basis. (Slight price differences translate into equally slight quality differences.) When price lines are properly drawn (that is, not too closely), customers can easily compare items.

An advantage of price lining is that the target market is fully aware of the price range of products in a given store, and this helps the store maintain its image. In addition, price lining makes merchandising and selling easier for salespeople, who can readily draw comparisons between floor and ceiling prices. The technique also helps salespeople trade up—that is, offer a higher-priced, better-quality item to a customer to better satisfy the customer's needs.

Psychological pricing takes many forms. Which ones are represented here?

400   Unit 8   *Pricing*

Odd-even (including the practice of setting prices just slightly below round amounts), multiple pricing (3 for $5), and promotional pricing (Valentine's Day, Presidents' Day, end of season).

The Right Stuff

Gift giving in Japan is practically an art form. The number of rules can be overwhelming to the average foreigner, and even the smallest overlooked detail can cause the opposite result from the one intended. Here are some guidelines.

To start, let your Japanese counterpart begin the process. Don't give a gift unless one is given to you. Then at a future meeting, present your gift—preferably something distinctively American and made in the United States. (Possibilities might include regional food specialties or crafts; books about your state or region; American CDs or magazine subscriptions, provided you know the recipient's interests and taste.) Don't overdo by spending too much on the gift. If you give a better gift than was given to you, this will cause your Japanese counterpart to lose face. It is best to shop at a prestigious store and have the gift wrapped there, in the store's own paper.

Discount Pricing

Discount pricing involves the seller's offering reductions from the usual price. Such reductions are generally granted for the buyer's performance of certain functions. These discounts include *cash, quantity, trade*, and *seasonal discounts*, as well as *promotional discounts* and *allowances*.

Cash Discounts Cash discounts are offered to buyers to encourage them to pay their bills quickly. Terms are generally written on the invoice. For example, *2/10, net 30* means that a 2 percent discount is granted if the bill is paid in 10 days. If the buyer does not take advantage of the discount, however, the full amount must be paid within 30 days.

Quantity Discounts Quantity discounts are offered to buyers for placing large orders. Sellers benefit from large orders through the lower selling costs involved in one transaction as opposed to several small transactions. Quantity discounts also offer buyers an incentive to purchase more merchandise than they originally intended to purchase.

There are two types of quantity discounts—*noncumulative* and *cumulative*. Noncumulative quantity discounts are offered on one order, while cumulative quantity discounts are offered on all orders over a specified period of time. Cumulative discounts may be granted for purchases made over six months, for example, in which case all purchases for that period are used to determine the quantity discount offered. In other cases, buyers may be

required to sign a contract that guarantees a certain level of business. For example, advertisers who agree to use a specified number of column inches in their newspaper ads might be charged contract rates that reflect usage. Generally, the more you advertise, the less you pay per column inch.

Trade Discounts Trade discounts are not really discounts at all but rather the way manufacturers quote prices to wholesalers and retailers. Since many manufacturers establish suggested retail prices for their items, they work off of those prices, which are called *list prices*. They grant members of the channel of distribution discounts from the list price for performing their respective functions. Thus, a manufacturer might grant wholesalers a 40 percent discount from the list price and retailers a 30 percent discount.

The manufacturer might also quote the discounts in series, such as 25 and 10 percent for retailers and wholesalers, respectively. Series, or chain, discounts are calculated in sequence, as shown below. The example is based on a list price of $50.

Retailer's discount	$50 \times .25 = \$12.50$
Cost to retailer	$50 - 12.50 = \$37.50$
Wholesaler's discount	$37.50 \times .10 = \$ 3.75$
Cost to wholesaler	$37.50 - \$3.75 = \$33.75$

In series discounts, note that the wholesaler's discount is based on the retailer's discount, not the original list price.

Seasonal Discounts Seasonal discounts are offered to buyers who are willing to buy in advance of the customary buying season. Manufacturers offer such discounts to obtain orders for seasonal merchandise early so that production facilities and labor can be utilized throughout the year. Manufacturers sometimes call these discounted purchases "early bird orders" because they encourage buyers to act before a certain date.

A variation on this device is used by resorts. They offer vacationers lower rates to encourage use of resort facilities during the off-season.

Other businesses use seasonal discounts to cut anticipated costs. Many retailers, for example, drastically reduce prices on Christmas cards and decorations the day after Christmas. Such retailers prefer to sell this merchandise at a lower markup than pay the costs of warehousing it until the following year.

Promotional Discounts and Allowances
Promotional discounts are offered to wholesalers and retailers who are willing to advertise or promote a manufacturer's products. The discount may take the form of a percentage reduction in price or free merchandise. The latter is called an allowance. Another alternative, discussed in Chapter 21, is cooperative advertising in which the manufacturer and the retailer share the costs of advertising, with the manufacturer paying the lion's share.

Some kinds of promotional discounts are offered directly to the consumer. As you learned in Chapter 19, a rebate is a partial refund on the cost of a particular item from the manufacturer. To receive the rebate, a customer

L3 Communication Skills

Ask students to develop a system for having all salespeople remind their customers of the special on sweat pants and sweat shirts. They are to prepare a memo to all salespeople explaining exactly what they want them to do to encourage the sale of the specially priced merchandise.

L1 Human Relations Skills

Have students assume that they work for a local retailer who is running a special end-of-season sale. All seasonal merchandise is reduced 25 percent or 50 percent off the original price. Unfortunately for the salespeople working with the sale items, some reflect markdowns that were taken prior to the sale. This is confusing customers. Some expect the 25 percent or 50 percent discount to be taken off the ticketed price instead of the original price.

Ask students how they would handle those customers. (Explain that even though some merchandise was marked down previously, today's sale stipulates that the markdown is a percentage off the original price, not a prior sales price.)

L2 Human Relations Skills

Tell students that to complicate matters, some of the nonseasonal merchandise has been found on the special sale racks. It seems that customers, belatedly seeing the rack with specially priced goods, have been leaving nonsale goods on the sale racks when they pick up sale items.

A customer who selected a misplaced item asks to receive the 25 percent discount, as noted on top of the rounder. Have students role-play this situation. The customer should get very annoyed when told that she has selected an item that is not on sale, even though she found it on the sale rack.

SECTION 30.2

L3 Human Relations Skills

Tell students to assume that they have observed a salesperson giving a customer the 25 percent discount on a nonsale item because the customer complained about finding it on the sale rack. Have students role-play the part of the salesperson's superior (assistant manager or store manager) who must address the mistake this employee is making, which is costing the store money.

Independent Practice

Have students visit several different retail stores in their community to investigate psychological pricing strategies discussed in this section. Tell them to provide examples of products and their prices to support their classifications in a written report.

Assess

Evaluation

Assign and review the Section 30.2 Review.

Reteaching

1. Assign and review the vocabulary terms for this section.
2. Assign and review Fact and Idea Review questions 6–10 from the Chapter Review.
3. To reteach the steps used in setting a price, ask students to recall all the research and decisions that helped them arrive at their final price for the wreaths, T-shirts, or jewelry. Write each step on the chalkboard, along with the students responses to reinforce their understanding.

Figure 30-4

WHAT PRICE COOKIES?

When setting the price of a new product, marketers must consider the competition's prices, estimated consumer demand, costs, and expenses, as well as the firm's pricing objectives and strategies. Here is the way a company like Continental would go through that process to arrive at a price for its new cookie (page 392).

Step 1—Determine ▲ Pricing Objectives

What is your purpose in setting a price for your product? Do you want to increase sales volume or sales revenue? establish a prestigious image for your product and your company? increase your market share and market position? Answering these questions will help you keep your prices in line with other marketing decisions.

Step 2—Study Costs ▶

Since the main reason for being in business is to make a profit, give careful consideration to the costs involved in making or acquiring the goods or services you will offer for sale. Determine whether and how you can reduce costs without affecting the quality or image of your product.

Step 3—Estimate Demand ▲

Employ market research techniques to estimate consumer demand. The key to pricing goods and services is to set prices at the level consumers expect to pay. In many cases, those prices are directly related to demand.

buys the product and then sends in a rebate form along with some proof of purchase.

Trade-in allowances also go directly to the buyer. Customers are offered a price reduction if they sell back an old model of the product they are purchasing. Consumers are generally offered trade-in allowances when purchasing cars or major appliances. Companies are usually granted such allowances when purchasing machinery or equipment.

402   Unit 8   *Pricing*

Steps in Setting Price

Now that you have studied pricing concepts, policies, and techniques, it is time to put all that information into a single process. Figure 30-4 describes the six steps for determining price.

Lifelong Learning

Pricing Strategies

Knowledge of how and why manufacturers and retailers set prices can motivate students as consumers to find the best products they can for the money. It can also convince them of the need to stay informed about the more technical aspects of marketing. Combined with good consumer habits, it can save students both time and money.

Step 4—Study Competition ▶

Investigate your competitors to see what prices they are charging for similar goods and services. Study the market leader. What is the range of prices from the ceiling price to the price floor? Will you price your goods lower than, equal to, or higher than your competitors'?

◀ Step 5—Decide on a Pricing Strategy

You may decide to price your product higher than the competition's because you believe your product is superior. You may decide to set a lower price with the understanding that you will raise it once the product is accepted in the marketplace.

◀ Step 6—Set Price

After you have evaluated all the foregoing factors, apply the pricing techniques that match your strategy and set an initial price. Be prepared to monitor that price and evaluate its effectiveness as conditions in the market change.

By applying all the principles you learned in this and the previous chapter, you should now be able to establish a price for a given good or service. So, turn to pages 404 and 405, and decide what price you think would be most appropriate for Coconut Surprise cookies. (See the Critical Thinking and Application Projects sections of the Chapter Review for activities that can guide you in your decision-making process.)

SECTION 30.2 *Review*

1. **Name five types of psychological pricing techniques and five types of discount pricing techniques.**
2. **List the steps in setting prices.**

Enrichment

1. Assign and review the appropriate activities in the Student Activity Workbook.
2. Assign and review the appropriate Critical Thinking questions from the Chapter Review.
3. Assign and review the Building Academic Skills Activities, Application Projects, Linking School to Work Activity, and Performance Assessment from the Chapter Review.
4. Have students skim their text looking for photos showing ads or displays that contain price data. Ask if all conform to the pricing rules and techniques discussed in this section. Have students point out any that do not, and explain or critique the variation. (One possible instance of the latter might be the Toyota ad in Chapter 3, the head and heart ad. The lease price cited— $259/mo.—is a bargain appeal using odd-even pricing; but the dynamic, arty photo (the sort that would usually appear without a price) is arguably a prestige appeal. There is a tension here between the two approaches—but that's the whole point of the ad.)

Close

Have students list the six steps in setting a price. (Determine pricing objectives, study costs, estimate demand, study competition, decide on pricing strategy, and set the price.)

Section Review Answers

1. Psychological: odd-even, prestige, multiple, promotional, and price lining. Discount: cash, quantity, trade, seasonal, and promotional.
2. Determine pricing objective, study costs, estimate demand, study competition, decide on pricing strategy, and set price.

Answers

Vocabulary Review

Sentences will vary. See Glossary for definitions.

Fact and Idea Review

1. Marketers first calculate the costs of acquiring or making a product and their expenses of doing business. Then they add their projected profit margin to these figures to arrive at a price. Markup pricing and cost-plus pricing are two of the most common methods of cost-oriented pricing.

2. They determine what present consumers are willing to pay for given goods and services. Two situations are theaters, which often charge different prices for tickets on the basis of location of seats, and telephone companies, which may charge higher rates for long-distance calls made at peak times.

3. Competition-oriented pricing does not take into account costs or customer demand. Two types are competitive bid and going-rate pricing.

4. Introduction, growth, maturity, and decline. Marketers want to keep a product in the growth stage as long as possible.

5. It should be lowered.

6. Odd numbers present a bargain image; even numbers present a quality image.

7. Advantages for customers: they are fully aware of the price range of products, which helps the store maintain its image. Advantages for salespeople: it makes merchandising easier and helps salespeople trade up to better satisfy customers' needs.

8. It encourages them to pay quickly.

Vocabulary Review

For each group of words listed below, write a sentence that reveals the relationship between the words in the group.

markup
cost-plus pricing

skimming pricing
penetration pricing

one-price policy
flexible-price policy

psychological pricing
prestige pricing
price lining

discount pricing
trade discounts
seasonal discounts

Fact and Idea Review

1. How does a marketer determine prices when using a cost-oriented approach? Name two common methods of cost-oriented pricing. (Sec. 30.1)

2. What do marketers who use demand-oriented pricing attempt to determine? Cite two situations in which demand-oriented pricing is used. (Sec. 30.1)

3. How does competition-oriented pricing differ from cost-oriented and demand-oriented pricing? Name two basic types of competition-oriented pricing strategies. (Sec. 30.1)

4. What are the four stages in a product life cycle? In which stage do marketers want to keep products? (Sec. 30.1)

5. Once sales begin to level off after a product has been introduced with skimming pricing, what should be done to the price? (Sec. 30.1)

6. What psychological principle is associated with odd-even pricing? (Sec. 30.2)

7. What are the advantages of price lining to customers and to salespeople? (Sec. 30.2)

8. Why are cash discounts offered to buyers? (Sec. 30.2)

9. Are trade discounts really discounts? Explain. (Sec. 30.2)

10. What are seasonal discounts? Why are they offered by manufacturers? by vacation resorts? by retailers? (Sec. 30.2)

Critical Thinking

1. As product manager at Continental Cookies, which method would you use to introduce the new Coconut Surprise cookies—skimming pricing or penetration pricing? Why?

2. Johnson & Johnson promoted its baby shampoo to adult male athletes by touting the product's

---

gentleness, even when used every day. At what stage in the shampoo's life cycle do you think this promotion took place? What do you think Johnson & Johnson was trying to accomplish by promoting its baby shampoo to adult males?

3. In establishing price lines for men's sweaters, which of the following would you select and why?
   a. $50, $52, $53, $55, $65, $67, $69, $72, $74, $77, $80
   b. $50, $65, $80

Building Academic Skills

Math

1. Determine the price a wholesaler would pay for an item with a list price of $100 if the series trade discounts were 40 percent and 10 percent for retailers and wholesalers, respectively.

2. A retail store is having a sale in which dresses are marked down 20 percent and suits are marked down 30 percent. What is the sale price of a dress priced at $120? What is the sale price of a suit priced at $215?

Communication

3. As a salesperson for a toy company, explain to a retail buyer why you are seeking an order in February for toys that will be sold in the retail store in November and December.

Human Relations

4. You work for a retail jeweler who has a flexible-price policy for a few selected customers. You are alone in the store and wait on a steady customer. When you ring up the sale, the customer tells you that you did not deduct the customary 20 percent discount. What would you do?

Technology

5. Set up a spreadsheet that will automatically calculate 20 percent, 30 percent, and 50 percent discounts during special promotions. Assume your work will be input into the sales terminal so salespeople will not have to do the calculations in their heads.

Application Projects

1. As product manager for Continental Cookies, you have ascertained the following facts:
   • Cost to make and market a one-pound tin of Coconut Surprise cookies is $1.

---

9. No, they are the way manufacturers quote prices to wholesalers and retailers.

10. Seasonal discounts are offered to buyers who are willing to buy in advance of the customary buying season. Manufacturers offer them to production facilities so labor can be utilized throughout the year. Vacation resorts offer them to get use out of resort facilities during the off-season. Retailers offer them to cut anticipated costs of warehousing seasonal products until the following year.

Critical Thinking

1. A case can be made for both methods. However, penetration pricing would be better if students see the product as one that is price-sensitive and highly competitive.

2. Shampoo was at the maturity stage. The company was trying to open a new market for the product—adult males.

3. b. Because the price differences must be great

- Market research indicates a strong demand for coconut cookies.
- Wholesalers and retailers both use a 40 percent markup on cookies.
- Most similar cookies retail for between $2.50 and $3.25 per pound.

Write a pricing memo to your boss. In it, answer these questions:

a. Considering costs, demand, and competition, as well as the effects of wholesalers and retailers on price, what should be the retail price of a pound of Continental's new Coconut Surprise cookies?

b. What should Continental charge wholesalers for the cookies?

c. What should it charge retailers?

2. Shop a discount store, a department store, a grocery store, and a specialty store. At each store, do the following:

a. Find two products that you would price forward to retail and two that you would price backward from retail. Explain why you would choose that particular method for the product.

b. Find two products that you would introduce by skimming pricing and two for which you would use penetration pricing. Explain why each pricing policy would effectively introduce the product to the market you want to reach and why it would be the best way to realize a profit.

c. Find two products that you would price using each of these techniques—odd-even pricing, prestige pricing, promotional pricing, and price lining. For each example, briefly explain the market you want to reach and why the particular pricing technique you have chosen would be effective.

Linking School to Work

Review the psychological and discount pricing techniques in this chapter in relation to the practices you have observed on your job. Cite examples of every concept used by your firm. Prepare written and oral reports on your findings.

Performance Assessment

Role Play

Situation. You are employed as a sales associate for a local department store. You are also a member of the store's teen advisory council. The women's accessories buyer makes a presentation to the teen council and asks for everyone's opinion of a new accessory. It's made of jeans material and lace and is designed to be worn like a necklace or scarf. Each neck piece, as the item is called, is unique. Everyone on the teen advisory council likes the way the neck piece looks on shirts and thinks it will sell well. The pricing of the item is more difficult because it is new. The buyer has requested that everyone on the teen council recommend a selling price for the new item. The items cost the store between $7.50 and $12.35. What price(s) will you recommend to the buyer, and how will you support your position?

Evaluation. You will be evaluated on how well you do the following:

- Distinguish between a one-price policy and a flexible-price policy.
- Explain the two main pricing policies that should be considered when introducing a new product.
- Apply the three basic pricing strategies (cost-oriented, demand-oriented, and competition-oriented) to pricing a product.
- Convince the buyer to use your plan for pricing the new product.

Creative Problem Solving

The student council is embarking on a fund-raising project and has asked for help from the local DECA chapter. The fund raiser involves selling T-shirts already purchased for $5.75 each. The problem is that there are three different styles, one of which they think will not sell well and another that they think will go fast. Unfortunately, the deal they made for the T-shirts will not permit them to order more of the latter design. (The purchase was a closeout, a whole lot, as is—100 shirts in each style.) The student council members have no idea how to determine a sale price for the T-shirts. As the person selected to work with the council, you must come up with a presentation that will educate them and help them decide on a price. What will you say?

Complete the Chapter 30 Computer Application that appears in the Student Activity Workbook.

1. Answers will vary, depending on the profit margin the manufacturer wants over and above the $1 cost to make and market the product. If the manufacturer wants a 10 percent profit margin, it would sell the cookies to wholesalers for $1.10. They would sell to retailers for $1.54, who would sell the cookies to consumers for $2.16. This last figure could be adjusted according to pricing strategies (*e.g.*, penetration pricing) and techniques.

   If the manufacturer wants a 40 percent profit margin, the price to wholesalers would be $1.40, to retailers to markup $1.96, and to consumers $2.74 (going-rate pricing). If students opt for skimming pricing based on high initial demand, the manufacturer's price to wholesalers could be even higher.

2. Products and prices will vary.

Linking School to Work

Answers depend on the work situation.

Performance Assessment

Refer to the *DECA Competitive Events Handbook* for evaluation guidelines.

Computer Application

Optional Activity. Refer to the *Marketing Software Binder* for the template and user information.

Evaluation

Administer the reproducible test for Chapter 30, or construct your own using the Testmaker software.

---

enough for customers to be able to differentiate among them.

Building Academic Skills

Math

1. Retailers: $100 \times .40 = $40; $100 - $40 = $60. Wholesalers: $60 \times .10 = $6; $60 - $6 = $54.

2. Dress: $120 x .80 = $96. Suit: $215 \times .70 = $150.50.

Communication

3. Answers will vary. One possibility is so that all orders can be processed in time for the holiday season.

Human Relations

4. Answers will vary.

Technology

5. Formula: retail price = (100 − discount percentage) = new sale price.

PRICING MATH

Pages 406–417

Chapter Overview

Chapter 31 presents the various mathematical formulas used to determine prices. It focuses on three principal areas—markup calculations, markdown calculations, and discount calculations.

Springboard

Pose this problem: Ollie's Gifts buys designer phones for $27.50 each and prices them at twice that amount. Cathy, a salesclerk, wants to buy one of the phones but can't spend more than $50. Determine the retail price of the phone ($55), how much Cathy will pay after a 15 percent employee discount ($46.75) and 4 percent sales tax ($48.62), and if she can afford the purchase (yes).

Prereading

List the section objectives to discuss with students. Have students skim the chapter, looking at the pictures, reading the captions, and noting the heads. Ask questions to ensure that students have a minimal understanding of the chapter structure.

Preteaching the Vocabulary

Before students begin reading the chapter, dictate each of the vocabulary terms and ask students to write them on a sheet of paper. When they finish, write the terms on the chalkboard. Then have students guess at the meaning of each. Write their guesses next to each term, but do not give the correct meaning. Leave this list on the chalkboard so that students can see how close their guesses were to the actual definitions as they work through the chapter.

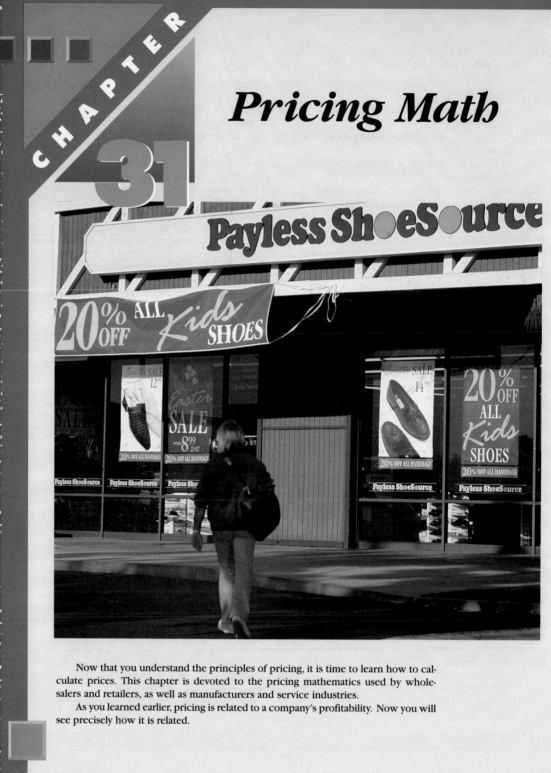

Pricing Math

Now that you understand the principles of pricing, it is time to learn how to calculate prices. This chapter is devoted to the pricing mathematics used by wholesalers and retailers, as well as manufacturers and service industries.

As you learned earlier, pricing is related to a company's profitability. Now you will see precisely how it is related.

Classroom Management

For the Teacher
- Teacher's Annotated Editions for all workbooks
- Teacher's Manual for *School-to-Work Handbook*
- *Testing Binder*
- *Transparency Binder*
- *Marketing Software Binder*
- *Marketing Career Portfolio*
- *Lesson Plans*

For the Student
- *Student Activity Workbook*
- *Marketing Math Workbook*
- *School-to-Work Handbook*
- *Student Software*
- *International Case Studies*
- *Marketing Career Portfolio*

SECTION 31.1

Objectives

After completing this section, you will be able to

- explain how a firm's net profit or loss is related to pricing;
- calculate dollar and percentage markup based on cost or retail; and
- calculate markdown in dollars, as well as determine sale price and maintained markup.

Terms to Know

- gross profit
- maintained markup

Profit vs. Markup

A businessperson makes the following statement: "We made a profit of $50—bought the whatsit for $100 and sold it for $150." The businessperson is only partially correct. The difference between the retail price ($150) and the cost ($100) is the markup, not the profit. Profit is the amount left from revenue after the costs of the merchandise *and expenses* have been paid.

Figure 31-1 makes this clear. It compares a profit and loss statement and the calculations for the retail price of an item. As you can see from the percentages, the markup on an item is similar to gross profit. **Gross profit** is the difference between sales revenue and the cost of goods sold. Expenses must still be deducted in order to get net, or actual, profit. Thus, for a business to be successful, its markup (like its gross profit) must be high enough both to cover expenses and provide the profit sought.

Basic Markup Calculations

Retailers and wholesalers use the same formulas to calculate markup. To make these formulas easy to understand, we will use only retail prices here. Note, however, that wholesale prices can be substituted in any of the formulas discussed.

The most basic pricing formula is the one for calculating retail price. It states in mathematical terms a relationship we have been discussing in the last two chapters: retail price is a combination of cost and markup. If you know these two figures (if, for example, a paperweight costs $10 and a retailer marks it up $4), you can calculate retail price. Here's how.

$$\text{Cost (C)} + \text{markup (MU)} = \text{retail price (RP)}$$
$$\$10 + \$4 = \$14$$

From this basic formula can be derived two others, those for finding cost and markup, respectively.

$$\text{Retail price (RP)} - \text{markup (MU)} = \text{cost (C)}$$
$$\$14 - \$4 = \$10$$
$$\text{Retail price (RP)} - \text{cost (C)} = \text{markup (MU)}$$
$$\$14 - \$10 = \$4$$

Profit and Markup Compared

Profit and Loss Statement

Sales revenue	$5,000	(100%)
Less cost of goods sold	2,750	(55%)
Gross profit on sales	2,250	(45%)
Expenses		
Salaries	250	
Advertising	150	
Utilities	400	
Rent	500	
Loan interest	100	
Depreciation	200	
Insurance	100	
Miscellaneous	50	
Total expenses	$1,750	(35%)
Net profit before taxes	$500	(10%)

Markup Pricing for One Item

Retail Price	$50.00	(100%)
Cost	27.50	(55%)
Markup	22.50	(45%)

Figure 31-1

Gross profit and markup are similar in that each must be sufficient to cover both expenses and net (or actual) profit. In the comparison being made here, how much of a single item's markup would go to expenses and how much to profit?

Chapter 31 *Pricing Math* **407**

FOCUS

Bell Ringer Activity

Ask students if profit and markup are one and the same.

Introducing the Section

Have students decide and commit to their answer for the Bell Ringer Activity. Then put an abbreviated profit and loss statement on the chalkboard. Next to it, put the retail price parts that correspond to items on the profit and loss statement. For example, next to Sales Revenue, put an arrow and note Price; next to Cost of Goods Sold, put an arrow and note Cost; and next to Gross Profit, put an arrow and note Markup.

Have students study the chalkboard comparison and decide if they want to change or keep their original response to the Bell Ringer Activity. Once you have all students committed to the correct answer, ask them how the markup of a product is related to the profit that the company expects to make. (Markup must be high enough to cover expenses and include profit if the company is to be financially successful.)

Note: To further reinforce this point, refer students to Figure 31-1 in their texts. Have them explain in their own words how it illustrates the same correspondences as the chalkboard diagram. Ask what new feature(s) it uses to bring home the same points. (Item figures that are directly proportional to the profit and loss statement entries, percentages in parentheses, and a substantial list of expenses that must be subtracted before an actual [or net] profit figure can be arrived at.)

Meeting Special Needs

Visually Impaired

Students with visual/spatial problems may have difficulty working with accounting-oriented content. You will need to describe accounting procedures and operations specifically with these students in mind. Do not simply assume that they can follow what you are saying while you perform calculations on the chalkboard. Take special care to name categories (i.e., accounting entries and spreadsheet cells) and to explain how figures are arrived at. Also, provide an opportunity for students to ask questions or request assistance with calculations.

Teach

Guided Practice

1. Read Section 31.1 with students.
2. Use the three transparencies for this section.
3. Have students read aloud the Case Study and review the answers in class.
4. To introduce the basic markup calculations, draw a circle on the chalkboard, and label it Retail Price. Then divide the circle into two parts, and label these Costs and Markup.

   Start assigning figures to these two parts. For example, make the markup 40 percent and the costs of the item 60 percent. Make the markup $2 and the costs $8. Provide several more variations to demonstrate that retail price equals cost plus markup.

   Once students understand that basic formula, provide them with two of the three numbers, and have them identify the third. For example, if the cost is $14 and the retail price $30, the markup is. . .($16.)

Discussion Starter

Remind students that they learned of the distinction between cost and retail figures back in Chapter 28 (page 371). To be sure they understand the significance of the distinction, help them cite some analogies (some similar situations they are already familiar with).

Begin by noting that the percentage markup on retail must only be applied to or used with other retail figures. Likewise, the percentage markup on cost must only be applied to or used with other cost figures. The two types of figures cannot be mixed.

Ask students to suggest some other math situations in which the same sort of general rule applies. (If you were figuring the area of a rectangle, you would have to convert all dimensions to the same unit of measure; you wouldn't multiply inches by feet,

408

Once again, notice that all three formulas are based on the principle that if you know two related variables, you can find a third. For example, if you know retail price and cost, you can find markup. If you know retail price and markup, you can find cost.

Throughout this chapter, you will rely on these three formulas. From this point on, when they (or their terms) are needed, we will cite them in abbreviated form (as $C + MU = RP$).

Practice 1

Use the retail price formula and its variations to do the following problems.

1. If a calculator costs AB Products $25 and the markup is $12, what is its retail price?
2. If a tennis racket retails for $135 and its markup is $75, what is its cost?

Note: Answers to all practice sets in this chapter appear on page 415.

Percentage Markup

In all of the examples and problems above, markup was expressed as a dollar amount. In most business situations, however, the markup figure is expressed as a percentage. From this point on, we shall distinguish between these two forms of markup (dollar and percentage). In calculations, we shall represent dollar markup with the abbreviation $MU(\$)$ and percentage markup with the abbreviation $MU(\%)$.

Expressing markup in either dollar or percentage form is not the only choice that wholesalers and retailers face in making markup calculations. If they choose to use the percentage form, they may also elect to compute their markup on either cost or retail price.

Most choose to do the latter for three reasons. First, the markup on the retail price sounds like a smaller amount and thus sounds better to customers. Second, future markdowns and discounts are calculated on a retail basis. Third, profits are generally calculated on sales revenue. Thus, it makes sense to use markup on retail prices when comparing and analyzing data that play a role in a firm's profits.

Here are the steps used to calculate the percentage markup on retail. They will be easier to follow if we have an example to work with. Assume that you want to calculate the percentage markup on a pair of bookends that Frump's Department Store stocks for $49.50 (cost) and sells for $82.50 (retail price).

Step 1   Determine the dollar markup.
$$RP - C = MU(\$)$$
$$\$82.50 - \$49.50 = \$33.00$$

Step 2   To change the dollar markup to the percentage markup, divide it by the retail price. The result will be a decimal.

408   Unit 8   *Pricing*

$$\frac{MU(\$)}{RP} = MU(\%) \text{ on retail}$$
$$\$33.00 \div \$82.50 = .4$$

Step 3   Change the decimal to a percentage. This figure is the percentage markup on retail.
$$.40 = 40\%$$

> Shift decimal point two places right.

Retailers may occasionally find the percentage markup on cost to be helpful. The calculation is the same, except for one step. In Step 2, you divide by cost instead of retail. Using the same facts as in the illustration above, you calculate the percentage markup on cost as follows:

Step 1   Determine the dollar markup.
$$RP - C = MU(\$)$$
$$\$82.50 - \$49.50 = \$33.00$$

Step 2   To change the dollar markup to the percentage markup, divide by cost.
$$\frac{MU(\$)}{C} = MU(\%) \text{ on cost}$$
$$\$33.00 \div \$49.50 = .6667$$

Step 3   Change the decimal to a percentage. This figure is the percentage markup on cost.
$$.6667 = 66.67\%$$

> Shift decimal point two places right.

Practice 2

Calculate the percentage markup in each of these situations.

1. If the retail price of a jar of jam is $2.50 and the cost is $1.25, what is the percentage markup based on cost price? based on retail price?
2. An electric sander costs $95, and its markup is $23.75. Find its percentage markup on cost price. Then calculate its percentage markup on retail price.
3. If a gallery sells a framed print for $100 and its markup is $25, what is its percentage markup on cost price? on retail price?

Markup Equivalents Table

If you calculated enough problems using the formulas for computing percentage markup based on cost and retail, you would begin to notice a correlation between the two figures. This fact led marketers to develop a calculation aid called a markup equivalents table, a portion of which is shown in Table 31-1. The table lists markup percentages based on retail and the equivalent percentages based on cost. To use the table, you locate the

---

More About

Markup

Keystone markup is a term commonly used in retailing circles. It refers to a 100 percent markup on cost.

percentage markup on retail and read its cost equivalent in the adjacent column or vice versa.

Markup Equivalents

Markup on Retail	Markup on Cost	Markup on Retail	Markup on Cost
4.8 %	5.0 %	25.0 %	33.3 %
5.0	5.3	26.0	35.0
6.0	6.4	27.0	37.0
7.0	7.5	27.3	37.5
8.0	8.7	28.0	39.0
9.0	10.0	28.5	40.0
10.0	11.1	29.0	40.9
10.7	12.0	30.0	42.9
11.0	12.4	31.0	45.0
11.1	12.5	32.0	47.1
12.0	13.6	33.3	50.0
12.5	14.3	34.0	51.5
13.0	15.0	35.0	53.9
14.0	16.3	35.5	55.0
15.0	17.7	36.0	56.3
16.0	19.1	37.0	58.8
16.7	20.0	37.5	60.0
17.0	20.5	38.0	61.3
17.5	21.2	39.0	64.0
18.0	22.0	39.5	65.5
18.5	22.7	40.0	66.7
19.0	23.5	41.0	70.0
20.0	25.0	42.0	72.4
21.0	26.6	42.8	75.0
22.0	28.2	44.4	80.0
22.5	29.0	46.1	85.0
23.0	29.9	47.5	90.0
23.1	30.0	48.7	95.0
24.0	31.6	50.0	100.0

Table 31–1

A markup equivalents table, one page of which is shown here, allows users to quickly convert markups on retail to markups on cost and vice versa. A 50 percent markup on retail is equal to what markup on cost?

Practice 3

Use the markup equivalents table to answer the following questions.

1. If the markup on retail is 25 percent, what is its equivalent markup on cost?
2. If the markup on cost is 60 percent, what is its equivalent markup on retail?

Cost Method of Pricing

Sometimes marketers know only the cost of an item and its markup on cost. In such a situation, they use the cost method of pricing.

As an example, consider a board game that a toy store buys for $8.50 and sells for cost plus a 40 percent markup on cost. To arrive at the retail price, follow these steps:

Step 1 Determine the dollar markup on cost. Multiply the cost by the percentage markup on cost in decimal form.
$$C \times MU(\%) = MU(\$)$$
$$\$8.50 \times .40 = \$3.40$$

Step 2 Add the dollar markup to the cost to get the retail price.
$$C + MU(\$) = RP$$
$$\$8.50 + \$3.40 = \$11.90$$

Often, however, the situation isn't that simple. Suppose, for example, you have the cost, but the only markup figure you know is the markup on retail. How do you proceed? The answer is you can't—at least, not without some adjustment. Markup on cost can only be applied to a cost figure; markup on retail, only to a retail figure. However, one kind of markup can be changed to the other by using the markup equivalents table.

Consider a sample problem. A marketer knows that the customary markup for a particular cosmetics firm is 33.3 percent on retail and that the cost of its best lipstick is $3.48. To project the lipstick's retail price, follow these steps:

Step 1 Use the markup equivalents table to get all the information in the same (cost) form. Find the cost equivalent of a 33.3 percent markup on retail.

Markup on Retail	Markup on Cost
32.0	47.1
33.3 →	50.0
34.0	51.5

Step 2 Apply the cost method to determine the retail price. First calculate the dollar markup on cost.
$$C \times MU(\%) = MU(\$)$$
$$\$3.48 \times .50 = \$1.74$$

Step 3 Then calculate the retail price.
$$C + MU(\$) = RP$$
$$\$3.48 + \$1.74 = \$5.22$$

Chapter 31 *Pricing Math* **409**

only inches by inches or feet by feet. If you were adding fractions you would convert them all to the lowest common denominator; if you had quarters, eighths, and sixteenths, you would probably convert them all to sixteenths.)

Critical Thinking

1. Ask: If you are given the markup percentage on retail and the only other figure you have is what an item cost the business, what options do you have to figure out the markup in dollars and the retail price? (Use the markup equivalents table or the retail method of pricing.)
2. To prove the reliability of the markup equivalents table, have students calculate the markup percentage on retail and the markup percentage on cost for three different situations:
   - RP $100 and C $80 [MU($) = $20; $20 ÷ $100 = .2 = 20%; $20 ÷ $80 = .25 = 25%]
   - RP $85 and C $68 [MU($) = $17; $17 ÷ $85 = .2 = 20%; $17 ÷ $68 = .25 = 25%]
   - RP $95 and C $76 [MU($) = $19; $19 ÷ $95 = .2 = 20%; $19 ÷ $76 = .25 = 25%]

Ask students what they noticed about the three problems they calculated. (All demonstrate that when the markup on retail is 20 percent, its equivalent markup on cost is always 25 percent.)

L1 Math Skills

Have students determine the retail price of a product that costs a business $75.49 and has a markup of $38.51. ($75.49 + $38.51 = $114)

L2 Math Skills

Have students determine the markup percentage based on the retail price of the item described in L1 Math Skills activity. ($38.51 ÷ $114 = .3378 = 33.78%)

L3 Math Skills

Tell students that the cost of purchasing the product identified in L1 and L2 Math Skills activities has gone up 10 percent, and the selling price must be increased accordingly. Have students determine the new selling price and markup by using the original retail markup percentage. [New C: $75.49 × 1.10 = $83.04. MU(%) on cost: 100 − 33.78% = 66.22%. New RP: $83.04 ÷.6622 = $125.40. New MU($): $125.40 − $83.04 = $42.36]

L1 Math Skills

Ask students to calculate the retail price of an item that cost the business $39.84. Tell them the markup is 55 percent on cost. ($39.84 × .55 = $21.91; $39.84 + $21.91 = $61.75)

L2 Math Skills

Tell students that the store ran a 20 percent off sale on the item in L1 Math Skills activity. Have students determine the sale price and the new maintained markup in dollars. [MD($): $61.75 × .20 = $12.35. SP: $61.75 − $12.35 = $49.40. Maintained markup ($): $49.40 − $39.84 = $9.56.]

L3 Math Skills

Have students calculate the maintained markup percent for the item dealt with in L1 and L2 Math Skills activities. ($9.56 ÷ $49.40 = .1935 =19.35%)

Retail Method of Pricing

Another way to compute the retail price when all you know are cost and the markup on retail is to use the retail method. This method is based on changing the information you have into retail figures.

Consider this problem. The owner of a sporting goods store wants to know what the markup and retail price should be for a sun visor that costs $6.75. His customary markup on retail is 40 percent. The steps in his calculation are as follows:

Step 1   Determine what percentage of the retail price is equal to cost. This is simply a matter of subtracting the known retail markup figure from 100 percent, which represents the retail price.

$$RP(\%) − MU(\%) = C(\%)$$
$$100\% − 40\% = 60\%$$

Step 2   To determine the retail price, divide the cost by the decimal equivalent of the percentage calculated in Step 1.

$$\$6.75 ÷ .60 = \$11.25$$

Step 3   Calculate the dollar markup.

$$RP − C = MU(\$)$$
$$\$11.25 − \$6.75 = \$4.50$$

Step 4   If you like, check your work by multiplying the retail price you calculated in Step 2 by the percentage markup on retail given originally. If your retail price is correct, the answer will match the dollar markup you calculated in Step 3.

$$RP × MU(\%) = MU(\$)$$
$$\$11.25 × .40 = \$4.50$$

You can use a visual device called the retail box (Figure 31-2) to help you remember this sequence of calculations.

Figure 31-2

To complete retail price using the retail method, fill in the boxes following the letter sequence (B–F). The amounts that go in B and D are usually known (given as part of the problem). The computations you must do are summarized below the diagrams. In the finished box, how do the entries at the top (E and A) relate to those below?

Practice 4

Calculate retail price and markup in these two problems by using the retail method.

1. Find the retail price and dollar markup for a handmade sweater that costs the Woolens Closet $90 and has a 40 percent markup on retail.
2. A machine-made sweater costs the Woolens Closet $35 and has a 60 percent markup on retail. Calculate this sweater's price and dollar markup.

Calculations for Lowering Prices

When a business lowers its prices, a new sale price must be calculated, as well as a new markup. Let's look at the steps used in calculating markdowns (lowered prices), maintained markups (new markup), and the actual sales prices derived from these calculations.

Markdowns

To reduce the quantity of goods in stock, a business will sometimes mark down merchandise by a certain percentage [MD(%)]. This reduction is based on the retail price. Consider as an example a record store that wants to mark down by 25 percent compact disks that originally sold for $16. The steps for calculating the sale price (SP) are as follows:

Retail Box

	$	%		$	%
Retail Price	E.	A. 100	Retail Price	E. 11.25	A. 100
Markup	F.	B.	Markup	F. 4.50	B. 40
Cost	D.	C.	Cost	D. 6.75	C. 60

Computation: $C = A − B$ $C = 100 − 40 = 60$
$E = \dfrac{D}{C}$ $E = 6.75 ÷ .60 = 11.25$
$F = E − D$ $F = 11.25 − 6.75 = 4.50$

Check: $E × B = F$ $11.25 × .40 = 4.50$

Caption Answer

E and A represent the totals of the boxes below them.

Everyday Low Prices— How Low Can They Go?

During the recession of the late 1980s, consumers learned how to shop for lower prices. They clipped coupons and bought in bulk. Even after the recession was over, well into the mid-1990s, consumers were still price conscious. Big manufacturers and retailers found that they had to offer special promotional discounts continually to lure customers to their products and businesses. Retailers and consumers would stock up on the item when the price was low and then wait until the next promotion before buying again. The result? Lower profit margins.

To phase out the deep discounts and wide price fluctuations, businesses turned to something called Everyday Low Prices (EDLP). This is a pricing method that keeps prices consistently low.

For example, Procter & Gamble reduced its Pamper diaper prices a total of 10 percent from 1990 to 1994. It reduced its Luvs brand prices 16 percent. To pay for these huge price reductions, P&G reduced the number of packaging options for Luvs and cut back on consumer promotions. The company expects its profits to grow as a result of increased sales volume.

The EDLP concept is most apparent in wholesale price clubs. Reduced costs allow the clubs to offer consumers lower prices than traditional supermarkets. Even though supermarkets enjoy an average gross margin of 25 percent vs. 11 percent for clubs, operating profits for clubs exceeded those for supermarkets by a substantial amount.

Spurred on by successes like these, other types of businesses are trying to implement EDLP. For example, magazine publishers have embraced the practice as a way to increase sales volume. Publishers of mass-market magazines typically expect 20 percent or more of their circulation to come from newsstand sales, but newsstand sales are down. Over the past 12 years, single-copy sales for the top 572 magazines fell by 24 percent. For example, newsstand sales for *Family Circle* dropped from 7.2 million in 1982 to 2.8 million in 1993; for *TV Guide*, 9.7 million to 5.6 million; for *Woman's Day*, 7 million to 3 million.

U.S. News and World Report's single-copy sales dropped 12.7 percent in one year, which led its publisher to do something drastic. It began testing lower cover prices in different parts of the country. It cut its $2.50 cover price to $1.50 in some regions and to $1 in others.

How low can prices go with EDLP? Manufacturers and retailers will continue to study the impact of this new pricing strategy for the answer.

Case Study Review

1. If a business wants to start using EDLP, what measures must it take so that it remains profitable?
2. How is it possible for supermarkets to enjoy an average gross margin of 25 percent versus 11 percent for warehouse clubs but still be unable to match the clubs' operating profits?

A MATTER OF ETHICS

3. If *U.S. News and World Report* could lower its $2.50 single-copy price to $1 in some regions of the country, should it still charge $1.50 in other parts of the country? Is that ethical?

5. To reteach how to calculate markdowns, have students draw on their personal experience in buying things on sale. Ask them how they calculate markdowns when they select something from a rack posted 20% Off Ticketed Prices. Show them that their methods are similar to, if not exactly the same as, the methods described in the text for calculating markdowns.

Enrichment

1. Assign and review the appropriate activities in the *Student Activity Workbook*.
2. Assign and review the appropriate Critical Thinking questions from the Chapter Review.
3. Arrange for students to have access to one of the new vehicle price lists that *Consumer Reports* makes available to the readers of its annual car issue. Have students locate the figure that represents how much the dealership pays to put the car on its lot (the cost). Then have them visit a local dealership and get a sticker price for the car (the retail price). Have them use these two figures to calculate the dealer's dollar and percentage markup. Then have them do the same set of calculations for the price *Consumer Reports* suggests they negotiate for.

Close

Ask students to complete the following statement: Retail price equals cost. . .(plus markup.)

Step 1 Determine the dollar markdown. Multiply the retail price by the percentage markdown.

$$RP \times MD(\%) = MD(\$)$$
$$\$16 \times .25 = \$4$$

Step 2 To determine the sale price, subtract the markdown from the retail price.

$$RP - MD(\$) = SP$$
$$\$16 - \$4 = \$12$$

Another way to arrive at the same answer is to consider what percentage of the original price will equal the sale price. The procedure is still two steps long, but the percentage calculation is so easy that you can probably do it in your head and thus save some time. Here are the steps involved.

Step 1 Determine what percentage of the original price will equal the sale price. This is simply a matter of subtracting the markdown percentage from 100 percent.

$$RP(\%) - MD(\%) = SP(\%)$$
$$100\% - 25\% = 75\%$$

Step 2 To find the sale price, multiply the retail price by the decimal equivalent of the percentage calculated in Step 1.

$$RP \times SP(\%) = SP$$
$$\$16 \times .75 = \$12$$

Practice 5

Calculate the sale price.

A suit that sells for $125 is to be marked down 40 percent. What is its new price?

Maintained Markup

When a marketer marks down goods, the markup and markup percentage change. The difference between an item's final sale price and its cost is called the **maintained markup.**

Let's consider an example. Assume that a cassette recorder that cost Zap Electronics $25 and originally sold for $50 is marked down 20 percent. The maintained markup (expressed in both dollars and as a percentage) is calculated as follows:

Step 1 Calculate the new sale price.

$$100\% - 20\% = 80\%$$
$$\$50 \times .80 = \$40$$

Step 2 To determine the maintained markup in dollars, subtract the cost from the sale price.

$$\$40 - \$25 = \$15$$

Step 3 To determine the maintained markup percentage, divide the maintained markup in dollars by the sale price.

$$\$15 \div \$40 = .375$$
$$.375 = 37.5\%$$

Practice 6

Now try the same type of computation on your own.

A computer that costs Compco Industries $150 to stock sells for $350 (retail price). The firm wants to mark down the computer 30 percent. Determine the sale price and maintained markup in dollars. Then calculate the maintained markup percentage.

Real World

Markdowns Go Wireless

These days large merchandisers are just as likely to do a markdown with a handheld scanner as a pen and an inventory list. The latter procedure, which often took days for a large inventory, can now be done quickly by one person.

The process requires bar-coded price tags and installation of a wireless radio-frequency network. (The latter enables the store computer to send and receive information through the handheld scanners.)

To do a markdown, an employee simply scans a price tag's bar code to verify that the item should be marked down. After that, the scanner takes over. It counts the merchandise, prints and applies a new label, and reports back to the office (that is, the computer). The result? Employees can do markdowns in half the time—and that means more time for selling.

SECTION 31.1

1. Explain how a firm's net profit or loss is related to pricing.
2. How are the dollar and percentage markups based on cost and based on retail calculated? Use the following information to illustrate the formulas: cost of a book is **$5.85**, and retail price is **$10.99**.
3. Assume that an item that cost $25 and currently retails for $59.99 is going to be marked down 20 percent for a special sale. Calculate markdown in dollars, as well as the sale price and maintained markup in dollars and as a percent.

Section Review Answers

1. For a firm to be successful, its markup (like its gross profit on a profit and loss statement) must be high enough both to cover its expenses and provide the profit sought.
2. Dollar markup is the difference between cost and retail price; percentage markup on cost/retail is calculated by dividing the dollar markup by cost/retail price. Example: MU($):

   $10.99 − $5.85 = $5.14; MU(%) on cost: $5.14 ÷ $5.85 = .8786 = 87.9%; MU(%) on retail: $5.14 ÷ $10.99 = .4676 = 46.8%.
3. Markdown: $59.99 × .20 = $12. Sale price: $59.99 − $12 = $47.99. Maintained markup in dollars: $47.99 − $25 = $22.99. Maintained markup percentage: $22.99 ÷ $47.99 = .479 = 47.9%.

SECTION 31.2

Objectives

After completing this section, you will be able to

- describe the general procedure for figuring discounts and
- calculate various kinds of discounts.

Term to Know

- employee discounts

Discounts

Recall that a discount is a reduction in the price of goods and services sold to customers. Retailers offer discounts to their employees as a job benefit. Manufacturers and distributors offer discounts to their customers to encourage prompt payment and stimulate business.

The general procedure for calculating discounts involves two steps:

Step 1   Multiply the price (P) by the discount percentage [D(%)] to get the dollar amount of the discount [D($)].
$$P \times D(\%) = D(\$)$$

Step 2   Subtract the discount from the price to get the net price (NP), or the amount that the customer will actually pay.
$$P - D(\$) = NP$$

Employee Discounts

Businesses offer **employee discounts** to encourage workers to buy the products they sell or manufacture. Employees who buy and use their company's products project confidence in and enthusiasm about them. Employee discounts can range from 10 percent to 30 percent for entry-level employees and as high as 50 percent or more for top-level executives.

Discounts from Manufacturers and Distributors

Some common types of discounts offered by manufacturers and distributors are *cash, trade, quantity, seasonal,* and *promotional discounts,* all of which were explained in Chapter 30. This section is devoted to explaining how each of these types is calculated.

Cash Discounts   Consider the invoice terms *3/15, net 60.* Recall that the first number (3) represents the percentage of the discount applicable to the invoice total. If that total is $1,000 and the customer takes advantage of the discount, the calculations are as follows:

Step 1   Determine the dollar discount.
$$P \times D(\%) = D(\$)$$
$$\$1,000 \times .03 = \$30$$

Step 2   Determine the net price.
$$P - D(\$) = NP$$
$$\$1,000 - \$30 = \$970$$

Cash discounts can be calculated on a unit basis as well. For example, if there are 100 items at (@) $10 each listed on the invoice, the net unit cost is figured as follows:

Step 1   Determine the dollar discount.
$$P \times D(\%) = D(\$)$$
$$\$10.00 \times .03 = \$.30$$

Step 2   Determine the net price.
$$P - D(\$) = NP$$
$$\$10.00 - \$.30 = \$9.70$$

The net amount payable by the customer would still be the same, of course—$970 ($9.70 × 100).

Trade Discounts   Recall that trade discounts are based on manufacturers' list prices. They are calculated in the same way as cash discounts. For example, to figure a 40 percent trade discount for an invoice totaling $5,789, you would do the following:

Step 1   Determine the dollar discount.
$$P \times D(\%) = D(\$)$$
$$\$5,789.00 \times .40 = \$2,315.60$$

Step 2   Determine the net price.
$$P - D(\$) = NP$$
$$\$5,789.00 - \$2,315.60 = \$3,473.40$$

If an invoice contains several items, the trade discount is applied to each item separately to determine its net unit cost to the business.

Practice 7

Determine the amounts payable by the following customers.

1. Southbend Trucking receives an invoice in the amount of $25,000 showing the terms *2/10, net 30.* The invoice lists five trucks at $5,000 each. If Southbend takes advantage of the discount, what will be the net amount due on the invoice? the net price per truck?

2. A manufacturer gives retailers a 25 percent trade discount. If an invoice received by Frump's Department Store totals $7,650, what is the amount of the store's discount? What is the amount payable to the manufacturer?

Chapter 31   *Pricing Math*   **413**

Lifelong Learning

Pricing Math

Understanding and performing basic pricing calculations enhances the student's confidence as a future employee and as a consumer. Students should be encouraged to use these equations and not avoid math calculations at school or work. Repetition will increase familiarity, speed, and accuracy. Checking the math on invoices received at home or on the job can serve as a source of practice outside of class.

Cooperative Learning

Have students work in groups to develop their own quantity discount plan for the school store. Tell them that the markets they will be targeting are school sports teams and the parents sport association.

Tell students to begin their plan with specialized T-shirts designed for each targeted group. Note that the cost of the T-shirts to the school store is $10. Finally, suggest that they first determine the retail price for one T-shirt and then work out the details for the quantity discounts.

Groups should summarize their discount pricing plans in chart form. They should prepare a written report as well, spelling out the rationale for the plan.

Independent Practice

Have students sign up to interview the managers or personnel directors of selected retail stores in the community to learn about their employee discount policies. Areas of inquiry should include the discount percentage for entry-level employees, conditions of the discount, and what the store gains by offering discounts. Students should report their findings in written form.

Assess

Evaluation

Assign and review the Section 31.2 Review.

Reteaching

1. Assign and review the vocabulary terms for this section.
2. Assign and review Fact and Idea Review questions 7–10 from the Chapter Review.

414

BRIGHT IDEAS

Reinvent the Light Bulb

While reinventing the light bulb might not appear to be an ideal use of an inventor's time, it actually was a bright idea for Intersource Technologies, Inc. It developed the E-Lamp, a bulb that provides 14 years of continuous service!

Of course, such longevity comes at a price—a $15-per-bulb price. Customers who balk at paying that much should give some attention to the mathematics of the situation. They would save $15 over the first 3 years of the bulb's life and then go on to more than double their savings in the remaining 11 years.

It pays to look at existing products continually with an eye to refining and improving them. Without this creative ability, we would all still be listening to gramophones and cooking on wood stoves.

Creativity Challenge Form teams of 3–5 people, and "reinvent" something of your own. Select a product and brainstorm possible improvements. Start with small refinements and move step-by-step to major innovations. Where the latter are concerned, dare to be extravagant and farfetched.

Quantity Discounts Quantity discounts may be quoted as either a percentage of price or as part of a quantity price list like this:

No. of items	1-24	25-48	49-72
Unit price	$.95	$.90	$.85

Using the above list, if you purchased 50 items, you would pay $.85 each. Your total bill would be $42.50 ($.85 × 50).

Sometimes businesses offer cumulative quantity discounts, whereby a certain minimum purchase must be made during a specified period of time for the discount to be activated. For example, a firm may offer a 2 percent cumulative quantity discount to any company that purchases $3,000 worth of products in a six-month period. If a firm's purchases total $2,500 during that period, no discount is permitted. If they total $4,000, however, the discount is allowed. It would be calculated in the following manner:

Step 1 Determine the dollar discount.
$$P \times D(\%) = D(\$)$$
$$\$4,000 \times .02 = \$80$$

414 Unit 8 *Pricing*

Step 2 Determine the net price.
$$P - D(\$) = NP$$
$$\$4,000 - \$80 = \$3,920$$

Promotional Discounts Promotional discounts are given to businesses that agree to advertise or in some other way promote a manufacturer's products. When the promotional discount is quoted as a percentage, it is calculated the same way as a cumulative discount.

Sometimes, however, marketers are granted a dollar amount as a promotional discount. In such cases, they may want to determine the net purchase price or the percentage of the promotional discount for themselves. Consider an example. The Cycle Shop buys Speedo bicycles for $10,000 and is granted a $250 promotional discount for displaying the bikes in its store window during the month of March. To determine the percentage discount, follow these steps:

Step 1 Divide the dollar discount by the original price. The answer will be a decimal.
$$D(\$) \div P = D(\%)$$
$$\$250 \div \$10,000 = .025$$

Step 2 Change the decimal to a percentage. This figure is the percentage discount.
$$.025 = 2.5\%$$

Shift decimal point two places right.

The Wrong Stuff

Is there such a thing as the wrong gift? Where gift giving crosses cultural boundaries, there certainly is.

For example, clocks are not welcome gifts in China. They remind people (especially the elderly) of the passing of time and the inevitability of death. Sharp objects like knives and letter openers are disfavored in both China and Japan. In China they symbolize severed friendship. In Japan they are tantamount to a suggestion of suicide.

Food items are gifts of choice in many cultures but likewise offer some opportunities for offense. Take along a bottle of wine for dinner? Not if your host is Muslim. What about some steaks? In Japan they would be appreciated. In India they would not be. (The cow is a sacred animal in India.)

Finally, what about wrapping? In Europe flowers are always unwrapped before giving. In Japan, however, all gifts are wrapped—but skip the bows and ribbons. Crossed ribbons are thought to symbolize bad luck.

Bright Ideas

Discuss other circumstances in which consumers can be "penny-wise and pound-foolish" when evaluating whether or not to buy an item based on the price. (Answers will vary. One possibility: failing to consider larger sizes of grocery items which usually offer better prices per ounce, pound, etc., than smaller sizes.)

More About

Promotional Discounts

To secure shelf space for new food products, manufacturers are charged a stocking (or slotting) fee by some supermarket chains. Even an older product may have such a fee, especially if the manufacturer wants it in a specific shelf location. The supermarket industry refers to these fees as promotional discounts from the manufacturer.

Seasonal Discounts Sellers offer seasonal discounts to encourage buyers to purchase goods long before the actual consumer buying season. For example, purchasing Halloween costumes before July 31 and ski apparel before May 1 might qualify retailers for seasonal discounts.

Seasonal discounts are calculated in the same way as other discounts. Here is an example. Lobo, Inc., offers an 8 percent seasonal discount to all buyers who purchase Christmas decorations before August 1. If an order is placed on July 30 for $1,500 worth of decorations, the net purchase price is calculated as follows:

Step 1 Determine the dollar discount.

$$P \times D(\%) = D(S)$$
$$\$1,500 \times .08 = \$120$$

Step 2 Determine the net price.

$$P - D(\$) = NP$$
$$\$1,500 - \$120 = \$1,380$$

Practice 8

Now try these problems involving quantity, promotional, and seasonal discounts.

1. Suppose a firm is required to buy $10,000 worth of goods by September 15 in order to qualify for a 10 percent cumulative quantity discount. Would a firm that purchased $5,000 worth of goods by that date get the discount? What about one that purchased $10,005 worth?
2. A manufacturer offers a retailer $375 as a promotional discount for advertising a certain product. What is the percentage discount if the total invoice was $37,500?
3. Regal Shoe Company offers retailers a 7 percent discount for placing orders by May 1. A retailer takes advantage of the offer and purchases $10,630 worth of shoes by the cutoff date. What is the net amount payable on the invoice?

SECTION 31.2

Review

1. What procedures are used to calculate the dollar amount of a discount and the final selling price?
2. Carlo's Ice Cream Specialties gives all of its employees a 15 percent discount on ice cream cakes. If the price of a chocolate ice cream roll is $12.50, what would an employee pay for it?

Answers to Practice Set Problems

Practice 1 (page 408)
1. $37
2. $60

Practice 2 (page 408)
1. 100% on cost
   50% on retail
2. 25% on cost
   20% on retail
3. 33⅓% on cost
   25% on retail

Practice 3 (page 409)
1. 33%
2. 37.5%

Practice 4 (page 410)
1. Retail price $150
   Dollar markup $60
2. Retail price $87.50
   Dollar markup $52.50

Practice 5 (page 412)
Sale price $75

Practice 6 (page 412)
Sale price $245
Maintained dollar markup $95
Maintained percentage markup 38.8%

Practice 7 (page 413)
1. Net amount due on invoice $24,500
   Net price per truck $4,900
2. Store discount $1,912.50
   Amount payable to the manufacturer $5,737.50

Practice 8 (page 415)
1. For $5,000 in purchases—no discount
   For $10,005—10% discount
2. 1%
3. Net amount payable $9,885.90

---

3. To reteach the various kinds of discounts, give students clues associated with each type, and use their responses to construct a chalkboard list. For example:
   - 1–12 items—8 cents each, 13–20 items—6 cents each (quantity discount)
   - 15 percent off if you buy your back-to-school stock in May (seasonal discount)
   - 30 percent off anything you can wear on the job (employee discount)

Enrichment

1. Assign and review the appropriate activities in the *Student Activity Workbook*.
2. Assign the Unit 8 Activity in the *Marketing Math Workbook*.
3. Assign and review the appropriate Critical Thinking questions from the Chapter Review.
4. Assign and review the Building Academic Skills Activities, Application Projects, Linking School to Work Activity, and Performance Assessment from the Chapter Review.
5. Have students visit or call a stationery store, an auto parts store, a building supply company, or any retailer that sells goods to tradespeople. Have students inquire if the business offers trade discounts. If so, ask about the rate and any proof required to obtain them. Tell students to prepare an oral report for the class based on their findings.

Close

Have students name as many of the discounts associated with pricing as they can think of. (Employee, cash, trade, quantity, seasonal, and promotional.)

Did You Know ❓

Seasonal discounts are offered in an attempt to even out the peaks and valleys of manufacturing or producing a product. If everyone waited until November to order holiday products, for example, the units sold during that month would likely have a higher cost as a result of expenditures for overtime labor or materials purchased on a rush basis.

Section Review Answers

1. Multiply price by discount percentage to get dollar amount of discount; subtract discount amount from price to get net price (amount customer actually pays).
2. Discount amount: $12.50 × .15 = $1.87.
   Employee pays: $12.50 − $1.87 = $10.63.

Answers

Vocabulary Review

Examples will vary. See Glossary for definitions.

Fact and Idea Review

1. Cost + markup = retail price

2. Markup on retail sounds like a smaller amount and thus sounds better to customers. Future markdowns and discounts will be calculated on retail basis. Profits are generally calculated on sales revenue (total retail sales).

3. Retail Price: RP − C = MU($); MU($) ÷ RP = MU(%) on retail. Cost: RP − C = MU($); MU($) ÷ C = MU(%) on cost.

4. *Step 1:* Determine the dollar markup on cost by multiplying the cost by the percentage markup on cost in decimal form.
Step 2: Add the dollar markup to the cost to get the retail price.

5. *Step 1:* Determine what percentage of the retail price is equal to cost by subtracting the known retail markup figure from 100 percent.
Step 2: Divide the cost by the decimal equivalent of the percentage calculated in Step 1 to get the retail price.
Step 3: Calculate the dollar markup by subtracting the cost from the retail price.
Step 4: Check by multiplying the retail price calculated in Step 2 by the percentage markup on retail given originally.

6. To determine the maintained markup in dollars, subtract cost from the sale price. To determine the maintained markup percentage, divide the maintained markup in dollars by the sale price.

7. *Step 1:* Multiply price by discount percentage to get the

Vocabulary Review

Explain the meanings of the following terms by giving an example of each.

gross profit
maintained markup
employee discounts

Fact and Idea Review

1. What is the most basic formula you need in order to calculate retail price? (Sec. 31.1)

2. List three reasons why most wholesalers and retailers elect to compute their markup on the selling price. (Sec. 31.1)

3. What is the formula for calculating the percentage markup on retail price? on cost? (Sec. 31.1)

4. What steps are used to calculate prices according to the cost method? (Sec. 31.1)

5. What steps do marketers follow when using the retail method? (Sec. 31.1)

6. What steps do you follow to calculate maintained dollar markup and maintained percentage markup? (Sec. 31.1)

7. What is the two-step procedure for calculating a discount? (Sec. 31.2)

8. How do you calculate the price for a $20 item when taking a 2 percent cash discount into account? (Sec. 31.2)

9. Company A offers a cumulative discount of 5 percent on orders of $10,000 in a six-month period. During that period Company B purchases $8,000 in one order and $4,000 in another. What would be the dollar discount, if any, to Company B? Explain. (Sec. 31.2)

10. What is the formula for determining the percent of a promotional discount? (Sec. 31.2)

Critical Thinking

1. Why is a firm's net profit or loss related to pricing?

2. If a buyer wanted to buy goods that cost $100 and the customary markup on retail was 40 percent, what two methods could the buyer use to calculate the retail price? Explain.

3. Is the initial markup calculated for an item sometimes the same as the maintained markup? Explain.

4. If you were given a trade discount of 30 percent and a seasonal discount of 10 percent and you also took advantage of a cash discount of 2 percent, would you be entitled to a 42 percent discount? Explain.

Building Academic Skills

Math

1. If a dress costs a business $72 and the markup is $45, what is the retail price?

2. If a pair of slacks retails for $110 and the cost is $50, what is the markup?

3. If a hammer sells for $16.95 and its markup is $6.75, what is the cost?

4. If a wallet costs a business $27 and sells for $45, what is the percentage markup on cost? the percentage markup on retail?

5. If a stationery store sells greeting cards for $3.50 and pays $1.60 each for them, what is the percentage markup on retail? the percentage markup on cost?

6. What is the equivalent markup on cost for the following percentage markups on retail?
   a. 25.0 percent   d. 50.0 percent
   b. 23.1 percent   e. 40.0 percent
   c. 33.3 percent   f. 28.5 percent

7. A pencil sharpener that costs a business $12.50 has a markup of 62 percent on retail price. Use a retail box to calculate the sharpener's retail price and check your answer.

8. Determine the maintained markup in dollars for a bracelet that is to be marked down 25 percent from its original retail price of $35.99. The bracelet cost the business $18.

9. The dating terms on a $3,000 invoice are 3/10, net 30. If the buyer takes advantage of the cash discount, what will be the net amount due?

Human Relations

10. Employees are not permitted to let friends use their employee discounts. A co-worker asks you to ring up a sale for her and to apply her employee discount to the purchase. Normally, that would be okay. However, you noticed that your co-worker had been talking to a friend and that the friend had picked out the item that your co-worker is buying. What would you do?

Technology

11. Design a spreadsheet that calculates the markdowns and maintained markups (in both dollars and percents) for items that are marked down 20 percent, 25 percent, 30 percent, 35 percent, 40 percent, 45 percent, and 50 percent, respectively. You will need to include the cost and original retail price in your speadsheet design.

---

dollar amount of the discount.
Step 2: Subtract the dollar amount of the discount from the price to get the price the customer will actually pay.

8. $20 × .02 = $.40; $20 − $.40 = $19.60.

9. Company B would receive $600 in discounts ($400 on the first order and $200 on the second) posted retroactively to its account at the end of the six-month period. Neither order in and of itself qualified for the discount, but the

combined order puts the company over the $10,000 requirement.

10. D($) ÷ P = D(%)

Critical Thinking

1. Because both profit and loss depend on markups. To make a profit, a firm's markups must be high enough not only to cover expenses but also to leave a residual amount for profit. Loss occurs when markups fail to leave

Application Projects

1. For a one-week period, look through current magazines and newspapers for advertisements and notices of consumer discounts—for example, promotional, introductory, holiday, and end-of-season sales. For each ad or notice, write down the name of the discounter, the item discounted, the amount of the discount, and the original retail price (when included). At the end of the week, share your list with the class and discuss what conclusions can be drawn from your and other students' lists. For example, are certain types of products—say, electronic items—frequently discounted? Are there more sales on certain days of the week than on others?

2. Prepare a quantity price list for cookies you sell in your school store. Assume your cost to make and market one cookie is $.25. At present, you sell one cookie for $.50. You would like to increase the sales volume by offering a quantity discount. Prepare a quantity price list for cookies sold in multiples of 1-12, 13-24, 25-36, 37-48, and 49-plus. Be sure your quantity prices still generate a profit for the store. Provide a rationale for your list.

Linking School to Work

Interview the owner/manager of the business where you work concerning the use of computers to calculate prices. For a manufacturing or service concern, ask if your firm uses special software to determine the price for an item or a job. If so, ask what information must be input for the system to work. In a retail concern, ask if markups and markdowns are incorporated into the firm's computer system. If so, ask who is responsible for inputting the information and checking it for accuracy. Report your findings in both written and oral forms.

Performance Assessment

Role Play

Situation. As a sales associate in the men's department of an upscale department store, you have been given the assignment of pricing new cotton slacks. You notice that the recommended price for the slacks is considerably lower than usual. You were told to price the slacks at $26. You know that the customary markup on apparel is around 50 percent based on the retail price. The invoice indicates that the store paid $18 for these slacks. Before you price all the slacks, you decide to do

some calculations to see what the retail price should be. Armed with your calculations, you plan what you are going to say to the menswear buyer (who is working in your store today). Since you want to be accepted into the management training program, you are determined to impress the buyer with your knowledge of pricing methods and calculations when you meet with her.

Evaluation. You will be evaluated on how well you do the following:

- Explain how a firm's net profit or loss is related to pricing.
- Calculate dollar and percentage markup based on cost or retail.
- Communicate your knowledge of pricing in an organized and articulate fashion.

Oral Presentation

Research all the different ways businesses present markdowns to consumers. Some run sales and advertise those sales in newspapers and direct mail pieces. Others use coupons and rebates. Compare the methods, language, and calculations used to demonstrate the savings a consumer is getting with these markdowns. Contrast those consumer markdown methods with the types of discounts manufacturers and distributors offer retailers (cash discount, trade discount, quantity discount, promotional discount, and seasonal discount). Report your findings in an oral presentation to the class.

COMPUTER APPLICATION

Complete the Chapter 31 Computer Application that appears in the Student Activity Workbook.

Portfolio

Consider the Application Projects that you have done for this unit. Select one that illustrates your mastery of the unit's content and might be of interest to potential employers. Reformat the activity as necessary, adding any explanatory text, and place it in your Portfolio. Consider using these activities:

- Chapter 29, Application Project 2
- Chapter 30, Application Projects 1 and 3 ■■

---

this residual amount or even cover expenses.
2. The cost method, with the assistance of the equivalents table, or the retail method, which equates all figures to retail.
3. Yes, when no markdowns have been taken and no price increases have been made.
4. No, because discounts are taken in a series.

Applying Academic Skills

Math

1. $72 + $45 = $117
2. $110 − $50 = $60
3. $16.95 − $6.75 = $10.20
4. Percentage markup on cost: $45 − $27 = $18; $18 ÷ $27 = 66.7%.
   Percentage markup on retail: $45 − $27 = $18; $18 ÷ $45 = 40%.

5. Percentage markup on retail: $3.50 − $1.60 = $1.90; $1.90 ÷ $3.50 = 54.3%. Percentage markup on cost: $3.50 − $1.60 = $1.90; $1.90 ÷ $1.60 = 119%.
6. **a.** 33.3% **d.** 100%
   b. 30% **e.** 66.7%
   c. 50% **f.** 40%
7. Retail price: $12.50 ÷ .38 = $32.89.
   Check: $32.89 × .62 = $20.39.
8. $35.99 × .25 = $9; $35.99 − $9 = $26.99; $26.99 − $18 = $8.99.
9. $3,000 × .03 = $90; $3,000 − $90 = $2,910.

Human Relations

10. Remind your co-worker of the policy and decline to ring up the sale.

Technology

11. Spreadsheet design must include columns for all items mentioned in the problem.

Application Projects

1. Conclusions will depend on ads collected and analyzed.
2. Quantity price lists will vary.

Linking School to Work

Answers depend on the work situation.

Performance Assessment

Refer to the *DECA Competitive Events Handbook* for evaluation guidelines.

Computer Application

Optional Activity. Refer to the *Marketing Software Binder* for the template and user information.

Evaluation

Administer the reproducible test for Chapter 31, or construct your own using the Testmaker software.

Portfolio

Refer to the *Marketing Career Portfolio* for development ideas and portfolio management and assessment.

Marketing Information Management

Unit Objectives

After completing this unit, students will be able to achieve the following outcomes:

- Discuss the importance of marketing research in planning and implementing marketing strategies.
- Explain the function of a marketing information system.
- Describe four important areas of marketing research.
- Describe the five steps in conducting marketing research.
- Write research instruments.

Chapter 32

Chapter 33

Teacher Classroom Resources

CHAPTER	32	33
Transparency Binder	Transparencies 51–52	Transparencies 53–55
Student Activity Workbook	pp. 197–204	pp. 205–212
Student Software	pp. 203–204	pp. 211–212
Marketing Math Workbook		Activity 9
School-to-Work Handbook	pp. 69–70	pp. 71–72
International Case Studies	pp. 69–70	pp. 71–72
Marketing Career Portfolio		Unit 9 activity, Student Text, p. 445
Test Booklet/ Testmaker Software	Chapter 32 test	Chapter 33 test, Unit 9 test

KEY TO BASIC SKILLS ACTIVITIES

L1 Level 1 activities are basic activities and should be within the range of all students.

L2 Level 2 activities are average activities and should be within the range of average and above average students.

L3 Level 3 activities are challenging activities designed for the ability range of above average students.

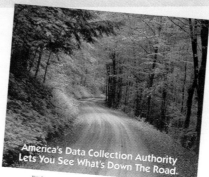

America's Data Collection Authority Lets You See What's Down The Road.

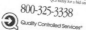

CHAPTER	PERFORMANCE OBJECTIVES
32 **Marketing Research**	**32.1** 1. Discuss the importance of marketing research. 2. Explain the function of a marketing information system. **32.2** 1. Describe four important areas of marketing research. 2. Define test marketing. 3. Identify several important trends affecting marketing research. 4. Explain the limitations of marketing research.
33 **Conducting Marketing Research**	**33.1** 1. Describe the five steps in conducting marketing research. 2. Explain the difference between primary and secondary data. 3. Name methods used to collect primary and secondary data. **33.2** 1. Write research instruments. 2. Describe the ways the computer is used in research.

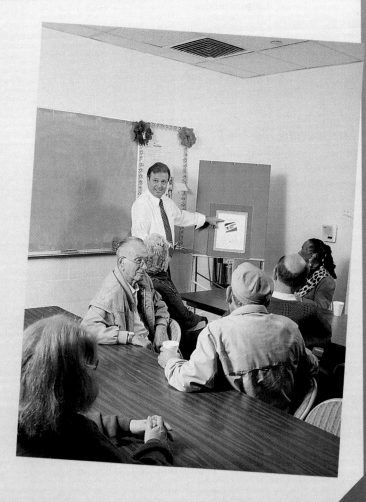

Unit Overview and Background Information

Unit 9 explores marketing information management—its importance, the major areas of marketing research, the steps performed in the marketing research process, and how marketing information systems can assist in the solution of problems businesses face today.

Chapter 32 introduces marketing research—the process of getting the marketing information needed to make sound business decisions through the systematic gathering, recording, and analyzing of data about problems relating to the marketing of products. Chapter 33 defines the five steps in the marketing research process: problem definition, obtaining data, data analysis, recommending solutions to the problem, and implementing the findings. The chapter also identifies the importance of marketing information systems.

Introducing the Unit

Ask students how they think their co-op training stations make decisions about when to introduce new products and delete old ones. Solicit answers from students working in various industries. For example, what factors made McDonald's investigate the possibility of adding low-calorie salads to its menu? Have students speculate on the ways that companies get information about their markets; make a chalkboard list of their answers.

Unit Project

If your program has a school store, have students develop a research study to determine the market potential for products to be offered in the store. They should develop the survey, conduct the research, analyze the data, and report the findings to the school administration.

418

Focus on the Photo/Cooperative Learning

Once students have completed this unit, divide the class into four teams. Assign each team one of the four specialized areas of marketing research: market research, advertising, product, and sales research. Ask each group to come up with a list of ten generic questions that could be used to gather information on a product (new or existing) from the point of view of their particular specialization.

Marketing Information Management

CHAPTERS

32
Marketing Research

33
Conducting Marketing Research

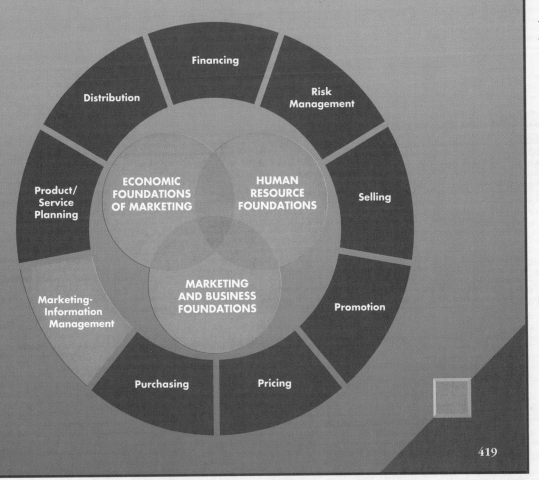

Financing

Distribution

Risk Management

Product/ Service Planning

ECONOMIC FOUNDATIONS OF MARKETING

HUMAN RESOURCE FOUNDATIONS

Selling

Marketing-Information Management

MARKETING AND BUSINESS FOUNDATIONS

Promotion

Purchasing

Pricing

419

Magazines/Journals

- *Advertising Age*
- *Business Week*
- *Fortune*
- *Grocery Marketing*
- *Inc.*
- *Journal of Advertising*
- *Journal of Marketing Research*
- *Marketing News*
- *Marketing Research Review*
- *Mass Market Retailers*
- *Research Alert*
- *Research in Marketing*
- *Sales and Marketing Management*
- *Stores*
- *The Wall Street Journal*

Associations

American Marketing Association
250 S. Wacker Drive, Ste. 200
Chicago, IL 60606
(312) 648-0536

Marketing Research Association
111 East Wacker Drive
Suite 600
Chicago, IL 60601
(312) 644-6610

Unit Closure

Make sure students understand the importance of marketing research in making sound business decisions, and that marketing research is a process in which the steps must be followed sequentially to obtain the best results. Have students create a visual representation of the marketing research process and the various types of marketing research. Display their work on the bulletin board.

Evaluation

Administer the printed test for Unit 9, or construct your own using the Testmaker software.

Guest Speaker Suggestions

- Have a representative from an industry trade association discuss how the association collects and uses industry data.
- Invite the marketing research director of a retail store or advertising agency to discuss recent marketing research studies conducted, data-gathering methods used, and solutions to marketing problems.

Field Trip Suggestions

- Have students observe a consumer test panel conducted by a local business.
- Have students visit a marketing research firm or marketing research department of a local business. They should have the opportunity to interview various personnel, discuss recent research projects and cost of services, and any other relevant information.

Chapter Overview

Chapter 32 introduces the world of marketing research and its increasing importance in our competitive marketplace.

 Springboard

Bring in several different brands of a commonly used product such as shampoo. Have students tell you the features, benefits, and target market of each. Ask students how the marketers of these products determined a marketplace need for them. (They use *marketing research.*)

Tell students that marketers use research (1) to determine the effectiveness of their advertising (*advertising research*), (2) to gauge customer acceptance of product design and usage (*product research*), (3) to obtain data through customer and market analysis (*market research*), and (4) to determine the potential sales for a product (*sales research*).

Prereading

List the section objectives to discuss with students. Have students skim the chapter, looking at the pictures, reading the captions, and noting the heads. Ask questions to ensure that the students have a minimal understanding of the chapter structure.

Preteaching the Vocabulary

Write the remaining vocabulary words that were not introduced in the Springboard Activity on the chalkboard. Students should generate definitions for each.

CHAPTER 32

Marketing Research

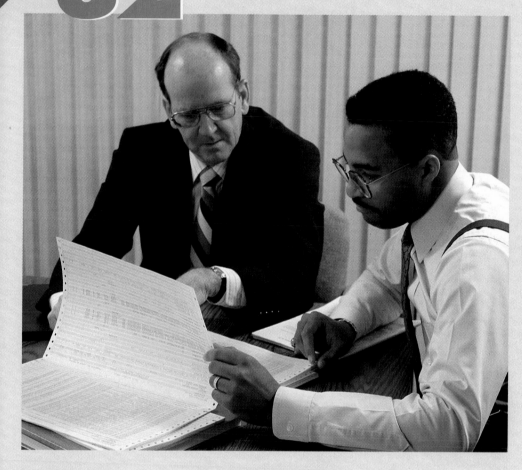

Successful business planning requires information about potential target markets, the competition, individual customers, and their reactions to products. As a result, more and more decisions in our increasingly competitive marketplace are being based on the results of marketing research.

Marketing research takes much of the guesswork out of business operations by providing pertinent information for making sound business decisions. In this chapter, you will read about marketing research. You will also learn about the various types of marketing research and why they are so important to business success.

420   Unit 9   *Marketing Information Management*

Classroom Management

For the Teacher

- Teacher's Annotated Editions of all workbooks
- Teacher's Manual for *School-to-Work Handbook*
- *Testing Binder*
- *Transparency Binder*
- *Marketing Software Binder*
- *Marketing Career Portfolio*
- *Lesson Plans*

For the Student

- *Student Activity Workbook*
- *Marketing Math Workbook*
- *School-to-Work Handbook*
- *Student Software*
- *International Case Studies*
- *Marketing Career Portfolio*

SECTION 32.1

Objectives

After completing this section, you will be able to

- discuss the importance of marketing research and
- explain the function of a marketing information system.

Terms to Know

- marketing research
- marketing information system
- database

What Is Marketing Research?

Marketing research involves the systematic gathering, recording, and analyzing of information about problems related to marketing goods and services. Marketing research can apply to any area of marketing. For example, an apparel manufacturer introducing a new product line might research the potential sales and market for the

Real World

MR Makes Mr. Clean Smile

Everyone sits and quietly molds figures out of modeling clay. This is not a scene from a kindergarten. It is a Motivational Research (MR) session at an ad agency. At this session, consumers have been asked to show their feelings toward a product by making a clay figure of the person they see the product to be. Does MR work? Well, when consumer feedback convinced makers of Mr. Clean to lose the character's menacing scowl, sales of the cleanser boomed.

product line. That same apparel manufacturer could determine the effectiveness of an advertising campaign for the new product line by researching customer response to its ads.

The primary emphasis of marketing research is to obtain information about the preferences, opinions, habits, trends, and plans of potential customers. Research helps businesses determine what customers want and need. This information helps marketers in many ways. For example, before developing a product, marketers can conduct research to determine the type of product customers want. The research can minimize losses or potential losses when introducing the new product. Gaining information about consumer likes and dislikes is significant since only one out of every ten new products introduced into the marketplace is accepted by consumers.

Why Is Marketing Research Important?

Given the huge failure rate of new products to gain consumer acceptance, marketing research can make or break a business. The major goal of any business is to increase sales and profits. Businesses that do not pay attention to what consumers are buying are likely to make costly marketing mistakes.

The information obtained from research helps businesses plan their future operations to try to increase sales and profits. Research helps to answer questions such as these: What products should be produced? Where should the products be sold? How will the products be promoted? At what price will the products sell?

Research also helps businesses solve marketing problems or anticipate future marketing problems. For example, a few years ago McDonald's changed its hamburger containers from space-age plastic boxes to paper wrappers in response to consumers who wanted packaging that was safer for the environment.

Research also helps a company keep track of what is happening in its markets. Through research, a company can determine its major competitors, what its competitors are offering, and what products consumers prefer.

Who Uses Marketing Research?

Marketing research is valuable for organizations of any size. The size of the business, though, may affect how it conducts the research. Small businesses that do less than $5 million in annual sales usually do not have separate

Discussion Starter

Ask students to determine what kind of customer information the following companies would maintain in their databases:

- a mail-order company offering gardening supplies and seeds (the seasonal climate where customers live, what types of seeds they buy at certain times of the year, whether they buy more flower seeds than vegetable seeds and vice versa, what types of supplies they buy most, what additional merchandise they request most);
- a small publisher that specializes in producing works of fiction (the type of fiction customers are buying—poetry, novels, mysteries, or short stories; which authors' books they buy most; whether they're buying softcover or hardback texts; how often they purchase books and in what quantities);
- a real estate office (customers' average incomes, the prices of their current homes, length of time in and size of their current homes, number of people in each family, the number of times they have purchased a new home in the past several years).

Independent Practice

1. Have students contact a local small business which is not their co-op work station to determine (1) what type of marketing research information the business maintains (for example, company records, competitors' records, customer profile data, and government data), and (2) how this information is stored and used. Have students write their findings in 150 to 200 words and share them with the class. Did they find that small businesses kept significantly less or significantly more information than they expected?

422

research departments. Here, marketing research is done informally by the owners, managers, or other employees.

Larger companies have formal research departments and specialists to plan and conduct marketing research. Some larger companies contract with marketing research companies to research special marketing related problems.

The top 50 marketing research firms in the United States had combined worldwide revenues of $3.7 billion in 1993. About $2.4 billion was spent that year on marketing research in the United States alone.

Individual businesses are not the only organizations that find marketing research valuable. Several departments in both the state and federal governments and trade associations representing various manufacturers, wholesalers, and retailers conduct marketing research. For example, industry trade associations, such as the National Retail Merchants Association, collect industry data to help their members understand the markets for their products. The Consumer Product Safety Commission, a government

America's Data Collection Authority Lets You See What's Down The Road.

How do you avoid those potholes? Is that a fork in the road ahead, or a dead end?

When you need to anticipate what's down the road, you need accurate research data. QCS gives you a road map of consistent, dependable information.

And now, QCS offers complete project management services, to make your job even easier!

With nearly 40 focus group suites, over 15 mall intercept locations, 500+ telephone interviewing stations, and more than 25 test kitchens, QCS is national in scope, but neighborhood-friendly when it comes to personal service.

At QCS, you won't get lost—and you'll get where you're going a lot faster. Call QCS today for a bid on your next project.

800-325-3338

Quality Controlled Services®

ADFAX INQUIRY #1110

*Some large companies **contract with marketing research companies, such as Quality Controlled Services, to help them solve marketing related problems. What special services does this particular company advertise?***

422 Unit 9 *Marketing Information Management*

agency, tests products to make certain they are safe for consumer use and to give consumers product information for use in making buying decisions.

Marketing Information Systems

In order to conduct marketing research, businesses need an organized way of collecting information. Many businesses have implemented sophisticated *marketing information systems* to organize, collect, and store marketing research data for future decisions. A **marketing information system** is a set of procedures and methods that regularly generates, stores, analyzes, and distributes marketing information.

Collecting useful marketing research data on a continuous basis provides marketers with information necessary to plan and implement marketing strategies. Data that should be a part of a marketing information system include:

- company records, such as sales results, expenses, and supplier data;
- competitors' records, such as their prices, location, and market share;
- customer profile data, such as the results of previous marketing studies regarding buying behavior, shopping patterns, and lifestyles research; and
- government data, such as price trends and future projections for the economy.

Marketing Databases

Computers have made the collection and analysis of data for marketing decision making much easier. For example, barcode scanners at point-of-sale terminals provide information not only on the merchandise that consumers are buying but also on inventory levels.

Information about consumers and their buying habits is stored in computer databases. A **database** is a collection (or file) of related information about a specific topic. For example, L. L. Bean, a sportswear and outdoor products retailer, has a database of the people to whom it sends its catalogs. American Express maintains a database not only of its card members and their addresses, but also of what they buy, where they buy it, restaurants they eat in, and how much they spend. The company uses the information to send their card members special offers on hotels, restaurants, and travel.

Many companies that collect information about their customers sell that information to others. For example, banks that provide mortgage loans might sell the names and addresses of the borrowers to insurance companies that then send information on buying mortgage insurance to the borrower. Such exchange of information among businesses has led to complaints of invasion of privacy since consumers don't know what information is

Did You Know

If students need the U.S. Census for a class project, and the document is not carried at a local library, instruct students to ask the local librarian for the location of the closest government depository library. Such libraries typically serve large academic publics and have a separate government librarian to organize the massive number of publications issued by the government.

contained about them in various databases. Marketers, however, defend the need to have information about their customers and their buying habits.

Difficulties of Marketing Information Systems

Setting up a marketing information system requires a significant investment of time and money. Trained personnel are needed to maintain them and to analyze the data collected for and kept in the system. Because computerized data collection is so easy, businesses sometimes have to wade through vast amounts of information to find something that is useful to their operations. However, even small businesses today are recognizing the need for marketing information systems if they are to remain competitive.

When in Paris—Have a Taco!

One of the fastest-growing trends in Paris is eating Tex-Mex cuisine. Where once there were only two Tex-Mex eateries in the city, today there are 200, with new ones opening every month.

Why the burst of popularity? It's not so much that the French like the taste of spicy Tex-Mex food but that they like the idea of it. They have taken to eating *fajitas* in the same way they have taken to wearing jeans and baseball caps—as a way to feel more American.

Interesting problems arise, however, when French diners are faced with the realities of Tex-Mex cuisine. Restaurants have learned to provide instructions for assembling *fajitas* and *tacos*, and illustrations showing how to eat them. They have also learned to cope with more awkward questions in a tactful manner. The most frequent question of this sort? "Where's the bread?" The answer? "Here it is. It's called a *tortilla*."

SECTION 32.1 *Review*

1. What is marketing research?
2. How does marketing research help businesses?
3. What is a marketing information system?

SECTION 32.2

Objectives

After completing this section, you will be able to

- describe four important areas of marketing research,
- identify several important trends affecting marketing research, and
- explain the limitations of marketing research.

Terms to Know

- advertising research
- product research
- test marketing
- market research
- sales research

Types of Marketing Research

The type of research marketers conduct depends on the problem they are trying to solve. Some of the most significant areas of research are

- advertising research,
- product research,
- market research, and
- sales research.

Sometimes more than one type of research must be conducted to solve a particular problem. In addition, data collected from one study can often be used to solve other business problems relating to the marketing of products.

Advertising Research

Advertising research focuses on the advertising message and media. It is designed to measure two things. One is the effectiveness of the advertising message. The other is the effectiveness of media placement.

Testing the Advertising Message The effectiveness of an advertising message can be tested before the ad is run. For example, marketing researchers can use

Chapter 32 *Marketing Research* **423**

SECTION 32.1

2. Assign and review the Chapter 32 Case Study in the *International Case Studies* workbook.

Assess

Evaluation

Assign and review the Section 32.1 Review.

Reteaching

1. Assign and review the vocabulary terms for this section.
2. Assign and review Fact and Idea Review questions 1–4 from the Chapter Review.
3. Have students tell you, in their own words, why marketing research is important.

Enrichment

1. Assign and review the appropriate activities in the *Student Activity Workbook*.
2. Assign and review the appropriate Critical Thinking questions from the Chapter Review.
3. Have students do library research on one of the top 50 marketing research firms in this country and report on the following: (1) where the firm is located, (2) its major clients or specific type of clients, (3) areas of marketing research specialization, and (4) recent marketing research campaigns.

Close

Have students complete this statement: Marketing research involves...(the systematic gathering, recording, and analyzing of information about problems related to marketing goods and services.)

Section Review Answers

1. Marketing research involves the systematic gathering, recording, and analyzing of information and data about problems related to marketing goods and services.
2. Research helps businesses to plan their future operations to try to increase sales and profits.
3. A marketing information system is a set of procedures and methods that regularly generates, stores, analyzes, and distributes marketing information.

Focus

Bell Ringer Activity

Tell students to imagine that they are a marketing research panel of consumers who are to evaluate the effectiveness of package design (as is done in product research). Hold up two different brands of the same product, each with different packaging. Ask students the following questions about each package: What do you like about the packaging? Color or lack of it? Artistic treatment? The fact that you immediately know the product's features and benefits? What specifically do you dislike about this packaging? Would you change anything about the packaging? If so, what? Would this packaging induce you to pick up this product over the other brands next to it? Why or why not?

Introducing the Section

Discuss students' answers to the Bell Ringer Activity. Consumer panels are used to test reactions to products, product packaging, and advertising. But this exercise shows how subjective customer preferences can be. Some of these panel members may offer entirely different responses to the marketers' questions on a different day. This is why marketers rely on three other types of marketing research in addition to product research.

Write the names of each type of research on the board. (Advertising research, product research, market research, and sales research.) Tell students that in this section they will learn in detail about each of these areas.

a consumer panel to get people's reactions to an advertisement. Consumer panels are groups of people who are questioned periodically or who provide information on research issues. For example, Chrysler Corporation used a consumer panel to evaluate its ads for the new Neon that were televised during the 1994 Super Bowl. The company wanted to know whether its message was being communicated in a way that helped viewers remember the details of the message.

A consumer panel can be composed of a cross section of people. It can also be composed of people who share common characteristics—senior citizens, single parents, college-educated adults, or teenagers, for example. Oral, written, or observed behavioral responses are recorded to indicate panel members' reactions to the ad.

A common technique to study how effectively a message has been delivered is asking panel members if they recall having seen or read an advertisement. They can also be asked how they were influenced by the ad and whether they were motivated to buy the advertised product as a result. For example, Farberware conducted advertising research for a new microwavable coffeemaker to help determine which product attributes should be the basis for its advertising campaign.

Researching the Medium Businesses also want to find out information about various types of media. Important data on broadcast advertising is assembled by the

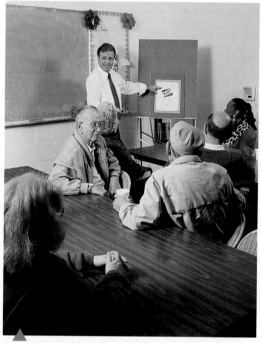

Consumer panels *can be used to test the effectiveness of an advertising message. What kinds of questions should the interviewer ask panel members if testing their reaction to this ad after it is run?*

Arbitron Ratings Company, a subsidiary of the Control Data Corporation. Arbitron produces radio, television, and cable audience measurements and advertising expenditure data. Continuous audience measurement in more than 260 markets makes it the largest radio audience service in the world. In TV audience measurement, the company measures over 200 U.S. markets by using people meter panels, household meter panels, and mail diaries at the local market level.

Mail diaries are records on which people report such viewer data as who is watching or listening to a station and what programs are tuned in. In meter-equipped households, devices attached to the television sets automatically monitor the type, time, and frequency of program viewing. By providing an estimate of the size and kind of audience that will be reached, Arbitron can help businesses decide on which television or radio program to advertise.

Magazines also collect information about their subscribers through surveys. Research can help determine which magazines are most effective for getting an advertising message to a particular market.

Product Research

Product research centers on evaluating product design and acceptance, competitive products, package design, and product usage. Many new products are designed, tested, changed, and introduced each year. Product research measures new and old product acceptance by consumers. It also identifies opportunities to meet changing customer needs.

Have you or your family ever received a small sample box of cereal in the mail? If so, you were participating in product research. Companies often send samples, usually accompanied by a cents-off coupon, to consumers to determine whether they like a product well enough to buy it.

One method of collecting data on products is through test marketing. **Test marketing** occurs when a new product is placed in one or more selected geographic areas. Test marketing allows marketers to test customer response to a product and to observe a product's sales performance. In the new product development stage, products are test marketed in limited areas. The results of the test marketing help the product manufacturer determine whether the product needs changes before it is introduced to the entire country. For example, Coca-Cola is using selected areas to test market a new soft drink, OK soda. This new soft drink is targeted toward 12- to 25-year-olds and will be expanded to a national market if the test market results are successful.

One concern that businesses have about test marketing is that it offers competitors a chance to see new products before they may be ready for a national introduction. Competitors can also try to influence the test results by running special advertising and promotions on their own products. Technology may offer the solution to that problem. A company called MarketWare Simulation Services has introduced a program called Visionary

---

Caption Answer

Have you ever seen this ad? Did you buy or avoid the product as a result of it?

More About

Marketing Research

To locate trade associations for class projects or to conduct actual marketing research, ask the librarian to locate a copy of *Encyclopedia of Associations* published by Gale Research Inc. of Detroit, MI on an annual basis. This source publishes an alphabetical list of trade associations both domestic and international.

Shopper. A computer program allows individuals in a research group to see many different products on screen, including existing products and the new test product. Viewers are able to read the sides and backs of packages and to make choices about which products to put in their on-screen shopping carts. The program tallies the group's responses to different products and gives its clients test market results via computer.

BRIGHT IDEAS

Ask Why

Du Pont, the chemical company, regularly uses marketing research to find out what customers think of its products. On one survey a researcher thought to ask, "Why did you choose our product over the competition's?" From the answers received, the company discovered that its products were bought by customers because they believed the products to be in some way better or purer than those of the competition's.

Du Pont decided to use this information to create a new advertising campaign. The advertising message was that Du Pont took special care to assure purity in the manufacture of its products. Print advertisements featured photos of white-coated scientists performing quality assurance checks in sparkling clean laboratories.

In the aftermath of the campaign, Du Pont's market share rose to a new high. The company had learned the pleasant way that if you ask why, you can be surprised by the answer. And if you're in a business that takes its marketing research seriously, you can turn what you learn into higher profits.

Creativity Challenge Break into teams of 3–5 people, and speculate about the kinds of distinctions consumers routinely make among similar products. Why do they choose a particular brand of batteries or canned vegetables or athletic shoes? Using one of these items or a product of your own choice, develop a list of reasons for a particular preference. Then, test that list. Devise a simple survey (written or oral) to find out what consumers really think. Use your classmates as a test group. Any surprises? Any ideas for capitalizing on them?

Market Research

Market research focuses on the customer and the market. It uses customer and market analysis to obtain data.

Customer analysis is the study of customer behavior. Questionnaires and interviews are used to gather information about customer attitudes, especially those relating to motivation to buy. Figure 32-1 on page 426 shows a questionnaire used in market research.

Market analysis is the study of the behavior of a consumer market. The goal of market analysis is to investigate the potential markets for a product and to define characteristics of the target market.

Market research also monitors major societal and population trends that can affect the development of new goods and services. To do this, researchers must note significant changes in population trends, lifestyles, and demographics. One significant recent trend is the increase in the over-55 segment of the U.S. population. Many goods and services are changing in response to this aging of the population. As people age, for example, they usually become increasingly health conscious and aware of diet. Food manufacturers have responded by producing foods that are low in fat, low in sodium, high in fiber, and calcium or vitamin enriched.

Sales Research

Sales research is the study of sales data. The goal of sales research is to determine the potential sales for a product and to solve problems related to future sales. Sales trends for various products may also be compared to determine whether a product's sales are increasing or declining.

Sales Forecasting *Sales forecasting* is an effort to estimate the future sales of a product. A total estimate of a market is calculated, and then an individual share is predicted for a business.

The share assigned to a business is called its *market share* or *sales penetration* of the market. Based on its research findings, the business can then try to increase its market share through changes in the product, pricing, promotion, or distribution.

Economic Forecasting *Economic forecasting* is an attempt to predict the future general economic conditions of a city, a region, the country, or another part of the world. This research requires extensive knowledge of economic statistics and trend indicators.

Several federal agencies collect information on key economic indicators, such as new building construction, inflation rates, money supply, and consumer and producer price indexes. Most businesses rely on government data to predict economic conditions and to adjust their business activities depending on the economic outlook.

Businesses use research on general economic conditions to help them plan for long-range expansion or to cut costs when unfavorable economic conditions, such as higher interest rates or raw materials costs, are forecast.

Chapter 32 *Marketing Research* **425**

Teach

Guided Practice

1. Read Section 32.2 with students.
2. Use the transparencies for this section.
3. Try to obtain copies of the following for students to peruse: a mail diary for recording television viewing, a magazine subscriber survey, a product sample with a cents-off coupon mailed to one's home.
4. Have students read aloud the Case Study and review the answers in class.
5. Assign and review the Chapter 32 Activity in the *School-to-Work Handbook*.

Discussion Starter

Have students imagine that they own a small business and don't have enough money to pay a marketing research firm. How would they conduct marketing research on their advertising? On trends in the community that they could address with their marketing mix? On demographics? On customer satisfaction with their product? (Answers could include casually talking to customers as they find merchandise in the store, asking customers to fill out comment cards or surveys before they leave the store, sending out informal customer surveys with an incentive to return them such as a percentage off of a product, asking customers as they check-out how they learned of the business, recording customers' zip codes when they check out so you can see where you may need to target more of your marketing effort, and monitoring customer response to coupons or specials in your newspaper advertising.)

Bright Ideas

The concept of purity and cleanliness is a useful marketing tool for companies specializing in food preparation and/or service, as well as drug manufacturers because consumers want to assume that their products are produced in a clean environment. Have students think of other companies who could use the Du Pont method of highlighting their standards of cleanliness in their marketing materials.

Critical Thinking

Have students name some positive and negative economic indicators in your community. Based on their answers, have them make some predictions about the future economic conditions in your town or city and region. What products are people in your community and in your region likely to need more of and less of in one year? In five years?

Cooperative Learning

Divide students into four groups: one for *advertising research*, one for *product research*, one for *market research*, and one for *sales research*. Each group will contribute to a marketing research bulletin board which features key terms, phrases, and visuals that combine to explain and illustrate the purpose of each type of marketing research.

Allow each group to generate five to ten key terms and visuals for the bulletin board. Give them magic markers and paper. Allow them to cut pictures and ads from magazines and newspapers. For example, to illustrate advertising research, they could (1) cut out an ad and (2) write the terms *effectiveness of the advertising message* and *effectiveness of media placement*, etc.

After all the information has been placed on the bulletin board, a spokesperson from each group should explain why each written element and visual element was chosen.

FMB - MAYNARD ALLEN BANK
Customer Satisfaction Survey

(1-4)

1) Do you consider FMB to be your primary or main banking institution?

Yes ☐1   No ☐2   (5)

2) Which of the following categories best describes how long you have been a customer of FMB? (✔ One Box)

Less than 1 year ☐1	10 to just under 15 years ☐5	
1 to just under 3 years ☐2	15 to just under 20 years ☐6	(6)
3 to just under 5 years ☐3	20 years or more ☐7	
5 to just under 10 years ☐4		

3A) What is the location of the FMB branch office which you use most often? (✔ One Box)

1235 E. Bridge Street, Portland ☐1   105 W. Main Street, Westphalia ☐4

175 Kent Street, Portland ☐2   Other (please list):

145 Main Street, Sunfield ☐3   _____ ☐5   (7)

3B) During a typical month, approximately how many times do you visit the FMB branch office which you use most often?

(IF NONE WRITE IN "0") _____ TIMES   (8-9)

3C) Is this branch office closest to: (✔ One Box)

Your Home ☐1   Your Work ☐2   Where You Shop ☐3   Other ☐4   (10)

3D) How do you usually access bank services? (✔ One Box)

Within the branch office ☐1	Walk-up ATM ☐4	
Drive-thru teller ☐2	Mail ☐5	(11)
Drive-thru ATM ☐3	Telephone ☐6	

4) Please ✔ no more than *two (2) boxes* that indicate the times you would most **prefer** to do business with your FMB branch office (such as deposits, withdrawals, account openings, or loan applications). (✔ Only Two Boxes)

	7:30 AM to 9:00 AM	9:00 AM to 12:00 Noon	12:00 Noon to 5:00 PM	5:00 PM to 6:00 PM	6:00 PM to 8:00 PM
Monday through Thursday	☐12	☐15	☐18	☐21	☐24
Friday	☐13	☐16	☐19	☐22	☐25
Saturday	☐14	☐17	☐20	☐23	☐26

5A) In general, how satisfied are you with the service provided at the FMB branch office you use most often? (✔ One Box)

Very Satisfied	☐4	Somewhat Dissatisfied	☐2
Somewhat Satisfied	☐3	Very Dissatisfied	☐1	(27)

5B) How has your level of satisfaction with your FMB branch office changed over the last 12 months? (✔ One Box)

Increased ☐1   Stayed The Same ☐2   Decreased ☐3   (28)

Figure 32–1

Questionnaires such as this are frequently used in customer analysis. What kinds of information can be provided to the bank through the use of this questionnaire?

Trends in Marketing Research

The nature and scope of marketing research are rapidly changing to keep pace with a changing marketplace. The United States is a huge market with many goods and services for almost any consumer need or want. The trend toward a global marketplace means increased international competition for U.S. companies, which must improve or change products frequently to hold on to their customers. In this environment, product quality and customer satisfaction are the key to business success. Research that measures these qualities has become the fastest growing form of marketing research.

Caption Answer

How satisfied customers are with the bank's services and ways in which the bank can improve its services along with information regarding how often the customer uses the bank's services and which location the customer is referring to in the survey.

CASE STUDY

CD-ROM: The Hot New Research Tool

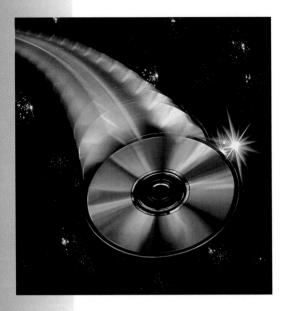

CD-ROM technology is the latest tool being used by marketing researchers. CD-ROM makes hard-to-find data easier to acquire. In addition, it can be obtained for less money than traditional marketing research studies.

Although CD-ROM publishing is a $1.7 billion industry, the technology is only a small part of the estimated $29 billion spent by marketers for business information. Compared to other forms of information delivery, though, CD-ROM is the second fastest growing medium.

CD-ROM is becoming increasingly popular with researchers because the cost of CD-ROM drives is decreasing, and there are more comprehensive marketing databases that are available on CD-ROM disks. In addition, information once stored on many diskettes or reels of computer tape can now be stored on a single compact disk.

Currently, more than 6,000 CD-ROM titles are available. These titles cover almost every marketing subject, including census data and demographics, advertising, telephone and mailing lists, and general marketing topics.

Companies, such as The Standard Rate and Data Service, have placed their business and consumer magazine directories on separate single compact disks. Now media buyers can find circulation numbers, reader demographics, and ad size specifications in minutes. This information is then used to buy advertising space in magazines targeted toward their customers.

The data on CD-ROMs can help companies learn more about their customers and the marketplace. Marketing researchers can find information on consumer purchase behavior and consumer attitudes. They can also search business data for Standard Industry Codes, employee size, sales volumes, and persons to contact for additional information. Reports that once took months to complete can now be done in a matter of hours.

Demographic and lifestyle information can be obtained by state, county, zip codes, and metropolitan statistical areas. Using commercially available Windows software with the CD-ROM databases, companies can conduct market research, advertising and media appraisals, site and territory evaluations, and direct marketing.

Business software titles can range from $200 to more than $5,000. Many can be purchased for a one-time fee or leased on a subscription basis.

While the costs of using sophisticated CD-ROM databases may be high, the ease and speed of obtaining the information needed may be worth the price. Many marketing researchers believe that CD-ROM technology is worth the cost because it saves time that would otherwise be spent in libraries or searching for information on online data services.

CD-ROMs are improving the way we conduct research. They allow researchers to access large databases, perform research, and ultimately, make more intelligent marketing decisions.

Case Study Review

1. What is the primary advantage to CD-ROM technology?
2. Why are some businesses willing to pay high costs for subscription service software systems coupled with CD-ROM technology?

A MATTER OF ETHICS

3. Many people are wary of marketers having vast databases on customer characteristics. What ethical obligations do you think the marketing research industry has to the public?

Chapter 32 *Marketing Research* **427**

Evaluation

Assign and review the Section 32.2 Review.

Reteaching

1. Assign and review the vocabulary terms for this section.
2. Assign and review Fact and Idea Review questions 5-10 from the Chapter Review.
3. Use the Concept Mapping Activity in the Chapter Review to help students identify the key concepts underlying marketing research.

Enrichment

1. Assign and review the appropriate activities in the *Student Activity Workbook*.
2. Assign and review the appropriate Critical Thinking questions from the Chapter Review.
3. Assign and review the Building Academic Skills Activities, Application Projects, Linking School to Work Activities, and Performance Assessment from the Chapter Review.

Figure 32-2

RESEARCH TRENDS

Business trends affect the nature of marketing research.

Data Integration ▼

Increasingly, marketing research is integrated with other data sources, such as legal, engineering, and manufacturing data, to create large databases of information.

Technology ▲ Advances

Advances in technology have resulted in the increased use of marketing research technologies, such as point-of-sale data collection and computerized database management programs.

The basic measure of business success in the future will be customer satisfaction, which is measured in continued sales. To maintain a high level of customer satisfaction, companies will need a thorough understanding of their customers' needs and information that tells them how well they are meeting those needs.

Another important trend is the use of both internal and external information in managing a business. Total Quality Management, or TQM, programs place a premium on gathering marketing and other information for use in improving business operations. Figure 32-2 lists additional trends that will affect the way businesses operate in the future.

Limitations of Marketing Research

Each of the major types of marketing research information is used to help businesses make sound business decisions. Few companies, though, can conduct as much marketing research as they would like. The amount of information that can be gathered is limited by the amount of money a company can afford to spend on the equipment and personnel needed to do the research. Often, there is too little time to do the research because

428 Unit 9 *Marketing Information Management*

Lifelong Learning

Marketing Research

There are many ways in which students can continue their study of marketing research. Most community colleges offer classes and seminars for those seeking to further their knowledge of the basics as well as more advanced topics such as questionnaire design, focus group technique, and analysis of findings. Many business owners, who conduct their own research, participate in these courses which are usually taught by principals in local market research firms. Have interested students check with your local college or university adult education department for availability of applicable courses.

Concern for Privacy ▲

Researchers, when collecting data, are showing a greater sensitivity to the public's concern for privacy.

Global Changes ▶

Global research alliances provide increased international marketing opportunities.

SECTION 32.2

4. Have each student contact the marketing department of a local community college, city college, or university for information on pursuing marketing research as an area of study within a marketing major. What specific courses would you take? What is the general content of each course? Are internships in marketing research available? If so, where are they and how long do they last? Where do most graduates with a marketing research emphasis find employment? If there are no post-secondary institutions available locally, have students consult a career resource (for example, the *Encyclopedia of Careers and Vocational Guidance*) for more information on marketing research as a career-sustaining occupation.

Close

Have students complete this statement: The four major areas of marketing research are… (advertising research, product research, market research, and sales research.)

decisions must sometimes be made before all possible data can be obtained.

Marketing research information also has its limitations. For example, customers in a test market situation may say they want a particular product, but there is no guarantee they will buy the product when it is actually produced for sale. In addition, fast-changing markets may not allow time for research. There is a time lag between identifying the need for a product, collecting the marketing research, and presenting the findings so the business can decide whether to produce the product. Business conditions, customer buying habits, and customer preferences can change over the time period of the study.

Despite these limitations, marketing research provides valuable information. Businesses will continue to rely on

marketing research to obtain the best possible information about customers and the marketplace.

SECTION 32.2 *Review*

1. **What are the four major areas of marketing research?**
2. **List at least four trends facing marketing researchers today.**
3. **What are two limitations of marketing research?**

Chapter 32   *Marketing Research*   **429**

Section Review Answers

1. Four major areas of marketing research are advertising research, product research, market research, and sales research.
2. Increased emphasis on customer satisfaction; emphasis on total quality management; more integration of marketing research data with other data sources, such as legal, engineering; quality assurance and manufacturing.

See text for additional possibilities.
3. The amount of information that can be gathered is limited by the amount of money there is to spend on equipment and personnel. Time constraints may force decisions to be made before all the data are collected. Customer information may be inaccurate.

Answers

Vocabulary Review

See Glossary for definitions.

Fact and Idea Review

1. Systematically gathering, recording, and analyzing data.
2. Obtaining information about the preferences, opinions, habits, trends, and plans of potential customers.
3. To generate, store, analyze, and distribute marketing information.
4. A collection of information on a specific topic.
5. Advertising research focuses on advertising message and media. This can help businesses by measuring the effectiveness of both the message and the media.
6. Product research is conducted to evaluate consumer acceptance, as well as to collect information about competitive products. Example: asking a consumer panel to describe what they like or dislike about a product.
7. Test marketing occurs when a product is placed in one or more selected geographic areas and its sales are monitored to test new products before they are distributed nationwide.
8. Market research: the collection of information about the customer and the market for a product. Example: to investigate a specific population group to determine consumer needs.
9. Sales research: how and where products are sold to determine potential sales for a product and to anticipate future sales. Example: calculate the total market for a type of product, then find the amount of that market held by a particular company. The result is the company's market share.

430

Vocabulary Review

Write the vocabulary terms below on 3" x 5" cards with the correct definition on the reverse. Review the terms and definitions by quizzing a classmate.

marketing research
marketing information system
database
advertising research
product research
test marketing
market research
sales research

Fact and Idea Review

1. What is involved in marketing research? (Sec. 32.1)
2. What is the major emphasis of marketing research? (Sec. 32.1)
3. What is the primary function of a marketing information system? (Sec. 32.1)
4. What is a marketing database? Give an example. (Sec. 32.1)
5. What is advertising research? How can it help businesses? (Sec. 32.2)
6. What is product research? Give an example. (Sec. 32.2)
7. What is test marketing? Why is it done? (Sec. 32.2)
8. What is market research? Give an example. (Sec. 32.2)
9. What is sales research? Give an example. (Sec. 32.2)
10. How has the global economy affected marketing research? (Sec. 32.2)

Critical Thinking

1. Recent consumer surveys indicate that only 34 percent of consumers surveyed trust marketers with regard to their use of consumer marketing information. What can the marketing research industry do to counteract consumer fears about trust and invasion of privacy?
2. Do you think there is a need for legislation to make a distinction between legitimate research and telemarketing sales? Explain.
3. Should every type of business engage in marketing research? Why or why not?
4. Explain what kind of marketing research should be done by a coin-operated car wash.

5. Explain why marketing researchers are concerned about consumer attitudes and lifestyles.
6. What are the advantages and disadvantages of test marketing?
7. What do you think marketing research would reveal about the differences between the lifestyles of dual-income families with children and the lifestyles of dual-income families without children? Consider time, income, product needs, shopping patterns, etc.

Building Academic Skills

Math

1. Assume that your company plans to send a marketing questionnaire to 30 percent of the names on a mailing list of 5,000 people. The mailing list was purchased from another company for $0.30 per name. If each questionnaire costs $0.10 to print; mailing costs are $0.36 (including the envelope and return envelope); and the cost of writing the questionnaire, analyzing the information, and preparing the report is $15,000, what is the total cost of this research?

Communication

2. Write a business letter requesting information from your local chamber of commerce on how it assists area businesses in conducting marketing surveys.

Human Relations

3. You have a part-time job in the marketing research department of a large corporation. You and three co-workers have been working on a project gathering information through telephone surveys. Your supervisor wants each of you to complete at least 30 surveys each day. Sometimes it is difficult to get 30 people to agree to respond to the survey questions. One of your co-workers has started making rude comments to people who do not agree to answer the questions and has told others that the survey is government-sponsored and they must answer the questions. What should you do?

Technology

4. Investigate database management computer software programs being used for marketing research by reviewing advertisements contained in business publications. Write a business letter requesting additional information.

10. International competition is forcing American companies to constantly improve products.

Critical Thinking

1. Individual companies must assure their consumers that the information collected will not be used in unscrupulous ways.
2. Answers will vary.
3. Marketing research is valuable for every size business.

4. A car wash would benefit from all the major types of marketing research discussed in the chapter.
5. By studying consumer attitudes and lifestyles, businesses are better able to suit their goods and services to consumers.
6. Advantages: Test marketing allows companies to measure the acceptance of new products on a limited basis. Disadvantages: The area selected as

Application Projects

1. Consult your library for current business publications such as *Inc., The Wall Street Journal, Business Week, Advertising Age,* and *Mass Market Retailers*. Find one current research activity being conducted by a company in the United States. Identify the activity and write a 200-word report that explains the scope and reasons for the research.

2. Prepare a 200-word report listing such market factors as population, income, education, trading area, and purchasing power that would make your city, area, region, or state an attractive place to locate a business. Consult city, county, or state offices, regional planning authorities, or the local chamber of commerce for detailed market information.

3. Assume that you are a marketing manager. Identify five questions that you would ask of a large research agency before you would contract for services related to advertising research.

4. Choose an existing consumer product that you think needs to be changed to make it more appealing to consumers (for example, sports shoes that need to be changed to fit better). Research any published information about your product and any proposed changes for it. Present these changes and the rationale for them in a five-minute oral report to the class.

5. Identify at least ten consumer goods that will require adaptation because of a generally aging population. Describe how the goal will need to be adapted.

6. Identify at least ten new or changed products that resulted from the change in consumers' attitudes toward products that are safer for the environment.

7. Use resources from your library to determine the demographics of your community (age, ethnic background, population, and income).

8. Select three businesses in the area. Locate them on a map and prepare a short oral report for the class on the geographical market each serves.

9. Research the characteristics of the 17- to 30-year old market. Write a 250-word report, identifying how to market to this group of people.

10. Prepare a 200-word report on the trends affecting marketing research within a particular industry, such as automotive, electronics, or communications.

Linking School to Work

Interview your training sponsor or current supervisor to find out how research is conducted at your place of employment. Report your findings to the class.

Performance Assessment

Role Play

Situation. You have been asked by your manager to present your ideas for conducting research on the feasibility of adding a new line of clothing to your small boutique. In your oral presentation to your manager, explain the types of research to be conducted.

Evaluation. You will be evaluated on how well you do the following:

- Recommend appropriate types of marketing research that should be conducted to determine whether the line of clothing should be added.
- Describe the importance of using marketing research to determine the feasibility of adding a new line of clothing.

Concept Mapping

Using poster paper, draw a map with the term "marketing research" in the center of the paper. Identify key concepts underlying marketing research that you learned about in reading the chapter.

COMPUTER APPLICATION

Complete the Chapter 32 Computer Application that appears in the Student Activity Workbook.

Communication
2. Letters should be written according to the business letter specifications described in Chapter 9.

Human Relations
3. Students' responses will vary.

Technology
4. Business letters should be written according to the specifications in Chapter 9.

Application Projects
1. Papers will vary.
2. Reports will depend on the students' community.
3. Students might ask: the companies data sources, computer technology, types of research it conducts, and references.
4. Example: to improve airline food by adding health food.
5. Examples: enlarged print books and easier to open containers.
6. Answers might include: fast-food, biodegradable plastic containers, coal-burning power plants that now have scrubbers, etc.
7.–8. Answers will vary.
9. Students should take into account the lifestyles of this market in terms of income, shopping patterns, and product needs.
10. Papers will vary depending on the industry students select.

Linking School to Work
Answers depend on the work situation.

Performance Assessment
Refer to the *DECA Competitive Events Handbook* for evaluation guidelines.

Computer Application
Optional activity. Refer to the *Marketing Software Binder* for template and user information.

Evaluation
Administer the reproducible test for Chapter 32, or construct you own using the Testmaker software.

---

a test market may not reflect consumer response for the entire country.

7. Students may suggest that families without children may have more time to shop, more discretionary income.

Building Academic Skills

Math

1. Cost of mailing list: $ 1,500

Number of questionnaires sent:
$$0.30 \times 5,000 = 1,500$$
Cost to print questionnaires:
$$0.10 \times 1,500 = 150$$
Mailing costs:
$$0.36 \times 1,500 = 540$$
Writing questionnaire $15,000
Total: $17,190

Chapter Overview

This chapter introduces students to the process of conducting marketing research.

 ## Springboard

Ask students the following question: *Could you frost a cake before you bake it?* Obviously, the answer to this question is no. You must go through a process to get a cake. You must mix the proper ingredients together, in the proper proportions, and bake the mixture for a specific time period. Then you can frost it!

Remind students that, like baking a cake, marketing research is a process in which many elements are brought together in order to arrive at a final product. To get the best results, the steps in the marketing research process must be done in order. In this chapter students will look at the process of marketing research.

Prereading

List the section objectives to discuss with students. Have students skim the chapter, looking at the pictures, reading the captions, and noting the heads. Ask questions to ensure that the students have a minimal understanding of the chapter structure.

Preteaching the Vocabulary

The night before you begin this chapter, have students skim through the chapter, paying particular attention to the boldface vocabulary terms. The day you begin this lesson, read the definitions for this chapter's vocabulary terms (but do not read them in order). Allow students to look at the vocabulary list to match the terms to the definitions.

432

CHAPTER 33

Conducting Marketing Research

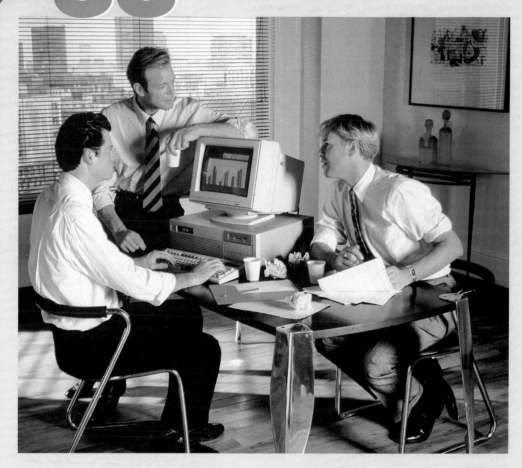

Marketing research is not a single act, but a series of activities performed to gather and analyze information. In this chapter you will review each step in the marketing research process. You will review techniques for writing research instruments. You will also learn about the impact computers are having on marketing research.

432   Unit 9   *Marketing Information Management*

Classroom Management

For the Teacher

- Teacher's Annotated Editions for all workbooks
- Teacher's Manual for *School-to-Work Handbook*
- *Testing Binder*
- *Transparency Binder*
- *Marketing Software Binder*
- *Marketing Career Portfolio*
- *Lesson Plans*

For the Student

- *Student Activity Workbook*
- *Marketing Math Workbook*
- *School-to-Work Handbook*
- *Student Software*
- *International Case Studies*
- *Marketing Career Portfolio*

Objectives

After completing this section, you will be able to

- describe the five steps in conducting marketing research,
- explain the difference between primary and secondary data, and
- name methods used to collect primary and secondary data.

Terms to Know

- problem definition
- primary data
- secondary data
- survey method
- sample
- online computer services
- observation method
- point-of-sale research
- experimental method
- data analysis

The Marketing Research Process

When engaging in marketing research, companies follow certain procedures. Five major steps are involved in the marketing research process:

1. defining the problem,
2. obtaining data,
3. analyzing the data,
4. recommending solutions to the problem, and
5. applying the results. (See Figure 33–1 on page 434.)

Each step is performed sequentially to arrive at a solution to a problem. Let's take a closer look at each step.

Step 1: Defining the Problem

The most difficult and yet a very important step in the marketing research process is defining the problem. **Problem definition** occurs when a business clearly identifies a problem and states the information needed to solve the problem. For example, a problem may be that sales have declined. The business needs to decide how to improve sales. To that end, it will want to know who is now buying its products, as well as why past customers are not buying the product now. The business will also need to know where the product sells and does not sell, and why. In addition, the business will need to know who its competitors are.

Research problems can focus on any part of the marketing mix. For example, to study the problem of decreased sales, marketers might pose the following questions for each part of the marketing mix:

- Are customers satisfied with our product?
- Are our prices competitive?
- Are our products distributed efficiently in the marketplace?
- Are our promotion activities effective?

Because money and time are limited, it is virtually impossible for marketing researchers to answer all the questions that confront a business. Each business has to determine which problems are the most important to solve at a given time. After the key problems have been selected for study, the next step of the marketing research process can begin.

Step 2: Obtaining Data

The second step in the marketing research process is to obtain data. During this second step, data are collected and examined in terms of the problem or problems being studied.

As you learned in Chapter 32, the word *data* means facts. There are two types of data used in marketing research: *primary* and *secondary*. **Primary data** are data obtained for the first time and used specifically for the particular problem under study. **Secondary data** have already been collected for some purpose other than the current study. Because secondary data is less expensive than collecting primary data, businesses try to use secondary data before they get primary data. So, let's look at secondary data first.

Chapter 33   *Conducting Marketing Research*   **433**

SECTION 33.1

FOCUS

Bell Ringer Activity

Divide students into groups of three or four and then pose this situation for them to discuss. For ten years, Patty-Cakes, a bakery specializing in "special occasion" cakes for events such as birthdays and weddings, has served the same market area whose demographics have changed relatively little in a decade. Most of the customers are middle-class, two-income families with children; some are retired "empty-nesters" on fixed incomes.

Recently, Patty Morris, the owner, decided that she would like to expand her business by adding a bistro-style breakfast/lunch restaurant. She wants to know if there are enough people in her target market area with the time and income to support her proposed breakfast/lunch restaurant business, and/or if she can draw people to her restaurant from other target areas. How would Patty Morris determine whether or not to make this addition to her current business?

Introducing the Section

List the five steps in the marketing research process on the board. After allowing students time for discussion, have each group report its results. Categorize students' suggestions under each of the five steps in the marketing research process. (Most of their suggestions will probably fall under #2, obtaining data).

Read with students the first section of this chapter entitled "The Marketing Research Process" and make sure they understand the five steps. Leave this information on the board and refer to it throughout this lesson. As students study each step in the marketing research process, have them brainstorm possible outcomes of the types of research Patty is likely to conduct, and possible solutions to her problem.

1. Read Section 33.1 with students.
2. Have students read aloud the Case Study and review the answers in class.
3. Use the transparencies for this section.
4. MarkEd Resource Center in Columbus, Ohio, (800) 448-0398, has materials appropriate for use with this chapter.
5. For further information on data collection and analysis, contact the Marketing Research Association, 111 East Wacker Drive, Suite 600, Chicago, IL 60601, (312) 644-6610.
6. The following publications are good supplemental resources to use in teaching this chapter:
   - *Advances in Consumer Research,* Association for Consumer Research, Brigham Young University, Graduate School of Management, 632 TNRB, Provo, UT 84602, (801) 378-2080 (a scholarly journal of new marketing research techniques and findings);
   - *Findex,* Cambridge Information Group Directories, Inc., 7200 Wisconsin Ave., Bethesda, MD 20814, (301) 961-6750 (a directory and description of thousands of published marketing research studies and reports about companies and industries);

Figure 33-1

THE MARKETING RESEARCH PROCESS

There are five steps in the problem solving process.

2. Obtaining Data:
Researchers obtain data from secondary and primary sources.

SURVEY
Did you buy Brand X?
☐ Yes   ☐ No

1. Defining the Problem:
The problem is identified and goals are set to solve the problem.

3. Analyzing Data:
Researchers compile, analyze, and interpret the data.

4. Recommending Solutions to the Problem:
Researchers come up with solutions to the problem and present them in a report.

5. Applying the Results:
The research results are put into action.

Lifelong Learning

Conducting Marketing Research

Conducting marketing research is a very specific skill and as a career is attractive to very detailed individuals who thrive on the challenge of predicting customer responses and utilizing technology and analytical skills to achieve a goal. The techniques described in this chapter have application in a wide variety of research tasks that the students will encounter in the future. Defining the problem to be studied and selecting data to aid in solving the problem are skills that will benefit students in the near future as they continue on their educational path. Encourage students to give careful consideration to how they can apply these valuable skills to their future.

How Secondary Data Are Obtained

Secondary data are obtained from both *internal sources* (sources within the company) and *external sources* (sources outside the company). Good sources of internal secondary data are employees and the records or reports of the business. Such records could include budgets, sales figures, income and expense records, customer records, and inventory records.

External secondary data can be obtained from five major sources:

1. *U.S. government agencies.* Information from government agencies can include demographics and reports on specific markets, industries, and products. The Small Business Administration, the U.S. Department of Commerce, and the U.S. Bureau of the Census are good sources for secondary data. Publications such as the *Census of the Population* and the *Statistical Abstract of the United States* contain hundreds of tables, graphs, and charts useful in analyzing business situations. Federal government studies are relatively inexpensive data sources that can provide useful information and statistics about markets, people, and business activities.
2. *Corporate, public, and university libraries.* There are about 6,000 corporate libraries in the United States, many of which specialize in secondary research. Some public and university libraries also offer research services.
3. *Consumer and business information companies.* An active and growing number of specialized research companies also offer data for business needs. Specialized companies sell demographic data, five-year forecasts, consumer purchase information, business data, census information, and consumer classification reports to businesses. These companies make data available in a wide variety of formats such as written reports, sourcebooks, CD-ROM, computer diskettes, and customized geographical maps of target markets.
4. *Business publications.* Good sources include such publications as *Inc., Forbes, Business Week, The Wall Street Journal,* and *Sales and Marketing Management.*
5. *Trade publications, books, and journals.* These publications can be obtained from trade associations such as the Food Marketing Institute and the National Retail Merchants Association.

Advantages of Secondary Data Secondary data has several advantages. It can be obtained quickly because most secondary data sources can be found in corporate, public, or college libraries. It can also be purchased from information companies. Obtaining secondary data is less expensive than primary data because the initial cost has already been paid by an agency or organization. In addition, some types of secondary data, such as nationwide population figures, are available through the U.S. Bureau of the Census. Any firm trying

▲ *Business publications* **are a valuable source of secondary data. Why do businesses try to use secondary data before they use primary data?**

to collect such data as this would have to spend a great deal of time and money.

Disadvantages of Secondary Data

There are two major disadvantages associated with secondary data. First, the existing data may not be suitable or available for the problem under study. This situation is most common for new and innovative products. For example, when manufacturers were trying to develop improved contact lenses, they found secondary data largely unavailable from government agencies because the product was fairly new. Primary research had to be used instead.

Second, the data may be dated. For example, federal census data is collected only every ten years. As a result, projections based on the current census may not always be accurate.

Despite these limitations, a business should try to find secondary data before collecting primary data. Secondary data may be readily available at little or no cost. Its use could avoid the need to collect primary data and thus save on research costs for the business.

How Primary Data Are Obtained

When marketing researchers cannot find the information they need from secondary data, they turn to the

Chapter 33 *Conducting Marketing Research* **435**

SECTION 33.1

- *Journal of Marketing Research,* American Marketing Association, 250 S. Wacker Dr., Ste. 200, Chicago, IL 60606, (312) 648-0536 (offers detailed information about the methods and analyses used in marketing research);
- *Research Alert,* Alert Publishing, Inc., 37-06 30th Ave., Long Island City, NY 11103-3808, (718) 626-3356 (reports on the results of consumer marketing studies); and
- *Research in Marketing,* JAI Press Inc., 55 Old Post Rd., No. 2, Greenwich, CT 06836 (203) 661-7602 (an annual compilation of marketing research).

Discussion Starter

Have students brainstorm five or six problems that need to be addressed in your school. By group consensus, choose the four most pressing problems.

Then divide students into four groups and assign one problem to each group. Have each group brainstorm types of primary and secondary data they would use in order to obtain information on the problem.

Critical Thinking

Ask students whether the following are examples of primary or secondary data:

- measuring three groups' responses to a new cereal packaging design (primary data);
- a U.S. government demographics report (secondary data);

Caption Answer

Secondary data is less expensive than primary data and may be more thorough than data that a company can afford to gather on its own.

- statistics from the SBA on the number of small business start-ups (secondary data);
- IBM's five-year sales figures (secondary data);
- marketing research conducted by Procter & Gamble for a new dishwashing liquid (primary data);
- a jewelry store's customer buying records (secondary data);
- census data from the state of Ohio (secondary data);
- an opinion research poll conducted by IBM for a new computer it plans to introduce two years from now (primary data);
- a table from the *Statistical Abstract of the United States* (secondary data);
- a personal interview conducted in a supermarket by a representative of a new ice cream manufacturer (primary data);
- a questionnaire sent to new home owners by their real estate agent's realty company (primary data);
- statistics from *Newsweek* on population growth in the Southwest (secondary data);
- observing customers interacting with salespeople in the housewares department of a local department store (primary data).

collection of primary data. Primary research data can be obtained through two sources:

1. *Individual company research.* Large companies frequently establish their own marketing research departments to conduct primary research.
2. *Commercial research organizations.* Research organizations provide marketing, advertising, and opinion research services under contract for other businesses and organizations. Nielsen, IMS International, Information Resources, and The Arbitron Ratings Company are some of the leading research organizations.

There are three basic methods used to collect primary data:

1. the survey method,
2. the observation method, and
3. the experimental method.

The Survey Method   The **survey method** is a research technique in which information is gathered from people directly through the use of interviews or questionnaires. It is the most frequently used method of collecting primary data. For example, have you ever noticed the questionnaires that some magazine publishers send subscribers when they bill them for subscriptions? These subscriber surveys are one example of primary research.

When conducting a survey, marketers must determine the number of people to include in their survey. If a target population is small, researchers can survey the entire target market. Usually, though, the target population is too large, and time and money are too limited to allow researchers to survey the entire target population. Researchers thus use a sample of the entire target population to get survey results. A **sample** is a part of the target population that is assumed to represent the entire population. The size of the sample depends upon the amount of money the company has to spend and the degree of accuracy that is needed. Generally speaking, the larger the sample, the greater the accuracy of the results.

After determining the size of the population to survey, you must create the data collection instrument. A *questionnaire* is a written list of questions designed to gain information about the identified problem. You will learn more about how to create a questionnaire in Section 33.2.

Once the questionnaire has been created, the survey can be conducted. Surveys can be conducted through a personal interview, by telephone, by mail, or via online computer services.

Perhaps the best way to conduct a survey is through a *personal interview.* The personal interview involves questioning people face-to-face. Examples of personal interviews include on-site interviews in retail stores or shopping malls.

A form of personal interview that is increasing in popularity is the *focus group interview.* A focus group interview involves six to ten people who are brought together

to informally discuss a particular situation under the direction of a skilled interviewer.

The interaction in a focus group interview stimulates thinking and gets immediate reaction to an idea or concept. Focus group facilities usually include conference rooms, observation rooms, and audiotape and videotape equipment.

A major advantage to personal interviews is that most people prefer to talk rather than to write. As a result, it is often easier to get people to respond to personal interviews than to written questionnaires.

A disadvantage is that it is more costly than mail or telephone surveys. Setting up personal interviews is costly because it requires hiring experienced interviewers who are skilled at asking nonbiased questions and interpreting the answers correctly.

The *telephone interview* is quick, efficient, and relatively inexpensive. However, a disadvantage of telephone interviews is that some people are unwilling to respond to questions over the telephone. People sometimes resist this approach to data collection because they do not know the caller or how their answers will be used. They may also resent the intrusion on their personal time at home.

A mail survey is a relatively inexpensive way to reach a potentially large audience. The average return rate, however, generally is only 10 to 20 percent. In recent years, some researchers have found that including a token payment, such as $1, with the questionnaire has resulted in higher rates of return. Another method that increases returns is to send postcards telling people that they will be

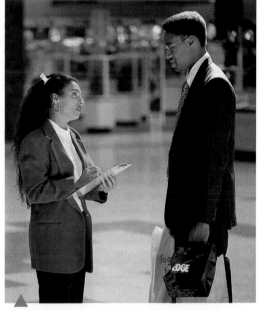

The personal interview **is one of the best ways to conduct a survey. Why?**

receiving a questionnaire within the next few days. Following the mailing of the questionnaire with a reminder postcard also helps improve the rate of return.

Research information can also be obtained through the use of **online computer services,** such as Internet. Online computer services are accessed through telephones and modems and allow users to communicate via computer. Similar services are offered through Prodigy and America Online. Users of these services may research online databases to find secondary information. They may

BRIGHT IDEAS

Consider Different Standards

Who among emerging nations is a potential customer for a business's goods? Can a nation whose per capita annual income is counted in hundreds rather than thousands of dollars possibly afford anything that industrialized nations have to offer?

The situation is not as bleak as it might at first appear, according to Futures Group, Inc., a Connecticut-based consulting firm. The firm helps would-be exporters identify potential markets in countries such as India and China, where per capita income is low by U.S. standards. It does this by analyzing purchasing power rather than income.

For example, China's per capita income of $400 a year becomes $2,500 when viewed this way. What the new standard takes into account is what income can buy in terms of housing, utilities, health care, and other necessities. Even though there are fewer than 3 million Chinese who earn middle-class wages of $10,000–$40,000, 80 million qualify for middle-class status when viewed in terms of their purchasing power.

Thus, it's not how much consumers have by U.S. standards that counts. It's what that amount will buy in the local economy.

Creativity Challenge Form teams of 3–5 people, and consider other situations governed by standards or rules. What other forms of evaluation are possible? For example, what alternatives are there to the grading system used in school? How else could a baseball or basketball game be scored? How else could clothing be sized? How would you approach the daily business or weather report on TV from a different perspective? Provide at least one alternative approach for each situation discussed.

also link into discussion groups and ask questions of other users. For example, questions may be posted on the computer "bulletin board" and answered by anyone who is interested. This type of research is probably most useful for companies seeking information about computers.

Another way online services are used to gain information is to review the comments made by people using the service. For example, software companies may monitor comments made about commercial software programs to gain information about how their software is used and how it could be improved.

The Observation Method The **observation method** is a research technique in which the actions of people are observed and recorded. This method is used primarily to get information about customer behavior or preferences. For example, toy manufacturers often develop models of several new toys. To decide which toys to market, the manufacturer brings in a group of children to play with the toys. Observers note which toys the children choose and how long they play with them. The toys that are popular are the ones that get marketed.

Another use of observation is to view the interaction between customers and employees. A retailer, for example, may want to know whether its employees are answering customers' questions correctly and in a friendly, helpful manner. The salespeople are observed on approach, sales presentation, product knowledge, and suggestion selling. This information can then be used to modify or improve employee training programs.

If an observation is properly performed and recorded, the results are often better than the survey technique. What people actually do is usually a better indicator than what they say they will do.

One disadvantage of the observation method is that it cannot measure attitude. Observation provides information on what the person does, but not why the person does it. If knowledge of attitude is important to the business in solving its research problem, additional information may need to be gathered using another research method.

The observation technique may use either *contrived* or *natural* situations. Contrived observations are set up by the researcher. The example given earlier of having children play with new toys is an example of a contrived observation. Contrived observations allow researchers to control a testing situation, but respondents may not make the same choices as they would in a real buying situation. For example, children faced with an entire store of toys might not choose the same toys as in the contrived observation.

With natural observation, customers or employees are viewed as they would normally act in a given situation. An example of natural observation is when customers are observed by people or hidden cameras as they shop, enter, or leave a store. Another form of natural observation is the *traffic count*—a count of people or cars as they pass by a store. For example, people can pass by without looking. They can stop, look, and walk on. They can stop, look, and enter the store.

Chapter 33 *Conducting Marketing Research*   **437**

Bright Ideas

How else could knowing about other countries standard of living be helpful to marketers? (By knowing how other people live, marketers can design products to meet their needs. For example, by knowing that space is at a premium in many other countries such as Japan, marketers can develop smaller appliances, folding beds, and smaller versions of other products.)

L1 Math Skills

(1) Patty Morris of Patty-Cakes sent customer questionnaires to 500 people in her target market area. Twenty-eight percent of these questionnaires were returned. How many people returned their questionnaires? (140. $500 \times .28 = 140$)

(2) What percentage did not return their questionnaires? ($1.00 - 28 = .72$)

L2 Math Skills

Here are Kmart Corporation's sales figures for 1987–1992.*

1987: $25,822,000

1988: $27,496,000

1989: $29,736,000

1990: $32,281,000

1991: $34,792,000

1992: $37,942,000

(1) What percentage of the highest sales figure is the lowest sales figure? (68%. $25,822,000 \div 37,942,000 = 0.68$)

(2) By what percentage did the company increase its sales from 1989 to 1990? From 1990 to 1991? (From 1989 to 1990, 8%. $32,281,000 - 29,736,000 = 2,545,000. $2,545,000 \div 32,281,000 = .078$ or 8%. From 1990 to 1991, 7%. $34,792,000 - 32,281,000 = 2,511,000. $2,511,000 \div 34,792,000 = .072$ or 7%)

* Statistics from *Hoover's Handbook of American Business.* Austin: Reference Press, 1993, p. 679.

L3 Math Skills

Have students make a bar graph or a line graph of Kmart Corporation's sales statistics in the L2 Math Activity. What conclusions can they draw about Kmart's growth from 1987 to 1992. (Kmart experienced steady growth with no decline in sales.)

Independent Practice

1. Assign and review the Chapter 33 Case Study in the *International Case Studies* workbook.
2. Have students use library and other resources to research careers in marketing research. They should include such information as:
   (1) the types of businesses that hire market researchers,
   (2) the qualifications and training required for this job,
   (3) the starting salary range,
   (4) the projected job availability in this field over the next five to ten years, and
   (5) what students can do now to prepare for a career in marketing research.

   Students' reports should be between 250 to 500 words.

Assess

Evaluation

Assign and review the Section 33.1 Review.

SKIPFIX Focuses on Focus Groups

Before marketing a new product, businesses often conduct focus groups to get first-hand reactions from potential consumers. SKIPFIX CD Skip Repair System, a product that repairs skips in compact discs, conducted several focus groups with potential customers. Participants were first given an education on the parts of a CD. They learned that a scratch in the play side of a CD causes a laser light to reflect improperly and the sound to "skip." If the scratch is small and runs in the same direction as the spiral pit tracks, the laser will lose its position.

Focus group participants were asked to bring to the session CDs that skipped. At the beginning of the session, the group members responded to general questions about their use of CDs and the need for such a product. They then had the opportunity to test the product's effectiveness on their damaged CDs. The company was interested in the participants' satisfaction with the product. It was also interested in the participants' reactions to the package design, directions, and proposed price. For example, participants were asked how difficult the directions were to follow and how much they were willing to spend for the product. They were also asked for suggestions for improving the package and directions.

SKIPFIX resulted from a nine-year research and development project that was to develop an environmentally safe and biodegradable product expressly made to remove scratches from plastic surfaces. The special formula was originally developed to repair the scratches in jet aircraft windows, ski goggles, eyeglasses, and aquariums.

The proposed SKIPFIX system contains a compact disc cleaning solution, super soft drying cloths, the repair solution, and application pads. The suggested retail price is $19.95.

Case Study Review

1. What do you think the SKIPFIX company learned from its focus group sessions that helped it market its new product?
2. What skills are needed to be an effective focus group leader?
3. What advantages may there be for SKIPFIX in holding a focus group rather than using a telephone survey?

A MATTER OF ETHICS

4. Suppose a competitor of SKIPFIX has developed a product to compete with SKIPFIX's CD repair kit. The competitor asks the same marketing research company that SKIPFIX used for its research to conduct a similar focus group study for its company. Is it ethical for the marketing research company to conduct the study for SKIPFIX's competitor? Explain.

Case Study Answers

1. They learned how much value participants placed on the product.
2. Good interpersonal and communication skills, as well as a solid understanding of the business.
3. Customers can actually see and use the product.
4. Some students might respond in a positive way by indicating how the marketing research company will be familiar with the product due to the work they had already done. However, SKIPFIX would probably not be pleased with the idea as it would potentially give their competitor a leg up in the market. Presumably, the marketing research company has to sign a confidentiality agreement with each client, so a lot depends on the ethics of the individuals involved.

Point-of-sale research is a powerful new form of research that combines natural observation with personal interviews to get people to explain buying behavior. Point-of-sale researchers observe shoppers in a retail store to decide which ones to choose as research subjects. For example, researchers may look for

- shoppers buying a specific type of product,
- shoppers buying a specific product brand, or
- shoppers who inspect a product but do not buy it.

After observation, researchers approach selected shoppers and ask them survey questions. Because point-of-sale research combines observation with personal interviews, it has many benefits for researchers. All participants in the research study are "qualified" respondents because they have been selected by observation. Participants can be chosen based on variables such as shopping time (morning, afternoon, or evening), product price, or any other variable that can be observed. Researchers can also get input from other family members or shopping companions. Participants can easily remember the reason why they purchased a product because the purchase has just been made.

Observation research is faster than other forms of research because participants do not have to be screened by telephone or scheduled for interviews or focus groups. This type of research can save money because businesses do not pay for postage or telephone costs, participant fees, or special interviewing facilities.

Whether researchers use a natural or contrived approach, they must record the data from the observation. For observation to be successful, customer actions must be identified and their behaviors noted.

The Experimental Method The **experimental method** is a research technique in which a researcher observes under controlled conditions the results of changing one or more marketing variables while keeping certain other variables constant. The experimental approach is often used to test new package designs, levels of media usage, and new promotions. For example, a candy company may want to compare the effectiveness of two different package designs for its new candy bar. To do so, the company researcher will select two similar groups of consumers. The first group is shown a proposed package for the candy bar. The other group is shown an identical package containing the same product information, except the colors of the package have been changed.

Each group's response is measured and the results determined. Since the researcher had control over the test environment and only the color of the packaging changed, if one package gets a better response the company can attribute it to the color.

The experimental method is used least often. One reason for this is the cost of setting up the research situation. In addition, people respond differently under controlled conditions in contrast to actual buying situations. This difference makes the research information less valuable. For situations where different approaches or ideas

Real World MARKETING

MR in the Palm of Your Hand

It used to be that survey data was laboriously collected, recorded, and tallied using paper and pencil. Then, with the advent of computers, the paper and pencil data was entered into a computer database for tallying and analysis. Now that same technology has made it possible to dispense with the paper and pencil entirely.

The newest application of computer technology to marketing research allows survey subjects to enter their responses themselves via a small, hand-held wireless keypad. The device totally eliminates the lag time between response and analysis. In fact, when used at conventions, the keypad has made it possible for survey results to be posted immediately on video screens. Some systems even present results in graph form for easier comprehension.

need to be compared, though, the experimental method offers the best source of information.

Step 3: Analyzing the Data

The third step in the marketing research process is *data analysis*. **Data analysis** is the compiling, analyzing, and interpreting of the results of primary and secondary data collection.

For example, XYZ Autos surveyed customers about the quality of the dealership's repair service. The number of customers returning the survey was 120. Answers to questions were organized so that the percentage of men and women responding to each question could be shown clearly. Data were cross-tabulated to determine such things as how men and women differ in their perceptions of the service. The answers to a question about the quality of service might be presented as follows. Note that the number of respondents is given in parentheses after the question. This number quickly tells the reader how many people responded to this question.

Question 3: How would you rate the quality of service provided by XYZ Autos? (N = 120)

Rating	Men	Women
Excellent	30%	60%
Good	15%	10%
Average	20%	20%
Fair	20%	5%
Poor	15%	5%

Chapter 33 *Conducting Marketing Research* **439**

SECTION 33.1

Reteach

1. Assign and review the vocabulary terms for this section.
2. Assign and review Fact and Idea Review questions 1-9 from the Chapter Review.
3. Write each step in the marketing research process as a column heading on the board. Divide students into five groups and assign each group one of the five steps. Have each student write one fact on the board about his or her groups' marketing research step. Have the students in each group explain their respective step in the marketing research process.

Enrichment

1. Assign and review the appropriate activities in the *Student Activity Workbook*.
2. Assign and review the appropriate Critical Thinking questions from the Chapter Review.
3. Assign the appropriate activities in the *Marketing Math Workbook*.
4. Invite the marketing research director of a shopping mall, department store, or advertising agency to discuss recent marketing research studies conducted, data-gathering methods used, and solutions to marketing problems. You may also wish to have this person discuss careers in marketing research.

 Did You Know

Recent immigrants may not speak or write English and therefore may not able to respond to survey questions unless written in their native language. However simply translating survey questions into other languages may not work because some of the concepts may not exist in other cultures due to lack of product exposure and/or lack of product choices. Also, recent immigrants may be reluctant to answer surveys because they fear that the information will go to the government and will be used against them at a later time.

5. If you know any small business owners, see if one of them has a marketing research issue that the class could work on as a project. For example, perhaps the business would like to open a second branch, but does not know where the best new location would be; or, perhaps, a new product line is being considered in a sporting goods store, and customer response is critical because a large cash outlay is necessary to bring the new line in to the store. Have students work in teams to propose surveys, questionnaires, and other marketing research tools that the business could use to get a handle on the information needed to make a decision.

There may not be a pressing need for this information on the part of the business owner. However, the exercise will be meaningful because it will require the students to think about real issues and design tools that theoretically could be used in the "real world" (whether the tools are ever implemented or not is incidental).

Close

Have students complete this statement: The most difficult and yet the most important step in the marketing research process is... (defining the problem.)

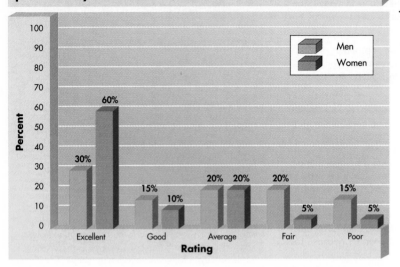

Question 3: How would you rate the quality of service provided by XYZ Autos? (N=120)

Figure 33–2

Charts, such as this one representing research results from the XYZ Autos survey, are typically included in research reports. Why are charts often included?

As you can see, female customers of XYZ Autos generally have a more favorable impression of the quality of service than the male customers. Using this information, the owner now knows that the dealership's image among its male customers needs to be improved.

Step 4: Recommending Solutions to the Problem

Successful research results in information that helps managers make decisions on how to solve a problem. The conclusions drawn from the research usually are presented in a report. The report must be well written and well organized so the appropriate business managers will understand them. Recommendations must be clear and well supported by the research data.

Let's use the example of the auto dealership. Looking at the table of percentages, the researcher would conclude that 55 percent of the male customers thought service was average or worse. The 55 percent is calculated by adding the percentages for average, fair, and poor. The percentage of women who answered that service was average or below was 30 percent. The conclusion to be drawn from these percentages is that service needs to be improved. Customers also need to be made aware of any improvements in service. A recommendation might be to provide additional training for repair staff. Another might be to develop a program to communicate better with customers about their repairs.

A typical research report includes these items:

- title page;
- acknowledgments to people who assisted in the research effort;
- table of contents;
- tables, figures, charts, and graphs (see Figure 33–2);
- introduction (includes the problem under study, its importance, definitions, limitations of the study, and basic assumptions);
- review of the research information (including the results of any secondary data reviewed for the research effort);
- procedures used (research technique or techniques used to obtain primary data);
- findings;
- recommendations;
- summary and conclusions;
- appendices; and
- bibliography.

Step 5: Applying the Results

The research report is used by managers to make decisions about their next actions in relation to the problem that was researched. In evaluating the research, managers may find that the research was inconclusive, additional research may be needed, or the research suggests specific courses of action.

Caption Answer

Charts are typically included because they help to clearly illustrate research results.

If the data gathered by research does not help to answer questions about the problem, the results are inconclusive. For example, suppose two different commercials for a new product are developed. The two new commercials, along with several old commercials, are shown to two groups of target customers. About the same number of customers choose each of the commercials, neither of which gets a large response. The results are inconclusive because one commercial did not win out over the other.

When results are inconclusive, the researchers may need to do more research. Sometimes the research also points out new areas of a problem that had not been anticipated before research was begun. That situation may also call for additional research. For example, in the case of the commercials the business may want to do more research to discover why neither commercial gained customers' attention. Perhaps the commercials were not interesting, or perhaps the target customers were not interested in the product. Further research would help to answer these issues.

Often research provides information that can be acted upon by decision makers. Let's use the example of the commercials again. If a large percentage of the target customers clearly remembered one commercial over the other, the decision would be made to use the favored commercial. Researchers could also conclude that the target market found the product interesting since they remembered the commercial relating to the product.

After the research has been completed and recommendations acted upon, a business should carefully monitor the results. A business needs to know whether the specific actions taken are successful. It also needs to know whether the information provided by the research was reliable; in other words, proved to be true. If decisions made as a result of the research lead to increased profits through better sales, increased efficiency, or reduced expenses, then the research effort has been worthwhile.

Marketing research is an ongoing process of problem solving. The results obtained through marketing research should become a part of the total information available to a business for making future decisions.

SECTION 33.1

Review

1. **What are the five steps in designing and conducting a research study?**
2. **Explain the difference between primary and secondary data.**
3. **Name the methods used most frequently to collect primary and secondary data.**

SECTION 33.2

Objectives

After completing this section, you will be able to

- **write research instruments and**
- **describe the ways the computer is used in research.**

Term to Know

- **forced-choice questions**

Constructing the Questionnaire

Questionnaires should provide data that have *validity*. In other words, the data should measure what it was intended to measure. For example, a researcher designs a questionnaire to measure a restaurant's customer service. If the questions are poorly written and do not address customer service, the questionnaire will not have validity.

Research questionnaires should also have *reliability*. That is, the questions should ask the same type of information from all the respondents. Questions should be clear and easily understood so that all participants understand the question in the same way. Questions that are unclear and poorly written will not gain reliable responses.

To be valid and reliable, a questionnaire must be properly written, formatted, and distributed. Let's take a look at how to do this.

Writing Questions

Survey questions can be either *open ended* or *forced choice*. Open-ended questions ask respondents to construct their own response to a question. "How can we serve you better?" is an example of an open-ended question. Open-ended questions generate a wide variety of responses that are sometimes difficult to categorize and tabulate. As a result, most researchers prefer forced-choice questions.

Forced-choice questions ask respondents to choose answers from possibilities given on a questionnaire. Forced-choice questions are the simplest questions to write and the easiest to tabulate. Forced-choice questions can be two-choice questions, multiple choice, or rating questions.

Chapter 33 *Conducting Marketing Research* **441**

SECTION 33.2

Focus

Bell Ringer Activity

Have students brainstorm a list of three problems for which a business might use marketing research. Write each problem as a column heading on the board. Have each student choose one of these problems and write three questions that could be asked about it on a research questionnaire.

Introducing the Section

Solicit students' answers from the Bell Ringer Activity. Write their questions under the appropriate headings. Ask students to identify the various types of questions they generated, categorizing each question in the board list as open-ended or forced-choice question. Have students discuss the value and the disadvantages of each type of question.

In this section, students will look at how to construct a marketing research questionnaire, including how to write good questions. They will also look at how the computer is used in research.

Teach

Guided Practice

1. Read Section 33.2 with students.
2. Use the transparency for this section.
3. As you explore the various types of forced-choice questions, give examples of poorly constructed questions and have students discuss how to improve them.
4. If you have a computer in your classroom, show students how database information is compiled and how useful such information is in marketing research.
5. Assign and review the Chapter 33 Activity in the *School-to-Work Handbook*.

Section Review Answers

1. Problem definition, obtaining data, analyzing the data, recommending solutions to the problem, and applying the results.
2. Primary data are data obtained for the first time and used specifically for the particular problem

under study. Secondary data have already been collected and are used for some other purpose than the current study.
3. Survey, observation, and experimental method.

Two-choice questions give the respondent only two options. For example, respondents may be asked to answer yes or no to whether they liked a certain brand. The following is an example of how a restaurant might ask yes-no questions.

Please answer *Yes* or *No* to the following questions:

Did your server make you feel welcome?	Yes	No
Were the daily specials suggested?	Yes	No
Was the service prompt?	Yes	No

Multiple choice questions give the respondent several choices from which to choose. For example, a restaurant might ask its customers the following question.

Please choose which of the following is most important to you when choosing a restaurant:

A. Price
B. Quality of the food
C. Location
D. Variety of food

Other forced-choice questions may ask respondents to rate a product based on a scale. A variety of scales may be used, such as a rating from strongly agree to strongly disagree or from very good to very poor. The following is an example of a rating question that might be used by a restaurant.

Please rate the following:

Cleanliness	Excellent	Good	Fair	Poor
Attitude	Excellent	Good	Fair	Poor
Quality	Excellent	Good	Fair	Poor
Value	Excellent	Good	Fair	Poor

As you perform secondary research, you may find examples of well-written questions. Use these examples to help you write your own questionnaires.

When a questionnaire is finished, it is a good idea to pretest the wording of the questions. Researchers commonly pretest written questionnaires with small groups in advance of a general mailing. This pretest allows for correction of any misleading questions, directions, or problems before the questionnaire is mailed.

Formatting

The format of the questionnaire should have the following features to increase the response rate:

1. The questionnaire should have different types of questions. For example, it may have 25 percent yes and no questions, 25 percent agree/disagree items, and 50 percent scaled-response questions.
2. Directions for completing the questionnaire must be clear for each section or group of questions. Do not assume that respondents will know how you want them to complete the questionnaire.
3. Questionnaires must have excellent visual appearance and design. You should use dark ink (usually black) on light paper and type that is easy to

Our Neighbor to the North

Life in the Multicultural MARKETPLACE

Despite our long common border and the fact that Canada is our biggest trading partner, many Americans are unaware of the most basic information about that nation's cultural makeup.

Fully 25 percent of Canadians consider French to be their first language. This figure rises to 80 percent in the province of Quebec. These individuals prefer to be called French-speaking Canadians rather than French-Canadians.

But not all Canadians are French. Like the United States, Canada was settled by a variety of people from around the world. Among them were the French, British, Irish, Germans, Scandinavians, Asians, Dutch, Ukrainians, Italians, and Poles. The original settlers included a variety of native American Indians.

read. Shading sections for contrast and using arrows to lead the reader through the questionnaire are also ways to improve the visual look of the questionnaire.

4. Numbers should be placed on all sections and on all questions. Respondents are more likely to respond to all items if they are numbered. Numbered questions are also easier to tabulate.
5. If your questionnaire requires more than one page, you may want to place a message at the bottom of each page to continue to the next page. (See Figure 33–3.)

Distributing the Questionnaire

Average response rates can be improved for questionnaires by following some simple suggestions. If a questionnaire is mailed, it should be sent as first-class mail with a hand-signed cover letter (personalized if the potential respondent is known). The cover letter should explain the purpose of the survey and the deadline for returning the questionnaire. A postage-paid return envelope should be included with the questionnaire. If the questionnaire is not mailed, a brief explanation of the survey's purpose should be placed on the questionnaire itself.

The Impact of the Computer on Marketing Research

Computers have had a tremendous impact on marketing research. Software programs allow researchers to analyze huge amounts of information. They also allow

---

More About

Computers and Marketing Research

On-line databases offer a quick way for individuals who don't work in a big market research department to access large amounts of information. For example, DataQuick (located in Marina del Rey, CA) offers a HomeData Report, which is a profile of any house or condo in the area, for $27.50. In addition, it offers on-line access to other secondary data sources such as the U.S. Census.

Figure 33-3

Questionnaires are used in the survey method to gather information from people directly. What elements have been included in the format of this survey to make it visually effective?

researchers to find secondary data in computer databases. The computer is used to prepare surveys and to generate lists of potential questionnaire respondents.

The following is a list of some marketing research activities that computers can help marketing researchers perform:

- *Data collection.* Computer databases are a source of information for researchers. Some databases are created electronically, such as those using scanner data.
- *Analysis.* Computers are used to analyze the information collected, such as competitive, demographic, site, and location data.
- *Forecasting.* Computer programs are available to use current market conditions and research data to forecast future sales by market segments.
- *Interviewing.* Computers can gain information directly from customers through special units that are set up to allow respondents to use touch-screen technology to answer questions.

- *Survey research.* Developing survey instruments is easier on the computer because changes are made easily.
- *Media research.* Electronic databases are available for defining television and radio audiences, as well as providing information on neighborhoods, targeted direct mail, and media planning.

SECTION 33.2 *Review*

1. **What are three steps that must be taken to construct a valid and reliable questionnaire?**
2. **Name six research activities that computers can help researchers perform.**

Chapter 33   *Conducting Marketing Research*   **443**

SECTION 33.2

Enrichment

1. Assign and review the appropriate activities in the *Student Activity Workbook*.
2. Assign and review the appropriate Critical Thinking questions from the Chapter Review.
3. Assign and review the Building Academic Skills Activities, Application Projects, Linking School to Work Activities, and Performance Assessment from the Chapter Review.
4. Have students research the services of one major marketing research firm to discover (1) in what type of research the firm specializes, (2) some of its major clients, and (3) the cost of its services. Students should write their findings in at least 150 words. Major marketing research firms include:
   - Burke Marketing Research, Inc., 800 Broadway, Cincinnati, OH 45202, (513) 852-8585 (marketing research);
   - I.M.S. International, Inc. (Subsidiary of Dun & Bradstreet Corp.), 1209 Orange St., Wilmington, DE 19801, (302) 834-5000 (marketing research and publishing);
   - Nielsen Marketing Research, 70 Seaview Ave., Stamford, CT 06902 (203) 353-7000 (marketing research);
   - Starch/Inra/Hooper, Inc., E. Boston Post Rd., Mamaroneck, NY 10543 (914) 698-0800 (marketing research and public opinion polls);

Close

Have students complete this statement: Research questionnaires should have two key things:... (validity and reliability.)

Caption Answer

Elements include directions, uses a type size and black ink so it can be read easily, and numbers are placed on all sections and questions.

Section Review Answers

1. Surveys must be properly written, formatted, and distributed.
2. Analysis, data collection, forecasting, interviewing, survey research, media research, statistical analysis.

Answers

Vocabulary Review

See Glossary for definitions.

Fact and Idea Review

1. Because they are readily available at little or no cost.
2. Advantages: They can be obtained quickly. They are less expensive. Disadvantages: The data may be unsuitable or out-of-date.
3. A research technique in which information is gathered from people directly through the use of questionnaires. Surveys can be conducted by mail, by telephone, or by personal interview.
4. With natural observation, customers or employees are viewed as they would normally act in a given situation. With contrived observation, the situation is not natural. Observers pose as customers to measure the effectiveness of an activity under study.
5. Survey research involves asking people directly. The observation method observes people in certain situations.
6. A research technique in which one or more marketing variables are observed under controlled conditions. It is used less frequently because of the high costs and because of such uncontrollable factors as people responding differently under controlled conditions than they normally would.
7. The compiling, analyzing, and interpreting of the result of primary and secondary collection.
8. Title page; acknowledgments; table of contents; lists of illustrations; introduction; review of the literature; procedures used to obtain primary data; findings; recommendations; summary and conclusions; appendices; and bibliography.

444

Vocabulary Review

Write two or three paragraphs on conducting marketing research, incorporating these vocabulary terms.

problem definition
primary data
secondary data
survey method
sample
online computer services
observation method
point-of-sale research
experimental method
data analysis
forced-choice questions

Fact and Idea Review

1. Why should secondary data be used first when trying to solve marketing research problems? (Sec. 33.1)
2. What are two advantages of using secondary data? What are two disadvantages of using secondary data? (Sec. 33.1)
3. What is the survey method of research? Describe three ways to conduct surveys. (Sec. 33.1)
4. What is the difference between a natural and contrived observation? (Sec. 33.1)
5. How does survey research differ from observation research? (Sec. 33.1)
6. What is the experimental method of marketing research? Why is this method of research used less frequently than the survey and observation methods? (Sec. 33.1)
7. What is data analysis? (Sec. 33.1)
8. Identify the elements in a final marketing research report. (Sec. 33.1)
9. Does the implementation of research findings end the research process? Why or why not? (Sec. 33.1)
10. What is the difference between an open-ended question and a forced-choice question? (Sec. 33.2)
11. Identify five steps in formatting a questionnaire. (Sec. 33.2)
12. Discuss the procedure for distributing a questionnaire. (Sec. 33.2)

Critical Thinking

1. Can business risks be eliminated by marketing research? Why or why not?

2. What sources of information would you use to identify the market for a new apparel and accessories store in your community?
3. Under natural observation, customers or employees do not know they are being observed. Do you think that this research technique is an invasion of privacy? Why or why not?
4. A store owner wants to know the effectiveness of window displays. Explain what variables the store owner would record during a natural observation.
5. Many restaurants ask businesspeople to leave their business card. How can these cards be used for marketing research?
6. Marketing research is growing in importance. What factors account for the increase in marketing research activities?

Building Academic Skills

Math

1. A retailer conducts a traffic study to estimate yearly sales. Use the following data to estimate yearly sales for the retailer: 1,200 people pass the store each day, 5 percent enter the store and spend an average of $12, the store is open 315 days during the year.
2. Research indicates that 80 percent of the customers for a pizza store live within 1 mile of the store, another 15 percent live within 2 miles of the store, and the remaining 5 percent live within 5 miles of the store. Compute the number of customers who live within the various trading areas if the population of the area is 12,540.

Communication

3. Write a 100-word memo to your instructor explaining the benefits of conducting marketing research prior to the introduction of a new line of merchandise for your school store.

Human Relations

4. You work for the manager of a marketing research department. You and five other employees conduct a number of surveys by telephone. Getting people to respond to questions over the telephone is increasingly difficult. The manager has asked each of you to provide suggestions for how the response rates to telephone surveys could be improved. What suggestions would you make?

9. No. A business should carefully monitor the results to measure the success of the specific actions taken and of the research method used.
10. Open-ended questions ask respondents to construct their own response to a question. Forced-choice questions ask respondents to choose answers from listed possibilities.
11. The five steps are outlined in Section 2.
12. If questionnaire is mailed, it should be sent as first class mail with a hand-signed, cover letter. If questionnaire is not mailed, a brief explanation of the survey's purpose should be placed on the questionnaire itself.

Critical Thinking

1. No. Despite the best marketing research and planning, some products fail in the marketplace.
2. Answers should reflect a combination of primary and secondary data.

Application Projects

1. Investigate recent advertising research in the area of *hermeneutics* (the science of interpretation), *ethnography* (the study of cultures), or *semiotics* (the study of symbols). Give your results in a 200-word written report.
2. Assume you are conducting research for a proposed frozen yogurt store in your community on the likes and dislikes of customers. Develop a list of ten survey questions to ask potential customers.
3. Choose a business to research. Identify at least two secondary data sources for each of the following items: size of market, characteristics of customers, income of customers, present sales volume of competitors, and information about trends in the industry.
4. You are the owner/operator of a local car wash. Design a ten-question survey to get information about your customers and their reactions to the services you provide.
5. Using the most recent *Survey of Buying Power* by Sales and Marketing Management, and U.S. Census data, determine the following about your community:
   a. population
   b. number of restaurants, retail stores, and gas stations, and the total sales for each
   c. number of households
   d. average family size
   e. average income
   f. estimated average age of the population
   g. average education level
6. Using the research information you found in Application Project 5, write a 200-word report on what new type of business might be successful in your community, including how the research supports your recommendation.
7. Interview customers in a mall or in your school store to determine how window displays affect their buying. Share your findings with the class.

Linking School to Work

1. Interview your training sponsor or immediate manager about any marketing research techniques used by your company to collect customer opinions on your products. If possible, bring a copy of any existing surveys to class.
2. Research how your business collects demographic information about its customers. Write a 250-word report on how customer information (name, address, occupation, age, etc.) is collected and used.

Performance Assessment

Role Play

Situation. You work in a small downtown floral shop. You have been asked by the owner to identify whether the shop should add a large assortment of greeting cards. Since the owner knows very little about marketing research, you will need to explain the steps used in marketing research. In addition, you are to recommend a marketing research method to determine the feasibility of adding greeting cards.

Evaluation. You will be evaluated on how well you do the following:
- Describe the five steps in conducting primary research.
- Detail research methods used in primary research.
- Recommend a research approach that is realistic and appropriate to the situation.

Develop a Survey

You are an employee of a family restaurant that has just recently added a bakery. Develop a written survey using forced-choice questions. The purpose is to determine whether your customers like the restaurant's services and its bakery products.

Complete the Chapter 33 Computer Application that appears in the Student Activity Workbook.

Portfolio

Consider the Application Projects that you have done for this unit. Select one that illustrates your mastery of the unit's content and might be of interest to potential employers. Reformat the activity as necessary, adding any explanatory text, and place it in your Portfolio. Consider using these activities:

- Chapter 32, Application Project 9
- Chapter 33, Application Project 4 ■ ■

3. Answers will vary. Some students may feel that this is an invasion of privacy. However, others may feel that the customer or employee is in public therefore there is no invasion of privacy issue as long as the research is ethical.
4. Answers will vary. Store owners might record how many people stop to look at the display and how many walked by without noticing the display.
5. Restaurants can use these cards to create mailing lists and then survey the customers on the list.
6. Answers to complex business problems can be found through marketing research.

Building Academic Skills

Math

1. $226,800 (1,200 × .05 = 60 people × $12 per person = $720 a day × 315 days = $226,800)
2. Within one mile: 10,032 (12,540 × .80 = 10,032) Between 1 and 2 miles: 1,881 (12,540 × .15 =

Communication

3. Memos should follow the format described in Chapter 9.

Human Relations

4. Ways to improve responses will vary.

Application Projects

1. Students should use library resources.
2. Survey questions will vary.
3. Answers will vary.
4. Questions vary.
5. Information will depend on the community that the students live in.
6. Types of businesses will depend on the results of students' research.
7. Students should determine an appropriate number of people to survey. They should write down any questions they will ask customers. They should write down all responses they receive.

Linking School to Work

Answers depend on the work situation.

Performance Assessment

Refer to the *DECA Competitive Events Handbook* for evaluation guidelines.

 ### Computer Application

Optional activity. Refer to the *Marketing Software Binder* for template and user information.

 ### Portfolio

Refer to the Marketing Career Portfolio for development ideas and portfolio management and assessment.

Evaluation

Administer the reproducible test for Chapter 33, or construct your own using the Testmaker software.

Product Planning

Unit Objectives

After completing this unit, students will be able to achieve the following outcomes:

- Explain how businesses plan what products to produce and sell and how they position and manage these products.
- Identify key product mix strategies.
- Explain the nature and scope of branding in product planning.
- Explain the importance of warranties and credit to product planning.

Chapter 36

Chapter 34

Chapter 35

Teacher Classroom Resources

CHAPTER	34	35	36
Transparency Binder	Transparencies 56–57	Transparencies 58–59	Transparencies 60–62
Student Activity Workbook	pp. 213–218	pp. 219–224	pp. 225–30
Student Software	pp. 217–218	pp. 223–224	pp. 225–230
Marketing Math Workbook			Activity 10
School-to-Work Handbook	pp. 73–74	pp. 75–76	pp. 77–78
International Case Studies	pp. 73–74	pp. 75–76	pp. 77–78
Marketing Career Portfolio			Unit 10 activity, Student Text, p. 485
Test Booklet/ Testmaker Software	Chapter 34 test	Chapter 35 test	Chapter 36 test, Unit 10 test

KEY TO BASIC SKILLS ACTIVITIES

L1 Level 1 activities are basic activities and should be within the range of all students.

L2 Level 2 activities are average activities and should be within the range of average and above average students.

L3 Level 3 activities are challenging activities designed for the ability range of above average students.

PERFORMANCE OBJECTIVES

Unit Overview and Background Information

Product planning involves all of the decisions a business makes in the production and sale of its products.

Chapter 34 explains how businesses plan what products to produce and sell. It also discusses how to position and manage products. Chapter 35 explores how branding, packaging, and labeling are incorporated into product planning strategy to create perceived product differences. Chapter 36 discusses extended product features and their role in product planning.

Introducing the Unit

The day you begin this unit, bring to class some "classic" products that have been on the market for a long time, such as Arm & Hammer Baking Soda and Dove soap. Place these classics next to some new products (perhaps a recently introduced breakfast cereal, or a recently introduced brand of sport shoe). Have students speculate on why the classic products have survived and what things the manufacturers have done to insure that they maintain a place in today's market.

Unit Project

By following your guidelines or guidelines developed by the National DECA Delta Epsilon Chi division for the Sales Representative Event, have students complete a 15-minute sales presentation for an item to be sold to a company for resale. Students should stress the product features, brands, warranties, packaging, labeling, and related extended product features during their presentations. Use the rating form provided by National DECA or develop your own.

Unit

10

446

Focus on the Photo/Cooperative Learning

After the students have completed the unit, divide the class into teams. Have each team study the unit opener photo and create a new brand name and/or brand mark for the basketballs featured in the photo. Ask each group to write a paragraph summarizing what led them to their choice and backing up why they think the cost of changing the brand name or mark would be worth the expense.

Product Planning

CHAPTERS

34
**What Is
Product Planning?**

35
**Branding, Packaging,
and Labeling**

36
Extended Product Features

Financing

Distribution

Risk
Management

Product/
Service
Planning

ECONOMIC
FOUNDATIONS
OF MARKETING

HUMAN
RESOURCE
FOUNDATIONS

Selling

Marketing-
Information
Management

MARKETING
AND BUSINESS
FOUNDATIONS

Promotion

Purchasing

Pricing

447

Resources for Enrichment of Unit Content

Magazines/Journals
- *Advertising Age*
- *Business Week*
- *Consumer Reports*
- *Forbes*
- *Grocery Marketing*
- *Inc.*
- *Mail Order Digest*
- *Mass Market Retailers*
- *Packaging*
- *Packaging Digest*
- *Stores*
- *Supermarket News*
- *The Wall Street Journal*

Associations

Center for Packaging Education
PO Box 020240
Brooklyn Heights, NY 11202-0005
(718) 624-6157
(Offers educational programs on the design and manufacture of packaging.)

Consumer Federation of America
1424 16th St., NW, Ste. 604
Washington, DC 20036
(202) 387-6121
(Represents consumer protection groups worldwide.)

Consumers' Research
800 Maryland Ave., NE
Washington, DC 20002
(202) 546-1713
(A service that analyzes and rates consumer products and collects information on consumer issues.)

Unit Closure

Conclude this unit with a general review of all elements of product planning, including packaging, labeling, warranties, guarantees, branding, and product mix. Have products available in your classroom to use as specific examples.

Evaluation

Administer the printed test for Unit 10, or construct your own using the Testmaker software.

Guest Speaker Suggestions

- Have a product developer from a local business discuss the steps his or her company takes to develop new products. If possible, have the person bring some recently developed products.
- Invite a package designer from an ad agency to discuss package/label design, and to show some recent examples of his or her work.

Field Trip Suggestion

Have students tour a local supermarket to discuss with a manager the product positioning used by several of the manufacturers whose goods are carried by the store.

Chapter Overview

This chapter introduces students to product planning.

 Springboard

Prior to the class, have students read through the chapter and write down the vocabulary definitions as homework. Break students into small groups. Provide each group with magazines and newspapers, along with large sheets of paper and colored markers. Have each group look through the magazines and newspapers, and choose product shots that illustrate the concepts presented in the Terms to Know. Have each group present its product shots/drawings and tell why each illustrates the appropriate vocabulary term.

Prereading

List the section objectives to discuss with the students. Have the students skim the chapter, looking at the pictures, reading the captions, and noting the heads. Ask questions to ensure that the students have a minimal understanding of the chapter structure.

Preteaching the Vocabulary

Have students ask you to define the vocabulary words with which they are unfamiliar. If no one asks for definitions, choose students at random to give a definition for each term.

CHAPTER
34

What Is Product Planning?

It's Saturday morning, and you have nothing for breakfast. You take a walk to your grocery store to buy some cereal. As you walk down the cereal aisle, you notice dozens of brands and varieties. As you head to the checkout register, you see the same company names appearing again and again on a variety of products ranging from soup to soap. Glancing back down the aisle, you wonder to yourself, "How did all these different types of products get to the store's shelves?"

In this chapter you will learn how businesses plan what products to produce and sell. You will also learn how they position and manage these products.

448   Unit 10   *Product Planning*

Classroom Management

For the Teacher
- Teacher's Annotated Editions for all workbooks
- Teacher's Manual for *School-to-Work Handbook*
- *Testing Binder*
- *Transparency Binder*
- *Marketing Software Binder*
- *Marketing Career Portfolio*
- *Lesson Plans*

For the Student
- *Student Activity Workbook*
- *Marketing Math Workbook*
- *School-to-Work Handbook*
- *Student Software*
- *International Case Studies*
- *Marketing Career Portfolio*

SECTION 34.1

Objectives

After completing this section, you will be able to

- explain the nature and scope of product planning,
- define product mix,
- describe product mix strategies, and
- identify the steps in new product development.

Terms to Know

- product planning
- product mix
- product line
- product item
- product width
- product depth
- product modification

What Is Product Planning?

Product planning involves making decisions about the production and sale of a business's products. These decisions relate to packaging, labeling, warranties, guarantees, branding, and product mix. A well-defined product plan allows a business to create sales opportunities, design appropriate marketing programs, and develop effective advertising campaigns. It also allows a business to coordinate the product mix offered to customers, add new products, and delete older products that no longer appeal to customers.

Product Mix

The **product mix** includes all the different products that a company makes or sells. A large manufacturer may have hundreds of products in its product mix. Procter &

Gamble for example, makes many different products. Some examples are hand soaps, body lotions, dish detergents, laundry detergents, shampoos, cosmetics, powders, and pain medications.

A retailer also has a product mix that is made up of all the different products the store stocks. Retail stores must plan their product mix carefully because they cannot offer all the possible products that customers may want. Stores need to offer a good selection of merchandise. Adding more products, though, may not result in increased sales if those are not the products the stores' customers want. In fact, sometimes adding too many new products can take away from existing sales.

The types and number of products to be carried must be based on the objectives of the business, the image the business wants to project, and the market it is trying to serve. Thus, product mixes are unique to each business. Even similar types of businesses offer different product mixes. For example, the product mix of Gap Kids, an apparel store, differs greatly from the product mix offered by Brooks Brothers, another apparel store. This product mix is different because each store serves a different market and wants to project a different image.

Product Items and Lines

A product mix is made up of all product lines and items offered by a company. A **product line** is a group of closely related products manufactured and/or sold by a business. Examples include all the car models produced by Ford, all the cereals produced by Kellogg's, and all the cake mixes produced by Pillsbury.

Retailers frequently sell more than one product line. A sporting goods store, for example, might carry both the Spalding and Wilson lines of tennis rackets. A supermarket might stock both the Libby and Del Monte canned fruit lines. A video store might sell the Kodak, Memorex, and Scotch videocassette product lines.

A **product item** is a specific model, brand, or size of a product within a product line. Typically, retailers carry several product items for each product line they sell. For example, a department store that carries the Guess? jeans product line will have an assortment of sizes and styles for both men and women. A computer store handling the Apple Computer product line would carry several Apple models. These models might include the Apple Classic and the Macintosh Performa, Powerbook, and Quadra.

Product Width and Depth

A product mix is defined by the *width* and *depth* of its product offerings. **Product width** refers to the number of different product lines a business manufactures or sells. **Product depth** refers to the number of product items offered within each product line.

Chapter 34   *What Is Product Planning?*   **449**

Focus

⏰ Bell Ringer Activity

Have students imagine that they are going to open a retail business and they must determine the types and number of products to be carried. Have them write the following on a separate sheet of paper:
(1) the type of retail business they would like to open (for example, a beauty supply store);
(2) four general categories of merchandise they would like to carry (for example, shampoo, hair coloring, nail polish, and cosmetic brushes); and
(3) the factors that would determine the type and number of products they will carry.

Introducing the Section

Review students' answers to #1 and #2 from the Bell Ringer Activity. From their prior reading of the chapter, students should be able to recall the types and number of products to be carried, which must be based on (1) the objectives of the business, (2) the image the business wants to project, and (3) the market it is trying to serve. List these factors on the chalkboard and keep them there for the remainder of this chapter.

Meeting Special Needs

Learning Disabled

Providing a positive learning environment for all the students in your class may require you to modify or rethink some of your teaching methods. If you have students in your class with learning disabilities, you may wish to consult with specialists in your school regarding techniques that have proven effective in teaching these particular students. You can

also consult such sources of information as *Journal of Learning Disabilities* or the *Learning Disability Quarterly*. Pairing students with peer helpers, when appropriate, can also serve to increase learning disabled students participation in class, provided a good pair match can be made.

Teach

Guided Practice

1. Read Section 34.1 with students.
2. Use the transparency for this section.
3. Have students read aloud the Case Study and review the answers in class.
4. If possible, invite a person from the product development division of a local company to discuss product development with your class. He or she may not be allowed to discuss products currently under development but should be able to give information on products developed and introduced in the recent past.

   Before the speaker comes to your class, tell students that product development in any company is a highly confidential process, so they should understand the speaker's limitations in discussing current products under development.
5. It may be helpful to obtain copies of the *Journal of Product Innovation Management* for students to peruse in your classroom.
6. MarkEd Resource Center in Columbus, Ohio, (800) 448-0398, offers materials that are appropriate for use with this chapter.

Discussion Starter

Have students analyze the width and depth of the products offered (1) in your school store, (2) in your school cafeteria, (3) in the candy sales in which they participate at school or through extracurricular activities outside of school.

Have students analyze both width and depth in terms of (1) the objectives of the organization, (2) the image the organization wants to project, and (3) the market the organization is trying to serve.

Let's look at some examples. A retailer that stocks several brands of jeans, such as Jordache, Levi's, Lee, and Wrangler, is demonstrating product width. The product depth is the number of sizes, price ranges, colors, and styles for each brand of jeans.

Both manufacturers and retailers must decide on the width and depth of their merchandise or product assortment. Assortment strategies vary with the type of business. For example, Red Lobster restaurants specialize in seafood dinners. They have great depth within a narrow product line. Other restaurants offer broader menus that include steak, chicken, and pasta dinners, as well as seafood. Their product assortment shows great width but less depth than Red Lobster's.

To determine its product mix, a business typically must answer several questions:

1. What is the business's target market?
2. What kind of product offerings do customers want?
3. What products are competitors offering?
4. How many product lines and product items are needed?
5. Should existing product lines be expanded, modified, contracted, or deleted?
6. What image does each product or product line project?
7. What image does the business want to project?

A business answers these questions by deciding its objectives. One objective might be to increase sales by adding new product lines and items. Another way to increase sales might be to create or identify a new use for an existing product. Businesses often have the objective of increasing their market share. One way to do this might be to develop new product lines to sell to their existing markets.

Product Mix Strategies

A product mix strategy is the plan for how the business determines which products it will make or stock. Depending upon their resources and their business objectives, businesses can use different product mix strategies. Some businesses develop completely new products to add to their existing product lines. Others expand or modify their current product lines. Sometimes businesses drop existing products to allow for new product offerings.

Developing New Products

New products can add substantially to a company's overall sales and boost its market share. For example, the

Figure 34–1

THE SIX STEPS IN NEW PRODUCT DEVELOPMENT
Developing new products involves six key steps.

1. Generating Ideas
Ideas are generated from a variety of sources.

A. Bad
B. Good

2. Screening Ideas
Ideas for new products are screened and evaluated. Ideas are eliminated. The best ideas are put through further evaluation. Finally, one or two ideas are selected for development.

More About

Generating Ideas
There are computer software programs available that are designed specifically to help companies generate new product ideas. These programs allow marketers to review a large database of ideas. They also include problem-solving questions to help marketers screen possible ideas.

board game Trivial Pursuit sold 20 million sets in 1984, its highest year. The game's maker has increased sales since that time by developing variations of the original game. It now offers travel packs, a children's version, and annual year-in-review editions. These new games continue to sell 1.5 million units each year.

According to one study, new products (those less than five years old) account for about 35 percent of total sales for major consumer and industrial goods companies. New products can also help a company's image by providing it with a reputation as an innovator and leader with its customers.

New products also increase markups and profits to sellers. This happens when new products are successful because they tend to be priced 10 to 15 percent higher than older, comparable products.

New products often become a major part of a company's product line. For example, Cabbage Patch dolls, first introduced as a novelty during the 1982 Christmas season, have become an ongoing product for Hasbro.

More than 75 million dolls have been sold since the doll was first introduced. Signed, special edition dolls sell today for as much as $650.

New product development generally involves six key steps:

1. generating ideas,
2. screening ideas,
3. developing the product,
4. testing the product,
5. introducing the product, and
6. evaluating customer acceptance of the product.

Let's take a closer look at each step. (See Figure 34-1.)

Generating Ideas New product ideas come from a variety of sources including customers, competitors, channel members, and company employees. Creativity is essential for new product development. Some companies sponsor idea sessions, which are designed to generate as many new ideas and new product concepts in as many product categories as possible.

3. Developing the Product

During the development stage a prototype is made. The prototype is tested and adjustments are made to improve the final product.

4. Testing the Product

Newly developed products are test marketed to obtain customers' responses.

GREAT TASTE!

$2.99

5. Introducing the Product

If customer response is favorable, the product is introduced into the marketplace.

6. Evaluating Customer Acceptance

After the product has been introduced, marketers track customer acceptance.

L1 Communication Skills

Have students research the product development of a now popular product—it could be a toy such as a Barbie Doll™, a food product such as a popular snack food, or a car—any product each student finds interesting. Students should take notes on the following:
(1) how the idea for the product came about;
(2) how ideas were evaluated, eliminated, and selected for development;
(3) how adjustments were made to the prototype;
(4) how the product was tested;
(5) how the product was introduced in the market; and
(6) how customer acceptance was evaluated (and continues to be evaluated).

Allow students library research time to choose a product. Discuss with each student his or her chosen product. Try to avoid repetition—each student should have a different product.

L2 Communication Skills

Have students present their findings in a five-minute oral presentation. Encourage students to use illustrations to augment their oral reports.

L3 Communication Skills

All students should take notes on each presentation. All notes should be typed into a final draft copy that has been spell-checked. Have students work in pairs to read each other's keyboarded final drafts, checking them for typos and grammatical errors.

Did You Know ?

Some good product ideas come from deep space. Due to the special needs of the astronauts, product innovations have been spurred on by necessity. Case in point: cordless home power tools such as those developed by Black and Decker, actually came out of the Apollo space program because astronauts had to have tools they could use both in and out of the spacecraft.

Teach (Cont'd.)

Independent Practice

1. Assign and review the Chapter 34 Case Study in the *International Case Studies* workbook.
2. Have students research the product mix of one of these corporations (or, of any other corporation of your choice that offers an extensive product mix): American Home Products Corp., Borden, Inc., Bristol-Myers Squibb Co., H. J. Heinz Co., PepsiCo, Inc., and Sara Lee Corp.

Students should list at least ten different brand-name products carried by each company. They should also research the history and background of the company to determine how and when the company came to produce such different types of products. (For example, PepsiCo acquired Frito-Lay in 1965 and thus got into the snack food business.) Students may be surprised at the variety of products these companies carry.

A good resource to use for this assignment and an excellent reference to have in your classroom is *Hoover's Handbook of American Business*, The Reference Press, 6448 Highway 290 East, Suite E-104, Austin, Texas 78723, (512) 454-7778. Other resources include *Directory of Corporate Affiliations*, *Million Dollar Directory, Standard and Poor's Register of Corporations, Thomas Register of American Manufacturers,* and *Macmillan Directory of Leading Private Companies.*

Review students' findings in class. Discuss the fact that many companies end up producing products far afield from their original product lines due to such things as mergers and acquisitions.

Screening Ideas During the screening stage in the new product planning process, ideas for products are evaluated. New product ideas are evaluated on general characteristics, such as the size of the market, the profit potential, and level of risk. New product ideas are also evaluated on their marketing impact, such as the possible effect on existing products and on the company image and the appeal to current and new markets.

The production requirements for new product ideas must also be considered. How long will it take to produce and introduce the new product? Can it be produced efficiently and at a competitive price? Each factor is weighed, and decisions are then made about which products to develop and market.

Developing the Product During product development, the new product idea takes a physical shape, and marketers develop a marketing strategy. Plans relating to production, packaging, labeling, branding, promotion, and distribution are made. Sometimes millions of dollars can be spent at this stage of development for testing, prototypes, and research. A *prototype* is a model of the product. Usually, only a few models are made at first, as the business tests the idea and makes changes to improve the final product.

Companies can experience long delays during this stage of product planning. For some products, such as prescription drugs and genetically engineered food products, government testing, requirements, and approval can add years to the product development stage.

Production difficulties can also delay the introduction of new products. For example, the ice cream company, Ben and Jerry's, ran into production difficulties when it first developed Cherry Garcia ice cream. The original idea was to use whole chocolate-coated cherries. The whole cherries were too large to go through the production machinery, which caused the chocolate to break off the cherries. After numerous tests, the company finally separated the cherries and the chocolate. Once the product was successfully produced and placed in the marketplace, it quickly became a success. Today the company earns about $150 million a year on all its ice cream and yogurt products.

Testing the Product After the product is developed, it is tested both in the lab and by consumers. As you learned in Chapter 32, new products are frequently test marketed in certain geographic areas to see whether they will be accepted by consumers. For example, PepsiCo developed a new soft drink for the European market to try to increase its market share. The cola is called Pepsi Max, a one-calorie cola, and it was made specifically for non-American tastes. International consumers typically do not like diet beverages, so the company spent more than two years testing different flavor combinations on the European market. Finally, one version met the company's goal of having at least 40 percent of the consumers in a taste test choose the new product over Coke.

Not every new product is test marketed in geographic areas. In some cases, the costs of testing may be too high.

Give Customers What They Like First

When the Coca-Cola Company decided to try to penetrate the Indonesian soft-drink market, it faced a dilemma. Prior to Coke's arrival, the favorite beverages of the average Indonesian were tea and tropical fruit juices. Carbonated beverages in general were not widely known. Thus, when Indonesians first tasted Coke, they were not impressed.

Rather than giving up, Coke decided to solve the problem with a phased-in marketing approach. To give Indonesians the time to develop a taste for carbonation, Coke developed strawberry-, pineapple-, and banana-flavored soft drinks for the market. In time, it plans to try again with Coke itself. Meanwhile, though, it will concentrate on building market share with beverages closer to current national tastes.

In others, marketers may forgo testing because they doubt the accuracy of test results. Sometimes companies fear that a time delay will allow competitors to enter the market before their product is ready.

Introducing the Product If a new product has been successfully test marketed, it is ready for full market introduction. The costs of introducing a new product often are quite high. The product must be advertised to introduce its benefits to consumers. A new or revised distribution network may be needed. The company may need to develop training programs for its sales force. To pay for these costs, the company needs to get its new products into the market as quickly as possible.

The earlier a product can be brought to market, the greater the chance that revenues and profits will be high. Fast product development is an important way to beat the competition and to establish leadership in the product category. The first company to introduce a new product has an advantage in acquiring customers and in building brand loyalty.

Evaluating Customer Acceptance After products have been introduced, marketers track new product performance. This step is done to evaluate customer acceptance of the product and the marketing strategies used to introduce the product.

One way to obtain customer responses is to study sales information. Scanning equipment and computer systems can be used to compile large amounts of sales and market data on existing and new products. From this information, customized reports on the performance of new products can be prepared. The information can be used to build a marketing database about customer responses

Did You Know

Sometimes new products are discovered by mistake. Ivory soap, for example was the result of a manufacturing mistake. A Procter soap and candle workman forgot to turn off his blending machine when he went to lunch. As a result, the batch of soap he was blending filled with air bubbles. The air bubbles made the soap float, giving the soap a new product feature and making "Ivory" a new product for the company.

and purchases. It can also help businesses answer key questions about new product development, such as:

- Who are the best customers for our new product?
- What new products are customers buying?
- How often do customers buy the new product?
- When did customers last buy the new product?

Expanding the Product Line

Companies can expand product mix by adding new product items and lines, which may or may not be related to current products. For example, General Mills introduced Yoplait Crunch 'N Yogurt (a cereal and yogurt combination) as an extension of its Yoplait Yogurt product line. Hershey Foods Corporation introduced Hershey's Hugs as a line extension to the traditional Hershey's Kiss.

Product expansions make good sense for many businesses. Companies often expand product lines as a way to build on an already established image, to increase sales and profits, and to appeal to new markets.

Build on Product or Company Image Companies that have successful product lines often add new products to those lines to take advantage of customers' positive attitudes toward the brand name. For

General Mills expanded its Yoplait product line by adding Yoplait Crunch 'N Yogurt. What are three reasons why companies might expand product lines?

example, Sony built on its image as a producer of high quality electronics products when it added the Walkman to its product line.

A company such as Sony builds its company image through advertising, making reliable products, and offering warranties for its products. Because it is often the first to offer a new consumer electronic product, Sony also has the image of being an innovator of such products.

Increase Sales and Profits Expanding a product line usually means increased sales and profits. For example, a few years ago Coke decided to make its cola slightly sweeter to compete for the market that prefers sweeter colas. While the sweeter coke drew new customers, Coke's traditional drinkers responded to the sweeter product with protest. They preferred their old, original Coke. The company soon decided to market two products instead of one. Coke Classic used the old formula, and Coke became the new, sweeter version. The company was able to increase its sales by holding on to its traditional market while gaining new customers for the new product.

Appeal to New Markets Expanding a product line can allow marketers to capture new markets. For example, the success of L'Oreal's Lancôme fragrances for women led the company to introduce a fragrance for men—a new market for the company. Ralph Lauren's Polo brand was extended to a new line of bedding and home furnishing products. General Motors, Chrysler, and Ford all expanded their truck lines to offer models that appealed to younger buyers.

Product expansions can have disadvantages. When a brand or corporate name is placed on a new product and it proves harmful or defective, all products with the corporate name suffer. In addition, adding products or product lines increases inventory, promotion, storage, and distribution costs. New products may also take sales away from existing product lines and may require additional training for sales representatives who sell the products to suppliers.

Modifying Product Lines

A **product modification** is an alteration in a company's existing product. Modified products may be offered in new and different varieties, formulations, colors, styles, features, or sizes.

Product modifications are a relatively quick and easy way to add new products to a company's product line. At a time when launching a new product can cost as much as $50 million, consumer products companies are turning to lower risk product modification. According to a recent study by Marketing Intelligence Service, Ltd., approximately 16,000 health, beauty, household, food, and pet products are introduced yearly. About 70 percent of these new products were product modifications. Product modifications are viewed as low-risk and low-cost ways to develop new products. Examples of product

Assess

Evaluation

Assign and review the Section 34.1 Review.

Reteaching

1. Assign and review the vocabulary terms for this section.
2. Assign and review Fact and Idea Review questions 1–10 from the Chapter Review.
3. To determine its product mix, a business must answer several questions, which are listed in the section. Review these seven questions with the students. Then choose two or three local businesses (for example, a fast-food restaurant, a retail store, and a service business) and have the students answer as many of these questions as possible about each business in order to analyze its product mix.

Enrichment

1. Assign and review the appropriate activities in the *Student Activity Workbook*.
2. Assign and review the appropriate Critical Thinking questions from the Chapter Review.

Caption Answer

Companies might expand product lines to build on an already established image, to increase sales and profits, to offer customers a complementary product, and to appeal to new markets.

More About

Expanding Product Lines

Technological breakthroughs can offer another reason to expand on a product line. Xerox has looked into the future and decided that its key to continued success is to develop digital copiers that will be compatible with other vendors' systems. It will expand its product line accordingly.

3. Have the students interview the manager or owner of a local retail store, discussing with him or her the choices made in the product mix. Students should summarize their findings in a 250-word report. Each student's report should tell what things are taken into consideration when new product lines are added, and when product lines are deleted. The manager or owner should give examples of product lines that have been added and deleted in this particular store, and tell why. How do the types and brands of products carried reflect the objectives of the business, the image the business wants to project, and the market the business is trying to serve?

The students can simplify their reports by narrowing their discussion to three or four types of products carried in the store (for example, in a retail drugstore, the students might discuss with the owner or manager types of pain relievers, vitamins, cotton balls, and cosmetics).

Close

Choose one local business with which all students are familiar—a business that you have not already discussed with the class. Have students describe its product mix in light of the objectives of the business, the image it wants to project, and the market it is trying to serve.

---

modifications are telephones in new colors and styles, and cars with airbags and antilock brakes.

Deleting a Product or Product Line

Sometimes companies decide that they will no longer produce or sell a particular product or perhaps even a whole product line. For example, a retailer who is trying to appeal to a younger customer may stop selling product lines that appealed to older customers.

Other reasons to drop a product or a product line include:

- The product has become obsolete.
- It has lost its appeal.
- It does not match current company objectives.
- It must be dropped to make room for other products.
- It is no longer profitable.
- It conflicts with another product in the same product line.

Let's take a closer look at each of these reasons.

The Product Is Obsolete Changing interests and technology have caused many products to be dropped. For example, older models of desktop computers have been dropped because newer models are faster and are less expensive to produce. Early computer games have been replaced by games that have more graphics and run on newer computers.

NCR is one company that suffered losses because it did not change its obsolete products. NCR stuck to its electromechanical cash registers instead of switching to the newer technology of electronic processing. As a result, the company lost significant market share. NCR was forced to write off $140 million of new, but obsolete, equipment and to cut the jobs of 20,000 workers.

The Product Has Lost Its Appeal As consumer tastes change, companies drop products that no longer appeal to the old tastes. For example, Brylcreem hair cream, Ovaltine hot chocolate, Lavoris mouthwash, and Lifebuoy bar soaps are products that have lost much of their former customer appeal. Although these products may have some lasting loyalties and may generate revenue, the makers of the products must decide whether to keep them in their product mixes.

Another example is black-and-white televisions. Many models have been dropped because customers today prefer color televisions.

The Product Does Not Match Current Company Objectives Sometimes a product does not match a company's current objectives. For example, Sears recently sold one of its subsidiaries, the Coldwell Banker real estate company. Over the past several years, Sears stores had lost market share to other retailers. The company decided to sell some unrelated businesses so it could focus more attention on its objective of regaining retail market share.

The Product Is Dropped to Make Room for Other Products Supermarkets, drugstores, department stores, and other retail outlets may change product mix frequently. As new products are developed, retailers must make shelf or display space for those they want to offer their customers. Since shelf space is limited and expensive, removing slow-moving products is a necessity. For example, a department store might decide to replace a brand of knit sweaters because its customers did not buy the sweaters very often.

Other products may be dropped because the store decides that it can make more money selling a different brand. For example, one manufacturer might offer better buying terms because the store can buy in volume. A store also may drop an unpopular brand for a more popular one. The store would make more profit because it would not have to mark the price down to get customers to buy the popular item.

The Product Is No Longer Profitable Seeking to increase profits, retailers will handle only fast-moving and profitable items. Often retailers will carry only those products whose stock turnover exceeds a certain number of turns per month.

Product developers may drop products when sales reach such a low level that the return on sales does not meet company objectives. Examples of products that have been dropped because they were no longer profitable are items such as typewriters or novelty products that were a quick-passing fad. For example, millions of pet rocks were sold in the 1980s, but the fad and the product are both gone now.

The Product Conflicts with Other Products in the Same Product Line Sometimes products take business away from other products in the same product line. Increased sales of one product can cause decreased sales of another product. For example, Procter & Gamble's decision to drop the many varieties of White Cloud bathroom tissue was made to avoid competition with its Charmin bathroom tissue.

1. What is product planning?
2. What is product mix?
3. Name four product mix strategies.
4. Identify the steps for new product development.
5. What is one disadvantage to expanding a product line?
6. What is a product modification?
7. List six reasons why companies drop a product or product line.

Section Review Answers

1. Decisions related to packaging, labeling, warranties, guarantees, branding, and product mix.
2. The different products a company makes.
3. Developing a new product, expanding, modifying, contracting, or deleting the product line.
4. Generating or screening ideas; developing, testing, introducing, evaluating product.
5. Increases inventory, promotion, storage, and distribution costs.
6. An alteration in an existing product.
7. Because a product is obsolete, has lost its appeal, no longer matches company objectives, has to be dropped to make room for newer ones, no longer is profitable, or conflicts with other products.

Objectives

After completing this section, you will be able to

- **define the product life cycle,**
- **explain the concept of product positioning, and**
- **describe the purpose of category management.**

Terms to Know

- **product life cycle**
- **product positioning**
- **category management**
- **planogram**

The Product Life Cycle

Products pass through a life cycle. A **product life cycle** represents the stages that a product goes through in its life. There are four stages of the life cycle: introduction, growth, maturity, and decline. As each stage in the product life cycle is reached, marketers must adjust their product mix and their marketing strategies to ensure continued sales.

Managing During the Introduction Stage

When the product is introduced to the market, the focus of the company's efforts is on promotion and production. The major goal is to draw the customer's attention to the new product. For example, compact disc players were introduced to the U.S. market in 1983. By 1985, 600,000 units had been sold.

The company works to build its sales by increasing product awareness. Special promotions may be tried to get the customer to try the new product. As you know, the costs of introducing a product are high, thus this is usually the least profitable stage of the life cycle.

Managing During the Growth Stage

During the growth phase of the product life cycle, the product is enjoying success as shown by increasing

Figure 34-2

The life cycle of a product can be divided into four stages: introduction, growth, maturity, and decline. Why are sales not at their highest during the introduction stage?

sales and profits. Much of the target market knows about and buys the product. Advertising may now focus on consumer satisfaction, rather than on the new product benefits. By this time, the competition is aware of the success of the product and is likely to offer new products, in order to compete. To keep its product sales growing, the company may have to introduce new models or modify the existing product to offer more than the competition.

Using the compact disc player example, by 1986 the product had entered its growth stage. Sales of CD players now amount to several million units a year, and several companies offer competing products.

Managing During the Maturity Stage

A product reaches the maturity stage when its sales level off or slow down. The product may have more competition now, or most of the target market may already own the product. For example, when a large proportion of potential buyers have a CD player, sales will slow and the product will enter the maturity stage.

During this stage, a company spends more of its marketing dollar fighting off the competition. Advertising expenses may climb, and the company may have to decide whether it can continue to improve the product to gain additional sales.

Chapter 34   *What Is Product Planning?*   **455**

Caption Answer

A product is in its infant stage during its introduction. At this stage, the product is new and unfamiliar to consumers. A great deal of money must be spent to get consumers to accept the product. Production, pricing, promotion, and distribution of the product are adjusted in this stage to ensure that the product gains recognition and becomes popular.

Focus

⏰ Bell Ringer Activity

Write the stages of the product life cycle on the board. Review the meaning of each. Then have students identify five products in your classroom and write on a separate sheet of paper where they think each product is in its product life cycle.

Introducing the Section

Review students' answers from the Bell Ringer Activity. Explain that product planning allows a business to create sales opportunities, design appropriate marketing materials, develop effective advertising campaigns, coordinate the product mix, add new products, and delete older products when necessary.

Point out that product planning is one of the broadest areas of marketing that students will encounter. If a product plan is well structured, a company can maintain successful products over a longer period of time than would be possible without product planning.

Ask students to imagine what happens to companies that ignore this step. (They can fold or go bankrupt even though they had an initial good product.) Relating product life cycle to products that students use daily will help them understand this concept.

Teach

Guided Practice

1. Read Section 34.2 with students.
2. Use the transparency for this section.
3. Invite a guest speaker from a local firm to talk to students on how it is managing several of its products which are at different phases of the product life cycle. If possible, have the speaker bring several of the products he or she will discuss with students.

Teach *(Cont'd.)*

4. Assign and review the Chapter 34 Activity in the *School-to-Work Handbook*.

Discussion Starter

Have each student generate a list of three products (they should not use the products they generated for the Bell Ringer Activity). Then have them discuss whether they think their products are positioned: (a) by price and quality, (b) by product features and benefits, (c) by unique characteristics, (d) in relation to competition, and/or (e) in relation to other products in a line. You may wish to let them look through magazines or newspapers to generate their products.

As this textbook went to press, several experimental products were introduced into the market. Are they now commonly available in the national market? If not, have students speculate on the reasons why they are not commonly available. For those products that did make it into the national market, where are they now in their product life cycles? Have students make some predictions about how these products will perform over the next few years:

1. Cars powered by electricity.
2. Virtual reality head-mounted displays which plug into PCs and TV sets. They immerse the wearer in the images they see. As the wearer moves his or her head, the images move, too.
3. Extremely user-friendly software from Microsoft entitled "Bob" that gives easy instructions to the licensee and can be customized to anticipate the licensee's use patterns.
4. Video-phones.
5. An edible slime called "Glop," manufactured by Catco, a specialty toymaker. (You may wish to add to this discussion by including additional recently introduced test products.)

Managing During the Decline Stage

During the decline stage, sales fall. Profits may reach a point where they are smaller than costs. Management will need to decide how long it will continue to support the product.

Besides dropping the product, the company can use other product mix strategies to try to gain further sales from a declining or failing product. These strategies include selling or licensing the product, recommitting to the product line, discounting the product, regionalizing the product, and modernizing or altering the product.

Sell or License the Product Many companies sell or license their poorer performing products to risk-taking companies. Risk-taking companies try to rejuvenate the product by changing the product's image or introducing it to a new market. For example, one of the latest toy fads is actually more than ten years old. The original Power Rangers were produced for Japanese TV. An entrepreneur bought distribution rights from the developer and now licenses toys and other Power Ranger products. The company expects to earn more than $80 million in licensing fees.

Recommit to the Product Line Some companies decide that a declining product has other uses that can help improve sales. For example, Knox gelatin lost sales, as people spent less time cooking and stopped making fancy gelatin desserts. The company found a new use for the product that appeals to a different market. Adding Knox gelatin to Jell-o mixes allows people to make gelatin desserts that can be held in the hand. Children, especially, like the new desserts.

However, even with recommitment and new advertising of new product uses, there is no guarantee that a product will continue to have enough sales. Eventually it may need to be dropped.

Discount the Product Many declining product lines can be saved from deletion by discounting them to compete with cheaper store or private brands. For example, Lever Brothers discounted Pepsodent toothpaste and Lifebuoy soap and advertised the products with phrases, such as "compare and save."

Regionalize the Product Sometimes companies decide to sell declining products only in the geographical areas where there is strong customer loyalty. For example, the Nabisco Food Group only markets its My-T-Fine soups in northeastern states because it still has a significant customer base there. By marketing its product only in that area, the company saves money by avoiding national advertising and distribution costs.

Modernize or Alter the Product Offering Some products can be altered or modernized to avoid deletion. Products can be completely redesigned, packaged differently, or reformulated. For example, Lavoris mouthwash—formerly available in red, green, and blue—was reformulated as a clear product. The new product now appeals to younger consumers who never used the original.

Companies spend large amounts of money to develop and promote consumer and industrial products. As a result, they are reluctant to delete products without trying one of the above strategies. If products must be dropped, a company needs to plan the move carefully to avoid disappointing customers and damaging the company's overall image.

Discounting the product is one way to handle a declining product. Lever Brothers discounted Pepsodent toothpaste to save it from deletion. What are four other strategies marketers can use to rejuvenate a declining product?

Caption Answer

Strategies include selling or licensing the product, recommitting to the product line, regionalize the product, and modernizing or altering the product.

Lifelong Learning

Product Planning

For students not pursuing a career in product development, the most relevant information may be understanding the product life cycle in terms of a planned purchase. The best time to buy a product may not be at the moment it is introduced. By keeping informed of new products in development students can learn to be educated consumers.

CASE STUDY

Audio Books…A Product Whose Time Has Come?

Some retailers and publishers believe that audio books are ready for the mass market. For years, audio books have been considered a minor product category in the publishing business. They have been targeted primarily to the blind and made available mainly through libraries. In the past, audio book sales usually represented only 10 percent of hardback book sales, with no audio book selling more than 70,000 copies. This sleepy little market, though, is changing as audio books become a growing product line.

According to a publisher's survey, retail sales of audio books hit about $1.2 billion in 1993. This figure is up from $250 million only five years ago. During 1993, Michael Crichton's "Jurassic Park" sold 175,000 audio books, and Rush Limbaugh's "The Way Things Ought To Be" sold 280,000 copies.

Major book publishers now release audio versions of hardcover books at the same time as the printed version. Audio-book publishers have also convinced mass merchandisers, such as Target, Kmart, and warehouse clubs, to stock audio versions of bestsellers.

The number of audio book specialty stores has also risen from 25 to 120. Audio bookstores typically carry between 3,000 and 7,000 titles. Audio books in shortened, abridged versions, sell for between $10 to $25. Unabridged versions sell for between $30 to $80. Many of the specialty stores also rent audiotapes.

Audio books appeal to regular book readers who do not have the time to sit and read books and to nonreaders who use them as secondary entertainment. Both customer types can listen to audio books while doing something else, such as driving to work or doing the laundry.

ReZound International of Minneapolis, a company that rents mostly abridged versions of audio books at low prices, has placed counter units in 2,000 convenience stores, gas stations, and video stores. Terry Lipelt, vice president for ReZound, states that the company is looking for the customer who wants a relatively short span of entertainment.

Book/music/video superstores, such as Barnes & Noble and Kmart's Borders, are also entering the audio book market. To promote sales, these superstores let customers sample two-minute segments of tapes with cliffhanger endings.

Bookstore competitors are skeptical about the market for audio books. According to a recent study, only 17 percent of U.S. households bought or listened to an audio book during the year. Blockbuster Entertainment recently dropped audio books from its video store product line because of poor sales.

Others, however, argue that since only 6 percent of U.S. households even shop at bookstores on a regular basis, the fact that 17 percent of them bought or listened to audio books is promising. They believe that if people who do not generally read books begin to use audio books, there will be a huge potential customer base in the future.

Case Study Review

1. Based upon the information presented, in what stage of the product life cycle are audio books? Explain.

2. Evaluate the strategy used by ReZound International to market audio books. Do you think they will be successful? Why or why not?

A MATTER OF ETHICS

3. Companies sometimes shorten, or abridge, books to enable them to fit onto an audiotape. If a company has to leave out only a small portion of the original book, is it ethical to leave the word "Abridged" off the packaging for the audio book? Explain your conclusion.

Chapter 34 *What Is Product Planning?* **457**

Critical Thinking

The text states that as consumer tastes change, companies drop products that no longer appeal to the old tastes. What things influence changes in customer taste? (Changes in customer taste are influenced by such things as (1) trends in hair style and clothing, (2) a need for more technologically advanced products and/or products with more features and benefits, (3) a need for products that can be prepared quickly [such as microwave dinners], and (4) a desire for products that reflect one's racial/cultural heritage.)

Have students give examples of products that have been dropped or whose sales are greatly diminished because they no longer suit customers' tastes and lifestyles, and thus are no longer profitable. (Answers include: record players, hula hoops [although, in recent years, these have been resurrected], eight-track tape players, rotary phones [these are made now only as novelty items], fountain pens [some pen companies still make them but they have gone out of common use], and glass baby bottles and cloth diapers.)

One of the reasons products are taken off the market is due to obsolescence. Ask students to define the term *obsolescence*.

Case Study Answers

1. Growth stage. Rationale: product has existed for a number of years and the market is growing based upon recent sales figures.
2. Answers will vary.
3. The truth-in-labeling laws require that consumers be told what they are buying. In the case of a published book, the consumer has a right to know that parts of the original are missing. Even without labeling laws, better customer relations will result if customers know what they are buying before they buy, rather than buying a product and then being disappointed. Disappointment in a product leads to fewer sales in the future.

Teach (Cont')

Cooperative Learning

Divide the class into four groups. Give each group colored markers and large sheets of paper. Have each group collaborate to create a visual/verbal representation of the phases of the product life cycle and how advertising and promotion are managed during each phase. Allow each group to display its completed work in your classroom.

Independent Practice

Have students generate a written list of at least three products that are no longer available, and tell the reasons why they think these products have been discontinued. Students should also tell whether these products have been replaced with other products from the same manufacturer that fill the same marketplace needs.

Have students share their lists in class. Also have students identify products that have just been introduced into the market, along with the consumer needs that these products appear to be filling.

Assess

Evaluation

Assign and review the Section 34.2 Review.

Reteaching

1. Assign and review the vocabulary terms for this section.
2. Assign and review Fact and Idea Review questions 11–16 from the Chapter Review.

BRIGHT IDEAS

Picture That!

In order to create a revolutionary new design, the makers of the Ford Taurus used the power of visual imagery to help them design the popular car. The design team members surrounded themselves with cutout pictures of any object they liked that they felt contained interesting visual shapes or lines. The products they chose were not by any means limited or necessarily related to cars. In fact, they used pictures of such diverse products as ski boots, refrigerators, and even door handles. What they were exposing their minds to were design trends, seeking a direction for their new car. While they did not use each and every element they had chosen to post on the walls, they did get an overall idea of what they wanted the car to look like, even before they began the actual design. The final results exceeded their wildest expectations. Sales of the Ford Taurus helped turn the company around.

Creativity Challenge Form teams of 3–5 people. Then select something you would like to re-design—a pair of shoes, a desk or an easy chair, the school lobby or auditorium, whatever. Use magazines, catalogs, newspapers, or brochures to compile a set of images whose elements or features you would like to include in your design. In each case, explain how and why you will include them in your design.

Product Positioning

Product positioning refers to the efforts a business makes to identify, place, and sell its products in the marketplace. It is an attempt to create an image of a product that appeals to customers. Product positioning is vital. Products that are not properly positioned will not be successful in the marketplace. Changing the image of unsuccessful products or repositioning them is costly.

To position their products, businesses need to identify customers' needs and to address how their product compares to the competition. For example, when Chrysler introduced the Plymouth Neon, it positioned the car both as a low-cost, affordable vehicle and as an alternative to other subcompact passenger cars.

A number of strategies are used to position products in the marketplace, including

- by price and quality,
- by product features and benefits,
- by unique characteristics,
- in relation to competition, and
- in relation to other products in a line.

Let's take a closer look at each of these strategies.

Positioning by Price and Quality

Companies frequently position their products in a product line based upon price and quality. For example, the Ford Motor Company deliberately positions its Escort as an economical passenger car while still emphasizing quality. It positions its Crown Victoria as a high-priced luxury passenger car. Promotional efforts are aimed at creating a price and quality image for each of these Ford products. This strategy enables Ford to give each of its products a unique position in the marketplace.

Positioning by Features and Benefits

Companies frequently position products by stressing their features and the resulting benefits to the buyer. For example, Oil of Olay was positioned as a premium facial moisturizer and cleanser to keep skin soft and young. Research indicated that consumers wanted not only a facial bar but also a bath bar with special moisturizing properties. In response, Procter & Gamble introduced the Oil of Olay Bath Bar. The company promoted the new bath bar by emphasizing its features and benefits. Advertisements proclaimed the product to be superior to other bath bars. It claimed to help the skin retain moisture better, to stay firm, to be less messy, and not to melt away like other skincare bath bars.

Real World

Meet the Beetle

In the 1950s, Detroit, the nation's car capital, was thinking big. However, Volkswagen, the new dream machine, was anything but big or flashy. How to position it to sell became Doyle Dane Bernbach's big puzzle. The agency's solution was to think small. Ads celebrated VW's economy and unchanging design. "VW," one copy tag read, "doesn't go in one year and out the other." Both agency and client came out big winners.

 Bright Ideas

Students need not have artistic backgrounds to trace design influences in the market. Having a sense of design is a skill that can be acquired and does not require the ability to actually produce a design. Students may or may not be aware that they are attracted to certain types of designs. Hold a product design award ceremony for the designs that are voted the most popular by the class.

Positioning by Unique Characteristics

Companies frequently position products to highlight their unique characteristics. The goal is to set the product apart from the competition. For example, when Apple Computer introduced the Newton MessagePad, it tried to position the product as a completely new way for people to access, manage, and communicate information. Apple encouraged consumers to try out the product at retail stores and at special demonstration events.

Positioning in Relation to the Competition

Some businesses position their products to compete directly with the products of other companies. For example, when the Warner-Lambert Company introduced Cool Mint Listerine, it did so by positioning its product against the competition. Traditionally, customers of mouthwashes chose between the "therapeutic" benefits of strong tasting, original Listerine or the "cosmetic" benefits of other brands like Scope. With its "cool mint" flavor, Listerine hoped to compete directly with other cosmetic brands. The company also hoped to retain those customers who believed that Listerine could fight germs, plaque, and gum infection better than other products.

Positioning in Relation to Other Products in a Line

Individual products may be positioned in relation to other products in the same line. For example, when Binney & Smith introduced washable crayons, it positioned them as a specialty item in the company's Crayola crayon line.

Car manufacturers often position their models in relation to each other. For example, models may range from the low-cost economy cars to the top-of-the-line luxury cars.

Category Management

Many manufacturers and retailers are adopting a new process for marketing and selling their products known as category management. **Category management** is a process that involves managing product categories as individual business units. A *category* may include a group of product lines that have the same target market and distribution channels. The process is designed to put manufacturers and retailers in closer touch with customer needs.

The manufacturer can customize this category's product mix, merchandising, and promotions according to customer preference on a store-by-store basis. Using scanning data on product sales and other market data, manufacturers assist retailers with their product mix. In examining product mix, a manufacturer determines which

Positioning in relation to other products **is a strategy Binney & Smith used when it introduced Crayola washable crayons. What are four other strategies a company might use to position its products?**

of its products a particular retailer does not carry. It also identifies products that would have strong sales potential for both the retailer and the manufacturer. This analysis helps the manufacturer to recommend an optimum product mix by projecting sales volume and profits for a retailer. Suggestions are then made to add certain items to its product mix and delete others.

Another way manufacturers can help retailers is through planograms. **Planograms** are computer-developed diagrams that show retailers how and where products within a category should be displayed on a shelf at individual stores. Manufacturers can even customize planograms for specific types of stores. Each store then can stock more of the products that appeal to people in its trading area and less of those that do not appeal to its customers.

SECTION 34.2 Review

1. What is a product life cycle? Name the four stages in the product life cycle.
2. Explain the concept of product positioning. Why is it important?
3. What is category management?

SECTION 34.2

3. Create a bulletin board display by first placing each of the four stages of the product life cycle on a separate sheet of paper and tacking each paper to the board.

Have students bring in a picture of one product from a magazine or newspaper, tell the class where the product is in its life cycle, tell how the product is positioned in the marketplace, and then place the picture under its appropriate category on the bulletin board.

Enrichment

1. Assign and review the appropriate activities in the *Student Activity Workbook*.
2. Assign and review the appropriate Critical Thinking questions from the Chapter Review.
3. Assign and review the Building Academic Skills Activities, Application Projects, Linking School to Work Activities, and Performance Assessment from the Chapter Review.
4. Have the students interview the manager of a local store to review a planogram for particular products in a category and discuss the management strategy behind the product placement. Students should write their findings in 150 to 200 words.

Close

Have students complete these statements: (a) A product life cycle represents… (the stages that a product goes through in its life.) (b) As each stage in the product life cycle is reached, marketers must adjust _____ and _____ to ensure continued sales. (their product mix and their marketing strategies)

Caption Answer

Companies may position by price and quality, by product features and benefits, by unique characteristics, and in relation to competition.

Section Review Answers

1. Product life cycle is the stages a product goes through during its life span. Four stages: introduction, growth, maturity, and decline.
2. The efforts of a business to identify, place, and sell its products in the marketplace.
3. Category management is a process that involves managing product categories as individual business units.

Answers

Vocabulary Review

See the Glossary for definitions.

Fact and Idea Review

1. A product item is a specific model, brand, or size of product within a product line. A product line is a group of closely related products manufactured and/or sold by a business.
2. Product width: the number of different product lines a business carries. Product depth: the number of product items offered within each product line.
3. It identifies the target market, creates an image for the business, affects the profits, and allows the business to meet its competition.
4. Customers, competitors, channel members, and company employees.
5. General product, marketing, and production characteristics.
6. Introducing a new product is expensive.
7. Marketers use research.
8. To build on an already established image, to increase sales and profits, to offer customers complementary products, and to appeal to new markets.
9. They are low risk and low cost ways to develop new products.
10. Because a product has lost its appeal, no longer matches company objectives, has to be dropped to make room for newer ones, is no longer profitable, or conflicts with other products.
11. Heavy advertising and other means of promotion, such as in-store displays, to draw customers' attention.
12. Company should be prepared to counter the effects of new products by offering new features.

460

Vocabulary Review

Using the vocabulary terms below, write a 150-word paper on product planning.

    product planning
    product mix
    product line
    product item
    product width
    product depth
    product modification
    product life cycle
    product positioning
    category management
    planogram

Fact and Idea Review

1. Explain the difference between a product item and a product line. (Sec. 34.1)
2. Explain the difference between product depth and product width. (Sec. 34.1)
3. List four reasons why product mix is important. (Sec. 34.1)
4. What are four sources that marketers turn to for new product ideas? (Sec. 34.1)
5. Summarize the types of criteria that marketers use to screen new product ideas. (Sec. 34.1)
6. Why must new products be introduced as quickly as possible? (Sec. 34.1)
7. How do marketers evaluate customer acceptance of a new product? (Sec. 34.1)
8. Identify four reasons for expanding a product line. (Sec. 34.1)
9. Explain the advantages of product modification. (Sec. 34.1)
10. Discuss the reasons why a business might delete its product lines. (Sec. 34.1)
11. What strategies might a business use during a product's introduction stage? (Sec. 34.2)
12. What strategies might a business use during a product's growth stage? (Sec. 34.2)
13. What strategies might a business use during a product's maturity stage? (Sec. 34.2)
14. List the strategies that a company can use during a product's decline stage. (Sec. 34.2)
15. List and describe five strategies used to position products in the marketplace. (Sec. 34.2)
16. How can manufacturers use category management to assist a retailer? (Sec. 34.2)

Critical Thinking

1. Identify a product item, product line, and product mix produced by one company.
2. If you owned a small retail store that sells party supplies to consumers, what are at least ten items you might have in your product mix?
3. Suppose a company is working on developing a new product, when a competitor introduces a new product that is similar. What are some things the company should consider in deciding whether to proceed with the development of its new product?
4. How do you think customers' perceptions affect the image a company tries to create for a product line?
5. In response to the "green movement," manufacturers are designing products that are safe for the environment. Choose a company and suggest ways the company could modify one of its products to be environmentally friendly.
6. For each of the items below, list a possible product modification or product extension.
   a. electric bread machine
   b. toothbrush
   c. animal crackers
7. Choose one of the following products and explain the strategies you would use to manage it during each stage of its life cycle.
   a. soup
   b. soap
   c. soda

Building Academic Skills

Math

1. Sales of a product that is in its growth stage are expected to continue growing at the rates of 10 percent for next year, 12 percent for the year following, and 14 percent for the third year. If 600,000 units were sold this year, how many units will be sold in each of the next three years?
2. The Griffin Company has two declining products. It is considering deleting one of them from its product line. Product A costs $68 per unit to produce and sells for $105. The storage, distribution, and promotion costs average $5.40 a unit. Last year, 18,000 units were sold. Product B costs $46 to produce and sells for $67. Its storage, distribution, and promotion costs average $8.50 a unit. Last year, 80,000 units were sold. Of the two products, which is the less profitable and should be deleted?

13. It must allocate more of its advertising budget to promoting the product.
14. Sell or license, recommit, discount, regionalize, and modernize or alter.
15. Stress price and quality, stress product features and benefits, stress unique characteristics, compare the product to the competition, show a relationship to other products in the line.
16. Manufacturers can customize product mix, merchandising, and promotions according to customer preference on a store-by-store basis.

Critical Thinking

1. Product item: Sony CD. Product line: Sony stereos, CD players, and tape decks. Product mix: Sony electronic equipment.
2. A party supplies store would have items such as paper plates, cups, and napkins, etc.
3. The company needs to study the competitor's product and compare its own product features.

Product A
$105 × 18,000 units = $1,890,000
$68 × 18,000 units = 1,224,000
Subtotal = $666,000
$5.40 × 18,000 units = 97,200
Total $568,800

Product B
$67 × 80,000 units = $5,360,000
$46 × 80,000 units = 3,680,000
Subtotal $1,680,000
$8.50 × 80,000 units = 680,000
Total = $1,000,000

Communication

3. Develop a 500-word written product plan for a truck manufacturer that is planning to diversify into the building and selling of buses. Identify possible target markets, product features, and considerations relating to pricing, sales, promotion, and placement.

Human Relations

4. You are a buyer of ready-to-wear clothing for a large, urban department store. Early one afternoon, you are confronted by an exasperated customer who is ready to walk out of the store because of the clutter of the merchandise. She complains that too many sizes, colors, and styles are jammed together on too many racks with too little space between them. "I came here to shop for a few bargains, not to arm wrestle with jogging suits," she fumes. How do you explain to her the dilemma retailers face in deciding just how much merchandise to stock? What is too much of an item? What is not enough? What are the costs and benefits for customers and retailers alike of carrying a large assortment of items?

Application Projects

1. Choose a retail business. Think about the mix of products you would choose to stock it. Write a 200-word report on your business, explaining your choices in terms of the market you want to reach and the image you want to project.

2. Choose a manufacturing business, such as an electronic equipment manufacturer. Describe the types of products it makes. Write a 200-word paper on the features of the products and the elements that should be included in a product plan.

3. Visit a grocery store or supermarket to obtain five examples of product line extensions. Write the name of the original product and the line extensions for the product. For example, the Cheerios product has extensions in Honey Nut Cheerios and Apple Cinnamon Cheerios.

4. Visit a store that carries a variety of items, such as a grocery store or electronics store. Choose three products, such as laundry detergent or tape recorders, and evaluate the width and depth of each product line. Explain how the selection increases or decreases the potential sales of those products.

5. Your store offers a wide but shallow product range. You think it will do better with more depth, but you only have so much capital to increase your inventory. Using what you have learned up to this point about advertising, display, marketing, and sales, write a 300-word paper explaining how you will decide which products you will cut and which you will add.

6. Select a general type of product, such as gasoline or food, to manufacture or sell. Identify how you would position the product. Explain your reason for your positioning choice.

Linking School to Work

1. Analyze the product mix of your cooperative training station or place of employment. Determine your target market and write a 250-word report on how your product mix appeals to your target market.

2. Select a new product offering at your place of employment. Analyze why customers may want to purchase this new product. Describe your conclusions in a 250-word report.

Performance Assessment

Role Play

Situation. You are working at an advertising agency that specializes in rejuvenating slow-moving products. You have been approached by Rufus General Foods regarding its Ricka brand of decaffeinated coffee. Recently, ads have featured gray-haired customers. This image does not appeal to Ricka's target market, which is customers between 40 and 50 years old who do not want to be reminded that they are aging. You have been asked to present a plan to reposition Ricka to give it a more contemporary image.

Evaluation. You will be evaluated on how well you can do the following:

• Develop an appropriate product mix strategy.
• Explain how you would position the product to achieve a more contemporary image.

Diagram

Select a product line from a business of your choice. Create a diagram of all the product items in one product line carried by the store. Identify each item by name, price, and at least two other distinguishing features.

COMPUTER APPLICATION

Complete the Chapter 34 Computer Application that appears in the Student Activity Workbook.

Communication

3. Students should include possible target market, product features, and considerations relating to advertising, sales, promotion, and staffing.

Human Relations

4. Students should be tactful in dealing with customers.

Application Projects

1. Products will depend on the business.
2. Product features will vary.
3. Examples include Haagen-Dazs ice cream's extension, Haagen-Dazs sorbet.
4. Students should evaluate the width and depth of their product.
5. Papers will vary.
6. Answers will vary.

Linking School to Work

Answers depend on the work situation.

Performance Assessment

Refer to the *DECA Competitive Events Handbook* for evaluation guidelines.

Computer Application

Optional activity. Refer to the *Marketing Software Binder* for template and user information.

Evaluation

Administer the reproducible test for Chapter 34, or construct your own using the Testmaker software.

---

4. A business must try to produce and promote a product that matches a customer's perceptions.
5. Possibilities: design packages that are recyclable, design products for disassembly after use, and use less harmful content in products.
6. Examples include: machine that makes bread and coffee; toothbrush with toothpaste that is attached; dinosaur or truck shaped crackers.
7. Examples will vary.

Building Academic Skills

Math

1. Year 1: 660,000 units (600,000 × 10% + 600,000)
   Year 2: 739,200 units (660,000 × 12% + 660,000)
   Year 3: 842,688 units (739,200 × 14% + 739,200)
2. Product B is the more profitable of the two, so product A should be dropped first. The calculations are as follows:

Chapter Overview

Chapter 35 introduces branding, packaging, and labeling, and their critical importance in product planning.

 ### Springboard

Write these products across the blackboard, as column headings: *breakfast cereal, hand soap, laundry detergent, instant coffee, toothpaste, cookies,* and *packaged meat.* (You should have one product for each row of students in your class.) The students in each row should generate five national and local brands for each product, and write them in the appropriate column on the board. Review the brands listed under each product.

Tell students that in this chapter they will look at each of these elements as they discuss the importance of branding, labeling, and packaging.

Prereading

List the section objectives to discuss with the students. Have the students skim the chapter, looking at the pictures, reading the captions, and noting the heads. Ask questions to ensure that the students have a minimal understanding of the chapter structure.

Preteaching the Vocabulary

List the vocabulary terms on the board. Have the class reach a consensus on a definition for each term.

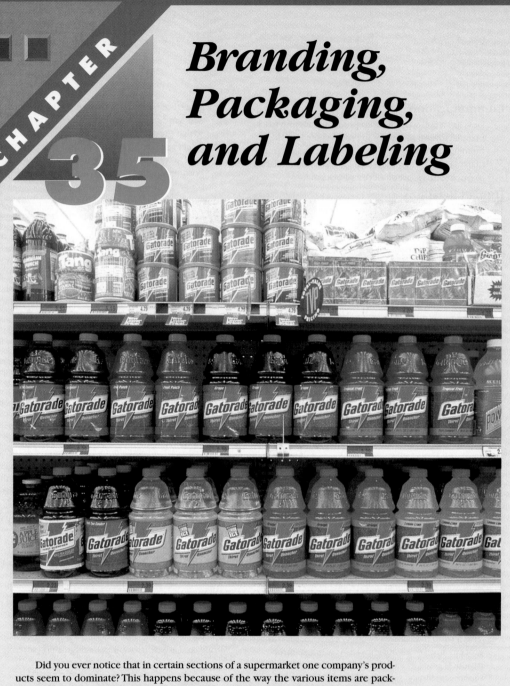

CHAPTER

35

Branding, Packaging, and Labeling

Did you ever notice that in certain sections of a supermarket one company's products seem to dominate? This happens because of the way the various items are packaged—the label is colorful; the brand name or logo stands out; the package sizes, shapes, and materials are what you expect and need for proper storage and convenient use.

What you have discovered is the importance of branding, packaging, and labeling to promotion and sales. In this chapter you will explore these three areas, with an emphasis on their importance to the product planning process.

Classroom Management

For the Teacher
- Teacher's Annotated Editions for all workbooks
- Teacher's Manual for *School-to-Work Handbook*
- *Testing Binder*
- *Transparency Binder*
- *Marketing Software Binder*
- *Marketing Career Portfolio*
- *Lesson Plans*

For the Student
- *Student Activity Workbook*
- *Marketing Math Workbook*
- *School-to-Work Handbook*
- *Student Software*
- *International Case Studies*
- *Marketing Career Portfolio*

SECTION 35.1

Objectives

After completing this section, you will be able to

- explain the nature and scope of branding in product planning,
- define branding elements,
- recognize the importance of branding in product planning,
- name three types of brands, and
- classify branding strategies.

Terms to Know

- brand
- brand name
- brand mark
- trade name
- trade character
- trademark
- national brand
- private brand
- generic products
- brand extension
- brand licensing
- co-branding strategy
- mixed-brand strategy

Branding

An important part of product planning is the use of brands. A **brand** is a name, design, or symbol that identifies the products of a company or group of companies.

Almost every product has a brand. Some brands are well known worldwide. For example, in a recent study of 10,000 consumers in Western Europe, Japan, and the United States, the most recognized and respected worldwide brands were (in order) Coca-Cola, Sony, Mercedes Benz, Kodak, Disney, Nestlé, Toyota, McDonald's, IBM, and Pepsi-Cola.

Because it identifies the products of a company and is often what sells a product, a brand can be a company's most important asset. *Financial World* magazine recently estimated the market value of some top worldwide brands to be in the billions. For example, it estimated the worth of Coca-Cola at $24.4 billion, Pepsi-Cola at $9.6 billion, and Nescafe instant coffee at $8.5 billion.

A brand can include a brand name, brand mark, trade name, trade character, and a trademark:

- A **brand name** is the word, group of words, letters, or numbers of a brand that can be spoken. Examples of brand names include Levi's, Nike, Coca-Cola Classic, Cover Girl, and Tylenol. Since brand-name products are advertised extensively, they usually cost more than similar unbranded merchandise.
- A **brand mark** is the part of the brand that is a symbol, design, or distinctive coloring or lettering. Some examples of brand marks are the U.S. Postal Service's eagle, Standard Oil's Amoco shield and torch, Disney World's castle, and Greyhound Bus Line's greyhound.
- A **trade name** identifies the company or a division of a particular corporation. Kellogg's is an example of a trade name.
- A **trade character** is a personified brand mark (that is, one given human form or characteristics). Some examples include the Pillsbury Doughboy, Bird's Eye's Jolly Green Giant, and the Keebler elves.
- A **trademark** is a brand name, brand mark, trade character, or a combination of these that is given legal protection. When used, it is followed by a registered trademark symbol (®). Examples include Frito-Lay's *Doritos®*, Kellogg's *Rice Krispies Treats®*

Real World

Ask for Sanka Brand

Listen carefully the next time you hear a commercial for Sanka decaffeinated coffee. You will notice it is always referred to as, "Sanka brand." Sanka is one of several products (like Kleenex, Band-Aid, and Q-Tips) whose names have become synonymous with the product itself. By adding the word brand, Sanka's promoters are hoping consumers will insist on Sanka, rather than settling for just any decaffeinated type of coffee. This also protects their exclusive right to use Sanka as a trademark.

Chapter 35 *Branding, Packaging, and Labeling* **463**

Discussion Starter

As the text states, private brands are now much better accepted by the buying public. Have students name some private brands that are available locally. Why were people in past decades sometimes reluctant to buy private brands? Why are private brands so popular now?

(In the past, many private brands—particularly food products—were inferior in quality to national-brand products. However, many private brands now rival the quality of national brands and are usually lower priced than national brands. Thus, consumers in our increasingly tough economy feel that private brands are a bargain.)

Ask students to name some products to which they are brand loyal. Why?

Critical Thinking

Generic drugs are some of the most popular generic products available today. Some generic medicines contain the same formulas and ingredients as brand-name medicines. Yet, the generics are considerably cheaper. Why? (Companies that research, develop, and manufacture medicine recoup their development and manufacturing costs in their product price. However, once a patent on the formula for a particular medicine expires, other pharmaceutical companies can reproduce the formula, manufacture the product, and offer a generic version at a lower price because they do not have to put money into the original R & D. Generics have become so widely accepted that many medical insurance companies will now only pay for patients' prescriptions if generics are used, or if no generics are available.)

A brand can include a brand name, brand mark, trade name, trade character, and a trademark. Can you identify each of these elements on this package?

cereal, and VISA®. When brand names, brand marks, and trade characters are registered, they cannot be used by competitors.

Brand names, brand marks, trade names, trade characters, and trademarks are often combined to form a firm's *corporate symbol*—a firm's name, logo, and/or trade characters.

Importance of Brands in Product Planning

The use of brands is important in product planning for several reasons. Brands help customers identify a product. Brands help to sell the product and establish customer loyalty. In a recent *Wall Street Journal* survey customers were found to be loyal to one particular brand in several categories:

- Branding helps to assure customers that products carrying the same brand are of a consistent quality. This reduces the risk that customers will be dissatisfied with their purchase.
- Branding identifies the firm that manufactured the product. When an identified company advertises a product, the customer already knows its general characteristics.
- Branding helps address new target markets. By simply extending the brands, different markets can be reached.
- Branding helps introduce new product lines and categories. Customers are more willing to try new products, if they carry a familiar brand name.
- Branding helps establish an image for a product or company (traditional or progressive, for example).

Generating Brands

According to a survey of communications and marketing executives at 400 U.S. firms, 75 percent of all companies in 1994 introduced a new name for a product or

the business itself. Some companies are finding it increasingly difficult to secure the right corporate or product names. This fact is not surprising when in the cosmetic and perfume business alone there are 72,100 registered names in the United States.

Brand names are often generated internally by employees or by using computer software programs. Computer software programs are available that specialize in generating brand names. Some programs check to see if a name is already owned and trademarked by another company. Sometimes companies hire ad agencies, naming consultants, or public relations firms to generate brand names. Branding is so important to product planning that 50 percent of all marketing firms do research to test new brand names before they are released.

Despite the high costs involved, marketers must sometimes change brand names. Names may change when a business adds new product lines; seeks new markets for its products; or seeks to modify, simplify, or improve its image. Approximately 50 percent of all corporate name changes occur because of company mergers and acquisitions. Brand names are also changed as a result of lawsuits and court decisions. For example, the breakdown of AT&T's Bell system into smaller regional Bell companies led to corporate name changes for the regional Bell companies.

Types of Brands

Manufacturers, wholesalers, and retailers may brand their own products. These products are classified by who owns them. Three classifications of brands are national brands, private brands, and generic brands.

National Brands   National brands, also called manufacturer brands, are owned and initiated by manufacturers. Some national brands are so popular that they help attract customers to a business that sells them. Examples of national brands include Pepsi, Kellogg's, and IBM.

National brands generate the majority of sales for most product categories. For example, 70 percent of all

---

Caption Answer

Brand name: Rainbow Chips Deluxe; brand mark: Keebler logo; trade name: Keebler; trade character: Keebler elf; trademark: the logo and the brand name.

food products, 65 percent of all appliances, 80 percent of all gasoline, and 100 percent of all automobiles are sold under national brands.

National brands not only identify a given product but also indicate a standard quality and price. They appeal to customers who want consistent quality, dependable product performance, status—and who will not take risks with unknown goods and services.

Private Brands Private brands are owned and initiated by wholesalers and retailers. The manufacturer's name does not appear on the product.

Private brands appeal to customers who want the quality and performance of national brands at a lower price. Many large supermarket and retail chains have private brands. At some major department stores, private brands amount to more than 40 percent of all merchandise carried.

Private brands are popular with retailers because they usually carry higher gross margins (and are thus more profitable for the seller) than national brands. They are better controlled by retailers because they cannot be sold by competitors and thus can lead to retailer, rather than to manufacturer, loyalty. Some private brands, such as Sears' Kenmore line of appliances and Craftsman tools, have become so popular and respected that they rival national brands in sales and customer recognition.

Generic Brands Generic products are "no frills" products that don't carry a brand name. They are generally sold in supermarkets and discount stores. Unbranded products are often priced 30–50 percent lower than nationally advertised brands and 10–15 percent lower than the private label brands offered by some retailers. Generics cost less because they are not heavily advertised or promoted.

Generic products were first introduced by the Jewel supermarkets in Chicago. Beginning with only a few products, they have now expanded into more than 320 product categories, including vitamins, auto parts, toys, and T-shirts. They have captured more than 10 percent of the sales volume for canned fruit cocktail, garbage bags, nondairy creamers, paper towels, frozen apple juice, butter, and vitamins. Generics are now offered in more than 250 retail chains throughout the United States. More than 75 percent of all U.S. supermarkets carry at least some generic items in their stores.

You can see that product planners must know their markets and their customers well. The makeup of the brands they carry (national, private, or generic) is a direct result of customer likes and dislikes. By understanding buyer preferences for certain products, a business can provide a proper balance of products for its target market.

Branding Strategies

Branding strategies are the ways companies use brands to meet sales and company objectives. Some of these strategies include brand extensions, brand licensing, co-branding, and mixed branding. Effective use of different brand strategies can increase sales of branded products and maximize company profits.

Brand Extension Brand extension is a branding strategy that uses an existing brand name for an improved or new product in the product line. For example, Nabisco extended its Fig Newton brand by adding Apple, Blueberry, Strawberry, and Cranberry Fig Newtons. As you learned in Chapter 34, launching new products is costly and the failure rate is high. By using an already established brand name, companies reduce the risk of failure. A potential problem with brand extensions is that by extending the product line too much, a company risks brand dilution. Brand dilution occurs when the original brand loses the strength of its brand identity because it has been stretched to encompass too many products or too varied a group of products. In this case, the original brand may lose its appeal with customers.

Brand Licensing Brand licensing is the legal authorization by a trademarked brand owner to allow another company (the licensee) to use its brand, brand mark, or trade character for a fee. The licensee pays the brand owner a royalty of about 5 percent of the wholesale price of the product.

Companies license their brands to enhance their company image and to sell more of their core products. For example, Caterpillar Corporation of Peoria, Illinois has licensed its name to more than 700 products, covering everything from marine apparel to scaled replicas of the company's machinery. Licensing must be carefully done, since licensed products must always parallel and support the core product's marketing strategy.

Co-Branding Sometimes companies use a co-branding strategy to sell their products. A co-branding strategy combines one or more brands to increase customer loyalty and sales for each individual brand. An example is *The GM Card* created by General Motors and MasterCard. GM wanted to find a marketing tool that would strengthen

▲ *Retailers usually stock a variety of national, private, and generic brands. Why would generic products appeal to consumers?*

Chapter 35 *Branding, Packaging, and Labeling*   **465**

SECTION 35.1

L1 Communication Skills
Hand write the label copy for a common product. Then produce a typed version of this same copy on your computer, but include several errors. Give a copy of your handwritten and your typeset copy to each student as a proofreading exercise. Students should use the proofreader's marks they entered in their notebooks when they studied Chapter 10.

L2 Communication Skills
The day before you assign this activity, have each student bring a product label to class. Divide students into pairs. Have each student read his or her label to the other student, who takes notes on the key information in the label's contents. How accurate was each student's note-taking? (If you want to make this a memory-skills activity, do not allow students to take notes.)

L3 Communication Skills
Have each student keyboard one product label that contains at least 100 words. Students should type the label exactly as it's typeset, using caps, caps/lower case, italic, and boldface. When students are finished, have them proofread their own work. Or, have them proofread each other's work.

Independent Practice

1. Assign and review the Chapter 35 Case Study in the *International Case Studies* workbook.
2. Using business magazines such as *Business Week, Fortune, Inc., Grocery Marketing, Supermarket News, Mass Market Retailers,* and *Stores,* have students identify five new products being introduced into the market. Have them identify the brand name, brand mark, trade name, trade character, and trademark.

Caption Answer

Generic products appeal to consumers because they cost less than national and private brands.

Assess

Evaluation

Assign and review the Section 35.1 Review.

Reteaching

1. Assign and review the vocabulary terms for this section.
2. Assign and review Fact and Idea Review questions 1–10 from the Chapter Review.
3. Have students write the terms *national brands, private brands,* and *generic brands* as three column headings across a sheet of paper. To help reinforce their understanding of each, have them review these three sections in the chapter and write down key points underneath each heading.

Enrichment

1. Assign and review the appropriate activities in the *Student Activity Workbook.*
2. Assign and review the appropriate Critical Thinking questions from the Chapter Review.
3. Have students research the brand name development on some key national brands (such as Pepsi-Cola) or on local brands with which people in your community or region are likely to be familiar (such as Jolt Cola).

Ask them to write a short report on how the name was developed, whether or not it's been changed over the years, and any other relevant information.

Close

For closure on this section, have students once again go through a magazine, choose an ad, and point out the following: the brand name, brand mark, trade name, trade character, trademark, and whether it's a national or a local brand.

466

BRIGHT IDEAS

The Name Game

What would you call a product that combines the stability and freedom of cross-country skis with the convenience of skates? "Snow skates" was what Snow Runner Inc., the manufacturer, called them. It was accurate, descriptive—and not particularly memorable. Snow Runner's president, John Sundit, decided his company's product needed a makeover. So, he hired an outside firm to come in and help rename and reposition it.

In the days that followed, consultants led Snow Runner's employees through a series of exercises designed to define and clarify the image of snow skates. They cut up magazines and made collages to characterize the product in pictorial form. They made extensive feature-benefit charts. They did market research on the likes and dislikes of winter sports enthusiasts.

It was the last exercise that provided the key. Outdoor sports enthusiasts were found to like animals. By narrowing the field to animals that tolerate and even like snow—and have universal appeal—they arrived at the answer. Dogs were widely loved. They worked with vigor and enthusiasm pulling sleds in snowy regions. And "dogs" just happened to be slang for feet. Snow skates became "Snow Dogs"!

Creativity Challenge Break into teams of 3–5 students, and try renaming a product yourselves. Select an item whose name, in the group's opinion, is either ineffective or less effective than it could be. Consider carefully the image that each new name projects and the needs of the target market.

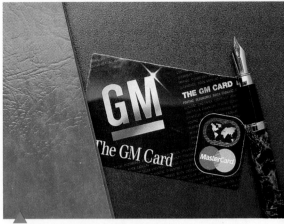

Co-branding is a branding strategy used by GM and MasterCard. Name two other companies that currently do or might benefit from co-branding. What brands do they or might they use to co-brand?

customer loyalty and provide prospective customers with a financial incentive to buy their next car or truck from GM. In 1993, GM and MasterCard joined in a partnership to develop a credit card with no annual fee. The GM Card offers a 5 percent cash rebate on each transaction toward the purchase or lease of a new GM car or truck. This co-branding strategy proved successful for both companies. After one month, 1 million new MasterCard customer accounts were opened and more than 130,000 card holders put their rebate earnings toward a new car purchase or lease.

Co-branding works well if both companies' brands complement each other and each brand receives equal billing in advertisements, direct mail, and other promotions. Of course, there must also be customer benefits to the arrangement in order for it to succeed. For more information on co-branding see the "Bright Ideas" feature in Chapter 36.

Mixed Brands Some manufacturers and retailers use a mixed-brand strategy to sell products. A **mixed-brand strategy** involves simultaneously offering a combination of national, private, and generic brands. For example, Union Carbide produces and sells generic and national brands of garbage bags. It advertises Glad bags, its national brand, as "superior to the thin, bargain bags." In this way, Union Carbide can maximize its profits by selling a generic product without damaging the reputation and the sales of its national brand product. A mixed-brand strategy allows a business to reach several target markets, maintain brand loyalty, and increase its overall product mix.

SECTION 35.1 *Review*

1. What is a brand?
2. What branding elements are frequently used in product branding?
3. Why is branding important to product planning?
4. Name three types of brands.
5. List four different branding strategies.

Section Review Answers

1. A name, design, or symbol that identifies the products of a company.
2. Brand name, brand mark, trade character, trademark, and corporate symbol.
3. It makes it easy to identify the product.
4. National, private, and generic.
5. Brand extension, brand licensing, co-branding, and mixed brands.

Caption Answer

Answers will vary. For example: TWA and VISA used co-branding to develop a credit card partnership. When customers use the card, they gain TWA flight miles.

Objectives

After completing this section, you will be able to

- list the principal functions of product packaging and
- describe the main functions of labels.

Terms to Know

- package
- label

Packaging

A **package** is the physical container or wrapping for a product. Because a package represents the size, shape, and final appearance of a product at the time of sale, it is important to product planning. In fact, it is estimated that some 10 percent of a product's retail price is spent on package development, design, and the package itself.

Functions of Packaging

A package does much more than hold a product. It has many functions, all of which will be explained below. Companies take great care in designing or redesigning the packages for their products. For example, Domino's Pizza chain changed from a square pizza delivery box to an eight-sided "octabox" container. It took two years of study and 50 prototypes to come up with a distinctive package that is cheaper to produce, keeps pizzas hotter longer, and prevents the pizza topping from sticking to the top of the box.

Promoting and Selling the Product Customer reaction to a product's package and brand name largely determines the success or failure of a product in the marketplace. A well-designed package, for example, is a powerful point-of-purchase selling device because it can make a product stand out from its competition. With stores becoming ever more self-service oriented in their layout, this function is especially important.

Attractive, colorful, and artistic packages have promotional value, too. Because a package carries a brand name, it serves as a constant reminder to the customer of the product's manufacturer.

A better container can even create new sales or help to minimize possible lost sales to competitors for the same products. For example, pump toothpaste containers were designed to be neater, cleaner, easier to use, and less wasteful than toothpaste tubes. The new containers have not replaced the tubes. However, they now provide a choice for people who prefer this type of package, and they appear along with toothpaste tubes on display shelves. Thus, pump type dispensers create new sales and also prevent lost sales, due to competitors offering similar new products.

Defining Product Identity Packages are often used to invoke prestige, convenience, status, or other positive product attributes in the eyes of the customer. Such packages can be a crucial part of an overall marketing strategy for a product—particularly its advertising component. Examples of such packaging include the use of egg-shaped containers for L'eggs stockings, Hunt's squeezable plastic ketchup bottle, and checkered lids for Smucker's jellies and preserves.

Providing Information The package also provides information for the customer. Many packages give directions for using the product and information about its contents, nutritional value (where applicable), and potential hazards.

For certain items, preprinted prices and inventory codes are placed on packages to assist with inventory control and management. An example of this is the Universal Product Code used in most retail settings.

Meeting Customer Needs Product packages often come in various sizes to meet the needs of different market segments. So-called family packs of food and grocery items are designed to meet the needs of larger families. Smaller packages are made for individuals. Specific examples include multipacks of beverages such as soda and juice, bulk sizes of paper packages, single-serving cans of soup, and family meals at fast-food outlets.

Packages and package design must also keep up with changing lifestyles. When designing packages, product planners analyze customer lifestyles. For example, two-income families and singles are two growing market segments, both of which place a premium on time and convenience. Knowing this has led product planners to design microwaveable dinners that can be prepared quickly in neatly designed packages. These packages minimize or even eliminate the use of other pans, pots, or dinnerware to make and serve the meal.

Ensuring Safe Use A package can improve product safety for the customer. Many products formerly packaged in glass, for example, now come in plastic containers. This eliminates potential injuries from breakage.

To avoid product tampering, many nonprescription drugs, cosmetics, and food items are now sold in tamper-resistant packages. These include jars and plastic containers with sealed lids and blisterpacks. Blisterpacks are packages with preformed plastic bubbles surrounding individual items arranged on a cardboard backing.

Countless other products are packaged in childproof containers. These have lids that make them more difficult to open. Thus, the chances of accidental spills and poisonings are reduced.

Chapter 35 *Branding, Packaging, and Labeling* **467**

Focus

 ### Bell Ringer Activity

Place the following on a table in front of the class: 12 pencils, 6 to 12 cookies, 4 rolls of tape, 25 paper clips or rubber bands, 20 to 30 loose Kleenex, 6 to 12 pickles or olives, and a glob of toothpaste—or display several products that are packaged differently. (Also have available the packaging for all of these products.)

Ask students to tell you how each of these products is normally packaged for retail sale, then place each product's package in front of the product. Ask students why each type of packaging material is used. Why, for example, are rubber bands packaged in cardboard boxes instead of in glass jars? Why are pickles and olives packaged in glass or plastic jars instead of in cellophane pouches? Why are pencils packaged in cardboard boxes or cardboard wrappers instead of in plastic bags?

Introducing the Section

Have students help you generate a chalkboard list of the purpose of packaging. Allow students to look closely at the product packaging and tell you the information contained on each product label. Then, have students brainstorm the reasons for product labels.

Given all the uses for packaging and product labels, it should be easy for students to see why both are so important in product planning.

Did You Know ?

Not everyone appreciates childproof containers. Seniors, especially those troubled by arthritis, are pressing manufacturers to develop senior-friendly caps that still remain childproof.

Guided Practice

1. Read Section 35.2 with students.
2. Have students read aloud the Case Study and review the answers in class.
3. Use the transparency for this section.
4. After you have finished reading this section, have students look once again at the product packaging you used for the Bell Ringer Activity. Have them speculate on why the colors and typeface were used on each label, and what total product image each label conveys. Remind them that a product label acts as an ad for a product; have them recall some of the fundamentals of good written ad preparation from Chapter 21.
5. Assign and review the Chapter 35 Activity in the *School-to-Work Handbook*.

Discussion Starter

Have students give examples of durable or nondurable goods whose labeling and packaging create the following product images: low-end, discount merchandise; average-priced merchandise; and high-end, prestige merchandise.

Critical Thinking

The manufacturers of some brand-name products such as baking powder and baking soda have changed their product labeling and packaging very little over the years, if at all. Why? (Some manufacturers seek to retain a product's identification with the past because consumers nostalgically associate the past not only with personal happiness but with product quality.)

Clearly a Matter of Choice

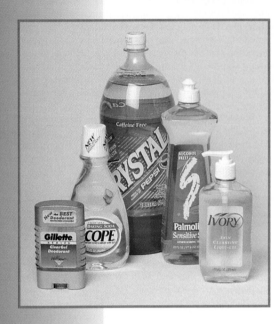

A recent trend in product planning and in packaging is transparency. It is the trend to make clear products and display them in clear containers. Marketers have decided that letting consumers see through their products gives them a natural and pure look. Amoco, Colgate-Palmolive, Procter & Gamble, Pepsi, and Coca-Cola are some of the companies that are either test marketing or launching new clear products.

The popularity of clear products and packaging is due to consumer perceptions. Many people look at water as being pure and clear. By making products that resemble the clarity of water, consumers believe that the product is free of harmful materials.

Clear products must meet perceived consumer benefits and must be properly positioned. For example, when Colgate-Palmolive introduced Palmolive Sensitive Skin it targeted people with sensitive skin. The product was marketed as a pure product to suggest to people that it was free of dyes and irritants.

Marketing a product without color is also an excellent way to differentiate your product from competitors. Since 1957, Procter & Gamble had been marketing Ivory Liquid dish detergent as a milky white liquid. In 1993, it decided to advertise an improved version of the product

with superior grease-cutting capabilities. Creating a clear version of the traditional dish detergent and placing it in a clear package got it instant recognition on supermarket shelves.

Clear deodorants and clear antiperspirants have also been well received by consumers. The clear deodorant products suggest that they have been formulated so that no trace of deodorant residue will remain on your clothing after use.

Another example of matching a clear product to perceived need is Conair's "Crystal Pure" hair conditioner. The product is positioned as a conditioner which was manageable and also gave a "crystal clear shine."

However, changing a product's appearance is not without risk. A product may jeopardize its original identity. Sometimes consumers need to see familiar characteristics in a product. For many customers, familiar characteristics, such as color, mean that the product will perform as expected. For example, most people associate cola drinks with the color brown. Therefore, when Coca-Cola introduced a clear, sugar-free, and calorie-free soda the company decided not to risk putting the Coke brand name on the new clear product. Instead, it used the less popular Tab brand name and created Clear Tab. Coca-Cola hopes that this new product will appeal to traditional soda drinkers, as well as to people who are looking for something different.

Look for more and more companies to jump on the clear product bandwagon. As long as clear products are seen as representing a product that means natural and pure, the trend in developing clear products should not just be a passing fancy.

■ ■ Case Study Review

1. What, in your opinion, will determine whether reformulating existing products as clear products will be successful?
2. What other products can you name that have been recently reformulated or introduced in a new clear form? How are clear products generally advertised?

A MATTER OF ETHICS

3. Do you think that marketing a clear product is a form of deception? Why or why not?

Case Study Answers

1. Clear products will be successful if they perform as expected in the eyes of the consumer.
2. Answers will vary, but most clear products will have to be advertised as clear, natural, pure, and not harmful to use.
3. Answers will vary. However, as long as people are getting the expected performance from the product it is acceptable. The lack of color does not have to mean lack of performance, it may simply mean that a new product category has been established.

A package does more than just hold the product. How do the containers shown here fulfill other key package functions?

Protecting the Product A package must protect a product during shipping, storage, and display. It must also protect the product from breakage and, in the case of food items, from spoilage.

Product planners know that a poorly designed package that does not protect the product will cost a business money for goods that can't be sold. Also, a damaged or spoiled product creates a bad image and leads to a reduction in future sales.

Basic protective materials for packages include cardboard, glass, metal, plastic, and wood. Food products, for example, are typically sold in boxes, metal cans, glass bottles and jars, and plastic containers. Variations on these basic forms include aerosol cans and pump dispensers.

Airtight containers retard spoilage. These include lidded containers and sealed wraps of foil or plastic. Products such as yogurt, cheese, lunch meat, and salad dressings are packaged this way.

Contemporary Packaging Issues

Product packaging allows companies unique opportunities to address social and political concerns. Companies are not only turning to environmentally friendly types of packaging but they are also using packaging to make social and political statements.

Environmental Packaging The environment is an important issue facing product planners today. Recent public opinion surveys show that most Americans support less wasteful packaging. They are even willing to pay more for products which reduce waste. In response to consumer concern, companies are making more packages that are reusable, recyclable, less wasteful, and safer for the environment. For example, Celestial Seasonings, a specialty tea company, uses recycled paperboard for its boxes. Most of Procter & Gamble's plastic laundry detergent containers are made with at least 25 percent recycled plastic. Budget Gourmet frozen dinners are packaged

in molded paper containers. The molded package avoids plastic trays, aluminum tops, and cardboard boxes that would otherwise be used to wrap around frozen dinners.

Cause Packaging As you learned earlier, packages perform a variety of functions to promote products. Packages can also be used to promote nonproduct issues. Some companies are using their packages to promote social and political causes. This practice is known as *cause packaging*. The issues that you might read about on the packages may be totally unrelated to the product you buy. For example, The Body Shop, which sells health and beauty products, wraps its customer purchases in bags that promote *Amnesty International*. Another example is Ben & Jerry's Homemade ice cream cartons which promote saving the rain forests and oppose the use of bovine growth hormone to stimulate milk production in cows. Other companies have included postcards to send to congressional representatives supporting or opposing certain legislative issues.

Printing messages on packages, bags, and bills encourages consumers to participate in politics. Some marketers believe that companies using cause packaging take an enormous risk promoting causes that not every consumer may agree with. Others feel that their views on social and political causes may actually help sell the product.

Labeling

A **label** is an information tag, wrapper, seal, or imprinted message that is attached to a product or its package. Labeling plays a major role in product planning strategy. Its main functions are to inform customers about a product's contents and directions for use and to protect businesses from legal liability for mishaps involving their products. Fear of litigation, consumer pressure, government regulations, and concern for consumer safety

Chapter 35 *Branding, Packaging, and Labeling* **469**

L1 Math Skills

The United States is producing more products for foreign markets and importing more foreign products. As a result, you will increasingly see metric measurements used on product labels. Here is a metric conversion chart.

When You Know	Multiply By	To Find
ounces	28.35	grams
pounds	0.454	kilograms
fluid ounces	29.573	milliliters
pints	0.473	liters
quarts	0.946	liters
gallons	3.785	liters

Ask students to make the following conversions. Round to the hundredth.

- How many grams are in five ounces? ($5 \times 28.35 = 141.75$ grams)
- How many kilograms are in 10 pounds? ($10 \times 0.454 = 4.54$ kilograms)
- How many milliliters are in 32 fluid ounces? ($32 \times 29.573 = 946.336$, which rounds to 946.34 milliliters)
- How many liters are in six pints? ($6 \times 0.473 = 2.838$, which rounds to 2.84 liters)
- How many liters are in 10 quarts? ($10 \times 0.946 = 9.46$ liters)

L2 Math Skills

Tell students: You have just received a shipment of the following items from Great Britain, and your boss wants you to convert them into English units for your customers. Round to the tenth.

- A package of cookies that weighs 510.3 grams. ($510.3 \div 28.35 = 18$ ounces)
- A container of coffee that weighs 226 grams. ($226 \div 28.35 = 7.97$ or 8 ounces)
- A package of cereal that weighs 382 grams ($382 \div 28.35 = 13.47$ or 13.5 oz)

L3 Math Skills

As a homework assignment, have students look at some of the product packaging in their homes and make a list of ten products and their metric weights. They should convert the weights to English units, put their answers on a separate sheet of paper, and exchange conversion problems with a person in class the next day. When students are finished, they should check each other's answers for accuracy.

Independent Practice

Have students compare the product packaging and labeling of a domestic product and an identical foreign product (for example, a domestic and a foreign brand of flour, tea, cookies, rice, etc.).

Using the information provided in this section as a guide, have students compare and contrast the quality of the packaging and the amount and type of information on the label, and speculate on the reasons for the similarities and differences. For example, do foreign brands offer less or more product and nutritional information than domestic brands? Have students discuss their findings in class.

Figure 35–1
LABELS

The information on food labels helps customers decide if the product is right for them.

Product Illustrations

must represent what the consumer finds in the package.

Product Guarantee

assures customer satisfaction.

Dates

include the packed on date (date food was packed), the sell by date (last date product should be used), the best if used by date (last date for use for top quality), and the expiration date (date after which the product should not be used).

Storage Information

tells how the product should be stored to have the least waste and best quality.

Weight Statements

give the "net weight" of the entire product minus the package or liquid it's packed in.

Manufacturer's Name and Address

is provided so consumers can write for more information or register a complaint.

The Universal Product Code

describes the merchandise.

Lifelong Learning

Branding, Packaging, and Labeling

Having the ability to wade through brand, packaging, and labeling issues will allow students to enter the marketplace with more acumen than the average consumer. The material presented in this chapter should actually encourage students to read and appreciate labels. Labels are designed to help the consumer make informed decisions as well as to promote the product. If students find that they are interested in working in the industry at this level, they will need to take further classes in both marketing and graphic arts in order to gain the needed skills to be employed in this area.

have all led manufacturers to place more information on their labels and packages.

Labels often contain a brand name, logo, ingredients, directions, and special promotional messages. Food labels include weight statements, dates, product illustrations, storage information, a universal product code, a product guarantee, and the manufacturer's name and address. (See Figure 35-1.)

Nonfood labels usually provide consumers with instructions for the proper use and care of products. They also give manufacturers a convenient place to communicate warranty information and product-use warnings. For example, notices of electrical hazard, flammability, and poisonous ingredients are required on the labels of certain categories of products.

Labeling Laws

Many package labels must meet local, state, and federal standards. These standards prevent manufacturers from misleading consumers.

The Federal Nutrition Labeling and Education Act The Federal Nutrition Labeling and Education Act (1994) was passed to protect consumers from deceptive labeling. This act, which is administered by the Federal Food and Drug Administration (FDA), is designed to provide universal and consistent nutritional information. It requires that labels give nutritional information on how a food fits into an overall daily diet, including its percentage of recommended daily amount of nutrients. The act also regulates seven health claims and defines descriptive terms to make them consistent on all products. These terms include *light* and *lite; free* (as in fat free, salt free, cholesterol free); *low; reduced;* and *good source*.

The Food and Drug Administration (FDA) also requires the manufacturers of certain products to place health warnings on their packages. For example, beginning in 1989, all alcoholic beverage labels had to carry the following statement: "According to the Surgeon General, women should not drink alcoholic beverages during pregnancy because of the risk of birth defects. Consumption of alcoholic beverages impairs the ability to drive a car or operate machinery and may cause health problems." Similar warnings of health risks have been required for years on cigarettes.

The Federal Food and Drug Administration is also proposing new regulations on over-the-counter drug labels to make the labels more understandable for consumers. Possibilities for regulations include changing the order in which information is presented and simplifying information describing warnings.

Federal Trade Commission Labeling Rules and Guidelines Another federal agency involved with product labeling is the Federal Trade Commission (FTC). The Care Labeling Rule, first passed by the Federal Trade Commission in 1972 and subsequently revised, requires that care labels be placed in textile clothing. The care labeling rules ensure that specific detailed infor-

Life in the Multicultural MARKETPLACE

50 Ways to Ask for Beans

Goya Foods, Inc., makes over 800 Hispanic food products. One problem the company regularly faces is the diversity of the Spanish language and the impact it has on product labels. For example, beans are called frijoles in Cuba and habichuelas in Puerto Rico. Orange juice is jugo de china to a Hispanic living in the Northeastern United States and jugo de naranja to those in Miami and the rest of the Southwest. Because such products must also be accessible to nonSpanish speakers, Goya already gives them bilingual labels. But how does it accommodate the Spanish language variations? It relies on the product photo to ensure that diverse groups can get past any language problems and find the products they want.

mation about the care of garments related to washing, ironing, and directions for cleaning be placed on labels.

Another area of interest for the FTC is environmental claims made for products. In 1992, the FTC released guidelines for companies to use when making environmental claims on labels. The FTC included definitions for environmental terms which could be used on labels. When using the term *recycled content,* the FTC requires that proof be given about the amount of material in a product or package that has been kept from a landfill or retrieved as manufacturing scraps. The term *recyclable* can be used only if the product or package can be reused as raw material for a new product or package. The terms *ozone safe* and *ozone friendly* can be used only if the products do not contain any ozone depleting chemicals. The terms *degradable, biodegradable,* and *photodegradable* can be used only if the product will decompose into elements found in nature within a reasonably short period of time after disposal.

As you can see, labeling is becoming a highly regulated and complex part of product planning. Marketers face the challenge of planning product packaging and labeling that conforms to regulations.

SECTION 35.2 *Review*

1. List the principal functions of product packaging.
2. What are the main functions of labels?

Assess

Evaluation

Assign and review the Section 35.2 Review.

Reteaching

1. Assign and review the vocabulary terms for this section.
2. Assign and review Fact and Idea Review questions 11–15 from the Chapter Review.
3. Have students list all of the reasons for the package design and the information presented on the package for a consumer product of their choice. Have them classify each feature under one of the functions of packaging.

Enrichment

1. Assign and review the appropriate activities in the *Student Activity Workbook*.
2. Assign and review the appropriate Critical Thinking questions from the Chapter Review.
3. Assign and review the Building Academic Skills Activities, Application Projects, Linking School to Work Activities, and Performance Assessment from the Chapter Review.

Close

Have students complete the following statements:
a) The purposes of packaging are... (to hold the product, to promote it, to help define its identity, to provide product information, to meet customer needs with various sizes available, to ensure safe use, and to protect the product.)
b) The main functions of labels are... (to give product contents and directions for use, and to protect businesses from legal liability for mishaps involving their products.)

More About

The FTC

Established in 1914, the FTC principally functions with respect to labeling in the following ways: to bring about the truthful labeling of textile, wool, and fur products; and to regulate other consumer commodities so as to prevent consumer deception and to facilitate value comparisons.

Section Review Answers

1. Promoting and selling the product, defining product identity, providing information, meeting customer needs, ensuring safe use, and protecting the product.
2. Their main function is to inform customers about a product's contents and directions for use, and to protect businesses from legal liability for mishaps involving their products.

35 CHAPTER *Review*

Answers

Vocabulary Review

See Glossary for definitions.

Fact and Idea Review

1. Brand name: a word or group of words that identifies a product and indicates a standard of quality and price. Brand mark: a symbol or design with distinctive coloring or lettering.
2. Trade character: a personified brand mark.
3. Trademark: a brand name, brand mark, trade character (or a combination) given legal protection.
4. Corporate symbol: a firm's name, logo, and/or trade characters.
5. Brands are generated by employees, software programs, ad agencies, public relations firms, and naming consultants.
6. A national brand is owned by the manufacturer. Private brands are owned by wholesalers and retailers.
7. Generic products are no-frills products that carry no brand name.
8. Brand extension uses a familiar or original brand name for other items in the product line. Brand licensing is the legal authorization by a brand owner to allow another company to use the brand, logo, or trademark for a fee.
9. Co-branding works well if the company's brands complement each other; there is a customer benefit to the arrangement; and each brand receives equal billing in advertisements, direct mail, and other promotions.
10. The simultaneous offering of national, private, and generic brands which allows a business to reach several target markets, maintain

Vocabulary Review

Select two products that your family regularly uses. Write one paragraph on each product describing the product characteristics by incorporating these vocabulary terms.

brand
brand name
brand mark
trade name
trade character
trademark
national brand
private brand
generic products
brand extension
brand licensing
co-branding strategy
mixed-brand strategy
package
label

Fact and Idea Review

1. What is the difference between a brand name and a brand mark? (Sec. 35.1)
2. What is a trade character? Name at least three trade characters with which you are familiar. (Sec. 35.1)
3. What is a trademark? (Sec. 35.1)
4. What are corporate symbols? (Sec. 35.1)
5. Describe how brands are generated. (Sec. 35.1)
6. What is the difference between a national brand and a private brand? (Sec. 35.1)
7. What are generic products? (Sec. 35.1)
8. How does brand extension differ from brand licensing? (Sec. 35.1)
9. When does a co-branding strategy work well for companies? (Sec. 35.1)
10. What is a mixed-brand strategy and why is it used? (Sec. 35.1)
11. What is the difference between a package and a label? (Sec. 35.2)
12. What are two contemporary packaging issues? (Sec. 35.2)
13. Identify three kinds of information commonly found on product labels. (Sec. 35.2)
14. What does the Nutrition Labeling and Education Act require? (Sec. 35.2)
15. Summarize the label guidelines released by the FTC concerning environmental claims. (Sec. 35.2)

Critical Thinking

1. Procter & Gamble, one of the nation's largest advertisers, introduced a new line of generic, lower-priced paper towels without advertising support. What was the company's strategy? What are the arguments in its favor? What are the arguments against it?
2. New product names must be chosen carefully. They should be aimed at a specific need and an existing market, rather than creating a market with a name. Explain this distinction by comparing the product name "Lean Cuisine" with the product name "Yuppie Yummies."
3. Child-proof packages have a problem: many of them tend to be adult proof, too. Do some supplemental product planning for an over-the-counter drug that is packaged in this manner—aspirin, for example. Address the problems of older people in opening the packages. Suggest some ways product manufacturers can help.
4. The ultimate product package is the grocery bag. Today, many supermarkets are switching from paper bags to biodegradable plastic bags. Try to reconstruct the product planning behind this move. What are the economic and environmental reasons for the switch?
5. Do you think putting political or social messages on packages is a wise marketing decision? Explain.
6. Why do many department stores carry both their own private label clothing lines and nationally recognized brands?
7. Co-branding is becoming a popular branding strategy. Explain the rationale behind this trend.

Building Academic Skills

Math

1. Robinson & Perry Advertising Agency billed Sky High Air Cargo Service $3,500 for the development of Sky High's corporate symbol. Robinson & Perry's designer was paid $1,500 for her creative work on this project. Her salary was what percentage of the entire amount?

Technology

2. Research the process used to recycle paper, glass, plastic, and aluminum packaging. Create a chart that illustrates and describes each type of recycling process.

---

brand loyalty, and increase the overall product mix offered by customers.
11. A package is the physical container or wrapping for a product. A label is an information tag, wrapper, seal, or imprinted message that is attached to a product or its package.
12. Cause packaging and environmental packaging.
13. Labels often contain a brand name, logo, ingredients, directions, and special promotional messages.
14. The law requires labels to give information on

how a food fits into an overall daily diet.
15. The guidelines included definitions for environmental terms which could be used on labels.

Critical Thinking

1. Strategy was to eliminate the advertising expense so that it could better compete with the price of generic paper towels that have captured more than 10 percent of the total sales volume for paper towels.

Communication

3. Company Z, maker of product X, packages its instant soups in plastic foam containers that cannot be recycled. Using the information you obtained from the Technology activity, write a letter to Company Z urging them to change their packaging. Suggest what you feel is the best alternative type of packaging and explain how it can be recycled.

Application Projects

1. Identify five household items commonly purchased in a grocery store or supermarket. Note the brand name, the elements of the product's corporate symbol, the packaging materials used, and any required labeling elements (health warnings, for example). Then write a 150-word paragraph description of how each product's package performs the basic package functions listed in this chapter.

2. Make a survey of grocery and drug products, noting any warning labels that appear. Try to find at least a dozen different types of products that carry such labels. Then write a 350-word report describing the nature of the warnings (and the products carrying them), their placement and prominence, and your evaluation of their effectiveness.

3. Visit a store that carries a variety of items, such as a grocery store or electronics store. Choose three products and evaluate the brand extensions that exist for the product. Explain how the brand extension might increase or decrease the potential sales of those products.

4. Some consumer groups say that generic prescription drugs are not as good as name brand prescription drugs. Research this issue and write a 200-word report describing your findings. Include your opinion on the subject and explain why you feel the way you do.

5. One of the hottest trends is ending a brand name with an *A* or using a *Z* in the name. Ending a product with an *A* often makes it sound enticing, friendly, and innovative. Using a *Z* stresses the image of advanced technology, scientific breakthrough, or superior performance. Create two lists of brand names ending in *A* and *Z*. Use business or personal magazines as a resource.

6. It is a trend to combine two words into one with a capital letter in the middle, for corporate and product names. For example, ComputerLand, PageMaker, MasterCard, and LaserJet. Using newspapers and professional and personal magazines, identify five examples of companies or products which have used this naming technique. Then create your own list of ten product brands and their uses.

7. Does your community have a product or waste packaging recycling program? If so, research the rules for recycling, the places where recycled products can be taken, and if any local retailers voluntarily participate.

Linking School to Work

1. Observe the types of brands produced by your employer. Identify the brand names, brand marks, trade characters, and trade names used.

2. If your employer is a wholesaler or retailer, ask him or her how they decide on the mix of national and private brands to carry. If your employer is a manufacturer, ask him or her how brand names at your company are generated.

Performance Assessment

Role Play

Situation. You are a brand manager for a large company. You have been asked to develop a brand name, brand mark, trade character, and corporate symbol for a new type of soup. You have also been asked to develop a package and label for your product. You will present your new brand in an upcoming meeting.

Evaluation. You will be evaluated on how well you can do the following:

- Define your branding elements.
- Create an appropriate package for your product and describe its functions.
- Create an appropriate label and describe its elements.

Research Report

Research and complete a 250-word report on current federal labeling requirements.

Complete the Chapter 35 Computer Application that appears in the Student Activity Workbook.

---

2. The name "Lean Cuisine" focuses on a specific market that will probably always be a market—diet-conscious people. The product name "Yuppie Yummies" appears to focus on a particular market (yuppies).

3. Students can indicate larger, easier to open lids, protective packaging and foil that are easier to remove, etc.

4. If supermarkets can switch to biodegradable plastic packaging, waste dumps will not run out of room as quickly.

5. Answers will vary.

6. Department stores carry private labels to compete with national brands.

7. By combining brand names with a single product offering, companies can provide greater value to demanding customers.

Chapter Overview

Chapter 36 introduces two key extended product features: warranties and credit.

 Springboard

Ask students to recall the definition for the term *product feature;* write this on the board. Have students define the word *extend;* write their answers on the chalkboard. Based strictly on the above information and without referring to their texts, have students define the term *extended product features.* Finally, have students brainstorm some ways a product's features could be extended.

Prereading

List the section objectives to discuss with the students. Have the students skim the chapter, looking at the pictures, reading the captions, and noting the heads. Ask questions to ensure that the students have a minimal understanding of the chapter structure.

Preteaching the Vocabulary

Before you start Section 36.1, write the vocabulary list on the chalkboard and ask if students are familiar with any of the terms. If they are, have them give brief definitions. As you study each term in the chapter, have students reach a consensus on phrases and/or symbols that will help them remember each term; write these on your chalkboard vocabulary list.

Extended Product Features

CHAPTER 36

One of the most common extended features that companies provide customers is a warranty. In this chapter you will learn about warranties and extended service contracts. You will study the principal federal and state statutes governing these and other product features. You will also learn about product liability suits.

Another important extended feature is credit. In this chapter you will learn about the importance of credit. You will read about types of credit extended to consumers and businesses and the role of credit in product planning. You will also learn about legislation affecting credit.

SECTION 36.1

Objectives

After completing this section, you will be able to

- **distinguish different types of warranties,**
- **explain the importance of warranties to product planning,**
- **identify additional extended product features,**
- **summarize the major provisions of product safety legislation, and**
- **describe consumer responsibilities and rights related to product performance.**

Terms to Know

- **warranty**
- **express warranty**
- **full warranty**
- **limited warranty**
- **implied warranty**
- **warranty of merchantability**
- **warranty of fitness for a particular purpose**
- **disclaimer**

Warranties

A **warranty** is a promise, or guarantee, given to a customer that a product will meet certain standards. Typically, these standards apply to materials, workmanship, and/or performance.

A *guarantee* is another term for warranty. The major difference in the use of the two terms is in the promotion of goods and services. For example, the term guarantee (or guaranteed) is usually used for promotional phrases, such as "money-back guarantee," "guaranteed not to shrink more than 3 percent," "guaranteed for 1,000 average hours," or "satisfaction guaranteed."

Warranty text is usually framed as a series of specific promises, such as "D & A Auto Body will repair any defects in workmanship billed on the repair invoice unless caused by or damaged from unreasonable use, maintenance, or care of the vehicle, excluding paint work if the vehicle's original finish is defective." Most warranties set time or use limits for coverage. The most familiar language is that usually found in auto warranties—"Warranty ends at 36 months or 36,000 miles, whichever occurs first." Finally, the typical warranty in some measure limits the seller's liability.

Businesses are not required by law to issue warranties. Most do, however, to convince their customers of the quality of their products. In fact, for some companies—notably automobile manufacturers—warranties are a key component of their product advertising.

Warranties come in two different forms—*express* and *implied*. These forms, in turn, can be divided into specific types.

Express Warranties

An **express warranty** is one that is explicitly stated, in either writing or spoken words, to induce a customer to buy. If the warranty is written, it can appear in a number of places—on the product packaging, in the product literature, in an advertisement, or as part of a point-of-purchase display. All that is required is that the location be convenient, or easily accessible to customers before purchase. Whether written or spoken, the warranty must be clearly worded so that customers can easily understand its terms. Spoken warranties, however, even if clearly worded, may not be enforceable unless they are in writing.

Here is an example of how an express warranty works. A written ad states that a portable stereo headset will operate when the user jogs. You purchase one of the headsets and discover almost immediately that it shorts out during jogging. You are entitled to whatever relief is specified in the warranty. Assume further that the package in which the headset came features a runner using the product in the rain. You find that the product shorts out in the rain. Once again, you are entitled to warranty relief because the illustration constitutes a promise of performance, even though the promise is not a written one.

There are two types of written warranties—a *full warranty* and a *limited warranty*. Under a **full warranty**, if a product is found to be defective within the warranty period, it will be repaired or replaced at no cost to the purchaser. All parts and labor are covered. Today, full warranties are rarely offered on consumer goods.

A **limited warranty** is one that offers less coverage than a full warranty. It may exclude certain parts of the product from coverage. It may also require the customer to bear some of the expense for repairs resulting from

🕐 Bell Ringer Activity

Most students should be familiar with the concept of product warranties and will thus be able to participate in this activity. Bring two or three products to class, such as a kitchen appliance, a fountain pen or ball-point pen, and a watch. Write the definition for *warranty* on the board. Read students a short sample warranty (see below), pointing out that it (1) promises to repair defects in materials, (2) under certain conditions, (3) within a certain period of time. Then have the class brainstorm limited warranty language for each product displayed.

(**Sample limited one-year warranty:** *This hand blender is warranted to be free from manufacturing defects for a period of one year from the date of purchase, subject to the following: that it is not misused and/or taken apart, and that it has not been used for commercial purposes. This warranty does not cover failure caused by build-up of food matter or water deposits. If this appliance becomes defective under the terms of the one-year warranty, we will repair it free of charge, including both materials and labor, provided it is returned prepaid to our nearest Authorized Service Center.*)

Introducing the Section

Read aloud with students the first head in this chapter entitled "Warranties." Make sure that students understand the general difference in the usage of *warranty* and *guarantee*. Also make sure that students now understand how a warranty is an extended product feature.

Meeting Special Needs

English as a Second Language

Students whose native language is other than English may find the legal terminology used in extended warranty features or in credit applications overwhelming. As these topics are of vital importance to students and consumers alike and contain information pertaining to the well-being and/or financial security of the consumer, you may wish to spend extra time going over this vocabulary and providing real life examples for students to read. Provide time for students to ask questions and receive clarification of any unfamiliar terminology.

Teach

Guided Practice

1. Read Section 36.1 with students.
2. Use the transparency for this section.
3. MarkEd Resource Center in Columbus, Ohio, (800) 448-0279, offers LAP Modules on warranties and guarantees, and on consumer protection in product planning.
4. To summarize the major provisions of consumer and product safety legislation, invite a guest speaker (lawyer, businessperson, state regulatory personnel, or Better Business Bureau staff member) to discuss consumer protection legislation and the rights of consumers in today's marketplace. If you have a representative from the Better Business Bureau, ask the person to give an overview of the Bureau's services.
5. Contact the United States Office of Consumer Affairs, Washington, D.C. 20201, and request a booklet entitled "How to Run a Consumer Week." Have students decide on an appropriate consumer education activity for your marketing education program, your school, or your community.

---

defects. It is not uncommon, for example, for a limited warranty to specify that the manufacturer will pay for replacement parts but charge the customer for labor or shipping.

Implied Warranties

Most major purchases that customers make are covered by written warranties provided by manufacturers. Where there is no written warranty, implied warranty laws apply.

An **implied warranty** is one that exists automatically by state law whenever a purchase takes place. There are two types of implied warranties—a *warranty of merchantability* and a *warranty of fitness for a particular purpose*.

A **warranty of merchantability** amounts to a promise from the seller that the product sold is fit for its intended purpose. For example, a can opener will open cans. A vacuum cleaner will clean carpets.

A **warranty of fitness for a particular purpose** arises when the seller advises a customer that a product is suitable for a particular use and the customer acts on that advice. For example, a customer buys a small truck based on a car salesperson's assurances that it will pull a trailer of a certain weight. If it turns out that the truck cannot tow the anticipated load, then the dealership must take back the truck and refund the buyer's money.

Warranty Disclaimers

Sometimes warranties have disclaimers to protect the businesses issuing them. A **disclaimer** is a statement that contains exceptions to and exclusions from a warranty. Disclaimers are often used to limit damages that can be recovered by a customer. A common form of disclaimer, for example, limits recovery to a refund of the purchase price. It also specifically excludes any other costs that may have been incurred by the owner as a result of the product's failure to operate properly. Another common disclaimer waives the customer's rights under implied-warranty laws.

Role of Warranties in Product Planning

Warranties are an important element of product planning. They are probably the major extended feature that customers expect when they make a purchase. From a business's viewpoint, however, warranties are significant because they

- force a company to focus on customer needs,
- set clear standards of performance,
- generate customer feedback,
- encourage quality control, and
- boost promotional efforts.

The importance of warranties is further demonstrated by widespread use among leading manufacturers and

476　Unit 10　*Product Planning*

---

retailers of extended warranties, which are also known as service contracts. *Extended warranties* or *service contracts* provide repair service or preventative maintenance for a specified length of time beyond a product's normal warranty period. Customers usually pay extra for such a contract at the time they purchase the covered product. Costs range from a few dollars on a low-cost item to hundreds of dollars on a higher-priced item, such as a car. In addition, there is often a deductible amount, which the customer pays before work is performed.

Such an arrangement has benefits for both businesses and customers. Businesses benefit by receiving additional money (and more profits, if the product performs as expected) on the original sale of a product. Customers benefit from the assurance of continued satisfactory product performance.

There are also disadvantages to service contracts. *Consumer Reports* magazine estimates that only 12 to 20 percent of people who buy extra repair or service protection ever use it. This happens because some service contracts overlap existing warranty coverage, meaning

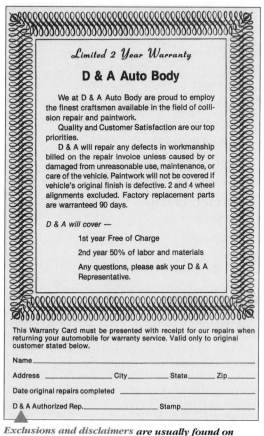

Exclusions and disclaimers are usually found on warranties. What exclusions or disclaimers are found on this warranty?

 More About

Full Warranties

Because full warranties are rare, they make news when they are offered. In 1992, Hyundai Electronics America drew peoples' attention when it offered a lifetime warranty for its personal computers. In contrast, most other computer companies offered only limited warranties. Hyundai's warranty helped it stand out amongst the crowd.

that a consumer is paying for something that is already available. In addition, most people either never need them or forget to use them.

Other Extended Product Features

Besides warranties product planners provide additional extended product features to help create customer satisfaction after the sale. These features include delivery, installation, billing, service after the sale, directions for use, technical assistance, and training.

Product planners must constantly evaluate a product's extended features from a customer's viewpoint. They should be able to answer yes to questions such as these:

1. Was the product delivered on time?
2. If installation was necessary, was it done properly?
3. Was the bill for the good or service accurate and timely?
4. If needed, was the service provided promptly, courteously, and correctly?
5. If needed, were technical assistance and training provided?
6. Were directions for use properly written?

Extended product features are so important because they are often remembered and used long after the price of the product has been forgotten.

Consumer Laws and Agencies

A working knowledge of relevant federal, state, and local laws is essential for businesspeople today. Manufacturers must be sure that their products meet all the requirements of the law—that they are safe, adequately labeled, and accurately advertised. If they are not, the manufacturer could face fines or costly recalls.

To keep abreast of statutory requirements, larger companies often employ consumer affairs or legislative specialists to advise management. Smaller companies often join industry trade associations to stay informed on existing and pending laws that affect their products. What follows is a brief survey of the kinds of laws that specialists concern themselves with.

Federal Statutes

Many of the warranty features already discussed in this chapter have their origins in a federal statute called the *Magnuson-Moss Consumer Product Warranty Act* of 1975. This statute governs written warranties for all consumer products costing $15 or more. It sets minimum standards for such warranties, rules for making them available before a product is sold, and provisions for lawsuits against manufacturers if they are not fulfilled.

Other federal statutes protect consumers by forcing companies to manufacture and sell safe products. The *Consumer Product Safety Act* of 1972, for example, established the Consumer Product Safety Commission (CPSC). This agency is responsible for monitoring the safety of more than 11,000 mostly nonfood items, such as toys, televisions, and appliances. The agency is empowered to issue standards for the construction, testing, packaging, and performance of these products.

If, in the course of its investigations, the CPSC finds any product that it believes to be defective or dangerous, it has three alternatives. It can:

1. require that warning labels be attached to the product,
2. recall the product and order repairs, or
3. prohibit the product's sale.

In December 1988, for example, the CPSC banned the sale of lawn darts, an outdoor game advertised as a form of family recreation. As a result of its investigation, the CPSC found that during a ten-year period, lawn darts caused nearly 6,700 injuries and three deaths.

The *Food, Drug, and Cosmetic Act* is another federal statute designated to assure consumers that the products they buy will be safe. "Safe" in this case means pure, wholesome, and effective, as well as informatively labeled and truthfully advertised. The act is enforced by the Food and Drug Administration, which certifies new drugs and inspects drug and food processing plants. The agency also regulates the advertising and sale of imported and exported foods, drugs, cosmetics, medical devices, animal drugs, animal feed, and products that emit radiation.

Other products are regulated by different federal agencies, and some are regulated by more than one agency. Cars and trucks, for example, have their emission

Life in the Multicultural MARKETPLACE

Am I Crazy or Do I Have a Phone Call?

If you're in the Netherlands and you want to signal someone across the room that he or she has a phone call, what do you do? You make a circular motion around your ear with your index finger. Of course, in many other places (including the United States), that could signify that a person was crazy or behaving in an irrational manner. In the Netherlands, however, if you wished to indicate that someone was crazy, you would simply tap the center of your forehead. But that gesture, too, has a very different meaning in the United States. Depending on how it's done, it could mean either, "Let me think," or, "Why didn't I think of that!" Imagine the confusion that could occur, if you got these signals crossed in a meeting with Dutch businesspeople!

SECTION 36.1

Discussion Starter

Have students name products that are usually covered by extended service contracts.

Ask students to speculate on the amount of money that extended service contracts can bring in to a retailer such as Sears if one out of four customers buys an extended service contract of $75 each. (Companies offer extended service contracts not only as good customer service but as major sources of revenue. As the text states, *Consumer Reports* estimates that only 12 to 20 percent of the people who buy extra repair or service protection ever use it. For a retailer such as Sears, this means that a large percentage of the money it brings in with service contracts is pure additional money.)

Cooperative Learning

Divide students into four groups. Have each group brainstorm at least four extended product features (in addition to a warranty) for one product. Have each group make its presentation to the class; have the entire class generate additional extended product features.

Independent Practice

Have students contact a service business in your community and discuss with the owner or manager the state and federal regulations that govern the business.

Students should write their findings in a 150- to 200-word report and include such things as training and licensure required, cost of licensure, regulations that govern how the business is run, etc.

Lifelong Learning

Extended Product Features

Becoming aware of the rationale behind extended product features is a significant step in the marketing education of each and every student in class. Those who will pursue marketing careers will find it the foundation they come back to time and time again as extended product features become increasingly important to retailers and manufacturers.

Students who end their marketing education with this class need to take with them the habit of reading the fine print and asking questions about anything they don't understand. Reading publications, such as *Consumer Reports* and other general business publications, on a regular basis can provide a lifetime of savings over a wide variety of purchases.

Evaluation

Assign and review the Section 36.1 Review.

Reteaching

1. Assign and review the vocabulary terms for this section.
2. Assign and review Fact and Idea Review questions 1–12 from the Chapter Review.
3. If the students are having a difficult time remembering these concepts, divide them into pairs and have them explain the concepts to each other, using their texts for reference.

Enrichment

1. Assign and review the appropriate activities in the *Student Activity Workbook*.
2. Assign and review the appropriate Critical Thinking questions from the Chapter Review.
3. Have the students look at product packaging in their homes or in local stores for product warnings and write at least three of the warnings in full. They should discuss these warnings in class. Do some or most of the warnings seem ridiculously obvious? Discuss the need for even obvious warnings. If the warning is not included, a customer can always say that he or she did not know about the potential hazards in using a product and can sue the manufacturer if injured while using it. Product warnings now even extend to food products, for just this reason.

Have students write a summary (without looking at their texts) of the key concepts they can recall from reading this section and doing the activities.

standards set by the Environmental Protection Agency (EPA), their window (price) stickers regulated by the Federal Trade Commission, and any potentially dangerous design flaws investigated by the National Highway Traffic Safety Administration. Making sure products meet this multiplicity of standards is an important function of product planning.

State Statutes

Many states have also passed consumer protection laws. Most are aimed at poorly made or poorly serviced products. For example, nearly all states have now passed so-called lemon laws.

Lemon laws are statutes designed to protect consumers from poorly built cars. Under most lemon laws, a car is a "lemon" if it is out of service at least 30 days during the first year of ownership or if four attempts have been made to fix the same problem. Lemon owners are entitled to a refund or a comparable replacement car.

Many states have incorporated *arbitration programs* into their lemon laws. In an arbitration, an impartial third party, such as a representative of the Better Business Bureau, decides the crucial issues—for example, whether a vehicle has met the standard of a lemon and, if so, how much of a refund is due. In most cases, the arbitrator's ruling is not binding on the parties. If the owner is not satisfied with the outcome, he or she can sue the carmaker in a court of law. The principal benefit of arbitration, however, is that it saves all parties the long delays and excessive costs often associated with a lawsuit.

The most common form of state regulation mainly affects service businesses. Most states require certain individuals—auto mechanics, realtors, building contractors, and barbers, for example—to meet special training requirements. Before they can legally practice their professions, these people must apply to the state for licensing or certification. The process frequently involves testing and the payment of a substantial fee.

Consumer Rights and Responsibilities

Consumers have a right to expect quality products at fair prices. What happens when the extended features that a business has built into a product fail—when, for example, buyers do not feel that the product's warranty has protected them adequately?

There are several steps that a consumer can take to resolve a problem:

1. First, the consumer should contact the retailer that sold the product.
2. If the retailer does not resolve the problem, the consumer should contact the manufacturer of the product.

3. If the problem is still unresolved, the consumer should contact the local, state, or federal offices that can assist with consumer complaints.
4. Finally, if the problem is still not resolved consumers can take legal action.

Consumers can sue manufacturers or retailers on at least three grounds—breach of federal law (written warranty), breach of state law (implied warranty), and negligence. *Negligence* means failure to take proper or reasonable care. In the area of product safety (defects resulting in personal injury), courts have held manufacturers and retailers liable for defects in products.

As part of product planning, businesses can take steps to minimize liability suits. To begin with, manufacturers should produce safe products. They should examine product design and look at what might go wrong. As part of this process, they should test their products thoroughly. They should give special attention to package design. Specifically, they should be sure that clear warnings are given on the package about any potential hazards involved in using the product.

Retailers can limit their liability by questioning manufacturers before accepting a product for sale. They should obtain the manufacturer's test data and determine the company's ability to stand behind the product before it is put on their shelves.

As a final line of defense against liability, businesses should encourage their customers to be responsible consumers. They should take every opportunity to remind their customers of their duty to be informed—especially to read and follow the directions provided on products.

Customers should also be reminded of their responsibility to be honest in their purchases and use of products. Shoplifting, switching price tags, shortchanging cashiers, and using coupons for products never purchased are all dishonest and illegal practices that raise prices for all consumers.

SECTION 36.1

Review

1. What are two forms of warranties?
2. Why are warranties important for product planning?
3. Identify three additional extended product features that are frequently part of product planning.
4. What are the basic provisions that product safety legislation requires of manufacturers?
5. What can consumers do when they do not feel that a product's warranty has protected them adequately?

Section Review Answers

1. Express and implied.
2. Warranties are important because they focus on customer needs, set clear standards of performance, generate customer feedback, encourage quality control, and boost promotional efforts.
3. Delivery, installation, billing, service after sale, directions for use, technical assistance, and training.
4. Products must be safe, adequately labeled, and accurately advertised.
5. Customers always have the option of suing.

SECTION 36.2

Objectives

After completing this section, you will be able to

- explain the importance of credit,
- list five sources of consumer credit,
- describe the four types of credit accounts extended to consumers,
- describe how businesses use trade credit, and
- summarize credit legislation.

Terms to Know

- credit
- regular, or 30-day, charge accounts
- installment accounts
- revolving accounts
- budget, or 90-day, accounts

Credit and Its Importance

Credit is an arrangement whereby businesses or individuals can obtain products or money in exchange for a promise to pay later. The use of credit is essential to our economy. In 1993, Americans charged $562 billion worth of purchases with credit cards. (See Figure 36–1).

Nearly everyone uses credit at some point in their lives. Credit allows most people to buy major purchases such as appliances, homes, autos, and recreational vehicles. Credit is also used by individuals for less costly purchases, such as meals, clothing, and gasoline.

Credit is used by businesses to purchase goods and services which are ultimately sold to consumers. Credit is also used between manufacturers, wholesalers, and retailers to buy such things as materials, equipment, supplies, and services for use either within their business or to sell to other businesses.

Without credit millions of people and thousands of businesses would not be able to buy goods and services when they are needed. This is because income (business or personal) often does not match buying needs when they occur. For example, if you need a new car, you will probably need to use your savings. While it is wise to save money from each paycheck, it is often difficult to save enough to buy a car. Credit allows you a convenient way to purchase a car on regular monthly payments. You, in effect, can buy a product and pay for it later. In today's economy, credit is a powerful financial tool.

Extending credit to customers gives consumers an incentive to purchase and thus increases businesses' sales and profits. It is one way for businesses to differentiate themselves, while encouraging customers to spend more on products.

Credit and the use of credit cards help build long-term relationships with customers. For example, Brooks Brothers, a clothing retailer, has incorporated special programs for its own credit card customers. The company sends mail-order catalogs, notices of special sales, and post-card mailings with special product offerings to its credit customers.

There are two major forms of credit—*consumer* and *business*. Let's take a closer look at each of these types of credit.

Discover 6%

Diners Club, Retail Cards, other 16%

CHARGE CARD

VISA 38%

American Express 16%

7751 466105 90083

1537
J B WATKINS

VALID THRU 08/94

MasterCard 24%

Figure 36–1

Americans charged $562 billion worth of goods and services on VISA, MasterCard, American Express, Discover, Diners Club, retail cards, and others in 1993. What dollar amount was charged on VISA cards?

Chapter 36 *Extended Product Features* **479**

More About

Credit and Its Importance

A person's credit history is an extremely important criteria used to determine credit worthiness by all those who issue credit. When people apply for a mortgage loan for a house or car loan, every detail of their credit history is examined. Stress the wise use of credit by young people.

Focus

Bell Ringer Activity

First, ask students to define the term *credit*. Ask them to brainstorm two lists: (1) things that people normally buy on credit and (2) things that businesses buy on credit. They may have a more difficult time with the latter since they perhaps have not considered the fact that businesses buy things on credit.

Introducing the Section

Tell students that credit—both consumer credit and business credit—is essential to our economy. Without it, many people and businesses would not be able to buy products when they need them. Ultimately, extending credit to consumers gives them an incentive to buy and thus increases a business's profits.

Teach

Guided Practice

1. Read Section 36.2 with students.
2. Have students read aloud the Case Study and review the answers in class.
3. Invite the following to be part of a panel to talk to your students about credit and its wise use: (a) a credit manager from a local bank, who can talk to students about the types of credit that banks commonly offer, (b) a credit manager from a local department store or other retail establishment to tell students how the store issues credit cards, (c) a representative from a consumer credit service, and (d) a representative from a local business to discuss which types of products his or her firm buys on trade credit.

4. MarkEd Resource Center offers materials on credit appropriate for use with this section.
5. Assign and review the Chapter 36 Activity in the *School-to-Work Handbook*.

Discussion Starters

Discuss with students the fact that credit card companies have made their cards into status symbols. For example, American Express offers three tiers of membership: the green card, the gold card, and the platinum card. While green card holders must pay off their charges each month and must pay extra for such services as flight insurance when booking airline tickets, gold and platinum card members receive flight insurance as a benefit of membership, as well as the option to revolve some of their monthly payments.

Does using credit encourage people to live beyond their means? (Some people definitely abuse credit cards. Others use credit cards responsibly. Some people over-spend on credit cards because they use them in financial emergencies. For example, medical emergencies can necessitate that some people might be driven to spend beyond their means.)

Critical Thinking

Ask students why some businesses set a minimum total dollar amount (for example, $15 or $20) before they will allow you to charge a purchase to a bank credit card, such as VISA or MasterCard. (Banks charge the business a service fee for processing each bank card purchase. Paying service fees on bank card purchases of very small amounts becomes cost prohibitive for a business. Thus, by setting a dollar minimum on bank card purchases, businesses are hoping to reduce their service fee costs.)

Consumer Credit

Companies who offer credit to consumers, such as banks, department stores, and oil companies, typically issue credit cards. Customers normally fill out credit applications in order to receive credit cards. Credit applications usually ask about customers' sources of income and how well they have repaid debts in the past. (See Figure 36-2).

Credit cards are issued with a credit limit based upon customers' ability to pay and their payment history. A *credit limit* is a preapproved dollar amount, which customers can use to purchase items on credit. Credit limits can range from several thousand dollars per card to as little as $500 for first time cardholders.

Purchases done by credit card are typically reviewed by computerized machines prior to a purchase. This is done to make sure a customer has not exceeded his or her credit limit and is able to make a purchase. If approved, the card is typically scanned by a point-of-sale terminal. The terminal prints a sales receipt for the customer and copies for the business. Some businesses record the amount of the purchase on a multicopy receipt form. Appropriate copies are kept by the business and given to the customer.

Bank Credit Cards   Bank credit cards are issued by banks. VISA and MasterCard are examples of

Figure 36-2

Customers must normally fill out a credit application in order to receive a credit card. What information on this application would be of most interest to a company extending credit?

480   Unit 10   *Product Planning*

Caption Answer

The financial information would be of most interest to a company extending credit.

More About

Consumer Credit

In order to verify customer credit histories, most companies use the services of companies such as TRW that compile information on consumer credit and resell it to those who issue credit. Because of TRW's computerized records, in some instances, credit can be approved on the same day or even within the same hour!

bank credit cards which are offered by banks such as Citibank, Chase Manhattan Bank, or Bank of America.

Customers sign a multipart charge form when they make a purchase using a bank credit card. Retailers who belong to a bank credit card system send these credit card forms, or receipts, to the bank for payment. The bank charges a service fee to process the amount of the purchase and sends the balance to the retailer. The bank, in turn, bills the customer for purchases made with the credit card. Banks that issue bank cards receive their income from finance charges, annual membership fees, and retailer servicing fees.

Retail Credit Cards Some businesses are large enough to offer their own credit cards, which are known as proprietary or retail credit cards. Examples of retail credit cards include J.C. Penney, Ann Taylor, Hudson's, and Shell. The individual retail company handles the processing and billing of all customer purchases.

Businesses that issue retail credit cards receive their income from finance charges. Finance charges on unpaid credit card balances are very expensive. In most states the legal annual percentage rates can go as high as 18 percent.

Credit Card Companies Credit card companies include American Express, Discover, and Diners Club. Credit card companies require that payments be made in full each month. They also usually charge their customers an annual fee or a service charge.

Credit card companies also charge retailers a service fee when retailers submit customers' charge slips to the credit card companies. This fee is payment for the service provided by the credit card company.

Debit Cards A variation of the credit card is a debit card. Debit cards allow consumers to enter a personal identification number into an automated teller machine (ATM). The ATM machine automatically deducts a customer's purchase from his or her bank checking or savings account.

Real World

The Origin of Modern Credit Cards

Credit cards have been circulating off and on since the beginning of this century. However, their main introduction began in 1950 when a New Yorker found himself short of cash in a Manhattan restaurant. That embarrassing moment prompted Frank McNamara to found Diners Club. The idea caught on like a shopping spree, and a year later it was billing more than $1 million. By 1981, when it was acquired by Citicorp, Diners Club had more than 4 million members.

Secured and Unsecured Loans Loans are also a form of credit. Consumers can obtain secured loans and unsecured loans for the purchase of goods and services. In secured loans, something of value, such as property, machinery, or stock is pledged as collateral, or security. The collateral helps to ensure that a loan will be repaid. If the loan is not repaid, the lender can keep the secured items to repay the debt.

Consumers can also obtain unsecured loans, which represent a written promise to repay a loan. Unsecured loans do not require any security. They rely on the excellent credit reputation of the borrower who pledges to repay the loan.

Types of Accounts

There are four major consumer credit plans in use today:

- regular, or 30-day, accounts;
- installment accounts;
- revolving accounts; and
- budget, or 90-day, accounts.

Let's take a closer look at each type.

Regular, or 30-Day, Accounts Regular charge accounts or 30-day accounts allow customers to charge purchases during a month and pay in full within 30 days after they are billed. There is no charge for this type of credit plan, if the bill is paid on time.

Installment Accounts Installment accounts, or time payment plans, allow for payment over a period of time. Installment accounts are normally used for large purchases, such as a college education, travel, automobiles, appliances, and furniture. Installment accounts offer a certain interest rate over a set period of time. Installment accounts sometimes require a down payment and a separate contract for each purchase.

Revolving Accounts With a revolving account, the retailer determines the credit limit and when payments are due. The minimum payment is usually a certain percentage on the balance owed or a minimum dollar amount, such as $15. However, the customer can choose to pay more than the minimum payment if he or she chooses to reduce the balance owed. A service charge is added to the balance each month.

Customers can make purchases up to the credit limit which is established when they apply for the card. Under most credit card arrangements, regular accounts become revolving accounts if the full amount is not paid for the billing period.

Budget, or 90-Day, Accounts Budget, or 90-day, accounts, allow for the payment of a purchased item over a 90-day period without a finance charge. Budget accounts are offered by some retailers who handle expensive products, such as furniture and appliances. Budget accounts do not require the customer to pay a service charge and ensure that the amount of credit offered will be repaid quickly.

Chapter 36 *Extended Product Features* **481**

L1 Decision-making Skills

Some credit card issuers send out solicitations to students after high school graduation. If you receive such a solicitation one or two years from now, what factors would determine whether or not you will apply for the card? (Answers should include consideration of one's employment situation, one's financial obligations, and one's needs [for example, if you are in vocational school or college, having a credit card may be a convenient way to pay for books and supplies on a quarterly or semi-annual basis].)

L2 Decision-making Skills

You need to purchase a couch, a television set, and a refrigerator, and you plan to buy them all at one store on a credit account. What factors would determine whether you would decide to put them on a 30-day account, an installment account, a revolving account, or a 90-day account? (Answers should include consideration of one's other financial obligations and ability to pay over a certain period of time, an ability to make a down payment on the merchandise [which is required of some installment accounts], the finance charge of the account, etc.)

L3 Decision-making Skills

Suppose that a business owner wants to purchase goods from you on trade credit. You do not know this business owner or his business. How will you decide whether or not to extend trade credit? (You could do the following: (1) obtain information about the business from a relevant trade organization, (2) contact a local bank, (3) talk to other people who have done business with this person, and (4) contact the Better Business Bureau.)

Independent Practice

1. Assign and review the Chapter 36 Case Study in the *International Case Studies* workbook.
2. Have students call credit representatives at three local business establishments (retail stores, gas stations, department stores, etc.) to determine what types of credit accounts they offer.

   Retailers, such as Sears and J. C. Penney, which offer a wide range of higher-ticket merchandise like furniture and appliances, are likely to have more types of credit accounts in addition to a standard revolving charge account. Have students report their findings to the class.

Assess

Evaluation

Assign and review the Section 36.2 Review.

Reteaching

1. Assign and review the vocabulary terms for this section.
2. Assign and review Fact and Idea Review questions 13–17 from the Chapter Review.
3. Have the students write one summary sentence for each "A" and "B" head section in this lesson. Or, have the students reread each section as a class and help you generate a chalkboard list of summary statements for each "A" and "B" head section.

■ CASE STUDY ■

Buying Groceries on Credit

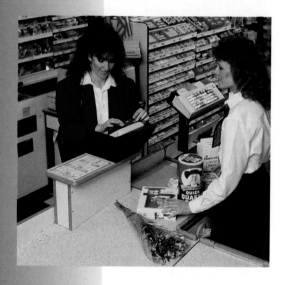

Cash may still be king in America, but supermarkets are now accepting credit cards for the payment of the weekly grocery bill. According to *Progressive Grocer* magazine, only 17 percent of U.S. supermarkets accepted credit cards in 1989. By 1992, this figure had grown to 39 percent. Because of aggressive marketing by credit card companies and the increased competition from specialty stores which accept credit cards, such as deli and flower shops, more supermarkets are allowing customers to charge their food bills.

Credit card companies believe offering credit has advantages for both consumers and retailers. Credit gives consumers an option for buying their groceries. Many consumers do not like to carry a lot of cash with them. Paying by credit card eliminates the need to carry cash. Credit card companies and supermarkets hope that the practice of accepting credit will lead to greater customer satisfaction and increased store profits. Some supermarkets hope the cards will create customer loyalty.

Some people, however, are appalled at the idea of purchasing food with credit cards. Consumer advocates aren't so sure that the benefits of this new service will outweigh the potential harm. They argue that paying for food with credit cards will lead to more consumer debt and bad spending habits.

Despite the protests and concerns of consumer advocates, supermarket research indicates that most shoppers are in favor of the change. One study of supermarket customers completed by VISA indicated that 49 percent of the people surveyed wanted to pay for their food electronically. In response to consumer complaints about consumer debt, VISA also conducted a study of current credit card customers. The company monitored supermarket customers who paid by credit card. They found that 55 percent of customers who used VISA at the supermarket paid their bills in full, when they were billed.

In 1994, 70 percent of U.S. customers purchasing products paid cash and only 9 percent paid by credit card. Thus, credit card companies face the challenge of converting a large cash market into credit consumers. Supermarkets that now accept credit are providing credit card companies with a tremendous opportunity to convert more consumers. For example, VISA has developed a marketing package especially for supermarkets. Its marketing package includes special advertising and promotional incentives to attract new customers to each store that accepts its card. MasterCard is also offering a supermarket package which includes sales promotions and advertising for retailers installing credit card processing equipment in their stores. Once a store decides to accept MasterCard, special incentives are frequently offered to customers to encourage them to pay by credit card. For example, customers who pay by credit card are offered a 5 percent promotional discount.

■ ■ *Case Study Review*

1. Why do consumer advocates believe that consumers should pay for essentials such as food, with cash, debit cards, or checks rather than with credit cards?
2. In your opinion, should credit cards be used for food purchases? Why or why not?

A MATTER OF ETHICS

3. Some consumer advocates have said that the practice of marketing credit cards to supermarkets is "extremely short sighted" and "in many ways immoral." What is the rationale behind these strong statements? Do you agree or disagree? Explain.

Case Study Answers

1. Advocates argue that credit cards will create an environment of bad spending habits. Consumers should rely on cash, rather than credit to avoid possibly overextending themselves on essentials, such as food.
2. Answers will vary.

3. Consumer advocates believe that using a credit card to pay for food is usually a warning sign that a consumer is having financial difficulties. These difficulties often lead to credit card bankruptcies.

BRIGHT IDEAS

Pick a Partner

When consumers use credit cards these days, there's a 20 percent chance that a second name follows VISA or MasterCard. General Motors, AT&T, and United Airlines, to name a few, are sharing logo space with credit card companies. This phenomenon, known as *co-branding*, has revolutionized the credit industry and pushed both VISA and MasterCard use up dramatically. This is because co-branders provide incentives to consumers that encourage them to pay by credit rather than cash. Usually these incentives include rebates or discounts on merchandise.

Even department stores and supermarket chains are beginning to co-brand with bank card companies. Kroger, an Ohio-based food store chain, offers consumers a MasterCard that rebates store credit on food purchases.

Industry experts estimate that co-branding will continue to grow. Such cards offer more profitability to the sponsoring financial institution because customers use them more often. For example, cards rebating frequent flier miles have ten times the volume of regular cards. Customers want the rebates and use the card even when they have the cash available.

Creativity Challenge Form teams of 3–5 students, and start putting together co-branding partnerships of your own. Look for pairings that, to the best of your knowledge, do not as yet exist. What about a bank card company and a sports team? a hospital? a temp service? Who would use such cards? What would be rebated or discounted?

Business Credit

Business credit, or trade credit, is similar to consumer credit in that money is loaned for goods and services. Suppliers provide raw materials, equipment, and inventory to businesses under an arrangement to pay later.

Unlike consumer credit, trade credit does not involve the use of credit cards. Credit memorandums, letters of credit, and credit drafts are used in trade credit arrangements. However, trade credit is similar to consumer credit, in that money is loaned with an agreement to pay later. As you learned in Chapter 18, cash discounts are frequently offered to businesses who promptly pay their bills.

Legislation Affecting Credit

Because of the tremendous impact that credit has on the economy and individuals, federal and state governments closely monitor its practice. There are many rules and regulations that protect consumers and their credit standing and provide information on the proper use of credit. The following are some of the principal credit laws:

- The *Truth in Lending Act* of 1968 requires that lenders disclose information about annual percentage rates, the name of the company extending credit, and the amount financed. It also requires lenders provide the total purchase price minus any down payments and taxes, the actual finance charge in dollars, a payment schedule, and late payment penalties.

- The *Fair Credit Reporting Act* of 1970 gives consumers the opportunity to check their credit histories for errors which may adversely affect them in obtaining credit. If a consumer is denied credit, the Act requires that a lender report the name and address of the credit bureau that was used by the lender.

- The *Equal Opportunity Acts* of 1975 and 1977 set guidelines for the review of applications for credit. In addition, these acts prohibit discrimination based upon age, sex, race, religion, or marital status.

- The *Fair Credit Billing Act* sets up procedures to resolve billing errors promptly.

- The *Credit and Charge Card Disclosure Act* of 1988 helps consumers by requiring credit card issuers to provide information about card costs.

In addition, the Federal Reserve Board in Washington, D.C., provides information on how to shop for credit cards. The Federal Reserve Board lists interest rates, grace periods, annual fees, and telephone numbers for 150 VISAs and MasterCards offered by the 25 largest card issuers, plus 125 other cards.

SECTION 36.2 *Review*

1. **Why is credit important to our economy?**
2. **List the types of consumer credit.**
3. **Identify the four major credit plans extended to consumers.**
4. **How do businesses use trade credit?**
5. **Why do federal and state governments pass legislation regulating credit?**

Chapter 36 *Extended Product Features* **483**

Enrichment

1. Assign and review the appropriate activities in the *Student Activity Workbook*.
2. Assign and review the appropriate Critical Thinking questions from the Chapter Review.
3. Assign and review the Building Academic Skills Activities, Application Projects, Linking School to Work Activities, and Performance Assessment from the Chapter Review.
4. Assign the appropriate activities in the *Marketing Math Workbook*.
5. Obtain a copy of a bank credit card statement and a retail credit card statement from a department store or oil company. Duplicate each, and give the students a copy of both. Review all parts of each statement, such as the account number, the statement closing date, the total credit line, cash advance limit, finance charge, interest rate, balance, etc.

    If possible, you may also wish to obtain statements from an installment account and a 90-day account. Allow the students to compare and contrast the terms, conditions, and payment requirements of each account. Discuss the advantages and disadvantages of each.

Close

Have students write a short statement that tells why credit is an extended product feature. (Answers should include a statement to the effect that credit allows consumers and businesses to buy goods and services when they are needed.)

Section Review Answers

1. Credit allows consumers and businesses to buy goods and services when they are needed in exchange for a promise to pay later.
2. Bank credit, retail credit, credit from credit card companies, loans, and debit cards.
3. Regular charge accounts, installment loans, revolving accounts, and budget or 90 day accounts.
4. Businesses use trade credit to purchase raw materials, equipment, and inventory from manufacturers, wholesalers, and retailers under an arrangement to pay later.
5. Legislation protecting consumers is necessary due to the tremendous impact credit has on the economy and individuals.

Answers

Vocabulary Review

See Glossary for definitions.

Fact and Idea Review

1. A warranty is a promise, or guarantee, given to a customer that a product will meet certain standards.
2. An express warranty is explicitly stated, in writing or in spoken words. An implied warranty is one that exists automatically by state law whenever a purchase takes place.
3. Under a full warranty, a product found to be defective within the warranty period will be repaired or replaced at no cost to the purchaser. A limited warranty offers less coverage than a full warranty (for example, it may exclude certain parts of the product from coverage).
4. To limit damages that can be recovered by a customer.
5. It provides parts and repair services for a specified length of time beyond a product's normal warranty period. Customers pay extra for such a contract.
6. Advantages: (1) Customers benefit from the assurance of continued satisfactory product performance and (2) peace of mind that comes with a preventative maintenance program. Disadvantages: (1) Some contracts overlap existing coverage while the manufacturer's warranty is in effect, meaning that a consumer is paying for something that is already available; and (2) most people either never need them or forget to use them.
7. It issues standards for the construction, testing, packaging, and performance of 11,000 mostly nonfood products.

484

Vocabulary Review

Divide into teams of four or five members for a game of marketing hangman. Your teacher will use the vocabulary terms below in creating hangman puzzles. Each team should take turns guessing the missing letters until a vocabulary term is identified. The team that correctly identifies and defines the term gets a point.

warranty
express warranty
full warranty
limited warranty
implied warranty
warranty of merchantability
warranty of fitness for a particular purpose
disclaimer
credit
regular, or 30-day, charge accounts
installment accounts
revolving accounts
budget, or 90-day, accounts

Fact and Idea Review

1. What is a warranty? (Sec. 36.1)
2. How does an express warranty differ from an implied warranty? (Sec. 36.1)
3. How does a full warranty differ from a limited warranty? (Sec. 36.1)
4. Why are warranty disclaimers used by businesses? (Sec. 36.1)
5. What is an extended warranty? Who pays for it, and how long does it last? (Sec. 36.1)
6. What are some advantages and disadvantages for consumers regarding extended warranties or service contracts? (Sec. 36.1)
7. What does the Consumer Product Safety Commission do? (Sec. 36.1)
8. What does the Food and Drug Administration do? (Sec. 36.1)
9. What are *lemon laws*? (Sec. 36.1)
10. What steps should consumers take to remedy a problem they have with a product? (Sec. 36.1)
11. Suggest three legal grounds on which businesses can be sued for product liability. (Sec. 36.1)
12. What responsibilities should businesses encourage their customers to assume? (Sec. 36.1)
13. Explain the difference between credit and credit limits. (Sec. 36.2)
14. Summarize how bank credit card and retail credit card issuers receive income. (Sec. 36.2)

484   Unit 10   *Product Planning*

15. How do credit card company charge cards differ from bank credit cards? (Sec. 36.2)
16. Explain the similarities and differences between consumer credit and business credit. (Sec. 36.2)
17. What does the *Truth in Lending Act* of 1968 require of lenders? (Sec. 36.2)

Critical Thinking

1. In your opinion, what criteria should be part of a good guarantee?
2. If in its advertising a company stresses the quality of its products, why does it sell extended warranties to its customers? Doesn't this imply that the company's products are subject to failure? Resolve this apparent contradiction.
3. It costs a retailer money to offer credit to customers. Identify some of the costs to a retailer.
4. Suppose you work in a clothing store. A customer wants to purchase a product with a credit card. What can you do to make sure his or her credit card hasn't reached its limit?

Building Academic Skills

Math

1. Your tire warranty reads as follows: "This limited warranty applies to all owners of the tire using it in noncommercial passenger service. If our examination shows that a passenger tire covered by this warranty has become unserviceable due to workmanship or materials defect during its tread life (*i.e.*, worn down to $3/32$ of an inch groove depth), it will be replaced on a "pro rata tread wear basis." A "pro rata" basis means that you will be given a discount proportional to the remaining tire life at the time of replacement. (In other words, if 70 percent of the tire's tread was gone when the tire failed, you would be given a 30 percent discount on a replacement.) Compute the remaining percentage of tire life and the cost of a replacement tire in the following circumstances:

Tread Depth	Tread Life Expired	Tread Life Remaining	New Tire Cost	Customer Cost
$4/32$	80%		$79.40	
$7/32$	50		57.25	
$8/32$	40		113.79	
$3/32$	90		65.00	
$2/32$	100		49.99	

8. It certifies new drugs and inspects drug- and food-processing plants. It also regulates the advertising and sale of medical devices.
9. It protects consumers from poorly built cars.
10. First, contact the seller. If the seller does not resolve the problem, contact the manufacturer. If the problem is still unresolved, contact the local, state, or Federal offices that can assist with consumer complaints. Finally if the problem is still not resolved, take legal action.

11. Breach of federal law (written warranty), breach of state law (implied warranty), and negligence.
12. Read and follow directions provided on packages, be honest in their purchases and use of the products, complain reasonably when seeking adjustments.
13. Credit is an arrangement whereby businesses or individuals can obtain products or money in exchange for a promise to pay later. A credit limit is a pre-approved dollar amount which you

Communication

2. Even though warranties are supposed to be written in clear, simple language, many consumers still find them difficult to understand. Find an example of a fairly long and detailed warranty—perhaps one for a major appliance or an automobile. Then rewrite it in your own words.

3. Write a business letter requesting a free copy of "Choosing a Credit Card" from the Federal Reserve Board. Address your letter to: Publications Services, MS-127, Board of Governors of the Federal Reserve System, Washington, D.C. 20551

Application Projects

1. Find a warranty for a small appliance and read the document carefully. Then answer the following questions.
   a. Is the warranty full or limited? How do you know?
   b. To what remedy is the purchaser entitled if a manufacturer's defect is found?
   c. Describe the required procedure for obtaining warranty repairs. Include the name and address of the nearest service center and note what, if any, charges the customer must pay.
   d. List any disclaimers that the warranty contains.
2. From newspapers, magazines, catalogs, and circulars, clip ads that use the words *warranty, warrant, guarantee,* or *guaranteed.* Assemble these ads into a bulletin board display on firms that use warranties as a key promotional element. *Note:* include tags and statements from product literature in the display, if these are available.
3. Develop a list of examples that would adversely affect a person's ability to obtain credit.
4. Obtain a credit application and use it to summarize in an outline the types of information asked for on a credit application.

Linking School to Work

1. Develop a report on the process used at your place of employment to honor product or service guarantees.
2. Investigate how credit is used at your place of employment. Report on any guidelines or rules, if available, which are used to grant credit to a customer.

Performance Assessment

Role Play

Situation. You are a service manager in an auto dealership. An angry customer is complaining about rattles and noises which are occurring in his car. His new car warranty has recently expired. The customer is complaining that prior to expiration, he requested the necessary repairs, but they were not done correctly. Your task is to represent the warranty conditions to the customer and to resolve the situation to the satisfaction of the customer.

Evaluation. You will be evaluated on how well you can do the following:

* Explain the type of warranty involved with your product.
* Describe consumer responsibilities and remedies related to product performance.
* Handle the situation with courtesy, tact, and professionalism.
* Resolve the situation to the satisfaction of the customer.

Create a Chart

Prepare a chart that shows the name and important features of each law that regulates the granting of credit.

COMPUTER APPLICATION

Complete the Chapter 36 Computer Application that appears in the Student Activity Workbook.

Portfolio

Consider the Application Projects you have done for this unit. Select one that illustrates your mastery of the unit's content and that might be of interest to potential employers. Reformat the activity as necessary. Add any explanatory text, and place it in your Portfolio. Consider using these activities:

* Chapter 34, Application Project 1
* Chapter 35, Application Project 2 ■ ■

Chapter 36 *Extended Product Features* **485**

---

can use to purchase items on credit.

14. Banks that issue bank cards receive their income from finance charges, annual membership fees, and retailer servicing fees. Retailers that issue retail credit cards receive their income from finance charges.

15. Credit cards require the payment in full of charges made during the month. Bank credit cards do not.

16. Business or trade credit is similar to consumer credit in that money is loaned for goods and services. Unlike consumer credit, trade credit does not involve the use of credit cards.

17. It requires that lenders disclose credit information.

Critical Thinking

1. A good guarantee should be unconditional and easy for the customer to use.

2. Sold to guard against rising repair costs after a product is used for several years, extended service contracts assure the customer of worry-free service and repairs.

3. Reasons are detailed in Section 36.2.

4. You can run the credit card through a computerized machine to make sure it hasn't reached its limit.

Building Academic Skills

Math

1. a. 20% $63.52 ($79.40 × .20 = $15.88) $79.40 – $15.88 = $63.52
   b. 50% $28.63
   c. 60% $45.52
   d. 10% $58.50
   e. 0% $45.99

Communications

2. Students should rewrite the warranties in clear language.
3. Write one letter as a class.

Application Projects

1. Answers will depend on the warranties they choose.
2. Review the completed bulletin board. Discuss which types of companies tend to offer warranties.
3. Answers vary.
4. Students should summarize the information required on a credit application.

Linking School to Work

Answers depend on the work situation.

Performance Assessment

Refer to the *DECA Competitive Events Handbook* for evaluation guidelines.

Computer Application

Optional activity. Refer to the *Marketing Software Binder* for template and user information.

Portfolio

Refer to the Marketing Career Portfolio for development ideas and portfolio management and assessment.

Evaluation

Administer the reproducible test for Chapter 36, or construct your own using the Testmaker software.

Entrepreneurship

Unit Objectives

After completing this unit, students will be able to achieve the following outcomes:

- Identify the risks, rewards, advantages, and disadvantages of entrepreneurship.
- Explain the scope of small business in the U.S. economy.
- Identify business risks and tell how businesses handle them.
- Explain each section of a business plan and prepare the appropriate documentation for each.

Chapter 39

Chapter 38

Chapter 37

Chapter 40

Teacher Classroom Resources

CHAPTER	37	38	39	40
Transparency Binder	Transparencies 63–64			Transparencies 65–70
Student Activity Workbook	pp. 231–238	pp. 239–246	pp. 247–254	pp. 255–262
Student Software	pp. 237–238	pp. 245–246	pp. 253–254	pp. 261–262
Marketing Math Workbook				Activity 11
School-to-Work Handbook	pp. 79–80	pp. 81–82	pp. 83–84	pp. 85–86
International Case Studies	pp. 79–80	pp. 81–82	pp. 83–84	pp. 85–86
Marketing Career Portfolio				Unit 11 activity, Student Text, p. 545
Test Booklet/ Testmaker Software	Chapter 37 test	Chapter 38 test	Chapter 39 test	Chapter 40 test, Unit 11 test

KEY TO BASIC SKILLS ACTIVITIES

L1 Level 1 activities are basic activities and should be within the range of all students.

L2 Level 2 activities are average activities and should be within the range of average and above average students.

L3 Level 3 activities are challenging activities designed for the ability range of above average students.

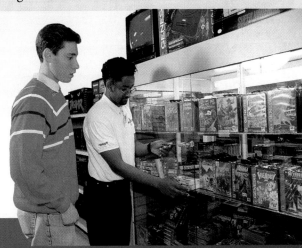

CHAPTER	PERFORMANCE OBJECTIVES	
37 **What Is Entrepreneurship?**	37.1	1. Define entrepreneurship. 2. Identify the risks involved in entrepreneurship. 3. Discuss the advantages and disadvantages of entrepreneurship. 4. Identify the personal characteristics and skills entrepreneurs need. 5. Explain the scope of small business in the American economy.
	37.2	1. Discuss business ownership opportunities. 2. Identify forms of business ownership. 3. Explain the legal steps to take in establishing a business.
38 **Risk Management**	38.1	1. Explain the nature of risk management. 2. Discuss the various types of business risks.
	38.2	1. Identify the ways businesses handle risks.
39 **Developing a Business Plan**	39.1	1. Discuss the importance and purpose of a business plan. 2. Identify the major sections of a business plan. 3. Describe and analyze a proposed business situation.
	39.2	1. Develop an organization plan. 2. Provide details related to goods or services to be offered. 3. Develop a marketing plan.
	39.3	1. Describe the elements found in the financial section of a business plan. 2. Identify sources of equity capital. 3. Identify sources of debt capital.
40 **Financing the Business**	40.1	1. Describe the purpose of preparing financial documents. 2. Develop a personal financial statement. 3. Determine start-up costs for a business.
	40.2	1. Estimate business income and expenses. 2. Prepare an income statement. 3. Calculate payroll and other expenses itemized on an income statement. 4. Prepare a balance sheet. 5. Prepare a cash flow statement.

Unit Overview and Background Information

Entrepreneurship is so highly stressed to marketing education students because it is so important to the U.S. economy.

Chapter 37 introduces students to the process of starting and managing a business. Chapter 38 discusses the economic, natural, and human risks inherent in business ownership and the steps business owners take to reduce and manage risk by careful planning. Chapter 39 discusses how potential business owners create a business plan to give an overall picture of a proposed business to potential investors and lenders. Chapter 40 shows students how to identify capital needs for a business and develop a financial plan that will meet those needs.

Introducing the Unit

Introduce the concept of entrepreneurship and ask students if they can generate the names of some modern-day entrepreneurs. Ask students to speculate on why some people prefer to work for themselves, when they initially sacrifice a great deal of security to do so, and what skills and abilities it takes to be your own boss. Also ask which students have already done some type of entrepreneurial endeavor, and which would consider working for themselves as a career move.

Unit Project

Have students research the role of small business ownership in our society since the 1700s. What roles is small business playing in the society of the late 1990s? What role will it probably play early in the twenty-first century? How is small business ownership reflective of current economic and sociological trends in our society?

Unit 11

486

Focus on the Photo/Cooperative Learning

Once students have completed this unit, divide the class into four groups and have each group discuss what they feel this picture says to them about entrepreneurship. What do they think the relationship is between entrepreneurship and the rest of the marketing world? Have each group write a caption for this photo that makes a statement about entrepreneurship. Allow time for the captions to be read aloud.

Entrepreneurship

CHAPTERS

37
**What Is
Entrepreneurship?**

38
**Risk
Management**

39
**Developing a
Business Plan**

40
**Financing the
Business**

Financing

Distribution

Risk
Management

Product/
Service
Planning

ECONOMIC
FOUNDATIONS
OF MARKETING

HUMAN
RESOURCE
FOUNDATIONS

Selling

Marketing-
Information
Management

MARKETING
AND BUSINESS
FOUNDATIONS

Promotion

Purchasing

Pricing

487

WHAT IS ENTREPRENEURSHIP?

Pages 488–499

Chapter Overview

This chapter introduces entrepreneurship and explores the types of business ownership.

Springboard

Ask which students have ever babysat, mowed lawns, cleaned pools, etc. What were the rewards in working for themselves? What were the drawbacks? Tell students that in working for themselves, they were acting in an entrepreneurial manner.

In this chapter, they will look at what it means to be an entrepreneur, including the aptitudes, abilities, and skills needed to manage an entrepreneurial business.

Prereading

List the section objectives to discuss with the students. Have the students skim the chapter, looking at the pictures, reading the captions, and noting the heads. Ask questions to ensure that the students have a minimal understanding of the chapter structure.

Preteaching the Vocabulary

Flip through the chapter with students. When you come to each **boldface** term, have one student read the definition aloud, then have students develop one visual symbol that will illustrate each term. Draw each symbol next to its corresponding term on the board.

CHAPTER 37

What Is Entrepreneurship?

Have you ever wished you were the boss? Did you ever think you had a good idea for a good or service? Do you like to plan your own day and make your own decisions? Then you might consider entrepreneurship.

This chapter introduces you to the process of starting and managing your own business. You will look at the advantages and disadvantages of business ownership. You will discover what special personal qualities and skills are needed for success. You will also learn about ways to enter into business and forms of business ownership.

Classroom Management

For the Teacher
- Teacher's Annotated Editions for all workbooks
- Teacher's Manual for *School-to-Work Handbook*
- *Testing Binder*
- *Transparency Binder*
- *Marketing Software Binder*
- *Marketing Career Portfolio*
- *Lesson Plans*

For the Student
- *Student Activity Workbook*
- *Marketing Math Workbook*
- *School-to-Work Handbook*
- *Student Software*
- *International Case Studies*
- *Marketing Career Portfolio*

SECTION 37.1

Objectives

After completing this section, you will be able to

- define entrepreneurship,
- identify the risks involved in entrepreneurship,
- discuss the advantages and disadvantages of entrepreneurship,
- identify the personal characteristics and skills entrepreneurs need, and
- explain the scope of small business in the American economy.

Terms to Know

- entrepreneurship
- entrepreneurs

What Is Entrepreneurship?

Entrepreneurship is the process of starting and managing your own business. As you know, everyone in the United States is free to start, own, and operate a business. **Entrepreneurs** are people who attempt to earn money and make profits by taking the risk of owning and operating a business. If you have ever provided baby-sitting services or cut someone's lawn, you have already been an entrepreneur.

Some entrepreneurs single-handedly make a major contribution to our economy. For example, Henry Ford introduced the mass production of automobiles, thus making them affordable to the average person. Ray Kroc made McDonald's the largest fast-food restaurant chain in the world. Former secretary Bette Graham developed Liquid Paper to paint over typing errors; the product is now sold worldwide. Steven Jobs and Steven Wozniak began Apple Computer, Inc., working mostly from their homes, and soon turned it into an international business.

These entrepreneurs became famous and wealthy. However, there are many entrepreneurs who do not dream of fame and riches. They are simply people who want to be their own bosses and make their own business decisions. They are willing to put in the effort and dedication it takes to be successful at running their own businesses.

The Risk of Entrepreneurship

Starting a new business is a risk because it is a major commitment of time, money, and effort. So, new business owners must be risk takers. Often, they quit their current jobs, work long hours, invest their savings, and borrow money—with no guarantee that the new business will succeed.

Some 60 percent of those who start a business are between the ages of 25 and 40. People between these ages usually have the work experience, the personal drive, the financial resources, and the willingness to take business risks. People over the age of 40 are usually established in life. They may have the money and experience it takes to start a business. However, they may be reluctant to do so because of family commitments or fear of losing what they have achieved.

The fear of losing money with a new business venture (or, at least, the fear of not making *enough* money) is very real. Most new businesses that survive employ only a few people and provide a living only for the business owner and his or her family. Some 8,400 new businesses are started each week. Studies show that two out of three new firms close their doors within four years of opening.

You can see, then, that owning and operating your own business can be risky. There are no guarantees of success. Nevertheless, being an entrepreneur has its advantages.

Real World

MARKETING

In the (Chocolate) Chips

The name *Mrs. Fields* summons up images of a sweet granny. Nevertheless, the queen of the chocolate chip cookie, Debbi Fields, is a trim, attractive young woman. A Palo Alto, California newlywed in search of a career, Debbi thought that if she offered the public freshly baked cookies, people just might bite. They did—to the tune of $30 million in the first six years.

Chapter 37 *What Is Entrepreneurship?* **489**

SECTION 37.1

FOCUS

Bell Ringer Activity

Give students five minutes to write a list of what they would consider to be the advantages and disadvantages of entrepreneurship.

Introducing the Section

Review students' answers from the Bell Ringer Activity. In this section they will look at the pros and cons of entrepreneurship and begin the process of exploring entrepreneurship as a career option.

Teach

Guided Practice

1. Read Section 37.1 with students.
2. Use the transparency for this section.
3. Encourage each student to shadow an entrepreneur for a day.
4. *Entrepreneurship*, one of Glencoe's Career Competencies in Marketing texts, is appropriate for use as a supplement to this chapter and for independent study in preparation for the National DECA Entrepreneurship Event. Also consult Glencoe's *Entrepreneurship and Small Business Management, Open for Business Video Series,* and *Entrepreneurial Endeavors* for more information on entrepreneurship and small business ownership.
5. *The Career Guide to Industries,* one of the Bureau of Labor Statistics' vocational guidance publications, will help students complete the lesson plan activities. It examines employment opportunities in 40 industries. Contact the Superintendent of Documents, P.O. Box 37194, Pittsburgh, PA 15250-7954, or the BLS Publications Sales Center, P.O. Box 2145, Chicago, IL 60690-2145.

Meeting Special Needs

Hearing Impaired

Students with hearing impairments may also have speech impairments or impediments ranging from problems with articulation or voice strength to being without ability to speak. These impairments can include stuttering, chronic hoarseness, or difficulty in expressing an appropriate word or phrase. Typically, such students refrain as much as possible from class participation. When speaking with a speech impaired student, use normal communication patterns and refrain from completing words or phrases for the student. Some students use electronic speaking machines or are adept at using body language to communicate. Your role as teacher is to create an environment that all students can participate in to the best of their abilities.

6. Additional career publications that will be helpful to students include the *Dictionary of Occupational Titles, Encyclopedia of Careers and Vocational Guidance, The Guide for Occupational Exploration, The Occupational Outlook Handbook,* and *The Occupational Outlook Quarterly.*

7. MarkEd Resource Center in Columbus, Ohio, (800) 448-0398, offers materials appropriate for use with this chapter.

8. If any students' parents or guardians are small business owners, encourage these students to share their observations about their parents' or guardians' work lives, including the amount of energy and commitment it takes to run the business, and the impact on one's personal life.

Discussion Starter

Many people have powerful altruistic motives for becoming entrepreneurs. First, make sure students understand the term *altruism* (unselfish regard for the welfare of others). Then have them discuss why altruism plays a part in some people's desire to be an entrepreneur. (Some people feel they are contributing to the local labor force and are thus making the community a better place to work and live.)

Critical Thinking

Have students discuss why small business ownership has become so important in our society.

BRIGHT IDEAS

Try Something Silly

Would you believe that Silly Putty started out as a government experiment? During World War II, General Electric began searching for an inexpensive substitute for rubber. When a chemical engineer mixed silicone oil and boric acid in a test tube, the result was a gooey substance that bounced.

Unfortunately, GE scientists couldn't find any practical use for the concoction, so in the laboratory it remained. There the scientists found many impractical uses for it. For example, they made special batches of the stuff for parties because it was fun to play with.

At one such party, an advertising consultant got his hands on some of the mixture. As he was playing with it, the term *silly putty* came to him. He bought 21 pounds of the substance from GE for $147 and began packaging it in small plastic eggs as a toy for adults. He was off to a brisk start, selling up to 300 eggs a day, when a feature in *New Yorker* magazine brought in orders totaling 230,000.

Although originally marketed to adults, Silly Putty found its biggest fans among children. Until recently, they accounted for over 80 percent of sales. Now, however, Silly Putty has begun to live up to GE's practical aspirations for it. Ironically, the substance that bounced so high on Earth now helps astronauts anchor items in the zero gravity of space.

Creativity Challenge Form teams of 3–5 people, and brainstorm a "silly" product that could be mass-marketed to children or adults. For inspiration, think of Play-Dough and Slime, Pet Rocks, and canned (San Francisco) fog. Remember, where novelty items like these are concerned, advertising, packaging, and promotion are often more important than the item itself.

Advantages of Entrepreneurship

If going into business for yourself is such a risky venture, why do so many people choose to do it? Here are some of the major reasons why people go into business for themselves.

Personal Freedom Entrepreneurs are not controlled by any other managers in their organizations. They

set their own work schedules. They make their own decisions, try out their own new ideas, and direct their energies into business activities as they see fit.

Personal Satisfaction Personal freedom leads to the personal satisfaction of doing what you enjoy each day. By being in control of their businesses and their work settings, entrepreneurs are much more in control of their lives.

Increased Income Personal satisfaction usually leads people to work hard at what they enjoy. Working hard usually results in making more money. Thus, the incentive to make money—coupled with the personal satisfaction that comes from doing so—is always present.

Self-esteem Freedom, satisfaction, and increased income add up to a greater feeling of self-esteem. People who work hard and are well rewarded for it, both personally and financially, are truly successful people.

Disadvantages of Entrepreneurship

The advantages of being an entrepreneur are definitely exciting and motivating. Nevertheless, there are some disadvantages, too.

Risk and Potential Loss of Income New businesses usually have a restricted cash flow because of start-up costs. This may mean that an entrepreneur's first year or more of operation does not meet his or her personal financial needs. Entrepreneurs enjoy improved earnings only if the business is successful. If they do not have the necessary personal or technical skills, their businesses will probably fail. With failures come a loss of employment, status, and invested money.

Long, Irregular Hours Entrepreneurs are not 40-hour-a-week people. It is quite possible that a new business will demand 12 to 16 hours a day in addition to weekends and holidays. Usually, new business owners do not even take vacations until the business proves successful.

Need for Daily Discipline Running a business may be personally and financially rewarding. However, it also requires doing many tedious, time-consuming tasks.

For example, the business owner may have to do general cleaning and maintenance because there is not enough money to hire someone else to do it. Also, there is usually a lot of paperwork involved in any business operation. Accounts payable, accounts receivable, payroll, and forms to fill out for all levels of government regulations require precise record keeping.

It takes a great deal of self-discipline to keep up with all these things on a daily, weekly, and monthly basis. They are just as important as actually selling the good or service.

Despite these disadvantages, the lure of being one's own boss attracts countless people each year. Those who are successful at it have certain personal characteristics that enable them to succeed where others fail. What are these personal qualities? Are you a budding entrepreneur?

Bright Ideas

Discuss with students why "silly" products can be so successful. The answers can be as varied as that such products are entertaining, they allow us to play which reminds us of our childhood, they distract us from our everyday problems, they give us something to talk about with others, and they can give us something to do with our hands. No one answer will always be correct. The reasons vary from person to person and even on the mood of the individual.

Self-Evaluation

The first seven questions consider your personality characteristics.	YES	NO
1. Do you like to make your own decisions?	____	____
2. Do you enjoy competition?	____	____
3. Do you have willpower and self-determination?	____	____
4. Do you plan ahead?	____	____
5. Do you like to get things done on time?	____	____
6. Can you take advice from others?	____	____
7. Can you adapt to changing conditions?	____	____
The next series of questions considers your physical, emotional, and financial well-being.		
8. Do you understand that owning your own business may entail working 12 to 16 hours a day, probably six days a week and maybe on holidays?	____	____
9. Do you have the physical stamina to handle a business?	____	____
10. Do you have the emotional strength to withstand the strain?	____	____
11. Are you prepared to lower your living standard for several months or years?	____	____
12. Are you prepared to lose your savings?	____	____
13. Do you know which skills and areas of expertise are critical to the success of your business?	____	____
14. Do you have these skills?	____	____
15. Does your idea for a business use these skills?	____	____
16. Can you find the people that have the expertise you lack?	____	____
17. Do you know why you are considering this business?	____	____
18. Will your business meet your career aspirations?	____	____

Figure 37–1

Take this self evaluation by answering each question honestly. As you do, ask yourself why each of these points could be important in running a small business.

Characteristics of a Successful Entrepreneur

To be a successful entrepreneur, you must have strong organizational skills, tremendous drive, and leadership ability. You must have the special skills and knowledge necessary to operate the business you have chosen. In addition, you must be in good physical and mental condition to work the hours the business will require.

It also helps to have parents or relatives who are already in business for themselves. Studies have shown that the family is a major influence on who becomes an entrepreneur. Being around people who are successful entrepreneurs positively influences children to feel that they can be successful entrepreneurs, too.

People who become entrepreneurs tend to think they are in control. They think that their hard work and determination—not luck or fate—will make their business successful.

They also have a spirit of adventure. They get a great deal of satisfaction from taking risks and achieving goals.

Do You Have What It Takes?

Before you think about owning your own business, you have to honestly ask yourself, "Do I have what it takes to go into business for myself?"

You can answer this question by doing a *self-evaluation*—an assessment of your personal qualities, abilities, interests, and skills. The self-evaluation in Figure 37–1 was developed by the Small Business Administration. Take a few minutes right now to answer each question on

Independent Practice

Many major corporations, such as Ford Motor Company, Gerber Products, J. C. Penney, Wendy's International, Inc., The Walt Disney Company, and Wm. Wrigley, Jr. Company, were started by entrepreneurs who had a dream of achieving a goal, who created a product to fill a market need, or who simply discovered or created a product accidentally and began to market it. Have students research information about the founder of one of these or any other U.S. corporations that started out as an entrepreneurial venture and write a character profile of the founder. Students should discuss the aptitudes, abilities, skills, and personal characteristics that made this person successful.

Assess

Evaluation

Assign and review the Section 37.1 Review.

Reteaching

1. Assign and review the vocabulary terms for this section.
2. Assign and review Fact and Idea Review question one from the Chapter Review.
3. Have each student rank the advantages and disadvantages of entrepreneurship and write a statement next to each one that tells why they ranked the item as they did. Have the students discuss their rankings in class.

Lifelong Learning

Entrepreneurship

Students who feel that they have entrepreneurial potential need to continue their education to gain the skills they need to run their own businesses. Many high schools, colleges, and adult education programs offer courses specific to entrepreneurship and small business management. Other helpful courses include accounting, computer classes, as well as additional marketing classes specifically for entrepreneurs. In addition, some individuals may also need to acquire further education in the profession of their choice. Joining a nonprofit organization that provides information to individuals, such as the National Business Association, can also be helpful.

Enrichment

1. Assign and review the appropriate activities in the *Student Activity Workbook*.

2. Assign and review the appropriate Critical Thinking questions from the Chapter Review.

3. Have the students research the structure of the workforce at this time and where employment growth is predicted to be the greatest. Have the students discuss their findings in class and brainstorm ideas for entrepreneurial endeavors based on the information. (The U.S. Department of Labor predicts that the bulk of the employment growth will be in health services, retail trade, and business services. These industries will account for 47 percent of total employment growth, down slightly from 50 percent in the 1980s.

    Services and professional occupations are gaining the most employment or growing the fastest.

    The economy will be more global, more service-oriented, and highly technology-based.

    Skilled workers will hold the fastest-growing jobs. These highlights of projections are from "The American Work Force: 1992-2005," i1, v37, *Occupational Outlook Quarterly*, Fall 1993, p.4.)

Close

Have students complete this statement: At this time, entrepreneurship interests me (or doesn't interest me) as a potential career option because...

Figure 37-2

The GNP of U.S. small business is higher than that of Canada, Australia, Korea, and Singapore. What percentage of the GNP do small businesses represent in the United States?

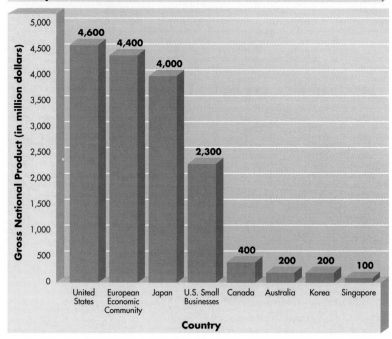

Output of Small Businesses in the United States Compared to Other Economies

Gross National Product (in million dollars)

- United States: 4,600
- European Economic Community: 4,400
- Japan: 4,000
- U.S. Small Businesses: 2,300
- Canada: 400
- Australia: 200
- Korea: 200
- Singapore: 100

Country

a separate piece of paper. Think before you answer—and be honest with yourself.

As you can see from answering the questions in Figure 37-1, starting a business requires careful self-evaluation. Answering yes to most or all of these questions should be an indication that you have the right characteristics for success. You should also consider the experiences of family, friends, and other businesspeople already in the same or a similar business. Find out about their experiences. Also, do library research on the type of business you wish to start. All this information taken together should give you a good indication of whether you are ready and able to join the ranks of America's millions of small businesspeople.

The Importance of Entrepreneurship in Our Economy

Small businesses are those with less than 500 employees in manufacturing and less than 100 in retailing. Small businesses make up the majority of U.S. businesses. In addition, they provide jobs for about 55 percent of the labor force. Eighty percent of the new jobs created came from businesses that were less than five years old.

Small businesses produce 50 percent of the Gross Domestic Product (GDP). (Recall from Chapter 4 that the GDP is a measure of the goods and services produced using labor and property located in this country.) Small businesses also represent 50 percent of the GNP. (See Figure 37-2.)

Small businesses benefit the economy and society in other ways, too. They offer consumers more choices of goods and services. They help improve products and processes. They challenge existing businesses to become more efficient and provide better goods and services. They also offer on-the-job training to many students who then use this valuable experience to open small businesses of their own.

SECTION 37.1 *Review*

1. What is entrepreneurship?

2. Why is starting a new business such a risk?

3. What are four advantages and three disadvantages of being an entrepreneur?

4. Give three characteristics of a successful entrepreneur.

5. Identify three reasons why small businesses are important to the economy.

Caption Answer

Small businesses represent 50 percent of the GNP.

Section Review Answers

1. Starting and managing a business.
2. It is a major commitment of time, money, and effort, with no guarantee of success.
3. See page 490 for a list of advantages and disadvantages.
4. Organizational skills, drive, leadership.
5. See the section "The Importance of Entrepreneurship in Our Economy."

Objectives

After completing this section, you will be able to

- **discuss business ownership opportunities,**
- **identify forms of business ownership, and**
- **explain the legal steps to take in establishing a business.**

Terms to Know

- **franchise**
- **sole proprietorship**
- **unlimited liability**
- **partnership**
- **general partnership**
- **limited partnership**
- **corporation**
- **stockholders**
- **foreign corporation**
- **Subchapter S corporation**
- **DBA**
- **Articles of Incorporation**

Business Ownership Opportunities

Some 420,000 businesses are started each year. There are four ways to enter business: develop a new business, purchase a franchise business, purchase an existing nonfranchise business, or take over the family business. (See Figure 37-3 on page 494.)

Forms of Business Organization

Just as you can choose which good or service to provide, you can also choose the legal organization or structure your business will take.

The legal form of business organization you select may make the difference between business success and business failure. It determines how fast you can get your business decisions implemented, how well you compete in the marketplace, and how quickly you can raise additional money for expansion.

As an entrepreneur, your choices of business organization are *sole proprietorship,* the *partnership,* and the *corporation.* The one you select depends on such circumstances as your financial condition, the type of business you want to start, the number of employees you will hire, the business risk involved, and your tax situation.

Remember that you can change your initial decision about the type of business organization you feel is best. As your business grows and prospers, your financial and tax situations may require you to change the form of organization.

The Sole Proprietorship

A **sole proprietorship** is a business owned and operated by one person. This is the most common form of business ownership. People usually become sole proprietors when they have a special skill by which they can earn a living. Plumbers, auto mechanics, and writers, for example, are often sole proprietors.

In addition to having a special skill, the sole proprietor must provide the money and management skill to run the business. In return for all this responsibility, the sole proprietor is entitled to all the profits.

There are several other advantages to a sole proprietorship, too. It is relatively easy to start. All business decisions made are your own. It is generally taxed less than other forms of business. It allows more freedom from government regulation.

If you choose this form of ownership, you have complete control over the business. However, you are also responsible for all business debts or legal judgments against the business.

For example, if the debts of your business exceed its assets (that is, all of its resources), your creditors can claim all of your own personal assets, such as your car, home, and savings. This responsibility is called unlimited liability. **Unlimited liability** means that your financial liability (responsibility) is not limited to your investment in the business, but extends to your total ability to make payments.

Problems can develop in a sole proprietorship when it becomes necessary to expand business operations but the only money available is the owner's personal assets. Also, making all the decisions yourself without the input and advice of others can be difficult.

The Partnership

A **partnership** is a legal agreement between two or more people to be jointly responsible for the success or failure of a business. A partnership agreement, usually prepared by an attorney, specifies the responsibilities of

Chapter 37 *What Is Entrepreneurship?* **493**

SECTION 37.2

Focus

Bell Ringer Activity

Clip several "business for sale" ads for sole proprietorships, franchises, and corporations from a local or national newspaper, or from business magazines. Read the ads to students. Ask them to help you generate a chalkboard list of things they would consider before buying each one of the enterprises mentioned.

Introducing the Section

Students' answers from the Bell Ringer Activity will vary but should include the following: (1) the amount of money they would have to invest in the business, (2) their general level of interest in and knowledge of the product(s) the business sells, (3) the legal requirements involved in business start-up and in taxation, (4) whether or not they want to have stockholders, (5) whether or not they want to answer to a corporate parent, and (6) the location of the business and its prior reputation and financial success.

In this section, students will look at the various forms of business ownership and the advantages and disadvantages of each.

Teach

Guided Practice

1. Read Section 37.2 with students.
2. Have students read aloud the Case Study and review the answers in class.
3. Use the transparency for this section.
4. Assign and review the Chapter 37 Activity in the *School-to-Work Handbook.*

More About

The SBA and Business Opportunities

Founded in 1953, the SBA is the federal agency that assists the small business sector by providing information and business counseling services, as well as loan programs. It serves as a representative of small business interests (the head of the SBA is a member of the cabinet), an advocate for small business, and as a collector of small business data. The SBA has helped launch many now familiar corporations such as Apple Computer, Nike, and Federal Express.

Discussion Starter

Discuss with students the value of networking. Entrepreneurs network constantly to keep up on innovations in their field, to keep building their list of resources and contacts, and to keep themselves visible in the community. Have students discuss ways that they can network now.

Discuss the value, as a professional, of belonging to associations which often sponsor national and regional conferences, provide publications, and act as a clearinghouse of information for members.

Have students prepare a networking card file using 3" x 5" index cards on which they write the names, addresses, phone numbers, and relevant information about their business contacts.

Cooperative Learning

Divide the class into four to six groups. Have each group choose one of the following career clusters: *Agribusiness, Environment, and Natural Resources; Business and Office; Communication; Construction; Consumer and Homemaking; Fine Arts and Humanities; Health, Hospitality and Recreation; Manufacturing; Marine Science; Marketing and Distribution; Personal Services; Public Services;* and *Transportation.*

Have each group research entrepreneurial opportunities by listing the following: (1) several small business' opportunities; (2) what the demand will be for jobs in the cluster; (3) emerging occupations in the cluster; (4) the skills, knowledge, and experience one needs to enter the field; (5) physical demands of working in the area; (6) work environment; (7) education and training necessary; and (8) part-time, volunteer and/or summer work that would help students prepare now for the entrepreneurial endeavor. Each group should present its findings to the class.

Figure 37–3

WAYS TO ENTER BUSINESS

The manner by which you choose to enter business will depend on your needs and your financial resources.

Starting Your Own Business ▼

Starting your own business allows you to start the business of your choice. You can decide where to locate your business and how you will set it up. You do not have to take on old bad debts, a bad reputation, or a poor location that you may inherit when you buy an existing business. However, you must establish every aspect of your business from the ground up. In addition, you must create and build a reputation with your customers.

Purchasing a Franchise Business ▼

A **franchise** is a legal agreement to operate a business in the name of a recognized company. The *franchisee* (the person purchasing the franchise) buys an existing business operation. All business planning is done by the *franchisor*, the owner of the recognized company. Planning generally includes management training and assistance with advertising, merchandising, and day-to-day operations. The biggest disadvantages of franchising are the large amount of capital needed to purchase most franchises and the high initial fees charged to begin operations. Also, the franchisor may limit the franchisee's choices as to how the business is run.

Purchasing an Existing ▲ Business

When you buy an existing nonfranchise business, you usually receive little or no help from the previous owner. Therefore, you must investigate why the business is being sold. You must carefully examine the business records and the condition of the property and inventory. You must also determine the reputation of the business in the community.

Taking Over the ▲ Family Business

Some of the same considerations for purchasing an existing business also apply for a family business. You must review business records and the overall condition of the property and inventory. You must determine the reputation of the business in the community. In addition, you need to explore potential conflicts and concerns with family members.

494   Unit 11   *Entrepreneurship*

▶ **More About**

Franchises

Franchise costs don't end when the business is up and running, but usually continue throughout the life of the agreement. The franchisee usually pays a percentage of sales or profits to the franchisor. In addition, many franchise agreements contain "buy back" language specifying at what point in time the franchisor has the right to "buy back" the franchise and the pay out to the franchisee.

each partner. Partners share the profits if the business is a success and share the losses if it fails.

Like a sole proprietorship, a partnership is subject to relatively little regulation and is fairly easy to establish. However, partnerships are a more complicated form of business ownership than the sole proprietorship.

There are two types of partnerships: *general* and *limited*. In a **general partnership,** each partner shares in the profits and losses. As in the sole proprietorship, each partner has unlimited liability for the company's debts. Also, each partner's share of the profits is taxed as personal income.

Because of the unlimited liability you face as a member of a general partnership, you might want to establish a *limited partnership*. In a **limited partnership,** each limited partner is liable for any debts only up to the amount of his or her investment in the company.

Every limited partnership, however, must have at least one general partner who has unlimited liability. In exchange for their limited liability, limited partners have no voice in the management of the partnership. The withdrawal of a limited partner does not dissolve the partnership, if you and your partners decide to continue doing business.

If you decide to establish a limited partnership, you must give public notice stating that one or more partners have limited liability. Otherwise, it is assumed that a general partnership exists and all partners have unlimited liability. You can get additional information regarding limited partnerships by contacting your state department of commerce.

There are several advantages to a partnership. It combines the skills of the owners. It may have access to more money and thus may operate and expand more easily. It allows each partner a voice in the management of the business. It is taxed and regulated less heavily than a corporation.

Despite these advantages, there are some disadvantages to partnerships, too. The owners may not always agree on business decisions. The actions of one partner are legally binding on the other partners. This means that all partners must assume their share of the business debt. They must also be responsible for the shares of the other partners, if they cannot pay. Finally, the business is dissolved, if one partner dies. It can be reorganized as a new partnership, but the process is time consuming and costly.

The Corporation

A **corporation** is a business that is chartered by a state and legally operates apart from the owner(s). It is the most complicated form of business organization we've looked at in this chapter.

Although a corporation can be any size, larger firms are usually organized as corporations. Those who work for a corporation are not necessarily the people who own it, although they may be.

The value of a corporation is divided into equal units called shares of stock. These shares of stock are sold through the *stock market* to individual investors called stockholders. **Stockholders** are the people who actually own the corporation. Stockholders have limited liability. They are liable for the losses of the corporation only to the extent of his or her individual investment. Stockholders are not responsible for debts incurred by the corporation. Corporations form governing bodies called *boards* who hire directors and officers to manage the affairs of the business and the interests of the stockholders.

A corporation can own assets, borrow money, and perform business functions without directly involving the shareholders. Therefore, it is subject to more government regulation than a sole proprietorship or a partnership.

Corporations can be *incorporated* (established) in the state where they will do business or in another state. It is best for most small businesses to incorporate in the state where they are going to do business. Otherwise, they may have to do business as a foreign corporation. A **foreign corporation** is incorporated under the laws of a different state from the one in which it does business. Foreign corporations must seek approval from and register with each state in which they intend to do business.

Some new businesses can also be established as Subchapter S corporations. A **Subchapter S corporation** is a small business that is taxed like a partnership or proprietorship.

There are strict provisions for Subchapter S corporations. The business, for example, can have no more than 35 shareholders. It must be incorporated in the United States. It can have no more than 20 percent of its gross revenues from investment income and no more than 80 percent of its gross revenues from foreign sources. You can learn more information about Subchapter S corporations by consulting IRS publication No. 589 or by calling your Internal Revenue office.

Give Me a Hand

Life in the **Multicultural** MARKETPLACE

The handshake is the common form of greeting in Europe and the Americas. However, as you travel around the world, greetings change enormously. In countries such as India and Sri Lanka, the traditional greeting involves placing one's palms together under the chin and bowing slightly. In Fiji, natives typically greet each other with a smile and an upward flick of the eyebrows. In Pakistan and other Muslim countries, the traditional greeting looks like a wave coupled with a twist of the hand. The gesture is made at eye level and always with the right hand. (To use the left hand, regarded as "unclean" in these cultures, would be insulting.) Meanwhile, in Japan, a bow from the waist is the most popular form of greeting.

Chapter 37 *What Is Entrepreneurship?* **495**

L1 Math Skills

The National Federation of Independent Business Foundation conducted a study of small business owners to determine where the idea for their small businesses originated. 45 percent said their business idea came from prior work experience, 6 percent said it came from a family business, 5 percent said it came from friends and relatives, 16 percent said it came from a personal interest/hobby, 7 percent said it came from a suggestion, 6 percent said it came from their education, 11 percent said it came from a chance happening, and 4 percent of the ideas came from other sources. Have students create a pie chart of these statistics.

L2 Math Skills

In the early 1990s, it would cost you $75,000 to obtain a franchise for a Pro Image sporting goods store. (1) The franchise fee would cost $13,500; (2) inventory, $35,000; (3) fixtures and equipment, $6,500; (4) leasehold improvements, $15,000; and (5) working capital, $5,000. What percentage of the $75,000 would go to the (a) franchise fee, (b) the inventory, (c) figures and equipment, (d) leasehold improvements, and (e) working capital?

(Answers: (a) 18 percent. $13,500 \div 75,000 = .18$. (b) 47 percent. $35,000 \div 75,000 = 0.466$ or 0.47. (c) 9 percent. $6,500 \div 75,000 = .086$ or .09. (d) 20 percent. $15,000 \div 75,000 = .2$. (e) 7 percent. $5,000 \div 75,000 = .066$ or .07.)

Have students create a pie chart of these percentages, labeling the chart and each slice of the pie.

Did You Know?

Many states now offer an alternative type of business form, known as the Limited Liability Corporation (LLC), which combines the benefit of limited liability without the heavy taxation of corporations. Even sole proprietors can often take advantage of this designation, resulting in savings not only in a business set-up but also in taxes over time.

L3 Math Skills

In the second Independent Practice Activity below, students are asked to research a franchise. Have students obtain a breakdown of the franchise fee costs as is done in the L2 Activity above. Next have them figure the percentage of the entire franchise fee cost for each increment. Then ask students to create a pie chart of these percentages, and label the chart and each slice of the pie.

Independent Practice

1. Assign and review the Chapter 37 Case Study in the *International Case Studies* workbook.
2. Have each student contact one company that offers franchises and write a 250-word summary of (1) the amount of money it takes to buy a franchise outlet and breakdown of the total cost, (2) training provided by the franchisor, (3) restrictions on the types of products one can sell in the franchise outlet, and (4) any other relevant information one would need to know about buying a franchise from this corporation.

Assess

Evaluation

Assign and review the Section 37.2 Review.

Reteaching

1. Assign and review the vocabulary terms for this section.
2. Assign and review Fact and Idea review questions 2–11.
3. Have the students create a chart that compares each type of business ownership with respect to such things as initial inevstment of capital, level of risk involved, taxation, ease or difficulty of starting business.

496

■ CASE STUDY ■

Outback Steakhouse Restaurants

The first Outback Steakhouse opened in 1988, in Tampa, Florida. By 1994 there were 210 Outback restaurants, including 42 franchises, with sales estimated at $544 million. Approximately 65 new Outback restaurants are opening each year. In addition to its impressive sales record and growth, the company has also created more than 14,000 jobs since it began.

In 1994, the company's founders, Bob Basham, Tim Gannon, and Chris Sullivan, received the Entrepreneur of the Year Award from *Inc.* magazine. Outback restaurants have been successful because of three things—a novel concept, decentralized management, and the founders' philosophy of allowing restaurant managers to become owners in the business.

Outback restaurants are designed as casual high-quality, medium-priced steakhouses with an Australian theme. The interior of each restaurant has an Australian motif outfitted with such things as boomerangs, aboriginal artwork, and Australian travel posters. Many of the drinks and entrées have Australian theme names, such as Aussie-Tizers, Kookaburra Wings, and the Melbourne.

Currently, Outback restaurants only serve dinner. The dinner-only policy ensures that food, made from first-rate ingredients, is always fresh and of high quality. Each restaurant is designed to support the careful preparation of first-rate food. Outback restaurants average about 6,000 square feet of space, of which more than half is dedicated to the kitchen. The emphasis on kitchen space versus restaurant space is designed to make certain that the service is fast and efficient.

One innovative management concept used by the company is decentralized control. Most restaurant chains

rely on four or five levels of management between the founders and restaurant managers. Outback restaurants rely on only one layer of management. There is no human resources department for the company. Hiring is done through joint venture partners who hire general managers who in turn, hire their own staff.

Job candidates for each restaurant have to take an aptitude test, complete a pattern interview with two managers, and complete a psychological test. Each general manager is ultimately responsible for training, motivating, and developing his or her personnel.

In addition to a unique concept and decentralized management, the founders believe in allowing general managers to share in the success of the company. Each Outback general manager signs a five-year contract and invests $25,000. In exchange for the investment, each manager receives 10 percent of the cash flow from his or her restaurant each month. The average general manager can expect to earn about $73,000 from this cash flow arrangement plus a base salary between $45,000 to $118,000 a year. In addition, each general manager receives 4,000 shares of stock that can be sold after five years of service.

This manager/owner concept has proven to be successful and ensures that the founders keep good general managers who also think like owners. As company founder Basham says, "We wanted to make sure that they (managers) had a big chunk of the action. They kind of have their life savings on the line, so they have that entrepreneurial flame burning inside them." By spreading this entrepreneurial flame Outback restaurants have become a $1 billion enterprise.

■ ■ *Case Study Review*

1. Speculate on why the company founders of the Outback restaurant rely only on dinner trade.
2. The company's ownership plan is unique to the industry, but profits have to be shared with others. Why do you think that the company founders believe that this is a good concept?

A MATTER OF ETHICS

3. Do you think it is appropriate that aptitude and psychological tests are given to future applicants? Why or why not?

Case Study Answers

1. Founders believe that the money that they may be losing at noon is made up for by making sure that the food is of high quality and that the restaurants are busy in the evening.
2. The founders believe that it is a good plan because (1) it reduces the management turnover rate—the industry average runs between 30 percent and 40 percent, while it is only 5.4 percent for Outback; (2) the ownership package attracts veteran managers to the business, which helps to insure continued success for the business.
3. Answers will vary. Students may point out that it depends on how the tests are used.

Whether or not you choose to file as a Subchapter S corporation, you must show your internal corporate organization when forming a corporation. This requirement includes the development of corporate bylaws, the selection of a board of directors, and the election of officers who will actually run the corporate operations. In small corporations, the members of the board of directors frequently are elected as the officers of the corporation.

There are four key advantages to this form of business organization. Each owner has limited liability. It is easier for a corporation to raise money for expansion than it is for other forms of business. People can easily enter and leave the business simply by buying or selling their shares of stock. Each operation area of the business can be professionally managed by an expert in that area.

Among the disadvantages to the corporation are the complexity of forming it, increased government regulation, and higher taxes on the profits of the corporation and on each stockholder. Also, accounting and record keeping are much more complex than for the other two major forms of business organization.

It is important to be flexible in approaching the legal form of ownership when establishing a new business. Often, a business starts out as a sole proprietorship, grows into a partnership, and ultimately ends up as a corporation. The entrepreneurs you read about at the beginning of the chapter—Henry Ford, Ray Kroc, Bette Graham, Steven Jobs, and Steven Wozniak—watched their businesses grow from sole proprietorships or partnerships to major corporations.

Legal Steps in Establishing Your Business

You will need to take specific legal steps to establish your business. The specific steps you will need to take will depend on whether you organize your business as a sole proprietorship, partnership, or corporation.

If you establish a sole proprietorship or partnership, you must file for a **DBA** (Doing Business As) at your local county clerk's office. A *DBA* is a registration process by which your county government officially recognizes that your business exists.

There is usually a filing fee for registration, but the process protects the name of your business for a certain number of years. However, this name protection applies only to the county where your business is registered.

Before you register, there is one thing you must do. Check with all the county clerks in your trading area and with your state department of commerce to see if any other business is using your chosen business name. This reduces the chances that someone will later sue you to prevent your use of their business name.

If you want to form a corporation, you must file **Articles of Incorporation** with the corporation and

securities bureau in your state department of commerce. *Articles of Incorporation* identify the name and address of your business, its purpose, the names of the initial directors, and the amount of stock that will be issued to each director.

There is a filing fee, but your business becomes protected and no other business may register under your name. The necessary forms, applications, and information on filing fees are also obtained from your state department of commerce.

The type of business organization is important to the overall success of your business. The decision is somewhat complicated, so you must get the best advice possible before starting operations. Discuss the advantages and disadvantages of each business form with an accountant, an attorney, or some other business advisor. If you elect to form a corporation, the laws of your state may require you to hire an attorney. Check your state laws for specific requirements regarding incorporation.

Depending on what business you enter and where you locate, you may have to obtain one or more licenses. Individual states license many businesses and occupations, such as doctors, accountants, cosmetologists, barbers, marriage counselors, and pharmacists. Licensing is done for these reasons:

- to protect the public from unscrupulous people,
- to establish minimum standards of education and training for people who practice a particular profession,
- to maintain the health and welfare of all citizens,
- to regulate where businesses can locate, and
- to protect neighborhoods and the environment.

In addition to state licenses, your community may require special local licenses or permits to comply with zoning ordinances, building codes, and safety standards. For example, most communities require you to obtain a license before you open a hotel, restaurant, or movie theater in the area. Be sure to check with your local government and your state department of licensing and regulation prior to starting your business.

SECTION 37.2 *Review*

1. What are four ways to enter into a business?
2. What are the three basic forms of business ownership?
3. What legal steps must you take to establish a sole proprietorship or partnership? What legal steps must you take to establish a corporation?

Chapter 37 *What Is Entrepreneurship?* **497**

SECTION 37.2

Enrichment

1. Assign and review the appropriate activities in the *Student Activity Workbook*.
2. Assign and review the appropriate Critical Thinking questions from the Chapter Review.
3. Assign and review the Building Academic Skills Activities, Application Projects, Linking School to Work Activities, and Performance Assessment from the Chapter Review.
4. Have the students identify at least three resources in your community that help small business owners and write a 50-word paragraph on each resource, discussing the type of help the resource offers. Also, have the students contact one of the following national organizations and write a paragraph on the benefits of membership in this organization:
   - American Society of Independent Business, 777 Main Street, Suite 1600, Fort Worth, TX 76102, (817) 870-1880;
   - National Association for the Self-Employed, 2328 Gravel Rd., Fort Worth, TX 76118, (800) 232-6273;
   - National Small Business Association, 1155 15th St., NW, #710, Washington, D.C. 20005-2706, (202) 293-8830; and
   - Small Business Service Bureau, 554 Main St., P.O. Box 1441, Worcester, MA 01601-1441, (508) 756-3513.

Close

Have students complete this statement: There are four main ways to enter business:... (start your own business, purchase an existing franchise, purchase an existing business, or take over a family business.)

Section Review Answers

1. Start your own business, purchase an existing franchise business, purchase an existing non-franchise business, or take over the family business.
2. The sole proprietorship, partnership, and corporation.
3. You must file for a DBA at your local county clerk's office. There is usually a filing fee for registration. Before you register you must check with all the county clerks in your trading area and with your state Department of Commerce to see if any other business is using your chosen business name. To form a corporation, you must file Articles of Incorporation with the Corporation and Securities Bureau in your state Department of Commerce.

Answers

Vocabulary Review

See Glossary for definitions.

Fact and Idea Review

1. It helps you assess whether you have the personal qualities, abilities, interests, and necessary skills.
2. A legal agreement to operate a business in the name of a recognized company.
3. Advantages: easy to start, all business decisions are your own, generally taxed less than other forms of business, allows more freedom from government regulation, and owner entitled to all profits.
   Disadvantages: harder to raise capital with only owner's funds, making decisions can be difficult, owner must provide all the money and management skills and must work long hours.
4. It means you are liable for all debts the business incurs to your total ability to make payments. Unlimited liability applies to sole proprietorships and general partnerships. Therefore, if you wanted to limit your liability, you might want to consider the limited partnership or corporate form.
5. In a general partnership, each partner shares in the profits and losses of the business. In a limited partnership, each partner is liable for any debts only up to the amount of his or her investment in the company.
6. Advantages: combines skill of the owners, access to more money, able to operate and expand easily because of more capital, etc. Disadvantages: owners may not always agree, actions of one partner are binding on the others, business is

498

Vocabulary Review

Divide the class into teams for a Marketing Quiz Bowl. Your teacher will call out the terms below. Teams should raise their hands when they feel they know the correct definition for the term. The team that raises its hand first has ten seconds to respond. If they incorrectly define the term, the other team then has ten seconds to respond. The team that correctly defines the term first gets a point.

entrepreneurship
entrepreneurs
franchise
sole proprietorship
unlimited liability
partnership
general partnership
limited partnership
corporation
stockholders
foreign corporation
Subchapter S corporation
DBA
Articles of Incorporation

Fact and Idea Review

1. Why should you do an honest self-evaluation if you are considering becoming an entrepreneur? (Sec. 37.1)
2. What is a franchise? How does franchising work? (Sec. 37.2)
3. List three advantages and three disadvantages of the sole proprietorship. (Sec. 37.2)
4. What is unlimited liability? How does unlimited liability affect the type of business organization selected by an entrepreneur? (Sec. 37.2)
5. What are the two different kinds of partnerships? Explain the difference between them. (Sec. 37.2)
6. List three advantages and three disadvantages of a partnership. (Sec. 37.2)
7. List three advantages and three disadvantages of a corporation. (Sec. 37.2)
8. What three groups of people are involved with the corporate form of ownership? (Sec. 37.2)
9. What is a foreign corporation? (Sec. 37.2)
10. What is a Subchapter S corporation? (Sec. 37.2)
11. What are five reasons for licensing certain occupations and businesses? (Sec. 37.2)

Critical Thinking

1. Do you think money and material gain are the most important reasons for becoming an entrepreneur? Explain. If you answer no to this question, what do you consider the most important reasons for becoming an entrepreneur?
2. What are the disadvantages of working for others as opposed to being your own boss? Would these disadvantages be enough to make you consider starting your own business? Why?
3. If a franchisee has a new product idea, who should get credit for it—the franchisee or the franchisor?
4. Which of the four ways to enter a business would you use to start your own business? Explain your decision.
5. Sole proprietorships and partnerships both have their advantages and disadvantages. If you were starting a restaurant, which type of business organization would you choose? Explain the reasons for your decision.

Building Academic Skills

Math

1. If 8,400 businesses are started each week, how many businesses are started in a two-year period?
2. If an entrepreneur works 11 hours a day, five days a week, 52 weeks a year, how many hours is the person working annually?

Communication

3. Prepare a three-minute speech on the information that should be included in a partnership agreement. Use library resources for information.
4. Write a 250-word report on the functions and services provided by the U.S. Small Business Administration.
5. Using this book and other sources, write a 250-word paper on why the entrepreneur is so important to the economy of the United States.
6. Write your local chamber of commerce to arrange for a resource speaker to talk to your class on "Small Business Opportunities in Our Community."

Human Relations

7. A very good friend of yours has an idea to start a small video rental business. She is very excited about this new venture. However, you have heard that small video stores are being replaced by superstores with 8,000 or more tapes in stock. You have also heard that the cost of opening a store has risen from

---

dissolved if one partner dies, etc.
7. Advantages: each owner has limited liability, easy to raise money for expansion, people can enter and leave simply by buying or selling shares. Disadvantages: harder to establish than the other two forms of business, increased government regulation, higher taxes on the corporation and on each shareholder.
8. Shareholders, directors, and officers.
9. A foreign corporation is incorporated under the

laws of a different state from the one in which it does business.
10. See Section 2 for discussion of various types of business ownership.
11. To protect the public from unscrupulous people, to establish minimum standards of education and training for people who practice a particular profession, to maintain the health and welfare of all citizens, etc.

$50,000 a few years ago to between $150,000 and $200,000 today. What would you tell your friend to do before she invests in this kind of business?

Application Projects

1. Obtain a copy of National DECA's Entrepreneurship Event (Organizing a Business). Identify the three main sections of the event. You will work more with this throughout this unit.
2. Complete a series of entrepreneurial aptitude tests provided by your teacher to find out about your interest in business ownership. In small groups of four to five students, discuss your personal qualities and aptitudes for business ownership.
3. Interview a small business owner in your community to discover why that person started his or her own business. In a 200-word report, write about the job duties and tasks typically performed on a daily, weekly, and/or monthly basis by the business owner.
4. Research and identify factors you need to know when you buy a franchise.
5. Identify your hobbies and interests. Then list as many business ideas relating to your hobbies and interests as you can identify.
6. Choose an entrepreneur. He or she may be a well-known historical or modern figure or someone in your community or family. Write a 200-word biography of the person and examine the characteristics that have made him or her successful.
7. Entrepreneurs often look into the future to see where new market needs will be. Describe the kinds of businesses that you think will boom in the next 25 years. Explain why you think they will do so and how you would go about getting the knowledge or training to enter one of them.
8. Research the companies already in one of the fields you listed in Application Project #7. Describe how you would compete with them if you were to enter the field. Tell whether your business would be a sole proprietorship, a partnership, or a corporation, and why this would be the most effective way to run your particular business.
9. Today, many professional people, such as doctors, attorneys, and chiropractors, are forming corporations themselves. Research the trend and give a five-minute oral report explaining why professionals are doing this.

Linking School to Work

1. Research whether your place of employment or current cooperative education training station was originally organized as a proprietorship, partnership, or a corporation. Write a 300-word report on how the business got started and whether it has changed its type of ownership over the years.
2. Interview your owner or immediate supervisor on the advantages and disadvantages of being an owner/manager and the type of preparation and/or training required for the position. Be prepared to give a five-minute talk on the results obtained during your interview.

Performance Assessment

Role Play

Situation. You own a convenience store. You have been invited to serve as a guest speaker at a local DECA chapter meeting. You have been asked to speak on the topic of entrepreneurship.

Evaluation. You will be evaluated on how well you are able to:

- Define entrepreneurship.
- Discuss the advantages and disadvantages of entrepreneurship.
- Identify the personal characteristics and skills entrepreneurs need.

Conduct an Information Interview

Conduct an information interview with someone who is a small business owner. Prior to your interview develop an interview script of at least ten questions to ask. Conduct the interview after receiving instructor approval of your questions. Write down or tape record the responses you receive to your questions.

Complete the Chapter 37 Computer Application that appears in the Student Activity Workbook.

Critical Thinking

1.–3. Answers will vary.
   4. Students' answers should be based on the chapter discussion.
   5. Students' answers should be based on the advantages and disadvantages discussed in the chapter, their own personalities and work experience.

Building Academic Skills

Math

1. $8,400 \times (52 \times 2) = 873,600$
2. $(11 \times 5) \times 52 = 2,860$

Communication

3. Students should research information on partnership agreements using library resources and by contacting the SBA.

---

4. Students should contact the SBA to obtain information.
5. Students should site reasons discussed in the chapter. They should also read current newspaper and magazine articles to find out more information. A suggested resource is *Innovation and Entrepreneurship* by Peter F. Drucker (© 1986).
6. Students should write a letter as a class.

Human Relations

7. Students should discuss the advantages and disadvantages of being an entrepreneur.

Application Projects

1. The class should obtain a copy of National DECA's Entrepreneurship Event by writing National DECA, 1908 Association Drive, Reston, VA 22091-1594.
2. Students should discuss the personal qualities and aptitudes they have for business ownership.
3. Students should share their findings with the class.
4. Students should use library resources to learn more about franchises.
5. For example, a student interested in sports may want to own a sports store.
6. Biographies will vary.
7. Possible trends will vary.
8. Answers will depend on the business the student chooses.
9. To limit their liability.

Linking School to Work

Answers depend on the work situation.

Performance Assessment

Refer to the *DECA Competitive Events Handbook* for evaluation guidelines.

Computer Application

Optional activity. Refer to the *Marketing Software Binder* for template and user information.

Evaluation

Administer the reproducible test for Chapter 37, or construct your own test using the Testmaker software.

Chapter Overview

This chapter introduces students to the concept of business risk and risk management.

Springboard

Recall with students the definition of an entrepreneur. Write the word *risk* on the board and have students define the term. Divide the class into groups. Each group is to compose its own tale about Sad Sam's Sorry Service Station—a business in which every conceivable thing that could go wrong does go wrong. Encourage students to incorporate a wide variety of disasters with employees, customers, the weather, etc., into their tales.

Have each group share its tale. As students mention the risks in their tales, categorize them on the board into three columns—*economic, natural,* and *human*—but do not actually write these column headings on the board.

Prereading

List the section objectives to discuss with students. Have students skim the chapter, looking at the pictures, reading the captions, and noting the heads. Ask questions to ensure that the students have a minimal understanding of the chapter structure.

Preteaching the Vocabulary

Write the terms for this chapter on the board. Without looking at their texts, have each group from the Springboard activity generate definitions for each term. Review all terms in class.

Risk Management

Businesses are constantly confronted with the possibility of loss or failure. A business can never be certain its products will sell. Customer preferences, lifestyles, and product demands change. Despite the best research and planning, some products simply fail in the marketplace. Other products may be damaged, stolen, destroyed, or lost.

In this chapter you will learn about the concept of risk and risk management. You will read about types of business risks and the methods businesspeople use to prevent or, at least, minimize them.

Classroom Management

For the Teacher

- Teacher's Annotated Editions for all workbooks
- Teacher's Manual for *School-to-Work Handbook*
- *Testing Binder*
- *Transparency Binder*
- *Marketing Software Binder*
- *Marketing Career Portfolio*
- *Lesson Plans*

For the Student

- *Student Activity Workbook*
- *Marketing Math Workbook*
- *School-to-Work Handbook*
- *Student Software*
- *International Case Studies*
- *Marketing Career Portfolio*

SECTION 38.1

Objectives

After completing this section, you will be able to

- explain the nature of risk management and

- discuss the various types of business risks.

Terms to Know

- risk
- business risk
- economic risks
- natural risks
- human risks

Risk Management

As a business owner, one of your primary goals will be to make a profit. However, there is no guarantee that this will happen. Your business may realize a lower return on investment than you expected. It may actually experience a loss after you have paid all your expenses. The possibility of financial loss is called **risk.**

While a business cannot totally eliminate all the risks of doing business, marketers can reduce and manage risks through careful planning. Risks are managed by using the best available marketing information, analyzing opportunities, and making decisions to balance risks with adequate monetary returns.

Kinds of Risks

Business risk is the possibility of business loss or failure. There are three kinds of business risks—*economic, natural,* and *human.* Let's take a closer look at each of these types of risks.

Economic Risks

Economic risks occur from changes in overall business conditions. These changes can include the amount or type of competition, changing consumer lifestyles, population changes, limited usefulness or stylishness of some products, product obsolescence, government regulation, inflation, or recession.

Businesses that fail to change their products when competitors offer more features and benefits experience economic risk through lost sales. Also, foreign competition is an economic risk for many U.S. companies. Foreign products often can be produced and sold for less than similar domestic products. However, foreign competition does force U.S. companies to improve productivity and efficiency to compete successfully in the marketplace.

Consumer lifestyles and population changes are other economic risks facing modern businesses. More single-parent households, dual-income families, the aging of the baby boom generation, and the increasing number of singles delaying marriage all present potential risks for businesses that fail to adapt products to meet changing needs.

The limited usefulness or stylishness of some products is another potential economic risk. If products are not sold before a new model year or before the new fashion styles or colors are introduced, prices have to be reduced to sell them. This obviously reduces sales volume and profits.

Some products inevitably become obsolete or outdated. This is called *product obsolescence*. It represents another type of economic risk for businesses that depend on fashion and the latest trends to market goods and services.

Real World

They're Less Bullish on Production Crews

During the classic TV ad for the investment firm Merrill Lynch, a bull carefully maneuvers through a china shop. The agency that created the ad, Ogilvy & Mather, took great pains to reduce business risks by ensuring that the animal was well trained. However, it should have taken as much care training the production crew. On the day of the filming, a butter-fingered set designer accidentally dropped and smashed a candelabra valued at $3,500.

Chapter 38   *Risk Management*   **501**

Have students maintain the same groups they were in for the Springboard activity and Preteaching the Vocabulary. Have all students study the three chalkboard lists generated during the Springboard activity and deduce the three categories into which you have divided the risks (*economic, natural,* and *human*).

Introducing the Section

Review students' Bell Ringer Activity answers. Tell students that while no business owner can eliminate all the risks of doing business, he or she can reduce and manage risks through careful planning, analysis, and decision making.

Teach

Guided Practice

1. Read Section 38.1 with students.
2. Have students read aloud the Case Study and review the answers in class.
3. MarkEd Resource Center in Columbus, Ohio, (800) 448-0398, offers materials appropriate for use with this chapter.

Discussion Starter

The text states that natural causes—floods, tornadoes, hurricanes, fires, lightning, droughts, earthquakes, and unexpected changes in normal weather conditions—can create risks. How can these natural causes financially ruin a business? (They can physically destroy the place of business, destroy off-site equipment like delivery trucks and service lines or cables, and destroy the homes or businesses of customers.)

Have students discuss natural disasters of the last few years and how they affected the economy in your area or in other areas of the country.

Independent Practice

Using the *Reader's Guide to Periodical Literature* and/or the newspaper/magazine database in your library, have students research and obtain a copy of an article on risk management. (The article should be at least 150 words.) They should write a 50- to 100-word abstract of the article, develop an outline of it, and bring it to class, prepared to deliver a five-minute oral presentation on the contents of the article.

"Risk management" is a broad category and should thus provide students the opportunity to report on many different aspects of this topic, such as how businesses responded to a natural disaster, steps being taken to prevent shoplifting, etc. Some of the content of these articles may be covered in Section 38.2. If so, students' findings will serve as a good preview to Section 38.2.

Assess

Evaluation

Assign and review the Section 38.1 Review.

Reteaching

1. Assign and review the vocabulary terms for this section.
2. Assign and review Fact and Idea Review questions 1–4 from the Chapter Review.
3. Write the terms *economic risk, natural risk*, and *human risk* on the chalkboard. Have each student give you one example of whatever type of risk you indicate.

CASE STUDY

Handling Bad Checks

Risk.

Risk Management.

TeleCheck

The term "risky business" is probably not what you had in mind when you opened your doors for business. ▪ But if you use TeleCheck, the world's largest check guarantee service, every check we approve is like money in the bank. Guaranteed. ▪ So whether you're faced with a low-numbered check or even an out-of-state check, you can rest assured that funds are there to back it up. How do we do this? With the industry's largest data base. And with frequent use of TeleCheck, you'll find that your discount rate is substantially less than the cost of credit card transactions. ▪ So get out of the risk management business and get back into what you know best, making the sale. Call TeleCheck today at 1-800-999-9770, Ext. 805.

Money In The Bank.
Guaranteed."

© TeleCheck Services, Inc. 1990

Circle 268 on Reader Service Card

Every year about 1.75 percent, or $10.2 billion worth, of checks that are written to retailers are bad or "bounce." Of the $10.2 billion in bad checks only 36 percent, or $3.7 billion, will be recovered. The rest, a staggering $6.5 billion, are lost by retailers!

Twenty-eight percent of these checks, or $2.9 billion worth, are fraudulent. Fraudulent checks are usually not collectable and represent a total loss to a business. They are checks written against nonexisting accounts or against stolen checks. Persons who write fraudulent checks often have phony aliases, drivers licenses, and social security numbers to fool cashiers into approving their checks.

As you can see, bad checks present a tremendous problem for retailers. To solve this problem, retailers could decide not to accept any checks. However, customers

expect stores to accept checks as a method of payment. A no-check policy could mean lost sales and customers.

Fortunately, there's a better alternative. To reduce the risk of bad checks, companies are now turning to check verification and guarantee companies, such as TeleCheck Services, Inc.

Members who use TeleCheck verification services input their bad-check information into their POS system. A master computer system picks up the information and adds it to its database. TeleCheck Services then shares that information with other retailers. Retailers can access the database and verify a check's validity. Until the mid-1980s most retailers did not conduct check authorizations. Each business had its own bad-check files but did not share them with any regional or national system. Databases such as TeleCheck's speed up check authorizations and make check cashing easier for both the customer and the business.

Check verification is fairly inexpensive. It only costs a few pennies for each transaction. An industry survey found that firms selling check verification services charge from 1 cent to 23 cents per authorization for an average of 11 cents per check.

TeleCheck Services, Inc. also guarantees checks. Every check that TeleCheck approves, even high risk out-of-state checks, are guaranteed to be paid by TeleCheck. Members pay TeleCheck a fee for this service.

Businesses who use check verification or guarantee services benefit by seeing a net reduction in bad check expenses. And, as TeleCheck advertises, these services "let you get out of the risk management business and get back into what you know best, making the sale."

Case Study Review

1. Why do you think the number of bad checks is so high?
2. What information should retailers request from customers to help reduce risks when accepting checks?

A MATTER OF ETHICS

3. Do you think some of the information that retailers require is an invasion of privacy? Why or why not?

Case Study Answers

1. If businesses don't verify a check it is easy for customers to get away with writing fraudulent checks.
2. Cashiers should ask for a driver's license number and a phone number.
3. Answers will vary, but discussion should focus around the fact that check acceptance is a privilege not a right. Because of this privilege, some personal information must be shared with the store.

*This building suffered earthquake damage. **What are two other types of natural risks that businesses face?***

Changes in the general business environment caused by inflation or recession can present economic risks. For example, all businesses in an area experiencing high unemployment will suffer through reduced product sales.

Government laws and regulations can also present economic risks. Laws requiring businesses to pay for such things as street and sewer improvements or parking and general maintenance reduce profits.

Product recalls or even the threat of recalls by the National Highway Traffic Safety Administration or other government agencies can affect sales and profits. Companies that have products recalled face high legal costs and expensive repairs and/or replacements. For example, in 1994 General Motors and the U.S. Department of Transportation made an out-of-court settlement on General Motor's C-K model pickup trucks manufactured between 1973 and 1987. The settlement cost General Motors $51 million. The trucks met federal safety standards for side mounted gasoline tanks when they were manufactured, but the government believed that they still presented an unreasonable risk. The company opted for an out-of-court settlement rather than face an even more costly legal battle in order to avoid a recall of General Motor's trucks.

Natural Risks

Natural risks are risks resulting from natural causes. Natural causes that create risks include floods, tornadoes, hurricanes, fires, lightning, droughts, earthquakes, and even unexpected changes in normal weather conditions.

Some products depend on predictable weather conditions for success. For example, a hardware store in the Midwest that sells snowblowers depends on a predictable season of heavy snow to sell the product. A mild or light snowfall during the winter represents a natural risk to the business. Conversely, a dry summer or a drought will affect the sales of lawnmowers. The sale of recreational products, such as boats, snow skis, motorcycles, swimming pools, snowmobiles, and related clothing items are all affected by weather conditions. These risks can spell financial ruin for a business.

Human Risks

Human risks are caused by human mistakes and the unpredictability of employees or customers. Some of the more common human risks are

- customer or employee dishonesty—taking goods or money;

Chapter 38   *Risk Management*   **503**

Enrichment

1. Assign and review the appropriate activities in the *Student Activity Workbook.*
2. Assign and review the appropriate Critical Thinking questions from the Chapter Review.
3. As this section states, foreign competition is a very real economic risk for many U.S. companies. Have students research the current impact of foreign competition on the American job market by using such resources as the newspaper/magazine database in your library; the *Reader's Guide to Periodical Literature*; trade, career, and business titles that very often discuss the factors influencing the American job market; and U.S. government publications.

   Students should present their findings in a 250-word report that includes a bibliography of sources, a title page, and a report cover. They should keyboard and spell-check their reports.

Close

Have students complete these statements: (a) A business risk is . . . (the possibility of business loss or failure.) (b) There are three kinds of business risks: . . . (economic, natural, and human.)

Caption Answer

Other types of natural risks include hurricanes, floods, lightning, droughts, and tornadoes.

Focus

Bell Ringer Activity

There are four basic ways that businesses can handle risks: *risk prevention and control, risk transfer, risk retention,* and *risk avoidance.* Write these terms on the board. Have students write a definition for them and give examples of each.

Introducing the Section

Review students' Bell Ringer Activity answers. Make sure they understand the concept behind each method of risk transfer. Write the examples on the board under each type of risk management. You can use your lists for reinforcement as you read through this section with students.

Teach

Guided Practice

1. Read Section 38.2 with students.
2. Invite a panel of experts to talk to your class about shoplifting and employee theft, and the security precautions businesses take to prevent both. Your experts could include the head of security or a security officer from a local business, an insurance agent, a police officer, a member of the fire department, a small business owner, and a representative from the Small Business Administration (the SBA offers many publications on crime prevention for small businesses).

   Make sure to have panel members discuss how to deal with shoplifters. Panel members should also discuss the fact that dealing with shoplifters can be potentially dangerous and is best left to security guards or police officers.

- employee carelessness—for example, failing to properly cook or handle food which eventually leads to customers becoming ill and hospitalized, or failing to properly store food products which eventually spoil;
- employee incompetence—for example, lacking the skills to do the job well;
- customer or employee accidents—for example, a customer falls over merchandise left in the aisle, breaks an arm, and sues the store, or an employee badly cuts his or her finger while creating a store display;
- employee illness—for example, becoming ill as a result of inhaling the toxic fumes from a chemical cleaner used at work; and
- customer nonpayment of accounts—for example, a customer pays for goods with a fraudulent check.

Whistle at Your Own Risk

In the United States, whistling is generally done as a sign of appreciation or approval. At sporting events or rock concert performances, whistling regularly accompanies a standing round of applause. In many other cultures, however, whistling conveys just the opposite sentiment. In Europe, it's the equivalent of being booed, whether the setting is a stadium, an opera house, or a political gathering. In India, whistling in public is considered rude. In the Middle East, whistling at a woman as a sign of interest or approval violates strictly observed social and religious taboos.

SECTION 38.1 Review

1. What is the difference between the concept of risk and risk management?
2. What is business risk?
3. Identify the three kinds of business risks and give an example of each.

Objective

After completing this section, you will be able to
- identify the ways businesses handle risks.

Terms to Know

- insurance policy
- extended coverage
- fidelity bonds
- performance bonds

Handling Business Risks

There are four basic ways that businesses can handle risks: *risk prevention and control, risk transfer, risk retention,* and *risk avoidance.* Let's take a closer look at each of these.

Risk Prevention and Control

Business risks can be handled through prevention and control. Risks can be prevented and controlled by screening and training employees, providing safe conditions and safety instruction, preventing external theft, and deterring employee theft.

Screening and Training Employees The best way to prevent the human risk of employee carelessness and incompetence is through employee screening and training. Many businesses have human resource development departments to screen, test, and train new employees to minimize the risk caused by improperly trained personnel.

In addition, more and more companies now require prospective employees to undergo a drug test before being hired. Drug testing and screening is done because drugs alter mental processes. Drug abuse can lead to increased human risk by

- making employees careless and more likely to forget safety rules;
- affecting perceptions about time, space, and distance, which can be especially dangerous when operating equipment;
- increasing the workload of other workers because of lateness or increased absenteeism; and

---

Section Review Answers

1. The possibility of financial loss is called risk. Risk management is the marketing function of managing risks.
2. Business risk is the possibility of business loss or failure.
3. Three kinds of business risks are economic, natural, and human.

- causing errors in work assignments which risks harming customers.

When employees begin a new job, some form of orientation, training, and instruction is normally provided. Depending on the marketing job, the training may be as brief as a few minutes of verbal instruction or as extensive as months or years of intensive academic work.

Effective orientation and training programs are essential in minimizing business risk. Properly trained personnel are better able to meet customer needs and wants and to prevent the risk of lost sales through human error.

An orientation and training program usually includes the following

- a description of what the company does;
- a description of what new workers in a department or area do;
- the names of the supervisors and co-workers and what they do;
- an explanation of job duties and how to do them;
- an explanation of job expectations;
- days and hours of work;
- times of breaks and where things are—restrooms, lockers, where to eat, etc.;
- employment policies, such as vacation, paid holidays, probation period, and benefits;
- the name and phone number of person to call if late or absent; and
- rules and regulations relating to safety.

Providing Safe Conditions and Safety Instruction Based on the number of workers who sustain job-related injuries and illness, safety and health information is sorely lacking in many training programs. The financial impact of workplace accidents is staggering. According to the National Safety Council, each year U.S. businesses lose an estimated $42 billion to work-related illness and injuries.

When employees have received safety instruction and are provided with safe work conditions, the potential for on-the-job accidents is greatly reduced. In marketing jobs, for example, common accidents include falls that occur while moving merchandise or injuries due to improper lifting techniques.

To prevent such risks, businesses can design storerooms and selling areas for efficient foot traffic and merchandise storage. They can also provide safety instruction on proper ways to lift and store merchandise.

Many companies address workplace safety by developing accident management programs which include

- creating a safety committee to check for hazards;
- developing plans to correct hazards before accidents occur;
- developing procedures to comply with all state and federal health and safety regulations;
- investigating and recording all workplace accidents;
- providing employees with protective clothing and equipment;

- making sure that first aid kits are near work stations;
- posting the address and phone number of the nearest hospital and clinic;
- offering employee classes in first aid and cardiopulmonary resuscitation;
- keeping track of how many work days were missed due to accidents or injuries;
- scheduling regular safety meetings;
- preparing written safety plans and circulating them to all employees; and
- offering incentives for improved safety records, such as prizes or bonuses for accident-free months.

Preventing External Theft One of the largest and most costly forms of human risk is external theft resulting from shoplifting and robberies. *Shoplifting* is the stealing of displayed merchandise from a business. Shoplifters conceal merchandise in purses, shopping bags, clothing, or through other means.

Shoplifting is one of the fastest growing crimes against property in the country. According to the Federal Bureau of Investigation (FBI), about 15 percent of all thefts committed in the United States involve shoplifting. For example, in 1992 the FBI reported that losses from retail shoplifting totaled close to $9 billion.

According to an annual Price Waterhouse *Shrinkage Survey*, 1.5 to 1.9 percent of mass merchandisers and discount store retailers' net sales and 2.4 percent of apparel specialty retailers' net sales are lost to shoplifting. This means that if a specialty retailer's net sales are $100 million, approximately $2.4 million are lost to shoplifters!

Businesses can help to deter shoplifting by

- educating employees about shoplifting prevention guidelines;
- planning effective store layouts with adequate lighting and orderly displays;

Real World

The Note with a Peel

Arthur Fry, an engineer at 3M Company, liked singing in his church choir. However, he didn't like losing his place in his hymnal every time his bookmark slipped out. Fry needed a page marker that would stay put. So, he invented one. Using glue left over from an unsuccessful experiment, Fry came up with Post-It Notes, little paper squares that can be pressed onto a page and easily peeled off again. Post-It Notes have given Fry peace of mind—and they have given 3M $50 million a year in sales.

Chapter 38 *Risk Management* **505**

3. Assign and review the Chapter 38 Activity in the *School-to-Work Handbook.*

Discussion Starter

Have students discuss the type of safety training they have received at their co-op training stations.

Someday, those students who open their own businesses or who are in a position to hire employees for a company may have job applicants who have been convicted of and served prison time for a felony.

Make sure that students understand the difference between a felony and a misdemeanor. A felony is a grave crime, such as auto theft or bank robbery; a misdemeanor is a less serious crime, such as shoplifting. State laws differ in their definitions of what constitutes a felony. Some states have much more stringent parameters than others.

Have students discuss the factors they would weigh before considering whether or not to interview a convicted felon for a particular position. (Handle the discussion carefully, acknowledging the fact that in the eyes of the law, a felon who has served time for his or her crime has paid a debt to society. However, as an employer, you must consider the type of position for which you are hiring when electing whether or not to interview a convicted felon. For example, if you are hiring a truck driver, you may not be able to insure a person who has been convicted and served time for felony manslaughter. If you are hiring someone who is to handle money daily, you may not be able to bond a person who has been convicted of crimes that involve funds or other fiduciary matters.

Lifelong Learning

Risk Management

Risk management is a huge specialty that offers employment opportunity for those interested in the field. Workplace safety can come under the jurisdiction of many departments, including Human Resource Management. Students interested in this field would benefit from taking courses in human resources, industrial and/or labor relations, and risk management. The Business department of your local community college is likely to offer classes on this subject. Following legislation pending in state and federal congressional committees can be another way to keep up with the field.

Teach (Cont'd.)

Thus, when considering whether or not to interview and/or hire a convicted felon, you need to look at such things as the type of position to be filled, versus the type of crime for which the person was convicted. Explain to students that the complexity of this matter requires the employer to review such matters with an attorney.)

Critical Thinking

1. Ask students why some states have banned lie detectors for job screening. (Possibilities include unreliability of equipment, misinterpretation of test results, invasion of privacy, and constitutional limits on self-incrimination.)
2. Employee theft can take many forms. Have students generate some methods of employee theft, other than outright stealing money from the business. (Answers could include theft of office supplies, parts, and/or raw materials; use of the telephone, photocopier and/or FAX machine for personal use; or use of the office mail for personal use.)

Businesses can deter shoplifters by locking up merchandise. What is one other way to deter shoplifters?

- keeping expensive items in locked display cases or tagged with electronic sensors that trigger alarms, if the merchandise is carried out of the store; and
- using security personnel and such security devices as two-way mirrors, closed circuit television, and wall and ceiling mirrors.

Some states have passed legislation to deal with the problem of shoplifting. For example, Michigan enacted several retail fraud laws that allow store personnel to make "citizen arrests" of those suspected of tag switching or seeking fraudulent refunds. The laws also make the parents of shoplifters, tag switchers, and fraudulent refund seekers who are minors liable in small-claims court.

It is important to remember that *everybody* is affected by shoplifting. Faced with increased costs of doing business and reduced sales from theft, businesses are forced to raise prices to compensate.

Robbery is the stealing of money or merchandise under threat or when left unattended. No matter where a business is located, it has a chance of being robbed. Many local police departments provide instruction on how to prevent and handle robberies. Sometimes businesses band together to form business watch programs similar to neighborhood watch programs.

Businesses can lower their risk from robberies by

- limiting the amount of money kept on hand and handling bank deposits discreetly,
- installing video cameras to help identify robbers,
- hiring extra employees so that no one is alone in a business at any time,
- hiring security guards,
- installing bulletproof glass in cashier cubicles,
- opening back doors only for freight or trash,
- installing switches near cash registers that allow employees to lock outside doors,
- increasing lighting inside and outside of the establishment, and
- making sure doors are locked and alarms are set at night.

A form of robbery is check fraud. Check fraud involves purchasing merchandise with fraudulent checks or with insufficient funds. This chapter's Case Study explores ways that companies deal with check fraud.

Controlling Employee Theft Another major problem for businesses is employee theft. Employee theft is the stealing of merchandise, funds, or other company property without purchasing it. Most employee theft occurs at the point-of-sale (POS) terminal, or cash

---

Caption Answer

Shoplifting can be reduced by educating employees about shoplifting prevention guidelines; planning effective store layouts with adequate lighting and orderly displays; keeping expensive items tagged with electronic sensors; and using security personnel, two-way mirrors, closed circuit television, and wall-to-ceiling mirrors.

Did You Know

There are many ways that companies can educate their employees on safe working techniques. One way is with the help of OSHA (Occupational Safety and Health Association) which is in charge of investigating violations of workplace safety. OSHA is ready to help employers plan workplace safety programs and, best of all, their service is free of charge.

register. To protect themselves from employee theft, many businesses have installed closed-circuit television systems and point-of-sale (POS) terminals that generate computerized reports.

POS computerized reports monitor void transfers, cash discrepancies, sales reports, refunds by employees, employees' discounts, and cash register transactions. By carefully analyzing these data, businesses improve the chances of apprehending dishonest employees.

Closed-circuit television systems used in conjunction with POS terminals lower the risk of employee theft. Closed-circuit systems include cameras concealed in mannequins, ceilings, or walls. Usually operated by security personnel in a control room, they are backed up with a video recorder.

Other prevention techniques include

- preemployment testing to detect attitudes about honesty (some states, however, have banned the use of lie detectors for preemployment screening);
- knowing all company policies and strictly adhering to them;
- incorporating policies to prosecute dishonest employees;
- internally talking about controls that prevent theft at business meetings;
- setting internal business standards of honest and dishonest behavior; and
- promoting open discussions dealing with employee honesty.

Risk Transfer

Some business risks can be handled by transferring the risk to another business or to another party. Three of the most common risk transfers are *insurance, guarantees and warranties,* and *transferring risks through business ownership.*

Purchasing Insurance Businesses can insure property and people against potential loss by purchasing insurance policies. An **insurance policy** is a contract between a business and an insurance company to cover a certain business risk.

Insurance companies estimate the probability of loss due to such risks as fire, theft, and natural disasters. Then the insurance company looks at the business's location, past experience, and type of business and determines an insurance rate.

The insurance rate charged depends on the degree of risk associated with an insurable feature, such as fire or theft. For example, if the risk of robbery is higher in a neighborhood where a business is located, the insurance company will charge higher rates for adequate coverage against theft. The business has a higher likelihood of being robbed and of thus making a claim against the insurance company for coverage of its losses.

Types of Insurance A business can buy a package of insurance that includes several types of insurance policies. The insurance policies protect a business against losses on its property or business operations.

One of the most common forms of business insurance is property insurance. *Property insurance* covers the loss of or damage to buildings, equipment, machinery, merchandise, furniture, and fixtures. In case of fire, for example, coverage can be purchased for the full replacement value of the building, merchandise, and other items or for a portion of the replacement value.

In addition, property insurance often covers off-premise accidents, outdoor property, loss of valuable

BRIGHT IDEAS

Try Something Practical

Lilly Pulitzer had nothing to do. Her husband, a publishing tycoon who owned some orange groves, suggested that she sell oranges to keep herself busy. So, Pulitzer bought a shop and went into the produce business. On the side, she sold orange juice.

Soon the sideline consumed the business. Pulitzer spent most of her time squeezing oranges. It was a dirty job—juice stains covered her clothing—but someone had to do it. Pulitzer got around the problem by wearing colorful print dresses to hide the juice stains. She had a Swiss dressmaker make the dresses for her out of fabric from Woolworth.

Then customers began asking about the dresses she wore. Soon Pulitzer was offering them for sale, too. For the second time, a sideline consumed her business. Pulitzer started selling more dresses than oranges. Her designs captivated the Palm Beach crowd. Even Jacqueline Kennedy wore them. What started out as a practical solution to a messy problem turned into a 1960s fashion statement.

Creativity Challenge Form teams of 3–5 students, and try your own hand at a thoroughly practical fashion statement. Design an article of clothing that solves a problem or answers a specific need. For example, you might create special clothing for pet groomers. If clothing doesn't inspire you, think about auto finish, auto upholstery, household carpeting, athletic footwear, or luggage. Describe your design's essentials in words, sketches, or collage form—whichever technique suits your group's talents.

Cooperative Learning

Divide the class into four groups and assign each group one or two types of insurance: (1) property insurance, (2) personal liability insurance and product liability insurance, (3) life insurance and credit insurance, and (4) workers' compensation insurance.

Give each group several magazines, a large sheet of poster board, several large sheets of paper, colored markers, and tape. Have each group use its materials to create a poster board on the types of insurance assigned to it. If students cannot find adequate pictures in the magazines, they can draw the pictures.

Have each group write a definition of each type of insurance on the poster board and tape the relevant pictures on the board, along with writing words or phrases that illustrate the type of insurance.

L1 Communication Skills

As mentioned under Guided Practice #2, the SBA offers numerous publications on crime prevention in small business. Have each student acquire one of these publications (or, have several copies of each publication available in your classroom), read it, and write a summary of the information. Have students review this information in class.

Bright Ideas

Point out that what happened to Lily Pulitzer isn't so unusual. Even when students work on reports, they may start out with one topic and be led by their interests to another, more interesting one. One key rule of business is to recognize when the side business is overshadowing the main business and to not stubbornly hold on to your first idea. What if Lily had stuck to selling oranges?

L2 Communication Skills

Using your dictionary, write the phonetic spelling of these words from Section 38.2.

beneficiary (be-nə-´fi-shē-,er-ē)

compensate (´käm-pən-,sāt)

deter (di-´tər)

discrepancy (dis-´kre-pən-sē)

fraudulent (´fro-jə-lənt)

guarantee (,gar-ən-´tē)

insurance (in-´shùr-ən(t)s)

legislation (,le-jəs-´lā-shən)

liability (,lī-ə-´bi-lə-tē)

orientation (,ōr-ē-ən-´tā-shən)

warranty (´wor-ən-tē)
　　　　(´wär-)

(All phonetic spellings are from *Merriam Webster's Collegiate Dictionary*, Tenth Edition, © 1993.)

L3 Communication Skills

Have students write the dictionary definitions for the above words and then write each in an original sentence related to chapter content. (Make sure that students do not merely rewrite a sentence from this section.)

Independent Practice

1. Assign and review the Chapter 38 Case Study in the *International Case Studies* workbook.
2. Many students may one day have to be bonded. Have students research this process. What must you do to become bonded? How does the bonding company determine how much money it will reimburse to a person who makes a claim against a bonded employee? Who is not eligible to become bonded? Under what circumstances is bonding revoked? Students should present their findings in a 250-word report.

---

papers and records, fire department service charges, and the personal property losses of others. Some policies provide added coverage for theft of personal property.

Typical property insurance includes the following features:

- *Replacement Cost Coverage.* This covers the replacement cost of buildings and other personal property. If the policy is written as a *coinsurance policy*, the insured business and the insurance company both share in the risk, if there is a loss. For example, a business may be insured for 80 percent of the replacement value. This means that, in case of a loss, the insurance company pays 80 percent of the covered items and the business pays 20 percent.
- *Automatic Increase Protection.* This policy feature automatically adjusts the coverage to compensate for inflation on both the building and the personal property.
- *Loss of Income.* This feature compensates a business for loss of income during the time repairs are being done to a building or property after a natural disaster.

Loss of income coverage also covers certain expenses that continue during the repair period, such as interest on loans, taxes, rent, advertising, telephone, and salaries.

Property insurance policies can be purchased with *extended coverage*. **Extended coverage** represents optional coverage on a basic property coverage policy. Extended coverage can be purchased to cover items that may not be covered on the basic property insurance policy, such as telephones and computers, rented cars, exterior glass, and outdoor signs.

Business liability insurance covers losses due to business operations. Business liability insurance is usually provided with up to $1 million limits. Included with this type of insurance are such features as

- premises and operations coverage;
- medical expense coverage;
- personal injury coverage;
- employee coverage; and
- advertising liability coverage.

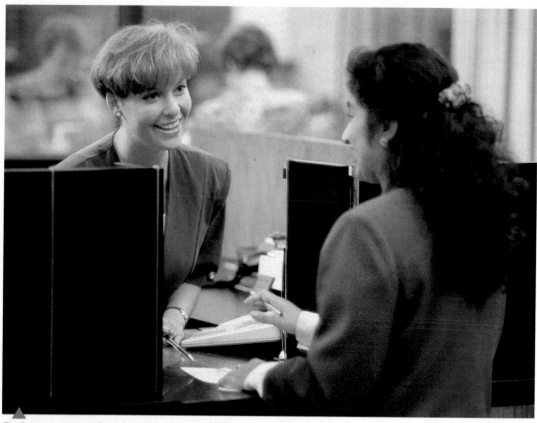

Businesses can purchase insurance to protect themselves against many forms of risk. What type of insurance would help protect a bank from employee theft?

Caption Answer

Fidelity bonds could protect the bank from employee theft.

More About

Purchasing Insurance

Insurance companies not only sell insurance, but also educate their clients about ways to reduce risk. They typically will assist business owners identify potential risks by conducting a walk through and recommending changes that can be easily made to warn customers and employees of potential hazards.

Personal liability insurance covers claims for damages suffered by customers and employees. The damages must have occurred near or in the business establishment.

Product liability insurance protects against business loss resulting from personal injury from products manufactured or sold by a business. For example, a product may cause skin infections, burns, or even injury or death because of defective parts or poor construction. Many businesses purchase product liability insurance to guarantee against losses even after products have been tested extensively by private companies and government agencies.

Fidelity bonds protect a business from employee dishonesty. Usually businesses require employees who handle money, such as bank tellers and cashiers, to be bonded. If a bonded employee steals money, the bonding company pays the loss. Individuals who are bonded undergo personal reviews of their character and background before they are bonded.

Performance bonds (also called surety bonds) insure against losses that might occur when work or a contract is not finished on time or as agreed. For example, a building contractor might be required to purchase a performance bond to guarantee completion of the job on time and according to specifications. The company that issues the performance bond is responsible for damages if the contract is not completed.

Life insurance is often purchased to protect the owners or managers of a business. For example, a sole proprietor (sole business owner) is usually required to have life insurance in order to borrow money. The policy will guarantee that there will be money to pay off the sole proprietor's debts and obligations, if he or she dies. Life insurance on a deceased partner can provide the money needed for other partners to continue the business (if named as *beneficiaries*—those who will receive the money from the policy).

Credit insurance protects a business from losses on credit extended to customers. *Credit life insurance* pays the balance of any loans granted by banks, credit unions, and other financial agencies in the event the borrower dies.

Workers' compensation insurance is a type of insurance paid by employers to cover employees that suffer job-related injuries and illness and to protect employers from being sued by an employee who is injured on the job. Most states require all public employers and those private employers who regularly employ a predetermined minimum number of employees for prescribed time periods to have workers' compensation insurance coverage.

Guarantees and Warranties *Guarantees* and *warranties* are promises by the seller or manufacturer concerning the performance and quality of a product and protection against loss. Guarantees and warranties were discussed in depth in Chapter 36.

Transferring Risks Through Business Ownership As you learned in Chapter 37, the amount of risk a business must handle depends in part on the type of business ownership. In a sole proprietorship, the individual owner assumes all risks. Partnerships enable the partners to share in the business risks. Corporations allow the stockholders, as owners, to share the business risks. The corporate form of ownership offers the most protection from losses.

Risk Retention

In some cases, it is impossible for businesses to prevent or transfer risks, so they *retain or* assume responsibility for them. This is called *risk retention*. For example, if customer trends change and merchandise remains unsold, the business has to assume the loss. That is, it retains the risk.

Businesses and businesspeople retain certain business risks because

- they are unaware of the risk (for example, they are unaware of internal theft);
- they underestimate the risk, as when merchandise is purchased in anticipation of high sales, but weather, trends, and customers' habits change; and
- they anticipate a profit by taking a risk, such as purchasing land for development and future profit on its sale for a subdivision.

Risk Avoidance

Certain risks can be avoided by anticipating them in advance. For example, market research can lead businesses to conclude that investment in a product is not worth the risk.

As you can see, businesses have several ways of handling risks. Owning and operating a business, however, always involves a degree of risk. The way a business manages its risks determines its success or failure.

SECTION 38.2

Review

1. **Identify the four ways businesses handle risk.**
2. **Name four ways that companies can prevent and control risks.**
3. **What are the three principal ways to transfer risk?**
4. **What is the difference between risk retention and risk avoidance?**

Assess

Evaluation

Assign and review the Section 38.2 Review.

Reteaching

1. Assign and review the vocabulary terms for this section.
2. Assign and review Fact and Idea Review questions 5–22 from the Chapter Review.
3. Divide students into six groups. Assign each group one of the following topics: (1) things included in employee orientation/training programs, (2) things included in accident management programs, (3) how businesses can deter shoplifting, (4) how businesses can lower their risk from robberies, (5) techniques for controlling employee theft, and (6) types of insurance and guarantees and warranties. Give each group five minutes to review its assigned information, then have all students close their texts while each group reteaches its assigned content.

Enrichment

1. Assign and review the appropriate activities in the *Student Activity Workbook*.
2. Assign and review the appropriate Critical Thinking questions from the Chapter Review.
3. Assign and review the Building Academic Skills Activities, Application Projects, Linking School to Work Activities, and Performance Assessment from the Chapter Review.

Close

Have students look through this section, choose the one or two concepts on which they still feel they need clarification, and write a 50-word summary of each concept to better reinforce it in their own minds.

Section Review Answers

1. Risk prevention and control, risk transfer, risk retention, and risk avoidance.
2. Providing safe working conditions and safety instruction, screening and training employees, preventing external theft, and controlling employee theft.
3. By purchasing insurance, providing warranties and guarantees, and by transferring risks.
4. Certain risks can be avoided by anticipating them in advance. Avoiding risks in advance is known as risk avoidance.

Answers

Vocabulary Review

See Glossary for definitions.

Fact and Idea Review

1. The marketing function of managing risks.
2. If products become out-of-date, businesses risk losing consumers.
3. It is costly to replace and/or repair defective products and pay legal fees.
4. Customer or employee dishonesty, employee carelessness, employee incompetence, etc.
5. Orientation topics are listed in Section 38.2.
6. By providing a safe working environment and safety instruction.
7. Through employee screening and training.
8. It can make employees careless and more likely to forget safety rules.
9. The removal of merchandise from a business without paying for it.
10. Ways to deter robberies are listed in Section 38.2.
11. Methods for controlling employee theft are listed in Section 38.2.
12. A contract between a business and an insurance company to cover a certain business risk.
13. Property coverage includes loss of, or damage to buildings and property. Business liability coverage covers losses due to close of business operations.
14. Replacement cost coverage, automatic increase protection, loss of income.
15. Coverage for: premises and operations, medical expense, personal injury, employees and advertising liability.
16. A fidelity bond protects a business from employee dishonesty. A performance bond

510

Vocabulary Review

Use the following vocabulary terms to create a rock song on how businesses can manage risks.

risk
business risk
economic risks
natural risks
human risks
insurance policy
extended coverage
fidelity bonds
performance bonds

Fact and Idea Review

1. Why is risk management an important marketing function? (Sec. 38.1)
2. Why is product obsolescence a type of economic risk for a business? (Sec. 38.1)
3. Why do companies fear product recalls? (Sec. 38.1)
4. Give three examples of human risks. (Sec. 38.1)
5. Identify a checklist of topics to cover in an employee orientation program. (Sec. 38.2)
6. How can businesses reduce the human risk of on-the-job injuries? (Sec. 38.2)
7. How can businesses reduce the human risk of carelessness and incompetence? (Sec. 38.2)
8. Why can drug abuse lead to increased human risk? (Sec. 38.2)
9. What is shoplifting? How can businesses deter shoplifting? (Sec. 38.2)
10. Explain procedures that can be used to deter the risk of armed robberies. (Sec. 38.2)
11. Explain procedures that can be used to control employee theft. (Sec. 38.2)
12. What is an insurance policy? (Sec. 38.2)
13. Explain the difference between property coverage and business liability coverage. (Sec. 38.2)
14. Identify some features and types of coverage found in property coverage policies. (Sec. 38.2)
15. Identify features commonly found in business liability policies. (Sec. 38.2)
16. Explain the difference between a fidelity bond and a performance bond. (Sec. 38.2)
17. Explain the difference between personal and product liability insurance. (Sec. 38.2)
18. Explain the difference between credit insurance and credit life insurance. (Sec. 38.2)

19. What is workers' compensation insurance? What are its two basic purposes? (Sec. 38.2)
20. How can the type of business ownership affect the risks of the owners of the business? (Sec. 38.2)
21. Why must some businesses retain risks? (Sec. 38.2)
22. What is risk avoidance? (Sec. 38.2)

Critical Thinking

1. Businesses face risks every day. Why are business owners willing to assume risks when it would be much easier to work for someone else?
2. Some people think that shoplifting only affects the retailer's business. Explain the consequences of shoplifting for the individual and for society.
3. Identify some factors that may affect the insurance rates charged to a retailer for fire protection.
4. How does a business determine what kinds of insurance to carry? Do you think it's possible for a business to carry too much insurance?
5. Insurance rates are partially based on past experience. Do you think it is appropriate to deny auto insurance to companies with poor driving records or robbery insurance to businesses in high crime areas? Analyze the two situations and be prepared to defend your answer.
6. Jury judgments on personal and product liability cases have led to huge cash settlements for injured parties. How do these claims affect businesses and you? Should there be set limits on the cash amounts given for injury or death? If so, how would you determine the settlement amounts?
7. What important factors should a business consider when selecting an insurance company?
8. "It's insured, so don't worry about it." What's wrong with this statement?
9. How can warranties and guarantees transfer business risks to other parties?

Building Academic Skills

Math

1. Given the following information, calculate the annual amount a small business pays for insurance.
   a. Property insurance of $716.18, paid semiannually
   b. Liability insurance of $76.25, paid quarterly
   c. Business interruption insurance of $205.50, paid annually

insures against losses when work on a contract is not completed as agreed.
17. Personal liability insurance covers claims for damages suffered by customers and employees near or in the business establishment. Product liability insurance protects against business loss resulting from personal injury from products manufactured or sold by a business.
18. Credit insurance protects a business from losses on credit extended to customers. Credit life

insurance pays the balance of any outstanding loans in case the borrower dies.
19. Insurance paid by employers to cover employees that suffer job-related injuries and illness and to protect employers from being sued by an employee who is injured on the job.
20. See Section 38.2 for discussion.
21. It is impossible to prevent or transfer the risks.
22. Anticipating risks in advance and deciding that the risk is not worth it.

d. Vehicle insurance of $315.00, paid quarterly

e. Employee group life and medical insurance of $524.15, paid quarterly

2. Calculate the amount of net sales lost to shoplifting in each of the following situations.

   a. Discount store with sales of $400 million with a shoplifting rate of 1.5%

   b. Mass merchandiser with sales of $600 million with a shoplifting rate of 1.9%

Communication

3. Write a 100-word paper on the responsibilities parents have to instill honesty and respect for personal property in their children so they do not shoplift.

4. Write a business letter to the National Safety Council, 444 N. Michigan Avenue, Chicago, Illinois 60611 requesting business safety information for your marketing class.

Human Relations

5. You are planning to start a small arts and crafts shop with a friend after graduation. You and your proposed partner believe that the business should be freed of risks through the purchase of insurance coverage on the building, vehicles, merchandise, staff etc. Identify the types of insurance you will need. Convince your friend of the logic behind your decisions.

Application Projects

1. List five products whose sales could be affected by seasonal changes. Identify the seasonal factor (for example snowfall or rain) and explain how this affects the sale of the product.

2. Contact your local chamber of commerce, Retail Merchants Association, police department, or state retail trade association for information about your state's legislation on shoplifting. Report your findings.

3. Develop a 200-word report on life insurance. Explain the difference between the various forms of life insurance and how life insurance rates are established.

4. Conduct a survey of retailers in your local community to determine the methods they use to prevent shoplifting.

5. Check with a local insurance agency to obtain sales brochures on business operations protection policies.

Linking School to Work

1. Write a report on your employer's company policies on observing a shoplifting incident. In your report explain the procedures and actions to take at your place of business when dealing with a shoplifter.

2. Report on the accident procedures used at your training station or place of employment.

3. Write a report on the orientation program used at your place of employment. Discuss the strengths and weaknesses in the program and any suggestions that you may have for improving it.

Performance Assessment

Role Play

Situation. You are an assistant manager for a large department store. You have been placed on special assignment to develop a risk management plan for your store. You are to describe the risks your business faces and develop a checklist of ways to handle these risks.

Evaluation. You will be evaluated on how well you do the following:

- Discuss the various types of business risks that affect your company.
- Describe ways of managing the business risks that affect your company.

Pictorial Essay

Create a chart using drawings, photos, and illustrations that shows types of business risks. Next to each illustration provide written explanation on how businesses can manage the risk.

COMPUTER APPLICATION

Complete the Chapter 38 Computer Application that appears in the Student Activity Workbook.

8. The cost of replacing individual losses is made up through higher premiums charged to all policyholders.

9. The risk is transferred to the seller or manufacturer.

Building Academic Skills

Math

1. (a) $1432.36
   ($716.18 × 2 = $1,432.36)
   (b) $305.00
   ($76.25 × 4 = $305.00)
   (c) 205.50
   ($205.50 × 1 = $205.50)
   (d) $1,260.00
   ($315.00 × 4 = $1,260.00)
   (e) $2,096.60
   ($524.15 × 4 = $2,096.60)

2. (a) $6,000,000
   ($400,000,000 × .015 = $6,000,000)
   (b) $11,400,000
   ($600,000,000 × .019 = $11,400,000)

Communication

3. Papers will vary.

4. Use the information received for a class discussion.

Human Relations

5. Answers include types of insurance discussed in chapter.

Application Projects

1. Examples include skis, bikes, and pools.

2. Material received will vary.

3. Reports will vary.

4. Students should share their survey findings in class.

5. Students should display the insurance brochures.

Linking School to Work

Answers depend on the work situation.

Performance Assessment

Refer to the *DECA Competitive Events Handbook* for evaluation guidelines.

Computer Application

Optional activity. Refer to the *Marketing Software Binder* for template and user information.

Evaluation

Administer the reproducible test for Chapter 38, or construct your own using the Testmaker software.

Critical Thinking

1. Some take risks for what they believe will be a larger profit or monetary gain.

2. Shoplifting causes everyone to pay higher prices.

3. The type of business; the age, condition, and type of construction of the building in which the business is housed; the location of the business relative to fire protection services; and any past experience the business may have had with fires.

4. A business must look at the degree of risk associated with each insurable feature.

5. Students might argue that all businesses should be entitled to some form of insurance.

6. Claims made against a business are eventually passed along to consumers in the form of higher prices.

7. The company's expertise in the field, its record for prompt payment in the event of loss, and its reliability.

Chapter Overview

This chapter introduces students to the business plan. It stresses the importance of business planning in developing a business idea and in evaluating results.

Springboard

Pose the following situation to students. In planning a road trip to a destination you have never visited, which method would be easiest and most efficient in reaching your goal: (A) using a road map, or (B) pointing your car in the general direction of your destination, relying on intuition, and following road signs? Some students may opt for the second choice because they, like many entrepreneurs, rely on intuition when making decisions.

Write *business plan* and *road map* on the board. Tell students that a business plan is a road map that helps them choose the best route, allows them to mark their progress, and helps them avoid futile side trips. The business planning process helps you determine whether your business idea will work.

Prereading

List the section objectives to discuss with students. Have students skim the chapter, looking at the pictures, reading the captions, and noting the heads. Ask questions to ensure that the students have a minimal understanding of the chapter structure.

Preteaching the Vocabulary

Give students 10 minutes to look through this chapter, find each vocabulary term, and make any notes that will help them remember the definitions. Review each term with the class.

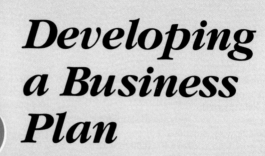

Developing a Business Plan

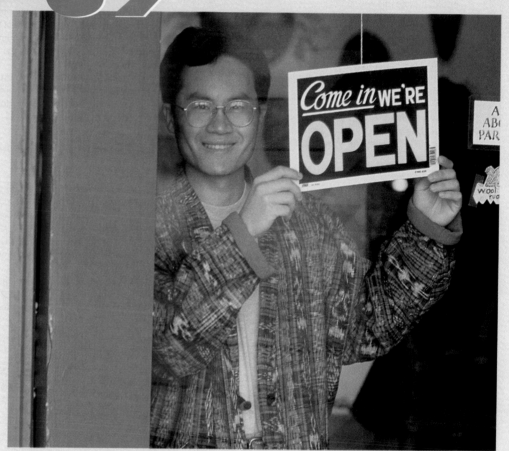

A business plan provides an overall picture of a proposed business to potential investors and lenders. It gives a description of the business, an organization and marketing plan, and a financial plan. When properly prepared, a good business plan not only helps you develop your ideas but also provides a way for you to evaluate your results.

In this chapter you will learn how to develop a business plan. Specifically, you will look at how to describe and analyze a business situation and develop the organization, marketing, and financial plan for your business.

Classroom Management

For the Teacher
- Teacher's Annotated Editions for all workbooks
- Teacher's Manual for *School-to-Work Handbook*
- *Testing Binder*
- *Transparency Binder*
- *Marketing Software Binder*
- *Marketing Career Portfolio*
- *Lesson Plans*

For the Student
- *Student Activity Workbook*
- *Marketing Math Workbook*
- *School-to-Work Handbook*
- *Student Software*
- *International Case Studies*
- *Marketing Career Portfolio*

SECTION 39.1

Objectives

After completing this section, you will be able to

- discuss the importance and purpose of a business plan,
- identify the major sections of a business plan, and
- describe and analyze a proposed business situation.

Terms to Know

- business plan
- business philosophy
- trading area
- buying behavior

Developing the Business Plan

Once you have determined that you want to establish your own business, you need to develop a business plan. A **business plan** is a proposal that describes every part of your new business to potential investors and lenders. Although business plan formats do vary somewhat, it is suggested that your business plan follow the outline identified in Figure 39–1 on page 514.

A business plan is important, because it maps out the course of your business and helps you do three things:

1. *Obtain financing.* It is expensive to open a business, and you will probably need financial assistance. Your business plan will help convince investors and lenders that your business idea will be profitable.
2. *Guide the opening of the business.* The plan identifies procedures necessary to legally establish the business.
3. *Manage the business successfully.* The plan is a management tool that helps you identify the month-to-month steps you must take to ensure that your business operates profitably.

A business plan must be well organized and easy to read. It should contain three main sections:

- a description and analysis of the proposed business situation,
- an organizational and marketing plan, and
- a financial plan.

Description and Analysis of the Proposed Business

The description and analysis section introduces the proposed business by describing it and the products it will sell. It includes your personal business philosophy. It contains a self-analysis which describes your business experience and training. This section of your business plan also includes a trading area analysis, a market segment analysis, and an analysis of potential locations.

Type of Business, Business Philosophy, and Type of Products

Begin your business plan with a description of the type of business you plan to open. Present data or significant trends that will influence the success of your business. Explain how a current or changing situation has created an unfulfilled consumer want that your business will address.

Next, give your *business philosophy*. A **business philosophy** tells how you think the business should be run and shows your understanding of your firm's role in the marketplace. It reveals your attitude toward your customers, employees, and competitors.

Once you start a business, your business philosophy will help you create a customer following. For example, part of the business philosophy of The Limited, Inc. is that the customer should always be happy with the merchandise. Thus, its principal customer policy is that no sale is ever final. Customers can always return merchandise if they are dissatisfied with it. This business philosophy has earned The Limited a loyal following of customers.

After you identify your business philosophy, describe the product you will offer. Tell the consumer benefits it will provide and why it will be successful. If you have sold your product before and thus know it well, tell about it here.

Include as many facts as you can obtain. Speculation and statements of belief do not in themselves convince investors and lenders to lend you money. Consult recent issues of *Business Week, Fortune, Inc., Money, The Wall Street Journal*, and other business publications for regional and national business information.

FOCUS

Bell Ringer Activity

First, have several copies of fairly detailed business plans available in your classroom. Allow students to sit in groups of three or four to thumb through several of the plans and get a feel for the contents of each. Then, get students' reactions to the plans. Does business planning seem like a great deal of perhaps unnecessary work? Would students rather just plunge into a business without taking the time to create the type of detailed plan they just reviewed?

Ask students to help you brainstorm a chalkboard list of reasons why business planning is important.

Introducing the Section

Business planning is important for three reasons:

(1) It helps in the obtaining of financing. Most potential lenders and investors will want to see a detailed business plan before lending or investing money.

(2) A business plan serves as a guide in opening a business. New business owners need a guide during business start-up to identify the legal procedures necessary to starting a business.

(3) Finally, a business plan helps in business management because it lays out the steps you must take to ensure profitable operation. Business owners review their business plans regularly to compare current business operation with original planning and projected financial information.

In this section, students will look at the first key section of a business plan: description and analysis of the proposed business.

Meeting Special Needs

Learning Disabled

Keep in mind that students with learning disabilities may require additional assistance completing some of the activities in this chapter. The scope of developing a business plan can be quiet complex and requires analytical ability and methodical work throughout the process. Break the task up into self-contained steps and provide additional assistance as needed. A variety of resources can come into play, including peer assistance or adult mentors. Students with learning disabilities require more support and structure. Clearly specify the scope of the assignment and review their work on a regular basis throughout the course of the project.

Teach

Guided Practice

1. Read Section 39.1 with students.
2. Have students read aloud the Case Study and review the answers in class.
3. Use the transparency for this section.
4. MarkEd Resource Center in Columbus, Ohio, (800) 448-0398, offers materials appropriate for use with this chapter, including a LAP module and *The Small Business Planning Guide*.
5. Here are some other references you may wish to use: (1) *An Entrepreneur's Guide to Developing a Business Plan*. Chicago: Arthur Anderson and Company, 1986. (2) Brooks, Julie K. *How to Write a Successful Business Plan*. New York: American Management Association, 1987. (3) Most accounting firms offer free booklets on preparing business plans.
6. In the first Application Project in the Chapter Review, students are asked to create a business plan. Help them to organize and prioritize information by developing a notebook that has one section devoted to each section of the business plan. Or, they can create a 3" x 5" card file, writing one or two related thoughts per card.

Discussion Starter

As the text mentions, part of The Limited's business philosophy is that the customer should always be happy with the merchandise; thus, no sale is ever final. Discuss with students the business philosophies of other businesses in your area. Also, have students compare the business philosophies of two similar businesses.

Outline for a Business Plan

I. Description and analysis of the proposed business situation
  A. Type of business
  B. Business philosophy
  C. Description of good or service
  D. Self-analysis
    1. Education and training
    2. Strengths and weaknesses
    3. Plan for personal development
  E. Trading area analysis
    1. Geographic, demographic, and economic data
    2. Competition
  F. Market segment analysis
    1. Target market
    2. Customer buying behavior
  G. Analysis of potential location

II. Organization and marketing plan
  A. Proposed organization
    1. Type of ownership
    2. Steps in establishing business
    3. Personnel needs
  B. Proposed good/service
    1. Manufacturing plans and inventory policies
    2. Suppliers
  C. Proposed marketing plan
    1. Pricing policies
    2. Promotional activities

III. Financial plan
  A. Sources of capital
    1. Personal sources
    2. External sources
  B. Projected income and expenses
    1. Personal financial statement
    2. Projected start-up costs
    3. Projected personal needs
    4. Projected business income
    5. Projected business expenses
    6. Projected income statement(s)
    7. Projected balance sheet
    8. Projected cash flow

Figure 39–1

A business plan describes every part of a proposed business to potential investors and lenders. Why do those who might give a potential entrepreneur financial backing want to know that the proposed business will make a profit?

Self-analysis

The next part of your business plan includes a *self-analysis*. A self-analysis is a description of your personal education, training, strengths, weaknesses, and a plan for personal development in your field.

For example, if you are interested in music and want to start an audio entertainment business, you must be able to accurately predict current music trends. You must also be able to buy, display, price, and advertise your merchandise correctly. In this part of the business plan, you would tell which skills you have in this area and which you do not. (If you do not have some of the skills you need, tell how other people will be able to help you or describe special training that will help you acquire the skills.)

Indicate the education and training you have had so far to prepare you for operating your new business. For example, in addition to your marketing education experience, you may have taken a bookkeeping course or worked part-time in the accounting department of a retail store. This shows you will be able to understand and interpret your business's financial statements.

Mention any future plans to continue your schooling—whether in a technical institute or college. Additionally, schooling plans should show that you intend to improve your skills for operating your business.

If you have a special license needed to open the business, mention that here, too. If you do not have the required license, you should be able to say here that you have applied for one. Examples of businesses frequently requiring special licenses for their owners or employees are hair salons and barbershops; construction companies; child-care facilities; and automotive, electrical, and mechanical repair businesses.

Finally, include the special personality traits and work habits you have that will help you to operate your proposed business. A statement about your motivation and willingness to work hard adds strength to your business plan.

Trading Area Analysis

Following an explanation of your personal strengths and skills, you should begin to define your trading area. A **trading area** is the geographical area from which a business draws its customers. Before going into business, you must completely analyze the trading area with respect to geographic, demographic, and economic data, as well as competition. Information about the population in your trading area is available from your local chamber of commerce or your state department of commerce. You can also consult the most recent local census data in your local library.

Geographic, Demographic, and Economic Data *Geographic data* includes population distribution. It tells how many people live in a certain area.

Demographics are such easily identified and measurable population statistics as age, gender, and marital

---

Caption Answer

Lenders need to know the potential entrepreneur will repay a loan.

BRIGHT IDEAS

Try a Hobby

Rolf Margenau's interest in restoring antique cars developed into something unexpected—a successful business. Tennatoys, his company, makes personalized antennas for cars, trucks, and boats. The antennas come in nine different designs, including a cowboy hat, a horse, a musical note, and the Chevrolet "bow tie." The last one is a big favorite with Chevy truck owners.

The idea for Tennatoys came from a friend's design that Margenau saw in 1993. Margenau immediately realized the potential of the product. He knew from his own experiences how restoration enthusiasts think when they customize a vehicle.

Today, Margenau concentrates on the marketing, and his friend still designs the antennae. His initial hunch proved correct. The Automotive Parts and Accessories Association reported that sales of auto accessories in 1993 were $11.3 billion. Tennatoys is reaching for a part of that lucrative market.

Creativity Challenge Form teams of 3–5 people, and put together a list of hobbies. Start with your own and expand the possibilities by including the hobbies of relatives, friends, and acquaintances. From your list choose the one hobby that your group thinks has the most (or, if you want a real challenge, the least) potential. Then try to come up with as many business ideas as possible, based on that hobby.

---

status. Knowing the demographics of your trading area will help you identify any trends happening now or in the future that will have a direct impact on your business. For example, if you plan to open a children's apparel store, and your trading area is fast becoming a family neighborhood, you will definitely want to note this.

Prevailing economic conditions are among the major factors affecting a business. *Economic factors* include economic growth projections, trends in pricing, interest rates, and government regulations. For example, tax increases or decreases levied by the local, state, or federal government will affect consumer buying power.

It is important to include how much *disposable income* the potential consumers in your trading area are likely to have. This means personal income from wages, salaries,

interest, and profits, minus federal, state, and local taxes. Disposable income is also referred to as *buying income*.

A special measurement called a *buying power index* has been developed to help new business owners determine the buying power for a given area. The index combines disposable income, population size, and retail sales figures into an overall indicator of an area's sales potential. These factors are then expressed as a percentage of total sales. Buying power indexes can be helpful in deciding where to locate your business. You can find more information on buying power indexes in the *Survey of Buying Power*, which is published annually by *Sales and Marketing Management* magazine.

National and international economic conditions can have an effect locally, too. For example, the North American Free Trade Agreement is expected to increase trade between Mexico and Canada. Such a trade agreement may affect your business by increasing or decreasing the demand for your product.

Will your business be affected by seasonal fluctuations? Are technological advancements happening now or in the future that could affect the demand or need for your product? You may not know the answers to these questions, but you should know how to find the information you need.

A good source of information on local economic conditions is your local bank. Bank officials often have business projections for major geographical areas and for most types of businesses located in their immediate area. In addition, many states have a department of commerce to assist new entrepreneurs in obtaining important information about economic trends within the state and within industries. Other good sources of information are related business publications available at schools, public libraries, colleges, and universities.

Competition As a new business operator, you must analyze your competition. List all the competitors in your trading area, along with their types of products, prices, locations, general quality of products, and their strengths and weaknesses. Determine your competition's sales volume and how they promote and sell their products. Show how your business will be superior to the competition based on these factors.

Some good sources of information about your competitors are the Yellow Pages, annual reports, trade associations, and business publications such as *Dun & Bradstreet* reports. Your local chamber of commerce should also be able to provide you with information.

Market Segment Analysis

The next part of your business plan should contain a market segment analysis. A market segment analysis is a description of your target market and the buying behavior of your potential customers.

Target Market As you know, your target market represents the specific group of people you want to

Critical Thinking

Services are intangible and thus are more difficult to describe than goods. Ask students what types of things they would include in a product description of a service such as a hair salon. (Possibilities: (1) special techniques or equipment which will be used to provide the service that other similar service providers might not offer, (2) descriptions of the service providers, (3) descriptions of ancillary products to be offered, and (4) customer benefits of receiving the service.) Provide students with other examples of service businesses (for example, restaurants, dry cleaners, and copy shops) and have them give sample product descriptions of each.

The more product knowledge you can convey to your customers, the more credibility you will have. Why? (Answers should indicate that if you convey a great deal of product knowledge, you portray yourself as the product expert. Thus, people will trust your product.)

Cooperative Learning

Divide students into four groups. Have each group research geographic, demographic, and economic data in your area. (Define for students what physical area you want them to research—for example, your town, your city, your county, etc. Also define the categories you wish them to research under demographic factors and economic factors.)

Have each group compile its research into a written report, or charts/graphs showing analysis and comparison of the statistics, or both.

Have all groups present their information and tell where they got their statistics. Then have students make predictions about what businesses your area could support and probably could not support, given their research.

Bright Ideas

If students seem stumped or are coming up with a very limited range of ideas, encourage them to look at providing related services for hobbyists as well as outlets for the product. For example, people who ride mountain bikes need maps of off-road trails in addition to access to pre-owned, reconditioned bikes.

Independent Practice

1. Assign and review the Chapter 39 Case Study in the *International Case Studies* workbook.
2. Have students research the current status of the North American Free Trade Agreement (NAFTA) and report on the economic implications and impact of the Agreement for businesses in your community, or in your region. (If the Agreement will not directly impact businesses in your community, at least make sure that students understand NAFTA and the intent of the Agreement with respect to its impact on our national economy.)
3. Have students list five different types of successful businesses in your community and analyze why each is located where it is. They should consider such things as (1) accessibility to the public, to suppliers, and to transit routes; and (2) each business's needs (manufacturers and wholesalers, for example, value low space costs and good access to transit routes over exposure to and accessibility by the public). Discuss students' findings in class.

Assess

Evaluation

Assign and review the Section 39.1 Review.

Reteaching

1. Assign and review the vocabulary terms for this section.
2. Assign and review Fact and Idea Review questions 1–8 from the Chapter Review.

CASE STUDY

Doing Business on the Internet

Ever thought about running a business without a store, salespeople, displays, inventory, and storage space? Well, this is exactly what Randy Adams and Bill Rollinson have done. The partners have opened a computer and software superstore on the Internet, a worldwide computer network.

Adams and Rollinson's business, known as the Internet Shopping Network (ISN), requires few of the traditional costs associated with running a business. ISN uses only a few computers and a small staff. Space is not that important because customer sales are done on computers not on a sales floor. ISN's store is open to 25 million people that currently use the Internet system.

ISN sells 20,000 computer hardware and software products. Customers review the product catalog by using their own computer. In addition, the computer catalog on-line service can also give product reviews before a customer places an order.

When a customer makes a purchase, the order is handled electronically by going to ISN's computers in California. The computer checks inventory, debits a customer's credit card, and sends the order electronically to a distributor. The customer receives order confirmation

through the Internet and receives the product within two days. Rollinson believes that the company's products are usually sold for the best prices available in the industry. Lower prices are possible because there are reduced selling costs. Selling expenses, such as operators, 800 toll-free numbers, and warehouse space are eliminated by using the computer.

Although companies have advertised products for years on private networks, such as Prodigy and CompuServe, businesses only began to market products on the Internet in the 1990s. Internet provides small businesses with many interesting business possibilities. An electronic business on the Internet can be open 24 hours a day, seven days a week, but operating costs may be as little as $1,000 a year. The Internet provides companies with an opportunity to advertise to more than 25 million people for a very low cost. Because the Internet is worldwide, companies can advertise their products internationally.

By using the Internet a small company, such as ISN, can compete effectively with larger companies. Since ISN does not have to invest in buildings, like a typical computer superstore, such as CompUSA, it can enter the business easily. Rather than build a new building, all ISN has to do is add another computer for about $25,000.

Experts do not really know whether sales and marketing through the Internet will ultimately be a boom or a bust. The challenge for new and existing businesses, however, is to explore the opportunities of using the Internet as a possible marketing tool for their products.

Case Study Review

1. Do you think that doing business on the Internet will be a boom or a bust?
2. Can you think of other businesses which might be able to sell their products on the Internet?
3. Who would you consider to be the typical user of the Internet?

A MATTER OF ETHICS

4. Although computer on-line services look promising, can you predict some possible problems with buying through computers?

Case Study Answers

1. Students should point out the reasons that some people prefer to shop in a real store and why some customers prefer shopping through computers.
2. Virtually any business could use the Internet. Examples include companies selling advertising services, business information services, florists, travel, magazines, art supplies, etc.
3. Nobody really knows for sure. Many more corporations are providing access to Internet to their employees and hundreds of thousands of people now access the system through their homes.
4. There are potential security problems because of computer hackers who might be able to gain access to credit card numbers and corporate accounts.

reach. You can identify your target market by common geographic characteristics, such as region, county size, size of city, density of population, and climate of the area. Or you can categorize it by demographic characteristics, such as age, gender, marital status, family size, income, occupation, education, religion, and culture or ethnic background.

You must carefully identify your target market because the needs and wants of different markets must be addressed differently in the marketing of goods and services. For example, families can live in the same city and have similar education levels, occupations, and incomes. However, their needs for entertainment, furniture, food, clothing, or personal services may vary greatly, depending on their religious or ethnic background. The latter, in fact, may define entirely different target markets.

Your task as an entrepreneur is to decide which market to target and how best to do it. The best way to make this decision is to be guided by the way the members of the target market perceive themselves and their own needs.

Customers' Buying Behavior   After you have identified your target market, you will also need to explain how the potential customer *buying behavior* associated with it will be good for your business.

Buying behavior is the process individuals use to decide what they will buy and from where and whom they will buy it. For example, if you plan to open a children's toy store, you have used demographic information to determine how many families with children are in your target market. You also know the approximate average family income. From your earlier analysis of the competition (other toy stores serving the same target market), you have an idea of how much disposable income these families spent on children's toys and which toys they bought. You also know which stores in which locations did the most business. This is your target market's buying behavior.

You can then put this information together to make decisions about how your store might best serve these same customers, given their buying behavior. Do you want to try to take business away from other toy stores, or do you want to try to sell items not offered in the other stores? Do you want to get your customers to buy a lot of low-priced items or a few high-priced ones?

Analysis of Potential Locations

After you have analyzed your trading area and your market segment including your target market and your competition, you are ready to select your location. Determining where to locate your business is one of your most important decisions because location has a direct effect on your sales.

Your analysis should include whether you will buy or rent the property, how you will control customer traffic, and the nearness to your competition. Your location will determine your hours of operation and the number of

customers who will see and patronize your business. For example, if you are located in a shopping mall or shopping center, your business hours will probably be set by the management association. In either place, you can also usually depend on fairly constant customer traffic generated by the other businesses in the same location.

Whether you locate in a mall, a neighborhood shopping center, or your own home depends upon available space and the nature of your business. If your business relies on impulse buying and thus needs many customers passing by, as do restaurants, it may be worthwhile to spend the extra money to rent the best available site. If customer count is not quite so crucial, site location is less important. The money you save on rent can be used to advertise or promote your business.

If you decide to locate in your home or in a separate location, consider these factors.

- Do you need to be in a commercial or a residential area?
- What, if any, restrictions exist which might prevent you from locating in a particular commercial or residential area?
- Is sufficient parking space available?
- Is the neighborhood safe?
- Will traffic congestion be a problem?
- On which side of the street will you locate?

In addition, you need to look at some personal issues about the location of your business. Do you want to be near family and friends? Do you want to locate in a neighborhood or city away from where you currently live?

After you have answered these questions, you are ready to find a specific site. Your first step should be to learn about any local ordinances or laws that may affect your business. For example, if you intend to build, you will need to get the necessary building permits. If you are planning to operate a regulated business, such as a child-care center or a service station, you will need to get the necessary approvals and permits required by your community to operate. If you are unsure about local regulations, meet with your local or county officials to find out what is required.

SECTION 39.1

Review

1. What is a business plan? Why is it important?
2. What are three sections of a business plan?
3. What are the seven major elements included in the description and analysis section of a business plan?

Enrichment

1. Assign and review the appropriate activities in the *Student Activity Workbook*.
2. Assign and review the appropriate Critical Thinking questions from the Chapter Review.
3. Have students interview the owners or managers of two small businesses in your community that are in direct competition (for example, two dry cleaners).

  Have students determine (1) what each business does to differentiate itself from the competition, (2) how each business "keeps tabs" on the competition's latest product offerings and on its level of success, and (3) what indirect competition each business faces. (Indirect competition is created by products that are the same as yours but offered through a different outlet, or through the use of new or newly applied technologies. For example, a moderately priced restaurant faces indirect competition from a take out food section in the supermarket.)

  Students should write their findings in 150 to 200 words. Have each student present his or her findings to the class.

Close

Have students complete this statement: The three key functions of a business plan are to: ... (obtain financing, guide the opening of the business, and manage the business successfully.)

Section Review Answers

1. A business plan is a proposal that describes every part of your new business to potential investors and financing agencies. It helps you obtain financing, it provides a guide to opening the business, and it is a management tool.
2. The description and analysis of the business situation, the organization and marketing plan, and the financial section.
3. Type of business, business philosophy, description of good or service, self-analysis, trading area analysis, market segment analysis, and analysis of potential location.

Focus

Bell Ringer Activity

Have each student pick a partner in the class. Together, each pair should brainstorm a list of the things that would be included in (1) the organization plan and (2) the marketing plan.

Introducing the Section

Review students' answers from The Bell Ringer Activity, creating a chalkboard list of their answers under column headings marked *organization plan* and *marketing plan*.

Tell students that this section explores the second part of a business plan, which tells how you would organize, manage, and develop your new business.

Teach

Guided Practice

1. Read Section 39.2 with students.
2. Assign and review the Chapter 39 Activity in the *School-to-Work Handbook*.

Discussion Starter

Discuss with students the current economic environment locally and nationally. What correlation do students see between the local and national economic environment, and local prices? For example, have fast-food restaurants cut prices on their standard fare, or are they offering extremely low-priced specials? Are health clubs offering two-for-one membership deals? What predictions can students make about how long such price-cutting will last? (Answers will vary.)

SECTION 39.2

Objectives

After completing this section, you will be able to

- develop an organization plan,
- provide details related to goods or services to be offered, and
- develop a marketing plan.

Terms to Know

- job descriptions
- organization chart

Organization and Marketing Plan

This section of the business plan tells how you plan to organize the new business. It contains a description of your current and anticipated staffing needs.

It also details how you plan to sell your product and how you intend to reach and satisfy customers with your product. The details of your proposed product are explained along with your potential suppliers, manufacturing or selling methods, and inventory policies.

Finally, it includes your marketing plan. Your marketing plan details your pricing strategies and promotional plans.

Proposed Organization

The organization part of your business plan is essentially a blueprint. It lays the foundation for the structure of your proposed business.

Types of Ownership   As you learned in Chapter 37, there are three main types of business ownership. In this part of the business plan you will need to identify the form of business ownership appropriate for your business and the rationale for your choice.

Steps in Establishing Your Business   Once you have detailed in your business plan what type of business ownership you have chosen, you need to show the steps you will take to establish your business. As you know from Chapter 37, the specific steps you will take will depend on whether you organize your business as a sole proprietorship, partnership, or corporation.

Personnel Needs   Whether you organize as a proprietorship, partnership, or a corporation, your business plan must show your personnel needs. Potential investors and lenders need to know that you can identify the essential jobs your business will need to run properly. They also will want you to identify, as much as you can, the people who will do those jobs.

Table 39-1 shows the typical functions in a business. Notice that some of the functions are repeated under more than one category. By identifying all the necessary functions, you will be able to begin planning an organizational structure for your business.

Most new businesses are one-person operations. If this is your case, then you will do all the business functions. However, if you plan to divide responsibilities among partners or hire people, you must identify how everyone fits into the organizational structure.

You need to prepare job descriptions for your partners, employees, and yourself. **Job descriptions** are written statements listing the requirements of a particular job. Each job description includes the purpose of the job, qualifications needed, duties to be performed, equipment to be used, and expected working conditions.

After various job descriptions have been prepared, you are ready to develop an organization chart. An **organization chart** is a diagram of the various jobs and functions that are found in a company. It should be drawn with the jobs and major duties identified and clear lines of authority shown.

Business Functions

Administration	Production	Marketing
Operations	Operations	Advertising
Personnel	Purchasing	Sales
Financial	Manufacturing	Public Relations
Legal	Distribution	Service
Public Relations	Service	

Table 39–1

Shown in this table are the typical functions performed in most businesses in three general categories: administration (running the business), production (making the product), and marketing (selling the product). Choose any of the above functions, such as purchasing. Name two positions you would find in that area.

Caption Answer

Answers will vary. For example, within the Personnel Department there could be a personnel director and an administrative assistant. In sales, you could have a sales manager and a sales representative.

Avoiding the N-Word

Life in the **Multicultural** MARKETPLACE

In Japan, saying unpleasant things (like no) indirectly is more than a social nicety. It's a cultural trait, one that can be misleading to foreigners—especially in business situations.

For example, in Tokyo, as a result of Western influence, the word *no* will emerge occasionally in business negotiations. In Osaka, however, Japan's second largest city, ambiguity and indirectness are the rule. There, a businessperson might say something like, "Since you made an effort, we'll consider your offer." This actually means no. However, foreigners unfamiliar with the country's customs frequently persist in trying to negotiate.

Sometimes outside professional help is needed to keep a business going and growing. Entrepreneurs are often afraid to spend money on such professional services as accounting. This can be a fatal mistake. These trained professionals will help you avoid making serious mistakes that can result in business failure. If you decide to use outside professionals, identify them and their responsibilities on your organization chart. Examples of professionals that can help you include accountants, attorneys, bankers, and insurance agents.

You can also use paid professional assistance to identify employment practices in your state or locality. For example, new business owners need to be familiar with laws regulating minimum wages, occupational health and safety, unemployment compensation, and worker's disability insurance. Another source of information about employment laws is your state department of labor. State agencies publish many inexpensive or free publications to help new entrepreneurs understand various employment laws, rules, and regulations.

Proposed Good or Service

This part of your business plan includes information on the types of goods and services you will offer, your potential suppliers, manufacturing plans, and inventory policies. Let's say you plan to introduce a new product, such as custom bumper stickers. Perhaps you are going to replicate and sell an existing product. In both cases, you would prepare a list of possible suppliers and a manufacturing plan that gives the purchasing and manufacturing requirements.

Closely related to your manufacturing plan is your inventory policy. You need to show how you will manage

the goods you purchase or manufacture. How much, for example, will you keep on hand? How will you keep track of what to order and what has been sold?

Your inventory system depends on the size and scope of your proposed business. You may not need an extensive system. Trade associations and many suppliers can give you suggestions for an inventory control system that is best for your business.

If you are planning a service business, you should come up with a plan that addresses how, when, and who will provide the service to your customers. State the services provided by your competitors, describe the additional services you will provide, and estimate their costs. By analyzing your competitors' expenses and your own expenses for providing a service, you can show how you will price your service without pricing yourself out of the market.

Proposed Marketing Plan

At this point in your business plan, you have selected your business organization, identified your staffing needs, and detailed your goods/services policies. You are now ready to develop your marketing policies—that is, the way you will price and promote your product.

Pricing Policies As you know, pricing your products is an important aspect of running a successful business. You must be able to set a price high enough to cover your costs and make a profit for your business but low enough to attract customers. Among the factors to consider in setting your prices are:

- your total cost for a product, including any delivery or service charges you must pay;
- your other expenses, such as rent, advertising and promotion costs, employee payroll, supplies, and any other recurring costs;
- the amount of profit you want to make on the product;
- the price being charged by your competitors (suppliers, competitors' catalogs and price lists, and advertising will keep you in touch with this); and
- your customers' wants and needs.

In a broader sense, your prices also need to reflect what is going on in the economy. During such poor economic times as a recession, customers tend to be more price conscious. So, your prices will need to stress value. During more prosperous times, your customer will probably be less price conscious and less resistant to higher prices. You will need to price your goods or services to match your customers' expectations of quality and value, while at the same time remaining competitive in the market.

If you are planning a service business, your prices should be based on the value of the service to your customer. The price you charge may have little relationship to your costs. For example, if you provide word processing services to clients who don't know how to type or

L1 Math Skills

Market share is a specific percentage of the sales volume of the total market. Give students the following scenario: Your marketing research revealed that the national market for Gadgets is $5.8 million. You plan to manufacture and introduce a new Gadget that you think will capture 5 percent of the national market during Year 1 of your product's introduction. What are your anticipated sales for Year 1? ($290,000. $5,800,000 × .05 = $290,000)

L2 Math Skills

Give students the following scenario: During Year 2 of business operation, your goal was to capture seven percent of the national market with your brand of Gadgets. If your year-end sales were $525,000, and the national market has increased to $7.3 million, did you meet your goal? (You made it! $525,000 ÷ $7,300,000 = .07) By what percentage did your sales increase from Year 1 to Year 2? (55 %. $290,000 ÷ $525,000 = .552, or 55%!)

L3 Math Skills

Give students the following scenario: Now that your Gadget has been on the market for two years, you feel you can only estimate an increase in sales for Year 3 of about 20 percent. What will be your sales figure for Year 3? ($630,000. $525,000 × .20 = $105,000. $525,000 + $105,000 = $630,000) If the national market for Gadgets is now $9.7 million, what is your market share at the end of Year 3? (7%. $630,000 ÷ $9,700,000 = .0649 or 7%)

Feature Note

This example shows that you must prepare not only for the country you plan to visit, but also for the city, as regional differences can and do occur frequently. Within Japan, numerous business styles exist, with Tokyo styles being the one most familiar to outsiders. Likewise, preparing for a trip to Kansas City, MO requires different preparation than a trip to Los Angeles, CA.

Did You Know ?

How long should a business plan be? Depending on who is being approached, anywhere from 10–40 pages. Banks are looking for tangible assets and evidence that the loan will be repaid. The version supplied to them can run from 10–20 pages. Investors, looking to predict growth, need to see more complex evidence of future success. For them, 40 pages are often necessary.

Independent Practice

Have students write a job description for the co-op job they now hold. (Tell them not to look at their actual job description, if they were given one.) The description should include the purpose of the job, qualifications needed, duties performed, equipment used, and working conditions. For those students who do not have co-op jobs, ask them to write a description of a job they perform at home or in school.

Assess

Evaluation

Assign and review the Section 39.2 Review.

Reteaching

1. Assign and review the vocabulary terms for this section.
2. Assign and review Fact and Idea Review questions 9–11 from the Chapter Review.

Enrichment

1. Assign and review the appropriate activities in the *Student Activity Workbook*.
2. Assign and review the appropriate Critical Thinking questions from the Chapter Review.
3. Have students contact the owners or managers of three service businesses to discuss how each sets his or her business's prices. For example, why does one hair salon charge $25 for a haircut, while another charges $45?

Close

Have students write a 50- to 100-word summary that tells the content of the organization and marketing section of a business plan.

The marketing plan section should contain a description of your promotional activities. Why is this information important to include?

use a computer, they may feel your prices are a bargain. However, you must make sure that your prices are not too high and that the quality of your services are similar to or better than your competitors' to keep your customers coming back to your company.

Promotional Activities   After you have discussed your pricing policies, you need to describe your promotional activities. Here you should identify ways you will reach the greatest number of potential customers in your target market with the most economical use of your time and money.

The simplest method of promoting your business is by providing quality products to your customers. If your present customers are satisfied, their word-of-mouth advertising will attract additional customers.

You will also need to advertise through other promotional methods. As you learned in Chapter 19, there are two categories of promotion: institutional and product. Institutional promotion creates a favorable impression and goodwill for your business. Product promotion is designed to sell a product. In this part of your business plan, you will need to identify the category of promotion you will use (institutional, product, or both) as well as the advertising media you will use. State why they are right for your business.

In addition, you should present a year-long budget for advertising. You should list the types of media you intend

to use and their costs in the budget. Answering these questions will help you develop promotional strategies:

- What is the best type of advertising to reach your target market—institutional advertising, product advertising, or both?
- What are the benefits of the various media in which you have chosen to advertise your business?
- What is your advertising budget?
- What other things do you need to include in your year-long plan?

SECTION 39.2

Review

1. What elements should be included in the proposed organization part of the business plan?
2. What information should be included in your proposed good or service part of the business plan?
3. What items should be covered in the marketing plan for a new business?

Section Review Answers

1. Ownership, steps in establishing business, and personal needs.
2. Details related to your proposed product or service to be offered including your manufacturing plans, inventory policies, and suppliers.
3. Proposed pricing policies, such as costs and markups compared to competition. Also promotional activities and your promotional plan.

Caption Answer

Describing your promotional activities shows investors or lenders how you intend to promote your product to the public. It also provides a guide to how to run this aspect of the business and helps determine how much money will be necessary for promotional activities.

SECTION 39.3

Objectives

After completing this section, you will be able to

- describe the elements found in the financial section of a business plan,
- identify sources of equity capital, and
- identify sources of debt capital.

Terms to Know

- equity capital
- debt capital
- collateral
- credit union

Financial Plan

As you know, it is expensive to start and operate a business. Unless you are already wealthy, you will need to borrow money to begin business operations. Potential investors and lenders will want to look at the financial estimates for your new business. They will want to know that their efforts will be as profitable for them as it will be for you.

The financial plan section shows lenders and investors what monies are needed to start the business. It includes statements of personal and external sources of capital. It also shows statements of projected income and expenses expected for at least the first year of operation.

Sources of Capital

Capital means the funds needed to finance the operation of a business. The term capital also includes all goods used to produce other goods. In business, capital may also include the property which you own and your cash resources. Nevertheless, when we refer to capital in this chapter, we are talking about anything that can be converted into money.

When entrepreneurs open their own businesses, they usually need a substantial amount of capital. There are

several ways to raise the capital for a new business. You can use money from your personal savings. You can also borrow money from banks, credit unions, relatives, friends, suppliers, and/or previous business owners.

The method you choose to raise money depends on the amount involved. Money needed for operating expenses is usually repaid within a year. A large amount of money borrowed to build a new facility, to purchase equipment, or to start an inventory will be repaid over a longer period of time.

Equity Capital

Raising money from within your company or by selling part of the interest in the business is called using **equity capital.** The advantage to using equity capital is that you do not need to repay the money or pay interest. However, the investor becomes a co-owner in your business. The larger the amount of interest in your business you sell, the greater degree of control you will lose to your investors.

Equity capital sources include

- personal savings,
- partners, and
- shareholders.

Personal Savings   The most common method of financing a business is using personal savings. Even though you might not want to do this, you probably cannot avoid investing all or part of your savings. As you know, starting any new business involves risk. Your prospective investors and lenders will expect you to share in that risk.

Partners   As you learned in Chapter 37, having partners is another way to raise money for your business. Partners may bring in their own money and have access to other sources unavailable to you. However, if you form a partnership, you lessen your degree of ownership. You may have to share control of the business with your partner.

Shareholders   If you form a corporation, you sell stock to shareholders as a way of raising capital. As you learned earlier in the chapter, you need to incorporate and obtain a charter to operate as a corporation.

Because each shareholder in a corporation has limited liability (that is, limited responsibility for debt), a corporation can raise large amounts of money from its shareholders. Although shareholders influence general corporate policy decisions, you can still control the corporation's daily activities by holding a majority of the shares.

Debt Capital

Raising funds by borrowing money is called using **debt capital.** Debt capital can work to your advantage. Borrowing money and repaying it builds your credit

Focus

Bell Ringer Activity

Have students brainstorm a list of the ways you can raise capital to start a business.

Introducing the Section

Review students' answers from the Bell Ringer Activity. It is often said that the financial section is the heart of a business plan. While a lender may only skim through the prior two sections, he or she will probably read every word of the financial section.

Recall with students the business plan/road map analogy. Your financial data gives you and your lenders and investors the "big picture." It shows all of you that the money put into the business will yield a profitable return. Thus, it's essential that your financial picture is in sharp focus.

Teach

Guided Practice

1. Read Section 39.3 with students.
2. MarkEd Resource Center, (800) 448-0398, offers materials on financing that are appropriate for use with this section.
3. Have a loan officer from a local lending institution speak about obtaining financing for a business start-up. Ask this person to bring to class copies of loan applications and/or transparencies for use with an overhead projector so students can become familiar with loan applications, the terminology, and the documentation necessary to begin the loan application process.

Lifelong Learning

Developing a Business Plan

Due to the importance of the business plan, students are advised to do further study on this area of marketing. Business magazines and books devoted to the subject, including *Inc.* magazine's *How to Write a Successful Business Plan,* are good supplementary reading. In addition, taking courses specifically geared to those involved in writing a business plan would be valuable for those pursuing entrepreneurial endeavors. However, even those who plan a corporate career should be encouraged to continue their studies in order to better evaluate potential businesses they might do business with during their careers.

Discussion Starters

Discuss with students the process of business planning. Does it seem tedious? Does it seem like too much time spent for not enough immediate reward?

Remind students that, like painting a picture or writing a book, creating a business plan is a cumulative, developmental process that takes time, energy, patience, and analytical skill. A potential businessperson who cannot go through with this process may not have what it takes to commit to a business.

If you were an investor who was asked to put money into a business that had no business plan, what factors would determine whether or not you would do it? (Possibilities include (1) whether the potential owner is starting a brand new business or buying the business from someone else, (2) if the latter, whether or not the existing business is successful, (3) the potential owner's experience with the type of business he or she proposes to buy, and (4) local market needs for the business.)

Independent Practice

Obtain from the SBA copies of the Business Plan for Retailers, the Business Plan for Small Manufacturers, and the Business Plan for Home-Based Businesses. Give each student a copy of each business plan. Have each student compare and contrast these plans, and prepare an analysis of how each plan is similar and how each is different with respect to the information included.

standing. This means it will be easier for you to borrow money in the future. While you must pay interest when you repay your loan, the interest you pay is a tax-deductible business expense. In addition, if you raise money by borrowing it, no ownership passes to the lender.

However, there is a major disadvantage to debt capital. If you cannot pay back your debt, you could be forced into bankruptcy. Investors or co-owners may not force this, but they will want to tell you how to run your business.

Debt capital sources include

- banks,
- credit unions,
- friends and relatives, and
- suppliers and previous owners.

Banks   Commercial banks, the most numerous and widespread lending agencies in the United States, are the most common sources of business financing. They know their local area and local economy well and offer a number of different loans and services on competitive and government-regulated terms.

Banks evaluate potential borrowers on criteria called the six *C's* of credit: *capital, collateral, capability, character, coverage,* and *circumstances.*

- *Capital.* How much of your own money or capital is to be invested in your new business? Banks, like other potential investors, will want to know how much capital you are willing to invest into your new venture.
- *Collateral.* What assets (things of monetary value) can be used as collateral for a loan? (We will talk more about assets in Chapter 40.) **Collateral** is something of value that a borrower pledges to a lender to ensure repayment of a loan. Some examples of collateral are jewelry, vehicles, bonds, stocks, machinery, the cash value of insurance policies, and real estate. Lenders will usually require the value of the collateral to be greater than the amount of the loan.

Some banks will require a guaranty of personal assets (in effect, a promise that you have the assets you claim to have) and a pledge that you will repay the loan. Banks want to know that your loan will be repaid, even if your business fails.

- *Capability and Character.* A resume of your previous training and related work experience, including professional and personal references, will answer questions about your capability and character.
- *Coverage and Circumstances.* Banks will want to know the amount of insurance coverage that you will carry and the general circumstances of your business as described in the description and analysis section of your business plan.

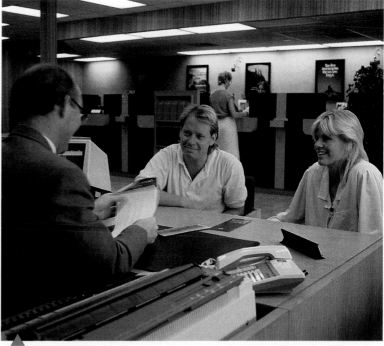

▲ *Banks are a common source **of business financing. What criteria do banks evaluate borrowers on?***

Capital

Ben and Jerry's raised $750,000 of investor capital in order to expand its business when it wrote its first business plan. A good business plan can be just as important as a good idea or a good product.

Six *C's* of credit: *capital, collateral, capability, character, coverage,* and *circumstances.*

Filling out loan application forms can be a lengthy and often tedious process. Contact a banker or the loan officer of your local bank. He or she will help you complete the necessary documentation.

Credit Unions   A credit union is a cooperative association formed by labor unions or groups of employees for the benefit of its members. Credit unions often charge lower interest rates on loans than banks do. To borrow money from a credit union, however, you must be a member. Check with your parents, guardians, and/or relatives to determine your eligibility, since credit unions often accept memberships for relatives. Credit unions also use the six *C*'s of credit to determine if they will accept your loan application.

Friends and Relatives   Many people begin their businesses with funds borrowed from relatives and friends. You should be cautious about doing this, however. An old saying tells us that two of the quickest ways to lose friends are to lend them money or to borrow money from them. You must consider whether starting a new business is worth the risk of losing or alienating people close to you.

If you do choose to borrow money from your family or friends, avoid future problems and misunderstandings by putting all agreements in writing. Identify the period of the loan, any interest to be paid, and your payment schedule.

If relatives or friends become investors in your business, determine the amount of control you will retain, whether you can buy back their interest at a later time, and how you will share the profits with them. Be sure that each person investing in your business can afford and is willing to possibly lose the money invested, if the business fails. Remember, no business, even yours, is guaranteed to succeed.

Suppliers and Previous Owners   Some suppliers may provide you with a low interest loan to purchase inventory, furniture, fixtures, and equipment on a delayed payment basis. This method of raising capital can improve your credit rating. It can also allow you to stretch your available cash. Also, as mentioned earlier, the interest on loan payments is a tax-deductible business expense.

If you are purchasing an existing business, consider the previous owner as a potential source of capital. Many sole proprietors want to see their businesses continue after their own retirement. They may be willing to provide you with a loan and a favorable repayment plan to get you started.

As you can see, there are many potential sources of capital to explore when seeking financing for your business. To make sure you have carefully researched all the available sources of capital, answer the following list of questions:

1. What amount of your own savings will you put into the business?

Real World

MARKETING

A Bird's-eye View of Success

The winter of 1916 was typically cold in the northern reaches of Canada. It was so cold, in fact, that the food supplies that reached a 30-year-old student of wildlife on assignment from America arrived frozen solid. Most people would curse frozen food. This man saw an opportunity in it. He went to work on a technique for quick-freezing vegetables, which he later sold to General Foods for $1 million. His name, which still appears on its frozen food line, was Clarence Birdseye.

2. Do you know the pros and cons of debt capital versus equity capital?
3. Did you check all of the available sources of capital?
4. Did you complete a personal financial statement?
5. Did you contact a banker or loan officer for a loan application?
6. Do you have a good rating on the six *C*'s of credit?
7. Did you contact a professional advisor, such as a lawyer or accountant, about ways to finance your business?

After you have identified your source or sources of capital, the last part of your business plan is to develop your financial statements. Your financial statements display your business income and expenses and help persuade investors to loan you money. These financial statements and the math needed to complete them will be discussed in Chapter 40.

SECTION 39.3 *Review*

1. Name the two major parts found in the financial section of a business plan.
2. Identify three main sources of equity capital.
3. Identify the main sources of debt capital.

Assess

Evaluation

Assign and review the Section 39.3 Review.

Reteaching

1. Assign and review the vocabulary terms for this section.
2. Assign and review Fact and Idea Review questions 12–15 from the Chapter Review.

Enrichment

1. Assign and review the appropriate activities in the *Student Activity Workbook.*
2. Assign and review the appropriate Critical Thinking questions from the Chapter Review.
3. Assign and review the Building Academic Skills Activities, Application Projects, Linking School to Work Activities, and Performance Assessment from the Chapter Review.
4. Have students contact one small business owner in your community and ask to thoroughly review his or her business plan. Then have students report on the following: (1) the difficulties the business owner encountered in creating the plan; (2) how these difficulties were overcome; and, (3) how the business owner uses his or her plan to find investors, recruit managers for the business, and form relationships with vendors. Students should write their findings in 250 words.

Close

Have students write a 25- to 50-word summary that tells the content of the financial section of a business plan.

Section Review Answers

1. Sources of capital and projected income and expenses.
2. Personal savings, partners, and shareholders.
3. Banks, credit unions, relatives and friends, suppliers and previous owners.

523

39 C H A P T E R *Review*

Answers

Vocabulary Review

See Glossary for definitions.

Fact and Idea Review

1. It tells how you think the business should be run and reveals your attitude toward your customers, employees, and competitors.
2. It identifies your personal education, strengths, weaknesses, and a plan for personal development.
3. The geographical area from which a business draws its customers. Because it will help you to identify the competition and any trends that will have an impact on your business.
4. Personal income minus taxes. You need to know if the area has enough customers with enough buying income to support your proposed business.
5. The Yellow Pages, annual reports, trade associations, your local Chamber of Commerce, and business publications.
6. The needs and wants of different groups of potential buyers must be addressed differently.
7. The process individuals use to decide what they will buy and from where and whom they will buy it. You can use this information to make decisions about how to best serve certain customers.
8. Whether you will buy or rent the property, how you will control customer traffic, and nearness to your competition.
9. Potential investors need to know that you can identify the essential jobs your business will need to run properly.
10. Manufacturing plans, inventory plans, and suppliers.

524

Vocabulary Review

Use each of the following terms in a sentence, based on your reading of the chapter content.

business plan
business philosophy
trading area
buying behavior
job descriptions
organization chart
equity capital
debt capital
collateral
credit union

Fact and Idea Review

1. What is a business philosophy? Why is it important? (Sec. 39.1)
2. Why is self-analysis critical to developing a business plan? (Sec. 39.1)
3. What is a trading area? Why is it important to analyze the trading area in your business plan? (Sec. 39.1)
4. What is meant by disposable income? Why is it important to know how much disposable income your potential customers have? (Sec. 39.1)
5. What sources can an entrepreneur use to find out about competition that already exists for a proposed product? (Sec. 39.1)
6. Why is the identification of your target market essential to your business plan? (Sec. 39.1)
7. What is buying behavior? Why is it important to understand customer buying behavior in your target market? (Sec. 39.1)
8. Identify at least three factors to consider when planning a location for a business. (Sec. 39.1)
9. Why is planning for personnel needs important for a new business? (Sec. 39.2)
10. What information is included in the proposed good or service part of the business plan? (Sec. 39.2)
11. Tell five things you should consider when setting your pricing policies. (Sec. 39.2)
12. What is the difference between debt capital and equity capital? (Sec. 39.3)
13. What is the most common method of financing a business? (Sec. 39.3)
14. How can a corporation raise capital? (Sec. 39.3)
15. What is a credit union? (Sec. 39.3)

Critical Thinking

1. How could a poorly written business plan hurt a new business venture?
2. React to this statement: "Employees are the most valued asset to a small business." Do you agree or disagree? Explain your answer.
3. What are some of the factors that a new business can control? What are some uncontrollable factors?
4. How can you determine a need for a product?
5. How would you determine which job positions you need to fill in your new business?
6. Under what conditions can a small business take the role of being a price-cutter?
7. Why would you have an accountant, attorney, or business advisor assist you in establishing your business?
8. What factors would you consider in selecting a lender for a business?

Building Academic Skills

Math

1. An employee was paid $5.75 an hour and double time on Sunday. What was the total weekly wage, if the employee worked 4 hours on Sunday, 4 hours on Wednesday, $3\frac{1}{2}$ hours on Thursday, and 6 hours on Saturday?

Communication

2. With the direction of your instructor, write a business letter inviting a local businessperson to speak on the importance of store location to a successful business.

Technology

3. Interview a small business owner about some of the new equipment or other technologies used in his or her business today, which were not available when he/she first started. Write a 100-word report on your findings.

Application Project

1. Begin to develop a business plan using instructor guidelines or those prepared by National DECA for the *Entrepreneurship Participating Event* by preparing a three-page section (Part I) entitled "Description and Analysis of the Business Situation." These activities will help you complete this project.

---

11. Your total cost for a product, your other expenses, the amount of profit you want to make.
12. Debt capital is money raised from lenders. Equity capital is money raised by selling part of the business.
13. With personal savings.
14. By selling shares of stock in the company.
15. Capital, collateral, capability, character, coverage, and circumstances.

16. A cooperative association formed by labor unions or groups of employees for the benefit of its members.

Critical Thinking

1. One possibility: if a plan is poorly prepared, it might prevent a lending agency from lending money to initiate the business.
2. Students should explain that the success of a business depends on an employee's performance.

a. Select a proposed business operation selling consumer products. Describe the type of business, the product involved, appealing factors about the business, factors you think will make it more successful, and proposed hours of operation.

b. Describe your aspirations and career objectives, educational experiences, and related work experiences that will help you be successful in the business. Make a chart of your competitors' strengths and weaknesses.

c. Analyze your competitors' goods, services, facilities, prices, selection, advertising, personnel, and distribution or delivery methods.

d. Use the *Survey of Buying Power* by Sales and Marketing Management along with U.S. census data to identify the economic data for the location of the proposed business.

e. Identify the target market for the proposed business by looking at potential customers' geographic and demographic characteristics.

f. Visit the city or township clerk and write a report about zoning regulations for your proposed site.

g. List all important factors for the proposed business location, such as traffic patterns and costs of renting or owning.

2. Continue the development of a business plan by preparing a three-page section (Part II) entitled "Organization and Marketing Plan." These activities will help you complete this section of your project.

a. Investigate which form of ownership you would select for a business. Write a report on the advantages and disadvantages that affected your decision.

b. Write your state department of commerce to get information about the steps required to establish a business in your state.

c. Prepare an organization chart for a new business. Explain the need for the positions and the reporting relationships that exist.

d. Prepare a written report on the advantages of using a certified public accountant to maintain records.

e. Prepare a written report on the pricing policies you will use in your selected business. Include information on price image, loss leaders, above-average markup, average markup, below average markup, special sales, and markdown policies.

f. Develop a one-month promotional plan for your business. The plan should contain a budget, selection of media, and a plan to evaluate its effectiveness.

g. Develop a list of special promotional events that would be conducted for each month of the year for your business.

h. Collect several employee application forms from area stores. Design a new application form for your business.

i. Investigate wage and salary data for jobs identified in your business plan. Explain the salary plan and benefit package that you would offer to new employees.

Linking School to Work

Select a product line available at your training station. Investigate the pricing policies used at your training station for selected items in the product line. Write a 100-word report on your investigation.

Performance Assessment

Role Play

Situation. You work in a restaurant. A co-worker plans to establish his own quick-serve restaurant. He believes that he will be successful because there is an available location and he is a good cook. He thinks he will have no trouble obtaining a loan because his proposed business has so much potential. He does not believe that it will be necessary to develop a business plan. Your task is to explain the importance of a business plan and convince your co-worker to develop one.

Evaluation. You will be evaluated on how well you do the following:

- Discuss the importance and purpose of the business plan.
- Identify the major sections of a business plan.
- Present a precise, well-organized presentation.

Written Report

By using available business magazines in school or at home, write a 150-word report on a successful new business venture.

Complete the Chapter 39 Computer Application that appears in the Student Activity Workbook.

and federal laws, rules and regulations.

8. Terms of the loan; reputation of the lender; ability to provide technical assistance; reputation for service location and ability to provide related business services such as money accounts.

Building Academic Skills

Math

1. $100.62. [($5.75 \times 4 \times 2) + ($5.75 \times 3.5) + ($5.75 \times 6) = $100.62]

Communication

2. Students should be prepared to ask the businessperson questions about store location.

Technology

3. Students should have a list of questions to ask the person they interview.

Application Project

1.–2. Students should use the information as outlined in the chapter to begin to construct their own business plan. The third section of the business plan will be completed in Chapter 40.

Linking School to Work

Answers depend on the work situation.

Performance Assessment

Refer to the *DECA Competitive Events Handbook* for evaluation guidelines.

 ## Computer Application

Optional activity. Refer to the *Marketing Software Binder* for template and user information.

Evaluation

Administer the reproducible test for Chapter 39, or construct your own using the Testmaker software.

3. Controllable factors: store location, merchandising techniques, pricing, store image and promotion, number of employees. Uncontrollable factors: competition, technology, economic conditions, seasons or climate, laws, rules, and regulations.

4. Answers will vary. Point out that entrepreneurs determine a need for a good or service by thoroughly studying the market.

5. Thorough analysis of tasks that must be done and decisions made by the owner of how many of

those tasks he or she can handle. Those tasks left must be analyzed and either contracted out or budget to hire.

6. Often when a business begins operation it can assume the role of a price-cutter because it has fewer expenses and may be willing to take a smaller profit margin initially to encourage repeat business and to attract new customers.

7. These professionals help to insure that the business will be in compliance with all local, state,

Chapter Overview

This chapter tells how to identify and plan for the capital needs of a proposed business by developing a well thought out financial section to a business plan.

Springboard

Begin by discussing all of the things for which a person is financially responsible when living on his or her own (for example, car payments, house or rent payments, child care, food, etc.). Then have students list the potential costs involved in maintaining a business (for example, rent, utilities, buying supplies, etc.). Finally, have students brainstorm some ways that good financial planning is achieved. (Answers should include such things as taking into account current and anticipated income and expenses.) Just as students' personal financial needs must be met, a business's financial needs must also be met. Both take good financial planning.

Prereading

List the section objectives to discuss with students. Have students skim the chapter, looking at the pictures, reading the captions, and noting the heads. Ask questions to ensure that the students have a minimal understanding of the chapter structure.

Preteaching the Vocabulary

Have students write each bold-faced term in the chapter and, based on its definition, generate their own personal symbol for the term. Review the vocabulary definitions before you begin reading the chapter and have several students share their personal symbols for each term.

Financing the Business

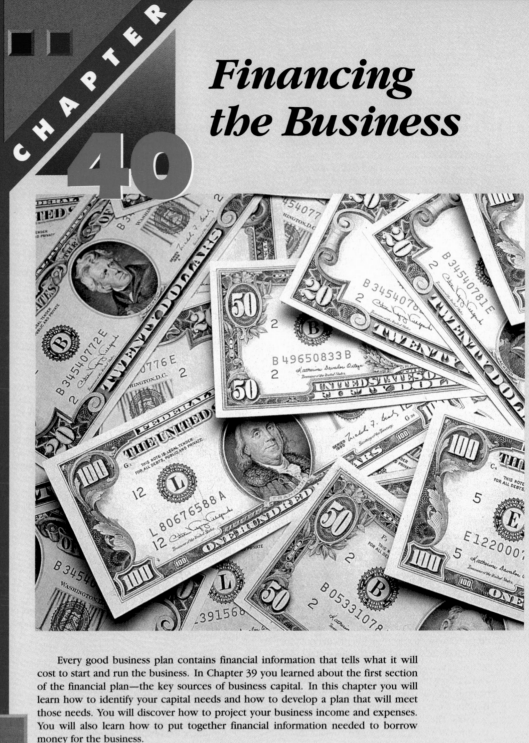

Every good business plan contains financial information that tells what it will cost to start and run the business. In Chapter 39 you learned about the first section of the financial plan—the key sources of business capital. In this chapter you will learn how to identify your capital needs and how to develop a plan that will meet those needs. You will discover how to project your business income and expenses. You will also learn how to put together financial information needed to borrow money for the business.

Classroom Management

For the Teacher
- Teacher's Annotated Editions for all workbooks
- Teacher's Manual for *School-to-Work Handbook*
- *Testing Binder*
- *Transparency Binder*
- *Marketing Software Binder*
- *Marketing Career Portfolio*
- *Lesson Plans*

For the Student
- *Student Activity Workbook*
- *Marketing Math Workbook*
- *School-to-Work Handbook*
- *Student Software*
- *International Case Studies*
- *Marketing Career Portfolio*

SECTION 40.1

Objectives

After completing this section, you will be able to

- describe the purpose of preparing financial documents,
- develop a personal financial statement, and
- determine start-up costs for a business.

Terms to Know

- personal financial statement
- asset
- liability
- start-up costs

The Financial Part of a Business Plan

The most common reason for writing a business plan is to obtain financing for the business. For example, if you want to start a small business providing equipment for making copies of documents, you will need to buy the copying equipment. You may need a loan to help you buy this equipment.

A major purpose of the business plan is to put together the financial information relating to your business. This information is presented on financial documents that describe your personal financial situation, as well as the financial needs of your business. Preparing financial statements helps you find out the amount of money you need to operate the business. It also helps you determine how much money you may need to borrow.

When you go to a lender to borrow money, the lender wants to know you will be able to repay a loan. A lender will look at your credit history, items you own that can be sold to pay off the loan (collateral), and your prospects for business success. Your financial documents give a potential lender a picture of you and your business.

Five important financial documents are the personal financial statement, the start-up cost estimate, the income statement, the balance sheet, and the cash flow statement.

In this section you will look at the first two financial statements.

The Personal Financial Statement

The **personal financial statement** is a summary of your current personal financial condition. A personal financial statement is like a snapshot of your finances. It is an important part of any loan application for a new business. It measures your financial progress to date and shows how well you have met your personal expenses in the past. It compares your *assets* to your *liabilities* on a specific date. An **asset** is anything of monetary value that you own. A **liability** is a debt you owe.

To develop a personal financial statement, you first list your assets. You should be realistic about the current value of your assets. For example, if you have a van worth $8,000, do not round it up to $10,000. Be sure to list all your cash assets (checking and savings accounts) and any investments (stocks, bonds, mutual funds, retirement funds) and personal assets (furniture, cars, clothes, and home). You will need to estimate the present value for each item. A lender will look for assets that you can sell to pay off the business loan, if your business does not do as well as expected.

Next, list your debts. Include such debts as your charge accounts, mortgage balance, and school and automobile loans. Add all your assets and all your debts to find a total for each. Then calculate your personal net worth by subtracting your debts from your assets. Figure 40–1 on page 528 shows an example of a personal financial statement.

Practice 1

1. If you have assets of $10,000 (car), $8,000 (savings), $1,000 (cash value of life insurance), $1,500 (cash), and personal property worth $1,500, what are your total assets?
2. If you have liabilities of $7,000 (car loan), $2,500 (student loan), and $500 (credit card balances), what are your total liabilities?
3. What is your net worth?

Note: Answers to all practice sets appear on page 543.

A lender will look at your personal financial statement as a part of determining whether you and your business are a good credit risk. In addition, a lender will require a copy of your personal tax returns. Your tax returns will

Chapter 40 *Financing the Business* **527**

SECTION 40.1

Focus

Bell Ringer Activity

Divide students into four groups and give each group a type of manufacturing or retail business. No two groups should have the same type of business. Give each group five to ten minutes to generate a list of the capital requirements they think that each business would need to start up a business.

Introducing the Section

Review each group's answers from the Bell Ringer Activity and list them on the chalkboard. Note the differences in the start-up needs for each type of business. Make sure students understand that start-up costs are either one-time costs or continuing costs. Also included in start-up costs are such things as the estimated time between starting the business and earning income from the first sales, and operating expenses that must be paid before cash is received from sales.

Teach

Guided Practice

1. Read Section 40.1 with students.
2. Use the transparencies for this section.
3. Invite a guest from a credit reporting agency to discuss credit reports and the importance of maintaining good credit. Ask the speaker to bring sample credit reports to use as visual aids so students understand how to read them. Also have the person discuss how erroneous reporting on credit reports can be corrected.

Meeting Special Needs

Gifted

For students who would benefit from the additional work of an independent project, assign the task of researching a successful business in the area and discovering through written reports and/or personal interviews how the concepts described in this chapter affected the business in its first few years.

For example, how did their initial estimates of profitability vary from paper to real numbers? What sources of financing did the business utilize and what would they recommend to other businesses in the start-up phase?

Have students generate a list of the one-time start-up costs and the continuing costs of running your school store. (Answers will vary. Possible one-time costs include renovation of and fixtures for an existing space in your school. Continuing costs include ongoing purchase of inventory and fixtures, purchase of supplies, repairs, etc.)

If you do not have a school store, choose a local business with which all students are familiar and have them generate a list of what they think were its start-up costs, and what are now its continuing costs.

Critical Thinking

Ask students why banks require collateral to be worth more than the amount of the loan, and why lenders prefer to be repaid rather than cashing in on collateral. (If the lender is forced to sell the collateral due to borrower default, the lender probably won't realize full value.)

Why would a bank require a borrower to insure the property that the bank will hold as collateral? (In case of the property's damage or loss, the lender will be repaid by the insurance company.)

Personal Financial Statement

August, 19 – –

Assets

Cash	$ 500.00
Savings accounts	1,500.00
Stocks, bonds, other securities	750.00
Life insurance cash value	0.00
Auto (1995 van)	18,000.00
Real estate (residence)	75,000.00
Vested pension plan	25,000.00
Other assets (lakefront property)	15,000.00
TOTAL ASSETS	$ 135,750.00

Liabilities

Accounts payable (credit cards)	1,875.00
Contracts payable	0.00
Notes payable (mortgage)	28,500.00
Taxes payable	2,500.00
Real estate loans	0.00
Other liabilities (1995 van)	15,500.00
TOTAL LIABILITIES	$ 48,375.00

TOTAL ASSETS	$ 135,750.00
TOTAL LIABILITIES	$ 48,375.00
NET WORTH	$ 87,375.00

Figure 40–1

A personal financial statement shows your financial condition to date. Based on the figures shown here, what is your total net worth?

show how you have earned money in the past. A credit report will also be requested. A credit report will show how well you have paid off debts in the past. If you plan to continue working at another job, the lender will also be interested in whether your other income can support your personal expenses until your new business becomes profitable.

Estimating Start-up Costs

Before starting your business, you need to know how much it will cost you. **Start-up costs** are a projection of how much money you will need for your first year of operation. You also need an estimate of operating costs after the first year.

Start-up costs vary for each type of business, but are based on factors such as the following:

528   Unit 11   *Entrepreneurship*

- *The nature of your proposed business*—manufacturing, wholesale, or retail businesses all have different needs and requirements. See Table 40-1.
- *The size of your business*—small businesses usually do not require as much money to start as big businesses.
- *The amount and kind of inventory needed*—for example, it is much more costly to purchase inventory for a large supermarket than for a neighborhood convenience store.
- *The estimated time between starting the business and earning income from the first sales.*
- *The operating expenses that must be paid before cash is received from sales.*

Business start-up costs may be one-time costs or continuing costs. *One-time costs* are expenses that will not be repeated after you begin operating the business. Examples of one-time costs include licenses and permits; deposits for telephone installation; and charges for installation of equipment, fixtures, and machinery.

More About

Start-up Costs

Many business consultants advise new businesses for a fee. Gaining practical advice and know-how from a consultant or from an accountant who works with similar businesses could actually save money. Many accountants will offer a free consultation to a new business owner to answer questions regarding start-up costs.

Caption Answer

$135,750 − $48,375 = $87,375

Start-up Costs

Table 40-1

Type of Business

Type of Costs	Manufacturing	Retail	Wholesale	Service
Deposits (rent, utilities, telephone)	7,500–20,300	3,900–35,300	7,400–17,700	4,200–14,000
Furniture and Equipment	20,100–42,000	21,300–42,300	22,500–54,900	19,700–54,100
Machinery and Equipment	10,000–60,000	5,000–32,500	19,900–33,900	——
Transportation Equipment	32,000–45,000	32,000–45,000	32,000–45,000	——
Building Improvements	11,300–42,000	11,300–52,500	15,000–30,000	15,000–60,000
Professional Fees	1,500–4,000	1,500–4,000	1,500–4,000	1,500–4,000
Advertising	3,000–10,000	10,000–15,000	3,000–10,000	3,000–10,000
Working Capital	9,900–45,000	3,800–93,700	25,200–75,000	9,900–35,100
Inventory	13,000–57,500	35,000–157,500	23,000–122,500	——
Totals	$108,300–326,300	$123,800–477,800	$149,500–393,000	$53,300–177,900

Table 40–1

Start-up costs vary depending on the type of business. Why is less money generally needed to establish a service business than to establish a manufacturing, retail, or wholesale business?

Continuing costs are operating expenses you will pay throughout the life of the business. Examples of continuing costs are such items as payroll, monthly rent, advertising, supplies, insurance, repairs, maintenance, and taxes. Most businesses are not profitable immediately, so estimate at least three months of continuing costs when deciding the amount of cash you will need for start-up costs.

You can find information to help you plan your financial needs from several sources. Your local library

Practice 2

If you have one-time costs of $18,000 and average monthly costs of $3,200, what are your total costs for the first quarter of operation? Using the same average monthly costs, what are total costs for the year?

Chapter 40   *Financing the Business*   **529**

L1 Math Skills

Give student's the following scenario: You estimate that your business start-up costs will be $10,200. You have saved $8,400.

(a) What percentage of the total amount do you have? (82%. $8,400 ÷ $10,200 = .82)

(b) What percentage of the total amount do you need? (18%. $10,200 − $8,400 = $1,800. $1,800 ÷ $10,200 = 0.1766 or .18. Or, 1.00 − .82 = .18)

L2 Math Skills

Ask students to complete the following:

(a) Subtract the decimals numbers you calculated for the L1(a) and L1(b) activities above. What is your answer? (.64. .82 − .18 5 = .64)

(b) Multiply the decimal numbers you calculated for the L1(a) and L1(b) activities above. What is your answer? (0.1476. .82 × .18 5 = 0.1476)

(c) Divide your answer for the L1(a) activity by your answer for the L1(b) activity. Round your answer to the hundredth. (4.56. .82 ÷ .18 = 4.55555 or 4.56)

L3 Math Skills

Tell students the following: You refigured your business start-up costs and determined that you will need about 15 percent more than you originally anticipated in the L1 Math Skills Activity. How much money will you need altogether to start your business? Write your answer in words. (Eleven Thousand Seven Hundred Thirty Dollars. $10,200 × .15 = $1,530. $10,200 + $1,530 = $11,730)

Independent Practice

1. Have students research types of software programs used to create financial statements. In your classroom discussion, give a demonstration of financial software on your classroom computer. You may also wish to review a personal financial manager software program such as "Quicken." Impress upon students that, even now, they should be managing their personal finances.

2. If you were not able to arrange for a guest speaker from a credit company to visit the class, assign students the task of researching what type of information is contained in a credit report.

   Students may not realize that even delinquent payments on a gasoline credit card can show up on a credit report. Also, there is always the possibility that information recorded on a credit report will belong to another person with a similar name. Consumers have varying rights in different states.

   Have students report on the rights in your state and on the way to go about verifying the information contained in a credit report.

Assess

Evaluation

Assign and review the Section 40.1 Review.

---

will have books on writing business plans and starting a new business. The Small Business Administration (SBA) provides information to people who want to start a new business. The SBA has developed a worksheet for estimating start-up costs and operating expenses for new businesses. (See Figure 40–2.)

Start-up Cost Worksheet

ESTIMATED MONTHLY EXPENSES

Item	Your estimate of monthly expenses based on sales of $_____ per year	Your estimate of how much cash you need to start your business (See column 3)	What to put in column 2. (These figures are typical for one kind of business. You will have to decide how many months to allow for in your business.)
	Column 1	Column 2	Column 3
Salary of owner	$	$	2 times column 1
All other salaries and wages			3 times column 1
Rent			3 times column 1
Advertising			3 times column 1
Delivery expense			3 times column 1
Supplies			3 times column 1
Telephone and telegraph			3 times column 1
Other utilities			3 times column 1
Insurance			Payment required by insurance company
Taxes, including Social Security			4 times column 1
Interest			3 times column 1
Maintenance			3 times column 1
Legal and other professional fees			3 times column 1
Miscellaneous			3 times column 1
STARTING COSTS YOU ONLY HAVE TO PAY ONCE			Leave column 2 blank
Fixtures and equipment			Fill in worksheet 3 on page 12 and put the total here
Decorating and remodeling			Talk it over with a contractor
Installation of fixtures and equipment			Talk to suppliers from whom you buy these
Starting inventory			Suppliers will probably help you estimate this
Deposits with public utilities			Find out from utility companies
Legal and other professional fees			Lawyer, accountant, and so on
Licenses and permits			Find out from city offices what you have to have
Advertising and promotion			Estimate what you'll use for opening
Accounts receivable			What you need in order to buy more stock until credit customers pay
Cash			For unexpected expenses or losses, special purchases, etc.
Other			Make a separate list and enter total
TOTAL ESTIMATED CASH YOU NEED TO START WITH	$	$	Add up all the numbers in column 2

Figure 40–2

The SBA provides worksheets to assist new business owners in estimating monthly expenses. Why is a worksheet helpful to beginning businesses?

Caption Answer

A worksheet is helpful because it provides a visual representation of continuing and one-time costs and the approximate amount of expense for each, and the total estimated cash to start a business.

More About

The SBA

The SBA does not have a "grant" program or make loans, but it does guarantee loans up to $75,000 to qualified small businesses by banks and other financial institutions. There is no stated minimum loan, but most lenders are hesitant to process loans of less than $25,000.

Real World

Head Count

Capital refers, among other things, to the money entrepreneurs need to start up or grow a new business. The term comes from the Latin word for head—caput. From ancient times to the present, nomadic herdsmen have measured their wealth by the number of cattle, sheep, or other animals they have. That number was determined by physically counting heads. That practice and its association with wealth are preserved to this day in the word capital.

You can also get estimates of start-up costs from people who are already in a similar business or from related trade associations. State and local government agencies, such as your state department of commerce and local chamber of commerce, are valuable sources of cost information. Here are some resources for information:

1. Small Business Administration
   Office of Business Development
   Washington, DC 20416

2. Dun & Bradstreet
   90 Church Street
   New York, NY 10007

3. Bank of America
   Small Business Reporter
   Department 3120
   P.O. Box 37000
   San Francisco, CA 94137

4. Robert Morris Associates
   Philadelphia National Bank Building
   Philadelphia, PA 19107

5. National Computing Resources Corporation
   Attention: Expense in Retailing
   3095 Kettering Blvd., 1st Floor
   Dayton, OH 45439

Other sources of information about start-up costs include public libraries and local, college, and university business libraries. Better Business Bureaus and business development agencies are also sources of information.

Personal Costs

Unless you are starting your new business while also working at another job, you will need money to live on during the start-up phase. Your *personal costs* are those expenses that are necessary for you to live. You will need to project your monthly living expenses and household cash needs for at least your first year of business. If you are starting a new business, you may be able to meet your personal expenses by working at another job or by relying on a spouse's income.

If you are not planning to work outside your business or do not have any other source of income, you must plan to have enough cash on hand to pay your personal expenses. Some experts suggest that you have enough start-up capital available to pay for up to six months of living expenses.

BRIGHT IDEAS

Take a Hint from Nature

In 1948 a Swiss engineer named George de Mestral went for a nature walk and got hooked on an idea. When he returned from his walk, Mestral found a number of burrs stuck to his clothing. They were so difficult to remove that he decided right then and there to find out what made them cling so tenaciously. When he examined them under a microscope, he discovered that they consisted of thin, strandlike hooks. It was the hooks that allowed the burrs to attach themselves to fabrics and animal fur alike. It struck Mestral at once that this might be a way to fasten two pieces of cloth together.

After eight years of research and development, what Mestral came up with was two strips of interlocking fabric. One contained thin, strandlike hooks; the other, bands of loops. When the two strips were pressed together, they adhered so thoroughly that they had to be ripped apart—or at least that was what it sounded like. Today, the characteristic "rip" of Velcro is heard when people take off their shoes, open their lunch sacks, or shift their possessions from earthquake-proofed shelves.

Creativity Challenge Form teams of 3–5 people. Then let your fingers do the walking through the pages of some nature-oriented publications like *Scientific American, Discovery, National Geographic,* or *Smithsonian.* Share the most interesting photos of nature subjects you find and see what product ideas they inspire.

Chapter 40 *Financing the Business* **531**

Reteaching

1. Assign and review the vocabulary terms for this section.
2. Assign and review Fact and Idea Review questions 1–3 from the Chapter Review.
3. Review each of the vocabulary terms for this section, using students' personal symbols from the Preteaching the Vocabulary section as a visual aid.

Enrichment

1. Assign and review the appropriate activities in the *Student Activity Workbook.*
2. Assign and review the appropriate Critical Thinking questions from the Chapter Review.
3. Have students develop a personal financial statement, listing their assets and their liabilities. If they don't actually know the value of some of their personal belongings (for example, personal items given to them as gifts, such as jewelry), have them make rough estimates. Students may use Figure 40-1 in the text as a model for their own statement. Be sure each student knows his or her own net worth, but you need not encourage students to share this personal material with others in the class.

Bright Ideas

What if Mestral had never stopped to notice the burrs stuck to his clothing, or if upon noticing them he had considered them merely annoying? Creative people have the tendency to look at things in a different way and to seek out new solutions or new ways of looking at the same old thing. Thomas Edison once remarked, "Make it a point to keep on the lookout for novel and interesting ideas that others have used successfully. Your idea has to be original only in its adaptation to the problem you are currently working on.

Assess (Cont'd.)

Remind students that the purpose of this exercise is to determine credit worthiness and that students in general do not qualify for large loans because they do not own anything of value such as real estate, stocks, bonds, securities, etc., nor do they typically have large savings accounts. Therefore, before they are able to qualify for a loan, they may need to work for a while in order to acquire the assets that would convince a bank to loan them money for a business venture. Another tactic is to start a business that requires very little capital and also work at a part-time job to pay living expenses until the student's business makes enough money to afford him or her a salary. (The students can use their financial statements to complete Application Project #1 in the Chapter Review.)

4. To determine personal income needs, have students develop a cost-of-living budget for themselves. Students should use Figure 40-3 as a model. They should pretend that they are living on their own in their immediate community.

Close

Have students complete this statement: The most common reason for writing a business plan is. . .(to obtain financing for the business.)

Estimating Personal Living Expenses

COST-OF-LIVING BUDGET
FOR AN AVERAGE MONTH
BASED ON AN AVERAGE INCOME OF $38,000

Regular Monthly Payments

Rent or mortgage (including taxes)	$ 550.00
Cars (including insurance)	350.00
Appliances/TV	0.00
Home improvement loan	200.00
Personal loan	55.00
Health plan	50.00
Life insurance premiums	15.00
Other insurance premiums	20.00
Miscellaneous (bank account service fees)	10.00
TOTAL	**$ 1,250.00**

Household Operating Expenses

Telephone	50.00
Gas and electricity	120.00
Water and garbage	30.00
Other household expenses, repairs, maintenance	20.00
TOTAL	**$ 220.00**

Food Expenses

Food—at home	500.00
Food—away from home	60.00
TOTAL	**$ 560.00**

Personal Expenses

Clothing, cleaning, laundry	$ 110.00
Medications	10.00
Doctors and dentists	50.00
Education	0.00
Dues	10.00
Gifts and contributions	40.00
Travel	50.00
Newspapers, magazines, books	10.00
Auto upkeep, gas, and parking	50.00
Spending money, allowances	20.00
TOTAL	**$ 350.00**

Tax Expenses

Federal and state income taxes	175.00
Personal property taxes	350.00
Other taxes	25.00
TOTAL	**$ 550.00**

BUDGET SUMMARY

Regular Monthly Payments	1,250.00
Household Operating Expenses	220.00
Food Expenses	560.00
Personal Expenses	350.00
Tax Expenses	$ 550.00
MONTHLY TOTAL	$

Figure 40-3

This form will help you estimate how much you need for your living expenses when you start your business. Based on the figures shown here, what is your monthly total for cost-of-living expenses?

Set aside the money for living expenses in a savings account. Do not use the money for any other purpose. This fund will help you get through the start-up period. The chart in Figure 40-3 will help you estimate how much money you should have in this account.

532 Unit 11 *Entrepreneurship*

Caption Answer

$1,250 + $220 + $560 + $350 + $550 = $2,930

Section Review Answers

1. Financial information helps determine how the business will operate financially. If you need a loan to help you finance a new business, lenders will also want to see financial documents.
2. Assets to liabilities on a specific date.
3. The two categories of business start-up costs are one-time costs and continuing costs.

SECTION 40.2

Objectives

After completing this section, you will be able to

- estimate business income and expenses,
- prepare an income statement,
- calculate payroll and other expenses itemized on an income statement,
- prepare a balance sheet, and
- prepare a cash flow statement.

Terms to Know

- income statement
- gross sales
- net sales
- net income
- interest
- principal
- balance sheet
- net worth
- cash flow statement

Estimating Business Income and Expenses

After estimating your start-up costs and personal living expenses, the next step is to estimate the money you expect to earn and to spend in operating your business. Many small businesses fail because they do not bring in enough profit to pay their costs and their owners' living expenses. Estimating your business income and expenses is a key part of your business plan. Lenders will want to see your estimates before deciding to loan you money.

If you are buying an existing business, you will have past operating results to use as a guide. If you are starting a new business, you will need to estimate your potential earnings and the costs of operating the business. The financial document that is used to calculate a business's earnings and expenses is the income statement.

The **income statement** is a summary of your business's income and expenses during a specific period, such as a month, a quarter, or a year. This statement is often called a *profit and loss statement*.

The income statement for an existing business shows the previous year's income and expenses. The income statement for a new or planned business estimates earnings and expenses for the first few months (or the first year) of operation. Figure 40-4 on page 534 shows a sample projected quarterly income statement. Refer to this figure as you read about the different parts of the income statement.

Income statements have several major parts: total and net sales, expenses of operating the business, net income from operations, net profit before income taxes, and net profit after income taxes. Each item on the income statement is added to or subtracted from total sales to find the amount of profit.

Total Sales
− Returns and Allowances
= Net Sales
− Cost of Goods Sold
= Gross Profit
− Expenses of Operating the Business
= Net Income from Operations
− Income Taxes
= Net Profit

Let's look at how you calculate the amounts for each part of the income statement.

Estimating Total Sales

The income businesses produce depends on the yearly volume of sales they generate. Most new businesses grow slowly in the beginning, so you should be conservative in estimating your first-year sales.

Most people who start a new business have some idea about where they will sell their products. For example, if you plan to manufacture a new product, you may already have discussed the product with potential buyers. You may even have a contract to produce a certain number. Suppose you are starting a new T-shirt printing business. You have a contract for 2,000 T-shirts, which you will sell at $6 wholesale. Your estimated total sales will be $12,000. If you think you can produce and sell ten times that amount during your first year, you would estimate your total sales at $120,000.

After calculating an estimated sales volume, you need to determine whether the amount is reasonable. You must verify your estimated sales volume by comparing it with projected industry figures for your size of business and location. Trade associations, bankers, other business-people, and industry business publications can all help you make sales and income estimates.

The accuracy of your sales estimates will also depend on the quality of your market analysis. Losses instead of profit are not uncommon during the first year or so in

Chapter 40 *Financing the Business* **533**

Focus

Bell Ringer Activity

Estimating expected earnings and expenses is a key part of writing the financial section of a business plan. Ask students to briefly write some of the ways that they would:

1. estimate income and expenses for an existing business; and
2. estimate income and expenses for a new business.

Then ask students what factors would help them estimate (project) income, particularly for a new business.

Introducing the Section

Review students' answers from the Bell Ringer Activity.

1. In estimating income and expenditures for an existing business, you can look at its prior operating results, figuring in your anticipated income and expenses if you plan to add additional products. You must consider why the owner is selling the business (strong businesses are rarely offered for sale) and how you will make the business more profitable, perhaps through better management or additional investment of cash for growth. You must also consider your overall goals and growth plans.

More About

Failure Rates

Some new businesses are riskier than others, and lenders will take this fact into consideration before granting a loan. Among the businesses with the highest failure rates are those providing recreation services and oil and gas extraction. Health services and private education services have one of the lowest failure rates.

2. For a new business, you must rely solely on estimating (projecting) your income and expenses. You must take into account such things as establishing the reputation of your business in the market, the costs involved in initial business start-up, the variable and fixed operating expenses in maintaining the business (paying employee salaries and advertising, for example), the immediate and anticipated market need for your product, and the direct and indirect competition in the market. And, as with an existing business, you must look at your overall goals and growth plans.

Have students practice estimating income and expenses by choosing a product students buy frequently, such as a music CD. Assume a royalty of 10 percent and a manufacturing cost of $1.80 per CD, including packaging. Ask students to estimate other expenses such as advertising and distribution. Estimate income based on the price students typically pay, considering that the wholesale price will be less. Remind students that some CDs will sell successfully, while others may not.

Teach

Guided Practice

1. Read Section 40.2 with students.
2. Use the transparencies for this section.
3. Assign and review the Chapter 40 Activity in the *School-to-Work Handbook*.

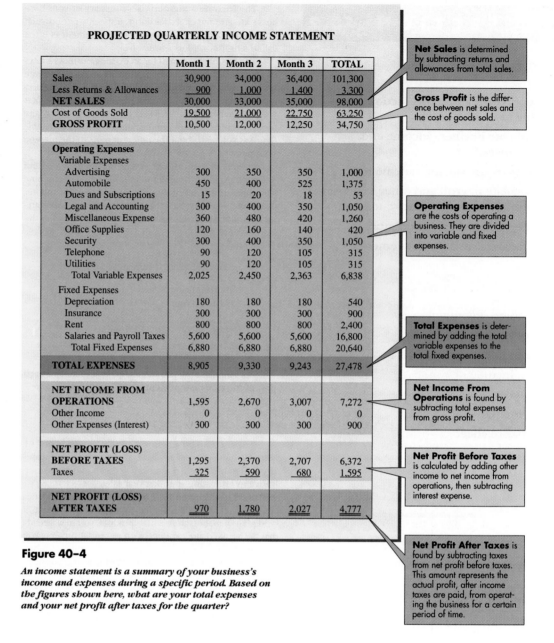

PROJECTED QUARTERLY INCOME STATEMENT

	Month 1	Month 2	Month 3	TOTAL
Sales	30,900	34,000	36,400	101,300
Less Returns & Allowances	900	1,000	1,400	3,300
NET SALES	30,000	33,000	35,000	98,000
Cost of Goods Sold	19,500	21,000	22,750	63,250
GROSS PROFIT	10,500	12,000	12,250	34,750
Operating Expenses				
Variable Expenses				
Advertising	300	350	350	1,000
Automobile	450	400	525	1,375
Dues and Subscriptions	15	20	18	53
Legal and Accounting	300	400	350	1,050
Miscellaneous Expense	360	480	420	1,260
Office Supplies	120	160	140	420
Security	300	400	350	1,050
Telephone	90	120	105	315
Utilities	90	120	105	315
Total Variable Expenses	2,025	2,450	2,363	6,838
Fixed Expenses				
Depreciation	180	180	180	540
Insurance	300	300	300	900
Rent	800	800	800	2,400
Salaries and Payroll Taxes	5,600	5,600	5,600	16,800
Total Fixed Expenses	6,880	6,880	6,880	20,640
TOTAL EXPENSES	8,905	9,330	9,243	27,478
NET INCOME FROM OPERATIONS	1,595	2,670	3,007	7,272
Other Income	0	0	0	0
Other Expenses (Interest)	300	300	300	900
NET PROFIT (LOSS) BEFORE TAXES	1,295	2,370	2,707	6,372
Taxes	325	590	680	1,595
NET PROFIT (LOSS) AFTER TAXES	970	1,780	2,027	4,777

Net Sales is determined by subtracting returns and allowances from total sales.

Gross Profit is the difference between net sales and the cost of goods sold.

Operating Expenses are the costs of operating a business. They are divided into variable and fixed expenses.

Total Expenses is determined by adding the total variable expenses to the total fixed expenses.

Net Income From Operations is found by subtracting total expenses from gross profit.

Net Profit Before Taxes is calculated by adding other income to net income from operations, then subtracting interest expense.

Net Profit After Taxes is found by subtracting taxes from net profit before taxes. This amount represents the actual profit, after income taxes are paid, from operating the business for a certain period of time.

Figure 40–4

An income statement is a summary of your business's income and expenses during a specific period. Based on the figures shown here, what are your total expenses and your net profit after taxes for the quarter?

business. In your business plan, you will need to show how you will support any losses. For example, you may need to show an ability to invest more capital or a way to reduce your operating expenses.

Calculating Net Sales

The total of all sales for any period of time is called **gross sales.** If your company sells only on a cash basis,

then your gross sales will simply be the total of all cash sales. If your company sells merchandise on account, accepts credit cards, and sells gift certificates, then all of these different types of sales must be totaled to arrive at gross sales.

Because most businesses have some customer returns and allowances (credit granted to customers for damaged

Total Expense = $27,478; Net Profit (Loss) After Taxes = $4,777 or defective goods kept by the customer), the gross sales figure does not reflect the actual income from sales. The total of all sales returns and allowances is subtracted from gross sales to get **net sales.** Net sales, then, represents the amount left after gross sales have been adjusted for returns and allowances. Look at Figure 40-4 to see the net sales line.

Determining Gross Profit

Gross profit on sales is the difference between the net sales and the cost of goods sold. The total amount spent to produce or to buy the goods sold is called the *cost of goods sold.*

The formula for calculating gross profit is:

$$\begin{array}{r} \text{Net Sales} \\ - \text{ Cost of Goods Sold} \\ \hline = \text{Gross Profit} \end{array}$$

Service businesses do not provide goods to their customers. Therefore, they don't have to determine their cost of goods sold. Their gross profit is the same as net sales. Other businesses that produce or buy products to sell must calculate the cost of goods sold.

To calculate cost of goods sold, add goods purchased during the year to the beginning inventory. Then subtract the amount of the ending inventory.

$$\begin{array}{r} \text{Beginning Inventory} \\ + \text{ Net Purchases} \\ - \text{ Ending Inventory} \\ \hline = \text{Cost of Goods Sold} \end{array}$$

As you learned in Chapter 27, beginning and ending inventory amounts are determined by figuring how much stock is on hand and calculating its value.

Once you know the cost of goods sold, you can calculate your gross profit by subtracting the cost of goods sold from net sales. For example, suppose you are employed by Seaside Surfboards, a company that sold $96,785 worth of surfboards last year. The company books show a total of $1,470 in sales returns and allowances. When you subtract the sales returns and allowances from total (gross) sales, you get net sales of $95,315. If the cost of goods sold for last year totals $53,769, your gross profit is:

$$\$95,315 - \$53,769 = \$41,546$$

Projecting Business Expenses

The next major part of the income statement are the operating expenses. *Operating expenses* are the costs of operating the business.

Operating expenses are either variable or fixed expenses. *Variable expenses* change from one month to the next, depending upon the needs of the business. Variable expenses include items such as advertising, office supplies, and utilities. *Fixed expenses* are costs that remain the same for a period of time. Expenses that are fixed for a certain period of time include items such as insurance, rent, and office salaries.

Projecting fixed expenses usually is easy because you simply add all your costs, such as rent, insurance, and so on. Variable expenses are often calculated as a percentage of some base amount. For example, advertising expenses may be planned to be 5 percent of total sales. Since employee wages may be a significant part of your business expenses, let's look at how to determine payroll costs.

Calculating Payroll Costs   To calculate payroll costs, you will need to estimate the number of employees you will need to help you operate your business. You will then need to determine typical salaries in your area for the work you will have the employees perform. You can get help on salary information by reviewing the help-wanted ads in the newspaper and finding similar jobs. You can also use the minimum wage as a starting point and decide how much more to pay for more skilled workers. For example, if the minimum wage is $4.75 for an unskilled worker, you may need to pay $8.50 an hour for a more skilled worker.

When setting up your business, you need to pay particular attention to your payroll records. Payroll records are important both to your employees and your company. They are used to prepare income tax returns, so the federal and state governments are interested in their accuracy, too.

Your payroll records may be part of the cash disbursements journal where you keep records of all cash payments. You may prefer to keep your payroll records in a separate payroll journal. If you use a separate journal for payroll records, you will want to use a separate page for each employee. Each page will show one employee's pay period, hours worked, earnings, deductions, and net pay. See Figure 40-5 on page 536 for a payroll journal that is used to record payroll information for employees.

The amount earned by an employee is that person's *gross pay. Net pay* is what the employee receives after deductions for taxes, insurance, and voluntary deductions. For example, if Nancy Baker earns $11 an hour and worked 40 hours during the week, her gross pay is $440 ($11 × 40 hours).

If Nancy's deductions total $94, you would calculate her net pay by subtracting the deductions from her gross pay:

$$\$440 - \$94 = \$346 \text{ (net pay)}$$

Tax tables are available for calculating the amount to be deducted from each employee's pay for state and federal income tax. The percentage of gross pay to be deducted for FICA (Social Security and Medicare taxes) changes almost every year. Get the latest information from your local social security office.

Example:
Find the net pay for Carmen Lopez, who worked a total of 44 hours during a week at $12 per hour. Carmen

Chapter 40   *Financing the Business*   **535**

4. MarkEd Resource Center in Columbus, Ohio, (800) 448-0398, has materials appropriate for use with this section. Also listed in the MarkEd catalog is another excellent supplement to small business planning entitled *The Business Planning Guide,* Sixth Edition, by David H. Bangs, Jr. It includes a section by section breakdown of the business plan, projected out to three years for Finestkind Seafoods, Inc., of York, Maine. (You may wish to contact Upstart directly for other titles, [800] 235-8866.)

5. Take students to your school and/or local library to make sure they understand how to use the available resources and industry publications on financial statistics that they can consult to create the financial section of a business plan.

6. Invite a local representative from the Small Business Administration to your class to discuss how to create the financial section of a business plan. Ask this person to bring selections of business plans for various types of businesses (if you do not already have samples of these in your classroom), comparing and contrasting the financial sections of each plan. When discussing how companies project future growth, you may wish to have available in your classroom the annual reports from some local, regional, and national businesses which discuss projections for growth. (See the Linking School to Work Activity in the Chapter Review.)

Did You Know ?

Some companies have found that sharing financial statements with employees can be a significant tool for motivating employee performance. To help employees who lack a financial background, the financial statements are annotated to explain the meaning of each line of the statements.

7. When discussing how to estimate cost of goods sold, take your students to a manufacturer's trade show (if possible) to have them get a feeling for the price of goods purchased for resale. If you don't have access to a trade show, obtain several copies of manufacturer's catalogs (for example, those from gift and/or card companies) to discuss this concept. Have students compare and contrast the purchase price for goods in various industries (manufacturing versus retail, for example). You may also wish to have manufacturers' representatives speak to the class on the cost of producing various types of goods.

Discussion Starter

After you have reviewed the concepts presented in this section, choose existing and new manufacturing and retail businesses in your community. Have students discuss what factors the owners of each business would have considered when estimating earnings and expenses.

Keep a list of students' answers on the chalkboard. Compare this list to their findings in the Cooperative Learning activity that follows.

Payroll Journal

Name _Nancy Baker_
Date of Birth _11-19-64_
Soc. Sec. No. _514-62-5254_
No. of Allowances _1_
Address _317 Sycamore_

Wage rate _$11.00/Hr_
Date employed _8-1-86_
Employee No. _9_
Department _B_

Pay Period Ending	Hours							Total Regular	Over-time	Earnings	Deductions					Net Pay
	S	M	T	W	T	F	S				Social Security	Medicare	Federal Income tax	State Income tax	Misc.	
8-14		8	8	8	8	8		40		440.00	27.28	6.38	53.00	22.00	17.00	312.34
8-21		7	8	8	8	8		39		429.00	26.60	6.22	50.00	21.45	17.00	

Figure 40–5

A payroll journal summarizes each employee's pay period, hours worked, earnings, deductions, and net pay. What is Nancy Baker's net pay for the period ending August 21?

is paid time and a half for overtime (hours worked beyond 40 hours in a week).

Step 1 Find the gross pay.
$480.00 ($12 × 40 hours)
+ 72.00 ($12 × 4 hours × 1.5)
$552.00

Step 2 Subtract the total deductions.
$552.00 (gross pay)
− 98.40 (total deductions)
$453.60 (net pay)

In estimating your total payroll costs, you will need to use current tax rates for local, state, and federal income and payroll taxes. Call your local chamber of commerce or obtain tax booklets from your state and federal tax agencies. Remember that as the employer, you will also pay FICA and unemployment payroll taxes on your employees' earnings. You will need to include those amounts in your total payroll expense estimate.

Calculating Total Expenses Once you have calculated all your fixed and variable expenses, you are ready to total your expenses. To calculate total operating expenses, add all the variable expenses to the fixed expenses.

Total Variable Expenses
+ Total Fixed Expenses
= Total Expenses

Net Income from Operations

After totaling your expenses, the next step is to calculate net income from operations. **Net income** is the amount left after operating expenses are subtracted from gross profit.

The formula for calculating net income from operations is:

Gross Profit on Sales
− Total Expenses
= Net Income from Operations

For example, suppose that you own Worldwide Travel Agency and had gross sales of $145,540 during the year. Your total operating expenses for the year were $79,630, so your net income from operations was:

$145,540 − $79,630 = $65,910

Especially in the early years of operation, a business may have a net loss from operations. A net loss results when expenses are larger than the gross profit on sales. If

Caption Answer

Nancy Baker's net pay is $307.73.

a loss is probable during the first months of operation, the financial plan should address how the business will pay its debts.

Calculating Other Income   In the "Net Income From Operations" section of the income statement, you should list money earned from sources other than sales or paid out for items that are not part of the operating expenses. For example, you may plan to earn interest on your cash deposits. **Interest** is the money paid for the use of money borrowed or invested. To estimate your interest earnings, check with local banks and find the current interest rate paid on similar accounts. Remember that you will also likely be using some of this money during the year, so you will need to calculate interest only on the amount actually on deposit. Unless the interest income you expect to earn is significant, you may want to list this amount as zero in your business plan.

Calculating Other Expenses   If you borrow money to start your business, you will also pay interest on that money. The amount you borrow is called the **principal.**

Interest is expressed as a percentage of the principal and is called the *rate* of interest. If you borrow $100 at 11 percent interest, the principal is $100 and the rate of interest is 11 percent. To find the amount of interest for one year, multiply the principal (p) times the rate of interest (r) times the length of time (t). This formula is stated as:

$$i = prt$$

For the example above you would pay $11 in interest:

$$\$100 \times 11\% \times 1 = \$11$$

The units in the rate of interest and time must agree. That is, if the rate of interest is expressed in years, then the time must be expressed in years as well. Both may be expressed in months. If the rate is given without reference to a time period, assume that it is for one year.

Suppose you are quoted a yearly rate and need to convert it to a monthly rate. Because there are 12 months in a year, divide the yearly rate by 12, and you will get the monthly rate. If you are quoted a monthly rate and want to convert it to a yearly rate, multiply the monthly rate by 12.

Once you decide how much money you will need to borrow and how long it will take you to repay the loan, you can calculate your total annual (or monthly) interest. This amount is listed on the financial statement as "Other Expenses."

Net Profit or Loss Before Taxes

Net profit or net loss before taxes is calculated by adding other income to net income from operations. Then subtracting other expenses from the total.

        Net Income from Operations
        + Other Income
        − Other Expenses
        ─────────────────────────────
        = Net profit (or loss) before taxes

Net Profit (or Loss) After Taxes

Net profit (or loss) after taxes is the amount of money left over after federal, state, and local taxes are subtracted. This amount represents the actual profit, after income taxes are paid, from operating the business for a certain period of time.

For new businesses, the projected income statement should be done on a monthly basis. After the first year, projected income statements can be prepared on a quarterly basis.

The steps that follow are a summary of how to prepare a monthly projected income statement.

Step 1   Estimate total sales.
Step 2   Subtract sales discounts, returns, and allowances from total sales to calculate net sales.
Step 3   List the estimated cost of goods sold.
Step 4   Subtract the cost of goods sold from net sales to find gross profit on sales.
Step 5   List each monthly operating expense, dividing them into variable and fixed expenses.
Step 6   Total the monthly operating expenses.
Step 7   Subtract total operating expenses from gross profit on sales to find net income from operations. If a loss is projected, put parentheses around the number. For example, a projected loss of $1,000 would be identified as ($1,000).
Step 8   Add other income such as interest on bank deposits and subtract other expenses, such as interest expense, from net income from operations. The result is net profit (or loss) before income taxes.
Step 9   Estimate total taxes on the net income and subtract that amount from net profit. The result is net profit (or loss) after taxes.

Know the Rules Before You Play the Game

You're in Germany on a business trip and want to entertain a client by taking him to dinner. Since you want your client to enjoy the meal, you're thinking about having him select the restaurant. Good idea or bad?

While it might seem considerate to allow your client to choose, he would probably not see it that way—on two counts. First, by having him make the choice, you would also be forcing him to set your budget. If he chooses incorrectly, it could be embarrassing—for both of you. Second, by turning the choice over to your guest, you would show yourself to be lacking in foresight. This is a trait that Germans value highly. Had you planned carefully, you would have asked a concierge to pick out a restaurant for you in advance.

Critical Thinking

Ask students the following:

If you were a banker or investor reviewing a business plan in anticipation of lending or investing money for a business start-up, what questions would you ask the potential business owner regarding how he or she will use your money? (Answers will vary but should include the following: How will the money make the business profitable? How will the money be repaid? How quickly will the money be repaid? Who will be making decisions regarding the use of the money? How qualified is this person to run a business? How knowledgeable about this particular business is this person? What experience does this person have in this area? How sound are the financial projections for this business? How do the projections compare to actual numbers of similar businesses?)

Cooperative Learning

Divide students into the same four groups they were in for the Bell Ringer Activity in Section 1: manufacturing and retail businesses.

Help each group make an appointment with the owner and/or general manager of each type of business that it is assigned. Each group should interview this person with respect to how income and expenses were initially projected, and how ongoing projections are made.

Each group should write a report of its findings and present it to the class.

Did You Know

Calculating sales volume for a service business involves establishing an hourly rate and multiplying that by the number of hours worked annually. Divide the result by 12 for a monthly income figure. Keep in mind industry averages and market trends. A service business cannot start out charging more than the industry average unless they offer something extra.

L1 Math Skills

Obtain tax tables for calculating the amount to be deducted from employees' pay for federal, state, and local taxes. Also obtain the gross pay to be deducted for FICA and unemployment.

Give students hourly or weekly salary amounts for imaginary employees at various skill levels (a nonskilled worker, a skilled worker, a supervisor, and an upper-level manager). Have them calculate each person's income for one month. Base an hourly employee's pay on a 40-hour week.

Depending on the level of your class, you may wish to have your students generate the salary amounts and work in pairs to solve the problems.

L2 Math Skills

Give each student a copy of a completed income statement that contains all of the elements in the income statement featured in the text. Ask each student to write a letter to a friend, describing the formula for how each of the following were achieved: *net sales, gross profit, operating expenses, total expenses, net income from operations, net profit before taxes,* and *net profit after taxes.*

L3 Math Skills

Have students research the current interest rate at three different financial institutions. Provide students with a loan amortization chart or table. Have them figure the fixed monthly payback amount for a five-year, ten-year, and fifteen-year $50,000 business loan, given the interest rate quoted at each financial institution.

Practice 3

Use a separate sheet of paper for your answers. The income statement for Mountain-Air Bikes is shown below.

1. How much did Mountain-Air pay for the bikes it sold?
2. How much was the gross profit for the year?
3. How much were total operating expenses?
4. Which operating expense was the most costly?
5. How much net income was earned during the year?

Mountain-Air Bikes
Income Statement
For the Year Ended December 31, 19--

Net Sales	$212,015
Cost of Goods Sold	109,614
Gross Profit	$?
Operating Expenses:	
Salaries	$ 24,019
Rent	11,211
Utilities	4,514
Advertising	2,422
Total Operating Expenses	$?
Net Income from Operations	$?

The Balance Sheet

A **balance sheet** is a summary of a business's assets, liabilities, and owner's equity. Figure 40–6 shows a typical balance sheet. Let's look at each part.

As you know, assets are anything of monetary value that you own. Assets are classified as either current or fixed. *Current assets* are expected to be converted into cash in the upcoming year. Examples of current assets include cash in the bank, accounts receivable (money owed to you by your customers), and inventory.

Fixed assets are used over a period of years to operate your business. Examples of fixed assets include land, buildings, equipment, furniture, and fixtures.

The assets of the business are important because they are needed to operate the business. If you are borrowing money to start a business, assets are also often used as collateral for the loan.

The next section of the balance sheet is used to report the liabilities of the business. Liabilities are amounts the business owes. Examples of liabilities include amounts owed for merchandise bought for resale or for taxes to be paid in the future.

Liabilities are classified as current or long-terms. *Current liabilities* are the debts the business expects to pay

538   Unit 11   *Entrepreneurship*

off during the upcoming business year. Some examples of current liabilities are accounts payable (money owed to suppliers), notes payable (money owed to a bank), taxes payable, and money owed to employees for salaries.

Long-term liabilities are debts that are not due to be paid in the coming year. Some examples of long-term liabilities are mortgages and loans.

The third section of the balance sheet is the equity, or net worth, section. When you start a new business, you will most likely invest some savings in the business. The amount of the savings is your equity, or ownership interest, in the business. The money invested will be used to buy assets and to operate the business. Your equity, then, is affected by the assets owned by the business and the debts the business owes. **Net worth** is the difference between the assets of a business and its liabilities:

Assets − Liabilities = Net Worth (Equity)

The balance sheet is prepared to show the amount of your ownership interest in the business on a given date. This information is used by a lender, for example, to determine whether the value of your business would be enough to pay off the amount of a loan.

Practice 4

Use a separate sheet of paper for your answers. The balance sheet for Mountain-Air Bikes is shown below.

1. How much are total assets for Mountain-Air Bikes?
2. How much are total liabilities?
3. What is Mountain-Air's net worth?

Mountain-Air Bikes
Balance Sheet
December 31, 19--

Current Assets	
Cash	$ 10,000
Accounts Receivable	15,000
Inventory	68,000
Fixed Assets	
Building	120,000
Equipment	80,000
Vehicles	30,000
Total Assets	$?
Current Liabilities	
Notes Payable	$ 3,000
Accounts Payable	12,000
Salaries Payable	5,000
Taxes Payable	1,000
Long-Term Liabilities	
Notes Payable	90,000
Total Liabilities	$?
Net Worth	$?

Lifelong Learning

Financing the Business

In order to enhance their knowledge of financial information related to business, students may wish to take additional business classes including accounting, small business management, entrepreneurship, and related computer classes to give them practical experience in using spreadsheets to perform a variety of financial calculations needed in business management. Such classes are offered at most community colleges, or by the SBA, and as regular university courses. In addition, reading from a variety of case studies in related books and magazines can help students further their understanding of the complexities of the financial side of business and marketing.

Balance Sheet

August, 19 – –

	Year 1	Year 2
Current Assets		
Cash	$ 7,000	$ 10,000
Accounts receivable	10,000	10,000
Inventory	150,000	265,000
Fixed Assets		
Real Estate	$ 100,000	$ 105,000
Fixtures and equipment	50,000	50,000
Vehicles	25,000	24,000
Other Assets		
Licenses	$ 100	$ 100
TOTAL ASSETS	$ 342,100	$ 464,100
Current Liabilities		
Notes payable (due within one year)	$ 125,000	$ 250,000
Accounts payable	10,000	15,000
Accrued expenses	5,000	5,000
Taxes owed	7,000	7,500
Long-Term Liabilities		
Notes payable (due after one year)	$ 75,000	$ 80,000
Other	15,000	20,000
TOTAL LIABILITIES	$ 237,000	$ 377,500
NET WORTH (ASSETS minus LIABILITIES)	$	$
TOTAL LIABILITIES plus NET WORTH should equal ASSETS		

Figure 40-6

A balance sheet is a dollars and cents description of your existing or projected business. Based on the figures shown here, what is the net worth of your business for year 1 and year 2?

Cash Flow Statement

A **cash flow statement** is a monthly plan that shows when you anticipate cash coming into the business and when you expect to pay out cash. A cash flow statement helps you to see if you will have enough money when you need it to pay your bills.

You probably already deal with cash flow in planning your personal expenses. For example, suppose you have a part-time job for which you earn take-home pay of $280 a month. If you have a car payment of $175 and car insurance of $85, that leaves you $20 a month for other expenses, such as meals and entertainment. You must plan your cash expenses so that you can pay your bills when they are due.

Businesses do the same type of planning by calculating cash flow. Businesses need cash to pay bills, their employees, and unexpected expenses. The cash flow statement tells you how much cash you started with, how and when you plan to spend cash, and how and when you plan to receive cash. It also tells you when you will need to find additional funds and when you will have cash left over. Figure 40-7 on page 540 shows a typical cash flow statement for the first three months of operation. Most lenders will require you to estimate cash flow for the first year of operation.

If you plan to operate a merchandising business, one of your largest payments of cash will be for your merchandise. You will most likely have to pay for part of the merchandise in cash, since new businesses often are not given large amounts of credit. When estimating sales for the income statement, you include both cash and credit

Chapter 40   *Financing the Business*   **539**

Caption Answer

Year 1: $342,100 − $237,000 = $105,100.
Year 2: $464,100 − $377,500 = $86,600.

More About

Cash Flow

The majority of new business start-ups that fail do so within the first three years of operation. One of the most common reasons for business failure is inadequate cash flow. Being successful means not only selling the product, but also collecting the money for it within a reasonable time.

Independent Practice

1. Assign and review the Chapter 40 Case Study in the *International Case Studies* workbook.
2. Have students research one of the following publications (or a publication of their choice) for an article on any aspect of small business financing discussed in this section: *American Journal of Small Business, Better Business Magazine, Black Enterprise, Cottage Connection, Entrepreneur Magazine, Executive Female, In Business, Inc. Magazine, Journal of Entrepreneurship, Journal of Small Business Finance,* or *Journal of Small Business Management.* Students should read the article, write a 100- to 200-word abstract of it, and be prepared to discuss it in class. The article may apply to all businesses or to a specific business.
3. Have the students write a major public company for a copy of its most recent annual report. Each student should develop a two-page paper summarizing the Chairman of the Board's letter to the stockholders, identifying any new goods and services planned for the future, the company's total sales, operating income and expenses, net income, and cash flow. Students should include any charts or graphs from the annual report that show these figures.

Projected Cash Flow Statement

Beginning of Month:	Startup	Month 1	Month 2	Month 3
Cash in Bank	$25,000			
Loans	5,000			
	$30,000			
Less Start-up Costs	20,000			
Total Beginning Cash	$10,000			
Income (during month):				
Cash Sales		$20,000	$20,000	$27,000
Credit Sales			10,000	13,000
Investment Income		200	200	200
Loans		0	0	0
Other Cash Income		0	0	0
TOTAL CASH INCOME		$20,200	$30,200	$40,200
Inventory Purchases				
Purchases for Cash		$15,000	$16,000	$14,750
Purchases for Credit		4,500	5,000	8,000
Total Inventory Purchases		$19,500	$21,000	$22,750
Expenses				
Variable Expenses				
Advertising		300	350	350
Automobile		450	400	525
Dues & Subscriptions		15	20	18
Legal & Accounting		300	400	350
Miscellaneous		360	480	420
Office Supplies		120	160	140
Security		300	400	350
Telephone		90	120	105
Utilities		90	120	105
Fixed Expenses				
Insurance		300	300	300
Rent		800	800	800
Salaries/Taxes (including owner's)		4,860	6,480	5,670
Total Expenses		$ 8,725	$ 9,150	$ 9,063
Capital Expenditures				
Purchase of Equipment and Other Assets		1,000		
Other Payments				
Loan Repayment		600	600	600
TOTAL CASH EXPENDITURES		$29,825	$30,750	$32,413
NET CASH FLOW (end of month)	$10,000	($ 9,625)	($ 550)	$ 7,787
CASH SURPLUS (monthly)	$10,000	$ 375	($ 175)	$ 7,162
CASH NEEDS	0	0	$ 175	0

Figure 40–7

A cash flow statement is a helpful financial tool for a business. What is the purpose behind completing a monthly cash flow statement?

Caption Answer

A cash flow statement helps avoid or plan for cash shortages or surpluses.

CASE STUDY

The Seeds of Business Success

At the age of 26, Sally Fox decided to become an entrepreneur. Her business idea was to grow natural brown cotton and to sell hand-spun cotton yarn. Fox started growing cotton by planting seeds in plastic pots in her mother's backyard.

Today Fox's business, Natural Cotton Colours, is a $5 million operation based in Wickenburg, Arizona. The road to business success was not easy for Fox, nor was it short. Fox spent seven years working at other jobs while she experimented with her cotton crops. Her early crops produced cotton fibers that were too short to be spun into yarn. Finally, Fox's efforts paid off and she was able to grow longer cotton fibers in natural colors of brown and green. Fox started a mail-order business selling raw cotton. Her first customers were hand spinners and weavers who liked to create their own cotton yarn. Her first year of operation gained Fox sales of just $1,000.

With such low sales, Fox realized that she would have to broaden her market beyond spinners and weavers. Fox was able to sign a contract with a Japanese textile mill which wanted her cotton for making naturally colored bath towels. Fox left her full-time job and concentrated on growing cotton. Her next crop weighed in at 100,000 pounds, which she sold to the Japanese mill for $279,000. With a loan of $100,000 from relatives, Fox finally was able to buy a farm in California in a region especially suited to growing cotton.

Fox's success seemed assured with an order for 800,000 pounds of cotton from the Japanese mill. For an order of this size, Fox needed to contract with nearby farmers to grow her cotton. An industry group refused permission for her to contract with local farmers because they were afraid her colored cotton would cross-pollinate with the local white cotton and ruin those crops. Fox was able to save part of the contract by finding farmers in another state who were willing to grow her cotton.

With money from the Japanese contract and from a small order by Levi Strauss & Co., Fox was able to earn her first profit—eight years after she started growing cotton in flower pots in the backyard. Two years later, in 1992, Fox's sales reached $1.6 million.

Today Fox operates from Arizona and has 5,000 acres under cultivation. Her cotton is used to make several different products—from table linens to clothing. Last year Fox's business had revenue of $5 million and a pretax profit of $1 million. Fox is already looking for new markets for her product, trying to stay one step ahead of the competition.

Case Study Review

1. During her first year of operating her mail-order business, Fox had sales of $1,000. How did Fox change her market focus to increase sales?
2. How was Fox able to finance her business growth?
3. What was the turning point for Fox in terms of financial success?

A MATTER OF ETHICS

4. Fox was not allowed to contract with farmers near her farm in California to grow her colored cotton because an industry group feared that the white cotton crops would be ruined. Do you think it is ethical for such a group to make decisions about which crops can be grown in an area and which cannot? Explain.

Chapter 40 *Financing the Business* **541**

Assess

Evaluation

Assign and review the Section 40.2 Review.

Reteaching

1. Assign and review the vocabulary terms for this section.
2. Assign and review Fact and Idea Review questions 4–12 from the Chapter Review.
3. Create 5" x 7" index cards with one of the following terms/concepts written on each card: *net sales, cost of goods sold, gross profit, operating expenses, total expenses, net income from operations, net profit before taxes, net profit after taxes, gross sales, operating expenses, variable expenses, fixed expenses, gross pay, net pay, balance sheet, current assets, fixed assets, current liabilities, long-term liabilities, cash flow* and *statement.* Choose any other terms/concepts from this section that you wish to have students review. Divide students into two teams. Flip a coin to determine which team goes first. Allow the first team to choose one index card from the stack. (Don't allow students to see the cards when they choose.) Allow the first team 30 seconds to give you a definition for the chosen term. If no team member can give a correct definition, allow the other team to try. Award ten points to the team that gives a correct definition for each term. Reward the winning team. Review the terms for which neither team could give a correct answer.

Case Study Answers

1. Fox contracted with a company that used cotton as one of its raw materials for making commercial products that were widely sold.
2. She borrowed money from relatives. Later, she was able to finance growth by signing contracts to deliver a certain amount of her cotton.
3. Either the improvement in fiber length that allowed Fox to sell her product in the commercial market or the signing of the contract with the Japanese company.
4. Some may say that a business person should have the right to sign a legal contract with another person without interference from such a group. Others may say the group was only protecting its interests and saving their crops from cross-pollination.

4. Give students several problems to complete on sample balance sheets and income statements. You may wish to use the financial statements from their annual reports that students obtain in the Independent Practice activity. Using these statements, eliminate several of the figures and then have students calculate what the missing figures are.

Enrichment

1. Assign and review the appropriate activities in the *Student Activity Workbook*.
2. Assign and review the appropriate Critical Thinking questions from the Chapter Review.
3. Assign and review the Building Academic Skills Activities, Application Projects, Linking School to Work Activities, and Performance Assessment from the Chapter Review.
4. Assign the appropriate activities in the *Marketing Math Workbook*.
5. Have the class review the sales from your school store during the last year. Given this information, have students project next year's income and expenses for the store.
6. To discuss projecting business expenses, have students analyze several examples of income statements and balance sheets from existing businesses to determine the current and fixed assets and current and long-term liabilities.

Close

Have each student write a 50-word summary that tells why the finance section of a business plan is so important.

---

sales. In contrast, the cash flow statement shows only the amount you expect to receive in cash (for cash sales and payments for credit sales) during the month. For example, you may receive payment for most of your credit sales 30 days after the sales.

You will also need to calculate your monthly costs for operating the business. Use the following steps to prepare a cash flow statement for your business.

Step 1 Add the total cash on hand (in bank accounts) and money received from any loans to find your total start-up money.

Step 2 Subtract the start-up costs to determine the amount of cash left over to operate the business.

Step 3 For each month during the first year, enter the estimated cash you expect to receive from cash sales and credit sales. If you have income from business investments or plan to take out additional loans, enter those amounts also.

Step 4 Add all sources of cash receipts to find total cash income for the month.

Step 5 List the cost of goods that you will buy for your inventory. This cost should be separated into purchases for which you will pay cash and purchases on credit, which you will pay for the next month. For example, the cash flow statement shows goods bought on credit in Month 1. This is a payment for items bought on credit prior to the opening of the business. Add the cash and credit purchases to find the total cost of inventory purchases.

Step 6 List the expenses you expect to pay during the month. These amounts are the same as those listed on the income statement, except for depreciation expense. Depreciation is a means of spreading the cost of an asset over a period of years. The amount of depreciation is not an actual payment made by the business, so it is not listed on the cash flow statement.

Step 7 Total all expenses for the month.

Step 8 List amounts that will be paid out for capital expenditures. A capital expenditure is money paid for an asset used to operate the business. For example, the purchase of a delivery truck would be a capital expenditure.

Step 9 List any other payments that will be made, such as repayment of the principal and interest for the loan.

Step 10 Add all the cash expenditures (cost of inventory purchased, expenses, capital expenditures, and other payments). Subtract the total cash payments from the total cash received during the month to determine net cash flow. If cash payments are higher than cash receipts, place the amount in parentheses.

Step 11 Add the beginning cash balance from the startup column to the net cash flow for the month. The result is the cash surplus for the month. If the

---

costs of operating the business are higher than income added to the beginning of the cash balance, the business will have a deficit rather than a surplus. In that case, the business will need additional cash for its operations. The amount is listed on the "Cash Needs" line. For example, in Figure 40–7 the cash flow projections show a need for additional cash of $175 by the end of month 2. If you compare month 2 on the income statement, you will see net profit for the month. What the income statement does not take into account is how long it may take a business to collect the cash from sales made on credit.

Practice 5

1. If you have total cash of $23,000 to start your business and start-up costs of $12,000, what amount of cash is available for operating the business?
2. Suppose income for the first three months is $100, $750, and $980. Total expenses for these same months are $4,800, $3,400, and $2,700. What is the cash flow for each month?
3. What is the cumulative amount of cash available at the end of each month?

What can you do if you project that you will need additional money during the year? If your business has potential and your balance sheet shows enough assets to serve as collateral, you will probably be able to borrow additional money. A loan can help you keep the business going during the start-up period and during slow sales months. If your cash flow projections indicate that you need to borrow money to meet monthly expenses, you will want to include monthly payments on the loan as a part of your cash needs for the rest of the year.

SECTION 40.2 Review

1. What financial document can you use to calculate a business's earnings and expenses?
2. What are the major categories that are calculated on the income statement?
3. How are payroll costs calculated?
4. What is the purpose of a balance sheet?
5. What is a cash flow statement? What is its purpose?

Section Review Answers

1. The key amounts calculated on an income statement are net sales, cost of goods sold, gross profit, net income from operations, and net income before and after taxes.
2. The balance sheet is a summary of your business assets, liabilities, and capital.
3. A cash flow statement is a budget forecast of the cash that you anticipate receiving and spending each month. It shows your expected revenue and expenses as well as such liabilities as loan payments, and thus allows you to see if you will have enough money to pay your bills.

Answers to Practice Problems

Practice 1 (page 527)

1. Total assets are $22,000 ($10,000 + $8,000 + $1,000 + $1,500 + $1,500 = $22,000).
2. Total liabilities are $10,000 ($7,000 + $2,500 + $500 = $10,000).
3. Net worth is $12,000 ($22,000 − $10,000 = $12,000).

Practice 2 (page 529)

1. Total costs for the first quarter are $27,600 [$18,000 + ($3,200 × 3) = $27,600].
2. Total costs for the year are $56,400 [$18,000 + ($3,200 × 12) = $56,400].

Practice 3 (page 538)

Mountain-Air Bikes
Income Statement
For the Year Ended December 31, 19--

Net Sales	$212,015
Cost of Goods Sold	109,614
Gross Profit	$102,401
Operating Expenses:	
Salaries	$ 24,019
Rent	11,211
Utilities	4,514
Advertising	2,422
Total Operating Expenses	$ 42,166
Net Income from Operations	$ 60,235

1. $109,614
2. $102,401 ($212,015 − $109,614 = $102,401)
3. $42,166 ($24,019 + $11,211 + $4,514 + $2,422 = $42,166)
4. Salaries
5. $60,235 ($102,401 − $42,166 = $60,235)

Practice 4 (page 538)

Mountain-Air Bikes
Balance Sheet
December 31, 19--

Current Assets	
Cash	$ 10,000
Accounts Receivable	15,000
Inventory	68,000
Fixed Assets	
Building	120,000
Equipment	80,000
Vehicles	30,000
Total Assets	$323,000
Current Liabilities	
Notes Payable	$ 3,000
Accounts Payable	12,000
Salaries Payable	5,000
Taxes Payable	1,000
Long-Term Liabilities	
Notes Payable	90,000
Total Liabilities	$111,000
Net Worth	$212,000

1. $323,000 ($10,000 + $15,000 + $68,000 + $120,000 + $80,000 + $30,000 = $323,000)
2. $111,000 ($3,000 + $12,000 + $5,000 + $1,000 + $90,000 = $111,000)
3. $212,000 ($323,000 − $111,000 = $212,000)

Practice 5 (page 542)

1. The amount of cash available for business operations is $11,000 ($23,000 − $12,000 = $11,000).
2. The cash flow is as follows:
   month 1; ($4,700) [$100 − $4,800 = ($4,700)];
   month 2; ($2,650) [$750 − $3,400 = ($2,650)];
   month 3; ($1,720) [$980 − $2,700 = ($1,720)].
3. The cumulative cash available at the end of each month is as follows:
   month 1; $6,300 ($11,000 − $4,700 = $6,300);
   month 2; $3,650 ($6,300 − $2,650 = $3,650);
   month 3;, $1,930 ($3,650 − $1,720 = $1,930).

Answers

Vocabulary Review

See Glossary for definitions.

Fact and Idea Review

1. They help determine how much capital will be needed to start/operate the business. Also required to obtain financing.
2. nature of proposed business, size of business, amount of inventory needed, time between using start-up funds from personal assets or from potential lenders and first sales, and the timing of cash revenues and your expenses.
3. Expenses that are necessary for you to live. To know how much you will need for personal expenses.
4. Net sales, expenses of operating the business, net income from operations, net profit before taxes, net profit after taxes.
5. Steps for projecting income are listed in Section 40.2.
6. Fixed expenses do not change for a given period of time. Variable expenses may change.
7. The assets, liabilities, and net worth of the business.
8. Anything of value owned by a business. Current assets are expected to be converted into cash in the upcoming year. Fixed assets are used over a period of years to operate a business.
9. A debt owed by the business. Current liabilities: debts paid off during the business year. Long-term liabilities: debts not due to be paid in the coming year.
10. The difference between the assets of a business and its liabilities.
11. The steps for preparing a cash flow statement are listed in Section 40.2.

Vocabulary Review

Using 3" x 5" cards, print a vocabulary word on one side and its definition on the other. With a classmate, review the term and definition for each of the following terms. Alternate between reading the terms and the definitions.

    personal financial statement
    asset
    liability
    start-up costs
    income statement
    gross sales
    net sales
    net income
    interest
    principal
    balance sheet
    net worth
    cash flow statement

Fact and Idea Review

1. Why are financial documents an important part of a business plan? (Sec. 40.1)
2. What factors determine start-up costs for a new business? (Sec. 40.1)
3. What are personal costs and why is it important to consider them when starting a new business? (Sec. 40.1)
4. What are the key components of an income statement? (Sec. 40.2)
5. List the steps in projecting income for a new business. (Sec. 40.2)
6. Explain the difference between fixed and variable expenses. (Sec. 40.2)
7. What three things does a balance sheet show? (Sec. 40.2)
8. What are assets? Explain the difference between current and fixed assets. (Sec. 40.2)
9. What is a liability? What is the difference between current liabilities and long-term liabilities? (Sec. 40.2)
10. What is net worth? (Sec. 40.2)
11. What are the steps in preparing a cash flow statement? (Sec. 40.2)
12. Explain the difference between an income statement, a balance sheet, and a cash flow statement in terms of the types of financial information each provides. (Sec. 40.2)

Critical Thinking

1. How would the financial aspects of financing a manufacturing, service, franchise, or retail business differ?
2. What sources could you use to determine the total cash needed to start a business?
3. What do you think are some of the legal issues new businesses have to handle?
4. What do you think a lender looks for in considering a loan application for a new business?

Building Academic Skills

Math

1. Total first-quarter sales for the Leon Company were $285,000. Goods returned by customers amounted to $4,100. The cost of goods sold to customers was $112,000. The company's total fixed and variable expenses were $84,500. Interest paid on a loan was $2,400. Taxes were estimated at a rate of 20 percent. Calculate the following amounts: net sales, gross profit, net income from operations, net profit before taxes, and net profit after taxes.

Communication

2. Write a letter to one of the following agencies to obtain financial information about starting a new business.

    Office of Minority Small Business
    U.S. Small Business Administration
    1441 L Street NW, Room 602
    Washington, DC 20416

    International Franchise Association
    1350 New York Avenue NW, Suite 900
    Washington, DC 20005

Human Relations

3. A friend has decided to open a carpet-cleaning business, which he feels will be immediately successful. Your friend believes that he will not need extra capital for personal costs. He feels that the business will generate enough revenue when it gets started to take care of his personal costs. What would you tell your friend about his lack of concern about personal costs?

Technology

4. Research how computers are used in the financial analysis of a business. Write your findings in a 150-word paper.

12. The income statement projects revenue and expenses. The balance sheet presents the assets and liabilities of the business. The cash flow statement shows how cash will flow into and out of the business.

Critical Thinking

1. Students' answers should be based on types of business information found in Chapter 37.

2. Lending agencies, previous owners, industry publications, suppliers, manufacturers, trade associations, local economic development authorities.
3. Understanding partnership agreements or articles of incorporation; permit requirements; zoning and licensing laws; local, state, and federal tax codes; FICA contributions; health and sanitation laws.

Application Projects

1. Develop a section for your business plan using instructor guidelines or guidelines and criteria prepared by National DECA for the *Entrepreneurship Written Event*. Prepare Part IV entitled "Planned Financing." The following activities will help you complete this section of your project.
   a. Develop your own personal financial statement.
   b. Based on an average month, project your personal living expenses.
   c. Project monthly sales for one year for your proposed business. Prepare a chart showing possible seasonal fluctuations in sales. Discuss how cash flow would be handled during the slower months.
   d. Identify the fixed and variable expenses of your proposed business.
   e. Determine the estimated profit for your proposed business. Interview a businessperson in your community who runs a similar business to help verify your profit estimate.
   f. Use Dun & Bradstreet or other available industry publications to get financial statistics for your business.
   g. Identify start-up costs for your proposed business, including the cost of equipment, supplies, and inventory.
   h. Develop an income statement for your business.
   i. List the assets to be used in your proposed business. Divide them into current and fixed assets.
   j. Develop a balance sheet for your business.
   k. Determine the capital that will be required to start your business. Calculate the monthly and yearly payments (including interest) for any financing you may require.
2. Write a 200-word paper on a successful entrepreneur using business publications in your marketing program or school media center.

Linking School to Work

Interview your supervisor or training station sponsor regarding the financial statement(s) that have proven to be most helpful to running the business. Identify the financial statement(s) and the reasons your supervisor has found them to be helpful.

Performance Assessment

Role Play

Situation. You have recently been hired to work part-time as a bookkeeper for a newly opened home repair service. The repair service has been started by an individual who has excellent technical skills. He has little experience with financial statements, however. He has asked you to explain the difference between an income statement, a balance sheet, and a cash flow statement. He also wants you to explain how to develop a cash flow statement for the business.

Evaluation. You will be evaluated on how well you do the following:

- Describe the purpose of preparing financial documents.
- Explain the income statement and how it is prepared.
- Explain a balance sheet and how it is prepared.
- Describe the procedure for developing a cash flow statement.

Construct a Chart

Using a large poster board, identify and label separate columns for the five financial documents discussed in this chapter. Under each column, identify the reasons for including a document as part of the financial section of a business plan.

 COMPUTER APPLICATION

Complete the Chapter 40 Computer Application that appears in the Student Activity Workbook.

 Portfolio

Consider the Application Projects that you have done for this unit. Select one that illustrates your mastery of the unit's content and might be of interest to potential employers. Reformat the activity as necessary, adding any explanatory text, and place it in your Portfolio. Consider using these activities:

- Chapter 37, Application Project 7, 8
- Chapter 39, Application Project 1, 2
- Chapter 40, Application Project 1 ■ ■

Communication
2. Letters should follow the business letter format.

Human Relations
3. Students should encourage the friend to complete the financial forms mentioned in the chapter.

Technology
4. Computers can assist with payroll processing, record-keeping, accounting, buying, financial analysis, inventory control and overall business operations.

Application Projects
1. Business plans should include a financial statement, personal living expenses, start-up costs, income statement, balance sheet, and cash flow statement.
2. Students should include information on how entrepreneurs started and financed their businesses.

Linking School to Work
Answers depend on the work situation.

Performance Assessment
Refer to the *DECA Competitive Events Handbook* for evaluation guidelines.

 ## Computer Application
Optional activity. Refer to the *Marketing Software Binder* for template and user information.

Portfolio
Refer to the *Marketing Career Portfolio* for development ideas and portfolio management and assessment.

Evaluation
Administer the reproducible test for Chapter 40, or construct your own using the Testmaker software.

---

4. Lenders want to be assured that their loans will be repaid.

Building Academic Skills

Math

1.

Total Sales	$285,000
− Returns & Allowances	4,100
= Net Sales	$280,900
− Cost of Goods Sold	112,000
= Gross Profit	$168,900
− Total Expenses	84,500
= Net Income from Operations	$ 84,400
− Interest Expense	2,400
= Net Profit Before Taxes	$ 82,000
− Taxes (at 20%)	16,400
= Net Profit After Taxes	$ 65,600

545

Career Planning

Unit Objectives

After completing this unit, students will be able to achieve the following outcomes:

- Discuss the importance of marketing careers to the U.S. economy.
- Describe current employment trends.
- Describe the 12 marketing occupational areas.
- Develop a plan to reach their career goals.
- Write a letter of application, a resume, and cover letter, and complete an application form.
- Prepare for and conduct themselves properly during a job interview.
- Follow up a job interview.

Chapter 41

Chapter 42

Chapter 43

Teacher Classroom Resources

CHAPTER	41	42	43
Transparency Binder	Transparency 71	Transparencies 72–74	Transparency 75
Student Activity Workbook	pp. 263–268	pp. 269–276	pp. 277–282
Student Software	pp. 267–268	pp. 275–276	pp. 281–282
Marketing Math Workbook			Activity 12
School-to-Work Handbook	pp. 87–88	pp. 89–90	pp. 91–92
International Case Studies	pp. 87–88	pp. 89–90	pp. 91–92
Marketing Career Portfolio			Unit 12 activity, Student Text, p. 591
Test Booklet/ Testmaker Software	Chapter 41 test	Chapter 42 test	Chapter 43 test, Unit 12 test, Final

KEY TO BASIC SKILLS ACTIVITIES

L1 Level 1 activities are basic activities and should be within the range of all students.

L2 Level 2 activities are average activities and should be within the range of average and above average students.

L3 Level 3 activities are challenging activities designed for the ability range of above average students.

CHAPTER	PERFORMANCE OBJECTIVES	
41 **Careers in Marketing**	**41.1**	1. Discuss the importance of marketing careers to the U.S. economy. 2. Describe current employment trends. 3. Explain the major benefits of working in marketing.
	41.2	1. Define the twelve marketing occupational areas. 2. Discuss marketing jobs at five skills levels. 3. Discuss possible career pathways in the marketing field.
42 **Making Your Career Decision**	**42.1**	1. Assess your values, lifestyle goals, interests, skills and aptitudes. 2. Describe your personality. 3. Describe your work environment and relationship preferences.
	42.2	1. Complete a career assessment. 2. Name career research resources.
	42.3	1. Match your own needs, wants, and potential qualifications with a realistic and satisfying career. 2. Develop a plan to reach your career goals.
43 **Finding and Applying for a Job**	**43.1**	1. Locate job leads from a variety of sources. 2. Name the legal document that you must have before you can begin working.
	43.2	1. Write a letter of application and complete an application form. 2. Write a resume and cover letter.
	43.3	1. Prepare for and conduct yourself properly during a job interview. 2. Follow up a job interview.

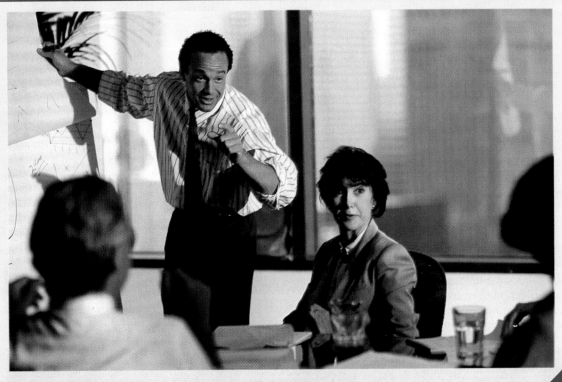

Unit Overview and Background Information

This unit is the logical conclusion to *Marketing Essentials*. After studying the marketing field and the skills necessary to succeed in it, students are ready to get down to the practical aspects of planning their future careers.

Chapter 41 looks at the place of marketing careers in the U.S. economy and describes current employment trends that will affect the employment outlook in marketing. Chapter 42 introduces a seven-step procedure to help guide students in making important career choices. Chapter 43 includes proven methods for conducting a job search.

Introducing the Unit

Ask how many students have seriously considered what career they will pursue after graduation from high school. For those students who have relatively little idea where they will direct their efforts, point out that such current hobbies and interests as sports, computers, and drawing could easily become the marketing jobs of tomorrow. Constantly reinforce how important it is for students to begin career planning now, even if their direction is not fully clear.

Unit Project

Have students write a report about the outlook for marketing jobs in your area. To do this, they can interview officials at local public employment agencies and they can go to company personnel offices. They should include in their questioning what starting salaries are, what level of education is required to start the job, whether there are company training programs, how many openings there are in an average year, and how many applicants there normally are for each opening.

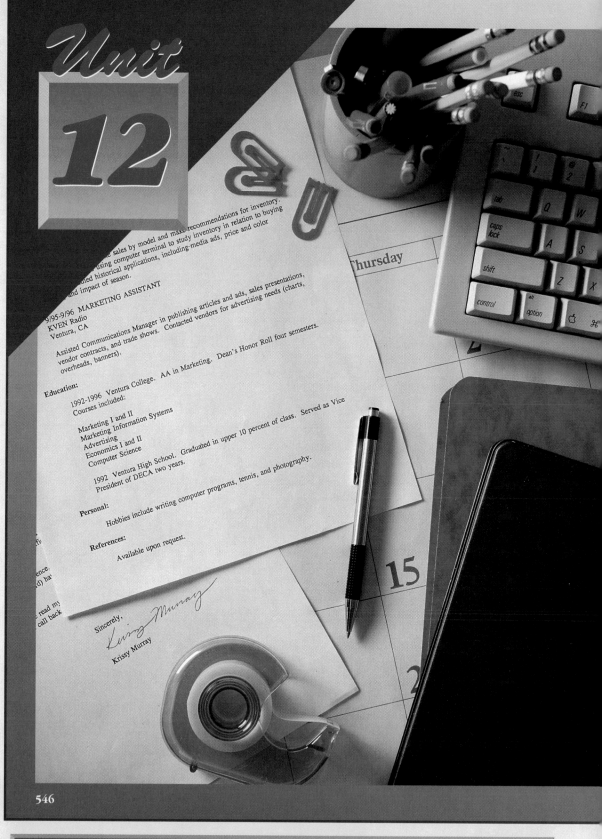

546

Focus on the Photo/Cooperative Learning

Before the class begins this unit, ask students to look at the above picture and list all the items they will need to conduct their job search. After the class has completed this unit, return to this photo and again ask students to come up with a list of items they will need for their job search. Compare and contrast the two lists and notice how much more detailed the second list is.

Career Planning

CHAPTERS

41
Careers in
Marketing

42
Making Your
Career Decision

43
Finding and
Applying for a Job

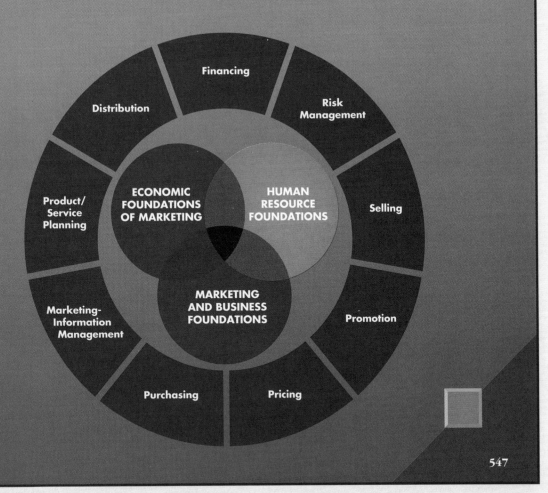

Resources for Enrichment of Unit Content

Books

- *Occupational Outlook Handbook*
- *Dictionary of Occupational Titles*
- *Dress Right for Business*, Glencoe
- *Encyclopedia of Careers and Vocational Guidance*
- *Guide for Occupational Exploration*
- *Independent Study for the World of Work*, Glencoe
- *Job Finding Fast*, Glencoe
- *Succeeding in the World of Work*, Glencoe
- *The Work Book*, Glencoe

Career Interest and Vocational Preference and Interest Surveys

- *Kuder Occupational Interest Survey, Kuder Preference Record*, CTB/McGraw-Hill (800) 538-9547
- *World of Work Career Interest Survey*, Glencoe/McGraw-Hill

Unit Closure

Meet with students individually to make sure that they leave this course with some type of career direction and an understanding of how to use career research resources.

Evaluation

Administer the printed test for Unit 12, or construct your own using the Testmaker software.

547

Guest Speaker Suggestions

- Have representatives from each of the marketing occupational areas form a panel to discuss career opportunities in their areas.
- Have representatives from community and civic organizations talk to students about volunteer opportunities that could prepare them for marketing jobs.

Field Trip Suggestion

Take students to your public library for an introduction to the career section and online career information services.

Chapter Overview

Chapter 41 introduces students to the importance of marketing as a career field.

 ### Springboard

Now that students are nearing the end of their Marketing class, they should be able to identify specific marketing jobs in many career interest areas. Give each student a current magazine or newspaper. Have them search through their publications to find as many examples of marketing jobs as they can. The jobs may not (and probably will not) be specifically cited; students will have to draw inferences from the articles and ads (for example, an article about a hospital may suggest a marketing job as a public relations officer).

Prereading

List the section objectives to discuss with students. Have students skim the chapter, looking at the pictures, reading the captions, and noting the heads. Ask questions to ensure that the students have a minimal understanding of the chapter structure.

Preteaching the Vocabulary

Students should be familiar with all vocabulary terms in this chapter. Have them reach a consensus on definitions for each term.

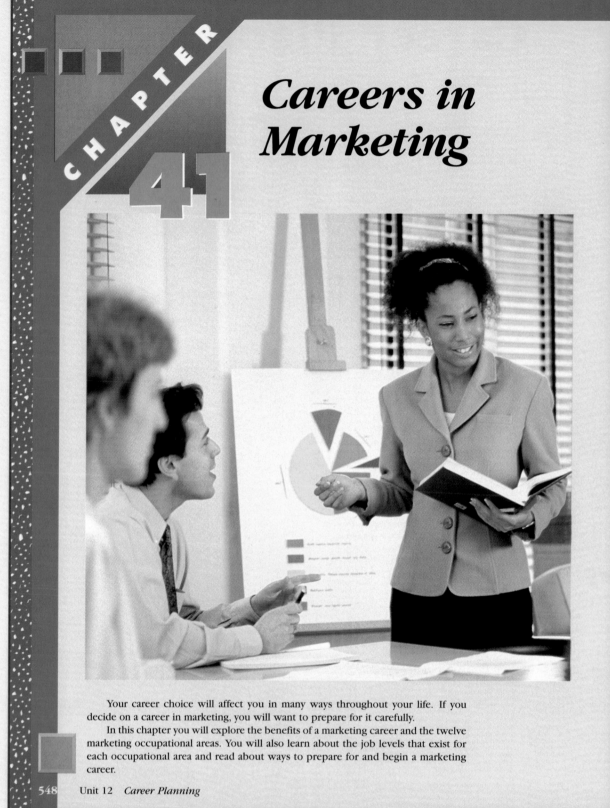

CHAPTER 41

Careers in Marketing

Your career choice will affect you in many ways throughout your life. If you decide on a career in marketing, you will want to prepare for it carefully.

In this chapter you will explore the benefits of a marketing career and the twelve marketing occupational areas. You will also learn about the job levels that exist for each occupational area and read about ways to prepare for and begin a marketing career.

548   Unit 12   *Career Planning*

Classroom Management

For the Teacher
- Teacher's Annotated Editions for all workbooks
- Teacher's Manual for *School-to-Work Handbook*
- *Testing Binder*
- *Transparency Binder*
- *Marketing Software Binder*
- *Marketing Career Portfolio*
- *Lesson Plans*

For the Student
- *Student Activity Workbook*
- *Marketing Math Workbook*
- *School-to-Work Handbook*
- *Student Software*
- *International Case Studies*
- *Marketing Career Portfolio*

SECTION 41.1

Objectives

After completing this section, you will be able to

- **discuss the importance of marketing careers to the U.S. economy,**
- **describe current employment trends, and**
- **explain the major benefits of working in marketing.**

Term to Know

- **fringe benefits**

An Overview of Marketing Careers

About 33 million Americans earn a living in marketing. Marketing provides perhaps the greatest diversity of opportunities of any career field—from buying merchandise to being the president of a company, from selling clothes to designing ads.

Careers in marketing include all the activities required to develop, promote, and distribute goods and services to consumers. When considered in this broad sense, marketing activities account for about one in every three American jobs.

Employment Trends

Of the two basic functions of business, production and marketing, job opportunities in marketing are growing, while those in production are shrinking. The reason for the change is obvious. Production jobs lend themselves to automation and mechanization. In recent years, this has reduced the number of production workers needed by many companies. Marketing, on the other hand, has not been mechanized nearly as much because it requires personal contact.

As an example, consider the use of computers. A single computer and a series of industrial robots can replace a whole production line of workers. A computer system installed in a marketing department, however, is far more likely to enhance the capabilities of its employees rather than replace them.

Indeed, changes in the marketplace have created the need for more rather than fewer marketing professionals. The changing gender roles, the rise in the number of single-person households, changing preferences in recreational activities, and the increase in foreign competition—all must be monitored through market research and marketing information systems. To track these and other quickly developing trends, companies are expanding their marketing programs and staffs.

Benefits of a Marketing Career

Perhaps the most obvious benefit of a career in marketing is the opportunity to make an above-average income. Of course, you probably won't earn any more money in an entry-level marketing job than you would in many other entry-level positions. For example, as a stock clerk in a retail store you will probably earn the minimum wage. Even in an entry-level job, however, it's nice to know that potential earnings in marketing are excellent.

Recent statistics show starting salaries for entry-level jobs in marketing range from $11,000 to $18,000 for high school graduates. New workers with an associate's degree earn between $14,000 and $27,000. New workers with a bachelor's degree in business administration earn between $28,000 and $60,000.

Besides earning you a good salary, a position in marketing may entitle you to some helpful and valuable extras. **Fringe benefits** (also called perquisites or "perks") are benefits, privileges, or monetary payments beyond salary or wages that go with a job. Examples include the use of a company car, an expense account, and bonuses for doing outstanding work.

In addition, most jobs in marketing, especially those beyond entry-level positions, are interesting and varied. Many involve a great deal of contact with people, and this in itself is often enjoyable and growth-producing.

You will usually have more opportunities to advance in a marketing career than in almost any other area of business. This is because of the high visibility that many marketing positions have.

Consider a few examples. People who work in marketing frequently present and shape their ideas in meetings with company managers and executives. People who work in sales get constant feedback on their efforts in the form of sales figures that are regularly reviewed by upper-level management. People who work in advertising may

Chapter 41 *Careers in Marketing* **549**

Focus

Bell Ringer Activity

Have students write one local, regional, statewide, national, or international trend in the marketplace or in the labor force that has been discussed in class over the course of studying this text, or one trend that students have observed through reading news publications, watching television, or observing the local economy.

Introducing the Section

Make a chalkboard list of the trends that students generate (for example, more women are entering the labor force). Then have students generate ways that marketers are responding to each trend. This section looks at the role of marketing in our economy and the benefits of a marketing career.

Teach

Guided Practice

1. Read Section 41.1 with students.
2. Have students read aloud the Case Study and review the answers in class.
3. MarkEd Resource Center in Columbus, Ohio (800) 448-0398, has materials appropriate for use with this chapter.

Discussion Starter

Have students identify some of the rewards and benefits of work, in addition to monetary rewards.

Meeting Special Needs

Physically Challenged

Career choices for the physically challenged students in your class need not be limited in any way other than by the interests and talents of the individual student. In order to help all students overcome preconceived notions of what career choices exist, invite a physically challenged marketer, entrepreneur, or other successful person to class to speak about his or her career. Invite him or her to discuss any obstacles he or she felt hindered his or her success and how he or she overcame them. Allow time for questions and encourage students to ask practical questions about physical barriers to entering buildings and prejudicial treatment.

Independent Practice

1. Assign and review the Chapter 41 Case Study in the *International Case Studies* workbook.
2. Whatever career area students eventually pursue, they should be aware of current and emerging trends in the economy (local, statewide, national, and international) that will affect the demand for people in marketing occupations.

   Give each student a choice of researching the local, statewide, national, or international economy. They should use such resources as a library's online information service, government statistics, statistics from local agencies, and any other resources they deem appropriate (1) to research what factors are positively or negatively affecting their chosen economy, and (2) how these factors will affect the demand for current marketing occupations and create new opportunities for marketers.

   Have all students share their information in class. At the end of the discussion, students should have an accurate picture of trends in the economy, how marketers are addressing those trends now, and how they will probably address them in the future.

Assess

Evaluation

Assign and review the Section 41.1 Review.

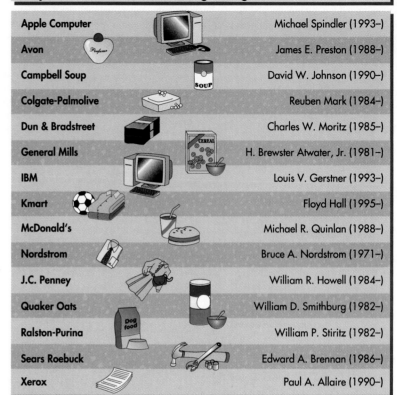

Corporate CEOs with Marketing Backgrounds

Apple Computer	Michael Spindler (1993–)
Avon	James E. Preston (1988–)
Campbell Soup	David W. Johnson (1990–)
Colgate-Palmolive	Reuben Mark (1984–)
Dun & Bradstreet	Charles W. Moritz (1985–)
General Mills	H. Brewster Atwater, Jr. (1981–)
IBM	Louis V. Gerstner (1993–)
Kmart	Floyd Hall (1995–)
McDonald's	Michael R. Quinlan (1988–)
Nordstrom	Bruce A. Nordstrom (1971–)
J.C. Penney	William R. Howell (1984–)
Quaker Oats	William D. Smithburg (1982–)
Ralston-Purina	William P. Stiritz (1982–)
Sears Roebuck	Edward A. Brennan (1986–)
Xerox	Paul A. Allaire (1990–)

Figure 41–1

Corporate CEOs are frequently drawn from the ranks of marketing professionals. Why do you think that marketing professionals make good candidates for CEOs?

develop ad campaigns that win critical acclaim from professional associations. What all these situations make clear is that people who work in marketing do the kinds of things that command attention, especially from management. If they do well, they are far more likely to be credited with their successes and rewarded for them. In terms of a job, this means winning promotions faster in marketing than in other careers.

In fact, because of their high visibility, marketing and sales careers offer the fastest route to middle and top management. A recent survey showed that more chief executive officers (CEOs) reach the top of their organizations through marketing and sales than through any other career area. Figure 41–1 lists just a few of the companies whose CEOs fit this description. All of these CEOs earn at least several hundred thousand dollars per year plus bonuses. Some earn millions.

Real World

Removing Barriers

Ron Mace was nine when polio put him in a wheelchair. He became an architect and designer with the goal of removing the everyday barriers that frustrate disabled people. His company, Barrier Free Environments, Inc., uses Mace's concept of "universal design" to design buildings and products that anyone can use, regardless of age or disability.

SECTION 41.1

Review

1. What proportion of the U.S. workforce is involved in marketing activities?
2. Name one employment trend.
3. List two major benefits of working in marketing.

Caption Answer

A marketing orientation provides the groundwork for business success.

Section Review Answers

1. One third of the work force.
2. Above-average beginning salary and opportunities for rapid advancement.
3. Marketing job opportunities are growing while those in production are shrinking.

CASE STUDY

Sun Financial Group's Clay Biddinger

It might seem crazy for a 26-year-old who has reached the level of sales manager to quit his job. However, that's exactly what Clay Biddinger did.

Biddinger worked for a computer and production equipment rental company. He cared about his customers' needs, and tried to fill them and his customers knew it. But Biddinger wanted to be an entrepreneur. He wanted to rent the same kinds of electronic equipment as his former employer—everything from computers to satellite dishes. He had given his previous customers such good service that one of them lent him $100,000 to get started.

Biddinger's original plan was to start his business with two other partners. Biddinger wasn't ready to put the money into the business right away. However, his two partners also had an industrial lighting company which was experiencing a cash flow problem. The partners asked Biddinger to loan them the money to help them with their financial problems. He loaned it to the business associates, and their business failed. Biddinger lost the money and he and the partners broke up.

Biddinger hadn't had a contract with the customer who loaned him the $100,000. He could have walked away from the loss. Instead, he worked hard, sometimes 20 hours a day, to repay the loan. He was determined to find enough customers to make the money back. At the end of his first year, he had done it—including a $16,000 profit.

Biddinger's successful leasing company is called Sun Financial Group, Inc. In 1993, it had income of more than $25 million and assets worth more than $350 million.

What is the secret of Sun Financial Group, Inc.'s success? Treating both customers and employees well is a big part of the answer. Helping customers to solve their equipment problems includes telling them where else to go, if Sun Financial Group, Inc. can't solve them. It also involves helping customers to get good prices for the equipment Sun Financial Group, Inc. is replacing for them. For example, a banking company in Florida was replacing its ATM machines with leased ones from Sun Financial Group, Inc. Biddinger looked all over the world for buyers for the ATMs. He found them in Czechoslovakia and Russia, where ATMs were a brand new idea. The bank sold its old ATMs for four times as much as it expected!

Biddinger knows that customer service also means listening to customer feedback. He spends one fifth of his time with his salespeople making customer calls. This keeps him up to date on what customers like and don't like about Sun Financial Group, Inc.'s services.

Biddinger thinks it's just as important for his employees to be satisfied. He knows that they will find more customers, if they are happy. The company matches all employee retirement contributions. It provides for employees to invest in company stock. It also sends employees back to college for further education—for free.

Sun Financial Group, Inc. attracts senior sales managers from larger companies. They like the fact that they are able to be entrepreneurs themselves. The company allows them to build their own business with their customers. It stands behind them as a resource, but they are able to act independently. There is no limit to the commissions that they make. Biddinger says he "hopes everyone makes five times more" than he does. The company can only become stronger that way.

Sun Financial Group, Inc. is a company built on the belief of its CEO that pleasing customers and pleasing employees go together to build success. Judging from its history since Biddinger quit his job in 1981 to start the company, that makes good business sense.

Case Study Review

1. Why would people at the marketing supervisor level accept a career-sustaining salesperson's job at Sun Financial Group, Inc.?
2. List some of the risks of leaving a secure position at a big company to start your own business.

A MATTER OF ETHICS

3. Biddinger derived the idea for his company from his previous employer. Do you feel this is an ethical means of deriving an idea? Explain.

Chapter 41   *Careers in Marketing*   **551**

551

Reteaching

1. Assign and review the vocabulary terms for this section.
2. Assign and review Fact and Idea Review questions 1 and 2 from the Chapter Review.
3. Ask students why they think marketing provides such a diversity of career opportunities. (Answers should include the fact that most businesses need product development, distribution, and promotion—key activities in marketing.)

Enrichment

1. Assign and review the appropriate activities in the *Student Activity Workbook*.
2. Assign and review the appropriate Critical Thinking questions from the Chapter Review.
3. Have two or three graduates of your school's marketing education program who are now working successfully in different areas of marketing talk to your students about their careers: (1) how they started, (2) where they are now, and (3) where they would like to be in five years.

   All speakers should discuss the advantages and disadvantages of their jobs, the duties and responsibilities, the fringe benefits, and how their marketing education classes helped them prepare for their careers.

Close

Have students list what they consider to be three to five major benefits of working in a marketing career.

Case Study Answers

1. Answers will vary. Though the salesperson job at Sun appears to be a lower level job, it offers opportunity to be an entrepreneur within the company. The income potential is great.
2. Answers will vary. Loss of job security, no guaranteed salary, losses of health and fringe benefits are some examples of risks.
3. Answers will vary.

Bell Ringer Activity

Write the 12 occupational areas on the board. Have students brainstorm at least three jobs in each area.

Introducing the Section

Survey the class to see how many students are working in each marketing area. (1) How many of them anticipate staying in this area? (2) How many of them have found another area of marketing more interesting? Opportunities for jobs in marketing exist in many areas, at many different skill levels. In this section, students will take a look at the broad range of marketing careers. (Leave your list of jobs on the board; you will use it for the Critical Thinking question in this section.)

Teach

Guided Practice

1. Read Section 41.2 with students.
2. Use the transparency for this section.
3. Your students will benefit from taking an occupational interest survey. California Testing Bureau/McGraw-Hill (CTB), (800) 538-9547, offers the *Kuder Occupational Interest Survey*, which is especially useful for high school students who are identifying potential careers, setting career goals, and making choices about advanced education. CTB also offers the *Kuder Preference Record* which measures students' preferences in ten broad career areas.

552

SECTION 41.2

Objectives

After completing this section, you will be able to

- **define the twelve marketing occupational areas,**
- **discuss marketing jobs at five skill levels, and**
- **discuss possible career pathways in the marketing field.**

Terms to Know

- **occupational area**
- **management training program**

Marketing Occupational Areas

Dividing occupations into areas makes it easier to see the thousands of jobs available in marketing. A marketing **occupational area** is a category of jobs that involves similar interests and skills. It's much easier to find information about the career area that most interests you, if you can focus on one or two areas. There are twelve generally accepted occupational areas within the field of marketing:

1. *Advertising and visual merchandising.* Examples of jobs in this area include copywriters, production assistants, and display specialists.
2. *Apparel and accessories marketing.* Sales of clothing and accessories account for a large fraction of the retail market. This area includes all the jobs that center on providing people with the opportunity to buy apparel and accessories. They include jobs such as manufacturer's showroom salespeople, stock clerks, and apparel retail buyers.
3. *Finance and credit services.* This occupational area includes jobs that involve finance and credit services. Examples of jobs include bank tellers, financial planners, bookkeepers, and financial controllers.
4. *Food marketing.* This area includes both wholesale and retail food sales and the transportation of food to market. (It does not include restaurant jobs, however.) Examples of jobs in this area include produce managers at supermarkets, food brokers, and dispatchers of supermarket chains' fleet of trucks.

552　Unit 12　*Career Planning*

---

5. *General merchandise retailing.* This area includes jobs that involve handling general merchandise and presenting it to customers. Examples of general merchandising and retailing jobs include stock handlers and store salespeople.
6. *Transportation and travel marketing.* This area involves jobs related to transportation and travel marketing. Travel agents, car rental agents, flight attendants, and airline ticket sellers are examples of jobs in this occupational area.
7. *Restaurant marketing.* This area involves jobs related to the restaurant business. It is sometimes divided into fast-food and full service restaurant areas. A chef at a small neighborhood restaurant, as well as the area manager for a national chain of drive-ins, are both involved in restaurant marketing.
8. *Entrepreneurship.* As you know from Chapter 37, an entrepreneur is a person who sets up and operates a business. Entrepreneurs must be knowledgeable about all aspects of the business they plan to manage and own, or they risk losing everything. They must be good planners, money managers, and marketers.
9. *Vehicle and petroleum marketing.* Jobs in tire shops, car dealerships, and the corner service station are involved in this area of marketing.
10. *Hospitality and recreation marketing.* Jobs in the hospitality and recreation area include hotel desk clerks and fitness club managers.
11. *General marketing.* This broad category requires skills that are essential in all areas of marketing. Usually, those preparing for general marketing jobs later move on to more specialized areas. Jobs related to this occupational area include marketing assistants and marketing researchers.
12. *Sales.* Like general marketing, this is a broad category that may include salespeople in any of the other marketing areas. Examples include telemarketers and manufacturer's sales representatives. Good salespeople can work in any of the occupational areas.

Job Levels in Marketing

Many jobs exist within each of the occupational areas of marketing. In apparel marketing, for instance, you might work as a cashier in a small shoe store, or as a women's sportswear buyer for a large department store chain. These two jobs would have different educational, skill level, and experience requirements.

Jobs in each marketing area can be categorized according to five skill levels:

1. *Entry level.* Entry-level jobs usually require no prior experience and involve limited decision-making skills. Jobs at this level include cashiers and stock clerks.
2. *Career sustaining.* Career sustaining jobs require a higher level of skill and more decision making than

---

entry-level jobs. Career-sustaining positions include sales representatives and head tellers.

3. *Marketing specialist.* Employees at the marketing specialist level must exhibit leadership ability and make many decisions on a daily basis. They need to be knowledgeable about many areas of the business that employs them. Being a marketing specialist is a long-term career goal for many in marketing. Examples of marketing-specialist jobs include buyers, loan officers, and cruise ship social directors.

4. *Marketing supervisor.* The fourth level in the marketing occupation hierarchy is the marketing supervisor level. Employees at the supervisory level must have good management skills, the ability to make many decisions on a daily basis, and excellent marketing skills. Sales managers and department managers work at this level. This is the highest career level many people aspire to. The prestige and income are generally quite high, and there is less risk involved than at the top management level.

5. *Manager/owner.* At the top level is the manager/owner. People at this level are competent to run a small business or a significant part of a large business. They must be highly skilled in a number of areas. They are responsible for the final success of the enterprise. Store managers, CEOs, vice presidents for sales, and the owners of small businesses fall under this heading.

Table 41–1 on page 554 shows possible job titles at the five levels in all twelve of the occupational areas.

Marketing Education and Career Pathways

Marketing offers opportunities to people with diverse educational backgrounds. Some people begin an entry-level job immediately after high school. Some take advantage of marketing education programs offered in high school before entering a marketing career. Some go on to a community college, technical institute, or vocational school for more training. Some will choose to earn a four-year degree from a college or university before entering the field.

Choosing your route from school to work is like following a path up a mountain. The path may branch, giving you many choices of routes. The route you choose should be one that prepares you best for the specific career goals you have chosen. It should also fit your own aptitudes. There are several traditional career pathways that you can examine to find the one that's best for you.

Entry-Level Path

There are several ways to train for an entry-level position. One way is to follow the standard high school curriculum. However, a combination of academic core classes,

BRIGHT IDEAS

Follow Your Nose

When percussionist Garry Kvistad went into business in 1979, his goal was to sell instruments and tuning services to other musicians. Along the way, he became interested in wind chimes. Specifically, he found himself annoyed by the poor quality of the chimes on the market. So, he made his own using precision-tuning technology and his own musical experience.

Kvistad's first set of chimes sold immediately. Subsequent orders encouraged him to begin manufacturing in quantity. The deeper he went into the manufacturing process, the more he realized that quality was the key to success. To this end, he developed a computer-aided process to give wind chimes perfect pitch.

In 1994 Kvistad employed 120 employees and had sales of $14 million. Had he stayed on his intended career path, he might have missed all of that. By being receptive to new possibilities and following up on opportunities as they appeared, he created his own distinctive business and quickly leaped to the top of his field.

Creativity Challenge Form teams of 3–5 people. Then try an experiment to duplicate Kvistad's roundabout route to a career.

- First, have each team member write down on a slip of paper a brief description of one noteworthy experience (positive or negative) that he or she has had. This might be a vacation abroad, a summer job, participation in an athletic event, or just a particularly memorable day with your friends or family. Fold the slips of paper and mix them together in a pile.
- Next, as a group, assume the identity of one person, a would-be marketer. Vote on the type of marketer you want to be and decide in which occupational area you will start a job search.
- Finally, "experience" each event submitted by choosing slips at random from the pile and reading them aloud. After each, determine how the experience might affect your career choice and how you will follow up on it. When all the slips have been read, compare the career you ended up with and the career you started with. Rate your ability to turn experiences into career opportunities.

4. Have your school guidance counselors discuss with your students the advantages of having a career goal. He or she should also discuss how to set short-term and long-range goals in anticipation of reaching a career goal. Finally, this person should discuss how the guidance department in your school can facilitate career exploration.

5. If you have not already done so, introduce students to such classic career resources as the *Occupational Outlook Handbook*. Take them to your school library or to a public library for an introduction to the career section and to online career information services.

6. Assign and review the Chapter 41 Activity in the *School-to-Work Handbook*.

Discussion Starter

Ask students how they can benefit now from having a career goal. (Having a career goal improves one's chances of choosing a satisfying career.)

Critical Thinking

Once you have read the section entitled "Job Levels in Marketing," return to the chalkboard list generated in the Bell Ringer Activity and have students classify each job according to its skill level.

Cooperative Learning

Divide students ideally into 12 groups, one for each marketing occupational area. Give each group large sheets of paper or poster board, markers, and several newspapers and magazines. Have each group create a poster that identifies jobs at each of the five skill levels in the group's respective occupational area. Each job should be labeled with the job title, the list of skills needed to do the job well, salary range, and outlook for the future.

More About

Entry-Level Positions

When selecting an entry-level position, students should look for companies that promote from within and that have demonstrated training programs. Many of the fast-food businesses offer this type of opportunity. Not all entry-level positions are equal. Some assume high turnover and hire management from other sources.

Bright Ideas

Ask students to explain how Kvistad's got interested in wind chimes. (Their poor quality.) How did he recognize the defect? (His prior musical training.) What other paths could he have chosen? (He could have ignored the wind chimes because of their poor quality and gone off in any other direction.)

One of the fringe benefits of Pedro's job is the ability to drive his company car for personal use. On his weekly expense reports, he can bill the company 28 cents per mile for each mile driven on company business. He cannot bill the company for personal mileage. Last week, he drove 784 miles. Of this amount, 230 miles were for personal business. How much did Pedro bill the company for mileage? ($155.12. 784 − 230 = 554. 554 × .28 = $155.12)

L2 Math Skills

Louise manages the housewares department at Wren's Department Store. She receives a one-half percent bonus of her department's annual sales, if annual sales exceed $600,000. First quarter sales were $105,678. Second quarter sales were $126,789. Third quarter sales were $200,220. Fourth quarter sales were $224,567. Did she meet her sales numbers? If so, what is her bonus?

(Yes, she met her sales numbers. Final sales were $657,254. [$105,678 + $126,789 + $200,220 + $224,567 = $657,254] Her bonus was $3,286.27. [$657,254 × .005 = $3,286.27])

L3 Math Skills

Tram's annual salary is $45,678. As of December 31, she received a $2,225 annual bonus, and a 5 percent salary increase. In addition to her salary of $45,678, how much more money did she receive? ($4,508.90. $2,225 + [$45,678 × .05] = $4,508.90)

Assuming that local, state, and federal taxes will take at least 30 percent of this amount, how much of her combined bonus and raise will Tram actually keep? ($3,156.23. $4,508.90 × .30 = $1,352.67. $4,508.90 − $1,352.67 = $3,156.23)

Job Titles at the Five Skill Levels in Marketing Occupation Areas

Occupational Areas	Skill Levels				
	Entry Level	Career Sustaining	Marketing Specialist	Marketing Supervisor	Manager/ Owner
Advertising and visual merchandising	proofreader, assistant display specialist	copywriter, display specialist	ad campaign manager	account executive	president
Apparel and accessories marketing	stock clerk, cashier	salesperson	buyer, manufacturer's showroom salesperson	district manager	store manager
Finance and credit services	bank teller bookkeeping clerk	bookkeeper	loan officer, accountant	accounting department manager	vice president
Food marketing	cashier	grocer checker	produce buyer, food broker	bakery manager	store manager
General merchandise retailing	cashier, stock clerk	salespeople, display designers	buyers, retail financial planners	assistant manager of discount store	store managers, corporate top management
Transportation and travel marketing	car rental service attendant	car rental agent, airline clerk	travel agent	car rental office manager	travel agency owner
Restaurant marketing	dishwasher, cashier	waiter, hostess, cook	wine steward, chef	assistant manager	restaurant manager
Entrepreneurship					sole proprietor of retail store
Vehicle and petroleum marketing	service station attendant, auto detailer	mechanic, truck driver, auto salesperson	department supervisor	sales manager	dealership owner, station owner
Hospitality and recreation marketing	maid, bellhop	desk clerk, tennis instructor, personal trainer	cruise ship or resort social director	hotel manager, ski shop manager	athletic club manager
General marketing	marketing assistant	salesperson	market researcher, business consultant	marketing supervisor	manager of consulting business
Sales	cashier, stock clerk	appliance sales, auto sales, insurance sales	real estate broker	department manager	owner of retail store, real estate office

Table 41–1

This table shows the examples of types of jobs in each occupational area, at each of the five skill levels. What skills are required at the marketing supervisor level?

marketing education classes, and participation in a cooperative education program is often a better choice because it prepares you specifically for a career in marketing.

Cooperative education programs give you work experience in marketing as part of your high school curriculum. You may work selling plants in a nursery, stocking shelves in a grocery store, or arranging bouquets at a florist shop. You will learn about business both on the job and in the classroom. When you leave high school, you will already have some marketing experience and knowledge.

Entry-level positions will usually lead to higher level positions. For example, many managers at McDonald's

In order to earn the $60,000 noted earlier in the chapter, very specialized skills are required including computer knowledge, sales skills, and work experience in the industry. Frequently, sales people earn these types of annual salaries based in part on commissions which change from year to year.

Employees at the marketing supervisor level must have good management skills, the ability to make many decisions on a daily basis, and excellent marketing skills.

restaurants start out as counter clerks. They learn as much as possible on the job and many go to McDonald's "Hamburger U" training facility in Chicago to learn more about the job. Then they move up to more responsible and better paying management jobs. Fred Turner, the senior chairman of McDonald's, began his career with the company as a fry cook!

When you enter the marketing field through an entry-level job, it is important to think about the possibilities for further education and training. The entry-level job market is limited. The pay is the lowest in the field, often at or just above minimum wage. Employers seek trained and knowledgeable employees for promotions. It will pay to become one of these.

Career-Sustaining Level Path

The path to a career-sustaining level job involves more education and training than the entry-level route. After graduation from high school, preferably with a marketing education and cooperative education background, you might need further education. For example, a job as an insurance agent will require a state-approved license. A real-estate agent needs a state certificate. Airline clerks are often expected to complete community college, as well as company sponsored training.

For a career-sustaining position, you should begin your study of marketing in high school. Then you can continue your marketing studies at a community college, technical institute, or vocational-technical school that participates in the program.

After two years of study at a community or junior college, you can earn an Associate of Arts (A.A.) degree in marketing. At a vocational-technical school, you can earn a certificate in an area of marketing.

Many programs are designed so that at a later date you can enter a four-year college to complete the work for a four-year degree, such as a Bachelor of Arts (B.A.) or Bachelor of Science (B.S.), depending on the course of study you choose. This allows you to prepare for a more demanding technical job or for a professional position.

Marketing-Specialist Level Path

You may want to begin a marketing career at the professional level. You may want to be a buyer for a big department store chain. Perhaps you'd like to be a hotel manager. These jobs usually require a bachelor's degree.

You will need to complete a solid academic program in high school. This should include courses in marketing and business. In the last year of high school, you can begin to take classes in your specialty area. You can then move on to a four-year college with a solid foundation that includes marketing education.

At the college or university, you will then major in your chosen field. For example, if you want a career in retail management, you will probably choose business administration. For a career in advertising and public relations, art, English, or communications would be good fields to choose. Combinations are also possible. For example, an entrepreneur wanting to open a private health club could major in both business administration and physical education.

Marketing Supervisor Level Path

If you want to advance in marketing research or consulting or move into top management, you will probably need even more than a bachelor's degree. You might need to earn a graduate degree in business or marketing. This usually means two or three more years of study beyond a four-year degree. Often marketing professionals pursue graduate degrees while they are employed. Sometimes their employers even help pay for the further education. It's very demanding working full time and going to school, but for many the rewards are worth it.

One route into the top ranks of marketing is a management training program. Usually, **management training programs** provide six months to two years of closely supervised on-the-job management training.

SECTION 41.2 *Review*

1. Name the 12 occupational areas.
2. Name the five skill levels.
3. Explain how a career pathway can lead to your ultimate career goal in marketing.

Chapter 41 *Careers in Marketing* **555**

SECTION 41.2

Independent Practice

Have students select a job in the marketing occupational area that they are interested in and research the future demand for this job; the skills, knowledge, and experience required; and the common characteristics of the job; and the physical demands of the job.

Assess

Evaluation

Assign and review the Section 41.2 Review.

Reteaching

1. Assign and review the vocabulary terms for this section.
2. Assign and review Fact and Idea Review questions 3–10 from the Chapter Review.
3. Review with students the 12 occupational areas within marketing.

Enrichment

1. Assign and review the appropriate activities in the *Student Activity Workbook*.
2. Assign and review the appropriate Critical Thinking questions from the Chapter Review.
3. Assign and review the Building Academic Skills Activities, Application Projects, Linking School to Work Activities, and Performance Assessment from the Chapter Review.
4. In the Independent Practice Activity, students choose a potential career. Now have students do a personal assessment to see how well their current skills and abilities match the position.

Close

Meet with each student and review and clarify his or her assessment from the #4 Enrichment Activity.

Section Review Answers

1. Occupational areas are listed on page 552.
2. The five levels are listed on page 552.
3. Answers will vary. One possible answer would be to enroll in a marketing program in high school and community college while working at an entry-level job in sales. After completion of a marketing program and additional experience at the entry-level job, one could move onto a career-sustaining job. This person might then enter college and earn a degree in marketing. After receiving a BA, this person might move onto the marketing specialist level.

41 CHAPTER *Review*

Answers

Vocabulary Review

See Glossary for definitions.

Fact and Idea Review

1. Jobs in production are decreasing, while jobs in marketing are increasing. Automation has affected production jobs, while massive changes in the way people live have made more market research necessary.
2. Marketing careers often lead to rapid advancement because of the high visibility that many marketing positions have.
3. Advertising and visual merchandising.
4. Hospitality marketing is related to the hotel and tourist businesses.
5. Examples will vary. Sample answers include salesperson and buyer.
6. High school curriculum, plus marketing education and cooperative learning.
7. High school, vocational college, and four-year college educational programs prepare students for technical jobs.
8. To prepare for a marketing specialist job students should obtain a bachelor's degree.
9. A bachelor's degree and usually a graduate degree in business or marketing.
10. A closely supervised on-the-job program of training in management skills that lasts from six months to two years.

Critical Thinking

1. The same basic interpersonal, communication, and math skills are important in sales positions at all levels and in all types of businesses.
2. Positive attitude, initiative and

Vocabulary Review

Pair up with another student and quiz each other on the meaning of the following vocabulary terms.

fringe benefit
occupational area
management training program

Fact and Idea Review

1. How do the trends in marketing and production jobs compare? What accounts for the differences in the trends? (Sec. 41.1)
2. Why do jobs in marketing often lead to rapid career advancement? (Sec. 41.1)
3. Which occupational area would you be working in if you were a copywriter? (Sec. 41.2)
4. What is hospitality marketing? (Sec. 41.2)
5. Give an example of a general merchandise retailing job. (Sec. 41.2)
6. What types of training will help you prepare for an entry-level marketing job? (Sec. 41.2)
7. What types of training will help you prepare for a career-sustaining level marketing job? (Sec. 41.2)
8. What educational background will help you prepare for a job at the marketing-specialist level? (Sec. 41.2)
9. What type of degree should you have to enter the marketing supervisor level? (Sec. 41.2)
10. What is a management training program? (Sec. 41.2)

Critical Thinking

1. Discuss how the marketing skills you would learn in a fast-food restaurant could be transferred to an industrial sales position.
2. If you decide to be a marketing entrepreneur, what kinds of character traits and interpersonal skills do you think you will need?
3. At which level of marketing do you think the most interesting jobs are? Explain why you believe this.
4. You have decided that you would like to start a business designing, producing, and selling women's sweaters. What kinds of courses would give you a good background for this?
5. Which occupational area in marketing are you most interested in? Why? Do you have work experience in this area? If not, explain how could you get work experience in this area.

Building Academic Skills

Math

1. In your entry-level job as a salesclerk, you made $12,000 a year. After many years of hard work and a long series of promotions, you became director of marketing at $120,000 a year. This is what percentage of your original salary?
2. Your salary as art director of Sell-Win Toys is $53,000. If, in addition, you earn a bonus of 5 percent of your annual salary, what would be your total earnings for the year?
3. Mike's Drum Shop wants to begin carrying a new line of congas from Brazil. Mike plans to borrow the money to buy 28 drums. The drums cost Mike $80 each, and he has to pay interest of 10 percent on the loan. How much will the drums cost Mike, including financing?

Communication

4. Many jobs in marketing involve a great deal of personal contact and require a high level of communication skills. Explain how and why such skills might be important in the following marketing careers.
   a. Personnel director for a large retail chain
   b. Advertising director
   c. Public relations specialist
5. Use a word processing program to write a plan for appropriate education and training for the marketing career of your choice.
6. Explain why someone working in the sales area of marketing would need to have good listening skills.

Human Relations

7. Suppose you have a sales position with a company. You enjoy the work and excel at it. In fact, you do so well that the company promotes you to sales manager. However, you soon find that supervising others does not suit you as well as sales did. What would you do?
8. How would you relate to a female supervisor? How would you relate to a male supervisor? If you feel that you would relate to each one differently because of his or her gender, tell why this would make a difference to you.
9. You have a friend who is planning to get a full-time job in a fast-food restaurant after high school. She thinks that something better will come along after

---

creativity, persuasive, willingness to take risks and accept responsibility, high self-esteem.
3. Answers will vary.
4. Examples include accounting and finance, management and business administration, selling, and clothing design.
5. Answers will vary.

Building Academic Skills

Math

1. 1000%
2. $55,650
3. $2464 (28 × $80 = $2240; $2240 × 10% = $224; $2240 + $224 = $2464)

Communication

4. Answers will vary.

she has gained some experience. How would you convince your friend that she would be better off getting more education?

Application Projects

1. List ten people you know who are employed. Do the work activities of these people involve marketing? How and to what extent? Compare your list with those of other students in your class.
2. Majoring in marketing in college could prepare you for a variety of careers, including work in television or radio. Find out what marketing opportunities exist in radio and television.
3. Ask your teacher or work coordinator to assist you in contacting a local businesswomen's organization and a minority businessperson's organization. See if you can get a representative from each group to come to speak to your class about the opportunities for women and minorities in the marketing field.
4. Research a local company's management training program. Report your findings to your classmates. Include the advantages and disadvantages of getting involved in such a program.
5. Read the classified section of your newspaper for one week. Bring to class five entry-level job positions that could lead to marketing careers.
6. Research a marketing career in warehouse management and visual merchandising. For each career, answer these questions:
   a. What are the employment trends in this area of marketing?
   b. What kind of education and training does this person need for this position?
   c. What would be the range of this person's job duties?
   d. What would be the advantages to having this job? the disadvantages?
   e. What would be the opportunities for advancement in this job?
   f. What would be the general salary range?
   g. Does this particular job in marketing appeal to you? Why or why not?
7. Research three marketing jobs, using U.S. government publications, such as the *Guide to Occupational Exploration, Dictionary of Titles,* and *The Occupational Outlook Handbook.* In addition to reporting on the educational and training requirements needed for each job, discuss the predicted outlook and the expected salary and promotions for each job. Report your findings to the class.
8. Write a short biography on a CEO of a large corporation. Choose someone whose background is in marketing. Be sure to include the person's education and a discussion of the jobs that led her or him to the top.

Linking School to Work

What levels of marketing jobs exist at your workplace? Describe the jobs at your workplace in terms of the five skill levels of marketing jobs.

Performance Assessment

Role Play

Situation. A friend of yours is starting an athletic fitness center and has asked you to serve as a business consultant. Your job is to develop a plan that includes a description of the marketing area the business is in; a proposal for the number of employees needed to staff the center; the title, skill level, and duties required of each position; and the training and education applicants need in order to obtain each position. Present your plan to your friend.

Evaluation. You will be evaluated on how well you can do the following:

- Identify occupational areas in marketing.
- Demonstrate your understanding of the five job levels in marketing.
- Discuss education options for marketing careers.
- Assess the staffing needs of a particular business.

Public Speaking

Choose a long-term career goal and design a course of study and on-the-job training that will lead you to your goal. Include the classes you should take in high school and a post secondary institution, an appropriate entry-level job, and possible management training programs. Present your findings in a five-minute speech to the class.

Complete the Chapter 41 Computer Application that appears in the Student Activity Workbook.

5. Answers will vary. Students should show familiarity with tech-prep and 2+2 programs in their plans.
6. Answers will vary. Salespeople need to understand customer desires and needs very well.

Human Relations

7. Answers will vary. Students might suggest that they talk to their supervisor about the situation. The student may also suggest that he or she take classes to learn management skills.
8. Answers will vary. Students should be aware of issues of discrimination. Would they discriminate against one gender or another?
9. Answers will vary. It is important to support the friend's self-esteem and encourage her to think she can succeed. Also, it is important to remind her that education gives her more career options.

Application Projects

1. Answers will vary. Have a class discussion about the ratio of marketing to non-marketing jobs in students' lists. Does the ratio indicate that marketing jobs are the national average of one in three?
2. Students can research radio and television careers in their library or they could call or write a local radio and television station and arrange for someone in the field to speak to the class.
3. Students should create a list of questions to ask the representative prior to the meeting.
4. Students should discuss the common elements that are used by all the companies presented.
5. Have students present their jobs they have selected and discuss why they selected these jobs.
6. Students should summarize their findings in a 250-word paper.
7. The teacher might list on the board or overhead projector, the information students report. Students can then compare the information on various marketing jobs.
8. Suggested resources for writing the papers include *Forbes, Business Week, Inc.,* and *Fortune.*

Linking School to Work

Answers depend on the work situation.

Performance Assessment

Refer to the *DECA Competitive Events Handbook* for evaluation guidelines.

Computer Application

Optional activity. Refer to the *Marketing Software Binder* for template and user information.

Evaluation

Administer the reproducible test for Chapter 41, or construct your own using the Testmaker software.

Chapter Overview

In this chapter, students look at the factors that will affect and influence their career decision.

Springboard

The day before you begin this chapter, have students create a sheet of paper with five columns:
(1) Jobs I would like to explore,
(2) My current skills and abilities that would be needed in this job,
(3) Current hobbies and interests that relate to this job,
(4) Educational preparation for this job, and
(5) Personal traits suited to this type of work.

Students should list at least three jobs and fill in the information requested. Have students bring their charts to class. Allow some of them to share the information they generated. This chapter will show them how to take all of these factors into consideration when making career decisions.

Prereading

List the section objectives to discuss with students. Have students skim the chapter, looking at the pictures, reading the captions, and noting the heads. Ask questions to ensure that the students have a minimal understanding of the chapter structure.

Preteaching the Vocabulary

Write the vocabulary terms on the board. Have each student silently choose two terms from the list and look up each term in the chapter without writing anything down. Have them close their texts and give the definition for each term to the person sitting next to them.

558

CHAPTER 42

Making Your Career Decision

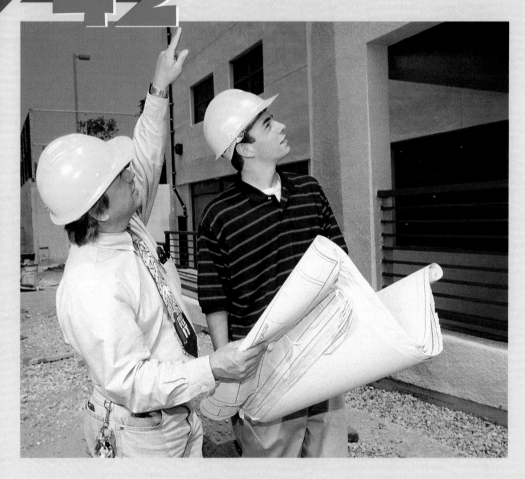

Your career choice will affect you in many ways throughout your entire life. So, you will want to give this decision careful consideration.

In this chapter you will discover how to assess your needs, wants, and personal qualifications. You will learn how to research careers by identifying your choices and gathering information on each choice. Finally, you will evaluate your choices, decide on a career, and develop a plan to achieve your career goal.

Classroom Management

For the Teacher
- Teacher's Annotated Editions for all workbooks
- Teacher's Manual for *School-to-Work Handbook*
- *Testing Binder*
- *Transparency Binder*
- *Marketing Software Binder*
- *Marketing Career Portfolio*
- *Lesson Plans*

For the Student
- *Student Activity Workbook*
- *Marketing Math Workbook*
- *School-to-Work Handbook*
- *Student Software*
- *International Case Studies*
- *Marketing Career Portfolio*

SECTION 42.1

Objectives

After completing this section, you will be able to

- **assess your values, lifestyle goals, interests, skills and aptitudes;**
- **describe your personality; and**
- **describe your work environment and relationship preferences.**

Terms to Know

- **values**
- **lifestyle goals**
- **aptitude**
- ***Dictionary of Occupational Titles (DOT)***

Choosing a Career

Choosing a career requires careful thought and preparation. The following procedure will help guide you in making important career choices:

1. Conduct a self-assessment.
2. Identify possible career choices.
3. Gather information on each choice.
4. Evaluate your choices.
5. Make your decision.
6. Plan how you will reach your goal.

Self-Assessment

The first step in your career search is to conduct a self-assessment. You can begin to do this by assessing your values, lifestyle goals, and interests. Then you can assess your skills and aptitudes, personality, work environment, and relationship preferences. As you make your assessment, record your findings in a special notebook or a section in a career planning notebook. Label it "Self-Assessment File." Summarize your various assessments in paragraph form or, where appropriate, use a rating scale.

Your Values

Things that are important to you are your **values**. Defining your system of values provides guideposts for your life and is essential in choosing a career. When you have clear values, you know what you want out of life. You can then choose a career that is suited to your values.

How do you know what your values are? The things and activities on which you spend your time and money are good indicators of your values.

Your Lifestyle Goals

The word *lifestyle* refers to the way you live. Dr. Arnold Mitchell, author of *The Nine American Lifestyles*, studied thousands of Americans over the age of 18. He learned a great deal about how people live and how satisfied they are with their lives. For example, he learned that the happiest, most satisfied people have the greatest control over how they spend their time. Most of these people are well educated, motivated to succeed, and have incomes well above the average. Dr. Mitchell's work showed the effect that a career has on total lifestyle.

Your lifestyle is made up of many things, including the following:

- where you live (city or rural area);
- the type of housing you live in;
- the school you attend;
- your favorite foods, clothing, and leisure activities;
- your relationships with your family and friends;
- your mode of transportation; and
- the work you do to earn a living.

Goal Setting The first step toward achieving the lifestyle you want is setting goals. Start by setting your long-range goals, those furthest in the future. Next, set the medium-range goals that will help move you closer to your long-range goals. Finally, set your short-range goals, the most immediate ones that will start you on your way toward your medium-range goals.

Your long-range goals are based on your dream lifestyle for some time in the future. These **lifestyle goals** reflect your vision of how you see yourself living in the future.

How do you want to be living, say, 20 years from now? Do you want to be married? Do you want children? What leisure activities will you pursue? Will you want to do a lot of entertaining? What type of home will you want? Once you picture these needs and wants, you can make plans for attaining them. These long-range goals will determine all the others.

The key to your dream lifestyle is the right career because your earnings will pay for your lifestyle. Remember, too, that your career not only supports your

SECTION 42.1

Focus

Bell Ringer Activity

Everybody knows people who are happy and people who are unhappy in their jobs. Begin this section by having students generate some examples of each (but do not allow them to give actual names). Then have students help you generate a chalkboard list of probable reasons that could help explain why these people enjoy/do not enjoy their work. Consider such things as personality type, aptitude for the type of work, whether or not the work agrees with each persons basic values, etc.

Write students' observations on the board, cautioning them that the purpose of this exercise is only to observe and not to make value judgments on others.

Introducing the Section

After you have finished the Bell Ringer Activity, have students consider the reasons why they are happy or unhappy in their co-op jobs or with any other activity in their lives such as participating in sports, school activities, or other extracurricular activities. Their reasons for being happy and/or unhappy will probably mesh with their observations generated in the Bell Ringer Activity.

This section will help them explore such considerations as personal values, skills, and aptitudes when setting career goals.

Meeting Special Needs

Visually Impaired

Students with visual challenges will require more detailed options than those presented in the chapter. Making career decisions for these individuals involves the same process described coupled with information about employers who have proven that they provide an optimum work environment for those who require special assistance.

As with the physically challenged students, there is no reason to limit choices. Only the fact that not all businesses have the resources to equip themselves for the visually challenged will limit the employment selections. Providing mentor opportunities is another viable method of offering assistance.

Guided Practice

1. Read Section 42.1 with students.
2. Use the transparency for this section.
3. MarkEd Resource Center in Columbus, Ohio, (800) 448-0398, has materials suitable for use with this chapter.
4. This section recommends the use of the *World of Work Career Interest Survey*. You can also contact CTB/McGraw-Hill, (800) 538-9547, for information on its vocational preference record and vocational interest surveys.
5. Invite one of your school's guidance counselors to discuss his or her services and resources available to help students research careers. In addition, you may wish to invite representatives of local, state, and federal government offices, along with military recruiters, to discuss how students can begin to research marketing-related careers in government and/or military service.

Discussion Starter

According to this section, the things and activities on which you spend your time and money are good indicators of your values. Ask students to consider the things and activities on which they, as a class in your marketing education program, have spent time and money. What do you, as a group, value?

---

lifestyle but is a part of it. The right career will be compatible with all the other elements in your life.

Goal Orientation A goal-oriented person is intellectually and emotionally directed toward achieving goals. How goal-oriented are you? Can you focus on achieving your goals even when it means giving up something else you would like? You probably know people who have difficulty achieving long-range goals because they are constantly distracted.

Suppose that your dream lifestyle depends on a career that requires a four-year degree. To achieve this goal, your study time will have to take the place of many fun activities you could be doing. You will also have to give up many things you could buy, if you were not spending money on tuition. However, if your goals are important to you, and if you are goal-oriented, you will make the necessary sacrifices.

If you do decide to pursue further education and training beyond high school, you will need to think about how you will pay the costs. Education is expensive, and the price goes up every year, but it is still an excellent investment.

Your Interests

You will probably spend 30 to 40 years working, so you will want to choose work that interests you. Of course, many jobs can become routine after a few years. That's when people hope to get promoted to a more challenging job.

When you research careers, you will make judgments about how interesting each career would be. Your judgments will probably be more accurate if you first survey your own interests.

To evaluate your interests, write down the things you like to do. Include interests such as leisure activities, school activities, and sports and social activities.

You may have a long list of interests. If your list is short, you may want to try out some new activities to learn whether you want to pursue them.

Your favorite classes in school, too, may suggest careers you would find interesting. List them according to the ones you like best.

Another way to find out about your interests is to take an interest survey. One of these, the *World of Work Career Interest Survey*, is similar to a test, but there are no right or wrong answers. You are given a long list of activities, and you decide how much you would like doing each of them. Then you score your own survey to learn which career areas you would find most interesting. Your school counselor or marketing teacher can probably arrange for you to take one of these surveys.

Your Skills and Aptitudes

Values and interests are important in self-assessment, because they help you picture what you want your life to become. They may even suggest certain careers. Beyond that, it takes certain skills to be successful in any career.

For a career goal to be realistic, you have to have an *aptitude* for the work. An **aptitude** is a knack, or a potential, for learning a certain skill. If you don't have an aptitude for skills required in a certain career, even a high level of interest won't help you succeed. For example, the person who can't describe the benefits of products won't have much success selling.

You can see, then, that it is important to identify your aptitudes before you choose a career. Begin a new page in your self-assessment file, and list all the things you have done well. Do you find it easy to sell cookies, candy bars, or whatever your DECA or marketing class sold to raise funds? Are you good at organizing committees and getting everyone to do their jobs? Is math easy for you? Have you won any prizes for your creative ability?

The grades you earn in school may indicate some of your aptitudes. If most of your written reports earned As and Bs, you probably have an aptitude for writing.

There are several tests that can help indicate areas of strength. If you want to take an aptitude test, ask your school counselor about it.

Perhaps you have already developed certain skills that will be useful in a career that interests you. If so, list them on a separate sheet of paper in your self-assessment file. Then add to your list as you develop new skills. Your skills list will be very helpful when you apply for a job.

Your Personality

Dr. John Holland identified six basic personality types and described how they relate to career choices. He also developed a personality test called *The Self-Directed Search* to help people learn to identify their personality types. Taking this test would provide another piece of information to help you make the right career choice. If you would like to take it, talk with your school counselor.

However, you may not need to take a test to learn about your own personality or how it will fit with certain careers. To assess your own personality traits, use a new page in your self-assessment file to list all the words that describe you. Then, as you research careers, try to find one that fits well with your own traits.

Your Work Environment

Your work environment refers to where you work—the place and the work conditions. Working conditions include sights, sounds, and smells.

Many factors affect working conditions—geographic location, for example. If you work outdoors, it makes a big difference whether you live and work in Syracuse, New York or Phoenix, Arizona. Whether you work during the day or at night also affects your working conditions.

You don't have to know all your preferences about working conditions now, but start thinking about them. Then, when you read about the working conditions of a certain career, you will have a better idea of whether you would prefer that career.

Lifelong Learning

Making Your Career Decision

Making a career choice is a lengthy process and does not always work out as planned. Explain that career development is not always an exact science and that it never actually ends. What meets a person's needs at one stage of life may not work at another. Having a family can impact greatly on career plans, as can health, the economy, world events, and new interests. Encourage students to think of career decisions as an ongoing process that will continue their entire adult life. Some students do not know yet where their strengths lie; others have a crystal clear mission. In either case, it is important to have an understanding of the career decision-making process.

Figure 42-1

DATA, PEOPLE, THINGS

All jobs involve working with data, people, or things.

◀ **Data**

A computer programmer works mostly with data. Do you like doing involved math problems? Do the hours pass quickly when you're working on a computer? If you answered yes, then you probably like working with data.

People ▲

This salesperson sells stereo equipment. Salespeople deal mostly with people. Think about your own preferences. Do you prefer working with large groups or with one person at a time? Do you get lonely working alone for hours on a project? A little reflection will probably tell you how much you like working with people.

Things ▲

A woodworker spends most of his or her time working with things. Do you enjoy spending Saturdays working on your car or fixing things around the house? If so, then you probably like working with things.

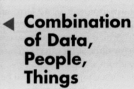

◀ **Combination of Data, People, Things**

In most marketing careers, you will work with more than one of the three. A travel agent works mostly with people and data.

Your Relationship Preferences

All jobs require working with data, people, or things—alone or in some combination. (See Figure 42-1.) Take some time to assess your preferences for data, people, and things. Talk with a family member about it, or rank your preferences on a scale of 1 to 10 (10 being the highest). Then consult some references. The *Dictionary of Occupational Titles (DOT),* for example, describes more than 20,000 jobs in terms of their relationships with data, people, and things. You can use the *DOT* to compare your preferences with the profiles of jobs you find interesting.

SECTION 42.1

Review

1. What area should you consider when conducting a self-assessment?
2. What are values?
3. What is the purpose of setting lifestyle goals?
4. Why is it important to know what skills and aptitudes you have?

Chapter 42 *Making Your Career Decision* **561**

Focus

Bell Ringer Activity

Ask students to answer these questions: (a) If you wanted to research one or several careers, what resources would you use? (b) In researching each career, what types of things would you want to know about each one and how they relate to your perception of what you are and what you want?

Introducing the Section

Make two lists of students' answers from the Bell Ringer Activity, based on (a) and (b) above. When discussing (b), encourage students to look beyond such things as duties and responsibilities, and include such things as values and lifestyle. Keep these lists on the board throughout this lesson and add to them as you discuss additional research resources and the things students would want to further explore.

Teach

Guided Practice

1. Read Section 42.2 with students.
2. When discussing the *DOT*, the *OOH*, and the *GOE*, reproduce and distribute pages from each so that students have a better idea of the content of each. Allow students to compare and contrast the similarities and differences between each resource.

■ SECTION 42.2

Objectives

After completing this section, you will be able to

- **complete a career assessment and**
- **name career research resources.**

Terms to Know

- **career outlook**
- *Occupational Outlook Handbook (OOH)*
- *Guide for Occupational Exploration (GOE)*
- **career consultation**

Career Assessment

Now begin a new section in your career planning notebook. Label it "Career Assessment File." Compare the information you write here with your self-assessment section to make a career decision.

Even if you have already chosen a career goal, select two or three other careers to research and assess. By learning about several careers now, you will save time later if your first choice turns out to be inappropriate.

If you have a career goal in mind, list it first. Then add any others you think might be possibilities.

Work Values

Certain values are important to success on the job. These include honesty, dependability, diligence, and team spirit.

In addition, however, each job and each career field have their own special work values. For example, most retail marketing careers would place a high value on working long hours, getting along with others, coping with stress, and being willing to work for lower pay initially.

As you research the careers you have selected, try to look beyond the duties and responsibilities. Consider the values that are important for success in each field.

Lifestyle Fit

Some careers will fit your lifestyle goals better than others. As you research each career, try to determine how

---

compatible it will be with the other elements of your lifestyle.

If spending time with your family is important to you, for example, then you probably wouldn't want a career that requires a lot of travel. If leisure time is important, then you probably wouldn't be happy working weekends.

Look for a career that enhances the other elements of your lifestyle. At least choose a career that doesn't conflict with them.

Salaries and Benefits

As you look at each career, ask whether it will provide the financial support for the lifestyle you want. Consider both salary and such fringe benefits as paid vacations, life insurance, health insurance, and a pension (or retirement) plan.

Everyone wants paid vacations, so you will no doubt look for this benefit. Life insurance is especially important for families. If your employer pays for this or if you can pay lower premiums through an employer-sponsored group plan, then you can save some money. The high cost of health care today makes health insurance a necessity. Some employers pay the premiums for all their employees. Others have group plans that save you money. You may not think a retirement plan is important since retirement seems a long way off. Nevertheless, many older workers continue working into their seventies because they are not covered by such a plan. Many others must rely on social security alone, which supports only the most basic lifestyle.

Some careers provide more fringe benefits than others. Some, for example, regularly pay bonuses or give discounts on merchandise. Some even make recreational facilities available to their employees.

Career Outlook

Suppose you find a career that seems interesting, one in which you could do well and one that will satisfy your lifestyle goals. You then need to see what the *career outlook* is in the field.

The availability of jobs is called the **career outlook.** Try to find a job in a field where the career outlook is good. This means one in an area that is growing and will therefore provide many job opportunities and many opportunities for advancement.

Education and Training

Every job requires a certain level of education and training. Some require only graduation from high school. Others require a year or two of post-high school education or training. Some require four or more years of college.

Look at the education and training requirements of various careers. For example, what if the career that fits your values, interests, aptitudes, and lifestyle goals requires more education and training than you are willing to pursue?

Did You Know

The average person can change jobs as many as six or seven times in a lifetime. It is also increasingly common to make complete career changes more than once in a work life. Often job changes are a result of economic downturns and a changing workplace. Other times people change careers simply to better suit their interests or lifestyle.

Duties and Responsibilities

More than anything else, jobs are distinguished by their duties and responsibilities. Job duties are the things you will be doing. Responsibilities are the things for which you must be accountable. For example, one of your duties may be to type business reports. Your responsibilities include completing the work neatly, correctly, and on time.

While you are researching careers, then, learn all you can about the duties and responsibilities of each job you are considering. That way, you can be more sure of matching yourself with a career that you will find interesting and can excel in.

Skills and Aptitudes Required

You know that it takes more than just an interest in a job or career to succeed. Every job requires different types and levels of skills.

As you research each career, note the skills needed to perform the required duties and exercise the required responsibilities. Then determine what aptitudes would be helpful in learning those skills. For example, suppose you are considering a career in advertising. When you look at the job description of an advertising copywriter, you learn that the skill used most is writing. If you haven't done much writing, you probably haven't developed much writing skill. The next question is, then, do you have an aptitude for writing?

Consider another example. When you look at the job description of an advertising layout artist, you learn that you would need good artistic skills. Perhaps you've done a lot of sketching and are developing your art skills further. If not, do you have an aptitude for sketching and design work?

Helpful Personality Traits

Personality is the total, complex mix of emotional and behavioral characteristics that makes each person unique. You have probably noticed that people in some careers seem to have similar personality traits. Does this mean that the type of work you do affects your personality, or do people with certain personality traits tend to choose specific careers? The answer to both questions, of course, is yes.

Your personality is affected, sometimes in minute ways, by all your life experiences. Since the work you do

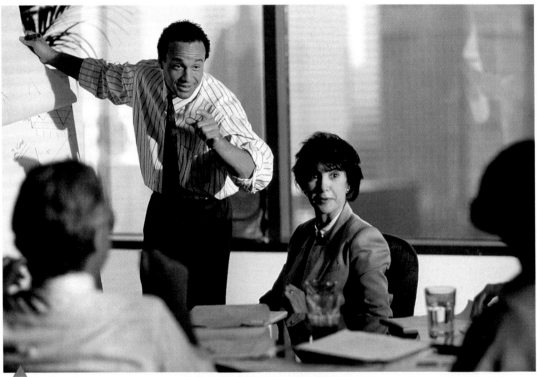

Personality traits **can help you succeed at certain jobs. For example, if your job involves public speaking, an exuberant personality will help you make your speeches more powerful. What personality traits do you have that would help you on the job of your choice?**

Chapter 42 *Making Your Career Decision* **563**

SECTION 42.2

3. There are numerous career texts available from trade publishers that give information on the current job market, specific careers, and trends for the future. Try to have some of these texts available in your classroom for independent student reading and/or for research. Many of them contain the latest projections from the Department of Labor and will help you maintain an accurate picture of national employment trends.
4. Assign and review the Chapter 42 Activity in the *School-to-Work Handbook*.

Discussion Starter

Discuss with students what they consider to be the most important fringe benefits in a job at this point in their lives. How will this change once they (a) live on their own, (b) have a family, (c) are not covered by their parents' or guardians' health insurance? (Answers will vary. You may wish to give students other variables to consider.)

Critical Thinking

Have students relate their observations on employment trends locally, regionally, and nationally, and tell how such trends will affect their preparation for pursuing their anticipated careers. They should consider such things as employment outlook, ability to work in certain areas of the country, initial and continuing education that it will take to keep abreast of developments in the field, and how they can prepare now for the current and anticipated changes.

Caption Answer

Answers will vary. An example might be. Good listening skills would be helpful in a managerial job.

Teach (Cont'd.)

Why are some people content to work in jobs where the salary is low when they have the skills and knowledge to be making more money elsewhere? (Answers should include a discussion of the non-material benefits of working at any job: enjoyment of the work, the joy of helping others, an alignment of one's personal values with the job and its requirements, an enjoyment of co-workers and/or the general atmosphere, a good "fit" with one's lifestyle, etc.)

L1 Math Skills

Give students the following scenario: Julia's company health insurance plan pays 80 percent of the first $1,000 worth of prescriptions and doctor's charges she incurs in a year. After this $1,000 limit is reached, the plan pays 95 percent. In 1999, her charges for prescriptions and doctor's visits were $1,765.60. How much did she pay out of pocket in 1999 for prescriptions and doctor's visits? ($238.28. $1,000 × .20 = $200. $765.50 × .05 = $38.28. $200 + $38.28 = $238.28)

L2 Math Skills

Give students the following scenario: Each paycheck, Julia has $7.65 deducted for health insurance, $2.50 deducted for life insurance, $1.75 deducted for dental insurance, and $5 deducted for a contribution to United Way. Julia receives 24 paychecks a year. How much is deducted from her paycheck over the course of a year for insurance and charitable contributions? ($404.40. $7.65 + $2.50 + $1.75 + $5 = $16.90. $16.90 × 24 = $405.60)

BRIGHT IDEAS

Do Your Homework

Imagine that it's 1957, and you're in an advanced English class. It's the night before the exam, and you haven't been able to finish your Shakespeare assignment. You contemplate your situation and envision a solution: "Gee, I wish someone else could read *King Lear* and explain it to me by tomorrow." But no help comes because Cliff Notes won't be invented until 1958.

Created by Cliff Hillegass in his Lincoln, Nebraska basement with an investment of $4,000, these controversial study aids originally consisted of titles on 16 Shakespearean works. They were always intended to accompany the reading of the text, not replace it.

Hillegass's idea obviously struck a chord with the buying public. Today the line consists of over 280 titles and sells 5 million study guides each year. Since 1993, the publisher has also offered a complete computer software line of study aids called Cliffs Study Ware.

Such products can be the bane of English professors, especially when students try to use them in place of reading the actual work. Students, for their part, are happy to have some help in getting through challenging works of literature and they don't mind paying for the service.

Creativity Challenge Form teams of 3–5 people, and compile a list of references you would like to have as *job search* aids—not titles but descriptions of content. Don't let yourselves be bound by what you *think* exists. Rather, let your imagination go and describe what you *wish* existed. After class, take your list to the school or public library and ask whether there are such references. You may be pleasantly surprised. (Remember, if you can imagine it, someone can write it and may already have done so. If not, then maybe you can do it in the future. Consider it another career opportunity!)

to earn a living will probably become the central activity in your life, it will certainly affect your personality. Your interpersonal relationships with other people at your workplace will have the greatest effect.

A popular belief about salespeople is that they must have outgoing personalities. That is not totally true, of

course. In reading the sales unit in this book, you learned that many successful salespeople do not have outgoing personalities. However, they enjoy helping other people. A very quiet person who is uncomfortable with strangers will have a difficult time on most sales jobs.

Work Environment

Working conditions vary from one job to another. For example, there are big differences in the work environments of an office, a department store, and a factory.

As you study the working conditions of the careers you have selected, try to learn these things about each job:

- Is the work done indoors or outdoors?
- Is the work done sitting down or standing up?
- Is the work environment dusty, smelly, or especially noisy?
- Is the work environment dangerous? If so, what are the risks?
- Is the work physically tiring (does it involve a lot of lifting, stretching, or walking)?
- Is the work done on a regular shift, such as 9–5, or must it be done at night or on weekends?

Work Relationships

As you research careers, note the data/people/things relationships in the specific jobs you have selected. Most jobs require working with other people to some extent. Some jobs—those in retail sales, for example—require you to work with people almost constantly. Other jobs require you to work almost constantly with data or things.

Research Resources

To research careers, you will need to gather information from a variety of sources. The best ones are *libraries, career consultations,* and actual *work experience.*

Libraries

You can find many good career information resources in your school or public library. Many school libraries have a special section, usually called the Career Information Center, devoted to career information. Others may simply carry career materials. In either case, you will find books, magazines, pamphlets, films, videos, and special references that will tell you more about your career choices.

The U.S. Department of Labor publishes three reference books that are especially helpful in career research. They are the *Dictionary of Occupational Titles,* the *Occupational Outlook Handbook,* and the *Guide for Occupational Exploration.* Most school and public libraries have these reference books.

Bright Ideas

Have students discuss the ethics of products such as Cliff Notes, which are generically referred to as "study aids." Ask if students have ever used such a product and if so, if they used it in addition to reading the material or in place of reading the material. Explain that the real benefit of these products is as an enhancement rather than a replacement.

*Working conditions **should be a key element in assessing any career. Which of these types of working conditions appeals to you? Why?***

L3 Math Skills

Give students the following scenario: Julia's monthly salary from January through June in 1999 was $2,765. After her raise in June, her monthly salary from July through December was $2,930. What percentage of her salary in 1999 went to deductions for health insurance, life insurance, dental insurance, and contributions to the United Way? (One percent. January through June salary was $2,765 × 6 = $16,590. July through December salary was $2,930 × 6 = $17,580. Her total salary for the year was $34,170. Percentage of deductions for insurance and contributions was $34,170 ÷ $405.60 = .01)

Independent Practice

1. Assign and review the Chapter 42 Case Study in the *International Case Studies* workbook.
2. Using your school library, the public library, and/or any other resources, have students list at least five additional career research resources. (These can include student vocational organizations, magazines such as *Inc.* or *Entrepreneur*, national educational/vocational associations, college career research centers, military recruiters, etc.) Have students share their resources in class.

Assess

Evaluation

Assign and review the Section 42.2 Review.

The *Dictionary of Occupational Titles (DOT)* (discussed earlier) describes about 20,000 jobs. Several hundred more jobs that have emerged since the publication of the dictionary are defined in the *DOT Supplement.* Following each job title you will find a nine-digit code number. Use this number to locate the job description you want in the front section of the *DOT.* The *DOT* number provides a sophisticated way of classifying jobs into career clusters and worker functions. For example, recall that every job requires a worker to function to some

degree in relation to data, people, and things. The middle three digits of the *DOT* number indicate the nature of this relationship for the given job title. This is explained fully in the *DOT* introduction.

Write down the *DOT* numbers of the jobs you are researching. This will save you some time because other sources also use these numbers to organize their information.

The *Occupational Outlook Handbook (OOH)* provides detailed information on more than two hundred

Chapter 42 *Making Your Career Decision* **565**

Caption Answer

Answers will vary depending on students' personalities, skills, and abilities.

Reteaching

1. Assign and review the vocabulary terms for this section.
2. Assign and review Fact and Idea Review questions 5–7 from the Chapter Review.
3. Review the following concepts to make sure students understand how they relate to their preferences in terms of a career: *work values, lifestyle fit, career outlook, skills, aptitudes, personality traits, work environment,* and *work relationships.*

Enrichment

1. Assign and review the appropriate activities in the *Student Activity Workbook.*
2. Assign and review the appropriate Critical Thinking questions from the Chapter Review.
3. Students should choose three marketing related jobs and, using any of the career resources discussed in this section plus additional resources, they should find the following information for each job: nature of the work, working conditions, education and training, job outlook, earnings, related occupations, and any additional information they choose to include.

Close

Application Project #1 in the Chapter Review can serve as ideal closure for this lesson. Encourage students to repeat this exercise periodically throughout their careers as their priorities shift with age, level and type of responsibilities both on and off the job, and changing goals.

occupations and is updated every two years. It is especially helpful and easy to use in locating such information as:

- education and training requirements,
- usual hours of work,
- working conditions,
- salaries,
- job or career outlook, and
- sources of additional information.

Such things as salaries and job outlook can change quickly. To avoid being misled by outdated information, be sure you use the latest edition of the *OOH.* For the latest information on recent changes, refer to the *Occupational Outlook Quarterly.* This is a supplement to the *OOH* that is published four times a year.

The *Guide for Occupational Exploration (GOE)* is a reference that organizes the world of work into 12 interest areas, which it then further subdivides into work groups and subgroups. For example, the interest area *Selling* is divided into the three work groups: *Sales Technology, General Sales,* and *Vending.* Each work group is then further divided into the subgroups *Wholesale, Retail, Demonstration and Sales,* and five others. The *GOE* includes the following types of career information:

- kind of work done,
- skills and abilities needed,
- interests and aptitudes, and
- required background or preparation.

The *GOE*'s 12 interest areas are also used in the *Career Interest Survey* and the *General Aptitude Test Battery (GATB).* The *GATB* is an aptitude test developed by the U.S. Department of Labor. Using these resources together provides a coordinated approach in your career planning process.

Career Consultations

A **career consultation** is an informational interview with someone who works in a career that interests you. You can learn a lot about the demands and opportunities of a career from someone with experience. Those who have met the challenges of a career are usually happy to talk about it.

Ask both your teacher and your counselor for suggestions about whom you should interview. They may have lists of people in the community who enjoy talking with young people about their work. Family members can also sometimes give you leads.

If you don't get some good suggestions from others, use the telephone directory to compile your own list of potential interviewees. For some careers, you will have to list companies and then call each to find out whom you should interview. For example, suppose you are interested in becoming a retail buyer. Buyers are not listed under their own category in the Yellow Pages, so you will have to call the store first to get the name of someone you can contact.

566   Unit 12   *Career Planning*

*Career consultations **often provide excellent insight to a job. What are three questions you could ask during this career consultation to find out more about this graphic artist's job?***

If possible, interview the person where he or she works. That's usually more convenient for the person, and it will give you a chance to see the workplace. You may even get to see others actively engaged in the work you want to learn about.

Before any career consultation, prepare a list of questions that you want to ask. Here are some suggestions.

- How do you spend most of your time on the job? Which work activities do you like most?
- What skills will I need to do this type of work? What skills will I need to advance?
- What education and training will I need? Can I complete some of the training after I begin working?
- How much time do you spend working with data? with people? with things?
- What are your hours of work? Do people in this career often work overtime? evenings? weekends?
- Is the work done mostly indoors or outdoors? Do most work activities require sitting, standing, or being on the move? Is the work environment sometimes hot, cold, noisy, or dusty? Is the work dangerous in any way?
- Will there be an increase in job opportunities in this field over the next several years? What impact will automation and new technology have on job opportunities in the next few years?

On-the-Job Experience

You can learn a great deal about a career by reading and by interviewing those who work in the field. There are many things, however, that you cannot learn about a job until you try it for yourself.

Many students work part-time after school, on weekends, or during the summer months. If you choose a job

Caption Answer

Answers will vary. Answers can include those listed under the heading "Career Consultation."

in a career field that interests you, you will benefit in the following ways:

- You can try out some of the work activities of your career and decide how much you like doing them.
- You can experience the work environment of the career.
- You can develop work habits that will help you succeed in your career.
- You can broaden your understanding of the world of work and smooth the transition from school to work.

Does your school have a work-experience program? You may know it by another name, such as cooperative education, cooperative work experience, work study, diversified occupations, or something similar. Many vocational work-experience programs include the word *cooperative* in their names because the programs represent a cooperative effort by schools and employers. In these programs, the teacher-coordinator teaches a class related to the job and also supervises students on the job.

SECTION 42.2 Review

1. What are the major areas you should assess when you investigate possible careers?
2. Name three sources for information about careers.

SECTION 42.3

Objectives

After completing this section, you will be able to

- **match your own needs, wants, and potential qualifications with a realistic and satisfying career and**
- **develop a plan to reach your career goals.**

Terms to Know

- **planning goals**
- **specific goal**
- **realistic goal**

Evaluating Your Choices

In the next step of the career planning process, you will match what you learned in your self-assessment with the career information you gathered. The best match should be the most logical career choice.

You will be more efficient in evaluating your choices, if you organize your task before you begin. Plan a time when you can spend at least an hour in this matching process. Of course, an hour probably won't be enough time to reach one of the most important decisions in your life—but allow at least that much time to get started.

Get out all the notes you made on self-assessment and all the information you gathered on careers. You may be able to take it all in and reach a logical decision without more writing. However, it will be easier if you do this matching process on paper. Create a *personal career profile*, an evaluation format that allows you to compare your self-assessment side by side with a particular career assessment. (See Figure 42-2 on page 568.)

On the left side of the profile, write the information about yourself just once. Then make several photocopies—one for each career that you researched. Using these copies, fill in the career information on the right by referring to your notes. After you complete each profile, reread all the information carefully. Then ask yourself the following questions:

- Does this career match my personal values? Do the work values important in this career match my personal values?

Chapter 42 *Making Your Career Decision* **567**

Bell Ringer Activity

Have students take a few minutes to answer these questions: "What is a plan of action?" "Does a plan of action guarantee success?"

Introducing the Section

Review students' answers from the Bell Ringer Activity. A plan of action is a series of steps taken to achieve a particular goal. It does not necessarily guarantee success, but it gives you a sense of direction by helping you outline the steps you need to follow in order to reach a goal. In this lesson, students will develop their final plan of action for choosing a career by formulating goals.

Teach

Guided Practice

1. Read Section 42.3 with students.
2. Have students read aloud the Case Study and review the answers in class.
3. Use the transparency for this section.
4. Some students may have difficulty in setting career goals because they need more time for career exploration and self-assessment. For those students experiencing such difficulty, meet with them individually to give them extra guidance and resources for research, or refer them to their counselors or to your school's career center. There are many vocational interest surveys in addition to those mentioned in the lesson plans for this chapter that will help students with self-assessment and career exploration.

Section Review Answers

1. Work values, lifestyle fit, salaries and benefits, career outlook, education and training, duties and responsibilities, skills and aptitudes required, helpful personality traits, work environment, and work relationships.
2. Libraries, career consultations, on-the-job experience.

Feature Note

Ask students if they can define Northern Ireland's relationship to England, Scotland, and Wales, given the information in the feature. (Although not part of Britain, Northern Ireland is part of the U.K.)

Teach *(Cont'd.)*

5. Invite a panel of marketing education graduates to talk to students about where they are in their marketing careers, where they anticipate being in five to ten years, and how their goals have helped them chart a course for success. They should also talk about how they overcame potential obstacles to their goals (for example, how did they get money for further education?).

Also have your guests discuss the adjustments they made when and/or if they found that their personal values, personality traits, etc., did not mesh with their careers.

Discussion Starter

This section says that you may often discover, through first-hand experience, that a career is just not for you. Discuss with students times that they tried such things as sports, school activities, or even their co-op jobs only to discover that they did not wish to pursue the activity further. Ask students the following questions:

- What have you learned about yourself from walking down a path and finding that it wasn't the best route for you to take after all?
- What skills and abilities did you learn that you were able to apply to something you did enjoy?

Personal Career Profile

Name Robert Woo   **Date** September 4, 19– –

Personal Information	Career Information	Match (1–5, with 5 being the best match)
Your Values: The value scales I took showed that I like to help other people (humanitarianism). I like to be a leader. Doing creative things is fun, too.	**Values:** As a teacher I would have a chance to help others—that's what it's all about. Teachers certainly have plenty of opportunities to be leaders, too. Teachers also need to be creative!	
Your Interests: My hobby interests have always been photography, reading, and theater. My career interest survey showed that I might like a career in leading/influencing, selling, the arts, or maybe a "humanitarian" career.	**Career Duties and Responsibilities:** As a teacher, I would present information, direct student discussions and activities in class. I would help each student individually, too. (Maybe I could teach marketing or general business.) A teacher's working conditions would be good in most schools. (Summers off!)	
My Personality: I like people, and I have a good attitude toward learning. I have an "open" mind. I'm enthusiastic, too. However, I don't have the energy and drive that some people have. I don't know if I could work night after night.	**Type of Personality Needed:** A teacher must like kids, even when they aren't very likeable. I would have to prepare my lesson every day—couldn't just forget about it. Teachers need to be organized, too.	
Data–People–Things Preferences: I think I like working with people most of all. I wouldn't want to be stuck in an office all day with only "data" to talk to. I also wouldn't like working only with things. Some data would be all right, though.	**Data–People–Things Relationships:** Teachers work mostly with people—their students, the principal, parents. They work with data (information), too, though. I don't think they work much with things.	
Skills and Aptitudes: I may have some natural teaching skills—the kids at the YMCA always come to me for help. I helped several kids in Miss Moore's class. Business classes are easy for me.	**Skills and Aptitudes Needed:** Being able to present information so students can understand it is a very important skill. Of course, you must know your subject. An appetite for learning new approaches to teaching is important, too.	
Education/Training Acceptable: I sure never thought I would go to college— I never even liked doing the homework in high school. However, here I am a senior with no real prospects of a good job. Maybe college is the answer.	**Education/Training Required:** Four years of college (it sounds like forever, but I guess it does go fast) is required before you can begin teaching in most states. Some states require course work beyond that.	

Figure 42–2

A personal career profile helps you compare your self-assessment with a particular career assessment. Based on this personal career profile, how does Robert Woo's personal information match the career information shown? Rank each category from 1–5.

Caption Answer

Rankings will vary. However, most students will likely agree that Robert's strongest matches for the career he has selected are the Values, Preferences, and Skills and Aptitudes sections. His weakest match is in Education/Training

- Does this career fit my lifestyle goals? Will it provide adequate income? Is the job outlook good for this career?
- Am I willing to continue my education and training as required for this career? Will I have the money to do so?
- Will the duties and responsibilities of this career interest me? Will I be able to perform them well?
- Will I have the skills required for this career? Do I have the aptitudes to learn the skills needed to advance in this career?
- How will my personality fit this career?
- Will I find the work environment and work relationships in this career satisfactory?

Using a personal career profile has a major advantage—you can refer to it again and again in the months and years ahead. Many people have doubts about their decision after they have made their choice. The profile makes it easy to review your evaluation, either to convince yourself of its wisdom or to change your decision based on your review.

Making Your Decision

You are now ready for the next-to-last step in the career planning process. It's time to make your choice! What career do you want to pursue?

You may feel that you aren't ready to make such an important decision. Perhaps you want more time. After all, you don't want to make a mistake that could affect you for years—maybe even the rest of your life!

Your choice of a career *is* important. In fact, it may be the most important decision you will ever make. However, don't wait until you are absolutely certain about a career choice before you make your decision. If you do that, you may be waiting for years! Make the best choice you can now, even if you think you may change it later. Even a flexible goal will give you something to aim for.

Do you know any recent high school graduates who have not made career choices? Do they have lifestyle goals? If they do, are they making any progress toward achieving them, or are they waiting for something to happen that will provide their dream lifestyle? Some 25-year-olds, for example, haven't made their first career decision; most of them will remain behind schedule in their careers all their lives. Making your first career decision now, even one you may change later, will be a positive influence on your life. It will give you a sense of direction. You can review your career planning process anytime. If you decide that another career is better for you, then it is no disgrace to change your goal. In fact, it's the right thing to do.

So don't be afraid of making the wrong career decision. Even a choice you have doubts about is better than no choice at all.

Developing a Plan of Action

Have you decided which of the marketing careers you researched is the best match with your self-assessment? If so, begin planning how you will achieve your career goal. A plan doesn't guarantee success, but it will outline the steps that you will need to follow to reach your ultimate goal.

Formulating Planning Goals

The small steps you take to get from where you are now to where you want to be are **planning goals**. They give your life a sense of direction and move you steadily toward your ultimate career goal. Every time you reach a planning goal, you gain confidence to move out boldly toward the next one.

Be Specific How do you know whether you are making progress toward your ultimate goal? The answer is, by making your planning goals specific. A **specific goal** is stated in exact terms and includes some details. The goal statement *I want to become a success* is not specific. *I want to complete my class in marketing this semester and earn at least a "B"* is specific. This is the type of planning goal that moves you along toward your ultimate goal.

Be Realistic Planning goals must also be realistic. A **realistic goal** is one that you have a reasonable chance of achieving. Few people can reasonably expect to become president of General Motors. If you have limited artistic talent, you can't reasonably expect to become a commercial artist. Think about your skills and aptitudes.

Real World

Have You Earned Your Salt Today?

Today salt is considered a kitchen staple, the kind of purchase that is so routine that consumers don't give it a second thought. It hasn't always been so, however.

Throughout history, salt has been a byword for something of great value because the mineral has had such varied and essential uses. More than a seasoning, it was used to preserve food and disinfect wounds. The Chinese valued salt so highly that they even made coins from it. The Romans gave their soldiers a special allowance for it called "salt money," or *salarium*. It's from this term that our modern word *salary* comes.

Cooperative Learning

Divide students into four to six groups. Give each group a list of three marketing jobs from various occupational interest areas. Each group should have different jobs. For each job, have students generate the following: (a) the personality type(s) that would probably be suited to this job, (b) the values a person would probably have if attracted to this career, (c) the aptitudes, abilities, and/or skills needed to do this job well, and (d) the necessary educational preparation. Review each group's answers.

Critical Thinking

One thing is certain: no matter what job you take or career you pursue, change is inevitable at your company, in your career field, or both.

Ask students to generate some basic strategies for coping with change and for keeping abreast of innovations in their chosen careers. (Strategies for coping with change include a willingness to develop new skills and flexibility in dealing with people and situations. Strategies for keeping abreast of innovations include reading trade journals; attending conferences, seminars, and educational presentations; keeping up on the daily news to determine how economic conditions, political conditions, and advances in technology will affect one's career field; and a willingness to pursue further education.)

Independent Practice

Have students write five of their planning goals, as suggested in the text. Then, since planning goals are so important, spend time with each student reviewing his or her planning goals. Help all students make their planning goals specific and realistic.

Assess

Evaluation

Assign and review the Section 42.2 Review.

Reteaching

1. Assign and review the vocabulary terms for this section.
2. Assign and review Fact and Idea Review questions 8–10 from the Chapter Review.
3. Review the following concepts to make sure students understand how they relate to their preferences in terms of a career: *ultimate career goal, short-range goals, medium-range goals,* and *long-range goals*.

Enrichment

1. Assign and review the appropriate activities in the *Student Activity Workbook*.
2. Assign and review the appropriate Critical Thinking questions from the Chapter Review.
3. Assign and review the Building Academic Skills Activities, Application Projects, Linking School to Work Activities, and Performance Assessment from the Chapter Review.

CASE STUDY

Glen Jones: The Cable King

It's not always easy to predict what career a person will be successful in. Sometimes someone's personality traits and aptitudes will seem to point in one direction. However, his or her career path will veer off into new territory—or territories.

Glenn Jones's self-assessment file would be an unusual one. Jones has been a bomb-disposal expert for the U.S. Navy, an attorney, and a candidate for Congress. He loves science fiction, and the novel *Dune* fascinates him. He writes poetry. He pays someone to read and summarize books for him. Many people call him a dreamer.

You might never guess from hearing about his interests what Jones's career is. He is the founder and major stockholder of a cable television empire. Its holdings include 55 cable providers with 1.3 million subscribers. He owns more than half of the Mind Extension University, a cable service that allows viewers to take college classes via television. He controls Jones Galactic Radio, which provides music services to cable subscribers. And he owns Jones Space Segment, which leases satellite time and transponders to his other companies. Jones Intercable is also one of the first cable companies to go to Europe, where cable TV is still a new idea.

By 1964, Jones had finished his careers disposing of bombs and practicing law. He was in debt from having run for Congress. He owned a beat up Volkswagen, and he wanted to go into the cable marketing business. So Jones borrowed $400 and made a down payment on a cable service in Colorado. He then bought two more small cable systems, borrowing the money again.

Soon Jones attracted investors in his growing cable business, who became limited partners. This method of financing his business allowed it to grow fast. One result is that Jones has been able to make a big investment in changing over from metal to fiber-optic cable. His companies have made this change way ahead of the competition. This means his systems are primed for the arrival of the information superhighway, which could bring big profits.

Many telephone companies are talking about sending video down the phone lines. But Jones is doing the reverse, sending phone service down the TV cables. It will be the first of its kind anywhere.

Not surprisingly, the corporate headquarters of Jones Intercable reflects Jones's quirky, innovative personality. There is a waterfall in the entry hall that is patterned after one in *Dune*. When it's time for employee meetings, bagpipers in kilts go through the halls, calling the participants. Employees who have excelled are awarded the title of "dragon-slayer."

Glenn Jones shows that it isn't necessary to give up all your odd personality traits to be successful in business. His success is a result of determination, creativity, and plenty of hard work. He's also had quite a lot of fun along the way, and you can be sure he plans to have more.

Case Study Review

1. What kind of education and training would you expect a cable TV entrepreneur to have?
2. How might Jones's hobby of reading science fiction be related to his career choice?

A MATTER OF ETHICS

3. It is hard for companies like Jones's to compete with huge telephone companies. Do you think it is ethical for phone companies to sell video service, if it could put cable companies out of business? Defend your position.

Case Study Answers

1. Answers will vary. Probably a college degree in marketing and communications.
2. Answers will vary. Fiber optic technology is cutting edge science. Satellite communication is a natural tie-in. Much in cable technology is new and exciting like fiction.
3. Answers will vary. Students should address idea of fair competition, monopolies, and employment. Probably larger companies can offer service more cheaply to consumers.

They will guide you in both your ultimate career goal and your planning goals.

Work Backward When you set your planning goals, begin with your ultimate career goal. Then decide what long-range goals you will need to reach to achieve your ultimate goal, what medium-range goals you will need to reach to achieve your long-range goals, and so on. Work backward, starting with your most distant objective and moving closer to your present position in time.

Planning goals can help you test your ultimate career goal. For example, suppose one of your medium-range goals is to work part-time in an advertising agency. Your work experience may reinforce your career decision, and you will be confident that it was a good one. There is also a possibility, however, that it will have the opposite effect. It may convince you that advertising isn't nearly as satisfying as you thought it would be. In this case, testing your decision may lead to your changing your ultimate career goal.

Choosing the Best Education for You

Whatever your career choice, your plan of action to reach your goal will include some education and training. The amount will vary from a few days of on-the-job training to four or more years of college.

Choosing education is much like choosing a career. Follow the complete decision-making process to select the best program and the best school for you. Your school counselor is a good place to start when you want information on vocational schools and centers, technical institutes, community colleges, and colleges and universities. Your school and public libraries are also likely to have information on them.

Choose the program and school that will best prepare you for your career. If you are not graduating this school year, there is still time to enroll in additional marketing classes and related courses that will help you toward your career goal. If you are planing education and training beyond high school, consider the following questions:

- What is my ultimate career goal?
- What course can I still take that will help me reach my career goal?
- What education and training beyond high school is required to reach my career goal?
- How much of this education and training must I complete before I enter this career?
- Where can I get this education and training?
- How much will this education and training cost, and how will I get the money?
- How much education and training can I get on the job? What part-time jobs will help?

Outlining Your Plan

After you have answered these questions, begin writing your personal plan of action—and it *is* important for

Personal Plan of Action

Goal	Date
Ultimate Career Goal:	
Vice President of Sales	2023
Long-Range Goals:	
2. Director of Sales	2018
1. Regional Sales Manager	2011
Medium-Range Goals:	
5. Begin job as District Sales Manager	2004
4. Complete university degree in marketing	2004
3. Begin job as Area Sales Representative	2001
2. Begin university courses in marketing (fall semester)	2000
1. Begin job as Sales Trainee	2000
Short-Range Goals:	
4. Complete two-year college program for A.A.	2000
3. Graduate from high school	1998
2. Take second year of marketing in high school	1998
1. Take part-time job in sales	1998

Figure 42–3

When written down, your personal plan of action for achieving your career goals should look something like this. Why are the entries numbered backwards?

you to write it down. Figure 42–3 provides an example. Begin with your long-range goals, then write down your medium-range goals and finish with your short-range goals. Write down the date that you plan to begin working toward and the date you expect to reach each goal. This will help keep you on track toward your ultimate career goal— the one that turns your dream lifestyle into reality!

SECTION 42.3 *Review*

1. How does a career profile help in evaluating careers?
2. After evaluating career choices, what is the next step to take in choosing a career?
3. What steps should be involved in developing a plan of action?

4. Have students keyboard their personal career profile for presentation to you. It should be spell-checked and written to your specifications (for example, specific margins, double columns, headers and/or footers).
5. Referring again to the job descriptions developed for the Cooperative Learning exercise in this section, students should now personally interview someone who works in the job for which they wrote the description. How closely does this person's job experience match the student's job description? Students should summarize their findings in at least 100 words, comparing their job description to their actual interview.
6. Allow students to meet in small groups to discuss what they learned about themselves by doing the work in this chapter and by completing the career profile.

Close

In the long run, only students themselves can take personal responsibility for their own progress. Conclude this chapter with a discussion of personal responsibility.

Students' success in their careers—and in their personal lives—depends on their ability to plan for themselves, guide themselves, set new and more appropriate goals, and ask for help when they need it.

Caption Answer

Because the plan is designed to be read from the bottom to the top. In other words, it's written in reverse chronological order.

Section Review Answers

1. A career profile helps to compare self assessment side by side with a particular career assessment.
2. The next step is make a career decision.
3. Formulate planning goals, fulfill educational requirements, choose the best education for the chosen career, outline the plan.

Answers

Vocabulary Review
See Glossary for definitions.

Fact and Idea Review
1. See Section 42.1 for lifestyle discussion.
2. It can help you make judgments about how interesting the jobs you are researching would be.
3. Identifying your personality type can help you find a career that fits well with your own traits.
4. Assessing your preferences for working with data, people, or things can help you choose a career that is compatible with those preferences. Careers mentioned will vary.
5. Health insurance, pension benefits, and the use of a company car. A job with many fringe benefits is likely to be a more attractive choice for a career.
6. Since your work will probably become the central activity in your life, it is important that the work fit well with your personality traits.
7. Some school libraries have a special section devoted to career information. Resources include books, magazines, pamphlets, films, video cassettes, special reference books.
8. Evaluating your choices, making your decision, planning to reach your goal.
9. "I want to earn a master's degree in business from Harvard.""I want to work in a large advertising company in New York City.""I want to own a retail store, selling sporting goods."
10. a. short-range
    b. mid-range
    c. short-range
    d. mid-range

572

Vocabulary Review
Use the following vocabulary terms in a paragraph on doing career research.

values
lifestyle goals
aptitude
Dictionary of Occupational Titles (DOT)
career outlook
Occupational Outlook Handbook (OOH)
Guide for Occupational Exploration (GOE)
career consultation
planning goals
specific goals
realistic goals

Fact and Idea Review
1. List seven elements of lifestyle. (Sec. 42.1)
2. How can making a list of your hobbies help you in the career planning process? (Sec. 42.1)
3. How does personality type relate to career research? (Sec. 42.1)
4. Why is it valuable to assess your preferences for working with data, people, or things? Give one example of a career that deals principally with each of these three areas. (Sec. 42.1)
5. Name three fringe benefits. How might the fringe benefits of a job or profession affect your career choice? (Sec. 42.2)
6. Why is it valuable to consider your personality traits when researching careers? (Sec. 42.2)
7. List the career resources you might find in a school or public library. (Sec. 42.2)
8. What are the three final steps in the career planning process as outlined in your text? (Sec. 42.3)
9. Give three examples of specific planning goals. (Sec. 42.3)
10. Suppose your long-range goal is to become a buyer for a chain of grocery stores. Identify the goals below as either short range or medium range:
    a. getting a summer job bagging groceries
    b. applying to a college to study retail business
    c. participating in a DECA chapter in high school
    d. getting your first job out of college as an assistant buyer (Sec. 42.3)

Critical Thinking
1. Think of your own hobbies or interests. Brainstorm ways that these could become professions.

572 Unit 12 *Career Planning*

2. How do you think your values were formed? What effect do you think your personal values will have on the career you choose?
3. Describe someone you know whose personality is a good match for the job he or she is in. Explain how the person's personality affects his or her work. Is the person happy in the job?
4. Child care has become a sought after fringe benefit. Why do you think this is so? What are the advantages for the companies who provide child care?
5. Why is it important to set goals? What is likely to happen to someone who does not set goals?
6. Describe the informal career planning process and the influences you have experienced as part of it.
7. If your long-range goal is to own a video production company, what are some short-range goals you could achieve while still in high school?
8. Discuss ways of getting on-the-job experience related to one of the career paths you are researching.
9. Why is it important that your plan of action be written down?

Building Academic Skills

Math
1. Suppose a company offers you a job paying $20,000 a year when you graduate from high school. This company pays college graduates 20 percent more than high school graduates. You estimate the total cost of attending college at $8,000 a year. If you graduate from college after four years, how long will it take to pay for your college education using your extra earnings? (Disregard the earnings you would give up while attending college.)
2. Use the *Occupational Outlook Handbook* to find the current salaries for two marketing careers that interest you. What is the annual difference in those two salaries? Disregarding pay increases over the years, how much more would you make in the higher paying job over a ten-year period?
3. In an entry-level management position, the wage for a person with a college degree is $23.22 per hour. Without a degree, the wage for the same job is $17.44 per hour.
    a. By what percentage does the college-educated individual's hourly wage exceed his/her fellow employee's?
    b. How much more would the person with the college degree make in a month, working 40 hours per week?

Critical Thinking
1. Hobbies indicate interests and also usually aptitudes and may have marketing tie-ins. If you are interested in mountain climbing, you might sell mountaineering equipment, teach climbing, open a wilderness excursion service.
2. Values usually formed in childhood and beyond, by parents and experience with other people and situations, religious training, etc.

3. Answers will vary.
4. In many households both parents work, making child care necessary. Companies with good child care might attract highly skilled employees, because of demand for the benefit.
5. Goals provide people with career direction. A person who doesn't have goals is more likely to end up in work he or she doesn't like and is less likely to be successful.
6. The process begins in childhood, includes

Communication

4. Write down what you would say in a telephone call requesting a career consultation. What impression would you want to make? Describe the tone of voice and manner of speaking you would use to make that impression.

5. In telling others about your career goals in the field of marketing, you use a great deal of jargon. Your listeners have little marketing experience and look at you with raised eyebrows. What does this response tell you? What can you do about it?

6. Select an area vocational school, technical institute, community college, college, or university in which you are interested. Write a letter requesting information about entrance requirements and courses of study. Conclude with a request for an application of admission.

Human Relations

7. You have always loved plants and flowers and have decided that your long-range goal is to own a retail garden shop. You have an opportunity to work in a local garden shop as soon as you graduate, get on-the-job training, work your way up, and eventually buy into the business. Your parents want you to go to college first. What should you do?

Application Projects

1. List the areas to look for when researching careers: work values, lifestyle goals, salary, fringe benefits, career outlook, duties and responsibilities, required skills and aptitudes, required education and training, personality traits, work environment, involvement with data/people/things. Rank these items according to how important they are to you in making a career choice. Compare your list with a partner's and discuss the reasons for any differences.

2. As in the previous question, list the important considerations in choosing a job. Interview two working people in the field of marketing. To what extent do each of the listed factors contribute to their liking or disliking their work? Did any of these factors affect their decisions to accept their present employment? What was most important to them when they were job hunting?

3. Conduct a career consultation in one of the career areas you are researching. Present your findings to the class.

4. Go to the library and find a magazine article about someone who has made a mid-life career change. Summarize the article orally or in writing for your classmates. Be sure to answer the following questions:
   a. What was the career change?
   b. Why did the person make it?
   c. How did the person feel afterward about his or her new career? about the process of change he or she had gone through?

Linking School to Work

Ask your employer to describe how he or she chose his or her career, and the steps taken to achieve his or her short-, medium-, and long-range goals. Share this information with the class, comparing different paths taken by different businesspeople. Use your class discussion to help you in your choice of a career pathway.

Performance Assessment

Role Play

Situation. You are a successful marketing manager for a large company. You have been asked to address a class of high school students on how to obtain a career of their choice. You will explain to the students the steps they should take to decide on a career and the plans they should make once they have made their career decision.

Evaluation. You will be evaluated on how well you do the following:

- Explain the seven-step career selection process.
- Describe ways to assess values, goals, and interests and match them with a career.
- Explain how to assess and research a career.
- Describe how to develop a plan of action.

Public Speaking

Choose a career that interests you and do library research about all the aspects of the job mentioned in the text, using the labor department references as well as other sources. Give a five-minute oral presentation to the class on your career.

Complete the Chapter 42 Computer Application that appears in the Student Activity Workbook.

They should be well prepared to ask questions about the career.

5. People outside a field often have trouble with jargon. To rectify the problem, use as little jargon as possible. When it is used, it should be defined for the listener.

6. Letters will vary, but should follow the standard letter format discussed in Chapter 9.

Human Relations

7. One possibility: a part time job in the garden shop while attending college.

Application Projects

1. Students should discuss why certain areas are more important than others.

2. Students should write down the information they obtain in these interviews and share their findings with the class.

3. Students may be able to obtain names from their career counselor of people within their career areas.

4. Papers will vary. Suggested resources include *Forbes, Business Week, Inc.*, and other professional journals.

Linking School to Work

Answers depend on the work situation.

Performance Assessment

Refer to the *DECA Competitive Events Handbook* for evaluation guidelines.

Computer Application

Optional activity. Refer to the *Marketing Software Binder* for template and user information.

Evaluation

Administer the reproducible test for Chapter 42, or construct your own using the Testmaker software.

---

everything you experience in the world—all influences on how you see life, your place in the world.

7. Possibilities include working as audio visual aide at school, taking photography courses, part-time work with a production company or film processing lab.

8. Answers depend on the choice of career path.

9. You may lose track of your plans if they are not written down.

Building Academic Skills

Math

1. 8 years.
2. Salaries will vary.
3. a. 33%
   b. $924.80

Communication

4. Students should convey a professional impression.

FINDING AND APPLYING
FOR A JOB

Pages 574–591

Chapter Overview

In this chapter students explore the job search process.

Springboard

Applying for a job is a process that begins with the job search and ends with the post-interview follow-up. Have students help you generate a chalkboard list of the things one must do in order to obtain and follow up on a job interview. (Answers include get a work permit; search for and follow up on job openings and leads through referrals, newspaper ads, employment agencies, company personnel offices, direct calling, and letters of inquiry; apply for a job with letters of application, resumes, and application forms; prepare for the job interview; interview; and follow up with a phone call or note.)

Prereading

List the section objectives to discuss with students. Have students skim the chapter, looking at the pictures, reading the captions, and noting the heads. Ask questions to ensure that the students have a minimal understanding of the chapter structure.

Preteaching the Vocabulary

Students should be familiar with all of the vocabulary terms in this chapter. Review them orally with the class. Write on the chalkboard those terms that students may not know or fully understand and reference them when you encounter them in discussing this chapter.

Finding and Applying for a Job

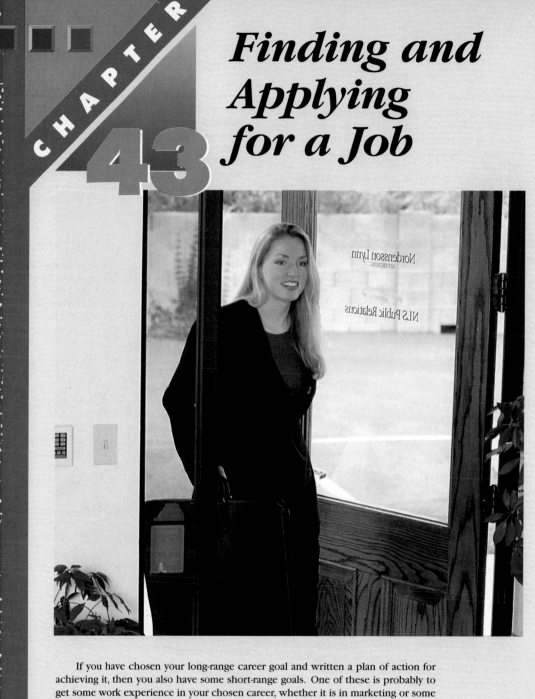

If you have chosen your long-range career goal and written a plan of action for achieving it, then you also have some short-range goals. One of these is probably to get some work experience in your chosen career, whether it is in marketing or some other field.

In this chapter you will learn about some proven methods of conducting a job search. Keep in mind that the same methods can be used to find a part-time job now and a full-time job when you are ready.

574   Unit 12   *Career Planning*

Classroom Management

For the Teacher
- Teacher's Annotated Editions for all workbooks
- Teacher's Annotated Edition for *School-to-Work Handbook*
- *Testing Binder*
- *Transparency Binder*
- *Marketing Software Binder*
- *Marketing Career Portfolio*
- *Lesson Plans*

For the Student
- *Student Activity Workbook*
- *Marketing Math Workbook*
- *School-to-Work Handbook*
- *Student Software*
- *International Case Studies*
- *Marketing Career Portfolio*

■ SECTION 43.1

Objectives

After completing this section, you will be able to

- locate job leads from a variety of sources and
- name the legal document that you must have before you can begin working.

Terms to Know

- job lead
- public employment agencies
- private employment agencies
- direct calling

Finding Job Openings

When you are ready for a full-time job, you will want one that matches your needs, wants, and qualifications. For now, though, your main interest in finding a job is probably to gain work experience and earn some money. Even so, you most likely won't be happy with just any job. You'll want one that you can enjoy and at which you can be successful.

How do you go about finding such a job? A productive first step is to contact all of the sources available to you that might produce a job lead. A **job lead** is information about a job opening. Sometimes the information is incomplete. For example, you may hear that a nearby department store is looking for part-time salespeople. You don't know which department needs workers or to whom you should apply. Sometimes you have to follow up skimpy leads and fill in the rest of the information yourself, like a detective would. Finding the right job requires getting as many job leads as possible and then promptly following up on each of them.

Exploring Sources of Job Leads

When there is low unemployment among adult workers, it is often easy to find leads for both full-time and part-time jobs. When the adult unemployment rate rises, leads are harder to find; and it may take a little longer to find the right job. In either situation, the available sources of leads are the same.

Your Counselor Retail stores and other businesses often call school counselors, asking them to refer qualified students for part-time or temporary jobs. Because school counselors usually have contacts in the business community, they sometimes hear about full-time jobs, too. Your counselor may know of a job that matches your interests and abilities.

Cooperative Education and Work Experience Programs Many high schools have a cooperative education program in which students work part-time on a job related to one of their classes. If the marketing class you are enrolled in is part of a cooperative program, you may already be working on a part-time job in marketing. Cooperative education teachers have contacts in the business community because they place and supervise students on part-time jobs. Therefore, if you have taken a cooperative education class or know the teacher of the class well, he or she may be a good source of job leads.

Many schools also offer a work experience program that is not limited to just one career area, such as marketing. In most schools, the work experience coordinator has hundreds of contacts in the business community. Therefore, he or she may be one of your best sources of job leads.

Schools have a good record of placing students in jobs that fit their interests and abilities. This is probably because teachers, counselors, and work experience coordinators know their students so well. Don't sit back and relax, however, thinking that a teacher or someone else in your school will find the right job for you. There are almost always more students looking for jobs than there are jobs to be filled. That means several well-qualified students will probably be referred for every job opening. Thus, you might follow up several good leads and still not get a job because of the competition.

Family and Friends One of your best sources of job leads often turns out to be members of your own family. Adult friends of your family and your own personal friends can be good sources, too.

Family members and friends often hear of job openings where they work. They may not immediately know of the perfect job for you, but they will ask their friends and co-workers about openings.

Do you have any friends who have started new jobs recently? If so, they may know of some job openings that weren't quite right for them but may be exactly what you are looking for. Ask them if they have any leads.

Make a list of family and personal friends who might help you find job leads. Do any of them own or manage their own business? They may need someone with your qualifications. If not, they probably have many business

Chapter 43 *Finding and Applying for a Job* **575**

SECTION 43.1

FOCUS

⏰ Bell Ringer Activity

Begin this lesson with a discussion of how students already have obtained jobs in which they are now employed. If most of them have obtained their part-time jobs with your help (thus foregoing more traditional routes such as following up on personal leads and newspaper ads), ask students how they obtained either a volunteer position, or a place on a sports team or in an extracurricular organization.

If any students have started some entrepreneurial activity such as a pet-sitting service, ask what methods they used to gain customers.

Introducing the Section

Make a chalkboard list of students' answers from the Bell Ringer Activity. Once you have a substantial list of ways to get jobs, ask students what skills they think it takes to get job interviews. (Answers will vary but could include perseverance and persistence, investigating the local job market, decision-making skills, deductive reasoning, memory skills, note-taking skills, and the ability to ask precise questions.)

Students should begin to see that getting good job interviews is not a matter of luck but a matter of having good skills and using them well. In this section they will look at how to get good job leads.

Meeting Special Needs

English as a Second Language

The job search process can be a monumental challenge to those whose native language is other than English especially if they are newcomers. In order for these individuals to meet their goals, extensive practice and role play dealing with the situations described in the chapter can make the difference between employment and despair. Peer partners selected for the role play should include one native speaker and one nonnative speaker if possible. Give extra attention to telephone situations and dealing with government agencies, both of which can be intimidating situations for those who feel uncertain about their use of the language.

Teach

Guided Practice

1. Read Section 43.1 with students.
2. MarkEd Resource Center in Columbus, Ohio, (800) 448-0398, has materials appropriate for use with this lesson.
3. Glencoe resources appropriate for use with this chapter include *Succeeding in the World of Work* (along with the live-action career videos correlated to this text), *Independent Study for the World of Work, Job Finding Fast, The Work Book,* and *Dress Right for Business. Entering the World of Work* and *Advancing in the World of Work* are available for special needs students. Call (800) 334-7344 for more information and a Glencoe Career Education catalog.

Discussion Starter

One additional source of finding job leads is working for a temporary employment agency. How could working temporary assignments provide job leads? (Answers will vary. With temporary assignments, you work daily, weekly, or monthly in a company or nonprofit organization for an hourly wage. You get the chance to demonstrate at least some of your skills, meet the "key players" in one or a number of departments, ask questions about the company, and experience the work environment. Depending on the length of a temporary assignment, you may also have access to job listings on an employment board, and to personnel in the employment office. Many people obtain full-time jobs through a temporary employment service.)

contacts, and one of them may be looking for a good worker like you.

Add to your list the names of friends who work for companies where you would like to work. Then add the names of school friends and neighbors who are somehow connected with a business that interests you. For example, perhaps a classmate's mother or father works for a company that has an opening that's just what you are looking for.

Most businesses welcome applications from friends of their employees. They know their employees would not recommend anyone who is not well qualified for the job.

Some young people are not comfortable asking friends for job leads. They want to get a job on their own. There is nothing wrong, however, with getting a job through a family member or friends, if you are qualified. Many jobs are never advertised because they are filled by friends of present employees. So, don't overlook this important source of job leads.

Former Employers   Have you ever held a job? Even if it was just a temporary job, such as babysitting or mowing lawns, your former employers may be good sources of job leads. If they were satisfied with your work, they will probably want to help you find a job.

Professional People in Your Personal Life   You probably have periodic contact with professional people in your personal life—doctors, dentists, or lawyers. If you have established a good rapport with these people, they will be happy to help you in your job search. Ask them for names of people that you can contact.

All of these people you know—family and friends, former employers, and professional people you know personally—form a network of individuals connected to you. Finding contacts among them is often called *networking*. It is a term you will come across often.

Newspaper Ads   Read the help-wanted ads in your local newspaper. Some papers separate jobs by type, such as sales jobs, accounting jobs, and so on. In most areas, the Sunday edition has the most ads.

The help-wanted ads are not only a good source of job leads, but they will also teach you a great deal about the local job market. You will learn the salaries offered and the qualifications required for different types of jobs.

Promptly follow up every ad that looks as though it could lead to the job you want. If you wait a day or two, the job will probably be filled. Be aware, however, that not every ad represents a legitimate job offer. Ads that require you to make a deposit of money are not usually genuine job offers but thinly disguised attempts to sell you something. Ads that require you to enroll in a course and pay a fee before you can be hired fall into the same category. People who place ads like these will take your money, but they don't usually have any jobs to offer.

Employment Agencies   The main function of employment agencies is to match workers with jobs. Most larger cities have two types of employment agencies—public and private. **Public employment agencies** are supported by state or federal taxes and offer services

The help-wanted ads in your local newspaper can give you a quick overview of the job market in your area. Check your own newspaper. How would you characterize the situation in your community? List the jobs that interest you. Why do they interest you?

free to both job applicants and employers. **Private employment agencies,** which are not supported by taxes, must earn a profit to stay in business. They charge a fee for their services, which is paid by either the job applicant or the employer.

Public employment agencies are identified by the names of the states in which they are located. The Texas Employment Commission and the California State Employment Development Department are examples. In some cities, the state employment service is the only one available.

When you fill out an application form at the public employment agency near you, you will be interviewed to determine your interests and qualifications. Then, when a job is listed that matches your interests and qualifications, the agency will call you. You will be told about the company and the job duties, then referred for an interview if you are still interested.

Private employment agencies often have job leads that are not listed with public agencies. So, if you aren't getting all the leads you want, consider applying at a private agency. Remember, however, that private agencies charge a fee, if they place you on a job. The fee for matching workers with higher-level jobs is often paid by the employer. The placement fee on entry-level jobs is usually paid by the employee. Thus, if you are a beginning worker, you will probably have to pay the fee yourself.

576   Unit 12   *Career Planning*

Employment Agencies

Employment agencies are moving away from employee fee-based services. Encourage students to not sign any documentation regarding such fees without having the document reviewed by a trusted advisor. Some such agencies are not endorsed by the Better Business Bureau.

Answers will vary. Students should list jobs that match their skills and abilities.

When you apply for placement through a private agency, you will have to sign a contract. Read it carefully. It will specify how much you will pay if you are referred to a job and hired. The amount is usually a percentage of your salary for the first several months or even the first full year of employment.

Company Personnel Offices Large companies have personnel offices to handle employment matters, including the hiring of new workers. You may check on job openings by telephoning that office or by making a personal visit. Some personnel offices list openings on a bulletin board. You can stop by at your convenience and see if anything new has been posted.

If you know that you would like to work for a certain company, and it has a personnel office, stop by often. Get to know the people who work there, and you will have a better chance of being hired.

Direct Calling The more job leads you have, the better your chances of finding a job that is right for you. If you don't have many leads, you may want to do some direct calling.

Direct calling is the process of contacting potential employers in person or on the telephone. Do this when you think you would like to work for certain companies but are unsure whether they have any openings. You can use the Yellow Pages to compile a list of company names, addresses, and telephone numbers.

With direct calling, you may get more consideration by calling in person than by inquiring about a job on the telephone. Either way, direct calling takes a lot of time. If you contact enough employers, though, you may find a job opening that interests you.

Letters of Inquiry Writing a letter of inquiry is a variation of direct calling. You use the technique under the same circumstances and for the same reason—when

you want to know whether a company has openings in the career area of your interest. Instead of making your inquiries by phone or in person, however, you write a letter.

How do you know to whom you should address your correspondence? You find out by doing a little research. You look up the company's number in the telephone directory. Then call and ask for the name of the individual who hires new employees. At that point you will learn whether the company has a personnel office or whether department heads do their own hiring. In the latter case, ask for the name of the head of the department in which you would like to work—marketing, for example. Confirm the spelling of any names you are given and the position of the person you will be contacting. Thank the person who gave them to you. Then verify the company's address, particularly asking for the correct zip code or any postal box, floor, or suite numbers.

Now you are ready to write your letter of inquiry. See page 130 of Chapter 9 to review the elements of a business letter. Figure 43-1 on page 578 provides an example.

Expanding Your List of Job Leads

Getting new job leads and following up the ones you already have should be overlapping processes. That is, as you follow up on existing leads, you should at the same time be looking for new ones. Here's how you do it. First you get as many job leads from your firsthand sources as possible. Then you expand your list by getting referrals from the people you see. Each time you follow up a lead that doesn't result in a job, ask your interviewer to suggest others you might contact. Try to get at least one or preferably two new leads from each interview.

Why should you do this? Consider it psychological insurance. Remember, many other people are looking for work, too. You may not get the job you want, or you may have to turn down a job that doesn't meet your expectations. Having other possibilities will keep you from getting discouraged in these circumstances. If you have a long list of leads, you can simply follow up the next one.

Real World

What the Smart Senior Wears

Burkhardt's Ltd., a Rhode Island clothing retailer, teaches college seniors how to dress on the job. In 90-minute seminars store personnel use mannequins to show what constitutes suitable business attire for men and women. They also tell students how to begin building a professional wardrobe and put a price tag on the process ($600–$700 suggested, to start).

Students who participate in the seminars receive a 10 percent discount if they shop at Burkhardt's—and 80 percent do. That's a figure that shows Burkhardt's knows how to build not only a wardrobe but a customer base as well.

Getting a Work Permit

If you're under the age of 18, most states require a work permit before you can legally begin working. However, in some states, such as Michigan, a cooperative education training agreement can serve as a legal work permit.

State and federal labor laws designate certain jobs as too dangerous for young workers. Most of these jobs are performed in hazardous environments or involve the use of power-driven machinery. The laws also limit the number of hours that young people can work in one day or one week. For example, more hours of work are allowed during summer vacations than during the school year.

Chapter 43 *Finding and Applying for a Job* **577**

Independent Practice

1. Have students generate at least five job leads from various sources. They should write each lead and tell how they found it.
2. Have students research the names and company addresses of three local personnel directors to whom they could write a letter of inquiry regarding an entry-level marketing job in the company or organization.

   Students should write a sentence or two telling how they found each person's name and address, and how they determined that this person was the appropriate company contact.

Assess

Evaluation

Assign and review the Section 43.1 Review.

Reteaching

1. Assign and review the vocabulary terms for this section.
2. Assign and review Fact and Idea Review questions 1–4 from the Chapter Review.
3. Review with students the sources of job leads. Add any additional sources that are not mentioned in this lesson (such as temporary job assignments), or sources that are specific to your area.

Enrichment

1. Assign and review the appropriate activities in the *Student Activity Workbook*.
2. Assign and review the appropriate Critical Thinking questions from the Chapter Review.
3. Have students write a letter of inquiry to one of the personnel directors they discovered in doing Independent Practice Activity 2. They should keyboard and spellcheck the letter. Have students work in pairs or in groups to share and critique their letters. Or, work with students individually.
4. The text states that looking through the help wanted section of the newspaper will teach you a great deal about your local job market. Have students study the Sunday classified ads from the newspaper in your town, city, or region, and write a 100-word summary of their observations about the local job market and the economic factors that are shaping it. You may wish to have students do this activity together as a class. (Many town and city newspapers will provide free copies of the paper for classroom use.)

Close

Have students complete these statements: (a) A job lead is... (information about a job opening.) (b) The most common sources of job leads are... (school counselors, cooperative education and work experience programs, family and friends, former employers, professional people in your personal life, employment agencies, company personnel offices, direct calling, letters of inquiry, newspaper ads, and suggestions from interviewers.)

Letter of Inquiry

735 North Fairfield
Dallas, Texas 75221
March 15, 19--

Mr. John Robinson
Sears Roebuck and Co.
5334 Ross Avenue
Dallas, TX 75206

Dear Mr. Robinson:

On May 17, I shall graduate from Sam Houston High School with a major emphasis in sales and marketing. While in high school, I have worked in sales part-time, but I am most eager to begin my first full-time job in sales.

As I have always been impressed by the courteous, efficient salespeople in your store, I am very interested in a job at Sears. If you anticipate a need for any full-time, permanent employees in the next several months, I would like to apply.

May I have an application form, or should I call for an interview at your convenience? My home telephone is 924-7884.

Sincerely,

Charlene J. Graham

Charlene J. Graham

Figure 43-1

You write a letter of inquiry when you want to know whether a company has openings in the career area of your interest. Why would you write a letter instead of making inquiries by phone or in person?

A work permit establishes for the employer that it is legal for a young worker to do the type of work offered. In some states, work permits must specify the *exact* job duties and hours of work. In these cases, both the employer and worker fill out sections of an application for the permit. The employer, worker, and the worker's parent must sign the application before a work permit is issued.

Ask your marketing teacher or counselor whether you will need a work permit and, if so, where you can get one. Work permits are usually issued by a designated school official. Check on this now, so you can avoid possible delays when you are ready to go to work.

SECTION 43.1

Review

1. List possible sources of job leads.
2. Explain how you can expand your list of job leads.
3. How old do you normally need to be to begin working without obtaining a work permit?

Caption Answer

In some situations this might be the most efficient way to proceed. Direct calling in person is extremely time consuming; direct calling by phone takes less time but can be expensive. A letter of inquiry accomplishes the same end of uncovering job openings without these drawbacks.

Section Review Answers

1. Counselor, cooperative education and work experience, family and friends, former employers, professional people, newspaper ads, employment agencies, company personnel offices, direct calling, and letters of inquiry.
2. Get as many job leads as possible. Expand your list with referrals from your interviewer.
3. 18

SECTION 43.2

Objectives

After completing this section, you will be able to

- write a letter of application and complete an application form and
- write a resume and cover letter.

Terms to Know

- standard English
- references
- resume
- cover letter

Applying for a Job

Employers look for the most qualified person to fill a job. They will decide whether to hire you based in part on how you look and what you say during an interview. More than anything else, though, they will want to know whether you have the ability to do the work.

Employers have several ways of getting this information. Many ask job seekers to fill out an application form. Some request additional documents—a separate letter of application or a resume. Finally, some employers administer one or more employment tests to applicants.

If you are qualified for a job, the way you present your qualifications may be the determining factor in whether you are hired. If you follow the suggestions on the next few pages, you will increase your chances of success.

Using Standard English

Everything you write and say to a prospective employer should be in standard English. **Standard English** is the formal style of writing and speaking that you have learned in school. It is standard because it means the same thing to everyone.

Most people do not use standard English for all their communication. In some situations, it isn't necessary. For example, when you write a letter to a close relative, you simply write what is on your mind, and you don't worry much about form. When you speak with a friend on the telephone, you may use slang or informal language. These practices make for comfortable and easy personal conversation, but they have no place in business. Most communication in business is formal, and that means standard English.

Standard English employs correct grammar, spelling, pronunciation, and usage. For example, "Marilyn *has* a job interview" is standard English. "Marilyn *have* a job interview" is not. The repeated use in conversation of the interjection *you know* is nonstandard English. Nonstandard pronunciations are another common lapse. (An accent, either regional or foreign, does not indicate nonstandard English.)

Employers will have several opportunities to evaluate your English. When they read your application form, they will notice whether you use and spell words correctly. If you write or type a letter of application or a resume, they will have another chance to evaluate your ability (or inability) to write. Finally, when you are interviewed, the employer will listen to you speak and will evaluate your grammar and pronunciation.

BRIGHT IDEAS

Get Physical

After Bryan Mattimore graduated from Dartmouth College, he began searching for a job but met with nothing but rejection. Discouraged, he turned his imagination to creating a wish list for the perfect job-hunting experience. It included interviewing with CEOs, not personnel directors; scheduling those meetings at his convenience, not theirs; being treated like a VIP, not someone of no consequence; setting up the meetings quickly and with many companies, without spending many futile hours on the phone; and being able to wear comfortable clothes, not a business suit, for all of these encounters.

Mattimore's next step was to create a publicity event called "Jogging for Jobs." He carried it out with other job seekers whom he found by advertising in the *New York Times*. The group jogged to 36 ad agencies in a three-day period. The stunt was creative enough to get media attention and thus indirectly benefit those companies he and his group had selected to receive their resumes. The results for Mattimore? Several job offers—and one great job.

Creativity Challenge Form teams of 3–5 people. Take 5–10 minutes for each person to create his or her own job-hunting wish list and share it with the group. Then, working together, brainstorm ways to help each person make his or her list a reality.

FOCUS

⏰ Bell Ringer Activity

Give each student a copy of a generic application form, or an application form from a familiar local business. Have students fill out the application for a specific job (for example, retail sales associate). Allow them to use any resources they have with them (such as address books). Allot 10 to 15 minutes for this activity.

Introducing the Section

In an employer's mind, filling out an employment application is not necessarily the same thing as applying for a job! Many employers use applications to screen potential interviewees. Thus, it's essential to make a good impression with a neat, complete application form.

After students have completed their forms, ask them the following questions: (1) What information should you have with you in order to fully complete an application form in an employment office? (2) What tools should you have with you in order to complete an application? (3) What instructions on the form did you find difficult to follow? Why? (4) What questions did you find difficult to answer? Why?

In this section, students will discover how to submit professional, completed application forms, along with well-composed resumes—two essential tools in a job search. Have students save their application forms. Refer to them as you discuss the section in this lesson on filling out application forms.

💡 Bright Ideas

Not all job hunting situations need to be as extravagant as the example in order to be successful. The key point to be gotten from Bryan Mattimore's campaign is that there is more than one way to approach the process. Allow time for students to share the ideas they developed with the whole class so that each person is exposed to a wide variety of imaginative job-hunting strategies.

Guided Practice

1. Read Section 43.2 with students.
2. Have students read aloud the Case Study and review the answers in class.
3. Use the transparencies for this section.
4. MarkEd Resource Center in Columbus, Ohio, (800) 448-0398, has materials appropriate for use with this lesson.
5. Provide good and poor examples of cover letters and resumes for overhead projection. Have students point out flaws in the poor examples, and tell why the good examples are better than the poor ones.
6. Provide students with copies of various resume formats for their notebooks. Project each format overhead and review the benefits of each.
7. Many students may be given employment tests when applying for marketing jobs. Obtain copies of common employment tests to administer to students for practice in such areas as math, spelling, proofreading, and filing.

   If your students have access to computers in your classroom or computer lab, have them test their knowledge of various word processing programs with some of the word processing tests available.

CASE STUDY

Selling Yourself Effectively

Many books have been written about how to prepare for and act in a job interview. There are seminars and courses devoted to the subject. As a matter of fact, helping people market themselves and their skills has become an industry itself.

One of the most well respected and popular of the interviewing experts is H. Anthony Medley. Medley is a California attorney who lectures throughout the country on interview techniques. He counsels job seekers and recruits for employers. Medley's book, *Sweaty Palms: The Neglected Art of Being Interviewed*, is a comprehensive guide to having a successful interview. In it Medley gives advice for handling most of the difficult questions and situations that can arise during a job interview. He stresses the importance of being prepared by knowing as much as possible about the company and about the interviewer. He discusses the meanings of different aspects of body language, advising interviewees to be natural.

Most of all, Medley emphasizes the importance of being enthusiastic about the interview itself, about the company, and about your possible place in the company. He says, "It is not enough to be interested or to say you are interested. You must show that you are interested through your actions." He points out that the interview is an event in itself, separate from a job offer or a job. It is the event where you sell yourself to an employer. Good salespeople have four important personality traits. These traits will help you sell yourself at the interview:

1. *Enthusiasm.* Medley defines enthusiasm as "the exhibition of fervent interest." You must let the interviewer see that the job really moves you.

2. *Sincerity.* False enthusiasm for a job will be evident to the interviewer. Find something about the job that really interests you and be enthusiastic about that.
3. *Tact.* Usually during an interview, the interviewer will say something controversial, or something he or she knows you disagree with. The interviewer does this to see how you will handle disagreement. Being tactful when you disagree involves validating the interviewer's position first and then disagreeing. You might say something like, "That's an interesting position, but I think…" This way you show respect for the interviewer's point of view, but still maintain your own opinion.
4. *Courtesy.* Medley defines courtesy as "consideration of the feelings of others." If you are not courteous to the interviewer, you will not get the job.

In order to be enthusiastic and sell yourself to the interviewer, you must have a positive attitude. Medley says, "You radiate what you feel. If you enter the interview with a chip on your shoulder, you'll be written off in a [second]." He describes interviews with candidates who were inappropriate for the job they were applying for but were so positive and enthusiastic that he recommended them for other, more appropriate positions. A positive attitude can take you a long way. Enthusiasm is contagious, and the interviewer will not be immune to your enthusiasm.

Case Study Review

1. If you feel your interview has gone well, and the interviewer seemed to be enthusiastic about you, but you learn you didn't get the job, what can you do?
2. What are some good ways to develop enthusiasm about a company you are applying to work for?

A MATTER OF ETHICS

3. Sometimes an interviewer will ask rude or personal questions to test how well you respond to stress. Sometimes he or she will even sit silently and stare at you. Do you think this is ethical behavior? Why or why not?

Case Study Answers

1. If you don't get the job, ask the interviewer if he or she can give any advice on how to present yourself better in future interviews. Ask the interviewer if he or she can suggest jobs either within or outside the company that you might be qualified for.
2. Learn as much about the company as possible in advance of the interview. Focus on the good things about the company and what you find interesting. Show enthusiasm during the interview.
3. Answers will vary. Some may feel that the rude behavior is misleading and deceitful behavior. Some may feel that it simply tests their ability to cope with difficult people and thus is acceptable behavior from the interviewer.

Filling Out Application Forms

Most employment application forms are short (from one to four pages), and most ask the same or similar questions. Because companies usually design their own forms, however, each one is a little different.

For the prospective employer, the application form provides information about your qualifications, so company personnel can decide whether to interview you. For you as an applicant, the form offers an opportunity to present your qualifications in a way that will make the employer want to talk with you in person.

The following is a list of suggestions for filling out an application form:

- Neatly fill out the application form. Spell all words correctly. If you fill out the form at home, use a dictionary to look up the spellings of any words you are unsure of. If you fill out the form at the place of employment, use words you know how to spell.
- If you can, take the application form home and fill it out on a typewriter. If you are not a good typist, make a photocopy of the form, fill out the copy, and get a friend who types well to complete the original. If you are asked to complete the form at the place of employment, use a pen with blue or black ink. Colored inks are considered nonserious and inappropriate.
- Answer every question that applies to you. If a question does not apply to you, write "NA" (meaning "Not Applicable") or draw a short line in the space. This will show that you did not overlook the item.
- Use your full name, not a nickname, on the form. On most applications, your first name, middle initial, and last name are requested. Provide your complete address, including your zip code.
- If there is a question on job preference, list a specific job title. Do not write "Anything" as an answer. Employers expect you to know what type of work you can and want to do.
- Most application forms include a section on education. Write the names of all the schools you have attended and the dates of attendance. If there are several, make a list for your own reference before you apply for a job.
- There will be a section on previous work experience on the form. You may not have had much experience, but you can include even short-term or unpaid jobs. Fill out this section in *reverse chronological order*. Begin with your current or most recent job and end with your first job.
- Be prepared to list several references. **References** are people who know your work habits and personal traits so well that they will recommend you for the job. Try to use professional references such as your teachers, friends established in business, or former employers. Make sure you ask permission to use your references before listing them on an application form. Do not list classmates, relatives, or personal friends.

- Sign your name using your first name, middle initial, and last name. Your signature should be written, never typed or printed.

An example of a completed application form is shown in Figure 43-2 on pages 582 and 583.

Writing Letters of Application

Most employers prefer application forms because they provide just the information employers need to reach a decision on interviews. However, some employers request that an applicant write a letter of application instead.

When you write a letter of application, you are essentially writing a sales pitch. You are trying to convince an employer that you are the best person to fill a specific job opening. So, tell why you are interested in the position and what your special qualifications for it are. Don't write a sad story about needing the job.

The following suggestions will help you write an impressive letter of application:

- Write a first draft to get down most of the main points. Then rewrite your letter, making changes and additions until it says exactly what you want it to say. Ask a teacher, parent or guardian, or friend in business to read and critique your letter. Then put the final touches on it and type a perfect copy.
- In your first sentence, describe how you learned about the job opening. If a friend who knows the employer gave you the lead, you might say, "At the suggestion of Mr. Charles Williams, I am writing about the job as mail-order clerk in your store." If you are writing in response to a newspaper ad, you might say, "I am responding to your ad in the *Daily News* for an advertising assistant."
- In your second sentence, state expressly that you are applying for the job. You might say, "I would like to be considered an applicant for this position."
- In the second paragraph, describe how your education and experience qualify you for the job. If you have a lot to say about both your education and your experience, use a separate paragraph for each. If you don't have much experience, just write about your education in more detail. Mention classes you have taken that are related to the job.
- List your references in the next paragraph. Be sure to ask the permission of these people before you list them in your letter.
- In your last paragraph, ask for a personal interview at the employer's convenience. If you are available for an interview only during certain hours or on certain days, state when these are. Then provide a telephone number where you can be reached.

Many businesses receive dozens of application letters every week. (If they advertised in the newspaper, they may receive hundreds of letters.) Businesses interview only a small portion of those who write. They interview

Discussion Starters

Ask students to give some alternative "high-tech" ways of submitting resumes that, while not traditional, may become more commonplace in the next century. Ask them also to speculate on some "high-tech" recruitment and screening measures now used by employers. (Answers will vary. According to an Atlanta-based out placement service called Enter-Change, some job seekers are experimenting with high-tech innovations to present themselves to employers in unusual ways, such as via diskette, e-mail, videotape, and audio cassettes. In order to recruit and screen applicants more efficiently, human resource managers now list jobs on the Internet and other computer networks, and use "interactive voice mail" software that asks applicants to use their touch-tone phones to submit qualifications. Source: "Paperless Resumes?," *Vocational Education Journal*, March 1995, page 55.)

Critical Thinking

Some companies, such as The Body Shop, require job applicants to write an essay on a particular topic related to the business. What would be the purpose of such a requirement? (Writing an essay is a way of screening out those who are not serious about applying for the position because they will not take the time to complete this task. Those applicants who do take the time to write the essay provide the potential employer with a way to evaluate their writing skills, their organizational skills, their knowledge of the business, and their sincerity in applying for the job.)

More About

Filling Out Application Forms

In addition to having students ask permission of their reference, they should also let the reference know to whom they have given their name and the position for which they have applied. This courtesy gives the reference time to prepare comments or reflect on the type of question that may be asked should the company call.

L1 Human Relations Skills

Give students the following scenario: Imagine you work in the human resource department of a large company. One of your duties is to review all applications for part-time employment. One day a young man calls to follow up on his application, which was done very poorly and is barely legible. What could students tell this man to help him with filling out applications in the future?

L2 Human Relations Skills

Give students the following scenario: After completing the L1 Activity, have students imagine that they receive a poorly done letter of application. For example, it does not specify the job the person wants or give work history or education. The letter is also written in slang. What could be said to this applicant in response to the person's inquiry?

L3 Human Relations Skills

Give students the following scenario: After completing both the L1 and L2 Activities, have students imagine that they receive a student's resume that has blatantly false information. (Some of the jobs listed call for post-high school training, for example, yet the student has not yet graduated from high school.) What could be said to this person about the impression a falsified work history would give a potential employer?

Job Application

SEARS, ROEBUCK AND CO.
APPLICATION FOR EMPLOYMENT

Date April 6, 19 - -

SEARS IS AN EQUAL OPPORTUNITY EMPLOYER and fully subscribes to the principles of Equal Opportunity unity. Sears has adopted an Affirmative Action Program to ensure that all applicants and employees are considered for hire, promotion and job status, without regard to race, color, religion, sex, national origin, age, handicap, or status as a disabled veteran or veteran of the Vietnam Era.

To protect the interests of all concerned, applicants for certain job assignments must pass a physical examination before they are hired.

PLEASE PRINT INFORMATION REQUESTED IN INK

NOTE: This application will be considered active for 90 days. If you have not been employed within this period and are still interested in employment at Sears, please contact the office where you applied and request that your application be reactivated.

Name Graham (Last) Charlene (First) Joan (Middle)   Social Security Number 541-62-6351 (Please present your Social Security Card for review.)

Address 753 (Number) North Fairfield Street (Street) Dallas (City) Texas (State) 75221 (Zip Code)

County Dallas

Current phone or nearest phone (214) 924-7486

Previous Address _____ (Number) _____ (Street) _____ (City) _____ (State) _____ (Zip Code)

Best time of day to contact after 4 p.m.

(Answer only if position for which you are applying requires driving.)

If hired, can you furnish proof of age? Yes ☒ No ☐   Licensed to drive car? YES ☐ NO ☐
If hired, can you furnish proof that you are legally entitled to work in U.S.? Yes ☒ No ☐   Is license valid in this state? YES ☐ NO ☐

Have you ever been employed by Sears or a subsidiary of Sears? YES ☐ NO ☒   If so when and where last employed? _____   Position _____

Former employees of Sears and certain Subsidiaries may be entitled to service credit under the Pension Plan based on prior employment with Sears, Roebuck and Co., Homart Development Co., Sears Investment Management Co., Sears Roebuck Acceptance Corp., Sears, Roebuck de Puerto Rico, Inc., Sears Roebuck Overseas, Inc., Sears Securities Sales, Inc., Terminal Freight Handling Co., Allstate Insurance Company and their Subsidiaries, Lifetime Foam Products, Pacific Installers, and Sears, S.A. (Central America), Dean Witter Reynolds Organization, Inc. and their Subsidiaries, Coldwell Banker and their Subsidiaries and Sears World Trade.

Have you a relative in the employ of Sears in the store or unit to which you are applying? _____ No

A PHYSICAL OR MENTAL DISABILITY WILL NOT CAUSE REJECTION IF IN SEARS MEDICAL OPINION YOU ARE ABLE TO SATISFACTORILY PERFORM IN THE POSITION FOR WHICH YOU ARE BEING CONSIDERED. Alternative placement, if available, of an applicant who does not meet the physical standards of the job for which he/she was originally considered is permitted.

Do you have any physical or mental impairment which may limit your ability to perform the job for which you are applying? _____ No

If yes, what can reasonably be done to accommodate your limitation? _____

EDUCATION	School Attended	No. of Years	Name of School	City/State	Graduate?	Course or College Major	Average Grades
	Grammar	7	Esperanza Elementary	Dallas, TX	Yes		B+
	Jr. High	3	Andrews Junior High	Dallas, TX	Yes		B
	Sr. High	3	Sam Houston High School	Dallas, TX	Yes	Marketing/Bus.	A–
	Other						
	College					Degree	

MILITARY SERVICE	BRANCH OF SERVICE	DATE ENTERED SERVICE*	DATE OF DISCHARGE*	HIGHEST RANK	SERVICE-RELATED SKILLS AND EXPERIENCE APPLICABLE TO CIVILIAN EMPLOYMENT

*Do not complete if applying in the state of California.

What experience or training have you had other than your work experience, military service and education? (Community activities, hobbies, etc.)

_____

I am interested in the type of work I have checked: ☒ Sales ☐ Office ☐ Mechanical ☐ Warehouse ☐ Other Specify _____

Or the following specific Job _____

I am seeking (check only one):

☐ Temporary employment (6 days or less)
☐ Seasonal employment (one season, e.g. Christmas)
☒ Regular employment (employment for indefinite period of time)
If temporary, indicate dates available _____

I am available for (check only one):

☐ Part Time
☒ Full-Time

If part-time, indicate maximum hours per week _____ and enter hours available in block to the right.

HOURS AVAILABLE FOR WORK	
Sun.	To
Mon.	8 a.m. To 6 p.m.
Tues.	8 a.m. To 6 p.m.
Wed.	8 a.m. To 6 p.m.
Thurs.	8 a.m. To 6 p.m.
Fri.	8 a.m. To 6 p.m.
Sat.	8 a.m. To 6 p.m.

Have you been convicted during the past seven years of a serious crime involving a person's life or property?
☒ NO ☐ YES   If yes explain _____

10534 Rev. 9/83

(SEE REVERSE SIDE)

REFERENCES

LIST BELOW YOUR FOUR MOST RECENT EMPLOYERS, BEGINNING WITH THE CURRENT OR MOST RECENT ONE. IF YOU HAD LESS THAN FOUR EMPLOYERS, USE THE REMAINING SPACES FOR PERSONAL REFERENCES. IF YOU WERE EMPLOYED UNDER A MAIDEN OR OTHER NAME, PLEASE ENTER THAT NAME IN THE RIGHT HAND MARGIN. IF APPLICABLE, ENTER SERVICE IN THE ARMED FORCES ON THE REVERSE SIDE.

NAMES AND ADDRESSES OF FORMER EMPLOYERS BEGINNING WITH THE CURRENT OR MOST RECENT	Nature of Employer's Business	Name of your Supervisor	What kind of work did you do?	Starting Date	Starting Pay	Date of Leaving	Pay at Leaving	Why did you leave? Give details
NOTE—State reason for and length of inactivity between present application date and last employer								
Name Merchandise Mart / Address 2800 Tyler Avenue Tel No 925-9021 / City Dallas, State Texas Zip Code 75221	Depart-ment Store	Mr. Travis	Sales	Month Nov. / Year 95	Month / Per Week	Month / Year / Per Week	Month / Per Week	Still employed part-time
NOTE—State reason for and length of inactivity between last employer and second last employer								
Name Chicken Annie's / Address 1700 S. Vernon Avenue Tel No 924-6318 / City Dallas, State Texas Zip Code 75221	Fast Food	Mrs. Riley	Sales	Month Jan. / Year 95	$80 / Per Week	Month Oct. / Year 95	$95 / Per Week	To accept a job with more hours
NOTE—State reason for and length of inactivity between second last employer and third last employer								
Name Mr. Paul Crawford (former teacher) / Address 3614 Rayburn Avenue Tel No 925-1163 / City Dallas, State Texas Zip Code 75221				Month / Year / Per Week		Month / Year / Per Week		
NOTE—State reason for and length of inactivity between third last employer and fourth last employer								
Name Miss Irene Jenkins / Address 1222 Oakwood Street Tel No 925-7611 / City Dallas State Texas Zip Code 75221				Month / Year / Per Week		Month / Year / Per Week		

I certify that the information contained in this application is correct to the best of my knowledge and understand that any misstatement or omission of information is grounds for dismissal in accordance with Sears, Roebuck and Co. policy. I authorize the references listed above to give you any and all information concerning my previous employment and any pertinent information they may have, personal or otherwise, and release all parties from all liability for any damage that may result from furnishing same to you. In consideration of my employment, I agree to conform to the rules and regulations of Sears, Roebuck and Co., and my employment and compensation can be terminated with or without cause, and with or without notice, at any time, at the option of either the Company or myself. I understand that no unit manager or representative of Sears, Roebuck and Co. other than the President or Vice-President of the Company, has any authority to enter into any agreement for employment for any specified period of time, or to make any agreement contrary to the foregoing, in some states, the law requires that Sears have my written permission before obtaining reports on me, and I hereby authorize Sears to obtain such reports.

Applicant's Signature _Charlene G. Graham_

NOT TO BE FILLED OUT BY APPLICANT

INTERVIEWER'S COMMENTS	Date of Emp.			Tested	(Store will enter dates as required)		Mailed	Completed
	Dept. or Division	Regular ☐ Part-Time ☐		Physical examination scheduled for		References Requests		
	Job Title			Physical examination form completed		Consumer Report		
	Job Title Code	Job Grade				With. Tax (W-4)		
	Compensation Arrangement					State With. Tax		
	Manager Approving			Review Card prepared	Minor's Work Permit			
Prospect for				Time card prepared	Proof of Birth			
1. 2.	Employee No.	Rack No.			Training Material Given to Employee			
				Unit Name and Number _____				

Figure 43-2

A job application form provides information about your qualifications, so company personnel can decide whether to interview you. How long did Charlene Graham work at Chicken Annie's? Why did she leave that company?

Critical Thinking

Have students brainstorm some additional sources of information when researching a company before an employment interview. (Answers will vary but could include annual reports, magazine and newspaper articles on the company, information from the Chamber of Commerce, and local media advertising.)

L1 Math Skills

Give students the following scenario: You decide you want to photocopy 35 copies of your resume. When you get to your local copy shop, you find that it charges seven cents per copy for the first 49 copies, and five cents per copy for 50 copies or more. How many copies would you have made of your resume? 35 or 50? Why? (It would be more economical to have 50 copies made. 35 copies will cost $2.45 [$35 \times .07 = 2.45$]. 50 copies will cost $2.50 [$50 \times .05 = 2.50$]. Thus, for an additional five cents, you can have 15 additional copies.)

L2 Math Skills

Give students the following scenario: You figure that you have about 20 hours of leisure time each week to spend as you wish. This week you have spent 15 hours of your leisure time writing cover letters to send out with resumes to potential employers. What percentage of your weekly leisure time was devoted to writing cover letters? (75%. $15 \div 20 = .75$)

Caption Answer

Graham worked at Chicken Annie's about ten months. She left to take a better-paying job.

L3 Math Skills

Give students the following scenario: One potential employer asked you to take a keyboarding test. She administered the test as an initial "warm up," and you keyboarded 55 words per minute. When she re-administered the test, you keyboarded 72 words per minute. By what percentage did you improve with the second test? (31%. 72 words − 55 words = 17-word improvement. 17 words ÷ 55 words = .309 or .31)

Independent Practice

1. Assign and review the Chapter 43 Case Study in the *International Case Studies* workbook.
2. Have students create a generic cover letter with a word processing program. Then have them create a cover letter for three different marketing jobs, using this generic letter as a basis for each.

   The jobs can be listings in the help-wanted section of your local newspaper, postings from a local job board or employment service, or any other source—as long as the job is legitimate and students use the correct company name and contact, etc.

   Review students' letters, helping them to discover additional ways to adapt their cover letters to these specific positions. Have students keep these letters in their notebooks for reference.

those people who have effectively presented their qualifications in a neatly written letter. If you can do this, you will have a big advantage over most applicants. Take the time to develop an effective letter of application that you are really proud of. Then you can use it as a model for other letters for other jobs. Of course, you will have to change the first paragraph, but most of the letter will need only minor changes.

As with any sales pitch, a good first impression counts, so type or word process your letter. If you are not a good typist, ask a friend to type it for you. If you don't have a friend who's a good typist, hire someone. If you use a computer, be sure to use the spell check to eliminate any spelling errors. Before you send your letter, make sure you have read it over for accuracy.

The sample letter shown in Figure 43-3 will give you some idea of how your finished letter should look. Be sure to include all the elements of a business letter. In particular, duplicate the salutation and complimentary closing as shown.

Letter of Application

> 1603 Loomis Street
> Winfield, Kansas 67156
> April 11, 19--
>
> Ms. DeEtta Clark
> North American Aircraft Co.
> 4000 Southwest Blvd.
> Wichita, KS 67202
>
> Dear Ms. Clark:
>
> Mr. Richard Crandell, my marketing instructor at Arkansas City Community College, advised me this morning of the commercial artist position that you have open. I wish to apply for this position.
>
> On May 17, I will graduate from Arkansas City Community College with a major in marketing and a special emphasis on advertising and commercial art. I have also taken commercial art courses during the past two summers at Southwestern College. My overall grade average in college is B+.
>
> For the past three years, I have assisted the advertising manager at Rubbermaid, here in Winfield, by preparing more than 30 ads that have run nationally. One of these ads, which I prepared myself, won an award at the recent advertising convention in Chicago.
>
> My father taught me to fly when I was in high school, so a job in advertising with an aircraft manufacturing company would combine my two greatest interests. It would be a dream come true! May I have an interview at your convenience? You can reach me most weekdays after 3 p.m. at (316) 221-5288.
>
> Yours truly,
>
> *Karen Anderson*
> Karen Anderson

Figure 43-3

A letter of application is a sales pitch telling an employer why you are the best person to fill a specific job opening. What things did Karen Anderson state in this letter that would qualify her for the commercial artist position at North American Aircraft Company?

Caption Answer

Anderson mentioned her academic work, including college courses in art; three years of experience working on national ads—one, which she personally prepared, an award winner—for a major company; and personal experience flying.

Preparing Resumes and Cover Letters

A good letter of application may convince an employer to grant you an interview. However, a resume and cover letter are even more impressive.

A **resume** is a brief summary of personal information, education, skills, work experience, activities, and interests. (See the sample in Figure 43-4.) It organizes all the facts about you that relate to the job you want. Thus, it saves the employer time before and during an interview.

Figure 43-4
RESUME

There are many variations in the format of resumes, but most are in short outline form (usually one or two pages). Most resumes include the information shown here.

1. Basic Identification—
provide name, address, and telephone number.

2. The Position for Which You Are Applying—
give a specific job title. If you use the same basic resume for several jobs, change this item.

3. Experience—
list any experience related to the job for which you are applying. This includes volunteer work. If you haven't any related experience, list such jobs as lawn mowing or delivering papers.

4. Education—
list the schools you attended, the years of attendance, and any courses taken that qualify you for the job. (This item also may need to be tailored to fit different jobs.)

5. Activities and Awards—
list school or other activities related to the job you want, along with any awards you have received.

6. References—
if your resume is short, list three; if your resume is a bit long, simply write "References available upon request." (In both cases, ask permission first from your references.)

Frank Johnson
1235 East Tenth Avenue
Ventura, CA 93003
(805) 964-6264

Objective:
Marketing Analyst

Experience:
9/96-present Assistant Marketing Analyst
Ventura Volvo
6580 Leland Street
Ventura, CA 93003

Used computer to estimate sales by model and make recommendations for inventory. Accessed databases using computer terminal to study inventory in relation to buying estimates. Studied historical applications, including media ads, price and color changes, and impact of season.

9/95-9/96 Marketing Assistant
KVEN Radio
Ventura, CA 93003

Assisted Communications Manager in publishing articles and ads, sales presentations, vendor contracts, and trade shows. Contacted vendors for advertising needs (charts, overheads, banners).

Education:
1992-1996 Ventura College. AA in Marketing. Dean's Honor Roll four semesters.

Courses included:
Marketing I and II
Marketing Information Systems
Advertising
Economics I and II
Computer Science

1989-1992 Ventura High School. Graduated in upper 10 percent of class. Served as Vice President of DECA two years.

Personal:
Hobbies include writing computer programs, tennis, and photography.

References:
Available upon request.

Assess

Evaluation

Assign and review the Section 43.2 Review.

Reteaching

1. Assign and review the vocabulary terms for this section.
2. Assign and review Fact and Idea Review questions 5–8 from the Chapter Review.
3. Review with students how they can enhance their chances of success in getting hired.

Enrichment

1. Assign and review the appropriate activities in the *Student Activity Workbook*.
2. Assign and review the appropriate Critical Thinking questions from the Chapter Review.
4. Assign the appropriate activities in the *Marketing Math Workbook*.
5. Provide a variety of application forms from local businesses. Allow students to fill out one or two forms from different businesses. Depending on the level of your class, have students work in pairs to review each other's forms for accuracy and completeness. Or, you can meet with each student individually to review his or her forms.
6. Have students use popular word processing programs to create their resume in various resume formats.

Did You Know

Evaluating and choosing a way of producing a resume is another important step students will take. Some may have the capability and equipment to do it themselves, or the school may have the equipment. Others will have to pay for the service. Prices can range from $10 for a word processed one page resume to hundreds of dollars for a "resume consultation." Advise students on the many different styles that can be used to lay out a resume.

7. Invite a personnel specialist to come to class and assist the students by offering a critique of their resumes and/or sample applications. If you are not familiar with such an individual, ask the school Guidance Counselors if they know of anyone who calls the school to recruit for entry-level positions and who might be willing as a community service to come to the classroom and spend time with the students giving them an overview of what interviewers are looking for in the way of introductory materials.

You may wish to arrange for a panel to speak to the class to present the different viewpoints and hiring practices of different types of companies. For example, a fast-food employer will be looking for different things than will a high-end retailer or a manufacturing environment. Students need to know that there are a variety of needs in the workplace and to structure their marketing tools to their desired target market.

Close

Have students complete this statement: Four ways in which employers can get information on the most qualified applicants for a job include:... (an application form, a separate letter of application, a resume, and employment tests.)

586

Cover Letter

Figure 43-5

A cover letter is an introductory letter of application without the information on education and experience. Why do you think a cover letter should accompany a resume?

1235 East Tenth Avenue
Ventura, CA 93003
April 6, 19--

Ms. Linda Morrison
Metromedia-West Television
3200 Beverly Drive
Beverly Hills, CA 90123

Dear Ms. Morrison:

Your ad for a marketing analyst in Sunday's *Los Angeles Times* described exactly the position that I am seeking. As you will see from the resume I have enclosed, my qualifications match up very well with the requirements listed in your ad.

My education, experience, and DECA participation (for which our school won a national award) have prepared me to fulfill your needs in marketing analysis.

After you have read my resume, I would appreciate an appointment for an interview. I will call back next week to arrange a time convenient to you.

Sincerely,

Frank Johnson

Frank Johnson

Because your resume outlines your qualifications for a particular job, you won't need a complete letter of application to accompany it. When you send an employer a resume, you enclose just a brief cover letter. A **cover letter** is a letter of application without the information on education and experience. (Figure 43-5 shows a sample cover letter.) It simply introduces you and allows you to say why you can do a good job for the company. You may want to emphasize one or two facts that make you especially well qualified for this particular job.

Although a resume is not required for many jobs, it is a polished and professional-looking document that can give you an edge over other applicants. It has a few other advantages as well. First, you can describe your qualifications. In a resume you have more freedom in describing your education and work experience than you have on an application form. Second, if you prepare your resume before you start applying for jobs, it will be much easier to fill out all those application forms. For this reason, some people prepare a resume as the first step in the

job application process. Third, even if you are not hired, many employers will keep your resume on file for a certain period of time. If they have an opening for which you qualify in the next several months, they may call you.

1. What are four important components of standard English?
2. Why do most employers prefer application forms?
3. What is the purpose of a letter of application?
4. List the basic types of information that are contained in a resume.
5. What is the purpose of a cover letter?

Caption Answer

The cover letter contains some material a resume does not, such as how you learned about the job opening. It also allows you to highlight some special aspect of your qualifications and ensures that your resume will still get to the right person should it be separated from its envelope.

Section Review Answers

1. Grammar, spelling, punctuation, and usage.
2. It contains specific information.
3. To tell why you are interested in the position and what your special qualifications for it are.
4. Identity, education, skills, experience, activities and awards, and references.
5. It introduces you to the employer.

SECTION 43.3

Objectives

After completing this section, you will be able to

- **prepare for and conduct yourself properly during a job interview and**
- **follow up a job interview.**

Interviewing for a Job

Application forms, letters of application, resumes, and cover letters are all important parts of the job application process. Their purpose is to make an employer interested enough that he or she will want to interview you. It is what happens during the interview that causes most employers to choose one applicant over others.

You, of course, want the interviewer to choose you for the job, so you will need to plan for a successful interview. Your plan should include three steps—*preparing for an interview, conducting yourself properly during an interview,* and *following up an interview.*

Preparing for an Interview

In every interview you will have, the employer's first impression of you will greatly affect whether you are offered a job. Remember, you never have a second chance to make a first impression. Appropriate grooming and dress, body language that shows confidence, and use of standard English all combine to make a good first impression. With some preparation, you can control all of these.

Dress and Grooming   In the past, employees in sales and office jobs followed a strict dress code. Men always wore suits, white shirts, ties, and leather shoes with dark socks. Women wore business suits or very conservative dresses, medium heeled shoes, and nylons. Today, employees in many stores and offices dress much more casually. This does not mean, however, that you can dress casually for every interview and still make a good impression.

Appropriate interview dress depends on the job. In sales, for instance, people dress more formally, in order to make a good impression on customers. In the interview, you will need to show that you are aware of that and can dress appropriately. If you are being interviewed for a job as a stock clerk, more casual wear is probably fine. However, your clothes should still be neat and clean.

Try to find out how employees dress at the company where you are interviewing. The standard will vary a great deal from one company to another. To make a good first impression, dress somewhat more formally than company employees do on the job. Many employers feel that if you don't care enough to dress up for the interview, then you don't care enough about the job.

Regardless of its style, your hair should be clean and neat. Many employers don't like beards or long hair on men. It may be unfair, but that's the way it is. Employers pay the bills—including the salaries. If you want a job, you will have to please the employer.

Wearing a great deal of jewelry can be distracting at an interview. Too much makeup can also be distracting. Also, employers will notice whether your hands are clean, your nails neatly trimmed.

Things to Know   Before you schedule an interview, find out information about the company. You will make a better impression if you can talk intelligently about the company's products. It will show that you are interested in the firm not just in the money you will earn as an employee. Some companies print brochures that explain the business they are in. Others print catalogs that describe their goods or services. You can also learn about a company's business from looking in the Yellow Pages or talking with family members or your teachers.

If you call for an interview appointment, write down the date and time and ask for the interviewer's name. Check the spelling after you write down the name and make sure you can pronounce it correctly.

Before your interview, carefully read your resume several times. Be ready to answer any questions about your education, work experience, or other qualifications.

The following questions are often asked of job applicants during interviews. If you practice answering them beforehand, you will feel more confident. Get a family member or friend to help you by asking the questions and giving you feedback on how you answer:

- Why do you want to work for this company?
- Do you want permanent or temporary work?
- Why do you think you can do this job?
- What jobs have you had? Why did you leave?
- What classes did you like best in school?

Let the Silverware Do the Talking

Around the world, eating utensils are used to send nonverbal signals. For example, in Sweden, placing a knife and fork crisscrossed one atop the other on an empty plate conveys the message that the diner would like seconds. In the United States that same signal means "I'm finished with my meal." In China, chopsticks placed parallel across a bowl or plate send the same message.

Lifelong Learning

Finding and Applying for a Job

At no point in the career process can an individual assume that the job search process is complete. Even employed individuals need to know that when companies are bought and sold, some people will be left looking for new positions. Company benefits are constantly changing, and what was once standard, such as paying for schooling, can be eliminated in the name of cost savings. It is up to the individual to keep informed, to read as many current publications as possible, and to constantly update skills and redefine goals. Encourage students to view this course as a launching pad to their voyage of career discovery.

Teach

Guided Practice

1. Read Section 43.3 with students.
2. MarkEd Resource Center in Columbus, Ohio, (800) 448-0398, has materials appropriate for use with this lesson.
3. Assign and review the Chapter 43 Activity in the *School-to-Work Handbook*.

Discussion Starter

In discussing job interviews, stress that employers today look for applicants who can demonstrate their ability to apply their academic and vocational knowledge and skills in the workplace. One of the best ways to show this in an interview is with a well-developed portfolio.

Have students discuss how they would use the portfolios they have developed during their study of *Marketing Essentials* in an employment interview. (For an excellent article on portfolio development and the use of portfolios in job interviews, see "Body of Evidence," *Vocational Education Journal*, March 1995.)

Cooperative Learning

Allow students to role play employment interviews in front of the entire class. Depending on the level of your class, you can act as an interviewer, or you can have students work in pairs, alternating turns as interviewer and interviewee. Give students the position applied for and the company. Have students dress appropriately on the day they will participate in this role play. Have the class evaluate the effectiveness of each interviewee.

- What school activities did you participate in?
- What do you want to be doing five years from now?
- Do you prefer working alone or with others?
- What is your main strength?
- How do you spend your spare time?
- What salary do you expect?
- What grades have you received in school?
- How do you feel about working overtime?
- How many days were you absent from school last year?
- Why should I hire you?
- When can you begin work?

Conducting Yourself Properly During an Interview

Always go alone for a job interview. Some young people take a friend along for moral support, but this is a mistake. Employers seldom hire anyone who can't handle an interview alone.

Plan to arrive for your interview about five to fifteen minutes early. If you have to travel across town, allow some extra time in case you run into traffic. If you are even a little late or rush in at the last minute, you will appear careless and thus make a bad impression. Don't be too early, though. Waiting outside the interviewer's door for half an hour is not comfortable for you or the employer.

Before you meet the interviewer, you may see a receptionist or personnel assistant. If you do, be very courteous and polite to this person. The interviewer may ask his or her opinion of you after you are gone.

If you have not already filled out an application form, the receptionist or assistant may give you one and ask you to complete it. In this case, you may have to complete the form before you are interviewed. Be prepared for this by always having a good pen with you. (Some people take two pens, just in case one runs out of ink.) If you have prepared a resume, take two copies to the interview—one to leave with your interviewer if he or she wants it and one to help you fill out an application form.

You may be introduced to the interviewer by the receptionist or assistant, or you may have to introduce yourself. In the latter case, say something like, "Good afternoon, I'm Lois Anderson, and I'm here about the sales associate position." Speak clearly and loudly enough to be heard, and smile.

Your body language is an important part of the interview. What do you think this applicant is telling the interviewer with his body language?

588 Unit 12 *Career Planning*

If the interviewer offers to shake hands, grasp the person's hand firmly. Don't give a limp handshake (it makes some people think you have a weak personality), but don't grab the interviewer's hand and crush it, either! If the interviewer doesn't offer to shake hands, don't offer your hand.

Remain standing until you are asked to sit down. If you are not asked to sit down, then stand for the interview—it will probably be a short one. When you do sit down, lean forward slightly toward the interviewer. This shows that you are interested in the job.

If you have a purse or briefcase with you, place it on the floor by your chair. Never put anything on the interviewer's desk, even if there is room. Don't let your eyes wander over papers on the interviewer's desk—it may look as though you are trying to read company correspondence.

It is normal to feel a little nervous at the beginning of an interview. You will relax as the interview progresses. Keep your hands in your lap, and try to keep them still. Of course, you should never chew gum during an interview. Look the interviewer in the eye most of the time and listen to him or her carefully. This, too, shows your interest. (Some people don't trust a person who can't look them in the eye.)

What to Say in an Interview Most interviewers begin by asking specific questions. Answer each question honestly. If you do not know the answer to a particular question, say so. (If you try to fake it, the interviewer will probably sense it.) Keep your answers short. No interviewer wants to listen to long stories, but don't be too brief, either. If many of the questions seem to call for a simple yes or no, then elaborate a little.

Two particular questions often cause problems for young job applicants. These questions are, "What type of work would you like to do?" and "What wage (or salary) do you expect?" You will probably answer the first question all right by giving the name of the specific job you want. The question about expected wage or salary is a little more difficult. If you specify a sum that's too high, you probably won't be offered the job. If you mention a figure that's too low, you may be paid less than other employees for the same type of work. Perhaps the best answer is something like, "I'm sure you know better than I do what a fair wage (or salary) would be. What do you usually pay for this type of work?" In other words, try to turn the question back to the interviewer. If you are pressed for an answer, mention a rate you know others get for the same type of work. So that you are prepared for this before the interview, find out what the going rate is for the type of work you want by checking with your marketing teacher.

In some cases, your interviewer will simply say something like, "Tell me about yourself." If that happens, you will have to do most of the talking. You will have to anticipate what the interviewer would like to know and present the information clearly. This type of interview is often difficult for the job applicant. If you have instant recall of everything on your application form or resume, you will probably handle the situation well. Just be sure to cover all your qualifications for the job and say why you would like to work for this particular company. (This is one of those instances in which knowing something about the company will help you in the interview.)

Your interviewer may not mention pay at all. In that case, wait until the interview is almost over, then ask how much the job pays. (If you ask about pay too early, it may appear that you are only interested in the money.)

If you are applying for a full-time, permanent job, you will probably receive some fringe benefits. These may include a paid vacation and insurance coverage. If your interviewer doesn't mention this, it's all right to ask—but wait until near the end of the interview. You don't want to sound too anxious to take a vacation from this job.

In most cases, the interviewer will expect you to ask some questions. If you don't, he or she will think you aren't interested in the job or the company. While your interviewer may answer some of your questions when discussing the job and the company, you will probably still have others you want answered. If your interviewer asks whether you have any questions, that, of course, is your cue to ask them. If your interviewer does not ask, he or she will probably pause after telling you about the job and asking about your qualifications. That is the time for you to ask your own questions. The questions listed below are among those most often asked by young applicants:

- What are the hours of work?
- What are the opportunities for advancement?
- What is the pay?
- When will I be notified if I am hired?

During the interview, be enthusiastic. Shift your eyes occasionally so that you don't stare, but look your interviewer in the eye most of the time.

You may be asked to a second interview with someone else in the company, such as a department head. This usually means you made a good impression in your first interview, and your chances of being offered the job are good.

Closing the Interview   At the close of the interview, one of several things can happen. You may be offered the job and accept, you may be offered the job but decline, or you may be told that you will not be hired. More likely, however, you will be told that a decision will be made later.

You will be able to sense when the interview is almost over. The interviewer will say something like, "Well, Mario, thank you for coming in" or "We'll decide by the end of the week." This is your cue to ask any last-minute questions. Then you should stand, smile, and thank your interviewer for his or her time. Usually, the interviewer will extend a hand for a handshake. Shake hands and go. Be sure to thank the receptionist or personnel assistant on your way out.

Following Up an Interview

After every interview, evaluate your performance. Do this whether you were offered the job or not. Which questions did you answer best? Which ones did you not answer very well? Were there any total disasters? Did you use standard English? Each interview is a learning experience that will help prepare you for the next one.

If an employer is interviewing several people, it is unlikely you will be offered the job the same day as your interview. The employer will want some time to consider all the applicants before making a decision. Many employers will check your references and call the school for a recommendation. This may take several days to a week or more. In the meantime, you can follow up your interview with a telephone call, a short thank-you letter sent a day or two after your interview, or a visit.

Unless you were told not to call, it is all right to telephone the employer five or six days after the interview. Ask to speak with the person who interviewed you. Then give your name and ask if he or she has made a decision on the job. This will let the employer know that you are still interested.

A thank-you letter is an appropriate way to follow up many interviews. Because most people don't bother to do this, you will make a good impression. Your letter should be brief and to the point. Simply thank the employer for the time given you and reaffirm your interest in the job. If you forgot to mention something during the interview that will help qualify you for the position, include it—but be brief. Your letter may be either handwritten or typed, but it must be neat.

If the company is nearby or if you know the employer personally, you may prefer to stop by rather than call or write. In that case, you can thank the employer in person for the time given you and ask when a decision is expected.

SECTION 43.3

Review

1. **What steps can you take to plan for a successful interview?**
2. **Why is it important to know something about the company before you interview?**
3. **How should you dress for a job interview?**
4. **How would you follow up a job interview?**

Chapter 43   *Finding and Applying for a Job*   **589**

SECTION 43.3

Assess

Evaluation

Assign and review the Section 43.3 Review.

Reteaching

1. Assign and review the vocabulary terms for this section.
2. Assign and review Fact and Idea Review questions 9–16 from the Chapter Review.
3. Review with students the highlights of good interview techniques. Also, ask students to answer some of the most commonly asked interview questions. Relate the latter to specific jobs (for example, "Why do you think you would make a good sales associate?")

Enrichment

1. Assign and review the appropriate activities in the *Student Activity Workbook*.
2. Assign and review the appropriate Critical Thinking questions from the Chapter Review.
3. Assign and review the Building Academic Skills Activities, Application Projects, Linking School to Work Activities, and Performance Assessment from the Chapter Review.
4. Have students write a thank-you note to a personnel director who has interviewed them for a real job recently.

Close

Have students complete this statement: Planning for a successful interview includes three steps: . . . (preparing for the interview, conducting yourself properly during the interview, and following up the interview.)

Section Review Answers

1. Preparation, conducting yourself properly during an interview, follow up.
2. So you can talk about the skills you have that fit the company's needs, and ask intelligent questions about the company.
3. A basic rule is to dress a little more formally than for the job itself. In any case, you should be clean, with clean and pressed clothes, your hair neatly groomed.
4. Follow up a job interview by evaluating your performance so that you can do a better job next time. Unless you are told not to call, it is all right to telephone the employer after five or six days to ask whether a decision has been made. A thank-you letter is also appropriate.

Answers

Vocabulary Review
See Glossary for definitions.

Fact and Idea Review

1. Some form of information about a job opening.
2. Your counselor, teachers or work-experience coordinator, family and friends, former employers, professional people in your personal life newspaper ads, employment agencies, personnel offices, direct calling, letters of inquiry.
3. They often hear of openings where they work.
4. You can expand your list of leads by getting new ones from the leads you already have.
5. The formal style of writing and speaking that you have learned in school. It should be used when communicating with an employer because most business is conducted using it.
6. Use professional references such as your teachers, friends established in business, or former employers.
7. Reverse chronological order.
8. One page is best.
9. Because you are trying to make a good impression, it is a good idea to dress more formally for an interview.
10. About five minutes early.
11. "Good afternoon, I'm Edward Earl. I'm here about the sales job."
12. Answer by naming the specific job you want.
13. "I'm sure you know better than I do what a fair wage would be. What do you usually pay for this type of work?"
14. If the interviewer does not ask specific questions but says, "Tell me about yourself," it is helpful to have recall of everything on your resume.

590

Vocabulary Review

Use the following vocabulary terms in a paragraph describing an effective job search.

job lead
public employment agencies
private employment agencies
direct calling
standard English
references
resume
cover letter

Fact and Idea Review

1. What is a job lead? (Sec. 43.1)
2. List seven sources of job leads. (Sec. 43.1)
3. How can family members and friends help you in a job search? (Sec. 43.1)
4. How do you use the job leads you already have to produce new ones? (Sec. 43.1)
5. What is standard English, and why is it advisable to use it when communicating with an employer? (Sec. 43.2)
6. Who are good people to list as references on a job application? (Sec. 43.2)
7. When listing your previous experience on a job application, what is the usual form? (Sec. 43.2)
8. How long should your resume be? (Sec. 43.2)
9. Given the choice of dressing casually or dressing up a bit for a job interview, which would you do and why? (Sec. 43.3)
10. When should you plan to arrive for a job interview? (Sec. 43.3)
11. Describe how you would introduce yourself to an interviewer. (Sec. 43.3)
12. What should you say if an interviewer asks you what kind of work you would like to do? (Sec. 43.3)
13. How should you respond if an interviewer asks you what wage or salary you want? (Sec. 43.3)
14. Why is it important to have studied your resume before a job interview? (Sec. 43.3)
15. How can you tell when an interview is over? (Sec. 43.3)
16. What is the purpose of following up a job interview? How is this done? (Sec. 43.3)

Critical Thinking

1. How would you respond if you applied for a job when you were 15 and the prospective employer

told you it wasn't important for you to have a work permit, even though the law requires one?
2. How would you feel about getting a job through a family or personal friend? Would you rather find a job on your own? Why or why not?
3. If you were interested in working for a particular company, would you prefer to visit the personnel office in person, call on the phone, or write a letter of inquiry? Why?
4. Who would make good references for you and why?
5. If you were an employer, what qualities do you think you would look for in a job seeker's application, application letter, or resume?
6. What do you think about a situation in which a potential employer denies an applicant a job because he has long hair or a beard?
7. After the interview, John feels pretty confident he will get the job at Dal Pozzo Tires. When he doesn't hear anything in a week, John calls back a couple of times, but the manager doesn't return his calls. What further follow-up should John do?

Building Academic Skills

Math

1. Your prospective employer tells you that you can have your choice of being paid two ways. Either you will be paid a straight salary of $400 per week or a base salary of $200 per week, plus commissions of 13 percent of your sales. In your last job, you sold $2,000 a week. Assuming you will continue to sell at least that amount, which salary option should you take? What is the difference between the two?

Communication

2. Assume you would like to work for a local mail-order company that sells electronic gadgets, but you don't know if there are any job openings. Write a letter of inquiry regarding summer employment.
3. Write a script for a direct call to a sporting goods store, inquiring about the availability of a part-time job. Practice aloud and then pretend to make your call in front of the class.

Human Relations

4. You are scheduled for a job interview. You arrive at the receptionist's desk terribly nervous and suddenly go completely blank. You can't remember the name of the person with whom you have the interview. What do you say to the receptionist? What might you have done to avoid this situation?

15. The interviewer will say something like, "Thank you for coming," or "We will decide by the next week and let you know."
16. To let the employer know that you are still interested. Following up can be done with a telephone call, a short thank you, or in person.

Critical Thinking

1. The interviewee may not trust the employer, may not want to take the job, or may think employer

would not follow the law in other instances.
2. Discuss the feelings, and reassure students that the practice is a good one, as long as they are qualified for the job.
3. Answers will depend on the student.
4. Employers who feel positively about the student's performance.
5. Answers may include command of standard English, ability to present qualifications, and willingness to work.

Application Projects

1. Find out from a teacher or counselor where you go to get a work permit. Investigate any restrictions on the type of job that can be held by students in your state. Present your findings in a 150-word paragraph.
2. Share any of your own letters of application or resumes with other students in your class. Assist each other in improving language, correcting grammar, and simplifying formats.
3. Make a list of questions you would want answered before a job interview was over.
4. With a classmate, devise and present a series of skits designed to show how body language and verbal communication can contribute to or detract from the success of a job interview. Consider including the following characters:
   a. the know-it-all applicant;
   b. the shy, nervous applicant who is unwilling (or unable) to provide information; and
   c. the applicant who does not speak standard English.
5. For one week, go through your newspaper's classified section and find jobs in the marketing field.
   a. Choose one company and research it.
   b. Prepare for an imaginary interview at this firm by writing out the answers to the list of questions commonly asked by interviewers.
   c. Working in groups of four to five with one student acting as the interviewer, interview for the job. Have the group members give you suggestions on ways to improve your performance.
6. Make a list of your special interests. Talk to your teacher or counselor about jobs available in an area of marketing that are compatible with your interests and your qualifications for those jobs. Discuss any extra skills you need to acquire.
7. Research the cooperative education and work experience programs available through your school. Write a 250-word paper on how they can help you achieve your goals in the field of marketing.
8. Make a list of all the professionals, friends, family members, and former employers who might be able to help you find work.
9. Prepare a letter of application and a resume for a marketing job of your choice.

Linking School to Work

Ask your employer what are the most important qualities he or she looks for when interviewing a prospective employee. Write them down in order of importance. Compare your list with your classmates'.

Performance Assessment

Role Play

Situation. You work in the personnel department of a company, interviewing and hiring applicants for jobs. One of your duties is to train others on the job applicant selection process. You must teach the new interviewer about all aspects of hiring—what to look for on job applications, how to conduct a good interview, and what to look for in those being interviewed.

Evaluation. You will be evaluated on how well you can do the following:

- Explain the purpose of a work permit.
- Explain what a properly completed application form should look like.
- Explain what to look for in a resume.
- Describe what good interview preparation and conduct includes for interviewees.
- List the kinds of questions that an interviewer should ask.

Public Speaking

Read John Mallory's *Dress For Success* or another book giving advice on how to present yourself well. Then give a five-minute oral report on the book to the class.

Complete the Chapter 43 Computer Application that appears in the Student Activity Workbook.

Portfolio

Consider the Application Projects that you have done for this unit. Select one that illustrates your mastery of the unit's content and might be of interest to potential employers. Reformat the activity as necessary, adding any explanatory text, and place it in your Porfolio. Consider using this activity:

- Chapter 43, Application Project 9 ■ ■

6. Students should understand that fair or not, some employers will demand their appearance be businesslike.
7. John might write a note thanking the manager for the interview and asking for a call, or he might stop in to the shop. He might decide to keep looking for a job.

Building Academic Skills

Math

1. Base salary option. $60 (13% × 2000 = $260. $260 + 200 = $460.)

Communication

2. Student letters should follow the format shown in the chapter.
3. Teachers should check for good phone voice, modulation, standard English, and courteous behavior.

Human Relations

4. Be honest with the receptionist. Bringing along notes with the interviewer's name and other information would prevent this situation.

Application Projects

1. Restrictions will vary depending on the state.
2. Students should check to make sure letters are professionally written.
3. Students should ask about working conditions, salaries and benefits, possibilities for advancement, and duties and responsibilities.
4. Skits will vary.
5. Have class write critiques so that they have a record of what they did well and where they need to improve.
6. If students' interests fall into groups, they might visit the counselor as a group.
7. Programs will vary.
8. Students should list those who might be able to help them find a job.
9. All elements discussed in the chapter should appear in the resume and letter of application.

Linking School to Work

Answers depend on the work situation.

Performance Assessment

Refer to the *DECA Competitive Events Handbook* for evaluation guidelines.

Computer Application

Optional activity. Refer to the *Marketing Software Binder* for template and user information.

Portfolio

Refer to the Marketing Career Portfolio for development ideas and portfolio management and assessment.

Evaluation

Administer the reproducible test for Chapter 43, or construct your own using the Testmaker software.

A

absolute advantage   Advantage a nation has when it possesses natural resources or capabilities that allow it to produce a given commodity at a lower cost than any other nation in the world.

adjacent colors   Colors located next to each other in the color wheel and contrast only slightly.

ad layout   A rough draft that shows the general arrangement and appearance of a finished ad.

advance dating   Indicates a date other than the invoice date from which dating terms take effect.

advertising   The nonpersonal presentation and promotion of ideas, goods, and services by an identified sponsor.

advertising agencies   Companies that exist solely to help clients sell their products.

advertising proof   A proof that shows exactly how an ad will appear when printed.

advertising research   Research that focuses on the advertising message and media.

agents   Intermediaries who negotiate title of goods but do not themselves take title.

agreements   A specific commitment that each member makes with the group.

allowance   Partial return of the sale price for merchandise that the customer has kept.

aptitude   A knack, or a potential, for learning a certain skill.

assertive   Standing up for your rights, beliefs, and ideas.

asset   Anything of monetary value that a person owns.

B

baby boomers   People born between the years 1946 and 1964.

Baby boomlet   People born in the 1980s and early 1990s (this generation peaked in 1991).

balance of trade   Difference in value between exports and imports of a nation.

balance sheet   A summary of a business's assets, liabilities, and owner's equity.

bar graph   A drawing made up of parallel bars whose lengths are proportional to the qualities being measured.

basic stock list   Buying plan used for items that should always be in stock.

blind check method   A method of checking merchandise using a list is made from an invoice of only style numbers and descriptions.

blocks   Interference to understanding a message.

body language   The physical movements and position of the body that communicate thoughts.

bonded warehouse   A warehouse that stores products that require the payment of a federal tax.

boomerang method   Objection comes back to the customer as a selling point.

brand   A name, design, or symbol that identifies the products of a company or group of companies.

brand extension   A branding strategy that uses an existing brand name for an improved or new product in the product line.

brand licensing   The legal authorization by a trade-marked brand owner to allow another company (the licensee) to use its brand, brand mark, or trade character for a fee.

brand mark   The part of the brand that is a symbol, design, or distinctive coloring or lettering.

brand name   The word, group of words, letters, or numbers of a brand that can be spoken.

break-even point   Point at which sales revenue equals the costs and expenses of making and distributing a product.

broadcast media   Includes radio and television.

budget, or 90-day, accounts   A type of credit plan that allows for the payment of a purchased item over a 90-day period without a finance charge.

business   All of the activities involved in producing and marketing goods and services.

business cycle   Movement of an economy through four recurring phases—prosperity, recession, depression, and recovery.

business philosophy   Tells how you think the business should be run and shows your understanding of your firm's role in the marketplace.

business plan   A proposal that describes every part of a new business to potential investors and lenders.

business risk   The possibility of business loss or failure.

buyers   People responsible for purchasing goods for resale.

buying behavior   The process individuals use to decide what they will buy and from where and whom they will buy it.

Glossary   **593**

buying signals Things a customer does or says to indicate a readiness to buy.

C

capital Goods, such as equipment or processed materials, used in a production process; also, money needed to start and operate a business.

capitalism Economic system characterized by private ownership of businesses and marketplace competition.

career consultation An informational interview with someone who works in a career that interests you.

career outlook The availability of jobs.

carload The minimum number of pounds of freight needed to fill a boxcar.

cash flow statement A monthly plan that shows when cash is anticipated to come into the business and when cash is expected to be paid out.

cash on delivery (COD) sale Transaction in which the customer pays for merchandise at the time of delivery.

cash sale Transaction in which the customer pays for his or her purchase with cash or a check.

CD-ROM A drive that provides high resolution graphics, animations, video, and digital sound.

channel of distribution Path a product takes from producer or manufacturer to final user.

channels The avenues by which the message is delivered.

circle graph A geometric representation of the relative sizes of the parts of a whole; also called a *pie chart*.

clip art Stock drawings, photographs, and headlines clipped from a printed sheet and pasted into an advertisement.

closing the sale Obtaining positive agreement from the customer to buy.

co-branding strategy A branding strategy that combines one or more brands to increase customer loyalty and sales for each individual brand.

cold canvasing Locating potential customers with little or no direct help other than a telephone directory.

collateral Something of value that a borrower pledges to a lender to ensure repayment of a loan.

command economy Economic system in which the government answers the three basic economic questions.

common carrier A motor carrier that provides transportation services to any business in its operating area for a fee.

communication The process of exchanging information, ideas, and feelings.

communications programs Software programs used to establish communication between your computer and other computers.

communist Describes a political system in which the government runs everything, and the Communist party runs the government.

community relations The activities that a business uses to acquire or maintain the respect of the community.

comparative advantage Advantage a nation gains by selling the goods it produces more efficiently than other goods.

competition Struggle between companies for customers.

complementary colors Colors that are found opposite each other in the color wheel and create the greatest contrasts.

consensus A decision that each member agrees to.

consignment buying Buying arrangement in which goods are paid for only after they are purchased by the final consumer.

consumer affairs specialists Specialists who handle customer complaints and serve as consumer advocates within the firm.

consumer market Market consisting of all people who make purchases for personal use.

Consumer Price Index (CPI) Measure of inflation based on change over a period in the prices of 400 goods and services used by the average urban family.

consumerism Societal effort to protect consumer rights by putting legal, moral, and economic pressure on business.

consumers Those who actually use a product.

contests Games or activities that require the participant to demonstrate a skill.

contract carrier A motor carrier that provides transportation services on a selective basis, according to agreements between the carrier and the shipper.

controlling The process of comparing what was planned with actual performance; involves three basic activities—setting employee standards, evaluating performance, and solving problems.

cooperative advertising An arrangement whereby advertising is paid for by both a manufacturer and a local advertiser.

copy The selling message in a written advertisement.

corporation A business that is chartered by state and legally operates apart from the owner(s).

cost per thousand (CPM) The media cost of exposing 1,000 readers to an ad.

cost What a retailer pays for merchandise.

cost-plus pricing All costs and expenses are calculated and then the desired profit is added to arrive at a price.

cover letter A letter of application without the information on education and experience.

credit An arrangement whereby businesses or individuals can obtain products or money in exchange for a promise to pay later.

credit union A cooperative association formed by labor unions or groups of employees for the benefit of its members.

customer advisory boards Panels of consumers who make suggestions on new products.

customer benefits Advantages or personal satisfaction a customer will get from a good or service.

customer profile Picture of a prospective customer based on geographic, demographic, and psychographic data.

customers Those who buy a product.

customs brokers Import specialists licensed by the U.S. Treasury Department.

D **data analysis** The compiling, analyzing, and interpreting of the results of primary and secondary data collection.

database A computerized collection (or file) of related information about a specific topic.

database programs Software programs used to collect related data, which can be sorted, searched through, and printed as needed.

debit card Card that allows the amount of a purchase to be debited, or subtracted, from a customer's bank account.

debt capital Raising funds by borrowing money.

decimal number A fraction or mixed number whose denominator is a multiple of 10.

demand Consumer willingness and ability to buy products.

demographics Statistics that describe a population in terms of personal characteristics like age, gender, income, ethnic background, education, and occupation.

denominator The bottom number in a fraction; represents how many parts in a whole or how many *total* parts are being considered.

derived demand Demand in one market that is based on demand in another; for example, demand in the industrial market is based on demand for goods and services in the consumer market.

desktop publishing programs Software programs used to design and produce professional printed materials.

Dictionary of Occupational Titles (DOT) A book that describes about 20,000 jobs in terms of their relationship with data, people, and things.

digits The ten basic symbols of our (Arabic) numbering system: 0, 1, 2, 3, 4, 5, 6, 7, 8, and 9.

direct calling The process of contacting potential employers in person or on the telephone.

direct check method A method of checking merchandise by checking directly against the actual invoice or purchase order.

direct close Close in which the salesperson asks for the sale.

direct distribution Goods or services are sold by the producer directly to the final user; no intermediaries are involved.

disclaimer A statement that contains exceptions to and exclusions from a warranty.

discount pricing Seller's offering reductions from the usual price.

discretionary income Money left after paying for basic living expenses such as food, shelter, and clothing.

disk drive Used to store information on a disk or read information from a disk.

display The visual and artistic aspects of presenting a product to a target group of customers.

disposable income Money left after taxes are taken out.

distractions Blocks to effective listening include noises and other environmental factors, interruptions by other people, and competing thoughts that creep into your mind.

distribution center A warehouse designed to speed delivery of goods and to minimize storage costs.

dollar control In inventory management, the planning and monitoring of the total inventory investment that a business makes during a stated period of time.

draft Exporter's authorization to a foreign bank to collect money owed for a shipment and release shipping documents to a foreign customer once payment is made.

dummy invoice check method A method of checking merchandise by counting on a form similar to an invoice, but sizes and styles are omitted.

E **E-mail** Electronic mail prepared on a computer and sent to someone else who has a computer.

economic risks Business risks that occur from changes in overall business conditions.

economy System by which a nation decides how to use its resources to produce and distribute goods and services.

elastic demand   Describes a situation in which a change in the price of a product creates a change in the demand for it.

electronic retail outlets   Retailers that sell goods to the ultimate consumer through special television programs and computer linkups.

embargo   Total ban on specific goods coming into and leaving a country.

emotional blocks   Biases against the opinions expressed by the sender that block your understanding.

emotional motive   Feeling experienced by a customer through association with a product.

empathize   To understand a person's situation or frame of mind.

employee discounts   Discounts given to workers to encourage them to buy the products they sell or manufacture.

empowerment   Encouraging team members to contribute to and take responsibility for the management process.

end-of-month (EOM) dating   Changes the date from which billing terms take effect to the end of the month.

endless chain method   Asking previous customers for names of potential customers.

entrepreneurs   People who attempt to earn money and make profits by taking the risk of owning and operating a business.

entrepreneurship   1. Factor of production consisting of the skills of people who are willing to risk their time and money to run a business. **2.** The process of starting and managing your own business.

equilibrium   Condition that exists when the amount of product supplied is equal to the amount of product demanded.

equity capital   Raising money from within a company or by selling part of the interest in the business.

ethics   Guidelines for good behavior, based on knowing the difference between right and wrong and doing what is right.

European Union (EU)   Europe's trading bloc; intended as a political as well as an economic union.

exchange   1. Merchandise brought back to be replaced by other merchandise. **2.** Sale of something in the marketplace.

exclusive distribution   Use of only one sales outlet for a product within a certain geographic area.

excuses   Insincere reasons for not buying or not seeing a salesperson.

exempt carrier   A motor carrier that is free from direct regulation of rates and operating procedures.

experimental method   A research technique in which a researcher observes under controlled conditions the results of changing one or more marketing variables while keeping certain other variables constant.

Export-Import Bank (Eximbank)   Independent agency of the U.S. government whose purpose is to foster trade between the United States and other countries.

exports   Goods and services sold to other countries.

express warranty   A warranty that is explicitly stated, in either writing or spoken words, to induce a customer to buy.

extended coverage   Optional insurance coverage on a basic property coverage policy.

extension   Result of multiplying the number of units by the cost per unit.

extensive decision making   Form of decision making used when there has been little or no previous experience with an item because it is infrequently purchased.

extra dating   Grants additional days before the dating terms take effect.

F

factors of production   Economist's term for resources.

family life cycle   Evolution of the family through traditional stages—single, newly married, full nest, empty nest, and sole survivor.

feature-benefit selling   Matching the features of a product to a customer's needs and wants.

feedback   The receiver's response to the message.

fidelity bonds   Bonds that protect a business from employee dishonesty.

finance   Money or anything that can be sold very quickly to get money; also, borrowing money.

fixtures   Store furnishings, such as display cases, counters, shelves, racks, and benches.

flexible-price policy   Pricing policy that permits customers to bargain for merchandise.

floor limit   Maximum amount a salesperson may allow a customer to charge without getting special authorization.

forced-choice question   A question that asks respondents to choose answers from possibilities given.

foreign corporation   A corporation that is incorporated under the laws of a different state from the one in which it does business.

foreign trade zones   Designated areas of a country where foreign businesses benefit from reduced tariffs.

form utility Value added by changing raw materials or putting parts together to make them more useful.

formal balance Placing large items with large items and small items with small items in a display.

fractions Numbers used to describe a part of some standard amount.

franchise A legal agreement to operate a business in the name of a recognized company.

free enterprise Economic system that encourages individuals to start and operate their own businesses without government involvement.

freight forwarders Private transportation service companies that combine shipments from several different businesses and deliver them to their destinations.

fringe benefits Benefits, privileges, or monetary payments beyond salary or wages that go with a job.

full warranty A warranty stating that a product is found to be defective within the warranty period, it will be repaired or replaced at no cost to the purchaser.

G **General Agreement on Tariffs and Trade (GATT)** International trade agreement designed to promote global free trade through the reduction of tariffs and the use of a common set of rules for trading.

general partnership A partnership in which each partner shares in the profits and losses.

Generation X People born between the years 1964 and 1980; also known as the baby bust generation.

generic products "No frills" products that carry no brand name.

geographics Segmentation of a market based on where people live.

goods Tangible products.

graphics and design programs Software programs used to produce drawings and designs.

greeting approach method Salesperson simply welcomes the customer to the store.

gross profit Difference between sales revenue and the cost of goods sold.

gross sales The total of all sales for any period of time.

Gross Domestic Product (GDP) Measure of the goods and services produced using labor and property located in a country; now the principal way of measuring output in the United States.

Gross National Product (GNP) Measure of the goods and services produced by labor and property supplied by a country's residents, whether there or abroad.

Guide for Occupational Education (GOE) A reference that organizes the world of work into 12 interest areas, which it then further subdivides into work groups and subgroups.

H **hardware** The equipment—the computer and all the other pieces attached to it that make up a computer system.

headline The lettering, slogan, or saying that gets the readers' attention, arouses their interest, and leads them to read the rest of the ad.

horizontal organization Nontraditional business structure characterized by self-managing teams, organization by process rather than function, and customer orientation.

human risks Risks caused by human mistakes and the unpredictability of employees or customers.

I **illustration** The photograph or drawing used in a print advertisement.

implied warranty A warranty that exists automatically by state law whenever a purchase takes place.

imports Goods and services purchased from other countries.

incentives Products that are more expensive than premiums that are earned and given through contests, or as sweepstakes awards.

income statement A summary of a business's income and expenses during a specific period, such as a month, a quarter, or a year

indirect distribution Goods or services are sold indirectly, through one or more intermediaries.

industrial market Market consisting of all customers who make purchases for business purposes; also called the business-to-business market.

inelastic demand Describes a situation in which a change in the price of a product has very little effect on the demand for it.

inflation Rising prices.

informal balance Balancing a large item with several small ones.

information utility Value added by communicating with the consumer.

infrastructure A country's physical development, including the state of its roads, ports, sanitation facilities, and utilities.

initiative Doing what needs to be done without being urged.

installment accounts A type of credit plan that allows for payment over a period of time.

institutional advertising Advertising that creates a favorable impression and goodwill for a business or an organization.

institutional promotion Promotion used to create a favorable image for a business or organization (especially in relation to competitors).

insurance policy A contract between a business and an insurance company to cover a certain business risk.

intensive distribution Use of all suitable sales outlets for a product.

interest The money paid for the use of money borrowed or invested.

intermediaries Channel members that help move products from the producer or manufacturer to the final user.

International Monetary Fund (IMF) Multinational agency whose purpose is to help stabilize exchange rates among the currencies of its member nations.

international trade Exchange of goods and services between nations.

invoice Bill.

jargon Technical or specialized vocabulary used by members of a particular profession or industry.

job descriptions Written statements listing the requirements of a particular job.

job lead Information about a job opening.

joint ventures Partnerships between foreign and domestic firms, frequently used or required to conduct business abroad.

just-in-time (JIT) Inventory control system in which companies are linked by computer to their suppliers to guarantee frequent shipments of goods that keep pace with production.

label An information tag, wrapper, seal, or imprinted message that is attached to a product or its package.

layaway Merchandise is removed from stock and kept in a separate storage area until the customer pays for it; also known as will-call.

layman's terms Words the average customer can understand.

letter of credit Guarantee of payment obtained by a foreign customer that allows a U.S. exporter to be paid by a U.S. bank as soon as goods have been shipped.

liability A debt owed by a business.

licensing A business arrangement whereby organizations license for a fee their logo, trademark, trade characters, names and likenesses, or personal endorsements to a business to be used in promoting the businesses's products.

licensing agreement Agreement that protects an originator's name and products.

lifestyle goals Your vision of how you see yourself living in the future.

limited decision making Form of decision making used when a person buys goods and services that he or she has purchased before but not on a regular basis.

limited partnership A partnership in which each limited partner is liable for any debts only up to the amount of his or her investment in the company.

limited warranty A warranty that offers less coverage than a full warranty.

line graph Graph that uses a line to join points representing changes in a variable quantity over a specific period of time.

local radio advertising Radio advertising done by a local business for its target market.

loss leader Item priced at cost to draw customers into a store.

mainframe The largest and most powerful type of computer.

maintained markup Difference between an item's final sale price and its cost.

management The process of achieving company goals by effective use of resources; involves planning, organizing, and controlling.

management training program Closely supervised on-the-job management training.

market The group of all potential customers who share common needs and wants, and who have the ability and willingness to buy the product.

market economy Economic system in which the market answers the three basic economic questions, without no government involvement.

marketing Process of developing, promoting, and distributing products in order to satisfy customers' needs and wants.

marketing concept Idea that to make a profit a business must focus all of its efforts on satisfying the needs and wants of its customers.

marketing information system A set of procedures and methods that regularly generates, stores, analyzes, and distributes marketing information.

marketing mix Combination of marketing decisions involving product, price, place, and promotion; also called the four P's.

marketing research The systematic gathering, recording, and analyzing of information about problems related to marketing goods and services.

marketplace Wherever a product is sold to a buyer.

market position A firm's relative standing in relation to its competitors.

market research Research that focuses on the customer and the market.

market segmentation Dividing the total market into smaller groups of people who share specific needs and characteristics.

market share A firm's percentage of the total sales volume generated by all competitors in a given market.

markup Difference between the price of an item and its cost.

marquee A sign used to display the store's name.

mass-marketing Using a single marketing plan to reach all the consumers.

media The agencies, means, or instruments used to convey messages.

memorandum buying Buying arrangement in which the supplier agrees to take back any unsold goods by a certain date.

merchandise approach method Salesperson makes a comment or asks questions about a product that the customer is looking at.

microcomputer The smallest type of computer or personal computer.

middle management In a traditionally organized company, the people who carry out top management's decisions and motivate supervisory personnel so the company can meet its goals.

mini-nationals Midsized and smaller companies that have operations in foreign countries.

mission statement Formal statement of a company's ultimate goals.

mixed-brand strategy The simultaneous offering of a combination of national, private, and generic brands.

mixed number A whole number and fraction together.

model stock list Buying plan used for fashionable merchandise and other items that change rapidly.

monopoly Exclusive control over a product or the means of producing it.

most-favored-nation status (MFNS) Status the United States grants to countries with which it wants to encourage trade.

multinationals Large corporations that have operations in several countries.

N

national brand A brand owned and initiated by a manufacturer.

national spot radio advertising Radio advertising used by national firms to advertise on a local station-by-station basis.

nationalize To take ownership by government action and without compensation.

natural risks Risks resulting from natural causes.

net income The difference between total expenses and gross profit.

net sales The total of all sales, after subtracting sales returns and allowances.

net worth The difference between the assets of a business and its liabilities.

network radio advertising Radio advertising broadcast from a studio to all affiliated radio stations throughout the country.

never-out list Buying plan used for best-selling products that make up a large percentage of sales volume.

news release A prewritten story about a company that is sent to the various media.

nonprice competition Form of competition that focuses on factors that are not related to price, like product quality, service and financing, business location, and reputation.

nonprofit organizations Service organizations operated with no intention of earning a profit for those who initiate or manage them; all income earned goes to the charitable cause outlined in the organization's charter.

nonverbal communication Expressing oneself through body language.

North American Free Trade Agreement (NAFTA) International trade agreement among the United States, Canada, and Mexico.

numerator The top number in a fraction; represents the number of parts being considered.

O

objection analysis sheet Sheet that enumerates common objections and possible responses to them.

objections Concerns, hesitations, doubts, or other honest reasons a customer has for not making a purchase.

observation method A research technique in which the actions of people are observed and recorded.

occupational area A category of jobs that involves similar interests and skills.

Occupational Outlook Handbook (OOH) A book that provides detailed information on more than two hundred occupations and is updated every two years.

on-approval sale Agreement that permits a customer to take merchandise (usually clothing) home for further consideration.

one-price policy Pricing policy under which all customers are charged the same price for goods and services offered for sale.

online computer services Research information that can be accessed through telephones and modems and allow users to communicate via computer.

online services Computer services that allow people to use their computers to access services and information.

open-ended questions Questions that require more than a yes or no answer.

open-to-buy (OTB) Amount of money available for buying goods.

opening cash fund Coins and currency designated for a cash register for a given day's business.

organization chart A diagram of the various jobs and functions that are found in a company.

organizing A coordinated effort to reach a company's planning goals; involves assigning responsibility, establishing working relationships, staffing, and directing the work of employees.

P

package The physical container or wrapping for a product.

paraphrase Restating in a different way, not word for word.

parcel post Standard surface package delivery provided by the U.S. Postal Service.

parliamentary procedure A structure for holding group meetings and making decisions.

partnership A legal agreement between two or more people to be jointly responsible for the success or failure of a business.

penetration pricing Pricing policy that sets a very low price for a new product to encourage as many people as possible to buy it.

percent Number of parts per hundred.

performance bonds Bonds insure against losses that might occur when work or a contract is not finished on time or as agreed.

perpetual inventory system A method of keeping track of the number of items in inventory on a constant basis.

personal financial statement A summary of a person's current personal financial condition.

physical distribution The process of transporting, storing, and handling goods to make them available to customers.

physical inventory system A method of counting stock by visually inspecting or actually counting it to determine the quantity on hand.

pie chart Another name for a circle graph.

place utility Value added by having a product where customers can buy it.

planning The first step in the management process; involves deciding what will be done and how it will be accomplished.

planning goals The small steps you take to get from where you are now to where you want to be.

planogram Computer-developed diagrams that show retailers how and where products within a category should be displayed on a shelf at individual stores.

point-of-sale (POS) system A computerized system that uses light pens, hand-held laser guns, stationary lasers, or slot scanners to feed information directly from merchandise tags or product labels into a computer.

point-of-sale research A powerful form of research that combines natural observation with personal interviews to get people to explain buying behavior.

positioning Getting consumers to think of a product in a certain way.

possession utility Value added by exchanging a product for some monetary value.

preapproach Getting ready to sell.

premiums Prizes or rewards offered to a customer as an added inducement to make a purchase.

preretailing marking method A method of marking merchandise pricing information marked in advance by the seller, or the buyer, on the retailer's copy of the purchase order.

press conference A meeting in which media members are invited by a business or organization to hear an announcement about a newsworthy event.

press kit A folder containing articles, news releases, features stories, and photographs about a company, product, or person.

prestige pricing Setting higher-than-average prices to suggest status and prestige to the consumer.

price competition Form of competition that focuses on the sale price of a product.

price discrimination Charging different prices to similar customers in similar situations.

price fixing Agreement of competitors to set their prices within a certain range.

price lining Offering all merchandise in a given category at certain prices (as offering all blouses at $25, $35, and $50).

price Value of money (or its equivalent) placed on a good or service.

primary data Facts obtained for the first time and used specifically for the particular problem under study.

principal   The amount of money borrowed.

print media   Print means or instruments used to convey messages, such as newspapers, magazines, direct mail pieces, signs, and billboards.

private brand   A brand owned and initiated by wholesalers and retailers.

private carrier   A motor carrier owned and operated by an individiual business that transports only its own goods.

private employment agencies   Agencies not supported by taxes and must earn a profit to stay in business. They charge a fee for their services, which is paid by either the job applicant or the employer.

private sector   Businesses not associated with government agencies.

private warehouse   A warehouse facility owned by a business for its own use.

privatization   Process of selling government-owned businesses to private individuals.

problem definition   Clearly identifying a problem and stating the information needed to solve the problem.

product depth   The number of product items offered within each product line.

product feature   Physical characteristic or quality of a good or service that explains what it is.

product item   A specific model, brand, or size of a product within a product line.

product life cycle   The stages that a product goes through in its life.

product line   A group of closely related products manufactured and/or sold by a business.

product mix   All the different products that a company makes or sells.

product modification   An alteration in a company's existing product.

product obsolescence   Products that become outdated.

product planning   All the decisions a business makes about the production and sale of its products.

product positioning   The efforts a business makes to identify, place, and sell its products in the marketplace.

product promotion   Promotion used by a business to convince potential customers to buy products from it instead of from a competitor.

product research   Research that centers on evaluating product design and acceptance, competitive products, package design, and product usage.

product width   The number of different product lines a business manufactures or sells.

production   Creating, growing, manufacturing, or improving on something produced by someone else.

productivity   Output per worker hour.

products   Goods and services.

profit   Money earned from conducting business after all costs and expenses have been paid.

promotion   Any form of communication a business or organization uses to inform, persuade, or remind people about its products and improve its public image.

promotional advertising   Advertising designed to increase sales.

promotional mix   The combination of different types of promotion a business uses to persuade customers to buy its products.

promotional tie-ins   Sales promotional arrangements between one or more retailers or manufacturers which combine their resources (advertising and sales promotional activities) to do a promotion that creates additional sales for each partner.

proportion   The relationship between and among objects in a display.

prospect   Potential customer; also called a lead.

psychographics   Study of consumers based on their lifestyle, and the attitudes and values that shape it.

psychological pricing   Pricing techniques that create an illusion for customers or that make shopping easier for them.

public employment agencies   Employment agencies that are supported by state or federal taxes and offer services free to both job applicants and employers.

public relations   Any activity designed to create goodwill toward a business.

public sector   Government agencies and services that operate as businesses but are not intended to earn a profit.

public warehouse   A warehouse facility available to any business that will pay for its use.

publicity   Creating demand for a business or product by placing news about it in publications or on radio, television, or stage.

purchase order   Legal contract between a buyer and a supplier that specifies the terms of the agreement.

purchasing agent   Person responsible for buying goods used in service and manufacturing businesses.

Q

quorum   A proportion of the membership—usually more than half.

quota   Limit on either the quantity or monetary value of a product that may be imported.

R

rational motive   Conscious, factual reason for a purchase.

realistic goal   A goal that you have a reasonable chance of achieving.

rebates   Discounts offered by manufacturers for purchasing items during a given time period.

receipt-of-goods (ROG) dating   Terms begin when the buyer's firm receives the goods.

receiving record   A form that is used to describe the goods received by a business. Also called a log.

references   People who know your work habits and personal traits so well that they will recommend you for the job.

referrals   Names provided by satisfied customers of other people who might buy a product.

regular, or 30-day, charge accounts   A type of credit plan that allows customers to charge purchases during a month and pay in full within 30 days after they are billed.

relationship marketing   Strategies businesses use to stay close to their customers.

resident buying offices   Retailers' representatives in a central market.

resources   All the things used in producing goods and services: land, labor, capital, and entrepreneurship; also called factors of production.

resume   A brief summary of personal information, education, skills, work experience, activities, and interests.

retail   Refers to what a retailer is paid for merchandise.

retailers   Businesses that buy goods from wholesalers or directly from manufacturers and resell them to the final consumer.

return   Merchandise brought back for a cash refund or credit.

return on investment   Calculation used to determine the relative profitability of a product; profit divided by investment.

revolving accounts   A type of credit plan where the retailer determines the credit limit and when payments are due.

risk   Potential for loss or failure.

routine decision making   Form of decision making used when a person needs little information about a product because of a high degree of prior experience with it or a low perceived risk.

S

sales associates   Salespeople who know their products and how to sell.

salesclerks   Salespeople who are simply order takers or cashiers.

sales incentives   Awards given to managers and employees who successfully meet or exceed their company's set sales quota for a particular product or line or products.

sales promotion   The use of marketing devices, such as displays, premiums, and contests to stimulate purchases.

sales research   Research that focuses on sales data.

sales transaction   Process of recording a sale and presenting the customer with proof of payment.

sample   A part of the target population that is assumed to represent the entire population.

scarcity   Condition that exists when people's wants and needs exceed their resources.

seasonal discounts   Discounts offered to buyers who are willing to buy in advance of the customary buying season.

secondary data   Facts that have already been collected for some purpose other than the current study.

selective distribution   Use of a limited number of sales outlets for a product in a given geographic area.

selling   Helping customers make satisfying buying decisions.

service approach method   Salesperson asks the customer if he or she needs assistance.

service close   Close that explains services that overcome obstacles to a sale.

services   Intangible products; usually a series of tasks performed for a customer.

setting   Where communication takes place.

shortages   Excesses of demand over supply.

signature   The distinctive identification symbol for a business.

six-month merchandise plan   Budget that estimates planned purchases for a six-month period.

skimming pricing   Pricing policy that sets a very high price for a new product to capitalize on the high demand for it during its introductory period.

slogan   A catch phrase or small group of words that are combined in a special way to present an advertising message.

slotting allowance   A cash premium paid by the manufacturer to a retail chain for the costs involved in placing a new product on its shelves.

socialist   Describes a political system in which there is increased government involvement in people lives and the economy.

software   Controls the functioning of the hardware and directs its operation.

sole proprietorship   A business owned and operated by one person.

source marking   A method of marking merchandise in which the seller or manufacturer marks the price before delivering merchandise to the retailer.

specialty media   Relatively inexpensive, useful items with an advertiser's name printed on them.

specific goal   The type of planning goal that moves you along toward your ultimate goal.

spreadsheet programs   Software programs used to organize, calculate, and analyze numerical data.

spot check method   A method of checking merchandise by randomly checking one carton in a shipment.

standard English   The formal style of writing and speaking that you have learned in school.

standard of living   Measurement of the amount of goods and services that a nation's people have.

standing-room-only close   Close used when a product is in short supply or when the price will be going up in the near future.

start-up costs   A projection of how much money a person will need the first year of business operation.

stockholders   The people who actually own the corporation.

stockkeeping unit (sku)   Each item or a group of related items in a unit control inventory system.

stock turnover   Number of times the average stock has been sold and replaced in a given period of time.

storage   The marketing function of holding goods until they are sold.

storefront   The total exterior of a business.

store layout   The way floor space is allocated to facilitate sales and serve the customer.

Subchapter S corporation   A small business that is taxed like a partnership or proprietorship.

suggestion selling   Selling additional goods or services to a customer.

supervisory-level management   In a traditionally organized company, the people who carry out the plans of middle management by directly assigning work duties to and supervising employees on the job.

supply   Amount of goods producers are willing to make and sell.

surpluses   Excesses of supply over demand.

survey method   A research technique in which information is gathered from people directly through the use of interviews or questionnaires.

sweepstakes   Games of chance.

T

tariff   A tax on imports; also called a duty.

telemarketing   Process of selling over the telephone.

test marketing   Placing a product in one or more selected geographic areas.

third party method   Using a previous customer or neutral person to give a testimonial about a product.

till   Cash drawer of a cash register.

time draft   Document that allows a foreign customer to take delivery of goods without payment; essentially a promise to pay in the future.

time utility   Value added by having a product available at a certain time of year or a convenient time of day.

ton-mile   The movement of one ton of freight one mile.

top management   In a traditionally organized company, the people with the greatest responsibility; includes the chief executive officer, president, and vice president(s).

trade character   A personified brand mark (that is, one given human form or characteristics).

trade discounts   Not really discounts but rather the way manufacturers quote prices to wholesalers and retailers.

trademark   A brand name, brand mark, trade character, or a combination of these that is given legal protection.

trading area   The geographical area from which a business draws its customers.

transportation of goods   The marketing function of moving goods from a seller to a buyer.

trial close   An initial effort to close a sale.

U

unit control   In inventory management, planning and monitoring the quantities of merchandise that a business handles during a stated period of time.

unit pricing   Form of pricing that allows consumers to compare prices in relation to a standard unit or measure, such as an ounce or a pound.

Universal Product Code (UPC)   Bar code used for electronic entry and recording of sales.

Universal Vendor Marketing (UVM) code   Series of numbers on a price tag, designed to be read by an electronic wand.

unlimited liability   Your financial liability is not limited to your investment in the business, but extends to your total ability to make payments.

utility   Added economic value.

V

value   Personal satisfaction gained from use of a good or service.

values   Things that are important to you.

vending service companies   Retailers that buy manufacturers' products and sell them through machines that dispense goods to consumers.

vertical organization Traditional business structure characterized by three levels of management—top, middle, and supervisory level.

visual merchandising The coordination of all physical elements in a place of business so that it projects the right image to its customers.

W————

warranty A promise, or guarantee, given to a customer that a product will meet certain standards.

warranty of fitness for a particular purpose An implied warranty arising when the seller advises a customer that a product is suitable for a particular use and the customer acts on that advice.

warranty of merchantability A promise from the seller that the product sold is fit for its intended purpose.

which close Close that encourages a customer to make a decision between two items.

wholesalers Businesses that obtain goods from manufacturers and resell them to industrial users, other wholesalers, and retailers.

whoopies Well-heeled older persons; the 50-plus generation.

word processing programs Software programs used to create text documents.

Index

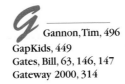

611

Cover Photo

James Porto/FPG International

Photography Credits

Munshi Ahmed 58; Almhult/IKEA U.S. West 287; Glen Allison/Tony Stone Images xx, v(tr); Arnold & Brown Photography 134; C. Aurness/Westlight 28; Bruce Ayers/Tony Stone Images 385t, 402l; BT Pictures 212; Bachman/Uniphoto 62bl; Big 5 Sporting Goods, Inc. 400m; Dan Bosler/Tony Stone Images 193, 563, 580; Edward W. Bower/The Image Bank 44, vi(tl); Robert Brenner/Photo Edit 69bl; California Tree Fruit Association 273; Cindy Carp/Black Star 48; Melanie Carr/Uniphoto 150, vii(m); John Carr & Son, Inc. 95; Robert Cerri/The Stock Market 22tr, v(br); Ron Chapple/FPG International 68bl; Chevrolet Motor Division x(bl), 242; Chrysler Corp. 275; David Conklin/Uniphoto xv(tl), 474; Gary Conner/Index Stock Photography 6tr; Michael K. Daly/The Stock Market 24; Dana Perfumes 22tl, 23bl; The Dannon Company, Inc. 25; De Beers 180; Deere & Company 190, 299; DMSI 332(2), 354, 355(2); Mary Kate Denny/Photo Edit 64; Department of Industrial & Commercial Developement, Yucatan Mexico 99; DKNY, Inc. 277; Myron J. Dorf/The Stock Market xiv(tl), 427; Steve Dunwell/The Image Bank 46m; Jon Feingers/The Stock Market 183; Ken Fisher/Tony Stone Images 102, vii(tl); Florsheim, Inc. 292; Gerald French/FPG International 482; Tim Fuller Photography viii(br), ix(m, br), xvi(tl), xvii(br) 178(2), 179(2), 186, 191, 196, 198, 200, 201, 206, 211, 216, 218, 219, 222, 223, 228, 237, 384b, 436, 512, 561tr, 561br, 574, 588; Jane Garnes iii(tr); General Mills 250; Rober Ginn/Photo Edit 68tl; Goodyear 383; Larry Dale Gordon/The Image Bank 128; Charles Gupton/Tony Stone Images 319, 358; Charles Gupton/Uniphoto 68bl, 80tl; Mark Harmel/FPG International 522; Henley & Savage/Uniphoto 6l; Frank Herholdt/Tony Stone Images 418; Christina Koci Herandez 516; Walter Hodges/Tony Stone Images 47; Ted Horowitz/The Stock Market xii(m), 356; Julie Houck/Tony Stone Images 576; IBM 314; Illinois Special Olympics 300; Index Stock Photography xvi(bl), 80bl, 104, 306, 526, 565br; Internet Shopping Network 143; Gary Irving/Tony Stone Images 500; Izzo Systems, Inc. 34; J 2 Marketing Services 174; Zigy Kaluzny/Tony Stone Images 68tr, 91; David Kaolubowski 551; Keebler Company 403m; Kentucky Fried Chicken Corp. 260; Anne Klein, Inc. x(m), 272; Michael Krasowitz/FPG International 120; Don Kushnick 202; Erica Langsmer/Black Star 50; Freda Leinwand 69tl; Levi Strauss & Co. 156; Life Fitness 147; John Lund/Tony Stone Images 86; Maybelline, Inc. 19; Phil McCarten/Photo Edit 71; Tom & Dee Ann McCarthy/The Stock Market 162t; Tom McCarthy/Photo Edit 123, 298; McDonald's Corporation v(m), 4(3), 5bl, 74l; Will & Deni McIntyre/Alcoa 60; McNeil Consumer Products Co. 74m; Paul Merideth/Tony Stone Images xii(bl), 336; Microsoft Corporation 146; Ted Mishima Photography 566; Liana Miuccio Photography 347, 399; Mountasia Entertainment International, Inc. 18; National Aerial Advertising, Inc. 263; National Wildlife Federation 274; New Products Showcase & Learning Center 35(3); Michael Newman/Photo Edit 37, 127, 169, 296, 503; Newman's Own, Inc. 66, vi(m); Ray Ng 570; Oshman's Sporting Goods Co. Inc. 400b; Gabe Palmer/The Stock Market 420; Eligio Paoni/Saba 163; Greg Pease/Tony Stone Images 325; Pepsico, Inc x(tl), 51, 92, 259; Luis Pidilla/The Image Bank 46b; James Porto/FPG International i; Quality Controlled Services 422; Duncan Raban/Retna Ltd. NYC 113; Radio Shack/Division of Tandy Corp. 322; Jon Riley/Tony Stone Images 81l, 360, 508; Roadway Services Company 82, 333; Bill Ross/Westlight 39r; Ross Laboratories 74r; SMH Group xiii(tl), 386; James Schnepf Photography 496; Sears, Roebuck & Co. 372; Sharp Electronics Corporation 203bl; Ron Sherman/Tony Stone Images 361; Eric Leigh Simmons/The Image Bank 162b; Wayne Simpson 10; Frank Siteman/Tony Stone Images 488; Don Smetzer/Tony Stone Images xv(br), 172, 486; The Softad Group ix(tr), 203tr; Spalding Company 446; Sprint/World Cup USA94 247; Steiner/FPG International 182; Harald Sund/The Image Bank x(tr), 244;, Sunshine Biscuits, Inc. 402b; Superstock 19(t), 329; Target Stores/A Division of Dayton Hudson Corporation 400t; TeleCheck Services, Inc. 502; Telegraph Colour Library/FPG International 126, 352, 432; Tennessee Valley Authority 39l; Tiffany & Co. xiii(m), 392; Toyota Motor Sales, USA, Inc. 32; Roger Tully/Tony Stone Images 326; Pete Turner/The Image Bank 46t; Uniphoto Inc. xvi(br), xvii(tl), 62tl, 253, 548, 561tl, 561bl, 565tr; United Parcel Service of America, Inc. 328; United States Postal Service 213; Terry Vine/Tony Stone Images 565tl; Vivitar Corporation 176; Cary S. Welinsky/Natural Cotton Colours, Inc. 541; Dana C. White/Dana White Productions vii(bl), viii(tl, m), xi(m, bl), xiii(br), xiv(m), 2, 5tl, 8(3), 9(2), 14, 38, 63, 72, 76, 77, 81r, 137, 141, 142, 145, 152, 154, 157, 160, 162m, 166, 167, 168, 256, 262, 270, 285, 286(3), 209(4), 308, 364, 378, 384m, 389(3), 396, 402t, 424, 506, 558; Lee White Photography vi(bl), xi(tl), xiv(br), 22bl, 23tl, 80tl, 138, 140, 188(2), 189(2), 224, 278, 282, 287b, 289, 293, 230, 377, 384t, 385, 406, 411, 435, 438, 448, 453, 456, 457, 459, 462, 464, 465, 466, 468, 469, 470, 494(4), 520, 546; Chris Windsor/Tony Stone Images 30; Wm. Wrigley Jr. Company 17; David Young-Wolff/Photo Edit 303.

Glencoe would like to thank and acknowledge the following companies, institutions and individuals for their contributions with some of the photography in this book:
Adray's; Blockbuster; Boulevard Camera; Broadway Department Stores; Crescent Jewelers; Domino's Pizza; Executive Cleaners; Federal Express; Footlocker; Hughes Market; Lawrence Company; Maya Shoe Repair; Martin Minkardo; Paper Mate; Pavilions Market; Pepperdine University School of Business & Management; Claude Pepper Senior Center; Santa Monica College; Santa Monica High School; Sulka; Venice Family Clinic; Wherehouse; Natalie, Michael & Andrew White; Wilshire West Stationers.

Acknowledgements

Figure 4-3 (top) From the *1994 Investor's Guide*. Reprinted by permission of *Fortune*.

Figure 4-3 (bottom) Reprinted from June 27, 1994 issue of *Business Week* by special permission, copyright © 1994 by McGraw-Hill, Inc.

Figure 4-4 From *Fortune*, February 7, 1994. © 1994 Time Inc. All rights reserved.

Figure 4-5 From *Fortune*, October 4, 1993. © 1993 Time Inc. All rights reserved.

Figure 6-1 Source: *American Demographics* magazine, © 1992. Reprinted with permission.

Figure 6-2 Source: *American Demographics* magazine, © 1994. Reprinted with permission.

Figure 6-3 From *Sales & Marketing Management's 1993 Survey of Buying Power*.

Table 7-1 From *Fortune*, June 14, 1993. © 1993 Time Inc. All rights reserved.

Figure 19-2 (bottom right) Used by permission of Merriam-Webster, Inc.

Figure 19-2 (left) Reprinted by permission of the McDonald's Corporation.

Figure 23-1 Reprinted by permission of the Saturn Corporation.

Figure 29-1 © 1994 ASM Communications, Inc. Used with permission from *Brandweek*.

Figure 33-3 Reprinted by permission of the McDonald's Corporation.

Page 476 D&A Auto Body. Used with permission.

Figure 36-1 Used with permission from Citibank.